D0488137

The Biographical Dictionary of World War II Generals and Flag Officers

The Biographical Dictionary of World War II Generals and Flag Officers

The U.S. Armed Forces

R. Manning Ancell
with Christine M. Miller

Greenwood Press
Westport, Connecticut • London

Library of Congress Cataloging-in-Publication Data

Ancell, R. Manning.
    The biographical dictionary of World War II generals and flag officers
    :   the U.S. Armed Forces / R. Manning Ancell with Christine M.
Miller.
        p.   cm.
    Includes bibliographical references and index.
    ISBN 0–313–29546–8 (alk. paper)
    1. World War, 1939–1945—Biography—Dictionaries.   2. United
States—Armed Forces—Biography—Dictionaries.   3. Generals—United
States—Biography—Dictionaries.   4. Admirals—United States—
Biography—Dictionaries.   I. Miller, Christine Marie.
II. Title.
D736.A63   1996
940.53′092′20—dc20   95–50450

British Library Cataloguing in Publication Data is available.

Library of Congress Catalog Card Number: 95–50450
ISBN: 0–313–29546–8

First published in 1996

Greenwood Press, 88 Post Road West, Westport, CT 06881
An imprint of Greenwood Publishing Group, Inc.

Printed in the United States of America

The paper used in this book complies with the
Permanent Paper Standard issued by the National
Information Standards Organization (Z39.48–1984).

10 9 8 7 6 5 4 3 2 1

For the families of the generals
and admirals of the Armed Forces
who selflessly served their
country from December 7, 1941
to September 2, 1945

Contents

Preface

This book should have been written fifty years ago just after the war ended, when information was readily available and the memories of participants at their keenest. Unfortunately, compilations of this type have traditionally held little interest for historians and the general public when the event they chronicle is still fresh in their memory. As a result, many years later determined authors often struggle to acquire bits and pieces of information on people who were relegated to relative obscurity by the passage of time and about whom little or no substantive material survived. Imagine the enormous challenge, for example, of putting together today a collection of reminiscences of all the participants in the War of 1812.

The enormous popularity of all aspects of World War II over the last half century has produced thousands of books but no single collection of biographies of American military and naval leaders during the war. That is precisely why we undertook to produce the first definitive book containing biographical material on all our country's generals and flag officers who served any amount of active duty between December 7, 1941 and September 2, 1945. This includes general officers of the U.S. Army, the U.S. Army Air Force, the National Guard and the U.S. Marine Corps and flag officers of the U.S. Navy and Coast Guard. In addition to regular officers we included officers called to active duty from the Reserves, officers brought from retirement to temporary active duty, and officers promoted to high rank directly from civilian life.

The task of assembling appropriate data on these gentlemen was aided somewhat by technology — the mimeograph machine, then the copier are good examples — but hampered by inattention over many years. At war's end biographical sketches written in preceding years were largely relegated to file folders and, for the most part, not updated. The only exception was those officers who remained in the service and rose to much higher rank and responsibility, but that was a very small percentage. Our task, therefore, was one of locating bits and pieces of information from a variety of sources in order to compile biographical entries that contained the information we felt was both relevant and necessary.

    In deciding what material to include in each biographical entry we considered first what the reader would want to find and second how we would acquire that information. We found all too soon that a small number of the individuals profiled in the book were well known and the preparation of their entries was completed quickly, but the preponderance of those who qualified for inclusion in the book represented a collective challenge of the first order. In the end we were able to collect the necessary material on ninety-nine percent of the generals and flag officers whom we identified through official sources, including official registers and wartime lists issued by the personnel establishments of each Service. For the one percent that is incomplete or eluded us entirely and is missing, we apologize with the hope the reader will understand why.

Acknowledgments

A book of this size and complexity could not have gotten off the ground without the assistance of many people to whom we are grateful. To a few, however, we wish to extend special appreciation.

Historian Dennis Vetock and the staff of the library at the Institute for Military History at Carlisle Barracks guided us through the wealth of material housed in that vast storehouse of military knowledge, particularly the many file cabinets of biographical sketches housed in the basement.

Bruce Jacobs, a retired major general in the National Guard and a first-rate historian and writer, spent an inestimable amount of time helping us piece together the information that forms the chapter on wartime National Guard general officers. Without his guidance the chapter could never have been written.

Dr. Don Carter and Dr. Walt Moody and their helpful staffs at the U.S. Army Military History Center and the Air Force History Division, respectively, opened their files and assisted us in collecting hundreds of pages of biographical information on former general officers.

On the sea service side, Kathy Lloyd and her people were invaluable assets as we waded through countless files in the archives at the Naval Historical Center, while across the street at the office of Marine Corps History, Dan Crawford made certain the extensive and exceptionally well-kept records on its general officers met our needs. If not, he found answers to our many questions. We received exceptional responsiveness from Dr. Bob Browning, the Coast Guard historian, no matter how complex our request.

The offices that administer to the needs of the general officers of the Army and Air Force contain a wealth of information that was made available to us, particularly the dates when officers passed away.

Arlington National Cemetery, certainly well down on anyone's list of viable sources of biographical material, turned out to be a wellspring of information. Our sincere thanks to the members of the visitor's center who went out of their way to be responsive to our needs well past the eleventh hour.

Many others earned a special thanks for their contribution. To Dr. Vincent Transano, David Moore, John Tyree, Tim Trant, Rear Admiral Frank J. Allston, Major Ken Huxley, and Fred Carr, a special tip of the hat. To the many other unnamed people whose enthusiastic contributions helped us meet our deadline, we will always be grateful.

1

The United States Army

Abbott, Oscar Bergstrom (1890-1969) Born in San Antonio, Texas, on October 8, 1890. Attended the Agricultural and Mechanical College of Texas. Enlisted service in Texas National Guard May 1916-June 1917. Commissioned in the cavalry. Graduated from Command and General Staff School in 1931 and the Army War College in 1933. Instructor with the Texas National Guard July 1937-August 1940. Staff officer, later chief of the miscellaneous branch, War Department General Staff August 1940-June 1942. With headquarters of Services of Supply June 1942-May 1944. Brigadier general in April 1943. Commanding general of Camp Beale, California, May 1944-February 1946. Reverted to colonel in 1946 and retired in October 1950. Decorations included the Legion of Merit. Died on October 1, 1969.

Abraham, Clyde Rush (1883-1955) Born in Farmington, Pennsylvania, on July 17, 1883. Commissioned in the infantry from West Point in 1906. Duty with 81st Division in France in World War I. Graduated from Command and General Staff School in 1927 and the Army War College in 1933. Commanding officer of 17th Infantry 1936-1939. Inspector general of the Puerto Rican Department 1939-1940. Brigadier general in October 1940. Assistant division commander of 5th Division October 1940-May 1942. Reverted to colonel in May 1942. Retired in July 1943. Brigadier general on the retired list in October 1948. Died on March 25, 1955.

Adams, Claude Mitchell (1895-1958) Born in Humboldt, Tennessee, on October 2, 1895. Enlisted service in Tennessee National Guard and the Regular Army 1916-1917. Commissioned in the infantry in April 1917. Duty with 119th Infantry in France, including the Ypres-Lys and Somme offensives October 1917-May 1919. Professor of military science and tactics at Punahou Academy 1928-1931 and University of Florida 1934-1937. Graduated from Command and General Staff School in 1940. Aide to General George C. Marshall 1940-1941. Professor of military science and tactics at Staunton Military Academy 1941-1942 and Augusta Military Academy 1942. Brigadier general in March 1943. Military attache in Brazil 1942-1944. Retired in July 1944. Decorations included the Legion of Merit. Died on March 26, 1958.

Adams, Clayton Sinnot (1890-1965) Born in Champaign, Illinois, on December 7, 1890. Commissioned in the infantry reserve following attendance at Officer's Training Camp, Fort Sheridan in 1917. Called to active duty in September 1940. Served in the office of the adjutant general 1940-1942. Brigadier general in September 1942. Head of Army Postal Service 1942-1943. Duty with Army Service Forces December 1943 until released from active duty in July 1944. Decorations included the Legion of Merit. Died on April 6, 1965.

Adams, Emory Sherwood (1881-1967) Born in Manhattan, Kansas, on February 6, 1881. B.S. from Kansas State Agricultural College in 1898. Enlisted service in 20th Kansas Infantry and Regular Army 1898-1902. Commissioned in the infantry in October 1902. Overseas duty in the Philippines 1903-1904 and again 1908-1909, in China 1911-1913, and France during World War I, 1918-1919. Extended duty with the adjutant general department 1922-1938. Appointed the adjutant general, U.S. Army with the rank of major general in May 1938. Retired on February 28, 1942. Recalled to active duty in March 1942, serving until August 1945. Decorations included the Distinguished Service Medal. Died on November 30, 1967.

Adams, Paul De Witt (1906-1987) Born on October 6, 1906, in Heflin, Alabama. Commissioned in the infantry from West Point in 1928. With 34th Infantry, 8th Infantry Division, 1940-1942. Executive officer of 1st Special Service Force 1942-1944. Commanding officer of 143rd Infantry January 1944-January 1945. Brigadier general in March 1945. Assistant division commander of 45th Infantry Division January 1945-January 1946. Reverted to colonel in June 1946. Assignments after the war included commanding general of 101st Airborne Division June-October 1953, V Corps 1959-1960, Third Army October 1960-October 1961 and commander in chief of Strike Command 1961-1966. Retired as general in 1966. Decorations included two Distinguished Service Medals, the Silver Star, two Legions of Merit and four Bronze Stars. Died on October 31, 1987.

Adcock, Clarence Lionel (1895-1967) Born on October 23, 1895, in Waltham, Massachusetts. Commissioned in the Corps of Engineers from West Point in 1918. Graduated from Command and General Staff School in 1935, then instructor until 1938. Graduated from the Army War College in 1939. Deputy chief of staff for supply at I Corps, Fifth Army, Allied Force Headquarters at Algiers and Sixth Army Group June 1942-June 1945. Brigadier general in March 1943. Deputy chief of staff for civil affairs at SHAEF, then U.S. Forces European Theater of Operations June 1945-March 1946. Retired in January 1947 as colonel, recalled to active duty and retired again in 1949 as major general. Decorations included three Distinguished Service Medals and two Legions of Merit. Died on January 9, 1967.

Adler, Julius Ochs (1892-1955) Born in Chattanooga, Tennessee, on December 3, 1892. Graduated from Princeton University in 1914. Employed by the *New York Times* 1914-1917. Attended the first Business and Professional Men's Training Camp at Plattsburg, New York, in 1916. Commissioned in the cavalry in 1917 and ordered to active duty. Served with the 306th Infantry, 77th Division in the Lorraine, Aisne-Marne, Vesle and Meuse-Argonne offensives in World War I. Returned to the *New York Times* in May 1919, becoming general manager in 1935. Ordered to active duty again in October 1940. Duty with 113th Infantry and 4th Motorized Division 1940-1941. Brigadier general in July 1941. With 6th Infantry Division 1941-1944. Reverted to inactive status in November 1944 as a result of illness while in New Guinea. Major general, Army Reserve, in January 1948. Decorations included the Distinguished Service Cross, Silver Star, Legion of Merit and Purple Heart. Died on October 4, 1955.

Ahern, Leo James (1886-1974) Born in Miller, South Dakota, on July 17, 1886. Commissioned in the field artillery from West Point in 1909. Duty in Hawaii with 1st Field Artillery 1915-1917. Graduated from School of the Line in 1922, Command and General Staff School in 1923 and the Army War College in 1924. Staff officer with the Philippine Department 1924-1926. Attended Babson Institute in 1929. Duty in office of the inspector general, U.S. Army June 1940-January 1945. Brigadier general in March 1943. Reverted to colonel in June 1946 and retired that September. Died on July 25, 1974.

Akin, Spencer Ball (1889-1973) Born in Greenville, Mississippi, on February 13, 1889. Commissioned in the infantry from Virginia Military Institute in 1910. Extensive assignments with the Signal Corps beginning in 1919. Graduated from Command and General Staff School in 1928 and the Army War College in 1936. Brigadier general in December 1941. Signal officer for Third Army May-November 1941. Chief signal officer of Army forces Far East November 1941-March 1942. Chief signal officer in the Southwest Pacific Area 1942-1945. Major general in November 1943. Chief signal officer of U.S. Army Forces Pacific 1945-1946. Retired in March 1951. Decorations included the Distinguished Service Cross, two Distinguished Service Medals, two Silver Stars and the Legion of Merit. Retired March 31, 1951. Died on October 6, 1973.

Alexander, Clyde Charles (1892-1965) Born in Fresno, California, on July 1, 1892. Commissioned in the field artillery, National Guard, in June 1915 and the Regular Army in August 1917. With the 18th field artillery in France during World War I. Participated in the Aisne-Marne, Champagne-Marne, St. Mihiel and Meuse-Argonne offensives. Professor of military science and tactics at the University of Illinois 1921-1925 and the University of Florida 1928-1932. Graduated from Command and General Staff School in 1934 and the Army Industrial College in 1936. Assistant, then chief of supply division, National Guard Bureau 1938-1941. Deputy chief of staff, acting chief of staff and chief of staff at headquarters Services of Supply, Southwest Pacific Area 1942-1945. Brigadier general in February 1943. Reverted to colonel in July 1946. Retired in July 1952. Decorations included the Distinguished Service Medal. Died on January 4, 1965.

Alfonte, James Raymond (1886-1951) Born in Fortville, Indiana, on December 7, 1886. Attended Purdue. Commissioned in the infantry in October 1911. With the 7th Infantry in the Punitive Expedition to Mexico in 1914. Underwent flying training 1916-1917. Extensive duty with the Quartermaster Corps 1921-1945. Graduated from Command and General Staff School in 1930, the Army Industrial College in 1932 and the Army War College in 1938. Quartermaster at the Infantry School 1938-1942. Brigadier general in June 1942. Duty at headquarters of the quartermaster general 1942-1943. Commanding general of New Cumberland, Pennsylvania, Army Service Forces Depot 1943-1945. Commanding general of Utah Army Service Forces Depot 1945-1946. Retired in August 1946. Decorations included the Legion of Merit. Died in February 8, 1951.

Allen, Frank Albert Jr. (1896-1979) Born in Cleveland, Ohio, on June 19, 1896. Attended Kenyon College 1914-1917. Commissioned in the infantry reserve in August 1917. With the 77th Field Artillery in France during World War I, participating in the Aisne-Marne, St. Mihiel and Meuse-Argonne offensives. Professor of military science and tactics at Norwich University 1921-1923. Aide to Major General Dennis E. Nolan April 1926-July 1933. Graduated from Command and General Staff School in 1936 and the Army War College in 1940. Battalion and regimental commander in 5th Armored Division October 1941-August 1942. Commander of Combat Command "A" in 9th Armored Division August 1942-June 1943. Brigadier general in September 1942. Commander of Combat Command "B" in North Africa June 1943-July 1944. Chief of public relations at General Eisenhower's headquarters September 1944-July 1945. Commanding general of 3rd Armored Division July 1945-November 1945. Retired in November 1956. Decorations included the Distinguished Service Medal, Legion of Merit, three Silver Stars, the Distinguished Flying Cross, two Bronze Stars and two Purple Hearts. Died on November 20, 1979.

Allen, Harvey Clark (1888-1963) Born in Craftsburg, Vermont, on March 21, 1888. B.S. from the University of Vermont in 1909. Commissioned in the Coast Artillery Corps in September 1910. M.S. from Michigan State University in 1921. Graduated from Command and General Staff School in 1927 and the Army War College in 1928. With the War Department General Staff 1928-1932 and again 1935-1939. Brigadier general in October 1940. Commanded 33rd Coast Artillery Brigade February 1941-December 1941. Commander of Antiaircraft Artillery Training Center December 1941-November 1944. Retired in August 1945. Decorations included the Legion of Merit. Died on December 12, 1963.

Allen, Leven Cooper (1894-1979) Born in Fort Douglas, Utah, on March 29, 1894. Attended the University of San Francisco 1912-1916. Commissioned in the infantry in November 1916. Served in France during World War I. Graduated from Command and General Staff School in 1931 and the Army War College in

1935. With war plans division of the War Department General Staff May 1941-February 1942. Commandant of the Infantry School February 1942-October 1943. Brigadier general in January 1942, major general in September 1942. Chief of staff of First Army Group, renamed 12th Army Group, 1943-1945. Retired in 1951. Decorations included two Distinguished Service Medals, the Legion of Merit, Bronze Star and Purple Heart. Died on September 27, 1979.

Allen, Roderick R. (1894-1970) Born in Marshall, Texas, on January 29, 1894. B.S. from Agriculture and Mechanical College of Texas in 1915. Commissioned in the cavalry in November 1916. Served in France with 3rd Cavalry during World War I. Graduated from Command and General Staff School in 1928, the instructor there 1932-1934. Graduated from the Army War College in 1935 and the Naval War College in 1936. With War Department General Staff 1936-1940. Duty with 1st Armored Regiment, 3rd Armored Division, 32nd Armored Regiment, 6th Armored Division and 4th Armored Division July 1940-October 1943. Brigadier general in May 1942, major general in February 1944. Commanding general of 20th Armored Division October 1943-September 1944, then 12th Armored Division September 1944-August 1945 and 1st Armored Division August 1945-February 1946. Assignments after the war included commanding general of 3rd Armored Division 1948-1950, XVI Corps, then 9th Infantry Division 1951-1952. Retired in May 1954. Decorations included the two Distinguished Service Medals, the Silver Star, Legion of Merit and Bronze Star. Died on February 1, 1970.

Allen, Terry de la Mesa (1888-1969) Born on April 1, 1888, at Fort Douglas, Utah. Commissioned in the cavalry following graduation from Catholic University of America in 1912. Saw combat in World War I with the 358th Infantry of the 90th Division, earning the nickname "Terrible Terry" for his prowess. Graduated from Command and General Staff School in 1924 and the Army War College in 1935. Brigadier general in October 1940. Commanded the 3rd Cavalry Brigade 1940-1941 and 2nd Cavalry Division 1941-1942. Major general in June 1942. Allen was the only general in World War II to train and lead two different divisions: the 1st Infantry Division in the North African campaign in 1942 and the 104th Infantry Division in France 1944-1946. Retired in August 1946. Decorations included two Distinguished Service Medals, the Silver Star, Legion of Merit, Bronze Star and two Purple Hearts. Died on September 12, 1969.

Allen, Wayne Russell (1899-1975) Born in Denver, Colorado, on January 28, 1899. Enlisted service in the California National Guard 1915-1917. Commissioned in the infantry in December 1917. Served with the 5th, 159th, and 372nd Infantry in France during World War I. Returned to inactive status in October 1920. Recalled to active duty as colonel in 1941 with subsequent assignments in the Services of Supply in Washington, DC, and Europe. Brigadier general in September 1944. Released from active duty in March 1946. Decorations included the Distinguished Service Medal, Legion of Merit and Bronze Star. Died on December 6, 1975.

Allin, George R. (1880-1956) Born in Iowa City, Iowa, on February 15, 1880. Commissioned in the field artillery from West Point in 1904. Served briefly with the AEF in France during World War I. Graduated from Command and General Staff School in 1923 and the Army War College in 1924. Brigadier general in October 1940. Commandant of the Field Artillery School January 1941 until retirement in June 1942. Decorations included the Distinguished Service Medal and Legion of Merit. Died on June 2, 1956.

Almond, Edward Mallory (1892-1979) Born in Luray, Virginia, on December 12, 1892. B.S. from Virginia Military Institute in 1915. Commissioned in the infantry in 1916. Served with 4th Division in France during World War I, taking part in the Meuse-Argonne and Aisne-Marne offensives. Graduated from Command and General Staff School in 1930, the Army War College in 1934, and the Naval War College in 1940. Brigadier general in March 1942. Assistant division commander, then commanding general of 93rd Infantry Division March 1942-August 1945. Major general in September 1942. Assignments after the war included commanding general of 2nd Infantry Division September 1945-June 1946, X Corps in Korea August 1950-July 1951 and commandant of the Army War College July 1951-December 1952. Retired as lieutenant general in January 1953. Decorations included the Distinguished Service Cross, two Distinguished Service Medals, two Silver Stars, three Distinguished Flying Crosses, two Bronze Stars, sixteen Air Medals, three Commendation Ribbons and the Purple Heart. Died on June 11, 1979.

Althaus, Kenneth George (1893-n/a) Born in Cincinnati, Ohio, on June 13, 1893. Attended Queen City College. Commissioned in the 1st Infantry, Ohio National Guard in August 1916 and the Regular Army in July 1917. Professor of military science and tactics at Alabama Polytechnic Institute 1923-1927 and North Carolina State College 1935-1940. Graduated from Command and General Staff School in 1932. Instructor at field artillery School December 1941-October 1942. Assistant commander of Combat Command "E" October 1942-January 1943. Commanding officer of 11th Armored Regiment January 1943-June 1943. Brigadier general in June 1943. Combat commander "A" of 10th Armored Division June 1943-April 1945. Retired in March 1946. Decorations included the Bronze Star.

Anderson, John Benjamin (1891-1976) Born on March 10, 1891, in Waxabachie, Iowa. Commissioned in the field artillery from West Point in 1914. Served in France during World War I. Graduated from Command and General Staff School in 1925 and the Army War College in 1928. With the War Department General Staff 1928-1932. In the office of the chief of field artillery 1938-1941. Brigadier general in October 1941, major general August 1942. Commanding general of 102nd Infantry Division September 1942-December 1943. Commanding general of XVI Corps December 1943-October 1945. Retired in 1946. Decorations included the Distinguished Service Medal, Legion of Merit and Bronze Star. Died on September 1, 1976.

Anderson, Jonathan Waverly (1890-1967) Born in Lookout Mountain, Tennessee, on June 7, 1890. Commissioned from USNA in 1911. Served on active duty in the Navy, accepting a commission in the Regular Army in March 1912. Battalion commander in the 10th Field Artillery in France during World War I, taking part in the Champagne-Marne, Aisne-Marne and St. Mihiel offensives. Graduated from Command and General Staff School in 1925, the Army War College in 1930, and the Naval War College in 1938. With war plans division of the War Department General Staff 1938-1941. Brigadier general in July 1941. Artillery commander, then commanding general of 3rd Infantry Division July 1941-February 1943. Major general in March 1942. Commanded X Corps and I Corps 1943-1945. Retired in June 1950. Decorations included the Distinguished Service Medal, Silver Star and Legion of Merit. Died on June 15, 1967.

Andrus, Clift (1890-1968) Born in Fort Leavenworth, Kansas, on October 12, 1890. Commissioned in the field artillery in 1912. Graduated from Command and General Staff School in 1930, the Army War College in 1934, and the Naval War College in 1935. Duty with Hawaiian Department August 1941-March 1942. Brigadier general in May 1942. Commanding general of 1st Infantry Division Artillery May 1942-December 1944. Commanding general of 1st Infantry Division December 1944-May 1946. Major general in March 1945. Retired in October 1952. Decorations included the Distinguished Service Cross, Distinguished Service Medal, two Silver Stars, two Legions of Merit and two Bronze Stars. Died on September 30, 1968.

Ankcorn, Charles Morris (1893-1955) Born in Palouse, Washington, on September 11, 1893. Attended the University of Idaho and Ohio State University. Commissioned in the infantry in October 1917. Professor of military science and tactics at the State College of Washington 1924-1929. Graduated from Command and General Staff School in 1934. Commander of 157th Infantry Regiment September 1940-September 1943. Brigadier general in September 1943. Injured by a mine that month and returned to the U.S. in January 1944. Retired in December 1944. Decorations included the Distinguished Service Cross. Died on October 1, 1955.

Appleton, John Adams (1892-1966) Born in New York City on December 24, 1891. B.S. from Yale University in 1914. Employed by Locomobile Company of America and the Pennsylvania Railroad Company 1914-1917. Commissioned in the Corps of Engineers, Officers Reserve Corps, in September 1917 and in the Transportation Corps, Regular Army, in June 1918. Served with the AEF in France 1918-1919. Discharged in 1919 and rejoined Pennsylvania Railroad Company until 1942. Recalled to active duty with Army Service Forces in the China-Burma-India Theater of Operations and European Theater of Operations 1943-1945. Brigadier general in November 1944. Retired in 1946. Decorations included two Legions of Merit. Died on December 5, 1966.

Arms, Thomas Seelye (1893-1970) Born in Cleveland, Ohio, on March 22, 1893. B.S. from VMI in 1915. Commissioned in the infantry in 1916. Served in Tientsin, China 1921-1922. Graduated from Command and General Staff School in 1931. Instructor at the Infantry School 1931-1935 and Ohio National Guard 1935-1940. Commanding officer of 159th Infantry December 1941-October 1942. Instructor in India, then China November 1942-February 1945. Brigadier general in April 1943. Commanding general of Replacement and Training Command in 1945. Retired in September 1946. Decorations included the Legion of Merit. Died on September 30, 1970.

Armstrong, Clare Hibbs (1894-1969) Born in Albert Lea, Minnesota, on January 23, 1894. Commissioned in the infantry from West Point in 1917. Graduated from Command and General Staff School in 1936. Duty at West Point 1938-1942. Commanded the 109th Coast Artillery Group and 50th Antiaircraft Brigade May 1942-August 1945. Brigadier general in March 1943. Reverted to colonel in April 1946. Retired in March 1952. Decorations included the Distinguished Service Medal and two Bronze Stars. Died on July 12, 1969.

Armstrong, Donald (1889-1984) Born in Stapleton, New York, in April 1889. B.A. from Columbia in 1909, M.A. in 1910. Commissioned in the Coast Artillery Corps in September 1910. Served in France during World War I, taking part in Champagne and Meuse-Argonne offensives. Graduated from the Army Industrial College in 1927. Brigadier general in May 1942. Commanding general of Tank Automotive Center August 1942-December 1942. Commanding general of Ordnance Replacement Training Center December 1942-September 1944. Commandant of Army Industrial College September 1944 until retirement in October 1946. Decorations included the Distinguished Service Medal and Legion of Merit. Died on January 11, 1984.

Arnold, Archibald Vincent (1889-1973) Born in Collinsville, Connecticut, on February 24, 1889. Commissioned in the infantry from West Point in 1912, where he was an All-American football player. Graduated from Command and General Staff School in 1930 and the Army War College in 1935. Chief of staff of I Army Corps May 1941-September 1941. Brigadier general in September 1941. Commander of 69th field artillery Brigade, then Division Artillery, 44th Division September 1941-February 1943. Commander of 7th Infantry Division Artillery February 1943-February 1944. Major general in May 1944. Commanding general of 7th Infantry Division 1944-1946. Military governor of Korea 1945-1946. Retired in May 1948. Decorations included two Distinguished Service Medals, the Silver Star, Legion of Merit, Air Medal and Commendation Ribbon. Died on January 4, 1973.

Arnold, Calvert Hinton (1894-1963) Born in Swainsboro, Georgia, on November 23, 1894. B.S. from Mercer University in 1915, B.A. in 1922. Enlisted service with Georgia National Guard 1916-1917. Commissioned in the infantry in August 1917. Graduated from the Army Industrial College in 1927, the Command and

General Staff School in 1936, and the Army War College in 1938. Chief signal officer in the Netherlands East Indies, then Southwest Pacific Area January 1942-May 1943. Commandant of Central Signal Corps School June 1943-June 1945. Brigadier general in January 1945. Duty in office of the chief signal officer 1945-1949. Retired in October 1949. Decorations included the Legion of Merit. Died on May 18, 1963.

Arnold, William Howard (1901-1976) Born in Dyersburg, Tennessee, on January 18, 1901. Commissioned in the infantry from West Point in 1924. Served in Tientsin, China with 15th Infantry 1934-1936. Graduated from Command and General Staff School in 1938. Aide to Brigadier General Oscar W. Griswold 1940-1941. Deputy chief of staff, then deputy chief of staff of IV Corps February 1942-April 1943. Brigadier general in September 1943. Chief of staff of XIV Corps April 1943-November 1944. Major general in November 1944. Commanding general of the Americal Division November 1944-December 1945. Assignments after the war included commanding general of U.S. Forces Austria 1953-1955 and Fifth Army 1955-1961. Retired as lieutenant general in February 1961. Decorations included two Distinguished Service Medals, the Silver Star, two Legions of Merit and two Bronze Stars. Died on September 30, 1976.

Arnold, William Richard (1881-1965) Born in Wooster, Ohio, on June 10, 1881. B.A. from St. Joseph's College in 1908. Graduated from St. Bernard's Seminary and ordained a priest of the Roman Catholic Church in June 1908. Parish priest 1908-1913. Commissioned in the Chaplain Corps in May 1913. Duty as chaplain in U.S. and abroad 1913-1937. Chief of chaplains 1937-1945. Brigadier general in November 1941, major general in November 1944. Retired in June 1945. Decorations included the Distinguished Service Medal. Died on January 7, 1965.

Arrowsmith, John Caraway (1894-1985) Born in Reno, Nevada, on June 4, 1894. B.S. from Case School of Applied Science in 1917. Graduated from the Army Industrial College in 1930 and the Command and General Staff School in 1938. Commissioned in the Corps of Engineers in July 1918. Professor of military science and tactics at Carnegie Institute of Technology 1925-1929. Graduated from Army Industrial College in 1930. Graduated from the Command and General Staff School in 1938. Commander of 45th Engineers March 1942-January 1944. Brigadier general in June 1943. Reverted to colonel in January 1944 and retired in May 1953. Decorations included the Legion of Merit and Bronze Star. Died on June 1, 1985.

Augur, Wayland Bixby (1894-1982) Born in Detroit, Michigan, on March 5, 1894. B.S.from the University of California in 1916. Commissioned in the cavalry in August 1917. Instructor at Cavalry School 1929-1932. Graduated from Command and General Staff School in 1934, then instructor there 1935-1939. Chief of staff of 88th Infantry Division July 1942-December 1942. Brigadier general in December 1942. Commanding general of 56th Cavalry Brigade December 1942-

April 1944. Combat commander "B" of 13th Armored Division April 1944-February 1946. Reverted to colonel in February 1946. Retired in July 1953. Decorations included the Bronze Star and Commendation Ribbon. Died on February 4, 1982.

Aurand, Henry Spiese (1894-1980) Born on April 21, 1894, in Tamaqua, Pennsylvania. Commissioned in the Coast Artillery Corps from West Point in 1915. Graduated from Command and General Staff School in 1928, the Army War College in 1931 and the Army Industrial College in 1940. Brigadier general in January 1942, major general in September 1942. Commanding general of 6th Service Command 1942-1944. Deputy chief ordnance officer in the European Theater of Operations in 1944. Commanding general of Services of Supply in the China Theater of Operations in 1945. Assignments after the war included. commanding general of U.S. Army Pacific 1949 until retirement as lieutenant general in August 1952. Decorations included three Distinguished Service Medals and the Bronze Star. Died on June 18, 1980.

Avery, Ray Longfellow (1884-1965) Born on July 15, 1884, in Manchester, New Hampshire. Commissioned in the Coast Artillery Corps from West Point in 1908. Instructor at West Point 1912-1915. Duty with the 2nd Division of AEF in World War I, including the St. Mihiel campaign. Again instructor at West Point 1919-1921. Graduated from Command and General Staff School in 1932, the Army Industrial College in 1935 and the Army War College in 1936. Brigadier general in October 1940. Commander of Edgewood Arsenal, Maryland 1940-1946. Retired in July 1946. Decorations included the Distinguished Service Medal. Died on June 9, 1965.

Ayres, Leonard Porter (1879-1946) Born in Niantic, Connecticut, on September 15, 1879. B.A. from Boston University in 1902, M.A in 1909 and Ph.D. in 1910. Commissioned colonel as chief statistical officer of U.S. Army during World War I. He returned to various endeavors in Cleveland between the wars. Recalled to active duty in October 1940 as coordinator of statistics in the office of the under secretary of war. Brigadier general in July 1941. Duty with the Services of Supply until retirement in June 1942. The author of numerous books on economics 1905-1939. Decorations included the Distinguished Service Medal. Died on October 29, 1946.

Baade, Paul William (1889-1959) Born in Fort Wayne, Indiana, on April 16, 1889. Commissioned in the infantry from West Point in 1911. Served with the 322nd Infantry in France during World War I. Graduated from Command and General Staff School in 1924 and the Army War College in 1929. Staff officer, then commanding officer of 16th Infantry 1939-1941. Brigadier general in July 1941. Assistant division commander, then commanding general of 35th Infantry Division July 1942-December 1945. Major general in February 1943. Retired in September 1946. Decorations included the Distinguished Service Medal, two Silver Stars, three Bronze Stars and the Purple Heart. Died on October 9, 1959.

Babcock, Franklin (1885-1972) Born in Stonington, Connecticut, on August 11, 1885. Graduate of Rensselaer Polytechnic Institute in 1907. Commissioned in the Coast Artillery Corps in 1910. Served with the 51st Artillery in France in World War I, seeing action in St. Mihiel, Pont-a-Mousson and Aisne-Marne offensives. Graduated from Command and General Staff School in 1928 and the Army Industrial College in 1937. Chief of the investigations division, office of the inspector general, 1937-1941 and 1942-1946. Brigadier general in September 1944. Retired in August 1946. Decorations included the Distinguished Service Medal. Died on September 1, 1972.

Back, George Irving (1894-1972) Born on February 25, 1894, in Sioux City, Iowa. B.S. from Morningside College of Iowa in 1921. Commissioned in the Signal Corps in 1920. Graduated from Command and General Staff School in 1939. Signal officer at the Army War College 1941-1942 and Signal Corps headquarters in Washington 1942-1944. Brigadier general in June 1945. Deputy, then chief signal officer in the Mediterranean Theater of Operations August 1944-November 1945. Assignments after the war included chief signal officer of the U.S. Army 1951-1955. Retired as major general in June 1955. Decorations included two Distinguished Service Medals, the Silver Star and Legion of Merit. Died on September 28, 1972.

Badger, George Maurice (1897-1970) Born in Ohio Falls, Indiana, on August 14, 1897. Commissioned in the Coast Artillery Corps from West Point in 1918. Instructor at West Point 1929-1934. Graduated from Command and General Staff School in 1936 and the Army War College in 1940. Served with the personnel division of War Department General Staff October 1940-June 1942. At headquarters of Army Service Forces June 1942-September 1943. Commander of 62nd Antiaircraft Artillery Brigade September 1943-March 1944. Brigadier general in January 1944. Commanding general of 56th Antiaircraft Artillery Brigade March 1944-September 1945. Retired in June 1949. Decorations included two Legions of Merit and the Bronze Star. Died on September 23, 1970.

Baehr, Carl Adolph (1885-1959) Born in Minneapolis, Minnesota, on July 28, 1885. Commissioned in the infantry from West Point in 1909. Commanded a battalion of the 3rd Field Artillery in France during World War I. Graduated from Command and General Staff School in 1923 and the Army War College in 1926. Chief of staff of the Philippine Division 1938-1940. Commander of 71st Field Artillery Brigade April 1941-February 1944. Brigadier general in December 1941. Artillery commander of VI Corps 1944-1945. Retired in June 1946. Decorations included the Distinguished Service Medal, Silver Star, Legion of Merit and Bronze Star. Died on December 22, 1959.

Baer, Joseph Augustus (1878-1958) Born in Kutztown, Pennsylvania, on April 29, 1878. Commissioned in the cavalry from West Point in 1900. Served in the Boxer Rebellion 1900-1901. Instructor at West Point 1903-1907 and 1910-1915. Duty with inspector general of the AEF in World War I. Graduated from the

Army War College in 1921 and the Command and General Staff School in 1923. Military attache in Vienna 1929-1933. Acting chief of staff, then chief of staff of Second Service Command October 1940 until retirement on April 30, 1942. Recalled to active duty the following day in the same position. Brigadier general in April 1943. Retired again in January 1944. Decorations included the Distinguished Service Medal, Silver Star and Legion of Merit. Died on August 30, 1958.

Baird, Harry Howard (1893-1969) Born in Hurley, Wisconsin, on November 30, 1893. Enlisted service with Minnesota National Guard 1916-1917. Commissioned in the cavalry in 1917. Graduated from Command and General Staff School in 1934. Deputy chief of staff of U.S. Army forces in Australia 1942-1943. Brigadier general in November 1944. Deputy chief of staff of U.S. Army forces in the Far East 1943-1945. Commanding general of special troops, U.S. Army forces in the Pacific 1945-1946. Reverted to colonel in February 1946. Retired in March 1950 as brigadier general. Decorations included the Distinguished Service Medal, Legion of Merit and Purple Heart. Died on January 4, 1969.

Baird, Henry Welles (1881-1963) Born in Kent Island, Maryland, on August 13, 1881. Enlisted service with 15th Cavalry 1904-1907. Commissioned in the cavalry in 1907. Graduated from Command and General Staff School in 1923. Commanding officer of 1st Cavalry November 1938-October 1940. Brigadier general in October 1940, major general in July 1941. Commanding general of 4th Armored Division March 1941-May 1942 and again June 1942-November 1942. Retired as colonel in November 1942. Major general on the retired list in 1948. Died on October 10, 1963.

Baker, Walter Campbell (1877-1957) Born on September 22, 1877, in Chester, Pennsylvania. Enlisted service May-October 1898. Commissioned in the Artillery in 1901. Graduated from the Army War College in 1923 and Command and General Staff School in 1924. Commandant of the Chemical Warfare School 1927-1929. Major general in May 1937 as chief of the Chemical Warfare Service. Retired in April 1941. Recalled to active duty in June 1941 for duty in the office of the under secretary of war until March 1942. Thereafter with the War Production Board. Retired again in February 1944. Decorations included the Distinguished Service Medal. Died on February 20, 1957.

Baldwin, Geoffrey Prescott (1892-1951) Born in Madison Barracks, New York, on May 10, 1892. Commissioned in the infantry from West Point in 1916. Battalion commander in 60th Infantry in the St. Mihiel and Meuse-Argonne offensives in World War I. Graduated from Command and General Staff School in 1926 and the Army War College in 1928. Professor of military science and tactics at West Virginia University 1932-1936. Member of the Infantry Board at Fort Benning 1936-1940. Duty with supply division of the War Department General Staff May 1941-April 1942. Brigadier general in April 1942. Assistant division commander of 79th Division 1942-1943. Retired in 1943. Recalled to active duty with the War Department Board 1943-1946. Decorations included the Distinguished Service Cross, Silver Star and Commendation Ribbon. Died on August 25, 1951.

Balmer, Jesmond Dene (1895-1979) Born in Pullman, Washington, on March 30, 1895. Attended the University of Washington. Enlisted service with 346th Field Artillery September 1917-June 1918. Commissioned in the field artillery in 1918. Duty with 4th Field Artillery Brigade in World War I, including battles of St. Mihiel and Meuse-Argonne. Professor of military science and tactics at Purdue 1935-1936 and the University of Florida 1937-1938. Staff officer in operations division of the War Department General Staff March 1942-June 1942. Commandant of the Artillery School June 1942-January 1944. Artillery commander of XXI Corps January 1944-August 1945. Retired in January 1953. Served with the CIA 1953-1965. Decorations included the Distinguished Service Medal, Legion of Merit, Bronze Star and Commendation Ribbon. Died on November 24, 1979.

Bank, Carl Conrad (1889-1979) Born on October 13, 1889, in Donnellson, Iowa. Commissioned in the cavalry from West Point in 1915. With 76th Field Artillery of the 3rd Division in France in World War I, participating in the Champagne-Marne and Aisne-Marne campaigns. Graduated from Command and General Staff School in 1931. Professor of military science and tactics at the University of Utah 1935-1939. Duty with the Hawaii Department 1940-1941. Artillery officer of I Corps, then Allied Forces Headquarters, North Africa Theater of Operations 1941-1944. Brigadier general in May 1944. Commanding general of 13th Field Artillery Brigade 1944-1945. Reverted to colonel in March 1946 and retired in September 1947. Brigadier general on the retired list in 1948. Decorations included two Legions of Merit. Died on January 20, 1979.

Barber, Henry Anson Jr. (1896-1956) Born in Fort Reno, Oklahoma, on July 31, 1896. Commissioned in the infantry from West Point in 1917. Saw action in the Marne and St. Mihiel offensives and operations along the Vesle River in World War I. Served with 15th Infantry at Tientsin 1927-1928. Graduated from Command and General Staff School in 1933 and the Army War College in 1937. Military attache in Cuba 1938-1941. With the war plans division of the War Department General Staff July 1941-May 1943. Assistant division commander of 65th Infantry Division, then 4th Infantry Division, May 1943-January 1944. Brigadier general in September 1943. Deputy commander of Chinese Combat Command January-May 1945. Retired in December 1949. Decorations included the Distinguished Service Cross and Legion of Merit. Died on April 29, 1956.

Barkalow, Russell Gilbert (1893-n/a) Born in Wapakoneta, Ohio, on December 7, 1893. Attended Ohio State University. Enlisted service in the Ohio National Guard 1916-1917. Commissioned in the field artillery, Regular Army, in 1920. Graduated from Command and General Staff School in 1936. Professor of military science and tactics at the University of Nebraska 1936-1940. Executive officer of 7th Division Artillery October 1940-February 1941. With Fourth Army, then headquaarters of Army Ground Forces until May 1942. Brigadier general in April 1942. Commanding general of 74th Field Artillery Brigade May 1942-December 1942. Artillery commander of 87th Infantry Division December 1942-March 1944. Reverted to lieutenant colonel in March 1944. Retired in July 1951 as colonel.

Barker, Ray Wehnes (1889-1974) Born on December 10, 1889, in New York City. Enlisted service with the 15th Cavalry 1910-1913. Commissioned in the cavalry in 1913. Served with the Punitive Expedition into Mexico 1916-1917. Transferred to the field artillery and accompanied the 13th Field Artillery to France in World War I, taking part in the Marne-Vesle and Meuse-Argonne offensives. Graduated from Command and General Staff School in 1928 and the Army War College in 1940. Commanding officer of 31st Field Artillery June 1940-April 1941 and 30th Field Artillery June 1941-April 1942. Brigadier general in July 1942. Deputy chief of staff, then assistant chief of staff of European Theater of Operations 1942-1945. Major general in June 1943. Retired in February 1947. Decorations included the Distinguished Service Medal, Legion of Merit and Bronze Star. Died on June 1, 1974.

Barnes, Gladeon Marcus (1887-1961) Born in Vermontsville, Michigan, on June 15, 1887. B.C.E. from the University of Michigan in 1910. Commissioned in the Coast Artillery Corps in 1910. Graduated from the Army Industrial College in 1936 and the Army War College in 1938. Involved in the design, testing and implementation of numerous artillery weapons and ordnance 1910-1936. Brigadier general in October 1940, major general in March 1943. Chief of research and engineering, then chief of the research and development service, office of the chief of ordnance 1938-1946. Retired in April 1946. Decorations included the Distinguished Service Medal. Died on November 15, 1961.

Barnes, Harold Arthur (1887-1953) Born in Oneida, New York, on August 7, 1887. Enlisted service with 74th Company, Coast Artillery Corps 1908-1917. Commissioned in the Quartermaster Corps in 1917. Executive to the quartermaster general for civilian personnel affairs December 1940-April 1942. Chief of the organized planning and control division April 1942-March 1943. Brigadier general in April 1943. Deputy quartermaster general March 1943 until retirement in February 1946 as colonel. Brigadier general on the retired list in June 1948. Decorations included the Distinguished Service Medal. Died on August 7, 1953.

Barnes, Julian Francis (1889-1961) Born in Washington, DC, on October 14, 1889. Commissioned in the field artillery in 1912. Graduated from Command and General Staff School in 1925 and the Army War College in 1930. Executive officer of 4th Division Artillery October 1940-February 1941. Commanding officer of 35th Field Artillery February 1941-December 1941. Brigadier general in September 1941. At headquarters of Army Ground Forces in 1942. Major general in January 1942. Artillery commander of 97th Infantry Division February 1943-July 1944. Commander of 61st Field Artillery Brigade July 1944-January 1946. Commanding general of 153rd Field Artillery Group for one month then reverted to colonel in February 1946. Retired in October 1947 as colonel. Major general on the retired list in 1948. Decorations included the Bronze Star. Died on December 23, 1961.

Barnett, Allison Joseph (1892-1971) Born in Kentucky, on April 2, 1892. Attended Hartford College and the University of Kentucky. Enlisted service with Kentucky National Guard 1907-1913. Commissioned in the infantry in 1920. Graduated from Command and General Staff School in 1933. Executive officer of the Infantry Replacement Training Center, Camp Croft December 1940-August 1941. Served with Air Support Command of GHQ Air Force August 1941-May 1942. Brigadier general in July 1942. Assistant division commander of 93rd Infantry Division July 1942-December 1942. Chief of staff of U.S. forces in the South Pacific Area December 1942-August 1944. Major general in January 1944. Commanding general of 70th Infantry Division August 1944-August 1945 and the 94th Division August 1945-January 1946. Retire in October 1947. Decorations included the Distinguished Service Medal, Legion of Merit and Bronze Star. Died on October 7, 1971.

Barnett, James Washington (1892-1983) Born in Clinton, Alaska, on October 15, 1892. Enlisted service 1914-1916. Commissioned in the cavalry in 1916. With Services of Supply in France May 1918-July 1919. Graduated from Command and General Staff School in 1927. Instructor at Cavalry School 1927-1931 and 1932-1934, then Command and General Staff School 1934-1936. Graduated from the Army War College 1936, then instructor there 1937-1940. Aide to Lieutenant General John L. DeWitt November 1940-July 1941. Supply officer, then deputy chief of staff and finally chief of staff of Western Defense Command July 1941-October 1943. Assistant division commander of 93rd Division October 1943-January 1945. Commander of U.S. Army forces on New Caledonia January-October 1945. Reverted to colonel in February 1946 and retired in June 1949 as brigadier general. Decorations included the Distinguished Service Medal and Legion of Merit. Died on April 17, 1983.

Barnwell, Charles Heyward Jr. (1894-n/a) Born in Dalton, Georgia, on November 17, 1894. Graduated from the University of Alabama in 1915. Commissioned in the infantry in 1917. Assistant inspector general of VI Corps Area, February 1941-January 1942. Inspector general at headquarters of Services of Supply in the Southwest Pacific Area, January 1942-February 1943. Inspector general at headquarters U.S. Army Forces Far East February 1943-June 1945. Reverted to colonel in February 1946. Retired in June 1952 as brigadier general. Decorations included the Distinguished Service Medal and two Legions of Merit.

Barr, David Goodwin (1895-1970) Born in Myrtlewood, Alabama, on June 16, 1895. Attended Alabama Presbyterian College. Graduated from Command and General Staff School in 1936 and the Army War College in 1939. Commissioned in the infantry reserve in 1917. Saw action in France with the 18th Infantry, 1st

Division 1918-1919. With Washington Provisional Brigade 1936-1938 and again 1939-1940. Executive officer to the supply officer, then supply officer of I Armored Corps July 1940-June 1942. Brigadier general in June 1942. Chief of staff of the Armored Force June 1942-July 1943. Chief of staff at headquarters of North African Theater of Operations January-September 1944. Major general in February 1944. Chief of staff of Sixth Army Group September 1944-July 1945. Chief of personnel for Army Ground Forces July 1945-January 1948. Assignments after the war included commanding general of 7th Infantry Division May 1949-February 1951 and the Armored Center, Fort Knox February 1951 until retirement in February 1952. Decorations included the Distinguished Service Cross, three Distinguished Service Medals, two Silver Stars, the Legion of Merit and Distinguished Flying Cross. Died on September 26, 1970.

Barrett, Charles Joseph (1900-1963) Born in South Orange, New Jersey, on February 15, 1900. Enlisted service July 1917-November 1918. Commissioned in the Corps of Engineers from West Point in 1922. Instructor at West Point 1928-1931. Graduated from Command and General Staff School in 1937. Instructor at West Point again 1937-1941. With the War Department General Staff 1941-1942. Chief of staff, then artillery commander of 84th Infantry Division 1944-1945. Brigadier general in March 1945. Professor at West Point 1947-1963. Retired in 1963. Decorations included the Silver Star, Legion of Merit and Bronze Star. Died on June 30, 1963.

Barron, William Andros Jr. (1892-1964) Born on December 16, 1892, at Newburyport, Massachusetts. B.A. from Harvard in 1914. Commissioned in the field artillery, Officers Reserve Corps in 1917. Duty with 303rd Field Artillery in the AEF July 1918-April 1919, including Meuse-Argonne offensive. Resigned in 1926. Returned to active duty as lieutenant colonel, General Staff Corps, in June 1942. Assigned to headquarters of First Service Command 1942-1943, then chief of staff 1943-1945. Brigadier general in November 1944. Returned to inactive status after the war. Decorations included the Legion of Merit. Died on September 29, 1964.

Barth, Charles Henry Jr. (1903-1943) Born on October 1, 1903, in Leavenworth, Kansas. Commissioned in the Corps of Engineers from West Point in 1925. Graduated from Command and General Staff School in 1940. Duty with the War Department General Staff November 1942-February 1943. Chief of staff of the European Theater of Operations February 1943-May 1943. Brigadier general in March 1943. Killed in an airplane accident in Iceland on May 3, 1943. Decorations included the Distinguished Service Medal and Legion of Merit.

Barton, Raymond Oscar (1889-1963) Born in Granada, Colorado, on August 22, 1889. Commissioned in the infantry from West Point in 1912. Graduated from Command and General Staff School in 1924 and the Army War College in 1933. Instructor at the Command and General Staff School 1928-1932. Professor of military science and tactics at Georgetown University 1933-1937. Chief of staff of

4th Division July 1940-October 1941, then IV Corps October 1941-June 1942. Brigadier general in March 1942, major general in August 1942. Commanding general of 4th Infantry Division June 1942-March 1945. Head of infantry training March 1945 until retirement in February 1946. Decorations included two Distinguished Service Medals, the Silver Star, Bronze Star and Commendation Ribbon. Died on February 27, 1963.

Barzynski, Joseph Edward (1884-1972) Born in St. Paul, Nebraska, on March 13, 1884. Commissioned in the infantry from West Point in 1905. With the Punitive Expedition into Mexico 1916-1917. Quartermaster of 32nd Division in France during World War I. Graduated from Command and General Staff School in 1933. Duty in the office of the quartermaster general 1936-1941. Brigadier general in August 1940. Commander of Chicago Quartermaster Depot October 1941 until retirement in July 1944. Decorations included the Legion of Merit. Died on August 11, 1972.

Bastion, Joseph Edward (1883-1971) Born in Pittsfield, Massachusetts, on March 27, 1883. M.D. from Georgetown University in 1906. Graduated from Army Medical School in 1909. Commissioned in the medical reserve in July 1908. Served with the Punitive Expeditionary Force in Mexico in 1916. Graduated from Command and General Staff School in 1924 and the Army War College in 1929. Surgeon for VI Corps Area 1940-1943. Brigadier general in June 1943. Commander of Percy Jones General Hospital 1943 until retirement in February 1947. Decorations included the Distinguished Service Medal and Legion of Merit. Died on January 1, 1971.

Bathurst, Robert Marks (1893-1964) Born on August 28, 1893, in Huntington, Pennsylvania. Commissioned in the field artillery from West Point in 1917. Commanded 2nd and 1st Battalions, 3rd Field Artillery, AEF 1918-1919. Graduated from Command and General Staff School in 1931. Battalion commander with the 25th Infantry in Hawaii 1939-1942. Chief of staff of Western Defense Command 1943-1944. Brigadier general in June 1944. Chief of staff of the Alaskan Department 1944-1946. Retired in 1953. Decorations included two Legions of Merit and two Commendation Ribbons. Died on April 15, 1964.

Battley, Joseph Franklin (1893-1970) Born in Norfolk, Virginia, on December 19, 1893. Enlisted service with Virginia National Guard 1917-1918. Commissioned in the engineer reserve in May 1918. Active duty in Chemical Warfare Service 1920-1938, then assignments in Selective Service and Army Service Forces. Served in the office of the under secretary of war 1940-1942. Chief of the service command division at headquarters of Army Service Forces 1942-1943. Deputy chief of staff for service commands 1943-1945. Brigadier general in February 1944. Head of public relations for Army Service Forces 1945-1947. Retired in July 1947. Decorations included the Distinguished Service Medal and Legion of Merit. Died on December 18, 1970.

Baylis, James Ernest (1884-1964) Born in Estabuchie, Mississippi, on March 20, 1884. B.S. from Mississippi A&M in 1905 and M.D. from Tulane in 1910. Graduated from Army Medical School in 1912. Commissioned in the Medical Corps in 1912. Graduated from Command and General Staff School in 1927 and the Army War College in 1931. Staff officer, later commanding officer of Medical Replacement Training Center, Camp Robinson December 1941-September 1943. Brigadier general in February 1942. Commanding general of Medical Replacement Centers at Camp Grant and Fort Lewis September 1943-February 1945. Theater surgeon for the China-Burma-India Theater of Operations February 1945-November 1945. Chief surgeon of Seventh Army November 1945 until retirement in October 1947. Decorations included two Legions of Merit. Died on July 3, 1964.

Bayne-Jones, Stanhope (1888-1970) Born in New Orleans, Louisiana, on November 6, 1888. A.B. from Yale in 1910 and M.D. from Johns Hopkins in 1914. Professor, then dean of Yale Medical School 1932-1942. Called to active duty in the office of the surgeon general, U.S. Army, 1942-1946. Brigadier general in February 1944. Returned to inactive status in 1946. Decorations included the Distinguished Service Medal and three Silver Stars. Died in Washington on February 20, 1970.

Beach, George Corwin Jr. (1888-1948) Born in Topeka, Kansas, on October 28, 1888. M.D. from Kansas City University Medical College in 1911. Graduated from Army Medical School in 1917. Commissioned in the Medical Corps in 1917. Commanding officer of station hospital at Fort Sam Houston July 1941-November 1942. Brigadier general in April 1943. Commanding general of Brooke Medical Center, Fort Sam Houston November 1942-February 1946. Commanding general of Walter Reed Army Medical Center at his death on November 18, 1948. Decorations included the Distinguished Service Medal and Legion of Merit.

Beasley, Rex Webb (1892-1961) Born on October 16, 1892, in Linden, Tennessee. Commissioned in the field artillery from West Point in 1917. Personnel officer at headquarters of AEF then duty with 1st Division at the second Marne offensive, St. Mihiel and Meuse-Argonne in World War I. Graduated from Command and General Staff School in 1933 and the Army War College in 1934. Chief of the materiel section in the office of the chief of field artillery July 1938-March 1942. Brigadier general in April 1942. Served at headquarters of Army Ground Forces in 1942. Commanding general of 81st Infantry Division Artillery 1942-1945. In the military government office on the staff of Eighth Army 1945-1947. Retired as major general in October 1952. Decorations included the Silver Star, two Legions of Merit and the Purple Heart. Died on February 26, 1961.

Beebe, Lewis C. (1891-1951) Born in Ashton, Iowa, on December 7, 1891. Commissioned in the Coast Artillery Corps, Oregon National Guard in 1916. Served with the 30th Infantry in the AEF, participating in the Aisne, Champagne-Marne, Aisne-Marne, St. Mihiel and Meuse-Argonne offensives. Instructor at the

Infantry School 1927-1930. Graduated from Command and General Staff School in 1932. Professor of military science and tactics at Shattuck School (Minnesota) 1932-1938. Graduated from the Army War College in 1939. In the Philippines as a battalion commander, staff officer at the Philippine Department, assistant chief of staff for supply under General MacArthur and chief of staff of U.S. forces under General Wainwright 1940-1942. Brigadier general in March 1942. Taken prisoner of war on May 6, 1942 and liberated on August 27, 1945. Retired in September 1950. Decorations included the Distinguished Service Cross, Distinguished Service Medal and Purple Heart. Died on February 17, 1951.

Beiderlinden, William Arthur (1895-1981) Born in Springfield, Missouri, on March 4, 1895. B.S. from Drury College in 1917. Commissioned in the field artillery in 1917. With the AEF in France December 1917-March 1919. Graduated from Command and General Staff School in 1939. Staff officer with 4th Motorized Division June 1940-May 1942. Deputy chief of staff of X Corps May 1942-February 1943. Brigadier general in March 1943. Artillery commander of 44th Infantry Division February 1943-November 1945. Retire as major general in June 1955. Decorations included the Distinguished Service Medal, Legion of Merit and Bronze Star. Died on April 12, 1981.

Bell, Marcus Brenneman (1893-1981) Born in Fredonia, Kansas, on February 22, 1893. B.S. from University of Missouri in 1916. Enlisted service with Maryland National Guard 1916-1917. Commissioned in the infantry, Regular Army in 1917. Professor of military science and tactics at Lehigh University 1921-1924. Graduated from Command and General Staff School in 1934. Instructor at the Infantry School 1934-1938. Mobilization officer for V Corps Area 1940-1941. Assistant to the assistant chief of staff for supply, War Department General Staff in 1941. Chief of staff of 80th Infantry Division in 1942. Brigadier general in December 1942. Assistant division commander of 81st Infantry Division December 1942-January 1946. Reverted to colonel in February 1946. Retired as brigadier general in October 1951. Decorations included the Silver Star and two Legions of Merit. Died on May 18, 1981.

Benedict, Jay Leland (1882-1953) Born in Hastings, Nebraska, on April 14, 1882. Enlisted service in Nebraska National Guard 1898-1899. Commissioned in the field artillery from West Point in 1904. Instructor at West Point 1908-1912 and 1916-1917. With the War Department General Staff 1920-1924. Graduated from Command and General Staff School in 1925 and the Army War College in 1926. Returned to the War Department General Staff 1926-1930. Brigadier general in January 1938. Superintendent of West Point 1938-1940. Major general in September 1940. Commanding general of IV Corps 1940-1941. Again with the War Department General Staff 1942-1946. Retired in April 1946. Decorations included the Distinguished Service Medal and Legion of Merit. Died in September 16, 1953.

Bergin, William Edward (1892-1978) Born in Pueblo, Colorado, on May 18, 1892. Attended Benedictine College 1905-1908 and St. Mary's College 1908-1910. Commissioned in the infantry in 1917. Duty with 20th Infantry 1917-1919. Professor of military science and tactics at Georgetown University 1921-1925. Graduated from Command and General Staff School in 1934. Adjutant general at III Army Corps December 1940-February 1942. Chief of staff of headquarters detachment, Chinese Training and Combat Command in the China-Burma-India Theater of Operations 1942-1945. Brigadier general in March 1943. Duty at Army Ground Forces, then with Tenth Army at Okinawa in 1945. Assignments after the war included the adjutant general, U.S. Army July 1951 until retirement in March 1954. Decorations included the Distinguished Service Medal and Legion of Merit. Died on January 23, 1978.

Berry, Robert Ward (1902-1960) Born on March 20, 1902, in Hackensack, New Jersey. Commissioned in the Coast Artillery Corps from West Point in 1924. Instructor there 1928-1932 and again 1936-1939. Graduated from Command and General Staff School in 1940. In the personnel division of the War Department General Staff 1940-1944. Brigadier general in November 1944. Commanding general of 76th Antiaircraft Artillery Brigade 1945-1946. Commanding general of the 1st Region, U.S. Army Air Defense Command at his death on April 1, 1960. Decorations included the Distinguished Service Medal and Legion of Merit.

Bessell, William Weston Jr. (1901-1977) Born on May 17, 1901 in San Juan, Puerto Rico. Commissioned in the Corps of Engineers from West Point in 1920. Graduated from Command and General Staff School in 1940. In the office of the chief of engineers 1940-1942. With the War Deparement General Staff 1942-1946. Brigadier general in May 1944. Dean of the Academic Board at West Point 1959 at his retirement in 1965. Decorations included two Distinguished Service Medals and the Legion of Merit. Died on January 13, 1977.

Besson, Frank S. Jr. (1910-1985) Born on May 30, 1910, in Detroit, Michigan. Commissioned in the Corps of Engineers from West Point in 1932. M.S. from Massachusetts Institute of Technology in 1935. With the Military Railroad Service in the Persian Gulf Theater of Operations, then the Western Pacific 1943-1946. Brigadier general in January 1945. Assignments after the war included chief of the Transportation Corps 1958-1962 and commanding general of Army Materiel Command 1962-1969. Retired as general in 1970. Decorations included three Distinguished Service Medals, two Legions of Merit and the Commendation Ribbon. Died on July 15, 1985.

Bethea, James Albertus (1887-1984) Born on October 30, 1887, in Marion County, South Carolina. M.D. from Tulane in 1913. Commissioned in the Medical Reserve Corps in 1915. Director of field hospital in 4th Division, AEF in World War I. Chief of surgical services at Fort Sam Houston Hospital 1940-1942. Commander of McCloskey General Hospital, Temple, Texas 1942-1946. Brigadier general in November 1943. Commanding general of Brooks General Hospital

1946-1948. Major general in April 1948. Chief surgeon of Far East Command 1948-1949. Retired in October 1949. Decorations included the Legion of Merit. Died on November 6, 1984.

Betts, Edward C. (1890-1946) Born in Alabama on June 9, 1890. LL.B. from the University of Alabama in 1911. Commissioned in the infantry in 1917. With 47th Division, AEF 1918-1919. Professor of law at West Point 1938-1942. Judge advocate of the European Theater of Operations April 1942 until his death there on May 6, 1946. Brigadier general in September 1943. Decorations included the Legion of Merit and Bronze Star

Betts, Thomas Jeffries (1894-1977) Born in Baltimore, Maryland, on June 14, 1894. B.S. from the University of Virginia in 1916. Commissioned in the Coast Artillery Corps in 1917. Served with the 49th Artillery, AEF in 1918. In the military intelligence division at the War Department General Staff 1929-1933 and again 1938-1943. Brigadier general in November 1943. Deputy assistant chief of staff for intelligence at SHAEF 1943-1945. Chief intelligence officer at the Bikini atomic tests 1946. Reverted to colonel in April 1946. Retired as brigadier general in July 1953. Decorations included the Distinguished Service Medal, Bronze Star and Purple Heart. Died on May 23, 1977.

Beyette, Hubert Ward (1891-1968) Born in Texas on September 21, 1891. Commissioned in the Quartermaster Corps in 1917. Subsistence officer for the 1st Replacement Depot, AEF 1918-1919. Quartermaster supply officer at Memphis General Depot March 1942-July 1942. Commander of Schenectady General Depot July 1942-January 1945. Brigadier general in September 1943. Special assistant to the director of supply at Army Service Forces January-August 1945. Chief of graves registration in the office of the quartermaster general in 1945. Retired in October 1946. Decorations included the Legion of Merit. Died on July 8, 1968.

Bickelhaupt, Carroll Owen (1888-1954) Born in Roscoe, South Dakota, on December 15, 1888. B.S. from the University of Wisconsin in 1911. With AT&T and Southern Bell 1911-1930 except for service with the Signal Corps in World War I. Called to active duty as colonel in 1941. Director of communications, then chief signal officer for the Europen Theater of Operations, then the U.S. military government in Germany 1941 until 1949, when he went inactive. Brigadier general in August 1944. Decorations included the Distinguished Service Medal, Legion of Merit, Bronze Star and Commendation Ribbon. Died on May 6, 1954.

Birks, Hammond Davies (1896-1973) Born in Chicago, Illinois on February 5, 1896. Attended the University of Chicago 1915-1917. Commissioned in the infantry, Officers Reserve Corps in 1917. Participated in battle of St. Mihiel in World War I. Graduated from Command and General Staff School in 1940. Commanding officer of the reception center at Fort Custer 1940-1941. Commander of 120th Infantry Combat Team, 30th Infantry Division 1942-1944. Assistant division commander of 9th Division November 1944-June 1945. Brigadier general in

January 1945. Commanding general of the War Department Personnel Center June 1945 until retirement in November 1946. Decorations included the Silver Star, Legion of Merit, Bronze Star and Purple Heart. Died on January 30, 1973.

Bissell, John Ter Bush (1893-1976) Born on November 18, 1893, in Allegheny, Pennsylvania. B.A. from Hamilton College in 1914. Commissioned in the infantry from West Point in 1917. Served with the 7th Machine Gun Battalion, AEF at the Aisne defense and Chateau-Thierry campaign 1917-1918. Attended the Ecole d'Application d'Artillerie in France 1920-1921. Instructor, then assistant professor at West Point 1924-1928. Aide-de-camp to Major General Fred W. Sladen 1929-1931. Graduated from Command and General Staff School in 1933. Assistant professor of military science and tactics at Princeton July 1936-September 1939. Graduated from the Army War College in 1940. In the counterintelligence branch at the War Department General Staff 1940-1943. Commanding officer of 112th Field Artillery Group in 1943. Executive officer, then commander of XXI Corps Artillery in 1944. Brigadier general in November 1944. Commanding general of 89th Division Artillery December 1944-August 1945. Retired in February 1946. Decorations included the Silver Star, Legion of Merit and Bronze Star. Died on July 14, 1976.

Bixby, Ernest Aaron (1899-1965) Born on February 22, 1899, in North Charlestown, New Hampshire. Commissioned in the field artillery from West Point in 1919. Assistant professor of military science and tactics at Princeton 1926-1928. Instructor with the organized reserves in Kentucky 1928-1931 then at West Point 1934-1936. Graduated from Command and General Staff School in 1937. Again assistant professor of military science and tactics at Princeton 1937-1939. Graduated from the Army Industrial College in 1940. Duty in the office of the assistant secretary of war in 1941. In the operations division at the War Department General Staff 1941-1942. Assistant chief of staff for operations at Army Ground Forces 1942-1943. Commanding officer of 4th Armored Division Artillery March 1943-September 1944. Brigadier general in November 1944. Commanding general of 90th Division Artillery 1944-1945 then the Army Personnel Center at Camp Atterbury 1945-1946. Reverted to colonel in February 1946. Retired as brigadier general in November 1955. Decorations included three Silver Stars, the Legion of Merit and two Bronze Stars. Died on March 1, 1965.

Black, Frederick Harry (1894-1986) Born in Meadville, Missouri, on April 17, 1894. Commissioned in the field artillery in 1917. Instructor at the School of Fire 1918-1920 and the Field Artillery School 1932-1936. Graduated from Command and General Staff School in 1939. Instructor with the New York National Guard 1939-1941. In the supply division at the War Department General Staff 1941-1942. Commander of 26th Infantry Division Artillery 1942-1943, then 99th Infantry Division Artillery 1943-1945. Brigadier general in September 1944. Commanding general of Infantry Replacement Training Center at Camp Blanding November 1945-February 1946. Reverted to colonel in February 1946. Retired in

June 1950. Decorations included the Silver Star, Legion of Merit and two Bronze Stars. Died on July 2, 1986.

Black, Garland Cuzorte (1894-1951) Born in Dayton, Ohio, on November 14, 1894. B.S. from the University of Missouri in 1917. Commissioned in the cavalry in 1917. With 12th Cavalry at Columbus, New Mexico in 1918. Graduated from Command and General Staff School in 1937. Instructor at the Signal School 1937-1941. Executive officer at the Army War College 1941-1942. Signal officer for Second Army March 1942-December 1942. Ground signal officer at the Army War College 1942-1943. Chief of the signal section at Army Ground Forces 1943-1944. Signal officer for First Army Group, then Twelfth Army Group 1944-1945. Brigadier general in January 1945. Commander of Army Service Forces Training Center 1945 until retirement in September 1946. Decorations included the Legion of Merit. Died on January 23, 1951.

Blackmore, Philip Guillou (1890-1974) Born in Bristol, Virginia, on January 18, 1890. B.S. from Virginia Military Institute in 1911. Commissioned in the Coast Artillery Corps in 1911. Served in Hawaii 1916-1919. Assistant professor of military science and tactics at Yale 1920-1921. Member of the Infantry Board 1931-1936. Graduated from Command and General Staff School in 1937. Ordnance officer at headquarters of VII Corps Area, then IX Corps Area 1940-1941. Ordnance officer at Third Army, then Sixth Army 1941-1947. Brigadier general in September 1944. Commanding general of White Sands Proving Ground August 1947 until retirement in January 1950. Decorations included the Distinguished Service Medal, Legion of Merit and Bronze Star. Died on April 7, 1974.

Blakeley, Harold Whittle (1893-1966) Born in Malden, Massachusetts, on December 29, 1893. Attended Boston University 1915-1917. Commissioned in the field artillery in 1917. Graduated from Command and General Staff School in 1936. Instructor at the Field Artillery School 1936-1938. Graduated from the Army War College in 1939. Instructor at the Command and General Staff School 1939-1940. Commander of 6th Field Artillery 1940-1941. Commander of 5th Armored Division Artillery 1941-1942. Brigadier general in June 1942. Commanding general of Combat Command "A," 5th Armored Division 1942-1943. Commanding general of 4th Infantry Division Artillery, then 4th Infantry Division 1944-1946. Major general in March 1945. Retired in April 1946. Decorations included the Silver Star, Legion of Merit and Bronze Star. Died on May 10, 1966.

Blakelock, David Hazen (1895-1975) Born in Washington, DC, on June 1, 1895. Commissioned in the District of Columbia National Guard in 1917 and the Cavalry in 1918. Served with the 17th Cavalry in Hawaii 1919-1922. Graduated from Command and General Staff School in 1928 and the Army War College in 1936. Commanding officer of Services of Supply Force 51 in Washington, DC 1942-1943. Held logistical assignments in the South Pacific Area and Pacific Ocean Area 1943-1945. Brigadier general in Janaury 1945. With the readjustment division of Army Service Forces 1945-1946. Retired in June 1950. Decorations included the Distinguished Service Medal and three Legions of Merit. Died on May 26, 1975.

Bledsoe, William Pinckney (1892-1972) Born in Beulah, Alabama, on April 22, 1892. Attended Howard College. Commissioned in the field artillery reserve in 1917. Served with the 6th Field Artillery, AEF at Toul and Soissons 1918-1919. Commissioned in the field artillery, Regular Army, in 1920. Professor of military science and tactics at the University of Utah 1924-1928. Graduated from Command and General Staff School in 1935 and the Army War College in 1938. Instructor at the Command and General Staff School 1938-1941. Battalion commander in, then chief of staff of 25th Infantry Division, Hawaii October 1941-1945. Brigadier general in June 1943. Retired in June 1946. Decorations included the Legion of Merit, Bronze Star and Purple Heart. Died on October 1, 1972.

Blesse, Frederick Arthur (1888-1954) Born in Illinois on November 12, 1888. M.D. from Hahnemann College in 1913. Commissioned in the Medical Section in 1918. Graduated from Army Medical School in 1925. Instructor at Medical Field Service School 1926-1930. Graduated from Command and General Staff School in 1932 and the Army War College in 1936. Medical advisor to MacArthur while he was military advisor to the Philippine government 1936-1939. Surgeon at 3rd Division 1939-1940. In the support section of the War Department General Staff 1940-1941. Chief of planning and research in the office of the chief of the War Department morale branch in 1941. Chief surgeon for Army Ground Forces 1941-1942. Brigadier general in December 1942. Chief surgeon for Fifth Army and the North African Theater of Operations 1943-1944. Chief surgeon for Army Ground Forces, then Army Field Forces April 1944 until retirement in November 1948. Decorations included the Distinguished Service Medal and Legion of Merit. Died on June 4, 1954.

Bliss, Raymond Whitcomb (1888-1965) Born in Chelsea, Massachusetts, on May 17, 1888. M.D. from Tufts College in 1910. Commissioned in the Medical Reserve Corps in 1911. Graduated from Army Medical School in 1913. Military observer in London 1940-1941. Commanding officer of Fort Sill hospital in 1941. Surgeon for the Eastern Defense Command 1942-1943. Chief of operations service in the office of the surgeon general 1943-1944. Brigadier general in September 1943. Deputy surgeon general of the Army January 1945-June 1947. Assignments after the war included surgeon general of the Army June 1947 until retirement in June 1951. Decorations included the Distinguished Service Medal and Legion of Merit. Died on December 12, 1965.

Blood, Kenneth Thompson (1888-1979) Born in Petterell, Massachusetts, on February 6, 1888. B.S. from Massachusetts Institute of Technology in 1909. Commissioned in the Coast Artillery Corps in 1911. Duty at the Torpedo School 1916-1919. In the Philippine Islands 1921-1924. Graduated from Command and General Staff School in 1927. Instructor at the Coast Artillery Corps School 1931-1935. Graduated from the Army War College in 1936. Executive officer to the chief of coast artillery 1938-1941. Brigadier general in April 1941. Commanding officer of harbor defenses at Boston, then IV Corps Area Coast Artillery District 1941-1942. Major general in September 1942. Commander of New England sector 1942-1944. Member of the War Department Personnel Board 1944-1945. Retired in February 1948. Decorations included two Legions of Merit. Died on January 29, 1979.

Blount, Roy Eugene (1889-1969) Born in Crawford, Texas, on June 13, 1889. Commissioned in the infantry, Texas National Guard in 1912 and the Cavalry, Regular Army in 1920. Served with the 1st Squadron Cavalry, Texas National Guard 1916-1917. Graduated from Command and General Staff School in 1932 and the Army Industrial College in 1933. Assistant chief of staff of 3rd Division 1933-1937. Executive officer, then commanding officer of 5th Cavalry 1938-1939. Instructor at the Cavalry School in 1940. Assistant chief of staff for supply at 1st Cavalry Division 1940-1941. Assistant, then chief of staff of VII Corps in 1942. Assistant chief of staff of the Hawaii Department in 1943. Commanding general of Army Port and Service Command, Central Pacific Theater of Operations from 1943. Brigadier general in January 1944. Retired in October 1947. Decorations included the Distinguished Service Medal, Legion of Merit and Bronze Star. Died on December 26, 1969.

Bluemel, Clifford (1885-1973) Born in Trenton, New Jersey, on November 9, 1885. Commissioned in the infantry from West Point in 1909. Served in the U.S. in World War I. Graduated from Command and General Staff School in 1918 and the Army War College in 1927. Support officer for III Corps Area 1936-1940. Commander of 45th Infantry 1940-1941. Commandant of the Staff School at Camp Allen, Philippines in 1941. Brigadier general in December 1941. Commander of 31st Division, Philippine Army 1941-1942. Taken prisoner of war at the fall of Bataan in April 1942. Released in August 1945. Commanding general of Fort Benjamin Harrison at his retirement in October 1947. Decorations included the Distinguished Service Cross, Distinguished Service Medal and Silver Star. Died on June 27, 1973.

Boatner, Haydon Lemaire (1900-1977) Born in New Orleans, Louisiana, on October 8, 1900. Commissioned in the infantry from the West Point in 1924. Graduated from Command and General Staff School in 1939. Commanding officer of the forward echelon in Burma 1942. Brigadier general in November 1942. Chief of staff of the Chinese Army in Burma 1942-1943. Commanding general of combat troops in northwest Burma 1943-1944. Chief of staff of Chinese Combat Command 1944-1945. Assignments after the war included commanding general of 3rd Division 1954-1955 and provost marshal general, U.S. Army 1957-1960. Retired as major general in November 1960. Decorations include three Distinguished Service Medals, the Silver Star, Legion of Merit, Bronze Star and Commendation Ribbon. Died on May 29, 1977.

Boatwright, Walter Putney (1886-1957) Born in Buckingham County, Virginia, on March 17, 1886. B.S. from Virginia Polytechnic Institute in 1907. Commissioned in the Coast Artillery Corps in 1908. Attended Massachusetts Institute of Technology 1914-1916. Combat service with the AEF in World War I at Aisne-Marne, Oise-Aisne and Argonne. Graduated from Command and General Staff School in 1926. Commanding officer of Frankford Arsenal December 1939-June 1942. Brigadier general in October 1940. Deputy chief of the New York Ordnance District, then chief June-September 1942. In the office of the chief of ordnance September 1942-February 1943. Again in New York February-July 1943. Chief of the Ordnance Tank Automotive Center in Detroit 1943-1945. Duty in the office of the chief of ordnance August 1945 until retirement in February 1946. Decorations included the Distinguished Service Medal, Legion of Merit and Purple Heart. Died on January 7, 1957.

Bohn, John James (1889-1983) Born in St. Paul, Minnesota, on April 3, 1889. Attended the University of Minnesota 1908-1909. Enlisted service 1914-1916. Commissioned in the cavalry in 1916. Served with the Punitive Expedition into Mexico in 1916 and the AEF in World War I. Instructor at the Alabama National Guard 1923-1927. Graduated from Command and General Staff School in 1929 and the Army War College in 1932. Executive officer of the Cavalry School 1939-1941. Trains commander, then chief of staff of 3rd Armored Division 1941-1942. Chief of staff of II Corps in 1942. Combat commander in 8th Armored Division, then 3rd Armored Division 1942-1944. Brigadier general in July 1944. Retired in February 1945. Decorations included the Silver Star and Bronze Star. Died on April 21, 1983.

Bolling, Alexander Russell (1895-1964) Born in Philadelphia on August 28, 1895. Attended USNA 1915-1916. Commissioned in the infantry, Officers Reserve Corps in 1917. Served with 3rd Infantry Division, AEF at Aisne-Marne, Champagne-Marne, St. Mihiel and Argonne engagements in 1918. Graduated from Command and General Staff School in 1935 and the Army War College in 1938. Assistant chief of staff for intelligence at I Corps Area 1938-1940, then assistant chief of staff for personnel at Army Ground Forces 1940-1943. Brigadier general in August 1942. Assistant division commander of 8th Infantry Division, then 84th Division 1943-1944. Major general in January 1945. Commanding general of 84th Division in 1945. Assignments after the war included commanding general of Third Army 1952-1955. Retired as lieutenant general in July 1955. Decorations included the Distinguished Service Cross, two Distinguished Service Medals, the Silver Star, Legion of Merit, Bronze Star and Purple Heart. Died on June 3, 1964.

Bolte, Charles Lawrence (1895-1989) Born in Chicago on May 8, 1895. B.S. from Armour Institute of Technology in 1917. Commissioned in the Officers Reserve Corps in 1916 and entered active duty the following year. Graduated from Command and General Staff School in 1932 and the Army War College in 1937. Brigadier general in January 1942. Chief of staff of U.S. Forces in the British Isles

1942-1943. Major general in April 1943. Commanding general of the 34th Infantry Division 1944-1946. Assignments after the war included irector of plans, then assistant chief of staff for operations, finally deputy chief of plans, U.S. Army 1949-1951 and commanding general of Seventh Army in Europe in 1952. General in 1953 as vice chief of staff, U.S. Army 1952-1955. Retired in April 1955. Decorations included two Distinguished Service Medals, the Silver Star, Legion of Merit and Purple Heart. Died on February 13, 1989.

Bonesteel, Charles Hartwell (1885-1964) Born in Fort Sidney, Nebraska, on April 9, 1885. Commissioned in the infantry from West Point in 1908. Served with 7th Division, AEF in 1918. Instructor at West Point 1919-1924. Graduated from Command and General Staff School in 1926 and the Army War College in 1932. Instructor at the Infantry School 1932-1935. Brigadier general in September 1940. Chief of staff of VI Corps Area 1940-1941. Major general in April 1941. Commanding general of 5th Infantry Division in 1941. Commander of Iceland Base Command August 1941-June 1943. Commandant of the Infantry School 1943-1944. Commanding general of Western Defense Command in 1944. With 12th Army Group, then inspector general in the European Theater of Operations 1944-1945. President of the War Department Manpower Board 1945-1947. Retired in January 1947. Decorations included the Distinguished Service Medal, Legion of Merit and Bronze Star. Died on June 5, 1964.

Boone, Milton Orme (1891-1985) Born in Oakland, New Jersey, on June 15, 1891. Enlisted service with Virginia National Guard 1916-1917. Commissioned in the Quartermaster Corps in 1917. Served with 2nd Division, AEF in World War I. Attended Harvard 1930-1931. Commander of New Cumberland General, Pennsylvania, Depot 1938-1942. At the San Francisco Port of Embarkation in 1942. Commanding general of California Quartermaster Depot 1942-1946. Brigadier general in January 1944. Retired in May 1948. Decorations included two Silver Stars and the Legion of Merit. Died on August 10, 1985.

Booth, Donald Prentice (1902-) Born in Albany, New York, on December 21, 1902. Commissioned in the Corps of Engineers from West Point in 1926. Instructor at West Point 1935-1939. Graduated from Command and General Staff School in 1940. With 2nd Engineers at Fort Sam Houston in 1940. Assistant to the district engineer in Seattle 1940-1942. Director of ports, then chief of staff, finally commanding general of the Persian Gulf Command October 1942-August 1945. Brigadier general in May 1944. Assignments after the war included commanding general of 28th Infantry Division 1953-1954, commanding general of 9th Infantry Division in 1954. Deputy assistant chief of staff, then assistant chief of staff, finally deputy chief of staff for personnel, U.S. Army 1954-1957, high commissioner of the Ryukyu Islands 1958-1961 and ommanding general of Fourth Army 1961-1962. Retired as lieutenant general on February 28, 1962. Decorations include three Distinguished Service Medals.

Borden, William A. (1890-1967) Born in San Antonio, Texas, on March 20, 1890. M.E. from Cornell in 1912. Commissioned in the ordnance in 1918. Graduated from the Army Industrial College in 1925. M.B.A. from Harvard in 1928. Graduated from the Army War College in 1933. Brigadier general in January 1944. Director of new development division in the War Department and member of the joint committee on new weapons and equipment, Joint Chiefs of Staff 1944-1946. Retired as colonel in August 1946. Decorations included the Distinguished Service Medal and Legion of Merit. Died on September 23, 1967.

Boudinot, Truman Everett (1895-1945) Born in Hamilton, Iowa, on September 2, 1895. Commissioned in the Cavalry in 1917. Duty with the 8th Cavalry in Texas 1917-1919. Served in the Philippine Islands 1925-1927. Graduated from Command and General Staff School in 1937. Commanding officer of 32nd Armored Regiment, 3rd Armored Division 1942-1943. Brigadier general in September 1944. Commanding general of Combat Command "B," 3rd Armored Division 1944-1945, then 7th Armored Division September 1945 until his death on December 11, 1945.

Bowen, Frank Sayles Jr. (1905-1976) Born on March 4, 1905, in Fort William McKinley, Philippine Islands. Commissioned in the infantry from West Point in 1926. Assistant chief of staff for operations at I Corps, then U.S. Army forces in the Southwest Pacific, finally at Eighth Army December 1942-May 1947. Brigadier general in June 1945 but reverted to colonel in March 1946. Assignments after the war included deputy commanding general, then commanding general of 6th Armored Division 1954-1955, commanding general of 101st Airborne Division 1955-1956, commanding general of XII Corps 1958-1960, then deputy commander in chief of naval forces in the Eastern Atlantic and Mediterranean 1960-1962. Retired in Ocotober 1962. Decorations included two Distinguished Service Crosses, three Distinguished Service Medals, four Silver Stars, the Legion of Merit, two Bronze Stars, the Air Medal, Commendation Ribbon and Purple Heart. Died on September 24, 1976.

Bowman, Frank Otto (1896-1978) Born on July 27, 1896, in Mesilla Park, New Mexico. Commissioned in the Corps of Engineers from West Point in 1918. Chief engineer at II Corps and engineer at the European Theater of Operations in 1942. Engineer at Fifth Army 1943-1945. Brigadier general in February 1944. Assignments after the war included chief of staff, then commanding general of the engineer center, Fort Belvoir 1949-1953 and commanding general of U.S. Army Training Center, Fort Leonard Wood December 1954 until retirement as major general in June 1956. Decorations included the Distinguished Service Medal, three Legions of Merit and the Purple Heart. Died on March 13, 1978.

Bowman, Harwood Christian (1895-1962) Born in Alabama on January 14, 1895. LL.B. from the University of Alabama. Commissioned in the field artillery, Alabama National Guard in 1917. Graduated from Command and General Staff School in 1937. Brigadier general in May 1945. Reverted to colonel in April

1946. Retired in June 1948. Decorations included the Distinguished Service Medal, Legion of Merit and Bronze Star. Died on November 29, 1962.

Boyd, Leonard Russell (1891-1977) Born in Lebanon, Oregon, on November 26, 1891. Attended the University of California 1915-1916. Commissioned in the infantry in 1916. Served with the 16th Infantry, AEF at St. Mihiel, Montdidier-Noyen, Aisne-Marne and Meuse-Argonne engagements 1917-1919. Instructor at the Infantry School 1925-1929. Graduated from Command and General Staff School in 1935 and the Army War College in 1938. Instructor at the Command and General Staff School 1938-1940. Plans and training officer with deputy chief of staff for operations, IX Corps 1940-1942. Brigadier general in May 1942. Chief of staff of the Hawaiian Department June 1942-August 1943. Assistant division commander of 93rd Infantry Division August 1943-February 1946. Reverted to colonel in July 1946. Retired in November 1951. Decorations included the Distinguished Service Medal, three Silver Stars, the Legion of Merit, two Bronze Stars, the Air Medal and Commendation Ribbon. Died on January 17, 1977.

Boye, Frederic William (1891-1970) Born on October 19, 1891, in New York City. Commissioned in the cavalry from West Point in 1915. Duty with the Punitive Expedition into Mexico in 1916. Served with the 12th Division in 1918. Graduated from Command and General Staff School in 1926. Assigned to to West Point 1929-1933. Served with the National Guard Bureau 1937-1940. Executive officer of 7th Cavalry, then assistant chief of staff of 1st Cavalry Division, finally commanding officer of 12th Cavalry 1940-1943. Served in China 1944-1945. Brigadier general in March 1945. Assigned to the War Department Personnel Center at Fort Sam Houston 1945-1946. Reverted to colonel in April 1946. Retired in 1950. Decorations included the Distinguished Service Medal, Legion of Merit and Commendation Ribbon. Died on October 6, 1970.

Bradford, Karl Slaughter (1889-1972) Born in Washington, DC, on June 28, 1889. Commissioned in the cavalry from West Point in 1911. Served in the operations division of the War Department General Staff 1918-1919. Graduated from Command and General Staff School in 1926. Professor of military science and tactics at Massachusetts Agricultural College 1930-1931. Instructor at the Cavalry School 1934-1936. Graduated from the Army War College in 1937. Brigadier general in April 1941. Commanding general of 1st Cavalry Brigade 1941-1943. Deputy director of the War Department Manpower Board 1943-1946. Retired in December 1946. Decorations included the Legion of Merit. Died on August 15, 1972.

Bradford, William Brooks (1896-1965) Born in Tallahassee, Florida, on March 15, 1896. B.S. from VMI in 1916. Commissioned in the cavalry in 1917. Graduated from Command and General Staff School in 1934. Director of department of tactics at the Cavalry School 1939-1941. Chief of staff of 2nd Cavalry Division, 83rd Infantry Division and 33rd Infantry Division 1941-1943. Brigadier general in

April 1943. Assistant division commander of 99th Infantry Division, then 25th Infantry Division 1943-1944. Commanding general of 1st Cavalry Brigade 1945-1949. Retired in March 1953. Decorations included the Legion of Merit and Bronze Star. Died on January 17, 1965.

Bradley, James Lester (1891-1957) Born in Doniphan, Missouri, on May 18, 1891. Commissioned in the infantry from West Point in 1914. With 19th Infantry at Vera Cruz in 1914. Served in the U.S. in World War I. Graduated from Command and General Staff School in 1926. Instructor at the Infantry School 1926-1930. Graduated from the Army War College in 1931. Instructor at Command and General Staff School 1932-1936. Served at headquarters of IX Corps Area in San Francisco 1938-1940. Assistant chief of staff for plans and operations, then chief of staff at Fourth Army 1940-1942. Brigadier general in September 1941, major general in June 1942. Commanding general of 96th Division 1942-1946. Retired in January 1947. Decorations included the Distinguished Service Medal, Legion of Merit and Bronze Star. Died on July 30, 1957.

Bradley, Joseph Sladen (1900-1961) Born in Vancouver, Washington, on June 9, 1900. Commissioned in the infantry from West Point in 1919. Graduated from Command and General Staff School in 1937. Held numerous positions with 126th Infantry of 32nd Division 1942-1944. Brigadier general in September 1944. Served with the War Department General Staff 1944-1946. Assignments after the war included commanding general of 25th Division in the Korean War. Retired as major general in May 1956. Decorations included two Distinguished Service Crosses, two Distinguished Service Medals, four Silver Stars and two Bronze Stars. Died on January 17, 1961.

Bradley, Omar Nelson (1893-1981). Born on February 12, 1893, in Clark, Missouri. Commissioned in the infantry from West Point in 1915. Professor of military science and tactics at South Dakota State College 1919-1920. Instructor at West Point 1920-1924. Graduated from Command and General Staff School in 1929. Instructor at the Infantry School 1929-1933. Graduated from the Army War College in 1934 then instructor at West Point again until 1938. With War Department General Staff June 1938-February 1941. Brigadier general in February 1941. Commandant of the Infantry School March 1941-February 1942. Major general in February 1942. Commander of the 82nd Infantry Division February-June 1942 and the 28th Infantry Division June 1942-January 1943. Lieutenant general in June 1943. Commanding general of I Corps April-September 1943, First U.S. Army Group (including First Army) October 1943-August 1944 and 12th Army Group August 1944-July 1945. General in March 1945. As commanding general of 12th Army Group he commanded more uniformed American troops than any officer in history. Assignments after the war included director of the Veterans Administration 1945-1947 then chief of staff, U.S. Army 1948-1949. General of the Army in September 1950 as the first chairman of the Joint Chiefs of Staff 1949-1953. Author of *A Soldier's Story* (1951). Decorations included the Defense Distinguished Service Medal, four Distinguished Service Medals, the

Silver Star, two Legions of Merit and the Bronze Star. Recipient of the Thayer Award in 1973. Died on April 9, 1981.

Bradshaw, Aaron Jr. (1894-1976) Born in Washington, DC, on July 1, 1894. Commissioned in the Coast Artillery Corps from West Point in 1917. Chief of antiaircraft artillery in North African Theater of Operations 1941-1943. Brigadier general in April 1943. Commanding general of antiaircraft artillery for Seventh and Fifth Army 1943-1945. Retired as major general in January 1953. Decorations included the Distinguished Service Medal, Silver Star, two Legions of Merit, the Bronze Star and two Commendation Ribbons. Died on November 8, 1976.

Bragdon, John Stewart (1893-1964) Born in Pittsburgh, Pennsylvania, on May 21, 1893. Commissioned in the Corps of Engineers from West Point in 1915. Wounded while serving with First Army in the AEF. Graduated from Command and General Staff School in 1928. Division engineer in South Atlantic 1941-1944. Brigadier general in March 1943. Assistant chief of military construction in the office of the chief of engineers 1945-1949. Assignments after the war included deputy chief of engineers 1950-1951. Retired as major general in June 1951. Decorations included two Distinguished Service Medals and the Purple Heart. Member of the council of economic advisors to President Eisenhower, then special assistant 1954-1960. Died on January 7, 1964.

Brann, Donald W. (1895-1945) Born in Rushville, Indiana, on September 26, 1895. Commissioned in the infantry, Officers Reserve Corps in 1917. Served in Tientsin, China with the 15th Infantry 1923-1927. Instructor at the Infantry School 1931-1933. Graduated from Command and General Staff School in 1935. Professor of military science and tactics at the University of Hawaii 1935-1937. Graduated from the Army War College in 1938 then instructor again at the Infantry School 1938-1939. With the operations and training divisiion of the War Department General Staff 1939-1942. Chief of staff of 95th Infantry Division 1942-1943. Brigadier general in September 1943. Assistant chief of staff for operations at Fifth Army in 1943. Deputy chief of staff for operations at 15th Army Group December 1944-December 1945. Major general in June 1945. Died on December 29, 1945, in the European Theater of Operations. Decorations included two Distinguished Service Medals and the Legion of Merit.

Braun, Gustav J. Jr. (1895-1945) Born on January 15, 1895, in Buffalo, New York. Commissioned in the infantry in 1917. Served with the 47th Infantry Division, AEF in 1918. Instructor at the Infantry School 1920-1924 and again 1926-1927. Duty with the 15th Infantry in China 1930-1933. Assistant editor of the "Review of Military Literature" at the Command and General Staff School 1935-1938. Assistant professor of military science and tactics at the University of California 1938-1939. Assistant chief of staff of IX Corps Area, then VII Army Corps 1941-1942. Commanding officer of II Armored Corps Special Troops in 1942. Chief of staff of 69th Infantry Division in 1943. Chief of staff, then regimental commander of 133rd Infantry, 34th Infantry Division, finally assistant division commander of the 34th July 1944 until reported missing in action during fighting in the Mediterranean area on March 17, 1945. Brigadier general in January 1945. Decorations included the Distinguished Service Cross and two Purple Hearts.

Bresnahan, Thomas Francis (1892-1971) Born in Fitchburg, Massachusetts, on July 4, 1892. B.S. from Middlebury College in 1917. Commissioned in the infantry in 1917. Signal officer with the 38th Infantry, AEF 1918-1919. Saw action at Aisne, Champagne-Marne, Aisne-Marne, Vesle, St. Mihiel and Meuse-Argonne campaigns. Professor of military science and tactics at Pennsylvania State College 1924-1929. Duty in the Canal Zone 1931-1936. Instructor with the Massachusetts National Guard in 1936. Graduated from Command and General Staff School in 1938. Again instructor with the Massachusetts National Guard 1938-1940. Assistant chief of the training division in the National Guard Bureau 1940-1941. Commanding officer of headquarters company at GHQ U.S. Army then Army Ground Forces 1941-1943. Duty with Third Army in 1943. Brigadier general in September 1943. Commanding general of Infantry Replacement Training Center at Camp Hood, then Army Ground Forces Replacement Training Center at Fort Meade 1944-1945. Retired in March 1948. Decorations included the Distinguished Service Cross, Legion of Merit and two Purple Hearts. Died on December 11, 1971.

Brett, Sereno Elmer (1891-1952) Born in Portland, Oregon, on October 31, 1891. B.S. from Oregon State in 1916. Commissioned in the infantry in 1916. Transferred to the Tank Corps in 1918. Led the first American tank attack in World War I at St. Mihiel with the 326th Battalion, 1st Division September 12-15, 1918. Graduated from Command and General Staff School in 1927. Instructor at the Infantry School 1927-1930. Member of the Infantry Board 1931-1933. Graduated from the Army War College in 1934. Again member of the Infantry Board 1935-1938. Instructor at Command and General Staff School 1938-1940. Brigadier general in February 1942. Commanding general of 5th Armored Division 1942-1943. Retired in October 1943. Decorations included the Distinguished Service Cross, Distinguished Service Medal and two Silver Stars. Died on September 9, 1952.

Brewer, Carlos (1890-1976) Born in Mayfield, Kentucky, on December 5, 1890. Commissioned in the field artillery from West Point in 1913. Instructor, then assistant professor at West Point 1916-1921. Graduated from Command and General Staff School in 1928. Instructor at the Field Artillery School 1928-1932. Graduated from the Army War College in 1933. Assistant chief of staff at 9th Division 1941-1942, then 6th Armored Division in 1942. Brigadier general in February 1942, major general in August 1942. Commanding general of 12th Armored Division 1942-1944. Reverted to colonel in September 1944. Commander of 46th Field Artillery Group, Seventh Army 1945-1946. Retired in December 1950. Decorations included the Legion of Merit, Bronze Star and Commendation Ribbon. Died on September 29, 1976.

Bricker, Edwin Dyson (1875-1967) Born in Chambersburg, Pennsylvania, on November 24, 1875. Commissioned in the infantry from West Point in 1898. Served during the Spanish-American War in the Santiago campaign and in the Philippines during the resurrection 1899-1901. Chief purchasing officer in the ordnance department, AEF during World War I. Graduated from the Army War College in 1923. Brigadier general in September 1930. Assistant to the chief of ordnance 1930-1934. Commander of Frankford Arsenal (Philadelphia) 1934-1939. Retired in November 1939. Recalled to active duty in November 1940. Chief of the requisitioning section in the Board of Economic Warfare until retirement again in June 1943. Decorations included the Distinguished Service Medal and two Silver Stars. Died on April 7, 1967.

Briggs, Raymond Westcott (1878-1959) Born in Beaver, Pennsylvania, on July 19, 1878. Commissioned in the infantry in 1900. Transferred to the Artillery in 1901. Assisted in dynamiting of San Francisco to stop the spread of fires following the earthquake in April 1906. Brigadier general on the battlefield in 1918. Commanding general of 304th Field Artillery, New York 77th Division in 1918. Reverted to colonel after the war. Graduated from Command and General Staff School in 1920 and the Army War College in 1921. Duty with the War Department General Staff 1921-1925. Chief of staff of the Philippine Department 1936-1938. Retired in June 1942. Recalled to active duty in July 1942 as brigadier general. Commandant of St. Thomas Military Academy 1943 through retirement a second time in 1947. Decorations included the Distinguished Service Medal. Died on December 23, 1959.

Brink, Francis G. (1893-1952) Born in Marathon, New York, on August 22, 1893. B.A. from Cornell in 1916. Commissioned in the infantry, Officers Reserve Corps in 1917. Instructor at the Infantry School 1921-1923. Assistant Professor of military science and tactics at Louisiana State University 1928-1934. Graduated from Command and General Staff School in 1936. Commander of 31st Infantry, Philippine Islands 1938-1941. On the staff of General Wavell, the British Allied commander in Burma, 1941-1942. Staff officer in the China-Burma-India Theater of Operations 1942-1944. Brigadier general in November 1944. Chief of the operations division, Southeast Asia Command 1944-1945. At headquarters of U.S. Army forces in China 1945-1946. Chief of the military advisory group in Saigon at the time of his death on June 24, 1952. Decorations included the Distinguished Service Medal, two Legions of Merit, the Commendation Ribbon and Purple Heart.

Brittingham, James Francis (1894-1983) Born in Princess Anne, Maryland, on July 4, 1894. B.S. from the University of Missouri in 1915. Enlisted service with the District of Columbia National Guard on the Mexican border 1916-1917. Commissioned in the field artillery in 1917. Served with the 12th Field Artillery, AEF 1917-1919. Saw action in the Toulon Sector, the Aisne defense, and Chateau-Thierry, St. Mihiel and Meuse-Argonne campaigns. Instructor with the Pennsylvania National Guard 1923-1928 then at the Field Artillery School 1929-

1933. Graduated from the Command and General Staff School in 1937. Member of the Field Artillery Board 1939-1942. Brigadier general in May 1942. Commanding general of 89th Infantry Division Artillery May 1942-September 1943, then IV Corps Artillery 1943-1944. Artillery officer at Seventh Army 1944-1945. Commanding general of VIII Corps Artillery, then 4th Division Artillery, finally Third Army Artillery June 1945-May 1946. Reverted to colonel in April 1946. Retired as brigadier general in June 1954. Decorations included two Distinguished Service Medals, the Silver Star, Legion of Merit, Bronze Star and Purple Heart. Died on January 19, 1983.

Brooks, Edward Hale (1893-1978) Born in Concord, New Hampshire, on April 25, 1893. B.S. from Norwich University in 1916. Commissioned in the cavalry in 1917. Participated in the second Battle of the Marne and the Aisne-Marne, St. Mihiel and Meuse-Argonne campaigns in World War I. Graduated from Command and General Staff School in 1934 and the Army War College in 1937. Chief of the statistics branch at the War Department General Staff 1939-1941. Brigadier general in December 1941. Artillery officer at the Armored Force 1941-1942. Major general in August 1942. Commanding general of 11th Armored Division, then the 2nd Armored Division 1942-1944. Commanding general of VI Corps October 1944-March 1945. Commanding general of 4th Service Command 1945-1947. Assignments after the war included commanding general of Second Army June 1951 until retirement as lieutenant general in April 1953. Decorations included the Distinguished Service Cross, two Distinguished Service Medals, two Silver Stars, two Legions of Merit and the Bronze Star. Died on October 10, 1978.

Brougher, William Edward (1889-1965) Born in Jackson, Mississippi, on February 17, 1889. B.S. from Mississippi Agricultural and Mechanical School in 1910. Commissioned in the infantry in 1911. Served with the AEF 1918-1919. Graduated from Command and General Staff School in 1923. Professor of military science and tactics at Louisiana State University 1925-1930. Graduated from the Army Industrial College in 1933. Instructor with the West Virginia National Guard 1936-1937. Graduated from the Army War College in 1938. Commanding officer of 57th Infantry in the Philippines 1940-1941. At headquarters of U.S. Army forces in the Far East in September 1941, then promoted to brigadier general by MacArthur in December 1941 as commanding general of 11th Division, Philippine Army. Taken prisoner by the Japanese at the fall of Bataan in April 1942. Liberated in Manchuria in August 1945. Assignments after the war included commanding general of Fort McClellan 1946-1947 and Camp Gordon 1947-1949. Retired in February 1949. Decorations included the Distinguished Service Medal. Died on March 6, 1965.

Brown, Albert Eger (1889-1984) Born on June 13, 1889, in Charleston, South Carolina. Commissioned in the infantry from West Point in 1912. Served at Vera Cruz, Mexico in 1914 and with the 8th and 183rd Brigades, AEF 1918-1919, including the Aisne-Marne offensive. Professor of military science and tactics at the

University of North Dakota 1919-1923. Graduated from the Command and General Staff School in 1925, the Army War College in 1930 and the Naval War College in 1931. Duty at the War Department General Staff 1931-1935. Member of the Infantry Board 1935-1938. Again at the War Department General Staff 1940-1941. Brigadier general in August 1941, major general in May 1942. Commanding general of 7th Infantry Division in the Aleutians May 1942-June 1943. Commanding general of Infantry Replacement Training Center at Camp Wheadle in 1943 then 5th Division 1943-1945. Assignments after the war included commanding general of 6th Infantry Division June-September 1946. Retired in June 1949. Decorations included two Legions of Merit and the Bronze Star. Died on October 12, 1984.

Brown, Charles Conrad (1890-1971) Born in Houston, Texas, on January 3, 1890. Graduated from VMI in 1910. Commissioned in the infantry, Officer Reserve Corps 1917. Served with the 317th Ammunition Train, AEF 1918-1919. Saw action at Meuse-Argonne. Transferred to the Quartermaster Corps in 1920. Instructor at the University of Tennessee 1923-1924. Duty in the Philippine Islands 1925-1927. Instructor at the Field Artillery School 1927-1931 and with the Virginia National Guard 1935-1937. Assistant chief of staff for operations at 1st Military Area 1939-1940. Assistant chief of staff for intelligence at IV Corps 1940-1942. Executive officer of 90th Division Artillery February-August 1942. Artillery officer at XII Corps, then Fourth Army 1942-1944. Commander of XVI Corps Artillery January 1944-August 1945. Brigadier general in September 1944. Retired in May 1947. Decorations included the Distinguished Service Medal, Legion of Merit and Bronze Star. Died on January 10, 1971.

Brown, Everett Ernest (1889-1974) Born in Vinton County, Ohio, on December 15, 1889. Commissioned in the infantry, Ohio National Guard in 1910. With 166th Infantry in France 1917-1918, including the Champagne-Marne, Aisne-Marne and Chateau-Thierry offensives. Transferred to the Regular Army in 1920. Professor of military science and tactics at Denison University 1921-1925. Aide-de-camp to Major General Paul B. Malone at headquarters of III Corps Area 1933-1935. Graduated from Command and General Staff School in 1938. Instructor with Kansas State College ROTC 1938-1940. Assistant chief of staff for supply at VII Corps Area 1941-1942. Assistant chief of staff for intelligence at VIII Corps, then XIV Corps 1942-1943. Commanding officer of 35th Infantry in 1943. Brigadier general in February 1944. Assistant division commander of 25th Infantry Division February 1944-May 1948. Retired in December 1949. Decorations included the Silver Star and three Legions of Merit. Died on October 3, 1974.

Brown, Homer Caffee (1893-1950) Born in Carthage, Missouri, on September 25, 1893. Commissioned in the infantry from West Point in 1917. Served with the 3rd Infantry in Texas 1917-1920. Professor of military science and tactics at Mancius School 1924-1929. Graduated from Command and General Staff School in 1934 and the Army War College in 1935. Instructor at the Command and General Staff School 1935-1939. Assistant to the assistant chief of staff for operations at Third Army 1940-1941. Commanding officer of 9th Infantry 1941-1942. Served in the Southwest Pacific Area 1942-1946. Brigadier general in May 1944. Reverted to colonel in February 1946. Retired in 1948. Decorations included the Legion of Merit and Bronze Star. Died in San Antonio on February 18, 1950.

Brown, Lloyd Davidson (1892-1950) Born in Sharon, Georgia, on July 28, 1892. B.A. from the University of Georgia in 1912. Commissioned in the infantry in 1917. With the 61st Infantry in the AEF in 1918. Professor of military science and tactics at Riverside Military Academy (Georgia) 1920-1922. Instructor at the Infantry School 1923-1927. Graduated from Command and General Staff School in 1930. Chief of the administrative division at the National Guard Bureau in 1940. Assistant to the assistant chief of staff for personnel, then operations 1941-1942. Brigadier general in May 1942. Assistant division commander of 102nd Infantry Division June 1942-February 1943. Major general in April 1943. Commanding general of 28th Infantry Division 1943-1944. Reverted to colonel in August 1944. Retired in December 1948. Decorations included the Silver Star, Legion of Merit and Commendation Ribbon. Died on February 17, 1950.

Brown, Philip Edward (1896-1978) Born in Virginia, Minnesota, on January 7, 1896. Attended the University of West Virginia 1913-1917. Commissioned in the infantry, Officers Reserve Corps in 1917. Professor of military science and tactics at City College of New York 1925-1929. Graduated from Command and General Staff School in 1935 and the Army War College in 1937. Duty in the office of the inspector general, U.S. Army 1937-1941. Operations and training officer at IV Corps in 1941. Brigadier general in April 1942. Deputy inspector general May 1942-June 1945. Major general in January 1945. Retired in December 1945. Decorations included the Distinguished Service Medal and Legion of Merit. Died on January 1, 1978.

Brown, Robert Quinney (1907-1973) Born in Warren, Arkansas, on July 15, 1907. Commissioned in the field artillery from West Point in 1931. Commanding officer of support troops, then commandant at headquarters command of SHAEF 1942-1946. Brigadier general in June 1945. Reverted to colonel in April 1946. Assignments after the war included commanding general of I Corps Artillery 1956-1958, then 2nd Armored Division Artillery 1958-1961. Retired as brigadier general in July 1961. Decorations included the Distinguished Service Medal, Legion of Merit and Bronze Star. Died on November 13, 1973.

Brown, Thoburn Kaye (1888-1958) Born on October 26, 1888, in Clyde, North Carolina. Attended the University of Tennessee 1906-1908. Commissioned in the cavalry from West Point in 1913. Instructor, then assistant professor at West Point 1916-1922. Graduated from Command and General Staff School in 1924. Again at West Point 1928-1932. Graduated from the Army War College in 1933. Brigadier general in May 1942. Commanding general of 4th Cavalry Brigade 1942-1944. Commanding general of Allied Command in Rome 1944-1945. Reverted to colonel in February 1946. Retired in October 1948. Decorations included the Legion of Merit and Bronze Star. Died on September 11, 1958.

Brown, Wyburn Dwight (1899-1981) Born in Marion, South Carolina, on June 23, 1899. Commissioned in the field artillery from West Point in 1919. Instructor there 1924-1929, then professor 1932-1936. Graduated from Command and General Staff School in 1937. Instructor at the Field Artillery School 1937-1941. With operations division at the War Department General Staff 1941-1942. Commanding general of 11th Airborne Division Artillery December 1942-March 1944. Brigadier general in February 1943. Commanding general of 33rd Field Artillery Brigade March 1944-January 1945. Chief of the U.S. military mission to Colombia 1945-1946. Reverted to colonel in July 1946. Retired in June 1951. Decorations included the Bronze Star. Died on April 3, 1981.

Browne, Frederick William (1875-1960) Born in St. Charles, Iowa, on October 25, 1875. LL.B. from George Washington University in 1901, LL.M. from National University in 1902. Commissioned in the Corps of Engineers in 1918. Served with the War Department General Staff 1925-1933. Retired as colonel in 1938. Recalled to active duty in January 1939. Assistant budget officer for the War Department 1939-1944. Brigadier general in February 1942. Retired in January 1944. Decorations included the Legion of Merit. Died on December 16, 1960.

Browning, Albert Jesse (1899-1948) Born in Ogden, Utah, on September 27, 1899. B.S. from Massachusetts Institute of Technology in 1922. Commissioned in the Coast Artillery Corps, Officers Reserve Corps in 1922. Volunteered for active duty in May 1942 and appointed colonel. Served with the purchases branch, Services of Supply until October 1942. Director of the purchases division at Army Service Forces, then assistant director of materiel October 1942 until February 1945, when he returned to inactive duty. Brigadier general in June 1943. Decorations included the Distinguished Service Medal. Died on July 3, 1948.

Bruce, Andrew Davis (1894-1969) Born in St. Louis, Missouri, on September 14, 1894. B.S. from Texas A&M in 1916. Commissioned in the infantry in 1918. With 2nd Division in World War I in Verdun, Aisne-Marne, San Miguel, Champagne and Meuse-Argonne offensives. Graduated from Command and General Staff School in 1933, the Army War College in 1936 and the Naval War College in 1937. Brigadier general in February 1942, major general in September 1942. Commanding general of Tank Destroyer Command 1942-1943. Commanding general of 77th Infantry Division May 1943-1946. Assignments after the war included commanding general of 7th Infantry Division 1946-1947, deputy commanding general of Fourth Army 1947-1951 and commandant of Armed Forces Staff College 1951-1954. Retired as lieutenant general in August 1954. Decorations included the Distinguished Service Cross, three Distinguished Service Medals, the Legion of Merit, Bronze Star and Purple Heart. Died on July 1, 1969.

Brush, Rapp (1889-1958) Born at Fort D.A. Russell, Wyoming, on November 7, 1889. Attended the University of Illinois 1909-1911. Commissioned in the infantry in 1918. Graduated from Command and General Staff School in 1923 and the Army War College in 1926. With the operations and training division at the War Department General Staff 1927-1931. Chief of the arms, equipment and finance sections in the office of the chief of infantry 1935-1939. Executive officer of 30th Infantry in 1939. Commanding officer of 21st Infantry July 1940-May 1942. Brigadier general in April 1941, major general in May 1942. Commanding general of 40th Infantry Division May 1942-September 1945. Retired in December 1945. Decorations included the Distinguished Service Medal, Silver Star, Legion of Merit, Bronze Star and Air Medal. Died on March 6, 1958.

Bruton, Philip Gilstrap (1891-1960) Born in San Francisco on April 17, 1891. Enlisted service in the California National Guard 1910-1915. Attended Polytechnic College of Engineering. Commissioned in the Corps of Engineers in 1920. Graduated from Command and General Staff School in 1937. District engineer in the Newfoundland Engineer District May 1941-April 1943. Executive office of the North Atlantic Division in 1943. Director of labor in the War Food Administration 1943-1945. Brigadier general in May 1944. Duty in the office of the chief of engineers 1945-1946. Retired in September 1946. Decorations included two Legions of Merit. Died on November 6, 1960.

Bryan, Blackshear Morrison (1900-1977) Born in Alexandria, Louisiana, on February 8, 1900. Commissioned in the field artillery from West Point in 1922. With the War Department General Staff 1940-1942. In the office of the provost marshal general 1942-1946. Brigadier general in December 1942. Assignments after the war included commanding general of XVI Corps 1952-1953, senior member of the United Nations Command Military Armistice Commission in 1953, commanding general of I Corps 1953-1954, superintendent of West Point 1954-1956, commanding general of U.S. Army Pacific 1956-1957 and commanding general of First Army 1957-1960. Retired as lieutenant general in 1960. Decorations included the Distinguished Service Medal, Air Medal and Commendation Ribbon. Died on March 2, 1977.

Bryden, William (1880-1972) Born in Hartford, Connecticut, on February 3, 1880. Commissioned in the field artillery from West Point in 1904. Instructor at West Point 1908-1912. Aide to Major General Thomas H. Berry 1916-1917. Brigadier general in October 1918 as commanding general of 15th Field Artillery Brigade, then 9th Field Artillery Brigade in World War I. Reverted to major in February 1919. Graduated from the Command and General Staff School in 1923, then instructor there until 1927. Graduated from the Army War College in 1928. Executive officer of 11th and 13th Field Artillery Brigades 1931-1934. With the operations and training division at the War Department General Staff 1935-1937. Brigadier general again in September 1937. Commanding general of 16th Infantry Brigade September 1937-May 1938. Deputy chief of staff, U.S. Army June 1940-March 1942. Major general in September 1940. Commanding general of IV

Corps Area 1942-1944. Retired in February 1944. Decorations included three Distinguished Service Medals. Died on January 20, 1972.

Bucher, Oliver Boone (1890-1962) Born in Bridgewater, Virginia, on December 5, 1890. Graduated from VMI in 1917. Commissioned in the Coast Artillery Corps in 1917. Duty in the Canal Zone 1920-1923. Professor of military science and tactics at Virginia Polytechnic Institute 1927-1931. Graduated from the Command and General Staff School in 1938. Plans and training officer in the 2nd Military Area, New York in 1939. Executive officer of the antiaircraft section at First Army in 1940. Chief of the equipment division at headquarters of the Anti-aircraft Command in 1941. Regimental commander of 608th Coast Artillery in 1942. Commanding officer of 117th Coast Artillery Group, then 29th Antiaircraft Group in 1943. Brigadier general in June 1943. Commanding general of Antiaircraft Artillery Training Center at Camp Callen December 1943-May 1944. Commanding general of Caribbean Defense Command 1944-1946. Reverted to colonel in April 1946. Assignments after the war included commandant of VMI 1947-1950. Retired in December 1950. Decorations included the Legion of Merit and Commendation Ribbon. Died on March 17, 1962.

Buckner, Simon Bolivar Jr. (1886-1945) Born on July 18, 1886, in Munfordville, Kentucky. Commissioned in the infantry from West Point in 1908. Commanded training units at Kelly Field, Texas during World War I. Instructor at West Point 1918-1919 and 1932-1936. Graduated from Command and General Staff School in 1925, then continued as instructor 1925-1928. Graduated from the Army War College in 1929, then instructor 1929-1932. Commandant of Cadets at West Point 1933-1936. With 23rd Infantry August 1936-May 1937. Commanding officer of 66th Infantry 1937-1938. Duty with the Civilian Conservation Corps in Alabama 1938-1939. Chief of staff of 6th Infantry Division 1939-1940. Brigadier general in October 1940. Commander of Alaska Defense Force July 1940-March 1944. Major general in August 1941, lieutenant general in May 1943. Organized and commanded Tenth Army from June 1944. Killed by a Japanese artillery shell during the Battle of Okinawa on June 18, 1945. Decorations included the Distinguished Service Medal. General posthumously in July 1954.

Buechler, Theodore Earl (1893-1980) Born on October 26, 1893, in Grand Island, Nebraska. Commissioned in the field artillery from West Point in 1917. Graduated from Command and General Staff School in 1933. Brigadier general in October 1942. Commanding general of 100th Division Artillery 1942-1943. Commanding general of XVI Airborne Corps Artillery 1943-1944. Artillery officer in the European Theater of Operations in 1945. Retired in July 1953. Decorations included the Legion of Merit and Commendation Ribbon. Died on November 6, 1980.

Bull, Harold Roe (1893-1976) Born on January 6, 1893, in Springfield, Massachusetts. Commissioned in the infantry from West Point in 1914. Served with AEF in World War I. Instructor at West Point 1921-1924. Graduated from

Command and General Staff School in 1928. Instructor at the Infantry School 1928-1932. Graduated from the Army War College in 1933 and the Naval War College in 1934. Secretary of the War Department General Staff 1938-1939. Brigadier general in July 1941. Assistant division commander of 4th Division in 1941. Assistant chief of staff for operations on the War Department General Staff in 1942. Major general in March 1942. Commanding general of the Replacement and School Command 1942-1943 then III Corps in 1943. Deputy chief of staff for operations, then chief of staff of Allied Command in Europe, then commanding general of 4th Division, finally deputy chief of staff for operations at SHAEF 1944-1945. Chief of staff of U.S. Forces European Theater of Operations 1945-1946. Assignments after the war included commandant of the National War College 1949-1952. Retired in July 1952 as lieutenant general. Decorations included three Distinguished Service Medals, the Silver Star, Legion of Merit and Bronze Star. Died on November 1, 1976.

Bullene, Egbert Frank (1895-1958) Born in Salinas, California, on January 25, 1895. Graduated from USNA in 1917 and transferred that year to the U.S. Army. Battery commander in the 4th Division in World War I, seeing action in the Marne, St. Mihiel and Meuse-Argonne offensives. Transferred to the Chemical Warfare Service in 1925. Graduated from the Army Industrial College in 1928. Graduated from the Command and General Staff School in 1937 then instructor there until 1939. Graduated from the Army War College in 1940. Chemical officer for the Armored Force January-September 1942. Chief of the training division in the office of the chief of the Chemical Warfare Service 1942-1943. Brigadier general in April 1943. Commander of the Chemical Warfare Service Unit Training Center at Camp Sibert 1943-1944. With the San Jose Project in Panama 1944-1945. Assignments after the war included deputy chief, then chief of the Chemical Warfare Service February 1951 until retirement in March 1954 as major general. Decorations included the Legion of Merit, Bronze Star and Purple Heart. Died on February 21, 1958.

Burgin, Henry Tocitus (1882-1958) Born in North Middletown, New York, on October 9, 1882. Commissioned in the Artillery from West Point in 1905. Served in the Philippine Islands 1913-1915. Ordnance officer with the 41st Division, AEF in 1918. Graduated from Command and General Staff School in 1922 and the Army War College in 1923. Brigadier general in October 1938, major general in October 1940. Coastal defense and antiaircraft commander for the Hawaiian Department, then chief of Hawaiian Artillery, then commanding general of Central Pacific Area Base Command, finally commanding general of Hawaiian Artillery Command July 1941-April 1946. Retired in August 1946. Decorations included the Distinguished Service Medal, Legion of Merit and Purple Heart. Died on July 31, 1958.

Burnell, Nathaniel Alanson (1897-1976) Born on September 13, 1897, in Westbrook, Maine, the brother of Ray Lawrence Burnell. Commissioned in the Coast Artillery Corps from West Point in 1919. Served in the Philippine Islands 1921-

1923. Instructor at the Coast Artillery School 1933-1938. Graduated from Command and General Staff School in 1939 and the Naval War College in 1940. Commanding officer of 613th Coast Artillery 1942-1943. Brigadier general in September 1943. Commanding general of 74th Antiaircraft Artillery Brigade, then 52nd Antiaircraft Artillery Brigade, finally 31st Antiaircraft Artillery Brigade January 1943-March 1946. Reverted to colonel in March 1946. Retired as brigadier general in August 1957. Decorations included the Distinguished Service Medal, Legion of Merit and Bronze Star. Died on June 27, 1976.

Burnell, Ray Lawrence (1891-1968) Born in Westbrook, Maine, on June 28, 1891, the brother of Nathaniel Alanson Burnell. Enlisted service with the Rhode Island National Guard 1916-1917. Commissioned in the Coast Artillery in 1917. Served with the 79th Field Artillery in France 1918-1919. Professor of military science and tactics at Iowa State College of Agriculture and Mechanical Arts 1924-1929, from which he earned a B.S. in 1928. Professor of military science and tactics at the University of Illinois 1933-1937. Instructor at the Command and General Staff School 1940-1942. Chief of staff of 98th Infantry Division 1942-1943. Commander of 409th Field Artillery Group from 1943. Brigadier general in March 1945. Reverted to colonel in February 1946. Retired as brigadier general in February 1948. Decorations included the Legion of Merit, Bronze Star and Commendation Ribbon. Died on December 24, 1968.

Burns, James Henry (1885-1972) Born on September 13, 1885, in Pawling, New York. Commissioned in the field artillery from West Point in 1908. Served at Vera Cruz in 1914. Duty in the office of the chief ordnance officer, AEF in 1918. Graduated from the Army Industrial College in 1926 and the Army War College in 1927. Ordnance officer in the Philippine Department August 1932-August 1935. In the office of the chief of staff, U.S. Army 1935-1936. Executive officer to the assistant secretary of war, then the under secretary of war 1936-1942. Major general in October 1940. Chief of the Army Ordnance Corps March 1942-September 1944. Retired in December 1944. Decorations included two Distinguished Service Medals. Died on November 27, 1972.

Burpee, Clarence Lemar (1894-n/a) Born in Jackson, Georgia, on September 12, 1894. Enlisted service with the Marine Corps 1918-1919. Discharged in 1919. With Atlantic Coast Line Railroad 1920-1941. Appointed lieutenant colonel in the engineer reserve in July 1941. Called to active duty as colonel in June 1942. Commanding officer of 703rd Railway Grand-Division June 1942-October 1943. Director of military railways in Italy in 1943. With the 2nd Military Railway Service at Army Service Forces Unit Training Center 1943-1944. Brigadier general in February 1944. Assistant chief of transportation in the Military Railways Division at the European Theater of Operations June 1944-February 1945. Returned to inactive status. Decorations included the Distinguished Service Medal and Legion of Merit.

Burress, Withers A. (1894–1977) Born in Richmond, Virginia, on November 24, 1894. Graduated from VMI in 1914. Commissioned in the infantry in 1916. Served with 23rd Infantry, 2nd Division in the AEF in World War I. Instructor at the Infantry School 1920-1922. Graduated from Command and General Staff School in 1931, then instructor there until 1933. Graduated from the Army War College in 1935. Professor, then commandant of cadets at West Point 1935-1940. At the War Department General Staff 1940-1941. Brigadier general in March 1942, major general in August 1942. Commanding general of 100th Infantry Division 1942-1945. Commanding general of VI Corps 1945-1946. Assignments after the war included commanding general of the Infantry School 1948-1951, VII Corps 1951-1953 and First Army 1953-1954. Retired as lieutenant general in November 1954. Decorations included the Distinguished Service Medal, Silver Star, Legion of Merit and two Bronze Stars. Died on June 13, 1977.

Burt, Ernest Hill (1892–1984) Born in New Haven, Connecticut, on June 29, 1892. B.S. from Michigan State in 1914. With the 14th Infantry in the U.S. during World War I. Commissioned in the field artillery, Connecticut National Guard in 1916 and the infantry, Regular Army, in 1917. LL.B. from Yale in 1919. Instructor at West Point 1923-1926. Transferred to the Judge Advocate General Corps in 1928. Graduated from Command and General Staff School in 1931. Legal advisor to Major General Johnson Hagood and Major General Frank McCoy 1931-1934. LL.M. from George Washington University in 1940. Graduated from the Army War College in 1941. Chief of the military justice section in the office of the judge advocate general, U.S. Army 1941-1942. Brigadier general in December 1942. Judge advocate general representative at headquarters of U.S. Army forces in the Far East May 1944 until retirement in October 1946. Decorations included the Legion of Merit. Died on February 26, 1984.

Busbee, Charles Manly (1893–1970) Born on July 3, 1893, in Raleigh, North Carolina. Commissioned in the field artillery from West Point in 1915. Served with the Punitive Expedition into Mexico 1916-1917. Graduated from Command and General Staff School in 1926. Instructor at General Service Schools 1926-1928. Graduated from the Army War College in 1930. Commanding officer of 79th Field Artillery May-December 1941. Assistant chief of staff for operations at Eastern Defense Command in 1942. Brigadier general in July 1942. Commanding general of 102nd Division Artillery August 1942-1946. Reverted to colonel in April 1946. Retired in July 1953. Decorations included the Legion of Merit, two Bronze Stars and the Commendation Ribbon. Died on January 19, 1970, in Salem, Virginia.

Butcher, Edwin (1879–1950) Born in Staten Island, New York, on June 28, 1879. Commissioned in the infantry from West Point in 1904. Served in the Philippines 1907-1911 and Panama 1915-1918. Graduated from Command and General Staff School in 1924 and the Army War College in 1929. Chief of staff of the Philippine Division October 1936-October 1938. Member of the Infantry Board 1938-1940. Assistant chief of staff, then chief of staff at III Corps Area 1940 until retirement in June 1942. Recalled to active duty in July 1942 in the same position. Brigadier general in April 1943. Retired again in January 1944. Decorations included two Silver Stars and the Legion of Merit. Died on July 29, 1950.

Butler, Frederic Bates (1896-1987) Born on October 5, 1896, in San Francisco, California. Commissioned in the Corps of Engineers from West Point in 1918. Aide to Brigadier General William D. Connor in China 1923-1926. Instructor at West Point 1926-1927. Again aide to Major General Connor, now superintendent of West Point 1933-1935. Commanding officer of 1st Engineers 1940-1942 then 168th Infantry in 1943. Brigadier general in January 1944. Assistant division commander of 34th Infantry Division, then deputy commanding general of VI Corps, finally assistant division commander of 45th Division 1944-1945. Commanding general of the Infantry Replacement Training Center at Camp Fannin in 1945. Retired in April 1953. Decorations included the Distinguished Service Cross, two Legions of Merit, the Bronze Star and Purple Heart. Died on June 20, 1987.

Byers, Clovis Ethelbert (1899-1973) Born on November 5, 1899, in Columbus, Ohio. Commissioned in the cavalry from West Point in 1920. Graduated from Command and General Staff School in 1936 and the Army War College in 1940. Chief of staff of 77th Division in 1942. Brigadier general in October 1942. Chief of staff of I Corps 1942-1943. Chief of staff of Eighth Army 1944-1948. Major general in June 1945. Assignments after the war included commanding general of the 82nd Airborne Division 1948-1949, commanding general of XVI Corps in 1952, chief of staff of Allied Forces Southern Europe 1952-1954, commanding general of X Corps in 1954, deputy commandant of the National War College 1954-1955 and commandant of the NATO Defense College in Paris 1955-1957. Retired as lieutenant general in June 1959. Decorations included the Distinguished Service Cross, two Distinguished Service Medals, two Silver Stars, two Legions of Merit, three Bronze Stars and the Purple Heart. Died on December 13, 1973.

Byron, Joseph Wilson (1892-1951) Born on June 3, 1892, in Fort Meade, South Dakota. Commissioned in the cavalry from West Point in 1914. Served with 304th Tank Battalion in AEF December 1918-February 1919. Resigned in 1919. Called to active duty in July 1942 as colonel at one dollar per year pay. Brigadier general in August 1942. Chief of the Army Exchange Service August 1942-August 1945. Major general in September 1944. Returned to civilian status after the war. Decorations included the Distinguished Service Medal. Died on April 12, 1951 while on a Caribbean cruise.

Caffey, Benjamin Franklin Jr. (1893-1972) Born in Salt Lake City, Utah, on July 20, 1893. LL.B. from the University of Michigan in 1916. Commissioned in the infantry in 1917. Served with the 16th Infantry, AEF at Aisne-Marne, St. Mihiel and Meuse-Argonne 1917-1918. Aide-de-camp to Major General Robert L. Bullard, then briefly Major General Harry C. Hale, and Bullard again 1920-1924. Aide-de-camp to Major General William R. Smith June 1925-March 1928. Instructor at the Infantry School 1928-1929. Instructor, then assistant professor at West Point 1929-1933. Instructor with the 34th National Guard Division 1935-1937. Duty in the Philippines 1937-1938. Aide to Lieutenant General Hugh A. Drum 1940-1941. Commanding officer of 39th Infantry, then 29th Combat Team in 1942. Brigadier general in November 1942. Assistant division commander of 34th Division 1942-1943. With the special operations section at Allied Force Headquarters in the Mediterranean, then in the North African Theater of Operations in 1944. Commanding general of Special Troops, Fourth Army September 1944-April 1945. In the office of the chief of staff, U.S. Army in 1945. Patient in Walter Reed Army Hospital September 1949 until retirement in March 1950. Decorations included the Distinguished Service Medal, two Legions of Merit and the Bronze Star. Died on July 9, 1972.

Callender, George Russell (1884-1973) Born in Everett, Massachusetts, on May 13, 1884. M.D. from Tufts College in 1908. Commissioned in the Medical Reserve Corps in 1912. Graduated from Army Medical School in 1913. Served in the Hawaii Department 1916-1918. Pathalogist at Army Medical Center in 1939. Assistant commandant, then commandant of Medical Department Professional Service Schools 1940-1946. Retired in November 1946. Brigadier general in March 1945. Decorations included the Distinguished Service Medal. Author of *Malaria in Panama* (1929). Died on February 26, 1973.

Camm, Frank (1895-1976) Born in Lynchburg, Virginia, on January 8, 1895. LL.B. from the University of Virginia in 1917. Commissioned in the field artillery in 1917. Served with the 55th Artillery, AEF in World War I and saw action at Meuse-Argonne and Aisne-Marne. Assistant professor at Harvard 1926-30, then Xavier University 1936-1940. Graduated from Command and General Staff School in 1941. Commander of 56th Field Artillery 1941-1942. Executive officer of 78th Division Artillery 1942-1943. Brigadier general in April 1943. Commanding general of 15th Field Artillery Brigade, then XIII Corps Artillery, then 78th Division Artillery, finally 31st Antiaircraft Artillery Brigade 1943-1946. Retired in August 1954. Decorations included the Legion of Merit, two Bronze Stars and the Commendation Ribbon. Died on December 15, 1976.

Camp, Thomas James (1886-1973) Born in Seymour, Connecticut, on November 10, 1886. B.A. and M.A. from Yale in 1908 and 1915. Commissioned in the infantry in 1912. Instructor at the first officers training camp in 1917. Battalion commander in France in 1918. Graduated from Command and General Staff School in 1926, then instructor there until 1930. Graduated from the Army War College in 1931 and the Naval War College in 1935. With the War Department General Staff 1937-1941. Organized and commanded the 51st Armored Infantry 1941-1942. Brigadier general in March 1942. With 1st Armored Division in 1942. Commanding general of Combat Command "A" in 12th Armored Division 1942-1943. Commanding general of Armored Replacement Training Command, then Panama Mobile Force and Security Command 1943-1946. Retired in October 1946. Decorations included two Legions of Merit. Died on December 23, 1973.

Campbell, Arthur Griffith (1884-1957) Born in Lexington, Virginia, on November 15, 1884. Graduated from Virginia Military Institute in 1906. Commissioned in the Coast Artillery Corps in 1908. Battery commander in 52nd Artillery, AEF in 1918. With the military intelligence division at the War Department General Staff 1918-1921. Duty in Panama 1924-1927. Graduated from Command and General Staff School in 1924 and the Army War College in 1928. Brigadier general in October 1940. Commanding general of Camp Pendleton November 1940-November 1941. Commanding general of 2nd Coast Artillery District, Fort Hamilton November 1941-December 1941. Commander of the Newport Subsector, New England Sector of North Atlantic Coastal Frontier December 1941 until retirement in August 1944. Died on January 25, 1957.

Campbell, Boniface (1895-1988) Born in Colby, Washington, on September 27, 1895. B.S. from Bowdoin College in 1917. Commissioned in the infantry in 1917. Served in the Philippines 1919-1923. Professor of military science and tactics at Purdue 1927-1931, then instructor at Field Artillery School 1931-1935. Graduated from Command and General Staff School in 1936. Professor of military science and tactics at Arkansas State College 1936-1938. Graduated from the Army War College in 1939. In the operations and training divisiion of the War Department General Staff 1939-1942. Brigadier general in August 1942. Commanding general of 98th Infantry Division Artillery, then IX Corps Artillery August 1942-October 1945. Reverted to colonel in March 1946. Retired in December 1956. Decorations included two Legions of Merit. Died on March 25, 1988.

Campbell, Levin Hicks Jr. (1886-1976) Born in Washington, DC, on November 23, 1886. Graduated from USNA in 1909. Resigned to accept a commission in the Coast Artillery Corps. Served in the office of the chief of ordnance in World War I and again 1940-1941. Brigadier general in October 1940. Assistant chief of industrial service in the office of the chief of ordnance January-June 1942. Major general in April 1942. Chief of ordnance 1942-1946. Lieutenant general in April 1945. Retired in May 1946. Decorations included the Distinguished Service Medal. Died on November 1, 1976.

Campbell, William Archibald (1887-1971) Born in Salt Lake City on December 27, 1887. Commissioned in the infantry, Utah National Guard in 1908. Served with the 146th Field Artillery, AEF in the Battle of Marne in 1918. Transferred to the field artillery in 1920. Instructor at the Field Artillery School 1928-1932. Graduated from Command and General Staff School in 1934. Instructor with the Utah National Guard 1934-1936. Graduated from the Army War College in 1937. Instructor at the Command and General Staff School 1937-1941. With 49th Field Artillery in 1941. Brigadier general in April 1942. Commander of 3rd Infantry Division Artillery 1942-1944. At headquarters of Army Ground Forces, then director of ground force instruction at the Command and General Staff School August 1944-1946. Reverted to colonel in March 1946. Retired in February 1948.

Decorations included the Distinguished Service Medal, Legion of Merit and Bronze Star. Died on August 18, 1971.

Campbell, William Franklin (1892-1964) Born in Olney, Illinois, on February 7, 1892. B.S. from the University of Illinois in 1917. Commissioned in the infantry in 1917. Instructor at the Quartermaster Corps School 1927-1930. Graduated from Command and General Staff School in 1932 and the Army War College in 1933. Finance officer in the intelligence division of the War Department General Staff 1933-1937. Instructor at the Command and General Staff School 1937-1941. Duty in the office of the quartermaster general July 1941-October 1942. Ground quartermaster at the Army War College October 1942-December 1943. Deputy chief quartermaster, then chief at Services of Supply in the Southwest Pacific Area December 1943-April 1945. Brigadier general in November 1944. Commanding general of 76th Quartermaster Base Depot in the Philippine Islands in 1945. Chief quartermaster for U.S. Army forces in the Pacific August 1945-June 1946. Reverted to colonel in June 1946 and retired in June 1949. Decorations included two Legions of Merit and the Bronze Star. Died on November 28, 1964.

Canham, Charles Draper Willliam (1901-1963) Born in Kola, Mississippi, on January 26, 1901. Enlisted service in the Regular Army 1919-1920. Commissioned in the infantry from West Point in 1926. Duty in the Philippines 1931-1935. Graduated from Command and General Staff School in 1939. With the 18th Infantry 1939-1941. Deputy chief of staff, then commanding officer of 116th Infantry, 29th Infantry Division September 1942-July 1944. Wounded during the invasion of Normandy. Brigadier general on the battlefield in August 1944. Assistant division commander of 8th Infantry Division, then 4th Infantry Division 1944-1946. Assignments after the war included commanding general of 82nd Airborne Division in 1952, deputy commanding general of Third Army October 1952-July 1953, commanding general of 3rd Infantry Division November 1953-August 1954. Deputy commanding general of IX Corps in 1954 then commanding general of XI Corps (Reserve) January 1958 until retirement in January 1961. Decorations included the Distinguished Service Cross, Silver Star, three Legions of Merit, two Bronze Stars and the Purple Heart. Died on August 21, 1963.

Canine, Ralph Julian (1895-1969) Born in Flora, Indiana, on November 9, 1895. B.S. from Northwestern in 1916. Commissioned in the field artillery in 1917. Served with 8th Field Artillery and 7th Artillery Brigade, AEF 1918-1919. Assistant professor of military science and tactics at Purdue University 1921-1924. Duty in the Philippines 1925-1927. Graduated from Command and General Staff School in 1938. Assistant professor of military science and tactics at Ohio State University 1938-1941. Commanding officer of 99th Field Artillery Battalion May 1941-February 1942. Executive officer of 77th Division Artillery in 1942. Assistant chief of staff for operations, then chief of staff of XII Corps February 1942-September 1945. Brigadier general in November 1944. Assignments after the war included chief of staff of V Corps 1946-1947, commanding general of 1st Infantry Division Artillery, then division commander September 1947-October 1949 and commanding general of Armed Forces Security Agency, later renamed National Security Agency, September 1950 until retirement as lieutenant general in April 1957. Decorations included two Distinguished Service Medals, the Silver Star, Legion of Merit and two Bronze Stars. Died on March 8, 1969.

Cannon, Robert Milchrist (1901-1976) Born in Salt Lake City, Utah, on August 16, 1901. Commissioned in the field artillery from West Point in 1925. Graduated from Command and General Staff School in 1938. Instructor at the Field Artillery School 1938-1942, then with Chinese troops in the China-Burma-India Theater of Operations 1942-1943. Chief of staff of the China-Burma-India Theater of Operations March 1943-May 1945. Brigadier general in August 1944. Commanding general of XXXII Corps Artillery in 1945. Assistant chief of staff for transportation in Tenth Army, then assistant chief of staff for supply in Sixth Army 1945-1948. Assignments after the war included Deputy Commander in Chief U.S. Army Pacific 1959-1961. Retired in August 1961 as lieutenant general. Decorations included two Distinguished Service Medals, the Bronze Star and Air Medal. Died on September 3, 1976.

Caraway, Paul Wyatt (1905-1985) Born on December 23, 1905, in Jonesboro, Arkansas. Commissioned in the infantry from West Point in 1929. LL.B. from Georgetown University in 1933. Stationed in Tientsin with the 15th Regiment 1935-1937. Instructor at West Point 1938-1942. Graduated from Command and General Staff School in 1942. In the operations division of the War Department General Staff 1942-1944. Deputy chief of staff for plans in the China Theater of Operations 1944-1945. Brigadier general in May 1945. Commanding general of the Chunking Liaison Group, China Theater of Operations 1945-1946. Reverted to colonel in April 1946. Assignments after the war included commanding general of 7th Infantry Division 1955-1956 and high commissioner of the Ryukyu Islands 1961-1964. Retired as lieutenant general in July 1964. Decorations included two Distinguished Service Medals and two Legions of Merit. Died on December 13, 1985.

Carleton, Don Emerson (1899-1977) Born in LaCrosse, Wisconsin, on October 22, 1899. Enlisted service with 2nd Battalion, Chemical Warfare Service 1918-1919. Commissioned in the cavalry in 1923. Served in the Philippines 1930-1932. Instructor with the New Jersey National Guard 1936-1940. Plans and training officer with 8th Cavalry 1940-1941. Commanding officer of the Anti-Tank Troop, 1st Cavalry Division in 1941. Graduated from Command and General Staff School in 1942. Executive officer of 5th Cavalry in 1942. Secretary of the general staff at Allied Force Headquarters North Africa October 1942-March 1943. Chief of staff of 3rd Infantry Division, then VI Corps, finally Fifth Army March 1943-May 1945. Brigadier general in September 1944. Chief of staff of Third Army 1945-1946. Reverted to colonel in April 1946. Retired in August 1954. Awards included the Distinguished Service Medal, two Legions of Merit and the Bronze Star. Died on August 19, 1977.

Carrington, Gordon De L. (1894-1944) Born in Evansville, Indiana, on November 15, 1894. Attended San Diego Junior College 1914-1915 and the University of California 1915-1916. Commissioned in the Coast Artillery Corps in 1916. Instructor at the Coast Artillery School in 1918. Served in Panama 1919-1921. Instructor with the California National Guard 1922-1925. Graduated from Command and General Staff School in 1932 and the Army War College in 1936. Instructor at the Army War College 1938-1939. In the office of the chief of the Air Corps in 1940. Assistant chief of staff for personnel at the Army War College 1941-1942. Brigadier general in February 1942. Commanding general of Coast Artillery Replacement Training Center, Camp Wallace in 1942. Inspector of training, then assistant chief of staff for operations at Antiartillery Command July 1942-August 1943. Commanding general of 62nd Antiaircraft Artillery Brigade August 1943 until his death on August 21, 1944.

Carroll, Percy James (1891-1987) Born in East St. Louis, Illinois, on February 8, 1891. M.D. from St. Louis University in 1914. Commissioned in the Medical Corps in 1917. Post surgeon at Fort Stotsenburg, the Philippines in 1940. Commanding officer of Sternberg General Hospital 1941-1942. Chief surgeon for U.S. Army Forces Southwest Pacific Area February 1942-December 1943. Brigadier general in June 1943. Commanding general of Vaughn General Hospital 1944 until retirement in September 1946. Decorations included the Distinguished Service Medal and Legion of Merit. Died on December 22, 1987.

Carter, Arthur Hazelton (1884-1965) Born in Hillsboro, Kansas, on January 6, 1884. Commissioned in the field artillery from West Point in 1905. Resigned to enter the Officers Reserve Corps. Served on active duty in ordnance and field artillery units 1917-1919. Discharged in 1919. Ordered to active duty in October 1941 as brigadier general. Served in the office of the under secretary of war October 1941-March 1942. Director of the fiscal division at Services of Supply March 1942-February 1946. Major general in April 1943. Returned to civilian life as senior partner with Haskins and Sells in New York City. Decorations included the Distinguished Service Medal. Died on January 4, 1965.

Carter, William Vaulx (1883-1971) Born in Fort Lowell, Arizona, on January 30, 1883. Commissioned in the cavalry from West Point in 1904. Aide to his father, Brigadier General W.H. Carter, in 1907. Duty with 7th Cavalry in the Philippines October 1913-November 1915. Professor of military science and tactics at Bingham School, Asheville, North Carolina 1916-1917. Transferred to the Adjutant General Department in 1922. Adjutant general of the Hawaiian Coast Artillery Brigade 1931-1935 then at III Corps Area 1935-1940. Brigadier general in October 1940. Assistant adjutant general of the Army October 1940 until retirement in August 1942. Died on January 26, 1971.

Case, Homer (1894-n/a) Born in Elkland, Missouri, on December 8, 1894. B.S. from Drury College in 1915. Attended Washington University 1915-1917. Commissioned in the Coast Artillery Corps in 1917. Served with 54th Artillery, AEF in the St. Mihiel and Argonne engagements and wounded at Verdun in 1918. Duty in the Philippines 1923-1926. Instructor at Coast Artillery School 1927-1931. Graduated from Command and General Staff School in 1933. In the Philippines again 1934-1936. Graduated from the Army War College in 1937. With the intelligence division at the War Department General Staff 1937-1941. Assistant chief of staff for intelligence with the Special Army Observers Group in London May-July 1941. Duty with the Washington Provisional Brigade 1941-1942. Brigadier general in December 1942. Commanding general of the 31st Coast Artillery Brigade December 1942-February 1943, then 32nd Coast Artillery 1943-1945. Commanding general of 102nd Antiaircraft Artillery Brigade July-November 1945. Assistant to the chief of ground developments division at Army Ground Forces November 1945-July 1946. Retired in August 1954. Decorations included the Distinguished Service Medal and two Legions of Merit.

Case, Rolland Webster (1882-1957) Born in Manchester, Michigan, on May 26, 1882. Commissioned in the infantry from West Point in 1905. Graduated from Command and General Staff School in 1923 and the Army War College in 1929. Brigadier general in October 1940. Commander of Aberdeen Proving Ground and Watertown Arsenal 1942-1943. Retired in August 1943. Decorations included the Legion of Merit. Died on December 16, 1957.

Casey, Hugh John (1898-1981) Born on June 7, 1898, in Brooklyn, New York. Commissioned in the Corps of Engineers from West Point in 1918. Served in the U.S. in World War I. Professor of military science and tactics at the University of Kansas 1922-1926. Engineering assistant to General MacArthur 1937-1940. Chief of the design and engineering section in the office of the quartermaster general, U.S. Army 1940-1941. Chief engineer for U.S. Army forces in the Far East, then at general headquarters of the Southwest Pacific Area 1941-1944. Brigadier general in January 1942, major general in February 1944. Commanding general of Army Service Command in Pacific Ocean Areas 1944-1945. Chief engineer of Army forces in the Pacific Area 1945-1946. Retired in December 1949. Decorations included the Distinguished Service Cross, two Distinguished Service Medals, the Silver Star, Legion of Merit and Bronze Star. Died on August 30, 1981.

Catron, Thomas Benton (1888-1973) Born in Santa Fe, New Mexico, on May 15, 1888, the son of U.S. Senator Thomas Benton. Commissioned in the infantry from West Point in 1909. Director of the Army Intelligence School in the AEF 1918-1919. Instructor at General Service Schools 1919-1923. Director of instruction at West Point 1923-1927. Editor of the "Infantry Journal" in the office of the chief of infantry 1927-1931. Duty in Hawaii September 1934-March 1936. Retired in March 1936. Involved in the oil business and sheep ranching 1936-1941. Returned to active duty in February 1941. Commanding officer of 1611th Corps Area 1941-1943. Executive officer of the Women's Army Corps 1943-1944. Director of personnel at 3rd Service Command January 1944 until retirement again in February 1946. Brigadier general in January 1945. Decorations included the Distinguished Service Medal, two Legions of Merit and the Commendation Ribbon. Died on April 18, 1973.

Chamberlain, Edwin William (1903-1966) Born on August 30, 1903, in Challis, Idaho. Commissioned in the field artillery from West Point in 1927. Duty with the 59th Coast Artillery in the Philippines November 1927-October 1929. Member of the Coast Artillery Board June 1937-August 1938. Intelligence officer, office of the assistant chief of staff for intelligence at Fort Bragg 1938-1939. Assistant to the intelligence officer, office of the deputy chief of staff for intelligence at IX Corps February-July 1940. Graduated from Command and General Staff School in 1940. Assigned to 70th Coast Artillery July-August 1940. Duty in the operations and training division at the War Department General Staff August 1940-October 1942. Brigadier general in June 1945. Retired in September 1946. Decorations included the Distinguished Service Medal. Died on May 1, 1966.

Chamberlin, Harry Dwight (1887-1944) Born in Elgin, Illinois, on May 20, 1887. Commissioned in the cavalry from West Point in 1910. Attended the French Cavalry School in 1923 and the Italian Cavalry School in 1924. Graduated from Command and General Staff School in 1928. Captain of U.S. Olympic Equestrian Team in 1932. Graduated from the Army War College in 1933. Chief of staff of 1st Cavalry Division 1938-1939. Commander of 2nd Cavalry 1939-1941. Brigadier general in April 1941. Commander of a task force in the invasion of New Hebrides Islands in 1942. Hospitalized in the U.S. in late 1942. Commanding general of Fort Ord at the time of his death on September 29, 1944.

Chamberlin, Stephen J. (1889-1971) Born on December 23, 1889, in Spring Hill, Kansas. Commissioned in the infantry from West Point in 1912. Served in the U.S. during World War I. Graduated from Command and General Staff School in 1925. In the office of the chief of information, War Department 1926-1930. Graduated from the Army War College in 1933. Chief of construction division in the War Department General Staff 1938-1941. Deputy chief of staff, then chief of staff of U.S. Army forces in Australia in 1942. Brigadier general in February 1942. Deputy chief of staff for operations in the Southwest Pacific Area 1942-1945. Major general in September 1943. Director of the intelligence division, U.S. Army General Staff 1946-1948. Assignments after the war commanding general of Fifth Army as lieutenant general 1948-1951. Retired in September 1951. Decorations included the Navy Cross, four Distinguished Service Medals and the Silver Star. Died on October 23, 1971.

Chambers, William Earl (1892-1952) Born on February 9, 1892, in Chicago, Illinois. Commissioned in the infantry from West Point in 1916. In the tactical department of West Point 1917-1919. Graduated from Command and General Staff School in 1926 and returned as instructor 1929-1933. Graduated from the Army War College in 1934. Brigadier general in June 1942. With Iceland Base Command 1942-1943. In operations section of headquarters of European Theater of Operations 1944-1946. Retired in 1946. Decorations included the Distinguished

Service Medal and Legion of Merit. Died in an aircraft accident in Nogales, Mexico, on February 11, 1952.

Chandler, Rex Eugene (1901-1964) Born on July 24, 1901, in Gazette, Maryland. Commissioned in the field artillery from West Point in 1923. Aide-de-camp to Brigadier General George Van Horn Mosely in 1927. Instructor at West Point 1928-1932, then the Field Artillery School 1933-1936. Graduated from Command and General Staff School in 1937. Instructor again at the Field Artillery School 1937-1940. Duty in the office of the chief of field artillery June 1940-March 1942. Commanding officer of the 328th Field Artillery Battalion in 1942. Deputy chief of staff of I Corps 1942-1943. Brigadier general in May 1944. Commanding general of 1st Cavalry Division Artillery 1944-1945. Reverted to colonel in March 1946 and retired in July 1947 Brigadier general on the retired list in 1948. Decorations included the Silver Star, two Legions of Merit and two Bronze Stars. Died on September 6, 1964.

Chapin, Willis McDonald (1893-1960) Born on June 27, 1893, in St. Johns, Michigan. Commissioned in the Coast Artillery Corps from West Point in 1916. Instructor at West Point 1918-1919. Professor of military science and tactics at Virginia Polytechnic Institute 1926-1929. Graduated from Command and General Staff School in 1934. Instructor with the Maine National Guard 1934-1939. Antiaircraft officer for the Canal Zone 1939-1942. Commanding officer of Antiaircraft Artillery Brigade in North African Theater of Operations 1943-1944. Brigadier general in January 1944. Commanding general of 31st Antiaircraft Artillery Brigade 1944-1945. Reverted to colonel in December 1945 and retired in December 1949. Decorations included the Bronze Star and two Legions of Merit. Died on October 15, 1960.

Chapman, Elbridge Gerry Jr. (1895-1954) Born in Denver on November 20, 1895. B.A. from the University of Colorado in 1917. Enlisted service in Colorado National Guard 1916-1917. Commissioned in the infantry, Officers Reserve Corps in 1917. Served with the 5th Machine Gun Battalion in World War Two, seeing action at Chateau-Thierry, St. Mihiel, Champagne and Meuse-Argonne, where he was wounded. LL.B. from the University of Colorado in 1920. Professor of military science and tactics at Northwestern 1923-1928. Duty with 45th Infantry in the Philippines April 1931-August 1935. Aide to Major General Paul B. Malone at headquarters of IX Corps Area 1935-1936. Graduated from the Command and General Staff School in 1938. Instructor at the Infantry School 1938-1941. Commanding officer of 88th Airborne Infantry Battalion September 1941-March 1942. Brigadier general in July 1942. Executive officer at headquarters of Airborne Command 1942-1943. Major general in March 1943. Commanding general of Airborne Command in 1943, then Airborne Division 1943-1945. Commandant of the Parachute School January 1946 until retired in November 1946. Decorations included the Distinguished Service Cross, Distinguished Service Medal, two Silver Stars and the Purple Heart. Died on July 6, 1954.

Chase, William Curtis (1895-1986) Born in Providence, Rhode Island, on March 9, 1895. Enlisted service with Rhode Island National Guard 1913-1916. B.A. from Brown University in 1916. Commissioned in the cavalry in November 1916. Served on the Mexican border in 1916 and with the 4th Division in World War I. Graduated from Command and General Staff School in 1931 and the Army War College in 1935. Instructor at the Cavalry School 1935-1938 then Command and General Staff School 1938-1940. With the War Department General Staff 1940-1942. Assistant division commander, then commanding general of 1st Cavalry Division 1942-1945. Brigadier general in March 1943, major general in March 1945. Assignments after the war included chief of staff, then deputy commanding general of Third Army 1949-1951. Retired in February 1955. Decorations included the Distinguished Service Cross, two Distinguished Service Medals, the Legion of Merit, four Bronze Stars, the Commendation Ribbon and Purple Heart. Died on August 21, 1986.

Chavin, Raphael Saul (1894-1974) Born in New York City on July 19, 1894. B.A. from Cornell in 1916. Enlisted service with Texas National Guard 1916-1917. Commissioned in the Coast Artillery Corps in 1917. Commanding officer of 54th Ammunition Train, AEF 1918-1919. Attended Massachusetts Institute of Technology 1921-1922. M.B.A. from Harvard in 1931. Graduated from the Army Industrial College in 1935. Commanding officer of Ravenna (Ohio) Ordnance Plant 1940-1942. Brigadier general in December 1942. Duty in the office of the chief of ordnance 1942-1943. Commanding general of Stockton Ordnance Depot August 1943-February 1946. Reverted to colonel in February 1946. Retired in December 1952. Decorations included the Legion of Merit. Died on June 3, 1974.

Cheadle, Henry Barlow (1891-1959) Born on May 1, 1891, in Cannon Falls, Minnesota. Commissioned in the infantry from West Point in 1913. Served as an observer in the AEF in World War I. With the 28th Infantry at Vera Cruz March-November 1914. Aide-de-camp to Brigadier General S.H. Plummer 1916-1918. Instructor at the Infantry School October 1918-September 1921. Duty in the Philippine Islands 1922-1925. Graduated from the Command and General Staff School in 1927. In the military intelligence division at the War Department General Staff 1928-1929. Graduated from the Army War College in 1931. In the operations and training division at the War Department General Staff 1931-1934. Military attache in Spain, Portugal and Hungary 1938-1940. With 16th Infantry 1941-1942. Brigadier general in December 1942. Assistant division commander of 94th Division 1943-1945. Reverted to colonel in February 1946. Retired in April 1951. Decorations included the Distinguished Service Medal, two Bronze Stars and the Commendation Ribbon. Died on December 16, 1959.

Cheves, Gilbert Xavier (1895-1985) Born in Richardson, Georgia, on March 5, 1895. Attended Catholic University 1913-1915. B.S. from the University of Georgia in 1917. Commissioned in the cavalry in 1917. Served with the 6th Cavalry, AEF at Rochefort, Laprice, La Vernelle and Gievres 1918-1919. Instructor, then adjutant at the Cavalry School 1922-1927. Graduated from Command and

General Staff School in 1935. Duty in the office of the chief of cavalry 1938-1940. Liaison officer with the Armored Force 1940-1942. Commanding officer of 36th Armored Regiment July 1942-March 1943. Brigadier general in April 1943. Chief of staff of Army Service Forces in the Middle East Theater of Operations March 1943-January 1944. Commanding general of Base Section, then Services of Supply, finally Services of Supply for the China-Burma-India Theater of Operations and the Pacific Theater of Operations 1944-1945. Major general in September 1944. Reverted to colonel in 1946. Retired in June 1947. Decorations included the Distinguished Service Medal and Legion of Merit. Died on November 15, 1985.

Chickering, William Elbridge (1895-1959) Born in Smithville, New Jersey, on January 8, 1895. Commissioned in the infantry in 1917. Served with the 7th Infantry, AEF at Champagne-Marne, Aisne-Marne, St. Mihiel and Meuse-Argonne 1917-1918. Wounded and taken prisoner on October 3, 1918. Aide-de-camp to Brigadier General Fred W. Sladen in 1921. Transferred to the Adjutant General's Department in 1927. Assistant adjutant general in the Philippine Department July 1933-May 1936. Graduated from Command and General Staff School in 1937. Duty in the adjutant general's office 1938-1940. Deputy administrator of export control in the War Department 1940-1941, then with the Army Group in the War Department 1941-1942. Adjutant general, then chief of staff at headquarters of Services of Supply, U.S. Army forces in the Middle East July 1942-November 1943. Director of the Army Postal Service 1943-1946. Brigadier general in January 1944. Retired in February 1946. Decorations included the Silver Star, two Legions of Merit and the Purple Heart. Died on March 2, 1959.

Christian, Thomas Jonathan Jackson (1888-1952) Born in San Diego on August 29, 1888. Commissioned in the cavalry from West Point in 1911. Served with the 7th Cavalry in the Philippine Islands in 1915, then the 16th Cavalry on the Mexican border 1916-1917. Professor of military science and tactics at Colorado State Agricultural College in 1917. Instructor with Cornell University ROTC 1918-1923. Graduated from the Command and General Staff School in 1927. Professor of military science and tactics at the University of Chicago 1927-1933. Graduated from the the Army War College in 1934. With the war plans division at the War Department General Staff 1934-1938. Post executive officer at West Point 1939-1940. Commanding officer of Field Artillery Replacement Center, Camp Roberts 1940-1941. Brigadier general in April 1941. Commanding general of 73rd Field Artillery Brigade 1941-1942. Reverted to colonel June 1942. Retired in August 1948. Died on September 15, 1952.

Christiansen, James George (1897-1982) Born on September 23, 1897, in Portland, Oregon. Attended the University of California 1915-1916. Commissioned in the Corps of Engineers from West Point in 1918. Assistant professor of military science and tactics at Oregon Agricultural College 1921-1925. Instructor at West Point 1932-1936. Graduated from Command and General Staff School in 1937 and the Army War College in 1940. Duty at GHQ U.S. Army 1940-1942.

Deputy chief of staff, then chief of staff of Army Ground Forces June 1942-September 1945. Brigadier general in March 1943, major general in August 1944. Assignments after the war included commanding general of 2nd Armored Division September 1947-August 1949 and commanding general of 6th Armored Division March 1952-March 1953. Retired in September 1954. Decorations included two Distinguished Service Medals and the Silver Star. Died on July 6, 1982.

Christmas, John Kay (1895-1962) Born in Pittsburgh, Pennsylvania, on March 4, 1895. B.S. from Lafayette College in 1917. Commissioned in the Coast Artillery Corps in 1917. Served with 60th Artillery at St. Mihiel and Argonne offensives in 1918. Graduated from Command and General Staff School in 1934 and the Army War College in 1935. Officer in charge of the automotive division at Aberdeen Proving Ground 1939-1941. Chief of the tank and combat vehicle division in the office of the chief of ordnance 1941-1942. Brigadier general in May 1942. Assistant chief of the Tank-Automotive Center in Detroit 1942-1945. Major general in October 1943. Assistant to the chief of ordnance in 1945. Retired in January 1954. Decorations included the Distinguished Service Medal and Commendation Ribbon. Died on March 8, 1962.

Christy, William Canou (1885-1957) Born in Phoenix, Arizona, on November 25, 1885. Commissioned in the cavalry from West Point in 1907. Served in Philippine Islands 1915-1917. Duty as motor transport officer with 4th and 8th Corps, AEF in 1918. Graduated from Command and General Staff School in 1925 and the Army War College in 1928. With the War Department General Staff June 1928-July 1932. Executive officer of the Cavalry School 1932-1935. Inspector general, then chief of staff of the Panama Canal Department 1940-1945. Brigadier general in September 1943. Retired in October 1946. Decorations included the Distinguished Service Medal, Legion of Merit and Commendation Ribbon. Died on January 31, 1957.

Church, John Huston (1892-1953) Born in Glen Iron, Pennsylvania, on June 28, 1892. Attended New York University 1915-1917. Commissioned in the infantry in 1917. Served with the 28th Infantry, AEF at Cantigny, Montdidier-Noyon, Aisne-Marne and Meuse-Argonne in 1918. Aide-de-camp to Brigadier General F.C. Marshall in 1920. Instructor with the Maryland National Guard 1922-1926 and again 1929-1933. Duty in the Philippine Islands 1933-1936. Graduated from Command and General Staff School in 1937. Instructor with the Arizona National Guard 1938-1940. Assistant chief of staff for operations, then chief of staff at 45th Division October 1940-September 1943. Commanding officer of 157th Infantry 1943-1944. Assistant division commander of 45th Infantry Division, then 84th Infantry Division August 1944-January 1946. Brigadier general in August 1944. Assignments after the war included commanding general of 24th Infantry Division in the Korean War in 1950 and commanding general of the Infantry Center, Fort Benning 1951-1952. Retired in June 1952. Decorations included the Distinguished Service Cross, Silver Star, Legion of Merit and three Purple Hearts. Died on November 4, 1953.

Chynoweth, Bradford Grethen (1890-1985) Born on July 20, 1890, in Fort Warren, Wyoming. Commissioned in the Corps of Engineers from West Point in 1912. Graduated from Command and General Staff School in 1928 and the Army War College in 1932. With 66th Infantry October 1939-July 1940 and 53rd Infantry July 1940-December 1941. Brigadier general in December 1941. Commanding general of the Visayan Force 1941-1942. Prisoner of war 1942-1945. Retired in October 1947. Decorations included the Distinguished Service Medal. Died on February 8, 1985.

Clark, Frank Sheldon (1885-1975) Born in Greenfield, Massachusetts, on August 2, 1885. B.S. from Norwich University in 1909. Commissioned in the Coast Artillery Corps in 1909. Served in the Philippines 1911-1914. Professor of military science and tactics at the University of Maine 1914-1917. With the AEF 1917-1919. Graduated from Command and General Staff School in 1925, the Army War College in 1930 and the Naval War College in 1931. With the war plans division of the War Department General Staff 1931-1935 and again 1938-1940. Brigadier general in October 1940. Commandant of the Coast Artillery School October 1940-January 1942. Commanding general of 41st Coast Artillery Brigade in 1942, then Seacoast Artillery Replacement Center at Camp McQuaide 1942-1943. Commanding general of Boston Sub-Sector and Harbor Defenses March 1943-January 1944. Member of the Joint Post War Separation Committee Board, office of the secretary of war and office of the chief of staff, U.S. Army January 1944 until retired in November 1945. Decorations included the Legion of Merit. Died on February 6, 1975.

Clark, Mark Wayne (1896-1984). Born on May 1, 1896, at Madison Barracks, New York. Commissioned in the infantry from West Point in 1917. Wounded in combat while commanding a battalion in France during World War I. With the War Department General Staff 1921-1924. Graduated from Command and General Staff School in 1935. Graduated from the Army War College in 1937. Staff officer with 3rd Infantry Division 1937-1940. Instructor at the Army War College 1940, then duty at GHQ, later Army Ground Forces, 1940-1942. Brigadier general in August 1941. Major general in April 1942. Commander of I Corps, Europe, July-October 1942. Lieutenant general in November 1942. Deputy commander of Allied Forces in North Africa, November 1942-January 1943. Commanded Fifth Army January 1943-December 1944. Commander of Fifth Army Group December 1944-June 1945. General in March 1945. Allied High Commissioner for Austria 1945-1947. Assignments after the war included commanding general of Sixth Army 1947-1949, commander of Army Field Forces 1949-1952 and Commander in Chief United Nations Command Korea 1952-1953. Retired in 1953. Decorations included the Distinguished Service Cross, four Distinguished Service Medals, the Legion of Merit, Bronze Star and Purple Heart. President of The Citadel 1954-1960. Author of *Calculated Risk* (1950) and *From the Danube to the Yalu* (1954). Died on April 17, 1984.

Clarke, Bruce Cooper (1901-1988) Born on April 29, 1901, in Adams, New York. Commissioned in the Corps of Engineers from West Point in 1925. Graduated from Command and General Staff School in 1940. Member of the General Staff Corps 1942-1943. Combat commander in 7th and 4th Armored Divisions 1943-1945. Brigadier general in November 1944. Staff officer at headquarters of Army Ground Forces 1945-1948. Assignments after the war included commanding general of 1st Armored Division 1951-1953, I Corps in the Korean War in 1953, U.S. Army Pacific 1954-1956, Seventh Army 1956-1958 and Continental Army Command 1958-1960. Commander in Chief U.S. Army Europe 1960-1962. Retired as general in 1962. Decorations included the Distinguished Service Cross, three Distinguished Service Medals, three Silver Stars, the Legion of Merit, three Bronze Stars, the Air Medal and Commendation Ribbon. Died on March 17, 1988.

Clarke, Carter Weldon (1896-1987) Born in Smithland, Kentucky, on September 20, 1896. Attended the University of Kentucky 1913-1916. Enlisted service in the Kentucky National Guard 1915-1918. Commissioned in the Signal Corps in 1918. Instructor at the Signal School 1929-1933. Graduated from Command and General Staff School in 1936. Chief of the War Department message center, office of the chief signal officer 1936-1939. Graduated from the Army War College in 1940. Signal officer at Second Air Force 1940-1941. Chief of the military intelligence section at the War Department General Staff, then deputy chief of the Military Intelligence Service, finally deputy director of the intelligence division at the War Department General Staff July 1941-January 1949. Brigadier general in November 1944, then reverted to colonel in 1946. Assignments after the war included chief of the Army Security Agency 1949-1950. Retired in August 1954. Decorations included the Distinguished Service Medal, Legion of Merit and two Bronze Stars. Died on January 9, 1987.

Clarkson, Herbert Slayden (1891-n/a) Born in San Antonio, Texas, May 19, 1891. Graduated from USNA in 1913. Resigned from the Navy and commissioned in the field artillery in 1913. Served with the 2nd Field Artillery in the Philippine Islands 1914-1915, with the Punitive Expedition into Mexico in 1916, and as a brigade adjutant in the AEF in 1918, seeing action at St. Mihiel and Meuse-Argonne offensives. Instructor with the Pennsylvania National Guard, then the Texas national Guard 1922-1926. Graduated from Command and General Staff School in 1928. In the operations and training division of the National Guard Bureau 1928-1930. Instructor again with the Texas National Guard 1930-1932, then at the Field Artillery School 1934-1938. Assistant inspector general at the VI Corps Area 1939-1940. Chief of the executive division, office of the inspector general, U.S. Army 1941-1943. Brigadier general in September 1943. Inspector general in the North African Theater of Operations 1943-1944. Chief of the inspector general section in the Mediterranean Theater of Operations 1944-1945. Retired in May 1946. Decorations included the Distinguished Service Medal.

Clarkson, Percy William (1893-1962) Born in San Antonio on December 9, 1893. B.S. from Texas A&M in 1915. Commissioned in the infantry in 1916. Served with the 26th Infantry, 1st Division, AEF in World War I. Graduated from Command and General Staff School in 1928. Assistant professor at West Point 1928-1933. Graduated from the Army War College in 1934. With the War Department General Staff 1940-1941. Chief of staff of 36th Infantry Division in 1941. Brigadier general in June 1942. Assistant division commander of 91st Infantry Division in 1942. Major general in December 1942. Commanding general of 87th Infantry Division 1942-1943, then 33rd Infantry Division 1943-1945. Assignments after the war included commanding general of X Corps November 1945-January 1946, 3rd Infantry Division March 1947-August 1950 and Deputy Commanding General U.S. Army Pacific 1950-1953. Retired in December 1953. Decorations included three Distinguished Service Medals, two Silver Stars, the Legion of Merit, Bronze Star, two Air Medals, the Commendation Ribbon and Purple Heart. Died on September 14, 1962.

Clay, Lucius Du Bignon (1897-1978) Born on April 23, 1897, in Marietta, Georgia. Commissioned in the Corps of Engineers from West Point in 1918. Instructor at West Point 1924-1928. On MacArthur's staff in the Philippines 1937-1938. Oversaw Red River Dam project 1938-1940. Brigadier general in March 1942. With the War Department General Staff 1942-1944. Major general in December 1942. Deputy director for war programs, office of War Mobilization and Reconversion 1944-1945. Lieutenant general in April 1945. Deputy, then military governor of American Zone in occupied Germany 1945-1949, overseeing the resupplying of food and materials during the Berlin Blockade. General in March 1947. Retired in May 1949. Decorations included three Distinguished Service Medals, the Legion of Merit and Bronze Star. Clay was active in business in New York City after retirement. His son, Lucius D. Clay Jr., became a four-star general in the U.S. Air Force. Died on April 16, 1978.

Cleland, Joseph Pringle (1902-1975) Born in Holdredge, Nebraska, on March 2, 1902. Commissioned in the infantry from West Point in 1925. Served in the Philippines with 31st Infantry 1929-1932. Professor of military science and tactics at Kemper Military School 1936-1938. Graduated from Command and General Staff School in 1939. Duty in Panama 1939-1941. In the military intelligence division at the War Department General Staff 1941-1942. Chief of staff, then regimental commander, and finally assistant division commander of 43rd Division 1942-1946. Brigadier general in June 1945. Reverted to colonel on March 1946. Assignments after the war included commanding general of 40th Division in the Korean War 1952-1953, 1st Cavalry Division in 1953 and XVII Airborne Corps 1953-1955. Retired in June 1955. Decorations included the Distinguished Service Medal, Silver Star, two Legions of Merit, two Bronze Stars and the Commendation Ribbon. Died on March 28, 1975.

Clewell, Edgar Lewis (1896-1973) Born in Bethesda, Minnesota, on July 22, 1896. B.A. from Moravian College in 1916. Commissioned in the infantry in 1917. M.A. from Columbia University in 1922. Transferred to the Signal Corps in 1925. Served in Hawaii 1925-1928. Instructor with the Pennsylvania National Guard 1936-1939. Graduated from Command and General Staff School in 1940. Commanding officer of Signal Corps Replacement Training Center, Fort Monmouth February 1942-July 1943. Brigadier general in August 1942. Commanding general of Chicago Signal Depot 1943-1944. Assistant chief of the procurement and distribution service, office of the chief signal officer December 1944 until retirement in November 1946. Decorations included the Legion of Merit and Commendation Ribbon. Died on May 27, 1973.

Cobbs, Nicholas Hamner (1896-1968) Born in Montgomery, Alabama, on March 6, 1896. B.A. from University of the South in 1914. Commissioned in the Finance Department in 1917. Graduated from Command and General Staff School in 1926. M.B.A. from Harvard in 1935. Fiscal director of the Army June 1942-February 1946. Brigadier general in May 1944. Retired in August 1946. Decorations included the Distinguished Service Medal, Legion of Merit and Bronze Star. Died on February 1, 1968.

Coburn, Henry Clay Jr. (1879-1958) Born in Washington, DC, on Augusr 5, 1879. B.S. from Columbian College in 1900, M.D. from George Washington University in 1903. Commissioned in the Medical Reserve Corps in 1908. Graduated from Army Medical School in 1910. Served in the Philippine Islands 1910-1913. Commanding officer of Base Hospital Numbers 17 and 2 in the AEF 1917-1919. Chief of medical service at Fort Sam Houston General Hospital, then Walter Reed General Hospitlal 1930-1939. Assistant to the surgeon, then surgeon at Fort Bragg Station Hospital April 1939 until retirement in November 1945. Brigadier general in April 1941. Decorations included the Legion of Merit. Died on October 22, 1958.

Code, James Arthur Jr. (1893-1971) Born on January 17, 1893, in San Francisco, California. Commissioned in the Coast Artillery Corps from West Point in 1917. Served with 1st Division of AEF in 1918. M.S. from Yale in 1920. Attended Ohio State University 1920-1923. Attended the University of California 1934-1938. Brigadier general in January 1942, major general December 1942. Assistant chief, then chief signal officer of U.S. Army 1941-1946. Retired in 1946 as colonel. Major general on the retired list in 1948. Decorations included the Distinguished Service Medal and Bronze Star. Died on October 29, 1971.

Coffey, John Will (1897-1951) Born on January 12, 1897, in New York City. Commissioned in the Coast Artillery Corps from West Point in 1917. Instructor at West Point 1924-1928. Duty in Panama 1929-1931. Graduated from the Command and General Staff School in 1933. Instructor at the Ordnance School 1933-1935 then the Command and General Staff School 1935-1939. Graduated from the Army War College in 1940. Brigadier general in September 1943. Chief ordnance officer at AAF headquarters in Italy 1943-1945. Reverted to colonel in December 1945. Killed in an aircraft accident in Germany on March 8, 1951. Decorations included the Distinguished Service Medal and Legion of Merit.

Colbern, William Henry (1895-1959) Born on June 26, 1895, in Lee's Summit, Maryland. Commissioned in the infantry in 1917. Transferred to the field artillery in 1923. Instructor at the Field Artillery School 1929-1931. Graduated from the Polish Cavalry School in 1932. Graduated from Command and General Staff School in 1937. Professor of military science and tactics at the University of Illinois 1937-1938. Military attache in Warsaw, then The Hague 1938-1940. With the plans and training division of the War Department General Staff 1940-1941. Commanding officer of 7th Field Artillery Battery March 1941-February 1942. Executive officer of 1st Infantry Division Artillery in 1942. Brigadier general in September 1942. Commanding general of 92nd Infantry Division Artillery 1942-1945. Commanding general of Camp Chaffee 1945-1946. Retired as major general in June 1956. Decorations included the Distinguished Service Medal, Legion of Merit, Bronze Star and Commendation Ribbon. Died on April 30, 1959.

Cole, William Edward (1874-1953) Born on September 22, 1874, in Willard, Utah. Attended the University of Utah 1892-1893. Commissioned in the Artillery from West Point in 1899. Served in the Canal Zone 1914-1917. Brigadier general in August 1918. Commanding general of 11th Field Artillery Brigade and 153rd Field Artillery at St. Mihiel 1918-1919. Reverted to colonel in 1920. Graduated from General Staff College in 1920. Brigadier general again in January 1930. Commanding general of 1st Coast Artillery District 1930-1931. Major general in December 1935. Commander of V Corps Area 1935-1938. Retired in December 1938. Recalled to active duty immediately after Pearl Harbor. Member of the War Department Personnel Board December 1941 until retirement again in September 1944. Decorations included the Distinguished Service Medal. Died on May 18, 1953.

Colladay, Edgar Bergman (1885-1971) Born in Madison, Wisconsin, on January 8, 1885. B.S. from the University of Wisconsin in 1909. Commissioned in the Coast Artillery Corps in 1910. Graduated from the Army War College in 1930 and the Army Industrial College in 1933. Brigadier general in October 1940. Retired in August 1946. Decorations included the Distinguished Service Medal and two Legions of Merit. Died on August 14, 1971.

Collier, John Howell (1898-1980) Born on September 8, 1898, in Uvalde, Texas. Enlisted service with Texas National Guard 1916-1917. Commissioned in the cavalry from West Point, where he earned the nickname "Peewee," in 1919. Assistant professor of military science and tactics at New Mexico Military Institute 1931-1936. Graduated from Command and General Staff School in 1941. Battery commander in 68th, then 66th Armored Regiment of the 2nd Armored Division 1941-1943. Commanding officer of the 66th, then commanding general of Combat Command "A" 1944-1945. Brigadier general in November 1944. Assignments after the war included commandant of the Armor School 1952-1954 then commanding general of I Corps July 1954-June 1955 and Fourth Army 1955-1958. Retired as lieutenant general in October 1958. Decorations included two Distinguished Service Medals, three Silver Stars, the Legion of Merit and two Bronze Stars. Died on April 21, 1980.

Collins, Harry John (1895-1963) Born in Chicago on December 7, 1895. Attended the University of Chicago. Commissioned in the infantry in 1917. Instructor at the Infantry School 1926-1929. Graduated from Command and General Staff School in 1934 and the Army War College in 1935. Staff officer with 6th Division 1939-1941 then IV Corps in 1942. Commanding officer of 354th Infantry, 89th Division in 1942. Brigadier general in October 1942. Assistant division commander of 99th Division 1942-1943. Major general in September 1943. Commanding general of 42nd (Rainbow) Division 1943-1946. Assignments after the war included commanding general of 2nd Infantry Division July 1948-April 1950, 8th Division January 1951-January 1952 and 31st Infantry Division October 1952 until retirement in September 1954. Decorations included the Distinguished Service Medal, Silver Star, Bronze Star and Commendation Ribbon. Died on March 8, 1963.

Collins, James Francis (1905-1989) Born in New York City on September 2, 1905. Commissioned in the field artillery from West Point in 1927. Assistant artillery officer, then executive officer of I Corps Artillery 1941-1944. Deputy chief of staff, then chief of staff of I Corps 1944-1945. Brigadier general in January 1945. Commanding general of I Corps Artillery 1945-1946. Reverted to colonel in February 1946. Assignments after the war included commanding general of U.S. Army Alaska 1954-1957, deputy chief of staff for personnel, U.S. Army 1958-1961 and Commander in Chief U.S. Army Pacific 1961-1964. Retired as general in March 1964. Decorations included the Distinguished Service Medal, Legion of Merit, Bronze Star and Air Medal. Died on January 22, 1989.

Collins, James Lawton (1882-1963) Born in New Orleans on December 10, 1882, the brother of Joseph Lawton Collins. Commissioned in the cavalry from West Point in 1907. Aide to Pershing in the Philippines 1911-1913, again 1916-1917 during the Punitive Expedition into Mexico, and in the first weeks after the AEF arrived in France. Transferred to the field artillery. Commanded 7th Field Artillery at Meuse-Argonne. Served with the War Department General Staff 1920-1924 during Pershing's tenure as chief of staff. Graduated from Command and General Staff School in 1926. Military attache in Rome 1928-1932. Attended the coronation of King George VI of England as aide to Pershing in 1937. Commanding officer of 6th Field Artillery 1937-1938. Brigadier general in February 1939. Commanded 2nd Field Artillery Brigade 1939-1940. Major general in October 1940. Commanding general of 2nd Division 1940-1941, then the Puerto Rico Department 1941-1943. Director of administration at the War Department 1943-1944. Commanding general of 5th Service Command 1944-1946. Retired in

August 1946. Decorations included two Distinguished Service Medals and the Silver Star. Died on June 30, 1963.

Collins, Joseph Lawton (1896-1987) Born on May 1, 1896, in New Orleans, Louisiana, the brother of James Lawton Collins. Attended Louisiana State University 1912-1913. Commissioned in the infantry from West Point in 1917. With American forces in Germany 1919-1921. Instructor at West Point 1921-1925 and the Infantry School 1927-1931. Graduated from Command and General Staff School in 1933, the Army Industrial College in 1937 and the Army War College 1938, where he remained as instructor until 1941. Chief of staff of Hawaiian Department 1941-1942. Brigadier general in February 1942, major general May 1942. Commanding general of 25th Division 1942-1943. Commanded VI Corps 1944-1945. Lieutenant general in April 1945. Assignments after the war included vice chief of staff, then chief of staff of the army 1947-1953 then U.S. representative on the NATO military committee 1953-1955 and special representative of the United States to the Republic of Vietnam 1955-1956. Retirement in 1956. Decorations included four Distinguished Service Medals, two Silver Stars, two Legions of Merit and the Bronze Star. Author of War *in Peacetime* (1969). Died on September 12, 1987.

Collins, Leroy Pierce (1883-1981) Born in Troy, New York, on March 4, 1883. Attended Union College 1901-1904. Enlisted service 1904-1907. Commissioned in the field artillery in 1907. Duty with 4th Field Artillery in the Philippines 1907-1909. In Panama 1916-1917. Professor of military science and tactics at Stanford University 1919-1923. Instructor at the Field Artillery School 1924-1927. Graduated from the Army War College in 1929 and the Naval War College in 1930. Assistant chief of staff for military intelligence at I Corps Area 1936-1938. Staff officer, then assistant commandant of the Field Artillery School 1939-1941. Brigadier general in January 1941. Commanding general of 18th Field Artillery Brigade, then 59th Field Artillery Brigade February-November 1942. Commander of American forces in Ireland 1942-1945. Retired in March 1945. Decorations included the Legion of Merit and Bronze Star. Died on May 14, 1981.

Colson, Charles Frederick (1896-1970) Born in Charleston, South Carolina, on November 17, 1896. Commissioned in the infantry from West Point in 1918. Served with the 45th, 57th and 15th Infantry in the Philippines November 1926-October 1929. Graduated from Command and General Staff School in 1937. Infantry liaison officer at 480th Armored Regiment, 20th Armored Division in 1943. Deputy chief of staff of XXII Corps in 1944. Brigadier general in November 1944. Assistant division commander of 88th Infantry Division in 1944. Commanding general of Combat Command "A" in 8th Armored Division 1944-1945. Reverted to colonel in April 1946. Assignments after the war included commanding general of the Military District of Washington 1952-1953. Retired in July 1953. Decorations included the Silver Star and two Bronze Stars. Died on August 22, 1970.

Colton, Roger Baldwin (1887-1978) Born on December 15, 1887, in Jonesborough, North Carolina. Ph.B. from Yale in 1908. Commissioned in the Coast Artillery Corps in 1910. Served aboard the cable steamer *Joseph Henry* in the Atlantic 1916-1917. M.S. from Massachusetts Institute of Technology in 1920. Instructor at the Coast Artillery School, then a member of the Coast Artillery Board 1921-1924. Duty in the Philippines 1924-1926. Graduated from Command and General Staff School in 1928. Signal officer in the Panama Department 1930-1932. Graduated from the Army War College in 1938. Director of Signal Corps laboratories 1938-1941. In the office of the chief signal officer, U.S. Army August 1941-September 1944. Brigadier general in January 1942 and major general in August 1942. Served at AAF headquarters, then Wright Field, finally as air communications officer at Air Technical Service Command September 1944 until retirement in January 1946. Decorations included the Distinguished Service Medal and Legion of Merit. Died on January 24, 1978.

Conklin, John French (1891-1973) Born on April 20, 1891, in Fort Leavenworth, Kansas. Commissioned in the Corps of Engineers from West Point in 1915. With the Punitive Expedition into Mexico 1916-1917. Graduated from Command and General Staff School in 1927 and the Army War College in 1934. Engineer with Third Army 1942-1945. Brigadier general in January 1945. Retired in April 1951. Decorations included the Distinguished Service Medal, Legion of Merit and Bronze Star. Died on January 25, 1973.

Connolly, Donald Hilary (1886-1969) Born in Fort Mojave, Arizona, on February 11, 1886. Attended the University of California 1905-1906. Commissioned in the Corps of Engineers from West Point in 1910. Graduated from Command and General Staff School in 1923 and the Army War College in 1929. Instructor at Command and General Staff School 1929-1934. Officer in charge of the WPA in Southern California 1935-1939. Commander of 2nd Engineers 1939-1940. Administrator of civil aeronautics in the Department of Commerce 1940-1941. Brigadier general in January 1941. At headquarters of AAF in 1942. Major general in October 1942. Commander of Persian Gulf Command 1942-1944. Member of the Army-Navy Liquidation Commission 1945-1946. Retired in February 1948. Decorations included the Distinguished Service Medal and Legion of Merit. Died on June 18, 1969.

Connor, William Durward (1874-1960) Born in Beloit, Wisconsin, on February 22, 1874. Commissioned in the Corps of Engineers from West Point in 1897. Graduated from the Army War College in 1909. With the War Department General Staff 1912-1916. Deputy chief of staff of AEF 1917-1918. Brigadier general in June 1918. Chief of staff of 32nd Division, then commanding general of 63rd Brigade 1918-1919. Commanding general of American forces in France 1919-1920. Chief of Transportation Service 1920-1921. Deputy chief of staff, U.S. Army 1921-1922. Commanding general of U.S. Army forces in China 1923-1926. Major general in September 1925. Commanding general of 2nd Division 1926-1927. Commandant of the Army War College 1927-1932. Superintendent of West

Point 1932-1938. Retired in February 1938. Recalled to active duty in May 1941 as chairman of the Construction Advisory Committee in the War Department. Retired again in March 1942. Decorations included the Distinguished Service Medal and two Silver Stars. Died on June 16, 1960.

Conrad, George Bryan (1898-1976) Born in Waynesville, North Carolina, on November 2, 1898. Commissioned in the infantry from West Point in 1918. Instructor at West Point 1927-1931 and again September 1933-November 1937. Assistant military attache in London, then chief of the operations branch at the European Theater of Operations October 1939-October 1943. Served with General Staff Corps 1942-1944. Deputy chief of staff for intelligence in the European Theater of Operations 1944-1945. Brigadier general in March 1945. Deputy chief of staff for intelligence in First Army Group in 1944 then intelligence staff officer at SHAEF until retirement in December 1946. Decorations included the Distinguished Service Medal, Legion of Merit and Bronze Star. Died on December 11, 1976.

Cook, Gilbert Richard (1889-1963) Born on December 30, 1889, in Texarkana, Arkansas. Attended the University of Arkansas 1905-1906. Commissioned in the infantry from West Point in 1912. Served with the 58th Infantry in the AEF in World War I at St. Mihiel, Meuse-Argonne, Aisne-Marne, Vesle River and Marne-Ourcq engagements. Instructor at the Infantry School 1919-1921. Graduated from Command and General Staff School in 1925. Professor of military science and tactics at Georgia Institute of Technology 1925-1926. Instructor at the Infantry School 1926-1930. Graduated from the Army War College in 1932. Member of the staff at Command and General Staff School 1938-1941. Commanding officer of 21st Infantry 1941-1942. Brigadier general in May 1942. Assistant division commander of 25th Infantry Division in 1942. Major general in August 1942. Commanding general of 104th Infantry Division 1942-1943. Commanding general of XII Corps, then deputy commanding general of Third Army 1943-1944. At headquarters of Army Ground Forces 1945 until retirement in May 1946. Decorations included two Distinguished Service Medals and two Silver Stars. Died on September 19, 1963.

Cooke, Elliott Duncan (1891-1961) Born in Staten Island, New York, on August 15, 1891. Commissioned in the infantry in 1917. Served as a battalion commander in the 9th Infantry in the AEF at Verdun, Belleau Woods, Blanc Mont and Meuse-Argonne engagements. Professor of military science and tactics at Oklahoma Agricultural and Mechanical College 1927-1931. Graduated from Command and General Staff School in 1936. Instructor at the Infantry School 1936-1938. Graduated from the Army War College in 1939. Assistant inspector general of IX Corps Area June 1939-August 1941. In the office of the inspector general, U.S. Army 1941-1942. Brigadier general in March 1943. Chief of the overseas inspection division, office of the inspector general 1942-1946. Retired in October 1950. Decorations included the Legion of Merit and two Bronze Stars. Author of *Americans vs Germans* (1942). Died on February 18, 1961.

Copeland, John Eubank (1891-1978) Born in Birmingham, Alabama, on February 28, 1891. B.S. from Vanderbilt University in 1913. Commissioned in the infantry in 1916. Served in the AEF 1918-1919. Graduated from Command and General Staff School in 1928. Instructor at the Infantry School 1928-1930. Instructor at the Washington National Guard 1930-1934. Graduated from the Army War College in 1940. Commanding officer of 15th Infantry in 1941. Commanding officer of Fort Ray, Alabama 1941-1942. Brigadier general in September 1942. Assistant division commander of 65th Infantry Division 1943 until retirement in April 1946. Decorations included two Legions of Merit and the Bronze Star. Died on September 16, 1978.

Corbin, Clifford Lee (1883-1966) Born in Dayton, Ohio, on February 12, 1883. Commissioned in the artillery from West Point in 1905. Commanding officer of the mine planted "Ringgold" 1908-1910. Military attache in Santiago 1916-1917. Adjutant with 7th Brigade, AEF in World War I. Transferred to the Quartermaster Corps in 1920. Graduated from Army Industrial College in 1925. Duty in the Philippines 1927-1929. Quartermaster at the Hawaiian Department 1936-1938. Quartermaster supply officer at the New York General Depot 1938-1940. Brigadier general in April 1940. Assistant to the quartermaster general and director of procurement for the Quartermaster Corps 1940-1945. Major general in September 1942. Retired in November 1946. Decorations included the Distinguished Service Medal. Died on January 20, 1966.

Corderman, William Preston (1904-) Born in Hagerstown, Maryland, on December 1, 1904. Commissioned in the Signal Corps from West Point in 1926. M.S. from Yale in 1927. Graduated from Command and General Staff School in 1939. With the War Department General Staff 1939-1942. Assistant director of censorship 1941-1943. Commanding general of Army Security Agency 1943-1946. Brigadier general in June 1945. Reverted to colonel in April 1946. Assignments after the war included commanding general of Fort Monmouth 1957-1958. Retired in September 1958. Decorations included two Distinguished Service Medals and the Legion of Merit.

Corlett, Charles Harrison (1889-1971) Born on July 31, 1889, in Burchard, Nebraska. Commissioned in the infantry from West Point in 1913. Duty with the Signal Corps, AEF in World War I. Resigned in May 1919. Manager of Quemado Sheep and Cattle Company until he returned to active duty in July 1920. Instructor at Coast Artillery School 1925-1926 then the Command and General Staff School 1927-1931. With the War Department General Staff 1934-1938. Assistant to the provost marshal, then provost marshal for the Hawaiian Department 1938-1940. Commanding officer of 30th Infantry, then chief of staff of IX Corps July 1940-October 1941. Brigadier general in September 1941. Major general in September 1942. Commanding general of Task Force Kiska 1942-1943. Commanding general of 7th Division on Kwajalein in 1944. Commander of XIX Corps in 1944. With 12th Army Group October 1944-January 1955. Commanding general of XXXVI Corps January 1945 until retirement in May 1946. Decorations included three Distinguished Service Medals, the Silver Star and Legion of Merit. Died on October 14, 1971.

Cort, Hugh (1897-1974) Born on August 3, 1897, in Sabillasville, Maryland. B.A. from Johns Hopkins University in 1917. Commissioned in the field artillery in 1918. Graduated from Command and General Staff School in 1938. Executive officer of 22nd Field Artillery Battery 1941-1942. Assistant chief of staff for supply, then chief of staff of 77th Infantry Division 1942-1943. Chief of staff at headquarters of the European Theater of Operations, then at XIX Corps 1943-1944. Chief of staff, then artillery commander of 24th Infantry Division 1944-1946. Brigadier general in May 1945. Retired in August 1954. Decorations included the Silver Star, three Legions of Merit, two Bronze Stars, the Air Medal and Commendation Ribbon. Died on September 26, 1974.

Cota, Norman Daniel (1893-1971) Born in Chelsea, Massachusetts, on May 30, 1893. Commissioned in the infantry from West Point in 1917 then instructor there 1918-1920. Duty in Hawaii 1924-1928. Graduated from Command and General Staff School in 1931. Instructor at the Infantry School 1932-1933. Graduated from the Army War College in 1936. Instructor at the Command and General Staff School July 1938-November 1940. Assistant chief of staff for military intelligence, then plans and training at 1st Division March 1941-June 1942. Chief of staff of 1st Division 1942-1943. Brigadier general in February 1943. U.S. adviser to the combined operations branch of the European Theater of Operations in 1943. Assistant division commander of 29th Division 1943-1944. Major general in September 1944. Commanding general of 28th Division 1944-1945. Retired in 1946. Decorations included the Distinguished Service Cross, Distinguished Service Medal, two Silver Stars, two Legions of Merit, the Bronze Star, Distinguished Flying Cross, two Air Medals and the Purple Heart. Died on October 4, 1971.

Coulter, John Breitling (1891-1983) Born in San Antonio, Texas, on April 27, 1891. Commissioned in the cavalry in 1912. Aide-de-camp to Brigadier General William A. Mann in 1916. In 1917-1918 served in France with 808th Infantry, seeing action at St. Mihiel, then aide again to Major General Mann. Graduated from Command and General Staff School in 1927, the Army War College in 1933 and the Naval War College in 1934. With the military intelligence division of the War Department General Staff 1934-1938. Executive officer, then commanding officer of 4th Cavalry 1938-1941. Brigadier general in October 1941. Commanding general of 3rd Cavalry Brigade, 2nd Cavalry Division October 1941-July 1942 then 2nd Cavalry Division 1942-1943. Major general in March 1943. Commanding general of 85th Infantry Division 1943-1945. Assignments after the war included deputy commander, then commanding general of U.S. Army Forces Korea and XXIV Corps 1948-1949 then commanding general of I Corps 1949-1950 and IX Corps 1950-1952. Retired in January 1952. Lieutenant general in February 1951. Decorations included three Distinguished Service Medals, two Silver Stars, the Distinguished Flying Cross, Bronze Star and six Air Medals. Died on March 6, 1983.

Covell, William Edward Raab (1892-1975) Born November 29, 1892, in Washington, DC. Commissioned in the Corps of Engineers from West Point in 1915. Commanding officer of 2nd Engineer Regiment, 2nd Division, AEF in 1918. Graduate of the Command and General Staff School in 1930. Retired as lieutenant colonel in 1940. Recalled to active duty in June 1941. In the construction division, office of the quartermaster general 1941-1942. Division engineer in the Caribbean Division 1942-1943. Brigadier general in June 1943. Director of fuels and lubricants in the office of the quartermaster general 1943-1944. Major general in November 1943. Commanding general of Services of Supply in China-Burma-India Theater of Operations May 1944 until relieved from active duty in October 1945. Decorations included two Distinguished Service Medals. Died on August 16, 1975.

Cowles, Miles Andrew (1894-1974) Born on May 19, 1894, in Wilkesboro, North Carolina. Attended Davidson College 1912-1913. Commissioned in the field artillery from West Point in 1917. Served with the 13th Field Artillery, AEF in 1918 at Aisne-Marne, St. Mihiel and Meuse-Argonne. Attended the University of Chicago 1923-1925. Instructor at West Point 1929-1934. Graduated from Command and General Staff School in 1936. Duty in Hawaii with 13th Field Artillery then at headquarters of the Hawaiian Department 1936-1939. Instructor at the Field Artillery School 1940-1943. Brigadier general in March 1943. Commanding general of 36th Division Artillery 1943-1944. Commandant of Tank Destroyer School 1944-1945. Reverted to colonel in February 1946. Retired as brigadier general in July 1953. Decorations included the Silver Star. Died on May 21, 1974.

Cox, Albert Lyman (1883-1965) Born in Raleigh, North Carolina, on December 1, 1883. B.A. from the University of North Carolina 1904. LL.D. from Harvard Law School 1907. Commissioned in the 3rd North Carolina Infantry in 1916. With the 3rd on the Mexican border in 1916. Judge of the Superior Court of North Carolina, 7th Judicial District 1916-1917. Commanding officer of 113rd and 55th Field Artillery in World War I. Discharged in 1919 then appointed colonel in the field artillery reserve in August 1919 and brigadier general in November 1922 as commanding general of the 156th Brigade, organized reserves. Civilian aide to the secretary of the army for North Carolina 1923-1934. Director of Selective Service for Washington, DC, 1940-1941. Ordered to active duty in July 1941 as commanding general of Provisional Brigade, District of Columbia then the military district of Washington March 1942 until returned to inactive status in September 1942. Decorations included the Distinguished Service Medal. Died on April 17, 1965.

Cox, Richard Ferguson (1886-1964) Born in Graceville, Minnesota, on February 26, 1886. Attended the University of Minnesota. Commissioned in the Coast

Artillery Corps in 1910. Assistant to the chief of coast artillery 1917-1921. Duty in the Philippines 1921-1923. Graduated from Command and General Staff School in 1927 and the Army War College in 1930. In the personnel division at the War Department General Staff 1930-1933. Graduated from the Naval War College in 1935. Director of the department of tactics at the Coast Artillery School 1936-1939. Commanding officer of 70th Coast Artillery 1939-1940. Brigadier general in October 1940. Commanding general of Antiaircraft Artillery Training Center at Hinesville, Georgia 1940-1941. Commanding general of 38th Coast Artillery Brigade, then 4th Coast Artillery District February 1941-March 1942. Commanding general of harbor defenses at Boston 1942-1944. Retired in February 1944. Died on May 12, 1964.

Craig, Charles Frost (1895-1982) Born in Shelbyville, Tennessee, on October 21, 1895. Commissioned in the infantry in 1917. Served with the 53rd Infantry, AEF 1918-1919 and saw action in the Vosges Mountains and at Meuse-Argonne. Assistant professor of military science and tactics at the University of Tennessee 1924-1928. Duty in Hawaii 1928-1931. Assistant professor of military science and tactics at Oklahoma Agricultural and Mechanical College 1936-1939. Instructor with the Ohio National Guard 1939-1940. Plans and training officer, then chief of staff, finally assistant division commander of 37th Infantry Division October 1940-December 1945. Brigadier general in October 1942. Reverted to colonel in February 1946. Retired as brigadier general in September 1955. Decorations included the Distinguished Service Medal, Silver Star, three Legions of Merit, two Bronze Stars, the Commendation Ribbon and three Purple Hearts. Died on January 23, 1982.

Craig, Louis Aleck (1891-1984) Born on July 29, 1891, in West Point, New York. Commissioned in the cavalry from West Point in 1913. Duty in Panama in 1916. Battery commander in the 5th Field Artillery, then assistant plans and training officer at I Corps and 4th Division in World War I. Professor of military science and tactics at Harvard 1924-1929. Graduated from the Command and General Staff School in 1931. Instructor with the Georgia National Guard 1931-1933. Graduated from the Army War College in 1939. Commanding officer of 18th Field Artillery 1941-1942. Brigadier general in February 1942. Commanding general of 72nd Field Artillery Brigade 1942-1943. Major general in February 1943. Commanding general of 97th Infantry Division then XXIII Corps 1943-1944. Commanding general of 9th Infantry Division, then XX Corps, finally Third Army August 1944-October 1945. Assignments after the war included deputy commanding general of Fifth Army 1946-1947 and inspector general of U.S. Army 1948-1952. Retired in May 1952. Decorations included the Distinguished Service Medal, Silver Star, Legion of Merit and Bronze Star. Died on January 3, 1984.

Craig, Malin (1875-1945) Born on August 5, 1875, in St. Joseph, Missouri. Commissioned in the infantry from West Point in 1898. Served in the Santiago campaign in the Spanish-American War, the expedition to Peking in 1900 and in the Philippines 1900-1904. Aide to Major General J. Franklin Bell 1903-1904. Graduated from the Infantry and Cavalry School in 1905. Graduated from the Army War College in 1910. Chief of staff of 41st Division, then I Corps during the Aisne-Marne, St. Mihiel and Meuse-Argonne offensives. Brigadier general in February 1918. Reverted to major in August 1919. Brigadier general again in April 1921, major general in July 1924. Chief of cavalry, U.S. Army 1924-1926. Commanding general of the Panama Canal Division, then IX Corps Area 1927-1935. General in October 1935. Chief of staff, U.S. Army 1935-1939. Retired in August 1939. Recalled to active duty in September 1941 as chairman of the War Department Personnel Board. Decorations included two Distinguished Service Medals. Died on July 25, 1945.

Crain, James Kerr (1879-1972) Born in Concord, New Hampshire, on January 26, 1879. Commissioned in the Coast Artillery Corps from West Point in 1904. Instructor at the Artillery School 1906-1907. Duty in the Philippines 1908-1910. Instructor at West Point 1911-1912. Chief ordnance officer at I Corps, Second Army and Third Army, AEF in the Aisne-Marne, St. Mihiel and Meuse-Argonne engagements 1918-1919. Graduated from the Army War College in 1926. Ordnance officer in the VIII Corps Area 1934-1939. In the office of the chief of ordnance July 1939-October 1940. Brigadier general in October 1939. Head of field service in the Ordnance Department October 1940 until retirement in June 1942. Recalled to active duty as Assistant military attache in London and member of the London Munitions Assignments Board August 1942 until retirement a second time in December 1945. Decorations included two Distinguished Service Medals, the Legion of Merit and Bronze Star. Died on July 29, 1972.

Cramer, Myron Cady (1881-1966) Born in Portland, Connecticut, on November 6, 1881. B.A. from Wesleyan University in 1904, LL.B. from Harvard in 1907. Commissioned in the cavalry, Washington National Guard in 1910. Commissioned in the Judge Advocate General Department in 1920. Graduated from Command and General Staff School in 1930. Major general in December 1941 as the judge advocate general, U.S. Army December 1941-November 1945. Retired in November 1945. Decorations included the Distinguished Service Medal and Legion of Merit. Died on March 25, 1966.

Crane, John Alden (1885-1951) Born in St. George, Maryland, on December 2, 1885. B.A. from Johns Hopkins in 1907. Commissioned in the field artillery in 1907. Served with 1st Division, AEF at the Aisne-Marne offensive and with 6th Field Artillery. Duty in the Philippines 1919-1921. Graduated from Command and General Staff School in 1923 and the Army War College in 1928. Instructor at the Field Artillery School 1931-1932. Military attache in Istanbul 1932-1936. Foreign liaison officer at the War Department General Staff 1938-1940, then chief of the military attache and foreign liaison section in 1940. Brigadier general in October 1940. Commanding general of 13th Field Artillery Brigade October 1940-January 1944. Major general in September 1943. Retired in October 1946. Decorations included the Distinguished Service Cross, Distinguished Service Medal, two Silver Stars, the Legion of Merit and Purple Heart. Died on March 11, 1951.

Crane, William Carey (1891-1978) Born on March 25, 1891, in Fort Thomas, Kentucky. Commissioned in the field artillery from West Point in 1913. Graduated from Command and General Staff School in 1927 and the Army War College in 1928. Brigadier general in December 1942. Chief of staff of Southern Defense Command 1942-1944. Commanding general of IV Corps Artillery 1944-1945, then Fort Devens 1945-1946. Retired in February 1947. Decorations included the Distinguished Service Medal, Legion of Merit, Bronze Star and Commendation Ribbon. Died on April 20, 1978.

Cranston, Joseph Alfred (1898-1973) Born in Leavenworth, Kansas, on September 8, 1898. Commissioned in the infantry from West Point in 1919. Member of the Olympic boxing team in 1920. Instructor at West Point 1922-1926. Aide to the commanding general of the Philippine Department 1926-1928. Instructor at West Point again 1929-1933. Graduated from Command and General Staff School in 1935 and the Army War College in 1938. With the War Department General Staff 1940-1942. Staff officer at Army Ground Forces 1942-1943. Brigadier general in March 1943. With Services of Supply, China-Burma-India Theater of Operations 1944-1945. Retired in July 1948. Decorations included the Distinguished Service Medal, Bronze Star and Commendation Ribbon. Died on December 2, 1973.

Crawford, David McLean (1889-1963) Born on October 10, 1889, in Flushing, New York. Commissioned in the Coast Artillery Corps from West Point in 1912. Instructor at West Point 1916-1921. M.S. from Yale in 1922. Chief of the war plans and training division in the office of the chief signal officer 1928-1932. Graduated from Command and General Staff School in 1934 and the Army War College in 1940. Signal officer at headquarters of II Corps Area, then VII Corps 1940-1941. Air defense officer at GHQ Air Force 1941-1942. Brigadier general in December 1942. Chairman of the Army Communication Board in the War Department 1942-1943. Communications coordinator on the U.S. Joint Army-Navy Communication Board and Inter-Allied Combined Communication Board 1943 until retirement in June 1946. Died on May 1, 1963.

Crawford, James Blanchard (1888-1974) Born in New York City on November 27, 1888. Commissioned in the Coast Artillery Corps from West Point in 1911. Instructor at West Point 1914-1918 and again 1924-1925. Graduated from Command and General Staff School in 1926. Served in Panama 1926-1929. Graduated from the Army War College in 1933. Instructor at the Command and General Staff School 1933-1937. Duty in the Philippines October 1937-April 1940. Commanding officer of 65th Coast Artillery 1940-1941. Brigadier general in April 1941. Commanding officer of Coast Artillery Replacement Training Center, Camp Davis in 1941. Commanding general of Antiaircraft Artillery Training Center, Fort Bliss December 1941-April 1943. Commanding general of 39th Antiaircraft

Artillery Brigade 1943-1944. Member of the secretary of war's Separation Board, then president of the Discharge Review Board 1944-1946. Retired in June 1946. Decorations included the Legion of Merit. Died on August 4, 1974.

Crawford, Robert Walter (1891-1981) Born on September 17, 1891, in Warsaw, New York. Commissioned in the Corps of Engineers from West Point in 1914. Instructor at the Engineer School 1916-1917. Duty with 1st Engineers, AEF in 1918. B.S. from Cornell in 1921. District engineer in Hawaii 1928-1931. Instructor again at the Engineer School 1931-1932. Graduated from the Army War College in 1936. District engineer in New Orleans 1936-1939. Chief of the supply and projects section at the War Department General Staff March 1939-June 1942. Brigadier general in December 1941. At headquarters of the Armored Force in 1942. Commanding general of Services of Supply in the Middle East 1942-1943. Major general in February 1943. Deputy commanding general of Services of Supply in European Theater of Operations 1943-1944. Assistant chief of staff for supply at SHAEF 1944-1945. Division engineer for the Lower Mississippi Valley Engineer Division 1945-1946. Retired in December 1948. Decorations included two Distinguished Service Medals, two Legions of Merit and the Bronze Star. Died on November 27, 1981.

Crawford, Roscoe Campbell (1887-1980) Born on November 1, 1887 in Bridgewater, Pennsylvania. Commissioned in the Corps of Engineers from West Point in 1912. Graduated from Command and General Staff School in 1927, the Army War College in 1928. Commandant of the Engineer School 1940-1943. President of the Engineer Board, U.S. Army 1940-1941. Brigadier general in July 1941. Division engineer in the Missouri River Division, U.S. Engineers 1943-1946. Assignments after the war included deputy chief of engineers 1946-1949. Major general in 1948. Retired in November 1949. Decorations included the Distinguished Service Medal and Legion of Merit. Died on January 2, 1980.

Crichlow, Robert William Jr. (1897-1972) Born in Murfreesboro, Tennessee, on October 6, 1897. Commissioned in the Coast Artillery Corps from West Point in 1919. Graduated from Command and General Staff School in 1937. President of the Antiaircraft Artillery Board 1942-1943. Brigadier general in June 1943. Commanding general of 57th Antiaircraft Brigade 1943-1944. Deputy chief of requirements section, Army Ground Forces 1944-1945. Patient at Walter Reed Army Hospital September 1953 until retirement as major general in February 1954. Decorations included two Legions of Merit. Died on August 30, 1972.

Crist, William Earl (1898-1985) Born in Harrisburg, Pennsylvania, on August 10, 1898. Commissioned in the infantry from West Point in 1920. Instructor at the Infantry School 1921-1923. Stationed with the 15th Infantry in Tientsin 1923-1926. Commandant of cadets at West Point 1929-1932. Special attache to Nanking 1935-1936. Graduated from Command and General Staff School in 1938. In the military intelligence division of the War Department General Staff 1939-1943. Brigadier general in March 1943. Assistant division commander of 91st Division in 1943. Member of the U.S. military mission to Moscow in 1944. With the civil affairs division of Tenth Army 1944-1945. Retired in November 1955. Decorations included two Legions of Merit. Died on March 18, 1985.

Crittenberger, Willis Dale (1890-1980) Born on December 2, 1890, in Anderson, Indiana. Commissioned in the cavalry from West Point in 1913. Graduated from Command and General Staff School in 1925. Graduated from the Army War College in 1930. Duty in the office of the chief of cavalry 1938-1940. Chief of staff of 1st Armored Division July 1940-August 1941. Brigadier general in July 1941. Commanding general of 2nd Armored Brigade in 2nd Armored Division, then division commander August 1941-July 1942. Major general in February 1942. Commanding general of I Armored Corps, II Armored Corps and IV Corps 1942-1945. The IV Corps fought against the Germans for 401 days between March 1944 and October 1945. Lieutenant general in June 1945. Commander in chief of Caribbean Command 1945-1948. Assignments after the war included U.S. representative on the Inter-American Defense Board in 1948 and commanding general of First Army 1950-1952. Retired in December 1952. Decorations included two Distinguished Service Medals and three Bronze Stars. Died on August 4, 1980.

Crockett, James Cave (1888-1962) Born in Troy, Indiana, on August 16, 1888. B.A. from University of the South in 1912. Commissioned in the infantry, Officers Reserve Corps in 1917. Served with the AEF at St. Mihiel and Meuse-Argonne in 1918. Aide-de-camp to Major Preston Brown in 1926. Graduated from the Command and General Staff School in 1927. Aide to General Brown again June 1927-March 1930 and October 1930-August 1932 in Panama. Graduated from the Army War College in 1933. Assistant military attache in Berlin 1933-1937. Instructor at the Command and General Staff School September 1939-April 1941. Assistant chief of staff for intelligence at I Armored Corps 1941-1943. Brigadier general in February 1943, then reverted to lieutenant colonel in October 1943. Colonel in September 1944. Retired in August 1948. Decorations included the Bronze Star. Died on May 9, 1962.

Crowell, Evans Read (1895-1982) Born on December 7, 1895, in Morristown, Tennessee. Commissioned in the Coast Artillery Corps, Officers Reserve Corps in 1917. Duty in Panama 1919-1921. Instructor at the Coast Artillery School 1924-1926. In the Philippine Islands 1927-1929. Assistant professor of military science and tactics at the University of Alabama 1931-1935. Served in Hawaii 1935-1938. Graduated from Command and General Staff School in 1939. Battalion commander in 6th Coast Artillery 1939-1940. Plans and training officer in the Coast Artillery Replacement Training Center, Camp Callan in 1941. Executive officer of 34th Coast Artillery Brigade October 1941-February 1942. With the 38th Coast Artillery Brigade 1942-1943. Commander of 65th Antiaircraft Artillery Brigade November 1943-November 1944. Brigadier general in August 1944. Commanding general of Antiaircraft Artillery School November 1944-1946. Reverted to colonel in March 1946. Retired in August 1954. Decorations included the Legion of Merit. Died on March 2, 1982.

Cubbison, Donald Cameron (1882-1968) Born in Kansas City, Kansas, on May 8, 1882. Commissioned in the field artillery from West Point in 1904. Served in the Philippines in 1914-1916 and with the 4th Field Artillery in the Punitive Expedition into Mexico in 1916. Duty with artillery schools in the AEF 1917-1919, seeing action in the Champagne-Marne, Aisne-Marne and St. Mihiel campaigns. Graduated from School of the Line in 1921 and Army General Staff School in 1922. Treasurer at West Point 1922-1926. Graduated from the Army War College in 1927. Professor of military science and tactics at Stanford University 1930-1935. Instructor at the Field Artillery School 1937-1938. Brigadier general in August 1938. Served in Hawaii as commanding general of 11th Field Artillery Brigade 1939-1940. At the Field Artillery School in 1940. Major general in January 1941. Commanding general of 1st Division January 1941-May 1942 then the Field Artillery Replacement Training Center, Fort Bragg May 1942 until retirement in February 1946. Decorations included the Distinguished Service Medal and Legion of Merit. Died on December 25, 1968.

Culin, Frank Lewis Jr. (1892-1967) Born on March 31, 1892, in Seattle, Washington. B.S. from the University of Arizona in 1915, M.S. in 1916. Commissioned in the infantry in 1916. Served with the Punitive Expedition into Mexico 1916-1917. Professor of military science and tactics at Spring Hill College, then the University of Florida 1919-1921. Duty in the Philippine Islands 1921-1923. Professor of military science and tactics at the University of Oregon 1923-1927. Graduated from Command and General Staff School in 1930. Instructor with the Connecticut National Guard 1934-1937. At headquarters of National Guard Bureau 1937-1939. Graduated from the Army War College in 1940. Commanding officer of 32nd Infantry, 7th Division 1941-1943. Brigadier general in June 1943. Commanding general of 87th Division 1944-1946. Major general in March 1945. Retired in November 1946. Decorations included the Distinguished Service Medal, three Silver Stars, the Bronze Star and Air Medal. Died on December 31, 1967.

Cummins, Joseph Michael (1881-1959) Born in St. Louis, Missouri, on July 21, 1881. B.A. from St. Louis University in 1901. Commissioned in the infantry in 1903. Graduated from Command and General Staff School in 1923. Instructor at General Service Schools 1923-1926. Graduated from the Army War College in 1927. Duty with the War Department General Staff 1930-1934. Director of the Infantry Board 1934-1936. Director of the war plans division at the Army War College 1936-1938. Brigadier general in February 1938. Commanding general of 18th Brigade 1938-1939. Commanding general of the Atlantic sector in the Panama Canal Department in 1939. Commanding general of 5th Division in 1940. Major general in October 1940. Commanding general of XI Corps Area 1941-1942. Retired in December 1942. Died on October 16, 1959.

Cunningham, James Hutchings (1886-1963) Born on June 15, 1886, in Annisquam, Massachusetts. Commissioned in the Coast Artillery Corps from West Point in 1908. Instructor at West Point 1912-1916. Served with the AEF 1917-1919. In the military intelligence division of the War Department General Staff 1919-1923. Graduated from Command and General Staff School in 1925 and the Army War College in 1932. In the war plans division of the War Department General Staff August 1932-October 1936. Commanding officer of 14th Coast Artillery May 1939-July 1941. Brigadier general in July 1941. Commanding general of harbor defenses at Puget Sound July 1941-June 1945. Retired in April 1946. Died on May 27, 1963.

Cunningham, Julian Wallace (1893-1972) Born in Blairsville, Pennsylvania, on May 1, 1893. B.A. from George Washington University in 1916. Commissioned in the cavalry in 1917. Professor of military science and tactics at the University of Georgia 1921-1922. Instructor with the Massachusetts National Guard 1922-1923. Duty in the Philippine Islands 1933-1935. Graduated from Command and General Staff School in 1936. Instructor with the Connecticut National Guard 1936-1940. Assistant to the assistant chief of staff for operations at Third Army in 1941. Commanding officer of 112th Cavalry November 1941-October 1943. Brigadier general in September 1943. Commander of a task force in the miscellaneous group, U.S. Army Forces Far East October 1943-June 1944. Commanding general of 112th Cavalry Combat Team June 1944-December 1945. Reverted to colonel in July 1946. Retired as major general in May 1952. Decorations included the Distinguished Service Medal, Legion of Merit, Bronze Star and Purple Heart. Died on August 22, 1972.

Curtis, James Washington (1888-n/a) Born on October 3, 1888, in Jefferson City, Missouri. B.A. from Kentucky Military Institute in 1908. Commissioned in the infantry, Officers Reserve Corps in 1917. Served with the 1st Division, AEF 1917-1918, including the second battle of Marne. Instructor with the New York National Guard 1924-1927. Graduated from Command and General Staff School in 1928. Instructor at Cornell University ROTC 1928-1932. Duty in the Philippines 1932-1934. Instructor at the Infantry School July 1936-August 1939. With the training section in the office of the chief of infantry 1939-1942. Chief of the operations and plans division, then assistant chief of staff, finally chief of staff at headquarters of the Replacement and School Command May 1942-June 1945 Brigadier general in April 1943. Reverted to colonel in March 1946 and retired in October 1948. Decorations included the Distinguished Service Medal and Silver Star.

Cutler, Elliott Carr (1888-1947) Born in Bangor, Maine, on July 30, 1888. B.A. from Harvard in 1909, M.D. in 1913. Commissioned in the Medical Corps in 1917. Served with field hospitals of the AEF during World War I. Saw action at Belleau Wood, Chateau-Thierry, St. Mihiel and Meuse-Argonne. Discharged in 1919. Professor of surgery at Harvard Medical School 1932-1942. Called to active duty in July 1942. Chief consultant in surgery in the medical section, Services of Supply in the European Theater of Operations 1942-1945. Brigadier general in June 1945. Served at the Veterans Administration July 1945 until retirement in April 1946. Decorations included the Distinguished Service Medal. Died on August 16, 1947.

Cutler, Stuart (1896-1986) Born on February 10, 1896 in Dobbs Ferry, New York. Commissioned in the infantry, Officers Reserve Corps in 1917. Served with the 23rd Infantry, AEF in 1918. Professor of military science and tactics at Pennsylvania State College 1928-1930. Duty in the Philippine Islands 1930-1933 and with the Civilian Conservation Corps 1934-1940. Executive officer of 22nd Infantry in 1941. Commanding officer of Camp Gordon December 1941-February 1942. Commanding officer of 326th Infantry 1942-1943. Brigadier general in September 1943. Assistant division commander of 13th Airborne Division September 1943-May 1944. Chief of the airborne section at 12th Army Group May-September 1944. Deputy chief of staff for plans at First Allied Airborne Army 1944-1945. Retired in November 1946. Decorations included the Distinguished Service Medal, Legion of Merit and Bronze Star. Died on June 25, 1986.

Dager, Holmes Ely (1893-1973) Born in Asbury Park, New Jersey, on June 24, 1893. Commissioned in the infantry, New Jersey National Guard in 1912 and Regular Army in 1917. Served on the Mexican border in 1916. With the 51st Infantry, AEF, including the Meuse-Argonne offensive, 1918-1919. Professor of military science and tactics at Clason Point (New York) Military Academy 1920-1924. Graduated from Command and General Staff School in 1931 and the Army War College in 1936. Instructor at Command and General Staff School 1936-1940. With the 18th Infantry 1940-1941. Assistant chief of staff for operations at First Army 1941-1942. Commander of 41st Armored Infantry, 2nd Armored Division January-June 1942. Brigadier general in June 1942. Commanding general of Combat Command "B," 8th Armored Division 1942-1945. Major general in May 1945. Assignments after the war included commanding general of 11th Armored Division September 1945-February 1946 and U.S. Army Forces Austria 1946-1947. Retired in October 1947. Decorations included the Distinguished Service Cross, Distinguished Service Medal, two Silver Stars, the Legion of Merit and three Bronze Stars. Died on July 24, 1973.

Dahlquist, John Ernest (1896-1975) Born on March 12, 1896 in Minneapolis, Minnesota. Commissioned in the infantry, Officers Reserve Corps in 1917. Instructor at the Infantry School 1924-1928. Graduated from Command and General Staff School in 1931. Duty in the Philippines 1931-1934. Graduated from the Army War College in 1936. With the personnel division of the War Department General Staff 1937-1941. Assistant chief of staff of the European Theater of Operations in 1942. Brigadier general in April 1942. Assistant division commander of 76th Infantry Division October 1942-February 1943. Major general in June 1943. Commanding general of 70th Infantry Division 1943-1944, then 36th Infantry Division July 1944-October 1945. Assignments after the war commanding general of 1st Infantry Division 1949-1951, V Corps August 1951-March 1953 and Fourth Army in 1953. Chief of Army Field Forces August 1953-February 1955 and commanding general of Continental Army Command 1955-1956. Retired in February 1956 as general. Decorations included the Distinguished Service Cross, two Distinguished Service Medals, the Silver Star, two Legions of Merit and three Bronze Stars. Died on June 30, 1975.

Dalbey, Josiah Toney (1898-1964) Born on January 10, 1898, in Eufaula, Alabama. Enlisted service with Louisiana National Guard 1916-1917. Commissioned in the infantry from West Point in 1919. Instructor with the Louisiana National Guard 1921-1924. Duty in the Philippines 1925-1927. Served with the 15th Infantry in Tientsin 1931-1933. Graduated from Command and General Staff School in 1940. Duty in the operations and training divisions of the War Department General Staff 1940-1942. Chief of staff of the Airborne Command, then commanding general of the Airborne Center, Camp Mackall 1942-1945. Brigadier general in November 1944. Deputy commander of the American sector in Berlin 1945-1946. Retired in July 1952. Decorations include the Bronze Star. Died on May 12, 1964.

Daley, Edmund Leo (1883-1968) Born in Worcester, Massachusetts, on November 1, 1883. Commissioned in the Corps of Engineers from West Point in 1906. Instructor at West Point 1911-1915. Commanding officer of 6th Engineers, then division engineer with 3rd Division, AEF, including the St. Mihiel and Meuse-Argonne offensives 1918-1919. Professor at West Point 1920-1922. Graduated from the Army War College in 1936. Brigadier general in October 1938. Deputy commander of the Puerto Rico Department 1939-1941. Major general in September 1940. Commanding general of V Corps April 1941-May 1942. Retired in September 1942. Decorations included the Distinguished Service Medal and Silver Star. Died on December 19, 1968.

Dalton, James Leo II (1910-1945) Born on January 20, 1910, in New Britain, Connecticut. Commissioned in the cavalry from West Point in 1933. Company commander, battalion commander and regimental executive officer in 35th Infantry at Hawaii then in the Pacific 1940-1943. Commanding officer of 161st Infantry 1943-1945. Brigadier general in March 1945. Assistant division commander of 25th Division March-May 1945. Killed by a sniper at Balete Pass, Luzon, on May 16, 1945. Decorations included the Distinguished Service Cross, two Silver Stars, the Legion of Merit, two Bronze Stars, the Air Medal and Purple Heart.

Dalton, Joseph Nicholas (1892-1961) Born in Winston-Salem, North Carolina, on June 27, 1892. B.S. from VMI in 1912. Assistant commandant, then commandant of cadets at Sewanee Military Academy 1912-1916. Commissioned in the infantry in 1916. Battalion commander with 55th Infantry in the AEF in World War I. Aide-de-camp to Major General Hanson Ely 1928-1931. Graduated from Command and General Staff School in 1934. Adjutant general of IV Corps, then I Corps, finally at the Puerto Rico Department 1940-1942. Brigadier general in July 1942. Director of administration, then personnel at Army Service Forces 1942-

1945. Major general in September 1943. Retired in November 1946. Decorations included the Distinguished Service Medal and Legion of Merit. Died on November 24, 1961.

Daly, Cornelius Martin (1891-1974) Born on August 3, 1891, in Washington, DC. Attended U.S. Revenue Cutter School in 1914. Commissioned in the cavalry in 1916. Troop commander with 3rd Cavalry, AEF 1917-1919. Graduated from Command and General Staff School in 1928. Instructor at the Cavalry School 1930-1934 then at Command and General Staff School 1934-1938. Graduated from the Army War College in 1939. Commanding officer of 13th Cavalry Regiment, 7th Brigade 1939-1940. Assistant chief of staff for operations at 1st Armored Division, then I Armored Corps 1940-1941. Chief of staff of 5th Armored Division 1941-1942. Brigadier general in March 1943. Combat commander "A" at 20th Armored Division March 1943-March 1945 then assistant division commander March 1945-March 1946. Reverted to colonel in March 1946. Retired in November 1946. Decorations included the Bronze Star and Purple Heart. Died on August 11, 1974.

Danford, Robert Melville (1879-1974) Born in New Boston, Illinois, on July 7, 1879. Commissioned in the field artillery from West Point in 1904. Served in the Philippine Islands 1907-1908. Instructor at the Mounted Service School 1908-1912, then the School of Fire 1912-1915. M.A. from Yale in 1917. Brigadier general in August 1918 as commanding general of Field Artillery Replacement Depot, Camp Jackson. Reverted to major after the war. Commandant of cadets at West Point 1919-1923. Graduated from Command and General Staff School in 1924 and the Army War College in 1929. Chief of staff of VI Corps Area 1937-1938. Major general in March 1938 as chief of field artillery. Retired in February 1942. Decorations included the Distinguished Service Medal. Died on September 12, 1974.

Danforth, Edward Courtney Bullock (1894-1974) Born in Augusta, Georgia, on August 20, 1894. B.S. from Harvard in 1915. Commissioned in the infantry in 1917. Company commander in 328th Infantry, 82nd Division 1917-1919, the same unit that Sergeant Alvin York served in. Discharged in 1919. Representative for Mutual Benefit Life Insurance Company 1920-1940. Called to active duty as lieutenant colonel in November 1940. Supply officer at Fort Jackson 1940-1941. Assistant executive of the Columbia (South Carolina) District May 1941-May 1942. Duty with 4th Service Command in 1942. Graduated from the Command and General Staff School in September 1942. Commander of 4th Service Command Rehabilitation Center December 1942-May 1944. Member of the secretary of war's Separation Board then the Disability Review Board 1942-1949. Brigadier general in February 1945. Retired in 1954. Decorations included the Silver Star. Died on September 6, 1974.

Daniel, Maurice Wiley (1896-1986) Born on October 1, 1896, in New Albany, Indiana. B.S. from the University of Louisville in 1918. Commissioned in the infantry in 1920. Duty in Hawaii with 13th Field Artillery 1923-1926. Assistant Professor of military science and tactics at Oregon Agricultural College 1926-1930. M.S. from Purdue in 1931. Instructor at Field Artillery School 1932-1936. Graduated from Command and General Staff School in 1937. Assistant liaison officer for the Armored Force September 1941-March 1942. In the requirements division of Army Ground Forces in 1942. Commander of 10th Armored Division Artillery, then 1st Armored Division Artillery June 1942-June 1944. Brigadier general in August 1944. Assistant division commander of 1st Armored Division 1944-1945. Reverted to colonel in February 1946. Retired as brigadier general in August 1954. Decorations included the Silver Star, two Legions of Merit and two Bronze Stars. Died in 1986.

Danielson, Clarence Hagbart (1889-1952) Born on August 7, 1889, in Lead, South Dakota. Commissioned in the infantry from West Point in 1913. With the Punitive Expedition into Mexico in 1917. Duty in the office of the adjutant general 1926-1930. Graduated from Command and General Staff School in 1932. Again in the office of the adjutant general 1933-1936. Graduated from the Army War College in 1938. Adjutant general of West Point 1938-1941, then First Army 1941-1942. Again at the office of the adjutant general 1942-1943. Brigadier general in March 1943. Major general in January 1944. Commanding general of 7th Service Command 1944-1945. Adjutant general of U.S. Army forces, Western Pacific 1945-1946. Retired in 1946. Decorations included the Distinguished Service Medal and two Legions of Merit. Died on May 22, 1952.

Danielson, Wilmot Alfred (1884-1966) Born in Des Moines, Iowa, on July 25, 1884. B.S. from Iowa State College in 1907. Enlisted service with the Iowa National Guard 1905-1908. Commissioned in the field artillery in 1918. Served with the 131st and 133rd Field Artillery in France October 1918-March 1919 then in the Philippines July 1919-July 1922. M.S. from Massachusetts Institute of Technology in 1926. Quartermaster at Fort Knox July 1937-March 1940. Constructing quartermaster at the Panama Canal Zone March 1940-November 1941. Brigadier general in April 1941. Commander of Memphis General Depot 1941-1944. Retired in July 1946. Decorations included the Legion of Merit. Died on March 3, 1966.

Darby, William Orlando (1911-1945) Born on February 8, 1911, in Fort Smith, Arkansas. Commissioned in the field artillery from West Point in 1933. With 80th Field Artillery October 1939-August 1940. Battery commander in 99th Field Artillery 1941-1942. Commanding officer of 1st Ranger Battalion January 1942-April 1944. With operations division of the War Department General Staff April 1944-March 1945. Assistant division commander of 10th Mountain Division in April 1945. Killed in action in northern Italy by an exploding shell on April 30, 1945. That day his name appeared on the list of nominees for promotion to brigadier general. Secretary of War Henry L. Stimson recommended to the President on May 2 that Darby's name be kept on the list and he was promoted posthumously on May 15, 1945 with an effective date of April 30, 1945. Decorations included two Distinguished Service Crosses, the Distinguished Service Medal, Silver Star, Legion of Merit, Bronze Star and three Purple Hearts.

Dasher, Charles Lanier (1900-1968) Born on July 11, 1900, in Savannah, Georgia. Commissioned in the field artillery from West Point in 1924. With the 11th Field Artillery in Hawaii 1926-1929. Instructor at West Point 1932-1937. Graduated from the Command and General Staff School in 1940. Instructor then executive officer at the Field Artillery School October 1940-August 1943. Assistant artillery officer with XIX Corps 1943-1944. Commander of 32nd Field Artillery Brigade, then 75th Division Artillery July 1944-July 1945. Brigadier general in March 1945. Artillery officer with XVIII Corps July-November 1945. Assignments after the war included assistant division commander of 3rd Division in 1952 and commanding general of 24th Division 1952-1953 in the Korean War, deputy commanding general of Fifth Army 1953-1955 and commanding general of U.S. Army Caribbean June 1958 until retirement as major general in August 1960. Decorations included the Distinguished Service Medal, three Legions of Merit, three Bronze Stars, two Commendation Ribbons and the Purple Heart. Died on October 31, 1968.

Daugherty, Lester Amiel (1891-n/a) Born on September 5, 1891, in Jackson, California. Commissioned in the Coast Artillery Corps, California National Guard in 1915. B.A. from the University of California in 1916. Commissioned in the Regular Army in 1917. Served with occupation forces in Germany July 1919-October 1921. Professor of military science and tactics at the University of Illinois June 1929-April 1933. Duty with the 11th Field Artillery 1933-1936. District inspector with the Civilian Conservation Corps October 1937-May 1941. Assigned to 30th Field Artillery 1941-1944. Brigadier general in June 1943. Commander of 30th Field Artillery June-August 1944 and U.S. Army Alaska August-October 1944. Assistant chief of staff with Commander in Chief Pacific Fleet October 1944-January 1946. Retired in September 1951. Decorations included the Legion of Merit.

Davidson, Garrison Holt (1904-1992) Born on April 24, 1904, in New York, New York. Commissioned in the Corps of Engineers from West Point in 1927. Engineer with western task force in North African Theater of Operations 1942-1943. Brigadier general in September 1943. Engineer for Seventh Army 1943-1945. Member of the War Crimes Commission in 1945. Engineer with Fifteenth Army, then Army Ground Forces, finally Sixth Army 1945-1947. Assignments after the war included commandant of the Command and General Staff College July 1954-July 1956, superintendent of West Point 1956-1960 and commanding general of Seventh Army July 1960-March 1962 then First Army April 1952 until retirement in May 1964 as lieutenant general. Decorations included three Distinguished Service Medals, the Silver Star, Legion of Merit and Bronze Star. Died on December 25, 1992.

Davis, Addison Dimmitt (1883-1965) Born on January 23, 1883, in New Richmond, Ohio. Attended Miami University of Ohio 1900-1902 and the University of Cincinnati 1902-1904. M.D. from Jefferson Medical College in 1906. Commissioned in the Medical Reserve Corps in 1908. Graduated from Army Medical School in 1909. Served as medical officer in the Punitive Expedition into Mexico 1916-1917 and in the AEF in World War I. Assistant to the surgeon at the Philippine Department 1930-1932. Surgeon with U.S. Army troops in China March-June 1942 then commanding officer of Sternberg General Hospital in Manila August-October 1942. Executive officer of the Army Medical Center in Washington, DC 1938-1941. Brigadier general in December 1940. Commandant of Medical Field Service School May 1941-May 1945. Retired in September 1946. Decorations included the Legion of Merit. Died on June 8, 1965.

Davis, Benjamin Oliver (1877-1970) Born on July 1, 1877, in Washington. Student at Howard University 1897. Left to serve in the Spanish-American War as a first lieutenant. At conclusion of war mustered out and enlisted as a private in the 9th Cavalry, eventually earning a commission in 1901. Served in the Philippines during World War I. Extensive service as professor of military science and technology at Tuskegee Institute and Wilberforce University 1920-1938. Brigadier general in October 1940, the first black general officer in the Army's history. Brigade commander in 2nd Cavalry Division from January 1941 until retirement in June 1941. Decorations included the Distinguished Service Medal and Bronze Star. Recalled to active duty during World War II, first with the inspector general, U.S. Army then as an adviser on race relations in the European Theater of Operations. Died on November 26, 1970.

Davis, George Arthur (1892-1969) Born in Lynn, Massachusetts, on December 19, 1892. Commissioned in the infantry, Officers Reserve Corps in 1917. Served with the 9th Infantry, AEF 1917-1918, including the Aisne-Marne campaign. Professor of military science and tactics at Boston University 1920-1924. Plans and training officer with 15th Infantry, Tientsin 1929-1931. Graduated from Command and General Staff School in 1933. Professor of military science and tactics at Ripon College 1933-1935. Graduated from the Army War College in 1936 and the Army Industrial College in 1937. B.S. from Georgetown University in 1937. Instructor, then assistant director of training at the Infantry School 1937-1941. Duty in the office of the chief of infantry 1941-1942. Chief of staff of X Corps, then Third Army May 1942-April 1944. Brigadier general in March 1943. Assistant division commander of 28th Infantry Division April 1944-March 1945. Commanding general of 6960th Reinforcement Depot, Ground Reinforcement Command in France March 1945 until retirement in February 1946. Decorations included two Silver Stars, two Legions of Merit and two Bronze Stars. Died on January 10, 1969.

Davis, John Fuller (1892-1978) Born on May 2, 1892, in Augusta, Georgia. Commissioned in the cavalry from West Point in 1915. Served with the AEF 1917-1919. Graduated from Command and General Staff School in 1926 and the

Army War College in 1931. Chief of staff of 6th Service Command 1942-1944. Brigadier general in November 1943. Deputy director of the information and education division of the War Department August 1944-November 1945. Reverted to colonel in February 1946. Decorations included two Legions of Merit. Died on July 17, 1978.

Davis, Leonard Louis (1894-1975) Born on January 13, 1894, in Freeport, Illinois. B.S. from the University of Illinois in 1917. Commissioned in the Coast Artillery Corps in 1917. Served in the Philippines 1921-1922. Instructor, then member of the board at Coast Artillery School 1931-1936. Graduated from Command and General Staff School in 1937. In the fiscal section, office of the chief of coast artillery 1939-1942. Assistant to the chief of the ground requirements section at Army Ground Forces March 1942-May 1943. Commanding general of 61st Antiaircraft Artillery Brigade, then 48th Antiaircraft Artillery Brigade 1943-1944, finally 48th Division 1944-1946. Brigadier general in January 1944. Reverted to colonel in February 1946. Retired in October 1948. Decorations included the Bronze Star. Died on March 12, 1975.

Davis, Thomas Jefferson (1893-n/a) Born in West Union, South Carolina, on October 19, 1893. Enlisted service in the Georgia National Guard 1916-1918, including duty on the Mexican border and with the 31st Division in the AEF. Commissioned in the infantry in 1920. Transferred to the Adjutant General Department in 1933. Brigadier general in December 1942. Adjutant general for Allied Forces North Africa 1942-1943. Adjutant general at SHAEF headquarters 1944-1945. Retired in October 1946. Decorations included the Distinguished Service Medal, Legion of Merit and Bronze Star.

Davison, Donald Angus (1893-1944) Born on October 26, 1892, in San Carlos, Arizona. Commissioned in the Corps of Engineers from West Point in 1915. Served with engineer training schools in the U.S. 1918-1919. Graduated from the Command and General Staff School in 1928. Instructor there 1932-1936. Graduated from the Army War College in 1937. Engineer at headquarters of Services of Supply in England in 1942. Brigadier general in April 1942. Aviation engineer 1943-1944. Observer at headquarters of 12th Air Force 1944. Died in Bangalore, India, on May 6, 1944. Decorations included two Legions of Merit.

Dawley, Ernest Joseph (1886-1973) Born in Antigo, Wisconsin, on February 17, 1886. Commissioned in the field artillery from West Point in 1910. Served in the Philippines 1910-1911 and again 1913-1915. With the Punitive Expedition into Mexico in 1916. Aide-de-camp to Brigadier General E.S.J. Greble in 1917. Served with the AEF 1918-1919. Instructor at West Point 1919-1924. Graduated from Command and General Staff School in 1927. In the office of the chief of field artillery 1927-1930. Graduated from the Army War College in 1934. Instructor at the Infantry School 1934-1939. Commanding officer of 82nd Field Artillery 1939-1940. Brigadier general in October 1940. Commanding general of 7th Division Artillery October 1940-July 1941. Commanding general of 40th Infantry Division 1941-1942, then VI Corps 1942-1943. Major general in September 1941. Commandant of Tank Destroyer School, then commanding general of Tank Destroyer Center February 1944-March 1945. Commanding general of Ground Force Reinforcement Command in the European Theater of Operations in 1945. Retired in September 1947. Decorations included the Distinguished Service Medal, Silver Star and two Purple Hearts. Died on September 8, 1973.

Dean, William Frishe (1899-1981) Born in Carlyle, Illinois, on August 1, 1899. Graduated from the University of California in 1922. Commissioned in the infantry in 1923. Graduated from Command and General Staff School in 1936, the Army Industrial College in 1939, and the the Army War College in 1940. With the War Department General Staff 1941-1944. Brigadier general in December 1942. Assistant division commander, then commanding general of 44th Infantry Division 1944-1945. Major general in March 1945. Member of staff at the Command and General Staff School 1945-1947. Assignments after the war included military governor of Korea 1947-1948, commanding general of 7th Infantry Division 1948-1949 then 24th Infantry Division from October 1949. The division was the first to meet the North Koreans in June 1950. During a skirmish at Taejon, on July 20-21, Dean became separated from the division and was captured by North Korean troops after several days of wandering. He was liberated in September 1953 and awarded the Medal of Honor. Deputy commanding general of Sixth Army at the time of his retirement in October 1955. Author of *General Dean's Story* (1954). Decorations included the Medal of Honor, Distinguished Service Cross, Distinguished Service Medal, Legion of Merit and Bronze Star. Died on August 24, 1981.

Deane, John Russell (1896-1982) Born in San Francisco on March 18, 1896. Attended the University of California. Commissioned in the infantry in 1917. Served in Panama 1920-1923 and with the 15th Infantry in Tientsin 1932-1934. Secretary of the War Department General Staff 1941-1943. Brigadier general in September 1943. Commander of the U.S. Military Mission to Moscow 1943-1945. Retired in September 1946. President of Italian Swiss Colony Wine Company for several years thereafter. Decorations included the Distinguished Service Medal and Legion of Merit. Author of *The Strange Alliance* (1947). Died on July 14, 1982.

Dear, William Richard (1883-1956) Born on December 7, 1883, in Hamilton, Virginia. M.D. from the University of Pennsylvania in 1906. Commissioned in the Medical Corps in 1908. Graduated from Army Medical School in 1909. Professor of military science and tactics at the University of Pennsylvania 1926-1932. Brigadier general in April 1941. Commanding general of Medical Replacement Training Center, Camp Pickett April 1941-October 1943. Commanding general of Northington General Hospital, Tuscaloosa October 1943-April 1946. Retired in August 1946. Decorations included the Legion of Merit. Died on September 7, 1956.

Decker, George Henry (1902-1980) Born on February 16, 1902, in Catskill, New York. B.S. from Lafayette College in 1924. Commissioned in the infantry in 1924. Graduated from Command and General Staff School in 1937. Deputy chief of staff of Third Army, then Sixth Army 1942-1943. Chief of staff of Sixth Army 1943-1946. Brigadier general in August 1944, major general June 1945. Assignments after the war included commanding general of 5th Infantry Division 1948-1950, comptroller of the Army 1950-1955 and commander of VI Corps 1955-1956. General in June 1956. Deputy commander of U.S. European Command 1956-1957, commander in chief of United Nations Command Korea 1957-1959, then vice chief of staff and chief of staff, U.S. Army 1959-1962. Retired in October 1962. Decorations included the Distinguished Service Medal, Silver Star, Legion of Merit and Bronze Star. Died on February 6, 1980.

Denit, Guy Blair (1891-1976) Born in Salem, Virginia, on September 28, 1891. Attended Virginia Polytechnic Institute. M.D. from the Medical College of Virginia in 1914. Commissioned in the Medical Corps, Virginia National Guard in 1915. Served on the Mexican border 1916-1917. Assistant division surgeon with 29th Division in 1918. Graduated from Army Medical School in 1921. Graduated from the Army War College in 1936. Instructor at the Command and General Staff School 1938-1942. Surgeon in the North African Theater of Operations, then chief surgeon on General MacArthur's staff 1943-1946. Brigadier general in January 1944. Assignments after the war included chief surgeon of the European Command 1948-1952 and U.S. Army Europe 1952-1953. Retired in September 1953. Decorations included the Distinguished Service Medal, Legion of Merit and Bronze Star. Died on March 1, 1976.

Denson, Eley Parker (1884-1970) Born on August 29, 1884 in Trinity, North Carolina. Attended the University of North Carolina 1903-1905. Commissioned in the infantry from West Point in 1909. Served with the AEF 1918-1919. Graduated from the School of the Line in 1922 and Army General Staff School in 1923. Member of the Infantry Board 1923-1926. Graduated from the Army War College in 1927. In the operations and training division at the War Department General Staff 1928-1932. Professor of military science and tactics at Valley Forge Military Academy 1932-1935 and Montana State University 1937-1939. Commanding officer of 39th Infantry 1939-1941, then Camp Shelby August-December 1941. Commander of the Seattle Port of Embarkation 1941-1946. Brigadier general in September 1942. Retired in August 1946. Decorations included the Distinguished Service Medal and Legion of Merit. Died on February 13, 1970.

Denton, Frank Richard (1899-) Born in Arkansas City, Kansas, on July 16, 1899. Commissioned in the field artillery in 1918 and served in World War I, receiving a discharge in 1919. Attended the University of Kansas 1920-1922. Worked in banking in Pittsburgh 1922-1942. Called to active duty in 1942 and served in the General Staff Corps until 1945. Brigadier general in June 1945. Decorations included the Distinguished Service Medal.

Devers, Jacob Loucks (1887-1979). Born on September 8, 1887, in York, Pennsylvania. Commissioned in the Artillery from West Point in 1909. Staff duty with the School of Fire (later the Field Artillery School) during World War I, attaining temporary rank of colonel. Instructor at West Point 1912-1916 and 1919-1924. Graduated from Command and General Staff School in 1925 and the Army War College in 1933. Instructor again at West Point 1936-1939. Brigadier general in May 1940, Major general in October 1940. Commanded the 9th Infantry Division October 1940-July 1941 and the Armored Force July 1941-May 1943. Lieutenant general in September 1942. Commander of the European Theater of Operations, U.S. Army, May 1943-January 1944. Deputy supreme allied commander of Mediterranean Theater of Operations, January-October 1944, then commanding general, Sixth Army Group until World War I ended. General in March 1945. Assignments after the war included chief of Army Ground Forces from 1945 until retirement in 1949. Decorations included four Distinguished Service Medals and the Bronze Star. Died on October 17, 1979.

Devine, James Gasper (1895-1972) Born on April 19, 1895, in San Francisco, California. Commissioned in the Coast Artillery Corps, California National Guard in 1915. Served with the AEF 1918-1919 and with the 65th Coast Artillery in Panama June 1924-July 1927. Professor of military science and tactics at high schools in Denver, Colorado 1935-1939 then instructor with the Massachusetts National Guard 1939-1940. Graduated from Command and General Staff School in 1942. Commander of harbor defenses in Long Island Sound 1942-1943. Brigadier general in March 1943. Commanding general of 43rd then 37th Antiaircraft Artillery Brigades March 1943-August 1945. Commanding general of 4th Antiaircraft Command 1945-1946. Reverted to colonel in March 1946. Retired as brigadier general in August 1954. Decorations included the Legion of Merit. Died on July 24, 1972.

Devine, John Matthew (1895-1971) Born in Providence, Rhode Island, on June 18, 1895. Commissioned in the field artillery from West Point in 1917. Served with the 3rd Field Artillery in the AEF in 1919. M.S. from Yale in 1922. Instructor at West Point 1932-1936. Graduated from Command and General Staff School in 1938. Professor of military science and tactics at Yale 1938-1940. With the 1st Armored Division 1940-1941. Deputy chief of staff for intelligence, then chief of staff of I Armored Corps 1941-1942. Brigadier general in May 1942. Combat command commander in 6th Armored Division 1942-1943. Commanding general of 90th Division Artillery 1943-1944. Commanding general of 8th Armored Division 1944-1945. Major general in May 1945. Commanding general of 2nd Armored Division 1945-1946. Assignments after the war included chief of staff of Army Ground Forces in 1948 and commanding general of 1st Cavalry Division 1949-1950. Retired in July 1952. Decorations included the Distinguished Service Medal, Silver Star, Legion of Merit and two Bronze Stars. Died on March 8, 1971.

DeVoe, Ralph Godwin (1883-1966) Born on June 15, 1883, in Indiana, Pennsylvania. M.D. from the University of Pennsylvania in 1908. Commissioned in the Medical Reserve Corps in 1909. Graduated from Army Medical School in 1910. Served in the Philippines 1911-1914. Commanding officer of Base Hospital 34, AEF 1918-1919. Professor of military science and tactics at New York University 1921-1924. Graduated from Command and General Staff School in 1925. Surgeon at Fort Bliss, then Fort Monroe 1934-1940. Corps surgeon with II Corps 1940-1942, then post surgeon at Fort Dix January-October 1942. Commanding officer of Halloran General Hospital, New York October 1942 until retired in September 1946. Brigadier general in May 1944. Decorations included the Legion of Merit. Died on July 29, 1966.

DeWitt, Calvin Jr. (1894-1989) Born on August 25, 1894, in Fort Leavenworth, Kansas, the son of Brigadier General Calvin DeWitt. Commissioned in the cavalry from West Point in 1916. Served with the Services of Supply, AEF 1917-1919. Instructor with New York National Guard 1921-1922, then at West Point 1922-1926. Graduated from Command and General Staff School in 1928. Attended the French Cavalry School 1930-1931. Graduated from the Army War College in 1938. With the War Department General Staff 1940-1942. Chief of staff of New York Port of Embarkation, then commanding general of Boston Port of Embarkation 1942-1945. Brigadier general in April 1943. Commander of Nagoya and Kobe Bases 1945-1946. Reverted to colonel in March 1946. Retired in 1954 as brigadier general. Decorations included the Distinguished Service Medal, two Legions of Merit and the Commendation Ribbon. Died on January 10, 1989.

DeWitt, John Lesesne (1880-1962) Born on January 9, 1880, at Fort Sidney, Nebraska. Student at Princeton University two years, leaving to serve in the Spanish-American War. Commissioned in the infantry from the ranks in 1898. Deputy chief of staff for supply of I Corps February-July 1918 and of First Army August 1918-January 1919. Quartermaster general of the Army 1930-1934 in statutory rank of major general. Reverted to brigadier general March 1934. Commander of 1st Brigade, 1st Division 1934-1935, then 23rd Brigade 1935-1936. Major general in again December 1936. Commander of the Philippines Division January-July 1937. Commandant of the the Army War College July 1937-December 1939. Lieutenant general in December 1939. Commander of Fourth Army December 1939-September 1943 and, concurrently, commander of the Western Defense Command in San Francisco from March 1941. Following the Pearl Harbor attack DeWitt was given unprecedented authority to oversee the relocation of persons of Japanese ancestry to detention camps in the Southwest and Midwest. Commandant of the Army and Navy Staff College September 1943-November 1945. Retired in June 1947. General on the retired list in July 1954. Decorations included four Distinguished Service Medals. Died on June 20, 1962.

DeWitt, Wallace (1878-1949) Born in Fort Steele, New York, on June 1, 1878. M.D. from the University of Pennsylvania in 1900. Commissioned in the Medical Corps in 1906. Brigadier general in December 1935. Assistant to the surgeon general of the Army December 1935-December 1939. Retired in June 1942. Recalled to active duty July 1942-February 1945. Died on December 15, 1949.

Diller, LeGrande Albert (1901-1987) Born on February 16, 1901, in North Lonawanda, NewYork. Commissioned in the infantry in 1923. B.S. from Syracuse University in 1924. Served at Fort Clayton, Canal Zone April 1925-June 1927, Schofield Barracks, Hawaii 1931-1934. Graduated from Command and General Staff School in 1937. Duty at Fort McKinley, Philippines July 1939-December 1940. Assistant to the assistant chief of staff for intelligence in the Philippine Division 1940-1942. Aide to General MacArthur from 1942. Brigadier general in January 1945. Reverted to colonel in April 1946. Retired in September 1954. Decorations included the Distinguished Service Medal, Silver Star and Legion of Merit. Died on September 2, 1987.

Dillon, Theodore Harwood (1884-1961) Born in Center Valley, Indiana, on January 6, 1884. Commissioned in the Corps of Engineers from West Point in 1904. Commanding officer of 37th Engineers, and deputy chief engineer in First Army, AEF 1918-1919. Discharged at the end of the war. Professor at Massachusetts Institute of Technology, then Harvard 1920-1926. With Carnegie Institute of Technology 1939-1941. Recalled to active duty as colonel in the Quartermaster Corps in 1941. Brigadier general in February 1942. Deputy chief of the transportation department February 1942 until he returned to inactive status in June 1943. Decorations included the Distinguished Service Medal. Died on July 11, 1961.

Disque, Brice Pursell (1879-1960) Born in California, Ohio, on July 19, 1879. Commissioned in the cavalry, Officers Reserve Corps in 1901. Graduated from Infantry and Cavalry School in 1906 and Army Staff College in 1907. Organized and commanded the Spruce Division 1917-1919 in World War I. Reverted to inactive status at the end of 1919. Brigadier general, Officers Reserve Corps in February 1921. Business executive in California 1920-1942. Recalled to active duty in the War Department in September 1941. Served in the Morale Branch until January 1942. Decorations included the Distinguished Service Medal. Died on February 28, 1960.

Dissinger, Charles Edward (1894-n/a) Born on September 7, 1894, in Sunbury, Pennsylvania. Commissioned in the cavalry, Officers Reserve Corps in 1917. Assistant Pmst at Norwich University 1924-1928. B.S. from Pennsylvania State College in 1926. M.S. from Norwich University in 1928. Graduated from Command and General Staff School in 1936. Instructor with Wisconsin National Guard 1936-1939. Duty in the National Guard Bureau 1939-1942. Director of the mobilization division 1942-1944, then plans and operations 1944-1946 at Army Service Forces. Brigadier general in March 1945. Reverted to colonel in February 1946. Retired in August 1953. Decorations included the Distinguished Service Medal.

Ditto, Rollo Curtin (1886-1947) Born on September 27, 1886 in Mercersberg, Pennsylvania. Enlisted service in the Coast Artillery Corps 1907-1909. Commissioned in the infantry in 1909. Professor of military science and tactics at South Dakota College of Agricultural and Mechanical Arts 1914-1915. Served with the 7th Infantry, AEF at the Aisne-Marne, Marne, St. Mihiel and Meuse-Argonne offensives and wounded on July 23, 1918. Instructor at the Infantry School in 1921. Graduated from Command and General Staff School in 1923. Graduated from the Army War College in 1927. Brigadier general in September 1941. Duty at Huntsville Arsenal August 1941-May 1943 Assistant chief of the Chemical Warfare Service for materiel 1943-1946. Retired in April 1946. Decorations included the Distinguished Service Medal, two Silver Stars and the Purple Heart. Died on January 7, 1947.

Doe, Jens Anderson (1891-1971) Born in Chicago, Illinois, on June 20, 1891. Commissioned in the infantry from West Point in 1915. Wounded at St. Mihiel while serving with 5th Division, AEF in 1918. Instructor at the Infantry School 1919-1921. Graduated from Command and General Staff School in 1926. Duty with the 15th Infantry 1926-1930. Graduated from the Army War College in 1933. Instructor at the Command and General Staff School 1933-1937. Professor of military science and tactics at the University of California 1937-1940. Commanding officer of 17th Infantry February 1941-June 1942 then 163rd June 1942-February 1943. Brigadier general in February 1943. Assistant division commander, then commanding general of 41st Infantry Division 1943-1946. Major general in August 1944. Assignments after the war included commanding general of 5th Division, then 3rd Division 1946-1949 Retired in February 1949. Decorations included the Distinguished Service Cross, two Distinguished Service Medals, four Silver Stars, the Air Medal and Purple Heart. Died on February 25, 1971.

Donaldson, William Henry Jr. (1894-1948) Born on April 28, 1894, in Watertown, South Dakota. Commissioned in the Coast Artillery Corps from West Point in 1917. Instructor at West Point 1932-1933. Graduated from Command and General Staff School in 1935. Brigadier general in February 1943. Commanding general of Services of Supply in New Guinea 1943-1944. Commanding general of Services of Supply in Australia 1944-1946. Reverted to colonel in February 1946. Commanding officer of the Seattle Port of Embarkation at the time of his death on December 8, 1948. Decorations included the Distinguished Service Medal and Legion of Merit.

Donovan, Leo (1895-1950) Born on December 6, 1895, in Selma, Alabama. B.S. from Alabama Polytechnic Institute in 1917. Commissioned in the infantry, Officers Reserve Corps in 1917. Served with the 56th Infantry, AEF 1918-1919. In the Philippines 1928-1930. Graduated from the Command and General Staff School in 1936 and the Army War College in 1939. Instructor at the Command and General Staff School September 1939-June 1942. Commanding officer of 309th Infantry, 78th Infantry Division in 1942. Brigadier general in April 1943.

Commander of 1st Airborne Infantry Brigade in 1943. Commanding general of the Airborne Command November 1943-February 1944. Assistant chief of staff for plans and training at Army Ground Forces February 1944-August 1945. Major general in November 1944. Retired as colonel in December 1946. Decorations included the Distinguished Service Medal and Legion of Merit. Died on May 21, 1950.

Donovan, Richard (1885-1949) Born on December 2, 1885, in Paducah, Kentucky. Commissioned in the Coast Artillery Corps from West Point in 1908, then instructor there 1910-1914. Duty in the Philippine Islands 1916-1919. M.S. from Massachusetts Institute of Technology in 1921. Instructor at Coast Artillery School 1921-1923. Graduated from Command and General Staff School in 1926. Graduated from the Army War College in 1931. Duty in Panama 1931-1934. Brigadier general in October 1940. Commanding general of VIII Corps Area 1940-1945. Major general in April 1941. Deputy chief of staff at headquarters of Army Service Forces May 1945 until retirement in April 1947. Decorations included the Distinguished Service Medal. Died on February 7, 1949.

Donovan, William Joseph (1883-1959) Born on January 1, 1883, in Buffalo, New York. B.A., Columbia University in 1905, LL.D. in 1907. Organized a cavalry troop for the New York National Guard and took it to Mexico to participate in the Punitive Expedition 1916-1917. Commander of the 165th Infantry in World War I. Wounded three times in the battle at Landres-et-St. Georges October 1918 and awarded the Medal of Honor. Practiced law in New York 1920-1942. Defeated by Herbert H. Lehman in the 1932 governor's election. Appointed by President Roosevelt to draw up plans for a worldwide military intelligence network, then named director of the Office of Strategic Services upon its creation in June 1942. Brigadier general in March 1943. Major general in November 1944. Returned to private practice in 1946. Ambassador to Thailand 1953-1954. Decorations included the Medal of Honor, Distinguished Service Cross, and two Distinguished Service Medals. Died on February 8, 1959.

Dooling, Henry Chessman (1887-1972) Born in Clayton, New Jersey, on June 23, 1887. M.D. from Medical-Surgical College in 1908. Commissioned in the Medical Section, Officers Reserve Corps in 1917. Graduated from Army Medical School in 1917. Served with the 89th Division, AEF at St. Mihiel and Meuse-Argonne in World War I. Assistant to the chief of medical services at Walter Reed General Hospital 1923-1926. Chief of medical services at Gorgas Hospital 1926-1931, then William Beaumont General Hospital 1931-1936, finally the Station Hospital at Fort Riley 1936-1940. Superintendent of Colon Hospital, Panama, Gorgas General Hospital, William Beaumont General Hospital and the station hospital at Fort Riley 1940-1946. Brigadier general in May 1944. Reverted to colonel in July 1946. Retired in July 1947. Decorations included the Legion of Merit. Died on November 22, 1972.

Doran, Charles Richard (1892-1984) Born on August 14, 1892. B.S. from Louisiana State University in 1916. Commissioned in the field artillery in 1917. Served with the 18th Field Artillery, AEF at Chateau-Thierry, Champagne-Marne, Aisne-Marne, St. Mihiel and Meuse-Argonne 1918-1919. In Hawaii 1924-1929. Graduated from Command and General Staff School in 1935. Instructor with the Louisiana National Guard 1935-1940. Commanding officer of 18th Field Artillery 1941-1942. Staff officer at Field Artillery School in 1942. Brigadier general in March 1943. Commanding general of 17th Field Artillery Brigade (later renamed VII Corps Artillery) 1943-1946. Reverted to colonel in July 1946. Retired in May 1948. Decorations included two Legions of Merit, the Bronze Star and Purple Heart. Died on July 22, 1984.

Doriot, Georges Frederic (1899-n/a) Born on September 24, 1899, in Paris, France. Graduated from the University of Paris in 1915. Served with the French Army in World War I then immigrated to the United States. Attended Harvard University. Professor at Harvard 1929-1941. Became a U.S. citizen on January 8, 1940. Commissioned lieutenant colonel in the Quartermaster Corps Reserve and called to active duty in July 1941. Served in the office of the quartermaster general 1941-1942, then chief of the research and development branch in the military planning division 1942-1943 and finally director of the military planning office 1943-1946. Brigadier general in January 1945.

Dorn, Frank (1901-1981) Born on June 25, 1901, in San Francisco, California. Commissioned in the field artillery from West Point in 1923. Served in the Philippines 1926-1929. Instructor at Field Artillery School 1930-1933. Student of the Chinese language in Beijing 1934-1939. Aide to Brigadier General (later major general and lieutenant general) Joseph W. Stilwell 1939-1942. Member of U.S. mission to Burma 1942. Artillery officer, then deputy chief of staff at U.S. Army forces in the China-Burma-India Theater of Operations July 1942-November 1944. Brigadier general in November 1943. Commanding general of China Training and Combat Command 1944-1945. Commanding general of 11th Airborne Division Artillery, then at headquarters of Army Ground Forces in 1945. Reverted to colonel in March 1946. Retired as brigadier general in November 1953. Decorations included the Distinguished Service Medal, Silver Star and Bronze Star. Died on July 26, 1981.

Downs, Sylvester DeWitt Jr. (1889-1957) Born on February 28, 1889, in Greenville, Pennsylvania. Commissioned in the cavalry from West Point in 1914. Transferred to the field artillery in 1917. With the Punitive Expedition into Mexico 1916-1917. Served in the U.S. training field artillery units in World War I. Instructor at Field Artillery School 1923-1926. Graduated from Command and General Staff School in 1927. Instructor with the New York National Guard 1932-1935. Returned to Command and General Staff School as instructor 1935-1939. Served in Alaska 1940-1944, including command of Fort Richardson 1943-1944. Brigadier general in March 1943. Reverted to colonel in September 1944.

Deputy chief of staff of IX Corps 1945-1946. Retired in November 1946. Died on April 20, 1957.

Drain, Jesse Cyrus (1883-1974) Born in Braddock, Pennsylvania, on September 25, 1883. Commissioned in the infantry from West Point in 1907. With the 15th Infantry in the Philippines and China 1911-1915. Served on the Mexican border 1916-1917 and in the AEF in World War I. Instructor at the Infantry School 1918-1921. Graduated from Command and General Staff School in 1922 and the Army War College in 1925. Instructor at Command and General Staff School 1926-1934. Professor of military science and tactics at Georgetown University 1936-1938. Commanding officer of 31st Infantry in the Philippines 1938-1940. Commanding officer of 81st Infantry Brigade 1940-1941. Brigadier general in January 1941. Commanding general of the Atlantic Zone, Panama Mobile Force then the Mobile Force February 1942-April 1943. With the War Department Manpower Board 1943-1945. Retired in September 1945. Died on January 12, 1974.

Drake, Charles Chisholm (1887-1984) Born on November 2, 1887, in Brockton, Massachusetts. Commissioned in the infantry from West Point in 1912. Served with the expedition to Vera Cruz, Mexico in 1914. Duty with the 59th Infantry, AEF in the Aisne-Marne, St. Mihiel and Meuse-Argonne offensives in 1918. Transferred to the Quartermaster Corps in 1920. Graduated from the Army War College in 1925. Instructor at the Quartermaster School 1927-1930. Quartermaster at GHQ Air Force 1935-1940. Superintendent of transport service in the Philippine Department in 1940. Brigadier general in December 1941. With U.S. Army forces in the Far East 1941-1942. Prisoner of war 1942-1945. Retired in October 1946. Decorations included the Distinguished Service Medal. Died on July 16, 1984.

Draper, William H. Jr. (1894-1974) Born in New York City on August 10, 1894. B.A. from New York University in 1916, M.A. in 1917. Commissioned in the infantry, Officers Reserve Corps in Active duty as battalion commander at Campt Upton, New York during World War I. Rejoined the ORC after the war. Investment banker in New York City 1919-1940. Vice president of Dillon Read and Company when called to active duty in 1940. At Camp Clipper, then Camp Forrest 1940-1943. Commanding officer of the 136th Infantry Regiment in the Pacific Theater of Operations 1943-1944. Head of the contract termination division at the War Department in 1944. Brigadier general in January 1945. Chief of the economic division of the Control Council for Germany 1945-1946. Assignments after the war included duty at headquarters of the American military government in Germany as head of the economic division, with promotion to major general in 1947. While there he formulated the "Draper Plan" to rejuvenate German industry. Appointed under secretary of the army in 1947, serving until February 1949. U.S. permanent representative to the NATO Council 1952-1953. Decorations included the Distinguished Service Medal and two Legions of Merit. Died on December 26, 1974.

Drewry, Guy Humphrey (1894-1973) Born on October 16, 1894, in La Crosse, Virginia. B.S. from Virginia Military Institute in 1916. Commissioned in the Coast Artillery Corps in 1917. Served in the Philippine Islands 1918-1921. Transferred to ordnance in 1921. In the office of the chief of ordnance 1936-1942. Brigadier general in September 1942. Commanding general of Springfield Ordnance District 1942-1945. Duty in the office of the director of materiel at headquarters of Army Service Forces 1945-1946. Retired in August 1946. Decorations included two Legions of Merit. Died on April 6, 1973.

Drum, Hugh Aloysius (1879-1951) Born on September 19, 1879, in Fort Brady, Michigan. Commissioned from the ranks in the infantry in 1898. Graduated from Army Staff College in 1912. Deputy chief of staff, later chief of staff of First Army in World War I, attaining temporary rank of brigadier general in October 1918. Promoted again to brigadier general in December 1922. Assistant chief of staff, U.S. Army 1923-1926. Commander of 1st Infantry Brigade 1926-1927, then 1st Infantry Division 1927-1930. Inspector general of the Army 1930-1931. Major general in December 1931. Commanding general of First Army 1931-1933. Deputy chief of staff of the Army 1933-1935. Commander of Hawaiian Department 1935-1937. Commanding general of Second Army 1937-1938. Lieutenant general in August 1939. Commanded First Army August 1939 until retirement in September 1943. Decorations included two Distinguished Service Medals and the Silver Star. Died on October 3, 1951.

Duff, Robinson Earl (1895-1979) Born on January 18, 1895, in El Paso, Illinois. Commissioned in the infantry, Officers Reserve Corps in 1917. Assistant professor of military science and tactics at the University of Oklahoma 1921-1923. Duty in Hawaii 1923-1927. Instructor at the Infantry School 1927-1931. Graduated from Command and General Staff School in 1933. Instructor with the Arizona National Guard 1933-1935. Graduated from the Army War College in 1936. In the construction branch of the War Department General Staff July 1938-March 1942. Assistant division commander of 10th Mountain Division May 1944-June 1945. Brigadier general in November 1944. With occupation forces in Japan in 1945. Assignments after the war included commander of the Army Security Agency 1951-1953. Retired in January 1953. Decorations included the Distinguished Service Cross, Silver Star, Legion of Merit, two Bronze Stars and the Purple Heart. Died on September 27, 1979.

Duke, James Thomas (1893-1970) Born on June 10, 1893, in California, Maryland. B.S. from the University of Maryland in 1916. Commissioned in the cavalry in 1917. Instructor at the Cavalry School 1924-1927 and again 1928-1932. Graduated from Command and General Staff School in 1934 and the Army Industrial College in 1940. In the training division, office of the chief of cavalry 1941-1942. Staff officer with Army Ground Forces in 1942. Commanding general of Charleston Port of Embarkation May 1942-August 1945. Brigadier general in March 1943. Duty with U.S. Army Forces Pacific 1945-1946. Reverted to colonel in February 1946. Retired in June 1953. Decorations included the Distinguished Service Medal. Died on December 9, 1970.

Dulaney, Robert Leroy (1902-1984) Born on March 4, 1902, in Marshall, Illinois. Commissioned in the infantry from West Point in 1923. Duty in the Philippines with 31st Infantry 1925-1927. Graduated from Command and General Staff School in 1941. With 23rd Infantry, 2nd Infantry Division 1941-1942. Commanding officer of 645th Tank Destroyer Battalion October 1942-October 1943. Executive officer, then commanding officer of 180th Infantry, 45th Division 1943-1945. Brigadier general in March 1945. Assistant division commander of 44th Division 1945-1946. Assignments after the war included commanding general of 3rd Division in the Korean War in 1952 and 47th Division 1953-1954. Retired in January 1954 as major general. Decorations included two Silver Stars, two Legions of Merit, two Bronze Stars and the Air Medal. Died on November 7, 1984.

Dumas, Walter Alexander (1893-1952) Born in Sherman, Texas, on November 25, 1893. B.S. from Davidson College in 1915, M.A. in 1916. Commissioned in the infantry, Officers Reserve Corps in 1917. Instructor at the Infantry School 1923-1927. Member of faculty at West Point 1927-1931. Graduated from Command and General Staff School in 1933, the Army War College in 1936. Duty with general staff of Ninth Corps Area 1936-1940. Instructor again at the Infantry School 1940-1941. Staff officer with Western Defense Command 1941-1942. Commander of Tank Destroyer Replacement Training Center 1942-1943. Brigadier general in June 1943. Director of plans and operations for U.S. Army forces in the South Pacific, then at Tenth Army 1943-1945. In the operations section of the Far East Command 1945-1947. Reverted to colonel in July 1946. Retired in October 1947. Decorations included the Distinguished Service Medal, three Legions of Merit and the Purple Heart. Died on September 13, 1952.

Dunckel, William Caldwell (1893-1977) Born in Springfield, Missouri, on October 12, 1893. B.S. from the University of Missouri in 1915. Commissioned in the field artillery in 1917. Served with 21st Field Artillery, AEF in Frapelle and St. Mihiel offensives in 1918. Professor of military science and tactics at the University of Missouri 1921-1924. Duty in the Philippines 1928-1930. Graduated from the Command and General Staff School in 1935, the Army War College in 1938 and the Naval War College in 1939. Assistant to the military advisor to the government of the Philippine Islands (General MacArthur) 1939-1941. Commanding officer of 48th Field Artillery Battalion in 1941. Brigadier general in August 1942. Commander of 104th Infantry Division Artillery 1942-1943, then the Americal Division 1943-1944. Chief of the planning division at headquarters of the Southwest Pacific Area 1944-1945. Major general in January 1945. Retired in October 1945. Decorations included the Distinguished Service Medal, two Silver Stars, the Bronze Star and two Purple Hearts. Died in August 1977.

Dunham, George Clark (1887-1954) Born in Mitchell, South Dakota, on July 27, 1887. M.D. from the University of Oregon in 1914. Commissioned in the

Medical Reserve Corps in 1915. Graduated from Army Medical School in 1917. Instructor at Army Medical School 1919-1921. Ph.D. from Johns Hopkins in 1921. M.A. from George Washington University in 1925. Graduated from the Army War College in 1926. Adviser on public health to the governor general of the Philippines 1931-1935. Director of laboratories at Army Medical School, then director of the school 1936-1940. Brigadier general in February 1942. Director of the division of health and sanitation at the Institute of Inter-American Affairs February 1942-June 1945. Major general in February 1944. Retired in October 1945. Decorations included the Distinguished Service Medal and Purple Heart. Died on October 4, 1954.

Dunkelberg, Wilbur Eugene (1898-1987) Born on August 6, 1898, in Rockford, Iowa. Commissioned in the infantry from West Point in 1918. Served in China 1919-1921 and the Philippine Islands 1929-1931. Instructor at the Infantry School 1935-1936. Graduated from Command and General Staff School in 1937 and the Army War College in 1940. Again instructor at the Infantry School 1941-1942. At headquarters of Army Ground Forces and the War Department General Staff in 1942. Brigadier general in February 1943. Assistant division commander of 95th Infantry Division 1943-1944. Commanding general of U.S. forces on Attu Island, Alaskan Command 1944-1945. Assignments after the war included assistant division commander of 24th Division May-October 1952, then 3rd Division in the Korean War 1952-1953, finally 6th Division 1954-1955. Retired in November 1955. Decorations included three Legions of Merit. Died on April 13, 1987.

Dunlop, Robert Horace (1886-1970) Born on October 2, 1886, in Poultney, Vermont. Commissioned in the infantry from West Point in 1910. Served in China 1916-1917, including duty in Peking during the revolution in July 1917. Transferred to the adjutant general department in 1922. Graduated from Command and General Staff School in 1925 and the Army War College in 1933. Assistant chief of staff for personnel, then military intelligence at headquarters of IV Corps Area 1935-1939. Adjutant general at the Hawaii Division, then the Hawaiian Department August 1939-June 1942. Brigadier general in July 1942. Director of the civilian personnel division, office of the adjutant general, U.S. Army 1942-1946. Retired in March 1946. Decorations included two Legions of Merit. Died on January 18, 1970.

Dunn, Beverly Charles (1888-1970) Born on July 16, 1888, in Fort Monroe, Virginia. Commissioned in the Corps of Engineers from West Point in 1907. Duty in the Philippines 1915-1916. Instructor, then assistant professor at West Point 1917-1918, then instructor at the Engineer School 1919-1921. Graduated from the Army Industrial College in 1928 and the Army War College in 1938. District engineer in Seattle July 1940-March 1942. At the North Atlantic Engineering Division 1942-1943. Brigadier general in March 1943. Deputy chief engineer at the European Theater of Operations, then SHAEF 1944-1945. Reverted to colonel in February 1946. Retired in July 1948. Decorations included two Distinguished Service Medals. Died on August 21, 1970.

Eager, John Macaulay (1889-1956) Born in Baltimore, Maryland, on August 20, 1889. B.A. from Harvard in 1912. Commissioned in the field artillery in 1918. Military attache in Rome 1919-1923. Graduated from the Command and General Staff School in 1925. Duty in the Canal Zone 1925-1928. Chief of staff of V Corps Area October 1940-March 1944. Brigadier general in September 1943. Commander of Italian Service Units at Fort Wadsworth 1944-1945. Retired in March 1946. Decorations included the Legion of Merit. Died on November 15, 1956.

Eagles, William Willis (1895-1988) Born on January 12, 1895, in Albion, Indiana. Commissioned in the infantry from West Point in 1917. Instructor at the Infantry School 1921-1923 and again 1931-1935. Professor of military science and tactics at Ripon College 1925-1930. Graduated from the Command and General Staff School in 1936. With VII Corps 1940-1942. Brigadier general in July 1942. Assistant division commander of 3rd Infantry Division 1942-1943. Major general in November 1943. Commanding general of 45th Infantry Division 1943-1945. Commanding general of the Infantry Replacement Training Center at Camp Hood June 1945-January 1946. Retired in January 1953. Decorations included two Distinguished Service Medals, the Bronze Star and Purple Heart. Died on February 19, 1988.

Earnest, Herbert Ludwell (1895-1970) Born in Richmond, Virginia, on November 11, 1895. Attended the Medical College of Virginia 1915-1916. Commissioned in the cavalry, Officers Reserve Corps in 1917. Served in France 1918-1919. Instructor at the Cavalry School 1923-1925, then the Command and General Staff School 1926-1929. Graduated from the Command and General Staff School in 1934. Instructor at the Chemical Warfare School 1936-1938. Graduated from Army Industrial College in 1939. In the operations and training division at the War Department General Staff June 1939-June 1942. Executive officer of Tank Destroyer Center at Camp Hood in 1942. Commander of 1st Tank Destroyer Brigade November 1942-August 1944. Brigadier general in February 1943. Commanding general of Task Force "A" in Third Army in 1944, then Combat Command "A" in 4th Armored Division November 1944-January 1945. Commanding general of 90th Infantry Division January-December 1945. Major general in May 1945. Retired in September 1947. Decorations included the Distinguished Service Medal, Silver Star, Legion of Merit and three Bronze Stars. Died on June 11, 1970.

Easley, Claudius Miller (1891-1945) Born in Thorp Spring, Texas, on July 11, 1891. Commissioned in the Texas National Guard in 1912. B.S. from Texas A&M in 1916. Served with the 31st Infantry in the Philippines 1921-1924. Graduated from the Command and General Staff School in 1930. Instructor at the Infantry School 1930-1934. Graduated from the Army War College in 1940. Duty in the storage division of the War Department General Staff June 1940-February 1942. Brigadier general in July 1942. Assistant division commander of 96th Infantry Division August 1942 until he was killed in action on Okinawa on June 19, 1945.

Eastwood, Harold Eugene (1892-1973) Born in New York City on July 28, 1892. Enlisted service in the Illinois National Guard 1911-1914. Commissioned in the cavalry, Illinois National Guard in 1914 and the Regular Army in 1920. Served with the 17th Cavalry at Schofield Barracks, Hawaii December 1920-September 1921. Graduated from the Command and General Staff School in 1938. Instructor at the Cavalry School June 1938-April 1941. Duty with the War Department General Staff April 1941-July 1942 then Services of Supply July-October 1942. Deputy director of the resources division at Services of Supply October 1942-April 1943. Duty with the operations section of U.S. Army Forces Southwest Pacific Area April 1943-May 1945. Brigadier general in November 1944. Deputy to the assistant chief of staff at Southwest Pacific Area May 1945-June 1946. Retired in July 1952. Decorations included the Distinguished Service Medal and Legion of Merit. Died on November 1, 1973.

Eaton, Ralph Parker (1898-1986) Born on August 5, 1898, in Bloomington, Illinois. Commissioned in the infantry from West Point in 1924. Assistant professor of military science and tactics at Ohio State 1930-1932. Duty with 45th Infantry in the Philippines 1932-1934. Graduated from the Command and General Staff School in 1938. Assistant adjutant general in IV Corps 1940-1942. Deputy chief of staff for personnel, then chief of staff of 82nd Airborne Division, then chief of staff of XVII Airborne Corps 1942-1945. Brigadier general in January 1945. Reverted to colonel in February 1946. Retired in August 1954. Decorations included the Distinguished Service Medal, two Legions of Merit, the Bronze Star and Purple Heart. Died on May 16, 1986.

Eberle, George Leland (1894-1978) Born on January 23, 1894, in Des Moines, Iowa. Enlisted service in the Arizona National Guard 1916-1917. Commissioned in the infantry in 1917. Duty with 57th Infantry in the Philippines 1927-1929. Graduated from the Command and General Staff School in 1934 and the Army War College in 1935. Instructor at the Command and General Staff School 1935-1939. Duty with the operations and training division at the War Department General Staff February 1940-August 1942. Brigadier general in July 1942. Assistant division commander of 98th Infantry Division August 1942-April 1944. Chief of plans at Allied Force Headquarters, North African Theater of Operations 1944-1945. Chief of staff of the Mediterranean Theater of Operations November 1945-February 1946. Assignments after the war included deputy commandant of National War College July 1952 until retirement as major general in July 1954. Decorations included two Distinguished Service Medals and the Legion of Merit. Died on June 7, 1978.

Eddleman, Clyde Davis (1902-1992) Born in Orange, Texas, on January 17, 1902. Commissioned in the infantry from West Point in 1924. Graduated from the Command and General in Staff School in 1938 and the Army War College in

1955. Chief of training division, then assistant chief of staff of Third Army November 1941-January 1943. Deputy chief of staff of Sixth Army January 1943-
December 1945. Assignments after the war included commanding general of 4th
Infantry Division May 1954-October 1955, commandant of the Army War College May-October 1955, deputy chief of staff for plans, then deputy chief of staff
for millitary operations, U.S. Army, October 1955-July 1958, commanding general of Seventh Army July 1958-March 1959, commander in chief of U.S. Army
Europe April 1959-October 1960 and vice chief of staff, U.S. Army November
1960-March 1962. Retired in 1962. Decorations included two Distinguished
Service Medals, the Silver Star, Legion of Merit and Bronze Star. Died on
August 19, 1992.

Eddy, Manton Sprague (1892-1962) Born on May 16, 1892, in Chicago, Illinois. Commissioned in the infantry in 1918. Served with the 4th Division of the
AEF in World War I and saw action at Aisne-Marne and near the Vesle River,
where he was wounded in August 1918. Member of the Infantry Board 1921-
1924. Professor of military science and tactics at Riverside Military Academy
1925-1929. Graduated from the Command and General Staff School in 1934 then
instructor there until 1939. Assistant chief of staff for intelligence at the III Corps
Area 1940-1942. Commander of 114th Infantry, 44th Division 1941-1942.
Brigadier general in March 1942, major general in August 1942. Assistant division commander of 9th Infantry Division, then commanding general 1942-1944.
Commanding general of XII Corps 1944-1945. Assignments after the war included commanding general of the Command and General Staff School 1948-
1950 and deputy commander of U.S. European Command, then commanding
general of Seventh Army July 1950 until retirement in March 1953 as lieutenant
general. Decorations included the Distinguished Service Cross, two Distinguished
Service Medals, the Silver Star, two Legions of Merit, two Bronze Stars, the Air
Medal, Commendation Ribbon and Purple Heart. Died in April 1962.

Edgerton, Glen Edgar (1887-1976) Born on April 17, 1887, in Parkerville, Kan-
sas. B.S. from Kansas State Agricultural College in 1904. Commissioned in the
Corps of Engineers from West Point in 1908. Division engineer in 14th Division
in World War I. Graduated from the Command and General Staff School in 1924.
Assistant to the chief of engineers 1933-1936. Engineer of maintenance at the
Panama Canal 1936-1940. Brigadier general in October 1940. Governor of the
Panama Canal July 1940-May 1944. Major general in March 1942. Director of
materiel at Army Service Forces 1944-1945. Retired in April 1949. Decorations
included two Distinguished Service Medals and the Legion of Merit. Died on
April 9, 1976.

Edward, Harvey (1893-1947) Born on October 1, 1893, in New York City.
Commissioned in the cavalry, Officers Reserve Corps in 1917. Graduated from
Army Industrial College in 1931, the Command and General Staff School in 1934
and the Army War College in 1938. Brigadier general in June 1945. Reverted to

colonel in April 1946. Decorations included the Legion of Merit. Died on March 5, 1947.

Eichelberger, Robert Lawrence (1886-1961) Born on March 9, 1886, in Urbana, Ohio. Attended Ohio State University 1903-1905. Commissioned in the infantry from West Point in 1909. Deputy chief of staff of the American Expeditionary Force in Siberia 1918. Secretary of the the the War Department General Staff 1935-1938. Commanding officer of 30th Infantry 1938-1940. Brigadier general in 1940. Superintendent of West Point 1940-1942. Major general in March 1942. Commanding general of 77th Infantry Division, then XI Corps March-September 1942. Commanding general of I Corps September 1942-September 1944. Lieutenant general in October 1942. Commanding general of 8th Army September 1944 until retirement in September 1948. Decorations included two Distinguished Service Crosses, five Distinguished Service Medals, three Silver Stars, the Legion of Merit, Bronze Star and Air Medal. Author of *Our Jungle Road to Tokyo* (1950). General on the retired list in July 1954. Died on September 26, 1961.

Eisenhower, Dwight David (1890-1969) Born on October 14, 1890, in Denison, Texas. Commissioned in the infantry from West Point in 1915, where he acquired the nickname "Ike." Engaged in training duties in World War I. Graduated from the Command and General Staff School in 1926. Duty with the American Battle Monuments Commission in 1927. Graduated from the Army War College in 1928. Assistant executive to the assistant secretary of war 1929-1932, and special assistant to General Douglas MacArthur in Washington and the Philippines 1933-1939. Regimental executive officer in the 15th Infantry, then chief of staff of 3rd Infantry Division in 1940. Chief of staff of IX Corps then Third Army March 1941-September 1941. Brigadier general in September 1941. With war plans division of the War Department General Staff December 1941-May 1942. Major general in April 1942. Commander of U.S. Forces Europe June 1942-November 1943. Lieutenant general in July 1942, general in February 1943. Supreme Commander Allied Expeditionary Force December 1943-November 1945. General of the Army in December 1944. Assignments after the war included chief of staff, U.S. Army 1945-1948. President of Columbia University 1948-1950. Recalled to active duty as Supreme Allied Commander in Europe in 1950. President of the United States 1953-1961. Decorations included six Distinguished Service Medals and the Legion of Merit. Author of *Crusade in Europe* (1949) and *Mandate for Change* (1963). Died on March 28, 1969.

Elliott, Dabney Otey (1890-1976) Born on October 13, 1890, in Sewanee, Tennessee. Commissioned in the Corps of Engineers from West Point in 1914. Chief of staff of IX Corps 1941-1942. Brigadier general in June 1943. Chief engineer for Allied Forces in the North African Theater of Operations 1943-1944. Commanding general of engineers in the China Theater of Operations 1944-1946. Retired in 1950. Decorations included the Distinguished Service Medal and two Legions of Merit. Died on June 20, 1976.

Elmore, John Archer (1902-1971) Born on December 29, 1902, in Montgomery, Alabama. Commissioned in the infantry from West Point in 1924. Duty with 19th Infantry in Hawaii 1926-1929. Instructor at the Infantry School in 1930. Served with the 15th Infantry in China 1936-1938. Aide to Brigadier General Charles P. Hall in 1941. Graduated from the Command and General Staff School in 1942. Operations officer in 93rd Infantry Division in 1942. Assistant chief of staff, then chief of staff of XI Corps November 1942-February 1946. Brigadier general in January 1945. Reverted to colonel in March 1946. Assignments after the war included assistant division commander of 47th Infantry Division, then 1st Infantry Division 1954-1955. Retired in January 1956. Decorations included the Distinguished Service Medal, Silver Star, Legion of Merit and Bronze Star. Died on November 11, 1971.

Embick, Stanley Dunbar (1877-1957) Born in Franklin County, Pennsylvania, on January 22, 1877. Attended Dickinson College 1893-1895. Commissioned in the Coast Artillery Corps from West Point in 1899. Chief of staff of the American section, Supreme War Council at Versailles 1917-1918. Delegate to the Paris peace conference 1918-1919. Instructor at the Army War College 1921-1923. With the War Department General Staff 1926-1930. Brigadier general in September 1930. Commandant of the Coast Artillery School 1930-1932. Commander of harbor defenses at Manila 1932-1935. Assistant chief of staff, then deputy chief of staff at the War Department General Staff 1935-1938. Major general in May 1936. Commanding general of IV Corps Area, then Third Army 1938-1940. Lieutenant general in August 1939. Member of the Joint Defense Board 1940-1941. Retired in January 1941. Recalled to active duty in February 1941. Member of the Joint Defense Board 1941-1942. With the Joint Chiefs of Staff 1942-1945 while concurrently chairman of the Inter-American Defense Board 1942-1946. Decorations included two Distinguished Service Medals. Died on October 23, 1957.

Emery, Ambrose Robert (1883-1945) Born on July 26, 1883, in Bloomfield, Indiana. B.S. from Georgia Institute of Technology in 1904. Commissioned in the infantry in 1905. Duty with 15th Infantry in Tientsin, China 1916-1918. Graduated from the Command and General Staff School in 1926 and the Army War College in 1932. Professor of military science and tactics at Texas A&M 1932-1936. Commanding officer of 27th Infantry in Hawaii 1936-1938. Professor of military science and tactics at Pennsylvania State College October 1938-December 1940. Commander of Infantry Replacement Training Center at Macon, Georgia December 1940 until retirement in February 1944. Brigadier general in October 1941. Decorations included the Legion of Merit. Died on November 28, 1945.

Englehart, Francis Augustus (1890-1969) Born on March 1, 1890, in Laclede, Missouri. Commissioned in the Coast Artillery Corps from West Point in 1913. Instructor at West Point 1916-1919 then the Coast Artillery School 1920-1921. Graduated from Army Industrial College in 1933. M.B.A. from Harvard in 1935.

Duty in the office of the chief of ordnance 1941-1944. Brigadier general in November 1944. Ordnance officer for U.S. Army Forces in the Middle Pacific 1944-1945. Retired in August 1946. Decorations included the Legion of Merit. Died on January 13, 1969.

English, Paul Xavier (1888-1964) Born in Richmond, Virginia, on September 29, 1888. B.S. from Virginia Military Institute in 1911. Commissioned in the infantry in 1912. Duty in the Canal Zone 1915-1917. Professor of military science and tactics at the University of Texas at El Paso 1920-1924. Graduated from the Command and General Staff School in 1928 and the Army War College in 1933. Chemical officer in the Philippine Department February 1936-February 1938. Chief of the manufacturing and supply division, then chief of the industrial division, office of the chief of the Chemical Warfare Service 1938-1944. Brigadier general in January 1942. Assistant chief of staff, then commanding officer of 7th Service Command February 1944 until retirement in July 1946. Decorations included two Legions of Merit. Died on June 25, 1964.

Ennis, Riley Finley (1897-1963) Born on April 23, 1897, in Paulding, Ohio. Attended Ohio State and Miami University of Ohio. Commissioned in the infantry in 1918. Served with 35th Infantry in Hawaii 1921-1924. Assistant professor of military science and tactics at Knox College 1928-1932. Graduated from the Command and General Staff School in 1936. Instructor at the Infantry School 1936-1938. Graduated from the Army War College in 1939. Military observer in London and Cairo December 1940-October 1941. Assistant to the plans and training officer, U.S. Army 1941-1942. Duty in the training division of Army Ground Forces March 1942-March 1944. Commander of Combat Command "A" in 12th Armored Division 1944-1945. Brigadier general in August 1944. Assignments after the war included commanding general of 101st Airborne Division 1954-1955 and deputy commanding general of Sixth Army August 1955 until retirement in March 1957. Decorations included the Distinguished Service Medal, two Legions of Merit and the Bronze Star. Died on September 11, 1963.

Erickson, Sidney (1885-n/a) Born in Lakefield, Minnesota, on July 28, 1885. Enlisted service February 1907-March 1914. Commissioned in the Philippine Scouts in 1914. Served in the Philippines March 1914-April 1921. Professor of military science and tactics at the University of Nebraska 1921-1925. Graduated from Command and General Staff School in 1927 then instructor there 1929-1933. Graduated from the Army War College in 1934. Duty with the Organized Reserves in Minneapolis October 1935-January 1940 then 7th Service Command 1941-1942. Chief of staff of 7th Service Command April 1942-February 1944. Brigadier general in April 1943. Chief of staff of 4th Service Command 1944-1945.

Evans, Edward Arthur (1895-n/a) Born in Muskogee, Oklahoma, on September 17, 1895. Commissioned in the Coast Artillery Corps, Officers Reserve Corps in 1918. Called to active duty in November 1940. Served with the 9th Coast Artillery District 1941-1942. Duty at headquarters of III Corps February-May 1942. Brigadier general in May 1942. Commander of the Florida Subsection, Eastern Defense Command 1942-1944. Duty in the office of the secretary of war January-October 1944 then with the War Department General Staff October 1944-May 1945.

Evans, Vernon (1893-1987) Born on August 21, 1893, in Detroit, Michigan. Commissioned in the infantry from West Point in 1915. Commanding officer of 1st Machine Gun Battalion, 1st Division in AEF in World War I. Instructor at the Infantry School 1920-1923. Graduated from the Command and General Staff School in 1926 and the Army War College in 1928. Executive officer of 19th Brigade in the Canal Zone 1928-1931. Instructor at the Infantry School 1931-1935. Assistant professor of military science and tactics at Georgetown University 1935-1938. Chief of the Infantry Tank School at Fort Benning 1940-1941. Commanding officer of 81st Tank Regiment, 5th Armored Division September 1941-July 1942. Combat command commander in 13th Armored Divison 1942-1943. Brigadier general in September 1942. Deputy chief of staff, then chief of staff of China-Burma-India Theater of Operations 1943-1945. Major general in January 1945. Retired in January 1953. Decorations included the Distinguished Service Medal. Died on November 4, 1987.

Eyster, George Senseny (1895-1951) Born on August 8, 1895, in Halltown, West Virginia. Commissioned in the infantry from West Point in 1917. Graduated from the Command and General Staff School in 1938. Head of the defense housing section at the Federal Works Administration in 1940. Served with the War Department General Staff 1940-1942. Chief of the unit training branch at Services of Supply 1942-1943. Chief of staff of 76th Infantry Division January-August 1943. Deputy chief of staff for operations at European Theater of Operations 1944-1945. Brigadier general in May 1944. Retired in 1950. Decorations included the Distinguished Service Medal, two Legions of Merit and the Bronze Star. Died on March 9, 1951.

Fairbank, Leigh Cole (1889-1966) Born in Genesee County, Michigan, on November 14, 1889. Attended Detroit College of Medicine 1908-1909. D.DS. from Georgetown University in 1912. Commissioned in the Dental Corps in 1916. Attended Washington University in 1928. Graduated from Army Dental School in 1935. Brigadier general in 1938 as the assistant surgeon general and the first Dental Corps general officer. Served until retirement in February 1942. Died on June 28, 1966 following an automobile accident eleven days earlier.

Faith, Don Carlos (1896-1963) Born in Washington, Indiana, on February 13, 1896. Attended the University of Wisconsin 1915-1918. Commissioned in the infantry in 1917. In the Philippines with 57th Infantry 1919-1923. Instructor with Wisconsin National Guard 1926-1930. Duty in Tientsin, China with 15th Infantry 1930-1931. Graduated from Command and General Staff School in 1936 and the Army War College in 1939. At the National Guard Bureau 1939-1940 then the

War Department General Staff 1941-1942. Brigadier general in December 1942. Commanding general of WAC Training Command 1942-1943. Assistant division commander of 95th Infantry Division 1944-1945. Assignments after the war included assistant commandant of the Command and General Staff School 1946-1948. Retired in October 1948. Decorations included the Distinguished Service Medal, Silver Star, Legion of Merit and two Bronze Stars. B.A. and M.A. from George Washington University in 1949, Ph.D. in 1951. Died on August 8, 1963.

Fales, Eugene Warren (1887-1963) Born in Niagara County, New York, on September 16, 1887. Attended Rutgers University 1906-1909. Commissioned in the infantry in 1912. With Pershing in the Punitive Expedition into Mexico 1916-1917. Served in the AEF 1918-1919. Graduated from Command and General Staff School in 1926 and the Army War College in 1928. Attended the French tank school in 1933. Member of the Infantry Board 1934-1936. Commandant of Tank and Motor School 1936-1938. Executive officer in the office of the chief of infantry 1939-1941. Brigadier general in July 1941. Commanding general of Infantry Replacement Center, Camp Roberts 1941-1943. Commanding general of Infantry Replacement Center, Camp Blanding July 1943-September 1945. Major general in September 1944. Retired in August 1946. Decorations included the Legion of Merit. Died on March 23, 1963.

Farmer, Archie Arrington (1892-1963) Born in Wilson, North Carolina, on April 2, 1892. B.S. from the University of North Carolina in 1914. Commissioned in the infantry in 1917. Duty in Hawaii 1919-1922. Transferred to the Signal Corps in 1923. Graduated from the Command and General Staff School in 1932. In the office of the chief signal officer as chief of the supply and procurement divisions July 1938-December 1941. Commanding officer of Philadelphia Signal Depot 1941-1942. Brigadier general in July 1942. Commanding general of Signal Corps Eastern Signal Service from 1942. Retired in March 1946. Decorations included the Legion of Merit. Died on May 5, 1963.

Farrell, Francis William (1900-1981) Born on May 28, 1900, in Chicago, Illinois. Commissioned in the infantry from West Point in 1920. Duty with 35th Infantry in Hawaii 1923-1926. Instructor at West Point 1928-1935. Graduated from the Command and General Staff School in 1939. Instructor at the Field Artillery School 1939-1943. Chief of staff of 11th Airborne Division 1943-1944. Brigadier general in January 1944. Commanding general of 11th Airborne Division Artillery 1944-1945. Assignments after the war included deputy chief of staff for operations, U.S. Army 1952-1953, commanding general of 82nd Airborne Division 1953-1955, commanding general of V Corps 1957-1959 and Seventh Army 1959-1960. Retired in July 1960. Decorations included two Distinguished Service Medals, the Silver Star, Legion of Merit, two Bronze Stars and the Air Medal. Died on January 27, 1981.

Farrell, Thomas Francis (1891-1967) Born in Rensselear County, New York, on December 3, 1891. C.E. from Rensselear Polytechnic Institute in 1912. Commissioned in the Corps of Engineers, Officers Reserve Corps in 1916. Engaged as an engineer at the Panama Canal 1913-1917. Served with 1st Engineers, AEF at Cantigny, Aisne-Marne, Montdidier-Noyon, St. Mihiel and Meuse-Argonne 1917-1918. Instructor at the Engineer School 1921-1924, then West Point 1924-1926. Chief engineer for the New York State Department of Public Works 1930-1941. Called to active duty in the Corps of Engineers as colonel February 1941-January 1944. Brigadier general in January 1944. Chief engineer at the China-Burma-India Theater of Operations 1944-1945. Major general in October 1945. Deputy commander of the Manhattan Project 1945-1946. Released from active duty in April 1946. Decorations included the Distinguished Service Cross, Distinguished Service Medal, two Legions of Merit and the Purple Heart. Died on April 11, 1967.

Faymonville, Philip Ries (1888-1962) Born on April 30, 1888, in California. Commissioned in the Coast Artillery Corps from West Point in 1912. Ordnance officer with the AEF in Siberia during World War I. Graduated from Army Industrial College in 1933 and the Army War College in 1934. Military attache in Russia 1934-1939. Served in the office of the chief of ordnance 1939-1940. Ordnance officer at Fourth Army October 1940-September 1941. Member of the special war supplies mission to the USSR September-December 1941. Duty with the War Department General Staff 1941-1943. Brigadier general in January 1942. Reverted to colonel.in November 1943 and retired in April 1948. Decorations included the Legion of Merit. Died on March 29, 1962.

Feldman, Herman (1889-1969) Born in New York City on September 10, 1889. Enlisted service 1907-1917. Commissioned in the field artillery in 1917. Served with the 2nd Field Artillery in the Philippines 1917-1918. Chief of the general supplies section in the office of the assistant chief of staff for supply 1941-1942. At headquarters of Army Service Forces in 1942. Assistant chief of staff for supply at Services of Supply, European Theater of Operations, then Mediterranean base section in North African Theater of Operations 1942-1943. Deputy quartermaster general, the quartermaster general of the U.S. Army August 1943 until retirement in September 1951. Brigadier general in January 1944, major general in January 1948. Decorations included the Distinguished Service Medal, Legion of Merit and Commendation Ribbon. Died on September 27, 1969.

Fellers, Bonner Frank (1896-1973) Born on February 7, 1896, in Ridge Farm, Illinois. Commissioned in the Coast Artillery Corps from West Point in 1918. Graduated from Command and General Staff School in 1935 and the Army War College in 1939. Military attache in Egypt 1940-1942. Brigadier general in December 1942. Member of General MacArthur's staff in the Pacific 1943-1946. Retired in November 1946. Decorations included two Distinguished Service Medals and the Legion of Merit. Died on October 7, 1973.

Fenn, Clarence Charles (1890-1971) Born in Ashland, Wisconsin, on February 26, 1890. LL.B. from Georgetown University in 1914. Graduate studies at the University of Wisconsin. Commissioned in the infantry in 1917. Duty in the Hawaiian Division 1922-1925. Judge advocate in the Philippine Division 1930-1933. Graduated from Army Industrial College in 1936 and the Army War College in 1940. Judge advocate general for VI Corps in 1941. Theater of Operations judge advocate with U.S. Army forces in the China-Burma-India Theater of Operations February 1942-1945. Brigadier general in January 1945. Retired in February 1950. Decorations included two Legions of Merit. Died on July 20, 1971.

Fenton, Chauncey Lee (1880-1962) Born on January 14, 1880, in Edinburgh, Pennsylvania. Graduated from West Point and commissioned in the Coast Artillery Corps in 1904. Served with the AEF at the Aisne-Marne, St. Mihiel, Somme and Meuse-Argonne offensives in 1918. Graduated from the Army War College in 1923 and the Command and General Staff School in 1928. Professor at West Point 1928-1944. Retired in January 1944. Returned to active duty in February 1944 and served until June 1946. Decorations included the Distinguished Service Medal and Legion of Merit. Died on February 8, 1962.

Ferenbaugh, Claude Birkett (1899-1975) Born on March 16, 1899, in Dresden, New York. Commissioned in the infantry from West Point in 1919. Duty in Hawaii 1922-1925. Graduated from the Command and General Staff School in 1937. Served with the 57th Infantry in the Philippines 1937-1939. Graduated from the Army War College in 1940. At the War Department General Staff 1941-1942. Deputy chief of staff for operations at I Corps, North African Theater of Operations in 1942. With the War Department General Staff again 1943-1944. Brigadier general in May 1944. Assistant division commander of 83rd Division 1944-1945. Assigned to the War Department General Staff, then commander of the Military District of Washington 1945-1948. Assignments after the war included commanding general of 5th Armored Division 1950-1951 and 7th Infantry Division in 1951. Deputy commanding general of Eighth Army December 1954 until retirement as lieutenant general in September 1955. Decorations included two Distinguished Service Medals, two Silver Stars, two Legions of Merit and two Bronze Stars. Died on September 10, 1975.

Ferrin, Charles Sabin (1892-1976) Born in Montpelier, Vermont, on November 28, 1892. B.S. from the University of Vermont. Commissioned in the infantry in 1917. Served in the AEF in 1918. Instructor with the Vermont and Massachusetts National Guard 1922-1923. Graduated from Command and General Staff School in 1932, Army Industrial College in 1938 and the Naval War College in 1939. Brigadier general in January 1945. Retired in November 1952. Decorations included the Legion of Merit, Bronze Star, two Air Medals and the Commendation Ribbon. Died on July 25, 1976.

Ferris, Benjamin Greeley (1892-1982) Born on September 20, 1892, in Pawling, New York. Commissioned in the infantry from West Point in 1915. Professor of military science and tactics at Connecticut Agricultural College 1919-1920, then Boston University 1920-1921. Graduated from the Command and General Staff School in 1927 and the Army War College in 1936. Supply officer at First Army

April-December 1941. With 5th Infantry Division 1942-1943. Brigadier general in October 1942. Deputy chief of staff of U.S. Army Forces China-Burma-India Theater of Operations December 1943-December 1944. Member of the Equipment Review Board at Army Ground Forces in 1945. Retired in September 1951. Decorations included two Legions of Merit, the Bronze Star and Commendation Ribbon. Died on September 2, 1982.

Fielder, Kendall Jordan (1893-1981) Born in Cedartown, Georgia, on August 1, 1893. B.S. from Georgia Institute of Technology in 1916. Commissioned in the infantry in 1917. Served with a machine gun battalion in World War I. Plans and training officer, then executive officer of 22nd Infantry Brigade at Schofield Barracks, Hawaii 1938-1941. Officer in charge of military intelligence and counterintelligence in Hawaii and Pacific Ocean Areas 1941-1945. Brigadier general in November 1944. Reverted to colonel in March 1946 and retired in July 1953. Decorations included the Distinguished Service Medal, two Legions of Merit, the Bronze Star and Commendation Ribbon. Died on April 13, 1981.

Finley, Thomas Dewees (1895-1984) Born on June 2, 1895, in Annapolis, Maryland. Commissioned in the Corps of Engineers from West Point in 1916. With 7th Engineers, 5th Division, AEF 1918-1919. Instructor at West Point 1927-1931. Graduated from Command and General Staff School and the Army War College in 1935. At the military intelligence division of the War Department General Staff 1935-1941. Duty with general staff corps at Second Army 1941-1942. Brigadier general in May 1942. Assistant division commander of 89th Infantry Division May 1942-February 1943. Major general in March 1943. Commanding general of 89th Infantry Division 1943-1945. Retired in September 1946. Decorations included the Distinguished Service Medal, two Legions of Merit and the Bronze Star. Died on Decemeber 19, 1984.

Fitch, Burdette Mase (1896-1977) Born in Delphos, Kansas, on February 12, 1896. Attended the University of Kansas 1913-1916. Enlisted service 1917-1918 attached to General Pershing's staff at general headquarters of AEF. Commissioned in the field artillery in 1920. Instructor with Rhode Island National Guard 1929-1935. Duty with 24th Field Artillery in the Philippines 1935-1938. Staff officer at headquarters of U.S. Army forces in Australia 1941-1942. Adjutant general on General MacArthur's staff 1942-1945. Brigadier general in August 1944. Adjutant general for Supreme Commander Allied Powers in Tokyo 1945-1946. Retired in July 1953. Decorations included the Distinguished Service Medal, Legion of Merit and Purple Heart. Died on November 6, 1977.

Fleming, Philip Bracken (1887-1955) Born in Burlington, Iowa, on October 15, 1887. Attended the University of Wisconsin 1905-1907. Commissioned in the Corps of Engineers from West Point in 1910. Duty in Panama 1911-1912 and again 1915-1917. Senior instructor at West Point 1926-1933. Executive officer then deputy administrator in the office of the Administrator of Public Works May 1933-June 1935. Administrator of the wage and hour division of the Department of Labor 1939-1941. Brigadier general in January 1941. Federal Works Administrator 1941-1949. Major general in October 1942. Retired in February 1947. Decorations included the Distinguished Service Medal. Chairman of the U.S. Maritime Commission 1949-1950. Under secretary of commerce 1950-1951. Died on October 6, 1955.

Flory, Lester De Long (1899-1990) Born on June 10, 1899, in Ashley, Pennsylvania. Commissioned in the Coast Artillery Corps from West Point in 1919. Served in Panama 1921-1924. Instructor at West Point 1925-1927. Graduated from the Command and General Staff School in 1936 and the Army War College in 1940. At headquarters of Army Service Forces 1942-1943. Commander of 63rd Antiaircraft Artillery Brigade 1943-1944. Brigadier general in January 1944. At headquarters of U.S. Forces in Austria 1945-1946. Reverted to colonel in April 1946. Retired in June 1949. Decorations included the Distinguished Service Medal and Legion of Merit. Died on January 2, 1990.

Ford, Elbert Louis (1892-1990) Born on December 2, 1892, in Milford, Connecticut. Commissioned in the Coast Artillery Corps from West Point in 1917. Professor of military science and tactics at Yale September 1921-December 1924. Graduated from Army Industrial College in 1932 and the Army War College in 1934. Duty at Springfield Armory 1937-1942. Chief of staff at headquarters of North African Theater of Operations 1943-1944. Brigadier general in June 1943. In the office of the chief of ordnance 1944-1946. Assignments after the war included chief of ordnance, U.S. Army 1949-1953. Retired as major general in October 1953. Decorations included the Distinguished Service Medal, two Legions of Merit and the Commendation Ribbon. Died on February 25, 1990.

Ford, William Wallace (1898-1986) Born on October 2, 1898, in Waverly, Virginia. Commissioned in the field artillery from West Point in 1920. Aide-de-camp to Brigadier General Edgar Russell in 1922. Duty with 11th Field Artillery in Hawaii 1923-1926. Instructor at East Kentucky State Teachers College ROTC 1936-1939. Instructor, then director of communications and airborne training departments at the Field Artillery School May 1941-January 1944. Commanding general of 87th Infantry Division Artillery 1944-1945. Brigadier general in August 1944. Reverted to colonel in February 1946. Retired in August 1954. Decorations included two Legions of Merit, the Bronze Star, Air Medal and Commendation Ribbon. Died on November 9, 1986.

Forster, George Jacob (1891-1979) Born in Wisconsin on April 24, 1891. Commissioned in the infantry reserve in 1917. Served with the 26th Infantry, AEF 1917-1919 at Cantigny, Soissons, St. Mihiel and Meuse-Argonne engagements. Aide-de-camp to Major General Charles P. Summerall August 1919-November 1930. Duty in Iceland September 1941-February 1944. Brigadier general in September 1942. Assistant division commander of 66th Infantry Division February 1944-September 1945. Reverted to colonel in February 1946. Retired in April 1951. Decorations included the Distinguished Service Cross, Silver Star, Legion of Merit, two Bronze Stars and the Commendation Ribbon. Died on December 24, 1979.

Fort, Guy O. (1879-1942) Born in Keelersville, Michigan in 1879. Enlisted service with the 4th Cavalry 1899-1902. Commissioned in the Philippine Constabulary, the national police force, in 1904. Resigned in 1917, then commissioned again in 1921. Took command of the 81st Division, Philippine Army and commissioned brigadier general on December 20, 1941. The division was moved to Mindanao in 1942 and designated the Lanao Force. Taken prisoner of war in May 1942. Refusing to cooperate with his captors, he was executed by firing squad on November 9 or 13, 1942 (records are inconclusive) in Mindanao, the only American-born general officer executed by the enemy in World War II.

Fortier, Louis Joseph (1892-1974) Born in Gretna, Louisiana, on April 8, 1892. B.C.E. from Tulane in 1913. Commissioned in the field artillery in 1917. Served with the 17th Field Artillery, 2nd Division of AEF 1917-1918. M.S. from Alabama Polytechnic Institute in 1923. Graduated from Command and General Staff School in 1933 and the Army War College in 1936. Military attache in Belgrade 1939-1941. Brigadier general in August 1942. Commanding general of 94th Division Artillery 1942-1945. Member of the United Nations Military Staff Committee 1945-1946. Retired in December 1950. Decorations included the Distinguished Service Medal, Legion of Merit, Bronze Star and Commendation Ribbon. Died on November 6, 1974.

Foster, George Burgess Jr. (1884-1949) Born in Salem, Massachusetts, on July 27, 1884. M.D. from Jefferson Medical College in 1909. Commissioned in the Medical Corps in 1909. Graduated from Army Medical School in 1910. Duty in the Philippine Islands 1913-1915. D.P.H. from Harvard Medical School in 1917. Served with the AEF 1917-1919. Instructor at Army Medical School 1919-1920. Commanding officer of Tripler General Hospital, Hawaii July 1939-May 1941. Chief of medical services, then commanding general at O'Reilly General Hospital, Springfield, Missouri 1941-1946. Brigadier general in May 1944. Retired in 1946. Decorations included the Legion of Merit. Died on December 31, 1949.

Foster, Ivan Leon (1896-1965) Born in Yates, Missouri, on April 23, 1896. Commissioned in the field artillery in 1917. Served with the 124th Field Artillery in World War I in the Meuse-Argonne and Lorraine campaigns. Professor of military science and tactics at the University of Illinois 1922-1927. Graduated from Command and General Staff School in 1936 and the Army War College in 1938. At headquarters of AAF 1940-1942. Brigadier general in September 1942. Commanding general of 84th Infantry Division Artillery 1942-1944. Deputy assistant chief of staff for operations at Allied Forces Headquarters for the North African Theater of Operations April 1944-September 1945. Retired in July 1948. Decorations included the Legion of Merit. Died on November 26, 1965.

Fowler, Raymond Foster (1884-1949) Born in Alexandria, Nebraska, on October 14, 1884. Attended the University of Nebraska 1904-1906. Commissioned in the Corps of Engineers from West Point in 1910. Section engineer in the AEF 1917-1918. Graduated from Command and General Staff School in 1925 and the Army War College in 1935. Chief of the supply division in the office of the chief of engineers 1941-1942. Brigadier general in June 1942. Division engineer in the South Atlantic Division then engineer on the staff of 4th Service Command from 1942. Retired in December 1945. Decorations included the Distinguished Service Medal. Died on January 19, 1949.

Fox, Alonzo P. (1895-1984) Born in St. Louis, Missouri, on November 11, 1895. B.C.S. from St. Louis University in 1917. Commissioned in the infantry in 1917. Overseas duty in the Philippines 1923-1924 and with the 19th Infantry in Hawaii 1932-1935. Professor of military science and tactics at the University of Maine September 1935-January 1936. Graduated from the Command and General Staff School in 1938. Instructor at the Infantry School 1938-1942. Assistant chief of staff for operations at X Corps September 1942-January 1943. Brigadier general in March 1943. Assistant division commander of 102nd Infantry Division 1943-1945. Commanding general of War Department Personnel Center at Fort Sam Houston June 1945-June 1946. Assignments after the war included duty in the office of the assistant secretary of defense for internal security affairs 1955-1957. Retired as lieutenant general in July 1957. Decorations included two Distinguished Service Medals, the Silver Star, Legion of Merit, three Bronze Stars and the Commendation Ribbon. Died on December 16, 1984.

Fox, Leon Alexander (1890-1965) Born in Birmingham, Alabama, on November 2, 1890. M.D. from Cincinnati University in 1912. In private practice 1913-1916. Commissioned in the Medical Corps in 1916. Graduated from Army Medical School in 1917. Chief health officer in the Caribbean and North Atlantic Division 1941-1942. Field director of the U.S. Typhus Commission 1943-1944. Brigadier general in March 1943. Chief medical officer in the North Atlantic Division 1945-1946. Retired in April 1946. Decorations included the Distinguished Service Medal and Legion of Merit. Died on June 5, 1965.

Frank, Selby Harney (1891-1974) Born on August 15, 1891, in Louisville, Kentucky. Commissioned in the Coast Artillery Corps from West Point in 1913. Served at headquarters of the First Army, AEF as officer in charge of automotive parts and supplies in 1918. Graduated from the Command and General Staff School in 1931. Duty in Puerto Rico 1939-1941. In the office of the chief of ordnance 1941-1842. Ordnance assignments in Texas, Louisiana and Maryland in 1943. Deputy, then chief ordnance officer at European and Mediterranean Theaters of Operation 1944-1945. Brigadier general in January 1945. In the office of the chief of ordnance 1945-1946. Reverted to colonel in February 1946. Retired as brigadier general in August 1951. Decorations included two Legions of Merit, two Bronze Stars and the Commendation Ribbon. Died on September 4, 1974.

Franke, Gustav Henry (1888-1953) Born in Manning, Iowa, on September 7, 1888. Commissioned in the Coast Artillery Corps from West Point in 1911. Instructor at West Point 1915-1917. Served with the 1st Division and general headquarters of AEF in 1918. Professor of military science and tactics at Colorado Agricultural and Mechanical College 1922-1924. Graduated from Command and General Staff School in 1926. Professor of military science and tactics at Alabama Polytechnic Institute 1931-1936. Graduated from the Army War College in 1937. Command of 2nd Field Artillery 1937-1940. Commanding officer of the Field Artillery Replacement Center, Fort Bragg in 1941. Brigadier general in April 1941. Commanding general of 6th Division Artillery 1941-1942. Major general in April 1942. Commanding general of 81st Division in 1942. Member of the War Department Dependency Board in 1943. Retired in January 1944. Died on March 19, 1953.

Franklin, John Merryman (1895-1975) Born in Cockeysville, Maryland, on June 18, 1895. B.A. from Harvard in 1918. Vice president of Roosevelt Steamship Company 1927-1931. President of United States Lines 1936-1942. Entered active duty as colonel in 1942. Transportation officer in the office of the quartermaster general in 1942. Chief of the water division in the office of the chief of transportation in 1942. Brigadier general in March 1943. Assistant chief of transportation 1943-1946. Major general in June 1945. Returned to the presidency of United States Lines after the war. Decorations included the Distinguished Service Medal and Bronze Star. Died on June 2, 1975.

Franks, John Brandon (1890-1946) Born in Leavenworth, Kansas, on March 10, 1890. B.S. from the University of Michigan in 1917. Commissioned in the field artillery in 1917. Served with the AEF 1918-1919. M.S. from Massachusetts Institute of Technology in 1925. Duty in Hawaii 1927-1930. Graduated from Army Industrial College in 1936. Executive officer in the defense aid section, office of the undersecretary of war July 1940-November 1941. With the Services of Supply 1941-1943. Served in the European Theater of Operations as chief of plans and training in the Forward Echelon Communications Zone, then commanding officer of 67th Headquarters Company at Quartermaster Base Depot, finally deputy chief quartermaster in the Communications Zone 1943-1945. Brigadier general in January 1945. Returned to the U.S. and died on November 13, 1946. Decorations included two Legions of Merit and the Bronze Star.

Fredendall, Lloyd Ralston (1883-1963) Born in Cheyenne, Wyoming, on December 28, 1883. Attended West Point 1902-1903. Commissioned in the infantry in 1907. Overseas duty with 2nd Infantry in the Philippines 1907-1908, in Hawaii 1911-1913, again in the Philippine Islands 1914-1917, and with the AEF 1917-1919. Instructor at the Infantry School 1920-1922. Graduated from Command and General Staff School in 1923 and the Army War College in 1925. Professor of military science and tactics at the University of Minnesota 1933-1934. Commanding officer of 57th Infantry in the Philippines 1936-1938. Executive officer in the office of the chief of infantry August 1938-December 1939. Brigadier general in December 1939. With the 5th Division in 1940. Major general in October 1940. Commanding general of 4th Division October 1940-July 1941. Commanding general of II Corps July 1941-June 1942, then XI Corps 1942-1943. Deputy commanding general, then commanding general of Second Army March 1943 until retirement in March 1946. Lieutenant general in June 1943. Decorations included the Distinguished Service Medal. Died on October 4, 1963.

Frederick, Robert Tryon (1907-1970) Born on March 14, 1907, in San Francisco, California. Commissioned in the Coast Artillery Corps from West Point in 1928. Graduated from the Command and General Staff School in 1939. With the War Department General Staff 1941-1942. Commander of 1st Special Service Force in Mediterranean and Pacific Theater of Operationss 1942-1944. Brigadier general in January 1944, major general in August 1944. Commanding general of 1st Airborne Division, then 45th Division 1944-1945. Assignments after the war included commanding general of 4th Division, then 6th Division 1949-1951. Retired in March 1952. Decorations included two Distinguished Service Crosses, two Distinguished Service Medals, the Silver Star, two Legions of Merit, two Bronze Stars, the Air Medal and eight Purple Hearts. Died on November 29, 1970.

French, Charles Augustus (1888-1982) Born in Sunol, California, on February 9, 1888. B.S. from Oregon Agricultural College in 1911. Commissioned in the Coast Artillery Corps in 1912. Overseas duty in the Philippines 1915-1917, with the Motor Transport Corps, AEF 1918-1919, and with 55th Artillery in Hawaii 1919-1924. Graduated from the Command and General Staff School in 1926. Professor of military science and tactics at New Bedford, Massachusetts high schools 1932-1932 and the University of Minnesota September 1939-July 1941. Executive officer of 34th Coast Artillery Brigade 1941-1943. Chief of staff of 4th Island Command in the Southwest Pacific Area February 1943-August 1943. Commanding general of 68th Antiaircraft Artillery Brigade 1943-1945. Brigadier general in November 1943. Reverted to colonel in March 1946. Retired in February 1948. Decorations included the Legion of Merit, Bronze Star, Air Medal and Commendation Ribbon. Died on April 13, 1982.

Frink, James Luke (1885-1977) Born in Ida Grove, Iowa on March 10, 1885. Attended Drury College 1904-1905. Enlisted service 1906-1908. Commissioned in the infantry in 1908. Served with the AEF in the Somme defense and Meuse-Argonne offensive in World War I. Graduated from Army Industrial College in 1925, the Army War College in 1926 and Command and General Staff School in 1929. Quartermaster for IV Corps Area 1940-1942. Brigadier general in October 1940. Deputy quartermaster general, U.S. Army 1942-1943. Major general in September 1943. Commanding general of Services of Supply in Japan June-November 1945. Retired in August 1946. Decorations included two Distinguished Service Medals, the Legion of Merit, Air Medal and Purple Heart. City manager of Greensboro, North Carolina 1946-1947. Died on April 30, 1977.

Fry, James Clyde (1897-1982) Born on December 25, 1897, in Sandpoint, Idaho. Commissioned in the infantry from West Point in 1922. Duty in Hawaii with 27th Infantry 1925-1928. Company commander with 31st Infantry in the Philippine Islands 1937-1939. Operations officer at 80th Armored Regiment April-September 1941. Assistant military attache in Ankara and Cairo September 1941-July 1942. Duty with the War Department General Staff in 1942. Executive officer of 2nd Armored Regiment in 1942. Commanding officer of 69th Armored Regiment, then aassistant chief of staff for operations at the Armored Command 1943-1944. Commanding officer of 350th Infantry, 88th Division then assistant division commander of the 88th April 1944-December 1945. Brigadier general in June 1945. Assignments after the war included commanding general of 2nd Division in the Korean War May 1952-May 1953. Retired in December 1957. Decorations included the Distinguished Service Cross, Distinguished Service Medal, Silver Star, two Legions of Merit, the Bronze Star and Purple Heart. Died on October 27, 1982.

Fuller, Horace Hayes (1886-1966) Born on August 10, 1886, in Fort Meade, South Dakota. Commissioned in the cavalry from West Point in 1909. Duty in the Philippines 1914-1916. With 108th Field Artillery, AEF 1918-1919. Graduated from Command and General Staff School in 1923 then instructor there 1923-1927. Graduated from the Army War College in 1928. Military attache in Paris 1935-1940. Brigadier general in October 1940. Commandant of the Command and General Staff School in 1941. Major general in December 1941. Commanding general of 41st Infantry Division December 1941-August 1944. President of U.S. Army Forces Far East Board August-November 1944. Deputy chief of staff of Southeast Asia Command November 1944 until retirement in August 1946. Decorations included the Distinguished Service Medal, Silver Star and Legion of Merit. Died on September 18, 1966.

Fulton, Walter Scott (1879-1950) Born in Lyndoch, Ontario, on March 23, 1879. Commissioned in the infantry from West Point in 1904. Duty in the Philippines 1906-1908. Aide to Brigadier General Daniel H. Brush 1908-1911. With the 4th Infantry at Vera Cruz in 1914. Instructor with the Minnesota National Guard 1920-1924. Graduated from the Command and General Staff School in 1925 and the Army War College in 1929. With the War Department General Staff 1929-1933. Instructor with the Louisiana National Guard 1933-1936. Instructor at the Infantry School in 1940. Executive officer, then commanding general of Fort Benning December 1940 until retirement in January 1944. Brigadier general in September 1942. Decorations included the Legion of Merit. Died on June 24, 1950.

Funk, Arnold John (1895-1980) Born in Stayton, Oregon, on August 13, 1895. B.S. from Oregon State College in 1916. Commissioned in the infantry in 1917. Instructor at Boston University ROTC 1924-1928 and the University of Georgia ROTC 1936-1938. Graduated from Command and General Staff School in 1939. Executive officer and plans and training officer in 45th Infantry, Philippine Scouts

1939-1941. Assistant chief of staff for operations at U.S. Army forces in the Far East in 1941. Commanding officer of 57th Combat Team in 1941. Chief of staff of Luzon Force 1941-1942. Brigadier general in January 1942. Reported missing in action, later found to be a prisoner of war in Formosa, Japan and Manchuria. Released in August 1945. Commanding general of Camp Edwards at retirement in May 1952. Decorations included two Distinguished Service Medals, the Silver Star, two Bronze Stars and the Purple Heart. Died on December 29, 1980.

Futch, Theodore Leslie (1895-1992) Born on January 19, 1895, in Monroe, North Carolina. Commissioned in the field artillery from West Point in 1917. Aide-de-camp to Brigadier General Harry G. Bishop 1918-1919. Professor of military science and tactics at Iowa State College 1921-1925. Instructor at the Field Artillery School 1926-1930. Professor of military science and tactics at Alabama Polytechnic Institute 1935-1938. Executive officer, then assistant commandant of the Field Artillery School December 1940-December 1942. Artillery officer at XIII Corps, then 35th Division December 1942-September 1945. Brigadier general in November 1943. Commanding general of Fort Bragg September 1945-February 1946. Retired in August 1954. Decorations included the Legion of Merit and four Bronze Stars. Died on January 18, 1992.

Gaffey, Hugh J. (1895-1946) Born in Hartford, Connecticut, on November 18, 1895. Attended the University of Pennsylvania 1916-1917. Commissioned in the field artillery in 1917. Served with 312th Field Artillery, AEF 1918-1919. Graduated from Command and General Staff School in 1936. Assistant to plans and training officer, then plans and training officer at I Armored Corps July 1940-January 1942. With 2nd Armored Division 1942-1944. Brigadier general in August 1942, major general in April 1943. Chief of staff of Third Army Arpil-December 1944. Commanding general of 4th Armored Division December 1944-September 1945. Commanding general of the Armored School September 1945 until his death on June 16, 1946, in the crash of a B-25 north of Godman Field at Fort Knox. Decorations included the Distinguished Service Medal and Silver Star.

Gage, Philip Stearns (1885-1982) Born in Detroit, Michigan, on November 13, 1885. Commissioned in the Coast Artillery Corps from West Point in 1909. Served with the 92nd Division in France in 1918, including the Vosges defense and the Meuse-Argonne offensive. Instructor at West Point 1919-1923. Graduated from Command and General Staff School in June 1925. Commanding officer of 55th Coast Artillery in Hawaii 1925-1927 then Fort Derussy, Hawaii August 1927-October 1930. Graduated from Army Industrial College in June 1937. Commander of harbor defense at Charleston 1937-1940. Brief duty with 7th Coast Artillery October 1940-April 1941. Brigadier general in April 1941. Commanding general of harbor defenses in New Jersey 1941-1943. Commander of the New Jersey Sub-Sector at Fort Hancock August 1943-March 1944. Commanding general of harbor defenses at Boston 1944-1945. Decorations included the Legion of Merit. Died on January 13, 1982.

Gailey, Charles Kenon Jr. (1901-1966) Born on May 14, 1901, in Conyers, Georgia. Commissioned in the infantry from West Point in 1920. Attended Massachusetts Institute of Technology 1929-1930. Instructor in the Tank School 1930-1931. Graduated from the Command and General Staff School in 1937. Aide to the commanding general of IX Corps Area 1937-1938. Executive officer of war plans division, the War Department General Staff 1940-1945. Brigadier general in January 1945. Assignments after the war included assistant division commander, then commanding general of 43rd Division 1952-1954 and commanding general of the Military District of Washington 1959-1961. Retired in June 1961. Decorations included two Distinguished Service Medals. Died on May 21, 1966.

Gaither, Ridgely (1903-1992) Born in Baltimore, Maryland, on February 23, 1903. B.A. from St. Johns College in 1924. Commissioned in the infantry in 1924. With 7th Infantry in Alaska 1926-1929. Duty with 15th Infantry in China 1935-1937. Graduated from the Command and General Staff School in 1939. In the training section, office of the chief of infantry 1939-1942 then the operations section, Army Ground Forces March 1942-July 1943. Commandant of the Parachute School 1943-1944. Brigadier general in November 1943. Assistant division commander of 86th and 88th Infantry Divisions 1945-1947. Assignments after the war included commanding general of 11th Airborne Division, then 40th Infantry Division 1952-1954, commanding general of XVIII Airborne Corps July-August 1955, deputy commanding general of Continental Army Command August 1956-April 1958, Commander in Chief U.S. Caribbean Command 1958-1960 and commanding general of Second Army August 1960 until retirement in April 1962. Decorations included two Distinguished Service Medals, the Legion of Merit and Bronze Star. Died on October 26, 1992.

Gallagher, Philip Edward (1897-1976) Born on March 13, 1897, in Fort Myer, Virginia. Commissioned in the infantry from West Point in 1918. Instructor at the Infantry School 1918-1923. Stationed with the 15th Infantry in Tientsin 1923-1926. Assistant Professor of military science and tactics at Lafayette College 1926-1928. Instructor at West Point 1928-1933. Graduated from Command and General Staff School in 1935, then instructor there until 1938. Graduated from the Army War College in 1939. At the Infantry School 1939-1940. Member of the Infantry Board 1940-1942. Commandant of cadets at West Point 1942-1943. Brigadier general in February 1943. Assistant division commander of 89th Division 1943-1944. Commanding general of Panama Mobile Force and Section Command 1944-1945. Commanding general of Southern Command in the 1st Chinese Combat Command June-December 1945. Assignments after the war in cluded commanding general of 14th Division in 1946 and commanding general of Fort Gordon 1956-1957. Retired in February 1957. Decorations included the Distinguished Service Medal and Legion of Merit. Died on July 18, 1976.

Gard, Robert Gibbins (1899-1983) Born on November 17, 1899, in Frankfurt, Indiana. Commissioned in the field artillery from West Point in 1919. Duty in

Hawaii 1924-1926. Instructor at West Point 1926-1930 then assistant professor 1932-1937. Graduated from the Command and General Staff School in 1939. Instructor at the Field Artillery School 1939-1943. Commanding general of 96th Division Artillery 1944-1945. Brigadier general in August 1944. Member of the commission prosecuting Japanese war criminals 1945-1946. Assignments after the war included deputy commander of Third Army October 1954-April 1956, member of the United Nations Armistice Commission in Korea in 1956 and commanding general of VII Corps 1957-1959. Retired in December 1959. Decorations included the Distinguished Service Medal, Silver Star and Legion of Merit. Died on May 19, 1983.

Gardner, Fulton Quintus Cincinnatus (1882-1963) Born in Layefette Springs, Mississippi, on November 8, 1882. Commissioned in the artillery from West Point in 1904. Attended Massachusetts Institute of Technology 1910-1911. Assistant to the chief of Coast Artillery Corps 1911-1912. Officer in charge of installing submarine nets in U.S. harbors during World War I. Graduated from the Army War College in 1922 and Command and General Staff School in 1928. Assistant commandant of the Coast Artillery School 1937-1938. Brigadier general in May 1938. Commander of the Provisional Coast Artillery Brigade in 1938 and the Hawaii Separate Coast Artillery Brigade 1938-1941. Major general in October 1940. Commanding general of 4th Antiaircraft Command January 1942- April 1944. Commanding general of Northeastern Sector, Eastern Defense Command 1944-1945. Retired in November 1946. Decorations included the Distinguished Service Medal. Died on August 30, 1963.

Gardner, John Henry (1893-1944) Born in Meadowdale, New York, on October 10, 1893. B.S. from Union College in 1913, M.S. in 1915. Commissioned in the field artillery in 1917. Served with the 18th Field Artillery in the AEF 1918-1921 at Champagne-Marne, Aisne-Marne, St. Mihiel and Meuse-Argonne offensives. Transferred to the Signal Corps in 1923. M.S. from Yale in 1924. Graduated from the Command and General Staff School in 1939. Executive officer, then director of the Aircraft Radio Laboratory 1939-1942. Director of the Aircraft Signal Service July 1942-August 1943. Brigadier general in April 1943. Commanding general of Signal Corps Aircraft Signal Service in 1943. Assistant chief of procurement and distribution in the office of the chief signal officer August 1943 until his death on October 11, 1944. Decorations included the Legion of Merit.

Garlington, Creswell (1887-1945) Born in Rock Island, Illinois, on June 23, 1887. Commissioned in the Corps of Engineers from West Point in 1910. Duty at the Panama Canal 1913-1916. Instructor at West Point 1916-1917. Assistant chief of staff of 77th Division, AEF in the Vesle Sector and Oise-Aisne offensive in 1918. Instructor at Army General Staff College, AEF 1918-1919. Graduated from Ecole Superieure de Guerre in 1923, the Command and General Staff School in 1925 and the Army War College in 1928. Assistant commandant of the Engineer School 1936-1940. Duty in the office of the chief of engineers in 1941. War Department liaison with the U.S. Navy 1942-1943. Brigadier general in July

1942. Commanding general of Engineer Replacement Training Center, Fort Leonard Wood January January 1943-November 1944. At headquarters 7th Service Command 15-30 November 1944 then on sick leave until his death on March 11, 1945. Decorations included the Distinguished Service Cross and Purple Heart.

Garrett, Robert C. (1886-1981) Born in Logan, Ohio, on March 9, 1886. Graduated from New Mexico Military Institute in 1907. Service as lieutenant in New Mexico Territorial National Guard 1907-1909. Commissioned in the Coast Artillery Corps in 1909. With 44th Coast Artillery, AEF at St. Mihiel in 1918. Senior instructor with New York National Guard 1921-1925. Graduated from the Command and General Staff School in 1927. Harbor defense artillery engineer at Panama Canal 1927-1930. Graduated from the Army War College in 1935. Commanding officer of harbor defenses at Portland, Maine 1939-1941. Brigadier general in October 1940. Commander of Hawaiian Seacoast Artillery Command November 1941-May 1945. Retired in June 1946. Decorations included the Legion of Merit and Commendation Ribbon. Died on November 29, 1981.

Garvin, Crump (1898-1980) Born on December 1, 1898, in Harrison, Arkansas. Commissioned in the infantry from West Point in 1920. Duty in Hawaii with the 45th Infantry 1924-1926 and again with 22nd Infantry 1931-1933. In the personnel and miscellaneous sections, office of the chief of infantry August 1941-July 1942. Chief of the news division at Army Ground Forces in 1942. Assistant chief of staff for personnel at VII and XIV Corps in 1942. Chief of staff of the Americal Division on Guadalcanal December 1942-April 1943. Commanding officer of 164th Infantry June 1943-April 1944. Chief of staff of XXIV Corps April 1944-August 1946. Brigadier general in November 1944. Assignments after the war included chief of the logistics division at SHAPE February 1953-December 1954 and deputy commandant of Armed Forces Staff College 1955-1956. Retired in January 1959 as major general. Decorations included two Distinguished Service Medals, two Legions of Merit and two Bronze Stars. Died on September 5, 1980.

Gasser, Lorenzo Dow (1876-1955) Born in Lykins, Ohio, on May 3, 1876. Served as captain in the 2nd Ohio Infantry 1898-1899. Officer in volunteer service in Spanish-American War and 43rd Infantry, Philippine Islands during the insurrection November 1899-June 1901. Commissioned in the infantry, Regular Army in 1901. Duty in the Philippines with 21st Infantry 1902-1904 and in Cuba 1906-1909. Served with the Punitive Expedition into Mexico in 1916. Assistant chief of staff for personnel at III Corps, First Army and GHQ AEF 1918-1919, including the Chateau-Thierry, St. Mihiel and Meuse-Argonne campaigns. Graduated from the Army War College in 1921. Brigadier general in June 1936. Deputy chief of staff, U.S. Army August 1939 until retirement in May 1940. Recalled to active duty in May 1941. Served with the War Department Manpower Board May 1941-December 1945. Major general in January 1942. Decorations included three Distinguished Service Medals and the Legion of Merit. Died on October 30, 1955.

Gavin, James Maurice (1907-1990) Born in Brooklyn, New York, on March 22, 1907. Dropped out of school in 1922 and worked at various jobs. Enlisted service 1924-1925. Commissioned in the infantry from West Point in 1929. Instructor at West Point 1940-1941. Graduated from the Command and General Staff School in 1942. Commanding officer of 505th Parachute Infantry Regiment 1942-1944. Brigadier general in September 1943. Assistant division commander of 82nd Airborne Division. Parachuted with the division commander, General Ridgway, into Normandy on June 6, 1944. Commanding general of 82nd Airborne Division August 1944-March 1948; Gavin was the youngest division commander in World War II. Major general in October 1944. Assignments after the war included commander of VI Corps 1952-1954 and deputy chief of staff, U.S. Army 1954-1958. Retired as lieutenant general in January 1958. Decorations included two Distinguished Service Crosses, the Distinguished Service Medal, two Silver Stars, the Bronze Star and Purple Heart. Died on February 23, 1990.

Gay, Hobart R. (1894-n/a) Born in Rockport, Illinois, on May 16, 1894. B.A. from Knox College in 1917. Commissioned in the cavalry in 1917. Instructor at the Cavalry School 1925-1929. Duty at Fort Clayton, Canal Zone 1936-1938. Graduated from Army Industrial College in 1940. Quartermaster officer, the chief of staff of I Armored Corps 1941-1943. Chief of staff of Seventh, Third and Fifteenth Armies July 1943-December 1945. While serving as chief of staff to General George S. Patton's Third Army he accompanied Patton on a hunting trip just before the controversial general was to return to the United States. A freak accident in his staff car left Patton paralyzed and he died four days before Christmas. Brigadier general in June 1943, major general in March 1945. Assignments after the war included commanding general of Fifteenth Army January-February 1946, 1st Armored Division February-April 1946, 1st Cavalry Division in the Korean War 1949-1951, deputy commanding general of Fourth Army February 1951-July 1952, commanding general of VI Corps and III Corps 1952-1954 and commanding general of Fifth Army September 1954 until retirement in August 1955. Decorations included two Distinguished Service Crosses, two Distinguished Service Medals, two Silver Stars, two Legions of Merit, the Distinguished Flying Cross, two Bronze Stars, two Air Medals and two Purple Hearts.

George, Charles Peaslee (1886-1946) Born on August 10, 1886, in Fort Concho, Texas. Enlisted service in the Regular Army 1905-1908. Commissioned in the field artillery in 1908. Duty with 5th Field Artillery in the Philippines 1908-1911. With the Punitive Expedition into Mexico in 1916 and the 6th Field Artillery, then the 61st Field Artillery Brigade, AEF 1917-1918. At the War Department General Staff 1918-1921. Graduated from the Command and General Staff School in 1925 and the Army War College in 1927. Member of the U.S. Olympic Equestrian Team at the Olympic Games in Holland in 1928. Commanding officer of 18th Field Artillery 1939-1941. Brigadier general in April 1941.Commanding general of Field Artillery Training Center April-October 1941 then 73rd and 76th Field Artillery Brigades 1942-1943. At Brooke General Hospital July 1943-January 1944. Commanding general of XXII Corps Artillery January-November

1944. Served with Fourth Army 1944-1946. Retired in October 1946. Died on December 30, 1946.

Gerhardt, Charles Hunter (1895-1976) Born on June 6, 1895, in Lebanon, Tennessee, son of Brigadier General Charles Gerhardt. Commissioned in the cavalry from West Point in 1917. Saw action with the AEF at St. Mihiel and Meuse-Argonne in World War I. Aide-de-camp to Brigadier General William M. Wright 1918-1919. Instructor at the Cavalry School 1923-1924 then West Point 1926-1931. Graduated from the Command and General Staff School in 1933. Duty in the Philippines 1934-1936. Brigadier general in July 1941, major general in June 1942. Commanding general of 91st Infantry Division 1942-1943. Commanding general of 29th Division 1943-1946. Retired in September 1952. Decorations included the Distinguished Service Medal, Silver Star, Legion of Merit and Bronze Star. Died on October 9, 1976.

Gerow, Lee Saunders (1891-1982) Born in Petersburg, Virginia, on March 29, 1891. B.S. from Virginia Military Institute in 1913. Commissioned in the infantry in 1913. Professor of military science and tactics at the University of Wisconsin 1924-1925, then Western Military Academy 1925-1928. Graduated from the Command and General Staff School in 1931. Professor of military science and tactics at the University of Washington 1937-1938. Graduated from the Army War College in 1939 and Army Industrial College in 1940. With the war plans division at the War Department General Staff July 1940-April 1942. Commanding officer of 338th Infantry, 86th Infantry Division 1942-1943. Brigadier general in March 1943. Assistant division commander of 85th Infantry Division 1943-1945. Reverted to colonel in February 1946. Retired in July 1949. Decorations included the Silver Star, Legion of Merit, two Bronze Stars and two Commendation Ribbons. Died on May 19, 1982.

Gerow, Leonard Townsend (1888-1972) Born in Petersburg, Virginia, on July 13, 1888. Commissioned in the infantry following graduation from Virginia Military Institute in 1911. Served during the occupation of Vera Cruz, Mexico 1914. Graduated from the Command and General Staff School in 1926 and the Army War College in 1931. With war plans division of the War Department General Staff 1935-1942. Brigadier general in October 1940. Major general in February 1942. Commanding general of 29th Infantry Division 1942-1943 then V Corps 1943-1945. Elements of V Corps liberated Paris and Gerow was the first American general to reenter that city. Lieutenant general in January 1945. Commander of Fifteenth Army January-July 1945. President of the Theater of Operations General Board July-October 1945. Assignments after the war included commandant of the Command and General Staff School October 1945-January 1948 and commanding general of Second Army 1948-1950. Retired in July 1950. General on the retired list in July 1954. Decorations included three Distinguished Service Medals, the Silver Star, two Legions of Merit and the Bronze Star. Died on October 12, 1972.

Gibbons, Lloyd H. (1895-1945) It is a matter of record that Gibbons was born in 1895, but very little information is available on his early life. It is known that he had enlisted service in World War I and rose from private to sergeant major. Commissioned in the infantry in 1918, he served during the rest of World War I and was released from active duty in 1920. It is unclear what relationship he maintained with the Army between the world wars but he was called to active service as lieutenant colonel in June 1941. After holding a number of commands Gibbons was promoted to brigadier general. He died on April 7, 1945, the circumstances of his death unknown.

Gibson, Herbert Daskum (1891-1980) Born in Schenectady, New York, on October 27, 1891. Commissioned in the infantry in 1917. Served with the 23rd Infantry, AEF at Verdun, Aisne, Chateau-Thierry, Aisne-Marne, St. Mihiel and Meuse-Argonne 1917-1919. Wounded in April 1918, gassed in June 1918 and wounded again in October 1918. Assistant professor at Georgia Institute of Technology ROTC 1921-1922, University of Pennsylvania 1922-1923, Western Maryland College 1923-1925 and Cornell University 1937-1940. Commander of a U.S. Army task force on Canton Island in Febraury 1942. Brigadier general in August 1942. Representative of the military governor of Hawaii 1942-1944. Commanding general of the Replacement Training Command at U.S. Army Forces Pacific Ocean Areas 1944-1946. Retired in September 1946. Decorations included the Distinguished Service Cross, Silver Star, two Legions of Merit, the Bronze Star and three Purple Hearts. Died on March 17, 1980.

Gilbert, Harold Napoleon (1896-1966) Born in Halifax, Pennsylvania, on March 10, 1896. Attended Pennsylvania State College 1915-1916 and Bucknell College 1916-1917. Commissioned in the infantry in 1917, Gilbert served with the AEF in 1918. He saw duty with the 45th Infantry in the Philippines 1929-1930 and again 1934-1936. He served in the office of the adjutant general, U.S. Army 1936-1942 as chief of the enlistment division and officer in charge of the U.S. Army Recruiting and Induction Service 1938-1941. He coined the phrase "Keep 'Em Flying," which was widely used during the early months of World War II. Member of War Department Dependency Board 1942-1945. Brigadier general in April 1943, major general in October 1945. Served in the office of the adjutant general as director of the Military Personnel Procurement Service September 1945 until retirement in December 1946. Decorations included the Distinguished Service Cross, two Distinguished Service Medals, the Commendation Ribbon and Purple Heart. Died on November 16, 1966.

Gilbreath, Frederick (1888-1969) Born in Dayton, Washington, on February 21, 1888. Commissioned in the cavalry from West Point in 1911. Duty in the Philippines with 14th Cavalry 1911-1914. Served on the Mexican border 1916-1917 and in World War I. Graduated from the Staff School in 1923 and the Army War College in 1927. Staff officer with the War Department General Staff 1928-1932. Assistant commandant of the Cavalry School 1939-1940. Served with the 7th Cavalry 1940-1941. Commander of the San Francisco Port of Embarkation November 1941-June 1944. Brigadier general in December 1941, major general in September 1942. Commanding general of Army Service Forces Training Center at Fort Lewis June-August 1944. Commanding general of South Pacific Base Command 1944-1945. Retired in August 1946. Decorations included the Distinguished Service Medal and Purple Heart. Died on February 28, 1969.

Gill, William Hanson (1886-1976) Born in Unison, Virginia, on August 7, 1886. B.S. from VMI in 1907. Commissioned in the infantry in 1907. Saw action with the 5th Division, AEF at St. Mihiel and Meuse-Argonne 1918-1919. Instructor at Command and General Staff School 1925-1929. Graduated from the Army War College in 1930. Executive officer of 27th Infantry 1936-1938. Instructor at the Army War College in 1940. Chief of staff of 8th Division 1940-1941. Brigadier general in October 1941. Commanding general of 55th Brigade, 28th Infantry October 1941-April 1942. Major general in May 1942. Commanding general of 89th Division 1942-1943 and 32nd Infantry Division February 1943 until retirement in May 1946. Decorations included the Distinguished Service Cross, Distinguished Service Medal, two Silver Stars, the Legion of Merit and Bronze Star. Died on January 17, 1976.

Gilland, Morris Williams (1898-1985) Born on September 8, 1898, in Brooklyn, New York. Commissioned in the Corps of Engineers from West Point in 1918. Assistant to the engineer at the Panama Canal 1933-1935. Served with Services of Supply in the European Theater of Operations in 1942. Chief of staff of Services of Supply, North African Theater of Operations 1943-1944. Brigadier general in February 1944. Signal officer in the communications zone of the European Theater of Operations 1944-1945. Reverted to colonel in April 1946. Retired in September 1948. Decorations included two Distinguished Service Medals, the Legion of Merit and Bronze Star. Died on August 19, 1985.

Gillem, Alvan Cullon Jr. (1888-1973) Born in Nashville, Tennessee, on August 8, 1888. Attended the University of Arizona in 1908 and the University of the South 1908-1909. Enlisted service 1910-1911. Commissioned in the infantry in 1911. Duty in the Philippines 1911-1912. Professor of military science and tactics at the University of Montana in 1919. Duty with the 27th Infantry in Siberia 1919-1920. Again in the Philippines 1920-1921, then Hawaii 1921-1922. Graduated from the Army War College in 1926. Professor of military science and tactics at the University of Maryland August 1930-June 1935. Instructor at the Infantry School 1935-1940. Brigadier general in January 1941, major general in July 1941. Commanding general of II Armored Corps, then commander of the Desert Training Center in 1942. Commanding general of the Armored Force May 1943-November 1943. Commanding general of XIII Corps November 1943-August 1945. Lieutenant general in June 1945. Assignments after the war included commander of VII Corps August 1945-April 1946 and commanding general of Third Army June 1947 until retirement in August 1950. Decorations included two Distinguished Service Medals, the Legion of Merit and Bronze Star. Died on February 13, 1973.

Gillespie, Alexander Garfield (1881-1956) Born in Gaines, Michigan, on August 19, 1881. Commissioned in the artillery from West Point in 1906. Instructor at the Coast Artillery School 1914-1915. Duty in the Philippine Islands 1915-1917. Wounded in action with the AEF in World War I. Assistant military attache in Tokyo 1920-1922. Graduated from the Command and General Staff School in 1924 and the Army War College in 1929. Professor at West Point 1929-1933. Commanding officer of Rock Island Arsenal 1934-1937. Duty in the office of the chief of ordnance 1937-1940. Brigadier general in October 1940. Commander of Watervliet Arsenal (New York) 1940-1945. Chairman of the Industrial Service Ordnance Department 1945-1946. Retired in 1947. Decorations included the Distinguished Service Medal, Legion of Merit, Commendation Ribbon and Purple Heart. Died on January 17, 1956.

Gillmore, William Nelson (1903-1990) Born in Monterey, California, on March 25, 1903. Commissioned in the field artillery from West Point in 1925. Instructor at the Field Artillery School 1934-1938. Graduated from the Command and General Staff School in 1939. Assistant artillery officer at the Armored Force in 1942. Commanding officer of 11th Airborne Division Artillery, then 101st Airborne Division Artillery 1943-1945. Brigadier general in May 1945. Assignments after the war included commanding general of 82nd Airborne Division Artillery 1945-1948, 11th Airborne Division Artillery 1948-1949 and 7th Infantry Division Artillery 1949-1950. Chief of the Army Security Agency 1950-1951. Commanding general of IX Corps Artillery in the Korean War in 1951, commanding general of 4th Armored Division, then II Corps 1955-1957 and XV Corps 1959-1961. Retired in May 1962. Decorations included two Distinguished Service Medals, the Legion of Merit and Bronze Star. Died on September 19, 1990.

Gjelsteen, Einar Bernard (1900-1985) Born on October 18, 1900, in Menominee, Michigan. Commissioned in the field artillery from West Point in 1923. Duty in Hawaii 1928-1930. Instructor at West Point 1936-1939. Graduated from the Command and General Staff School in 1940. Instructor, then assistant commandant of the Field Artillery School 1940-1944. Commanding general of 86th Division Artillery 1944-1945. Brigadier general in January 1945. Reverted to colonel in March 1946. Retired as major general in September 1957. Decorations included two Legions of Merit and the Bronze Star. Died on February 10, 1985.

Glancy, Alfred Robinson (1881-1959) Born in Miamiville, Ohio, on July 17, 1881. M.E. from Lehigh University in 1903. In the mining industry 1903-1926. Vice president of General Motors 1926-1930. Commissioned colonel in the Officers Reserve Corps in July 1942 and called to active duty in August 1942 in the office of product management, chief of ordnance. Brigadier general in September 1942. Chief of the Tank-Automobile Center 1942-1943. Reverted to civilian status in July 1943. Decorations included the Legion of Merit. Died on August 4, 1959.

Godfrey, Stuart Chapin (1886-1945) Born in Milford, Massachusetts, on January 1, 1886. Attended Massachusetts Institute of Technology 1904-1905. Commissioned in the Corps of Engineers from West Point in 1909. Instructor, then associate professor at West Point 1912-1917. Commanding officer of 318th Engineers, AEF in 1918. Assistant to the chief of engineers 1921-1923. Graduated from the Command and General Staff School in 1926 then instructor there 1928-1932. Graduated from the Army War College in 1933. Duty as department engineer in the Canal Zone August 1935-July 1937. Chief of the operations and training section, office of the chief of engineers 1937-1941. At headquarters of Air Force Combat Command in 1942. Brigadier general in March 1942. Air engineer with Air Service Command, China-Burma-India Theater of Operations then India-Burma Theater of Operations 1943-1944. Commanding general of Aviation Engineering Training Center July 1945 until his death on October 19, 1945, in a plane crash north of Geiger Field.

Goldthwaite, Ralph Harvard (1882-1969) Born in Holbrook, Massachusetts, on September 17, 1882. B.A. from Harvard in 1903, M.D. in 1906. Commissioned in the Army Medical Corps. Graduated from the Army Medical School in 1909. Duty in the Philippines 1912-1913. Served as colonel, Medical Corps, AEF in World War I. Graduated from Medical Field Service School in 1934. At Gorgas Hospital in the Canal Zone 1935-1938. Surgeon at the Field Artillery School 1938-1940. Commanding officer of Army-Navy General Hospital at Hot Springs National Park 1941-1945. Brigadier general in April 1943. Retired in May 1946. Decorations included the Legion of Merit. Died on February 2, 1969.

Goodman, John Forest (1891-1947) Born on August 22, 1891, in Waco, Texas. Commissioned in the infantry from West Point in 1916. Served with the 26th Infantry Division, AEF in World War I. Prisoner of war July 22 to December 18, 1918. Instructor with the Massachusetts National Guard 1922-1927. Graduated from the Command and General Staff School in June 1931. Instructor at the Command and General Staff School 1933-1935 and with the national guard December 1937-September 1939. Graduated from the Army War College in June 1940. Again instructor with the national guard 1940-1941. Executive officer of 52nd Infantry Brigade 1941-1942. Commanding officer of 364th Infantry 1944-1945. Brigadier general in June 1945. Retired as colonel in September 1946. Decorations included the Silver Star, Legion of Merit and Purple Heart. Died on March 6, 1947.

Goodman, William Moses (1892-1958) Born in Norfolk, Virginia, on September 8, 1892. B.S. from VMI in 1912. Commissioned in the infantry in 1916. Served with the 40th Artillery Brigade, AEF 1918-1919. Graduated from the Command and General Staff School in 1931, the Army War College in 1936 and the Naval War College in 1937. With the supply division of the War Department General Staff July 1937-February 1942. Brigadier general in February 1942. Commander of antiaircraft defenses in Los Angeles in 1942. Head of the overseas supply division, then deputy commanding general at Army Base, Brooklyn July

1942 until retirement in September 1946. Major general in February 1944. Decorations included the Distinguished Service Medal and Bronze Star. Died on December 13, 1958.

Gorder, Alexander Oscar (1893-1973) Born in Bottineau, North Dakota, on December 15, 1893. Attended North Dakota State School of Forrestry 1914-1915 and North Dakota University 1915-1916. Enlisted service with 1st North Dakota Infantry on the Mexican border 1916-1917. Commissioned in the infantry, North Dakota National Guard in 1917. Transferred to the Regular Army. Served in Panama Canal Zone 1932-1935. Graduated from the Command and General Staff School in 1937. Assistant chief of staff for supply at the Tank Destroyer Center, Camp Hood 1941-1942. Commanding general of the 2nd Tank Destroyer Brigade January 1943-February 1944 then the Tank Destroyer Replacement Training Center at Camp Hood February 1944-January 1946. Brigadier general in February 1943. Retired in May 1948. Decorations included the Legion of Merit and Commendation Ribbon. Died on October 5, 1973.

Graham, Roy Charles Lemach (1892-1980) Born in Minneapolis, Minnesota, on September 1, 1892. B.S. from New Hampshire College in 1917. Commissioned in the infantry in 1917. Instructor at the Quartermaster School 1928-1930. Graduated from the Command and General Staff School in 1932 and the Army War College in 1933. Instructor at the Command and General Staff School 1933-1937. Chief quartermaster at the Army War College 1941-1942. Director of the plans divisiion at Army Service Forces in 1942. Assistant chief of staff for supply at the Persian Gulf Command 1942-1945. Brigadier general in August 1944. Deputy assistant chief of staff, then assistant chief of staff for supply at U.S. Army Forces Pacific May 1945-June 1946. Retired in September 1952. Decorations included two Distinguished Service Medals. Died on January 1, 1980.

Grant, Ulysses Simpson II (1881-1968) Born on July 4, 1881, in Chicago, Illinois, the son of Major General Frederick D. Grant and grandson of President U.S. Grant. Attended Columbia University in 1898. Commissioned in the Corps of Engineers from West Point in 1903. Duty in the Philippines 1903-1904. Served in Vera Cruz, Mexico in 1914 and on the Mexican border 1916-1917. Member of the General Staff Corps 1917-1920 with duty on the Supreme War Council at Versailles 1918-1919. Graduated from the Command and General Staff School in 1934. Chief of staff of 2nd Coast Artillery at Governor's Island 1936-1940. Brigadier general in October 1940. Division engineer at Great Lakes 1940-1941. Commander of Engineer Replacement Training Center, Fort Leonard Wood April 1941-June 1942. Chief of the production branch in the office of civilian defense, War Department July 1942-April 1946. Major general in February 1943. Retired in July 1945. Decorations included the Distinguished Service Medal and Legion of Merit. Died on August 29, 1968.

Grant, Walter Schuyler (1878-1956) Born in Ithaca, New York, on January 24, 1878. Commissioned in the cavalry from West Point in 1900. Served in the Boxer

Rebellion in 1900, the Philippine Insurrection 1900-1902, and at various times on the Mexican border 1912-1917. Graduated from the School of the Line in 1914 and the General Staff School in 1915. Deputy chief of staff of First Army and chief of staff of I Corps, AEF 1918-1919. Instructor at General Service Schools 1921-1923 then the Army War College 1923-1927. Chief of staff of 1st Corps Area 1931-1933. Assistant commandant, then commandant of the Army War College 1935-1937. Brigadier general in March 1936. Commander of New York Port of Embarkation 1937-1938. Major general in October 1938. Commander of the Philippine Department July 1939-May 1940. Commanding general of III Corps Area October 1940-August 1941. Retired in January 1942. Recalled to active duty in February 1942 to sit on various boards of general officers in the War Department through the end of the war. Decorations included the Distinguished Service Medal and Legion of Merit. Died on March 4, 1956.

Gray, Carl Raymond Jr. (1889-1955) Born in Wichita, Kansas, on April 14, 1889. B.A. from the University of Illinois in 1911. In the railroad industry 1911-1916. Active duty in the Corps of Engineers as zone supply officer, Atlanta 1917-1919. Member of the Corps of Engineers, Officers Reserve Corps 1921-1942. Called to active duty in command of railway transportation in the European Theater of Operations in 1942. Brigadier general in June 1942, major general in September 1945. Returned to inactive status in February 1946. Appointed by President Truman to relieve General Omar Bradley as Administrator of Veterans Affairs in December 1947, serving until 1953. Decorations included the Distinguished Service Medal, two Legions of Merit, the Bronze Star and Commendation Ribbon. Died on December 3, 1955.

Greely, John Nesmith (1885-1965) Born in Washington, DC, on June 6, 1885. B.A. from Yale in 1906. Commissioned in the field artillery in 1906. Graduated from the Command and General Staff School in 1932 and the Army War College in 1936. Military attache in Madrid 1939-1940. Brigadier general in June 1940. Commanding general of the Provisional Brigade 1940-1941. Major general in July 1941. Commanding general of 2nd Division 1941-1942. Chief of the military mission to Iran 1941-1942. Analyst in the office of the coordinator of Inter-American affairs in 1943. Retired in February 1943. Decorations included the Distinguished Service Medal. Author of *War Breaks Down Doors* (1929). Died on June 13, 1965.

Green, Joseph Andrew (1881-1963) Born in Cherokee, Iowa, on January 14, 1881. Attended the University of Wisconsin 1901-1902. Commissioned in the Coast Artillery Corps from West Point in 1906. Commanding officer of 1st Battalion, 57th Coast Artillery, AEF at Chalons, Verdun, St. Mihiel and Racicourt 1917-1919. Graduated from the Command and General Staff School in 1923 and the Army War College in 1926. Major general in April 1940 as chief of the Coast Artillery Corps. Commanding general of Antiaircraft Command in Army Ground Forces March 1942 until retirement in March 1944. Decorations included the Distinguished Service Medal and Legion of Merit. Died on October 27, 1963.

Green, Thomas Henry (1889-1971) Born in Cambridge, Massachusetts, on April 22, 1889. LL.B. from Boston University in 1915. Commissioned in the cavalry in 1917. LL.M. from George Washington University in 1923. Brigadier general in May 1942. Assistant judge advocate general, U.S. Army April 1943-December 1945. Assignments after the war included the judge advocate general as major general December 1945 until retirement in November 1949. Decorations included two Distinguished Service Medals. Died on March 27, 1971.

Greenbaum, Edward S. (1890-1970) Born in New York City on April 13, 1890. B.A. from Williams College in 1910. LL.B. from Columbia Law School in 1913. Practiced law in New York City 1913-1940 with the exception of World War I service 1917-1919. Called to active duty as colonel in 1941. Executive officer to the under secretary of war 1941-1946. Brigadier general in March 1943. Returned to civilian status in 1946. Decorations included the Distinguished Service Medal. Died on June 12, 1970.

Greene, Douglass Taft (1891-1964) Born on April 24, 1891, in Fort Logan, Colorado. Commissioned in the infantry from West Point in 1913. Duty in Hawaii with the 2nd Infantry 1913-1916. Graduated from the Command and General Staff School in 1929 and the Army War College in 1934. Professor of military science and tactics at Drexel Institute of Technology 1934-1940. Commanding officer of 67th Armored Regiment August 1940-March 1942. Brigadier general in March 1942. With 7th Armored Division 1942-1943. Commanding general of 16th, then 12th Armored Division March 1943-September 1944. Major general in September 1943. Deputy commanding general of Second Army September-October 1944. With Replacement and School Command October 1944-February 1945. Commander of the Infantry Replacement Training Center at Camp Gordon February 1945 until retirement in February 1946. Died on June 13, 1964.

Greer, Frank Upton (1895-1949) Born on September 24, 1895, in Washington, DC. Attended Catholic University 1915-1918. Commissioned in the infantry in 1917. With 318th Infantry, AEF in 1918. LL.B. from George Washington University in 1925. Duty in the Canal Zone 1926-1929. Instructor with the organized reserves in Pennsylvania 1929-1932. Graduated from the Command and General Staff School in 1934 and the Army War College in 1936. Professor of military science and tactics at Rhode Island State College 1938-1941. With the 18th Infantry 1941-1943. Brigadier general in June 1943. Assistant division commander of 79th Infantry Division 1943-1945. Duty in the War Department bureau of public relations in 1945. Retired in August 1946. Decorations included the Silver Star, Bronze Star and two Purple Hearts. Died on May 17, 1949.

Gregory, Edmund Bristol (1882-1961) Born in Storm Lake, Iowa, on July 4, 1882. Commissioned in the infantry from West Point in 1904. Served with the 14th Infantry in the Philippines 1904-1905 and again 1908-1910. Instructor at West Point 1911-1912. Served in Shanghai, China 1922-1924. Instructor with the

New York National Guard 1924-1927. M.B.A. from Harvard in 1929. Graduated from the Army War College in 1937. Duty in the office of the quartermaster general, U.S. Army 1937-1940. Major general in April 1940 as quartermaster general of the Army 1940-1946. Lieutenant general in April 1945. Retired in June 1946. Decorations included two Distinguished Service Medals. Died on January 26, 1961.

Grimes, William Middleton (1889-1951) Born on March 4, 1889, in Fort Barrancas, Florida. Commissioned in the cavalry in 1911. Duty with the 9th Cavalry in the Philippine Islands 1916-1917. Served with the 14th Machine Gun Battalion, AEF in 1918. Instructor at the Infantry School 1919-1920. Instructor at the Cavalry School 1920-1924. Graduated from the Command and General Staff School in 1925. Secretary of the Cavalry School 1925-1929. Graduated from the Army War College in 1933, then instructor there 1933-1936. Served in the operations and training division at the War Department General Staff 1938-1940. Duty with 1st Armored Regiment, then 4th Armored Division 1940-1942. Brigadier general in September 1941, major general in May 1942. Commanding general of 8th Armored Division May 1942-October 1944, then the Cavalry School 1944-1945. Commanding general of the Antilles Department, Puerto Rico June 1945 until retirement in October 1946. Decorations included the Silver Star, three Legions of Merit and two Commendation Ribbons. Died on April 2, 1951.

Griner, George Wesley Jr. (1895-1975) Born in Carrol County, Georgia, on September 28, 1895. Attended Emory College 1912-1915. B.A. from Southern Methodist University in 1917. Commissioned in the infantry in 1917. Served with 15th Machine Gun Battalion at St. Mihiel and Meuse-Argonne in World War I. Professor of military science and tactics at Allen Academy 1924-1928 and again 1929-1931. With the 57th Infantry in the Philippines 1933-1935. In the supply division, then assistant chief of staff for supply on the War Department General Staff 1939-1942. Assistant chief of staff for supply in the European Theater of Operations January-December 1942. Brigadier general in May 1942. Assistant division commander of 77th Infantry Division January-March 1943. Commanding general of 13th Airborne Division March-November 1943. Major general in September 1943. Commanding general of 98th Infantry Division, then 27th Infantry Division 1943-1944. Retired in August 1946. Decorations included the Distinguished Service Medal, Silver Star and Legion of Merit. Died on October 3, 1975.

Griswold, Oscar Woolverton (1886-1959) Born in Ruby Valley, Nevada, on October 22, 1886. Attended the University of Nevada 1905-1906. Commissioned in the infantry from West Point in 1910. Served in China 1914-1917 and with the AEF 1918-1919. Graduated from the Command and General Staff School in 1925 and the Army War College in 1929. With the War Department General Staff 1929-1931. Member of the Infantry Board July 1932-May 1936. Duty in the office of the chief of infantry 1936-1939. Commanding officer of 29th Infantry September 1939-October 1940. Brigadier general in October 1940. With 4th Infantry Division 1940-1941. Major general in August 1941. Commanding general of Infantry Replacement Training Center at Camp Croft in 1941. Commanding general of 4th Mechanized Division, IV Corps and XIV Corps August 1941-August 1945. Lieutenant general in April 1945. Assignments after the war included commanding general of 4th Infantry Division 1945-1947. Retired in October 1947. Decorations included three Distinguished Service Medals, two Silver Stars, the Legion of Merit, Bronze Star, Air Medal and Purple Heart. Died on September 28, 1959.

Groninger, Homer McLaughlin (1884-1963) Born in Port Royal, Pennsylvania, on July 24, 1884. Commissioned in the cavalry from West Point in 1908. Served with the Punitive Expedition into Mexico in 1916. Staff officer at headquarters of the AEF then machine gun officer in 2nd Division at Meuse-Argonne 1918-1919. Graduated from the Command and General Staff School in 1923. Instructor at the Cavalry School 1923-1925. Graduated from the Army War College in 1926. Instructor at West Point 1926-1930 and the Command and General Staff School 1930-1935. Instructor with Pennsylvania National Guard 1935-1938. Commanding officer of 11th Cavalry June 1938-October 1940. Brigadier general in October 1940. Commanding generalof the Brooklyn Port of Embarkation October 1940-June 1945. Major general in August 1942. Commanding general of the San Francisco Port of Embarkation June 1945 until retirement in December 1946. Decorations included the Distinguished Service Medal, Legion of Merit and Commendation Ribbon. Died on September 26, 1963.

Gross, Charles Philip (1889-1975) Born on March 14, 1889, in Brooklyn, New York. M.E. from Cornell University in 1910. Commissioned in the Corps of Engineers from West Point in 1914. Wounded at Meuse-Argonne while serving as commanding officer of 318th Engineers, AEF in World War I. Instructor at West Point 1922-1926. Graduated from the Command and General Staff School in 1927 and the Army War College in 1932. District engineer at Rock Island, Illinois 1940-1941. Engineer with VI Corps, then chief of transportation for Army Service Forces in 1941. Brigadier general in March 1942, major general in August 1942. Member of the combined staff, Combined Chiefs of Staff 1942-1945. Attended conferences at Washington, Quebec, Malta, Yalta and Potsdam. Retired as colonel in Novemeber 1945. Major general on the retired list in August 1948. Recalled to active duty in the office of the high commissioner to Germany 1948-1952. Decorations included the Distinguished Service Medal, Legion of Merit and Purple Heart. Died on July 18, 1975.

Groves, Leslie Richard (1896-1970) Born on August 17, 1896, in Albany, New York. Commissioned in the Corps of Engineers from West Point in 1918. Graduated from the Command and General Staff School in 1936 and the Army War College in 1939. With the War Department General Staff 1939-1940. In office of the quartermaster general, then chief of engineers 1940-1942. Brigadier general in September 1942. Head of the "Manhattan Engineer District," a code name for America's atomic bomb development project that led to the explosion of the first nuclear device on July 16, 1945, in Alamogordo, New Mexico. Major general in February 1944. Assignments after the war included head of the Army's Special Weapons Project 1947-1948. Retired as lieutenant general in February 1948. Decorations included the Distinguished Service Medal and Legion of Merit. Author of *Now It Can Be Told: The Story of the Manhattan Project* (1962). Died on July 13, 1970.

Grow, Robert Walker (1895-1985) Born in Sibley, Iowa, on February 14, 1895. B.S. from the University of Minnesota in 1916. Commissioned in the infantry, Minnesota National Guard in 1916. Assistant professor of military science and tactics at the University of Illinois 1919-1923. Instructor at the Cavalry School 1925-1926. Graduated from the Command and General Staff School in 1929 and instructor there 1934-1935. Graduated from the Army War College in 1936. Deputy chief of staff for operations at 2nd Armored Division July 1940-September 1941. Commanding officer of 34th Armored Regiment 1941-1942. Commander of Combat Command "B" in 8th Armored Division. Brigadier general in March 1942. Commander of Combat Command "A" in 19th Armored Division April 1942-May 1943. Major general in September 1943. Commanding general of 6th and 3rd Armored Divisions 1943-1945. Assignments after the war included commanding general of 26th Infantry Division 1945-1946. Military attache in Moscow 1950-1951. Sometime in July 1951 Soviet agents stole from his bedroom a diary in which he kept secret notations in violation of Army regulations. He was convicted by court martial in July 1952 and retired in January 1953. An Appeals Court upheld his conviction in July 1953. Decorations included the Distinguished Service Cross, Distinguished Service Medal, two Silver Stars, the Legion of Merit and Bronze Star. Died on March 11, 1985.

Grower, Roy William (1890-1957) Born in Richmond, New York, on January 27, 1890. B.S. from the University of Syracuse in 1913. Commissioned in the Corps of Engineers in 1920. Assistant professor of military science and tactics at the University of Cincinnati 1920-1921 and Alabama Polytechnic Institute 1929-1930. Instructor at Fort Benning 1930-1935. Duty in the Canal Zone 1937-1939. District engineer in the Upper Missouri Valley Division June 1939-August 1942. Commanding officer of 351st Engineer General Service Regiment 1942-1944. Engineer in the east base section, Services of Supply and commander of base section one, communications zone in the European Theater of Operations in 1944. Brigadier general in November 1944. Commander of Brittany Base Section and Burgundy District Continenal Advance Section in the European Theater of Operations in 1945. Retired in March 1946. Decorations included the Legion of Merit. Died on January 31, 1957.

Gruber, William Rudolph (1890-1979) Born in Cincinnati, Ohio, on December 17, 1890. Commissioned in the infantry in 1912. Transfwerred to the field artillery in 1917. Served with 13th and 17th Field Artillery, AEF at Aisne-Marne, St. Mihiel, Champagne and Meuse-Argonne in 1918. Professor of military science and tactics at St. John's School 1919-1920, instructor at the Field Artillery School

1920-1922, then Professor of military science and tactics at the University of Oklahoma 1922-1923. Graduated from the Command and General Staff School in 1925. Graduated from the Army War College in 1929 and the Naval War College in 1936. Supply officer, then acting chief of staff of the Hawaiian Division September 1938-March 1941. With the 85th Field Artillery 1941-1942. Brigadier general in February 1942. Commanding general of 38th Infantry Division Artillery 1942-1944 then 24th Infantry Division Artillery August 1944 until retirement in August 1946. Decorations included three Silver Stars. Died on January 27, 1979.

Gruenther, Alfred Maximillian (1899-1983) Born on March 3, 1899, in Platte Center, Nebraska. Commissioned in the field artillery from West Point in 1919. Graduated from the Command and General Staff School in 1937 and the Army War College in 1939. At the War Department General Staff 1939-1941. Deputy chief of staff, then chief of staff of Third Army 1941-1942. Brigadier general in August 1942. Deputy chief of staff at Allied headquarters in London August 1942-January 1943. Chief of staff of Fifth Army 1943-1944. Major general in February 1943. Chief of staff of Fifteenth Army Group 1944-1945. Assignments after the war included deputy commandant of National War College 1946-1947, first director of the joint staff, Joint Chiefs of Staff 1947-1949, deputy chief of staff for plans, U.S. Army 1949-1950, chief of staff at SHAPE 1950-1953 and Supreme Allied Commander in Europe 1953-1956. Retired in November 1956. Decorations included two Distinguished Service Medals, the Legion of Merit and Bronze Star. Died on May 30, 1983.

Grunert, George (1881-1971) Born in White Haven, Pennsylvania, on July 21, 1880. Enlisted service 1898-1901 including the Spanish-American War. Commissioned in the cavalry in 1901. Served in the Philippines during the early months of the insurrection 1901-1902. Professor of military science and tactics at Shattuck School (Minnesota) 1912-1916. With the Punitive Expedition into Mexico 1916-1917 and the I Corps, AEF in World War I. Graduated from the Army War College in 1921 and the the Command and General Staff School in 1932. Director of military intelligence, then war plans at the Army War College 1935-1936. Commander of the 26th Cavalry, then the 23rd Brigade 1938-1940. Brigadier general in November 1936, major general in December 1939. Commanding general of the Philippine Department 1940-1942 and VI Corps Area in 1942. Deputy chief of staff for service commands, Army Service Forces May-August 1943 then commanding general of First Army August-October 1943. Lieutenant general in October 1943. Commanding general of Eastern Defense Command October 1943 until retirement in July 1945. Decorations included two Distinguished Service Medals, the Legion of Merit and Purple Heart. Died on January 13, 1971.

Gullion, Allen W. (1880-1946) Born in Carrollton, Kentucky, on December 14, 1880. B.A. from Centre College in 1901. Commissioned in the infantry from West Point in 1905. Professor of military science and tactics at the University of Kentucky 1912-1914. LL.B. from the University of Kentucky in 1914. Served as colonel in the 2nd Kentucky Infantry with the Punitive Expedition into Mexico in

1916. Chief of the mobile division at National Selective Service in 1917. Judge advocate with the III Corps, AEF in 1918. Senior War Department representative at the Geneva conference in 1929. Graduated from the Army War College in 1931 and the Naval War College in 1932. Assistant judge advocate general of the U.S. Army in 1936, then judge advocate general as major general December 1937-July 1941. Provost marshal general of the U.S. Army July 1941 until retirement in December 1944. Decorations included the Distinguished Service Medal. Died on June 19, 1946.

Gunner, Matthew John (1886-1985) Born in Dallas, Texas, on March 31, 1886. C.E. from the University of Texas in 1909. Enlisted service in the Texas National Guard 1909-1912. Commissioned in 1912. Served with the 8th Infantry in the Philippine Islands May 1915-February 1916 then the 10th Infantry in the Panama Canal Zone 1916-1917. Headquarters commandant at the port of Antwerp, Belgium, July 1920-January 1921. Graduated from the Command and General Staff School in 1924 and the Army War College in 1930. Assigned to the War Department General Staff June 1930-August 1934. Duty with the 57th Infantry in the Philippines August 1934-October 1936. Professor of military science and tactics at the University of Tennessee October 1936-July 1939. Assistant chief of staff for personnel with IV Corps 1939-1941. Commanding officer of 10th Infantry March 1941-July 1942. Director of the Infantry Board July 1942-March 1943. Secretary of the Joint Strategic Survey Committee March 1943-March 1944. Duty in the office of the deputy chief of staff of U.S. Army Forces Far East March 1944-April 1945. Assistant chief of staff to General MacArthur 1945-1946. Retired in 1949. Decorations included the Distinguished Service Medal and Legion of Merit. Died on September 10, 1985.

Gurney, Augustus Milton (1895-1967) Born on February 18, 1895, in Oneonta, New York. Commissioned in the field artillery from West Point in 1917. Served in AEF with 91st French Balloon Company and 5th Field Artillery at Argonne in 1918. Instructor at West Point 1919-1924. M.S. from Yale in 1927. Instructor at the Field Artillery School 1928-1931. Graduated from the Command and General Staff School in 1933 and the Army War College in 1937. Instructor at the Command and General Staff School 1937-1940. Duty with II Corps 1940-1942. Brigadier general in April 1942. Commanding general of 79th Infantry Division Artillery 1942-1944. Chief of staff of Second Army 1944-1945. Retired in April 1954. Decorations included the Legion of Merit. Died on April 10, 1967.

Guthrie, John Simpson (1908-) Born on June 12, 1908, in Washington, DC. Commissioned in the infantry from West Point in 1930. Deputy chief of staff for operations at Seventh Army 1944-1946. Brigadier general in June 1945. Reverted to colonel in April 1946. Assignments after the war included commanding general of XIV Corps (Reserve) September 1959 until retirement in June 1961. Decorations included two Distinguished Service Medals, two Silver Stars, two Legions of Merit, the Bronze Star, two Commendation Ribbons and the Purple Heart.

Hagins, William Archer (1888-n/a) Born in Halcyondale, Georgia, on August 8, 1888. M.D. from the University of Georgia in 1914. Commissioned in the Medical Corps in 1917. Graduated from Army Medican School in 1917. Served with Field Hospital 13, 1st Division and regimental surgeon in 18th Infantry in 1918. Camp surgeon at Fort Benning, then Camp Wheeler 1940-1942. Surgeon at VII Corps, then assistant surgeon at Third Army 1942-1943. Surgeon at Southwest Pacific Area 1943-1945. Brigadier general in January 1945. Retired in April 1948. Decorations included the Distinguished Service Medal, three Silver Stars, the Legion of Merit and Bronze Star.

Haines, Oliver Lincoln (1891-1982) Born in Chula Vista, California, on September 13, 1891. B.S. from the University of California in 1914. Commissioned in the field artillery in 1914. Served with 6350th and 79th Field Artillery, AEF 1917-1919 Instructor at the Cavalry School 1922-1926. Graduated from Air Corps Tactical School in 1927. White House aide August 1929-June 1931. Graduated from the Command and General Staff School in 1934 then instructor there 1935-1938. Graduated from the Army War College in 1939. Inspector general at 3rd Armored Division, the Armored Force and headquarters of the European Theater of Operations April 1941-December 1945. Brigadier general in November 1943. With VII Corps January-February 1946. Reverted to colonel in February 1946. Retired in September 1951. Decorations included the Legion of Merit and Bronze Star. Died on June 6, 1982.

Haines, Ralph E. (1883-1976) Born on August 4, 1883, in Vinton, Iowa. Attended Pomona College 1902-1904. B.S. from the University of California in 1907. Commissioned in the Coast Artillery Corps in 1910. Duty in the Philippines 1915-1919. Instructor at the Coast Artillery School 1919-1923. Graduated from the Command and General Staff School in 1924 and the Army War College in 1927. Commanding officer of 70th Coast Artillery 1938-1941. Brigadier general in January 1941. Commander of harbor defenses at Narragansett Bay, then San Francisco from September 1942. Retired in August 1945. Died on June 1, 1976.

Haislip, Wade Hampton (1889-1971) Born on July 9, 1889, in Woodstock, Virginia. Commissioned in the infantry from West Point in 1912. Served on the Mexican border with the 19th Infantry 1915-1916 and the V Corps and 3rd Division, AEF in the St. Mihiel and Meuse-Argonne offensives in 1918. Instructor at West Point 1921-1923. Graduated from the Command and General Staff School in 1925. Graduated from the Army War College in 1932. Instructor at the Command and General Staff School 1932-1936. Served with the budget and legislative planning division of the War Department General Staff 1938-1941. Brigadier general in January 1941, major general in March 1942. Commanding general of the 85th Division 1942-1943. Commanding general of IX Corps 1944-1945. Commanding general of Seventh Army in 1945. Lieutenant general in April 1945.

President of the secretary of war's Personnel Board 1945-1946. Assignments after the war included deputy chief of staff and vice chief of staff, U.S. Army 1948-1951. Retired as general in July 1951. Decorations included four Distinguished Service Medals, the Legion of Merit and two Bronze Stars. Died on December 23, 1971.

Hall, Charles Philip (1886-1953) Born in Sardis, Mississippi on December 12, 1886. Attended the University of Mississippi 1905-1907. Commissioned in the infantry from West Point in 1911. Instructor there 1914-1917. Served with the 2nd Division, AEF in World War I. Saw action at Aisne, Chateau-Thierry, Aisne-Marne, St. Mihiel, Champagne and Meuse-Argonne campaigns. Member of the Infantry Board 1922-1923. Graduated from the Command and General Staff School in 1925. Instructor at the Infantry School 1925-1927. Graduated from the Army War College in 1930. Duty in the Philippines 1930-1932. Instructor at the Infantry School 1932-1937. Brigadier general in January 1941. With 3rd Division in 1941-1942. Major general in March 1942. Commanding general of 93rd Infantry Division March-October 1942. Commanding general of XI Corps 1942-1948. Lieutenant general in June 1945. Retired in December 1948. Decorations included the Distinguished Service Cross, three Silver Stars, the Bronze Star and Purple Heart. Died on January 26, 1953.

Hall, Gene William (1898-1951) Born in Brooklyn, New York, on November 25, 1898. Engineer and developer in New York City 1919-1942. Commissioned colonel in the Corps of Engineers in March 1942. Executive officer of the Caribbean Engineer Division in New York City, Miami and San Juan 1942-1944. Brigadier general in January 1945. Died on November 30, 1951.

Halloran, George Matthew (1889-1965). Born in Fort Abe Lincoln, North Dakota, on January 19, 1889. Attended Pennsylvania State College 1908-1910. Commissioned in the infantry in 1911. Served with the 23rd Infantry 1917-1918. Graduated from the Army War College in 1926 and Army Industrial College in 1927. Professor of military science and tactics at the University of Wyoming 1936-1940. Assistant executive at 1st Military Area, Knoxville 1940-1941. Acting chief of staff of 81st Division July-December 1941. Commanding officer of Camp Shelby December 1941-June 1946. Brigadier general in October 1942. Reverted to colonel in March 1946. Retired in July 1948. Decorations included the Legion of Merit. Died on December 5, 1965.

Halsey, Milton Baldridge (1894-1990) Born on March 6, 1894, in Huntsville, Alabama. Attended the University of Alabama 1912-1913. Commissioned in the infantry from West Point in 1917. In the personnel division of the War Department General Staff 1924-1928. Graduated from the Command and General Staff School in 1933. In the Hawaiian Department September 1937-June 1940. Duty with the War Department General Staff in 1940. Chief of staff of 29th Infantry Division 1941-1942. Brigadier general in May 1942. Assistant division commander of 44th Infantry Division 1942-1944. Commanding general of 97th Infantry Division 1944-1945. Assignments after the war included deputy commander of Sixth Army February 1951 until retirement as major general in January 1953. Decorations included the Distinguished Service Medal. Died on October 24, 1990.

Hamblen, Archelaus Lewis (1894-1971) Born in Gorham, Maine, on July 24, 1894. B.S. from the University of Maine in 1916. Commissioned in the infantry in 1916. Saw action with the 15th Machine Gun Battalion, AEF in 1918. Assistant professor of military science and tactics, then professor of military science and tactics at the University of Arkansas 1928-1932. Graduated from the Command and General Staff School in 1934 and the Army War College in 1937. Duty with the War Department General Staff July 1941-July 1942. Brigadier general in December 1942. Assistant chief of staff for supply at Allied Forces Headquarters in England 1942-1943. Assistant chief of staff for supply, then assistant to the plans officer at Allied Forces Headquarters in North Africa 1943-1944. Assistant chief of staff for supply at the U.S. component, Allied Armies in Italy 1944-1945. Assistant chief of staff for plans in the Mediterranean Theater of Operations 1945-1946. Reverted to colonel in June 1946. Retired in July 1954. Decorations included two Distinguished Service Medals, the Legion of Merit, Bronze Star and Commendation Ribbon. Died on October 8, 1971.

Handwerk, Morris Clinton (1891-1967) Born in Pennsylvania on February 17, 1891. Enlisted service in the Coast Artillery Corps 1913-1917. Commissioned in the Coast Artillery Corps in 1917. Graduated from the Command and General Staff School in 1937 and the Army War College in 1940. In the war plans division of WDGS in 1940. At GHQ U.S. Army 1940-1942. Commander of the Antiaircraft Training Center at Camp Edwards from April 1942. Brigadier general in August 1942. Reverted to colonel in April 1946. Retired in February 1951. Decorations included two Legions of Merit and two Bronze Stars. Died on August 28, 1967.

Handy, Thomas Troy (1892-1982). Born on March 11, 1892, in Spring City, Tennessee. B.S. from VMI in 1914. Commissioned in the field artillery in 1916. Served with 5th Field Artillery, 42nd (Rainbow) Division and 151st Field Artillery in France during World War I. Graduated from the Command and General Staff School in 1927 and the Army War College in 1935. Instructor at VMI 1921-1925, Fort Sill 1931-1934, and the Naval War College 1935-1936. Brigadier general in December 1941, major general in June 1942. With the War Department General Staff 1936-1940 and 1942-1945. Lieutenant general in September 1944, general in March 1945. Assignments after the war included commander of Fourth Army 1947-1949, commander of the U.S. European Command 1949-1952 and Deputy Supreme Allied Commander in Europe 1952-1953. Retired in February 1954. Decorations included the Distinguished Service Cross, three Distinguished Service Medals and the Legion of Merit. Died on April 17, 1982.

Haney, Harold (1894-1973) Born in Brazil, Indiana, on January 2, 1894. Enlisted service 1914-1917. Commissioned in the infantry in 1917. Assistant professor of military science and tactics at Ohio State University 1925-1930. Duty with the 15th Infantry in Tientsin, China 1933-1935. Assistant professor of military science and tactics at the University of Alabama 1937-1938. Graduated from the Command and General Staff School in 1939. Section chief at the Infantry School 1939-1942. Commandant of officers candidate school in the Southwest Pacific Area 1943-1945. Brigadier general in January 1945. Retired in July 1953. Decorations included two Silver Stars, two Legions of Merit, the Bronze Star and Air Medal. Died on February 25, 1973.

Hannum, Warren Thomas (1880-1956) Born in Pottsville, Pennsylvania, on March 8, 1880. Commissioned in the Corps of Engineers from West Point in 1902. Served overseas in the Philippine Islands 1902-1904, Cuba 1906-1908 and Hawaii 1912-1915. Graduated from the Command and General Staff School in 1916. In Mexico with the Punitive Expedition 1916-1917. In the civil affairs section of the general staff at headquarters AEF in 1918. Assistant commandant of the Engineer School in 1919. Instructor at the Command and General Staff School 1920-1922. Duty at the War Department General Staff 1922-1925. Graduated from the Army War College in 1926. Division engineer in the South Pacific Division 1938-1942. Brigadier general in May 1942. Division engineer in the Pacific Division in 1942. Retired in June 1942, then recalled in July 1942 in the same position. Division engineer at Salt Lake City 1943-1944. Retired again in January 1944. Decorations included the Distinguished Service Medal and Legion of Merit. Died on August 14, 1956.

Hardaway, Francis Page (1888-1981) Born in St. Louis, Missouri, on April 26, 1888. B.A. from Washington University in 1909. Commissioned in the Coast Artillery Corps in 1909. Professor of military science and tactics at Peacock Military College, San Antonio 1916-1917. Battalion commander in the 53rd Heavy Artillery Regiment, AEF at Champagne-Marne and Meuse-Argonne offensives in 1918. Professor of military science and tactics at Washington University 1919-1923. Graduated from the Command and General Staff School in 1925. Instructor at the Coast Artillery School 1925-1929. Graduated from the Army War College in 1936. Commanding officer of 51st Coast Artillery, then Chesapeake Bay harbor defenses 1938-1940. Commander of Antiaircraft Artillery Replace Training Center at Camp Callan December 1940-April 1943. Brigadier general in April 1941. Commanding general of 37th Antiaircraft Artillery Brigade 1943-1945. Commanding general of Panama Coast Artillery Command 1945-1946. Retired in August 1948. Decorations included the Legion of Merit and Commendation Ribbon. Died on September 18, 1981.

Hardaway, Robert Morris II (1887-1978) Born in Marion, Kentucky, on February 5, 1887. M.D. from Washington University in 1910. Graduated from Army Medical School in 1911. Commissioned in the Medical Corps in 1912. Served at Vera Cruz in 1914. Surgeon in the Philippine Islands 1915-1917. With the AEF in

World War I. Chief medical officer at Fitzsimon General Hospital 1932-1938 and Gorgas Hospital, Panama 1938-1940. Commanding officer of the station hospital at Fort Bliss in 1941 and Bushnell General Hospital in Brigham City, Utah 1942-1948. Retired in August 1948. Brigadier general in September 1945. Decorations included the Legion of Merit and Commendation Ribbon. Died on March 25, 1978.

Hardigg, Carl Adolphus (1890-1967) Born in Uniontown, Kentucky, on June 28, 1890. Commissioned in the infantry in 1913. Graduated from the Command and General Staff School in 1925 and the Army War College in 1929. With the War Department General Staff 1929-1933. In the office of the quartermaster general 1936-1944. Brigadier general in February 1942, major general in Novermber 1944. Chief of the subsistence section at headquarters of the Quartermaster Corps 1944-1946. Retired in October 1946. Decorations included the Distinguished Service Medal. Died on January 30, 1967.

Harding, Edwin Forrest (1886-1970) Born in Franklin, Ohio, on September 18, 1886. Commissioned in the infantry from West Point in 1909. Instructor at West Point 1919-1923. Graduated from the Command and General Staff School in 1929. Instructor at the Infantry School 1929-1933. Graduated from the Army War College in 1934. Secretary of the U.S. Infantry Association 1934-1938. Commanding officer of 27th Infantry 1938-1940. Brigadier general in October 1940. Assistant division commander of 9th Infantry Division in 1941. Major general in February 1942. Commanding general of 32nd Infantry Division 1942-1943 and the Mobile Force, Panama Canal Zone March 1943-August 1944. Commanding general of the Antilles Department 1944-1946. Retired in October 1946. Decorations included the Silver Star and Legion of Merit. Died on June 5, 1970.

Harding, Horace (1896-1991) Born on May 29, 1896, in Washington, DC. Commissioned in the infantry from West Point in 1917. Saw action at St. Mihiel and Meuse-Argonne with the AEF in World War I. Transferred to the field artillery in 1920. Instructor with the Pennsylvania National Guard 1922-1924. Instructor at the Field Artillery School 1930-1934. Artillery officer in I Corps, then commanding officer of I Corps Artillery 1942-1945. Commanding general of Eighth Army Area Command in 1945. Brigadier general in February 1943. Reverted to colonel in March 1946. Assignments after the war included commanding general, as brigadier general, of 40th Division Artillery in the Korean War 1951-1952. Retired in June 1953. Decorations included the Distinguished Service Cross, two Legions of Merit and the Bronze Star. Died on December 29, 1991.

Hardy, Rosswell Eric (1893-1961) Born in Troy, New York, on December 18, 1893. C.E. from Rensselaer in 1914. Commissioned in the infantry in 1917. M.B.A. from Harvard in 1934. Graduated from the Command and General Staff School in 1939. Commanding officer of Indiana and Hoosier Ordnance Plants, Charleston, Indiana 1940-1941. Deputy chief of St. Louis Ordnance District 1941-1942. Brigadier general in May 1942. Duty at the office of the chief of ordnance 1942-1948. Retired in June 1951. Decorations included the Distinguished Service Medal and Commendation Ribbon. Died on January 10, 1961.

Harmon, Ernest Nason (1894-1979) Born on February 26, 1894, in Lowell, Massachusetts. Commissioned in the cavalry from West Point in 1917. Served with the AEF 1918-1919. Instructor at West Point 1921-1925. Professor of military science and tactics at Norwich University 1927-1931. Graduated from the Command and General Staff School in 1933 and the Army War College in 1934. Assistant chief of staff for supply, then chief of staff of the Armored Force 1939-1941. Brigadier general in March 1942, major general in August 1942. Commanding general of 2nd Armored Division 1942-1943, 1st Armored Division 1943-1944 and the 2nd again 1944-1945. Commander of XXI Corps 1945-1946. Assignments after the war included commanding general of the constabulary in Germany 1946-1947 and deputy commander of Army Ground Forces 1947-1948. Retired in February 1948. Decorations included the Distinguished Service Cross, four Distinguished Service Medals, two Silver Stars, four Legions of Merit, the Bronze Star and Purple Heart. President of Norwich University 1950-1965. Died on November 13, 1979.

Harper, Arthur McKinley (1893-1972) Born on December 23, 1893, in Minneapolis, Minnesota. Commissioned in the cavalry from West Point in 1917. Duty in the Canal Zone with 4th Field Artillery 1921-1924. Professor of military science and tactics at Iowa State College 1925-1929. Graduated from the Command and General Staff School in 1936. Professor of military science and tactics at Xavier University 1936-1940. Commanding officer of 60th Field Artillery Battalion 1940-1942. Brigadier general in May 1942. With 30th Infantry Division April 1942-September 1943. Commanding general of III Corps Artillery 1943-1944. Commanding general of XXIV Corps Artillery 1944-1945. Major general in January 1945. Commanding general of 98th Division 1945-1946. Retired in December 1953. Decorations included three Legions of Merit, the Bronze Star and Commendation Ribbon. Died on February 23, 1972.

Harriman, Joseph Eugene (1900-1963) Born on April 17, 1900, in Appleton, Wisconsin. Attended Lawrence College 1916-1917 and Northwestern University 1917-1918. Commissioned in the Coast Artillery Corps from West Point in 1920. Stationed in the Philippines 1923-1925. Graduated from the Command and General Staff School in 1936 and the Army War College in 1939. Antiaircraft officer in the North African and European Theater of Operationss 1942-1943. Brigadier general in April 1943. Commanding general of 52nd Antiaircraft Artillery Brigade 1943-1944. Military attache in Turkey in 1945. Reverted to colonel in February 1946. Retired in August 1950. Decorations included the Legion of Merit, Commendation Ribbon and Purple Heart. Died on December 11, 1963.

Harris, Arthur Ringland (1890-1968) Born in Norfolk, Nebraska, on August 1, 1890. Attended the University of Nevada 1908-1910. Commissioned in the field artillery from West Point in 1914. Served with the AEF in World War I. Military attache to several Central American republics 1931-1935. Professor of military science and tactics at Harvard 1935-1939. On the War Department General Staff 1939-1941. Deputy chief of staff for intelligence, First Army 1941-1943. Brigadier general in March 1943. Military attache in Mexico, then Argentina 1943-1946. Retired in April 1948. Decorations included the Legion of Merit. Died on March 20, 1968.

Harris, Charles Spurgeon (1894-1993) Born in Harrisville, North Carolina, on January 28, 1894. B.A. from the University of North Carolina in 1917. Commissioned in the coast artillery corps in 1917. Served with the heavy artillery in World War I. Instructor at the Coast Artillery School 1924-1927. Member of the Coast Artillery Board 1933-1935. Graduated from the Command and General Staff School in 1939. Antiaircraft officer for Third Army 1940-1941, then at GHQ U.S. Army 1941-1942. Brigadier general in March 1942. Commander of 42nd Antiaircraft Artillery then 42nd Coast Antiaircraft Artillery Brigade April 1942-April 1944. Staff officer with Tenth Army 1944-1945. Commanding general of Tenth Army Antiaircraft Artillery April-August 1945. Reverted to colonel in June 1946. Retired in July 1953. Decorations included the Bronze Star and Commendation Ribbon. Died on February 11, 1993.

Harris, Charles Tillman Jr. (1884-1961) Born in Mexia, Texas, on March 31, 1884. Attended the University of Texas 1902-1903. Commissioned in the Coast Artillery Corps in 1907. Served in the ammunition production office of the War Department during World War I. Graduated from the Army War College in 1924 and Army Industrial College in 1926. Director of the planning branch in the office of the assistant secretary of war 1934-1938. Brigadier general in September 1938. Assistant chief of ordnance 1938-1942. Major general in August 1941. Commanding general of Aberdeen Proving Ground 1942-1946. Retired in June 1946. Decorations included three Distinguished Service Medals, the Legion of Merit and Bronze Star. Died on December 24, 1961.

Harris, Frederick Mixon (1900-1969) Born on June 29, 1900, in Rockmart, Georgia. Commissioned in the infantry from West Point in 1920. Served with the 15th Infantry in China 1926-1929. Professor of military science and tactics at Drexel Institute 1931-1936. Stationed at Camp Paraiso, Canal Zone October 1939-September 1941. Executive officer in the office of the deputy chief of staff for intelligence, Panama Canal Department 1941-1942. On the War Department General Staff 1942-1943. Brigadier general in June 1943. Assistant division commander, then commanding general of 63rd Division 1943-1945. Reverted to colonel in February 1946. Retired in August 1954. Decorations included the Silver Star and three Bronze Stars. Died on April 10, 1969.

Harrison, Eugene Lynch (1898-1981) Born on August 20, 1898, in San Augustine, Texas. Attended the Agricultural and Mechanical College of Texas 1916-1918. Commissioned in the cavalry from West Point in 1923. Graduated from the Command and General Staff School in 1937. Aide-de-camp to the secretary of war 1940-1942. Commanding officer of 47th Armored Regiment, 14th Armored Division 1942-1943. Staff officer with Lieutenant General Jacob L. Devers, commander of the European Theater of Operations 1943-1944. Assistant chief of staff for operations, IV Corps in 1944, then assistant chief of staff for intelligence at Sixth Army Group 1944-1945. Brigadier general in January 1945. Retired in October 1953. Decorations included the Distinguished Service Medal, Legion of Merit and Bronze Star. Died on June 14, 1981.

Harrison, William Henry (1892-1956) Born in Brooklyn, New York, on June 11, 1892. Attended Pratt Institute 1913-1915. With New York Telephone, Western Electric and AT&T 1909-1941. Called to active duty in 1941 as colonel and chief of the shipbuilding, construction and supplies branch in the office of production management. Brigadier general in 1942 and major general in 1943. Director of procurement and distribution service in the office of the chief signal officer, then head of priorities and allocations division in the Department of Commerce until he returned to civilian status at the end of the war. Decorations included the Distinguished Service Medal. Died on April 21, 1956.

Harrison, William Kelly Jr. (1895-1987) Born on September 7, 1895, in Washington, DC. Commissioned in the cavalry from West Point in 1917. Instructor there 1919-1922. Graduated from the Command and General Staff School in 1934 and the Army War College in 1938. On the War Department General Staff 1939-1942. Brigadier general in June 1942. Assistant division commander of 78th Infantry Division, then 30th Division 1942-1945. Assignments after the war included deputy commanding general of Army Forces Far East 1952-1953, senior delegate to the truce team in the Korean War 1952-1953, chief of staff of Far East Command 1953-1954 and commander in chief of the Caribbean Command 1954 until retirement in 1957. Decorations included the Distinguished Service Cross, three Distinguished Service Medals, the Silver Star, Legion of Merit, two Bronze Stars and the Purple Heart. Died on May 25, 1987.

Harrold, Thomas L. (1902-1973) Born in San Diego, California, on June 21, 1902. Commissioned in the cavalry from West Point in 1925. Served in the Philippine Islands 1930-1932. Instructor at West Point December 1932-August 1938. Assigned to 11th Cavalry 1938-1942. Graduated from Command and General Staff School in 1942. Executive officer of 2nd Cavalry February-July 1942. Commanding officer of 52nd Armored Infantry Regiment July 1942-December 1943. Commander of Combat Command "A," 9th Armored Division 1943-1945. Brigadier general in May 1945. Assignments after the war include deputy commanding general of I Corps, then the 1st Cavalry Division in the Korean War, commanding general of XVI Corps 1952-1953 and 10th Division 1953-1954, and commandant of the National War College 1958-1961. Retired as lieutenant general in 1961. Decorations included the Distinguished Service Medal, two Silver Stars, the Legion of Merit, four Bronze Stars and the Commendation Ribbon. Died on June 16, 1973.

Hart, Charles Edward (1900-1991) Born on June 17, 1900, in Fort Washington, Maryland. Commissioned in the field artillery from West Point in 1924. Instructor at West Point 1935-1940, then at the Field Artillery School 1940-1942. Graduated from the Command and General Staff School in 1942. Artillery officer for I Corps 1942-1943, then First Army 1943-1946. Brigadier general in August 1944. Assignments after the war included commandant of the Artillery 1953-1954, commanding general of V Corps 1954-1956 then Second Army 1956-1957 and commander of Army Air Defense Command 1957-1960. Retired in August 1960. Decorations included two Distinguished Service Medals, two Legions of Merit and the Commendation Ribbon. Died on December 9, 1991.

Hart, William Lee (1881-1957) Born in Yorkville, South Carolina, on January 27, 1881. Enlisted service in the South Carolina Militia and National Guard 1898-1908. M.D. from the University of Maryland in 1906. Commissioned in the Medical Corps in 1908. Graduated from Army Medical School in 1908. Served with the Punitive Expedition into Mexico in 1916. Chief of the overseas division, office of the surgeon general in the AEF. Graduated from the Command and General Staff School in 1926, Army Industrial College in 1927 and the Army War College in 1931. Surgeon with the Philippine Division 1935-1936. Surgeon, then chief of the medical branch in the IV Corps Area, Fort Sam Houston 1940-1944. Retired in January 1945. Recalled to active duty in February 1945. Brigadier general in March 1945. Retired again in March 1946. Died on December 22, 1957.

Hartle, Russell Peter (1889-1961) Born on June 26, 1889, in Chernsville, Maryland. B.A. from the University of Maryland in 1910. Commissioned in the infantry in 1910. Served in the Philippines 1910-1912. Professor of military science and tactics at Utah State Agricultural College 1919-1921 then Oregon Agricultural College in 1921 and Salt Lake City high schools 1921-1923. Graduated from the Command and General Staff School in 1925. Instructor at the Command and General Staff School 1925-1928. Graduated from the Army War College in 1930. Served with 31st Infantry in the Philippines 1930-1933. Graduated from the Naval War College in 1934. In the war plans division of the War Department General Staff 1934-1937. Executive officer, then commanding officer of 65th Infantry in Puerto Rico 1939-1940. Brigadier general in October 1940. Commander of Puerto Rico Mobile Force 1940-1941. With 6th and 34th Infantry Divisions in 1941. Major general in October 1941. Commanding general of U.S. forces in the United Kingdom January 1942-July 1943. Commanding general of Branch Immaterial Replacement Training Center at Camp Fannin 1943-1945. Retired in June 1946. Decorations included the Distinguished Service Medal and Legion of Merit. Died on November 23, 1961.

Hartman, Charles Dudley (1886-1962) Born in Brookhaven, Mississippi, on August 22, 1886. Commissioned in the infantry from West Point in 1908. Served with the Quartermaster Corps in World War I, responsible for constructing all housing for troops. M.B.A. from Harvard in 1929. At the War Department General Staff 1935-1938. Executive officer in the construction division, office of the quartermaster general 1938-1939. Superintendent of the Army Transport Service in 1939. Chief of the construction division, office of the quartermaster general 1940-1941. Brigadier general in August 1940. Commander of the Quartermaster Reserve Training Camp at Camp Lee 1941-1942. Commanding general of Forth Worth Quartermaster Depot September 1942-January 1943. Retired in April 1943. Decorations included the Distinguished Service Medal. Died on February 14, 1962.

Hartman, George Eitle (1895-1968) Born in Brookhaven, Mississippi, on January 4, 1895. Attended Southwest Presbyterian College 1913-1915. B.S. from Mississippi State College in 1917. Commissioned in the Mississippi National Guard in 1917. Graduated from Army Law School in 1924 and Army Industrial College in 1927. Brigadier general in April 1943. Served at Army Service Force Training Center, Camp Ellis 1943-1946. Reverted to colonel in March 1946. Retired in April 1954. Decorations included two Legions of Merit, the Bronze Star and Commendation Ribbon. Died on July 1, 1968.

Hartness, Harlan Nelson (1898-1986) Born on March 28, 1898, in Claremont, Virginia. Attended the University of Virginia 1916-1917. Commissioned in the infantry from West Point in 1919. B.A. from Columbia University in 1923. Instructor at West Point 1923-1926. Duty at Fort Clayton in the Canal Zone 1926-1929. Professor of military science and tactics at the University of Minnesota 1929-1933. Attended Kriegsakademie in Berlin 1935-1937. Instructor at the Command and General Staff School 1937-1940. At the War Department General Staff 1940-1942, then headquarters of Army Ground Forces 1942-1944. Brigadier general in August 1, 1942. Assistant division commander of 26th Division August 1943-September 1945. Deputy assistant chief of staff for operations with 15th Army Group in 1945. Assignments after the war included commanding general of 7th Division 1946-1948, assistant commandant of the Command and General Staff College 1948-1950 and commanding general of 4th Division October 1950-April 1953. Retired in October 1954 as major general. Decorations included the Silver Star, Legion of Merit and two Bronze Stars. Died on June 13, 1986.

Hasbrouck, Robert Wilson (1896-1985) Born on February 2, 1896, in Kingston, New York. Commissioned in the Coast Artillery Corps from West Point in 1917. Served with the 62nd Coast Artillery, AEF in 1918. Instructor at Field Artillery School 1921-1924. Professor of military science and tactics at Princeton 1927-1932. Graduated from the Command and General Staff School in 1934 and the Army War College in 1937. Duty in the operations and training division of the War Department General Staff 1937-1941. Battery commander, then executive officer of division artillery in 4th Armored Division April 1941-March 1942. Chief of staff of 1st Armored Division March-August 1942. Brigadier general in September 1942. Combat commander with 8th Armored Division August 1942-August 1943. Deputy chief of staff of Twelfth Army Group 1943-1944. Commanding general of 7th Armored Division 1944-1945 in the Battle of the Bulge. Major general in January 1945. Retired in September 1947. Decorations included the Distinguished Service Medal, Silver Star, Legion of Merit and Bronze Star. Died on August 19, 1985.

Hasbrouck, Sherman Vitus (1898-) Born on June 18, 1898, in Stone Ridge, New York. Commissioned in the infantry from West Point in 1920. Served in the Philippines 1921-1924. Aide to Major General Frank R. McCoy in 1927. Instructor at West Point 1936-1939. Graduated from the Command and General Staff School in 1940. Instructor at the Field Artillery School July 1940-March 1942. Assigned to the military personnel division at headquarters of Services of Supply March 1942-June 1944. Deputy commander of XXIII Corps Artillery in 1944. Brigadier general in January 1945. Commanding general of 97th Infantry Division Artillery March 1945-February 1946. Reverted to colonel in March 1946. Retired in August 1955. Decorations included the Legion of Merit, Bronze Star and Commendation Ribbon.

Hatcher, Julian Sommerville (1888-1963) Born in Winchester, Virginia, on June 26, 1888. B.S. from USNA in 1909. Resigned to accept a commission in the U.S. Army in 1910. Invented the breech mechanism for Army guns in 1914. Established and first commanding officer of Army Machine Gun School 1916-1917. At headquarters of the AEF in 1918. Chief of the small arms division of the Ordnance Department 1929-1933. Commandant of the Ordnance School, then chief of ordnance training 1937-1942. Brigadier general in July 1941. Chief of the Ordnance Field Service 1943-1945. Major general in November 1944. Retired in May 1946. Decorations included the Distinguished Service Medal and Legion of Merit. Author of several books on rifles and marksmanship. Died on December 4, 1963.

Hawkins, Hamilton S. (1872-1950) Born in Dakota Territory on September 25, 1872, the son of Brigadier General Hamilton S. Hawkins. Commissioned in the 4th Cavalry from West Point in 1894. Graduated from School of the Line in 1911 and Army Staff College in 1912. Chief of staff of 35th Division at Meuse-Argonne in World War I. Assistant commandant of Cavalry and Mounted Service Schools 1919-1923. Chief of staff of the Philippine Division 1926-1928. Brigadier general in September 1928. Commanding general of 14th Infantry Brigade, then 1st Cavalry Brigade 1928-1934. Commanding general of 1st Cavalry Division 1934-1936. Retired in September 1936. Recalled to active duty in September 1941. Retired again in November 1943. Decorations included the Purple Heart. Died on October 19, 1950.

Hauseman, David Nathaniel (1895-1981) Born in Pottstown, Pennsylvania, on March 4, 1895. Enlisted service in the Ordnance Department 1917-1918. B.S. from the University of Pennsylvania in 1918. Commissioned in the ordnance in 1918. B.S. from Massachusetts Institute of Technology in 1928 and M.B.S. from Harvard in 1935. Graduated from Army Industrial College in 1939. Chief of the Philadelphia Ordnance District 1940-1943. Director of the readjustment division, Army Service Forces 1943-1946. D.Sc. from Temple University in 1944. Brigadier general in September 1944. Retired in September 1946. Decorations included the Distinguished Service Medal, Legion of Merit and Commendation Ribbon. Vice president of Temple University 1946-1948. Died on December 19, 1981.

Hawley, Paul Ramsey (1891-1965) Born in West College Corner, Indiana, on January 31, 1891. B.S. from Indiana University in 1912 and M.D. from the University of Cincinnati in 1914. Commissioned in the Medical Corps in 1916. Graduated from Army Medical School in 1917. Ph.D. from Johns Hopkins in 1923. Graduated from the Command and General Staff School in 1936 and the Army War College in 1939. Commander of Medical Department Replacement Training Center at Camp Lee January-May 1941 then commandant of Medical Field Service School May-September 1941. Chief surgeon at Special Observers Group in London, then with U.S. Army Forces in the European Theater of Operations September 1941-July 1943. Brigadier general in September 1942. Chief medical director at the Veterans Administration 1943-1947. Major general in February 1944. Retired in June 1946. Decorations included the Distinguished Service Medal, Legion of Merit and Bronze Star. Died on November 24, 1965.

Hayden, Frederic Lord (1901-1969) Born on February 12, 1901, at Fort Screven, Georgia. Commissioned in the Coast Artillery Corps from West Point in 1920. Instructor at West Point 1930-1936. At headquarters of VI Corps Area 1939-1941, then Army Service Forces 1942-1944. Chief of staff of 5th Service Command 1944-1945. Brigadier general in June 1945. Deputy chief of staff for personnel at Army Forces Western Pacific in 1945. Retired in 1955. Decorations included two Distinguished Service Medals, the Legion of Merit, Bronze Star and Commendation Ribbon. Died on July 29, 1969.

Hayes, Philip (1887-1949) Born in Portage, Wisconsin, on June 16, 1887. Commissioned in the infantry from West Point in 1909. Instructor at West Point 1912-1917. Served in the Philippines and with the war plans division of the War Department General Staff 1917-1919. Graduated from the Command and General Staff School in 1924. Instructor, then executive officer at the Field Artillery School 1924-1929. Graduated from the Army War College in 1930. Instructor at the Command and General Staff School 1930-1935. Assistant chief of staff for operations and training, then chief of staff of the Hawaii Department 1937-1941. Professor of military science and tactics at Harvard December 1941-March 1942. Chief of staff of I Corps Area 1942-1943. Brigadier general in June 1943. Deputy chief of staff for Service Commands August-December 1943. Commanding general of 3rd Service Command December 1943-January 1946. Major general in January 1944. Retired in May 1946. Decorations included the Distinguished Service Medal, Legion of Merit and Commendation Ribbon. Died on November 25, 1949.

Hayes, Thomas Jay (1888-1967) Born on September 18, 1888, in Ironton, Ohio. Commissioned in the infantry from West Point in 1912. Served at the invasion of Vera Cruz in 1914 and with the 5th Division, AEF in World War I. Graduated from Army Industrial College in 1931 and the Army War College in 1932. Professor at West Point 1933-1938. Works manager at Springfield Armory 1938-1940. Duty in the office of the under secretary of war 1941-1942. Brigadier general in September 1941, major general in February 1942. Chief of production division, Services of Supply in 1942. Chief of Ordnance Department, Army Service Forces 1942-1945. Retired in September 1945. Decorations included the Distinguished Service Medal and Legion of Merit. Died on March 18, 1967.

Hayford, Bertram Francis (1899-1985) Born on January 8, 1899, in Chicago, Illinois. Commissioned in the field artillery from West Point in 1919. Duty in Hawaii with 11th Field Artillery 1920-1923. Instructor at West Point 1924-1929. Assistant professor of military science and tactics at Purdue 1934-1939. Graduated from the Command and General Staff School in 1940. Served with the Hawaii Department Service Command 1940-1945 as officer in charge of the transportation section, assistant to the assistant chief of staff for supply and director of the supply division. Brigadier general in March 1945. Assistant chief, then chief of the planning section on the staff of the commander in chief, Pacific Ocean Areas 1945-1946. Reverted to colonel in April 1946. Retired in November 1955. Decorations included two Legions of Merit. Died on December 9, 1985.

Haynes, Loyal Moyer (1895-1974) Born in Lorimor, Iowa, on March 3, 1895. Attended Western Union College 1913-1914. B.S. from Knox College in 1917. Commissioned in the field artillery in 1917. Served with the 4th Division, AEF 1918-1919. Graduated from the Command and General Staff School in 1937. Assistant chief of staff for supply at Third Army 1941-1942. Chief of staff of Southern Defense Command 1942-1943. Brigadier general in March 1943. Assistant chief of staff for supply at Army Ground Forces 1943-1945. Deputy chief of staff at U.S. Forces Austria 1945-1946. Retired in July 1954. Decorations included the Distinguished Service Medal, Silver Star and Legion of Merit. Died on February 7, 1974.

Hays, George Price (1892-1978) Born in China on September 27, 1892. Attended Oklahoma Agricultural and Mechanical College. Commissioned in the 10th Field Artillery in 1917. Served with the AEF in 1918 at the second battle of the Marne, where he won the Medal of Honor, and the Meuse-Argonne offensive. Professor of military science and tactics at Cornell University 1922-1926. Graduated from the Command and General Staff School in 1934. Duty with the Civilian Conservation Corps 1934-1935. Graduated from the Army War College in 1940. With the 99th Field Artillery in 1940. Commanding officer of the Field Artillery Battalion at Edgewood Arsenal in 1941. Assistant to the plans and training officer on the War Department General Staff in 1941. At headquarters of Army Ground Forces in 1942. Brigadier general in August 1942. Assistant division commander of 85th Division, then 2nd Infantry Division 1942-1945. Major general in January 1945. Assignments after the war included commanding general of 2nd Infantry Division 1945-1949, U.S. high commissioner for Germany December 1949-April 1952 and commanding general of U.S. Forces Austria April 1952-1953. Retired as lieutenant general in April 1953. Decorations included the Medal of Honor, two Distinguished Service Medals, two Silver Stars, the Legion of Merit, Bronze Star and Purple Heart. Died on September 7, 1978.

Hazlett, Harry Fouts (1884-1960) Born in Deersville, Ohio, on April 17, 1884. Ph.B. from Mt. Union College in 1904. Commissioned in the Ohio National Guard in 1904 and the Regular Army in 1920. Graduated from the Command and General Staff School in 1927 and the Army War College in 1933. Brigadier general in September 1942. Chief of staff, then commander of the Replacement and School Command, Army Ground Forces 1942-1946. Major general in March 1943. Assignments after the war included commanding general of 86th Infantry Division 1946-1947. Retired in October 1947. Decorations included the Distinguished Service Medal. Died on September 27, 1960.

Heard, Jack Whitehead (1887-1976) Born in New York City on March 6, 1887, the son of Brigadier General John W. Heard and brother of Ralph Townsend Heard. Commissioned in the cavalry from West Point in 1910. Served with the aviation section of the Signal Corps 1915-1919. Graduated from the Command and General Staff School in 1924, the Army War College in 1931, the Naval War College in 1932 and Army Industrial College in 1934. Brigadier general in October 1940. Duty with the Armored Force 1940-1943. Major general in February 1942. Member of the War Department Manpower Board 1943-1946. Retired in September 1946. Decorations included the Legion of Merit. Died on October 25, 1976.

Heard, Ralph Townsend (1895-1993) Born in Fort Ethan Allen, Vermont, on August 15, 1895, the son of Brigadier General John W. Heard and brother of Jack Whitehead Heard. Attended Stanford University 1915-1916 and the University of Texas 1916-1917. Commissioned in the field artillery in 1916. Served on the Mexican border 1916-1917 and with the 6th Field Artillery, 1st Division in the AEF 1917-1918. On the morning of October 23, 1917, he was the first American to fire against the enemy in World War I. Shell casings were presented to President Wilson and General Pershing. Attended the Ecole d'application d'artillerie 1920-1922. Instructor in field artillery in the I Corps Area 1928-1933. Organized and commanded the 1st U.S. Anti-Tank Force 1937-1938. Graduated from the Command and General Staff School in 1940. Chief of the U.S. mission to countries in Central and South America in 1941. Headed American Intelligence Command 1942-1943. Assistant chief of staff at U.S. Army Forces Pacific Ocean Areas October 1943-June 1945. Brigadier general in January 1945. Retired in November 1946. Decorations included the Distinguished Service Medal, two Silver Stars, two Legions of Merit, the Bronze Star, Air Medal and Purple Heart. Died on December 28, 1993.

Hearn, Thomas Guerdon (1890-1980) Born on November 14, 1890, in Tuskegee, Alabama. Commissioned in the infantry from West Point in 1915. Served with the Punitive Expedition into Mexico 1916-1917 and with the AEF in World War I. Graduated from the Command and General Staff School in 1928 and the

Army War College on 1936. Chief of staff of II Corps 1941-1942. Brigadier general in February 1942. Chief of staff to the commanding general of China-Burma-India Theater of Operations 1942-1944. Major general in June 1943. Chief of staff of China Theater of Operations in 1944. Commanding general of Infantry Replacement Training Center 1945-1946. Retired in August 1946. Decorations included the Distinguished Service Medal. Died on June 4, 1980.

Heavey, William Francis (1896-1974) Born on January 29, 1896, in Fort McPherson, Georgia. Commissioned in the Corps of Engineers from West Point in 1917. Wounded while serving with the 3rd Division, AEF in World War I. B.S. from Massachusetts Institute of Technology in 1922. Graduated from the Command and General Staff School in 1938. Engineer for IV Corps 1941-1942. Brigadier general in September 1942. Commanding general of the Engineer Brigade at Admiral Halsey's South Pacific Command 1942-1946. Retired in January 1948. Decorations included the Distinguished Service Medal, Legion of Merit, Bronze Star, Commendation Ribbon and two Purple Hearts. Died on March 11, 1974.

Hedrick, Lawrence Hyskell (1880-1958) Born in Warren City, Indiana, on November 22, 1880. LL.B. from the University of Missouri in 1905. Commissioned in the 4th Infantry, South Dakota National Guard in 1908. Served with the Punitive Expedition into Mexico 1916-1917, the 147th and 121st Field Artillery in 1918 and at the School of Fire in 1919. Transferred to the Judge Advocate General Department, Regular Army in 1920. Graduated from the School of the Line in 1922, the Army Staff School in 1923 and the Army War College in 1927. On the War Department General Staff 1931-1935. With the Hawaii Department 1935-1937. Chief of the claims and litigation section in the office of the judge advocate general, U.S. Army 1940-1942. Brigadier general in June 1942. Retired in November 1942 as colonel. Recalled to active duty in December 1942. Judge advocate general of the European Theater of Operations December 1942-April 1943. Air judge advocate general at headquarters of AAF July 1943-January 1946. Decorations included two Legions of Merit. Died on March 17, 1958.

Heflebower, Roy Cleveland (1884-1973) Born in Washington, DC, on October 25, 1884. M.D. from George Washington University in 1906. Commissioned in the Medical Reserve Corps in 1909. Graduated from Army Medical School in 1910. Served in the Philippines 1913-1915, with the Punitive Expedition into Mexico in 1916 and with base hospital number 68, AEF in 1918. Graduated from the School of the Line in 1922, the Army War College in 1924 and Army Industrial College in 1927. Instructor at the Command and General Staff School 1931-1935. Brigadier general in December 1941. Commander of Medical Replacement Training Center at Camp Berkeley August 1941-March 1945 then Army Convalescent and General Hospital at Camp Butler March 1945 until retirement in August 1946. Decorations included the Legion of Merit and Commendation Ribbon. Died on October 28, 1973.

Heileman, Frank August (1891-1961) Born in St. Louis, Missouri, on March 13, 1891. B.S. from the University of Missouri in 1914. Enlisted service with the Missouri National Guard 1916-1917. Commissioned in the infantry in 1917. Served with the 18th Machine Gun Battalion, AEF in the Meuse-Argonne offensive in 1918. Transferred to the Corps of Engineers in 1923. Graduated from the Command and General Staff School in 1931. Graduated from the Army War College in 1940 and transferred to the General Staff Corps. Served as director of supply at headquarters of Army Service Forces 1943-1945. Brigadier general in June 1943, major general in March 1945. Assistant chief of staff for supply at headquarters of Army Forces Western Pacific 1945-1947. Assignments after the war included assistant chief, then chief of transportation, U.S. Army September 1947 until retirement in March 1953. Decorations included the Distinguished Service Medal, Legion of Merit, Bronze Star and Commendation Ribbon. Died on September 24, 1961.

Helmick, Charles Gardiner (1892-1991) Born in Fort Sherman, Idaho, on July 7, 1892, the son of Major General Ely A. Helmick. B.S. from USNA in 1913. Resigned to accept appointment in the field artillery, U.S. Army that year. Duty in the Philippine Islands 1913-1915. With 15th Field Artillery, 2nd Division in the AEF 1917-1918 and participated in the Marne and Aisne-Marne campaigns. Graduated from the Command and General Staff School in 1926 and the Army War College in 1933. Graduated from Air Corps Tactical School in 1938. Chief of the budget branch at the War Department General Staff then at Services of Supply 1941-1942. Brigadier general in April 1942. Commanding general of 35th Infantry Division Artillery 1942-1943 then the 76th Field Artillery Brigade, later designated V Corps Artillery, at Normandy and the Battle of the Bulge 1943-1945. Commanding general of Fort Meade 1945-1946. Retired as major general in July 1952. Decorations included the Distinguished Service Medal, four Silver Stars, three Legions of Merit, the Bronze Star, Air Medal and Commendation Ribbon. Died on December 19, 1991.

Hendrix, Raleigh Raymond (1897-) Born in Skeedee, Oklahoma, on September 7, 1897. Enlisted service with the Oklahoma National Guard 1917-1919. Commissioned in the Coast Artillery Corps in 1924. Served with the 64th Coast Artillery in Hawaii 1924-1927 and again 1930-1932. With 63rd Coast Artillery 1940-1942. Assistant antiaircraft officer at Allied Force headquarters of the European Theater of Operations July 1942-October 1943. Brigadier general in September 1943. Commanding general of 71st Antiaircraft Artillery Brigade 1943-1944 then II Corps Artillery August 1944-September 1945. Commander of War Department Persosnnel Center at Camp Grant 1945-1946. Reverted to colonel in April 1946. Retired in September 1961. Decorations included the Distinguished Service Medal, three Legions of Merit and the Bronze Star.

Henning, Frank Andrew Jr. (1896-1983) Born on July 13, 1896, in Lakota, North Dakota. Attended the University of North Dakota. Commissioned in the field artillery from West Point in 1920. Duty with 13th Field Artillery in Hawaii

1923-1927. Assistant professor of military science and tactics at Purdue 1927-1932. Instructor at the Field Artillery School 1935-1937. In the planning and equipment branches of the War Department General Staff 1939-1941. In the office of the assistant chief of staff for supply, U.S. Army 1941-1942. Chief of the liaison branch, Army Service Forces 1942-1943. Commanding general of 71st Division Artillery 1943-1945. Brigadier general in May 1944. Assignments after the war included deputy commanding general of XVIII Airborne Corps April 1954 until retirement in July 1954. Decorations included the Legion of Merit, Bronze Star and Commendation Ribbon. Died on November 4, 1983.

Henry, Guy Vernor (1875-1967) Born in Fort Robinson, Nebraska, on January 28, 1875. Commissioned in the infantry from West Point in 1898. Served in the Spanish-American War and the Philippine Insurrection 1900-1901. Commandant of cadets at West Point 1916-1917. Attained the rank of brigadier general in World War I. Graduated from the Army War College in 1921, School of the Line in 1922 and the General Staff School in 1923. Chief of cavalry as major general March 1930-March 1934. Reverted to brigadier general in March 1934. Commanding general of 7th Cavalry Brigade 1934-1935. Commandant of the Cavalry School 1935-1939. Major general in September 1937. Retired in January 1939. Recalled to active duty in September 1941 as head of the Inter-Allied Personnel Board and senior Army member of the U.S. Canadian and Mexican Defense Commission until the end of the war. Decorations included two Distinguished Service Medals and the Silver Star. Died on November 29, 1967.

Henry, Stephen Garrett (1894-1973) Born in Melrose, Louisiana, on November 23, 1894. Commissioned in the infantry in 1917. B.S. from Louisiana State University in 1917. Commanding officer of 140th Machine Gun Battery, AEF in 1918. Attended Massachusetts Institute of Technology in 1922. Instructor at the Tank School 1923-1926. Graduated from the Command and General Staff School in 1928. Again istructor at the Tank School 1928-1932. Instructor at the Infantry School 1932-1933. Graduated from the Army War College in 1934. Battalion commander with 65th Infantry in Puerto Rico 1934-1936. In the operations division of the War Department General Staff 1936-1940. Conceived, established and then commanded the Armored Force School 1940-1943. Brigadier general in July 1941. Major general in March 1943. Commanding general of 20th Armored Division February-October 1943. Established the research and development division at the War Department General Staff then assistant chief of staff for personnel 1943-1946. Retired in October 1946. Decorations included two Distinguished Service Medals and the Legion of Merit. Died on January 5, 1973.

Herr, John Knowles (1878-1955) Born in White House, New Jersey, on October 1, 1878. Attended Lafayette College 1895-1898. Commissioned in the cavalry from West Point in 1902. Instructor at West Point 1911-1913. Chief of staff of 30th Division 1918-1919. Graduated from the Command and General Staff School in 1926 and the Army War College in 1927. Instructor at the Army War College 1929-1931. Commanding officer of 7th Cavalry 1935-1938. Chief of cavalry as major general 1938-1942. Retired in February 1942. Decorations included the Distinguished Service Medal. Died on March 12, 1955.

Herren, Thomas Wade (1895-1985) Born in Dadeville, Alabama, on August 9, 1895. B.A. from the University of Alabama in 1917. Commissioned in the field artillery in 1917. Served with the 78th Field Artillery, AEF 1918-1919. Graduated from the Command and General Staff School in 1936. Instructor at the Cavalry School 1936-1942. Commanding officer of 106th Cavalry Regiment 1942-1943. Commandant of the Cavalry School January 1943-October 1944. Brigadier general in September 1944. Assistant division commander of 70th Infantry Division 1944-1945. Deputy chief of staff for operations at Fourth Army 1945-1946. Assignments after the war included commanding general of the Military District of Washington 1950-1952 and commanding general of First Army December 1954 until retirement in July 1957. Decorations included the Distinguished Service Medal and two Legions of Merit. Died on June 4, 1985.

Herrick, Hugh Nathan (1892-n/a) Born in Annandale, Minnesota, on May 31, 1892. Commissioned in the Coast Artillery Corps in 1917. Served with the AEF 1918-1919. B.S. from the University of California in 1920. In the Panama Canal Zone with 2nd Coast Artillery 1923-1927. Duty in the office of the chief of coast artillery 1927-1931. Graduated from the Command and General Staff School in 1933. With 91st Coast Artillery in the Philippines 1933-1936. Graduated from Air Corps Tactical School in 1937. Member of the Coast Artillery Board 1937-1940. Executive officer in the office of the chief of coast artillery July 1940-March 1942. At headquarters of the Antiaircraft Command 1942-1943. Brigadier general in February 1943. Commander of Antiaircraft Replacement Training Center at Camp Wallace January 1943 until retirement in January 1944.

Herron, Charles Douglas (1877-1977) Born on March 13, 1877, in Crawfordsville, Indiana. Attended Wabash College in 1896. Commissioned in the infantry from West Point in 1899. Served in the Philippine Islands 1899-1901. Graduated from Army School of the Line in 1907 and Army Staff School in 1908. M.A. from Wabash College in 1908. Instructor at West Point 1908-1910. Chief of staff of 78th Division in 1918. Graduated from the Army War College in 1920. Chief of staff of the Philippine Department 1927-1929. Executive for reserve officer affairs in the War Department 1930-1935. Brigadier general in October 1934, major general in March 1937. Commanding general of the Hawaiian Department 1938-1941. Retired in March 1941. Lieutenant general in July 1940. Retired in March 1941. Recalled to active duty for the period September 1941-April 1944. Decorations included two Distinguished Service Medals. Died on April 23, 1977.

Hershey, Lewis Blaine (1893-1977) Born on September 12, 1893, near Angola, Indiana. Attended Tri-State College 1910-1914. Enlisted and commissioned service in the Indiana National Guard 1911-1917. Service in France with the AEF in 1918. Commissioned in the field artillery, Regular Army in 1920. Graduated from the Command and General Staff School in 1932 and the Army War College in 1934. Secretary of the Joint Army and Navy Selective Service Committee 1936-1940. Brigadier general in October 1940. Deputy director, then director of Selective Service 1940-1970. Major general in April 1942, lieutenant general in June 1956 and general in November 1969. Retired in March 1973. Decorations included the Distinguished Service Medal Died on May 20, 1977.

Hertford, Kenner Fisher (1900-) Born on September 25, 1900, in Galveston, Texas. Commissioned in the Corps of Engineers from West Point in 1923. Administrative officer for the European office of the Battle Monuments Commission 1938-1941. Duty in the operations and training branch, office of the chief of engineers in 1941. Brigadier general in September 1944. With operations division of the War Department General Staff 1945-1946. Reverted to colonel in April 1946. Assignments after the war included hief of research and development, U.S. Army as major general 1954-1955. Retired in July 1955. Decorations included two Distinguished Service Medals and the Legion of Merit.

Hesketh, William (1895-1986) Born in England on November 11, 1895. Naturalized in 1906. Commissioned in the Coast Artillery Corps in 1917. Instructor with the Connecticut National Guard 1937-1939. Graduated from the Command and General Staff School in 1940. Supply officer at IX Corps in 1940. Commanding officer of 74th Coast Artillery July 1940-April 1941. Plans and training officer at Chesapeake Bay harbor defenses in 1941. Commanding officer of 1st Antiaircraft Command December 1941-July 1942. Commanding general of 45th Coast Artillery Brigade July-September 1942. Brigadier general in August 1942. Commanding general of 46th Antiaircraft Artillery Brigade September 1942-March 1944. Commanding general of Antiaircraft Replacement Training Center at Camp Stewart, then Fort Bliss 1944-1945. Retired in June 1948. Died on December 6, 1986.

Hess, Walter Wood Jr. (1892-1972) Born on March 17, 1892, in Philadelphia, Pennsylvania. Commissioned in the Coast Artillery Corps from West Point in 1915. Served with the AEF as battalion commander in the 107th Field Artillery at Meuse-Argonne, the 53rd Field Artillery Brigade, 28th Division at Meuse-Argonne and Ypres-Lys, and the 16th Field Artillery, 4th Division at Aisne-Marne and Somme offensives. Instructor with the Pennsylvania National Guard 1923-1928. Graduated from the Command and General Staff School in 1930. Instructor at the Field Artillery School 1930-1934. Commanding officer of 36th Field Artillery, 13th Field Artillery Brigade 1938-1943. Commanding general of 36th Division Artillery 1943-1945. Brigadier general in January 1944. Commanding general of the Replacement Training Center at Fort Bragg 1945-1946. Commanding general of the U.S. military liaison mission in the Soviet zone of Potsdam 1946-1949. Commander of Camp Carson 1950-1952. Retired in March 1952. Decorations included two Legions of Merit, two Bronze Stars and the Commendation Ribbon. Died on April 10, 1972.

Hester, Hugh Bryan (1895-1983) Born in Hester, North Carolina, on August 5, 1895. B.A. from the University of North Carolina in 1916 and LL.B. in 1917. Commissioned in the field artillery in 1917. Graduated from Army Industrial College in 1939. Executive to the director of the procurement division, office of the secretary of war 1939-1941. Chief of procurement control in the office of the quartermaster general 1941-1942. Deputy chief quartermaster, then chief of the subsistence depot, finally director of procurement at the Southwest Pacific Theater of Operations 1943-1944. Brigadier general in November 1944. Commanding general of the Australian base section, U.S. Army Services of Supply 1944-1945. Director of the food and agriculture division in the office of the military governor, U.S. Army in Germany 1945-1947. Reverted to colonel in February 1946. Retired in August 1951. Decorations included the Distinguished Service Medal, Silver Star and Commendation Ribbon. Died on November 25, 1983.

Hester, John Hutchinson (1886-1976) Born in Albany, Georgia, on September 11, 1886. Attended the University of Georgia 1903-1904. Commissioned in the infantry from West Point in 1908. Served in the Philippenes with 24th Infantry 1913-1915 and the Punitive Expedition into Mexico in 1916. Graduated from School of the Line in 1922, the Command and General Staff School in 1923 and the Army War College in 1927. Professor of military science and tactics at the University of Minnesota 1929-1933. Executive officer of the 65th Infantry in Puerto Rico 1933-1935. In the operations and training division of the War Department General Staff 1935-1939. Brigadier general in September 1940. Executive to the chief of staff for reserve officer affairs, War Department 1940-1941. Commanding general of Camp Wheeler in 1941, then 43rd Infantry Division October 1941-October 1943. Major general in February 1942. Commanding general of the Tank Destroyer Center October 1943-June 1944, then the Infantry Replacement Training Center 1944-1945. Retired in February 1946. Decorations included two Legions of Merit. Died on February 11, 1976.

Hewett, Hobart (1900-1967) Born on March 21, 1900, in Canton, Massachusetts. Commissioned in the Coast Artillery Corps from West Point in 1919. Duty in the Panama Canal Zone 1921-1924. Instructor at the Coast Artillery School 1930-1934, then member of the Coast Artillery Board 1936-1938. Served in Hawaii 1939-1942. Commanding officer of 509th Coast Artillery in 1942. Brigadier general in December 1942. Commander of 32nd and 31st Coast Artillery Brigades December 1942-December 1944. Assistant commanding general of the Infantry Replacement Training Center at Camp Gordon February-September 1945. In the development section, office of the chief of Army Ground Forces September 1945-March 1946. Reverted to colonel in March 1946. Assignments after the war included commanding general of 3rd Division Artillery 1953-1954 and Deputy Commander in Chief U.S. Army Europe 1958-1959. Retired in April 1960. Decorations included the Distinguished Service Medal and Legion of Merit. Died on March 18, 1967.

Hibbs, Louis Emerson (1893-1970) Born on October 3, 1893, in Washington, DC. Commissioned in the field artillery from West Point in 1916. Twice wounded in combat as a battery commander with the 1st Division, AEF in World War I. Aide to Brigadier General Douglas MacArthur 1919-1922. Instructor at Field Artillery School 1923-1926. Graduated from the Command and General Staff School in 1927. With 13th Field Artillery in Hawaii 1927-1930. Manager of athletics at West Point 1938-1942. Brigadier general in March 1942. Commanding general of 36th Infantry Division Artillery March 1942-February 1943. Major general in June 1943. Commanding general of 63rd Infantry Division 1943-1945. Assignments after the war included commandant of the Field Artillery School 1945-1946 and commanding general of 12th Infantry Division in the Philippines June-September 1946. Retired in January 1947. Decorations included the Distinguished Service Medal, Silver Star and two Purple Hearts. Died on April 28, 1970.

Hickey, Daniel Webster Jr. (1895-1980) Born in Chicago, Illinois, on August 2, 1895. Attended the University of Illinois 1914-1917. Commissioned in the Coast Artillery Corps in 1917. Served with the 1st Antiaircraft Battery, AEF in World War I, participating in the Meuse-Argonne, St. Mihiel and Verdun engagements. In the Philippines 1921-1922. Instructor with the Arkansas National Guard 1923-1927. Duty in the Panama Canal Zone 1933-1938. Graduated from the Command and General Staff School in 1938. With 65th Coast Artillery 1938-1940. Training officer with 9th Coast Artillery District 1940-1941. Chief of the materiel section in the office of the chief of coast artillery July 1941-March 1942. With Army Ground Forces March-December 1942. Brigadier general in December 1942. Commanding general of 54th Coast Artillery Brigade December 1942-July 1945 then 38th Antiaircraft Artillery Brigade July 1945-March 1946. Reverted to colonel in March 1946. Retired in June 1954. Decorations included the Legion of Merit and two Bronze Stars. Died on November 13, 1980.

Hickey, Doyle Overton (1891-1961) Born in Rector, Arkansas, on July 27, 1891. B.A. from Hendrix College in 1913. Commissioned in the field artillery, Officers Reserve Corps in 1917. Served with the 31st Division, AEF in World War I. Transferred to the Regular Army in 1920. Duty in the Philippines 1928-1930. Graduated from the Command and General Staff School in 1936. In the Philippines again as aide to Brigadier General Francis W. Honeycutt 1938-1940. Executive officer of the Field Artillery Replacement Training Center at Fort Bragg 1940-1941. In the training section, office of the chief of field artillery May 1941-March 1942. Combat commander with 3rd Armored Division 1942-1945. Brigadier general in September 1942. Commanding general of 3rd Armored Division March-August 1945. Assignments after the war included chief of staff of Far East Command 1950-1953. Retired in July 1953 as lieutenant general. Decorations included two Distinguished Service Medals, four Silver Stars, the Legion of Merit, Bronze Star and Air Medal. Died on October 20, 1961.

Hickey, Thomas Francis (1898-1983) Born in South Boston, Massachusetts, on April 1, 1898. Enlisted service 1916-1917. Commissioned in the infantry in 1917. Served with 341st Machine Gun Battalion and 27th Division, AEF at St. Mihiel and Meuse-Argonne in 1918. Assistant secretary, then secretary of the Field Artillery School 1926-1929. Instructor with the Massachusetts National Guard 1929-1933. Graduated from the Command and General Staff School in 1938. Instructor there November 1940-February 1942. Assistant chief of staff for operations at II Corps in 1942. Chief of staff of XI Corps 1942-1943. Commanding general of 42nd Infantry Division Artillery, then X Corps Artillery, finally 31st Infantry Division Artillery April 1943-October 1945. Brigadier general in September 1943. Assignments after the war included commanding general of 82nd Airborne Division 1950-1952, XVIII Airborne Corps February 1952-August 1953 and IX Corps 1953-1954. Deputy commander of U.S. Forces Far East January-November 1954. Again commanding general of IX Corps 1954-1955 and Third Army 1955-1958. Retired in April 1958. Decorations included two Distinguished Service Medals, the Silver Star, Legion of Merit, Air Medal, Commendation Ribbon and Purple Heart. Died on November 18, 1983.

Higgins, Gerald Joseph (1909-) Born on August 29, 1909, in Chicago, Illinois. Commissioned in the infantry from West Point in 1934. Instructor at the Infantry School in 1938. Company commander, operations officer and executive officer with 501st Parachute Battalion March-December 1941. Plans and training officer in the Provisional Parachute Group December 1941-April 1942. Deputy chief of staff for operations of the Airborne Command, then 101st Airborne Division April 1942-February 1943. Brigadier general in August 1944. Assistant division commander of 101st Airborne Division 1944-1945. Assignments after the war included commandant of Cadets at West Point 1946-1948, assistant division commander of 11th Airborne Division, then 24th and 4th Infantry Divisions July 1948-October 1950 and commanding general of 82nd Airborne Division 1952-1953. Retired in August 1955. Decorations included the Silver Star, Legion of Merit, Bronze Star and Commendation Ribbon.

Hill, Francis (1909-1973) Born in Boston, Massachusetts, on March 5, 1909. Enlisted service with the Massachusetts National Guard 1927-1929. Commissioned in the field artillery from West Point in 1933. Duty with 1st Battalion, 13th Field Artillery in Hawaii July 1939-March 1941. Field artillery instructor at Chinese Training Center, India 1942-1943. Deputy chief of staff for operations at China-Burma-India Theater of Operations, then India Burma Theater of Operationss 1943-1946. Brigadier general in June 1945. Reverted to colonel in April 1946. Assignments after the war included commanding general of 3rd Armored Division Artillery 1959-1961 and V Corps Artillery 1961-1963. Retired as brigadier general in July 1963. Decorations included two Distinguished Service Medals, the Legion of Merit, Bronze Star and Commendation Ribbon. Died on December 1, 1973.

Hill, Milton Abram (1892-1976) Born in Killmaster, Michigan, on July 12, 1892. Commissioned in the infantry in 1917. Duty in Puerto Rico 1917-1920. Again in Puerto Rico as professor of military science and tactics at the College of Agricultural and Mechanical Arts 1927-1931. Instructor in the Philippine Army 1937-1939 then commandant of General Service School in the Philippine Army 1939-1941. Inspector at headquarters of U.S. Army forces in the Far East October 1941-August 1942. Inspector general in the North African Theater of Operations 1942-1943. Inspector of training at the Infantry Replacement Training Center, Camp Roberts April-July 1943. Secretary of the Joint Brazil-U.S. Defense Committee in 1944. Military attache in Santaigo, Chile, October 1944-1946. Brigadier general in March 1945. Retired in October 1946. Decorations included the Legion of Merit. Died on April 1, 1976.

Hilldring, John Henry (1895-1974) Born in New Rochelle, New York, on March 27, 1895. Attended Columbia University, B.S. from the University of Connecticut in 1917. Commissioned in the infantry reserve in 1917. Saw action with the 38th Infantry Regiment in the AEF 1918-1919. Instructor at the Medical Field Service School 1932-1934. Graduated from the Command and General Staff School in 1936. At the War Department General Staff 1939-1941. Assistant chief of staff for personnel at the War Department December 1941-June 1942. Brigadier general in January 1942. Commanding general of 84th Infantry Division July 1942-April 1943. Major general in September 1942. Director of the civil affairs division at the War Department May 1943 until retirement in July 1946. Decorations included the Distinguished Service Cross and two Distinguished Service Medals. Assistant secretary of state 1946-1947. Died on January 20, 1974.

Hillman, Charles Clark (1887-1979) Born in Almyra, Arkansas, on August 27, 1887. B.S. from the University of Arkansas in 1907. Attended Tulane Medical School 1907-1908 and the University of Chicago in 1908. M.D. from Rush Medical College in 1911. Commissioned in the Medical Corps in 1913. Chief of professional services in the office of the surgeon general, U.S. Army 1939-1944. Brigadier general in January 1942. Commanding general of Letterman General Hospital 1944-1946. Retired in January 1947. Decorations included two Legions of Merit. Died on June 13, 1979.

Hinds, John Hamilton (1898-1993) Born on February 9, 1898, in Fort Monroe, Virginia. Commissioned in the field artillery from West Point in 1918. B.S. from Massachusetts Institute of Technology in 1923. Graduated from the Command and General Staff School in 1937 and the Army War College in 1939. On the War Department General Staff 1939-1942. Commanding general of 71st Division Artillery, then XIII Corps Artillery, finally XXI Corps Artillery 1942-1944. Brigadier general in September 1943. Artillery officer for First, then Twelfth Army Group, finally commanding general of 2nd Division Artillery 1944-1946. Assignments after the war included civil administrator of the Ryukyu Islands 1950-1951 and commanding general of 1st Cavalry Division in the Korean War in 1951. Retired in March 1956. Decorations included the Distinguished Service Medal, two Silver Stars, the Legion of Merit, three Bronze Stars, the Air Medal and Commendation Ribbon. Died on January 18, 1993.

Hinds, Sidney Rae (1900-1991) Born on May 14, 1900, in Newton, Illinois. Commissioned in the infantry from West Point in 1920. Member of 1924 Olympic shooting team. Commanding officer of 41st Armored Infantry, 2nd Armored Division 1942-1945. Brigadier general in March 1945. Commanding general of Combat Command "B," 2nd Armored Division 1945. Commanding general of the Armored Replacement Training Center at Fort Knox 1945-1946. Retired in February 1947. Decorations included the Distinguished Service Medal, four Silver Stars, the Legion of Merit, three Bronze Stars, two Commendation Ribbons and the Purple Heart. Died on February 17, 1991.

Hines, Charles (1888-1966) Born in Salt Lake City, Utah, on December 25, 1888. Commissioned in the Coast Artillery Corps from West Point in 1910. Served with 44th Coast Artillery and 39th Artillery Brigade, AEF at St. Mihiel and Meuse-Argonne in 1918. Instructor at West Point 1919-1924. Duty in the Philippines 1924-1926. Graduated from the Command and General Staff School in 1931, the Army War College in 1937 and Army Industrial College in 1938. Secretary of the Army-Navy Munitions Board 1939-1942. Brigadier general in April 1941. Director of the resources division at Services of Supply March-August 1942. Commanding general of 43rd and 38th Coast Artillery Brigades August 1942-July 1945. Reverted to colonel in February 1946. Retired in October 1946. Decorations included the Legion of Merit. Died on October 17, 1966.

Hinman, Dale Durkee (1891-1949) Born in Cherokee, Iowa, on November 4, 1891. M.E. from Colorado School of Mines in 1915. Commissioned in the Coast Artillery Corps in 1916. Duty in the Canal Zone 1917-1918. Instructor at the Coast Artillery School 1921-1924, then member of the Coast Artillery Board 1924-1925. Graduated from the Command and General Staff School in 1927. Duty in the Philippines 1927-1929. Graduated from the Army War College in 1934. Commanding officer of 71st Coast Artillery August 1940-May 1941. Brigadier general in October 1941. Commanding general of 38th Coast Artillery Brigade November 1941-February 1942. Inspector of training at headquarters of Antiaircraft Command 1942-1943. Commanding general of Antiaircraft Artillery Training Center, Fort Bliss April 1943-November 1943. Retired in November 1944. Decorations included two Legions of Merit. Died on December 26, 1949.

Hobbs, Leland Stanford (1892-1966) Born on February 24, 1892, in Gloucester, Massachusetts. Commissioned in the infantry from West Point in 1915. Served with the Punitive Expedition into Mexico 1916-1917. Aide-de-camp to Major General Arthur Murray, then Brigadier General George G. Trent in 1918. Instructor at West Point 1920-1924. Graduated from the Command and General Staff School in 1934 and the Army War College in 1935. Chief of staff of Third Army 1937-1939. Graduated from the the Naval War College in 1940. Chief of staff of the Trinidad Sector 1941-1942. Brigadier general in May 1942. With 80th Infantry Division in 1942. Major general in September 1942. Commanding general of 30th Infantry Division September 1942-September 1945. Assignments after the war included commanding general of III Corps, then 2nd Armored Division 1946-1947, deputy commanding general of Third Army 1947-1949, commander of IX Corps 1949-1950 and deputy commanding general of First Army 1951-1953. Retired in January 1953. Decorations included the Distinguished Service Medal, two Silver Stars and three Bronze Stars. Died on March 6, 1966.

Hobson, William Horace (1888-1960) Born on September 5, 1888, in Somerville, Tennessee. Commissioned in the infantry from West Point in 1912. Served in Panama, Canal Zone and the Philippines 1917-1919. Professor of military science and tactics at Georgetown University 1919-1923. Graduated from the Command and General Staff School in 1924. Professor of military science and tactics at Georgetown again 1929-1933. Graduated from the Army War College in 1935. Instructor, then assistant commandant at the Infantry School 1939-1941. Commanding officer of 30th Infantry 1941-1942. Member of National Munitions Board 1942-1943. Commanding general of Fort Benning 1943-1945. Brigadier general in February 1944. Retired in June 1946. Decorations included the Distinguished Service Medal and Commendation Ribbon. Died on July 4, 1960.

Hodes, Henry Irving (1899-1962) Born on March 19, 1899, in Washington, DC. Commissioned in the infantry from West Point in 1920. In the Philippine Islands with 26th Cavalry 1933-1936. Graduated from the Command and General Staff School in 1937 and the Army War College in 1940. With the War Department General Staff 1940-1944. Commanding officer of 112th Infantry, 28th Division in 1944. Brigadier general in January 1945. Assistant deputy chief of staff, U.S. Army 1945-1949. Assignments after the war included assistant division commander of 1st Cavalry Division, then 7th Infantry Division 1949-1950, deputy commander of Eighth Army then commanding general of 24th Division in the Korean War 1951-1952, commandant of the Command and General Staff College 1952-1954, commanding general of Seventh Army 1954-1956 and Commander in Chief U.S. Army Europe May 1956 until retirement as general in April 1959. Decorations included two Distinguished Service Medals, two Silver Stars, two Legions of Merit, two Bronze Stars, the Air Medal and two Purple Hearts. Died on February 14, 1962.

Hodge, John Reed (1893-1963) Born on June 12, 1893, in Golconda, Illinois. Attended Southern Illinois Teachers College and the University of Illinois 1911-1917. Commissioned in the infantry in 1917. Graduated from the Command and General Staff School in 1934 and the Army War College in 1935. With the War Department General Staff 1936-1941. Chief of staff of VII Corps in 1941. Brigadier general in June 1942. Assistant division commander of 25th Infantry Division 1942-1943. Major general in April 1943. Commanding general of Americal Division 1943-1944. Commander of XXIV Corps 1944-1948, including the Okinawa campaign as an element of Tenth Army. Lieutenant general in June 1945. Assignments after the war included commanding general of V Corps 1948-1950, commander of Third Army 1950-1952 and chief of Army Field Forces 1952-1953. Retired as general in June 1953. Decorations included four Distinguished Service Medals, the Legion of Merit, Air Medal and Purple Heart. Died on November 12, 1963.

Hodges, Courtney Hicks (1887-1966) Born in Perry, Georgia, on January 5, 1887. Attended West Point 1904-1905. Enlisted service 1906-1909. Commissioned in the infantry in 1909. Served with the Punitive Expedition into Mexico 1916-1917. Saw action with the 6th Infantry, AEF in the St. Mihiel and Meuse-Argonne offensives. Graduated from the Command and General Staff School in 1925. Member of the Infanatry Board at Fort Benning 1929-1933. Graduated from the Army War College in 1934. Assistant commandant, then commandant of the Infantry School 1938-1941. Brigadier general in May 1940. Major general in May 1941 as chief of infantry until March 1942. Commander of X Corps 1942-1943. Lieutenant general in February 1943. Commanding general of Third Army 1943-1944. Deputy commander, then commanding general of First Army 1944-1949. As an element of Bradley's Twelfth Army Group, First Army liberated Paris, fought in the Battle of the Bulge, reached the Rhine River and captured the Remagen Bridge intact, and was the first American force to link up with the Russians. General in April 1945. Retired in March 1949. Decorations included three Distinguished Service Crosses, three Distinguished Service Medals, the Silver Star and Bronze Star. Died on January 16, 1966.

Hodson, Fremont Byron (1894-n/a) Born in Marshfield, Oregon, on February 26, 1894. Attended the University of Oregon 1914-1917. Enlisted service with the 44th Infantry and 3rd Infantry Replacement Regiment in 1917-1918 then the 161st Infantry in the AEF 1918-1919. Commissioned in 1920. Assistant to the officer in charge of the Civilian Conservation Corps division in the office of the adjutant general, U.S. Army 1940-1941. Executive officer of the transportation branch in the office of the chief of transportation 1941-1942. Assistant chief of transportation for personnel and training 1942-1943. Commanding general of the New Orleans Port of Embarkation from September 1943.

Hoffman, Hugh French Thomason (1896-1951) Born on November 27, 1896, in Van Buren, Arkansas. Commissioned in the cavalry from West Point in 1919. Instructor there 1924-1926. Commanding officer of 5th Cavalry April 1942-August 1944. Brigadier general in August 1944. Commanding general of 2nd Brigade, 1st Cavalry Division August 1944-February 1945, then 1st Cavalry Division February-August 1945, finally 2nd Cavalry Brigade August 1945-January 1949. Chief of staff of Fourth Army when he died on April 19, 1951. Decorations included the Distinguished Service Medal, two Silver Stars, the Legion of Merit, Bronze Star and Air Medal.

Hoge, William Morris (1894-1979) Born on January 13, 1894, in Boonville, Missouri. Commissioned in the Corps of Engineers from West Point in 1916.

Served with the 1st and 7th Engineers, AEF in World War I. Instructor at VMI 1919-1921. B.S. from Massachusetts Institute of Technology in 1922. Instructor at the Engineer School, then Infantry School 1924-1931. Assistant to General MacArthur and chief engineer organizing the Corps of Engineers in the Philippine Army in 1937. District engineer in Omaha 1938-1940. Commanding officer of the Engineer Replacement Training Center at Fort Belvoir in 1941. Brigadier general in March 1942. Commanding general of Alaska military highway in 1942. Commanding general of the Armored Force 1942-1943. Commanding general of 5th and 6th Engineer Special Brigades November 1943-July 1944 then 9th Armored Division October 1944-March 1945. Major general in May 1945. Commanding general of 4th Armored Division in 1945. Assignments after the war included commanding general of U.S. Forces Trieste 1948-1951, IX Corps in the Korean War in 1951, Fourth Army then Seventh Army 1952-1953 and Commander in Chief U.S. Army Europe 1954-1955. Retired in January 1955. Decorations included two Distinguished Service Crosses, three Distinguished Service Medals, three Silver Stars, the Legion of Merit, Bronze Star, Air Medal, Commendation Ribbon and Purple Heart. Died on October 29, 1979.

Holbrook, Willard Ames Jr. (1898-1988) Born on May 31, 1898, in Fort Grant, Arizona, the son of Major General William A. Holbrook. Commissioned in the cavalry from West Point in 1918. Aide-de-camp to Brigadier General L.R. Holbrook 1926-1927 and Brigadier General Edward L. King 1927-1929. Graduated from the Command and General Staff School in 1929. Instructor at West Point 1934-1938. Graduated from the Army War College in 1940. In the intelligence division at the War Department General Staff 1940-1942. Commander of 11th Armored Division trains, then Combat Command "A," 11th Armored Division 1942-1946. Brigadier general in September 1944. Reverted to colonel in February 1946 and retired in November 1946. Brigadier general on the retired list in 1948. Decorations included two Silver Stars, the Legion of Merit and Bronze Star. Died on July 1, 1988.

Holcombe, William Henry (1891-1980) Born on September 21, 1891, in Washington, DC. Commissioned in the Corps of Engineers from West Point in 1914. Served with the AEF in World War I 1918. Graduated from the Command and General Staff School in 1936. Chief engineer in Burma 1942. Brigadier general in October 1942. Deputy commanding general of Services of Supply in China-Burma-India Theater of Operations 1942-1943. Commanding general of Army Service Forces Training Center at Camp Gordon Johnston 1944-1946. Reverted to colonel and retired in December 1946. Brigadier general on the retired list in 1948. Decorations include the Legion of Merit and Bronze Star. Died on November 6, 1980.

Holdridge, Herbert Charles (1892-1974) Born on March 6, 1892, in Wyandotte, Michigan. Commissioned in the cavalry from West Point in 1917. Instructor, then assistant professor at West Point 1918-1919 and 1925-1929. M.A. from Columbia in 1929. Transferred to the adjutant general branch in 1930. Graduated from the Command and General Staff School in 1938. Commandant of the Adjutant General School 1941-1942. Brigadier general in December 1942. Head of branch schools in the War Department 1942 until retirement in February 1944. Died on September 29, 1974.

Holland, Thomas Leroy (1879-1944) Born in Straughan, Indiana, on August 10, 1879. LL.B. from St. Lawrence University in 1906, LL.M. in 1907. Commissioned in the Quartermaster Corps, Officers Reserve Corps in 1917. Duty in Hawaii 1924-1927. Commanding officer of IV Corps Quartermaster Depot January 1940-July 1941. Commanding officer of Atlanta Quartermaster Depot 1941-1943. Retired as lieutenant colonel in June 1942, then recalled to active duty the following month. Brigadier general in March 1943. Chief of the depot operations branch, office of the quartermaster general May-October 1943. With the Atlanta Army Service Forces Depot October 1943 until retirement in December 1943. Died on August 19, 1944.

Holly, Joseph Andrew (1896-1987) Born on September 25, 1896, in Chicago, Illinois. Commissioned in the infantry from West Point in 1919. Duty in the Philippine Islands 1923-1925. Professor of military science and tactics at the University of Illinois 1925-1929. Graduated from the Command and General Staff School in 1937. Instructor at the Infantry School 1932-1936. Member of the Armored Force Board 1942-1943. Brigadier general in March 1943. Commandant of the Armored School 1943-1944. Deputy chief of staff for operations in Assembly Area Command, European Theater of Operations 1945-1946. Retired in January 1951. Decorations included the Legion of Merit and Bronze Star. Died on August 19, 1987.

Holman, Jonathan Lane (1897-1975) Born on December 6, 1897, in La Grange, Texas. Commissioned in the cavalry from West Point in 1918. Served with the field artillery in France 1919-1921. M.S. from Massachusetts Institute of Technology in 1925. Instructor at West Point 1931-1936. Graduated from the Command and General Staff School in 1937 and Army Industrial College in 1940. Chief of the planning section, office of the chief of ordnance 1940-1941. Chief ordnance officer, Services of Supply in Southwest Pacific Theater of Operations 1942-1943. Brigadier general in February 1943. Chief of staff, Services of Supply in Southwest Pacific Theater of Operations 1943-1944. Deputy to the assistant chief of staff for supply with the War Department General Staff 1945-1946. Retired as major general in June 1956. Decorations included the Distinguished Service Medal, Bronze Star and Commendation Ribbon. Died on April 3, 1975.

Holmes, Henry Benjamin Jr. (1892-1976) Born in East Lexington, Virginia, on August 8, 1892. B.S. from VMI in 1916. Commissioned in the Coast Artillery Corps in 1916. Served in Hawaii 1919-1922. Instructor at the Coast Artillery School 1923-1927. Graduated from the Command and General Staff School in 1930. Duty with 59th Coast Artillery in the Philippines 1930-1933. Graduated from the Army War College in 1936. Chief of the materiel and finance section, office of the chief of Coast Artillery Corps 1938-1940. Professor of military science and tactics at VMI 1940-1941. Brigadier general in February 1942. Commanding general of 46th Coast Artillery Brigade 1942-1943. Chief of staff of the Hawaiian Department 1943-1944. Reverted to colonel in March 1946. Retired in August 1947. Decorations included the Distinguished Service Medal, Legion of Merit and Commendation Ribbon. Died on December 19, 1976.

Holmes, Julius Cecil (1899-1968) Born in Pleasanton, Kansas, on April 24, 1899. Attended the University of Kansas 1917-1922. Commissioned in the infantry, Kansas National Guard in 1919. Served in the Foreign Service 1925-1937. Vice president of the New York World's Fair 1937-1940. Called to active duty as lieutenant colonel in February 1942. Duty with the Joint Chiefs of Staff February-September 1942. Assistant chief of staff for personnel at Allied Force Headquarters September 1942-December 1944. Brigadier general in June 1943. Released from active duty in December 1944. Decorations included the Distinguished Service Medal and Legion of Merit. Assistant secretary of state for administration and personnel December 1944-August 1945. Died on July 14, 1968.

Homer, John Louis (1888-1961) Born on September 16, 1888, in Mt. Olive, Illinois. Commissioned in the Coast Artillery Corps from West Point in 1911. Graduated from the Command and General Staff School in 1925, Army Industrial College in 1935 and the Army War College in 1939. Commanding officer of 61st Coast Artillery June 1939-April 1941. Brigadier general in April 1941. Commanding general of 40th Coast Artillery Brigade April 1941-September 1942. Major general in August 1942. Commanding general of the New York-Philadelphia Sector, then the Southeast Sector of the Eastern Defense Command 1942-1944. Commanding general of the 4th Antiaircraft Command April-December 1944. Deputy commanding general of the Panama Canal Department in 1945. Retired in September 1950. Decorations included the Distinguished Service Medal, Legion of Merit and Commendation Ribbon. Died on September 27, 1961.

Honnen, George (1897-1974) Born on November 16, 1897, in Philadelphia. Commissioned in the infantry from West Point in 1920. Graduated from the Command and General Staff School in 1938. Chief of staff of Third Army 1941-1942. Brigadier general in September 1942. Chief of staff of Sixth Army 1942-1943. Commandant of Cadets at West Point 1943-1946. Reverted to colonel in March 1946. Retired in November 1957. Decorations included two Distinguished Service Medals and the Legion of Merit. Died on January 23, 1974.

Hopping, Andrew Daniel (1894-1951) Born in Lima, Ohio, on January 3, 1894. B.A. from Butler University in 1917. Enlisted service with the Indiana National Guard in 1917. Commissioned in the infantry in 1918. Served with the 38th Division, AEF in World War I. M.B.A. from Harvard in 1935. Graduated from Army Industrial College in 1940. Duty with the supply division of the War Department General Staff 1940-1942. Staff officer with Army Service Forces 1942-1944.

Deputy quartermaster general 1944-1946. Brigadier general in June 1945. Died on January 11, 1951. Decorations included two Legions of Merit.

Horkan, George Anthony (1894-1974) Born in Augusta, Georgia, on July 1, 1894. B.A. from Georgetown University in 1915. Commissioned in the infantry in 1917. Served with 55th Infantry, AEF in the Second Army offensive in 1918. M.B.A. from Babson Institute in 1925. Graduated from Army Industrial College in 1932. Director of mobilization at the Quartermaster School 1938-1941. Instructor, then commandant of the Quartermaster School 1941-1944. Brigadier general in April 1943. Commanding general of Camp Lee 1944-1946. Assignments after the war included chief quartermaster at the U.S. European Command 1948-1951 during the Berlin Airlift and the quartermaster general, U.S. Army October 1951 until retirement as major general in January 1954. Decorations included the Distinguished Service Medal and two Commendation Ribbons. Died on November 2, 1974.

Hospital, Ralph (1891-1972) Born in Washington, DC, on January 27, 1891. B.A. from George Washington University in 1913. Commissioned in the cavalry in 1913. Served with the cavalry in World War I. Assistant Professor of military science and tactics at Cornell University 1919-1922. Graduated from the Command and General Staff School in 1917. Assistant Professor of military science and tactics at Cornell again 1927-1932. Graduated from Army Industrial College in 1933. Instructor with the New Jersey National Guard 1933-1938. Battalion commander in the 84th Field Artillery 1938-1941. Commanding general of 2nd Cavalry Division Artillery July 1941-December 1941, then 75th Field Artillery Brigade December 1941-September 1943, finally 91st Infantry Division Artillery September 1943-November 1945. Brigadier general in February 1942. Reverted to colonel in 1946. Retired as brigadier general in January 1951. Decorations included the Silver Star, Legion of Merit, Bronze Star and Commendation Ribbon. Died on December 20, 1972.

Howard, Edwin Britain (1901-1993) Born on December 26, 1901, in Harlan, Kentucky. Commissioned in the infantry from West Point in 1923. Graduated from the Command and General Staff School in 1938. Deputy chief of staff for intelligence at XI Corps, then U.S. Forces in Austria 1942-1947. Brigadier general in May 1944. Reverted to colonel in April 1946. Retired in September 1954. Decorations included the Distinguished Service Medal and Legion of Merit. Died on January 29, 1993.

Howell, George Pierce Jr. (1901-1979) Born in Maryland on November 1, 1901. Commissioned in the infantry from West Point in 1923. Duty with 31st Infantry inthe Philippines 1926-1928. Aide to Brigadier General Alfred T. Smith in the Philippines and at Fort Lewis 1935-1938. Executive officer of 501st Parachute Battalion, then commanding officer of 502nd Parachute Battalion October 1940-May 1942. At the Parachute School, Airborne Command, Fort Benning May 1942-June 1943. Brigadier general in August 1942. Commanding general of

2nd Airborne Infantry Brigade 1943-1944. Chief of the military mission to Holland at Supreme Headquaraters Allied Expeditionary Forces 1944-1945. Retired in December 1945. Decorations included the Legion of Merit and Bronze Star. Died on June 10, 1979.

Howell, Reese Maughan (1889-1967) Born on October 9, 1889, in Wellsville, Vermont. Attended the University of Vermont 1909-1911. Commissioned in the cavalry from West Point in 1915. Battery commander with 24th Field Artillery in the Philippines 1921-1923. Instructor with the Louisiana National Guard 1923-1928. Graduated from the Command and General Staff School in 1931. Professor of military science and tactics at the University of Oklahoma 1935-1939. Graduated from the Army War College in 1940. Commanding officer of 4th, then 17th Field Artillery, 13th Field Artillery Brigade 1940-1944. Brigadier general in June 1943. Assistant division commander of 82nd Airborne Division September-December 1944, then commanding general of 9th Division Artillery December 1944 until retirement as colonel in June 1946. Brigadier general on the retired list in 1948. Decorations included the Silver Star, Legion of Merit and Bronze Star. Died on March 5, 1967.

Hoyle, Rene E. DeRussy (1883-1981) Born in West Point, New York, on September 16, 1883, the son of Brigadier General Eli D. Hoyle. Commissioned in the 6th Field Artillery from West Point in 1906. Served on the Mexican border 1914-1916. Assistant commandant of the School of Fire 1918-1919. Served with the AEF in 1919. Professor of military science and tactics at Yale University 1919-1923. Graduated from the Command and General Staff School in 1924 and the Army War College in 1927. Faculty member at the Field Artillery School 1930-1935. Commanding officer of Fort Hoyle (named after his father) then 6th Field Artillery Regiment 1939-1940. Brigadier general in October 1940. Artillery commander, then commanding general of 9th Infantry Division September 1940-July 1942. Major general in February 1942. Commanding general of Field Artillery Replacement Training Center at Camp Roberts 1942-1944. Duty at headquarters of Army Ground Forces December 1944 until retirement in August 1945. Decorations included the Distinguished Service Medal and Legion of Merit. Died on November 1, 1981.

Huebner, Clarence Ralph (1888-1972) Born in Bushton, Kansas, on November 24, 1888. Graduated from Grand Island (Nebraska) Business College in 1909. Enlisted service in the 18th Infantry 1910-1916. Commissioned in the infantry in 1916. Served with the 1st Division, AEF in World War I. Wounded in the Beaumont sector in April 1918 and again during the Aisne-Marne offensive in July 1918. Instructor at the Infantry School 1920-1922. Graduated from the Command and General Staff School in 1925. Instructor again at the Infantry School 1925-1928. Graduated from the Army War College in 1929. Instructor at the Command and General Staff School 1929-1933. Member of the Infantry Board 1933-1934. Duty in the office of the chief of infantry 1934-1938. With 19th Infantry in Hawaii August 1938-July 1940. Chief of the training branch at the War Department General Staff 1940-1942. Brigadier general in February 1942. Director of training at Services of Supply 1942-1943. Major general in March 1943. Commanding general of 1st Infantry Division August 1943-December 1944. Commanding general of V Corps January-September 1945. Assignments after the war included chief of staff of U.S. forces in the European Theater of Operations 1946-1947 and Deputy Commander in Chief U.S. European Command 1947-1950. Retired in November 1950. Decorations included two Distinguished Service Crosses, three Distinguished Service Medals, the Silver Star, Legion of Merit, Bronze Star and two Purple Hearts. Died on August 23, 1972.

Hueper, Remi Paul (1886-1964) Born in Louisville, Kentucky, on November 19, 1886. Enlisted service in the Navy 1902-1903. Attended Spencerian Business School (Louisiana). Commissioned in the Quartermaster Corps in 1917. Transferred to the Finance Corps in 1920. Duty with the Philippine Department 1924-1926. Graduated from the Command and General Staff School in 1932 and the Army War College in 1936. Served in Puerto Rico 1936-1938. Assistant chief of finance, U.S. Army November 1941 until retirement in August 1946. Brigadier general in September 1942. Decorations included the Distinguished Service Medal. Died on January 17, 1964.

Hunter, George Bowditch (1879-1965) Born on September 26, 1879, in Fort Fetterman, Wyoming. Commissioned in the cavalry from West Point in 1904. Served in the Philippines with 12th Cavalry 1904-1905 and again 1909-1911. Instructor at West Point 1911-1912. Commander of the U.S. School of Military Aeronautics in the office of the chief of the Air Service in World War I. Graduated from the Command and General Staff School in 1923. Instructor at the Field Artillery School 1923-1924. Graduated from the Army War College in 1926 then instructor there 1926-1930. Director of the supply division at the Army War College 1936-1940. Executive officer at Third Military Area, New Orleans 1940-1941. Commander of New Orleans Port of Embarkation July 1941 until retirement in June 1942. Brigadier general in March 1942. Recalled to active duty July 1942-March 1944. Decorations included the Distinguished Service Medal. Died on September 11, 1965.

Hughes, Everett Strait (1885-1957) Born on October 21, 1885, in Ipswich, South Dakota. Commissioned in the field artillery from West Point in 1908. Transferred to ordnance in 1911. Duty in the Philippine Islands 1912-1915. With the Punitive Expedition into Mexico in 1916. Served in the AEF in World War I. Graduated from School of the Line in 1922 and General Staff School in 1923, then instructor there 1923-1927. Graduated from the Army War College in 1928. Chief of the equipment division in the office of the chief of ordnance April 1940-May 1942. Chief ordnance officer at Services of Supply, European Theater of Operations May 1942-February 1943. Brigadier general in September 1942. Commanding general of Communications Zone, North African Theater of Operations 1943-1944. Major general in March 1943. Special assistant to General Eisenhower at SHAEF February 1944-September 1945. Assignments after the war included chief of ordnance, U.S. Army June 1946 until retirement in October 1949. Decorations included the Distinguished Service Medal, two Legions of Merit and the Bronze Star. Died on September 5, 1957.

Hughes, John Hendricken (1876-1953) Born in New York City on February 4, 1876. Commissioned in the infantry from West Point in 1897. Wounded in action during the Spanish-American War. Served in the Philippines during the insurrection and with the Services of Supply, AEF in World War I. Graduated from the School of the Line in 1920. Instructor at General Service School 1920-1922. Chief of staff of I Corps Area 1927-1931. Brigadier general in October 1931. Commanding general of 14th Brigade 1931-1933. Assistant chief of staff for operations and training at the War Department General Staff 1933-1937. Major general in October 1936. Commanding general of the Philippine Division, then Philippine Department 1937-1940. Retired in February 1940. Recalled to active duty. Served with the Army group 1941-1943 and in the office of the secretary of war 1943-1945. Decorations included the Distinguished Service Medal, Silver Star and Purple Heart. Died on August 6, 1953.

Hull, John E. (1895-1975) Born in Greenfield, Ohio, on May 26, 1895. B.A. from Miami University of Ohio in 1917. Commissioned in the infantry in 1917. Served with the 4th Division, AEF at the Aisne-Marne, St. Mihiel and Meuse-Argonne engegements in 1918. Professor of military science and tactics at the University of Wisconsin 1924-1928. Duty with 21st Infantry in Hawaii 1928-1930. Graduated from the Command and General Staff School in 1936. Professor of military science and tactics at Louisiana State University 1936-1937. Graduated from the Army War College in 1938. Instructor at the Command and General Staff School 1938-1941. Brigadier general in July 1942. Chief of the theater group, operations division, then assistant chief of staff in the operations division, finally assistant chief of staff for plans and operations at the War Department General Staff 1942-1946. Major general in January 1944, lieutenant general in June 1945. Assignments after the war included director of the Weapons Systems Evaluation Group, office of the secretary of defense 1949-1951, deputy chief of staff for operations, U.S. Army January-August 1951, vice chief of staff, U.S. Army 1951-1953 and Commander in Chief United Nations Forces Far East October 1953 until retirement in April 1955. Decorations included four Distinguished Service Medals, the Silver Star, Legion of Merit and Purple Heart. Died on June 10, 1975.

Hume, Edgar Erskine (1889-1952) Born in Frankfort, Kentucky, on December 26, 1889. B.A. from Centre College in 1908, M.A. in 1909. M.D. from Johns Hopkins in 1913, D.M. from the University of Munich and the University of Rome in 1914. Commissioned in the Medical Corps in 1916. Graduated from Army Medical School in 1917. Served with British Expeditionary Forces in World War I. Saw action at Meuse-Argonne and St. Mihiel. Wounded at Vittorio-Veneto in 1918. M.Ph. from Harvard and Massachusetts Institute of Technology in 1921, D.T.M. from Harvard in 1922 and Ph.D. from Johns Hopkins in 1924.

Director of administration at the Medical Field Service School 1937-1942. Commanding officer of Winter General Hospital, Topeka, Kansas 1942-1943. Chief of public health in Sicily in 1943. Wounded in the Italian campaign. Chief medical officer for Allied Military Government, Fifth Army 1943-1945. Brigadier general in January 1944. Assignments after the war included chief medical officer for the military government in the U.S. Zone of Austria 1945-1947 and chief surgeon in the Far East Command 1949-1951. Retired in December 1951. Decorations included three Distinguished Service Medals, four Silver Stars, the Legion of Merit, four Bronze Stars, the Air Medal, four Commendation Ribbons and four Purple Hearts as well as decorations from 41 countries. Died on January 24, 1952.

Hurdis, Charles Everett (1893-1977) Born on October 6, 1893, in Central Falls, Rhode Island. Commissioned in the field artillery from West Point in 1917. Served with 6th Field Artillery, 1st Division, AEF in World War I. Graduated from the Command and General Staff School in 1933 and the Army War College in 1934. Brigadier general in March 1942. Commanding general of Field Artillery Replacement Training Center, Camp Roberts in 1942, then 6th Division Artillery 1942-1945. Major general in May 1945. Commanding general of 6th Division 1945-1946. Retired in November 1946. Decorations included the Distinguished Service Medal, Legion of Merit and Bronze Star. Died on November 19, 1977.

Hurley, Patrick Jay (1883-1963) Born in the Choctaw nation, Indian territory (now Oklahoma) on January 8, 1883. Commissioned in the Indian Territory cavalry in 1904. B.A. from Indian University 1905. LL.B. from National University in 1908. Practiced law in Oklahoma. Served with the First Army, AEF in World War I, taking part in the Aisne-Marne, St. Mihiel and Meuse-Argonne offensives. Assistant secretary, then secretary of war in the Hoover administration 1928-1933. Called to active duty as colonel in August 1941. Brigadier general in January 1942. Minister to New Zealand 1942-1943. Special representative of President Roosevelt to the Cairo and Teheran conferences in 1943. Major general in December 1943. Ambassador to China 1943-1945. Retired in November 1945. Decorations included two Distinguished Service Medals, the Silver Star and Distinguished Flying Cross. Died on July 30, 1963.

Hurley, Thomas Dreux (1890-1963) Born in Arkansas on February 15, 1890. M.D. from the University of Arkansas in 1911. Commissioned in the Oklahoma National Guard in 1916 and the Medical Corps, Regular Army in 1917. Graduated from Army Medical School in 1917. Served with the American Ambulance Service 1917-1918. Brigadier general in March 1945. Retired in February 1946. Decorations included the Legion of Merit and Bronze Star. Died on May 2, 1963.

Hutchings, Henry Jr. (1892-1963) Born on February 3, 1892, in Austin, Texas. Commissioned in the Corps of Engineers from West Point in 1917. Served in the AEF in World War I. B.S. from Massachusetts Institute of Technology in 1921. Professor of military science and tactics at the Colorado School of Mines 1924-1929. Graduated from the Command and General Staff School in 1937. Commanding officer of Engineer Amphibian Command at Camp Edwards in 1943. Brigadier general in January 1944. Commanding general of 4th Engineer Brigade 1944-1945. Reverted to colonel in March 1946. Retired in 1949. Decorations included the Distinguished Service Medal, Silver Star and two Legions of Merit. Died on June 26, 1963.

Hyde, James Francis Clark (1894-1944) Born in Newton Highlands, Massachusetts, on April 29, 1894. Attended Massachusetts Institute of Technology 1912-1914. B.S. from Colorado College in 1916. Commissioned in the Corps of Engineers in 1916. Served with the 113th Engineers in the AEF 1918-1919. With the 3rd Engineers in Hawaii 1921-1925. Graduated from Air Corps Tactical School in 1931. Professor of military science and tactics at Massachusetts Institute of Technology 1933-1937. Duty in the Puerto Rican Department 1939-1942. Brigadier general in September 1942. Commander of Services of Supply for U.S. Army Forces Central Africa July 1942-June 1943. At headquarters of Services of Supply June-December 1943. Commanding general of Island Service Command December 1943-August 1944. Died of a heart attack on August 7, 1944 while on leave in the United States.

Hyssong, Clyde Lloyd (1896-1975) Born in Canon City, Colorado, on April 18, 1896. Enlisted service in the Colorado National Guard 1916-1920. Served with the AEF in World War I, including the Meuse-Argonne and St. Mihiel offensives. Commissioned in the infantry in 1920. Served with 15th and 45th Infantry in the Philippines 1927-1930. Graduated from the Command and General Staff School in 1939, the instructor there until 1940. Adjutant general of GHQ U.S. Army September 1940-March 1942. Adjutant general, then assistant chief of staff for personnel at GHQ Army Ground Forces 1943-1945. Brigadier general in June 1943, major general in November 1944. Retired in July 1949. Decorations included the Distinguished Service Medal and two Legions of Merit. Died on August 12, 1975.

Ingles, Harry Clyde (1888-1976) Born on March 12, 1888, in Pleasant Hill, Nebraska. Attended the University of Nebraska 1906-1909. Commissioned in the infantry from West Point in 1914. Served with the Signal Corps in World War I. Graduated from the Command and General Staff School in 1928 and the Army War College in 1931. Brigadier general in April 1941. Chief of staff of Caribbean Defense Command March-December 1942. Major general in December 1942. Commander of Panama Mobile Force December 1942-February 1943. Deputy commander of the European Theater of Operations in 1943. Chief signal officer, U.S. Army 1943-1947. Retired in March 1947. Decorations included two Distinguished Service Medals. Died on August 14, 1976.

Irvine, Willard Wadsworth (1892-1969) Born in Warrenton, Georgia, on April 11, 1892. B.S. from Emory University in 1913. Commissioned in the Coast Artillery Corps in 1917. Served in the Canal Zone 1919-1921. Graduated from Command and General Staff School in 1928. With the 59th Coast Artillery in the

Philippines 1928-1930. Instructor at the Coast Artillery School August 1932-August 1935. Graduated from the Army War College in 1936. Instructor at the Command and General Staff School August 1938-May 1941. Duty with the war plans division, the War Department General Staff 1941-1942. Brigadier general in July 1942. Commanding general of Norfolk Antiaircraft Artillery Region July 1942-March 1944. Deputy assistant chief of staff for operations at the War Department General Staff March 1944-May 1945. Retired as major general in April 1952. Decorations included three Legions of Merit. Died on October 4, 1969.

Irving, Frederick Augustus (1894-) Born on September 3, 1894, in Taunton, Massachusetts. Commissioned in the infantry from West Point in 1917. Wounded while serving with the 15th Machine Gun Battalion, 5th Division, AEF in World War I. Served with 19th Infantry in Hawaii 1926-1930. Graduated from the Command and General Staff School in 1938. Instructor at West Point 1938-1941 then commandant of cadets January 1941-February 1942. Brigadier general in March 1942, major general in August 1942. Commanding general of 24th Infantry Division, then 38th Infantry Division 1942-1945. Assignments after the war included deputy commander of Sixth Army 1950-1951 and superintendent of West Point 1951-1954. Retired in August 1954. Decorations included three Silver Stars, two Legions of Merit, the Bronze Star and Purple Heart.

Irwin, Constant Louis (1893-1977) Born in Montpelier, Idaho, on January 2, 1893. B.A. from the University of Wyoming in 1916. Commissioned in the infantry in 1916. Served with the 16th Infantry, 1st Division in the AEF in World War I and took part in the St. Mihiel, Aisne-Marne and Meuse-Argonne campaigns. Professor of military science and tactics at the University of Wyoming 1921-1924. Instructor with the Wisconsin National Guard 1930-1934. Graduated from the Army War College in 1935 then instructor at the Command and General Staff School 1935-1939. Executive officer of 31st Infantry in the Philippines October 1939-July 1940. Operations officer on the staff of General MacArthur, then Lieutenant General Wainwright 1941-1942. Commanding officer of 31st Infantry in 1942. Escaped from Corregidor three days before it fell to the Japanese. Chief of the school branch at headquarters of Services of Supply March-September 1943. Brigadier general in October 1943. Assistant division commander of 89th Division in 1943. Commanding general of Infantry Replacement Training Center at Camp Blanding September 1943 until retirement in March 1944. Decorations included the Distinguished Service Medal, Silver Star and Purple Heart. Died on July 26, 1977.

Irwin, Stafford Le Roy (1893-1955) Born on March 23, 1893, in Fort Monroe, Virginia, the son of Major General George L. Irwin. Commissioned in the cavalry from West Point in 1915. Served with the Punitive Expedition into Mexico 1916-1917. Instructor at the School of Fire 1918-1919. Professor of military science and tactics at Yale 1919-1920. Instructor with the Oklahoma National Guard 1920-1924. Graduated from the Command and General Staff School in 1927. Instructor at the Field Artillery School 1929-1933 then with the organized reserves

1933-1936. Graduated from the Army War College in 1937. Brigadier general in March 1942. Commanding general of 9th Division Artillery 1942-1943. Major general in June 1943. Commanding general of 5th Division 1944-1945 then XII Corps April-September 1945. Assignments after the war commander of V Corps 1946-1947 and U.S. Forces Austria 1950-1952. Retired in May 1952. Decorations included the Distinguished Service Medal, Silver Star, Legion of Merit and two Bronze Stars. Died on November 23, 1955.

Jackson, Harold Rufus (1894-1987) Born on January 9, 1894, in Lebanon, Indiana. Attended the University of Illinois 1912-1913. Commissioned in the Coast Artillery Corps from West Point in 1917. Instructor at West Point 1921-1925. Graduated from the Command and General Staff School in 1934. Instructor at the Coast Artillery School 1934-1938. Director of Antiaircraft Officer Candidate School at Camp Davis 1942-1943. Brigadier general in September 1943. Commanding general of Antiaircraft Replacement Training Center at Camp Wallace in 1943. Antiaircraft officer at the European Theater of Operations 1944-1945. Reverted to colonel in February 1946. Retired in 1953. Decorations included the Bronze Star and Commendation Ribbon. Died on May 4, 1987.

Jackson, Stonewall (1891-1943) Born on March 4, 1891, in Arlington, Kentucky. B.A. from the University of Kentucky in 1914. Commissioned in the infantry, Officers Reserve Corps in 1917. Professor of military science and tactics at Cornell University 1924-1928. Instructor at the Infantry School 1928-1931. Graduated from the Command and General Staff School in 1933. Served with the 31st Infantry in the Philippines 1933-1935. Professor of military science and tactics at Georgetown University September 1937-September 1939. Graduated from the Army War College in 1940. Instructor at the Infantry School June 1940-May 1942. Brigadier general in May 1942. Commanding general of 88th Infantry 1942-1943. Major general March 1943. Commanding general of 84th Infantry February-October 1943. Died on October 13, 1943, from injuries in an airplane crash.

Jacobs, Fenton Stratton (1892-1966) Born in Gordonsville, Virginia, on April 17, 1892. Enlisted service with the Virginia National Guard 1916-1917. Commissioned in the cavalry in 1917. Aide to Brigadier General Charles H. Gerhardt in the AEF 1917-1918. Assistant professor of military science and tactics at the University of Arizona 1923-1926. Graduated from the Command and General Staff School in 1935. Instructor at the Cavalry School 1935-1937. Assistant intelligence and operations officer in the office of the chief of cavalry July 1940-July 1942. Chief of staff of 91st Infantry Division 1942-1943. Chief of the equipment branch, then chief of staff of Western Base Section in the European Theater of Operations 1943-1944. Brigadier general in November 1944. Commanding general of the Channel Base Section in the European Theater of Operations 1944-1945. Retired in April 1952. Decorations included the Distinguished Service Medal, three Legions of Merit and the Bronze Star. Died on June 20, 1966.

Jarman, Sanderford (1884-1954) Born in Boatner, Louisiana, on November 24, 1884. Attended Louisiana State University 1901-1904. Commissioned in the Coast Artillert Corps from West Point in 1908. Served with the Coast Artillery in World War I. With the War Department General Staff 1934-1938. Commanding officer of 64th Coast Artillery in Hawaii, then Coast Artillery and Antiaircraft Command at Panama, Canal Zone 1939-1941. Brigadier general in February 1939 and major general in October 1940. Commanding general of Camp Stewart in 1941. Commanding general of Antiaircraft Command, Eastern Defense Command December 1941-1944. Governor general of Saipan 1944-1945. Retired in February 1946. Decorations included the Distinguished Service Medal and Legion of Merit. Died on October 15, 1954.

Jay, Henry Davis (1891-1979) Born in Fallbrook, California, on March 17, 1891. M.E. from Lehigh University in 1915. Served with the Ohio National Guard 1916-1917. Commissioned in the cavalry in 1917. Served in the AEF 1918-1919. Graduated from the Command and General Staff School in 1932 and the Army War College in 1936. Duty with 11th Field Artillery in Hawaii 1936-1939. Professor of military science and tactics at Harvard 1939-1941. Chief of staff of IV Corps 1942-1943. Commanding officer of 36th Field Artillery 1943-1944. Brigadier general in September 1944. Commanding general of II Corps Artillery 1944-1945. Retired in October 1948. Decorations included the Legion of Merit. Died on June 27, 1979.

Jaynes, Lawrence C. (1891-1977) Born in Coalton, Ohio, on August 10, 1891. Commissioned in the ordnance, Officers Reserve Corps in 1918. Transferred to the Tank Corps and then the infantry in 1920. Saw action at Meuse-Argonne with the AEF in World War I. Graduated from the Command and General Staff School in 1935 and the Army War College in 1939. Brigadier general in September 1942. Commanding general of Combat Command "A," 13th Armored Division 1942-1944. Commanding general of Replacement and Training Command Mediterranean Theater of Operations 1944-1945, then inspector general in 1945. Major general in June 1945. Deputy commander of the Mediterranean Theater of Operations 1945-1946, then chief of staff 1946-1947, and commanding general in 1947. Commanding general of the New York-New Jersey-Delaware Military District December 1947-March 1950. Special assistant to the chief of staff, U.S. Army March 1950-1953. Retired in July 1953. Decorations included the Distinguished Service Medal, two Legions of Merit, the Bronze Star and Commendation Ribbon. Died on June 20, 1977.

Jeffe, Ephraim Franklin (1897-1986) Born in St. Louis, Missouri, on February 22, 1897. E.E. from Polytechnic Institute of Brooklyn in 1916. Commissioned in the Signal Corps in 1917. Served with 403rd Telegraph Battery in the AEF 1918-1919. Discharged in 1920. With Consolidated Edison 1932-1942. Commissioned major when ordered to active duty in May 1942. Duty in the civilian personnel bureau, office of the chief signal officer in 1942 then at Philadelphia Signal Depot December 1942-February 1943. Executive officer to the vice chairman of the War

Production Board 1943-1944. Brigadier general in June 1944. Duty at headquarters of Army Service Forces 1944-1945. Died on November 29, 1986.

Jenkins, Reuben Ellis (1896-1975) Born in Cartersville, Georgia, on February 14, 1896. Commissioned in the infantry in 1918. Served with the AEF in World War I and saw action at Argonne Forest. Served in China with the 15th Infantry 1928-1931. Graduated from the Command and General Staff School in 1936 and the Army War College in 1938. Instructor at the Command and General Staff School 1938-1941. With the personnel division of the War Department General Staff September 1941-August 1943. Duty with Allied Force Headquarters in North Africa in 1943. Assistant chief of staff for operations at Sixth Army Group 1944-1945. Brigadier general in May 1944. With Army Ground Forces 1945-1946 then the War Department General Staff in 1946. President of the Army Ground Forces Board November 1946-April 1948. Assistant director, then director of the Joint U.S. Military Advancement and Planning Group in Athens 1948-1951. Assistant chief of staff for operations, Army General Staff 1951-1952. Major general in May 1952. Commanding general of IX Corps in the Korean War August 1952-August 1953. Lieutenant general in March 1953. Commanding general of X Corps in the Korean War August-October 1953. Retired in February 1954. Decorations included the Distinguished Service Cross, three Distinguished Service Medals, the Legion of Merit and Commendation Ribbon. Died on July 29, 1975.

Johns, Dwight Frederick (1894-1977) Born on May 16, 1894, in Rockford, Illinois. Commissioned in the Corps of Engineers from West Point in 1916. With the Punitive Expedition into Mexico 1916-1917. B.S. from Massachusetts Institute of Technology in 1922. Graduated from the Command and General Staff School in 1933 and the Army War College in 1938. Commanding officer of 21st Engineer Regiment 1940-1942. Brigadier general in February 1942. Chief of staff of Services of Supply in the Southwest Pacific Theater of Operations 1942-1943. Commanding general of Service Command in New Guinea 1943. Commandant of the Engineer School 1944-1945. Assistant chief of engineers 1945-1946. Reverted to colonel in March 1946 and retired in 1949. Decorations included the Distinguished Service Medal and Legion of Merit. Died on November 8, 1977.

Johnson, Bernhard Alfred (1898-) Born in Chicago, Illinois, on April 25, 1898. Commissioned in the infantry, Officers Reserve Corps in 1922. B.A. from Luther College in 1919. In the banking industry 1919-1933. Served with the Civilian Conservation Corps 1933-1940. Called to active duty in December 1940 and transferred to the Quartermaster Corps in July 1941. Assistant quartermaster in the Western Defense Command 1941-1942. Executive officer to the director of ports at the Port of Embarkation at New Orleans, then Camp Stoneman in 1942. Commanding officer of 9th Port, then executive officer of Gulf District, Persian Gulf Service 1942-1945. Brigadier general in January 1945. Served with Army-Navy Liquidation Commission January-August 1945. Commanding general of 9th

Port, Army Service Forces Training Center from August 1945. Decorations included two Legions of Merit.

Johnson, James Harve (1887-1964) Born in Kentucky on May 12, 1887. Commissioned in the Coast Artillery Corps from West Point in 1912. Graduated from Command and General Staff School in 1928, the Chemical Warfare School in 1929 and the Army Industrial College in 1935. Instructor at West Point 1941-1944. Brigadier general in January 1945. Commander of Army Service Forces Training Center at Camp Lee 1945-1946. Retired as colonel in 1946. Brigadier general on the retired list in 1948. Decoration included the Legion of Merit. Died on January 23, 1964.

Johnson, Neal Creighton (1892-1979) Born in Los Angeles, California, on January 17, 1892. Enlisted service with the California National Guard 1913-1917. Served on the Mexican border in 1916. Commissioned in the infantry in 1917. With 8th Infantry in Germany 1919-1923. Graduated from the Command and General Staff School in 1930. Instructor at the Infantry School 1930-1934. Duty in Hawaii with the 35th Infantry then the Hawaiian Department 1934-1937. Instructor at the Cavalry School 1939-1942. Brigadier general in October 1942. Assistant division commander of 42nd Infantry Division 1944-1945. Commanding general of Infantry Advanced Replacement Training Center at Camp Shelby February-June 1945, then commanding general of Infantry Replacement Training Center at Camp Roberts June 1945-April 1946. Reverted to colonel in April 1946. Retired in January 1952. Decorations included the Legion of Merit, Bronze Star and Commendation Ribbon. Died on February 12, 1979.

Johnson, Robert Wood (1893-1968) Born in New Brunswick, New Jersey, on April 4, 1893. Entered Johnson & Johnson, the family business founded by his father and uncle, in 1910. Chief executive officer, except for a brief period of active duty, 1932-1963. Commissioned in the ordnance department in May 1942 and promoted to colonel later that month. Chief of the New York Ordnance District 1942-1943. Brigadier general in May 1943. Vice chairman of the War Production Board until the end of the war, when he returned to civilian status. Died on January 30, 1968.

Johnston, Paul William (1892-n/a) Born in Transfer, Pennsylvania, on July 5, 1892. B.A. from Allegheny College in 1914. Graduate student at Boston University 1916-1917. Executive with Erie Railroad 1918-1942. Commissioned colonel, U.S. Army in 1942. Sent to Australia to conduct surveys of railroads and other transportation systems in that country. Brigadier general in September 1944. Chairman of the General Purchasing Board until the end of the war, when he returned to Erie Railroad. Vice president 1945-1949, president 1949-1956 and chairman 1956-1960. Decorations included the Distinguished Service Medal.

Jones, Alan Walter (1894-1969) Born on October 6, 1894, in Goldendale, Washington. Attended the University of Washington 1914-1917. Commissioned in the infantry in 1917. Duty with 45th Infantry in the Philippine Islands 1922-1923. Instructor at the Infantry School 1924-1929. Graduated from the Command and General Staff School in 1936 and the Army War College in 1938. With 19th Infantry in Hawaii 1938-1941. In the operations and training division of the War Department General Staff June 1941-March 1942. Assistant division commander of 90th Infantry Division March 1942-February 1943. Brigadier general in June 1942. Commanding general of 106th Infantry Division February 1943-July 1945. Major general in March 1943. Hospitalized from wounds in July 1945 and retired as lieutenant colonel in October 1945. Major general on the retired list in 1948. Decorations included the Purple Heart. Died on January 22, 1969.

Jones, Albert Monmouth (1890-1967) Born in Quincy, Massachusetts, on July 20, 1890. Attended Massachusetts Institute of Technology 1909-1911. Commissioned in the infantry in 1911. Duty in the Panama Canal Zone 1912-1915 and Mexico in 1916. Professor of military science and tactics at Oregon Agricultural College in 1920. Graduated from the Command and General Staff School in 1924 and the Army War College in 1932. Senior instructor to the Massachusetts National Guard 1936-1940. Commanding officer of 31st U.S. Infantry in the Philippines 1940-1941. Brigadier general in December 1941. Major general in March 1942. Commanding general of 51st Division, Philippine Army then I Philippine Corps during the battles for South Luzon and Bataan 1941-1942. Taken brisonor after the fall of Corregidor and participated in the Bataan death march. Prisoner of war until liberated by the Russians in 1945. Commanding general of Camp Beale in 1946. Chief of the U.S. military assistance group to the Philippines 1946-1949. President of the Army Personnel Board, office of the secretary of the army 1949-1951. Retired in July 1952. Decorations included the Distinguished Service Cross, Distinguished Service Medal, two Silver Stars, the Legion of Merit, two Bronze Stars and the Commendation Ribbon. Died on May 12, 1967.

Jones, Henry Lawrence Cullem (1887-1969) Born in Brokenbow, Nebraska, on August 20, 1887. B.S. from the University of Nevada in 1906. Commissioned in the cavalry in 1911. Served with the field artillery at Fort Sill in World War I. Graduated from the Command and General Staff School in 1924 and the Army War College in 1931. Instructor at the Command and General Staff School 1933-1937. Director of the gunnery department at the Field Artillery School 1939-1941. Brigadier general in July 1941, major general in May 1942. Commanding general of 38th Infantry Division 1942-1945. Retired in February 1946. Died on January 22, 1969.

Jones, Lloyd E. (1889-1958) Born in Columbia, Missouri, on June 17, 1889. Attended the University of Missouri 1909-1911. Commissioned in the field artillery in 1911. Regimental executive officer with the 5th Field Artillery, AEF in World War I. Graduated from the Command and General Staff School in 1924 and the Army War College in 1930. Faculty member at the Field Artillery School 1935-1938. Professor of military science and tactics at the University of Missouri 1939-1940. Chief of staff of I Corps 1940-1941. Brigadier general in May 1941.

Commanding general of 76th Field Artillery Brigade 1941-1942. Commanding
general of Cold Bay, Aleutian Islands 1942-1943. Major general in September
1943. Commanding general of 10th Mountain Division in 1943. With Army
Ground Forces 1944-1946. Retired in April 1946. Decorations included the Distinguished Service Medal. Died on January 3, 1958.

Jones, Thomas H. (1885-1947) Born on October 29, 1885, in Norcross, Georgia. Commissioned from Annapolis in 1909. Resigned to accept appointment in
the Coast Artillery Corps, U.S. Army in 1910. Duty at Fort Mills, Philippine Islands 1913-1915. Attached to Seventh French Army, then 59th Artillery, AEF
1917-1919 at the St. Mihiel and Meuse-Argonne offensives. Instructor with the
New York National Guard 1921-1924. Graduated from the Command and General Staff School in 1926. Instructor at the Coast Artillery School 1926-1930.
Graduated from the Army War College in 1931. Battery commander with 91st
Coast Artillery at Fort Mills, Philippine Islands 1931-1934. Professor of military
science and tactics at Georgia Institute of Technology 1934-1939. Commander of
harbor defenses at Fort Wright, New York, Long Island Sound, and Portland,
Maine, October 1939-July 1944. Brigadier general in July 1941. Commanding
general of U.S. Army Forces Bermuda 1944-1946. Retired in November 1946.
Died on June 4, 1947.

Joyce, Kenyon Ashe (1879-1960) Born in New York City on November 3,
1879. Served in the Spanish-American War in 1898 and the Philippine Insurrection 1900-1901. Commissioned in the cavalry in 1901. Fought in Montana in operations against Ute Indians in 1906. Chief of staff of the 87th, then the 83rd Division, AEF in World War I, seeing action in the Meuse-Argonne offensive. Military attache in London 1924-1927. Brigadier general in November 1936. Commander of 1st Cavalry Division 1938-1940. Major general in November 1939.
Commanding general of IX Corps 1941-1942 then 9th Service Command in 1943.
President of the Allied Control Commission for Italy until retirement in November
1943. Decorations included two Distinguished Service Medals and the Purple
Heart. Died on January 11, 1960.

Kabrich, William Camillus (1895-1947) Born in Pocahontas, Virginia, on September 19, 1895. B.S. from Virginia Polytechnic Institute in 1917. Commissioned
in the Coast Artillery Corps in 1917. Transferred to the Chemical Warfare Service
in 1929. M.S. from Massachusetts Institute of Technology in 1933. In the office
of the chief of the Chemical Warfare Service, then commanding general of
Chemical Warfare Service Technical Command 1942-1945. Brigadier general in
December 1942. Commanding general of Pine Bluff Arsenal 1945-1947. Died
while on active duty on January 27, 1947. Decorations included the Commendation Ribbon.

Kane, Paul Vincent (1892-1959) Born on July 19, 1892, in Worcester, Massa-
chusetts. Commissioned in the Coast Artillery Corps from West Point in 1916.
Battery and battalion commander in the AEF in World War I. Aide to Brigadier
General Grote Hutcheson 1919-1920. Instructor at West Point 1920-1924 and

again 1931-1936. Graduated from the Army War College in 1937. Professor of military science and tactics at the University of Oklahoma 1939-1941. Brigadier general in June 1942. Assistant division commander of 96th Infantry Division 1942-1944. Commanding general of III Corps 1944-1946. Reverted to colonel in March 1946. Retired in 1949. Decorations included the Distinguished Service Medal, Silver Star, Legion of Merit, Bronze Star and Commendation Ribbon. Died on July 1, 1959.

Karlstad, Charles Herbert (1894-1960) Born in Castlewood, South Dakota, on January 26, 1894. Commissioned in the infantry, Officers Reserve Corps in 1917. B.S. from South Dakota State College in 1917. Commanding officer of 338th Machine Gun Battalion in World War I. Instructor at the Infantry School 1922-1926. Duty with 45th Infantry in the Philippines 1927-1929. Graduated from the Command and General Staff School in 1933 and the Army War College in 1936. Instructor at the Command and General Staff School 1938-1940. Head of mobilization section at the War Department General Staff 1940-1942. Commanding officer of 62nd Armored Infantry 1942-1943 then headquarters combat command at 14th Armored Division 1943-1944. Chief of staff of XXII Corps 1944-1945. Brigadier general in March 1945. Commander of 4th Service Command Recreation Center in 1945. Retired in July 1953. Decorations included the Silver Star, Legion of Merit and Bronze Star. Died on December 22, 1960.

Kasten, William Henry (1891-1963) Born in Schenectady, New York, on July 15, 1891. B.S. from the University of Illinois in 1916. Commissioned in the field artillery, Illinois National Guard in 1916. Duty with 12th Cavalry in the Panama Canal Zone 1920-1921. Graduated from the Command and General Staff School in 1929. Quartermaster at the Hawaiian Division then assistant to the commander of the Hawaii Quartermaster Depot 1931-1933. Graduated from Army Industrial College in 1938. Finance officer in the Puerto Rico Department 1939-1941. Staff finance officer with Army Air Force Combat Command 1941-1942. Air finance officer, then deputy for air finance, finally budget and fiscal officer at headquarters AAF April 1942-July 1945. Appointed chief of finance, U.S. Army, as major general, in July 1945. Retired from that position in January 1949. Decorations included the Distinguished Service Medal and two Commendation Ribbons. Died on December 19, 1963.

Kean, William Benjamin (1897-1981) Born on July 9, 1897, in Buffalo, New York. Commissioned in the infantry from West Point in 1918. Served with the 43rd and 45th Infantry in the Philippines 1921-1923. Professor of military science and tactics at Punahou Academy, Hawaii 1931-1935. Graduated from the Command and General Staff School in 1939. Served in the office of the chief of infantry 1939-1942. Duty with the Replacement School Command March-September 1942. Chief of staff for the 28th Infantry Division Brigadier general in April 1943. Chief of staff of II Corps 1943. Chief of staff of First Army 1943-1947. Assignments after the war included commanding general of 5th Division 1947-1948 and 25th Division 1948-1951 in the Korean War, commanding general of III Corps

1951-1952 and commanding general of Fifth Army 1952-1954. Retired as lieutenant general in September 1954. Decorations included three Distinguished Service Medals, the Silver Star, two Legions of Merit, the Distinguished Flying Cross, Bronze Star and four Air Medals. Died on March 10, 1981.

Keating, Frank Augustus (1895-1973) Born in New York City on February 4, 1895. Commissioned in the infantry, New Jersey National Guard in 1917. Instructor with the Ohio National Guard 1922-1924. Duty in the Philippines 1925-1926 and with the Hawaiian Division 1930-1933. Executive officer, then commanding officer of 15th Infantry 1939-1941. Chief of staff of 2nd Division 1941-1942. Brigadier general in July 1942. Commanding general of Amphibious Training Center at Camp Edwards 1942-1943. Commanding general of 102nd Infantry Division 1944-1945. Major general in January 1945. Retired in August 1950. Decorations included two Distinguished Service Medals, two Legions of Merit, the Bronze Star and Commendation Ribbon. Died on April 28, 1973.

Keerans, Charles Leslie Jr. (1899-1943) Born on Januaury 14, 1899, in Charlotte, North Carolina. Attended North Carolina College of Engineering and VMI. Commissioned in the infantry from West Point in 1920. Graduated from the Command and General Staff School in 1938. Instructor at the 24th Infantry 1938-1941. Supply officer for Headquarters Company, Airborne Command at Fort Bragg 1941-1942. Chief of staff of 101st Airborne Division 1942-1943. Brigadier general in February 1943. Assistant division commander of 82nd Airborne Division January 1943 until July 11, 1943, when he was killed on an air mission over Sicily. Decorations included the Purple Heart.

Keliher, John (1891-1964) Born on March 19, 1891, in Boston, Massachusetts. Commissioned in the infantry from West Point in 1915. Served on the Mexican border 1916-1919. Professor of military science and tactics at the University of Wisconsin 1919-1920. With 8th Field Artillery in Hawaii 1921-1925. Professor of military science and tactics at Stanford University 1925-1928. Graduated from the Command and General Staff School in 1932. Executive officer of 8th Field Artillery in Hawaii 1932-1935. Commanding officer of 8th Field Artillery in Hawaii 1940-1941. Deputy chief of staff for operations at headquarters of U.S. Army Forces Mid Pacific 1942-1944. Deputy chief of staff for civil affairs at headquarters of U.S. Army Forces Pacific Ocean Area 1944-1945. Brigadier general in January 1945. Retired in December 1950. Decorations included the Distinguished Service Medal, Legion of Merit and Commendation Ribbon. Died on June 8, 1964.

Kells, Clarence Howard (1892-1954) Born on October 9, 1892, in Kennockee, Michigan. Commissioned in the infantry in 1917. Served with 7th Division in the AEF 1918-1919. Instructor with the Ohio National Guard 1925-1930 and 8th Infantry in 1933. Graduated from the Command and General Staff School in 1936. Adjutant at Hawaiian quartermaster department 1937-1939. Instructor at the Quartermaster School 1939-1940. With the water transportation branch in the office of the quartermaster general 1940-1942. Duty at Boston Port of Embarkation October 1942-June 1944. Brigadier general in February 1943. Commanding general of San Francisco Port of Embarkation 1944-1945 then New York Port of Embarkation 1945-1946. Major general in January 1945. Retired in August 1946. Decorations included the Distinguished Service Medal. Died on March 24, 1954.

Kelly, Paul Boyle (1896-1971) Born on January 24, 1896, in Washington, DC. Attended Baltimore Polytechnic Institute 1911-1915. Enlisted in the Maryland National Guard in 1913 and served on the Mexican border 1916-1917. Commissioned in the Coast Artillery Corps from West Point in 1918. Aide to Major General William Lassiter in the Panama Canal Department 1924-1926 then Brigadier General R.E. Callan 1927-1928. Served in Hawaii 1929-1932. Graduated from the Command and General Staff School in 1937. Aide to Brigadier General Philip B. Peyton at Fort Sheridan, with 21st Infantry Brigade in Hawaii, and at the Army War College 1937-1940. Brigadier general in June 1943. Staff officer with 8th Infantry Division 1940-1942. Commanding officer of 1st Antiaircraft Group 1942-1943. Commander of 56th Antiaircraft Artillery Brigade 1943-1944. Antiaircraft officer for Seventh Army 1944-1945 then Army Ground Forces 1945-1946. Retired in May 1951. Decorations included two Legions of Merit and the Bronze Star. Died on October 9, 1971.

Kelser, Raymond Alexander (1892-1952) Born in Washington, DC, on December 2, 1892. D.V.M. from George Washington University in 1914. Commissioned in the Veterinary Corps in 1918. Chief of the veterinary laboratory at Letterman General Hospital in 1918. M.A. from American University in 1922, Ph.D. in 1923. Instructor at Army Medical School 1928-1933. Resident fellow in bacteriology at Harvard Medical School 1933-1935. Director of the veterinary division in the office of the surgeon general 1938 until retirement in 1946. Brigadier general in March 1942. Died on April 16, 1952.

Kendall, Paul Wilkins (1898-1983) Born on July 17, 1898, in Baldwin, Kansas. Commissioned in the infantry from West Point in 1918. Served with the 27th Infantry Regiment in Siberia 1919-1920. Instructor at West Point 1924-1929. Professor of military science and tactics at Western Military and Naval Academy 1929-1934. Graduated from the Command and General Staff School in 1936. In China with the 15th Infantry 1936-1938. Chief of staff of 85th Division 1942-1943. Brigadier general in March 1943. Assistant division commander, then commanding general of 88th Division 1943-1945. Major general in January 1945. Assignments after the war included commanding general of 2nd Infantry Division 1946-1948, deputy commanding general of U.S. Forces Austria 1948-1950. Inspector of infantry at headquarters of Army Field Forces in 1951. Lieutenant general in September 1952. Commanding general of I Corps in the Korean War 1952-1953. Deputy commanding general of Army Forces Far East 1953-1954. Commanding general of Allied Land Forces in Southeastern Europe 1954-1955. Commanding general of Sixth Army July 1955 until retirement in September 1957. Decorations included the Distinguished Service Cross, two Distinguished

Service Medals, three Silver Stars, the Legion of Merit, Bronze Star and Purple Heart. Died on October 3, 1983.

Kennedy, John Thomas (1885-1969) Born in Hendersonville, South Carolina, on July 22, 1885. Commissioned in the cavalry from West Point in 1908. Awarded the Medal of Honor for heroism on Patian Island on July 4, 1909, during the Moro insurrection in the Philippines. Served at Vera Cruz in 1914 and with the Punitive Expedition into Mexico in 1916. With 5th Field Artillery, AEF 1917-1918 at St. Mihiel and Meuse-Argonne offensives. Instructor at the Field Artillery School 1919-1922, the Cavalry School 1922-1923 and again at the Field Artillery School in 1923. Graduated from the Command and General Staff School in 1924. Professor of military science and tactics at Alabama Polytechnic Institute 1926-1931. Graduated from the Army War College in 1932. Duty in the operations branch of the War Department General Staff 1932-1936. With I Corps 1941-1942. Brigadier general in May 1942. Commanding general of Fort Bragg 1942-1945. Retired in February 1946. Decorations included the MH, Distinguished Service Medal, Silver Star and Purple Heart. Died on September 26, 1969.

Kenner, Albert Walton (1889-1959) Born in Holyoke, Massachusetts, on December 15, 1889. Ph.D. from George Washington University in 1910 and M.D. in 1915. Commissioned in the Medical Reserve Corps in 1916. Transferred to the Regular Army in 1917 and graduated from the Army Medical School. Served as surgeon with 26th Infantry, 1st Infantry Division, AEF in World War I. Instructor at West Point 1920-1922. Post surgeon at Fort Myer 1937-1941. Surgeon for the Armored Force 1941-1942. Chief surgeon for the Western Task Force in North Africa in 1942. With the Army Group, U.S. Army 1942-1943. Brigadier general in December 1942. Major general in September 1943. Chief training and inspection officer in the office of the surgeon general 1943-1949. Retired in June 1949. Decorations included the Distinguished Service Cross, two Distinguished Service Medals, three Silver Stars, the Legion of Merit and Purple Heart. Died on November 12, 1959.

Kerr, Francis Rusher (1890-1975) Born on December 2, 1890, in Rhode Island. Commissioned in the infantry from West Point in 1914. Served in France during World War I. Instructor at West Point 1919-1920. Resigned in 1920. Member of the Officers Reserve Corps 1926-1940. Called to active duty in January 1940 as chief of the claims division, then the export control branch, office of the administrator of export control 1940-1942. Chief of the Army Exchange Service, War Department as brigadier general 1943-1945. Retired in 1950. Decorations included the Legion of Merit. Died on February 8, 1975.

Keyes, Geoffrey (1888-1967) Born on October 30, 1888, in Fort Bayard, New Mexico. Commissioned in the cavalry from West Point in 1913. Graduated from the Command and General Staff School in 1926 and the Ecole Superieure de Guerre in Paris in 1933. Head of the tactics department at the Cavalry School

1933-1936. Graduated from the Army War College in 1937. Executive officer of 13th Cavalry, 7th Cavalry Brigade 1938-1939. Chief of the supply and transportation branch at the War Department General Staff 1939-1940. Chief of staff of 2nd Armored Division 1940-1942. Brigadier general in January 1942. Deputy commanding general I Armored Corps 1942-1943. Major general in June 1942. Deputy commanding general of I Armored Corps in the North African Theater of Operations in 1943. Commanding general of II Corps 1943-1946. Lieutenant general in April 1945. Assignments after the war included commanding general of Third Army 1946-1947 and high commissioner for U.S. Forces in Austria 1947 until retirement in 1950. Decorations included three Distinguished Service Medals, two Silver Stars, the Legion of Merit and Bronze Star. Died on September 17, 1967.

Keyser, George Vernon (1895-1972) Born on March 22, 1895, in Black Rock, Arkansas. Attended Wabash College 1913-1915. Commissioned in the field artillery from West Point in 1918. Instructor at West Point 1924-1928 and the Field Artillery School 1931-1936. Graduated from the Command and General Staff School in 1937. Served with 24th Field Artillery in the Philippine Islands 1937-1938. Assistant to the plans and training officer for the Philippine Department 1938-1939. Instructor, then faculty member at the Field Artillery School 1939-1942. Brigadier general in October 1942. Commanding general of XI Corps Artillery 1943-1945. Retired in March 1954. Decorations included two Legions of Merit, the Bronze Star and Commendation Ribbon. Died on July 5, 1972.

Kibler, Abram Franklin (1891-1955) Born in Staunton, Virginia, on July 10, 1891. B.S. from VMI in 1912. Graduate studies at the University of Wisconsin 1914-1915. Commissioned in the field artillery in 1917. Battalion commander in World War I. Graduated from the Command and General Staff School in 1935 and the Army War College in 1938. At the War Department General Staff 1939-1942. Brigadier general in June 1942. Commanding general of 78th Division Artillery 1942-1943, then XIII Corps Artillery in 1943. Deputy chief of staff for operations at Twelfth Army Group 1943-1945. Major general in November 1944. Chief of the operations division at the General Board in the European Theater of Operations 1945-1946. Retired in June 1952. Decorations included two Distinguished Service Medals, the Legion of Merit, Bronze Star and Commendation Ribbon. Died on January 24, 1955.

Kiefer, Homer Watson (1898-1976) Born on November 20, 1898, in Attica, Ohio. Enlisted service with the Ohio National Guard 1917-1918. Commissioned in the field artillery from West Point in 1920. Instructor at Field Artillery School 1921-1923. Duty with 13th and 6th Field Artillery in Hawaii 1923-1929. Aide to Major General L.R. Holbrook at Fort Hamilton 1934-1935. Assistant professor of military science and tactics at Princeton 1939-1941. Executive officer of 11th Field Artillery then 24th Division Artillery in Hawaii 1941-1944. Artillery officer for Sixth Army June 1944-November 1945. Brigadier general in March 1945. Assignments after the war included commanding general of V Corps Artillery

March 1948-August 1950, assistant division commander of 9th Infantry Division 1951-1952 and commanding general of 9th Infantry Division 1952-1953. Retired in July 1953. Decorations included the Distinguished Service Medal, Silver Star, three Legions of Merit, the Distinguished Flying Cross and two Bronze Stars. Died on September 22, 1976.

Kilburn, Charles Solomon (1895-1978) Born on January 2, 1895, in Silver City, New Mexico. Commissioned in the cavalry from West Point in 1917. Aide-de-camp to Brigadier General Willard A. Holbrook 1917-1919, Brigadier General DeRosey C. Cabell in 1919, Major General Joseph T. Dickman in 1921, Major General John L. Hines in 1921, Brigadier General Edward N. Lewis in 1921, Major General John L. Hines at the Presidio 1926-1930 and General Malin Craig at the Presidio 1930-1931. Graduated from the Command and General Staff School in 1935 and the Army War College in 1937. Duty in the office of the chief of cavalry 1937-1941. With 1st Cavalry Division 1941-1942. Brigadier general in June 1942. Assistant division commander, then commanding general of 11th Armored Division 1942-1946. Retired as colonel in November 1946. Decorations included the Legion of Merit. Brigadier general on the retired list in 1948. Died on December 28, 1978.

Kilpatrick, John Reed (1889-1960) Born in New York City on June 15, 1889. B.A. from Yale in 1911. Enlisted service with the New York State Guard 1912-1917. Chief of the regulating office, AEF as colonel in World War I. Discharged in 1919. President of Madison Square Garden 1933-1942. Called to active duty in March 1942. Brigadier general in July 1942. Commanding general of Newport News Port of Embarkation 1942-1945. Released from active duty in October 1945. Decorations included two Distinguished Service Medals. Died on May 7, 1960.

Kimball, Allen Russell (1886-1951) Born in Oneida, New York, on June 20, 1886. Commissioned in the infantry from West Point in 1911. Served in the Philippines in 1912 and on the Mexican border in 1916. Professor of military science and tactics at Castle Heights Military Academy 1916-1917. Duty in the Panama Canal Zone 1919-1920 and again 1924-1927. Graduated from the Command and General Staff School in 1928, Army Industrial College in 1933 and the Army War College in 1934. Assistant secretary of war and member of the War Department Budget Advisory Committee September 1938-June 1940. Quartermaster at West Point 1940-1942. Brigadier general in June 1942. Commanding general of Jeffersonville Quartermaster Depot May1942-March 1944. Deputy chief quartermaster in the European Theater of Operations March-July 1944. Headquarters commandant in the European Theater of Operations 1944-1946. Retired in June 1946. Decorations included two Legions of Merit, two Bronze Stars and the Commendation Ribbon. Died on December 6, 1951.

King, Edgar (1884-1970) Born on August 1, 1884, in Van Buren, Arkansas. M.D. from the University of Arkansas in 1906. Commissioned in the Medical

Corps in 1907. Graduated from Army Medical School in 1907. Brigadier general in October 1942. Served in the office of the surgeon general as specialist in treating mental illness as related to problems of military discipline 1942-1946. Retired as colonel in January 1946. Decorations included the Distinguished Service Medal and Legion of Merit. Died on October 17, 1970.

King, Edward Postell Jr. (1884-1958) Born in Atlanta, Georgia, on July 4, 1884. B.L. from the University of Georgia in 1903. Commissioned in the 6th Field Artillery in 1908. Served with 2nd Field Artillery in the Philippines 1915-1917. Graduated from the Command and General Staff School in 1923. Instructor at the Infantry School 1923-1925. Graduated from the Army War College in 1930. Instructor at the Command and General Staff School 1930-1935. Graduated from the Naval War College in 1937. Instructor at the Army War College 1937-1940. Brigadier general in December 1940. Commander of Fort Stotsenberg, Philippine Islands 1940-1942. Major general in December 1941. Prisoner of war April 1942-August 1945. Retired in November 1946. Decorations included two Distinguished Service Medals. Died on August 31, 1958.

King, Henry Lord Page (1895-1952) Born in Macon, Georgia, on April 17, 1895. B.S. from Alabama Polytechnic Institute in 1916. Commissioned in the infantry, Officers Reserve Corps in 1917. Instructor at Signal Corps School 1925-1928. Graduated from the Command and General Staff School in 1933. In the war plans and training division, office of the chief signal officer 1933-1936. Graduated from the Army War College in 1937. Again in the office of the chief signal officer 1937-1938. Instructor at the Command and General Staff School 1940-1941. Officer in charge of military personnel division at War Department General Staff 1941-1944. Brigadier general in December 1942. Reverted to lieutenant colonel in September 1944 and retired as colonel in June 1946. Died on October 29, 1952.

Kingman, Allen Frederick (1893-1988) Born in New Bedford, Massachusetts, on December 18, 1893. Attended Massachusetts Institute of Technology 1915-1916. B.A. from Harvard in 1916. Commissioned in the infantry in 1916. Instructor at U.S. Tank School 1924-1927. Graduated from the Command and General Staff School in 1930 and the Army War College in 1934. Instructor at the Command and General Staff School 1934-1938 then inspector general 1939-1940. At the War Department General Staff 1940-1942. Commanding officer of 67th Armored Regiment Combat Command in 1942. Brigadier general in June 1942. Commanding general of 2nd Armored Division in 1943. Staff officer with Fifth Army 1943-1945. Reverted to colonel in February 1946. Retired in May 1953. Decorations included the Legion of Merit and Purple Heart. Died on August 1, 1988.

Kingman, John J. (1882-1948) Born in Omaha, Nebraska, on June 18, 1882, the son of Brigadier General Dan C. Kingman. Commissioned in the Corps of Engineers from West Point in 1904. Duty in the Philippine Islands 1907-1910. Served as chief of staff of 90th Division, AEF in World War I. Division engineer in the South Pacific 1936-1938. Brigadier general in January 1938. Assistant chief of enginners 1938-1941. Retired in November 1941. Recalled to active duty until the end of the war. Decorations included the Distinguished Service Medal and Legion of Merit. Died on July 21, 1948.

Kirk, James (1890-1972) Born on February 24, 1890, in Jacksonville, Florida. Commissioned in the Coast Artillery Corps from West Point in 1912. Graduated from Air Corps Tactical School in 1932, Army Industrial College in 1933 and the Army War College in 1934. Works manager at Watertown Arsenal 1934-1938. Officer in charge of the small arms ammunition factory at Frankford Arsenal 1938-1942. Brigadier general in July 1942. Chief of the small arms branch in the Ordnance Department 1942-1946. Retired as major general in February 1952. Decorations included the Distinguished Service Medal, Legion of Merit and Commendation Ribbon. Died on July 20, 1972.

Kirk, Norman Thomas (1888-1960) Born on January 3, 1888, in Rising Sun, Maryland. M.D. from the University of Maryland in 1910. Commissioned in the Medical Corps in 1912. Graduated from Army Medical School in 1913. Served at Vera Cruz in 1914. Chief of surgical service at Letterman General Hospital 1936-1941 and Walter Reed General Hospital 1941-1942. Commanding officer of Percy Jones General Hospital 1942-1943. Major general in June 1943. Surgeon general of the U.S. Army 1943-1947. Retired in June 1947. Decorations included the Distinguished Service Medal and Legion of Merit. Died on August 13, 1960.

Knudsen, William Signius (1879-1948) Born in Denmark on March 25, 1879. Apprenticed as a bicycle mechanic, then held a variety of positions in the United States with Ford Motor Company and Chevrolet Motor Company. Vice president, then president of General Motors 1933-1942. Appointed lieutenant general on January 28, 1942 as director of production in the office of the under secretary of war. Director of Army Air Forces Materiel and Services July 1944-May 1945. Returned to private industry June 1, 1945. Decorations included the Distinguished Service Medal. Died on April 27, 1948.

Koenig, Egmont Francis (1892-1974) Born in New York City on April 23, 1892. B.A. from Columbia University in 1912. Enlisted service as a private in the British Army 1914-1915. Commissioned in the infantry in 1916. Served with the 21st Infantry in World War I. Instructor at the Army Industrial College 1923-1924 and the Cavalry School 1928-1929. Graduated from the Command and General Staff School in 1933, then instructor there 1935-1940. Commandant of the AAF Intelligence School 1942-1944. Brigadier general in May 1944. Commander of all base sections in North Africa in 1944, then the United Kingdom, Normandy and the English Channel in 1945. Reverted to colonel in March 1946. Retired in May 1948. Decorations included the Distinguished Service Medal, two Legions of Merit and the Bronze Star. Died on March 29, 1974.

Kramer, Hans (1894-1957) Born on December 12, 1894 in Magdeburg, Germany. Attended the University of Michigan 1912-1913. Commissioned in the Corps of Engineers from West Point in 1918. M.S. from the University of Pennsylvania in 1928 and D.Eng. from the Technical University of Dresden in 1932. Brigadier general in September 1942. Chief engineer at headquarters of U.S. Army Forces Mid Pacific 1942-1944. Retired in February 1945. Decorations included the Legion of Merit. Died on February 16, 1957.

Kramer, Herman Frederick (1892-1964) Born in Lincoln, Nebraska, on November 27, 1892. B.S. from the University of Nebraska in 1914. Enlisted service in the Nebraska National Guard 1910-1917. Commissioned in the infantry in 1917. Instructor at the University of Illinois 1927-1931. Graduated from the Command and General Staff School in 1933. Instructor at the General Staff School 1933-1937. Attended the Kriegsakademie in Berlin 1937-1939. Military observer in Germany and Poland 1939-1941. Duty at the War Department General Staff 1941-1942. Brigadier general in July 1942. Assistant division commander of 104th Division 1942-1943. Major general in March 1943. Commanding general of 66th Infantry Division 1943-1945. Military governor of Koblenz, Germany in 1945. Commanding general of 97th Division 1945-1946. Retired in December 1946. Decorations included the Distinguished Service Medal, Legion of Merit and two Bronze Stars. Died on October 12, 1964.

Kroner, Hayes Adlai (1890-1975) Born in Winterville, Georgia, on October 20, 1890. B.C.E. from Georgia Institute of Technology in 1911 and M.E. in 1912. Commissioned in the infantry in 1912. Graduated from the Command and General Staff School in 1928 and the Army War College in 1933. Assistant miltary attache in London 1934-1939. Commanding officer of Fort Brody January-November 1939, then 3rd Battery, 2nd Infantry 1939-1940 and 2nd Infantry 1940-1941. Duty in the office of the inspector general, U.S. Army, then military observer in London, finally chief of the British Empire Section of the War Department General Staff in 1941. Brigadier general in May 1942. Chief of the military intelligence section at the War Department General Staff 1942-1943. Military attache in Brazil 1944-1945. Retired in January 1947. Decorations included two Legions of Merit and the Bronze Star. Died on November 27, 1975.

Krueger, Walter (1881-1967) Born on January 26, 1881, in Flatow, West Prussia. Came to the U.S. in 1889. Enlisted in the U.S. Army in 1898. Commissioned in the infantry from the ranks in 1901. Graduated from the Staff College in Fort Leavenworth in 1907. With Pershing in the punitive expedition to Mexico 1916-1917. Served as assistant chief of staff of the 26th Division, then the 84th Division, and finally chief of staff of the Tank Corps in World War I. Graduated from the Army War College in 1921, then instructor there 1921-1922. Graduated from the Naval War College in 1926, then instructor there 1928-1932. Chief of the war plans divisiion, the War Department General Staff May 1936-June 1938. Brigadier general in October 1936. Commander of 6th Infantry Brigade June 1938-February 1939. Major general in February 1939. Commanding general of 2nd Infantry Division February 1939-October 1940, then VIII Corps October 1940-May 1941. Lieutenant general in May 1941. Commanding general of Third Army May 1941-February 1943, then Sixth Army through the end of the war. General in March 1945. Retired in July 1946. Decorations included the Distinguished Service Cross, four Distinguished Service Medals and the Legion of Merit. Author of *From Down Under to Nippon: the Story of the Sixth Army in World War II* 1953. Died on August 20, 1967.

Kuldell, Rudolph Charles (1889-1973) Born on February 20, 1889, in Pittsburgh, Pennsylvania. Commissioned in the Corps of Engineers from West Point in 1912. Assistant to the chief of engineers in 1918. Resigned in 1920. With Hughes Tool Company 1920-1939. Volunteered for active duty in December 1941 and commissioned lieutenant colonel in February 1942 as assistant to the division engineer in the Southwest Division. Director of engineer support in the office of the chief of engineers 1942-1946. Brigadier general in November 1944. Assignments after the war included commanding general of 406th Engineer Special Brigade 1947 until returning to civilian status in 1949. Decorations included the Distinguished Service Medal. Died on August 30, 1973.

Kunzig, Louis A. (1882-1956) Born in Altoona, Pennsylvania, on January 6, 1882. Commissioned in the infantry from West Point in 1905. Graduated from the Command and General Staff School in 1926 and the Army War College in 1931. Duty with III Corps 1934-1937. Commanding officer of 11th Infantry 1937-1940. Professor of military science and tactics at the University of Pennsylvania in 1940. Commanding officer of the Infantry Replacement Training Center at Spartansburg, South Carolina 1940-1941 then Camp Blanding June 1941-1944. Brigadier general in May 1942. Retired in January 1944. Decorations included the Legion of Merit. Died on August 7, 1956.

Kurtz, Guy Orth (1894-1969) Born in Davis, Illinois, on February 18, 1894. B.S. from the University of Colorado in 1917. Commissioned in the field artillery in 1917. Professor of military science and tactics at Colorado Agricultural College in 1919. Duty with 11th Field Artillery in Hawaii 1923-1926. Instructor at Field Artillery School 1927-1931. Graduated from the Command and General Staff School in 1936. Professor of military science and tactics at Purdue 1936-1938. Graduated from the Army War College in 1939. In the training section, office of the chief of field artillery 1939-1941. With Army Ground Forces in 1942. Brigadier general in August 1942. Assistant division commander, then artillery commander of 88th Infantry Division August 1942-January 1945. Commanding general of Fifth Army Artillery in 1945. President of the Artillery Board August 1945-February 1946. Reverted to colonel in February 1946. Retired in July 1953. Decorations included the Silver Star, Legion of Merit, two Bronze Stars and the Air Medal. Died on October 5, 1969.

Kutschko, Emerick (1892-1969) Born on January 5, 1892, in Chicago, Illinois. Enlisted service 1914-1918, including the punitive expedition into Mexico 1916-

1917. Commissioned in the infantry in 1918. Served in the AEF during World War I and saw action at St. Mihiel and Meuse-Argonne offensives. Instructor at the Infantry School 1921-1922. Professor of military science and tactics at the University of Georgia 1923-1925. Instructor at the Tank School 1927-1928. Graduated from the Command and General Staff School in 1935. Instructor at the Infantry School 1935-1936. Graduated from the Army War College in 1937. Duty in the operations and training division of the War Department General Staff October 1939-March 1942. Executive officer, then chief of the operations division at Army Ground Forces in 1942. Commander of the 34th Armored Regiment 1942-1943. Deputy chief of staff for intelligence at IX Corps July-October 1943. Deputy director of the new developments division on the War Department Special Staff 1943-1945. Brigadier general in March 1945. Retired in August 1946. Decorations included the Distinguished Service Medal, Silver Star and Legion of Merit. Died on October 1, 1969.

Kutz, Harry Russell (1889-1976) Born in Pottstown, Pennsylvania, on January 29, 1889. Commissioned in the infantry from West Point in 1911. Served on the Mexican border 1916-1917 and with the AEF in World War I. Graduated from Army Industrial College in 1939. Brigadier general in June 1942. Chief of Military Plans and Training Service in the Ordnance Department 1942-1946. Retired in June 1946. Decorations included the Distinguished Service Medal, Legion of Merit and Purple Heart. Died on March 3, 1976.

Ladd, Jesse Amos (1887-1957) Born on September 21, 1887, in Bradner, Ohio. Commissioned in the infantry from West Point in 1911. Served with the 34th Infantry in the Punitive Expedition into Mexico 1916-1917. Instructor at the Infantry School 1921-1922 then West Point 1922-1925. Graduated from the Command and General Staff School in 1926. Instructor at the Infantry School 1926-1930. Member of the Infantry Board 1931-1935. Graduated from the Army War College in 1938. Commanding officer of 2nd Infantry and 15th Infantry then Fort Glenn, Alaska 1939-1943. Brigadier general in August 1941. Commanding general of Camp Reynold November 1943-December 1944, Indiantown Gap Military Reservation 1944-1945 and 9th Infantry Division 1945-1946. Reverted to colonel in March 1946. Retired in September 1947. Died on December 14, 1957.

Ladue, Laurence Knight (1903-1951) Born on June 14, 1903, in Missouri. Commissioned in the cavalry from West Point in 1924. Graduated from the Command and General Staff School in 1941. Deputy chief of staff for operations at Fifth Army, then chief of staff of IV Corps 1944-1945. Brigadier general in June 1945. Deputy chief of staff of U.S. forces in Austria 1946-1948. Graduated from National War College in 1948. With the Joint Chiefs of Staff 1948-1951. Deputy commanding general of X Corps in the Korean War in 1951. Killed in action in Korea on May 24, 1951. Decorations included the Distinguished Service Medal, Legion of Merit and two Bronze Stars.

Lanahan, Francis Henry (1897-1975) Born on October 28, 1897, in Trenton, New Jersey. Enlisted service in the New Jersey National Guard 1917-1920. Commissioned in the Coast Artillery Corps from West Point in 1920. Transferred to the Signal Corps in 19126. Graduated from the Command and General Staff School in 1936, then instructor there until 1940. Duty with the War Department General Staff 1940-1943. Brigadier general in September 1943. Chief signal officer for SHAEF 1943-1947. Major general in March 1945. Retired in 1955. Decorations included the Distinguished Service Medal, two Legions of Merit and the Bronze Star. Died on December 4, 1975.

Landrum, Eugene Manuel (1891-1967) Born in Pensacola, Florida, on February 6, 1891. Enlisted service in the Regular Army 1910-1916. Commissioned in the infantry in 1916. Duty in Hawaii in 1917 and the Philippines 1917-1918. Graduated from the Command and General Staff School in 1933 and the Army War College in 1936. Instructor, then executive officer at the Infantry School June 1936-March 1941. Staff officer with 3rd Infantry Division 1941-1942, then the Alaskan Defense Command June 1942-October 1943. Brigadier general in March 1942, major general in March 1943. Commanding general of 87th and 71st Infantry Divisions 1943-1944. Commanding general of Infantry Advance Replacement Training Center at Cam Maxey October 1944-March 1946. Reverted to colonel in March 1946. Retired in February 1951. Decorations included three Distinguished Service Medals. Died on July 24, 1967.

Lane, Arthur Willis (1883-1983) Born on August 22, 1883, in Gorham, North Carolina. Commissioned in the infantry from West Point in 1905. Duty in the Philippines 1908-1909 and again 1913-1916. Graduated from General Staff School in 1922, the the Naval War College in 1927 and the Army War College in 1928. Instructor at the Command and General Staff School 1929-1934. Served in the office of the chief of infantry 1934-1937. Commanding officer of the 23rd Infantry 1937-1939. Chief of staff of Fourth Army 1940-1941. Brigadier general in October 1940. Commanding general of IX Corps Area in 1941 and Camp Roberts in 1942. Chairman of the ninth section, War Department Manpower Board 1943-1945. Retired in August 1945. Decorations included the Legion of Merit. Died on February 15, 1983.

Lang, John Walton (1883-1967) Born in Pass Christian, Mississippi, on February 26, 1883. Commissioned in the 23rd Infantry from West Point in 1907. Military attache in Madrid 1917-1919. Professor of military science and tactics at Lehigh University in 1919. Instructor at the Infantry School 1924-1926. Graduated from the Command and General Staff School in 1927. Chief of public relations at the War Department 1929-1930. Graduated from the Army War College in 1931. Professor of military science and tactics at the Citadel 1931-1936. Commanding officer of 22nd Infantry 1936-1938. Faculty member at the Command and General Staff School 1938-1939. Chief of U.S. Mission to Colombia 1939-1941. Military attache in Buenos Aires 1941-1945 then Mexico City July-November 1945. Brigadier general in November 1943. Retired in February 1946. Decorations included the Legion of Merit. Author of *Manual of Military Training* (1921). Died on July 22, 1967.

Lange, Otto Frederick (1891-1965) Born on March 28, 1891, in St. Paul, Minnesota. Commissioned in the infantry from West Point in 1916. Served with the 2nd Division, AEF in World War I. Assistant professor at West Point 1921-1925. Graduated from the Command and General Staff School in 1927. Instructor at the Infantry School 1927-1931. Professor of military science and tactics at University of Florida 1931-1937. Executive officer of 11th Infantry 1937-1939. Graduated from the Army War College in 1940. Brigadier general in October 1941. Assistant division commander of 36th Division 1942-1943. Commander of Infantry Replacement Training Center units at Camp Blanding, Camp Maxey and Camp Roberts 1943-1947. Retired in 1948. Decorations included the Silver Star and Commendation Ribbon. Died on May 5, 1965.

Lanham, Charles Trueman (1902-1978) Born in Washington, DC, on September 14, 1902. Commissioned in the infantry from West Point in 1924. Duty in the Panama Canal Zone 1927-1930. Instructor at the Infantry School 1932-1934. With the National Guard Bureau 1935-1938. Graduated from the Command and General Staff School in 1939. At the training branch of the War Department 1941-1942. Head of visual aids at headquarters of Army Ground Forces in 1942. Commanding officer of 272nd Infantry, 69th Infantry Division 1943-1944, then 22nd Infantry, 4th Infantry Division 1944-1945. Brigadier general in March 1945. Assistant division commander of 104th Division in 1945. Assignments after the war included commanding general of 1st Infantry Division 1953-1954 and deputy commandant of Armed Forces Staff College July 1954 until retirement as major general in December 1954. Decorations included the Distinguished Service Cross, two Silver Stars, the Legion of Merit, Bronze Star and Purple Heart. Died on July 20, 1978.

Larkin, Thomas Bernard (1890-1968) Born on December 15, 1890, in Louisburg, Wisconsin. B.A. from Gonzaga University in 1910. Commissioned in the Corps of Engineers from West Point in 1915. With the Punitive Expedition into Mexico 1916-1917. Served with the AEF in World War I. Assistant military attache in Tokyo 1921-1923. Graduated from Army Industrial College in 1927, the Command and General Staff School in 1929, the Army War College in 1938 and the Naval War College in 1939. Officer in charge of the third locks project at the Panama Canal 1939-1942. Brigadier general in May 1942. Chief engineer, then chief of staff at Services of Supply in the Mediterranean Theater of Operations 1942-1943. Major general in April 1943. Commanding general of 2nd Service Command, Mediterranean Theater of Operations 1945-1946. Assignments after the war included the quartermaster general of the Army 1946-1949 and deputy chief of staff for logistics, U.S. Army 1949-1952. Retired in December 1952. Decorations included three Distinguished Service Medals, the Silver Star and Legion of Merit. Died on October 17, 1968.

Larned, William Edmund (1888-1965) Born in West Point, New York, on January 27, 1888. Commissioned in the infantry from West Point in 1911. Served with 5th Infantry in the Panama Canal Zone 1914-1917. Instructor at the School of Fire 1917-1918. With 8th Field Artillery Brigade in France 1918-1919. In the war plans division of the War Department General Staff 1919-1920. Brigadier general in February 1942. Commanding general of Picatinny Arsenal February-July 1942. Reverted to colonel in July 1942. Retired in February 1948. Decorations included the Legion of Merit and Commendation Ribbon. Died on June 4, 1965.

Lastayo, Edward Haviland (1897-1973) Born on October 4, 1897, in West Hoboken, New Jersey. Enlisted service in the New Jersey National Guard 1917-1918. Commissioned in the field artillery from West Point in 1920. Duty in the Philippines 1922-1924. Instructor at West Point 1925-1929. With 8th Field Artillery in Hawaii 1934-1936. Instructor with Cornell Univesity ROTC 1939-1940. Operations officer, then executive officer of 1st Division Artillery March 1941-June 1942. Chief transportation officer in Mediterranean Theater of Operations 1942-1945. Brigadier general in June 1945. Retired in August 1953. Decorations included two Distinguished Service Medals, the Legion of Merit and Commendation Ribbon. Died on December 10, 1973.

Lauer, Walter Ernst (1893-1966) Born in Brooklyn, New York, on June 20, 1893. Attended Cornell University 1915-1917. Commissioned in the infantry in 1917. Served with the AEF in World War I. Graduated from the Command and General Staff School in 1938. Served in the North African Theater of Operations 1942-1943. Brigadier general in February 1943. Assistant division commander of 93rd Infantry Division in 1943. Commanding general of 99th Infantry Division 1943-1945, 66th Infantry Division August-October 1945 and 80th Infantry Division 1945-1946. Major general in January 1944. Retired in March 1946. Decorations included the Distinguished Service Cross, two Silver Stars, the Legion of Merit, three Bronze Stars and the Purple Heart. Died on October 13, 1966.

Lawes, Herbert Joseph (1891-1964) Born in St. Paul, Minnesota, on May 2, 1891. Attended the College of St. Thomas 1907-1911. Commissioned in the infantry in 1912. Served at Vera Cruz, Mexico in 1914. Graduated from the Command and General Staff School in 1933 and the Army War College in 1934. Commanding officer of Holabird Quartermaster Depot August 1938-April 1943. Brigadier general in March 1943. Commander of Letterkenny Ordnance Depot 1943-1944. In the office of the chief of ordnance in 1944. Commanding general of Army Service Forces Technical Center at Aberdeen Proving Ground 1944-1945. Retired in August 1947. Decorations included the Legion of Merit and Commendation Ribbon. Died on November 4, 1964.

Lawrence, Thompson (1889-1973) Born in Nashville, Tennessee, on March 11, 1889. Commissioned in the infantry from West Point in 1911. Instructor at West Point 1916-1918 and 1919-1923. Graduated from the Army War College in 1933. Instructor at the Command and General Staff School 1933-1937. Instructor at the

Army War College 1939-1941. Brigadier general in October 1941. Commanding general of the Armored Force Replacement Training Center at Fort Knox 1941-1942. Major general in December 1942. Commanding general of 99th Infantry Division December 1942-August 1943. Commanding general of Infantry Replacement Training Center at Camp Roberts August 1943-August 1945. Retired in December 1945. Died in 1978.

Lawton, William Stevens (1900-1993) Born on May 16, 1900, in Newport, Rhode Island. Commissioned in the Air Corps from West Point in 1922, then transferred to the Coast Artillery Corps. Assistant deputy chief of staff for operations at the Hawaiian Department 1941-1943. Deputy chief of staff of U.S. Army Forces in the Mid Pacific 1943-1946. Brigadier general in September 1944. Assignments after the war included chief of staff of Army Field Forces 1950-1951, deputy chief of staff of Far East Command 1952-1953 and comptroller of the Army 1957-1960. Retired as lieutenant general in June 1960. Decorations included three Distinguished Service Medals, two Legions of Merit and the Bronze Star. Died on February 26, 1993.

Layman, Walter G. (1888-1944) Born on September 17, 1888, in Parkersburg, West Virginia. Attended Virginia Polytechnic Institute. Commissioned in the infantry in 1917. Served with the 329th Infantry, AEF 1918-1919. Graduated from the Command and General Staff School in 1928. Student, then instructor at the Air Corps Tactical School 1932-1934. Graduated from the Army War College in 1935. Duty in China with the 15th Infantry 1935-1938. In the office of the chief of infantry 1939-1942. Assistant chief of staff for operations, Services of Supply in the European Theater of Operations 1942-1944. Brigadier general in May 1944. Died of a heart attack in Cheltenham, England on September 24, 1944. Decorations included the Distinguished Service Medal and Legion of Merit.

Lear, Ben (1879-1966) Born in Hamilton, Ontario, on May 12, 1879. Commissioned in the 1st Colorado Infantry Volunteers in 1899 and the cavalry, Regular Army in 1901. Duty in the Philippine Islands in 1903. Participated in the Olympic Games in Stockholm June-July 1912. With the War Department General Staff in 1918. Graduated from School of the Line in 1922 and Army General Staff School in 1923. Instructor at General Service Schools 1923-1925. Graduated from the Army War College in 1926. Brigadier general in May 1936. Commanding general of 1st Cavalry Division 1936-1938. Major general in October 1938. Commanding general of the Pacific Sector of the Panama Canal Zone 1938-1940, then Second Army October 1940-April 1943. Lieutenant general in May 1943. Retired in May 1943 and immediately recalled to active duty. Member of the secretary of war's Personnel Board 1943-1944. Commanding general of Army Ground Forces July 1944-January 1945. Deputy commander of U.S. Army forces in the European Theater of Operations January-July 1945. Retired again at the end of the war. Decorations included two Distinguished Service Medals and the Silver Star. General on the retired list in July 1954. Died on November 2, 1966.

Leavey, Edmond Harrison (1894-1980) Born on July 21, 1894, in Longview, Texas. Commissioned in the Corps of Engineers from West Point in 1917. Assistant Professor of military science and tactics at Rensselaer 1922-1926. Graduated from the Command and General Staff School in 1938. With construction division, office of the quartermaster general 1940-1942. Chief of staff of U.S. Army Forces in Ireland in 1942. Commanding officer of North African Theater of Operations base section 1942-1943. Brigadier general in April 1943. Deputy chief of staff for supply at headquarters of Pacific Ocean Areas 1943-1945. Major general in February 1944. Chief of staff of U.S. Army Forces in the Western Pacific in 1945, Received the surrender of Japanese forces in the Philippines on September 3, 1945. Assignments after the war included chief of the Transportation Corps, U.S. Army 1945-1948 and comptroller of the Army 1948-1949. Retired in 1949. Recalled to active duty at SHAPE 1951-1952. Decorations included the Distinguished Service Medal and four Legions of Merit. Vice president, then president of ITT 1952-1959. Died on February 11, 1980.

Lee, John Clifford Hodges (1887-1958) Born in Junction City, Kansas, on August 1, 1887. Commissioned in the Corps of Engineers from West Point in 1909. Aide to Major General in Leonard Wood 1917-1918. Staff officer with 89th Division, AEF 1918-1919. Saw action at St. Mihiel and Meuse-Argonne offensives. Graduated from the Army War College in 1932. Instructor at Army Industrial College 1932-1933. Brigadier general in October 1940. Commander of the Fort Mason, California Port of Embarkation 1940-1941. Commanding general of 2nd Infantry Division November 1941-May 1942. Major general in February 1942. Chief of the Services of Supply in the European Theater of Operations 1942-1945, with additional responsibility as deputy commander of U.S. forces in the Theater of Operations from January 1944. Lieutenant general in February 1944. Assignments after the war included commander of U.S. forces in the Mediterranean Theater of Operations December 1945-September 1947. Retired in December 1947. Decorations included three Distinguished Service Medals, the Silver Star, Legion of Merit and Bronze Star. Died on August 30, 1958.

Lee, Raymond Eliot (1886-1958) Born in St. Louis, Missouri, on March 26, 1886. C.E. from the University of Missouri in 1909. Commissioned in the Coast Artillery Corps in 1909. Instructor at West Point 1913-1917. Served with the 15th Field Artillery, AEF in 1918. Graduated from the Command and General Staff School in 1923. Duty in the Philippines 1923-1926. Graduated from the Army War College in 1927. With the operations and training division at the War Department General Staff 1928-1932. Military attache in England 1935-1939 and again 1940-1941. Brigadier general in October 1940. Acting assistant chief of staff for intelligence at the War Department General Staff 1941-1942. Commanding general of 15th Field Artillery Brigade June 1942-April 1943. Duty with 4th Service Command in 1943. Commanding general of Field Artillery Replacement Training Center at Fort Sill 1944-1945. Retired in February 1946. Decorations included the Distinguished Service Medal. Died on April 8, 1958.

Lee, William Carey (1895-1948) Born on March 12, 1895, in Dunn, North Carolina. Attended Wake Forest College and North Carolina State College. Commissioned in the infantry reserve in 1917. Served with the 81st Division, AEF 1918-1919, seeing action at Meuse-Argonne. Professor of military science and tactics at North Carolina State College 1922-1926. Instructor at the Tank School 1931-1933. Instructor at the Infantry School 1935-1937. Graduated from the Command and General Staff School in 1938. In the training section, office of the chief of infantry 1939-1941. Duty with the Provisional Parachute Group 1941-1942. Commanding general of the Airborne Command March-August 1942. Brigadier general in April 1942, major general in August 1942. The 82nd Airborne Division was divided into two divisions on August 16, 1942, and Lee became commanding general of the new 101st Airborne Division. On February 5, 1944, while in England, he suffered a heart attack and was sent back to the U.S. and retired on April 9, 1944. The new commander, Major General Maxwell D. Taylor, told the men of the division just before D-Day to shout "Bill Lee" as they jumped from the airplane instead of the traditional "Geronimo" in his memory. Decorations included the Distinguished Service Medal. Died on June 25, 1948.

Legge, Barnwell Rhett (1891-1949) Born in Charleston, South Carolina, on July 9, 1891. B.S. from the Citadel in 1911. Commissioned in the field artillery in 1916. Served with the 26th Infantry in the AEF 1917-1918, including the Montdidier-Noyon, Aisne-Marne, St. Mihiel and Meuse-Argonne engagements. Instructor at the Infantry School 1920-1922. Graduated from Ecole Superieure de Guerre in 1925 and the Command and General Staff School in 1929. Battalion commander in the 15th Infantry, Tientsin 1933-1935. Graduated from the Army War College in 1936. Instructor at the Command and General Staff School 1936-1939. Assistant military attache in Paris, then military attache in Bern in 1939. Brigadier general in May 1942. Retired in January 1948. Decorations included the Distinguished Service Cross, Distinguished Service Medal, four Silver Stars and the Purple Heart. Died on June 7, 1949.

Lehman, Raymond Godfrey (1895-1964) Born on October 26, 1895, in Sleepy Eye, Montana. Commissioned in the infantry, Officers Reserve Corps in 1917. Instructor at the University of Nebraska ROTC 1927-1932. Graduated from the Command and General Staff School in 1934. Instructor at the Infantry School 1934-1939. Duty with 15th Infantry in Tientsin 1939-1940. Served on general staff of IX Corps October 1940-April 1942. Assistant division commander of 87th and 8th Infantry Divisions 1942-1943. Brigadier general in December 1942. Commanding general of 93rd Infantry Division May 1943 until retirement in August 1945. Major general in June 1943. Decorations included the Commendation Ribbon. Died on October 20, 1964.

Lehner, Charles Royal (1893-1979) Born in Brooklyn, New York, on October 27, 1893. Enlisted service in the field artillery 1913-1917. Served in the AEF in 1918. Commissioned in the field artillery in 1917. Instructor with the Michigan National Guard 1924-1928. Assistant professor of military science and tactics at

Colorado State College 1936-1937. Supply officer at Camp Murray, then commanding officer of 3rd Quartermaster Battalion, 3rd Infantry Division in 1941. Quartermaster at Sixth Army in the Philippines 1943-1949. Brigadier general in January 1945. Retired in March 1949. Decorations included the Distinguished Service Medal, Legion of Merit, Bronze Star and Purple Heart. Died on April 24, 1979.

Lemnitzer, Lyman Louis (1899-1988) Born on August 29, 1899, in Honesdale, Pennsylvania. Commissioned in the Coast Artillery Corps from West Point in 1920. Instructor at West Point 1926-1930 and 1934-1935. Graduated from the Command and General Staff School in 1936 and the Army War College in 1940. Duty with war plans division and the staff of Army Ground Forces May 1941-June 1942. Brigadier general in June 1942. Briefly commander of 34th Antiaircraft Brigade, then assistant chief of staff of Allied Forces in Europe under General in Eisenhower to aid in the planning of the North African invasion. Again commander of 34th February 1943-July 1943. Deputy chief of staff of Allied 15th Army Group July 1943-November 1945. Major general in November 1944. Assignments after the war included deputy commandant of National War College August 1947-October 1949. He underwent parachute training October-November 1950 then served as commanding general of 11th Airborne Division December 1950-November 1951. Commanding general of 7th Infantry Division in the Korean War November 1951-August 1952, deputy chief of staff for plans, U.S. Army August 1952-March 1955, commander-in-chief United Nations Command Korea March 1955-July 1957, vice chief of staff, U.S. Army, July 1957-July 1959, chief of staff July 1959-September 1960, chairman of the Joint Chiefs of Staff September 1960-November 1962, commander of U.S. Forces in Europe November 1962-January 1963 and Supreme Allied Commander in Europe January 1963 until retirement in July 1969. Decorations included six Distinguished Service Medals, the Silver Star and two Legions of Merit. Died on November 12, 1988.

Lentz, John M. (1896-1989) Born in Florence, Kentucky, on January 30, 1896. B.A. from Gettysburg College in 1917. Commissioned in the field artillery, Officers Reserve Corps in 1917. Served with 77th Field Artillery, AEF at the Aisne-Marne, St. Mihiel and Meuse-Argonne offensives in 1918. Instructor at the Field Artillery School 1931-1934. Graduated from the Command and General Staff School in 1936 and the Army War College in 1940. Commanding officer of 24th Field Artillery 1940-1941. Field artillery officer at GHQ U.S. Army June 1941-June 1942. Brigadier general in September 1942. Assistant chief of staff for operations at Army Ground Forces 1942-1944. Commanding general of XII and XV Corps Artillery February 1944-February 1946. Reverted to colonel in February 1946. Retired in January 1955 as major general. Decorations included two Distinguished Service Medals, the Silver Star, Legion of Merit, two Bronze Stars, two Air Medals and two Commendation Ribbons. Died on February 25, 1989.

Lenzner, Emil (1899-1980) Born on June 30, 1899, in Felytz, Germany. Enlisted service 1917-1920. Commissioned in the Signal Corps from West Point in 1924. Duty in Hawaii September 1925-September 1929. Instructor with Illinois National Guard 1933-1935. Assistant to the signal officer at Army Ground Forces October 1941-September 1942. Chief signal officer in the Western Task Force September 1942-January 1943. Chief of the plans division, signal section then chief of the communications branch at Allied Force Headquarters in London 1943-1944. Brigadier general in November 1944. Chief of the signal section at Sixth Army Group then at Army Ground Forces August 1944-June 1946. Reverted to colonel in June 1946. Retired in August 1958. Decorations included three Distinguished Service Medals, the Legion of Merit and Commendation Ribbon. Died on April 7, 1980.

Leonard, John William (1890-1974) Born on January 25, 1890, in Toldeo, Ohio. Commissioned in the infantry from West Point in 1915, where he acquired the nickname "Peewee." Served with the Punitive Expedition into Mexico in 1916 and the 6th Infantry, AEF at St. Mihiel and Meuse-Argonne in 1918. Graduated from the Command and General Staff School in 1928. Professor of military science and tactics at Pennsylvania Military College 1928-1933. Duty with 15th Infantry in China 1933-1936. Brigadier general in June 1942, major general in October 1942. Commanding general of 9th Armored Division 1942-1945. Assignments after the war included commandant of the Armor School 1946-1948, military attache in London 1948-1951 and commanding general of V Corps and XVIII Airborne Corps 1951-1952. Retired in January 1952. Decorations included the Distinguished Service Cross, Distinguished Service Medal, Silver Star, Legion of Merit, Bronze Star, Purple Heart and two Commendation Ribbons. Died on October 26, 1974.

Lerch, Archer Lynn (1894-1947) Born on January 12, 1894, in Sumner, Nebraska. B.A. from the University of California in 1917. Commissioned in the infantry in 1917. Served with the 63rd Infantry, AEF in 1918. Professor of military science and tactics at the University of California 1926-1931. Graduated from the Command and General Staff School in 1937. Professor of military science and tactics at the University of Florida 1937-1938. Commanding officer of the Provost Marshal General Training Center at Fort Oglethorpe, then Fort Custer in 1942. Brigadier general in December 1942. In the office of the provost marshal general, U.S. Army December 1942-May 1944. Major general in May 1944. Provost marshal general, U.S. Army 1944-1945. Military governor of Korea at the time of his death on September 11, 1947. Decorations included the Distinguished Service Medal and Legion of Merit.

Lester, James Allen (1891-1958) Born on October 13, 1891, in Prosperity, South Carolina. Commissioned in the field artillery from West Point in 1915. Commanded a battery and battalion in the field artillery, 4th Division, AEF at Champagne, Aisne-Marne, St. Mihiel and Meuse-Argonne campaigns. Graduated from the Command and General Staff School in 1927 and Ecole Superieure de

Guerre in 1929. Assistant military attache in Paris 1932-1936. Graduated from the Army War College in 1940. Assistant commandant of the Field Artillery School 1941-1942. Brigadier general in March 1942. Commanding general of 24th Division Artillery, then XIV Corps Artillery, finally commanding general of 24th Division 1942-1948. Major general in March 1945. Retired in January 1953. Decorations included the Distinguished Service Medal, Legion of Merit and Commendation Ribbon. Died on March 10, 1958.

Lewis, Burton Oliver (1889-1977) Born in Cleveland, Ohio, on April 1, 1889. Commissioned in the field artillery from West Point in 1910. Served in the office of the chief of ordnance for the AEF 1917-1918. Graduated from Army Industrial College in 1929 and the Army War College in 1939. In the office of the chief of ordnance, U.S. Army June 1940-May 1942. Brigadier general in October 1940. Commanding general of Boston Ordnance District May 1942-January 1944. Assistant chief of transportation January 1944 until retirement in July 1947. Decorations included the Distinguished Service Medal, Legion of Merit and Purple Heart. Died on July 9, 1977.

Lewis, Henry Balding (1889-1966) Born on May 8, 1889, in Bedloe's Island, New York. Commissioned in the infantry from West Point in 1913. Adjutant general of Western Defense Command 1940-1942. Brigadier general in June 1942. Assistant adjutant general of the Army 1942-1943. Adjutant general and assistant chief of staff of 12th Army Group 1943-1945. Administrative adviser to the administrator of veteran's affairs 1945-1946. Assistant adjutant general of the Army 1946-1949. Retired in May 1949. Major general in January 1948. Decorations included the Distinguished Service Medal, Legion of Merit and Bronze Star. Died on May 21, 1966.

Lewis, James Malcolm (1898-1954) Born on February 17, 1898, in Moundsville, West Virginia. Commissioned in the field artillery from West Point in 1920. Instructor at the University of Illinois ROTC 1926-1930. Aide to Brigadier General Andrew Moses 1930-1931. Instructor at West Point 1931-1933. Graduated from the Command and General Staff School in 1936. Member of the Field Artillery Board 1938-1942. Executive office of 83rd Division Artillery in 1942. Commanding Officer of 203rd Field Artillery 1943-1944. Brigadier general in May 1944. Commanding general of 32nd Field Artillery Brigade, then 30th Division Artillery 1944-1945. Reverted to colonel in February 1946. Brigadier general again in June 1951. Commanding general of Camp Stoneman at the time of his death on April 19, 1954. Decorations included the Legion of Merit and two Bronze Stars.

Lewis, John Earle (1887-1966) Born on April 27, 1887, in Emporia, Kansas. Commissioned in the cavalry from West Point in 1912. With the 10th Cavalry on the Mexican border December 1913-December 1914 and again during the Punitive Expedition in 1916. Instructor at the Field Artillery School 1922-1925. Graduated from the Command and General Staff School in 1926, Air Corps Tactical School in 1930, Army Industrial College in 1937 and the Army War College in 1938. Instructor, then assistant commandant and commandant of Army Industrial College 1938-1941. Brigadier general in February 1942. Commanding general of 73rd Artillery Brigade, then 30th Division Artillery 1942-1944. Artillery officer for the European Theater of Operations 1944. Member of U.S. Group Control Council in the European Theater of Operations February 1945 until retirement in November 1946. Decorations included the Legion of Merit. Died on July 5, 1966.

Lewis, John Taylor (1894-1983) Born in Rockford, Illinois, on October 23, 1894. B.S. from the University of Illinois in 1917. Commissioned in the infantry, Officers Reserve Corps, then the Coast Artillery Corps, Regular Army in 1917. Battery commander in the 69th Coast Artillery of the AEF in 1918. M.S. from Yale in 1925. Instructor at Coast Artillery School 1929-1930 then member of the Coast Artillery Board 1930-1933. Graduated from the Command and General Staff School in 1935 and the Army War College in 1938. Chief of the materiel and finance section, then the fiscal section in the office of the chief of coast artillery 1940-1941. Secretary of the the War Department General Staff 1941-1942. Brigadier general in February 1942. Commanding general of the military district of Washington May 1942-September 1944. Major general in March 1943. Commanding general of the AEF mission to France, then the French mission to U.S. forces in the European Theater of Operations 1944-1945. Retired as lieutenant general in September 1954. Decorations included three Distinguished Service Medals. Died on December 5, 1983.

Lewis, Robert Henry (1884-1965) Born in Cleveland, Ohio, on February 21, 1884. Commissioned in the artillery from West Point in 1905. Duty in the Philippines 1913-1915. Liaison officer between U.S. forces in First Army and French units in the AEF during World War I. Graduated from Ecole Superieure de Guerre in 1923 and the Command and General Staff School in 1928. Brigadier general in March 1940. Commanding general of Panama Mobile Forces 1940-1942. Major general in March 1942. Duty at Panama Canal Department March-December 1942. Commanding general of the northwestern sector of Western Defense Command 1943-1945. Retired in May 1946. Decorations included the Distinguished Service Medal and Legion of Merit. Died on October 28, 1965.

Lewis, Thomas Edward (1898-1976) Born on October 16, 1898, in Milwaukee, Wisconsin. Commissioned in the infantry from West Point in 1922. Instructor at the Field Artillery School 1934-1936. Graduated from the Command and General Staff School in 1937. Aide to the commandant of the Command and General Staff School 1939-1940. Member of the staff at the Army War College 1940-1941. Artillery officer at II Corps, then Fifth Army June 1942-January 1945. Brigadier general in June 1943. Commanding general of 88th Division Artillery 1945-1946. Reverted to colonel in June 1946. Assignments after the war included commanding general of I Corps Artillery in the Korean War 1952-1953. Retired in June

1953. Decorations included the Distinguished Service Medal, Silver Star, two Legions of Merit, the Bronze Star and two Purple Hearts. Died on June 14, 1976.

Lim, Vicente (1889-1945) Born in the Philippine Islands in 1889. Commissioned in the Philippine Scouts from West Point in 1915. Retired as lieutenant colonel in 1936. Called back to active duty as brigadier general and deputy chief of staff of the Philippine Army in 1939. In command of the 41st Division, Philippine Army on Bataan when overrun and captured by Japanese forces early in 1942. Held as a prisoner of war until released. Led a guerrilla force until captured again in 1944. Executed in Manila sometime between November 1944 and January 1945. Decorations included the Legion of Merit and the Purple Heart.

Lincoln, George Arthur (1907-1975) Born on July 20, 1907, in Harbor Beach, Michigan. Commissioned in the Corps of Engineers from West Point in 1929. Rhodes scholar 1929-1932. M.A. from Oxford. Instructor at West Point 1937-1941. Duty at headquarters of the European Theater of Operations 1942-1943. In the operations division of the War Department General Staff 1943-1947. Brigadier general in January 1945. Assignments after the war included special assistant to the secretary of the amy, then the secretary of defense 1948-1952. Professor at West Point 1947-1969. Retired in January 1969. Decorations included two Distinguished Service Medals and two Legions of Merit. Director of the office of emergency preparedness 1969-1973. Died on May 24, 1975.

Linden, Henning (1892-1984) Born on September 3, 1892, in Minneapolis, Minnesota. B.S. from the University of Minnesota. Commissioned in the infantry in 1917. Duty in the Canal Zone 1918-1921. Professor of military science and tactics at the University of Maryland 1921-1925. Graduated from the Command and General Staff School in 1936. Professor of military science and tactics at Boston University 1938-1940. With the Alaska Defense Command 1942-1944. Brigadier general in June 1943. Assistant division commander of 42nd Infantry Division 1944-1945. Reverted to colonel in March 1946. Retired in September 1952. Decorations included the Silver Star, two Legions of Merit, two Bronze Stars and two Commendation Ribbons. Died on March 15, 1984.

Lindsey, Malcolm Fraser (1891-1975) Born on July 22, 1891, in Waco, Texas. Attended the University of Texas. Commissioned in the infantry, Officers Reserve Corps in 1917. Served with 31st Infantry, AEF in Siberia 1919-1920. Instructor at the Infantry School 1922-1925. Graduated from the Command and General Staff School in 1932. Instructor at the Infantry School 1932-1934. Graduated from the Army War College in 1935 and Air Corps Tactical School in 1936. With 32nd Infantry 1940-1941 then commanding officer of Army forces in Kodiak, Alaska, and Fort Greeley 1941-1942. Liaison officer with U.S. Army forces in the China-Burma-India Theater of Operations December 1942-February 1945. Brigadier general in November 1943. Commanding general of 3rd Service Command February 1945-February 1946. Reverted to colonel in February 1946. Retired in July 1951. Decorations included two Legions of Merit and the Commendation Ribbon. Died on December 10, 1975.

Littlejohn, Robert McGowan (1890-1982) Born on October 23, 1890, in Jonesville, South Carolina. Commissioned in the cavalry from West Point in 1912. Instructor at West Point 1917-1918. Served with the AEF in World War I. Graduated from the Command and General Staff School in 1926 then instructor there until 1929. Graduated from the Army War College in 1930. Quartermaster at West Point 1934-1938. Quartermaster of the Philippine Department 1939-1940. Chief of the clothing division, office of the quartermaster general 1940-1941. Brigadier general in January 1942. Chief quartermaster in the European Theater of Operations 1942-1945. Major general in November 1943. Commanding general of American Graves Registration Command 1945-1946. Retired in July 1946. Decorations included two Distinguished Service Medals, the Legion of Merit and Bronze Star. Died on May 6, 1982.

Livesay, William G. (1895-1979) Born on March 2, 1895, in Benton, Illinois. Enlisted service in the Regular Army 1915-1916. Commissioned in the infantry in 1916. Served with the 30th Infantry in the Punitive Expedition into Mexico 1916-1917 and the 28th Infantry, then the 2nd Infantry Brigade, in the AEF in 1918, including the campaigns at Montdidier-Noyon, Aisne-Marne, St. Mihiel and Meuse-Argonne. Graduated from the Command and General Staff School in 1926. Instructor at the Infantry School 1926-1930. Graduated from the Army War College in 1933. Member of the Infantry Board 1933-1936. Operations officer with 2nd Division January-July 1941. Chief of staff of the Puerto Rican Department July 1941-March 1942. Brigadier general in April 1942. With 35th Infantry Division in 1942. Commanding general of the Puerto Rican Mobile Force August 1942-July 1943. Major general in October 1942. Commanding general of 91st Infantry Division 1943-1945. Assignments after the war included commanding general of the Armored Center and School 1948-1950. Retired in June 1950. Decorations included the Distinguished Service Medal, five Silver Stars and the Legion of Merit. Died on June 7, 1979.

Llewellyn, Fred Warde (1878-1955) Born in Hillsboro, Oregon, on May 8, 1878. Attended Pacific University 1892-1897. Commissioned in the infantry, Washington National Guard in 1903. Brigadier general in Washington National Guard January 1911-April 1914. Commissioned in the infantry, Regular Army in 1920. Graduated from the Command and General Staff School in 1926 and the Army War College in 1930. Assistant judge advocate general of the army 1941-1943. Retired in May 1942 but continued on active duty. Brigadier general in July 1942. Retired again in March 1944. Decorations included the Distinguished Service Medal and Legion of Merit. Died on August 22, 1955.

Lockwood, Benjamin Curtis Jr. (1888-1980) Born in Columbus, Ohio, on June 14, 1888. Commissioned in the infantry from West Point in 1911. Instructor there 1914-1917 then at the Infantry School 1921-1923. Graduated from the Command

and General Staff School in 1924 and the Army War College in 1931, then instructor there 1935-1939. Commander of 69th Infantry Brigade October-December 1941. Brigadier general in December 1941. Assistant division commander of 35th Infantry Division in 1942. Commanding general of bases at Tongabatu and Espiritu Santo in the South Pacific Theater of Operations 1942-1943. Commanding general of Army ground Forces Replacement Depot at Fort Ord July 1943-May 1946. Retired in March 1948. Decorations included the Distinguished Service Medal and Legion of Merit. Died on April 3, 1980.

Loome, James Thomas (1901-1979) Born on October 20, 1901, in Massachusetts. Commissioned in the field artillery from West Point in 1924. Commanding officer of 318th Field Artillery Battalion, executive officer of 81st Division Artillery and commander of 98th Division Artillery 1944-1946. Brigadier general in June 1945. Retired in December 1946. Decorations included the Legion of Merit and Bronze Star. Died on November 21, 1979.

Loomis, Harold Francis (1890-1970) Born in Rockville, Connecticut, on June 19, 1890. Commissioned in the cavalry from West Point in 1914. Instructor at the Coast Artillery School 1918-1919 and West Point 1920-1924. Graduated from the Command and General Staff School in 1928. Instructor again at the Coast Artillery School 1928-1932. Graduated from the Ecole Superieure de Guerre in 1934 and the Army War College in 1939. With the war plans division of the War Department General Staff 1939-1941. Brigadier general in October 1941. Commanding general of harbor defenses at Portland, Maine 1941-1942. Commander of the southern sector at New Orleans 1942-1943. Chairman of the joint rearmament committee, Mediterranean Theater of Operations then chief of the rearmament division at SHAEF 1943-1945. Retired in November 1946. Decorations included the Distinguished Service Medal and Legion of Merit. Died on October 21, 1970.

Loper, Herbert Bernard (1896-1989) Born on October 22, 1896, in Norcatur, Kansas. B.A. from Washburn College in 1916. Commissioned in the Corps of Engineers from West Point in 1919. B.S. from Massachusetts Institute of Technology in 1921. Instructor at the Chemical Warfare School 1930-1934. Graduated from the Command and General Staff School in 1940. Assistant chief of staff for supply, then operations at 5th Division in 1940. Assistant to the chief of the intelligence division, then chief of the intelligence division in the office of the chief of engineers 1941-1943. Engineer for U.S. Army Forces in Pacific Ocean Areas 1944-1945. Brigadier general in November 1944. Deputy chief engineer at U.S. Army Forces Pacific 1945-1946. Assignments after the war included chief of the Armed Forces Special Weapons Project 1952-1955. Retired as major general in February 1955. Decorations included the Distinguished Service Medal and two Legions of Merit. Died on August 25, 1989.

Lord, Kenneth Prince (1888-1957) Born in Rockland, Maine, on December 11, 1888, the son of Brigadier General Herbert A. Lord. Commissioned in the cavalry in 1911. Served with the 2nd Cavalry in the Punitive Expedition into Mexico in 1916. Battery commander in the 77th Field Artillery, AEF in 1918, including the Aisne-Marne, St. Mihiel and Meuse-Argonne offensives. Instructor with the Connecticut National Guard 1922-1924. B.S. from Tufts College in 1929. Graduated from the Command and General Staff School in 1930 and Army Industrial College in 1931. Assistant chief of staff of II Corps in 1940. Chief of staff of First Army 1941-1944. Brigadier general in September 1941. Chief of staff, then acting commanding general of Eastern Defense Command 1944-1946. Retired in September 1946. Decorations included the Silver Star and two Legions of Merit. Died on April 27, 1957.

Lord, Royal Bertrand (1899-1963) Born on September 19, 1899, in Worcester, Massachusetts. B.S. from Brown University in 1919. Commissioned in the Corps of Engineers from West Point in 1923. Served with 3rd Engineers in Hawaii 1923-1926. Instructor at West Point 1927-1931. Again with 3rd Engineers in 1939. Deputy director, then director of the Bureau of Public relations in the War Department in 1941. Chief of operations on the Board of Economic Warfare 1941-1942. Duty with the General Staff Corps, then chief of staff to the commanding general of Services of Supply in the European Theater of Operations in 1942. Chief of staff of the communications zone, then deputy chief of staff at headquarters of European Theater of Operations 1942-1946. Brigadier general in February 1944, major general in November 1944. Retired as major in April 1946. Major general on the retired list in 1948. Decorations included the Distinguished Service Medal, Legion of Merit and Bronze Star. Died on October 21, 1963.

Loucks, Charles Ernest (1895-1987) Born on June 29, 1895, in Mayfield, California. Commissioned in the Coast Artillery Corps, Officers Reserve Corps in 1917. B.A. from Stanford in 1921. M.S. from Massachusetts Institute of Technology in 1931. Assistant military attache in Paris, then London 1940-1941. Executive officer in the office of the chief of the Chemical Warfare Service 1941-1942. Brigadier general in December 1942. Commanding general of Rocky Mountain Arsenal 1942-1944. Chief of the industrial division, then the research and development division of the Chemical Wafare Service 1944-1948. Retired as major general in May 1955. Decorations included the Distinguished Service Medal, Legion of Merit and Commendation Ribbon. Died on December 16, 1987.

Lough, Maxon Spafford (1886-1964) Born on September 15, 1886, in Fargo, North Dakota. Commissioned in the infantry in 1911. Served with 38th Infantry, AEF in 1918, including the Champagne-Marne, Aisne-Marne and Meuse-Argonne campaigns. Graduated from the Command and General Staff School in 1924. Instructor at the Infantry School 1924-1927. Graduated from the Army War College in 1928. Member of the Infantry Board 1933-1937. Commanded the 38th Infantry August 1937-January 1939. Chief of the personnel section in the office of the chief of infantry July-October 1941. Brigadier general in September 1941. With U.S. Army Forces Far East October 1941-April 1942. Prisoner of war April 1942-August 1945. Retired in August 1946. Decorations included the Distinguished Service Cross, Distinguished Service Medal and two Purple Hearts. Died on July 13, 1964.

Loughry, Howard Kendall (1882-1965) Born on March 21, 1882, in Monticello, Indiana. Served with the 161st Indiana Volunteer Infantry in the Spanish-American War. Commissioned in the infantry from West Point in 1906. Transferred to the Coast Artillery Corps in 1907. Assistant adjutant, then adjutant, finally adjutant general in First Army, AEF 1917-1918. Participtaed in the Nolon-Montdidier, second Marne, St. Mihiel and Meuse-Argonne engagements. Instructor at the Coast Artillery School 1921-1922. Graduated from the Command and General Staff School in 1923. Instructor again at the Coast Artillery School 1923-1926. Graduated from the Army War College in 1927 and the Naval War College in 1928. In the war plans division of the War Department General Staff 1928-1932. Commanding officer of 60th Coast Artillery Regiment in the Philippine Islands 1933-1935. Chief of the budget and legislative planning branch at the War Department General Staff 1936-1940. Chief of finance, U.S. Army as major general April 1940-April 1945. Governor of the U.S. Soldier's Home April 1945 until retirement in October 1945. Decorations included the Distinguished Service Medal. Died on October 9, 1965.

Lovett, Ralph Brundidge (1890-1977) Born on October 16, 1890, in Altoona, Kansas. Attended the University of Kansas and Oklahoma Baptist College. Commissioned in the infantry, Officers Reserve Corps in 1917. Transferred to the adjutant general branch in 1935. Duty in the office of the adjutant general, U.S. Army 1938-1939. Executive officer of the public relations branch in the intelligence division of the War Department General Staff 1939-1940. With the public relations branch in the office of the deputy chief of staff, U.S. Army then the secretary of war 1940-1942. Brigadier general in August 1942. Director of operations and training in the office of the adjutant general, U.S. Army 1942-1943. Adjutant general in the European Theater of Operations 1944-1946. Retired in February 1947. Decorations included the Legion of Merit, Bronze Star and Commendation Ribbon. Died on December 4, 1977.

Lowe, Frank E. (1885-1968) Born on September 20, 1885, in Springfield, Massachusetts. B.S. from Worcester Polytechnic Institute in 1908. Commissioned in the field artillery, Officers Reserve Corps in 1917. Battery commander in the II Corps, AEF 1918-1919. Participated in the Meuse-Argonne offensive. Discharged in June 1919. Continued affiliation with the ORC, reaching colonel by 1938. Active duty in the office of the chief of staff, U.S. Army 1940-1941, then the assistant chief of staff for intelligence at the War Department General Staff 1941-1942. Brigadier general in July 1941. Special duty in the office of the chief of staff, U.S. Army with the U.S. Senate special committee investigating the national defense program, known as the Truman Committee 1942-1946. Major general in September 1943. Returned to inactive status in September 1946. Recalled to active duty by President Truman in August 1950 as his personal representative and observer in the Korean War. Retired in May 1951. Died on December 27, 1968.

Luberoff, George (1879-1961) Born on December 14, 1879, in New York City. Enlisted service during the Spanish-American War and with the infantry 1902-1917. Commissioned in the quartermaster reserve in 1917. Quartermaster for First Army Artillery, then First Army, AEF 1917-1919. Graduated from Army Industrial College in 1927. Commanding officer of Boston Quartermaster Depot 1934-1940, then Jeffersonville Quartermaster Depot June 1940-May 1942. Brigadier general in April 1941. Retired in May 1942. Returned to active duty June 1942-January 1944. Decorations included the Distinguished Service Medal and Commendation Ribbon. Died on May 28, 1961.

Lucas, John Porter (1890-1949) Born on January 14, 1890, in Kearneysville, West Virginia. Commissioned in the cavalry from West Point in 1911. Commanding officer of a machine gun troop of 13th Cavalry at Columbus, New Mexico when Villa attacked on March 9, 1916. Served with the Punitive Expedition 1916-1917. Aide-de-camp to Brigadier General George Bell, Jr., in 1917. Wounded near Amiens, France, in June 1918. Professor of military science and tactics at the University of Michigan 1919-1920. Transferred to the field artillery in 1920. Instructor at the Field Artillery School 1921-1923. Professor of military science and tactics at Colorado Agricultural College 1924-1929. In the persosnnel division of the War Department General Staff 1932-1936. Brigadier general in October 1940. Commanding general of 2nd Division Artillery 1940-1941. Major general in August 1941. Commanding general of 3rd Infantry Division 1941-1942 then III Corps April 1942-May 1943. Commanding general of VI Corps at landings in Sicily and at Anzio 1943-1944. Deputy commanding general of Fourth Army 1944-1946. Chief of the Army Advisory Group in Nanking, China at the time of his death on December 24, 1949. Decorations included three Distinguished Service Medals, the Silver Star and Purple Heart.

Lull, George Fairless (1887-1976) Born on March 10, 1887, in Scranton, Pennsylvania. M.D. from Jefferson Medical College in 1912. Commissioned in the Medical Corps in 1912. Graduated from Army Medical School in 1913. Served with base hospital number 35 in the AEF during World War I. Medical adviser to the governor general of the Philippine Islands 1930-1932. Commanding officer of 1st Medical Regiment and instructor at Medical Field Service School 1936-1940. Chief of the military personnel division in the office of the surgeon general, U.S. Army July 1940-June 1943. Brigadier general in March 1943. Deputy surgeon general June 1943-April 1946. Major general in September 1943. Retired in April 1946. Decorations included the Distinguished Service Medal, Legion of Merit and Purple Heart. Died on February 7, 1976.

Lutes, Leroy (1890-1980) Born on October 4, 1890, in Cairo, Illinois. Commissioned in the infantry, Illinois National Guard in 1914 and the Regular Army in 1917. Served with the 21st Infantry on the Mexican border 1917-1918. Duty in Panama 1921-1924. Graduated from the Command and General Staff School in 1930 and the Army War College in 1935. In the National Guard Bureau 1935-1939. Assistant chief of staff for supply with Third Army January 1940-November

1941. Brigadier general in November 1941. Commanding general of 37th Antiair-craft Artillery Brigade 1941-1942. Director of operations at Services of Supply March 1942-January 1943. Major general in October 1942. Director of plans and operations, then chief of staff, finally commanding general of Army Service Forces January 1943-June 1946. Lieutenant general in June 1945. Assignments after the war included commanding general of Fourth Army October 1949 until retirement in January 1952. Decorations included two Distinguished Service Medals, the Legion of Merit and Bronze Star. Died on January 30, 1980.

Lyman, Albert Kualli Brickwood (1885-1942) born in Homaltua, Hawaii, on May 5, 1885. Commissioned in the Corps of Engineers from West Point in 1909. Duty at Fort Shafter, Hawaii 1913-1916. Served with 60nd Engineers in France in 1918. Instructor at the Engineer School 1918-1920. Military attache in Cuba 1921-1923. Commanding officer of 14th Engineers at Fort William McKinley, Philippine Islands 1930-1932. Graduated from Army Industrial College in 1936. District engineer in Boston 1936-1940. Commanding officer of 3rd Engineers at Schofield Barracks, Hawaii July 1940-August 1942. Brigadier general on August 10, 1942. Died on August 13, 1942.

Lyman, Charles Bishop (1888-1981) Born on August 20, 1888, in Harakua, Hawaii. Commissioned in the infantry from West Point in 1913. Graduated from the Command and General Staff School in 1927 and the Army War College in 1936. Commander of Maui District 1941-1942. Commanding officer of 21st In-fantry, 24th Infantry Division 1942-1944. Brigadier general in September 1944. Assistant division commander of 32nd Division 1944-1945. Retired as colonel in March 1946. Brigadier general on the retired list 1948. Decorations included the Silver Star, two Legions of Merit and two Bronze Stars. Died on April 15, 1981.

MacArthur, Douglas (1880-1964) Born on January 26, 1880, at an Army post near Little Rock, Arkansas, the son of Captain (later lieutenant general) Arthur MacArthur. Commissioned in the Corps of Engineers from West Point in 1903. Aide to President Theodore Roosevelt 1906-1907. Chief of staff, later command-ing general, of 42nd (Rainbow) Division in World War I, attaining temporary rank of brigadier general. Superintendent of West Point 1919-1922. Brigadier general in January 1920, major general in January 1925, general in November 1930 upon appointment as chief of staff, U.S. Army. Served 1930-1935. In the Philippines 1935-1941, earning promotion to field marshal, Philippine Army in 1936. Re-signed from U.S. Army in 1937. Recalled to active duty in U.S. Army in July 1941 as lieutenant general and named commander of U.S. Army Forces in the Far East. Escaped from Corregidor in February 1942, earning the Medal of Honor. General again in December 1941. In October 1944 he fulfilled his promise "I shall return" when his forces landed in the Philippines. General of the Army in Decem-ber 1944. Commander of Far East Command 1947-1950. Named supreme com-mander, United Nations Forces Korea following the invasion of South Korea by North Korea in June 1950. Recalled by President Truman on April 11, 1951. Re-turned to the United States and gave his famous "Old soldiers never die, they just fade away". speech before a joint session of Congress. Author of *Reminiscences* (1964). Died in Washington on April 5, 1964.

MacKelvie, Jay Ward (1890-1985) Born in Esmond, South Dakota, on September 23, 1890. Enlisted service with 7th Cavalry 1913-1917. Commissioned in the cavalry in 1917. Served with 28th Field Artillery, AEF 1918-1919 including the St. Mihiel offensive. Professor of military science and tactics at Colorado Agricultural College 1926-1928. Graduated from the Command and General Staff School in 1932. Instructor at the Field Artillery School 1932-1933 and again 1933-1935. Graduated from the Army War College in 1936. In the materiel division, office of the chief of field artillery 1938-1941. Duty in the war plans division of the War Department General Staff February-April 1942. Brigadier general in March 1942. Commander of 85th Infantry Division Artillery 1942-1943 then XII Corps Artillery September 1943-January 1944. Commanding general of 90th Infantry Division January-June 1944. At headquarters of the European Theater of Operations in 1944. Commanding general of 80th Infantry Division Artillery September 1944-June 1945 then V Corps Artillery June 1945 until retirement in September 1946. Decorations included the Legion of Merit, two Bronze Stars and the Purple Heart. Died on December 5, 1985.

MacMorland, Edward Elliott (1892-n/a) Born in Kansas City, Missouri, on July 22, 1892. B.A. from the University of Missouri in 1914, M.A. in 1915. Attended Princeton 1915-1916. Commissioned in 1916. Served in the AEF in France and Germany during World War I. Graduated from Army Industrial College in 1925. Chief of the maintenance branch, office of the chief of ordnance from 1941. Brigadier general in March 1943. Served in the China Theater 1943-1945. Retired in July 1952. Decorations included two Legions of Merit, the Commendation Ribbon and Purple Heart.

MacNider, Hanford (1889-1968) Born in Mason City, Iowa, on October 2, 1889. B.A. from Harvard in 1911, M.S. from Norwich in 1926 and LL.D. from Syracuse University in 1932. Enlisted service on the Mexican border with the 2nd Infantry, Iowa National Guard 1916-1917. Commissioned in the infantry in 1917. Served with 9th Infantry, 2nd Division, AEF in World War I. Resigned in 1919. Assistant secretary of war 1925-1928. Minister to Canada 1930-1932. Active duty as assistant division commander of 32nd Division and 1st Cavalry Division, then commander of 158th Recruit Training Command January 1942-February 1946. Brigadier general in August 1942. Returned to inactive status in 1946. Decorations included three Distinguished Service Crosses, the Distinguished Service Medal, three Silver Stars, the Legion of Merit, two Bronze Stars, the Air Medal and two Purple Hearts. Died on February 17, 1968.

Macon, Robert Chauncey (1890-1980) Born in Washington, DC, on July 12, 1890. B.S. from Virginia Polytechnic Institute in 1912, M.E. in 1913. Commissioned in the infantry in 1916. Served with the 15th Infantry in China 1920-1922. Professor of military science and tactics at Virginia Polytechnic Institute 1924-

1928. Graduated from the Command and General Staff School in 1931. Assistant chief of staff for supply, then plans at the Panama Canal Department 1931-1933. Graduated from the Army War College in 1934. Instructor at the Infantry School 1934-1939. Assistant chief of staff for plans at VII Corps Area March-August 1940. Duty with 6th Armored Infantry 1940-1941. Assistant chief of staff for supply at 4th Armored Division 1941-1942. Commanding officer of 7th Infantry, 3rd Infantry Division in the North African invasion April 1942-April 1943. Brigadier general in February 1943. Assistant division commander, then commanding general of 83rd Infantry Division April 1943-April 1946. Major general in June 1944. Assignments after the war included military attache in Moscow 1946-1948 and deputy chief of Army Field Forces 1949-1952. Retired in July 1952. Decorations included the Distinguished Service Medal, Silver Star, Legion of Merit and two Bronze Stars. Died on October 20, 1980.

Maddocks, Ray Tyson (1895-1973) Born in Silver City, Iowa, on September 21, 1895. B.S. from Knox College in 1916. Commissioned in the cavalry 1917. Served with the AEF 1917-1919. Instructor at the Cavalry School 1920-1930. Graduated from German cavalry school in 1931. Again instructor at the Cavalry School 1931-1937. Graduated from the Command and General Staff School in 1938. Duty in the war plans division at the War Department General Staff 1941-1943. Brigadier general in November 1943. Served in the China-Burma-India Theater of Operations as chief of U.S. Army planners in the Southeast Asia Command and assistant chief of staff then chief of staff of U.S. Forces China 1943-1946. Major general in June 1945. Retired in June 1951. Decorations included two Distinguished Service Medals, the Legion of Merit, Bronze Star and Commendation Ribbon. Died on June 5, 1973.

Maddox, Halley Grey (1899-1977) Born in Kentucky on January 29, 1899. Commissioned in the infantry from West Point in 1920. Deputy chief of staff for intelligence with I Armored Corps, Seventh Army and Third Army 1942-1945. Brigadier general in November 1944. Assignments after the war included commanding general of 25th Division 1953-1954 and deputy commanding general of U.S. Army Europe and Second Army 1956-1959. Retired as major general in 1959. Decorations included two Distinguished Service Medals, the Legion of Merit and two Bronze Stars. Died on May 26, 1977.

Maddox, Louis Wilson (1891-1956) Born in Lamar, Missouri, on April 22, 1891. Commissioned in the infantry, Officers Reserve Corps in 1917. Served with 27th Infantry in Siberia, the Philippines and Hawaii August 1919-November 1922. Instructor at the Infantry School 1928-1931. Post finance officer at Fort Bragg July 1938-June 1942. Chief finance officer for Southwest Pacific Area Services of Supply 1942-1943 then U.S. Army Forces Far East February 1943-September 1945. Brigadier general in June 1945. Retired in August 1946. Decorations included the Distinguished Service Medal. Died on July 1, 1956.

Magee, James Carre (1883-1975) Born on January 23, 1883, in Ireland. M.D. from Jefferson Medical College in 1905. Commissioned in the Medical Corps in 1909. Duty on the Mexian border in 1916-1917. Regimental surgeon with AEF 1917-1919. Executive officer at Walter Reed Medical Center 1935-1939. Major general in June 1939. Surgeon general of the Army 1939-1943. Retired in October 1943. Decorations included the Distinguished Service Medal and Purple Heart. Died on October 15, 1975.

Magruder, Bruce (1882-1953) Born in Washington, DC, on December 3, 1882. Enlisted service in the coastal Artillery Corps 1904-1907. Commissioned in the infantry in 1907. Served in the Philippine Islands 1907-1911, on the Mexican border 1912-1914, and again in the Philippines November 1914-September 1917. Executive officer of the intelligence section at GHQ, AEF 1917-1919. Instructor at the Infantry School 1923-1926. Graduated from the Command and General Staff School in 1927. Professor of military science and tactics at North Carolina State College August 1931-October 1936. Executive officer at the Infantry School 1937-1940. Brigadier general in November 1939. Commanding general of 1st Armored Division July 1940-March 1942. Major general in October 1940. Commander, Infantry Replacement Training Center, Camp Wolters March 1942-1946. Retired in May 1946. Decorations included the Distinguished Service Medal and Legion of Merit. Died on July 23, 1953.

Magruder, Carter Bowie (1900-1988) Born on April 3, 1900, in London, England. Commissioned in the field artillery from West Point in 1923. M.S. from Purdue in 1932. Instructor at the Field Artillery School 1932-1933. Graduated from the Command and General Staff School in 1935. Again instructor at the Field Artillery School 1935-1938. Graduated from the Army War College in 1939. Assistant chief of staff for operations at 3rd Infantry Division 1939-1941. Duty with the War Department General Staff 1941-1942. Director of the plans division at headquarters of Army Service Forces 1942-1944. Assistant chief of staff for supply in the Mediterranean Theater of Operations July-November 1944. Brigadier general in August 1944. Chief of staff, then commanding general of troop support, Far East Theater of Operations 1945-1946. Major general in March 1945. Assignments after the war included commanding general of 24th Infantry Division 1953-1954 then IX Corps January 1954-April 1954, chief of staff of Far East Command 1954-1955, deputy chief of staff for logistics, U.S. Army and Commander in Chief United Nations Command Korea 1959-1961. Retired in 1961. Decorations included three Distinguished Service Medals. Died on March 14, 1988.

Magruder, John (1887-1958) Born in Woodstock, Virginia, on June 3, 1887. Graduate of VMI in 1909. Commissioned in the infantry in 1910. Transferred to the field artillery in 1911. With 120th Field Artillery, AEF during World War I 1918-1919. Assistant military attache in Peking 1920-1924. Graduated from the Command and General Staff School in 1926. Again in Peking as military attache 1926-1930. Graduated from the Army War College in 1931. Professor of military science and tactics at VMI 1932-1935. Military attache in Switzerland May 1935-June 1939. Brigadier general in October 1940. Commanding general of 1st Division Artillery January 1941-July 1942. Duty at headquarters of Services of Supply 1942-1943. Deputy director of the OSS October 1943-May 1944. Duty in the War Department bureau of public relations May-August 1944. Again with the OSS 1944-1945. Director of the strategic services unit at the War Department 1945-1946. Retired in October 1946. Decorations included the Distinguished Service Medal. Died on April 30, 1958.

Magruder, Marshall (1885-1956) Born in Washington, DC, on October 12, 1885. Attended George Washington University 1904-1907. Commissioned in the field artillery in 1908. Served in the Philippines 1915-1917 then with 1st Division in France in World War I. Graduated from the Command and General Staff School in 1924. Professor of military science and tactics at the University of Illinois 1924-1928. Graduated from the Army War College in 1932 and the Naval War College in 1933. Regimental commander at Schofield Barracks, Hawaii 1935-1937. Organized and commanded the first armored cavalry artillery regiment in the Army 1939-1940. Brigadier general in October 1940. Artillery officer at headquarters of the Armored Force 1940-1942. Commanding general of 14th Field Artillery Brigade March 1942-January 1943. Duty with special troops of Third Army January-March 1943. Served with the War Department Manpower Board March 1943 until retirement in August 1946. Died on July 4, 1956.

Maguire, Hamilton Ewing (1891-1971) Born on November 24, 1891, in Detroit, Michigan. Attended the University of Michigan 1010-1912. Commissioned in the field artillery from West Point in 1916. Served in the Punitive Expedition into Mexico 1916-1917. Graduated from the Command and General Staff School in 1930 and the Army War College in 1938. Brigadier general in September 1944. Chief of staff of XIX Corps 1944-1945. Chief of staff of 3rd Service Command 1945-1946. Retired in 1948. Decorations included the Distinguished Service Medal, Legion of Merit and two Bronze Stars. Died on February 20, 1971.

Mahin, Frank C. (1887-1942) born in Clinton, Iowa, on May 27, 1887. Attended Harvard 1905-1907. Enlisted service 1910-1912. Commissioned in the infantry in 1912. Served with 15th and 31st Infantry in the Philippine islands 1915-1917 and 11th Infantry in 1918 with the AEF at St. Mihiel and meuse-Argonne offensives. Wounded in action on September 12 and October 15, 1918. Graduated from the Command and General Staff School in 1925. Instructor at Field Artillery School 1925-1927. Graduated from the Army War College in 1929. Acting inspector general at the Panama Canal Department in 1934. Commanded the 60th Infantry November 1940-May 1942. Brigadier general in October 1941. Commanding general of 33rd Division as major general in May 1942. Died on July 24, 1942 in a plane crash near Waynesboro, Tennessee, while on an observation flight. Decorations included the Purple Heart.

Mallett, Pierre (1893-n/a) Born in Brooklyn, New York on March 14, 1893. Attended North Carolina State University 1913-1917. Commissioned in the infantry, Officers Reserve Corps in 1917. Served with 103rd Infantry, 16th Infantry and the 7th Machine Gun Battalion, AEF at Aisne-Marne, St. Mihiel and Meuse-Argonne 1917-1918. Professor of military science and tactics at the University of Illinois 1922-1926. Instructor at the Field Artillery School July 1937-October 1941. Commanding officer of 138th Field Artillery 1941-1942 then 1st Cavalry February 1942-January 1943. Brigadier general in February 1943. Commanding general of 16th Field Artillery Brigade January-August 1943. Commanding general of 85th Infantry Division Artillery September 1943-November 1945. Reverted to colonel in February 1946. Retired in May 1950. Decorations included the Silver Star, Legion of Merit, two Bronze Stars and the Commendation Ribbon.

Mallon, Francis Bernard (1886-1983) Born in Middletown, New York, on September 17, 1886. Attended West Point 1908-1909. Enlisted service with 5th Infantry 1909-1912. Commissioned in the infantry in 1912. Served in the Philippine Islands 1914-1917. Graduated from the Command and General Staff School in 1923 and the Army War College in 1927. With the War Department General Staff 1927-1930 and again 1939-1941. Brigadier general in January 1942. Commanding general of Replacement Training Center at Camp Joseph T. Robinson 1942-1943 then Army Ground Forces Depot Number One at Fort Meade July 1943-July 1945. Major general in September 1944. Commanding general of Army Ground Forces Depot Number Four at Camp Adair July 1945-March 1946. Retired in September 1946. Decorations included the Purple Heart. Died on December 18, 1983.

Malony, Harry James (1889-1971) Born on August 24, 1889, in Lakemont, New York. Commissioned in the infantry from West Point in 1912. Served with the AEF in World War I. Graduated from the Command and General Staff School in 1926. Professor of military science and tactics at the University of Oklahoma 1931-1935. Graduated from the Army War College in 1936, then instructor there until 1940. Member of Atlantic Bases Board 1940-1942. Brigadier general in January 1941, major general in August 1942. Commanding general of 94th Infantry Division 1942-1945. Retired in 1949. Decorations included three Distinguished Service Medals, the Silver Star, Bronze Star and two Commendation Ribbons. Died on March 23, 1971.

Mandell, Harold Chittenden (1892-1959) Born in Hailey, Idaho, on November 30, 1892. B.S. from the University of Utah in 1916. Commissioned in the field artillery, Utah National Guard in 1916. Served with the 2nd Cavalry in France 1918. Instructor with the New York National Guard July 1920-September 1922. Graduated from the Command and General Staff School in 1926. Instructor at the Cavalry School 1926-1930, with the Wyoming National Guard 1930-1934 and at the Command and General Staff School 1934-1935. Graduated from the Army War College in 1936. Again instructor at the Command and General Staff School 1936-1940. Assistant chief of staff for operations, then intelligence at 1st Infantry

Division 1940-1941. Chief of staff of 1st Infantry Division July 1941-July 1942, then 104th Infantry Division July 1942-July 1943. Assistant to the chief of the plans section at headquarters U.S. Pacific Fleet July 1943-May 1945. Brigadier general in May 1944. Retired in September 1946. Decorations included the Legion of Merit. Died on May 19, 1959.

Manley, Frederick Willis (1881-1958) Born in Minneapolis, Minnesota, on May 2, 1881. Commissioned in the infantry from West Point in 1905. Duty with 13th Infantry in the Philippines 1905-1908. Served at the occupation of Vera Cruz in 1914 and with GHQ, AEF at St. Mihiel and Meuse-Argonne in World War I. Instructor at West Point 1919-1920. Graduated from the Command and General Staff School in 1925. Military attache in Madrid February 1926-January 1930. Graduated from the Army War College in 1933. Duty at the Philippine Department 1933-1935 then in the office of the high commissioner to the Philippines 1935-1936. Acting chief of staff of 31st Division 1940-1942. At 4th Service Command March 1942-December 1943. Brigadier general in October 1942. Retired in January 1944. Decorations included the Distinguished Service Medal and Purple Heart. Died on December 10, 1958.

Maraist, Robert Victor (1893-1961) Born in St. Martinsville, LA, on February 28, 1893. Attended Southwestern University 1914-1915 and Louisiana State University 1915-1917. Commissioned in the field artillery in 1917. Served with 10th Field Artillery, AEF including the Aisne-Marne, St. Mihiel and Meuse-Argonne offensives 1918-1920. Professor of military science and tactics at Cornell University 1924-1928. Graduated from the Command and General Staff School in 1934. Instructor with the organized reserves in Indianapolis 1936-1940. Executive officer, then commanding officer of 27th Armored Field Artillery Battalion December 1940-February 1942. Staff officer, then artillery commander at 1st Armored Division February 1942-June 1943. Brigadier general in June 1943. Combat commander at 16th Armored Division June 1943-October 1944. Commanding general of 69th Infantry Division Artillery October 1944-November 1945. Reverted to colonel in January 1946. Retired in February 1953. Decorations included two Silver Stars, two Legions of Merit, two Bronze Stars and two Commendation Ribbons. Died on February 18, 1961.

March, Francis Andrew (1895-1967) Born on November 2, 1895, in Easton, Pennsylvania. Commissioned in the field artillery from West Point in 1918. Instructor at the University of Illinois 1927-1931. Duty at Schofield Barracks, Hawaii 1931-1934. Public relations officer at West Point April 1936-July 1940. Intelligence officer at 47th Field Artillery in 1941. Commander of 320th Field Artillery Battalion February 1942-January 1943. Executive officer of 82nd Airborne Division Artillery January 1943-November 1945. Brigadier general in November 1944. Assistant division commander of 82nd Airborne Division November 1945-February 1946. Reverted to colonel in February 1946. Retired in May 1953. Decorations included the Silver Star, Legion of Merit and Commendation Ribbon. Died on November 2, 1967.

Marietta, Shelley Uriah (1881-1974) Born in Palmyra, Iowa, on January 5, 1881. DDS from Drake University in 1902, M.D. from the University of Illinois in 1909. Commissioned in the Medical Corps in 1910. Served on the Mexican border in 1912 and in the AEF in 1918. Commander of Tripler General Hospital 1935-1937. Brigadier general in December 1939. Commanding general of Walter Reed General in Hospital 1939-1940, then Walter Reed Medical Center March 1940-December 1943. Major general in September 1943. Assistant to the surgeon general, U.S. Army 1943-1945. Retired in January 1945. Decorations included the Distinguished Service Medal. Died on November 22, 1974.

Maris, Ward Hale (1892-1978) Born in Carthage, Indiana, on November 18, 1892. Attended the University of Kansas 1910-1913. B.S. from the University of Chicago in 1915. Commissioned in the field artillery in 1917. With 10th Field Artillery and 3rd Field Artillery Brigades in France in 1918. Assistant Professor of military science and tactics at Colorado State University 1923-1928. Graduated from the Command and General Staff School in 1934. Professor of military science and tactics at Purdue 1934-1936. Graduated from the Army War College in 1937. Instructor at the Command and General Staff School 1937-1939. Duty at the War Department General Staff 1940-1942. Brigadier general in May 1942. Commanding general of 95th Infantry Division Artillery 1942-1944, XXI Corps Artillery April 1944-August 1945, and 8th Division Artillery in 1945. Commanding general of Camp Fannin 1945-1946. Retired as major general in November 1952. Decorations included the Distinguished Service Medal, Silver Star, Legion of Merit, Bronze Star and two Commendation Ribbons. Died on May 9, 1978.

Marks, Edwin Hall (1887-1967) Born in Wilmington, Delaware, on July 2, 1887. Commissioned in the Corps of Engineers from West Point in 1909. Served in Guam 1913-1914 and the Philippines 1914-1915. Instructor at West Point 1916-1917. Served with 20th Engineers in the AEF in 1918. Graduated from the Command and General Staff School in 1926 and the Army War College in 1929. Division engineer in the Ohio River Division 1938-1941. Brigadier general in April 1941. Commanding general of Engineer Replacement Training Center April 1941-June 1944 then the Southwest Engineer Division June 1944-March 1946. Reverted to colonel in March 1946. Retired in July 1947. Decorations included the Distinguished Service Medal and Legion of Merit. Died on December 19, 1967.

Marley, James Preston (1882-1952) Born in Slayden, Texas, on November 20, 1882. Commissioned in the field artillery from West Point in 1907. Served with 1st then 6th Field Artillery in the Philippines 1910-1913. Instructor at General Service Schools 1923-1927. Graduated from the Army War College in 1928 and the Naval War College in 1929. Staff officer with the Panama Canal Department 1935-1937. Duty in the office of the inspector general, U.S. Army June 1939-October 1940. Brigadier general in October 1940. Assistant division commander of 8th Division 1940-1941. Major general in April 1941. Commanding general of

8th Motorized Division April 1941 until retirement in November 1942. Recalled to active duty December 1942-January 1944. Died on November 27, 1952.

Marquat, William Frederick (1894-1960) Born in St. Louis on March 4, 1894. Commissioned in the Coast Artillery Corps in 1920. With 55th Coast Artillery in Hawaii June 1921-May 1926. Graduated from the Command and General Staff School in 1933. Instructor with the New Hampshire National Guard 1933-1935. Served in the Philippines at Fort Mills, then commanding officer of Fort Wint, finally assistant to the military adviser to the Philippine government September 1937-December 1940. Again in the Philippines as assistant to the military adviser, then chief of staff of the Philippine Coast Artillery Command May 1941-March 1942. Brigadier general in January 1942. Antiaircraft officer in the Southwest Pacific Area 1942-1943. Commander of 14th Antiaircraft Command November 1943-January 1946. Retired in September 1955. Decorations included the Distinguished Service Cross, three Distinguished Service Medals, two Silver Stars and the Air Medal. Died on May 29, 1960.

Marshall, George Catlett (1880-1959). Born on December 31, 1880, in Uniontown, Pennsylvania. Graduate of VMI in 1902. Commissioned in the infantry in 1902. Graduated from Army Staff College in 1908. Staff officer with First Army, then VIII Corps, in France during World War I, attaining temporary rank of colonel. Reverted to captain after the war. Served as aide to General in John J. Pershing 1919-1924. Battalion commander in 15th Infantry, Tientsin, China, 1924-1927. Assistant commandant of the Infantry School 1927-1932. Commanding officer of 8th Infantry 1932-1933. Senior instructor with Illinois National Guard 1933-1936. Brigadier general in July 1936 With the War Department General Staff 1938-1939. Major general in July 1939. Deputy chief of staff, then acting chief of staff July-September 1939. General in September 1939. Chief of staff, U.S. Army 1939-1945. General of the Army in December 1944. Resigned from the Army in November 1945. Decorations included two Distinguished Service Medals and the Silver Star. Personal representative of President Truman to mediate peace between the Nationalist and communist Chinese in 1946. Secretary of State 1947-1949. Secretary of Defense 1950-1951. Proponent of the "Marshall Plan" for the economic recovery of Europe, to which the U.S. contributed more than $112 billion. Presented a gold medal from Congress. Awarded the Nobel Peace Prize in 1953. Died on October 16, 1959.

Marshall, James Creel (1897-1977) Born on October 14, 1897, in Plattsburg, Missouri. Commissioned in the Corps of Engineers from West Point in 1918. Graduated from the Command and General Staff School in 1940. With the atomic bomb project 1942-1943. Brigadier general in November 1944. Assistant chief of staff for supply, Services of Supply 1944. Commanding general of Boston Port of Embarkation 1945-1946. Retired as colonel in 1947. Brigadier general on the retired list in 1948. Decorations included the Legion of Merit and Bronze Star. Died on July 19, 1977.

Marshall, Richard Jaquelin (1895-1973) Born in Markham, Virginia, on June 16, 1895. Graduate of Virginia Military Institute in 1915. Commissioned in the field artillery in 1916. Served as battery commander in 6th Field Artillery, AEF 1917-1919 including participation in the St. Mihiel and Meuse-Argonne offensives. Duty in the Philippines as head of the supply division, office of the quartermaster of the Philippine Department 1929-1932. Graduated from the Command and General Staff School in 1934, Army Industrial College in 1935 and the Army War College in 1936. Assistant to Douglas MacArthur in the Philippines October 1939-July 1941. Deputy chief of staff of U.S. Army Forces in the Far East July 1941-April 1942. Brigadier general in December 1941. Deputy chief of staff at headquarters of Southwest Pacific Area April 1942-July 1942. Commanding general of Services of Supply in the Southwest Pacific Area July 1942-September 1943. Major general in August 1942. Deputy chief of staff to MacArthur 1943-1944. Deputy chief of staff then chief of staff of U.S. Army Forces Far East 1944-1946. Retired in November 1946. Decorations included the Distinguished Service Cross, two Distinguished Service Medals, the Silver Star and Legion of Merit. Died on August 3, 1973.

Marston, Morrill Watson (1896-n/a) Born in Ames, Iowa, on January 30, 1896. B.S. from Iowa State University in 1917. Commissioned in the infantry in 1917. Duty in the Panama Canal Zone 1922-1925. Instructor at the Engineer School 1928-1932. Graduated from Command and General Staff School in 1936 and the Army War College in 1939. Assistant chief of staff for intelligence with the Hawaiian Department 1939-1941. Assistant chief of staff for supply with the Hawaiian Department, the Central Pacific Area and with U.S. Army Forces Pacific Ocean Areas 1941-1947. Decorations included the Distinguished Service Medal, Legion of Merit, Bronze Star and the Army Commendation Ribbon.

Martin, Clarence Ames (1896-1986) Born in Belle Haven, Virginia, on September 13, 1896. Graduate of Virginia Military Institute in 1917. Commissioned in the infantry in 1917. Served with the AEF in 1918. Professor of military science and tactics at Tennessee Military Institute 1922-1927. With the 45th Infantry, Philippine Scouts May 1927-August 1929. Professor of military science and tactics at Virginia Military Institute 1932-1936. Graduated from the Command and General Staff School in 1937 and the Army War College in 1940. Instructor with the Tennessee National Guard in 1940. Staff officer with 30th Division June 1940-January 1942. Assistant chief of staff for supply, then intelligence at I Corps in 1942. Commanding officer of 128th Infantry January-February 1953. Brigadier general in February 1943. Assistant division commander of 32nd Division 1943-1944. Commanding general of 31st Division September 1944-December 1945. Major general in November 1944. Retired in July 1947. Decorations included the Distinguished Service Cross, Distinguished Service Medal, three Silver Stars, the Legion of Merit and Air Medal. Died on December 11, 1986.

Martin, Joseph Ignatius (1894-1957) Born in Chicago, Illinois, on February 1, 1894. M.D. from Chicago Hospital College of Medicine in 1918. Commissioned in the Medical Corps in 1920. Served at Sternberg General Hospital in the Philippines 1921-1923. Graduated from Army Medical School in 1925, the Command and General Staff School in 1934. Post surgeon at Fort Sherman, then assistant to the surgeon at the Panama Department September 1934-October 1936. Graduated from the Army War College in 1940. Executive officer of Medical Department Replacement Center at Camp Grant December 1940-March 1943. Chief surgeon at Fifth Army, Army Forces Western Pacific and Army Forces Pacific March 1943-August 1946. Brigadier general in January 1944. Deputy commandant of Brooke Army Medical Center 1946-1947. Commandant of Medical Field Service School July 1947-August 1953. Surgeon at U.S. Army Europe 1953-1955. Duty in the office of the surgeon general August-November 1955. Retired in November 1955. Decorations included the Distinguished Service Medal and Legion of Merit. Died on April 13, 1957.

Martin, Thomas Lyle (1891-1984) Born on May 18, 1891, in Forrest City, Arkansas. Commissioned in the infantry from West Point in 1916. With the Punitive Expedition into Mexico. Served as commanding officer of 19th Machine Gun Battalion, AEF in World War I. Instructor at the Infantry School 1919-1921 and again 1922-1925. Graduated from the Command and General Staff School in 1927. Duty with 21st Infantry at Schofield Barracks, Hawaii June 1927-August 1930. Instructor at the Cavalry School 1930-1935 then with the Louisiana National Guard 1937-1938. Graduated from the Army War College in 1939. Executive office of Washington (DC) Provisional Brigade June 1939-April 1940. Supply officer at Fourth Army 1940-1941. Duty at headquarters of Western Defense Command April 1941-June 1942. Brigadier general in June 1942. Assistant division commander of 2nd Division 1942-1944. Reverted to colonel in July 1944. Retired in April 1951. Decorations included the Legion of Merit, Bronze Star and Commendation Ribbon. Died on April 26, 1984.

Massey, Clyde (1902-1990) Born on August 1, 1902, in Morrill, Kansas. Commissioned in the Air Service from West Point in 1924. Transferred to the Quartermaster Corps. Served in the Philippine Islands with the 26th Cavalry 1934-1937. Graduated from the Command and General Staff School in 1941. In North African Theater of Operations 1942-1943. Quartermaster of Seventh Army 1943-1945. Brigadier general in November 1944. With U.S. Air Forces Pacific Area August 1945-January 1946. Reverted to colonel in February 1946. Retired in 1954. Decorations included the Distinguished Service Medal, two Legions of Merit and the Bronze Star. Died on March 17, 1990.

Matchett, Henry Jeffrey (1891-1984) Born in Toronto, Canada, on January 7, 1891. Graduated from the University of Minnesota in 1913. Enlisted service with the Minnesota National Guard 1916-1917. Commissioned in the infantry in 1917. Served in Hawaii with 27th Infantry at Schofield Barracks July 1925-May 1927. Graduated from the Command and General Staff School in 1930. Instructor at the Infantry School 1930-1934. Graduated from the Army War College in 1940. Duty in the personnel section, office of the chief of infantry 1940-1941. Assistant chief of staff for intelligence, then chief of staff at IV Corps October 1941-June 1942. Commanding officer of 314th Infantry June-August 1942. Chief of the training branch at the War Department General Staff 1942-1943. Chief of staff of V Corps October 1943-October 1944. Brigadier general in September 1944. Commander of Ground Forces Replacement System in the European Theater of Operations 1944-1945. Duty at headquarters of Fifteenth Army May 1945-March 1946. Reverted to colonel in March 1946. Retired in February 1950. Decorations included the Distinguished Service Medal, Legion of Merit and two Commendation Ribbons. Died on April 26, 1984.

Matejka, Jerry Vrchlicky (1894-1980) Born in Nelsonville, Texas, on August 18, 1894. B.S. from Texas University in 1917. Commissioned in the Coast Artillery Corps in 1917. Assistant signal officer in the Panama Canal Department 1920-1921. Graduated from Army Industrial College in 1926, the Command and General Staff School in 1934 and the Army War College in 1935. Duty at GHQ U.S. Army August 1940-May 1941. Chief signal officer for U.S. Forces British isles then at Allied Forces Headquarters in North Africa 1941-1943. Brigadier general in August 1942. Chief of personnel and training, office of the chief signal officer 1943-1945. Commanding general of Fort Monmouth 1945-1947. Retired in October 1955. Decorations included three Legions of Merit. Died on May 22, 1980.

Mather, John (1883-1965) Born on September 15, 1883, in Lowell, Massachusetts. Commissioned in the Coast Artillery Corps in 1908. Served with 143rd Coast Artillery in Hawaii 1913-1916. Instructor at the Coast Artillery School 1917-1918. Battalion commander with 60th Coast Artillery, AEF in 1918, including the Meuse-Argonne offensive. Graduated from Army Industrial College in 1927. Production manager then commanding general of Watertown Arsenal January 1938-July 1942. Brigadier general temporarily from December 1941 to July 1942. Retired in September 1943. Died on February 19, 1965.

Mathewson, Lemuel (1899-1970) Born on March 29, 1899, in Bath, New York. Commissioned in the infantry from West Point in 1922. Served with 31st Infantry in the Philippines 1925-1927. Instructor at West Point 1931-1936. Graduated from the Command and General Staff School in 1939. Instructor at the Artillery School September 1939-November 1940. At the War Department General Staff 1940-1943. Aide to President Roosevelt 1943-1944. Assistant commander of 7th Corps Artillery 1944. Commanding general of XVIII Airborne Corps Artillery 1944-1945. Brigadier general in March 1945. Assignments after the war included chief of staff of Caribbean Defense Command August 1945-November 1948, commanding general of 11th Airborne Division Artillery 1949-1951, commanding general of Berlin Command 1951-1953, director of the joint staff, Joint Chiefs of Staff 1954-1955, commanding general of V Corps 1956-1957 and Sixth Army 1957-1958. Retired in April 1958. Decorations included the Distinguished Service Medal, three Legions of Merit and the Bronze Star. Died on February 26, 1970.

Maxwell, Russell Lamonte (1890-1968) Born on December 28, 1890, in Oak-dale, Illinois. Commissioned in the Field Artilllery from West Point in 1912. Served with 1st Field Artillery in Hawaii 1912-1915. Chief of ammunition service in the AEF in 1919. Graduated from the Command and General Staff School in 1924, Army Industrial College in 1925 and the Army War College in 1934. Served on the staff of the assistant secretary of war 1939-1940. Administrator of export control 1940-1941. Brigadier general in February 1941. Chief of U.S. Military Mission to Cairo 1941-1942. Major general in March 1942. Commanding general of U.S. Army Forces in the Middle East 1942-1943 Commanding general of Army Service Forces Unit Training Center April-September 1943. Assistant chief of staff for supply, the War Department General Staff 1943-1946. Retired as colonel in September 1946. Major general on the retired list in 1948. Decorations included two Distinguished Service Medals. Died on November 24, 1968.

Mayberry, Hugh Tullock (1892-1970) Born in Farmington, Missouri, on December 1, 1892. B.A. from William Jewell College in 1914. Attended Rensselaer Polytechnic Institute 1916-1917. Commissioned in the infantry in 1919. Assistant professor of military science and tactics at Boston University 1925-1926. Instructor with the New York National Guard 1926-1927. Graduated from the Command and General Staff School in 1933. Duty with 19th Infantry in Hawaii 1933-1935. Assistant instructor with the Georgia National Guard 1935-1937. Instructor at the Infantry School October 1938-December 1941. Assistant commandant then commandant of Tank Destroyer School February 1942-February 1944. Brigadier general in November 1942. Assistant division commander of 99th Infantry Division February 1944-June 1945. Commanding general of War Department Personnel Center at Camp Shelby June 1945-March 1946. Reverted to colonel in March 1946. Retired in December 1952. Decorations included the Silver Star, two Legions of Merit and the Bronze Star. Died on April 28, 1970.

Maynard, John Blackwell (1887-1945) Born in Portsmouth, Virginia, on August 12, 1887. B.S. from Virginia Polytechnic Institute in 1907. Attended Colorado School of Mines 1907-1908. Served with 17th Field Artillery, AEF at Chateau-Thierry and Aisne-Marne 1917-1919. Graduated from the Command and General Staff School in 1924. Instructor at the General Service Schools 1924-1928. Graduated from the Army War College in 1929. Professor of military science and tactics at Virginia Polytechnic Institute 1929-1935. Battery commander with 15th Coast Artillery in Hawaii 1935-1937. Brigadier general in April 1941. Duty at Coast Artillery Replacement Training Center, Camp Wallace April 1941-February 1942. Commander of Barrage Balloon Training Center at Camp Tyson 1942-1943. Commanding general of Antiaircraft Replacement Training Center at Fort Eustis July 1943 until retirement in August 1944. Died on February 2, 1945.

McAfee, Larry Benjamin (1883-1950) Born in Delphi, Indiana, on July 3, 1883. M.D. from George Washington University in 1906. Commissioned in the Medical Corps in 1909. Graduated from Army Medical School in 1910. Served in Hawaii 1911-1915 and as surgeon in AEF base hospitals 1917-1919. Graduated from

Army Industrial College in 1925 and the Army War College in 1930. Executive officer to the suregon general, U.S. Army March 1940-May 1941. Brigadier general in May 1941. Assistant to the surgeon general May 1941-May 1945. Commanding general of Burns General Hospital in Santa fe July 1945-November 1946. Retired in November 1946. Decorations included the Distinguished Service Medal and Legion of Merit. Died on July 8, 1950.

McAuliffe, Anthony Clement (1898-1975) Born on July 2, 1898, in Washington, DC. Attended West Virginia University 1916-1917. Commissioned in the field artillery from West Point in 1919. Graduated from the Command and General Staff School in 1937 and the Army War College in 1940. Brigadier general in August 1942. Commanding general of 101st Airborne Division Artillery 1942-1944. Assistant division commander of 101st Airborne Division June 1944-January 1945. When the division was surrounded at Bastogne by advancing German troop in late December 1944, during the Battle of the Bulge, he replied to a demand for surrender with "Nuts" and rallied his troops to hold on until relieved by elements of Patton's Third Army. Major general in January 1945. Commanding general of 103rd Division, then 79th Division January-September 1945. Assignments after the war included deputy director of research and development, later chief of the Chemical Corps, U.S. Army 1947-1953, deputy chief of staff for operations, U.S. Army February-September 1953, commanding general of Seventh Army 1953-1955 and commander of U.Ss. Army Europe March 1955 until retirement in May 1956. Decorations included the Distinguished Service Cross, two Distinguished Service Medals, the Silver Star and Bronze Star. Chairman of the New York State Civil Defense Commission 1959-1963. Died on August 11, 1975.

McBride, Allan Clay (1885-1944) Born in Frederick, Maryland, on June 30, 1885. Graduated from St. John's College in 1908. Commissioned in the field artillery in 1908. Served with 4th Field Artillery at vera Cruz in 1914, in the Philippines 1916-1917 and as battery commander with the 349th Field Artillery, AEF 1918-1919. Instructor at the Field Artillery School 1920-1922. Graduated from the Command and General Staff School in 1923 and the Army War College in 1926. Instructor at the Command and General Staff School 1930-1935. Commanding officer of 12th Field Artillery 1939-1940. Inspector general at Third Army 1940-1941. Plans and training officer at the Philippine Department February 1941 until taken prisoner by the Japanese shortly after the fall of Bataan in early April 1942. Brigadier general in December 1941. Died on May 9, 1944, at Japanese prison camp Taiwan-Formosa, Philippine Islands. Decorations included the Distinguished Service Medal.

McBride, Horace Logan (1894-1962) Born on June 28, 1894, in Madison, Nebraska. Attended the University of Nebraska 1910-1911. Served as battery commander in 347th Field Artillery, AEF in World War I, including the Meuse-Argonne offensive. Commissioned in the field artillery from West Point in 1916. Assistant military attache at The Hague then Warsaw in 1919. Professor of military science and tactics at Yale University 1923-1927. Graduated from the Command and General Staff School in 1928. Instructor at Field Artillery School June 1928-July 1932. Served in the Philippine Islands 1932-1935. Graduated from the Army War College in 1936. Instructor at the Command and General Staff School 1936-1940. At the Panama Canal Zone 1940-1942. Commanding general of 80th Infantry Division Artillery April 1942-March 1943. Brigadier general in May 1942. Commanding general of 80th Division 1943-1944. Major general in March 1943. Commanding general of XX Corps 1945-1946. Assignments after the war included Commanding general of 9th Division 1946-1947, commandant of the Command and General Staff College 1950-1952 commander-in-chief of the Caribbean Command 1952-1954. Retired in June 1954. Decorations included the Distinguished Service Medal, two Silver Stars, the Legion of Merit, Bronze Star and Commendation Ribbon. Died on November 14, 1962.

McBride, Robert Bruce Jr. (1892-1981) Born on July 7, 1892, in Bridgeport, Alabama. Commissioned in the Coast Artillery Corps from West Point in 1916. Served with 2nd Field Artillery in the Philippines 1917-1918. Instructor at Field Artillery School 1922-1926. Graduated from the Command and General Staff School in 1928. Instructor with the organized reserves in Indianapolis 1928-1933. Battalion commander with 11th Field Artillery at Schofield Barracks, Hawaii 1933-1934. Instructor with the Indiana National Guard 1934-1939. Chief of the historical section at the Army War College January 1939-October 1940. Assistant chief of staff for operations at Second Army 1940-1942. Assistant chief of staff for operations at the San Francisco Port of Embarkation in 1942-1943. Brigadier general in June 1943. Commanding general of 32nd Division Artillery 1943-1945. Commanding general of 32nd Division in 1945. Reverted to colonel in March 1946. Retired in July 1952. Decorations included the Silver Star, two Legions of Merit, two Bronze Stars and the AM. Died on September 24, 1981

McCabe, Edward Raynsford Warner (1876-1960) Born in Petersburg, Virginia, on July 12, 1876. Attended University School (Petersburg) 1889-1896 and the University of Virginia 1900. Commissioned in the infantry in 1900. Served in the Punitive Expedition into Mexico 1916-1917. Military attache in Prague 1920-1922, then Rome 1924-1926. Professor of military science and tactics at Stanford 1927-1930. Graduated from the Army War College in 1931. Military attache in Rome again 1931-1933. Chief of military intelligence division, the War Department General Staff 1937-1940. Retired in July 1940. Superintendent of Staunton Military Academy 1941-1943. Recalled to active duty in May 1943. Brigadier general in January 1944. Commandant of the School of Military Government January 1944-June 1946. Decorations included the Legion of Merit. Died on February 15, 1960.

McCabe, Frederick (1891-1973) Born in Portland, Oregon, on February 9, 1891. Attended Oregon State College 1912-1914. Enlisted service with 21st Infantry 1914-1916. Commissioned in the infantry in 1916. Duty on the Mexican border 1916-1917. Assistant professor of military science and tactics at the University of California 1919-1922. Served with 65th Infantry in Puerto Rico 1925-1928. Graduated from the Command and General Staff School in 1931. Instructor at the Infantry School July 1933-July 1936 then secretary 1936-1937. Graduated from the Army War College in 1940. Deputy chief of staff for intelligence at 7th Division 1940-1941 then III Corps 1941-1942. Brigadier general in October 1942. Liaison officer with Sixth Chinese Army in Burma 1942-1945. Commanding general of Infantry Replacement Training Center at Camp Robinson 1945-1946. Retired in September 1947. Decorations included the Distinguished Service Medal and Bronze Star. Died on January 16, 1973.

McCain, William Alexander (1878-1960) Born on August 25, 1878, in Carroll County, Mississippi. Attended the University of Mississippi 1895-1896. Commissioned in the cavalry from West Point in 1902. Duty with 8th Cavalry in the Philippine Islands 1905-1907 and again March 1911-February 1914. With 13th Cavalry in the Punitive Expedition into Mexico in 1916. Served in Germany 1920-1922. Graduated from Army Industrial College in 1924 and the Army War College in 1928. Commanding officer of Philadelphia Quartermaster Depot July 1934-June 1942. Brigadier general in November 1940. Retired as colonel in June 1942. Decorations included the Distinguished Service Medal. Died on May 13, 1960.

McChrystal, Arthur John (1893-1980) Born on November 25, 1893, in San Jose, California. B.A. from Stanford University in 1915, M.S. from the University of Utah in 1916. Commissioned in the infantry, Officers Reserve Corps in 1917. Served with 15th Infantry in China 1921-1924. Professor of military science and tactics at Georgia School of Technology 1926-1928. Duty at the Presidio of San Francisco 1928-1936 Retired in August 1937. Recalled to active duty as assistant military attache to London November 1940-February 1942. Adjutant general at the San Francisco Port of Embarkation April-October 1942. Executive officer in the office of the military attache to London October 1942-May 1943. Director of press relations, propoganda and censorship at Allied Force Headquarters of the North African Theater of Operations 1943-1945. Brigadier general in February 1944. Decorations included the Distinguished Service Medal. Died on June 19, 1980.

McClure, Mark (1898-1990) Born on February 6, 1898, in Anderson, Indiana. Commissioned in the field artillery from West Point in 1922. Instructor at West Point July 1930-August 1935. Served with 13th Field Artillery in Hawaii 1935-1938. Graduated from the Command and General Staff School in 1939. Duty in the office of the chief of field artillery 1939-1942. Assistant chief of staff for intelligence at 95th Infantry Division May-October 1942. Chief of staff of 100th Infantry Division October 1942-May 1944. Commanding general of 95th Division Artillery 1944-1945. Brigadier general in March 1945. Assignments after the war included chief of staff of Eighth Army in 1954, commanding general of 24th Division 1954-1955 and deputy commanding general of Fourth Army 1955-1957. Retired in September 1957. Decorations included the Distinguished Service

Medal, Silver Star, Legion of Merit, two Bronze Stars and the Purple Heart. Died on October 2, 1990.

McClure, Robert A. (1897-1957) Born in Mattoon, Illinois, on March 4, 1897. Attended West Point. Commissioned in the infantry in 1917. Instructor at the Infantry School 1926-1930. Graduated from the Command and General Staff School in 1932 and the Army War College in 1936. Instructor there 1936-1940. Military attache in London 1941-1942. Brigadier general in March 1942. Chief of intelligence in the European Theater of Operations in 1942, then at Allied Forces headquarters 1942-1943. Major general in March 1944. Chief of psychological warfare division at SHAEF 1944-1945. Director of information control division in the military government in Germany 1945-1947. Retired in May 1957. Decorations included two Distinguished Service Medals, two Legions of Merit and the Bronze Star. Died on January 1, 1957.

McClure, Robert Battey (1896-1973) Born in Rome, Georgia, on September 15, 1896. Attended USNA 1916-1917. Commissioned in the infantry in 1917. Served with the AEF during World War I. Professor of military science and tactics at New York Military Academy 1919-1924. Attended Chemical Warfare School in 1928. Duty in Tientsin 1929-1931. Graduated from the Command and General Staff School in 1936 and the Army War College in 1940. Duty in Hawaii 1940-1942 and the South Pacific 1942-1944. Brigadier general in 1943. Chief of staff of U.S. forces in the China Theater of Operations in 1944. Commanding general of Chinese Combat Command and deputy chief of staff to Chiang Kai-shek 1945-1946. Retired as major general in May 1954. Decorations included the Distinguished Service Cross, two Distinguished Service Medals, the Legion of Merit, two Bronze Stars and two Purple Hearts. Died on September 15, 1973.

McCoach, David Jr. (1887-1951) Born in Philadelphia, Pennsylvania, on January 27, 1887. Commissioned in the Corps of Engineers from West Point in 1910. Served in the Panama Canal Zone 1910-1911 and again 1915-1917. Staff officer with 27th Division, AEF in 1918. Graduated from the Command and General Staff School in 1923 and the Army War College in 1928. Engineer commissioner in Washington 1938-1941. Executive officer in the office of the chief of engineers May 1941-October 1943. Brigadier general in January 1942, major general in September 1943. Commanding general of 9th Service Command October 1943-September 1944. Chief of the engineer section at Allied Forces North Africa Theater of Operations 1944-1945. Commanding general of 6th Service Command May 1945 until retirement in April 1946. Decorations included two Distinguished Service Medals and the Legion of Merit. Died on December 15, 1951.

McConnell, Frank Charles (1898-1981) Born in Cicero, Indiana, on June 21, 1898. B.S. from Purdue in 1920. Commissioned in the Coast Artillery Corps in 1921. Served with 92nd Coast Artillery in the Philippines 1925-1927 and 64th Coast Artillery in Hawaii 1931-1932. Graduated from the Command and General Staff School in 1937. Duty with 1st Coast Artillery, Panama Canal Zone 1937-

1939. Executive officer of 39th Coast Artillery Brigade 1941-1942. Duty at headquarters of Antiaircraft Command, Army Ground Forces 1942-1945. Brigadier general in September 1943. Commanding general of 32nd Antiaircraft Artillery Brigade 1945-1946. Deputy commander of Philippine Ground Forces Command in 1946. Reverted to colonel in May 1946. Retired in September 1957. Decorations included two Legions of Merit and two Bronze Stars. Died on August 23, 1981.

McCornack, Condon Carlton (1880-1944) Born on May 7, 1880, in St. Helena, California. B.S. from the University of Oregon in 1901. M.D. from Jefferson Medical College in 1904. Commissioned in the Medical Corps in 1910. Graduated from Army Medical School in 1910. Served in the Philippine Islands 1912-1913 and China 1913-1915. Student then instructor at the Command and General Staff School 1920-1924. Graduated from the Army War College in 1925, then instructor there until 1929. Assistant commandant of Medical Field Service School 1929-1932. Post surgeon at Schofield Barracks, Hawaii then surgeon for Hawaiian Department June 1936-May 1939. Surgeon at IX Corps Area 1939-40, then Fourth Army 1940-1943. Deputy chief of staff of Western Defense Command January 1943 until retirement in May 1944. Brigadier general in February 1944. Decorations included the Legion of Merit. Died on November 5, 1944.

McCoy, Frank Ross (1874 -1954) Born in Lewistown, Pennsylvania, on October 29, 1874, the son of Major General Thomas F. McCoy. Commissioned in the cavalry from West Point in 1897. Aide-de-camp to Major General Leonard Wood 1900-1901, President Theodore Roosevelt in 1902, Secretary of War William H. Taft in 1906 and Roosevelt again 1907-1908. Graduated from the Army War College in 1908. Commanding officer of a cavalry patrol on the Mexican border 1915-1916. Military attache in Mexico City in 1917. Member of the general staff at GHQ AEF 1917-1918. Brigadier general in August 1918. Commanding general of 63rd Infantry Brigade, AEF in 1918. Director general of transportation in the AEF 1918-1919. Reverted to colonel after the war. Assistant to Leonard Wood, governor general of the Philippines 1921-1925. Brigadier general again in September 1923. Brigade commander in 2nd Infantry Division 1925-1927. Served in Nicaragua 1927-1928. Major general in September 1929. Commanding general of IV Corps Area 1929-1932. Commanding general of 1st Cavalry Division March-October 1933, VII Corps Area 1933-1935, VI Corps Area 1935-1936 and II Corps Area May 1936 until retirement in October 1938. Returned to active duty in December 1941 as a member of the Roberts Commission investigating the Pearl Harbor disaster, then chairman of a military commission trying Nazi saboteurs and spies in 1942. Chairman of the Far Eastern Commission 1945-1949. Decorations included two Distinguished Service Medals, two Silver Stars and the Purple Heart. Died on June 4, 1954.

McCroskey, Samuel Lusker (1893-1960) Born in Colfax, Washington, on February 4, 1893. B.A. from Washington State College in 1916. Commissioned in the Coast Artillery Corps in 1917. Duty at Fort Amador, Canal Zone 1921-1924. Instructor at Coast Artillery School 1925-1928. Graduated from the Command and General Staff School in 1936. Executive officer of Camp Davis January-July 1941 then the 16th Coast Artillery Training Group July-December 1941. Member of the Coast Artillery Board December 1941-March 1942. Commanding officer of 38th Coast Artillery Brigade May-June 1942. Brigadier general in June 1942. Commanding general, 55th Coast Artillery Brigade June 1942-February 1945. Reverted to colonel in February 1946. Retired in September 1950. Decorations included two Legions of Merit and the Bronze Star. Died on June 3, 1960.

McCulloch, William Alexander (1889-1959) Born on February 10, 1889, in Rensselaer, New York. Commissioned in the infantry from West Point in 1913. Commanding officer of 199th Machine Gun Battalion, 32nd Division in World War I. Wounded twice, in August and September 1918. Member of tactical department at West Point 1923-1927. Graduated from the Command and General Staff School in 1928. Professor of military science and tactics at Drexel Institute 1928-1935. Instructor with the South Carolina National Guard 1936-1940. Commanding officer of 24th Infantry in Hawaii 1940-1941 then 27th Infantry, 25th Division 1941-1943. Brigadier general in March 1943. Assistant division commander of Americal Division 1943-1944. Commanding general of War Department Personnel Center at Fort Bragg in 1945. Reverted to colonel in November 1945.. Retired in February 1949. Decorations included the Legion of Merit, two Bronze Stars and two Purple Hearts. Died on December 2, 1959.

McCunniff, Dennis Edward (1889-1960) Born on October 31, 1889, in La Jara, Colorado. Commissioned in the infantry from West Point in 1913. With Pershing on the Punitive Expedition into Mexico. Aide to Brigadier General F.J. Kernan, commanding general of Services of Supply in the AEF in World War I. Instructor with the Colorado National Guard 1919-1922 then at West Point 1922-1923. Served in China with 15th Infantry 1923-1926. Instructor at the Infantry School 1928-1932. Instructor, then commandant of cadets at West Point 1932-1937. Chief of staff of 2nd Division December 1940-November 1941. Duty with 34th Infantry in 1941 and U.S. Army Forces Central Pacific in 1942. Brigadier general in February 1943. Commanding general of combat command "A," Pacific Ocean Areas 1943-1945. Reverted to colonel in March 1946. Retired in October 1949. Decorations included the Legion of Merit. Died on April 3, 1960.

McDonald, Robert Clarence (1881-1958) Born on February 18, 1881, in Bells, Tennessee. M.D. from Tulane University in 1909. Commissioned in the Medical Corps in 1911. Graduated from AMS in 1911. Served in Hawaii 1911-1916 and with the AEF in 1918. Graduated from the Command and General Staff School in 1926 and the Army War College in 1930. Surgeon at Thrid Army 1940-1942. Chief of the medical branch at 3rd Service Command 1942-1943. Commanding officer of England General Hospital 1943-1944. Surgeon with 4th Service Command July 1944 until retirement in February 1945. Brigadier general in January 1945. Decorations included the Legion of Merit. Died on March 17, 1958.

McDowell, Rex McKinley (1893-n/a) Born on July 14, 1893, in Dayton, Ohio. D.D.S. from Ohio State University in 1916. Commissioned a dental surgeon in 1916. Dental surgeon with 42nd Division, AEF 1918-1919 and at the station hospital, Camp Stotsenberg, Philippine Islands 1925-1927. Graduated from Army Industrial College in 1932. Dental surgeon at Fort Kamehameha, Hawaii 1937-1939. Assistant chief of the dental division, than assistant director, office of the surgeon general, U.S. Army 1939-1945. Brigadier general in January 1945. Retired in December 1948. Decorations included the Legion of Merit.

McFarland, Andrew Jackson (1888-1965) Born on May 7, 1888, in Robinson Springs, Alabama. Served as an officer with the Alabama National Guard July 1913-October 1919. Commissioned in the infantry in 1920. Duty with 57th Infantry in the Philippines 1924-1927. Professor of military science and tactics at the University of Maine 1930-1932. Instructor with the organized reserves in Wichita 1934-1935. Graduated from the Army War College in 1936. Instructor at the Command and General Staff School 1938-1942. Served with the Combined Chiefs of Staff as secretary of combined staff planners then secretary of the Combined Chiefs from September 1942. Brigadier general in May 1944. Retired in May 1947. Decorations included the Distinguished Service Medal. Died on September 10, 1965.

McFarland, Earl (1883-1972) Born in Topeka, Kansas, on July 7, 1883. M.E. from Worcester Polytechnic Institute in 1923. Commissioned in the artillery from West Point in 1906. Professor at West Point 1924-1929. Graduated from the Command and General Staff School in 1931, Army Industrial College in 1933 and the Army War College in 1934. Brigadier general in June 1938. Assistant to the chief of ordnance 1938-1942. Commander of Springfield Armory June 1942 until retirement in July 1943. Decorations included the Distinguished Service Medal. Died on January 19, 1972.

McGaw, Edward John (1901-1972) Born on February 13, 1901, in Philadelphia, Pennsylvania. Commissioned in the field artillery from West Point in 1920. Instructor at West Point 1925-1930. Graduated from the Command and General Staff School in 1936. Again at West Point as instructor 1936-1939. Graduated from the Army War College in 1940. Commanding officer of the 7th Field Artillery Observation Battalion 1941-1942. Commanding general of 63rd Division Artillery 1943-1945. Brigadier general in June 1943. Deputy chief of staff for operations with Army Forces Western Pacific 1945-1947. Assignments after the war included commanding general of 11th Airborne Division Artillery in 1947 and VI Corps Artillery 1952-1953 and commanding general of 1st Cavalry Division 1955-1956. Retired as major general in February 1961. Decorations included the Distinguished Service Medal, two Legions of Merit, three Bronze Stars, the Air Medal and two Commendation Ribbons. Died on March 19, 1972.

McGinley, Eugene (1900-1972) Born on January 28, 1900, in Hamilton, Ohio. Commissioned in the Coast Artillery Corps from West Point in 1919. Aide-de-camp to Major General Ernest Hinds July 1923-October 1924. Duty with 13th Field Artillery in Hawaii 1927-1930. Aide to Brigadier General Paul A. Wolf June 1930-July 1932. Graduated from the Command and General Staff School in 1937. With the supply division of the War Department General Staff 1940-1942. Chief of the operations division at Services of Supply March 1942-November 1943. Artillery officer at Second Army 1943-1944 and Eighth Army 1944-1946. Brigadier general in June 1945. Reverted to colonel in March 1946. Retired as major general in October 1955. Decorations included the Distinguished Service Medal, Legion of Merit and Bronze Star. Died on February 12, 1972.

McIntyre, Andrew Frank (1892-1974) Born in Canandaigua, New York, on April 4, 1892. With Pennsylvania Railroad 1909-1942. Called to active duty in January 1942 as colonel and chief of the railroad section, office of the assistant chief of staff for supply, the War Department General Staff. Brigadier general in August 1944. Returned to civilian status in January 1946. Recalled to temporary active duty as assistant chief of army transportation during the threatened railroad strike in 1948 and again in 1950. Decorations included the Distinguished Service Medal. Died on October 23, 1974.

McKay, Neal Henry (1896-1951) Born in Troupe, Texas, on June 10, 1896. Commissioned in the Quartermaster Corps in 1920. Graduated from the Army Industrial College in 1940. Brigadier general in November 1944. Retired in March 1948. Decorations included the Distinguished Service Medal, Legion of Merit, Bronze Star and the Commendation Ribbon. Died on June 11, 1951.

McKee, John Lloyd (1895-1963) Born in Pittsburgh, Pennsylvania, on December 8, 1895. Attended Virginia Military Institute 1911-1913 and Richmond College 1913-1915. Enlisted service in the Virginia National Guard 1913-1915. Commissioned in the infantry in 1915. Served on the Mexican border in 1916 and in the AEF 1917-1918 in the Second Marne, Belleau Woods, Champagne-Marne and Aisne-Marne engagements. Aide to Brigadier General G.B. Duncan 1920-1921. Duty in Hawaii 1924-1927. Graduated from the Command and General Staff School in 1932. Professor of military science and tactics at Louisiana State University 1932-1934. Graduated from the Army War College in 1935. Again in Hawaii, duty with the Hawaiian Department 1935-1937. Professor of military science and tactics at Valley Forge Military Academy 1939-1941. With the war plans division at the War Department General Staff 1941-1942. Brigadier general in September 1942. Assistant division commander of 8th Motorized Division in 1942, then 87th Infantry Division 1942-1945. Reverted to colonel in January 1946. Retired in April 1953. Decorations included the Silver Star, Legion of Merit and two Bronze Stars. Died on November 18, 1963.

McKenzie, Henry Ray (1904-1992) Born on July 25, 1904, in Hamilton, Texas. Commissioned in the Coast Artillery Corps from West Point in 1929. Asssistant quartermaster at the Army Medical Center, Washington, DC 1936-1937. Graduated from Army Industrial College and MBA from Harvard in 1940. Brigadier general in March 1945. Chief quartermaster for U.S. Army forces in the Mid Pacific 1945-1946. Retired in September 1958. Decorations included three Legions of Merit. Died on December 27, 1992.

McKinley, Edward Brigham (1895-1963) Born on December 20, 1895, in Washington, DC. Commissioned in the Sanitary Corps in 1917. Served with the AEF in 1918. B.S. from Maryland State College in 1920. Duty at Schofield Barracks, Hawaii 1932-1935. M.B.A. from Harvard in 1937. Graduated from Army Industrial College in 1938 and the Army War College in 1939. Chief fiscal officer in the office of the quartermaster general June 1939-January 1945. Brigadier general in April 1943. Deputy vice president of the Allied Commission in Italy January-September 1945. Retired in March 1948. Decorations included two Legions of Merit and the Commendation Ribbon. Died on July 15, 1963.

McMahon, John Eugene Jr. (1890-1971) Born on September 11, 1890, in West Point, New York. Commissioned in the field artillery from West Point in 1913. Instructor at West Point 1916-1918. Professor of military science and tactics at Princeton University 1918-1923. Served with the 8th Field Artillery in Hawaii 1923-1926. Graduated from the Command and General Staff School in 1928. Professor of military science and tactics at Purdue 1928-1933. Graduated from the Army War College in 1934. Assistant executive in the office of the assistant secretary of war 1934-1938. Duty at headquarters of 7th Division 1940-1942. Brigadier general in February 1942. Commanding general of 77th Infantry Division Artillery 1942-1943. Commanding general of VIII Corps Artillery 1943-1945. Commanding general of 5th Service Command 1945-1946. Reverted to colonel in March 1946. Retired in September 1950. Decorations included the Distinguished Service Medal, two Legions of Merit and the Bronze Star. Died on June 27, 1971.

McMahon, Leo Thomas (1893-1987) Born on July 31, 1893, in Rome, New York. Attended Union College 1915-1916. Commissioned in the cavalry in 1918. Served with the AEF in 1918 and American occupation forces in Germany in 1919. Transferred to the field artillery in 1920. Aide-de-camp to Brigadier General Robert Alexander 1922-1923. Instructor with Kansas National Guard 1923-1927 and Pennsylvania National Guard 1933-1934. Graduated from the Command and General Staff School in 1936. Again with Pennsylvania National Guard 1936-1941. Assistant chief of staff for operations at 28th Division, II Army Corps, XI Corps and Second Army December 1941-August 1943. Brigadier general in September 1943. Commanding general of 65th Division Artillery September-November 1943 then 106th Division Artillery November 1943-April 1945. Commanding general of 106th Division April-August 1945 then XXIII Corps Artillery August-October 1945. Reverted to colonel in February 1946. Retired in February 1948. Decorations included the Legion of Merit and Bronze Star. Died on September 28, 1987.

McMahon, William Claude (1895-1990) Born on January 10, 1895, in Brooklyn, New York. Commissioned in the infantry from West Point in 1917. Served with First Army, AEF in World War I. Attended Columbia Law School 1924-1927. Assistant professor at West Point 1925-1929. Graduated from the Command and General Staff School in 1934. Instructor at the Infantry School 1934-1935. Graduated from the Army War College in 1936. Instructor at the Command and General Staff School 1936-1940. Assistant chief of staff for supply at 4th Motorized Division July 1940-January 1943. Brigadier general in June 1942. Major general in February 1943. Commanding general of 8th Motorized Division 1943-1944. Deputy chief of staff for personnel at 15th Army Group 1944-1945. Chief of staff of U.S. forces in Austria 1945-1946. Retired in September 1949. Decorations included the Distinguished Service Medal and Legion of Merit. Died on March 30, 1990.

McNair, Lesley James (1883-1944) Born in Verndale, Minnesota, on May 25, 1883. Commissioned in the Artillery from West Point in 1904. Saw duty with the Funston Expedition to Vera Cruz in 1914 and the Pershing Punitive Expedition into Mexico in 1917. Served with the 1st Division, then at general headquarters of the AEF 1917-1919. Professor of military science and tactics at Purdue University 1924-1928. Graduated from the Army War College in 1929. Brigadier general in January 1937. Commander of 2nd Field Artillery Brigade March 1937-April 1939. Commandant of the Command and General Staff School April 1939-July 1940. Chief of staff at GHQ, U.S. Army, July 1940-March 1942. Major general in September 1940 and lieutenant general in June 1941. Commanding general of Army Ground Forces March 1942-June 1944. Assigned to the European Theater of Operations in the summer of 1944 as commander of a diversionary, nonexistant army. Killed in his foxhole near St. Lo by an errant Allied bomb on July 23, 1944. Decorations included three Distinguished Service Medals. Posthumous promotion to general in July 1954.

McNaught, Warren Henry (1894-1984) Born on January 24, 1894, in Plymouth, Massachusetts. Attended Massachusetts Agricultural College. Commissioned in the field artillery, Officers Reserve Corps in 1917. Served with the 77th Field Artillery, AEF at Meuse-Argonne in 1918. Duty at Fort Stotsenburg, Philippines with 24th Field Artillery July 1928-August 1930. Instructor with the New York National Guard 1930-1933 then the organized reserves in Wisconsin 1937-1939. Adjutant, then executive officer for the Wisconsin Military Area August 1939-November 1941. Executive officer of 5th Infantry Division Artillery 1941-1942 then 93rd Infantry Division Artillery from February 1942. Brigadier general in June 1945. Reverted to colonel in April 1946. Retired in July 1951. Decorations included the Legion of Merit, Bronze Star, and Air Medal. Died on February 21, 1984.

McNeil, Edwin Colyer (1882-1965) Born in Alexandria, Minnesota, on November 13, 1882. Attended the University of Minnesota 1900-1901. Commissioned in the infantry from West Point in 1907. Instructor at West Point 1910-1913. LL.B.

from Columbia in 1916. Graduated from Army General Staff School in 1918. Served as assistant judge advocate general at headquarters of AEF in 1918. Graduated from the Army War College in 1923. Professor at West Point 1923-1929. Assistant to the hudge advocate general, U.S. Army 1936-1942. Brigadier general in January 1942. Assistant judge advocate general in the European Theater of Operations 1943-1944. Retired in November 1944. Recalled to active duty the following day in the same position and served there until 1946. Decorations included the Distinguished Service Medal and Legion of Merit. Died on October 1, 1965.

McQuillin, Raymond Eugene (1887-1982) Born on December 24, 1887, in Britton, South Dakota. B.S. from the University of Minnesota in 1911. Commissioned in the cavalry in 1912. Duty on the Mexican border 1912-1916. Attended Yale 1919-1920. Instructor at the Cavalry School 1920-1923. Graduated from the Command and General Staff School in 1925. Military aide in the White House 1927-1931. Graduated from the Army War College in 1931. Instructor at the Command and General Staff School 1936-1940. Combat Commander in 1st Armored Division February 1942-May 1943. Assistant sector commander of Western Defense Command 1943-1944. Brigadier general in March 1942. Commander of the gulf sector, Southern Defense Command 1944-1945. Commanding general of the southwest sector, Eastern Defense Command 1945-1946. Reverted to colonel in March 1946. Retired in February 1948. Decorations included the Silver Star and Commendation Ribbon. Died on March 31, 1982.

McReynolds, Wilbur Reece (1892-1957) Born in Spring Valley, Ohio, on September 9, 1892. A.B. and B.S. from Ohio University 1915 and 1916. Commissioned in the infantry in 1917. With 10th Division in France 1918. While commanding officer of the Subsistence School and Research Laboratory he developed "c rations" that were used extensively in World War II. Graduated from the Command and General Staff School in 1939. Quartermaster at Barksdale Field 1939-1940. Director of military training in the office of the chief of the Quartermaster Corps 1941-1944. Brigadier general in November 1943. Air quartermaster at headquarters AAF November 1944-May 1946. Retired in October 1947. Decorations included two Legions of Merit and the Commendation Ribbon. Died on April 3, 1957.

McSherry, Frank Johnson (1892-1980) Born on October 18, 1892, in Eldorado Springs, Missouri. B.S. from the University of Arizona in 1916, a second B.S. in 1917. Commissioned in the Coast Artillery Corps in 1917. Served with the 62nd Coast Artillery, AEF in World War I. Graduate study at Massachusetts Institute of Technology 1923-1924. Graduated from the Command and General Staff School in 1934 and the Army War College in 1937. War Department liaison with the Federal Security Administration 1938-1940, then the labor division's Advisory Commission to the Council of National Defense 1940-1941. Brigadier general in February 1942. Director of operations for the War Manpower Commission in 1942. Deputy chief of the Allied military government in the European Theater of

Operations 1943-1944. Deputy assistant chief of staff for civil affairs then director of the mapower division for Germany at SHAEF 1944-1946. Retired in October 1946. Decorations included the Distinguished Service Medal, Legion of Merit and Bronze Star. Died on August 1, 1980.

Mead, Armistead Davis (1901-1980) Born on October 16, 1901, in Charleston, West Virginia. Commissioned in the infantry from West Point in 1924. Assistant chief of the war plans division at headquarters of the Commander South Pacific Area in 1942. Assistant chief of staff for operations at Fourth Army 1943-1944 and Ninth Army 1944-1945. Brigadier general in June 1945. Assignments after the war included assistant division commander of 3rd Division in the Korean War 1950-1951, chief of staff of Third Army 1952-1953, commanding general of 1st Cavalry Division 1953-1954 and chief of civil affairs, Department of the Army 1959-1961. Retired in 1961. Decorations included two Distinguished Service Medals, three Silver Stars, the Legion of Merit and Bronze Star. Died on February 20, 1980.

Meade, Frank Celestine (1896-1978) Born on December 16, 1896, in Philadelphia, Pennsylvania. Commissioned in the Coast Artillery Corps from West Point in 1917. Instructor at West Point 1918-1919. Served with 55th Artillery in Hawaii 1923-1924. Professor of military science and tactics at the University of Wisconsin 1928-1932. M.S. from Yale in 1933. Graduated from the Command and General Staff School in 1938. In the office of the chief signal officer at war plans division, the War Department General Staff 1938-1942. Brigadier general in December 1942. Officer in charge of air communications divisions, then director of operations division at the War Department General Staff 1942-1944. Deputy for communications at headquarters of the European Theater of Operations October 1944-April 1946. Reverted to colonel in April 1946. Retired in October 1947. Decorations include two Legions of Merit. Died on December 24, 1978.

Mehaffey, Joseph Cowles (1889-1963) Born in Lima, Ohio, on November 20, 1889. Commissioned in the Corps of Engineers from West Point in 1911. Assistant to the chief of engineers 1917-1919. Graduated from the Command and General Staff School in 1935 and the Army War College in 1939. Commanding officer of 1st Engineers, 1st Infantry Division 1939-1940. Engineer at I Corps in 1941. Engineer of maintenance at the Panama Canal 1941-1944. Brigadier general in June 1942, major general in May 1944. Governor of the Panama Canal Zone 1944-1948. Retired in November 1949. Decorations included the Distinguished Service Medal and Legion of Merit. Died on February 18, 1963.

Melasky, Harris Marcy (1893-1972) Born on April 11, 1893, in Austin, Texas. Commissioned in the infantry from West Point in 1917. Served with the 12th Infantry, AEF in World War I in 1918. Duty in the Philippine Islands 1920-1921 then with the 15th Infantry in China 1921-1922. Graduated from the Command and General Staff School in 1935 and the Army War College in 1937. Chief of the test section on the Infantry Board 1939-1941. Assistant to the plans and training officer at the Caribbean Defense Command in 1942. Brigadier general in July 1942. Commanding general of 86th Infantry Division 1943-1945. Major general in February 1943. Retired in September 1946. Decorations included the Distinguished Service Cross, Distinguished Service Medal and Bronze Star. Died on October 24, 1972.

Menoher, Pearson (1892-1958) Born on November 14, 1892, in Fort Monroe, Virginia. Commissioned in the cavalry from West Point in 1915. With the Punitive Expedition into Mexico 1916-1917. Assistant chief of staff of 9th Division 1918-1919. Graduated from the Command and General Staff School in 1928 then instructor there until 1932. Chief of staff of XV Corps and Seventh Army 1943-1945. Brigadier general in January 1945. Assignments after the war included assistant division commander, then commanding general of 24th Division in the Korean War 1949-1950 and commanding general of V Corps 1950-1952. Retired in May 1952. Decorations included two Distinguished Service Medals, the Silver Star, Legion of Merit, three Bronze Stars and three Commendation Ribbons. Died on February 13, 1958.

Merrill, Frank Dow (1903-1955) Born on December 4, 1903, in Hopkinton, Massachusetts. Commissioned in the cavalry from West Point in 1929. B.S. from Massachusetts Institute of Technology in 1932. Instructor at the Cavalry School 1935-1938. Military attache in Tokyo 1938-1941. Deputy chief of staff for operations in the China-Burma-India Theater of Operations 1942-1943. Brigadier general in November 1943. In 1944 he organized and commanded "Merrill's Marauders," 3,000 volunteers who infiltrated behind enemy lines in Burma and won every engagement. Major general in September 1944. Chief of staff of Tenth Army 1945-1948, then Sixth Army briefly in 1948 until retiremen in June 1948. Decorations included the Distinguished Service Medal, two Legions of Merit, two Bronze Stars and the Purple Heart. Died on December 11, 1955.

Metcalfe, Raymond Franklin (1877-1957) Born in Salamanca, New York, on May 27, 1877. M.D. from the University of Buffalo in 1900. Commissioned in the Medical Corps in 1901. Served in the Philippines 1902-1905 and again 1907-1910. Division surgeon with the 36th Division, AEF in 1918. Commanding officer of Tripler General Hospital 1927-1930. Duty at Army Medical Center in Washington, DC 1935-1937. Brigadier general in December 1937. Assistant to the surgeon general of the Army March 1937 until retirement in May 1941. Recalled to active duty in December 1941. Duty at San Francisco Port of Embarkation then member of the Army Retiring Board until retirement again in February 1946. Decorations included the Distinguished Service Medal. Died on May 8, 1957.

Metzger, Earl Harrison (1889-1972) Born in Steelton, Pennsylvania, on August 14, 1889. B.S. from Pennsylvania State College in 1911. Commissioned in the Coast Artillery Corps in 1912. Served with the 52nd Coast Artillery, AEF at St. Mihiel and Meuse-Argonne in 1918. Graduated from the Command and General Staff School in 1925. Duty with 4th Coast Artillery at Fort Amador, Canal Zone

1925-1929. Graduated from the Army War College in 1935. Instructor with Rhode Island National Guard 1935-1938. Brigadier general in February 1942. Commanding general of Coast Artillery Antiaircraft Training Center at Camp Stewart February 1942-February 1943. Commander of 76th Antiaircraft Artillery Brigade in the Caribbean Defense Command 1943-1946. Reverted to colonel in March 1946. Retired in August 1949. Decorations included the Legion of Merit. Died on December 16, 1972.

Meyer, George Ralph (1886-1961) Born in Montgomery, Minnesota, on November 27, 1886. Attended the University of Minnesota 1904-1905. Commissioned from USNA in 1910. Resigned from the Navy and commissioned in the Coast Artillery Corps in 1911. Duty in Hawaii with 3rd Coast Artillery Company 1916-1918. Instructor at the Coast Artillery School 1918-1919. Graduated from the Command and General Staff School in 1925. Instructor at Coast Artillery School 1925-1929. Graduated from the Army War College in 1935 and the Naval War College in 1936. Instructor at the Command and General Staff School 1936-1940. Chief of staff of IX Corps 1940-1941. Brigadier general in August 1941. Commander of the Pacific Brigade of Panama Coast Artillery 1941-1943. Major general in March 1943. Commanding general of Panama Coast Artillery Command 1943-1945 then the Antiaircraft Command at Fort Bliss 1945-1946. Retired in August 1946. Decorations included the Distinguished Service Medal and Legion of Merit. Died on October 8, 1961.

Meyer, Henry John Dick (1899-1972) Born on September 20, 1899, in New York City. Commissioned in the field artillery from West Point in 1919. Duty at Schofield Barracks, Hawaii 1920-1923. Instructor at West Point 1925-1929. M.S. from Massachusetts Institute of Technology in 1933. Battalion commander in the Philippine Division 1938-1941. Executive officer of 13th Field Artillery Brigade, then commanding officer of 17th Field Artillery Regiment July 1942-May 1944. Brigadier general in September 1944. Commanding general of 45th Division Artillery 1944-1945. Retired in May 1957. Decorations included four Silver Stars, two Legions of Merit and the Purple Heart. Died on March 4, 1972.

Meyer, Vincent (1889-1974) Born in New York City on August 29, 1889. Commissioned from USNA in 1911. Resigned to accept a commission in the field artillery. Served in the Philippines 1913-1916, on the Mexican border 1916-1917 and with the AEF in World War I, where he saw action at Aisne-Marne, St. Mihiel and Meuse-Argonne. Instructor at Field Artillery School 1920-1923. Graduated from the Command and General Staff School in 1930 then instructor there until 1934. Graduated from the Army War College in 1937. Served with the supply division of the War Department General Staff 1937-1941. Brigadier general in October 1941. Commander of 18th Field Artillery Brigade November 1941-March 1944. Member of the European Advisory Committee, then Allied Control Council in Berlin 1944-1945. Retired in December 1945. Decorations included the Distinguished Service Medal. Died on July 28, 1974.

Meyers, Harry Frederick (1897-) Born on May 6, 1897, in Mason City, Iowa. B.A. from Des Moines University in 1920. Commissioned in the Coast Artillery Corps in 1920. Served at Fort Amador, Canal Zone 1921-1924. Assistant professor of military science and tactics at the University of Kansas 1925-1931. Duty with the 92nd Coast Artillery in the Philippines 1931-1933. Graduated from the Command and General Staff School in 1937. In Hawaii with 64th Coast Artillery 1939-1941. Secretary of the Coast Artillery School 1942-1943. Commander of 74th Antiaircraft Artillery Brigade September 1943-September 1945. Brigadier general in January 1944. Commanding general of the Antiaircraft Replacement Training Center at Fort Bliss 1945-1946. Reverted to colonel in March 1946. Retired in August 1954. Decorations included the Legion of Merit, Bronze Star, Commendation Ribbon and Purple Heart.

Michela, Joseph Anthony (1903-1949) Born on March 5, 1903, in Iron Mountain, Michigan. Commissioned in the cavalry from West Point in 1928. M.A. from Columbia in 1937. Graduated from the Command and General Staff School in 1940. Assistant military attache in Moscow 1940-1943. Brigadier general in December 1942. In the military intelligence division of the War Department 1943-1946. Reverted to colonel in 1946. Military attache in Prague at his death on June 12, 1949. Decorations included the Legion of Merit.

Mickelsen, Stanley Raymond (1895-1966) Born on October 8, 1895, in St. Paul, Minnesota. Commissioned in the Coast Artillery Corps in 1917. Duty in the Panama Canal Zone July 1918-November 1921. Instructor with the Connecticut National Guard 1923-1927. Instructor at the Coast Artillery School 1929-1933. Duty at Fort Mills, Philippine Islands 1933-1935. Graduated from the Command and General Staff School in 1936 and the Army War College in 1938. Commanding officer of 74th Coast Artillery October 1941-March 1942. Brigadier general in March 1942. Commanding general of 47th Artillery Brigade 1942-1943. Commanding general of Antiaircraft Artillery Training Center at Fort Bliss November 1943-November 1944. Duty at SHAEF 1944-1947. Reverted to colonel in March 1946. Retired as lieutenant general in October 1957. Decorations included two Distinguished Service Medals and the Legion of Merit. Died on March 28, 1966.

Mickle, Gerald St. Claire (1899-1972) Born on July 21, 1899, in Mobile, Alabama. Commissioned in the infantry from West Point in 1919. Served with 14th Infantry in the Panama Canal Zone 1923-1925. Instructor with Alabama National Guard 1930-1931. Again in the Canal Zone 1931-1933. Professor of military science and tactics at Riverside Academy 1935-1936. Graduated from the Command and General Staff School in 1936 and the Army War College in 1940. Assistant chief of staff for operations at 3rd Division then III Corps July 1940-January 1943. Brigadier general in March 1943. Assistant division commander of 75th Division in 1943 then 83rd Division 1943-1946. Retired in September 1946. Decorations included the Silver Star, Legion of Merit and Bronze Star. Died on September 16, 1972.

Middleton, John William (1897-1957) Born on May 10, 1897, in Broad Brook, Connecticut. Commissioned in the infantry from West Point in 1918. Served with 8th Infantry in France, Germany and Belgium 1919-1923. Instructor at West Point 1924-1929. Professor of military science and tactics at Ohio State University June 1930-August 1936. Graduated from the Command and General Staff School in 1937. Duty with 45th Infantry in the Philippines 1937-1939. At the Infantry School 1941-1942. With Army Ground Forces 1942-1943. In China 1943-1946. Brigadier general in March 1945. Retired in August 1954. Decorations included the Distinguished Service Medal, Legion of Merit and Bronze Star. Died on January 20, 1957.

Middleton, Troy Houston (1889-1976) Born on October 12, 1889, in Hazelhurst, Mississippi. B.S. from Mississippi Agricultural and Mechanical College in 1909. Enlisted service 1910-1912. Commissioned in the infantry in 1912. Served with the Punitive Expedition into Mexico in 1916 and the 47th and 39th Infantry in the AEF including the Aisne-Marne, St. Mihiel and Meuse-Argonne offensives. Instructor at the Infantry School 1919-1921. Graduated from the Command and General Staff School in 1924 and the Army War College in 1929. Professor of military science and tactics at Louisiana State University February 1930-September 1936. Retired as colonel in October 1937. Dean, then comptroller at Louisiana State University November 1937-January 1941. Recalled to active duty in January 1941. Duty at the Infantry Replacement Training Center 1941-1942. Assigned to the 4th Motorized Division March-April 1942 and the 36th Infantry Division April-May 1942. Brigadier general in June 1942, major general in October 1942. Commanding general of 45th Infantry Division 1942-1944. Commander of VIII Corps March 1944 until retirement as lieutenant general in August 1945. Decorations included two Distinguished Service Medals, the Silver Star, Legion of Merit and Bronze Star. President of Louisiana State University 1951-1962. Died on October 9, 1976.

Middleswart, William Herschel (1894-1964) Born in Portland, Oregon, on October 19, 1894. Attended Virginia Polytechnic Institute 1916-1917. Commissioned in the Quartermaster Corps in 1920. Attended George Washington University 1922-1924. Duty at the Philippine Quartermaster Depot 1927-1929. Graduated from Army Industrial College in 1937 and the Army War College in 1938. Commander of the Pacific Motor Pool at Fort Davis, Canal Zone 1938-1940. Served at the Philadelphia Quartermaster Depot 1940-1941. Chief quartermaster of the European Theater of Operations January-August 1942. At the Atlantic Base Section 1942-1943. Quartermaster of the Mediterranean Theater of Operations 1943-1945. Brigadier general in May 1944. Deputy chief quartermaster in the European Theater of Operations February-October 1945. Retired as major general in February 1954. Decorations included the Distinguished Service Medal, two Legions of Merit, the Bronze Star and Commendation Ribbon. Died on June 2, 1964.

Milburn, Bryan Lee (1896-1991) Born on July 2, 1896, in Fayetteville, Arkansas. B.A. from the University of Arkansas in 1917. Commissioned in the Coast Artillery Corps in 1917. Served in the Philippines and Hawaii. Graduated from the Command and General Staff School in 1935 and the Army War College in 1937. Instructor at the Command and General Staff School 1937-1940. Brigadier general in August 1942. Commandant of the Antiaircraft Artillery School, Camp Davis 1942-1944. Duty with the U.S. Group Control Council for Germany, then chief of staff to the military governor of Germany, finally commandant of the Berlin Command 1944-1948. Retired in November 1956. Decorations included the Distinguished Service Medal, two Legions of Merit and the Bronze Star. Died on July 27, 1991.

Milburn, Frank William (1892-1962) Born on January 11, 1892, in Jasper, Indiana. Commissioned in the infantry from West Point in 1914. Duty in the Canal Zone 1914-1918. Instructor at the Infantry School 1922-1926. Professor of military science and tactics at the University of Montana 1926-1931. Graduated from the Command and General Staff School in 1933 then instructor there 1934-1938. Plans and operations officer at 8th Division 1940-1941. Assistant division commander of 6th Division 1941-1942. Brigadier general in February 1942, major general in September 1942. Commanding general of 83rd Division, then XXI Corps 1942-1945. Assignments after the war included commander of V Corps 1945-1946, commanding general of 1st Infantry Division May 1946-August 1949. deputy commander of U.S. Army Europe 1949-1950 and commanding general of I Corps in the Korean War 1950-1951. Retired in April 1952. Decorations included the Distinguished Service Medal, Silver Star, Legion of Merit, Bronze Star and Air Medal. Football and basketball coach at Rocky Mountain College in Colorado Springs, Colorado after retirement. Died on October 25, 1962.

Miles, Sherman (1882-1966) Born in Washington, DC, on December 5, 1882, the son of Lieutenant General Nelson A. Miles. Commissioned in the cavalry from West Point in 1905. Served with 11th Cavalry in Cuba 1906-1907. Military attache in Bucharest, Romania 1912-1914 then Russia 1914-1916. Duty with I Corps at St. Mihiel and Meuse-Argonne offensives, then assistant chief of staff for military intelligence with IX Corps in the AEF 1918-1919. Graduated from the Army War College in 1922. Military attache in Turkey October 1922-April 1925. Graduated from the Command and General Staff School in 1927. Assistant chief of staff for operations and training in the Hawaiian Department 1929-1932. Served with the war plans division at the War Department General Staff July 1934-October 1938. Military attache in London and Ireland 1939-1940. Brigadier general in September 1939. Assistant chief of staff for military intelligence, then operations with the War Department General Staff April 1940-January 1942. Major general in January 1942. Commanding general of the I Corps Area 1942-1945. LL.D. from Bates College in 1943. Retired in February 1946. Decorations included the Distinguished Service Medal. Died on October 7, 1966.

Miley, William Maynadier (1897-) Born on December 26, 1897, in Fort Mason, California. Commissioned in the infantry from West Point in 1918. Professor of military science and tactics at Mississippi State College 1920-1924. Served in the Philippines 1926-1928. Instructor at West Point 1930-1934. Commanding officer of 501st Parachute Battalion then 503rd Parachute Infantry October 1940-January 1942. Commander of 1st Parachute Infantry Brigade in 1942. Brigadier general in June 1942. Assistant division commander of 82nd Infantry Division August 1942-April 1943. Major general in March 1943. Commanding general of 17th Airborne Division April 1943-September 1945. Assignments after the war included commanding general of 8th Division and the Infantry Replacement Training Center at Camp Croft 1945-1946, assistant division commander, then commanding general of 11th Airborne Division February 1947-May 1950, commander of U.S. Army Alaska 1952-1954 and chief of staff of Army Field Forces July 1954 until retirement in July 1955. Decorations included the Distinguished Service Medal, two Silver Stars and two Bronze Stars.

Miller, Fred W. (1891-1946) Born in Manchester, Iowa, on May 10, 1891. Commissioned in the Iowa National Guard in 1916. Served with the 50th Infantry in Germany 1919-1922. Instructor with the Iowa National Guard 1926-1929. Graduated from the Command and General Staff School in 1933 then instructor there until August 1937. Graduated from Army Industrial College in 1938 and the Army War College in 1940. Operations and training officer at VII Corps Area August 1940-July 1941, then VIII Corps Area July 1941-October 1942. Brigadier general in June 1942, major general in October 1942. Commanding general of 93rd Infantry Division October 1942-May 1943. Patient at Brooke General Hospital 1943-1944. Retired in June 1944. Died on July 1, 1946.

Miller, George Allen (1891-1978) Born on September 8, 1891. Commissioned in the infantry in 1917. Graduated from the Command and General Staff School in 1937. Brigadier general in June 1945. Retired in February 1948. Decorations included the Distinguished Service Medal and Legion of Merit. Died on June 20, 1978.

Miller, Lehman Wellington (1891-1973) Born on June 29, 1891, in Millerton, Pennsylvania. Attended Dartmouth 1908-1910. Commissioned in the Corps of Engineers from West Point in 1915. With the Punitive Expedition into Mexico 1916-1917. Graduated from the Command and General Staff School in 1932 and the Army War College in 1940. Chief of U.S. military mission to Brazil 1940-1941. Brigadier general in April 1941. Military attache in Rio de Janeiro 1941-1942. Commander of Engineer Replacement Training Center, Fort Belvoir 1942-1944. Retired in August 1944. Died on January 18, 1973.

Miller, Luther Deck (1890-1972) Born in Leachburg, Pennsylvania, on June 14, 1890. B.D. from Chicago Theological Seminary in 1917. Commissioned in the Chaplain Corps in 1918. Graduated from the Chaplain's School in 1922. Served in China 1925-1928, Hawaii 1937-1939 and at Fort Sam Houston 1939-1942.

Chaplain at I Corps 1942-1943 then Sixth Army May 1943-May 1945. Acting chief of chaplains May-July 1945, then chief of chaplains July 1945-November 1949. Brigadier general in March 1945. Decorations included the Legion of Merit and Bronze Star. Died on April 27, 1972.

Miller, Maurice Levi (1894-1976) Born on September 19, 1894, in Oronoco, Minnesota. Commissioned in the infantry from West Point in 1916. Wounded on October 15, 1918, during service with the AEF in World War I. Instructor at West Point 1924-1929. Duty with the 19th Infantry at Schofield Barracks, Hawaii 1930-1934. Graduated from the Command and General Staff School in 1936. Member of the Infantry Board 1938-1941. Assistant division commander of 100th Division 1942-1945. Brigadier general in October 1942. Assigned to the Infantry Replacement Training Center at Fort McClellan May 1945-January 1946. Reverted to colonel in March 1946. Retired in November 1950. Decorations included the Legion of Merit, Bronze Star, Purple Heart and two Commendation Ribbons. Died on September 11, 1976.

Miller, Troup (1879-1957) Born in Perry, Georgia, on February 10, 1879. Commissioned in the cavalry from West Point in 1902. Aide-de-camp to Brigadier General Charles Morton in the Philippines 1905-1907. Again in the Philippines with the 7th Cavalry 1911-1914. Professor of military science and tactics at Columbia Military Academy 1915-1917. Served with the AEF 1918-1919, participating in the St. Mihiel and Meuse-Argonne offensives. Instructor at the General Service Schools 1919-1921. Graduated from the Army War College in 1925 then instructor there 1926-1930. Instructor at the Command and General Staff School January 1932-February 1936. Inspector general at Eastern Defense Command 1941-1945. Retired in June 1942. Recalled to active duty in July 1942. Brigadier general in February 1943. Retired again in December 1945. Decorations included the Distinguished Service Medal, Legion of Merit and Commendation Ribbon. Died on January 26, 1957.

Milliken, Charles Morton (1888-1959) Born on August 4, 1888, in Bridgewater, Maine. Commissioned in the infantry from West Point in 1914. Served with the AEF April 1917-June 1918. Graduated from the Command and General Staff School in 1931, then faculty member until 1936. Graduated from the Army War College in 1937. Brigadier general in October 1941. Commanding general of Central Signal Corps Replacement Training Center, Camp Crowder 1941-1945, then Camp Crowder June 1945-April 1946. Retired in August 1948. Decorations included two Legions of Merit. Died on January 1959.

Millikin, John (1888-1970) Born on January 7, 1888, in Danville, Indiana. Commissioned in the cavalry from West Point in 1910. Served with the 5th Cavalry in the Punitive Expedition into Mexico 1916-1917. Professor of military science and tactics at St. John's College 1917-1918. With the 2nd Cavalry, AEF 1918-1919. Aide-de-camp to the secretary of war, then the chief of staff, U.S. Army June 1919-July 1921. Instructor and student at the Command and General

Staff School January 1924-July 1929. Graduated from the Army War College in 1931. Director of instruction at the Cavalry School 1931-1936. Commanding officer of 6th Cavalry 1939-1940. Brigadier general in October 1940. Commanding general of 6th Cavalry Brigade 1940-1941. Major general in July 1941. Commanding general of 83rd Division, then 33rd Division 1941-1943. Commanding general of III Corps October 1943-April 1945. Commanding general of 13th Armored Division in 1945. Retired in February 1948. Decorations included the Distinguished Service Medal, Silver Star and Bronze Star. Died on November 6, 1970.

Mills, Robert Hilliard (1883-1965) Born in Decatur County, Georgia, on July 29, 1883. Attended Southern Dental School 1904-1906. D.D.S. from the University of Maryland in 1907. Commissioned a dental surgeon in 1911. Duty in the Philippine Islands 1910-1913. Dental surgeon with 82nd Division and First Army, AEF 1918-1919, participating in the St. Mihiel and Meuse-Argonne offensives. Professor of military science and tactics at Northwestern University Dental School 1924-1925. Chief of dental service at Sternberg General Hospital, Philippine Islands 1925-1929. Dental surgeon at IX Corps Area 1940-1942. Brigadier general in May 1942. Director of the dental division, office of the surgeon general of the Army then assistant to the surgeon general 1942-1946. Major general in September 1943. Retired in September 1946. Decorations included the Distinguished Service Medal. Died on March 31, 1965.

Milton, Hugh Meglone II (1897-1987) Born in Lexington, Kentucky, on March 23, 1897. Enlisted service with the field artillery, AEF. Resigned at the end of World War I. B.S. from the University of Kentucky in 1919. Commissioned in the field artillery in 1919. Instructor, then assistant professor at Texas A&M 1919-1924. M.E. from the University of Kentucky in 1922. Joined the New Mexico National Guard in 1929. Graduated from the Command and General Staff School in 1937. Called to active duty in the Chemical Warfare Service as lieutenant colonel in 1941. Deputy chief of staff for supply, then chief of staff of XIV Corps in the Southwest Pacific Area 1942-1945. Brigadier general in June 1945. Released from active duty in 1946. Decorations included the Silver Star, Legion of Merit and two Bronze Stars. President of New Mexico Military Institute 1947-1951. Assistant secretary of the army 1953-1958, then under secretary 1958-1961. Died on January 27, 1987.

Minton, Hugh Chapman (1890-1963) Born in Smithfield, Virginia, on August 2, 1890. B.S. from Virginia Polytechnic Institute in 1911. Commissioned in the Virginia National Guard in 1916. Served on the Mexican border 1916-1917. Commissioned in the field artillery, Regular Army in 1917. Graduated from Army Industrial College in 1934. Executive officer to the chief of ordnance, U.S. Army July 1938-June 1942. Brigadier general in January 1942. District chief of the Pittsburgh Ordnance District in 1942. Deputy director then director of the resource and production division at headquarters of Army Service Forces November 1942-March 1945. Retired in April 1946. Decorations included the Distinguished Service Medal. Died on August 15, 1963.

Mitchell, William Lemuel (1897-1974) Born on December 6, 1897, at Mandeville, Louisiana. Commissioned in the infantry from West Point in 1920. Aide-de-camp to Major General William Lassiter in the Panama Canal Zone 1922-1924. Assistant professor of military science and tactics at Louisiana State University 1927-1932. Aide to Major General John M. Hughes in the Philippine Islands 1936-1939. Assistant to the assistant chief of staff for supply at GHQ U.S. Army then Army Ground Forces 1941-1942. At headquarters of Army Ground Forces 1942-1945. Brigadier general in January 1945. Assignments after the war included secretary general of the International Military Tribunal at Nurnberg, Germany November 1945-August 1946, deputy commanding general of IX Corps February-May 1951, assistant division commander of 25th Division in the Korean War May 1951-January 1952 and assistant division commander then commanding general of 5th Armored Division 1952-1955. Retired as major general in October 1955. Decorations included the Silver Star, two Legions of Merit and the Bronze Star. Died on February 10, 1974.

Molitor, Eric Spencer (1896-1985) Born on September 11, 1896, in Lansing, Michigan. Attended Michigan State College 1914-1915. Commissioned in the field artillery from West Point in 1918. Instructor at West Point 1924-1929 and 1934-1936. Graduated from the Command and General Staff School in 1937. Professor of military science and tactics at Princeton 1937-1940. Commanding officer of 14th Field Artillery, 2nd Armored Division 1940-1941. With the War Department General Staff 1941-1942. Member of the general staff at Army ground Forces in 1942. Artillery liaison officer at Fort Benning 1942-1943. Brigadier general in September 1943. Commanding general of 13th Airborne Division Artillery 1943-1946. Reverted to colonel in March 1946. Retired in August 1954. Decorations included the Legion of Merit. Died on December 27, 1985.

Monroe, Hammond McDougal (1894-1985) Born on February 7, 1894, in Eureka, California. Attended the University of California 1911-1915. Commissioned in the infantry from West Point in 1918. Instructor at West Point 1924-1928 then the Infantry School 1930-1934. Graduated from the Command and General Staff School in 1936. Duty at headquarters of Army Ground Forces 1940-1942. Chief of staff of 96th Division 1942-1944. Brigadier general in November 1944. Assistant division commander of 13th Airborne Division 1944-1946. Reverted to colonel in March 1946. Retired in July 1953. Decorations included the Commendation Ribbon. Died on January 25, 1985.

Montague, Robert Miller (1899-1958) Born on August 7, 1899, in Portland, Oregon. Attended the University of Oregon 1916-1917. Commissioned in the field artillery from West Point in 1919. Served in Hawaii 1923-1926. Instructor at West Point 1926-1932. Instructor at the Field Artillery School 1933-1937. Graduated from the Command and General Staff School in 1938. Associate professor at West Point 1940-1941. In the operations and training division of the War Department General Staff 1941-1942. Brigadier general in June 1942. Commanding general of 83rd Infantry Division Artillery June 1942-March 1946. Assignments after the war included deputy chief of Army Field Forces 1952-1955, commanding general of I Corps 1955-1956 and commander of Caribbean Defense Command until his death on February 20, 1958. Decorations included the Legion of Merit and two Bronze Stars.

Montgomery, Edward (1889-1962) Born in Omaha, Nebraska, on December 2, 1889. Attended Massachusetts Institute of Technology 1908-1911. Commissioned in the Coast Artillery Corps in 1912. Duty in the Philippine Islands 1916-1918. Instructor at the Field Artillery School during World War I. Served with occupation forces in France and Germany 1919-1922. Graduated from the Command and General Staff School in 1924. Professor of military science and tactics at the University of Minnesota 1924-1925. Graduated from the Army War College in 1931. Chemical officer at VIII Corps Area then Third Army 1939-1941. Chief of field service 1941-1942. Chief of Chemical Warfare Service in the European Theater of Operations in 1942. Air chemical officer at headquarters of AAF 1942-1946. Brigadier general in September 1943. Retired in August 1949. Decorations included the Distinguished Service Medal and Legion of Merit. Died on February 3, 1962.

Mood, Orlando Clarendon (1899-1953) Born in Summerton, South Carolina, on December 1, 1899. B.S. from the Citadel in 1921. Commissioned in the infantry in 1921. Duty with the 14th Infantry at the Panama Canal 1924-1927. Instructor at the Unfantry School 1928-1930. Graduated from the Command and General Staff School in 1937 and Army Industrial College in 1940. Served with the War Department General Staff 1940-1942. Duty with Services of Supply in the European Theater of Operations 1942-1944. Chief of staff of V Corps, then 15th Army 1944-1946. Brigadier general in June 1945. Reverted to colonel in March 1946. Died on May 2, 1953. Decorations included the Distinguished Service Medal, three Legions of Merit and the Commendation Ribbon.

Moore, Bryant Edward (1894-1951) Born on June 6, 1894, in Ellsworth, Maine. Commissioned in the infantry from West Point in 1917. Served with the AEF in World War I 1917-1918. Served with the 15th Infantry in Tientsin, China 1919-1921. Instructor at West Point 1924-1929. Duty with 35th Infantry in Hawaii 1933-1935. Professor of military science and tactics at City College of New York then the University of Illinois 1937-1942. Commanding officer of 164th Infantry in the Americal Division in 1942. Brigadier general in February 1943. Assistant division commander of 104th Division February 1943-February 1945. Major general in May 1945. Commanding general of 8th Division in 1945. Assignments after the war included commanding general of the 88th Division 1945-1948, superintendent of West Point 1949-1951 and commanding general of IX Corps in the Korean War until his death in combat on February 24, 1951. Decorations included three Distinguished Service Medals, two Silver Stars, the Legion of Merit and two Bronze Stars.

Moore, Cecil Ray (1894-1983) born in Grottoes, Virginia, on July 3, 1894. B.S. from Virginia Polytechnic Institute in 1916. Commissioned in the Coast Artillery Corps in 1917. Served with the AEF and occupation forces in Germany 1918-1922. Transferred to the Corps of Engineers in 1920. Graduated from the Command and General Staff School in 1933 and the Army War College in 1938. District engineer in Portland, Oregon 1938-1942. Chief engineer with Army Service Forces in the European Theater of Operations 1942-1946. Brigadier general in April 1943 and major general in March 1944. Retired in October 1946. Decorations included the Distinguished Service Medal, two Silver Stars, two Legions of Merit and the Bronze Star. Died on January 8, 1983.

Moore, George F. (1887-1949) Born on July 31, 1887, in Austin, Texas. B.S. from the Agricultural and Mechancial College of Texas in 1908. Commissioned in the Coast Artillery Corps in 1909. Instructor at the Coast Artillery School 1921-1923. Duty in the Philippine Islands August 1923-September 1925. Graduated from the Command and General Staff School in 1928. Again in the Philippines 1928-1930. Graduated from the Army War College in 1934. Professor of military science and tactics at Texas A&M 1937-1940. Again in the Philippines December 1940. Brigadier general in January 1941. Commanding general of harbor defenses at Manila and Subic Bay in January 1941. Major general in December 1941. Fought at Bataan and taken prisoner by the Japanese after its fall on May 6, 1942. Released in August 1945. Decorations included the Distinguished Service Medal. Died on December 2, 1949.

Moore, James Edward (1902-1986) Born on November 29, 1902, in Bedford, Massachusetts. Commissioned in the infantry from West Point in 1924. Served with 31st Infantry in the Philippines 1927-1929 then in China 1933-1936. Graduated from the Command and General Staff School in 1938. Aide to Brigadier General William H. Simpson November 1940-April 1941. Served in the budget and legislative branches of the War Department General Staff 1941-1942. Chief of staff of 35th Infantry Division, 30th Division, XII Corps, Fourth Army, Ninth Army and Second Army 1942-1946. Brigadier general in January 1944, major general in March 1945. Assignments after the war included secretary of the Army General Staff 1948-1950, commanding general of the 10th Division 1950-1951, commandant of the Army War College 1953-1955, commaning general of the Ryukyus Command 1955-1958, deputy chief of staff for operations, U.S. Army 1958-1959 and chief of staff of SHAPE 1959-1963. Retired as general in July 1963. Decorations included two Distinguished Service Medals, three Legions of Merit and the Bronze Star. Died on January 28, 1986.

Moore, Richard Curtis (1880-1966) Born on November 24, 1880, in California, Missouri. Attended Westminster College 1896-1899. Commissioned in the Corps of Engineers from West Point in 1903. Duty in the Philippine Islands 1903-1904 and Cuba 1906-1907. Served with 318th Engineers in the AEF 1918-1919. Graduated from the Command and General Staff School in 1921 then instructor at General Service Schools 1921-1924. Graduated from the Army War College in 1925. Served with U.S. naval mission to Peru 1928-1930. Brigadier general in March 1938. Commander of the Atlantic Sector, Panama Canal Department 1938-1939 then the 18th Infantry Brigade 1939-1940. Assistant chief of staff for supply at the War Department General Staff in 1940 then deputy chief of staff, U.S. Army July 1940-March 1942. Major general in February 1941. Assistant chief of staff for requirements at Army Ground Forces 1942-1943. Duty in the office of the Joint Chiefs of Staff 1943-1944. Retired in November 1944. Decorations included two Distinguished Service Medals. Died on August 20, 1966.

Moran, Richard Bartholomew (1895-1972) Born on November 22, 1895, in Florence, Colorado. Attended Colorado State University 1914-1917. Commissioned in the infantry reserve in 1917. Served in the AEF 1918-1919. Instructor at the Infantry School 1921-1922. Graduated from the Command and General Staff School in 1935. Instructor at the Signal School 1925-1929 and again in 1935. Signal officer of the Pacific Sector in the Panama Canal Zone 1935-1938. Graduated from the Army War College in 1939. Chief of the war plans and training divisions in the office of the chief signal officer, U.S. Army 1939-1941. Staff officer at GHQ, U.S. Army 1941-1942. Brigadier general in December 1942. Signal officer at Fifth Army 1942-1945. Reverted to colonel in April 1946. Retired in April 1950. Decorations included the Distinguished Service Medal, Legion of Merit and Commendation Ribbon. Died on February 13, 1972.

Morgan, Hugh Jackson (1893-1961) Born in Nashville, Tennessee, on January 25, 1893. B.S. from Vanderbilt University in 1914. Commissioned in the medical section, Officers Reserve Corps in 1918. Served as a private in the AEF 1917-1918. M.D. from Johns Hopkins in 1918. Released from active duty and joined the Army Reserve. Called to active duty as lieutenant colonel, Medical Corps Reserve in 1942. Brigadier general in December 1942. Chief consultant in medicine in the office of the surgeon general, U.S. Army 1943-1946. Returned to inactive duty in 1946. Decorations included the Distinguished Service Medal. Member of the Medical Advisory Commission to the secretary of war 1946-1948. Died on December 25, 1961.

Morris, William Henry Harrison Jr. (1890-1971) Born in Ocean Grove, New Jersey, on March 22, 1890. Commissioned in the infantry from West Point in 1911. Served in the Philippine Islands 1911-1912 and China 1912-1914. Professor of military science and tactics at Texas Agricultural and Mechanical School 1916-1917. Battery commander with the 90th Division, AEF in World War I, seeing action at St. Mihiel and Meuse-Argonne. Professor of military science and tactics at Bucknell University 1919-1923. Graduated from the Command and General Staff School in 1925 and the Army War College in 1930. Instructor at the Army War College 1930-1933. With the War Department General Staff 1938-1940. Brigadier general in January 1942. Commanding general of 6th Armored

Division January 1942-May 1943. Major general in May 1942. Commanding general of II Armored Corps May-September 1943, XVIII Corps October 1943-July 1944, 10th Armored Division July 1944-May 1945 and VI Corps in 1945. Assignments after the war included commander in chief of the Caribbean Command 1949-1952. Retired in March 1952 as lieutenant general. Decorations included the Distinguished Service Cross, Distinguished Service Medal, Silver Star, Legion of Merit, Bronze Star and Purple Heart. Died on March 30, 1971.

Morrisette, James Edward (1886-1973) Born in Newbern, Alabama, on January 17, 1886. Attended Southwestern Presbyterian University 1902-1903. B.A. from the University of Alabama in 1906, LL.B. in 1911. Professor of law at the University of Alabama 1911-1917. Commissioned in the field artillery in the field artillery in 1917. Assistant to the corps judge advocate at VII Corps, AEF 1918-1919. Transferred to the Judge Advocate General Department in 1920. Assistant judge advocate, then judge advocate at headquarters of American Forces in Germany 1920-1923. Instructor at West Point 1927-1930. Judge advocate at the Hawaiian Department August 1938-September 1940. Corps area judge advocate with VIII Corps Area 1940-1942. Chief of the military justice division, then assistant judge advocate general 1942-1944. Brigadier general in May 1944. Judge advocate general representative for U.S. Army Forces Pacific Ocean Areas 1944-1946. Died on December 27, 1973.

Morrissey, William Joseph (1888-1965) Born on February 3, 1888, in Philadelphia, Pennsylvania. Commissioned in the infantry from West Point in 1912. Wounded while serving with the 142nd Infantry, 36th Division, AEF in World War I. Professor of military science and tactics at Syracuse University 1920-1924. Graduated from the Command and General Staff School on 1925. Served with the General Staff Corps 1935-1937. Commanding officer of 35th Infantry, 25th Division 1940-1942. Deputy assistant chief of staff for supply at the War Department General Staff 1942-1946. Brigadier general in November 1944. Reverted to colonel in 1946. Retired in 1947. Brigadier general on the retired list in 1948. Decorations included the Silver Star, Legion of Merit, Bronze Star and Purple Heart. Died on April 2, 1965.

Moses, Raymond George (1891-1974) Born on December 26, 1891, in Buffalo, New York. Attended the University of Colorado 1909-1911. Commissioned in the Corps of Engineers from West Point in 1916. Served in the AEF 1917-1918. B.S. from Massachusetts Institute of Technology in 1921. Graduated from the Command and General Staff School in 1931 and Army Industrial College in 1934. Commanding officer of 5th Engineer Regiment 1940-1941. Brigadier general in March 1942. Assistant chief of staff for supply on the War Department General Staff 1942-1943 then with 12th Army Group 1943-1945. Retired in 1949. Decorations included two Distinguished Service Medals, the Legion of Merit, Bronze Star and Commendation Ribbon. Died on July 16, 1974.

Mudge, Verne Donald (1898-1957) Born on September 5, 1898, in Bantor, South Dakota. Attended the University of Florida. Commissioned in the cavalry from West Point in 1920. Graduated from the Command and General Staff School in 1935 and the Army War College in 1940. In the personnel division of the War Department General Staff 1940-1942. Chief of staff of 1st Cavalry Division in 1942. Brigadier general in February 1943. Commanding general of 5th Cavalry Brigade 1942-1943 and 2nd Cavalry Brigade 1943-1944. Major general in August 1944. Commanding general of 1st Cavalry Division August 1944 until retirement in November 1946. Wounded in action on February 28, 1945. Decorations included the Distinguished Service Cross, Distinguished Service Medal, Silver Star, Legion of Merit, Bronze Star, Air Medal and Purple Heart. Died on January 29, 1957.

Mueller, Paul John (1892-1964) Born on November 16, 1892, in Union, Missouri. Commissioned in the infantry from West Point in 1915. Battalion commander in the 64th Infantry, AEF in World War I. Occupation duty in Coblenz, Germany 1920-1922. Graduated from the Command and General Staff School in 1923 and the Army War College in 1928. With war plans division of the War Department General Staff 1931-1934.Instructor at the Command and General Staff School August 1935-July 1940. Chief of the training division, office of the chief of infantry 1940-1941. Chief of staff of Second Army 1941-1942. Brigadier general in October 1941, major general in September 1942. Commanding general of 81st Division 1942-1946. Retired in September 1954. Decorations included three Distinguished Service Medals, two Silver Stars and two Commendation Ribbons. Died on September 25, 1964.

Muir, James Irvin (1888-1964) Born in Fort Russell, Wyoming, on August 28, 1888. Commissioned in the infantry from West Point in 1910. Duty with 13th Infantry in the Philippine Islands 1914-1917. Graduated from the Command and General Staff School in 1925. Instructor with General Service Schools 1925-1929. Graduated from the Army War College in 1930. Served at Fort Shafter, Hawaii 1932-1935. Instructor at Cornell University ROTC August 1935-July 1939. Commanding officer of 26th Infantry 1940-1941. Brigadier general in April 1941. Duty with 44th Division, then commanding general of the division 1942-1944. Major general in February 1942. Commanding general of XXIII Corps August 1944-January 1945. Commanding general of Infantry Replacement Training Center at Camp Howze January-November 1945. Retired as colonel in November 1945. Died on May 8, 1964.

Muller, Walter Joseph (1895-1967) Born on September 29, 1895, in Fort D.A. Russell, Wyoming. Commissioned in the infantry from West Point in 1918. Assistant professor of military science and tactics at the Univeristy of Florida 1931-1936. Graduated from the Command and General Staff School in 1938. Assistant chief of staff for supply at the Armored Force March-May 1941. Assistant chief of staff for supply with I Armored Corps May 1941-March 1942. Served in North Africa Theater of Operations 1942-1943. Deputy chief of staff for supply at Seventh Army 1943-1944. Brigadier general in November 1944. Deputy chief of staff for supply at Third Army 1944-1945. Director of the Office of Military Government in Germany 1945-1947. Retired as major general in November 1956. Decorations included the Distinguished Service Medal, two Legions of Merit, two Bronze Stars and the Commendation Ribbon. Died on November 14, 1967.

Mullins, Charles Love Jr. (1892-1976) Born on September 7, 1892, in Gretna, Nebraska. Commissioned in the infantry from West Point in 1917. Professor of military science and tactics at the University of Illinois in 1919. Duty with 44th Infantry in Hawaii 1920-1922 then aide to the commander of the Hawaiian Department 1923-1924. Instructor at West Point 1925-1927. Graduated from the Command and General Staff School in 1934 and the Army War College in 1939. Established the National Military Academy in Nicaragua 1939-1942. Brigadier general in July 1942. Commanding general of 25th Division December 1942-May 1948. Major general in February 1944. Retired in January 1953. Decorations included the Distinguished Service Medal, Silver Star and Bronze Star. Died on March 1, 1976.

Mumma, Harlan Leslie (1894-1972) Born on December 6, 1894, in Findley, Ohio. Attended Ohio Northern University 1910-1911. Commissioned in the infantry from West Point in 1916. Professor of military science and tactics at the University of West Virginia 1919-1923. Duty with 42nd Infantry in the Panama Canal Zone 1923-1926. Instructor at West Point 1933-1934. Transferred to the Quartermaster Corps in 1937. Deputy quartermaster, then department quartermaster at the Panama Canal Department 1941-1946. Brigadier general in September 1944. Retired in April 1948. Decorations included two Legions of Merit. Died on April 2, 1972

Munnikhuysen, Henry Dorsey F. (1886-1955) Born on December 28, 1886, in Belair, Maryland. Commissioned in the cavalry from West Point in 1909. Served with the 7th Cavalry in the Philippines 1914-1915 and the AEF in France 1918-1919. Instructor at the Quartermaster Corps School 1926-1927. Graduated from the Command and General Staff School in 1928. Again instructor at the Quartermaster Corps School 1928-1931. Graduated from Army Industrial College in 1932 and the Army War College in 1933. Assistant post and division quartermaster at Schofield Barracks, Hawaii 1930-1940. Brigadier general in October 1940. Assistant to the quartermaster general 1940-1943 then director of the personnel division, office of the quartermaster general 1943-1946. Retired in April 1946. Decorations included the Legion of Merit and Purple Heart. Died on March 22, 1955.

Munson, Edward Lyman Jr. (1904-1967) Born on August 26, 1904, at Fort Bayard, New Mexico. Commissioned in the infantry from West Point in 1926. Served with the 35th Infantry in Hawaii August 1928-December 1930 and the 19th Infantry May 1935-July 1937. Instructor at West Point 1937-1941. Chief of Army Picture Service, Army Service Forces 1941-1944. Chief of Army Picture

Service in the office of the chief signal officer 1944-1945. Brigadier general in June 1945. Retired as major in December 1945. Brigadier general on the retired list in 1948. Decorations included two Legions of Merit. Died on June 29, 1967.

Murphy, John Bartlett (1898-1984) Born on June 16, 1898, the son of Brigadier General Edward Murphy, in Macedonia, Iowa. Attended Texas A&M 1916-1917. Commissioned in the field artillery from West Point in 1919. Professor of military science and tactics at the University of Vermont 1922-1923 and Ohio State University 1930-1935. Graduated from the Command and General Staff School in 1939. With the general staff at the Armored Force 1941-1943 and 7th Armored Division in 1943. Brigadier general in April 1943. Commanding general of 100th Division Artillery 1943-1945. Reverted to colonel in March 1946. Retired as major general in July 1958. Decorations included the Distinguished Service Medal, Silver Star, Legion of Merit, two Bronze Stars and the Commendation Ribbon. Died on September 5, 1984.

Murray, John Trott (1892-1960) Born on November 14, 1892, in Meridian, Mississippi. Commissioned in the infantry from West Point in 1917. Instructor at West Point 1918-1920. Duty with 44th Infantry in Hawaii 1920-1923. Professor of military science and tactics at the University of Oregon 1923-1926. Instructor at the Infantry School then with the Oregon National Guard 1937-1940. Chief of staff of 41st Division September 1940-February 1942. Commander of 186th Infantry 1942-1945. Brigadier general in September 1943. Retired as colonel in November 1947. Brigadier general on the retired list in October 1948. Decorations included the Distinguished Service Medal, Silver Star and Bronze Star. Died on November 27, 1960.

Murray, Maxwell (1885-1948) Born on June 19, 1885, in West Point, New York, the son of Major General Arthur Murray. Commissioned in the Coast Artillery Corps from West Point in 1907. Duty in the Philippine Islands 1908-1911. Instructor at West Point 1915-1917. Served with 5th Field Artillery, 1st Division, AEF 1917-1918. Attended MIT 1919-1920. Graduated from the Command and General Staff School in 1926 and the Army War College in 1929. Assistant and aide to Dwight F. Davis, governor general of the Philippine Islands 1929-1932. Member of the Field Artillery Board 1932-1936. Commanding officer of 5th Field Artillery 1936-1938. Brigadier general in December 1938. Commanding general of the Washington, DC Provisional Brigade December 1938-July 1940. Commanding general of 11th Field Artillery Brigade in Hawaii 1940-1941 then commandant of the Hawaii Division 1941-1942. Major general in July 1941. Commanding general of 35th Infantry Division April 1942-January 1943 then Southern California Sector, Western Defense Command January-June 1943. Retired in September 1946. Decorations included the Distinguished Service Medal and Silver Star. Died on August 4, 1948.

Myers, Donald Johnson (1893-1958) Born in Red Cloud, Nebraska, on April 9, 1893. B.A. from the University of Colorado in 1917. Commissioned in the infantry in 1917. Professor of military science and tactics at the University of West Virginia 1921-1923. Duty with 14th Infantry and 19th Infantry Brigade in the Panama Canal Zone 1923-1926. Professor of military science and tactics at the University of Indiana 1928-1932. Graduated from the Command and General Staff School in 1934 and the Army War College in 1935. In the supply division of the War Department General Staff July 1936-January 1940. Duty with 35th Infantry then executive officer of 22nd Infantry Brigade in Hawaii May 1940-October 1941. Chief of staff of 40th Infantry Division April 1942-February 1943. Brigadier general in September 1942. Assistant division commander of 33rd Infantry Division 1943-1945. Commanding general of 40th Infantry Division July 1945 until retirement in September 1946. Decorations included the Silver Star, two Legions of Merit and the Bronze Star. Died on August 13, 1958.

Nelson, Otto Lauren Jr. (1902-1985) Born on November 2, 1902, in Omaha, Nebraska. Commissioned in the infantry from West Point in 1924. Instructor at West Point 1929-1935. M.A. from Columbia in 1932. Graduated from the Command and General Staff School in 1938. Assistant professor at West Point 1939-1941. Ph.D. from Harvard in 1940. Assistant deputy chief of staff, U.S. Army 1942-1944. Brigadier general in January 1944. Major general in November 1944. Deputy commanding general of the Mediterranean Theater of Operations January 1945-August 1945. Retired in March 1946. Decorations included two Distinguished Service Medals. Died on June 25, 1985.

Nevins, Arthur Seymour (1891-1979) Born in Camp Point, Illinois, on July 19, 1891. B.A. from the University of Illinois in 1913. Commissioned in the infantry in 1917. Duty with 57th Infantry in the Philippines July 1920-January 1923. Assistant professor of military science and tactics at the University of Illinois April 1923-August 1925. Instructor at the Infantry School July 1928-August 1931. Graduated from the Command and General Staff School in 1933 and the Army War College in 1936. Again in the Philippines 1936-1939. Instructor at the Command and General Staff School October 1939-August 1940. Deputy chief of staff of VIII Corps 1940-1942. In the plans division of the War Department General Staff in 1942. Brigadier general in December 1942. Assistant chief of staff of Fifth Army January-October 1943. Deputy chief of staff for intelligence at SHAEF October 1943-January 1945 then chief of the plans and operations section 1945-1946. Reverted to colonel in March 1946. Retired in August 1946. Decorations included the Distinguished Service Medal, two Legions of Merit and the Bronze Star. Died on January 19, 1979.

Newcomer, Francis Kosier (1889-1967) Born on September 14, 1889, in Bryon, Illinois. Commissioned in the Corps of Engineers from West Point in 1913. Assistant commandant of the Engineer School, AEF 1918-1919. Associate professor at West Point 1919-1924. Graduated from the Command and General Staff School in 1935 and the Army War College in 1940. Assistant to the president of the Mississippi River Commission 1940-1941. Engineer at Third Army 1942. Chief engineer at China-Burma-India Theater of Operations 1943-1944.

Brigadier general in November 1944. Engineer of maintenance at the Panama Canal 1944-1948. Retired from the Army in 1949 but continued as governor of the Panama Canal until 1952. Decorations included the Distinguished Service Cross and Legion of Merit. Died on August 16, 1967.

Newgarden, Paul Woolever (1892-1944) Born on February 24, 1892, in Philadelphia, Pennsylvania. Commissioned in the infantry from West Point in 1913. Instructor at West Point 1917-1921. Served with 27th Infantry, then inspector at the Hawaiian Division 1923-1925. Graduated from the Command and General Staff School in 1926. Instructor at the Field Artillery School 1927-1931. Graduated from the Army War College in 1932. Organized, trained and commanded 41st Armored Infantry 1941-1942. Commander of Combat Combat "A," 2nd Armored Division in 1942. Organized, trained and commanded 10th Armored Division 1942-1944. Brigadier general in January 1942, major general in June 1942. Killed in an airplane accident near Chattanooga, Tennessee, on July 14, 1944. Decorations included the Legion of Merit.

Neyland, Robert Reese Jr. (1892-1962) Born on February 17, 1892, in Greenville, Texas. Attended Burleson College 1909-1910 and Texas A&M 1910-1911. Commissioned in the Corps of Engineers from West Point in 1916. B.S. from Massachusetts Institute of Technology in 1921. Professor of military science and tactics and head football coach at the University of Tennessee 1926-1933. Retired as major in February 1936. Recalled to active duty as district engineer, then division engineer at Norfolk and Dallas 1941-1944. Brigadier general in November 1944. Commanding general of base section, Services of Supply in India Burma Theater of Operations 1944-1946. Retired in 1948. Decorations included the Distinguished Service Medal and three Legions of Merit. Died on March 28, 1962.

Niblo, Urban (1897-1957) Born on November 20, 1897, in Galveston, Texas. Commissioned in the field artillery from West Point in 1919. B.S. and M.S. from Massachusetts Institute of Technology in 1928. Ordnance officer at II Corps 1942-1943. Ordnance officer at Fifth Army and the Mediterranean Theater of Operations 1943-1945. Brigadier general in November 1944. Ordnance officer at Fourth Army 1945-1946. Retired in 1955. Decorations included two Distinguished Service Medals, the Silver Star and Legion of Merit. Died on August 11, 1957.

Nicholas, Richard Ulysses (1890-1953) Born on November 16, 1890, in York, Pennsylvania. Commissioned in the Corps of Engineers from West Point in 1913. Served with training units in the U.S. 1918-1919. Duty in Hawaii 1922-1924 and the Canal Zone 1925-1927. Graduated from the Command and General Staff School in 1935. Assistant engineer att the Panama Canal Department 1936-1939. Graduated from the Army War College in 1940. Engineer at IX Corps, then the Presidio 1940-1942. Engineer at Western Defense Command and Fourth Army 1942-1943. Engineer at Ninth Army 1944-1945. Brigadier general in March

1945. Retired in September 1946. Decorations included the Bronze Star. Died on May 7, 1953.

Nichols, Harold F. (1888-1983) Born on April 13, 1888, in Rockford, Illinois. Commissioned in the Coast Artillery Corps from West Point in 1911. Instructor at West Point 1915-1917. Served with the 53rd Coast Artillery, AEF in the Meuse-Argonne offensive in 1918. Instructor at the Coast Artillery School 1919-1920 then at West Point 1920-1924. Graduated from the Command and General Staff School in 1926 then instructor there 1928-1932. Graduated from the Army War College in 1933. Director of tactics, then assistant commandant of the Coast Artillery School August 1938-November 1940. Commander of Antiaircraft Artillery Replacement Training Center, Fort Eustis 1940-1941. Brigadier general in April 1941. Commander of Hawaiian Antiaircraft Artillery Command 1941-1944. Commanding general of Antiaircraft Artillery Replacement Training Center at Camp Haan April 1944-January 1945. Assistant commander of Southern, then Northern California sectors of the Western Defense Command January-September 1945. Retired in July 1947. Decorations included the Legion of Merit. Died on September 10, 1983.

Nichols, William Robert (1885-1950) Born in Petersburg, Virginia, on July 25, 1885. B.S. from VMI in 1906. Captain in the Virginia Volunteers 1907-1908. Attended Massachusetts Institute of Technology 1908-1909. Commissioned in the Coast Artillery Corps in 1909. Served in France 1919-1922. Graduated from the Command and General Staff School in 1924. Professor of military science and tactics at Virginia Polytechnic Institute 1924-1929. Graduated from the Army War College in 1930. Duty in Hawaii 1930-1932. Instructor at the Command and General Staff School 1932-1935. Served in Panama as commanding officer of Fort Amador harbor defenses 1939-1940. Chief of staff of 4th Service Command December 1940-February 1944. Brigadier general in September 1943. Commanding general of Fort Hood February 1944 until retirement in February 1945. Decorations included the Legion of Merit. Died on July 12, 1950.

Nisley, Harold Albert (1892-1963) Born on January 16, 1892, in Washington Court House, Ohio. Commissioned in the field artillery from West Point in 1917. M.S. from Massachusetts Institute of Technology in 1923. Assistant professor at West Point 1926-1930. Graduated from Army Industrial College in 1931 and the Army War College in 1936. Ordnance officer of the Armored Force 1940-1942. Chief of the automotive maintenance section, field service, office of the chief of ordnance 1942-1943. Deputy to the chief ordnance officer in the European Theater of Operations October 1943-March 1944. Ordnance officer for 12th Army Group 1944-1945. Brigadier general in January 1945. Retired in August 1948. Decorations included the Distinguished Service Medal, Legion of Merit and Bronze Star. Died on December 23, 1963.

Noce, Daniel (1894-1976) Born on November 3, 1894, in Denver, Colorado. Student at Colorado State College of Agricultural and Mechanical Arts 1912-

1913. Enlisted service with Colorado National Guard 1912-1913. Commissioned in the Corps of Engineers from West Point in 1917. Regimental commander of 602nd Engineers, AEF in World War I, including the St. Mihiel and Meuse-Argonne offensives. B.S. from Massachusetts Institute of Technology in 1921. Instructor at the Engineer School 1921-1923. Engineer in charge of harbor defenses in Manila and Subic Bay, Philippine Islands 1928-1930. Graduated from the Command and General Staff School in 1933. Again instructor at the Engineer School 1933-1935. Graduated from the Army War College in 1937. Commanding officer of Engineer Amphibious Command 1942. Brigadier general in July 1942. Deputy chief of staff for operations at the European Theater of Operations 1943-1944. Major general in February 1944. Deputy chief of staff for operations at headquarters of Army Forces in the Mediterranean Theater of Operations 1944-1945. Chief of staff of Army Service Forces, U.S. Army 1945-1946. Assignments after the war included chief of staff of U.S. European Command 1949-1952, inspector general of the Army 1952-1954. Retired in October 1954. Decorations included three Distinguished Service Medals and the Legion of Merit. Died on February 17, 1976.

Nold, George Jacob (1893-1962) Born in Nappanee, Indiana, on October 13, 1893. B.S. from Purdue in 1917. Commissioned in the Corps of Engineers in 1917. Duty with 3rd Engineers in Hawaii 1919-1921. Instructor at the Engineer School 1922-1924. Professor of military science and tactics at the University of Kansas 1926-1930. Engineer at the Alaskan Department 1941-June 1944. Brigadier general in September 1943. Engineer at Tenth Army 1944-1946. Retired in July 1955. Decorations included three Legions of Merit. Died on June 3, 1962.

North, Thomas (1893-1990) Born in London, England, on April 28, 1893. Attended King's College 1910-1911. Enlisted service 1917-1918 on the Somme front in France. Commissioned in the Corps of Engineers in 1918. Transferred to the field artillery in 1920. Officer in charge of the Paris office of American Battle Monuments Commission 1924-1929. Aide to Brigadier General Lucius Holbrook 1929-1931. Again with American Battle Monuments Commission 1931-1933. Graduated from the Command and General Staff School in 1935. Duty with the training section in the office of the chief of field artillery July 1940-March 1942. In operations department of the War Department General Staff 1942-1946. Brigadier general in January 1944. Decorations included the Distinguished Service Medal and Purple Heart. Died on June 26, 1990.

Nulsen, Charles Kilbourne (1886-1959) Born in Kilbourne, Louisiana, on July 9, 1886. Attended Georgetown College (Kilbourne) 1901-1902. Commissioned in the infantry from West Point in 1908. Served in Alaska with the 16th Infantry 1910-1912 and with the Punitive Expedition into Mexico 1916-1917. With 13th Infantry in World War I 1917-1918. Graduated from the Command and General Staff School in 1927. Senior instructor at West Point 1927-1931. Graduated from the Army War College in 1932. In the military intelligence division of the War Department General Staff 1932-1936. Commanding officer of 23rd Infantry

1940-1941. Commanding general of Fort Sam Houston July 1941-May 1946. Brigadier general in March 1943. Retired in October 1947. Decorations included the Legion of Merit. Died on March 13, 1959.

O'Brien, John Joseph (1904-) Born in Havre, Montana, on March 8, 1904. Attended St. Thomas College 1917-1919. LL.B. St. Paul College of Law in 1928. Practiced law in St. Paul, Minnesota, 1928-1935. With the Department of Justice 1936-1941. Commissioned colonel in 1941, brigadier general in January 1945.

O'Connor, James A. (1885-1952) Born in Bay City, Michigan, on July 19, 1885. Attended Notre Dame 1902-1903. Commissioned in the Corps of Engineers from West Point in 1907. Served in Hawaii 1909-1912 and with the Punitive Expedition into Mexico 1916-1917. Commanding officer of 303rd Engineers, AEF at St. Mihiel and Argonne 1918-1919. Instructor at the Engineer School 1920-1921. Graduated from the Command and General Staff School in 1923 and the Army War College in 1927. Instructor at the Command and General Staff School 1927-1931. Department engineer in the Philippine Department August 1931-June 1934. Commandant of the Engineer School 1939-1940. Commander of Northwest Service Command December 1941-February 1944. Brigadier general in September 1942. Commanding general of Army Service Forces Training Center at Fort Devens in 1944. Engineer for U.S. Army forces in the China-Burma-India Theater of Operations May 1944-February 1945. Division engineer with New England Engineer Division February 1945 until retirement in May 1946. Decorations included the Distinguished Service Medal and Legion of Merit. Died on March 23, 1952.

O'Daniel, John Wilson (1894-1975) Born in Newark, Delaware, on February 15, 1894. Enlisted service in the Delaware National Guard 1912-1917. Attended Delaware College. Commissioned in the infantry in 1917. Wounded in action while serving with the 11th Infantry, AEF in the St. Mihiel and Meuse-Argonne offensives in 1918. With the Civilian Conservation Corps 1933-1936. Professor of military science and tactics at the Academy of Richmond County 1936-1938. Graduated from the Command and General Staff School in 1939. Commanding officer of 2nd Battalion, 24th Infantry in 1941. Deputy chief of staff for plans and training at Third Army in 1942. Brigadier general in November 1942. Commanding general of 3rd Infantry Division February 1944-July 1945, where he earned the nickname "Iron Mike." Major general in May 1944. Assignments after the war included commandant of the Infantry School 1945-1948, military attache in Moscow June 1948-August 1950 and commanding general of I Corps 1951-1952 then U.S. Army Pacific 1952-1954. Retired in February 1956. Decorations included the Distinguished Service Cross, four Distinguished Service Medals, two Silver Stars, four Bronze Stars, two Air Medals, the Commendation Ribbon and Purple Heart. Died on March 29, 1975.

O'Dwyer, William (1890-1964) Born in County Mayo, Ireland, on July 11, 1890. Immigrated to New York in 1910. Worked as a laborer and longshoreman and attended evening classes at Fordham University Law School, from which he graduated with an LL.B. in 1923. Practiced law 1926-1932. District attorney for King's County, New York 1937-1939, then Brooklyn 1940-1941. Prosecuted Murder, Inc. in 1940. Commissioned major in the judge advocate general branch, Regular Army in 1942. Served with the II Corps and the Air Corps Materiel Command in New York and Washington, D.C. 1942-1943. At headquarters of AAF 1943-1945. Brigadier general in August 1944. Returned to civilian life in 1945. Elected mayor of New York and served 1946-1950. Ambassador to Mexico 1950-1952. Died on November 24, 1964.

Ogden, David Ayres Depue (1897-1969) Born on October 16, 1897, in Newark, New Jersey. Attended Princeton 1914-1916. Commissioned in the Corps of Engineers from West Point in 1918. Served with 11th Engineers in the Canal Zone 1925-1928. District engineer in Trinidad 1940-1942. Brigadier general in September 1942. Commanding general of 3rd Brigade, Special Engineers August 1942-July 1945. Assignments after the war included commanding general of the Ryukyus Command 1951-1955, deputy inspector general, then inspector general, U.S. Army May 1955-October 1957. Retired as lieutenant general in October 1957. Decorations included three Distinguished Service Medals, the Bronze Star, Legion of Merit and Commendation Ribbon. Died on November 26, 1969.

O'Hare, Joseph James (1893-1961) Born on February 19, 1893, in Boston, Massachusetts. Commissioned in the Coast Artillery Corps from West Point in 1916. Instructor at West Point 1920-1925. Military attache in Havana 1929-1933. Commanding officer of U.S. troops at the New York World's Fair 1939-1940. Assistant chief of staff for personnel at First Army 1940-1944. Brigadier general in November 1944. Assistant chief of staff for personnel at 12th Army Group 1944-1945. Deputy chief of staff for personnel at Army Service Forces in the European Theater of Operations 1945-1946. Retired in February 1953. Decorations included the Distinguished Service Medal, Legion of Merit, two Bronze Stars and the Commendation Ribbon. Died on April 2, 1961.

Oldfield, Homer Ray (1887-1974) Born in Bethlehem, Iowa, on May 15, 1887. Attended Drake University 1904-1905. Commissioned in the Coast Artillery Corps from West Point in 1909. Served with the artillery reserve, AEF in World War I. Member of the Coast Artillery Board 1919-1921. Graduated from the Command and General Staff School in 1923 and the Army War College in 1925. Commanding officer of 65th Coast Artillery, Panama Canal 1925-1928. At the War Department General Staff 1928-1932. With the general staff at IX Corps Area 1937-1940. Commanding officer of 72nd Coast Artillery 1940-1941. Brigadier general in August 1941. Commanding general of the Atlantic Brigade, Panama Coast Artillery Command 1941-1942. Major general in May 1942. Commanding general of Panama Coast Artillery Command 1942-1943. Commanding general of Antiaircraft Training Center at Camp Davis, then Camp Hood 1943-1946. Retired in October 1946. Decorations included the Distinguished Service Medal and Purple Heart. Died on December 22, 1974.

Oliver, Lunsford Errett (1889-1978) Born on March 17, 1889, in Nemaha, Nebraska. Commissioned in the Corps of Engineers from West Point in 1913. Engineer with Alaska road commission 1924-1927. Graduated from the Command and General Staff School in 1928 and the Army War College in 1938. Instructor at the Command and General Staff School 1938-1940. With 1st Armored Corps 1940-1941. At headquarters of the Armored Force, Fort Knox 1941-1942. Brigadier general in February 1942. Assistant division commander of 1st Armored Division February-December 1942. Major general in November 1942. Commanding general of 5th Armored Division 1943-1945. Commanding general of 4rh Armored Division July-September 1945. Retired in May 1948. Decorations included two Distinguished Service Medals, the Silver Star, two Legions of Merit and three Bronze Stars. Died on October 13, 1978.

Olmstead, Dawson (1884-1965) Born on May 21, 1884, in Corry, Pennsylvania. Commissioned in the cavalry from West Point in 1906. Served in Cuba with the 15th Cavalry 1906-1907. Assigned to GHQ, AEF in 1918. Graduated from the Command and General Staff School in 1924. Signal officer for the Hawaii Division 1924-1927. Graduated from the Army War College in 1934. Commander of the Signal School 1938-1941. Major general in October 1941. Chief signal officer of the Army October 1941- June 1943. War Department representative on the Telecommunications Board in the Department of State 1943-1944. Retired in January 1944. Decorations included the Distinguished Service Medal. Died on September 2, 1965.

Olmsted, George Hamden (1901-) Born on March 18, 1901, in Des Moines, Iowa. Commissioned in the field artillery from West Point in 1922. Resigned in 1923 and joined the Iowa National Guard. Transferred to the cavalry, Officers Reserve Corps in 1936. Insurance executive 1923-1940. Appointed major U.S. Army in March 1942. Member of War Department Special Staff 1942-1944. Served with General Staff Corps in China Theater of Operations 1944-1945. Brigadier general in January 1945. Assignments after the war included command of the 103rd Division 1951-1959. Decorations included the Distinguished Service Medal, Legion of Merit and Bronze Star.

Ord, James Garesche (1886-1960) Born in Fort Lewis, Colorado, on October 18, 1886. Commissioned in the infantry from West Point in 1909, fourth in a direct line of Army officers. With the Punitive Expedition into Mexico 1916-1917. Served in the AEF in World War I and fought in the Aisne-Marne, St. Mihiel and Meuse-Argonne campaigns. Graduated from the Command and General Staff School in 1924 and the Army War College in 1929. Director of the Infantry Board at Fort Benning 1936-1938. Commanding officer of 57th Infantry 1938-1940. Instructor with Pennsylvania National Guard June-October 1940. Brigadier general in October 1940. With the 1st Division 1940-1942. Major general in February 1942. Commanding general of 28th Infantry Division February-June 1942. Chief of the Joint Brazil-U.S. Defense Commission June 1942-October 1945.

Hospitalized in October 1945 and retired in February 1946. Decorations included the Legion of Merit and Commendation Ribbon. Died on April 17, 1960.

Osborn, Frederick Henry (1889-n/a) Born in New York, New York, on March 21, 1889. B.A. from Princeton in 1910. In the banking industry in New York City 1921-1938. Commissioned colonel in September 1940 as chairman of the President's Advisory Commission on Selective Service. Brigadier general in January 1941 as chairman of the War Department Committee on Education, Recreation and Community Service. Major general in September 1943. Director of the Information and Education Division of Army Service Forces 1943-1945. Returned to civilian life in September 1945.

Osborne, Theodore Morrison (1899-1986) Born on November 13, 1899, in Teton, Montana. Commissioned in the Coast Artillery Corps from West Point in 1923. Served with 3rd Engineers in Hawaii 1931-1935. Graduated from the Command and General Staff School in 1936. Assistant professor at West Point 1936-1940. Executive assistant to the division engineer at North Pacific Division July 1940-May 1941. District engineer in the Great Lakes Division in 1941. Commanding officer of Midwest Air Depot sub-office in 1941. District engineer in the Southwest Division in 1942. Director of contruction, then assistant chief of staff for operations, finally commanding officer of the Persian Gulf Service Command October 1942-October 1944. Brigadier general in February 1944. At headquarters of Army Service Forces 1944-1945. Retired as lieutenant colonel in October 1947. Brigadier general on the retired list in 1948. Decorations included two Distinguished Service Medals. Died on June 24, 1986.

Osmun, Russel Alger (1887-1954) Born on May 19, 1887, in Detroit, Michigan. Graduated from USNA in 1910. Resigned in 1911. Commissioned in the Coast Artillery Corps in 1914. Served with the field artillery in World War I. Graduated from the Command and General Staff School in 1930. Supply officer with the Hawaii Division 1930-1932. Graduated from Army Industrial College in 1933 and the Army War College in 1934. Director of the department of tactics and technique, then assistant commandant of the Quartermaster School August 1937-February 1941. Duty in the general services division, office of the quartermaster general, U.S. Army 1941-1942. In the Army section of the Joint U.S. Army-U.S. Navy Intelligence Collection Agency, U.S. Army Forces Mideast 1943-1944. Brigadier general in September 1943. Chief of the Military Intelligence Service May 1944-April 1945. Commanding general of Kansas City Quartermaster Depot 1945-1946. Retired in September 1946. Decorations included the Legion of Merit. Died on August 9, 1954.

Ostrander, Lester Smith (1895-1965) Born in Warren, Ohio, on September 1, 1895. B.A. from Western Reserve University in 1917. Commissioned in the infantry in 1917. Instructor at the Infantry School of Arms 1918-1919 then the Infantry School 1919-1922. Duty at Schofield Barracks, Hawaii 1923-1926. Instructor with the West Virginia National Guard 1926-1931. Served in the office of the adjutant general, U.S. Army 1939-1942. Brigadier general in February 1943. Adjutant general at headquarters of U.S. Army Forces at Brisbane, Australia February 1943-January 1945. Director of operations and training division, then publications division in the office of the adjutant general, U.S. Army January-December 1945. Retired in December 1946. Decorations included the Distinguished Service Medal and Legion of Merit. Died on May 23, 1965.

Ostrom, Charles Douglas Yelverton (1890-1980) Born in Alturas, California, on April 26, 1890. B.S. from the University of California in 1912. Enlisted service in California National Guard 1910-1915. Commissioned in the Coast Artillery Corps in 1916. Served with the 64th Artillery, AEF in World War I. Professor of military science and tactics at the University of California 1922-1926. Duty with 92nd Coast Artillery in the Philippine Islands 1926-1929. Graduated from the Command and General Staff School in 1935 and the Army War College in 1939. Instructor at the Command and General Staff School 1939-1942. Brigadier general in February 1942. Served in the South Pacific Area 1942-1943. Commanding general of the Coast Artillery Seacoast Replacement Training Center at Camp McQuaide March-October 1943 then the Southern Sector of Eastern Defense Command October 1943-March 1944. Commanding general of harbor defenses in New York 1944-1945. Reverted to colonel in December 1945. Retired in October 1950. Decorations included the Legion of Merit and Commendation Ribbon. Died on February 8, 1980.

Ott, Edward Stanley (1893-1982) Born on December 30, 1893, in Mt. Hermon, Louisiana. Attended the University of Illinois 1913-1914. B.A. from Louisiana State University in 1917. Commissioned in the field artillery in 1917. Graduated from the Command and General Staff School in 1935 and the Army War College in 1938. With the War Department General Staff 1939-1942. Staff officer with Army Ground Forces 1942. Brigadier general in June 1942. Commanding general of 91st Infantry Division Artillery June 1942-September 1943. Commander of XV Corps Artillery September 1943-September 1945. Retired in February 1947. Decorations included the Distinguished Service Medal, Silver Star, Legion of Merit, two Bronze Stars, the Air Medal and two Purple Hearts. Died on November 4, 1982.

Owens, Alexander Mitchell (1887-1970) Born in Anne Arundel County, Maryland, on January 21, 1887. Enlisted service 1906-1917. Commissioned in the cavalry, Officers Reserve Corps in 1917. Station quartermaster at Albrook Field 1934-1936. Quartermaster at 8th Division, then I Corps 1940-1941. Assistant to the quartermaster general, U.S. Army January-April 1942. Deputy director of the storage and distribution division, office of the quartermaster general 1942-1946. Brigadier general in May 1944. Retired in February 1946. Decorations included the Distinguished Service Medal. Died on December 27, 1970.

Oxx, Francis Hudson (1898-1956) Born on September 13, 1898, in Jamestown, Rhode Island. Commissioned in the Corps of Engineers from West Point in 1920.

Instructor at West Point 1924-1929, then associate professor 1936-1940. Engineer on the Missouri River war construction project 1940-1942. Enginnering officer at North African Theater of Operations September 1942-March 1943. Deputy chief of staff, then chief of staff for North African Theater of Operations 1943. Chief of staff, then commanding officer of the peninsula base section, North African Theater of Operations 1943-1945. Brigadier general in January 1945. Commanding officer of the peninsula base section, Mediterranean Theater of Operations January 1945-June 1946. Retired in 1951. Decorations included the Distinguished Service Medal and two Legions of Merit. Died on February 15, 1956.

Paine, George Harris (1884-1949) Born in Scranton, Pennsylvania, on July 14, 1884. Commissioned in the infantry from West Point in 1906. Served with the 3rd and 9th Field Artillery in Hawaii 1915-1917 then the 2nd Division at Verdun in 1918. Assistant commandant of the Field Artillery School 1918-1921. Graduated from the Army War College in 1924. Duty with the Philippine Department 1924-1927 and the Hawaii Department 1931-1936. With the military intelligence division at the War Department General Staff in 1936. Military attache in Rome 1936-1941. Brigadier general in April 1941. Commander of 46th and 31st Field Artillery Brigades 1941-1945. Commanding general of the School Troops Field Artillery School at Fort Sill February 1945 until retirement in April 1946. Died on May 11, 1949.

Palmer, Charles Day (1902-) Born in Chicago, Illinois, on February 20, 1902, brother of Williston Birkhimer Palmer. Commissioned in the field artillery from West Point in 1924. With 11th Field Artillery in Hawaii 1929-1932. Instructor at Harvard University ROTC 1932-1937. Graduated from the Command and General Staff School in 1938. Served in the British West Indies 1941-1942. Chief of staff of 11th and 2nd Armored Divisions, then V and VI Corps 1944-1945. Brigadier general in February 1945. Chief of staff of 4th Service Command then Seventh and Third Army 1945-1947. Assignments after the war included commander of 1st Cavalry Division Artillery December 1947-August 1951, chief of staff of the U.S. European Command 1954-1955, deputy commander of Army Forces Far East 1955-1957, deputy commander of Eighth Army 1957-1958, commanding general of Sixth Army March 1958-September 1959 and deputy Commander in Chief U.S. European Command 1959-1962. Retired in March 1962. Decorations included three Distinguished Service Medals, two Silver Stars, two Legions of Merit, two Distinguished Flying Crosses and the Bronze Star.

Palmer, John McAuley (1870-1955) Born in Carlinville, Illinois, on April 23, 1870. Commissioned in the infantry from West Point in 1892. Aide-de-camp to Brigadier General E.V. Sumner 1898-1899. Served in Cuba in 1899 and the Boxer Rebellion in 1900. Instructor at West Point 1901-1906. Duty in the Philippines with 15th Infantry 1906-1907. Graduated from the General Staff College in 1910. Duty in the Philippines again 1914-1915. Deputy chief of staff of the AEF 1917-1918 in the Meuse-Argonne, Grande Montague and Bois d'Etraye engagements. Commanding officer of 58th Infantry in the Meuse-Argonne campaign.

Aide to Pershing 1921-1923. Brigadier general in December 1922. Commander of 19th Infantry Brigade in the Canal Zone 1923-1925. Retired in January 1926. Recalled to active duty in November 1941. Served as adviser to the the War Department General Staff until retirement again in September 1946. Decorations included two Distinguished Service Medals. Died on October 26, 1955.

Palmer, Williston Birkhimer (1899-1973) Born on November 11, 1899, in Chicago, Illinois, brother of Charles Day Palmer. Commissioned in the field artillery from West Point in 1919. Served in the Canal Zone with 4th Field Artillery 1920-1926. Aide-de-camp to Major Grneral Andrew J. Bowley 1931-1935. Assistant to the artillery officer, then artillery officer at the Armored Force in 1942. Brigadier general in August 1942. Artillery officer for First Army Group in 1943. Commanding general of VII Corps Artillery 1944-1945. Commanding general of school troops at the Artillery School in 1945. Assignments after the war included commanding general of 82nd Airborne Division, then 2nd Armored Division 1949-1951, commanding general of X Corps January-August 1952, vice chief of staff, U.S. Army May 1955-May 1957 and Deputy Commander in Chief U.S. European Command 1957-1959. Retired in December 1959. Decorations included three Distinguished Service Medals, the Silver Star, Legion of Merit, Bronze Star and Air Medal.. Died on November 10, 1973.

Pape, Robin Bernard (1903-) Born on January 6, 1903, in Waterbury, Connecticut. Commissioned in the Air Service from West Point in 1924. Graduated from Command and General Staff School in 1938. Assistant military attache in Tokyo 1938-1941. Military observer with the China-Burma-India Theater of Operations 1941-1942 then director of operations 1942-1943. Assigned to Southeast Asia Command 1943-1945. Brigadier general in January 1944. Retired in June 1954. Decorations included the Legion of Merit.

Parker, Cortlandt (1884-1960) Born in Fort Apache, Arizona, on December 10, 1884, the son of Major General James Parker. Commissioned in the cavalry from West Point in 1906. In the Philippines with 2nd Field Artillery 1907-1909. Served with the 6th Field Artillery and 1st Field Artillery Brigade in the AEF in World War I. Graduated from the School of the Line in 1922, General staff School in 1923 and the Army War College in 1924. Duty with the War Department General Staff 1924-1928. Military attache in London 1931-1935. Again at Schofield Barracks as commanding officer of 8th Field Artillery 1936-1939. Commanding officer of Army troops at the New York World's Fair 1939. Commander of 19th Field Artillery November 1939-October 1940. Brigadier general in October 1940. Commanding general of 5th Division Artillery 1940-1942. Major general in August 1942. Commanding general of 5th Division 1942-1943. Commanding general of the Southern California Sector, Western Defense Command 1943-1946. Retired in August 1946. Decorations included the Distinguished Service Medal, Silver Star and Legion of Merit. Died on January 19, 1960.

Parker, Edwin Pearson Jr. (1891-1983) Born in Wytheville, Virginia, on July 27, 1891. Attended George Washington University 1909-1911. Commissioned in the field artillery in 1913. Duty in the Panama Canal Zone 1916-1918. Assistant professor of military science and tactics at Ohio State University then Harvard 1919-1923. Graduated from the Command and General Staff School in 1925. Professor of military science and tactics at the University of Oklahoma 1927-1931. Graduated from the Army War College in 1937. Instructor with Virginia National Guard 1937-1941. Commander of the Field Artillery Replacement Training Center at Fort Bragg January 1941-May 1942. Brigadier general in October 1941, major general in June 1942. Commanding general of 78th Infantry Division 1942-1945. Assignments after the war included commanding general of XXIII Corps September 1945-February 1946, commander of Third Army April-August 1946, deputy commander of Fifth Army 1948-1949 and provost marshal general, U.S. Army April 1949-1953. Retired in January 1953. Decorations included the Distinguished Service Medal, Silver Star, Legion of Merit, two Bronze Stars and the Commendation Ribbon. Died on June 5, 1983.

Parker, George Marshall Jr. (1889-1968) Born in Sac City, Iowa, on April 17, 1889. Commissioned in the infantry in 1910. Served with the 21st Infantry in the Philippines 1910-1912 and on the Mexican border 1916-1917. Instructor at the Infantry School of Arms 1917-1918. Duty in the Panama Canal Zone 1919-1922. Graduated from the Command and General Staff School in 1923 and the Army War College in 1925. Instructor at the Infantry School 1935-1939. Commander of the 7th Infantry 1939-1941. Brigadier general in April 1941. Commander of the Post of Manila, Philippine Islands April 1941-April 1942. Major general in December 1941. Prisoner of war April 1942-August 1945. Retired in September 1946. Decorations included the Distinguished Service Medal. Died on October 25, 1968.

Parks, Floyd Lavinius (1896-1959) Born in Louisville, Kentucky, on February 9, 1896. Attended Cumberland College 1912-1913. B.S. from Clemson College in 1917. Commissioned in the infantry in 1918. Duty with 65th Engineers, the first Tank Corps unit in the U.S. Army (commanded by Captain Dwight D. Eisenhower) in 1918. Aide-de-camp to Major General E.F. McGlachlin 1921-1923. M.S. from Yale in 1924. In Hawaii with 11th Tank Company 1925-1926 then aide to Major General while commander of the Hawaiian Department 1927-1928 and superintendent at West Point 1928-1932. Graduated from the Command and General Staff School in 1935. Instructor at the Infantry School 1935-1937. Aide to General Malin Craig 1937-1939. Graduated from the Army War College in 1940. Plans and training officer in 2nd Armored Brigade 1940-1941. Briefly with 2nd Armored Division then secretary of the War Department General Staff July 1941-March 1942. Deputy chief of staff, then chief of staff of Army Ground Forces March 1942-May 1943. Brigadier general in June 1942. Assistant division commander of 69th Infantry Division May 1943-July 1944. Chief of staff of First Allied Airborne Army 1944-1945. Major general in March 1945. Duty with the military government in Berlin then in the office of the chief of staff, U.S. Army

July 1945-January 1946. Assignments after the war included chief of information, Department of the Army 1949-1953 and commanding general of Second Army August 1953 until retirement as lieutenant general in February 1956. Decorations included two Distinguished Service Medals, the Legion of Merit, Bronze Star, Air Medal and Commendation Ribbon. Died on March 11, 1959.

Partridge, Frank Huber (1893-1994) Born in Scranton, Pennsylvania, on December 1, 1893. Attended the University of Pennsylvania. Commissioned in the infantry in 1917. Duty in the Philippine Islands 1922-1924. Graduated from the Command and General Staff School in 1933. Assistant chief of staff for personnel and supply with the Philippine Division 1934-1936. Served with the Civilian Conservation Corps 1936-1940. Duty at the War Department General Staff then chief of administrative branch at Services of Supply 1940-1942. Commanding officer of 355th Infantry June-December 1942. Assistant division commander of 97th Infantry Division December 1942-1946. Brigadier general in February 1943. Reverted to colonel in March 1946. Retired in December 1953. Decorations included the Legion of Merit and Bronze Star. Died on June 28, 1994.

Partridge, Richard Clare (1899-1976) Born on February 15, 1899, in Boston, Massachusetts. B.A. from Harvard in 1919. Commissioned in the field artillery from West Point in 1920. Graduated from the Command and General Staff School in 1936. Military attache in Budapest 1940-1942. Interned in Lisbon January-May 1942. Deputy chief of staff for operations at Allied Forces headquarters and 15th Army Group 1942-1943, then 1st Army Group and VII Corps 1943-1945. Wounded at Normandy on D-Day. Brigadier general in March 1945. Commanding officer of 358th Infantry, 90th Division in 1945. Assignments after the war included military attache in Yugoslavia 1946-1949 and commanding general of 5th Division 1954-1955. Retired in March 1959. Decorations included two Distinguished Service Medals, two Legions of Merit, two Bronze Stars and the Purple Heart. Died on July 23, 1976.

Paschal, Paul Clarence (1892-1964) Born on April 3, 1892, in Silver City, North Carolina. Commissioned in the infantry from West Point in 1914. Wounded while serving with the 3rd Division in the AEF in World War I. Graduated from the Command and General Staff School in 1924 then instructor there until 1928. Graduated from the Army War College in 1929. Duty with 14th Infantry in the Panama Canal Zone 1929-1932. In the military intelligence division at the War Department General Staff 1932-1935. Instructor at the Infantry School 1935-1939 and the Army War College 1939-1940. Commanding officer of 38th Infantry 1940-1942. Professor of military science and tactics at the University of Kentucky December 1942-March 1943. Commanding officer of 313th Regiment March-August 1943. Assistant division commander of 45th Division 1943-1944. Brigadier general in November 1943. Commanding general of the Infantry Replacement Training Command 1944-1945. Duty at headquarters of Caribbean Defense Command April-September 1945. Hospitalized until retirement in June

1946. Decorations included the Distinguished Service Cross and Purple Heart. Died on April 25, 1964.

Patch, Alexander McCarrell (1889-1945) Born on November 23, 1889, at Fort Huachuca, Arizona. Attended Lehigh University 1908-1909. Commissioned in the infantry from West Point in 1913. Served on the Mexican border in 1916. Commanded a machine gun battalion in the AEF in World War I. Professor of military science and tactics at Staunton Military Academy 1920-1924 and again 1925-1928 following graduation from the Command and General Staff School in 1925. Graduated from the Army War College in 1932. Brigadier general in December 1940. Training duty at Fort Bragg 1941-1942. Major general in March 1942. Organized and trained the Americal Division in 1942, taking part in the first offensive in the Pacific at Guadalcanal October 1942-February 1943. Commander of the III Corps area 1943-1944. Commanding general of Seventh Army March 1944-June 1945. Lieutenant general in August 1944. Commander of Fourth Army June 1945 until his death on November 21, 1945. Decorations included four Distinguished Service Medals. Posthumous promotion to general in July 1954.

Patch, Joseph Dorst (1885-1966) Born in Fort Huachuca, Arizona, on December 8, 1885. Enlisted service with 9th Infantry 1909-1911. Commissioned in the infantry in 1911. Served in the Philippine Islands in 1910 and the Panama Canal Zone 1911-1914. Saw action with the 26th and 18th Infantry, AEF at Cantigny, Montdidier-Noyon and Aisne-Marne offensives. Wounded in action on July 18, 1918. Instructor at the Infantry School 1919-1922. Professor of military science and tactics at Lehigh University 1922-1924. Graduated from the Command and General Staff School in 1925. Again instructor at the Infantry School 1925-1928. Graduated from the Army War College in 1935. Professor of military science and tactics at the University of Maryland 1935-1939. Instructor at the Army War College July 1939-June 1940. Commander of 34th Infantry June 1940-May 1942. Brigadier general in October 1941, major general in May 1942. Commanding general of 80th Infantry Division May 1942-March 1943 then the Trinidad Sector at Caribbean Defense Command 1943-1944. Commanding general of the Army Service Forces Training Center at Fort Lewis July 1944 until retirement in December 1945. Decorations included the Distinguished Service Cross and Purple Heart. Died on November 21, 1966.

Patrick, Edwin Davies (1894-1945) Born in Tell City, Indiana, on January 11, 1894. Attended Indiana University 1912-1915 and the University of Michigan 1915-1916. Commissioned in the infantry in 1917. Served on the Mexican border 1917-1918 and saw action at St. Mihiel and Meuse-Argonne with the 14th Machine Gun Battalion, AEF in World War I 1918-1919. Instructor at the Infantry School 1920-1922. Duty with 15th Infantry in Tientsin 1926-1929. Again instructor at the Infantry School 1929-1932. Graduated from the Command and General Staff School in 1934. Instructor with the Washington National Guard 1934-1936. Graduated from the Army War College in 1937 and the Naval War College in 1938. Assistant chief of staff for intelligence in the VIII Corps Area 1938-1942.

Commanding officer of 357th Infantry March-November 1942. Staff officer with the commander of the South Pacific area December 1942-June 1943. Chief of staff of Sixth Army 1943-1944. Brigadier general in May 1943, major general in September 1944. Commanding general of 6th Infantry Division September 1944 until his death from battle wounds on Luzon Island, Philippines on March 14, 1945. Decorations included the Silver Star and Legion of Merit.

Patton, George Smith Jr. (1885-1945) Born on November 11, 1885, in San Gabriel, California. Attended Virginia Military Institute in 1904. Commissioned in the cavalry from West Point in 1909. Represented the United States in the military pentathlon events at the 1912 Olympic games in Stockholm. Served with Pershing on the Mexican border in 1916 and in France 1916-1917. Commanding officer of the 304th Tank Brigade at the St. Mihiel and Meuse-Argonne offensives. Graduated from the Command and General Staff School in 1924 and the Army War College in 1932. Commanding officer of 3rd Cavalry 1938-1940. Commander of 2nd Armored Division 1940-1942. Brigadier general in October 1940 and major general in April 1941. Commanding general of I Armored Corps, then II Armored Corps 1942-1943, taking part in the invasion of North Africa. Commander of Seventh Army in the invasion of Sicily in 1943. Involved in the widely publicised slapping of a soldier at the end of the Sicily campaign. Lieutenant general in April 1943. Commander of Third Army 1944-1945. The Third Army fought in much of the Battle of the Bulge, during which Patton became known as "Old Blood and Guts." General in April 1945. Briefly commander of U.S. forces in Europe in November 1945. Died following an automobile accident on December 21, 1945. Decorations included two Distinguished Service Crosses, three Distinguished Service Medals, the Silver Star, Legion of Merit, Bronze Star and Purple Heart. Author of *War as I Knew It* (1947).

Paul, Willard Stewart (1894-1966) Born in Worcester, Massachusetts, on February 28, 1894. Enlisted service with 1st Colorado Field Artillery 1916-1917. Commissioned in the infantry in 1917. Attended Dartmouth University. Professor of military science and tactics at Johns Hopkins 1921-1924, from which he received a B.S. in 1924. Duty with 27th Infantry in Hawaii 1924-1928. Instructor at the Infantry School 1930-1933. Graduated from the Command and General Staff School in 1935. Assistant professor of military science and tactics at Culver Academy 1935-1936. Graduated from the Army War College in 1937. Served with the Adjutant General Department 1937-1941 then at GHQ U.S. Army 1941-1942 and GHQ Army Ground Forces 1942-1943. Brigadier general in June 1942. M.S. from American University in 1942. Commanding general of 75th and 26th Infantry Divisions 1943-1945. Major general in March 1943. Deputy chief of staff for personnel at SHAEF then deputy chief of staff at headquarters of the European Theater of Operations in 1945. Assistant chief of staff for personnel, U.S. Army 1945-1948. Retired in December 1948. Decorations included two Distinguished Service Medals, the Silver Star, Legion of Merit and two Bronze Stars. Died on March 21, 1966.

Peabody, Paul Everton (1892-1979) Born on May 1, 1892, in Chicago, Illinois. B.A. from the University of California, Berkley in 1915. Enlisted service with the California National Guard 1916-1917. Commissioned in the infantry in 1917. Served with the 1st Division, AEF in World War I 1917-1919. Graduated from the Command and General Staff School in 1928, the Army War College in 1933 and the Naval War College in 1939. Chief of staff of Alaska Defense Command 1940-1942. Brigadier general in May 1942, major general in August 1942. Commanding general of 8th Motorized Division in 1942. Military attache in London 1943-1944. With the War Department General Staff 1945-1946. Retired in March 1950. Decorations included the Distinguished Service Medal and three Legions of Merit. Died on June 19, 1979.

Pearson, Madison (1890-1968) Born in Dadeville, Alabama, on January 12, 1890. Enlisted service 1908-1909. Commissioned in the Philippine Scouts in 1913 and the infantry in 1917. Served with the 4th Machine Gun Battalion, First Army and the 3rd Division, AEF at Champagne-Marne, Aisne-Marne, St. Mihiel and Meuse-Argonne engagements 1918-1919. Professor of military science and tactics at Clemson Agricultural College 1919-1925. Graduated from the Command and General Staff School in 1926. Duty at the Hawaiian Department 1937-1939. Graduated from the Army War College in 1940. With the 2nd Armored Division 1940-1941. Member of the Adjutant General's Board in 1941. Deputy director of administrative services division of Services of Supply June 1942-September 1943. Brigadier general in December 1942. Commanding general of Pine Camp 1943-1944 then Fort Dix 1944-1946. Retired in May 1946. Decorations included the Distinguished Service Medal, Silver Star, Legion of Merit and Purple Heart. Died on July 21, 1968.

Peckham, Howard Louis (1897-1972) Born on May 29, 1897, in Norwich, Connecticut. Commissioned in the Corps of Engineers from West Point in 1918. Professor of military science and tactics at Missouri School of Mines 1920-1926. Instructor at West Point 1926-1930. Duty in Puerto Rico 1933-1935. Graduated from the Command and General Staff School in 1940. Chief of staff of 8th Armored Division April-July 1942. Brigadier general in August 1942. Commanding general of Combat Command, 12th Armored Division 1942-1943. Director of fuels and lubricants in the office of the quartermaster general October 1943-March 1946. Retired in 1956. Decorations included the Distinguished Service Medal and two Commendation Ribbons. Died on October 8, 1972.

Peek, Ernest Dichmann (1878-1950) Born in Oshkosh, Wisconsin, on November 19, 1878. Commissioned in the Corps of Engineers from West Point in 1901. Graduated from School of the Line in 1909. Commanding officer of 21st Engineers with the AEF in World War I, taking part in the Meuse-Argonne and St. Mihiel offensives. Graduated from the Army War College in 1920 then instructor there until 1921. Duty with the Panama Canal Department 1921-1924. Attended Babson Institute 1929-1930. Brigadier general in July 1937. Commander of 4th Brigade 1937-1940. Major general in October 1940. Chief of staff of IX Corps

Area 1940-1941 then commanding general 1941-1942. Retired in October 1942. Decorations included the Distinguished Service Medal and Silver Star. Died on April 24, 1950.

Pence, Arthur William (1898-1954) Born on July 18, 1898, in Fort Monroe, Virginia. Commissioned in the Corps of Engineers from West Point in 1918. Duty with 14th Engineers in the Philippines 1926-1928. Professor of military science and tactics at the University of Alabama 1928-1932. Graduated from the Command and General Staff School in 1938. Instructor at the Engineer School 1938-1940. Deputy engineer for Services of Supply in the European Theater of Operations in 1942. Engineer officer of Mediterranean Base Sector in the North African Theater of Operations November 1942-April 1943. Brigadier general in April 1943. Commanding general of base sectors in the Mediterranean Theater of Operations 1943-1944. Faculty member at the Command and General Staff School 1944-1948, having reverted to colonel in April 1946. Commanding general of 6th Armored Division at his death on November 8, 1954. Decorations included the Distinguished Service Medal, two Legions of Merit and the Bronze Star.

Pence, George Dunbar (1902-1977) Born on July 13, 1902, in Fort Morgan, Alabama. Commissioned in the field artillery from West Point in 1924. Aide-de-camp to Brigadier General C.E. Kilbourne in the Philippines 1929-1932. Instructor at West Point 1934-1938. Graduated from the Command and General Staff School in 1941. Duty with the War Department General Staff 1941-1942. Assistant chief of staff at Services of Supply, European Theater of Operations in 1942. Again at the War Department General Staff 1943-1944. Brigadier general in August 1944. Chief of staff of the Mediterranean Theater of Operations 1944-1945. Major general in January 1945. Duty in the office of the chief of staff, U.S. Army June 1945 until retirement in February 1946. Decorations included the Distinguished Service Medal and Legion of Merit. Died on February 24, 1977.

Pendleton, Randolph Tucker (1889-1973) Born in Lexington, Virginia, on August 23, 1889. B.A. from Virginia Military Institute in 1908. Commissioned in the Coast Artillery Corps in 1911. Duty in the Philippines 1914-1915. Instructor at Coast Artillery School 1917-1918. Commanding officer of the 1st Trench Mortar with the I Corps, AEF at St. Mihiel and Meuse-Argonne offensives 1918-1919. Professor of military science and tactics at Massachusetts Institute of Technology 1920-1924. Graduated from the Command and General Staff School in 1926. Again instructor at Coast Artillery School 1926-1930. Graduated from the Army War College in 1933. Once again at Coast Artillery School 1936-1941. Commander of 10th Coast Artillery March 1941-June 1942. Brigadier general in May 1942. Commanding general of Atlantic Coast Artillery Brigade, Caribbean Defense Command 1942-1944 then 57th Antiaircraft Artillery Brigade October-November 1944. Commanding general of Antiaircraft Artillery Training Center 1944-1945. Retired in August 1949. Decorations included the Legion of Merit. Died on January 13, 1973.

Pennell, Ralph McTyeire (1882-1973) Born in Anderson City, South Carolina, on August 18, 1882. Commissioned in the field artillery from West Point in 1906. Duty with 2nd Field Artillery in the Philippines 1915-1917. Graduated from the Command and General Staff School in 1923, the Army War College in 1927 and Naval War College in 1928. Served with the Hawaiian Division 1928-1930. Member then president of the Field Artillery Board 1935-1939. Duty with 27th Division 1940-1942. Brigadier general in January 1941, major general in February 1942. Commanding general of 27th Division March-October 1942. Member of the War Department Dependency Board, then commander of Field Artillery Replacement Training Center at Fort Sill 1942-1944. Commandant of the Field Artillery School October 1944 until retirement in March 1946. Decorations included two Distinguished Service Medals and the Legion of Merit. Died on May 17, 1973.

Perkins, Robert Meredith (1887-1960) Born on September 26, 1887, in Norfolk, Virginia. Commissioned in the Coast Artillery Corps from West Point in 1913. Instructor at West Point 1922-1926. Graduated from the Command and General Staff School in 1928. Secretary of Coast Artillery Corps School 1928-1931. Graduated from the Army War College in 1935. Brigadier general in March 1942. Commanded 53rd Antiaircraft Brigade 1942-1944. Commanding general of Hawaiian Antiaircraft Command 1944-1945. Retired in October 1947 as colonel. Brigadier general on the retired list in 1948. Decorations included two Legions of Merit. Died on January 15, 1960.

Perrin, Herbert Towle (1893-1962) Born on September 8, 1893, in Platville, Wisconsin. Attended Western Reserve University 1912-1915. Ph.B. from Kenyon College in 1916. M.A. from Princeton in 1917. Commissioned in the infantry in 1917. Served with 45th Infantry in the Philippines 1924-1926. Instructor at the Command and General Staff School 1928-1931 then student there, graduating in 1933. Assistant chief of staff for operations in the Philippine Department 1937-1940. With the war plans division of the War Department General Staff 1940-1942. Chief of staff of 76th Infantry Division in 1942. Brigadier general in March 1943. Assistant division commander of 106th Infantry Division 1942-1946. Retired in September 1946. Decorations included the Distinguished Service Cross and Legion of Merit. Died on June 9, 1962.

Perrine, Henry Pratt (1891-1953) Born on July 22, 1891, in Trenton, New Jersey. Commissioned in the infantry from West Point in 1913. M.B.A. from Harvard in 1931. Instructor, secretary, executive officer and commanding general of the Infantry School 1939-1944. Brigadier general in March 1943. Retired in 1951. Decorations included the Legion of Merit. Died on December 20, 1953.

Perry, Basil Harrison (1893-1960) Born on August 5, 1893, in Providence, Rhode Island. Attended Brown University 1911-1912. Commissioned in the field artillery from West Point in 1917. Served with the 7th Field Artillery in the AEF 1917-1918. Instructor at Field Artillery School 1919-1921. M.S. from Yale in

1922. Instructor at West Point 1926-1930. Graduated from the Command and General Staff School in 1932 and the Army War College in 1936. Instructor at the Command and General Staff School 1938-1940. Duty in the operations and training division of the War Department General Staff January 1940-March 1942. Brigadier general in March 1942. Commander of 28th Infantry Division Artillery 1942-1946. Reverted to colonel in February 1946. Retired in July 1953. Decorations included the Silver Star, two Legions of Merit, two Bronze Stars, the Air Medal and Commendation Ribbon. Died on April 10, 1960.

Persons, Wilton Burton (1896-1977) Born in Montgomery, Alabama, on January 10, 1896. B.S. from Alabama Polytechnic Institute in 1916. Commissioned in the Coast Artillery Corps in 1917. Served with the AEF in World War I. Professor of military science and tactics at the University of Minnesota 1924-1929. M.B.A. from Harvard in 1931. Graduated from the Command and General Staff School in 1938. Duty in the office of the chief of staff, U.S. Army as liaison officer with Congress 1939-1941. Chief of the legislative division in the office of the chief of staff, U.S. Army March 1942-1948. Brigadier general in June 1942, major general in November 1944. Retired in June 1949. Decorations included the Distinguished Service Medal and Legion of Merit. Superintendent of Staunton Military Academy 1949-1950. Returned to active duty as special assistant to General Eisenhower 1951-1952 then President Eisenhower 1953-1956. Died on September 5, 1977.

Peterson, Virgil Lee (1882-1956) Born on September 22, 1882, in Campbellsville, Kentucky. B.S. from Centre College in 1902. Commissioned in the Civil Engineer Corps from West Point in 1908. Served in the Philippines as aide to Major General J. Franklin Bell 1913-1914. Commandant of the Engineer School 1918-1920. Graduated from the Command and General Staff School in 1925 and the Army War College in 1933. Duty in Hawaii as commanding officer of 3rd Engineers 1934-1935 then division engineer with the Hawaiian Division 1935-1936. Major general in December 1939 as inspector general of the War Department 1939-1945. Retired in February 1946. Decorations included the Distinguished Service Medal. Died on February 15, 1956.

Peyton, Philip B. (1881-1949) Born on January 22, 1881, in Nashville, Tennessee. B.S. from Virginia Military Institute in 1901. Commissioned in the infantry in 1904. Served in the Philippine Islands 1905-1907. Professor of military science and tactics at Drury College 1909-1911 then South Dakota Agricultural College 1911-1912. At Fort Seward, Alaska 1914-1916. Commanded 61st Infantry, AEF at St. Mihiel and Meuse-Argonne 1918-1919. Professor of military science and tactics at Shattuck School 1919-1923. Graduated from the Command and General Staff School in 1926. Instructor, then section chief at the Infantry School 1926-1928. Graduated from the Army War College in 1931. Duty with the War Department General Staff 1932-1936. Brigadier general in August 1937. Commander of 12th Infantry Brigade 1937-1938. Commanding general of the Hawaiian Separate Coast Artillery Brigade then the 21st Infantry Brigade April 1938-

December 1939. Commandant of the Army War College 1939-1940. Major general in October 1940. Commanding general of 8th Division then I Corps 1940-1942. Retired in February 1942. Decorations included the Distinguished Service Medal and Silver Star. Died on June 23, 1949.

Phelps, Joseph Vincil (1898-1981) Born on August 27, 1898, in Salisbury, Missouri. Commissioned in the field artillery from West Point in 1919. Duty with the AEF July-September 1919. Instructor at West Point 1924-1928. In Hawaii with 11th Field Artillery 1929-1931. Professor of military science and tactics at Alabama Polytechnic Institute 1931-1936. Graduated from the Command and General Staff School in 1938. Served with 2nd Field Artillery in the Panama Canal Zone 1938-1940. Duty at the Replacement and School Command March 1942-January 1943. Brigadier general in March 1943. Commanding general of 17th Airborne Division Artillery 1944-1945. Reverted to colonel in April 1946. Retired in May 1949. Decorations included the Silver Star, Legion of Merit and Bronze Star. Died on July 17, 1981.

Philips, Joseph Leon (1890-1960) Born on June 15, 1890, in Valley Forge, Pennsylvania. B.S. from State College of Washington in 1914. Commissioned in the cavalry in 1916. Served with the AEF in World War I 1917-1919. Graduated from the Command and General Staff School in 1928. Instructor at the Cavalry School 1930-1935. Graduated from Army Industrial College in 1938. Instructor with the Washington Military District 1938-1940. Instructor in the military district of Washington 1938-1940. In the office of the assistant secretary of war, then the under secretary 1940-1942. Brigadier general in July 1942. With the resource division of the Services of Supply in 1942. Member of the War Production Board, Army Group July 1942-March 1943. In the office of the chief of transportation in 1943. Served in the European Theater of Operations May 1943-September 1945. Retired in March 1946. Decorations included two Legions of Merit and the Bronze Star. Died on October 19, 1960.

Phillips, Thomas Raphael (1892-1965) Born in Black River Falls, Wisconsin, on January 27, 1892. Attended the University of Virginia. Commissioned in the Coast Artillery Corps in 1917. Served in the AEF 1919-1920. Graduated from the Command and General Staff School in 1936, then instructor there 1936-1940. Extended service in Puerto Rico as assistant to the assistant chief of staff for intelligence, assistant chief of staff for operations, chief of staff of the Puerto Rico Department and chief of staff of the Antilles Department July 1940-October 1945. Brigadier general in September 1942. Director of personnel services for the European Theater of Operations December 1945-March 1946. Reverted to colonel in March 1946. Retired in March 1950. Decorations included the Distinguished Service Medal and Legion of Merit. Died on July 29, 1965.

Phillipson, Irving Joseph (1882-1955) Born on April 3, 1882, in Dowagiac, Michigan. Commissioned in the infantry from West Point in 1904. Commanding officer of a battery, regiment and brigade in the 142nd and 143rd Infantry during the Meuse-Argonne offensive in World War I. Graduated from the Army War College in 1924. Commander of 30th Infantry 1935-1938. Brigadier general in July 1938. Commanding general of 2nd Brigade, 1st Division 1938-1940. Chief of staff of II Corps Area, Govenor's Island in 1940, then commanding general 1940-1942. Major general in April 1941. Executive director of Army Emergency Relief 1942-1944. Member of the War Department Board January 1944 until retirement in December 1944. Decorations included the Distinguished Service Medal. Died on April 4, 1955.

Philoon, Wallace Copeland (1883-1970) Born in Auburn, Maine, on October 13, 1883. B.S. from Bowdoin College in 1905. Commissioned in the infantry from West Point in 1909. Assistant military attache in Peking 1919-1923. Graduated from the Command and General Staff School in 1924 then instructor there 1928-1932. Graduated from the Army War College in 1933. Attached to the War Department General Staff 1935-1939. Chief of staff of the Panama Canal 1940-1941. Brigadier general in April 1941. Chief of staff of the Caribbean Defense Command 1941-1942. Commanding general of the Infantry Replacement Training Center at Fort McClellan 1942-1945. Major general in September 1945. Retired in October 1945. Decorations included the Legion of Merit. Died on January 16, 1970.

Piburn, Edwin William (1895-1958) Born in Kinsley, Kansas, on July 9, 1895. Attended Oklahoma Institute of Technology 1912-1914 and Iowa State University 1915-1917. Commissioned in the infantry in 1917. Served with the 18th Infantry in France 1919-1920 and 8th Infantry in Germany 1921-1922. Instructor at the Tank School 1924-1925, the Infantry School 1926-1927 and with the Colorado National Guard 1927-1932. Duty with 14th Infantry in the Panama Canal Zone 1936-1939. Professor of military science and tactics at South Dakota State College 1939-1940. Observer with the British forces in the Middle East 1941-1942. Brigadier general in September 1942. Combat Commander "B"with 14th Armored Division 1942-1944. Combat Commander "A" of 10th Armored Division November 1944-April 1945, including the Battle of the Bulge. Severely wounded near Ohrigen, Germany on April 17, 1945, and hospitalized for two years. Retired in October 1952. Decorations included the Silver Star, two Legions of Merit, two Bronze Stars, the Commendation Ribbon and Purple Heart. Died on September 28, 1958.

Pick, Lewis Andrew (1890-1956) Born in Brookneal, Virginia, on November 18, 1890. B.S. from Virginia Polytechnic Institute in 1914. Commissioned in the Corps of Engineers in 1917. Graduated from the Command and General Staff School in 1934. Instructor at the Command and General Staff School 1934-1938. Graduated from the Army War College in 1939. Executive officer to the division engineer of Ohio River division 1939-1941. Division engineer with the Missouri River division 1942-1943. Commander of the advance section at China-Burma-India Theater of Operations 1943-1945. Brigadier general in February 1944. Major general in March 1945. With the Missouri River division 1945-1949. Assignments after the war included chief of engineers, U.S. Army 1949-1952. Retired as lieutenant general in November 1952. Decorations included two Distinguished Service Medals. Died on December 2, 1956.

Pickering, James Arthur (1891-1983) Born on December 26, 1891, in Smith County, Mississippi. Attended the University of Mississippi 1909-1911. Commissioned in the Coast Artillery Corps from West Point in 1916. With the 318th Field Artillery, AEF 1918-1919. Instructor with the Wisconsin National Guard 1921-1922 then the Pennsylvania National Guard 1922-1924 and again 1926-1931. Graduated from the Command and General Staff School in 1935. Duty with 8th Field Artillery in hawaii 1935-1937. Professor of military science and tactics at Purdue University 1937-1940. Military intelligence officer with 2nd Armored Division 1940-1942. Brigadier general in May 1942. Commanding general of 8th Infantry Division Artillery 1942-1945. Assigned to Second Army August 1945 until retirement in September 1946. Decorations included the Silver Star, Legion of Merit and Bronze Star. Died on November 6, 1983.

Pierce, Clinton Albert (1894-1966) Born in Brooklyn, New York, on June 15, 1894. Enlisted service with Illinois National Guard 1916-1917. Commissioned in the cavalry in 1917. Instructor with the Tennessee National Guard 1923-1926 and at the Cavalry School 1933-1937. Commanding officer of 8th Cavalry at Fort Stotsenburg, Philippine Islands October 1941-January 1942. Brigadier general in January 1942. Taken prisoner of war by the Japanese in April 1942 and participated in the Bataan Death March. Liberated in August 1945. Retired in February 1951. Decorations included the Distinguished Service Medal, two Silver Stars and the Purple Heart. Died on August 22, 1966.

Pierce, John Leonard (1895-1959) Born in Dallas, Texas, on April 29, 1895. Attended Texas Agricultural and Mechanical College. Commissioned in the infantry in 1917. Served with the 49th Infantry then 8th Infantry in France 1918-1920. Professor of military science and tactics at Massey Military School 1923-1925. Graduated from the Command and General Staff School in 1938. Battalion commander in 67th Infantry November 1939-December 1940 then supply officer 1940-1941. Deputy chief of staff for supply at 3rd Armored Division 1941-1942. Chief of staff of II Armored Corps 1942-1943. Brigadier general in June 1943. Chief of staff of the Armored Command July 1943-March 1944. Combat Commander of the 16th Armored Division 1944-1945. President of the secretary of war's Discharge Review Board October 1945 until retirement in October 1946. Decorations included two Legions of Merit. Died on February 12, 1959.

Pierce, John Theodore (1892-1976) Born in Flagstaff, Arizona, on November 2, 1892. B.A. from the University of Wyoming in 1914, B.S. in 1915. Commissioned in the cavalry in 1916. In Hawaii with 17th Cavalry in 1921. Graduated from the Command and General Staff School in 1932. Instructor with the Texas National Guard 1933-1936. Graduated from the Army War College in 1937. Duty with the 26th Cavalry in the Philippines 1937-1939. Member of the Cavalry Board

1939-1941. Commanding officer of 14th Cavalry January 1941-May 1942. Commander of 2nd Cavalry Brigade May-September 1942. Brigadier general in June 1942. Assistant division commander of 103rd Infantry Division 1942-1945, including action in the Battle of the Bulge. Commanding general of War Department Personnel Center at Fort Sheridan June 1945-June 1946. Retired in November 1947. Decorations included the Silver Star, Legion of Merit and Bronze Star. Died on April 6, 1976.

Pierson, Albert (1899-) Born in Brooklyn, New York, on July 10, 1899. Attended Cornell University 1916-1918. Commissioned in the infantry in 1918. Attended Cornell University again 1919-1920. Assistant Professor of military science and tactics at Cornell 1922-1926. Graduated from the Command and General Staff School in 1937 and the Army War College in 1940. With the War Department General Staff 1940-1942. Brigadier general in February 1943. Assistant division commander of 11th Airborne Division February 1943-October 1945. Assignments after the war included chief of staff of U.S. Army Forces Far East 1954-1957 and onspector general, U.S. Army 1957-1959. Retired in August 1959. Decorations included the Silver Star, two Legions of Merit, the Bronze Star, Air Medal and Commendation Ribbon.

Pillsbury, Henry Church (1881-1955) Born in Lowell, Massachusetts, on May 27, 1881. B.A. from Dartmouth University in 1902. M.D. from Harvard in 1906. Commissioned in the Medical Corps in 1907. Graduated from Army Medical School in 1907. Division surgeon of the 11th Division 1918-1919. Instructor at Army Medical School 1919-1925. Assistant surgeon in the Philippine Department 1929-1930. Chief health officer at the Panama Canal 1936-1939. Surgeon for the III Corps area 1940. Surgeon at C.O. Lovell General Hospital, Fort Devens 1941-1943. Brigadier general in April 1941. Commanding officer of Thayer General Hospital, Nashville 1943-1945. Retired in May 1945.Died on July 17, 1955.

Plank, Ewart Gladstone (1897-1982) Born on November 4, 1897, in Garden City, Missouri. Enlisted service with 137th Infantry in World War I. Commissioned in the Coast Artillery Corps from West Point in 1920. C.E. from Rensselaer Polytechnic Institute in 1922. Duty in the Panama Canal Zone 1927-1929 then Nicaragua 1929-1930. Instructor with the New Mexico National Guard 1930-1932. Graduated from the Command and General Staff School in 1940. Deputy chief of staff at headquarters of Services of Supply in the European Theater of Operations July 1942-August 1943. Chief of staff, then commanding officer of the Eastern Base Section in the European Theater of Operations 1943-1944, then commander of the Advance Section, Communications Zone 1944-1945. Brigadier general in February 1944. Commanding general of the Base Section in the Philippine Islands 1945-1946. Major general in June 1945. Retired in May 1949. Decorations included two Distinguished Service Medals, the Legion of Merit and two Bronze Stars. Died on September 2, 1982.

Pope, Francis Horton (1879-1971) Born in Fort Leavenworth, Kansas, on May 7, 1879, the son of Major General John Pope. Commissioned in the cavalry from West Point in 1897. Served in the Spanish-American War and in the Punitive Expedition into Mexico 1916. Director of the division of motor transport service in the AEF in 1918. Deputy director of the Motor Transport Corps, AEF 1918-1919. Graduated from the Army War College in 1924. Brigadier general in January 1927. Assistant quartermaster general of the Army 1927-1931. Retired in May 1940. Recalled to active duty in January 1941. Retired a second time in December 1943. Decorations included the Distinguished Service Medal. Died on June 3, 1971.

Pope, George Van Wyck (1894-1972) Born on August 4, 1894, in Chicago, Illinois. Ph.B. from Hamilton College in 1916. Commissioned in the infantry, Officers Reserve Corps in 1917. Instructor at West Point 1918-1922. Served with the 27th Infantry in Hawaii 1922-1927. Instructor with the Organized Reserves in Illinois then at the Infantry School 1927-1935. Graduated from the Command and General Staff School in 1936. Duty with WDGS April 1941-January 1942. Chief of staff of 82nd Infantry Division, then 28th Infantry Division in 1942. Brigadier general in December 1942. Assistant division commander of 86th Infantrty Division from 1942. Retired in July 1954. Died on March 5, 1972.

Porter, John Andrew (1886-1950) Born in Allegheny County, Pennsylvania, on January 14, 1886. Enlisted service with 26th Infantry 1903-1917. Commissioned in the Quartermaster Corps in 1917. Served in the AEF 1918-1919. Instructor in the Quartermaster School 1928-1929. Graduated from the Command and General Staff School in 1931. Executive officer, then commanding officer of San Antonio General Depot April 1941-September 1943. Brigadier general in April 1943. Commanding general of Army Service Forces Depot, Fort Sam Houston 1943-1946. Retired in June 1946. Decorations included the Legion of Merit. Died on February 7, 1950.

Porter, Ray Edison (1891-1963) Born in Fordyce, Arkansas, on July 29, 1891. Attended the University of Arkansas 1906-1909. Commissioned in the infantry in 1917. Served with 34th Infantry in France in 1918-1919. Wounded in action on November 9, 1918. Professor of military science and tactics at Ouachita College August 1922-September 1927. Duty in Hawaii with 19th Infantry 1928-1931. Graduated from the Command and General Staff School in 1935 and the Army War College in 1937. Instructor at the Command and General Staff School June 1937-November 1940. Plans and training officer with V Corps 1940-1941. Chief of staff of 38th Infantry Division December 1941-May 1942. Commanding officer of 349th Infantry May 1942-August 1942. Brigadier general in August 1942. Assistant division commander of 34th Infantry Division August 1942-May 1943. Assistant chief of staff for operations at the War Department General Staff May 1943-December 1944. Major general in September 1943. Commanding general of 75th Infantry Division January-June 1945. Served in the office of the chief of staff, U.S. Army June 1945-August 1946. Assignments after the war included commanding general of 101st Airborne Division June 1951 until retirement in June 1953. Decorations included the Distinguished Service Cross, Distinguished Service Medal, Legion of Merit, Bronze Star, Commendation Ribbon and Purple Heart. Died in August 1963.

Porter, William Nichols (1886-1973) Born in Lima, Ohio, on March 15, 1886. Commissioned in the Navy following graduation from USNA in 1909. Resigned from the Navy in 1910 to accept a commission in the Coast Artillery Corps, U.S. Army. Commanding officer of 30th Artillery 1918-1919. Graduated from Army Industrial College in 1926, the Command and General Staff School in 1927 and the Army War College in 1938. Chemical officer at GHQ, U.S. Army April 1940-May 1941. Major general in May 1941. Chief of the Chemical Warfare Service 1941-1945. Retired in November 1945. Died on February 5, 1973.

Post, Elwyn Donald (1899-1961) Born on November 30, 1899, in Shelby, Ohio. Commissioned in the infantry from West Point in 1923. Served with the 35th Infantry in Hawaii 1925-1928. Instructor at West Point 1933-1937. Graduated from the Command and General Staff School in 1938. Operations officer, then chief of staff of the Alaskan Department 1940-1944 then chief of staff of Tenth Army 1944-1945. Brigadier general in March 1943. Reverted to colonel in February 1946. Assignments after the war included chief of the Military District of Washington 1957-1958. Retired as major general in June 1958. Decorations included the Distinguished Service Medal, two Silver Stars and three Legions of Merit. Died on September 29, 1961.

Potter, Waldo Charles (1885-1971) Born in La Moure, North Dakota, on August 27, 1885. Commissioned in the field artillery from West Point in 1907. Duty with the 1st Field Artillery in the Philippines 1911-1913 then at Schofield Barracks, Hawaii 1914-1915. Adjutant of the 2nd and 12th Field Artillery Brigades in the AEF in 1918. Saw action at the Aisne-Marne offensive. Graduated from the Command and General Staff School in 1923 and the Ecole superieure de Guerre in 1926. Instructor at the Command and General Staff School 1926-1930. Graduated from the Army War College in 1931. Professor of military science and tactics at Cornell University 1937-1940. Duty in the office of the chief of field artillery October 1940-October 1941. Brigadier general in October 1941. Commander of Field Artillery Replacement Center at Fort Sill 1941-1943. Member of the War Department Manpower Board March 1943 until retirement in March 1946. Decorations included the Legion of Merit. Died on July 21, 1971.

Powell, Carroll A. (1892-1948) Born on September 3, 1892, in Ohio. Graduated from the University of Cincinnati in 1917. Commissioned in the cavalry in 1917. M.S. from Yale University in 1922. Graduated from Army Industrial College in 1935. Brigadier general in November 1944. Retired in April 1947. Decorations included the Distinguished Service Medal, Legion of Merit and Bronze Star. Died on June 20, 1948.

Powell, William Dan (1893-1943) Born in Kansas City, Missouri, on November 11, 1893. B.S. from the University of Missouri in 1916. Commissioned in the infantry in 1917. Served in France during World War I. Served with occupation forces in Germany 1919-1922. Professor of military science and tactics at the University of South Dakota 1925-1931. Served with the 31st Infantry in the Philippines 1932-1935. Graduated from the Command and General Staff School in 1939. Assigned to the 20th Infantry 1939-1940. Personnel officer at III Corps headquarters 1940-1941. Assigned to the China Burma India Theater of Operations from 1942. Brigadier general in October 1942. Died on October 6, 1943, at Kunming Station Hospital in China.

Pratt, Don Forrester (1892-1944) Born in Brookfield, Missouri, on July 12, 1892. Attended the University of Wisconsin. Commissioned in the infantry in 1917. Graduated from the Command and General Staff School in 1932. Served in Tientsin with the 15th Infantry 1932-1936. Graduated from the Army War College in 1937. Instructor at the Infantry School 1937-1941. Chief of staff of 43rd Infantry Division 1941-1942. Brigadier general in August 1942. Assistant division commander of the 101st Airborne Division 1942-1944. Killed in France in the crash of his glider near Normandy the morning of D-Day, June 6, 1944.

Prentiss, Augustin Mitchell (1890-1977) Born in Chapel Hill, North Carolina, on January 4, 1890. B.S. from George Washington University in 1911. Commissioned in the cavalry in 1913. Commanding officer of the first ordnance base company sent overseas in World War I. Executive officer of the chemical warfare service, AEF 1917-1919. Ph.D. from George Washington University in 1923. Graduated from the Command and General Staff School in 1927 and the Army War College in 1932. Chemical officer at the Panama Canal 1937-1939 and the VI Corps area in 1940. Deputy chief of staff for personnel at VI Corps area 1940-1941. Commanding general of Pine Bluff Arsenal 1941-1946. Brigadier general in December 1942. Retired in August 1946. Decorations included the Distinguished Service Medal and Legion of Merit. Died on April 13, 1977.

Prichard, Vernon Edwin (1892-1949) Born on January 25, 1892, in Smithland, Iowa. Commissioned in the infantry from West Point in 1915. Served in the Punitive Expedition into Mexico 1916-1917 and with the AEF in World War I. Professor of military science and tactics at Yale 1925-1929. Aide-de-camp to Lieutenant General Hugh Drum 1936-1939. Graduated from the Army War College in 1940. Commander of 27th Field Artillery Battery June 1940-April 1941. Chief of staff of 4th Armored Division April 1941-September 1942. Brigadier general in February 1942, major general in September 1942. Commanding general of 14th Armored Division 1942-1944 and 1st Armored Division July 1944-September 1945. Died following an automobile accident in Washington, DC, on July 10, 1949. Decorations included the Distinguished Service Medal and Purple Heart.

Prickett, Fay Brink (1893-1982) Born on April 29, 1893, in Hutchinson, Kansas. Commissioned in the cavalry from West Point in 1916. Served in the Punitive

Expedition into Mexico 1916-1917 and as a battalion commander in the AEF in World War I during the Meuse-Argonne and St. Mihiel offensives. OMST at princeton 1924-1928. Graduated from the Command and General Staff School in 1930. Served in Hawaii with the 13th Field Artillery 1930-1932. Graduated from the Army War College in 1933. Duty with the plans division at the War Department General Staff 1933-1937. Member of the Field Artillery Board 1941-1942. Brigadier general in March 1942. Commander of 4th Division Artillery 1942-1943. Major general in January 1944. Commanding general of 75th Division 1943-1945, 10th Armored Division and 4th Armored Division 1945-1946. Retired in April 1953. Decorations included two Legions of Merit and the Bronze Star. Died on December 18, 1982.

Prosser, Walter Evans (1882-1981) Born on January 18, 1882, in New Albany, Indiana. Commissioned in the artillery from West Point in 1905. Served in Alaska 1911-1913 and with the Panama Canal Department in 1917. Commanding officer of the 350th Field Artillery in France in 1918. Graduated from the Army War College in 1923. Assistant chief of staff for military intelligence in the Philippines 1924-1926. Brigadier general in November 1937. Commander of 6th Infantry Brigade June-October 1939. Assigned to the 6th Division October 1939-May 1940. Commanding general of the 4th Division May-October 1940 then the Panama Canal Mobile Force 1940-1942. Major general in January 1941. Commandant of Midwestern Signal Corps School, then Training Center February 1942-June 1945. Retired in October 1945. Decorations included the Distinguished Service Medal. Died on September 11, 1981.

Pulsifer, Ralph (1903-1983) Born on March 14, 1903, in Leavenworth, Kansas. Commissioned in the infantry from West Point in 1924. Served in the Philippines 1927-1929 and with 27th Infantry at Schofield Barracks, Hawaii 1933-1935. Again in the Philippines 1938-1940. Assigned to the office of the adjutant general, U.S. Army 1940-1941. Duty with the War Department General Staff 1941-1942. Adjutant general at headquarters of European Theater of Operations 1942-1944. Brigadier general in September 1943. Retired in September 1945. Brigadier general on the retired list in 1948. Died on October 8, 1983.

Quade, Omar Heinrich (1886-1965) Born in St. Charles, Missouri, on August 18, 1886. M.D. from Washington University in 1909. Commissioned in the Medical Reserve Corps in 1911. Graduated from Army Medical School in 1912. Wounded while serving with the 1st Division of the AEF in World War I. Executive officer, then commanding officer of Sternberg General Hospital, Philippine Islands 1935-1937. Executive officer, then commanding general of Fitzsimons General Hospital July 1940 until retirement in August 1948. Brigadier general in May 1942. Decorations included the Legion of Merit and Purple Heart. Died on May 9, 1965.

Quinton, Alfred Bixby Jr. (1890-1968) Born in Topeka, Kansas, on August 17, 1890. Attended Washburn College 1907-1908 and Cornell University in 1912.

Commissioned in the Coast Artillery Corps in 1912. Served with the AEF 1918-1919. M.S. from Massachusetts Institute of Technology in 1921 and M.B.A. from Harvard in 1930. Instructor at Army Industrial College 1930-1934. Served in the office of the chief of ordnance 1938-1942. Chief of the Detroit ordnance district 1942-1946. Brigadier general in October 1942. Retired in August 1952. Decorations included the Distinguished Service Medal, Legion of Merit, Commendation Ribbon and Purple Heart. Died on September 25, 1968.

Ramey, Rufus Stanley (1893-1989) Born in Denver, Colorado, on September 15, 1893. B.A. from the University of Missouri in 1916. Commissioned in the cavalry in 1917. Instructor at the Cavalry School 1926-1929 and 1930-1932. Graduated from the Command and General Staff School in 1934 and the Army War College in 1938. Instructor at the Command and General Staff School 1938-1940. At the War Department General Staff 1940-1942. Commandant of the Cavalry School August 1942-December 1943. Brigadier general in September 1942. Commanding general of 5th Cavalry Brigade January-December 1944. Served at headquarters of Army Ground Forces 1944-1946. Reverted to colonel in February 1946. Retired in April 1953. Decorations included the Distinguished Service Medal, two Legions of Merit and the Bronze Star. Died on September 27, 1989.

Ramsey, Norman Foster (1882-1963) Born on July 9, 1882, in Oakdale, Illinois. Enlisted service with 20th Kansas Volunteer Infantry 1898-1899. LL.D. from St. Ambrose College in 1942. Commissioned in the infantry from West Point in 1905. Graduated from the Army War College in 1921 and the Command and General Staff School in 1927. Commanding officer of Rock Island Arsenal then commanding general of Rock Island Ordnance Center 1937-1944. Brigadier general in October 1940. LL.D. from St. Ambrose College in 1942. Retired in July 1944. Decorations included the Legion of Merit, Commendation Ribbon and Purple Heart. Died on April 11, 1963.

Ramsey, Thomas Harry (1895-1981) Born on March 2, 1895, in Ozona, Texas. Attended West Point 1916-1917. Commissioned in the infantry in 1917. Graduated from the Command and General Staff School in 1939 and the Army War College in 1940. Chief of the war plans branch, office of the quartermaster general, U.S. Army 1940-1942. Quartermaster for II Corps July-September 1942 then Allied Forces headquarters, North African Theater of Operations September 1942-October 1945. Brigadier general in September 1943. Retired in January 1950. Decorations included the Distinguished Service Medal and Legion of Merit. Died on October 9, 1981.

Randle, Edwin Hubert (1894-1990) Born on October 11, 1894, in Springfield, Illinois. B.A. from DePauw University in 1917. Commissioned in the infantry in 1917. Wounded in the Meuse-Argonne offensive in World War I. Assistant professor of military science and tactics, then professor of military science and tactics at Lafayette College 1927-1934. Served in Puerto Rico 1934-1936. Assistant professor of military science and tactics at Pennsylvania State College 1938-1940. Battalion commander then commanding officer of 47th Infantry, 9th Division July 1940-June 1943. Brigadier general in June 1943. Assistant division commander of 77th Infantry Division 1943-1945. Retired in June 1948. Decorations included the Distinguished Service Cross, three Silver Stars, three Legions of Merit, two Bronze Stars, two Commendation Ribbons and the Purple Heart. Died on March 30, 1990.

Randol, Marshall Guion (1882-1965) Born at the Presidio of San Francisco on October 18, 1882. Enlisted service with the field artillery May 1905-January 1908. Commissioned in the field artillery in 1908. Served in the Philippines 1915-1917. Rose to temporary colonel in World War I. Professor of military science and tactics at the University of Utah 1921-1922. Graduated from the Command and General Staff School in 1923. Professor of military science and tactics at the University of Missouri 1932-1937. Commanding officer of 1st Field Artillery August 1937-June 1940. Served with the 41st Division 1940-1942. Brigadier general in January 1941. Commanding general of Field Artillery Replacement Training Center March 1942 until retirement in October 1942. Died on December 14, 1965.

Randolph, Norman (1891-1953) Born on March 10, 1891, in Indianapolis, Indiana. Commissioned in the infantry from West Point in 1915. Instructor at West Point 1921-1925 and the Infantry School 1927-1931. Assistant chief of the bureau of insular affairs, then chief of personnel section in the office of the chief of infantry 1938-1941. Commanding officer of 28th Infantry 1941-1942. Brigadier general in September 1942. Chief of staff of Second Army 1942-1943, then 3rd Service Command 1943-1944. Commanding general of Pennsylvania district, 3rd Service Command 1944-1945. Retired in May 1945. Died on May 15, 1953.

Rankin, Fred Wharton (1886-n/a) Born in Mooresville, North Carolina, on December 20, 1886. B.S. from Davidson College in 1905. M.D. from the University of Maryland in 1909. Commissioned in the Medical Reserve Corps in 1917. Active duty with the AEF 1918-1919. Professor of surgery at the University of Louisville 1933-1942. Called to active duty in March 1942. Served in the office of the surgeon general 1942-1945. Brigadier general in December 1942.

Ransom, Paul Lewis (1894-1985) Born in Hartford, Vermont, on November 16, 1894. B.S. from Vermont University in 1916. Commissioned in the infantry in 1916. Served with the 2nd Machine Gun Battalion in the AEF at the Aisne-Marne, St. Mihiel and Meuse-Argonne offensives. Instructor at the Infantry School 1922-1925. Graduated from the Command and General Staff School in 1926. Professor of military science and tactics at Connecticut Agricultural College 1926-1928 and the Citadel 1931-1934. Graduated from the Army War College in 1935. With the War Department General Staff 1936-1940. Brigadier general in March 1942. Commanding general of 98th Infantry Division July 1942-November 1943. Assigned to headquarters of Second Army 1943-1944. Duty at Infantry

Replacement Training Centers at Camp Fannin January-August 1944 and Fort McClellan August-December 1944. Assistant division commander of 5th Infantry Division January-March 1945. Served with Fifteenth Army 1945-1946. Reverted to colonel in April 1946. Retired in May 1948. Decorations included two Silver Stars, the Legion of Merit, Bronze Star and Commendation Ribbon. Died on August 12, 1985.

Ratay, John Paul (1893-1980) Born in Posen, Germany, on January 21, 1893. Enlisted service in the Coast Artillery Corps 1914-1917. Commissioned in the field artillery in 1917. Served with 17th Field Artillery at Verdun, Aisne-Marne, St. Mihiel and Meuse-Argonne offensives in World War I. Assistant military attache in China 1924-1928. Military attache in Romania 1939-1942. Assistant chief of staff for intelligence with the Western Task Force in North Africa in 1942. Commanding general of Atlantic Base in Morocco in 1943, Northern Base in Corsica in 1944 and Delta Base in Southern France 1944-1946. Brigadier general in May 1944. Retired in April 1946 as colonel. Decorations included the Distinguished Service Medal, three Silver Stars, two Legions of Merit, the Bronze Star and two Purple Hearts. Died in 1980.

Ravdin, Isidor Schwaner (1894-1972) Born in Evansville, Indiana, on October 10, 1894. B.S. from Indiana University in 1916. M.D. from the University of Pennsylvania in 1918. Surgeon and college professor 1918-1940. Commissioned lieutenant colonel in the Medical Corps Reserve in 1940. Called to active duty in May 1942. Executive officer of the 20th General Hospital at Camp Claiborne May-December 1942. Served with the Services of Supply in the China-Burma-India Theater of Operations 1942-1945. Brigadier general in March 1945. Decorations included two Legions of Merit. Died on August 27, 1972.

Read, George Windle Jr. (1900-1974) Born in Fort Grant, Arizona, on July 29, 1900, the son of Major General George W. Read. Enlisted service with the 2nd Cavalry 1917-1919. Commissioned in the cavalry in 1919. Served with 7th Cavalry Brigade 1937-1941. Graduated from the Command and General Staff School in 1941. Observer with British forces in the Middle East in 1941. Assigned to 6th Armored Division February 1942-September 1945. Brigadier general in January 1945. Reverted to colonel in February 1946. Brigadier general again in July 1950. Assignments after the war included chief of staff of V Corps 1951-1952, commanding general of 2nd Armored Division 1952-1955, commander of Allied Land Forces Southeastern Europe 1955-1957 and commanding general of Second Army 1957-1960. Retired as lieutenant general in August 1960. Decorations included two Distinguished Service Medals, the Silver Star, Legion of Merit and two Bronze Stars. Died on December 15, 1974.

Ready, Joseph Louis (1895-1955) Born in Brighton, Massachusetts, on November 17, 1895. Commissioned in the infantry in 1917. Served with the 2nd Philippine Infantry 1919-1920. Professor of military science and tactics at the University of Maine 1923-1928. Duty with the 15th Infantry at Tientsin 1920-1922 and

1931-1933. Graduated from the Command and General Staff School in 1936 and the Army War College in 1939. Member of the Infantry Board 1939-1942. With the 85th Infantry Division February-August 1942. Brigadier general in August 1942. Assistant division commander of 7th Infantry Division August 1942-May 1943 and Amphibious Training Force Nine at Fort Ord May-September 1943. Assistant division commander of 7th Infantry Division from September 1943. Reverted to colonel in March 1946. Retired in June 1949. Decorations included the Silver Star, two Legions of Merit and the Bronze Star. Died on February 14, 1955.

Reber, Miles (1902-1976) Born on March 27, 1902, in Washington, DC. Commissioned in the Corps of Engineers from West Point in 1923. Duty with 3rd Engineers in Hawaii 1925-1929. White House aide 1930-1932. Instructor at West Point 1932-1936. Engineer with the Missouri and Mississippi River Divisions in 1943. Assistant chief of legislative division at the War Department General Staff 1943-1945, with a brief assignment at Army Service Forces in 1944. Brigadier general in May 1944. Deputy chief of legislative division at the War Department General Staff 1947-1948. Graduated from the National War College in 1949. Chief of legislative division at the War Department General Staff 1950-1953. Major general in February 1951. Commanding general of Western Area Command, USAREUR 1953-1955. Retired in December 1955. Decorations included the Distinguished Service Medal and Commendation Ribbon. Died on November 24, 1976.

Reed, Walter Lawrence (1877-1956) Born on December 4, 1877, in Fort Apache, Arizona. Enlisted service with the 2nd Artillery 1898-1900. Attended Randolph-Macon Academy. Commissioned in the infantry in 1900. Graduated from Army General Staff College in 1922, the Army War College in 1923 and the Naval War College in 1924. Major general in April 1938 as inspector general, U.S. Army 1938-1940. Retired in April 1940. Recalled to active duty from April 1942. Decorations included two Distinguished Service Medals. Died on May 1, 1956.

Reeder, William Oliver (1897-1985) Born on May 15, 1897, in Pittsburgh, Pennsylvania. Commissioned in the field artillery from West Point in 1917. Served with the 3rd Field Artillery, AEF 1918-1919. Instructor at West Point 1922-1925. M.S. from Yale in 1929. Graduated from the Command and General Staff School in 1940. Secretary, assistant commandant and commandant of the Signal School July 1940-June 1944. Brigadier general in April 1943. Signal officer and assistant chief of staff for supply at China-Burma-India Theater of Operations 1944-1946. Retired in January 1953. Decorations included two Legions of Merit. Died on October 25, 1985.

Regnier, Eugene Arthur (1893-1956) Born in Concordia, Kansas, on December 22, 1893. Commissioned in the cavalry, Officers Reserve Corps in 1917. Served with the 362nd Infantry in the AEF at St. Mihiel and Meuse-Argonne during

World War I. Aide to Major General E.F. McGlachlin 1919-1920, Major General Fox Conner 1926-1927 and the governor general of the Philippines, Henry L. Stimson, 1928-1932. Graduated from the Command and General Staff School in 1938. Instructor at the Cavalry School 1938-1940. Again aide to Stimson July 1940-March 1941. Commanding officer of 91st Reconaissance Squadron 1941-1942 then 6th Regiment, 6th Armored Division June-December 1942. Brigadier general in December 1942. Commander of Combat Command "B" 1942-1945. Director of the research and development division at Army Service Forces June 1945-March 1946. Retired in July 1954. Decorations included two Silver Stars, two Bronze Stars and the Commendation Ribbon. Died on December 7, 1956.

Reimel, Stewart Elvin (1892-1985) Born on April 24, 1892, in Stroudsburg, Pennsylvania. Attended Muhlenberg College 1912-1913 and Pennsylvania State College 1914-1917. Commissioned in the infantry in 1917. Served with the 4th Infantry in the AEF including the Aisne-Marne, St. Mihiel and Meuse-Argonne offensives 1917-1918. Executive assistant to the chief of ordnance 1940-1941. Assigned to the office of the under secretary of war January-July 1941. Duty with the resources division of Services of Supply 1941-1942. Chief of the maintenance division at the tank automotive center in Detroit July 1942-January 1944. Brigadier general in March 1943. Commander of Boston Ordnance District then New York Ordnance District 1944-1946. Retired in February 1946. Decorations included the Distinguished Service Medal. Died on July 24, 1985.

Reinhardt, Emil Fred (1888-1969) Born in Bay City, Michigan, on October 27, 1888. Commissioned in the infantry from West Point in 1910. Served with the 8th Infantry in the Philippine Islands October 1914-November 1917 and in Germany 1919-1922. Graduated from the Command and General Staff School in 1923. Professor of military science and tactics at the University of Dayton 1923-1928. Graduated from the Army War College in 1931. Brigadier general in April 1941. Commanding general of Camp Wolters October 1941-May 1942. Major general in April 1942. Commanding general of 76th Infantry Division May-November 1942, XIII Corps November 1943-September 1944 and 69th Infantry Division September 1944-August 1945. Retired in September 1946. Decorations included the Distinguished Service Medal and two Bronze Stars. Died on July 24, 1969.

Reinhart, Stanley Eric (1893-1975) Born on September 15, 1893, in Polk, Ohio. Commissioned in the field artillery from West Point in 1916. Served with the 17th Field Artillery, AEF in World War I. Instructor at West Point 1919-1922. Professor of military science and tactics at the University of Wisconsin 1923-1927. Graduated from the Command and General Staff School in 1932 and the Army War College in 1936. Treasurer at West Point 1936-1940. With the Hawaiian Department 1940-1942. Brigadier general in March 1942. Commanding general of 25th Division Artillery 1942-1943. Major general in September 1943. Commanding general of 65th Division 1943-1945 and 26th Infantry Division July-November 1945. Retired in September 1946. Decorations included two Distinguished Service Medals, the Silver Star, Legion of Merit and Bronze Star. Died on June 4, 1975.

Reybold, Eugene (1884-1961) Born in Delaware City, Delaware, on February 13, 1884. B.C.E. from Delaware College in 1903. Commissioned in the Coast Artillery Corps in 1908. Served in the Philippine Islands September 1910-September 1913. Commandant of the Coast Artillery School 1919-1920. Graduated from the Command and General Staff School in 1923. Instructor at General Service Schools 1923-1926. Graduated from the Army War College in 1927. Brigadier general in October 1940. Assistant chief of staff for supply with the War Department General Staff 1940-1941. Major general and chief of engineers October 1941-September 1945. Lieutenant general in April 1945. Retired in January 1946. Decorations included two Distinguished Service Medals. Died in November 1961.

Reynolds, Edward (1894-n/a) Born in Boston, Massachusetts, on March 27, 1894. B.A. from Harvard in 1915. Served with the Massachusetts National Guard on the Mexican border in 1916 and in the U.S. Navy in World War I. Executive vice president, then president of Columbia Gas and Electric Company 1930-1943. Served on active duty in the office of the surgeon general in charge of medical supplies November 1942-January 1946. Brigadier general in June 1945. Decorations included the Distinguished Service Medal.

Reynolds, Royal (1881-1971) Born in Elmira, New York, on October 14, 1881. M.D. from the University of Pennsylvania in 1906. Commissioned in the Medical Corps in 1909. Graduated from Army Medical School in June 1910. Served in the Philippine Islands 1911-1914. Commanding officer of Base Hospital 27 in the AEF 1917-1918. Duty at Sternberg General Hospital in the Philippines 1922-1924. Post surgeon at West Point 1939-1942. Brigadier general in May 1942. Commander of Army General Hospital in Memphis May 1942-April 1945. Hospitalized prior to retirement in October 1945. Decorations included the Legion of Merit. Died on April 25, 1971.

Reynolds, Russel Burton (1894-1970) Born in Dundee, Michigan, on December 24, 1894. Attended the University of Wisconsin 1913-1915. Commissioned in the infantry in 1917. Assistant Professor of military science and tactics at the University of Pennsylvania 1925-1929. Instructor at the Infantry School 1929-1933. Assistant Professor of military science and tactics at Ripon College 1936-1937. Graduated from the Command and General Staff School in 1938. Instructor at the Medical Field Service School 1938-1941. Director of the military personnel division, Army Service Forces 1942-1944. Brigadier general in March 1943. Major general in November 1944. Commanding general of 6th Service Command 1944-1945. Staff officer with U.S. Army Forces Western Pacific 1945-1946. Chief of special services at Department of the Army 1946-1949. Retired in August 1949. Decorations included two Distinguished Service Medals and the Commendation Ribbon. Died on December 8, 1970.

Rice, George William (1892-1962) Born in Cumberland, Maryland, on Ocotober 1, 1892. M.D. from the University of Maryland in 1916. Commissioned in the Medical Corps, Maryland National Guard in 1916. Served on the Mexican border 1916-1917. Graduated from Army Medical School in 1926, the Command and General Staff School in 1933 and the Army War College in 1937. Instructor with medical units in Baltimore 1937-1940. Surgeon for the Eighth Army 1944-1946. Brigadier general in June 1945. Reverted to colonel in March 1946. Retired in October 1952. Decorations included the Distinguished Service Medal, Legion of Merit, Bronze Star, Air Medal and Commendation Ribbon. Died on December 8, 1962.

Rice, John Kirkland (1896-1990) Born on May 16, 1896, in Leominster, Massachusetts. Attended the University of Michigan 1913-1914 and the University of Minnesota 1914-1915. Enlisted service with the Minnesota National Guard 1916-1917. Commissioned in the infantry in 1917. Served with the occupation forces in Germany 1919-1922. Battalion commander in the 27th Infantry Regiment at Schofield Barracks, Hawaii 1939-1941. Executive officer in the department of tactics at the Infantry School 1941-1942. Brigadier general in February 1943. Assistant division commander of 35th Division in 1943 and 78th Infantry Division 1943-1944. Commanding general of Camp McCoy 1945-1946. Retired in January 1953. Decorations included two Legions of Merit and two Bronze Stars. Died on July 19, 1990.

Richards, George Jacob (1891-1984) Born on April 12, 1891, in Easton, Pennsylvania. Commissioned in the Corps of Engineers from West Point in 1915. Served with the Punitive Expedition into Mexico 1916-1917. Graduated from the Command and General Staff School in 1930, the Army War College in 1933 and Naval War College in 1938. Brigadier general in March 1943. Member of War Department Special Staff 1943-1947. Major general in February 1944. Assignments after the war included the first comptroller of the U.S. Army 1947-1948. Retired in 1953. Decorations included the Distinguished Service Medal and Legion of Merit. Died on October 1, 1984

Richardson, Robert Charlwood Jr. (1882-1954) Born in Charleston, South Carolina, on October 27, 1882. Commissioned in the cavalry from West Point in 1904. Served with the 14th Cavalry in the Philippine Islands 1904-1905 and wounded at Cotta Usap in January 1905 during a battle with insurgents. Assistant instructor at West Point 1906-1911. Again in the Philippines with the 14th Cavalry 1911-1912. Assistant professor at West Point 1914-1917. Aide to Major General T.H. Berry 1917-1918. Duty with the Philippine Department 1921-1923. Graduated from the Command and General Staff School in 1924 and the Ecole Superieure de Guerre in 1926. Graduated from the Army War College in 1934. Brigadier general in June 1938. Commander of 2nd Cavalry Brigade June 1938-February 1939. Commandant of the Cavalry School 1939-1940. Major general in October 1940. Commanding general of 1st Cavalry Division October 1940-February 1941. Director of the bureau of public relations February-August 1941.

Commanding general of VII Corps 1941-1943. Lieutenant general in June 1943. Commander of the Hawaiian Department June-August 1943 then Pacific Ocean Areas 1943-1945. Retired in October 1946. Decorations included three Distinguished Service Medals, the Silver Star, two Legions of Merit, the AM and Purple Heart. Died on March 2, 1954. Posthumous promotion to general in July 1954.

Richart, Duncan Grant (1887-1950) Born in Ludys, Kentucky, on November 10, 1887. Commissioned in the cavalry from West Point in 1910. Resigned in 1914 but rejoined in 1916. Served with the 17th and 8th Cavalry in Hawaii 1921-1922. Graduated from the Command and General Staff School in 1926. Duty in the Canal Zone 1935-1937. Graduated from the Army War College in 1938. Commanding officer of 9th Cavalry December 1940-December 1941 and Fort Oglethorpe December 1941-August 1943. Commander of Fort Jackson from 1943. Brigadier general in February 1944. Retired in September 1946. Decorations included the Legion of Merit. Died on June 11, 1950.

Richmond, Adam (1889-1959) Born in Council Bluffs, Iowa, on September 24, 1889. B.A. from the University of Wisconsin in 1912, LL.B. in 1914. Commissioned in the infantry in 1920. Served in Hawaii 1922-1925 and the Canal Zone 1932-1935. Judge advocate in the 2nd Division July 1939-January 1941 and the Third Army January-July 1941. Brigadier general in March 1943. Retired in February 1947. Decorations included the Legion of Merit. Died December 1, 1959.

Rickard, Roy Victor (1891-1975) Born in Osseo, Wisconsin, on October 27, 1891. Attended Hunt Business College 1912-1913. Commissioned in the infantry, Officers Reserve Corps in 1917. Served with the 42nd Infantry in the Canal Zone 1922-1925. Duty with IX Corps Area 1940-1941. Executive officer of the supply section at headquarters Fourth Army April 1941-April 1942. Chief of staff of the Northern California Sector, Western Defense Command 1942-1943. Served in Alaska July-November 1943. Assistant chief of staff for supply at Fourth Army November 1943-May 1944 then Ninth Army 1944-1945. Brigadier general in January 1945. Retired in October 1951. Decorations included the Legion of Merit and Bronze Star. Died on January 7, 1975.

Ridgway, Matthew Bunker (1895-1993) Born on March 3, 1895, at Fort Monroe, Virginia. Commissioned in the infantry from West Point in 1917. Duty at West Point as instructor and head of athletics 1918-1924. Graduated from the Command and General Staff School in 1935 and the Army War College in 1937. Accompanied General Marshall on a special mission to Brazil in May 1939. With war plans division of the War Department General Staff September 1939-January 1942. Brigadier general in January 1942. Assistant division commander, then commanding general of 82nd Infantry Division, later 82nd Airborne Division, March 1942-August 1944. Major general in August 1942. Parachuted into Normandy on D-Day. Commanding general of XVIII Airborne Corps August 1944-September 1945. Lieutenant general in June 1945. Following the war served as

U.S. Army representative on the military staff committee of the United Nations 1946-1948. Deputy chief of staff for administration, U.S. Army 1949-1950. Commanding general of Eighth Army, later commander in chief of United Nations Command in Korea 1950-1952. General in May 1951. Supreme allied commander in Europe 1952-1953. Chief of staff, U.S. Army 1953-1955. Retired in June 1955. Decorations included two Distinguished Service Crosses, four Distinguished Service Medals, two Silver Stars, two Legions of Merit, two Bronze Stars and the Purple Heart. Author of *Soldier* (1956) and *The Korean War* (1967). Died on July 26, 1993.

Ridings, Eugene Ware (1899-1969) Born on January 9, 1899, in Grant County, Oklahoma. Commissioned in the infantry from West Point in 1923. Served in China with 15th Infantry 1926-1928. Instructor at West Point 1933-1936. Graduated from the Command and General Staff School in 1937 and the Army War College in 1940. Duty at the War Department General Staff 1940-1942. Assistant chief of staff for operations at VIII, then XIV Corps 1942-1945. Brigadier general in January 1945. Assistant division commander of the Americal Division July-December 1945. Reverted to colonel in March 1946. Assignments after the war included assistant division commander of 9th Division 1950-1951, then 31st Division 1951-1953, commanding general of 3rd Division in the Korean War in 1953, chief of the Military Assistance Advisory Group to Korea 1953-1954, deputy chief of staff of Army Field Forces 1954-1956. Deputy inspector general, U.S. Army 1957-1958. Retired as major general in February 1958. Decorations included the Distinguished Service Medal, two Silver Stars, two Legions of Merit, the Bronze Star, Air Medal and two Commendation Ribbons. Died on November 27, 1969.

Ridley, Clarence Self (1883-1969) Born in Corydon, Indiana, on June 22, 1883. Commissioned in the Corps of Engineers from West Point in 1905. Served in Hawaii and the Philippines November 1908-April 1912. Assistant maintenance engineer at the Panama Canal 1921-1924. Graduated from the Command and General Staff School in 1925, the Army War College in 1931 and Army Industrial College in 1932. Engineer of maintenance at the Panama Canal 1932-1936. Brigadier general in October 1938. Served with the 3rd Division 1940-1941. Major general in February 1941. Commanding general of 6th Division 1941-1942. Duty with the Army Group in 1942. Chief of the U.S. Military Mission to Iran 1943-1947. Retired in June 1947. Decorations included the Distinguished Service Medal. Died on July 26, 1969.

Ritter, William Leonard (1898-1971) Born in Hartford City, Indiana, on January 12, 1898. Commissioned in the infantry, Officers Reserve Corps in 1917. Served with the 4th Division in World War I. Brigadier general in August 1944. Deputy commanding general of U.S. Forces Africa and the Middle East 1944-1946. Reverted to colonel in March 1946. Retired in December 1950. Decorations included the Distinguished Service Medal, Bronze Star and two Purple Hearts. Died on July 6, 1971.

Rixey, George Foreman (1888-1974) Born in Jonesburg, Missouri, on March 2, 1888. Attended Central College 1904-1905, the University of Missouri 1905-1907, and Vanderbilt University 1907-1908. B.A. from Central Wesleyan College and ordained in the Methodist Episcopal Church in 1909. Commissioned in the coast artillery, Officers Reserve Corps in 1917. Served with the 26th Cavalry at Camp Stotsenburg, Philippine Islands and Sternberg General Hospital 1928-1930. Chaplain with U.S. Army Forces China at Tientsin 1935-1937. Executive officer in the office of the chief of chaplains 1940-1942 the deputy chief of chaplains 1942-1945. D.D. from American University in 1943. Brigadier general in November 1944. Assignments after the war included chaplain for Second Army 1946-1947 and chaplian for U.S. Forces Korea 1947-1948. Retired in March 1948. Decorations included the Distinguished Service Medal, Silver Star and Commendation Ribbon. Died on May 13, 1974.

Roberts, Frank Needham (1897-1975) Born on December 28, 1897, in Oskaloosa, Kansas. Commissioned in the infantry from West Point in 1920. Instructor at the Infantry School 1924-1927 then at West Point 1927-1931. Assistant miltary attache in China 1934-1938. Awarded the Navy Cross for heroism at the sinking of the *Panay* on December 12, 1937. Graduated from the Command and General Staff School in 1940. Duty with 20th Infantry 1940-1941. Served in the military intelligence division at the War Department General Staff 1942-1944. Brigadier general in November 1943. Chief of staff of the military mission to the Soviet Union 1945-1946. Retired as major general in November 1957. Decorations included the Navy Cross and three Distinguished Service Medals. Died on December 23, 1975.

Roberts, William Lynn (1890-1968) Born on September 17, 1890, in Ohio. Commissioned in the infantry from West Point in 1913. Served with the AEF in World War I at the St. Mihiel and Meuse-Argonne offensives. Graduated from the Command and General Staff School in 1926 then instructor there until 1930. Instructor at the Tank School 1931-1932. Executive officer of 21st Infantry Brigade in Hawaii November 1939-June 1940. Professor of military science and tactics at the Citadel 1940-1941. Instructor at the Command and General Staff School 1942-1943. Commanding officer of Combat Command in 10th Armored Division 1943-1945. Brigadier general in May 1945. Assistant division commander of 4th Armored Division 1945-1946. Retired in September 1950. Decorations included the Silver Star, Legion of Merit and two Bronze Stars. Died on November 27, 1968.

Robertson, Ralph K. (1883-n/a) Born in New York on April 24, 1883. B.A. from Cornell University in 1904, LL.B. in 1906. Commissioned in the infantry, New York National Guard in 1906. Served on the Mexican border 1916-1917 and in World War I. Brigadier general of the line in June 1937. Called to federal service in September 1940. Commander of the 87th Infantry Brigade, 44th Division 1940-1941. Duty at II Corps Area September 1941-October 1942. Commanding general of District One, 2nd Service Command 1942-1945.

Robertson, Walter Melville (1888-1954) Born on June 15, 1888, in Nelson County, Virginia. Commissioned in the infantry from West Point in 1912. Served in Hawaii 1912-1925 and with training units and the inspector general department of the AEF in World War I. Graduated from the Command and General Staff School in 1926 then instructor there until 1929. Graduated from the Army War College in 1930 then instructor there until 1933. With supply division of the War Department General Staff 1936-1940. Commanding officer of 9th Infantry November 1940-December 1941. Brigadier general in December 1941. Assistant division commander of 2nd Infantry Division 1941-1942. Major general in August 1942. Commanding general of 2nd Division 1944-1945, then IX Corps 1945-1946. Retired in 1950. Decorations included the Distinguished Service Cross, two Distinguished Service Medals, the Silver Star, Legion of Merit and Bronze Star. Died on November 22, 1954.

Robinett, Paul McDonald (1893-1975) Born in Mountain Grove, Missouri, on December 19, 1893. B.S. from the University of Missouri in 1917. Commissioned in the cavalry in 1917. Instructor at the Cavalry School 1922-1923. Aide to General Malin Craig July 1927-August 1932. Graduated from the Command and General Staff School in 1934. Again instructor at the Cavalry School 1934-1936. Graduated from the Army War College in 1937. Duty at the War Department General Staff 1937-1941. Deputy chief of staff for operations at GHQ 1941-1942. Commanding officer of 13th Armored Regiment 1942-1943. Brigadier general in November 1942. Commanding general of Combat Command "B" in 1st Armored Division January-May 1943. Commandant of the Armor School 1944-1945. Retired in August 1946. Decorations included the Distinguished Service Medal, Legion of Merit and Purple Heart. Died on February 5, 1975.

Robins, Thomas Matthews (1881-1965) Born in Snow Hill, Maryland, on March 14, 1881. Attended Dickinson College 1897-1899. Commissioned in the Corps of Engineers from West Point in 1904. Graduated from the Command and General Staff School in 1923 and the Army War College in 1926. Brigadier general in September 1939. Assistant to the chief of engineers 1939-1943. Major general in January 1942. Retired in March 1945. Decorations included two Distinguished Service Medals. Died on May 25, 1965.

Robinson, Bernard Linn (1901-) Born on May 1, 1901, in Sioux City, Iowa. Commissioned in the Corps of Engineers from West Point in 1920. Brigadier general in January 1945. Commanding general of 5201st Engineer Construction Brigade 1942-1945. Reverted to colonel in February 1946. Retired in 1957. Decorations included the Distinguished Service Medal, Legion of Merit and Bronze Star.

Robinson, Clinton Frederick (1902-1962) Born on August 21, 1902, in Danville, Ohio. Commissioned in the Corps of Engineers from West Point in 1924.

Served in the Panama Canal Zone November 1928-September 1929 and in Nicaragua September 1929-February 1931. Instructor at West Point 1931-1935. Director of operations for the Works Progress Administration July 1938-December 1940. Duty in the office of the quartermaster general 1940-1941. Member of the the War Department General Staff 1941-1942. Deputy chief of staff of Army Service Forces 1942-1946.Brigadier general in March 1943, major general in August 1944. Retired in December 1948. Decorations included the Distinguished Service Medal, Legion of Merit and the Bronze Star. Died on April 10, 1962.

Robinson, Donald Allister (1881-1958) Born in Chippewa Falls, Wisconsin, on March 29, 1881. Commissioned in the infantry from West Point in 1906. Served with 11th Infantry in Cuba 1907-1909. Duty in the Philippines 1915-1917. Assigned to the general staff at Services of Supply, AEF in 1918-1919 then at Coblenz, Germany 1920-1921. Graduated from the Command and General Staff School in 1925. Instructor at Oregon Agricultural College 1925-1927 then the Command and General Staff School 1928-1930. Graduated from the Army War College in 1933. Assistant chief of staff of the Philippine Department 1934-1937. Chief of staff of 1st Cavalry Division, IX Corps and Second Army 1939-1941. Brigadier general in January 1941. Commanding general of Cavalry Replacement Training Center at Fort Riley October 1941 until retirement in March 1943. Decorations included two Distinguished Service Medals. Died on October 30, 1958.

Robinson, John Nicholas (1893-1978) Born on May 8, 1893, in South Haven, Michigan. Commissioned in the infantry from West Point in 1915. Served with the Punitive Expedition into Mexico 1916-1917. Stationed at Fort Douglas 1917-1918. Professor of military science and tactics at Pennsylvania Military College 1923-1928. Graduated from the Command and General Staff School in 1930. Instructor at the Infantry School 1932-1937. Professor of military science and tactics at the University of Arkansas 1937-1940. Commanding officer of 201st Infantry 1940-1943. Commander of Fort Richardson 1943-1944. Brigadier general in January 1944. Assistant division commander of 89th Division 1944-1945. Reverted to colonel in April 1946. Retired in March 1949. Decorations included two Legions of Merit and the Bronze Star. Died on May 6, 1978.

Robinson, Joseph Stubbs (1898-1984) Born on May 1, 1898, in Cataumet, Massachusetts. Commissioned in the Coast Artillery Corps from West Point in 1918. Instructor there 1918-1921. Instructor with the Massachusetts National Guard 1928-1931. Duty with 4th Coast Artillery in the Canal Zone 1932-1935. Assistant professor of military science and tactics at the Citadel 1936-1939. Graduated from the Command and General Staff School in 1940. Plans and training officer with 69th Coast Artillery 1940-1941. Antiaircraft officer for V Corps then Fifth Army 1941-1944. Commander of the 34th Antiaircraft Artillery Brigade 1944-1945. Brigadier general in March 1945. Reverted to colonel in February 1946. Retired in August 1950. Decorations included two Legions of Merit and the Bronze Star. Died on November 17, 1984.

Roderick, Thomas Edison (1892-1944) Born on December 8, 1892, in Navarre, Ohio. Attended the College of Wooster. Commissioned in the infantry in 1917. Served with the 58th Infantry, AEF in the Aisne-Marne, Somme, St. Mihiel and Meuse-Argonne offensives in 1918. Wounded in action at Chery Chatreau in August 1918. Professor of military science and tactics at Clemson Agricultural College 1922-1923. Duty with 57th Infantry in the Philippine Islands 1929-1931. Graduated from the Command and General Staff School in 1937. Battalion commander in the 27th Infantry at Schofield Barracks, Hawaii 1937-1940. Assistant chief of staff for operations at 13th Infantry 1940-1941. Chief of the administrative branch, then group at the War Department General Staff 1941-1943. Deputy assistant chief of staff for operations at Allied Force Headquarters in the North African Theater of Operations 1943-1944. Brigadier general in February 1944. Died in North Africa on September 21, 1944. Decorations included the Silver Star and Purple Heart.

Rodes, Peter Powell (1890-1966) Born in Lexington, Kentucky, on October 10, 1890. Attended Annapolis 1910-1913. Commissioned in the field artillery in 1917. Served with the 90th Division, AEF in Germany in 1919. Duty at Schofield Barracks, Hawaii 1931-1933. Graduated from the Command and General Staff School in 1936. Instructor at the Field Artillery School 1936-1939. Graduated from the Army War College in 1940. Battalion commander with 16th Field Artillery 1940-1941. Commander of 2nd Cavalry Division Artillery December 1941-July 1942. Brigadier general in June 1943. Commanding general of 70th Infantry Division Artillery 1943-1945. Commander of the War Department Personnel Center at Fort Dix 1945-1946. Reverted to colonel in March 1946. Retired in October 1950. Decorations included the Legion of Merit and Bronze Star. Died on September 28, 1966.

Rodgers, Robert Clive (1887-1966) Born on March 17, 1887, in San Francisco, California. Commissioned in the cavalry from West Point in 1908. Assigned to Schofield Barracks, Hawaii 1912-1916. Served with the Punitive Expedition into Mexico 1916-1917. Duty with the Motor Transport Service, Services of Supply in AEF 1918-1919. Graduated from the Command and General Staff School in 1923. Instructor with the Utah National Guard 1924-1925. Commanding officer of 4th Cavalry 1938-1940. Brigadier general in October 1940. Commandant of the Cavalry School 1940-1942. Commanding general of 2nd Cavalry Brigade 1942-1943. Duty with the Army Group at Fort Sam Houston as member of the War Manpower Board in Dallas then duty with field agencies 1943-1946. Retired in March 1946. Decorations included the Legion of Merit and Bronze Star. Died on August 16, 1966.

Rodwell, James Stevenson (1896-1962) Born in Clyde, New York, on March 17, 1896. Enlisted service in the Regular Army 1916-1917. Commissioned in the cavalry in 1917. Served with the AEF in France and occupation forces in Germany 1918-1919. Graduated from the Command and General Staff School in

1939. Squadron commander in 8th Cavalry 1939-1940. Brigadier general in October 1940. Assistant chief of staff for operations at 4th Motorized Division then 4th Infantry Division 1940-1944. Assistant division commander of 4th Infantry Division 1944-1946. Retired in August 1946. Decorations included the Distinguished Service Cross, two Silver Stars, two Legions of Merit and the Bronze Star. Died on December 27, 1962.

Rogers, Arthur Henry (1892-1968) Born in Mitchell, South Dakota, on October 27, 1892. Enlisted service in the South Dakota Infantry 1909-1919. Attended Yankton College 1914-1917. Served on the Mexican border in 1917 and with the AEF in World War I. Commissioned in the infantry in 1920. Graduated from the Command and General Staff School in 1934. Duty in the Philippine Islands with the 31st Infantry 1934-1936. Graduated from the Army War College in 1940. Commanding officer of 30th Infantry July 1942-December 1943. Commander of the personnel center in the North African Theater of Operations 1943-1944. Brigadier general in January 1944. Duty with the Replacement Command, Mediterranean Theater of Operations 1944-1945. Retired in October 1946. Decorations included the Silver Star, two Legions of Merit, the Bronze Star and two Purple Hearts. Died on May 26, 1968.

Rogers, John Andrews (1889-1966) Born on February 7, 1889, in Nashua, New Hampshire. M.D. from Tufts University in 1914. Commissioned in the Medical Corps in 1917. Served with the AEF in France in World War I. Graduated from Army Medical School in 1921. Graduated from the Command and General Staff School in 1928 and the Army War College in 1933. Executive officer of the station hospital at Schofield Barracks, Hawaii 1937-1939. Executive officer to the surgeon general, U.S. Army 1941-1943. Surgeon for First Army September 1943-November 1945. Brigadier general in November 1944. Duty at headquarters of 6th Service Command 1945-1946. Retired in November 1946. Decorations included the Distinguished Service Medal and Legion of Merit. Died on December 11, 1966.

Rogers, Pleas Blair (1895-1974) Born in Alice, Texas, on November 14, 1895. Graduated from Wentworth Military Academy in 1915 and attended the University of Texas 1915-1916. Enlisted service with the 2nd Texas Infantry 1916-1917. Commissioned in the infantry in 1917. Served in a machine gun battalion of the 36th Division, AEF in World War I. Graduated from the Command and General Staff School in 1935 and the Army War College in 1938. Organized and commanded the Central Base Section in England April 1942-August 1944. Brigadier general in March 1943. Commanding general of the Seine Section August 1944-November 1945. Reverted to colonel in April 1946. Senior instructor for the Officers Reserve Corps in New York 1946-1947. Retired in January 1948. Decorations included the Distinguished Service Medal, Legion of Merit and Bronze Star. Died on December 25, 1974.

Rolfe, Onslow Sherburne (1895-1985) Born in Concord, New Hampshire, on January 6, 1895. Commissioned in the infantry from West Point in 1917. Wounded while serving with the 7th Infantry, 3rd Division in World War I. Instructor with ROTC at Rutgers University 1921-1925 and the Wisconsin National Guard 1930-1934. Graduated from the Command and General Staff School in 1936. Instructor at the Field Artillery School 1937-1941. Brigadier general in December 1942. Assistant division commander of 71st Division 1942-1946. Commanded 5th Infantry, U.S. Forces in Austria in 1946. Deputy to the assistant chief of staff for research and development, Army Field Forces 1947-1950, then assistant deputy chief of staff for operations 1951-1952. Commanding general of Northern Command in 1952. Commanding general of Headquarters and Service Command, then Central Command 1952-1953. Deputy chief of staff of Army Forces Far East in 1953-1954. Retired in August 1954. Decorations included the Distinguished Service Cross, Distinguished Service Medal, Legion of Merit and Purple Heart. Died on January 29, 1985.

Rollins, Francis W. (1893-n/a) Born on December 1, 1893, in Springfield, Massachusetts. Attended Brown University 1912-1914. Commissioned in the field artillery, Officers Reserve Corps in 1917. Served on the Mexican border in 1917 and in the AEF in World War I, seeing action at Aisne-Marne, St. Mihiel, Oise-Aisne and Meuse-Argonne. Brigadier general in September 1942. Commanding general of Field Artillery Replacement Training Center, Camp Roberts 1942-1943. In the European Theater of Operations 1944-1945. Returned to inactive status at the end of the war as commanding general of 66th Infantry Division, Officers Reserve Corps. Retired in June 1947. Decorations included two Bronze Stars.

Romulo, Carlos Peña (1901-1985) Born in the Philippine Islands on January 14, 1901. B.A. from the University of Manila in 1918. M.A. from Columbia University in 1921. Professor at the University of the Philippines 1923-1928. Awarded the Pulitzer Prize in 1941. Commissioned major, U.S. Army ten days after Pearl Harbor. Press aide, then aide to General MacArthur. Romulo was the last man out of Bataan before it fell to the Japanese. Toured the U.S. speaking on war issues July 1942-September 1944. Brigadier general in September 1944. Joined MacArthur in the Pacific and remained with him until the end of the war. Cofounder of the United Nations in 1945. President of the United Nations General Assembly 1949-1950. Foreign minister of the Philippines 1950-1952 and 1968-1984. Ambassador to the U.S. 1952-1953 and 1955-1962. Died on December 15, 1985.

Rooks, Lowell Ward (1893-1973) Born on April 11, 1893, in Colton, Washington. Attended State College of Washington 1913-1914 and the University of Washington 1914-1917. Commissioned in the infantry in 1917. Instructor at the Infantry School 1930-1933. Graduated from the Command and General Staff School in 1935 and the Army War College in 1937. Instructor at the Command and General Staff School 1937-1941. Chief of ground forces training division at the Army War College 1941-1942. Brigadier general in July 1942. Commanding general of 90th Division 1942-1945. Major general in June 1943. Retired in December 1945. Decorations included two Distinguished Service Medals, the Silver Star, Legion of Merit and Bronze Star. Died on January 17, 1973.

Roop, James Clawson (1888-1972) Born on October 3, 1888, in Upland, Pennsylvania. B.S. from the University of Pennsylvania in 1909. Served with the Engineer Corps in World War I as engineer support officer in the office of the general purchasing agent, AEF. Director, Bureau of the Budget in the Hoover administration August 1929-March 1933. Vice president of Pan American World Airways 1935-1942. Called to active duty in 1942 as colonel and promoted soon thereafter to brigadier general. General purchasing agent for U.S. Army Forces Australia, then the U.S. until the end of the war. Decorations included the Distinguished Service Medal. Died on January 23, 1972

Roosevelt, Theodore Jr. (1887-1944) Born in Oyster Bay, Long Island, New York, on September 13, 1887. Graduated from Harvard in 1908 and worked in the carpet and then banking industries. Joined his father and Major General Leonard Wood in organizing a summer training camp at Plattsburg, New York in 1915. Commissioned major in April 1917 and served with the 26th Infantry in France where he was twice wounded. Transferred to Army Reserve as colonel in 1919. Helped to organize the American Legion in 1919. Assistant secretary of the navy 1921-1922. In 1925 and again in 1928-1929 he and his younger brother Kermit led expeditions sponsored by the Field Museum in Chicago into central Asia to collect rare animals. Governor of Puerto Rico 1929-1932. Governor general in the Philippines 1932-1933. Chairman of the board of American Express Company 1934-1941. Recalled to active duty April 1941. Brigadier general in December 1941. Commander of 1st Division 1942-1944, leading it ashore on Utah Beach on D-Day. He was the only general officer in the first wave of the invasion. Died suddenly in Cherbourg on July 12, 1944. Recipient of the Medal of Honor posthumously.

Roper, Harry McKenzie (1901-1982) Born on July 30, 1901, in Washington, DC. Commissioned in the field artillery from the West Point in 1923. Graduated from the Command and General Staff School in 1940. Chief of staff of 3rd Division in North African Theater of Operations and X Corps in 1943. Commanding general of X Corps Artillery 1944-1946. Brigadier general in June 1945. Reverted to colonel in February 1946. Assignments after the war included commanding general of 7th Division Artillery in the Korean War 1951-1952. Retired as major general in August 1955. Decorations included the Distinguished Service Medal, Silver Star, Legion of Merit, Bronze Star and two Commendation Ribbons. Died on December 19, 1982.

Rose, Edward Chamberlin (1890-1967) Born in Colorado on December 12, 1890. Commissioned in the infantry from West Point in 1912. Graduated from the Command and General Staff School in 1928 and the Army War College in 1933. Commanding officer of Camp Blanding 1944-1945. Brigadier general in January

1945. Served in the adjutant general's office 1949-1950. Retired in December 1950 as colonel. Decorations included the Legion of Merit. Died on November 4, 1967.

Rose, John Bourisquot (1885-1966) Born on January 4, 1885, in Warrenton, Virginia. Commissioned in the Coast Artillery Corps from West Point in 1907. Served at Fort Mills, Philippine Islands in 1909 and in the AEF 1917-1918. Graduated from the Command and General Staff School in 1923 and the Army War College in 1928. Duty at the Panama Canal 1933-1935. Assigned to the War Department General Staff 1935-1939. Commanding officer of Aberdeen Proving Ground 1939-1941. Brigadier general in June 1940. Commanded Picatinny Arsenal in 1941. Served in the office of the chief of ordnance 1941-1943. Retired in January 1945. Decorations included the Legion of Merit. Died on January 13, 1966.

Rose, Maurice (1899-1945) Born on November 26, 1899, in Middletown, Connecticut. Enlisted service June-August 1916. Commissioned in the infantry in 1917. Served in the AEF 1918-1920. Professor of military science and tactics at Kansas State Agricultural College September 1927-September 1930. Duty in the Panama Canal Zone 1932-1935. Graduated from the Command and General Staff School in 1937. Instructor with the Pennsylvania National Guard October 1937-September 1939. Graduated from Army Industrial College in 1940. Battalion commander July 1940-July 1941. Executive officer of 1st Armored Brigade July 1941-January 1942. Chief of staff of 2nd Armored Division 1942-1943. Brigadier general in June 1943, major general in September 1944. Commanding general of 3rd Armored Division 1944-1945. Killed in action in Germany on March 30, 1945. Decorations included the Distinguished Service Medal, Silver Star and Purple Heart.

Rose, William Clayton (1889-1973) Born in Brooklyn, Alabama, on July 6, 1889. B.S. from Mississippi A&M College in 1910. Commissioned in the infantry in 1911. Served in the Punitive Expedition into Mexico 1916-1917. Graduated from the Command and General Staff School in 1929 and the Army War College in 1936. Brigadier general in April 1941. Assistant to the adjutant general, U.S. Army 1941-1942. Chief of the military division, then chief of executive services, finally vice chairman of the War Manpower Commission 1942-1945. Major general in September 1945. Chief of staff to the high commissioner to the Philippines 1945-1946. Retired in October 1946. Decorations included the Legion of Merit. Died on September 9, 1973.

Ross, David Marshall Ney (1896-1981) Born in New Orleans, Louisiana, on September 3, 1896. Attended the Citadel 1913-1915 and West Point 1916-1917. Commissioned in the infantry, Officers Reserve Corps in 1917 and the Regular Army in 1920. Served in the Philippines March 1929-August 1932. Professor of military science and tactics at the University of Alabama August 1933-June 1937. Assigned to the 5th Infantry September 1937-December 1938 and May-

September 1939. Aide to Major General J.A. Woodruff, commanding general I Corps Area September 1939-July 1942. Battalion commander with 321st Infantry July-September 1942. Served with 172nd Infantry 1942-1943. Brigadier general in September 1943. Retired in June 1944 as lieutenant colonel. Decorations included two Silver Stars and the Purple Heart. Died on April 20, 1981.

Ross, Frank Seymoure (1893-1970) Born in Aspen, Colorado, on March 9, 1893. Attended Texas University School of Mines 1912-1915. Enlisted service with the Texas National Guard May 1916-November 1917. Commissioned in the infantry in 1917. Served in the Philippine Islands November 1922-February 1925. Graduated from the Command and General Staff School in 1933 and the Army War College in 1936. Duty with the supply division of the War Department General Staff August 1938-April 1941 then executive officer of the transportation branch April-July 1941 and chief of the port and water section July 1941-March 1942. Chief of transportation with Army Service Forces, then at headquarters of the European Theater of Operations March 1942-March 1946. Brigadier general in June 1943, major general in June 1944. Retired in September 1946. Decorations included the Distinguished Service Medal, Silver Star, Legion of Merit and two Bronze Stars. Died on May 6, 1970.

Ross, Lewis Tenney (1896-1958) Born in Washington, DC, on March 16, 1896. Commissioned in the Corps of Engineers from West Point in 1918. Instructor with the Indiana National Guard 1926-1933. Duty with the district engineer in Honolulu May 1937-August 1939. Assistant to the chief of the operations and training section, office of the chief of engineers, U.S. Army August 1939-July 1941. Executive officer in the office of the chief of engineers, U.S. Army Forces Far East January 1943-January 1944. Chief engineer at headquarters of Services of Supply, Southwest Pacific Area January 1944-February 1945. Brigadier general in November 1944. Assigned to the military district of Washington, DC July 1945 until retirement in February 1946. Decorations included the Distinguished Service Medal and Bronze Star. Died on September 3, 1958.

Ross, Morrill (1895-1960) Born in Portland, Maine, on January 23, 1895. Commissioned in the field artillery in 1917. Served with the 17th Field Artillery, AEF November 1917-August 1919. Instructor at the Field Artillery School June 1923-August 1927. Graduated from the Command and General Staff School in 1936. Commanding officer of 66th Field Artillery April 1941-August 1942. Brigadier general in August 1942. Assigned to the 10th Armored Division August 1942-August 1943. Commanding general of 26th Infantry Division Artillery August 1943-August 1945. Reverted to colonel in March 1946. Retired in January 1950. Decorations included two Silver Stars, the Legion of Merit and two Bronze Stars. Died on December 18, 1960.

Rowan, Hugh Williamson (1894-1973) Born in Newport, Rhode Island, on March 16, 1894. Ph.B. from Yale in 1915. Attended Harvard 1915-1917. Commissioned in the Coast Artillery Corps in 1917. Division chemical officer with the 89th Division, AEF in World War I. Graduated from Army Industrial College in 1925. Chemical officer at headquarters of the European Theater of Operations 1942-1945. Brigadier general in May 1944. Reverted to colonel in April 1946. Retired in July 1953. Decorations included the Legion of Merit, Bronze Star and Commendation Ribbon. Died on May 7, 1973.

Rowe, Guy Ichabod (1886-1969) Born in Peacham, Vermont, on February 25, 1886. B.S. from Norwich University in 1909. Commissioned in the infantry in 1910. Served with the 13th Infantry in the Philippines September 1911-September 1914. Battalion commander with the 38th Infantry in France April-December 1918. Graduated from the Ecole de l'Intendence Militaire in September 1923 and the Command and General Staff School in June 1927. Instructor at the Quartermaster School June 1927-June 1931. Graduated from the Army War College in June 1932. Assigned to VI Corps Area July 1938-June 1940 then the office of the quartermaster general, U.S. Army June 1940-April 1942. Brigadier general in May 1942. Commander of Quartermaster Replacement Training Center April 1942-February 1944 then Jeffersonville Quartermaster Depot 1944-1945. Retired in August 1946. Decorations included the Distinguished Service Cross and Purple Heart. Died on December 29, 1969.

Royall, Kenneth Claiborne (1894-1971) Born in Goldsboro, North Carolina, on July 24, 1894. B.A. from the University of North Carolina in 1914. LL.B. from Harvard in 1917. Commissioned in the field artillery in 1917. Served with the AEF 1918-1919, then resigned to practice law in North Carolina. Called to active duty as colonel in 1942. Deputy fiscal director for Army Service Forces, then special assistant to the secretary of war, finally duty at headquarters of the European Theater of Operations until the end of the war. Brigadier general in November 1943. Decorations included the Distinguished Service Medal. Under secretary of war November 1945-July 1947, then secretary of war July-September 1947, finally secretary of the army 1947-1949. Died on May 27, 1971.

Rucker, Casper Bell (1886-1948) Born on September 9, 1886, in Missouri. Attended the University of Missouri. Enlisted service August 1909-October 1911. Commissioned in the infantry in 1911. Graduated from the Command and General Staff School in 1926. Instructor at the Infantry School June 1927-August 1931. Graduated from the Army War College in 1932. Assistant inspector general of the Philippine Department July 1938-November 1940. Chief of staff of 5th Division November 1940-December 1941. Deputy chief of staff of VIII Corps Area December 1941-January 1942. Chief of staff of 8th Service Command, Army Service Forces January 1942-June 1945. Brigadier general in June 1943. Retired in June 1946. Decorations included the Legion of Merit. Died on March 30, 1948.

Ruffner, Clark Louis (1903-1982) Born in Buffalo, New York, on January 12, 1903. B.S. from VMI in 1924. Commissioned in the cavalry in 1924. Assistant professor of military science and tactics at Norwich University in 1937. Graduated from the Command and General Staff School in 1941. Deputy chief of staff at VII Corps 1942-1943. Brigadier general in September 1943. Chief of staff of U.S. Army Forces Pacific Ocean Areas 1944-1946. Major general in March 1945. Assignments after the war included chief of staff of X Corps in 1950, commanding general of 2nd Infantry Division January-September 1951 and 2nd Armored Division November 1954-April 1956, commanding general of Third Army May 1958-February 1960 and U.S. representative to the NATO Military Committee March 1960 until retirement as general in October 1962. Decorations included the Distinguished Service Cross, three Distinguished Service Medals, two Silver Stars, two Legions of Merit, the Bronze Star, three AMs and Commendation Ribbon. Died on July 26, 1982.

Ruffner, David Lewis (1896-1973) Born in Charleston, West Virginia, on May 26, 1896. B.S. from VMI in 1917. Commissioned in the field artillery, Officers Reserve Corps in 1917. Instructor with the Missouri National Guard 1922-1924. Professor of military science and tactics at Harvard 1925-1929. Served in the Panama Canal Zone with 2nd Field Artillery 1932-1935. With the Civilian Conservation Corps 1935-1939. Graduated from the Command and General Staff School in 1940. Commanding officer of 183rd Field Artillery January-October 1942. Commanding officer of Mountain Training Center Artillery 1942-1943. Brigadier general in September 1943. Artillery commander of 10th Mountain Division September 1943-November 1945. Assignments after the war included commanding general of 5th Armored Division January 1951-May 1952 then 45th Infantry Division in the Korean War May 1952 until retirement as major general in June 1953. Decorations included the Distinguished Service Medal, Silver Star, two Legions of Merit, two Bronze Stars, the Commendation Ribbon and Purple Heart. Died on August 2, 1973.

Rumbough, David Sheridan (1894-1962) Born on September 7, 1894, in Washington, DC. Commissioned in the infantry from West Point in 1917. Served with the AEF in World War I. Instructor with the New York National Guard 1924-1929 then the Field Artillery School August 1929-July 1933. Professor of military science and tactics at VMI 1933-1934. Graduated from the Command and General Staff School in 1936. Assistant to the personnel officer at the Philippine Department October 1936-September 1938. Duty with 16th Field Artillery 1938-1939. Executive officer of the northern distruct, Civilian Conservation Corps July 1939-November 1940. Chief of the war plans section at headquarters of Army Ground Forces 1941-1942. Brigadier general in July 1942. Commander of 16th Field Artillery Brigade 1942-1943. Reverted to colonel in February 1943. Executive officer of 81st Infantry Division Artillery 1943-1945. Retired in June 1953. Decorations included the Legion of Merit and Bronze Star. Died on December 25, 1962.

Rumbough, William Samuel (1892-1980) Born in Lynchburg, Virginia, on November 2, 1892. Attended the University of Virginia 1910-1914. Enlisted service 1916-1917. Commissioned in the infantry in 1917. B.S. from George Washington

University in 1927. Graduated from the Command and General Staff School in 1931 and the Army War College in 1934. Served in the office of the chief signal officer July 1935-June 1939. Signal officer for the Hawaiian Division June 1939-February 1941. Duty at headquarters of IX Corps February-June 1941 then commanding officer of Signal Corps Replacement Training Center October 1941-May 1942. Brigadier general in December 1941. Chief signal officer in the European Theater of Operations May 1942-July 1945. Major general in May 1944. Retired in May 1946. Decorations included the Distinguished Service Medal, Legion of Merit and Bronze Star. Died on December 2, 1980.

Russell, Carl Austin (1892-1947) Born on April 6, 1892, in Minneapolis, Minnesota. B.S. from the University of Minnesota in 1916. Commissioned in the infantry in 1920. Served with the 31st Infantry in the Philippines December 1923-December 1926. Graduated from the Command and General Staff School in 1931. Professor of military science and tactics at Coe College June 1931-August 1935. Graduated from the Army War College in 1936 and Army Industrial College in 1937. Assigned to the 29th Infantry June 1937-July 1939. Deputy chief of the theater group for ground forces, the War Department General Staff July 1939-June 1945. Brigadier general in December 1942. Reverted to colonel in June 1946. Decorations included the Distinguished Service Medal. Died on August 16, 1947, in the Pacific area.

Rutherford, Harry Kenneth (1883-1964) Born on November 7, 1883, in Waddington, New York. Commissioned in the Coast Artillery Corps from West Point in 1907. Instructor at West Point January-December 1916. M.B.A. from Harvard in 1926. Graduated from Army Industrial College in 1927. Ordnance officer then commanding officer of the Hawaiian Ordnance Depot July 1930-April 1933. Executive assistant to the chief of the New York Ordnance District July 1933-June 1937. Director of the planning branch, office of the assistant secretary of war September 1937-April 1942. Brigadier general in October 1940, major general in December 1941. Assigned to the Services of Supply in 1943. Retired in November 1943. Died on March 15, 1964.

Rutledge, Paul Wolcott (1895-1973) Born in Greene, Ohio, on September 29, 1895. Attended Louisiana State University in 1917. Commissioned in the coast artillery reserve in 1917. Served with the 74th Coast Artillery in the AEF 1918-1919. Duty in the Panama Canal Zone 1921-1924. Assistant Professor of military science and tactics at the University of Alabama 1925-1930. Instructor with the South Carolina National Guard 1937-1939. Graduated from the Command and General Staff School in 1940. Assistant chief of staff for supply at IV Corps in 1940. Chief of the construction division at the National Guard Bureau 1940-1941. Commander of a task force occupying Christmas Island in 1942. Brigadier general in October 1942. Commanding general of 45th Antiaircraft Artillery Brigade 1942-1943 then the Antiaircraft Artillery Command with Fifth Army in 1944. Commanding general of 4th Antiaircraft Artillery Command 1944-1945. Antiaircraft artillery officer at U.S. Strategic Air Forces in 1945. Retired as major general in April 1956. Decorations included two Legions of Merit and two Commendation Ribbons. Died on September 8, 1973.

Ryan, Cornelius Edward (1896-1972) Born in Boston, Massachusetts, on May 13, 1896. B.S. from the University of Connecticut in 1917. Commissioned in the infantry in 1917. Served with the 49th Infantry in France July 1918-July 1919. Attended Massachusetts Institute of Technology 1924-1925. Graduated from Centre d'Etudes des Chars de Combat in 1928. Assistant professor of military science and tactics at the University of California May 1930-May 1936. Duty with the 23rd Infantry, 2nd Division May 1936-September 1938. Graduated from the Command and General Staff School in 1939. Instructor at the Infantry School June 1939-August 1945. Brigadier general in January 1945. Retired as major general in June 1957. Decorations included the Distinguished Service Medal, Legion of Merit, Bronze Star and four Commendation Ribbons. Died on June 6, 1972.

Ryder, Charles Wolcott (1892-1960) Born on January 16, 1892, in Topeka, Kansas. Commissioned in the infantry from West Point in 1915. Wounded while serving with the 16th Infantry Division, AEF in World War I. Saw action at Montdidier-Noyon, Aisne-Marne and Meuse-Argonne. Instructor at West Point 1921-1924. Graduated from the Command and General Staff School in 1926. Instructor at the Infantry School 1926-1929. Served in China with 15th Infantry 1929-1933. Graduated from the Army War College in 1934. With the military intelligence division of the War Department General Staff 1934-1937. Commandant of cadets at West Point 1937-1941. Chief of staff of VI Corps January 1941-January 1942. Brigadier general in January 1942. Assistant division commander of 90th and 34th Infantry Divisions in 1942. Major general in June 1942. Commanding general of the 34th Division 1942-1944. Commanding general of IX Corps 1944-1948. In the office of the chief of staff, U.S. Army in 1949. Retired in February 1950. Decorations included two Distinguished Service Crosses, the Distinguished Service Medal, two Silver Stars, two Legions of Merit and the Purple Heart. Died on August 17, 1960.

Sadler, Percy Lee (1893-n/a) Born on March 30, 1893, in Mobile, Alabama. Enlisted service in the Alabama National Guard 1916-1917. Commissioned in the infantry, Officers Reserve Corps in 1917. Duty with the 56th Infantry in France August 1918-July 1919. Served in Hawaii 1926-1929. Professor of military science and tactics at Lehigh University April 1929-July 1935. Served in the Panama Canal Zone May 1937-June 1939. Professor of military science and tactics at Western Maryland College 1939-1942. Commander of a composite force in Liberia May 1942-April 1944. Brigadier general in October 1942. Deputy commander of U.S. Army Forces Middle East April-June 1944. Commanding general of the U.S. contingent to the military headquarters fro Balkan affairs June 1944-May 1945. Reverted to colonel in March 1946. Retired in November 1946. Decorations included the Distinguished Service Medal and Legion of Merit.

Safford, Hermon French (1894-1988) Born in Leominster, Massachusetts, on August 19, 1894. B.S. from Worcester Polytechnic Institute in 1917. Commissioned in the Coast Artillery Corps in 1917. Served in the AEF in World War I. Attended Massachusetts Institute of Technology 1922-1923. Graduated from Army Industrial College in 1935. Works manager at Watervliet Arsenal 1935-1942. Brigadier general in September 1942. Chief of production services division in the office of the chief of ordnance 1942-1946. Retired in March 1946. Decorations included the Distinguished Service Medal and Legion of Merit. Died on October 7, 1988.

Sawbridge, Ben Menadue (1890-1974) Born in Port Townsend, Washington, on August 31, 1890. Attended Stanford University. Enlisted service in the Washington National Guard 1916-1917. Commissioned in the field artillery in 1917. Served with the 13th Field Artillery in France February 1918-September 1919. Duty at Schofield Barracks, Hawaii October 1920-October 1923. Instructor at the Field Artillery School June 1925-June 1928. Graduated from the Command and General Staff School in June 1934. Again with the 13th Field Artillery August 1934-July 1936. Graduated from the Army War College in 1937. Assigned to the War Department General Staff 1937-1941. At 45th Field Artillery Battalion, then 8th Division Artillery in 1941. Duty at Tank Destroyer Training and Firing Center November 1941-February 1942. Brigadier general in December 1942. Assistant chief of staff for personnel in the North African Theater of Operations February 1943-August 1944. Major General in August 1944. Assistant chief of staff for personnel with Sixth Army Group from August 1944. Retired in July 1946. Decorations included two Distinguished Service Medals and the Legion of Merit. Died on April 16, 1974.

Sayler, Henry Benton (1893-1970) Born on November 4, 1893, in Huntington, Indiana. Commissioned in the Coast Artillery Corps from West Point in 1915. Transferred to the Ordnance Corps in 1921. Attended Massachusetts Institute of Technology 1922-1923. Graduated from the Command and General Staff School in 1933. Chief ordnance officer of the European Theater of Operations 1942-1945. Brigadier general in April 1943, major general in June 1944. Director of research and development in the Ordnance Department in 1945. Retired in November 1949. Decorations included the Distinguished Service Medal, Legion of Merit, Bronze Star and Commendation Ribbon. Died on May 7, 1970.

Schabacker, Clarence Henry (1898-1968) Born on June 26, 1898, in Menomonie, Wisconsin. Commissioned in the Coast Artillery Corps from West Point in 1920. Served in the Panama Canal Zone January 1924-January 1927 and at Fort Kamehameha, Hawaii June 1930-November 1932. Graduated from the Command and General Staff School in 1938. Supply officer at West Point June 1938-April 1941. Duty with the War Department General Staff April 1941-July 1942 and at headquarters of Army Ground Forces 1942-1943. Commanding officer of 46th Antiaircraft Artillery Group June-September 1943. Brigadier general in January 1944. Commanding general of 55th Antiaircraft Artillery Brigade February-

October 1945. Reverted to colonel in March 1946. Retired in October 1953. Decorations included two Legions of Merit, the Bronze Star and two Commendation Ribbons. Died on October 8, 1968.

Schick, Lawrence Edward (1897-1967) Born in Chicago, Illinois, on September 24, 1897. Commissioned in the cavalry from West Point in 1920. Deputy chief of staff of Alaskan Department 1941-1944 then Tenth Army 1944-1945. Brigadier general in January 1945. Provost marshal general in Korea 1945-1946. Reverted to colonel in February 1946. Professor at West Point 1946-1961. Retired in October 1961. Decorations included two Distinguished Service Medals and the Legion of Merit. Died on October 14, 1967.

Schley, Julian Larcombe (1880-1965) Born on February 23, 1880, in Savannah, Georgia. Commissioned in the Corps of Engineers from West Point in 1903. Duty in Cuba 1906-1908. Instructor there 1909-1912. Served with the Corps of Engineers in the V Corps during World War I, including the St. Mihiel and Meuse-Argonne engagements. Engineer of maintenance at the Panama Canal 1928-1932 then governor of the Panama Canal 1932-1936. Commandant of the Engineer School 1936-1937. Chief of engineers, U.S. Army 1937-1941. Major general in April 1939. Retired in 1941. Recalled to active duty as director of transportation in the office of the coordinator of Inter-American Affairs until the end of the war, when he retired a second time. Died on March 29, 1965.

Schmidt, William Richard (1889-1966) Born on October 14, 1889, in Verdigre, Nebraska. Commissioned in the infantry from West Point in 1913. Served on the Mexican border 1913-1917. Instructor at West Point 1921-1923. Duty in Hawaii 1923-1926. Graduated from the Command and General Staff School in 1928, the Army War College in 1931 and Army Industrial College in 1932. Again in Hawaii 1938-1940. Commanding officer of 39th Infantry 1940-1941. Brigadier general in April 1942. Commanding general of 76th Division 1942-1945. Major general in December 1942. Assignments after the war included commanding general of 101st Airborne Division 1948-1949. Retired in October 1951. Decorations included the Distinguished Service Medal, Silver Star, Legion of Merit and Bronze Star. Died on July 18, 1966.

Schulz, John Wesley Niesz (1885-1965) Born in Wheeling, West Virginia, on May 14, 1885. Commissioned in the Corps of Engineers from West Point in 1908. Served with the 3rd Engineers in the Philippine Islands 1910-1914. Chief gas officer with First Army, AEF at St. Mihiel and Meuse-Argonne 1918-1919. Instructor at General Service Schools 1919-1923. Graduated from the Command and General Staff School in 1923, the Army War College in 1924. U.S. Army representative at Century of Progress in Chicago in 1933. Graduated from Army Industrial College in 1937. Director of purchases and contracts in the office of the under secretary of war 1940-1942. Brigadier general in January 1941. Commander of Engineer Unit Training Center at Camp Claiborne 1942-1943. President of the Engineer Board at Fort Belvoir 1943-1946. Retired in November 1946. Decorations included the Distinguished Service Medal and two Legions of Merit. Died on April 4, 1965.

Schuyler, Cortlandt Van Rensselaer (1900-1993) Born on December 22, 1900, in Arlington, New Jersey. Commissioned in the Coast Artillery Corps from West Point in 1922, where he acquired the nickname "alphabet" because of his long name. Instructor at West Point 1927-1931. Graduated from the Command and General Staff School in 1937. Duty in the office of the chief of the Coast Artillery Corps 1939-1942. With Army Ground Forces in 1942. Chief of staff of Antiair craft Command 1943. Brigadier general in June 1943. Commanding general of Antiaircraft Artillery Training Command December 1943-November 1944. Military chief of Allied Control Command in Romania 1944-1947. Assignments after the war included special assistant to the chief of staff of SHAPE 1951-1953, commanding general of 28th Division February-July 1953 and chief of staff of SHAPE 1953-1959. General in May 1956. Retired in November 1959. Decorations included two Distinguished Service Medals and the Legion of Merit. Died on December 6, 1993.

Schwien, Edwin E. (1894-1969) Born in St. Joseph, Missouri, on June 24, 1894. Attended Yale 1912-1915. Commissioned in the infantry in 1916. Served with the 48th Infantry in the AEF July 1917-August 1919. Professor of military science and tactics at the University of Oklahoma May 1924-August 1927. Graduated from the Command and General Staff School in 1928. Attended Ecole Superieure de Guerre 1930-1932. Instructor at the Command and General Staff School 1932-1936 then the Cavalry School in 1939. Assistant chief of staff for supply with 1st Cavalry Division August 1939-June 1940. Executive officer of 8th Cavalry June 1940-January 1941 then the Armored Force Replacement Training Center January 1941-December 1942. Commander of Combat Command "A" in 8th Armored Division December 1942-May 1944. Brigadier general in January 1943. Chief of the Military Mission to the French Committee of National Liberation May-August 1944. Assigned to the Allied Liaison Service in Italy August-October 1944 then with Sixth Army Group in France October 1944-April 1945. Retired in October 1945. Decorations included the Distinguished Service Cross and Purple Heart. Died on November 22, 1969.

Scott, Stanley Lonzo (1893-1984) Born on April 7, 1893, in New Albany, Indiana. Commissioned in the Corps of Engineers from West Point in 1916. Served with the AEF in World War I. B.S. from Massachusetts Institute of Technology in 1921. Instructor at West Point 1921-1924. Graduated from the Command and General Staff School in 1931. Director of engineers in the Southwest Division 1940-1942. Brigadier general in October 1942. Chief of staff of Persian Gulf Theater of Operations 1942-1944. At headquarters of Army Service Forces 1944-1946. Major general in June 1945. Retired in March 1954. Decorations included three Distinguished Service Medals and the Commendation Ribbon. Died on March 12, 1984.

Scowden, Frank Floyd (1886-1974) Born in Meadville, Pennsylvania, on August 18, 1886. Commissioned in the infantry from West Point in 1910. Duty in the Philippine Islands February 1912-June 1915, with the Punitive Expedition into Mexico in 1916 and in Fance September 1917-January 1920. M.B.A. from Harvard in 1928. Graduated from Army Industrial College in 1934 and the Army War College in 1935. Brigadier general in October 1940, major general in September 1942. Retired in November 1946. Decorations included the DSM, two Legions of Merit and the Bronze Star. Died on September 10, 1974.

Seals, Carl Herndon (1882-1955) Born in Eufaula, Alabama, on December 31, 1882. Commissioned in the infantry, Alabama National Guard in 1904 and the Regular Army in 1920. Served at Fort McKinley, Philippine Islands June 1921-April 1925. Graduated from the Command and General Staff School in 1926 and the Army War College in June 1931. Duty with the military intelligence division of WDGS 1931-1935. Adjutant general in the Philippine Islands 1935-1937. Assigned to the IV Corps Area 1937-1940. Adjutant general of the Philippine Department 1940-1942. Brigadier general in January 1942. Prisoner of war from the fall of Corregidor until September 1945. Died in 1955.

Searby, Edmund Wilson (1896-1944) Born on March 7, 1896, in Berkeley, California. Commissioned in the field artillery from West Point in 1918. Attended Ecole d'Application d'Artellerie 1920-1921. Graduated from the Command and General Staff School in 1940. Brigadier general in March 1943. Commanding general of 80th Infantry Division Artillery 1943-1944. Killed in action at Meurth et Moselle, France, on September 14, 1944. Decorations included the Silver Star, Legion of Merit and Purple Heart.

Searcy, Cyrus Higginson (1895-1963) Born in Waco, Texas, on August 12, 1895. Commissioned in the infantry in 1917. Stationed at the Panama Canal October 1920-October 1923. Graduated from the Command and General Staff School in 1930. Company commander with 57th Infantry in the Philippines October 1930-November 1932. Graduated from the Army War College in 1939. Assistant to the chief of the construction branch, the War Department General Staff July 1939-March 1942. Director of the requirements division at Services of Supply March-August 1942. Commanded the 362nd Infantry Regiment September 1942-August 1943. Chief of staff of VIII Corps August 1943-December 1945. Brigadier general in January 1945. Reverted to colonel in February 1946. Retired in July 1947. Decorations included the Distinguished Service Medal, two Legions of Merit and two Bronze Stars. Died on May 8, 1963.

Sebree, Edmund Bower (1898-1966) Born on January 7, 1898, in Olney, Illinois. Commissioned in the infantry from West Point in 1919. Professor of military science and tactics at Western Military Academy 1928-1932. Served with 45th Infantry in the Philippines 1932-1934. Graduated from the Command and General Staff School in 1937. Aide to Major General Herbert J. Brees 1937-1940. Staff officer with 9th Division 1940-1941. With the personnel division of the War Department General Staff 1941-1942. Brigadier general in August 1942. Assistant division commander of Americal Division 1942-1943 then 35th Infantry Division and 28th Infantry Division September 1943-September 1945. Assignments after the war included. commanding general of 5th Armored Division 1952-1953 and deputy commanding general of First Army 1953-1954. Retired in July 1957. Decorations included two Distinguished Service Medals, two Silver Stars, the Legion of Merit, Bronze Star and Purple Heart. Died on June 25, 1966.

Selleck, Clyde Andrew (1888-1973) Born on July 29, 1888, in Brandon, Vermont. Commissioned in the field artillery from West Point in 1910. Served with the 21st Field Artillery, AEC in 1918. Instructor with the New York National Guard 1921-1925. Graduated from the Command and General Staff School in 1927. Assigned to the National Guard Bureau 1927-1931. Graduated from the Army War College in 1935. Duty with the organized reserves 1939-1941. Brigadier general in December 1941. Served in Bataan 1941-1942. Reverted to colonel in January 1942. Captured by the Japanese Army in April 1942 and prisoner of war until September 1945. Retired in April 1947. Decorations included the Purple Heart. Died on January 9, 1973.

Sexton, William Thaddeus (1901-1983) Born on September 3, 1901, in Leavenworth, Kansas. Commissioned in the field artillery from West Point in 1924. Served with 24th Field Artillery in the Philippine Islands 1930-1933. Instructor at West Point 1936-1939. Graduated from the Command and General Staff School in 1940. Assistant secretary, then secretary of the War Department General Staff 1940-1944. Brigadier general in November 1944. Commanding general of 3rd Division Artillery 1944-1946. Reverted to colonel in February 1946. Assignments after the war included chief of staff of Sixth Army 1951-1954 and commanding general of 5th Infantry Division July 1955-March 1956. Retired as major general in August 1956. Decorations included the Legion of Merit and four Bronze Stars. Died on June 22, 1983.

Shadle, Charles Stricklen (1888-1985) Born in Altoona, Pennsylvania, on November 1, 1888. Enlisted service 1917-1918. Commissioned in the infantry in 1918. Wounded in action while serving with the AEF. Instructor at the Infantry School 1920-1921. Served in the Panama Canal Zone June 1931-April 1935. Chemical officer with 1st Cavalry Division June 1939-August 1941. Duty in the office of the chief of the Chemical Warfare Service August 1941-April 1942. Chemical officer in the European and North African Theater of Operationss April 1942-November 1945. Brigadier general in May 1944. Reverted to colonel in April 1946. Retired in October 1947. Decorations included the Distinguished Service Medal, Legion of Merit and Purple Heart. Died on March 1, 1985.

Sharp, William F. (1885-1947) Born on September 22, 1885, in Yankton, South Dakota. Enlisted service 1904-1907. Commissioned in the infantry in 1907. Served in the Philippine Islands 1910-1913. Instructor with the Colorado National Guard 1913-1917 then at the Command and General Staff School 1917-1918.

Commanding officer of 11th and 78th Field Artillery in the AEF at Meuse-Argonne in 1918. Professor of military science and tactics at Oregon Agricultural Colleege 1919-1921. Instructor at the Field Artillery School 1922-1923. Graduated from the Command and General Staff School in 1925. Duty at IX Corps Area 1940-1941. Brigadier general in December 1941. Assigned to the Philippine Department as commanding general of U.S. Forces in Mindanao December 1941-May 1942. Major general in April 1942. Surrendered to the Japanese Army in May 1942. Prisoner of war until released in August 1945. Retired in July 1946. Decorations included the Distinguished Service Medal. Died on March 30, 1947.

Shea, George David (1894-n/a) Born in Augusta, Georgia, on January 11, 1894. Enlisted service 1915-1917. Commissioned in the field artillery in 1917. Battery and battalion commander with 2nd Infantry Division in AEF in World War I. Instructor at the Field Artillery School July 1925-June 1929. Graduated from the Command and General Staff School in 1936. Director of the department of animal transportation 1936-1940. Assistant chief of staff for supply at 8th Division July 1940-October 1941 then chief of staff October 1941-August 1942. Brigadier general in July 1942. Commander of 90th Infantry Division Artillery August 1942-September 1943. Commanding general of 141st Field Artillery Brigade September 1943-May 1945 then the War Department Personnel Center June 1945-May 1946. Retired as major general in January 1953. Decorations included the Distinguished Service Medal, two Silver Stars, two Legions of Merit and two Bronze Stars.

Shedd, William Edgar (1885-1953) Born in Danville, Illinois, on February 25, 1885. Commissioned in the Coast Artillery Corps from West Point in 1907. Instructor at West Point 1911-1912. Served at Schofield Barracks, Hawaii 1915-1917 then as colonel on the staff of the chief of artillery in the AEF 1917-1919. Graduated from the Command and General Staff School in 1927 and the Army War College in 1928. Instructor at Coast Artillery School 1935-1938. Brigadier general in December 1938. Commanded 4th Artillery District December 1938-October 1939. Duty at the War Department General Staff October 1939-February 1941. Commanding general of coast defenses and antiaircraft, Panama Department, then deputy commander of the Panama Department 1941-1943. Major general in January 1941. Commanding general of the Antilles Department December 1943-September 1944 then 9th Service Command 1944-1946. Retired in August 1946. Decorations included three Distinguished Service Medals. Died on December 2, 1953.

Sheep, William Lloyd (1881-1952) Born on October 24, 1881, in Elizabeth City, North Carolina. M.D. from George Washington University in 1906. Commissioned in the Medical Corps in 1910. Assigned to Fort McKinley, Philippine Islands September 1914-August 1916. Assistant superintendent of Gorgas Hospital in the Canal Zone June 1931-September 1934. Chief of the military personnel division in the office of the surgeon general, U.S. Army 1936-1940. Brigadier general in October 1940. Commanding general of Lawson General Hospital in

Atlanta April 1941 until retirement in October 1945. Decorations included the Legion of Merit. Died on December 6, 1952.

Sheetz, Josef Robert (1895-1992) Born in Williamsport, Maryland, on November 30, 1895. Enlisted service in the Maryland National Guard 1914-1917. Commissioned in the field artillery in 1917. B.A. from St. John's College in 1918. Served with the 3rd Field Artillery in the AEF 1918-1919. Instructor at Field Artillery School September 1923-August 1927. Assistant professor at Princeton University August 1927-September 1931. Graduated from the Command and General Staff School in 1936 and the Army War College in 1939. Instructor at the Command and General Staff School September 1939-July 1941. Assistant chief of staff for supply at the War Department General Staff 1941-1942. Duty with British general staff May-December 1942. Brigadier general in December 1942. Assigned to 98th Division Artillery 1943-1945. Retired as major general in August 1950. Decorations included the Distinguished Service Medal and two Legions of Merit. Died on January 28, 1992.

Shekerjian, Haig (1886-1966) Born in Turkey on June 13, 1886. Emigrated to the U.S. in 1891. Attended Colgate University 1906-1907. Commissioned in the infantry from West Point in 1911. Served in Hawaii and Mexico 1916-1917 and the Balkans 1918-1919. Graduated from the Command and General Staff School in 1924. Assistant commandant of the Chemical Warfare School 1925-1926. Instructor at the Command and General Staff School 1926-1930. Graduated from the the Army War College in 1931. Executive in the office of the chief of the chemical warfare service 1936-1940. Brigadier general in January 1942. Chief of troops and training at Edgewood Arsenal in 1942. Commanding general of Chemical Warfare Replacement Training Center 1942-1943 then Camp Sibert 1943-1944. Deputy commander of the Army and Navy Liquidation Commission in the Middle East Theater of Operations 1945-1946. Retired in September 1946. Decorations included the Legion of Merit and Commendation Ribbon. Died on January 22, 1966.

Shepard, Whitfield Putnam (1894-n/a) Born in Syracuse, New York, on February 26, 1894. Attended Alexander Hamilton Institute. Enlisted service 1917-1918. Commissioned in the infantry in 1918. Served in the AEF at Meuse-Argonne offensive 1918-1919. Graduated from the Command and General Staff School in 1935 and the Army War College in 1937. Assistant chief then chief of the statistics branch at the War Department General Staff 1940-1942. Chief of staff of 7th Division 1942-1943. Commander of Combat Command "A" in 16th Armored Division 1943-1944. Brigadier general in February 1944. Assistant division commander of 3rd Infantry Division in 1944. Deputy chief of staff of Sixth Army Group 1944-1945. Assistant commandant of the Infantry School July 1945-January 1949. Retired as major general in January 1956. Decorations included the Distinguished Service Medal, Legion of Merit and Commendation Ribbon.

Sherman, Harry Benham (1894-1974) Born on April 25, 1894, in Honeyeye Falls, New York. Commissioned in the infantry from West Point in 1918. Served with the 50th Infantry in Germany October 1919-April 1922. Instructor at the University of South Dakota 1928-1932. Commanded 2nd Battalion in Panama October 1939-November 1941. Served with 15th Infantry as battalion commander then regimental commander 1941-1943. Commanding officer of 7th Infantry, 3rd Division 1943-1944. Brigadier general in June 1944. Assistant division commander of 3rd, 88th and 34th Divisions 1944-1945. Retired in January 1953. Decorations included the Distinguished Service Cross, Legion of Merit and Bronze Star. Died on January 21, 1974.

Sherrill, Stephen Huntting (1893-1956) Born on March 13, 1893, in East Hampton, Long Island, New York. Commissioned in the cavalry from West Point in 1917. Served with the AEF 1918-1919. Graduated from the Command and General Staff School in 1932 and the Army War College in 1939. Assigned to the War Department General Staff 1939-1942. Brigadier general in July 1942. Commanding general of Aircraft Warning Unit Training Center, Third Air Force 1943-1944. Retired in September 1944. Recalled to active duty as commanding general of Fort Monmouth 1944-1945. Decorations included two Legions of Merit. Died on June 28, 1956.

Shingler, Don Gilmore (1896-1963) Born in Perry Center, New York, on October 25, 1896. Commissioned in the Corps of Engineers from West Point in 1919. B.S. from Massachusetts Institute of Technology in 1921. Instructor at West Point 1925-1930 then the Engineer School 1930-1931. Graduated from the Command and General Staff School in 1936 and the Army War College in 1940. Chief of staff of U.S. military mission to Iran and oversaw development of Persian Gulf supply lines to the Soviet Union 1941-1943. Brigadier general in March 1943. Chief of the amphibious section at First Army in 1944. Director of the international division, Army Service Forces 1944-1946. Retired in April 1954. Decorations included the Distinguished Service Medal and Legion of Merit. Died on October 29, 1963.

Shinkle, Edward Marsh (1878-1966) Born in Higginsport, Ohio, on January 9, 1878. Attended Ohio Wesleyan University 1894-1895. Commissioned in the artillery from West Point in 1901. Graduated from the Army War College in 1920. Assistant to the chief of ordnance as brigadier general September 1934-August 1938. Brigadier general in October 1940. Commander of Picatinny Arsenal September 1941 until retirement in January 1942 then recalled to active duty as commander again February-October 1942. Decorations included the Distinguished Service Medal. Died on November 8, 1966.

Shoe, Robert Oliver (1891-1972) Born on March 15, 1891, in Wallingford, Pennsylvania. Attended Drexel Institute 1912-1913. Enlisted service in Pennsylvania National Guard 1916-1917. Commissioned in the cavalry, Officers Reserve Corps in 1917. Served with the 331st Battalion of the Tank Corps in France

August 1918-March 1919. Professor of military science and tactics at the University of South Dakota June 1923-September 1928. Graduated from the Command and General Staff School in 1937 and the Army War College in 1940. Assistant chief of staff for supply with II Corps December 1940-June 1942 then XI Corps June 1942-January 1943. Assigned to headquarters of Army Ground Forces January-October 1943. Chief of staff of Second Army October 1943-June 1944. Brigadier general in January 1944. Chief of staff of Eighth Army June-September 1944. Assistant division commander of 40th Infantry Division 1944-1945. Commander of Northern Forces, 108th RCT June 1945-January 1946. Retired as major general. Decorations included three Silver Stars, the Legion of Merit, Bronze Star, Air Medal and Purple Heart. Died in 1972.

Short, Walter Campbell (1880-1949) Born on March 30, 1880, in Fillmore, IL. Graduate of the University of Illinois in 1901. Commissioned in the infantry in 1902. Served with Pershing in the Mexican Punitive Expedition in 1916. Staff officer, later chief of staff of Third Army 1917-1919. Graduated from the Army War College in 1925. Brigadier general in December 1936. Assistant commandant of the Infantry School December 1936-December 1937. Brigade commander in 1st Division, December 1937-July 1938. Commanding general of 1st Division July 1938-October 1940. Major general in October 1940. Commander of I Corps October 1940-January 1941. Lieutenant general in February 1941. Commander of the Hawaiian Department January 1941-December 1941. Ten days after the Pearl Harbor attack Short was relieved of duty. Died on September 3, 1949.

Shugg, Roland Paget (1893-1989) Born on November 8, 1893, in Boston, Massachusetts. Commissioned in the cavalry from West Point in 1916. Served with the AEF August 1918-August 1919. Graduated from the Command and General Staff School in 1931. Professor of military science and tactics at Princeton University 1931-1935. Chief of staff of 3rd Armored Division April-December 1941. Chief of the motor section in the office of the chief of transportation December 1941-June 1942. Brigadier general in May 1942. Duty in the office of the chief of Ordnance 1942-1943. Commanding general of XI Corps Artillery 1943-1945. Reverted to colonel in March 1946. Assignments after the war included commanding general of 3rd Division Artillery in the Korean War 1950-1951. Retired as brigadier general in May 1952. Decorations included the Distinguished Service Medal, two Silver Stars, two Legions of Merit and two Bronze Stars. Died on July 28, 1989.

Sibert, Edwin Luther (1897-1977) Born on March 2, 1897, in Little Rock, Arkansas. Commissioned in the field artillery from West Point in 1918. Served with the 2nd Division in the AEF in 1919. Instructor at Cornell University ROTC 1922-1926 then the Field Artillery School 1927-1931. Graduated from the Command and General Staff School in 1935 and the Army War College in 1939. Military attache in Brazil 1940-1941. Chief of staff of 7th Division in 1942. Brigadier general in October 1942. Commanding general of 99th Division Artillery 1942-1943. Intelligence chief of 12th Army Group 1944-1945 and U.S. Forces, European Theater of Operations 1945-1946. Retired in January 1954. Decorations included three Distinguished Service Medals, the Legion of Merit and Bronze Star. Died on December 16, 1977.

Sibert, Franklin Cummings (1891-1980) Born on January 3, 1891, in Bowling Green, Kentucky. Commissioned in the infantry from West Point in 1912. Graduated from the Command and General Staff School in 1925 and the Army War College in 1929. Brigadier general in September 1941. Served as member of General Stilwell's staff in the China-Burma-India Theater of Operations 1941-1942. Accompanied Stilwell in the retreat from Burma in 1942. Major general in March 1942. Commanding general of 6th Division 1942-1944 then X Corps 1944-1946. Retired in June 1946. Decorations included the Distinguished Service Medal, Silver Star, two Legions of Merit, the Bronze Star and Air Medal. Died on June 24, 1980.

Silvester, Lindsay McDonald (1889-1963) Born in Portsmouth, Virginia, on September 30, 1889. B.S. from Maryland Agricultural College in 1911. Commissioned in the infantry in 1911. Served in Mexico with the Punitive Expedition in 1916 and the 30th and 7th Infantry in the Aisne-Marne, Champagne, St. Mihiel and Meuse-Argonne offensives of World War I. Wounded on October 11, 1918. Graduated from the Command and General Staff School in 1924, the Army War College in 1930. Professor of military science and tactics at North Carolina State College June 1930-August 1931. Brigadier general in July 1941. Commander of the 1st Tank Group July 1941-March 1942. Major general in March 1942. Commanding general of 7th Armored Division March 1942-November 1944. Reverted to colonel in November 1944. Retired in September 1949. Decorations included the Distinguished Service Cross, Silver Star, Distinguished Flying Cross, two Air Medals and the Purple Heart. Died on August 4, 1963.

Simmons, James Stevens (1890-1954) Born in Newton, North Carolina, on June 7, 1890. B.S. from Davidson College in 1911. Attended the University of North Carolina School of Medicine 1911-1913. M.D. from the University of Pennsylvania in 1915. Commissioned in the Medical Corps, Officers Reserve Corps in 1916. Graduated from Army Medical School in 1917. Chief of the department of bacteriology at Army Medical School 1930-1934. Ph.D. from George Washington University in 1934. President of the Army Medical Research Board in the Panama Canal Zone 1934-1935. Chief of preventive medical services in the office of the surgeon general, U.S. Army 1940-1946. Brigadier general in March 1943. Retired in 1946. Decorations included the Distinguished Service Medal. Died on July 31, 1954.

Simpson, Bethel Wood (1888-1955) Born in Lansing, Michigan, on July 11, 1888. Commissioned in the field artillery from West Point in 1911. Graduated from Army Industrial College in 1926 and the Command and General Staff School in 1927. M.B.A. from Harvard in 1936. Chief of the personnel division in the office of the chief of ordnance 1936-1941. Commander of Ordnance Replacement Training Center January 1941-February 1942. Brigadier general in February 1942. Commanding general of Ordnance Training Center February 1942-June 1944. Assigned to the ordnance office at headquarters Army Ground Forces June 1944-April 1945. Member of the Joint Production Survey Committee June-December 1945. Retired in November 1946. Decorations included the Legion of Merit. Died on February 17, 1955.

Simpson, William Hood (1888-1980) Born on May 19, 1888, in Weatherford, Texas. Commissioned in the infantry from West Point in 1909, where he earned the nickname "Texas Bill." Served in the Philippines 1909-1912, with the Punitive Expedition in 1916 and the 33rd Division in the AEF in World War I. Graduated from the Command and General Staff School in 1925 and the Army War College in 1928. Instructor at the Army War College 1936-1940. Brigadier general in October 1940. Commanding general of 30th Infantry Division, XII Army Corps, Fourth Army and Ninth Army in World War II. Lieutenant general in October 1943 and general on the retired list in July 1955. Died on August 15, 1980.

Sims, Leonard Henderson (1895-1971) Born in Chattanooga, Tennessee, on March 17, 1895. Attended the University of Chattanooga 1915-1917. Commissioned in the infantry, Officers Reserve Corps in 1917. Served with the AEF in France October 1917-September 1919. Duty with the 15th Infantry in Tientsin July 1930-July 1933. Finance officer at the Infantry School May 1937-July 1941 and headquarters IX Corps Area 1941-1943. Brigadier general in November 1943. Finance officer for the European Theater of Operations 1943-1945. Retired in August 1954. Decorations included the Distinguished Service Medal, Legion of Merit and Commendation Ribbon. Died on November 4, 1971.

Slack, Julius Easton (1898-1968) Born on November 21, 1898, in Hermansville, Michigan. Commissioned in the field artillery from West Point in 1919. Brigadier general in April 1943. Commanding general of XX Corps Artillery 1943-1945. Retired in September 1951. Decorations included the Silver Star, Legion of Merit, two Bronze Stars and two Air Medals. Died on May 31, 1968.

Sliney, George Wesley (1889-1966) Born on March 11, 1889, in Thermopolis, Wyoming. Commissioned in the cavalry from West Point in 1913. Instructor at West Point 1916-1918. Served with the 9th Cavalry in the Philippines 1920-1923. Graduated from the Command and General Staff School in 1925 then instructor there until 1929. Graduated from the Army War College in 1930. Instructor at Field Artillery School July 1937-March 1941. Artillery officer with Chinese Army and training units in the China-Burma-India Theater of Operations 1941-1944. Brigadier general in August 1944. Artillery officer for Northern Combat Area Command November 1944-March 1945. Commanding general of XXXVI Corps Artillery March-June 1945 then the War Department Personnel Center June 1945-March 1946. Retired in March 1949. Decorations included two Silver Stars, the Legion of Merit, Bronze Star, Air Medal and Commendation Ribbon. Died on January 27, 1966.

Sloan, John Emmet (1887-1972) Born in Greenville, South Carolina, on January 31, 1887. Graduated from USNA in 1910. Resigned in 1911. Commissioned in the field artillery in 1911. Served in the Panama Canal Zone January 1914-April 1917. Graduated from the Command and General Staff School in 1926. Professor of military science and tactics at Texas A&M 1926-1931. Graduated from the Army War College in 1932. Instructor at the Command and General Staff School 1932-1936. Professor of military science and tactics at Oregon State Agricultural College July 1938-June 1940. Duty with 76th Field Artillery and III Corps 1940-1942. Brigadier general in April 1941, major general in May 1942. Commanding general of 88th Infantry Division May 1942-October 1944. President of the War Department Decorations Board 1945-1946. Retired in October 1946. Decorations included the Distinguished Service Medal, Silver Star and Legion of Merit. Died on October 15, 1972.

Slocum, LeCount Haynes (1895-n/a) Born in Mare Island Navy Yard, California, on June 25, 1895. Attended Stanford University 1914-1917. Commissioned in the field artillery in 1917. Served with the AEF October 1918-August 1919. Instructor at the Field Artillery School June 1922-June 1925. Duty in Hawaii 1929-1931. Graduated from the Command and General Staff School in 1935, then instructor there 1935-1937. Graduated from the Army War College in 1938. Professor of military science and tactics at at Stanford University August 1938-July 1940. Field artillery liaison officer with the Corps of Engineers July 1940-February 1941. Assigned to the War Department General Staff 1941-1942. Brigadier general in December 1942. Commanding general of 72nd Field Artillery Brigade 1942-1943. Artillery commander at 89th Light Division 1943-1944 then the Americal Division January 1944-April 1946. Reverted to colonel in February 1946. Retired in July 1954. Decorations included the Silver Star, Legion of Merit, Bronze Star, Air Medal and Commendation Ribbon.

Smith, Albert Cowper (1894-1974) Born on June 5, 1894, in Warrentown, Virginia. Commissioned in the cavalry from West Point in 1917. Served with the 3rd Cavalry in France 1917-1918, including the Meuse-Argonne offensive, then with occupation forces in Germany in 1919. Instructor at West Point August 1922-September and again April 1929-August 1934. Graduated from the Command and General Staff School in 1937, then instructor there until 1940. Plans and training officer at the Armored Force Replacement Training Center, Fort Knox November 1940-April 1941 then with 4th Armored Division April 1941-July 1942. Commanded 37th Armored Regiment then Combat Command "A" in 14th Armored Division July 1942-July 1944. Brigadier general in March 1944. Commanding general of 14th Armored Division July 1944-September 1945. Major general in March 1945. Assignments after the war included command of 30th Infantry Division 1945-1946 and chief of military history 1953-1955. Retired in September 1955. Decorations included the Distinguished Service Medal, Silver Star and Bronze Star. Died on January 24, 1974.

Smith, Edward Ward (1895-1954) Born on October 23, 1895, in Livingston, Alabama. B.S. from Alabama Polytechnic Institute in 1916. Commissioned in the infantry from West Point in 1918. Instructor there in 1919. Graduated from Army Industrial College in 1934. Ordnance officer for 8th Division December 1940-January 1942, First Army January-August 1942, III Armored Corps September 1942-April 1943 and IV Corps 1943-1944. Assigned to headquarters Seventh Army 1944-1945. Brigadier general in January 1945. Retired in October 1946. Decorations included the Legion of Merit and Bronze Star. Died on May 19, 1954.

Smith, Edward White (1894-1967) Born in Humboldt, Tennessee, on January 16, 1894. Attended Memphis University 1909-1913. Commissioned in the field artillery in 1917. LL.B. from the University of Virginia in 1919. Resigned from the Army but recalled to active duty in 1942. Deputy chief of the legislative liaison division at the War Department General Staff 1942-1943. Brigadier general in December 1942. Executive for reserve and ROTC affairs at headquarters of Army Service Forces and duty in the office of the chief of staff, U.S. Army 1942-1945. Major general in October 1945. Returned to inactive status in 1946. Decorations included the Distinguished Service Medal. Died on September 3, 1967.

Smith, Frederic Harrison (1879-1961) Born on May 30, 1879, in Troy, Ohio. Commissioned in the Artillery from West Point in 1903. Wounded while serving as colonel in the field artillery, 77th Division in the AEF during World War I. Graduated from the Command and General Staff School in 1923 and the Army War College in 1925. Military attache to Turkey 1926-1928. Brigadier general in July 1937. Commandant of the Combined Arms Center 1938-1940. Major general in October 1940. Commanding general of VII Corps 1941-1943. Retired in May 1943. Decorations included the Purple Heart. Died on January 17, 1961.

Smith, George Stanley (1900-1968) Born on June 10, 1900, in Somerville, New Jersey. Commissioned in the field artillery from West Point in 1923. Graduated from the Command and General Staff School in 1937. Served in the intelligence section of the War Department General Staff 1940-1942. Intelligence chief of Fifteenth Army, then the Mediterranean Theater of Operations, finally at Allied Forces headquarters in the Mediterranean 1943-1946. Brigadier general in June 1945. Reverted to colonel in March 1946. Retired in June 1959. Decorations included the Distinguished Service Medal, Legion of Merit and Commendation Ribbon. Died on September 4, 1968.

Smith, John Piper (1883-1948) Born on January 28, 1883, in Hopewell, Pennsylvania. Graduated from Pennsylvania State College in 1907. Commissioned in the Coast Artillery Corps in 1908. Served with the AEF January 1918-May 1919 in the St. Mihiel and Meuse-Argonne offensives. Graduated from the Command and General Staff School in 1925 and the Army War College in 1926. Brigadier general in October 1940, major general in April 1941. Retired as colonel in November 1942. Active duty as major general December 1942-December 1945.

Decorations included two Distinguished Service Medals and the Purple Heart. Died on November 4, 1948.

Smith, Ralph Corbett (1893-n/a) Born in South Omaha, Nebraska, on November 27, 1893. B.S. from Colorado State College in 1916. Commissioned in the infantry in 1916. Served with the AEF in France 1917-1919. Instructor at West Point 1920-1923 then the Infantry School 1924-1927. Graduated from the Command and General Staff School in 1928 then instructor there 1930-1934. Graduated from the Army War College in 1935. Attended Ecole Superieure de Guerre 1935-1937. Assigned to the military intelligence division at the War Department General Staff 1938-1942. Brigadier general in April 1942. Assistant division commander of 76th Division in 1942. Major general in October 1942. Commanding general of 76th Division then 98th Division 1942-1944. Military attache in Paris 1945-1946. Retired in October 1946. Decorations included two Silver Stars and the Purple Heart.

Smith, Walter Bedell (1895-1961) Born in Indianapolis, Indiana, on October 5, 1895. Commissioned in the infantry, Indiana National Guard in 1917. Wounded while serving in France with AEF 1918. Graduated from the Command and General Staff School in 1935 and the Army War College in 1937. Instructor at the Infantry School 1937-1939. Duty with the War Department General Staff 1939-1941. Secretary of the War Department General Staff 1941-1942. Brigadier general in February 1942. Secretary of the Combined Chiefs of Staff February-September 1942. Major general in November 1942. Chief of staff of U.S. Army forces, European Theater of Operations, then SHAEF 1942-1945. Lieutenant general in January 1944. Assignments after the war included ambassador to the Soviet Union (retaining his military rank) 1946-1949, commanding general of First Army 1949-1950, director of CIA 1950-1953 and undersecretary of state 1953-1954. Retired as general in October 1954. Decorations included four Distinguished Service Medals, the Legion of Merit and Bronze Star. Author of *My Three Years in Moscow* (1950) and *Eisenhower's Six Great Decisions* (1956). Died on August 9, 1961.

Smith, Wayne Carleton (1901-1964) Born on December 4, 1901, in St. Joseph, Missouri. Commissioned in the infantry from West Point in 1925. Served with the 15th Infantry at Tientsin October 1931-December 1934. Company commander with 19th Infantry in Hawaii 1938-1939. Graduated from the Command and General Staff School in 1940. Assigned to 2nd Infantry Division July 1940-June 1941. Assistant chief of staff for supply with VII Corps June 1941-July 1943. Chief of staff of Central Pacific Base Command 1943-1945. Brigadier general in November 1944. Assignments after the war included assistant commander of IX Corps, then 45th Division in the Korean War 1952-1953, commanding general of 7th Division in Korea in 1953 and commanding general of 11th Airborne Division 1953-1955. Retired as major general in January 1957. Decorations included the Distinguished Service Cross, Distinguished Service Medal, Legion of Merit, Bronze Star and Air Medal. Died on November 13, 1964.

Smythe, George Winfred (1899-1969) Born on August 4, 1899, in Norristown, Pennsylvania. Commissioned in the infantry from West Point in 1924. Served with the Services of Supply in the North African Theater of Operations early in World War II. Commanding officer of 47th Infantry, 9th Division, then assistant division commander of 9th Division 1943-1945. Brigadier general in May 1945. Assignments after the war included assistant division commander of 1st Division 1949-1951, commanding general of 24th Division in 1952 and 3rd Division in the Korean War 1952-1953, and deputy commanding general of Second Army 1953-1955. Retired as major general in February 1957. Decorations included the Distinguished Service Cross, Distinguished Service Medal, two Silver Stars, the Legion of Merit, Bronze Star and two Purple Hearts. Died on January 16, 1969.

Snyder, Howard McCrum (1881-1970) Born in Cheyenne, Wyoming, on February 7, 1881. Attended the University of Colorado 1899-1901. M.D. from Jefferson Medical College in 1905. Commissioned in the Medical Corps in 1908. Graduated from Army Medical School in 1909. Served in the Philippine Islands 1909-1911 and Puerto Rico June 1929-September 1932. Instructor with the New York National Guard 1932-1936. Medical adviser to the National Guard Bureau 1936-1940. Brigadier general in October 1940. Assistant to the inspector general, U.S. Army 1940-1945. Major general in November 1943. Retired in February 1945. Died on September 22, 1970.

Solbert, Oscar Nathaniel (1885-1958) Born in Sweden on January 22, 1885. Commissioned in the Corps of Engineers from West Point in 1910. Military attache in Norway and Denmark 1918-1919. Resigned in 1926. Recalled to active duty in 1942. Served with SHAEF 1943-1945. Brigadier general in November 1944. Decorations included the Distinguished Service Medal. Died in 1958.

Somers, Richard Herbert (1881-1957) Born on December 8, 1881, in Mantua, New Jersey. Commissioned in the Coast Artillery Corps from West Point in 1907. Instructor there 1914-1916. Assigned to the office of the chief of ordnance 1921-1924. Graduated from Army Industrial College in 1924. M.B.A. from Harvard in 1928. Duty in the office of the chief of ordnance 1932-1936. Brigadier general in October 1940. Again in the office of the chief of ordnance 1940-1942. Retired in June 1942 as colonel. Decorations included the Legion of Merit. Died on January 22, 1957.

Somervell, Brehon Burke (1892-1955) Born on May 9, 1892 in Little Rock, Arkansas. Commissioned in the Corps of Engineers from West Point in 1914. Organized the 5th Reserve Engineers in 1916. Duty with the Punitive Expedition into Mexico 1916-1917. Involved with numerous engineering projects in France 1917-1918. Graduated from Command and General Staff School then the Army War College in 1926. Duty in Turkey 1933-1934 on a comprehensive survey for a five-year plan for the industrializatrion of Turkey. Headed the Works Projects Administration (WPA) in New York City August 1936-November 1940, which included construction of LaGuardia Airport. Assigned to the Quartermaster Corps in charge of the construction division December 1940-November 1941. Assistant chief of staff of the War Department General Staff 1941-1942. Commanding general of Army Service Forces (formerly Services of Supply) as lieutenant general 1942-1944. General in March 1945. Retired in 1948. Decorations included the Distinguished Service Cross, three Distinguished Service Medals and two Legions of Merit. Died on February 13, 1955.

Soule, Robert Homer (1900-1952) Born in Laramie, Wyoming, on February 10, 1900. Attended the University of Wyoming 1916-1918. Commissioned in the infantry in 1918. Served with the 31st Infantry in the AEF then the Philippine Islands 1918-1922. Military attache in Peking 1929-1933. Graduated from the Command and General Staff School in 1940. Assigned to the War Department General Staff 1941-1942. Commanding officer of 188th Paratroop Glider Infantry 1943-1945. Brigadier general in March 1945. Assistant division commander of 38th Infantry Division then 11th Airborne Division 1945-1946. Military attache in Nanking 1946-1950. Major general in August 1950. Commanding general of 3rd Infantry Division 1950-1951. Inspector of infantry at Army Field Forces November 1951 until his death on January 26, 1952. Decorations included the Distinguished Service Cross, two Legions of Merit, the Silver Star, Bronze Star, AM, Purple Heart and Commendation Ribbon.

Spalding, George Redfield (1877-1962) Born in Monroe, Michigan, on January 25, 1877. Commissioned in the Corps of Engineers from West Point in 1901. Duty in the Philippine Islands 1901-1903. Instructor at the Command and General Staff School 1911-1915. Served in the AEF in World War I as commanding officer of 305th Engineers, division engineer with 80th Division and chief engineer in First and Third Army. Graduated from the Army War College in 1920. Commander of Fort Belvoir 1933-1934. Brigadier general in May 1936. Assistant chief of staff at the War Department General Staff 1936-1938. Retired in July 1938. Recalled to active duty May 1941-January 1945 in the office of the chief of staff, U.S. Army then at headquarters of Army Service Forces. Decorations included two Distinguished Service Medals. Died on June 28, 1962.

Spalding, Isaac (1887-1977) Born on December 18, 1887, in Denton, Texas. Commissioned in the cavalry from West Point in 1912. Duty in the Philippine Islands October 1912-September 1915. Graduated from the Command and General Staff School in 1926, the Army War College in 1931 and Naval War College in 1932. Executive officer at 13th Field Artillery, Schofield Barracks, Hawaii September 1938-December 1940. Chief of the miscellaneous branch, personnel division at the War Department General Staff, January 1941-February 1942. Brigadier general in January 1942. Commanding general of 12th Field Artillery Brigade 1942-1943 then 77th Division Artillery 1943-1944. Hospitalized 1944-1945. Commanding general of Fort McPherson in 1946. Retired in July 1946. Decorations included the Legion of Merit and Bronze Star. Died on August 14, 1977.

Spalding, Sidney Parker (1889-1988) Born on August 5, 1889, in Lowell, Massachusetts. Commissioned in the Coast Artillery Corps from West Point in 1912. Wounded in combat while serving with the AEF in World War I. Graduated from Army Industrial College in 1935 and the Army War College in 1936. Duty in the office of the chief of ordnance 1936-1939. Executive officer at Springfield Arsenal 1939-1940. Duty in the office of the under secretary of War 1940-1943. Brigadier general in April 1941. Chief of supply division of the Military Mission to the U.S.S.R. 1943-1945. Major general in 1944. Member of Munitions Board 1945-1949. Retired in August 1949. Recalled to active duty in the office of the secretary of defense 1950-1951. Decorations included the Distinguished Service Medal, Legion of Merit and Purple Heart. Died on December 21, 1988.

Spence, William (1893-1984) Born on June 23, 1893, in Camilla, Georgia. Commissioned in the cavalry from West Point in 1916. Served on the Mexican border with the Punitive Expedition 1916-1917. Commanded a battery, battalion and regiment in the AEF 1917-1918. Instructor at West Point 1919-1923, then Harvard 1924-1928. Professor of military science and tactics at Oregon State Agricultural College 1934-1938. Commanding officer of 8th Field Artillery at Schofield Barracks, Hawaii 1938-1940. Brigadier general in March 1942. Commanding general of 93rd Infantry Division Artillery 1942-1944. Commanding general of 38th Division Artillery 1944-1945. Reverted to colonel in March 1946. Retired in September 1947. Brigadier general on the retired list in 1948. Decorations included two Legions of Merit, two Bronze Stars, the Air Medal and Purple Heart. Died on October 1, 1984.

Spiller, Oliver Loving (1887-1981) Born in Jacksboro, Texas, on November 15, 1887. Commissioned from USNA in 1909. Resigned in 1910. Commissioned in the Coast Artillery Corps in 1910. Duty in the Philippine Islands March 1914-February 1917. Instructor at the School of Fire July-October 1917. Served with the AEF in France April 1918-February 1919. Instructor at Coast Artillery School February 1919-January 1924. Graduated from the Command and General Staff School in 1925 and the Army War College in 1930. Duty in the Panama Canal Zone August 1936-January 1939. Commander of harbor defenses, Eastern New York October 1939-October 1940. Brigadier general in October 1940. Commander of the Antiaircraft Training Center October 1940-February 1941 and 39th Coast Artillery Brigade February 1941-April 1942. Commandant of the Antiaircraft Artillery School April 1942-February 1943 then Camp Stewart February-July 1943. Commanding general of Gulf Sector, Southern Defense Command July 1943-August 1944 and the Carribbean Defense Command August 1944-January 1945. Patient at Walter Reed Army Hospital, then retired in August 1945. Died on September 29, 1981.

Spofford, Charles Merville (1902-1991) Born on March 23, 1902, in St. Louis, Missouri. B.A. from Yale in 1924 and LL.B. from Harvard in 1928. Practiced law in New York City. Commissioned lieutenant colonel in 1942. Served in the European Theater of Operations as chairman of the Joint French-Allied Economic

Committee in 1942 then in the Mediterranean Theater of Operations as a member of the Allied Military Government of Occupied Territories in Sicily and Algiers 1943-1945. Brigadier general in September 1944. Returned to inactive status in December 1945. Decorations included the Distinguished Service Medal and Purple Heart. President of the Metropolitan Opera Association 1946-1950. Died on March 23, 1991.

Spragins, Robert Lily (1890-1964) Born on November 12, 1890, in Huntsville, Alabama. Commissioned in the infantry from West Point in 1913. Served at the invasion of Vera Cruz, Mexico in 1914. Executive officer of the 19th Brigade in the Canal Zone 1922-1925. Graduated from the Command and General Staff School in 1927. Duty in the plans and operations division of the Hawaiian Department 1939-1942. Brigadier general in May 1942. Assigned to the 95th Infantry Division 1942-1943. Major general in May 1943. Commanding general of 44th Division 1944-1945. Retired in August 1945. Decorations included two Distinguished Service Medals, the Silver Star and two Purple Hearts. Died on December 26, 1964.

Spruit, Charles Booth (1886-1954) Born in Council Bluffs, Iowa, on December 26, 1886. B.A. from Illinois College in 1908. M.D. from Harvard in 1915. Commissioned in the Medical Corps in 1920. Graduated from the Army Medical School in 1923. Served at Schofield Barracks, Hawaii 1923-1926. Graduated from the Command and General Staff School in 1937. Duty in the office of the surgeon general 1938-1942. Deputy chief of surgery in the European Theater of Operations May 1942-October 1944. Chief of surgery at the United States Base Sector, United Kingdom 1944-1945. Brigadier general in January 1945. Assigned to headquarters of Army Service Forces 1945-1946. Retired in October 1946. Decorations included the Distinguished Service Medal, Legion of Merit and Bronze Star. Died on July 3, 1954.

Stack, Robert Ignatius (1896-n/a) Born in Amsterdam, New York, on February 1, 1896. Attended Cornell 1916-1917. Commissioned in the infantry in 1917. Served with the 49th Infantry, AEF 1917-1919 and the 31st Infantry in Manila, Philippine Islands 1929-1931. Professor of military science and tactics at Oklahoma Agricultural and Mechanical College 1935-1937. Commanding officer of 4th Tank Company, 22nd Infantry 1937-1939. Battalion commander in 69th Armored Regiment 1940-1941. Combat commander with 1st Armored Division 1942-1944. Brigadier general in June 1943. Assistant division commander of 36th Infantry Division February 1944-December 1945. Reverted to colonel in February 1946. Retired in July 1953. Decorations included the Silver Star, two Legions of Merit, four Bronze Stars and the Purple Heart.

Stadler, John Harry Jr. (1903-1970) Born on February 10, 1903, in Bracketville, Texas. Commissioned in the cavalry from West Point in 1924. Aide to Major General George Grunert at headquarters of the Philippine Department 1937-1939. Graduated from the Command and General Staff School in 1940. Again aide to

Major General George Grunert at headquarters of the Philippine Department July 1940-July 1941. Duty at headquarters of Army Ground Forces 1941-1942. Commanding officer of 12th Cavalry, 1st Cavalry Division 1943-1944. Brigadier general in March 1945. Brigade commander with 1st Cavalry Division 1945-1946. Reverted to colonel in March 1946. Retired in January 1950. Decorations included the Silver Star, Legion of Merit, two Bronze Stars, the Commendation Ribbon and Purple Heart. Died on April 20, 1970.

Stanford, Albert Clinton (1895-1952) Born on March 25, 1895, in Chatsworth, Illinois. Commissioned in the cavalry from West Point in 1917. Instructor at West Point 1918-1919. Transferred to the Signal Corps in 1920. M.S. from Yale in 1926. Professor of military science and tactics at Michigan State University 1936-1940. Graduated from the Command and General Staff School in 1941. Personnel officer with I Corps June-September 1941 then at headquarters II Corps Area Septemeber 1941-April 1942. Brigadier general in July 1942. Commanding general of artillery in 34th and 75th Infantry Divisions August 1942-January 1946. Retired as colonel in January 1946. Brigadier general on the retired list in 1948. Decorations included the Legion of Merit and Bronze Star. Died on November 7, 1952.

Stark, Alexander Newton Jr. (1896-1968) Born in Fort Sam Houston, Texas, on January 4, 1896. Commissioned in the infantry in 1917. Served with the 18th and 61st Regiments in the AEF at the St. Mihiel and Meuse-Argonne offensives1918-1919, with the 15th Infantry in Tientsin 1920-1921 and the 31st Infantry in Manila March 1921-October 1922. Professor of military science and tactics at the University of California 1923-1926. Graduated from the Command and General Staff School in 1928. Instructor with the California National Guard 1936-1940. Executive officer, then commanding officer of 26th Infantry September 1940-July 1942. Brigadier general in March 1943. Commanding general of the Replacement Ground School, Birmingham, Alabama March in 1943. Assistant division commander of 42nd Infantry Division, then 43rd Infantry Division 1943-1945. Retired in February 1946. Decorations included the Distinguished Service Cross and two Silver Stars. Died on July 15, 1968.

Starr, Rupert Edison (1896-1976) Born in Angels Camp, California, on June 24, 1896. Attended the University of California 1915-1916. Commissioned in the Coast Artillery Corps, Officers Reserve Corps in 1918. Served with the 59th Coast Artillery in the Philippine Islands December 1920-August 1923 and the 64th Coast Artillery in Hawaii June 1927-December 1930. Graduated from the Command and General Staff School in 1936. Instructor at the Coast Artillery School June 1936-September 1938. Graduated from the Army War College in 1939 and the Naval War College in 1940. Duty in the office of the chief of coast artillery June 1940-March 1942 then at headquarters of Army Ground Forces March-June 1942 and the War Department General Staff June 1942-January 1943. Brigadier general in December 1942. Assigned to the 35th Antiaircraft Artillery Brigade in North Africa January-December 1943 then headquarters of

Army Ground Forces December 1943-June 1945. Antiaircraft officer for Far Eastern Air Forces June 1945-June 1946. Retired in May 1950. Decorations included the Legion of Merit and Commendation Ribbon. Died on November 15, 1976.

Stayer, Morrison Clay (1882-n/a) Born in Roaring Springs, Pennsylvania, on July 12, 1882. B.A. from Lafayette College in 1903. M.D. from Jefferson Medical College in 1906. Commissioned in the Medical Corps in 1908. Graduated from Army Medical School in 1909. Served in the Philippine Islands 1910-1912. Chief health officer for American Occupation Forces in Coblenz, Germany 1919-1921. Professor at the Medical Field Service School 1922-1926. Graduated from the Army War College in 1927. Instructor at the Infantry School 1927-1932. Assistant commandant of Carlisle Barracks 1932-1936. Post surgeon at Fort Riley 1936-1939. Health officer, then chief health officer in the Panama Canal Zone 1939-1941. Chief surgeon for the Caribbean Command 1941-1944 then the North African Theater of Operations 1944-1945. Major general in Novemeber 1943. Chief public health and welfare officer for the military government of Germany from 1945.

Stearns, Cuthbert Powell (1885-1969) Born on August 14, 1885, in Elizabeth New Jersey. Commissioned in the cavalry from West Point in 1909. Instructor at West Point November 1912-June 1916. Served with the 4th Cavalry in Hawaii April-October 1917. Graduated from the Command and General Staff School in 1923. Again instructor at West Point June 1923-June 1927. Instructor at the Field Artillery School November 1927-June 1929. Graduated from the Army War College in 1931. Chief of staff of 1st Cavalry Division February 1938-January 1939. Commanding officer of 5th Cavalry January 1939-July 1940. Chief of staff of 6th Infantry Division July 1940-Decemmber 1941. Assistant to the chief of staff, III Corps Area December 1941-July 1942. Military adviser in U.S. Army organization and problems at the School of Military Government July 1942-September 1943. Assigned to the European Theater of Operations September 1943-July 1945. Brigadier general in September 1944. Retired in February 1946. Decorations included the Distinguished Service Medal, Legion of Merit and Bronze Star. Died on June 6, 1969.

Stewart, George C. (1902-) Born in Selma, Alabama, on May 28, 1902. Commissioned in the infantry from West Point in 1923. Graduated from Command and General Staff School in 1938. Assigned to the War Department General Staff 1941-1942. Transferred to the Transportation Corps in 1942. Chief of transportation for U.S. Forces North Africa 1943-1945. Brigadier general in September 1943. Assignments after the war included assistant division commander of 2nd Infantry Division in the Korean War 1950-1951. Retired as major general in 1954. Decorations included two Distinguished Service Medals, two Silver Stars, the Legion of Merit and Bronze Star.

Stewart, Gilbert Henry (1878-1957) Born in Wichita, Kansas, on November 12, 1878. Commissioned in the infantry from West Point in 1902. Graduated from the Army War College in 1922. Commanding officer of Hawaii Ordnance Depot 1928-1931. Graduated from Army Industrial College in 1932. Commander of Watervliet (New York) Arsenal 1932-1938 then Springfield (Massachusetts) Armory 1938-1942. Brigadier general in October 1940. Retired in June 1942. Decorations included the Legion of Merit. Died on August 4, 1957.

Stewart, LeRoy Judson (1900-1983) Born on May 3, 1900, in South Carolina. Commissioned in the field artillery from West Point in 1922. Member of the Olympic riding team in 1932. Chief of staff of 7th Division 1943-1944. Brigadier general in May 1944. Commanding general of 7th Division Artillery 1944-1946. Reverted to colonel in March 1946. Retired in April 1951. Decorations included the Silver Star, three Legions of Merit and the Bronze Star. Died on January 13, 1983.

Stilwell, Joseph Warren (1883-1946) Born on March 19, 1883, in Palatka, Florida. Commissioned in the infantry from West Point in 1904. Served in the Philippines 1904-1906 and 1911-1912. Deputy chief of staff for intelligence in IV Corps, AEF in 1918. Studied Chinese language in Peking 1920-1923. Graduated from the Command and General Staff School in 1926. With 15th Infantry in Tientsin, China, 1926-1928. Chief of staff of U.S. Forces China 1928-1929. Instructor at the Infantry School under Lieutenant Colonel George C. Marshall 1929-1933. Military attache in China and Thailand 1935-1939. Brigadier general in May 1939. Commander of 3rd Infantry Brigade, then 7th Infantry Division 1939-1941. Major general in October 1940. Commander of II Corps July 1941-February 1942. Lieutenant general in February 1942. Commander of U.S. forces in China-Burma-India Theater of Operations and chief of staff to General in issimo Chiang Kai-shek, later deputy Supreme Allied Commander in China-Burma-India Theater of Operations March 1942-October 1944. General in August 1944. Relations between Stilwell and Chiang had been strained from the beginning and in October 1944 he was recalled to the U.S. at the insistence of the Nationalist Chinese leader. Chief of Army Ground Forces January-May 1945. Commanding general of Tenth Army June-October 1945. Assignments after the war included ommander of Western Defense Command December 1945-March 1946 and commanding general of Sixth Army March 1946 until his death on October 12, 1946. Decorations included the Distinguished Service Cross, two Distinguished Service Medals and the Legion of Merit.

Stivers, Charles Paul (1891-1966) Born in Downers Grove, Illinois, on October 10, 1891. B.S. from the University of Wisconsin in 1913. Commissioned in the infantry in 1916. Served in France in World War I July 1918-June 1919. Intelligence officer with the 27th Infantry in Hawaii March 1921-March 1924. Graduated from the Command and General Staff School in 1928. Instructor at the Infantry School June 1928-July 1932. Instructor at the Command and General Staff School July 1934-August 1935. Graduated from the Army War College in 1936.

Professor of military science and tactics at Ponoma College August 1936-February 1940. Personnel officer in the Philippine Department February 1940-March 1942. Accompanied General Douglas MacArthur to Australia in March 1942. Brigadier general in June 1942. Assistant chief of staff for personnel, then deputy chief of staff for U.S. Army Forces Far East 1942-1945. Major general in September 1943. Retired in September 1946. Decorations included two Distinguished Service Medals and the Silver Star. Died on June 2, 1966.

Stockton, Edward Alexander Jr. (1886-1948) Born in Philadelphia, Pennsylvania, on April 22, 1886. Commissioned in the Coast Artillery Corps from West Point in 1908. Served with the AEF 1917-1919. Graduated from the Command and General Staff School in 1928. Duty with the 59th Coast Artillery at Fort Mills, Hawaii October 1928-August 1930. Graduated from the Army War College in 1931. Commanding officer of Corozal Post, Canal Zone 1936-1937. Duty with 6th Coast Artillery October 1940-July 1941. Brigadier general in July 1941. Commander of harbor defenses in San Francisco 1941-1942. Commanding general of Antiaircraft Replacement Training Center at Camp Wallace July 1942-July 1943 then at Camp Stewart 1943-1944. Member of the secretary of war's Separation Board 1944-1945. Retired in March 1945. Died on July 13, 1948.

Stockton, Marcellus Lowry Jr. (1893-1985) Born on July 16, 1893, in Gridley, Kansas. Attended the University of Kansas in 1918. Commissioned in the cavalry in 1918. Assigned to the 4th Cavalry at Schofield Barracks, Hawaii 1918-1919. Professor of military science and tactics at Oregon Agricultural College 1927-1929. Instructor with the 106th Cavalry 1930-1934. Graduated from the Command and General Staff School in 1939. Assistant executive officer for supply at the Cavalry School October 1939-July 1940. Inspector general at 7th Division 1940-1941. Served with Fourth Army 1941-1942. Assistant commander of the Northwestern Sector, Western Defense Command at Fort Lewis December 1942 until retirement in June 1944. Brigadier general in February 1943.
Retired in June 1944. Died on February 11, 1985.

Stokes, John Harrison Jr. (1895-1968) Born on October 27, 1895, in Freehold, New Jersey. Commissioned in the infantry from West Point in 1918. Served with the 8th Infantry in Coblenz, Germany 1919-1923. Assistant Professor of military science and tactics at Mississippi State College 1935-1938. Assistant to the assistant chief of staff for intelligence at Third Army August 1940-December 1941. Assistant chief of staff, then chief of staff, finally assistant division commander of 2nd Division 1942-1945. Brigadier general in March 1945. Chief of staff of IX Corps July 1945-February 1946. Reverted to colonel in March 1946. Retired as major general in November 1956. Decorations included two Silver Stars, two Legions of Merit and the Bronze Star. Died on November 9, 1968.

Stoner, Frank Emil (1894-1966) Born in Vancouver, Washington on December 25, 1894. Attended West Point 1915-1916. Commissioned in the Philippine Scouts in 1917. Served in the Philippines 1917-1924. Professor of military science and tactics at Dallas High School 1922-1923. Headed the War department message center 1928-1932. Graduated from Command and General Staff School in 1939 and the Army Industrial College in 1940. Signal officer for V Corps in 1940 and Third Army in 1941. Assigned to the office of the chief signal officer as head of the Army Communications Service from February 1942. Major general in November 1944. Retired in 1948. Decorations included the Distinguished Service Medal. Died on October 27, 1966.

Stratton, James Hobson (1898-1984) Born on June 7, 1898, in Stonington, Connecticut. Commissioned in the Corps of Engineers from West Point in 1920. B.S. Rensselaer Polytechnic Institute in June 1922. Served in the Panama Canal Zone October 1924-September 1927. Instructor with the New Jersey National Guard September 1927-September 1931. Chief of the engineering branch, construction division, office of the chief of engineers December 1941-November 1943. Chief of operations at Services of Suppply, European Theater of Operations November 1943-February 1945. Brigadier general in May 1944. Deputy assistant chief of staff of the European Theater of Operations February-April 1945. Assistant chief of engineers, office of the chief of engineers April 1945-February 1946. Retired in July 1949. Decorations included the Distinguished Service Medal and Legion of Merit. Died on March 16, 1984.

Stroh, Donald Armpriester (1892-1953) Born in Harrisburg, Pennsylvania, on November 3, 1892. B.S. from Michigan Agricultural College in 1915. Commissioned in the cavalry in 1917. Intelligence officer with Fourth Army and aide to Lieutenant General John L. DeWitt July 1940-May 1941. Military observer in England May-July 1941. Again at Fourth Army July 1941-February 1942. With 85th Infantry Division February-August 1942. Brigadier general in July 1942. Assistant division commander of 9th Infantry Division August 1942-July 1944. Major general in August 1944. Commanding general of 106th Infantry Division 1945-1947. Retired in November 1947. Decorations included the Distinguished Service Medal, two Legions of Merit, the Bronze Star and Commendation Ribbon. Died on December 20, 1953.

Strong, Alden George (1885-1964) Born in Goddard, Kansas, on January 1, 1885. B.S. from Kansas State Agricultural College in 1911. Commissioned in the Coast Artillery Corps in 1911. Served with the Postal Express Service in France and the Depot Quartermaster in Germany January 1919-July 1922. Instructor in the Coast Artillery School September 1923-January 1924. Graduated from the Command and General Staff School in 1925. Instructor at the Command and General Staff School August 1928-August 1932. Graduated from the Army War College in 1933 and the Naval War College in 1934. Deptuy chief of staff of First Army July 1937-November 1938. Chief of the plans section in the office of the chief of coast artilley November 1938-April 1941. Commander of Bermuda Base Command April 1941-July 1944. Brigadier general in September 1941. Commanding general of harbor defenses at Portland, Maine July 1944-September

1946. Retired in September 1946. Decorations included the Legion of Merit. Died on August 4, 1964.

Strong, Frederick Smith Jr. (1887-1986) Born on May 16, 1887, in Orchard Lake, Michigan. Commissioned in the Corps of Engineers from West Point in 1910. Served with 7th and 2nd Divisions in the AEF in 1918. With the Services of Supply 1918-1919. Resigned in 1920. Colonel in the quartermaster reserve in 1941. Zone constructing quartermaster in the Fourth Zone in 1941. With the War Department General Staff in 1942. In the office of the chief of engineers 1942-1943. Chief engineer for Services of Supply in the China-Burma-India Theater of Operations in 1943. In the hospital on sick leave December 1943-March 1944. Commander of Northwest Service Command 1944-1945. Brigadier general in September 1944. At headquarters of Army Service Forces in 1945. Commanding general of United Kingdom Base Command August-December 1945. Returned to inactive status in June 1946. Decorations included the Distinguished Service Medal and Legion of Merit. Died in 1986.

Strong, George Veazey (1880-1946) Born in Chicago, Illinois, on March 4, 1880. Commissioned in the cavalry from West Point in 1904. LL.B. from Northwestern University in 1916. Graduated from the Army War College in 1924. Military adviser to the Disarmament Commission 1930-1934. Brigadier general in June 1938. Assistant chief of staff, U.S. Army 1938-1941. Major general in May 1941. Commanding general of VIII Corps May 1941-June 1942. Chief of military intelligence 1942- 1944. Retired in February 1944. Decorations included two Distinguished Service Medals, the Legion of Merit and Purple Heart. Died on January 10, 1946.

Strong, Robert William (1890-1975) Born on March 12, 1890, in Kingsville, Ohio. Commissioned in the cavalry from West Point in 1915. Commanded 1st Battalion, 77th Field Artillery through the St. Mihiel and Meuse-Argonne offensives and with the Army of Occupation in the Rhineland May 1918-July 1919. Instructor at West Point July 1919-June 1923. Graduated from the Command and General Staff School in June 1928 and the Army War College in June 1934. Served with the War Department General Staff August 1936-July 1940. Executive officer of 1st Armored Regiment, 1st Armored Division July 1940-April 1941. Commanding officer of 3rd Armored Regiment April-July 1942. Chief of staff of U.S. Army Forces in Africa in 1942. Brigadier general in February 1943. Commanding general of Cavalry Replacement Training Center February 1943-April 1945. Chief of U.S. Army Mission to Peru in 1945. Reverted to colonel April 30, 1946. Retired in March 1950. Decorations included the Legion of Merit. Died on October 16, 1975.

Stuart, LaRhett Livingston (1892-1967) Born January 17, 1892, in South Bethlehem, Pennsylvania. Commissioned in the Coast Artillery Corps from West Point in 1914. Instructor at West Point August 1917-August 1922. Served in the Panama Canal Zone June 1923-September 1926. Graduated from the Command

and General Staff School in June 1928. Duty with 60th Coast Artillery, then harbor defense supply officer in the Philippine Islands October 1932-January 1935. Graduated from the Army War College in June 1938. Assigned to the War Department General Staff June 1938-March 1942. Brigadier general in March 1942. Commanding general of 43rd Coast Artillery Brigade March-April 1942, Antiaircraft Artillery Training Center April 1942-February 1943, Antiaircraft Replacemnt Training Center February-December 1943, 66th Antiaircraft Artillery Brigade December 1943-1945. Duty at headquarters of Army Ground Forces August-September 1945. Reverted to colonel in February 1946. Retired in July 1951. Decorations included the Legion of Merit. Died on September 4, 1967.

Sturdevant, Clarence L. (1885-1958) Born on August 1, 1885, in Neillsville, Wisconsin. Commissioned in the Corps of Engineers from West Point in 1908. Served in the Panama Canal Zone October-December 1911, the Phillipine Islands December 1911-August 1913 and on Guam August 1913-August 1914. Assistant department engineer in the Philippine Department August-October 1914. Instructor at the Command and General Staff School June 1926-August 1930. Graduated from the Army War College in 1931. Department enginner in the Philippine Islands March 1935-March 1937. Brigadier general in October 1940. Assistant chief of the Corps of Engineers October 1940-May 1944. Commanding general of New Guinea Base Section, Services of Supply June 1944-July 1945. Major general in January 1945. Deputy chief of staff of U.S. Army Forces Western Pacific 1945-1946. Retired in September 1946. Decorations included the Legion of Merit and Bronze Star. Died on March 31, 1958.

Sturgis, Samuel Davis Jr. (1897-1964) Born on July 16, 1897, in St. Paul, Minnesota. Commissioned in the Corps of Engineers from West Point in 1918. Commander of 14th Engineers in the Philippines 1926-1929 and the 9th Engineers at Fort Riley 1929-1933. Chief engineer for Sixth Army early in the war. Brigadier general in November 1944. Assignments after the war included commanding general of 6th Armored Division 1951-1952 and chief of engineers, U.S. Army 1953-1955. Retired as lieutenant general in September 1956. Decorations included two Distinguished Sservice Medals, the Silver Star, Legion of Merit, Bronze Star and Air Medal. Died on July 5, 1964.

Styer, Wilhelm Delp (1893-1975) Born on July 22, 1893, in Salt Lake City, Utah. Commissioned in the Corps of Engineers from West Point in 1916. Served with the Punitive Expedition into Mexico 1916-1917 and the AEF 1917-1918. Assistant instructor with the New York National Guard in 1920 then the Massachusetts National Guard 1921-1922. B.S. from Massachusetts Institute of Technology in 1922. Engineer with the American Battle Monuments Commission in Europe 1928-1931. Assistant engineer at the Panama Canal 1936-1939. Deputy chief of construction at the War Department 1940-1942. Brigadier general in March 1942, major general in August 1942. Deputy commanding general and chief of staff of Army Service Forces 1942-1945. Lieutenant general in November 1944. Commanding general of U.S. Army Forces in the Western Pacific 1945-

1946. Retired in April 1947. Decorations included two Distinguished Service Medals. Died on February 26, 1975.

Sullivan, Joseph Pescia (1894-1977) Born on January 7, 1894, in San Francisco. Commissioned in the infantry from West Point in 1917. Served with 6th Infantry, AEF 1918-1919. Saw action at St. Mihiel and Meuse-Argonne and wounded at Romagne-Cunel. Military attache in Tokyo 1922-1925. M.B.A. from Harvard in 1934. Quartermaster supply officer at the Panama Canal 1934-1936. Camp quartermaster at Camp Shelby 1940-1942. Quartermaster for Fifth Army 1943-1945. Brigadier general in February 1944. Reverted to colonel in March 1946. Retired in December 1953. Decorations included the Distinguished Service Medal, Legion of Merit and Purple Heart. Died on November 30, 1977.

Sultan, Daniel Isom (1885-1947) Born on December 9, 1885, in Oxford, Mississippi. Attended the University of Mississippi. Commissioned in the Corps of Engineers from West Point in 1903. Instructor at West Point 1912-1916. Duty in Philippine Islands September 1916-March 1918. Assigned to the War Department General Staff March 1918-June 1919 and September 1919-August 1922. Graduated from the Command and General Staff School in 1923 and the Army War College in 1926. In charge of an interoceanic canal survey and in command of U.S. Army troops in Nicaragua August 1929-July 1931. Commanded 2nd Engineers August 1938-June 1939. Brigadier general in December 1938. Commander of 22nd Infantry Brigade in Hawaii June 1939-April 1941. Major general in April 1941. Commanding general of the Hawaiian Division March-April 1941 then the 38th Division May 1941-April 1942. Commanding general of VIII Army Corps April 1942-November 1943. Lieutenant general in September 1943. Deputy commander in chief of the China-Burma-India Theater of Operations November 1943-November 1944. Commander of Chinese armies in Burma November 1944-July 1945. Inspector general of the Army from July 1945. Sultan was the first Army man to receive four Distinguished Service Medals. Died on January 14, 1947.

Summers, Owen (1890-1971) Born in Portland, Oregon, on May 23, 1890, the son of Brigadier General Owen Summers. Commissioned in the infantry reserve in 1917. Served with the 364th Infantry in France in the Ypress-Lys, St. Mihiel and Meuse-Argonne engagements July 1918- March 1919. Aide to Major General William H. Johnston March 1919-July 1920. Assigned to the 45th Infantry in the Philippine Islands January 1928-February 1930. Professor of military science and tactics at Indiana University February 1930-August 1933. Graduated from the Command and General Staff School in June 1935. Professor of military science and tactics at Hill Military Academy September 1936-August 1938. Graduated from the Army War College in June 1939. Personnel officer at Trinidad Base Command in 1941. Brigadier general in September 1942. Assistant division commander of 80th Infantry Division November 1943-March 1945. Commanding general of Twelfth Reinforcement Depot in France March 1945 until he reverted to colonel in March 1946. Retired in June 1947. Decorations included the Silver

Star, two Legions of Merit, the Bronze Star and Purple Heart. Died on April 2, 1971.

Surles, Alexander Day (1886-1947) Born in Milwaukee, Wisconsin, on August 14, 1886. Attended the University of Michigan 1906-1907. Commissioned in the cavalry from West Point in 1911. Served with the 15th Cavalry in the Philippines 1915-1917. Instructor at West Point 1919-1923. Graduated from the Command and General Staff School in 1925 and the Army War College in 1935. Chief of the public relations branch, then the military intelligence division at the War Department General Staff 1935-1939. Commanding officer of the 1st Armored Regiment 1939-1940. With 1st Armored Division 1940-1941. Brigadier general in July 1941. Director of the bureau of public relations in the War Department 1941-1945. Major general in February 1942. Member of the chief of staff's advisory group 1945-1947. Died on December 5, 1947. Decorations included the Distinguished Service Medal.

Sutherland, Richard Kerens (1893-1966) Born in Hancock, Maryland, on November 27, 1893. B.A. from Yale in 1916. Commissioned in the infantry in 1916. Served with the 2nd Division in the AEF. Instructor at the Infantry School August 1920-May 1923. Professor of military science and tactics at the Shattuck School May 1923-August 1927. Graduated from the Command and General Staff School in 1928 and the Ecole Superieure de Guerre in Paris in July 1930 and the Army War College in 1933. Served at Tientsin, China July 1937-March 1938. Duty at the War Department General Staff 1933-1937. Chief of staff of the military mission to the Philippines 1938-1941. Brigadier general in July 1941, major general in December 1941. Chief of staff to MacArthur in the Pacific July 1941-December 1945. Lieutenant general in February 1944. Retired in November 1946. Decorations included two Distinguished Service Crosses, two Distinguished Service Medals and the Silver Star. Died on June 25, 1966.

Sverdrup, Leif John (1897-1976) Born on January 11, 1897, in Sulen, Norway. B.A. from Augsburg College in 1918 and B.S. from the University of Minnesota in 1921. Consulting engineer 1928-1942. Commissioned colonel in the Corps of Engineers in 1942. Chief of the construction section, office of the chief enginer, Southwest Pacific Area May-December 1942. Director of construction in the Southwest Pacific Area January 1943-February 1945. Brigadier general in May 1944. Commanding general of the Engineer Construction Command and consultant on engineer affairs, European Theater of Operations February 1945-April 1946. Major general in January 1945. Decorations included the Silver Star, Legion of Merit, Distinguished Service Medal and Purple Heart. Died on January 2, 1976.

Swartz, Charles Harlan (1898-1973) Born on November 27, 1898, in Pierre, South Dakota. Commissioned in the infantry from West Point in 1920. Served with the 11th Field Artillery, Schofield Barracks, Hawaii February 1924-February 1927. Instructor at the University of Utah ROTC September 1933-September

1938. Commanding officer of 1st Field Artillery Battalion September 1938-April 1941 and 53rd Field Artillery Battalion February-August 1942. Operations officer for 6th Infantry Division Artillery August 1942-January 1943. Executive officer of 6th Infantry Division 1943-1945. Brigadier general in May 1945. Commanding general of 25th Infantry Division Artillery 1945-1946. Reverted to colonel in February 1946. Retired in April 1957. Decorations included three Legions of Merit and the Commendation Ribbon. Died on August 23, 1973.

Swatland, Donald Clinton (1895-1962) Born on May 5, 1895, in Newark, New Jersey. B.A. from Princeton in 1916. Served in the AEF in World War I, then resigned and joined the Army Reserve. LL.B. from Harvard in 1921. Practiced law in New York City 1921-1942. Called to active duty as lieutenant colonel in 1942. Chief of the procurement division at Air Technical Service Command, Wright Field 1942-1945. Brigadier general in March 1945. Died in 1962.

Sweet, Joseph Burton (1892-1974) Born in Denver, Colorado, on October 22, 1892. B.S. from Kansas State Agricultural College in 1917. Commissioned in the infantry in 1917. Graduated from the Command and General Staff School in 1933 and the Army War College in 1937. Served at Fort William McKinley, Philippine Islands September 1920-August 1922. Professor of military science and tactics at Fairmount College, Kansas August 1922-August 1926. Instructor at the Infantry School May 1927-May 1931. Duty with the 21st Infantry Brigade in Hawaii in 1936. Assigned to headquarters of VIII Corps Area May 1937-July 1941. Duty in the office of the chief of infantry July 1941-March 1942, at headquarters of Army Ground Forces March-December 1942 and headquarters of Services of Supply December 1942-October 1943. Brigadier general in April 1943. Director of the motor transport service, Persian Gulf Command October 1943-January 1945. Assigned to headquarters of Army Ground Forces in 1945. Retired in June 1948. Decorations included the Legion of Merit. Died on January 16, 1974.

Swift, Innis Palmer (1882-1953) Born in Fort Laramie, Wyoming, on February 7, 1882. Commissioned in the cavalry from West Point in 1904. Served in Mexico during the Punitive Expedition 1916-1917 and in the AEF during World War I. Graduated from the Command and General Staff School in 1923, the Army War College in 1930 and Army Industrial College in 1931. Commanding officer of 8th Cavalry 1936-1939 then commander of 2nd Cavalry Brigade 1939-1941. Brigadier general in October 1940, major general in April 1941. Commanding general of 1st Cavalry Division 1941-1944 then I Corps 1944-1945. Retired in February 1946. Decorations included two Distinguished Service Medals, the Silver Star and Legion of Merit. Died on November 3, 1953.

Swift, Ira Platt (1898-1987) Born on February 8, 1898, in Chicara, Mississippi. Commissioned in the infantry from West Point in 1918. Served with the 8th and 26th Cavalry Regiments at Camp Stotsenburg, Philippine Islands May 1921-May 1924. Instructor at the Cavalry School 1928-1933. Graduated from the Command and General Staff School in August 1935. Instructor at West Point June 1936-

September 1938. Graduated from the Army War College in June 1939. Assigned to the War Department General Staff June 1939-July 1942. Commander of 14th Armored Regiment July 1942-November 1943. Chief of operations at 9th Armored Division 1943-1944. Deputy commander of 82nd Airborne Division 1944-1945. Brigadier general in March 1945. Duty with the War Department General Staff 1945-1947. Assignments after the war included commander of 25th Division 1951-1952 and commanding general of II Corps, then V Corps 1952-1954. Retired as major general in June 1954. Decorations included the Distinguished Service Medal, Silver Star, two Legions of Merit, two Bronze Stars and the Commendation Ribbon. Died on July 29, 1987.

Swing, Joseph May (1894-1984) Born on February 28, 1894, in Jersey City, New Jersey. Commissioned in the field artillery from West Point in 1915. Served with the Punitive Expedition into Mexico 1916-1917. During World War I assigned to the 1st Infantry Division and as aide-de-camp to General Peyton C. March 1918-1919. Duty with the 11th Field Artillery at Schoefield Barracks, Hawaii February 1921-March 1925. Graduated from the Command and General Staff School in 1927. Instructor at the Field Artillery School 1927-1931. Chief of the war plans section, office of the chief of field artillery July 1933-June 1934. Graduated from the Army War College in June 1935. Chief of staff of 2nd Division July 1938-December 1940. Commanding officer of 1st Cavalry Division Artillery January 1941-January 1942. Brigadier general in February 1942. Organized and commanded the artillery of the 82nd Division 1942-1943. Major general in February 1943. Activated and commanded the 11th Airborne Division 1943-1947, where he conducted the first airlift of a complete divison by parachute planes and gliders and the first mass landing at night of parachute and glider troops. This convinced the War Department that employment of airborne forces in division size was practicable and desirable. Assignments after the war included commanding general of I Corps February 1948-January 1949, commandant of the Army War College 1950-1951 and commanding general of Sixth Army as lieutenant general 1951-1954. Retired in February 1954. Decorations included the Distinguished Service Cross, Distinguished Service Medal, three Silver Stars, the Legion of Merit, three Bronze Stars, two AMs and the Commendation Ribbon. Served as head of the Bureau of Immigration and Naturalization 1954-1962. Died on December 9, 1984.

Talbot, Ralph Jr. (1884-1965) Born in Denver, Colorado, on June 18, 1884. Commissioned in the cavalry from West Point in 1905. Served on the Mexican border 1914-1915 and with the Motor Transport Corps in World War I. Duty with the army of occupation in Germany 1919-1923. Graduated from the Command and General Staff School in 1925 and the Army War College in 1928. Instructor at the Command and General Staff School in 1932. Chief of staff of 5th Division 1939-1940 then VI Corps in 1940. Brigadier general in October 1940. Commanding general of 6th Division Artillery 1940-1941. Commanding general of Trinidad Base Command from April 1941. Retired in March 1946. Decorations included the Legion of Merit and three Commendation Ribbons. Died on April 18, 1965.

Tansey, Patrick Henry (1894-1976) Born on January 26, 1894, in Mount Vernon, Indiana. B.A. from Christian Brothers College in 1914. Commissioned in the Corps of Engineers in 1918. Assistant professor of military science and tactics at Oregon State College 1920-1924. Instructor at West Point 1928-1932. Assistant public works administrator in Hawaii 1932-1935. Assistant engineer commissioner for the District of Columbia 1936-1940. Commander of 12th Engineers, 8th Division 1940-1941. Assistant engineer at GHQ, U.S. Army 1941-1942. Brigadier general in December 1942. At the War Department General Staff 1942-1943. Member of the Munitions Assignment Board in 1944. Deputy commander of the Ryukyus Islands in 1945. Retired as major general in May 1953. Decorations included the Distinguished Service Medal and Legion of Merit. Died on February 3, 1976.

Tate, Foster Joseph (1896-1985) Born on April 17, 1896, in Eunice, Alabama. Commissioned in the field artillery from West Point in 1919. Professor of military science and tactics at VMI August 1928-July 1933. Student, then instructor at the Command and General Staff School 1933-1937. Instructor at West Point 1939-1940. Duty in the operations and training divisions at the War Department General Staff 1940-1942. In the operations division at Army Ground Forces 1942-1943. Brigadier general in March 1943. Commanding general of 75th Division Artillery 1943-1944 then 34th Division Artillery 1944-1945. With the mobilization division of Army Service Forces 1945-1946. Military attache in Paris 1946-1949. Retired in July 1949. Decorations included two Legions of Merit, the Bronze Star and Commendation Ribbon. Died on March 11, 1985.

Tate, Ralph Hamilton (1899-1977) Born on June 27, 1899, in McBain, Michigan. Enlisted service during World War I. Commissioned in the Chemical Warfare Service in 1920. Served at Schofield Barracks, Hawaii August 1923-November 1925. Instructor at Chemical Warfare School August 1930-October 1931. Commanded a chemical company in the Philippine Islands October 1931-October 1932 then chemical officer of the Philippine Division and gas officer at Fort Mills 1932-1934. Graduated from Army Industrial College in July 1938 and the Army War College in June 1939. Assigned to the supply divison at the War Department General Staff June 1939-May 1941. Executive officer to the assistant secretary of war May 1941-September 1942. Chief of staff and deputy commander of the Atlantic Base Section in North Africa September 1942-August 1943. Assistant chief of staff for supply at headquarters Fifth Army August 1943-December 1944. Brigadier general in January 1944. Deputy chief of staff for supply with Fifteenth Army Group in Italy December 1944-June 1945. Deputy commanding general of U.S. Forces in Austria from June 1945. Retired in July 1947. Decorations included two Distinguished Service Medals, the Legion of Merit, Bronze Star and Commendation Ribbon. Died on June 18, 1977.

Taylor, George Arthur (1899-1969) Born on February 14, 1899, in Flat Rock, Illinois. Commissioned in the infantry from West Point in 1922. Served with the 35th Infantry at Schofield Barracks, Hawaii July 1924-September 1927. Graduated from the Command and General Staff School in June 1938. Duty with the 57th Infantry in the Philippine Islands 1938-November 1940. Intelligence officer for the 16th Infantry November 1940-June 1941. Assistant chief of staff of the Caribbean Force June-July 1941. Instructor at the Infantry School July 1941-August 1942. Assigned to the North African Theater of Operations August 1942-January 1943. Commanding officer of 26th Infantry, then 16th Infantry, 1st Infantry Division 1943-1944. Brigadier general in August 1944. Commanding general of 4th, then 1st Infantry Divisions 1944-1945. Retired in October 1946. Decorations included the Distinguished Service Medal, Legion of Merit, Bronze Star and Purple Heart. Died on December 3, 1969.

Taylor, James (1894-1969) Born in Milburn, New Jersey, on October 6, 1894. B.S. from VMI in 1917. Commissioned in the field artillery reserve in 1917. Served with the field artillery in the AEF in World War I. Professor of military science and tactics at the University of Kentucky 1924-1928. Graduated from the Command and General Staff School in 1933. Duty with 27th Infantry in Hawaii 1933-1935. Graduated from the Army War College in 1937. Assigned to the personnel division at the War Department General Staff 1939-1941. Brigadier general in June 1942. Chief of staff of 1st Armored Division August 1941-June 1942 then 6th Armored Division June 1942-September 1944. Reverted to lieutenant colonel in September 1944 and retired in August 1948. Decorations included the Bronze Star, Commendation Ribbon and Purple Heart. Died on May 22, 1969.

Taylor, Maxwell Davenport (1901-1987) Born on August 26, 1901, in Keytesville, Missouri. Commissioned in the Corps of Enginners from West Point in 1922. Instructor at West Point 1927-1932. Graduated from the Command and General Staff School in 1935 and the Army War College in 1940. Commander of the 12th Field Artillery Battalion 1940-1941. Assistant secretary of the War Department General Staff 1941-1942. Brigadier general in December 1942. Chief of staff of 82nd Infantry Division 1942-1943. Member of Allied Control Commission in Italy 1943-1944. Major general in May 1944. Commanding general of 101st Airborne Division 1944-1945. Assignments after the war included superintendent of West Point September 1945-January 1949, chief of staff of U.S. Forces in Europe 1949-1951, deputy chief of staff, U.S. Army 1951-1953, commanding general of Eighth Army in the Korean War 1953-1954, commander of U.S. Army Forces in the Far East 1954-1955, commander in chief of United Nations Command in Korea in 1955 and chief of staff, U.S. Army June 1955 until retirement in 1959. Recalled to active duty as military representative to President Kennedy, then chairman of the Joint Chiefs of Staff 1961-1964. Retired again to become ambassador to South Vietnam 1964-1965. Special consultant to the President 1965-1969. Decorations included the Distinguished Service Cross, three Distinguished Service Medals, two Silver Stars, the Legion of Merit, Bronze Star and

Purple Heart. Author *The Uncertain Trumpet* (1959), *Responsibility and Response* (1967) and *Swords and Plowshares* (1972). Died on April 19, 1987.

Taylor, Victor Vaughan (1893-1944) Born in Stockton, California, on July 24, 1893. Commissioned in the cavalry from West Point in 1915. Served with the Punitive Expedition into Mexico 1916-1917 and the 7th Division, AEF in World War I. Instructor at the Cavalry School February 1921-June 1922. Graduated from the Command and General Staff School in 1923. Instructor at West Point September 1923-January 1924. Duty at Fort Mills, Philippine Islands November 1926-September 1929. Graduated from the Army War College in June 1939. Adjutant general of the Puerto Rican Department June 1939-July 1941. Assigned to the War Department General Staff as deputy director of the international aid division 1941-1943. Brigadier general in September 1943. Duty with the Munitions Assignment Board August 1943 until retirement in May 1944. Decorations included the Legion of Merit. Died on September 22, 1944, near Kingman, Arizona.

Tenney, Clesen Henry (1892-1979) Born on August 24, 1892, in West Lebanon, New Hampshire. Commissioned in the Coast Artillery Corps from West Point in 1915. Instructor at West Point September 1919-December 1922. Duty with 55th Artillery then assistant to the assistant chief of staff of the Hawaiian Department December 1922-September 1926. Graduated from the Command and General Staff School in June 1928, the Army War College in June 1932 and the Naval War College in June 1933. Professor of military science and tactics at Virginia Polytechnic Institute June 1933-August 1938. Director of the statistics branch in the office of the assistant secretary of war 1938-1940. Executive officer of the statistical service in the Services of Supply July 1940-July 1942. Harbor defense commander for the Central Pacific Area July 1942-October 1943. Commanded the 55th Coast Artillery Regiment, Central Pacific Area February-August 1944. Brigadier general in May 1944. Commanding general of Kwajalein in 1944. Commanding general of 70th Antiaircraft Artillery Brigade in Hawaii in 1945. Retired in November 1946. Decorations included the Legion of Merit. Died on July 27, 1979.

Terrell, Henry Jr. (1890-1971) Born in San Antonio, Texas, on October 14, 1890. Attended the University of Texas 1908-1910. Commissioned in the infantry in 1912. Served with the 29th Infantry in the Panama Canal Zone February 1915-August 1917 and the 58th Infantry and 39th Infantry in France where he participated in Champagne-Marne defensive operations and the Marne-Aisne, St. Mihiel and Meuse-Argonne offensives 1917-1918. Professor of military science and tactics at West Texas Military Academy September 1919-September 1921. Graduated from the Command and General Staff School in 1925 and the Army War College in 1932. Instructor at the Infantry School June 1932-August 1936. Assigned to the War Department General Staff August 1938-February 1941. Brigadier general in January 1941. Duty with 8th Division February 1941-February 1942. Major general in February 1942. Commanding general of 90th Infantry Division February 1942-January 1944, XXII Corps January-November 1944 and the Infantry Advanced Replacement Training Center November 1944 until retirement in April 1946. Decorations included the Legion of Merit. Died on October 3, 1971.

Terry, Thomas Alexander (1885-1963) Born in Abbeville, Alabama, on November 22, 1885. Commissioned in the Coast Artillery Corps from West Point in 1908. Mine commander for the coast defenses of Cristobal, Panama Canal Zone September 1915-August 1917. Aide to Major General Adelbert Cronkhite, commanding general of 80th Division 1917-1918. Served with 58th Coast Artillery, AEF in World War I. Graduated from the Command and General Staff School in 1927. Instructor at West Point June 1927-August 1931. Graduated from the Army War College in 1932. Brigadier general in September 1940. Commanding general of 1st Coast Artillery District September 1940-June 1941. Major general in October 1940. Commanding general of I Corps Area and New England Frontier Defense Sector June 1941-May 1942 then Second Service Command May 1942-September 1945. Retired in September 1946. Decorations included two Distinguished Service Medals and the Legion of Merit. Died on April 23, 1963.

Textor, Gordon Edmund (1902-1955) Born on July 9, 1902, in Kasota, Minnesota. Commissioned in the Corps of Engineers from West Point in 1924. Instructor at West Point June 1928-August 1932. Served with 11th Engineers at Corozal, Panama Canal Zone November 1933-March 1936. Graduated from the Command and General Staff School in February 1940. District engineer in the office of the district engineer at Denison, Texas February 1940-February 1942. Member of the Board of Engineers for Rivers and Harbors February-August 1942. Duty with the Army Group, War Production Board August 1942-1943 and the War Department General Staff 1943-1946. Brigadier general in June 1945. Retired in May 1954. Decorations included the Distinguished Service Medal and Commendation Ribbon. Died on March 20, 1955.

Thiele, Claude Martin (1888-1976) Born in Danville, Kentucky, on September 25, 1888. C.E. from Cornell in 1911. Commissioned in the Coast Artillery Corps in 1911. Served with the AEF in France and Germany July 1919-March 1923. Instructor at the Coast Artillery School June 1925-June 1929. Graduated from the Command and General Staff School in 1925 and the Army War College in 1932. Assigned to the War Department General Staff 1932-1936. Commanding officer of 63rd Coast Artillery 1936-1938. Served in the Philippines 1938-1940. Commander of 77th Coast Artillery, 34th Coast Artillery Brigade 1941-1944. Brigadier general in April 1941. Chief antiaircraft officer with Army Service Forces in the European Theater of Operations June-August 1944 then antiaircraft officer for 12th Army Group in France August 1944-April 1946. Reverted to colonel in February 1946. Retired in September 1948. Decorations included two Legions of Merit, the Bronze Star and Commendation Ribbon. Died on October 25, 1976.

Thomas, Samuel Morgan (1903-1973) born in Searcy, Alabama, on December 12, 1903. B.S. from Georgia Institute of Technology in 1926. Employed as an electrical engineer by Allis Chalmers, Inc. 1926-1931 and the U.S. Army Corps of Engineers 1931-1940. Commissioned lieutenant colonel in the Corps of Engineers in 1940. Signal director then chief of staff at Persian Gulf Command 1942-1945. Brigadier general in March 1945. Returned to civilian status at conclusion of the war. Decorations included two Legions of Merit. Died on January 4, 1973.

Thompson, Charles Fullington (1882-1954) Born in Jamestown, North Dakota, on December 11, 1882. Attended the University of Michigan 1899-1900. Commissioned in the infantry from West Point in 1904. Duty in the Philippine Islands October 1905-August 1907 and December 1907-October 1914. Professor of military science and tactics at Cornell University November 1915-June 1917. Served with the AEF in France December 1917-May 1919 and participated in the Aisne-Marne and St. Mihiel offensives and the occupation of Toul Defensive Sector. Instructor at West Point May 1919-August 1920. Graduated from the Command and General Staff School in June 1925 and the Army War College in August 1926. Assistant chief of staff for operations and training with the Philippine Department September 1931-May 1934. Professor of military science and tactics at Oregon State Agricultural College September 1934-April 1936. Assistant commandant of the Infantry School January 1937-July 1938. Brigadier general in September 1938, major general in October 1940. Commanded the 3rd Division July 1940-July 1941, I Corps July 1941-June 1942 and Infantry Replacement Training Center June-October 1942. Island base commander in the South Pacific October 1942-June 1944. Commanding general of XVIII Corps June-September 1944 then the Military District of Washington September 1944-July 1945. Retired in November 1945. Decorations included two Distinguished Service Medals. Died on June 15, 1954.

Thompson, Harry Frank (1896-1980) Born in Ponca City, Oklahoma, on April 27, 1896. Attended the University of Kansas 1915-1917. Commissioned in the infantry in 1917. Served in World War I in France July 1918-June 1919. Instructor with the North Dakota National Guard May 1922-May 1926. Duty with the 14th Infantry at Panama Canal Zone September 1926-August 1929. Professor of military science and tactics at the University of Arkansas August 1929-August 1935. Graduated from the Command and General Staff School in June 1936 and the Army War College in 1940. Assigned to the War Department General Staff 1940-1942 and the Tank Destroyer Center May 1942-October 1943. Brigadier general in April 1943. Commanding general of United States troops in Adak, Alaska from October 1943. Retired in June 1946. Decorations included the Legion of Merit. Died on June 18, 1980.

Thompson, John Bellinger (1890-1957) Born on June 14, 1890, in Fort Davis, Texas. Commissioned in the infantry from West Point in 1914. Aide to Major General Arthur Murray 1917-1918. Graduated from the Command and General Staff School and the Army War College in 1938. Brigadier general in February

1942. Commander of Combat Command "B" in 7th Armored Division 1942-1944. Retired as colonel in May 1946. Brigadier general on the retired list 1948. Died on August 24, 1957.

Thompson, John Moore (1888-1963) Born on April 18, 1888, in Washington, DC. B.A. from St. John's College in 1907. Attended West Point 1907-1908. Commissioned in the cavalry in 1911. Instructor at the Cavalry School June 1923-January 1925. Graduated from the Command and General Staff School in 1925. Served with the 26th Cavalry in the Philippine Islands January 1925-June 1927. Instructor at the Infantry School July 1929-July 1933 then West Point July 1933-August 1937. Graduated from the Army War College in June 1938. Instructor at the Command and General Staff School June 1938-April 1941. Commanding officer of 4th Armored Division Train April 1941-March 1942. Assigned to 7th Armored Division March 1942-January 1946. Brigadier general in November 1944. Reverted to colonel in February 1946. Retired in April 1948. Decorations included two Legions of Merit, the AM and three Commendation Ribbons. Died on June 7, 1963.

Thompson, Orlen Nelson (1894-1960) Born on February 8, 1894, in Cleveland, Ohio. Commissioned in the infantry, Officers Reserve Corps in 1917. Served with the AEF in France during World War I. Duty at the American Barracks, Tientsin, China October 1929-February 1933. Assistant adjutant general of the Hawaiian Department July 1939-July 1941. Officer in charge of training and returns in the adjutant general office 1941-1943. Assistant adjutant general at headquarters of Third Army in 1943. Adjutant general of U.S. Army Forces Central Pacific Area July 1943-October 1945. Brigadier general in June 1945. Retired in November 1946. Decorations included the Distinguished Service Cross, Silver Star, two Legions of Merit, the Commendation Ribbon and Purple Heart. Died on July 7, 1960.

Thompson, Paul Williams (1906-) Born on December 19, 1906, in Alliance, Nebraska. Commissioned in the Corps of Engineers from West Point in 1929. B.S. from the University of Iowa in June 1932. Director of U.S. Waterways Experiment Station 1938-1939. Assistant to the chief of the intelligence section, office of the chief of engineers July 1940-July 1943. Commanding officer of the Assault Training Center in the European Theater of Operations 1943-1944. Commander of 6th Enginner Special Brigade in 1944. Assigned to the War Department General Staff in 1944 and Supreme Headquarters Allied Expeditionary Forces in 1945. Brigadier general in June 1945. Retired as major in June 1946. Brigadier general on the retired list in 1948. Decorations included the Distinguished Service Cross, two Legions of Merit, the Bronze Star and Purple Heart.

Thorpe, Elliott Raymond (1897-1989) Born in Stonington, Connecticut, on December 26, 1897. Attended Rhode Island State College in 1917. Commissioned in the infantry in 1918. Commander of the Maui District 1937-1939. Military attache in the Netherland East Indies 1940-1942. Assistant chief of staff for intelligence, then chief of counterintelligence at U.S. Army Forces Far East 1942-1946. Brigadier general in March 1945. Reverted to colonel in February 1946. Retired in January 1950. Decorations included two Distinguished Service Medals, the Legion of Merit, Bronze Star and Purple Heart. Died on June 27, 1989.

Thorson, Truman Casper (1895-1966) Born on January 23, 1895, in Scandinavia, Wisconsin. Commissioned in the infantry, Officers Reserve Corps in 1917 and the Regular Army in July 1920. Professor of military science and tactics at North Carolina State College 1930-1936. Instructor at the Infantry School in 1938. Regimental commander in the 28th Infantry Division July 1942-August 1943. Assistant chief of staff for intelligence in II Corps, North African Theater of Operations August-October 1943 then First Army, North African Theater of Operations October 1943-November 1947. Brigadier general in August 1944. Retired as major general in January 1953. Decorations included the Distinguished Service Medal, Legion of Merit and Bronze Star. Died on December 10, 1966.

Thrasher, Charles Orval (1886-1960) Born on December 9, 1886, in Paxton, Illinois. Attended the University of Illinois. Commissioned a second lieutenant during World War I, discharged on October 1919 and again commissioned in the Quartermaster Corps in 1920. Graduated from Army Industrial College in 1930. Served with the quartermaster department at headquarters of the Hawaiian Department September 1933-July 1936. Chief of the war plans and training division at San Francisco General Depot July-November 1940. Commanded Seattle Port of Embarkation and Seattle Quartermaster Depot November 1940-May 1942. Base section commander and later commander of the Loire Section, Communications Zone European Theater of Operations May 1942-June 1945. Brigadier general in February 1944. Retired in August 1946. Decorations included the Distinguished Service Medal, Legion of Merit and three Bronze Stars. Died on September 2, 1960.

Tilton, Rollin Larrabee (1888-1977) Born in Chicago, Illinois, on February 22, 1888. Attended Cornell University 1907-1909. Commissioned in the Coast Artillery Corps in 1909. Served with the Punitive Expedition into Mexico in 1916 and the AEF in World War I. Duty in Panama 1920-1923. Instructor at the Coast Artillery School 1929-1933. Graduated from the Command and General Staff School in 1935 and the Army War College in 1938. With the General Staff Corps in the Panama Canal Department 1938-1940. Brigadier general in October 1940. Commanding general of the 3rd Coast Artillery District 1940-1941. Commander of the Chesapeake Bay Sector December 1941-February 1944 then commander of harbor defenses at Chesapeake Bay Mar 1944-June 1946. Retired in February 1948. Decorations included the Legion of Merit and Commendation Ribbon. Died on August 21, 1977.

Timberlake, Edward Wrenne (1895-1980) Born on January 3, 1895, in Nashville, Tennessee. Commissioned in the infantry from West Point in 1917. Executive officer of 61st Antiaircraft Artillery Regiment in 1937. Military attache in

Cuba in 1938. Assistant professor of military science and tactics at the University of Illinois 1939-1942. Commanding officer of 71st and 89th Antiaircraft Artillery Regiments in 1942. Brigadier general in June 1943. Commanding general of 36th and 49th Antiaircraft Artillery Brigades 1943-1945. Commanding general of Antiaircraft Artillery, First Army 1945-1946. Reverted to colonel in February 1946. Professor of military science and tactics at Utah State University 1946 until retirement in 1950. Decorations included the Silver Star, Legion of Merit, Bronze Star, Commendation Ribbon and Purple Heart. Died on February 11, 1980.

Timberman, Thomas Sherman (1900-1989) Born on March 21, 1900, in Jamesburg, New Jersey. Commissioned in the infantry from West Point in 1923. Served with the 15th Infantry at American Barracks, Tientsin, China April 1925-May 1928 and the office of the military attache in Peking, China July 1931-April 1935. Aide to Major General H.B. Fiske, commanding general of the Panama Canal Department April-November 1935. Graduated from the Command and General Staff School in January 1940. Instructor at the Infantry School 1940-1941 and 1941-1942. Military observer in England August-November 1941. Assigned to the war plans division of the War Department General Staff 1942-1943. Brigadier general in January 1944. Commanding general of U.S. Forces Southeast Asia Command 1944-1946. Assignments after the war included commanding general of 1st Division 1951-1952, U.S. commander in Berlin 1952-1954 and chief of the Army Security Agency 1958-1960. Retired in April 1960. Decorations included three Distinguished Service Medals and two Legions of Merit. Died on August 2, 1989.

Timothy, Patrick Henry (1897-1981) Born on April 1, 1897, in Nashville, Tennessee. Commissioned in the Corps of Engineers from West Point in 1918. Instructor there 1918-1919 and 1929-1934. Served with the 14th Engineers and at the Topographical School in the Philippine Islands November 1921-January 1924. Graduated from the Command and General Staff School in August 1937. Duty in the office of the chief of engineers August 1937-November 1940. Commanding officer of 15th Engineer Battalion and Division Engineer of 9th Infantry Division November 1940-August 1941. Assigned to the War Department General Staff August 1941-January 1944. Engineer for First Army Group, European Theater of Operations January 1944-April 1945. Chief engineer for Twelfth Army Group April-June 1945. Commandant of the Engineer School from June 1945. Reverted to colonel in February 1946 and retired in October 1946. Decorations included the Distinguished Service Medal, Legion of Merit and Bronze Star. Died on October 27, 1981.

Tindall, Richard Gentry (1892-1984) Born in Columbia, Missouri, on April 22, 1892. B.A. from the University of Missouri in 1911. Commissioned in the infantry in 1916. Served with the AEF in World War I. Professor of military science and tactics at the University of Missouri July 1922-September 1926. Graduated from the Command and General Staff School in 1928. Instructor with the Texas National Guard June 1928-January 1930, at the Infantry School January 1930-July 1931 and at the Command and General Staff School August 1935-July 1938.

Duty in the office of the chief of infantry July 1938-September 1939. Graduated from the Army War College in June 1940. Assigned to the War Department General Staff November 1940-March 1941 Commanding officer of 93rd Anti-tank Battalion March 1941-June 1942. Brigadier general in September 1942. Military attache in Ankara 1943-1945. Duty with the Military Intelligence Service April 1945-August 1946. Retired in April 1952. Decorations included three Legions of Merit and the Commendation Ribbon. Died on June 29, 1984.

Tompkins, William Frazer (1892-1969) Born on September 22, 1892, in Richmond, Virginia. Commissioned in the Corps of Engineers from West Point in 1915. Served with the Punitive Expedition into Mexico 1916-1917. Wounded in battle as a battalion commander in the 56th Engineers, First Army, AEF in World War I. Graduated from the Command and General Staff School in 1929 and the Army War College in 1932. Duty with the War Department General Staff 1932-1935. District engineer in New Orleans 1936-1940. Brigadier general in July 1942. Member of the executive staff, Munitions Assignments Board 1942-1943. Director of special plans at War Department Special Staff 1943-1945. Major general in August 1944. Chief of staff of Service Command in Pacific Ocean areas in 1945 until retirement in 1946. Decorations included the Distinguished Service Medal, Legion of Merit and Purple Heart. Died on October 26, 1969.

Townsend, James Richard (1893-n/a) Born on July 27, 1893, in Burlington, North Carolina. B.E. from North Carolina College of Agriculture and Engineering in 1914. Commissioned in the Coast Artillery Corps in 1920. Served in the Panama Canal Zone February 1922-January 1925 and at Fort Shafter, Hawaii July 1931-July 1934. Instructor at the Coast Artillery School July 1934-September 1936. Graduated from the Command and General Staff School in 1939 and Army Industrial College in 1940. Served with the war plans division at the War Department General Staff 1940-1942. Brigadier general in March 1942. Commanding general of the Antiaircraft Training Center at Camp Haan 1942-1943 then the 35th Antiaircraft Artillery Brigade, North African Theater of Operations April 1944-July 1945. Assigned to Army Forces Western Pacific July 1945 until retirement in August 1946. Decorations included the Legion of Merit and Bronze Star.

Townsley, Clarence Page (1896-1975) Born on October 10, 1896, in Washington, DC. Commissioned in the field artillery from West Point in 1918. Instructor there 1919-1923. Assistant Professor of military science and tactics at Alabama Polytechnic Institute 1927-1931. Faculty member at the Field Artillery School 1931-1936. Assistant Professor of military science and tactics at Yale 1936-1937. Assigned to the I Corps Area 1940-1941 and the War Department General Staff 1941-1942. Brigadier general in December 1942. Commanding general of 86th Division Artillery 1942-1944. Commander of XXXVI Corps Artillery 1944-1945. Deputy commanding general of Ground Forces Replacement Center in France April 1945-January 1946. Retired in July 1953. Decorations included the Legion of Merit and Commendation Ribbon. Died on October 10, 1975.

Trott, Clement Augustus (1877-1950) Born in Milwaukee, Wisconsin, on December 14, 1877. Commissioned in the 7th Infantry from West Point in 1899. Duty in the Philippine Insurrection 1901-1903. Graduated from Infantry and Cavalry School in 1904 and Army Staff College in 1905. Served in Mexico with the Punitive Expedition in 1916. Colonel and chief of staff of 5th Division, AEF 1917-1918. Graduated from the Army War College in 1920. Brigadier general in September 1935. Commanding general of 6th, 18th, 22nd and 16th Brigades 1935-1939. Commander of 6th Division October 1939-October 1940 then V Corps Area November 1940-September 1941. Major general in April 1941. Retired on December 31, 1941. Decorations included the Distinguished Service Medal and Silver Star. Died on April 14, 1950.

Trudeau, Arthur Gilbert (1902-1991) Born on July 5, 1902, in Middlebury, Vermont. Commissioned in the Corps of Engineers from West Point in 1924. M.Sc. in civil engineering from the University of California in June 1928. Assistant administrator of the Works Projects Administration in New York City 1935-1936. Supervised river and harbor construction in the Pacific Northwest and Alaska 1936-1940. Graduated from Command and General Staff School in 1941 then instructor there until 1942. Chief of staff of the newly conceived Engineer Amphibian Command May 1942-April 1943. Overseas service in North Africa in 1944, where he was "borrowed" by General Dwight D. Eisenhower to break invasion bottlenecks in Normandy and southern France. Brigadier general in August 1944. Commanding officer of Base X, Manila, Philippines in 1945. Assignments after the war included commanding general of 7th Infantry Division in the Korean War in 1953, commander of I Corps September 1955-1958 and chief of Army Research and Development Command 1958-1962. Retired as lieutenant general in 1962. Decorations included two Distinguished Service Medals, two Silver Stars, the Legion of Merit, Bronze Star, Air Medal and Commendation Ribbon. Author of *Some Military Aspects of American Statecraft.* Died on June 5, 1991.

Truesdell, Karl (1882-n/a) Born August 27, 1882, in Moorhead, Minnesota. Enlisted service in U.S. Army 1901-1904. Commissioned in the infantry in 1904. Served with 33rd, 26th and 1st Divisions and V Army Corps, AEF in World War I. Graduated from Command and General Staff School in 1922, the Army War College in 1926 and the Naval War College in 1927. Chief of budget and legislation with the War Department General Staff 1927-1931. Served with the 15th Infantry at Tientsin, China 1932-1935. Director of the military intelligence department at the Army War College 1935-37. Commanding officer of Fort Jay and 16th Infantry 1937-1938. Brigadier general in 1938. Commanding general of 12th Brigade 1938-1939. Major general in October 1940. Commanding general of 1st Division in 1940 and VI Corps 1941-1942. Deputy commander of the Panama Department 1942-1943. Commandant of the Command and General Staff School from 1943. Decorations include the Distinguished Service Medal.

Truman, Ralph Emerson (1880-1962) Born in Kansas City, Missouri, on May 10, 1880. Enlisted service with 20th Infantry in the Spanish-American War. Attended Brown's Business and Technical School 1902-1903. Commissioned in the Missouri National Guard in 1916. Served with 4th Missouri Infantry during the Punitive Expedition into Mexico 1916-1917. Saw action at the Battle of the Argonne Forest in World War I. Commanded the 35th Division as major general 1938-1942. Retired in February 1942. Decorations included the Purple Heart. Died on April 30, 1962.

Truscott, Lucian King, Jr. (1895-1965) Born on January 9, 1895, in Chatfield, Texas. Studied for his teaching certificates from schools in Sapulpa in 1912 and Eufaula in 1913. Enlisted service during World War I. Commissioned in the cavalry, Officers Reserve Corps in August 1917. Duty at Schofield Barracks, Hawaii March 1919-October 1921. Instructor at the Cavalry School 1927-1931. Member of the U.S. Polo Team to Mexico in 1934. Graduated from Command and General Staff School in June 1936 then Instructor until 1940. Executive officer of 2nd Battalion, 13th Armored Regiment September 1940-July 1941. Member of the IX Corps general staff July 1941-May 1942. Brigadier general in May 1942. Duty with the combined operations staff of British Army, Navy and Air Force under command of Admiral Lord Louis Mountbatten in 1942, where he organized and trained the first American Ranger unit. Major general in November 1942. Field deputy to Allied Commander Dwight D. Eisenhower during the Battle of Tunisia the winter of 1942-1943. Commanding general of 3rd Infantry Division in 1943. Deputy commander then commander of VI Army Corps January-December 1944. Lieutenant general in September 1944. Commanding general of Fifth Army December 1944-October 1945 then Third Army and Eastern Military District, succeeding General George Patton. Unorthodox in his militaray dress, he wore a shiny enameled helmet, a weather-stained jacket, a white silk scarf and his "lucky" faded dress cavalry breeches. Decorations included the Distinguished Service Cross, Distinguished Service Medal and Legion of Merit. General on the retired list in July 1954. Died on September 12, 1965.

Tully, Joseph Merit (1893-1963) Born on October 4, 1893, in Kansas City, Missouri. Commissioned in the cavalry from West Point in 1916. Instructor at West Point 1918-1922. Graduated from the Command and General Staff School in June 1926 then instructor there 1927-1928. Served with the 26th Cavalry at Camp Stotsenburg, Philippine Islands 1928-1931. Professor of military science and tactics at Norwich University August 1931-June 1935. Executive officer of 4rd Cavalry Brigade December 1940-March 1941. Acting chief of staff of 2nd Cavalry Division March-November 1941. Commanding officer of 4th Cavalry 1941-1945. Brigadier general in March 1945. Assistant division commander of 90th Infantry Division in 1945. Commanding general of 80th Infantry Division 1945-1946. Reverted to colonel in March 1946. Retired in December 1951. Decorations included the Distinguished Service Medal, two Silver Stars, the Legion of Merit and Bronze Star. Died on May 1, 1963.

Tully, Terence John (1900-1978) Born in Old Point Comfort, Virgina, on January 12, 1900. Commissioned in the infantry from West Point in 1920. Served as information officer at Salt Lake City, in the Philippines, at Boston and Newport 1921-1930. Signal officer at Fort Monmouth, Fort Lewis and Fort Leavenworth 1931-1941. Signal officer for II Corps in the North African Theater of Operations 1942-1943. Chief signal officer for American Forces in the Mediterranean July 1943-September 1944. Duty in the office of the chief signal officer 1944-1945. Commanding general of Army Service Forces Training Center at Camp Crowder in 1945. Retired in 1954. Decorations included the Distinguished Service Medal and Legion of Merit. Died on March 27, 1978.

Twaddle, Harry Lewis (1888-1954) Born on June 2, 1888, in Clarksfield, Ohio. E.E. from Syracuse University in 1910. Commissioned in the infantry in 1912. Served at Fort Gibbon, Alaska 1917-1918. Instructor at the Infantry School 1921-1922. Graduated from the Command and General Staff School in 1923 and the Army War College in 1925. Assigned to the War Department General Staff 1926-1927. Instructor at the Command and General Staff School 1927-1932. Again in the operations and training division at the War Department General Staff August 1938-March 1942. Brigadier general in April 1941, major general in May 1942. Commanding general of 95th Infantry Division March 1942-October 1945. Retired in June 1948. Decorations included the Distinguished Service Medal, Silver Star, Legion of Merit and Bronze Star. Died on December 12, 1954.

Tychsen, Andrew Christian (1893-1986) Born on June 27, 1893, in Hoboken, New Jersey. Enlisted service in the Minnesota National Guard 1916-1917. Commissioned in the infantry, Officers Reserve Corps in 1920. Assistant Professor of military science and tactics at the University of Minnesota 1921-1925. Professor of military science and tactics at St. Thomas Military Academy, St. Paul, Minnesota 1927-1932. Served with the 27th Infantry at Schofield Barracks, Hawaii 1932-1935. Graduated from the Command and General Staff School in 1936. Executive officer of Camden Military District, 3rd Military Area 1938-1941. Battery commander of 1st Infantry Replacement Group 1941-1942. Regimental commander with 100th Infantry Division 1942-1944 then 399th Infantry Regiment from January 1944. Brigadier general in March 1945. Retired in June 1953. Decorations included the Distinguished Service Medal, two Legions of Merit, two Bronze Stars and the AM. Died on July 3, 1986.

Tyler, Max Clayton (1880-1974) Born on September 25, 1880, in Fargo, North Dakota. Commissioned in the cavalry from West Point in 1903. Served with the 3rd Battalion of Engineers in the Philippines in 1903 then the 2nd Battaltion of Engineers in Cuba 19067-1907. Instructor at Army Service Schools 1913-1916. Department engineer in the Philippine Department 1927-1929. Assistant to the chief of engineers 1936-1939. Brigadier general in September 1939. President of the Mississippi River Commission 1939-1945. Retired in September 1944. Decorations included two Distinguished Service Medals and the Legion of Merit. Died on August 22, 1974.

Uhl, Frederick Elwood (1886-1976) Born in Harrold, South Dakota, on March 30, 1886. Commissioned in the infantry from West Point in 1910. Served in the Philippine Islands 1910-1913. Instructor at West Point 1914-1917. With 38th Infantry, AEF 1917-1918 and member of AEF General Staff 1918-1920. Again at West Point as instructor 1920-1924. Staff member at the Infantry School 1925-1927. Graduated from the Command and General Staff School in 1928 and the Army War College in 1932. In the training section, office of the chief of infantry 1932-1935. Member of the Infantry Board 1937-1939. Commanding officer of 38th Infantry 1939-1940. Brigadier general in October 1940. Commanding general of Fort F.E. Warren 1940-1941 and VII Corps Area 1941-1944. Major general in February 1942. Commanding general of 4th Service Command January 1944-June 1945 then Replacement Command, Services of Supply Southwest Pacific Area 1945-1946. Retired in August 1946. Decorations included the Distinguished Service Medal, Legion of Merit and Purple Heart. Died on June 26, 1976.

Ulio, James Alexander (1882-1958) Born in Walla Walla, Washington, on June 29, 1882. Enlisted service 1900-1904. Commissioned in the infantry in 1904. Served with 1st Infantry in the Philippine Islands 1906-1908 then the Hawaiian islands 1912-1916. Assistant chief of staff with 35th Division in 1918. Graduated from the Command and General Staff School in 1921. Duty in the office of the adjutant general, U.S. Army 1926-1929 and again 1931-1935 with a year at the Army War College 1933-1934. In the Hawaii Department 1935-1937 as chief of the Service Command Section then chief of staff of Hawaii department. Executive officer in the adjutant general's office 1938-1939, then assistant adjutant general as brigadier general 1939-1942 and adjutant general as major general March 1942 until retirement in January 1946. Decorations included two Distinguished Service Medals. Died on August 2, 1958.

Uncles, John Francis (1898-1967) Born in Chillicothe, Missouri, on September 18, 1898. Enlisted service 1917-1918. Commissioned in the Field Artillery from West Point in 1922. Instructor at West Point 1930-1934. Duty with the 11th Field Artillery at Schofield Barracks 1934-1937. Graduated from the Command and general Staff School in 1938. Instructor at the Field Artillery School June 1938-July 1940. Assigned to the office of the chief of field artillery 1940-1942. Duty at Army Ground Forces headquarters in 1942. Commanding officer of the 404th Field Artillery Group 1943-1944. Commander of the 34th Field Artillery Brigade 1944-1945. Brigadier general in November 1944. Reverted to colonel in January 1946. Promoted to brigadier general again in October 1950, subsequent assignments included chief of staff of U.S. Army Europe 1954-1956 and commanding general of VII Corps 1956-1958. Retired in 1958 as lieutenant general. Decorations included two Distinguished Service Medals, the Legion of Merit and Bronze Star. Died on January 20, 1967.

Underwood, Edgar Harrison (1893-n/a) Born in Knoxville, Tennessee, on August 29, 1893. B.S. from the University of Tennessee in 1916. Commissioned in the Coast Artillery Corps in 1916. Served at Fort Mills, Philippine Islands 1919-1921. Assistant Professor of military science and tactics at the University of Washington 1922-1927. Duty with the 15th Cavalry in Hawaii 1927-1930. Professor of military science and tactics at the University of Alabama 1931-1939. Executive officer of 1st Coast Artillery at Fort Sherman, Canal Zone August 1939-December 1940. Commanding officer of 82nd Coast Artillery at Fort Randolph, Canal Zone 1940-1942. Brigadier general in March 1943. Commandant of the Antiaircraft Artillery School 1943-1944. Commanding general of the Atlantic Sector, Panama Canal Department 1944-1946. Retired in September 1946. Decorations included the Legion of Merit.

Vachon, Joseph Peter (1887-1961) Born in Westbrook, Maine, on January 23, 1887. Enlisted service 1908-1912. Commissioned in the Philippine Scouts in 1912, then the Regular Army in 1916. Served with the 15th Infantry in China 1917-1919. Graduated from the Command and General Staff School in 1929. Duty with the 19th Infantry at Schofield Barrcks in Hawaii 1931-1934. Assigned to the organized reserves 1934-1940. Instructor with the Connecticut National Guard 1940-1941. Brigadier general in December 1941. Commanding general of 43rd Infantry Division March-December 1941 then the 101st Philippine Army until taken prisoner of war on May 10, 1942. Released in August 1945. Retired in August 1946. Decorations included the Distinguished Service Medal and Silver Star. Died on December 31, 1961.

Van Brunt, Rinaldo (1901-1989) Born in Tallahassee, Florida, on December 13, 1901. Commissioned in the infantry from West Point in 1925. Chief of staff of 83rd Infantry Division 1942-1943, XXI Corps 1943-1945 and XXIII Corps in 1945. Brigadier general in June 1945. Assignments after the war included chief of staff of I Corps in the Korean War 1950-1952, commanding general of 4th Infantry Division 1954-1955 and deputy commanding general of Second Army 1959-1962. Retired as major general in 1962. Decorations included three Distinguished Service Medals, two Silver Stars and the Bronze Star. Died on June 18, 1989.

Vanderveer, Harold Cornelius (1889-1969) Born in Brooklyn, New York, on August 14, 1889. Enlisted service with the Marine Corps 1907-1911. Commissioned in the field artillery in 1912. Served with the 1st and 9th Field Artillery at Schofield Barracks, Hawaii 1915-1918. Graduated from the Command and General Staff School in 1926, Army Industrial College in 1934 and the Army War College in 1935. Duty with 9th Field Artillery 1939-1941. Artillery officer at IX Corps February 1941-February 1942. Brigadier general in February 1942. Assistant division commander of 38th Infantry Division February-September 1942. Commanding general of 5th Infantry Division Artillery 1942-1946. Reverted to colonel in February 1946. Retired in August 1949. Decorations included two Legions of Merit, the Bronze Star, Air Medal and Commendation Ribbon. Died on January 3, 1969.

Van Deusen, George Lane (1888-1977) Born in Passaic, New Jersey, on February 10, 1888. Commissioned from West Point in 1909. Commanded 105th Field Signal Battalion, 30th Division in France and Belgium in 1918. M.S. from Yale in 1921. Graduated from Command and General Staff School in 1925, the Army War College in 1936 and the Naval War College in 1937. Brigadier general in April 1941. Commanding general of Eastern Signal Corps Training Center at Fort Monmouth 1942-1944. Major general in May 1944. Retired in 1948. Died on January 12, 1977.

Van Fleet, James Alward (1892-1992) Born on March 19, 1892, in New Jersey. Commissioned in the infantry from West Point in 1915. Wounded while serving with the AEF in France in World War I. Commanding officer of 8th Infantry, 4th Division 1941-1944. Assistant division commander of 2nd Infantry Division as brigadier general and commanding general of 4th Division as major general in 1944. Commanding general of 90th Infantry Division 1944-1945 and III Corps 1945-1946. Assignments after the war included director of the U.S. Army Group for aid to Greece 1948-1950, commanding general of Second Army 1950-1951 and commanding general of Eighth Army in the Korean War 1951-1953. Retired as general in 1953. Decorations included three Distinguished Service Crosses, three Distinguished Service Medals, two Silver Stars, two Legions of Merit, three Bronze Stars, the Commendation Ribbon and two Purple Hearts. Died on September 23, 1992.

Van Volkenburgh, Robert Heber (1890-1972) Born February 5, 1890, in Detroit, Michigan. Commissioned in the Coast Artillery Corps from West Point in 1913. M.S. from Massachusetts Institute of Technology in 1920. Instructor at West Point 1920-1923. Adjutant and executive officer of the Panama Canal Department 1923-1926. Graduated from the Command and General Staff School in 1928. Instructor at the Coast Artillery School 1928-1932. Graduated from the Army War College in 1933 and the Naval War College in 1938. Brigadier general in September 1941. Commanding general of 40th Coast Artillery Brigade October 1941-June 1944 then 62nd Antiaircraft Artillery Brigade 1944-1945. Commandant of Antiaircraft Artillery School 1945-1946. Reverted to colonel in March 1946. Retired in 1950. Decorations included the Distinguished Service Medal and Commendation Ribbon. Died on March 6, 1972.

Van Voorhis, Daniel (1878-1956) Born in Zanesville, Ohio, on October 24, 1878. Attended Ohio Wesleyan University and Washington and Jefferson College. Enlisted service with 10th Pennsylvania Volunteer Infantry in the Spanish-American War. Commissioned in the cavalry in 1900. Aide-de-camp to Brigadier General J. Franklin Bell, commanding general of the 3rd Brigade in the Philippines 1900-1903 then the United States 1903-1905. Duty at Camp Stotsenburg, Philippines January 1906-January 1908 and again November 1910-December 1913. Served as a cavalry colonel in World War I. Graduated from the Army War College in 1929. Chief of staff of the Hawaiian Department 1934-1936. Brigadier general in February 1936. Commanding general of 7th Cavalry Brigade 1936-

1938. Major general in July 1938. Commanding general of V Corps Area 1938-1940. Lieutenant general in July 1940. Commanding general of the Panama Canal Department 1940-1941 then the V Corps Area until retirement in October 1942. Decorations included the Navy Cross, Distinguished Service Medal, Silver Star and Legion of Merit. Died on January 9, 1956.

Van Voorst, Marion (1897-1967) Born on August 13, 1897, in Indiana Commissioned in the Coast Artillery Corps from West Point in 1918. M.S. from Yale in 1933. Assistant military attache in London 1943-1946. Brigadier general in January 1945. Reverted to colonel in March 1946. Duty in the office of the chief signal officer, U.S. Army 1947-1948 then the office of the adjutant general 1948-1950 Retired in December 1950. Decorations included the Legion of Merit and Bronze Star. Died on September 27, 1967.

Vaughan, Harry Briggs (1888-n/a) Born in Norfolk, Virginia, on July 24, 1888. B.S. from Virginia Polytechnic Institute in 1911. Commissioned in the Corps of Engineers in 1917. Served in the AEF during World War I, including the Meuse-Argonne offensive. Professor of military science and tactics at the University of Illinois June 1924-September 1928. Graduated from Command and General Staff School in 1930. Duty with the 3rd Engineers at Schofield Barracks, Hawaii April 1935-May 1937. Assigned to the office of the chief of engineers 1937-1940. District engineer in Philadelphia February 1940-June 1943. Assigned to the European Theater of Operations 1943-1944. Brigadier general in February 1944, major general in November 1944. Commanding general of the United Kingdom Base Section 1944-1945 and the Bremen Post Command in 1945. Decorations included the Silver Star, Legion of Merit and Purple Heart.

Vaughan, Harry H. (1893-1981) Born on November 26, 1893, in Glasgow, Missouri. B.A. from Westminster College in 1916. Enlisted service in the Missouri National Guard 1917-1918. Commissioned in the field artillery in 1918. Served with the Missouri National Guard in Mexico in 1916. Commanding officer of 130th Field Artillery, 35th Division at Argonne, Vosges-Oisne, Marne, St.-Mihiel and Meuse-Argonne engagements 1917-1919. Discharged in 1919. Commissioned in the Officers Reserve Corps in 1924. Secretary to Senator Harry S. truman 1939-1942. Called to active duty as lieutenant colonel in January 1942. Served with U.S. Army forces in Australia 1942-1943. Liaison officer with the Truman-Mead Commission in 1944. Military aide to Vice President Truman in 1945 then President Truman 1945-1953. Brigadier general in June 1945, major general in June 1946. Retired in 1953. Decorations included two Silver Stars. Died on May 20, 1981.

Wahl, George Douglas (1895-1981) Born on October 15, 1895, in New Orleans, Louisiana. Commissioned in the field artillery from West Point in 1917. Served with the 3rd and 12th Field Artillery in the AEF in World War I, including the St. Mihiel and Meuse-Argonne offensives. Instructor at West Point 1919-1920 then the Field Artillery School 1920-1922. Graduated from the Command

and General Staff School in June 1930, Army Industrial College in June 1939 and the Naval War College in May 1940. Assistant chief of staff for intelligence at VII Corps Area 1940-1941. Commander of 191st Field Artillery 1941-1943 then XV Corps Artillery 1943-1944. Brigadier general in May 1944. Commanding general of 79th Division Artillery February 1944-March 1945 then assistant division commander of the 79th March-June 1945. Commanding general of the War Department Personnel Center at Indiantown Gap, Pennsylvania June 1945 until he reverted to colonel in March 1946. Retired in June 1949. Decorations included three Silver Stars, the Legion of Merit, two Bronze Stars, two Commendation Ribbons and two Purple Hearts. Died on March 24, 1981.

Wainwright, Jonathan Mayhew (1883-1953) Born on August 23, 1883, in Walla Walla, Washington. Commissioned in the cavalry from West Point in 1906. Assistant chief of staff of 82nd Infantry Division at St. Mihiel and Meuse-Argonne offensives in World War I. Graduated from the Command and General Staff School in 1931 and the Army War College in 1934. Brigadier general and commander of 1st Cavalry Brigade 1938-1940. Major general in September 1940. Commander of the Philippine Division 1940-1942. Lieutenant general in March 1942. Commander of U.S. Forces Far East in 1942. In command of American and Philippine forces on Bataan and Corregidor when overrun by the Japanese Army April-May 1942. Prisoner of war 1942-1945. General in September 1945. Commanding general of Fourth Army 1946-1947. Retired in August 1947. Decorations included the MH, Distinguished Service Cross and Distinguished Service Medal. Author of *General Wainwright's Story* (1945). Died on September 2, 1953.

Waite, Sumner (1988-1952) Born in Westbrook, Maine, on September 6, 1888. B.A. from the University of Maine in 1911. Commissioned in the 5th Infantry in 1911. Aide-de-camp to Major General Charles G. Morton 1916-1917. Served in World War I with the 3rd, 37th and 36th Divisions. Instructor at the Infantry School 1922-1925. Graduated from the Command and General Staff School in 1926, Ecole Superieure de Guerre in 1928 and the Army War College in 1932. Assistant military attache in Paris 1936-1940. Commander of 13th Infantry, 8th Infantry Division September 1940-July 1942. Commanding officer of Special Troops, Second Army in 1942. Deputy chief of staff for operations at headquarters of the European Theater of Operations in 1942. Assigned to the office of administrative services for Army Service Forces December 1942-October 1943. Chief of staff of 2nd Service Command 1943-1945. Brigadier general in November 1944. Retired in September 1948. Decorations included the Distinguished Service Medal, Legion of Merit and Commendation Ribbon. Died on June 6, 1952.

Waitt, Alden Hardy (1892-1981) Born in Orlando, Florida, on December 22, 1892. B.S. from Massachusetts Institute of Technology in 1915. Commissioned in the Chemical Warfare Service in 1920. Gas officer in the 29th Division, AEF in 1918. Instructor at Chemical Warfare School 1921-1924. M.S. from Massachusetts Institute of Technology in 1926. Instructor again at Chemical Warfare School 1933-1935. Graduated from the Command and General Staff School in 1936. Instructor at Air Corps Tactical School 1936-1940. Chemical officer with the Armored Force 1940-1941. Assistant chief of staff for operations on the War Department General Staff 1941-1942. Brigadier general in September 1942. Chief of the plans and training division, then assistant chief for field operations, finally acting chief of the Chemical Warfare Service 1942-1945. Retired as major general in September 1949. Decorations included the Distinguished Service Medal, Legion of Merit and two Commendation Ribbons. Died on February 11, 1981.

Waldron, Albert Whitney (1892-1961) Born on January 13, 1892, in Rochester, New York. Commissioned in the field artillery from West Point in 1915. Served with Pershing in the Punitive Expedition into Mexico 1916-1917. With the 1st Division, AEF in World War I. Plans and training officer with 5th Division in 1940. At the War Department General Staff 1940-1941. Duty with 7th Infantry Division 1941-1942. Brigadier general in February 1942, major general in December 1942. Field artillery representative in Army Ground Forces 1943 until retirement in 1946. Decorations included the Distinguished Service Medal. Died on June 21, 1961.

Walker, Fred Livingood (1887-1969) Born in Fairfield County, Ohio, on June 11, 1887. E.M. from Ohio State University in 1911. Commissioned in the infantry in 1911. Served with the 3rd Division, AEF in World War I, including the Aisne-Marne, St. Mihiel and Meuse-Argonne offensives. Wounded in action on July 21, 1918. Served in the Philippine Islands 1913-1914 and with the 17th Infantry in the Punitive Expedition into Mexico 1916-1917. Instructor at the Infantry School August 1920-September 1922. Graduated from the Command and General Staff School in 1927. Professor of military science and tactics at the Shattuck School 1927-1932. Graduated from the Army War College in 1933, remaining there as instructor until 1937. Commanding officer of the 15th Infantry at Tientsin, China 1937-1939. Duty on the staff of Second Army 1939-1941. Brigadier general in April 1941. Served with 2nd Division in 1941 then commanding general of 36th Division 1942-1944. Major general in January 1942. Director of military training for Army Service Forces 1945-1946. Retired in April 1946. Decorations included the Distinguished Service Cross and two Purple Hearts. Died on October 6, 1969.

Walker, James Hess (1900-1983) Born on November 15, 1900, in Carlsbad, New Mexico. Commissioned in the cavalry from West Point in 1920. Commanding officer of Machine Gun Troop, 12th Cavalry 1935-1939. In the personnel division at the War Department General Staff 1939-1943. Brigadier general in March 1943. Commanding general of 5th Cavalry Brigade in 1943. Commanding general of Redistribution Station for Army Air Forces, Army Ground Forces, and Army Service Forces 1944-1945. Retired in 1946. Decorations included two Legions of Merit. Died on May 5, 1983.

Walker, Walton Harris (1889-1950) Born on December 3, 1889, in Belton, Texas. Commissioned in the infantry from West Point in 1912. Served in the occupation of Vera Cruz, Mexico in 1914. With the 13th Machine Gun Battalion, 5th Division in AEF. Participated in the St. Mihiel and Meuse-Argonne offensives. Graduated from the Command and General Staff School in 1926. With the 15th Infantry in Tientsin, China, 1930-1933. Graduated from the Army War College in 1936. With war plans division, the War Department General Staff 1937-1940. Commanding officer of 36th Infantry February-July 1941. Brigadier general in July 1941. Commander of 3rd Armored Brigade July 1941-January 1942. Commanding general of 3rd Armored Division January-September 1942. Major general in March 1942. Commanding general of IV Armored Corps (renamed XX Corps) September 1942-June 1945. The XX Corps was an element of Patton's Third Army and it acquired the nickname "Ghost Corps" for the speed of its advances after landing in France in July 1944. Commander of 8th Service Command 1945-1946. Assignments after the war included commanding general of Fifth Army 1946-1948. Commander of Eighth Army during the early months of the Korean War 1948-1950. Killed in a jeep accident near Seoul, Korea, on December 23, 1950. Decorations included two Distinguished Service Crosses, two Distinguished Service Medals, three Silver Stars, the Legion of Merit and Bronze Star. Posthumous promotion to general in January 1951.

Walker, William George (1890-1974) Born in New York City on June 28, 1890. Enlisted service in the Minnesota National Guard 1912-1917. Commissioned in the infantry in 1917. Served with the 88th Division in World War I. Commissioned in the Regular Army in 1920. Duty with the 27th Infantry at Schofield Barracks, Hawaii 1925-1928. Professor of military science and tactics at the University of Minnesota 1928-1931. Graduated from the Command and General Staff School in 1935 and the Army War College in 1938. Assistant chief of staff for intelligence plans and training in the I Corps Area 1938-1941 then assistant to the assistant chief of staff for intelligence at Army Ground Forces September 1941-March 1942, finally assistant chief of staff for supply at Army Ground Forces 1942-1943. Brigadier general in March 1943. Member of the Joint Munitions Allocation Committee 1943-1944 then assigned to headquarters of U.S. Army Pacific 1945-1946. Retired in August 1946. Decorations included the Legion of Merit. Died on December 31, 1974.

Wallace, Fred Clute (1887-1959) Born in McMinnville, Tennessee, on July 1, 1887. Commissioned in the field artillery from West Point in 1910. Served with the 2nd and 3rd Field Artillery Regiments in the Philippine islands 1915-1917. Graduated from the Command and General Staff School in 1931. Member of the Field Artillery Board 1931-1935. Graduated from the Army War College in 1936. Commanding officer of ROTC at Alabama Polytechnic Institute 1936-1939. Executive officer in the office of the chief of field artillery 1939-1940. Brigadier general in October 1940. Commanding general of 4th Motorized Division Artillery in 1941 then the division October 1941-June 1942. Major general in January 1942. Commanding general of 4th Island Command 1943-1944 then Army Garrison Forces, Schofield Barracks November 194-May 1945. Island commander on Okinawa 1945-1946. Retired in April 1946. Decorations included two Distinguished Service Medals and two Legions of Merit. Died on July 30, 1959.

Wallender, Elmer Forrest (1889-1970) Born in Arthur City, Texas, on December 21, 1889. Attended Paris (Texas) Business College. Enlisted service 1914-1917. Commissioned in the infantry in 1917. Served in the Philippine Islands 1915-1917 and with the 15th Infantry in China 1917-1919. Served at Schofield Barracks in Hawaii 1932-1935. Graduated from Army Industrial College in June 1940. Quartermaster for IV Corps 1940-1942. Assistant to the quartermaster for IX Corps Area 1942-1943. Chief of staff of Army Service Command October 1943-September 1944. Brigadier general in September 1944. Commander of Headquarters Bases "K" and "G" in the Southwest Pacific Area 1944-1946. Reverted to colonel in March 1946. Retired in December 1949. Decorations included the Legion of Merit. Died on May 6, 1970.

Walsh, Roland Francis (1891-1956) Born in Charleston, South Carolina, on October 5, 1891. B.S. from the Citadel in 1912. Commissioned in the infantry in 1912. Served with the 24th Infantry at Fort Mills, Philippine islands 1914-1917 then the 8th Machine Gun Battalion in the AEF, seeing action at Aisne-Marne, St. Mihiel and Meuse-Argonne 1918-1919. Graduated from the Command and General Staff School in 1926. Instructor at the Quartermaster Corps School 1926-1927 and 1931-1933, with graduation from the Army War College in 1931. Assigned to the Hawaii Quartermaster Depot 1939-1942 then 4th Service Command June 1942-July 1943. Commander of the Philadelphia Quartermaster Depot 1943-1946. Brigadier general in September 1943. Retired in December 1946. Decorations included the Legion of Merit and two Commendation Ribbons. Died on August 12, 1956.

Walson, Charles Moore (1883-1959) Born on August 24, 1883, in Delaware. M.D. from Jefferson Medical College in 1906. Commissioned in the Medical Reserve Corps in 1911. Graduated from Army Medical School in 1912. Surgeon at Vera Cruz in 1914 and in Hawaii 1917-1918. Assistant to the chief surgeon for the AEF 1918-1919. Corps area surgeon 1940-1942 then service command surgeon August 1942-June 1946. Brigadier general in June 1945. Retired in August 1947. Decorations included the Legion of Merit. Died on May 14, 1959.

Wanamaker, William Wesley (1898-) Born on August 23, 1898, in Wakefield, Massachusetts. Commissioned in the Corps of Engineers from West Point in 1918. Served with the AEF 1918-1920. Instructor at Missouri School of Mines 1921-1925. Served with 14th Engineers at Fort McKinley, Philippine Islands 1930-1932. Executive assistant to the division engineer, Southwest Division 1939-1941. District engineer in Dennison, Texas, 1941-1943. Assistant engineer and chief transportation officer in the Southwest Pacific Theater of Operations 1944-1945. Brigadier general in June 1945. Reverted to colonel in March 1946.

Retired in 1949. Decorations included the Distinguished Service Medal, Legion of Merit and Bronze Star.

Ward, Orlando (1891-1972) Born on November 4, 1891, in Macon, Missouri. Commissioned in the cavalry from West Point in 1915. Served on the Mexican border and with the Punitive Expedition into Mexico 1914-1917 then with Third Army in the AEF 1917-1918. Instructor at the University of Wisconsin 1918-1922. Staff officer in the Philippine Department 1929-1931. Instructor at the Field Artillery School 1931-1935. Duty with the War Department General Staff 1937-1939 then secretary 1939-1941. Brigadier general in August 1941. Commanding general of 1st Armored Brigade 1941-1942. Major general in March 1942. Commanding general of 1st Armored Division in North African Theater of Operations 1942-1943. Commanding general of Tank Destroyer Center at Camp Hood May-October 1943. Commandant of Field Artillery School January-October 1944. Commanding general of 20th Armored Division 1944-1945. Assignments after the war included commanding general of V Corps in 1946, commander of 6th Division 1946-1949 and chief of military history, U.S. Army 1949-1953. Retired in January 1953. Decorations included the Distinguished Service Cross, Distinguished Service Medal, two Silver Stars, two Legions of Merit, the Bronze Star and Purple Heart. Died on February 5, 1972.

Warden, John Ashley (1886-1973) Born on July 31, 1886, in McKinney, Texas. B.S. from Agricultural and Mechanical College of Texas in 1908. Commissioned in the cavalry in 1908. Served with the 8th and 9th Cavalry at Fort McKinley, Philippine Islands 1914-1917. Graduated from the Command and General Staff School in June 1925, the Army War College in 1934 and the Naval War College in 1936. Quartermaster at IV Corps Area 1938-1941. Brigadier general in April 1941. Commanding general of Quartermaster Replacement Training Center, Fort F.E. Warren 1941-1943 then the Quartermaster School February-March 1943. Commanding general of Base Section One 1943-1945 then the Charlotte Quartermaster Depot 1945-1946. Retired in January 1947. Decorations included the Legion of Merit. Died on January 16, 1973.

Warnock, Aln Dudley (1894-1993) Born in San Antonio, Texas, on June 1, 1894. Enlisted service with the Arizona National Guard on the Mexican border in 1916-1917. Commissioned in the infantry, Arizona National Guard in 1920 and the Regular Army in 1920. Deputy sheriff in Pima City, Arizona 1919-1920. Assistant Professor of military science and tactics at the University of Oklahoma 1921-1925. Graduated from the Command and General Staff School in 1931. Executive officer of the 21st Brigade 1931-1935. Instructor with the Illinois National Guard 1935-1936. Graduated from the Army War College in 1937 then instructor at the Command and General Staff School 1937-1941. Deputy chief of staff at 16th Infantry 1941-1942. Brigadier general in December 1942. Assistant division commander of 5th Infantry Division then commanding general of Iceland Base Command 1942-1945. Retired in May 1946. Decorations included the Silver Star, two Legions of Merit and the Bronze Star. Died on September 1, 1993.

Waters, Jr. Jerome J. (1891-n/a) Born in Eagle Pass, Texas, on July 30, 1891. B.S. from Texas A&M in 1913. Commissioned in the field artillery in 1913. Served in France during World War I. Instructor at the Field Artillery School 1923-1926. Graduated from Command and General Staff School in 1936. Battery commander in the 8th Field Artillery at Schofield Barracks, Hawaii 1936-1938. Instructor with the Illinois National Guard 1938-1941. Commanding officer of 6th Training Regiment in 1941. Brigadier general in April 1942. Commanding general of 76th Division Artillery 1942-1944 then XXXII Corps Artillery November 1944-May 1945. Served in Central and South America 1945-1946. Decorations included two Silver Stars, two Legions of Merit and the Purple Heart.

Waters, William Edmund (1899-1956) Born on October 12, 1899, in Louisville, Kentucky. B.S. from Virginia Military Institute in 1921. Commissioned in the field artillery in 1921. Graduated from the Command and General Staff School in 1941. Saw action with the 1st Division in Europe 1943-1945. Brigadier general in March 1945. Reverted to colonel in February 1946. Decorations included the Legion of Merit and two Bronze Stars. Died on October 16, 1956.

Watson, Edwin Martin (1883-1945) Born in Eufala, Alabama, on December 10, 1883. Commissioned in the field artillery from West Point in 1908. Aide-de-camp to Brigadier General Frederick A. Smith 1910-1912. With the 24th Infantry in the Philippines 1912-1915. Military aide to President Woodrow Wilson 1915-1917. Served with the 12th Field Artillery, AEF at Toulon-Troyon, Aisne, Aisne-Marne, St. Mihiel and Meuse-Argonne in World War I. Junior aide to President Wilson 1918-1920. Graduated from the Command and General Staff School in 1927. Military attache in Brussels 1927-1931. Military aide, then secretary to President Franklin D. Roosevelt 1933-1945. Brigadier general in April 1939, major general in October 1940. Died on February 20, 1945, seven weeks before the death of Roosevelt. Decorations included two Silver Stars.

Watson, Leroy Hugh (1893-1975) Born on November 3, 1893, in St. Louis, Missouri. Commissioned in the infantry from West Point in 1915. Served with the 6th Division, AEF 1918-1920. Instructor at the Infantry School 1921-1925. Battalion commander with the 42nd then 32nd Infantry in Panama 1925-1928. Instructor at the Command and General Staff School 1930-1933. Battalion commander in the 33rd Infantry 1934-1936. At the War Department General Staff 1936-1940. Assistant chief of staff for personnel at 2nd Armored Division, the commanding officer of the division's 66th Armored Regiment 1940-1941. Commanding officer of 40th Armored Regiment, 3rd Armored Division 1941-1942. Brigadier general in February 1942. Commanding general of Combat Command 1, 3rd Armored Division 1942-1943, then commanding general of 3rd Armored Division 1943-1944. Major general in September 1942. Commanding general of 29th Division 1944-1945. Retired in November 1953. Decorations included two Silver Stars, two Legions of Merit and three Bronze Stars. Died on February 12, 1975.

Weart, Douglas Lafayette (1891-1975) Born on August 10, 1891, in Chicago, Illinois. Attended Armour Technical Institute 1909-1911. Commissioned in the Corps of Engineers from West Point in 1915. Served in Mexico with the Punitive Expedition in 1916 and the 1st Division, AEF in 1917-1918. Graduated from the Command and General Staff School, then instructor there 1934-1938. Graduated from the Army War College in 1939. Assistant engineer at the Panama Canal 1939-1942. Brigadier general in December 1942. Chief of staff of Caribbean Defense Command 1943-1944. Deputy commander of China Theater of Operations in 1945. Major general in May 1945. Retired in August 1951. Decorations included the Distinguished Service Medal and two Legions of Merit. Died on April 5, 1975.

Weaver, James Roy Newman (1888-1967) Born in Fremont, Ohio, on May 20, 1888. Attended Oberlin College 1906-1907. Commissioned in the infantry from West Point in 1911. Served with the 9th Infantry and 8th Infantry in the Philippines 1911-1912. Instructor at West Point 1917-1918 and 1920-1923. Graduated from the Command and General Staff School in 1926. Instructor at the Field Artillery School 1926-1930. Duty with the 5th Infantry at Fort McKinley, Philippine Islands 1930-1932. Commanding officer of 68th Armored Regiment August 1940-April 1941. Served in the Philippine Department as commander of the Provisional Tank Group October 1941 until captured as prisoner of war on Bataan April 9, 1942. Brigadier general in December 1941. Released from captivity in August 1945. Retired in May 1948. Decorations included the Distinguished Service Cross, Distinguished Service Medal, Silver Star and Bronze Star. Died on August 29, 1967.

Weaver, Theron DeWitt (1892-1986) Born in Detroit, Michigan, on December 2, 1892. B.S. from the University of Michigan in 1916. Commissioned in the Corps of Engineers in 1917. Served at headquarters of the AEF and in combat with British and French forces 1918-1919. Instructor at the Engineer School 1924-1928. Graduated from the Command and General Staff School in 1934 and the Army War College in 1935. Duty in the office of the assistant secretary of war 1939-1942. Brigadier general in August 1942. Duty on the staff of Army Service Forces 1942-1944. Assigned to headquarters of SHAEF December 1944-October 1945. Reverted to colonel in February 1946. Retired in December 1952. Decorations included the Distinguished Service Medal and Commendation Ribbon. Died on October 1, 1986.

Weaver, William Gaulbert (1888-1970) Born on November 24, 1888, in Louisville, Kentucky. Commissioned in the infantry from West Point in 1912. Served with the AEF in World War I. Professor of military science and tactics at the University of Wisconsin 1937-1941. Commanding officer of the Infantry Replacement Training Center at Camp Roberts in 1941. Assistant division commander of 90th Division, then commanding general of 8th Division 1942-1945. Brigadier general in April 1943, major general in January 1945. Retired in February 1946. Decorations included three Distinguished Service Crosses, the Distinguished

Service Medal, Silver Star, two Legions of Merit, two Bronze Stars, the Commendation Ribbon and three Purple Hearts. Died on November 25, 1970.

Weckerling, John (1896-n/a) Born in New Orleans, Louisiana, on November 21, 1896. Commissioned in the infantry in 1918. Served in the Philippine Islands 1924-1926. Studied the Japanese language in Tokyo 1928-1932. Assistant military attache in Tokyo 1935-1938. Served in the Panama Canal Zone 1939-1941. Assistant chief of staff for intelligence at Fourth Army 1942-1943. Assigned to the intelligence division at the War Department General Staff 1943-1944, then deputy assistant chief of staff for intelligence 1944-1946. Brigadier general in August 1944. Retired in September 1954. Decorations included the Distinguished Service Medal, Legion of Merit and Commendation Ribbon.

Wedemeyer, Albert Coady (1897-1989) Born on July 9, 1897, in Omaha, Nebraska. Commissioned in the infantry from West Point in 1919. Studied Chinese language in Tientsin 1930-1932. Graduated from the Command and General Staff School in 1936. Attended the Kriegsakademie, the German general staff school, 1936-1938. With war plans division, then plans and operations division of the War Department General Staff May 1941-October 1943. Brigadier general in July 1942, major general in September 1943. Deputy chief of staff to Lord Louis Mountbatten, Supreme Allied Commander Southeast Asia October 1943-October 1944. Commander of China Theater of Operations when Stilwell was recalled and the China-Burma-India Theater of Operations after it was divided October 1944-May 1946. Lieutenant general in January 1945. Assignments after the war included commander of Second Army June 1946-October 1947, director of the plans and operations division on the Army General Staff October 1947-November 1948 and commanding general of Sixth Army November 1948 until retirement in July 1951. General on the retired list in July 1954. Decorations included three Distinguished Service Medals and the Distinguished Flying Cross. Author of *Wedemeyer Reports* (1958). Died on December 17, 1989.

Weeks, Lawrence Babbitt (1888-1959) Born in Buffalo, New York, on October 16, 1888. Commissioned in the Coast Artillery Corps from West Point in 1913. Instructor at West Point 1922-1924 and with the New York National Guard 1930-1933. Assigned to the National Guard Bureau 1933-1937. Executive officer of 2nd Coast Artillery in 1938. Department head, assistant commandant and commandant of the Coast Artillery School 1939-1945. Brigadier general in February 1942. Retired in 1948. Decorations included the Legion of Merit. Died on November 29, 1959.

Weems, George Hatton (1891-1957) Born in Southside, Tennessee, on September 27, 1891. Commissioned in the infantry from West Point in 1917. Served with the 2nd Division in the AEF 1917-1919. Instructor at the Infantry School 1920-1923. Professor of military science and tactics at Davidson College 1923-1927. Graduated from Command and general Staff School in 1928. Instructor at West Point 1928-1929 and the Air Corps Tactical School 1929-1933. Graduated from the Army War College in 1934. Chief of the Military Mission to Haiti 1939-1941. Assistant commandant of the Infantry School from 1942. Retired in 1951. Decorations included the Distinguished Service Cross and the Silver Star. Died on February 25, 1957.

Weible, Walter Leo (1896-1980) Born at Waterbury, Connecticut, on June 2, 1896. Graduated from Pratt Institute in 1917. Enlisted service 1917-1918. Commissioned in the Coast Artillery Corps, Officers Reserve Corps in 1918. Served in Hawaii with the 10th Infantry 1922-1926 and again with the Honolulu Sector 1930-1933. Graduated from the Command and General Staff School in 1935, the Army War College in 1938 and Army Industrial College in 1939. Assigned to the operations and training division at the War Department General Staff July 1939-March 1942. Deputy director of training, then director of training for Army Service Forces March 1942-June 1945. Brigadier general in December 1942, major general in May 1944. Commander of Nagoya Base, Army Service Command June-September 1945. Assignments after the war included deputy commanding general of Fifth Army in 1953 and deputy chief of staff for personnel, U.S. Army 1953-1957. Retired as lieutenant general in January 1957. Decorations included two Distinguished Service Medals, the Legion of Merit, Bronze Star and Commendation Ribbon. Died on February 19, 1980.

Weir, John Merle (1891-1948) Born on September 6, 1891, in Indianapolis, Indiana. B.S. and LL.B. from John B. Stetson University in 1914, M.A. in 1917. Commissioned in the infantry, Officers Reserve Corps in 1917. Served with the 84th Division in the AEF 1918-1919. Instructor at West Point 1924-1928 and again 1934-1938. Judge advocate of the Puerto Rican Department 1939-1941. Executive officer then assistant judge advocate general in the office of the judge advocate general, U.S. Army 1941-1946. Brigadier general in September 1943. Retired in November 1946. Decorations included the Legion of Merit. Died on November 21, 1948.

Wells, Gordon Marshall (1895-n/a) Born in Mapleton, Iowa, on April 9, 1895. Attended the University of California. Commissioned in the Coast Artillery Corps in 1917. Duty at the Hawaii Ordnance Depot in 1931 and the Frankfort Arsenal 1937-1941. Chief of the artillery division in the ordnance department 1941-1945. Brigadier general in May 1942. Chief of the ordnance office in Detroit 1945-1946.

Wessels, Theodore Francis (1892-1974) Born in Philadelphia, Pennsylvania, on May 31, 1892. B.S. from Trinity College in 1914. Commissioned in the infantry, Officers Reserve Corps in 1917. Aide to Brigadier General Charles G. Treat June 1928-October 1920. Served with the 45th Infantry at Fort McKinley, Philippine Islands May 1926-November 1931. Graduated from the Command and General Staff School in 1934. Professor of military science and tactics at Indiana University 1934-1939, then instructor at the Infantry School 1939-1942. Duty with the 8th Armored Division 1942-1943. Brigadier general in March 1943. Commanding

general of Combat Command "B" in the 20th Armored Division February-
November 1943. Commandant of Yunan International Training Center at
Kunimg, China November 1943-May 1944. Chief of the U.S. Liaison Mission to
Ceylon May-November 1944. Senior liaison officer for Allied Forces Southeast
Asia 1944-1945. Deputy commander of Ground Forces Command February-July
1945. Reverted to colonel in February 1946. Retired in May 1952. Decorations
included the Silver Star, Legion of Merit and Bronze Star. Died on May 1, 1974.

Wesson, Charles Macon (1878-1956) Born in St. Louis, Missouri, on July 23,
1878. Commissioned in the cavalry from West Point in 1900. Duty with the 8th
Cavalry in Cuba August 1900-February 1902. Instructor at West Point 1903-
1907. Served with the AEF in World War I. Graduated from the Army War College in 1925. Assistant military attache in the United Kingdom April 1929-
September 1930. Chief of the technical staff in the office of the chief of ordnance
1930-1934. Major general in June 1938. Chief of ordnance 1938-1942. Duty in
the office of the Lend-Lease Administrator and the Foreign Economic Administrator Septemeber 1942-October 1945. Retired in December 1945. Decorations included two Distinguished Service Medals. Died on November 24, 1956.

Wheeler, Raymond Albert (1885-1974) Born in Peoria, Illinois, on July 31,
1885. Commissioned in the Corps of Engineers from West Point in 1911. Assigned to Isthmian Canal Commission, Canal Zone 1911-1912. Served with the
AEF at Aisne-Marne, St. Mihiel and Meuse-Argonne offensives 1918-1919. Instructor at the Infantry School 1919-1922. Graduated from the Command and
General Staff School in 1927. Assistant maintenance engineer in Panama 1927-
1930. Graduated from the Army War College in 1937. Member of the Board of
Engineers for Rivers and Harbors 1937-1940. Vice president of the Panama Railroad 1940-1941. Brigadier general in September 1941. Chief of the U.S. military
mission to Iraq, Iran and India 1941-1942. Major general in March 1942. Oversaw construction of "Ledo Road" linking China and India for the first time 1942-
1943. Staff officer then deputy commander at Allied Southeast Asia Command
1943-1945. Lieutenant general in February 1944. Chief of engineers, U.S. Army
October 1945 until retirement in February 1949. Decorations included three Distinguished Service Medals, the Silver Star, Legion of Merit and AM. Called from
retirement by the United Nations to oversee salvage efforts in the Suez Canal
1956-1957. Died on February 8, 1974.

Whisner, Emons Bertram (1895-1984) Born in Kansas City, Kansas, on August
24, 1895. Attended the University of Missouri 1915-1917. Commissioned in the
infantry in 1917. On occupation duty in France and germany 1919-1924. Instructor at the Infantry School 1927-1928. Liaison officer then aide to the governor
general of the Philippine Islands 1929-1932. Assistant professor of military science and tactics at Montana State University, State University of Iowa and Punahou Academy, Hawaii 1936-1942. Secretary to the general staff at Fort Shafter
1942-1944. Commander of the Replacement Depot, Pacific Ocean Area then 23rd
Replacement Depot, Hawaii 1944-1946. Brigadier general in January 1945. Re-

verted to colonel in March 1946 and retired in July 1953. Decorations included two Legions of Merit and the Bronze Star. Died on September 27, 1984.

White, Arthur Arnim (1889-1981) Born on October 21, 1889, in Coatsburg, Illinois. Commissioned in the infantry from West Point in 1915. Graduated from the Command and General Staff School in 1928. Assistant chief of staff for operations at VII Corps 1940-1942. Deputy chief of staff for supply at XIV Corps, then IV Corps 1943-1944. Brigadier general in May 1944. Chief of staff of Seventh Army 1944-1945. Major general in November 1944. Commanding general of 75th Division, then 71st Division 1945-1946. Assignments after the war included commanding general of V Corps Artillery 1946-1948 and commanding general of 9th Division 1948-1949. Retired in September 1949. Decorations included two Distinguished Service Medals, the Legion of Merit and Commendation Ribbon. Died on October 21, 1981.

White, Charles Henry (1883-1971) Born in Taunton, Massachusetts, on November 29, 1883. Commissioned in the infantry in 1907. Served in Cuba 1907-1909, the Philippine Islands 1914-1917 and Hawaii 1920-1923. Graduated from the Command and General Staff School in 1923 and the Army War College in 1930. Instructor with the organized reserves in Boston 1933-1936. Professor of military science and tactics at the University of California 1939-1940. Brigadier general in October 1940. Assigned to the 7th Division October 1940-March 1941. Commanding general of Replacement Training Center at Camp Roberts March-July 1941. Major General in August 1941. Commanding general of IX Corps April 1942-March 1944 then the Infantry Replacement Training Center at Camp Robinson March-October 1944. Member of the secretary of war's Personnel Board October 1944-March 1946. Retired in July 1946. Decorations included the Legion of Merit. Died on April 9, 1971.

White, Isaac Davis (1901-1990) Born in Peterborough, New Hampshire, on March 6, 1901. Commissioned in the cavalry following graduation from Norwich University in 1922. Graduated from the Command and General Staff School in 1939. With 2nd Armored Division August 1940-July 1945 as commander of a battalion, regiment, Combat Command "B" and commanding general. Brigadier general in May 1944, major general March 1945. Commandant of the Cavalry School July 1945-December 1946. Assignments after the war included deputy commanding general of Seventh Army November 1950-March 1951, chief of staff of First Army, March-August 1951, commanding general of X Corps August 1952-September 1953, commanding general of Fourth Army September 1953-June 1955, Commander-in-Chief United Nations Command Korea July 1955-June 1957 and Commander-in-Chief U. S. Army Pacific July 1957 until retirement as general in March 1961. Died on June 11, 1990.

White, William Robert (1887-1975) Born on January 14, 1887, in Portsmouth, Virginia. Attended Portsmouth Business College in 1906 and Dowd's Preparatory School 1911-1912. Commissioned in the infantry in 1912. Served with the 24th

Infantry in the Philippines June 1914-June 1916 and the 4th Machine Gun Battalion, 2nd Division in the AEF 1917-1918. Graduated from the Command and General Staff School in 1928 and the Army War College in 1933. Executive officer of the Hawaiian Quartermaster Depot January 1935-April 1937. Quartermaster at Fort Jay 1937-1940. Again in Hawaii as commanding officer of the 11th Quartermaster Regiment at Schofield Barracks May 1940-January 1944. Brigadier general in September 1942. Quartermaster of the Hawaiian Department 1944-1946. Retired in September 1946. Decorations included the Legion of Merit. Died on March 5, 1975.

Whitelaw, John Leonard (1899-1970) Born in Savannah, Georgia, on September 18, 1899. Attended the Citadel 1915-1917. Commissioned in the Coast Artillery Corps from West Point in 1919. Instructor at West Point 1932-1938. Graduated from Command and General Staff School in 1939. Assigned to the office of the chief of infantry 1941-1942 and headquarters of Army Ground Forces 1942-1943. Assistant division commander of 17th Airborne Division 1943-1945. Decorations included the Silver Star, Legion of Merit, Bronze Star, Commendation Ribbon and Purple Heart. Retired in 1955. Died on April 26, 1970.

Whitlock, Lester Johnson (1892-1971) Born in Piqua, Ohio, on October 27, 1892. B.A. from Miami of Ohio Unversity in 1914. Enlisted service 1916-1917. Commissioned in the field artillery in 1917. Professor of military science and tactics at the University of Oklahoma 1923-1927. Instructor with the New York National Guard 1929-1931. Graduated from the Command and General Staff School in 1938. Assigned to the construction branch of the supply division at the War Department General Staff 1938-1941. Assistant chief of staff for supply of the Southwest Pacific Area November 1941-October 1945. Brigadier general in June 1942, major general in January 1945. Retired in July 1954. Decorations included two Distinguished Service Medals and the Legion of Merit. Died on October 18, 1971.

Whitney, Courtney (1897-1969) Born in Washington, DC, on May 20, 1897. Enlisted service in the District of Columbia National Guard and the Signal Corps, aviation section reserve May 1917-March 1918. Commissioned in the aviation section reserve in 1918. LL.B. from National University in 1923. Served on active duty at Camp Nichols, Philippine Islands August 1925-November 1926. Resigned in June 1927 and practiced law for the next thirteen years. Returned to active duty as major in October 1940. Assigned as assistant chief of the legal division, then assistant air judge advocate at headquarters Army Air Corps until April 1943. Chief of the Philippine Regulatory Section of Allied Intelligence Bureau April 1943-November 1944. Brigadier general in January 1945. Chief of civil affairs security with U.S. Army Forces Pacific Ocean Area 1945-1946. Thereafter chief aide and confidant to General Douglas MacArthur. Resigned in May 1951, shortly after MacArthur was relieved by President Truman. Died on March 21, 1969.

Whittaker, Frank Lawrence (1893-1978) Born in Manchester, New Hampshire, on May 14, 1893. B.S. from Norwich University in 1915. Commissioned in the cavalry in 1916. Served on the Mexican border 1916-1917. Graduated from the Command and General Staff School in 1930 and the Army War College in 1936. Assistant chief of staff for supply at Western Defense Command 1941-1943. Brigadier general in February 1943. Deputy commander of the Alaskan Department February 1943-September 1944. Reverted to colonel in September 1944 and retired in November 1946. Decorations included two Legions of Merit. Died on June 7, 1978.

Whittaker, Horace Lincoln (1894-1973) Born in Marlboro, Massachusetts, on July 9, 1894. E.E. from Northeastern University in 1916. Commissioned in the Coast Artillery Corps in 1916. Served with the AEF in World War I. Duty in Hawaii 1921-1924 and again 1935-1938. Commandant of the Quartermaster School 1941-1943. Brigadier general in July 1942. Commanding general of the Quartermaster Unit Training Center, Fort F.E. Warren February 1943-February 1945. Commanding general of Fort Warren 1945-1946. Retired in November 1946. Decorations included the Legion of Merit and Commendation Ribbon. Died in 1973.

Wicks, Roger Manning (1894-1972) Born on November 7, 1894, in Utica, New York. Attended Yale 1914-1916. Commissioned in the field artillery from West Point in 1918. Served with the AEF in France, Belgium and Germany 1918-1922. Instructor at West Point 1924-1929, then the Field Artillery School 1929-1935. Graduated from the Command and General Staff School in 1936. Assistant Professor of military science and tactics at Yale 1936-1940. Duty with the 79th Field Artillery August 1940-December 1941. Assistant artillery officer, then artillery officer at IV Corps 1941-1942. Assigned to headquarters of Army ground Forces August-November 1942. Brigadier general in November 1942. Commanding general of 103rd Division Artillery November 1942-August 1945. Retired in May 1950. Decorations included the Legion of Merit and two Bronze Stars. Died on July 7, 1972.

Wilbur, William Hale (1888-1979) Born on September 24, 1888, in Palmer, Massachusetts. Attended Haverford College 1907-1908. Commissioned in the infantry from West Point in 1912. Attended Ecole Special Militaire 1919-1920 and Ecole Superieure de Guerre 1922-1924. Graduated from the Command and General Staff School in 1932 and the Army War College in 1935. Chief of staff of VI Corps Area 1940-1941, then I Armored Corps, North African Theater of Operations 1941-1942 where he earned the Medal of Honor. Brigadier general in December 1942. Assistant division commander of 36th Division 1943-1944. Chief of staff of Western Defense Command 1945-1946. Retired in March 1947. Decorations included the Medal of Honor, Silver Star, two Legions of Merit and the Bronze Star. Died on December 27, 1979.

Wilby, Francis Bowditch (1883-1965) Born in Detroit, Michigan, on April 24, 1883. Attended Harvard 1900-1901. Commissioned in the Corps of Engineers from West Point in 1905. Graduated from School of the Line in 1922, Army General Staff School in 1923 and the Army War College in 1924. Member of the Mississippi River Commission 1935-1938 and the Beach Erosion Board 1938-1939. Chief of staff of First Army 1939-1941. Brigadier general in October 1940, major general in September 1941. Superintendent of West Point January 1942-September 1945. Retired in January 1946. Decorations included two Distinguished Service Medals and the Legion of Merit. Died on November 20, 1965.

Willems, John Murphy (1901-1976) Born on December 24, 1901, at Fort Leavenworth, Kansas. Commissioned in the field artillery from West Point in 1925. Served at Camp Stotsenburg, Philippine Islands March 1927-June 1929. Graduated from the Command and General Staff School in 1939. Assistant artillery officer at Western Task Force, then artillery officer for Seventh Army and chief of staff of II Corps 1941-1945. Brigadier general in March 1945. Chief of staff of Seventh Army 1945-1946. Assignments after the war included commanding general of the 3rd Armored Division 1945-1946. Retired in December 1961. Decorations included two Distinguished Service Medals, two Legions of Merit and the Bronze Star. Died on September 14, 1976.

Willey, John Perry (1902-1976) Born in Hampton, Virginia, on April 22, 1902. B.S. from Virginia Polytechnic Institute in 1924. Commissioned in the cavalry in 1924. Graduated from the Command and General Staff School in 1939. Instructor at the Cavalry School 1939-1941. With 4th Armored Division 1941-1942. Instructor at the Armored Force School in 1943. Duty in the India-Burma Theater of Operations 1943-1945. Brigadier general in September 1944. Reverted to colonel in March 1946. Retired in August 1954. Decorations included the Legion of Merit, two Bronze Stars, the Air Medal and Commendation Ribbon. Died on December 9, 1976.

Williams, Edward Thomas (1901-1973) Born on February 6, 1901, in Detroit, Michigan. Commissioned in the infantry from West Point in 1920. Assistant professor of military science and tactics at Ohio State University 1930-1935. Graduated from the Command and General Staff School in June 1939. Instructor at the Field Artillery School 1939-1943. Artillery officer at Third Army 1943-1945. Brigadier general in March 1945. Assignments after the war included deputy chief of staff for operations at U.S. European Command 1950-1952, chief of staff of U.S. Army Europe 1952-1953, deputy commanding general of Third Army 1953-1954, deputy commander of Continental Army Command 1956-1958 and commanding general of Fourth Army 1959-1961. Retired in February 1961. Decorations included two Distinguished Service Medals, the Legion of Merit and Bronze Star. Died on October 14, 1973.

Williams, Lewis Kemper (1887-1971) Born in Patterson, Louisiana, on September 23, 1887. Graduated from the University of the South in 1908. Sugar and lumber manufacturer 1912-1940. Commissioned in the cavalry, Officers Reserve Corps in 1916. National president of the Reserve Officers Association 1931-1934. Ordered to active duty in November 1940 as officer in charge of the information division, Adjutant General Department and served there until September 1941. Commanding officer of the Louisiana Recreational District 1941-1942. Regimental commander at the Infantry Replacement Training Center, Fort McClellan July 1942-December 1943. Assigned to the Army Ground Forces Replacement Depot Number One at Fort Meade 1943-1944. Brigadier general in November 1944. Member of the secretary of war's Disability Board 1944-1945. Returned to inactive status at the end of the war. Died on November 17, 1971.

Williams, Samuel Tankersley (1897-1984) Born in Denton, Texas, on August 25, 1897. Enlisted service with 4th Texas Infantry 1916-1917. Commissioned in the infantry in 1920. Served with the 90th and 3rd Divisions in World War I. Transferred to the infantry, Regular Army in 1920. Member of the Infantry Board 1939-1942. Staff officer with 95th Infantry Division May-July 1942. Assistant division commander of 90th Motorized Division February 1943-August 1944. Brigadier general in March 1943. Assistant chief of staff for intelligence with XXII Corps September 1944-January 1945 then chief of staff February 1945-January 1946. Assignments after the war included commanding general of 25th Infantry Division in the Korean War 1952-1953, commanding general of XXVI Corps 1953-1954, IX Corps in 1954 and Fourth Army in 1955. Retired as lieutenant general in September 1960. Decorations included the Distinguished Service Cross, two Distinguished Service Medals, two Silver Stars, the Bronze Star, two Commendation Ribbons and two Purple Hearts. Died on April 26, 1984.

Williamson, Raymond Eccleston Serveira (1894-1957) Born on September 1, 1894, in Brooklyn, New York. Attended Amherst College 1913-1914. Commissioned in the cavalry from West Point in 1917. Served with the 82nd Division, AEF in 1918 including the Aisne-Marne, St. Mihiel and Meuse-Argonne offensives. Aide-de-camp to Major General C.D. Rhodes in Paris 1918-1919. Aide at the White House October 1921-September 1922. Instructor at West Point 1923-1927 and 1931-1935. Graduated from the Command and General Staff School in 1936 and the Army War College in 1940. Brigadier general in August 1942. Deputy chief of staff for personnel in Americal Division 1942-1943. Commanding general of the Service Command, South Pacific Theater of Operations 1943-1944. Deputy commanding general of 91st Division 1944-1945. Assignments after the war included commanding general of 3rd Armored Division 1950-1952. Retired in August 1954. Decorations included the Silver Star, Legion of Merit and three Bronze Stars. Died on September 27, 1957.

Williamson, William James (1884-n/a) Born on August 21, 1884, in Broadview, Sasketchewan. General traffic manager for Sears Roebuck and Company in Chicago 1929-1942. Commissioned in the AUS as colonel in July 1942. Duty in the office of the chief of transportation, Army Service Forces from 1942. Brigadier general in September 1944.

Williford, Forrest Estey (1882-1955) Born on January 22, 1882, in Coffeen, Illinois. Enlisted service with the Illinois National Guard 1900-1902. Commissioned in the Coast Artillery Corps from West Point in 1906. Instructor at West Point 1912-1914. Served in France 1917-1918. M.S. from Massachusetts Institute of Technology and Harvard in 1917. Graduated from the Army War College in 1920. Professor of military science and tactics at Virginia Polytechnic Institute 1920-1924. Graduated from the Command and General Staff School in 1926 then instructor there until 1929. Commander of the 91st Coast Artillery at Fort Mills, Philippine Islands 1930-1932. Served in the Canal Zone 1936-1938. Brigadier general in October 1940. Commander of the Coast Artillery Replacement Training Center, Fort Eustis November 1941-December 1942. Commanding general of harbor defense units in the South California Sector 1942-1944. Retired in January 1944. Decorations included the Distinguished Service Medal. Died on March 17, 1955.

Willis, John Mitchell (1886-1962) Born on November 25, 1886, in King George, Virginia. M.D. from George Washington University in 1909. Commissioned in the Medical Corps in 1910. Graduated from Army Medical School in 1911. Served in the Philippine Islands 1915-1917. Graduated from the Command and General Staff School in 1931 and the Army War College in 1935. Medical inspector of the Hawaiian Division 1935-1938. Assistant commandant of Medical Field Service School 1938-1941. Brigadier general in April 1941. Commanding general of Camp Grant 1941-1943. Chief of medical service at 9th Service Command October 1943-November 1944. Chief surgeon for U.S. Army Forces Pacific Ocean Areas 1944-1945. Retired in November 1948. Decorations included the Distinguished Service Medal, Legion of Merit and Commendation Ribbon. Died on July 23, 1962.

Willoughby, Charles Andrew (1892-1972) Born on March 8, 1892, in Heidelberg, Germany. Naturalized in 1910. B.A. from Gettysburg College in 1914. Commissioned in the infantry in 1915. Served on the Mexican border 1916-1917 then with 1st Division, AEF 1917-1918. Military attache in Venezuela, Columbia and Ecuador 1923-1927. Graduated from the Command and General Staff School in 1931. Graduate studies at the University of Kansas in 1933. Graduated from the Army War College in 1936. Instructor at the Infantry School 1936-1940. Assistant chief, then chief of intelligence on General MacArthur's staff in the Pacific 1941-1951. Brigadier general in June 1942, major general in March 1945. Retired in August 1951. Decorations included the Distinguished Service Cross, three Distinguished Service Medals, two Silver Stars, the Air Medal and Legion of Merit. Author of *Maneuver in War* (1939). Died on October 25, 1972.

Wilson, Alexander (1886-1952) Born on November 11, 1886, in Farmington, Missouri. Midshipman at United States Naval Academy 1906-1908. Commissioned in the infantry in 1911. Transferred to the Chemical Warfare Service in 1929. Chemical officer in the Hawaiian Department in 1933. President of the Chemical Warfare Board 1938-1941. With the AAF Combat Command at Bolling

Air Base July 1941-January 1942. Brigadier general in January 1942. Duty in the office of the chief of the Chemical Warfare Service February-October 1942. Commandant of the Chemical Warfare School October 1942-April 1944. Commander of Rocky Mountain Arsenal 1944-1945. Retired in August 1946. Decorations included two Legions of Merit. Died on July 1, 1952.

Wilson, Arthur Riehl (1894-1956) Born on July 18, 1894, in Cherokee, California. B.A. from the University of California in 1919. Commissioned in the field artillery in 1920. Professor of military science and tactics at the University of Missouri 1922-1926. Served with the 13th Field Artillery at Schofield Barracks 1926-1928. Graduated from the Command and General Staff School in 1934 and the Army War College in 1935. Instructor at the Command and General Staff School 1935-1937. Liaison officer with the WPA 1937-1939. Chief of the WPA branch at the War Department General Staff 1939-1940. Chief of the support division of Federal Works Agency June 1940-February 1942. Brigadier general in January 1942. Duty with the Army Group February-July 1942. Commanding general of Services of Supply Western Task Force 1942-1943. Commander of the Atlantic and Mediterranean Base Sections in the North African Theater of Operations 1943-1944. Major general in January 1944. Commanding general of the Continental Base Section in France in 1944. Chief of staff of Seventh Army 1944-1945. Retired in May 1946. Decorations included two Distinguished Service Medals, two Legions of Merit and the Bronze Star. Vice president of TWA 1946-1947. Died on August 11, 1956.

Wilson, Durward Saunders (1886-1970) Born on July 2, 1886, in Greenville, North Carolina. Commissioned in the infantry from West Point in 1910. Duty in the Philippine Islands 1914-1917. Commanding officer of 1st Replacement Battery at Camp Lee 1918-1920. Served with the Philippine Division 1920-1923. Instructor with the Mississippi National Guard 1923-1925. Graduated from the Command and General Staff School in 1927. Instructor at the Infantry School 1927-1931. Graduated from the Army War College in 1932 and the Naval War College in 1933. Executive officer of 16th Brigade 1934-1938. Duty on the staff of the Infantry School 1938-1940. Brigadier general in October 1940. Commanding general of 21st Infantry Brigade 1940-1941 then 24th Infantry Brigade October 1941-May 1942. Major general in May 1942. Commanding general of 24th Infantry Division May-September 1942, then 6th Motorized Division September-November 1942. Commanding general of the Infantry Replacement Training Center at Camp Croft 1942-1944. Commanding general of the Southeast Sector, Eastern Defense Command May 1944-May 1945. Served at headquarters of Army Ground Forces May 1945 until retirement in January 1946. Died on January 20, 1970.

Wilson, John Harold (1887-1970) Born on April 8, 1887, in Flint Stone, Maryland. Commissioned in the Coast Artillery Corps in 1920. Graduated from the Command and General Staff School in 1926. Served at Fort Mills, Philippine Islands 1926-1933 then with the 64th Coast Artillery at Fort Shafter, Hawaii 1933-

1935. Graduated from the Army War College in 1936. Instructor at the Command and General Staff School 1936-1940. Assistant chief of staff for operations at IX Corps Area 1940-1942. Deputy chief of staff, then chief of staff of 9th Service Command from May 1942. Brigadier general in November 1944. Retired in September 1946. Decorations included the Legion of Merit. Died on December 16, 1970.

Wilson, Robert Wilbur (1893-1964) Born in Harrisburg, Pennsylvania, on August 26, 1893. B.A. from Yale in 1916. Commissioned in the field artillery, Officers Reserve Corps in 1917. Served on active duty as assistant professor of military science and tactics at Texas A&M University 1919-1922. In the pharmaceutical industry 1922-1941. Called to active duty as lieutenant colonel of field artillery in June 1941. Graduated from the Command and General Staff School in 1941. Assistant to the chief of staff for supply at II Corps 1941-1942. Acting chief of staff for supply in the North African Theater of Operations 1942-1943. Assistant chief of staff for supply at First Army September 1943-August 1945. Brigadier general in November 1944. Decorations included the Distinguished Service Medal and two Legions of Merit. Died in 1964.

Wilson, Thomas Bayne (1892-1963) Born on May 26, 1892, in Williamstown, Kansas. Attended Oakland Polytechnic College. Employed by Southern Pacific Railroad, Pacific Greyhound Lines and Alaska Steamship Company 1911-1938 except for service with the Signal Corps 1917-1919. Called to active duty as colonel in 1942. Duty with the Transportation Corps February 1942-March 1943. Brigadier general in March 1943. Transportation officer for U.S. Army Forces Far East 1943-1944. Returned to inactive status in November 1944. Died on May 8, 1963.

Wilson, Walter King (1880-1954) Born on October 7, 1880, in Nashville, Tennessee. Commissioned in the artillery from West Point in 1902. Instructor at the Coast Artillery School 1911-1912. Served with the War Department General Staff during World War I. Graduated from the Army War College in 1922. Duty at Fort Ruger, Hawaii 1922-1925. Brigadier general in May 1937. Commander of 2nd Coast Artillery District 1937-1938 then harbor defenses of Manila, Philippines 1938-1941. Major general in October 1940. Commanding general of III Corps November 1940-July 1941, 9th Coast Artillery District 1941-1942 then Northern California Sector of Western Defense Command 1942-1944. Retired in June 1944. Decorations included two Distinguished Service Medals and the Legion of Merit. Executive director of Army Emergency Relief 1944-1946. Died on January 20, 1954.

Wilson, Walter King Jr. (1906-1985) Born on August 26, 1906, in Fort Barrancas, Florida, the son of Major General Walter K. Wilson. Attended the University of Hawaii in 1924. Commissioned in the Corps of Engineers from West Point in 1929. B.S. from the University of California in 1933. Instructor at West Point 1934-1938. Graduated from the Command and General Staff School in 1939 then instructor there 1941-1942. Commanding officer of 79th Engineer Combat Regiment 1942-1943. Deputy chief engineer in Southeast Asia Command 1943-1945. Brigadier general in February 1945. Commanding general of base sections in the India Burma Theater of Operations 1945-1946. Reverted to colonel in May 1946. Assignments after the war included commanding general of Fort Belvoir 1960-1961 and chief of engineers, U.S. Army 1961-1965. Retired as lieutenant general in June 1965. Decorations included the Distinguished Service Medal and two Legions of Merit. Died on December 6, 1985.

Wilson, William Henry (1877-1960) Born on December 26, 1877, in Mount Vernon, New York. Enlisted service with the 22nd Regiment, New York National Guard 1898-1899. Commissioned in the 43rd U.S. Volunteers in 1899. Served in the Spanish-American War and the Philippine insurrection. Transferred to the artillery, Regular Army in 1901. Assigned to general headquarters of the AEF 1917-1918. Assistant chief of staff for personnel at the Hawaiian Department December 1920-January 1924. Graduated from the Army War College in 1928 and the Naval War College in 1929. Chief of staff of I Corps Area 1935-1938. Brigadier general in October 1936. Major general in October 1938. Commanding general of I Corps Area September 1938-February 1939 then the Hawaiian Division February 1939-February 1941. Commander of Camp Stewart until July 1941. Retired on December 31, 1941. Decorations included the Distinguished Service Medal. Died on October 25, 1960.

Winn, John Sheridan Jr. (1898-1972) Born on December 18, 1898. Commissioned in the field artillery from West Point in 1918. Aide to Brigadier General D.H. Currie 1918-1919. Served with the 10th Field Artillery in Germany in 1919. Aide to Major General George Van Horn Moseley June 1922-September 1929, Brigadier General Charles J. Symonds 1929-1930 and Major General Malin Craig August 1932-August 1933. Executive officer of 4th Division Artillery September 1940-January 1942. Assigned to headquarters of Army Ground Forces 1942-1943. Brigadier general in September 1943. Commander of 19th Field Artillery Brigade July-September 1943. Commanding general of 42nd Infantry Division Artillery September 1943-October 1944. Assistant division commander of 36th Infantry Division 1944-1945. Assistant division commander, then artillery commander of 79th Division Artillery January-August 1945. Reverted to colonel in February 1946. Retired in November 1948. Decorations included three Legions of Merit, the Bronze Star and Commendation Ribbon. Died on March 9, 1972.

Winship, Blanton (1869-1947) Born on November 23, 1869, in Macon, Georgia. B.A. from Mercer University in 1889 and LL.B. from the University of Georgia in 1893. Served with 1st Georgia Infantry in the Spanish-American War and the Philippine insurrection 1899-1901. Commissioned in the artillery in 1901. Accompanied Major General Funston to Vera Cruz in 1914. Served with 42nd, 1st and 28th Divisions in the AEF 1917-1923. Military aide to the President May 1927-January 1928. Legal adviser to the governor general of the Philippines 1928-1930. Major general as judge advocate general, U.S. Army March 1931-

November 1933. Retired in November 1933. Recalled to active duty for the period March 1942-April 1944. Decorations included the Distinguished Service Cross, Distinguished Service Medal and Silver Star. Died on October 9, 1947.

Witsell, Edward Fuller (1891-1969) Born on March 29, 1891, in Charleston, South Carolina. B.S. from the Citadel in 1911. Commissioned in the infantry in 1912. Served with the 2nd Infantry September 1915-October 1917. Instructor with the Hawaiian National Guard 1917-1918. Language officer in Tokyo 1919-1923 then military attache 1926-1928. Graduated from the Army War College in 1929. Duty in the Canal Zone July 1934-September 1936 then the office of the adjutant general, U.S. Army 1937-1941. Assigned to Southeast Air Forces Training Center at Maxwell Field May 1941-March 1942. Adjutant general of III Corps Area in 1942. Director of the military personnel division, office of the adjutant general, U.S. Army 1943-1945. Brigadier general in January 1944, major general in July 1945. Acting adjutant general, then the adjutant general, U.S. Army 1945-1951. Retired in June 1951. Decorations included the Distinguished Service Medal and five Commendation Ribbons. Died on November 27, 1969.

Wogan, John Beugnot (1890-1968) Born on January 1, 1890, in New Orleans, Louisiana. Attended Spring Hill College 1906-1907. B.A. from College of Immaculate Conception in 1908. Commissioned in the Coast Artillery Corps from West Point in 1915. Served on the Mexican border in 1916 and with the Coast Artillery Corps, AEF 1917-1920, including the St. Mihiel and Meuse-Argonne engagements. Professor of military science and tactics at Harvard 1924-1928. Graduated from the Command and General Staff School in 1930. Commander of 2nd Field Artillery in the Panama Canal 1930-1932. Graduated from the Army War College in 1933. Member of the public relations staff at the War Department General Staff 1933-1937. Instructor at the Field Artillery School 1937-1940. Commanding officer of 68th Field Artillery Regiment 1940-1941. Chief of staff of 5th Armored Division August 1941-January 1942. Brigadier general in February 1942. Commanding general of Combat Command B, 2nd Armored Division February-September 1942. Major general in September 1942. Commanding general of 13th Armored Division 1942-1945. Severely wounded in the Ruhr battle on April 15, 1945, which forced retirement on October 31, 1946. Decorations included the Distinguished Service Medal, Silver Star, Legion of Merit and Purple Heart. Died on September 30, 1968.

Wolfe, Henry Charles (1896-1976) Born in Lewisburg, Pennsylvania, on May 21, 1896. B.S. from Bucknell University in 1916. Enlisted service in 1917. Commissioned in the Corps of Engineers in 1918. Served with the 535th Engineers in France 1918-1919. Instructor with the South Carolina National Guard 1922-1926. Graduated from Army Industrial College in 1931. Duty with 3rd Engineers at Schofield Barracks, Hawaii January 1935-July 1937. Graduated from the Command and General Staff School in 1940. Plans and training officer for the Engineer Replacement Training Center at Fort Belvoir December 1940-April 1941 then at Fort Leonard Wood 1941-1942. Brigadier general in September

1942. Commander of 1st Engineer Amphibious Brigade May 1942-May 1943. Assigned to the office of the chief of staff of Fifth Army August 1943-April 1944. Commanding general of the Invasion Training Center in the North African Theater of Operations April-August 1944. Chief of the engineer section in Sixth Army Group 1944-1945. Reverted to colonel in March 1946. Retired in May 1950. Decorations included the Distinguished Service Medal and two Legions of Merit. Died on July 6, 1976.

Wood, John Elliott (1891-1963) Born on February 23, 1891, in Hertford, North Carolina. B.S. from Massachusetts Institute of Technology in 1914. Commissioned in the Corps of Engineers in 1917. Served in the AEF 1917-1918 then with the army of occupation 1919-1920. Assistant departmental engineer in the Philippines 1934-1936. Officer in charge of the War Department map collection 1937-1940. Served in the North Africa Theater of Operations in 1942. Brigadier general in August 1942. Assistant division commander of 92nd Infantry Division 1943-1945. Reverted to colonel in March 1946. Retired in July 1949. Decorations included the Silver Star, Legion of Merit, Bronze Star and Commendation Ribbon. Died on October 1, 1963.

Wood, John Shirley (1888-1966) Born in Arkansas on January 11, 1888. Commissioned in the Coast Artillery Corps from West Point in 1912. Instructor at West Point 1916-1917. Served with the 3rd and 96th Divisions in the AEF in World War I. Professor of military science and tactics at the University of Wisconsin 1919-1923. Duty at Schofield Barracks, Hawaii 1927-1929. Graduated from Ecole Superieure de Guerre in 1931. Professor of military science and tactics at Culver Military Academy 1932-1937. Chief of staff of Third Army September 1939-November 1940. Artillery officer for 1st Division then November 1940-April 1941 then commanding general of 2nd Armored Division Artillery April-June 1941. Duty with I Armored Corps in 1941. Brigadier general in October 1941. Assigned to 5th Armored Division 1941-1942. Major general in June 1942. Commanding general of 4th Armored Division 1942-1944. Commander of the Replacement Training Center at Fort Knox 1945-1946. Retired in August 1946. Decorations included the Distinguished Service Cross, Distinguished Service Medal, Silver Star, Bronze Star, Air Medal and Commendation Ribbon. Died on July 2, 1966.

Wood, Walter Alexander Jr. (1894-1957) Born in Honesdale, Pennsylvania, on January 9, 1894. B.S. from John Hopkins in 1917. Commissioned in the Corps of Engineers in 1920. Served in the Philippines 1924-1926 then Hawaii 1932-1935. Graduated from the Command and General Staff School in 1936. Assistant professor of military science and tactics at the University of Nebraska 1936-1938. Duty in the supply division of the War Department General Staff 1938-1941. Assigned to headquarters Services of Supply in 1942. Brigadier general in September 1942. Director of the requirements division then deputy director of plans and operations at headquarters of Army Service Forces 1942-1945. Major general in

August 1944. Retired in September 1946. Decorations included two Distinguished Service Medals. Died on June 27, 1957.

Woodberry, John Henry (1889-1974) Born on February 22, 1889, in Johnsonville, South Carolina. Commissioned in the cavalry from West Point in 1914. Served with the 8th Cavalry in the Philippine Islands then with 15th Cavalry 1914-1916. Graduated from Army Industrial College in 1928, the Command and General Staff School in June 1930 and the Army War College in 1935. Chief of the statistical branch in the office of the deputy chief of staff, U.S. Army 1935-1939. Commanding officer of Raritan Arsenal 1940-1943. Chief ordnance officer for Services of Supply, Southwest Pacific Theater of Operations 1944-1945. Brigadier general in June 1945. Retired in August 1946. Decorations included the Legion of Merit and Bronze Star. Died on February 8, 1974.

Woodruff, Roscoe Barnett (1891-1975) Born in Oskaloosa, Iowa, on February 9, 1891. Commissioned in the infantry from West Point in 1915. Duty with the general staff at the Panama Canal Department 1921-1924. Member of the faculty at Command and General Staff School 1927-1931 and West Point 1932-1936. Graduated from the Army War College in 1932. Assigned to the operations and training division of the War Department General Staff 1936-1940. Assistant division commander of 2nd Infantry Division 1940-1942 and 77th Infantry Division January-June 1942. Major general in June 1942. Commanding general of 77th Infantry Division 1942-1943, VII Corps 1943-1944 and 24th Infantry Division 1944-1945. Assignments after the war included command of I Corps 1945-1948 and XV Corps 1951-1953. Retired in 1953. Decorations included two Distinguished Service Medals, three Silver Stars, two Bronze Stars, two Air Medals, the Commendation Ribbon and Purple Heart. Died on July 24, 1975.

Woodward, William Roscoe (1891-1994) Born on August 8, 1891, in Louisville, Mississippi. B.S. from Mississippi State College in 1911. Commissioned in the field artillery from West Point in 1916. Served with the AEF in World War I. Graduated from the Command and General Staff School in 1931. Brigadier general in December 1942. Commanding general of Americal Division Artillery 1942-1943. Commanding general of 104th Division Artillery 1943-1945. Reverted to colonel in March 1946. Retired in 1950. Decorations included the Silver Star, two Legions of Merit and the Bronze Star. Died on January 18, 1994.

Wooley, George Francis Jr. (1894-1978) Born on September 26, 1894, in Clinton, Iowa. Commissioned in the infantry from West Point in 1917. Aide-de-camp to Brigadier General Edmund Wittenmyer in 1922. M.S. from Yale in 1930. Instructor at the Field Artillery School 1930-1934. Served at Fort Stotsenburg, Philippine Islands 1934-1936. Artillery officer, then executive officer of 3rd Armored Division April 1941-July 1942. Signal officer at IV Corps, Fourth Army, then Seventh Army 1942-1945. Brigadier general in January 1945. Signal officer at Fourth Army 1945-1947. Reverted to colonel in February 1946. Retired in

April 1949. Decorations included the Distinguished Service Medal, Legion of Merit, Bronze Star and Commendation Ribbon. Died on August 7, 1978.

Woolfley, Francis Augustus (1893-n/a) Born on April 30, 1893, in New Orleans, Louisiana. Commissioned in the infantry in 1917. Professor of military science and tactics at Louisiana State University 1921-1925. Graduated from the Command and General Staff School in 1935 and the Army War College in 1938. Instructor, then director of training at the Infantry School 1938-1942. Organized, then commanded 377th Infantry, 95th Division May 1942-March 1943. Brigadier general in March 1943. Assistant division command of 76th Division in 1943. Commanding general of 106th Division 1944-1945. Reverted to colonel in February 1946. Retired in April 1953. Decorations included two Silver Stars, the Legion of Merit, two Bronze Stars and the Air Medal.

Worsham, Ludson Dixon (1891-1980) Born on October 22, 1891, in Evansville, Indiana. Commissioned in the Corps of Engineers from West Point in 1916. Served with the AEF in World War I. B.S. from Massachusetts Institute of Technology in 1921. Graduated from the Command and General Staff School in 1937. District engineer in Pittsburgh, Pennsylvania, then Mobile, Alabama, 1940-1941. Division engineer at Great Lakes, Illinois, then Northwest Service Command 1942-1944. Brigadier general in April 1943. Assistant chief engineer in the office of the chief of engineers 1944-1945. Engineer for Army Forces Western Pacific 1945-1946. Retired in November 1948. Decorations included the Distinguished Service Medal and two Legions of Merit. Died on April 1, 1980.

Wright, Boykin Cabell (1891-1956) Born in Richmond, Virginia, on September 20, 1891. B.A. from the University of Georgia in 1911 and LL.B. from Harvard Law School in 1914. Commissioned in the infantry in 1917. Served with the 82nd Division 1917-1918. Resigned to practice law in New York City in 1919. Called to active duty as brigadier general in March 1943. Director of the international division at Army Service Forces 1943-1944. Returned to inactive status in April 1944. Decorations included the Silver Star and Legion of Merit. Died on November 9, 1956.

Wyche, Ira Thomas (1887-1981) Born in Ocracoke, North Carolina, on October 16, 1887. Commissioned in the infantry from West Point in 1911. Served in France in 1918. Instructor at the Field Artillery School 1920-1922. Graduated from the Command and General Staff School in 1925. Instructor at the Cavalry School 1929-1933. Graduated from the Army War College in 1934. Duty in the office of the chief of field artillery July 1940-April 1941. Brigadier general in April 1941. Commander of 74th Field Artillery Brigade 1941-1942. Major general in April 1942. Commanding general of 79th Infantry Division May 1942-May 1945 then VIII Corps May-December 1945. Retired in September 1948. Decorations included the Distinguished Service Medal, Silver Star, Legion of Merit and two Bronze Stars. Died on July 8, 1981.

Wylie, Robert Howard (1899-1964) Born in Huntington, West Virginia, on February 24, 1899. Attended Virginia Military Institute 1917-1918. Commissioned in the infantry in 1918. Quartermaster at Fort Sherman, Canal Zone 1923-1924. Assistant superintendent of Army Transportation Service 1930-1931. Graduated from Army Industrial College in 1937. Again with Army Transportation Service 1938-1941. Assistant chief of the Transportation Corps March 1942-July 1945. Brigadier general in December 1942. Staff officer in the operations division of U.S. Army Forces Pacific in 1945. Retired in February 1947. Decorations included the Distinguished Service Medal and two Commendation Ribbons. Died on January 2, 1964.

Wyman, Willard Gordon (1898-1969) Born on March 21, 1898, in Augusta, Missouri. Attended Bowdoin College in 1917. Commissioned in the Coast Artillery Corps from West Point in 1919. Student of the Chinese language in Beijing 1928-1932. Graduated from the Command and General Staff School in 1937. Aide to the commanding general of 1st Cavalry Division then IX Corps July 1940-May 1941. Assistant chief of staff for persosnnel at IX Corps May-August 1941. Assigned to the plans division of the War Department General Staff 1941-1942. Deputy chief of staff for operations in the China-Burma-India Theater of Operations 1942. Deputy chief of staff for operations at Allied Force headquarters 1942-1943. Brigadier general in November 1943. Assistant division commander of 1st Division 1943-1944. Major general in November 1944. Commanding general of 71st Infantry Division 1944-1945. Assignments after the war included commanding general of IX Corps in the Korean War 1951-1952, Allied Land Forces in Southeastern Europe 1952-1954, Sixth Army 1954-1955 and Continental Army Command 1956-1958. Retired as general in 1958. Decorations included the Distinguished Service Cross, three Distinguished Service Medals, the Silver Star, Legion of Merit and two Bronze Stars. Died on March 29, 1969.

Yeager, Emer (1886-1956) Born in Prairie Creek, Indiana, on August 11, 1886. Enlisted service in the Regular Army 1908-1914. Commissioned in the Philippine Scouts in 1914. Transferred to the field artillery in 1916. Served in the Philippines 1914-1917 then the AEF 1918-1919. Graduated from the Command and General Staff School in 1924. Military attache in Poland, Czechoslovakia and Romania 1929-1933. Served with the Civilian Conservation Corps 1937-1942. Executive officer of the 2nd Port of Embarkation, Southwest Pacific Area 1942-1945. Brigadier general in September 1943. Duty at headquarters of Army Ground Forces February 1945 until retirement in September 1945. Decorations included the Legion of Merit. Died on November 24, 1956.

Young, Charles Duncanson (1878-1955) Born on May 19, 1878, in Washington, DC. Commissioned in the Engineer Corps Reserve in 1900. M.E. from Cornell University in 1902. Served with the Transportation Corps in World War I. Employed by the Pennsylvania Railroad 1902-1941. Called to active duty as colonel in 1940. Brigadier general in 1941 as director of procurement and distribution, Services of Supply 1941-1943. Deputy director of the office of defense transporation 1943-1945. Returned to inactive status after the war. Died on May 13, 1955.

Young, Gordon Russell (1891-1963) Born on December 14, 1891, in Philadelphia, Pennsylvania. Commissioned in the Corps of Engineers from West Point in 1913. Served with the Punitive Expedition into Mexico in 1916. Rose to colonel at age of 27 as a member of Pershing's staff in the AEF in 1918. Graduated from the Command and General Staff School in 1927 and the Army War College in 1935. Instructor at the Engineer School 1937-1938. Commanding officer of 11th Engineers 1939-1940. Department engineer in the Panama Canal Department in 1941-1942. Brigadier general in September 1942. Chief engineer at Caribbean Defense Command 1942-1944. Commanding general of Fort Belvoir 1944-1945. Retired in May 1951. Decorations included the Distinguished Service Medal and Legion of Merit. Died on May 25, 1963.

Young, Laurence W. (1877-1966) Born on August 18, 1877, in North Carolina. Commissioned in the North Carolina National Guard in 1905. Served as brigadier general 1913-1918. Adjutant general of North Carolina 1917-1918. Commissioned in the infantry, Regular Army in 1920. Graduated from the Command and General Staff School in 1927. Retired as colonel in August 1941. Recalled to active duty as brigadier general in September 1941 and served until January 1944. Died in 1966.

Young, Robert Nicholas (1900-1964) Born in Washington, DC, on January 14, 1900. B.A. from the University of Maryland in 1922. Commissioned in the infantry in 1923. Served with the 65th Infantry in Puerto Rico 1925-1928. Assistant professor of military science and tactics at the University of Maryland 1928-1932. Instructor at the Infantry School 1934-1937. Graduated from the Command and General Staff School in 1938. Assistant operations officer at Schofield Barracks, Hawaii 1938-1940. Aide to Major General Walter C. Short October 1940-January 1941. Duty in the supply division of the War Department General Staff January-June 1941. Assistant to the secretary of the War Department General Staff June-September 1942 then secretary of the War Department General Staff September 1942-March 1943. Brigadier general in June 1943. Assistant division commander of 70th Infantry Division March 1943-October 1944 then 3rd Infantry Division October 1944-July 1945. Commander of the Military District of Washington 1945-1946. Reverted to colonel in July 1946. Assignments after the war included commanding general of Sixth Army 1955-1957. Retired as lieutenant general in September 1957. Decorations included three Distinguished Service Medals, the Silver Star, Legion of Merit, two Bronze Stars and the Purple Heart. Died on October 19, 1964.

Younger, James Wellington (1894-1963) Born in Post Oak, Texas, on May 28, 1894. Commissioned in the infantry, Officers Reserve Corps in 1917. Served as railway transportation officer with the AEF in France 1917-1919. Transferred to the Transportation Corps in 1919. Assigned to the Quartermaster School 1931-

1939. Graduated from Army Industrial College in 1940. Chief of the administrative branch of the construction division in the office of the quartermaster general, U.S. Army December 1940-June 1941. Assistant quartermaster at Memphis, Tennessee, 1941-1943. Quartermaster of Second Army, then ground quartermaster for Army Ground Forces 1943-1944. Chief of the quartermaster section at 12th Army Group, European Theater of Operations 1944-1945. Brigadier general in March 1945. Reverted to colonel in March 1946. Retired in December 1946. Decorations included the Distinguished Service Medal and Legion of Merit. Died on January 12, 1963.

Yount, Paul Frailey (1908-1984) Born on September 9, 1908, in Alliance, Ohio. Commissioned in the Corps of Engineers from West Point in 1930. C.E. from Cornell University in 1933. Member of U.S. Military Mission to Iran 1941-1942. Commanding officer of Base Sector, Services of Supply in the China-Burma-India Theater of Operations in 1942. Brigadier general in May 1944. Commanding general of military railway service in India in 1944. Commander of Advance Sector, Services of Supply in India Burma Theater of Operations 1944-1945. Retired as major general in 1958. Decorations included three Distinguished Service Medals and two Legions of Merit. Died on November 28, 1984.

Zimmerman, Wayne Clifton (1897-1983) Born on January 15, 1897, in Wadena, Minnesota. Commissioned in the infantry from West Point in 1919. Graduated from the Command and General Staff School in 1940. Chief of staff of 7th Motorized Division 1942-1943. Commanding officer of 17th Infantry 1943-1944. Brigadier general in September 1944. Assistant division commander of 98th Division 1944-1946. Retired as major general in 1956. Decorations included the Distinguished Service Cross, Legion of Merit and two Bronze Stars. Died on December 23, 1983.

Zundel, Edwin Albert (1893-1985) Born on March 29, 1893, in Greensburg, Pennsylvania. Commissioned in the field artillery from West Point in 1915. Graduated from the Command and General Staff School in 1930. Artillery officer at I Corps, then XI Corps 1942-1943. Brigadier general in May 1944. Retired in 1953. Decorations included the Silver Star, three Legions of Merit and the Bronze Star. Died on February 13, 1985.

2

The United States Army Air Force

Acheson, George Robert (1904-1989) Born on January 21, 1904 in Lewiston, Maine. Enlisted service with 24th Pursuit Squadron February 1925-March 1926. Commissioned in the Air Corps in February 1927. Commanding officer of 67th Bombardment Squadron May 1941-September 1941. With 1st Air Support Service Command September 1941-July 1942. Commanding officer of 55th Bomber Wing June 1943-June 1945. Brigadier general in September 1944. Assignments after the war included commanding general of Alaskan Air Command February 1953-1956. Retired in January 1959 as major general. Decorations included the Distinguished Service Medal, Legion of Merit, Distinguished Flying Cross, two Air Medals and the Commendation Ribbon. Died on August 17, 1989.

Adler, Elmer E. (1892-1970) Born on January 30, 1892 in Buffalo, New York. Attended West Point. Commissioned in the Air Service in 1918. Graduated from Command and General Staff School in 1934 and the Army War College in 1935. Commanding general of 7th Bomb Group 1938-1939. Graduated from Air Corps Tactical School in 1939. Commanding officer of 9th Bomb Squadron 1929-1941. Group commander of 20th Bomb Group in 1941. Brigadier general in November 1941. Commanding general of Army Air Forces in the China-Burma-India Theater of Operations 1942-1943. Chief of the personnel and training division at Air Service Command 1943-1944. Chief of management control at Air Transport Command 1944-1946. Major general in January 1945. Retired in March 1946. Decorations included the Distinguished Service Medal, Legion of Merit and Commendation Ribbon. Died on August 13, 1970.

Agee, Walter Robertson (1905-1980) Born on June 25, 1905 in Silver City, New Mexico. Attended New Mexico Military Institute. Commissioned in the Air Corps in 1928. With 2nd Bomber Command October 1941-May 1942. Deputy chief of staff of Second Air Force May 1942-May 1943. Commanding officer of 16th Bomber Operational Training Wing May 1943-October 1943. With Second Air Force October 1943-December 1943. Air Inspector of Third Air Force December 1943-July 1944. Commanding officer of 89th Combat Crew Training

Wing July 1944-July 1945. Brigadier general in June 1945. Assignments after the war included commander of Civil Air Patrol January 1956-April 1959. Retired in April 1959. Decorations included the Legion of Merit, Bronze Star and Purple Heart. Died on January 16, 1980.

Alexander, Edward Harrison (1902-1978) Born in Watseka, Illinois, on January 4, 1902. B.A. from the University of Illinois in 1927. Commissioned in the Air Corps Reserve in June 1926 and the U.S. Army in May 1929. Duty at headquarters of the China-Burma-India Theater of Operations April 1942-December 1942. Brigadier general in June 1943. With Air Transport Command in China, the Caribbean and Australia 1943-1945. Assignments after the war included deputy commanding general of Eighteenth Air Force 1952-1956. Retired in June 1956. Decorations included the Legion of Merit and Distinguished Flying Cross. Died on November 14, 1978.

Allard, John Stetson (1897-1967) Born on January 16, 1897, in Boston, Massachusetts. Enlisted service 1917-1918. Commissioned in the Air Service, Officers Reserve Corps in 1918. Returned to inactive status following World War I. Vice president of Curtis-Wright Corp. 1929-1942. Recalled to active duty as colonel in July 1942 as assistant chief of staff of Twelfth Air Force. Deputy chief of staff of North African Strategic Air Force March-July 1943. With Seventh Bomber Command July 1943-March 1944. Deputy chief of staff, then chief of staff of Eighth Air Force March 1944-May 1945. Brigadier general in September 1944. Retired in January 1946. Decorations included the Legion of Merit. Died on October 3, 1967.

Andersen, James Roy (1904-1945) Born on May 10, 1904, in Racine, Wisconsin. Commissioned in the infantry from West Point in 1926. Earned his wings in 1936. Director of training at Army Air Force Basic Advanced Flying School March 1942-June 1943. With plans division of War Department General Staff June 1943-August 1944. At headquarters of Army Air Forces in Pacific Ocean Areas August 1944-February 1945. Brigadier general in January 1945. Killed in an aircraft accident near Kwajalein on February 26, 1945. Decorations included the Legion of Merit.

Anderson, Edward W. (1903-1979) Born in Manhattan, Kansas, on September 23, 1903. B.A. from Stanford University in 1928. Commissioned in the Air Corps in 1929. Commanding Officer of 20th Fighter Group March 1942-September 1942, then 4th Fighter Group September 1942-September 1943. Brigadier general in March 1944. Commanding general of 65th Fighter Wing September 1943-July 1945. Assignments after the war included deputy commander of Air Training Command April-November 1948 and assistant comptroller of the Air Force May 1950-July 1954. Retired as major general in October 1958. Decorations included the Silver Star, Legion of Merit, Bronze Star and three Air Medals. Died on April 12, 1979.

Anderson, Frederick Lewis (1905-1969) Born in Kingston, New York, on October 4, 1905. Commissioned in the cavalry from West Point in 1928. Earned his wings in the Air Corps in June 1929. Duty in the office of the chief of the Army Air Force 1941-1943. Brigadier general in February 1943, major general in November 1943. Commanding general of 8th Bomber Command 1943. Assistant chief of staff for operations at U.S. Strategic Air Forces in the European Theater of Operations February 1944-June 1945. Assistant chief of staff for personnel at headquarters Army Air Force 1945 until retirement in September 1947. Decorations included the Distinguished Service Cross, Distinguished Service Medal, Silver Star and Distinguished Flying Cross. U.S. ambassador to NATO 1952-1953. Died on March 2, 1969.

Anderson, Orvil Arson (1895-1965) Born in Springville, Utah, on May 2, 1895. Attended Brigham Young University. Commissioned in the Bureau of Military Aeronautics in August 1918. Became an airship pilot in 1920. Test pilot on semi-rigid airship *RS-1*, the only craft of its type built in America 1926-1927. Utilizing a canvas sea anchor which he designed, made the first successful anchoring of an airship at sea in 1933. Co-pilot of the balloon *Explorer I* in July 1934 and pilot of *Explorer II* in November 1935 which set an altitude record of 72,395 feet. Graduated from Command and General Staff School in 1938. Chief of plans division at headquarters of Army Air Force 1942-1943. Brigadier general in September 1942. Chairman of Combined Operational Planning Committee 1943-1945. Major general in November 1944. Assignments after the war included commandant of the Air War College 1946-1950. Retired in December 1950. Decorations included two Distinguished Service Medals, the Silver Star and two Distinguished Flying Crosses. Also awarded the Mackay Trophy. Died on August 23, 1965.

Anderson, Samuel Egbert (1906-1982) Born on January 6, 1906 in Greenboro, North Carolina. Commissioned in the Coast Artillery Corps following graduation from West Point in 1928. Transferred to the Air Corps in 1929. Instructor at Kelly Field and Chanute Field 1932-1939. With operations division of the War Department General Staff March 1942-May 1943. Commander of 3rd Medium Bomb Wing, then 9th Medium Bomb Command May 1943-May 1945. Brigadier general in November 1943, major general in August 1944. Chief of staff of Continental Air Force May 1945-February 1946. Assignments after the war included commanding general of Eighth Air Force August 1950-May 1953, commanding general of Fifth Air Force May 1953-May 1954, and commander of Air Research and Development Command August 1957-July 1963. Retired as general in July 1963. Decorations included four Distinguished Service Medals, the Silver Star, Distinguished Flying Cross and Bronze Star. Died on September 12, 1982.

Andrews, Frank Maxwell (1884-1943) Born on February 3, 1884, in Nashville, Tennessee. Commissioned in the Cavalry from West Point in 1906. Transferred to the aviation section of the Signal Corps in 1917. Served in the southern United States during World War I. Graduated from Command and General Staff School in 1929 and the Army War College in 1933. Brigadier general in March 1935.

Commander of GHQ Air Force March 1935-March 1939. Major general in February 1938. Reverted to colonel, then promoted once again to brigadier general in August 1939. Assistant chief of staff, U.S. Army August 1939-November 1940. Major general in October 1940. Commander of Panama Canal Air Force (later Caribbean Air Force) November 1940-September 1941, then Caribbean Defense Command September 1941-November 1942. Lieutenant general in September 1941. From November 1942-February 1943 commander of U.S. Forces Middle East, then commander U.S. Army Forces Europe. Killed in an aircraft accident in Iceland on May 3, 1943. Decorations included two Distinguished Service Medals and the Distinguished Flying Cross.

Ankenbrandt, Francis LeRoy (1904-1976) Born in Chicago, Illinois, on January 27, 1904. Commissioned in the Signal Corps from West Point in 1926. M.S. from Yale in 1927. Instructor at West Point 1929-1934. Theater of Operations signal officer in the South Pacific Area July 1942-July 1944. Director of communications of Army Air Forces Pacific Ocean Area July 1944-August 1945. Brigadier general in January 1945. Assignments after the war included director of communications-electronics in the office of the Joint Chiefs of Staff 1955-1956. Retired as major general in October 1956. Decorations included the Distinguished Service Medal, Legion of Merit and Bronze Star. Died on December 1, 1976.

Armstrong, Frank Alton Jr. (1902-1969) Born in Hamilton, North Carolina, on May 24, 1902. LL.B. from Wake Forest College in 1923, B.S. in 1925. Enlisted service as flying cadet February 1928-February 1929. Commissioned in the Air Reserve in February 1929. Duty at headquarters of Army Air Force August 1941-February 1942. With 8th Bomber Command in England February 1942-August 1943. Brigadier general in February 1943. Commanding general of 17th Bomber Operational Training Wing and 315th Bomber Wing 1943-1946. Led the first non-stop flight from Japan to Washington, DC in a B-29 in November 1945. Assignments after the war included commanding general of Second Air Force 1952-1956, commander of Alaskan Air Command, then Commander in Chief Alaska July 1956-July 1961. Retired as lieutenant general in July 1961. Decorations included the Distinguished Service Cross, Distinguished Service Medal, Silver Star and four Distinguished Flying Crosses. Died on August 20, 1969.

Arnold, Henry Harley (1886-1950) Born on June 25, 1886, in Gladwyne, Pennsylvania. Commissioned in the infantry from West Point in 1907, where he acquired the nickname "Hap." Pioneer aviator, learning to fly from Orville Wright in 1911 and earning several decorations including two Mackay trophies. Flew the first U.S. Air Mail in September 1911. Oversaw the Army's aviation training program in Washington, DC during World War I. Graduated from Command and General Staff School in 1929. Commanding officer of March Field 1931-1935. Brigadier general in February 1935, major general in September 1938. Chief of the Air Corps (later Army Air Force) 1938-1946. Lieutenant general in December 1941, general in March 1943. General of the Army in December 1944. Retired in June 1946. Decorations included three Distinguished Service Medals and the Distinguished Flying Cross. General of the Air Force in 1949, the only officer so honored. Author of three books with General Ira C. Eaker and an autobiography, *Global Mission* (1949). Died on January 15, 1950.

Arnold, Milton Wylie (1907-) Born in Troup County, Georgia, on May 23, 1907. Commissioned in the Air Corps from West Point in 1931. M.S. from California Institute of Technology in 1937. With the Directorate of Weather 1941-1942. Oversaw development of North Atlantic ferry route 1942. Chief of staff of North Atlantic Division, Air Transport Command 1943. Held numerous positions with Eighth Air Force 1943-1945. Brigadier general in June 1945. Chief of staff of Air Transport Command 1945-1946. Retired in April 1946. Decorations included the Silver Star, four Distinguished Flying Crosses, the Legion of Merit, Bronze Star and five Air Medals. Resides in Palm Beach, Florida.

Atkinson, Joseph Hampton (1900-1984) Born in Dublin, Texas, on February 5, 1900. Commissioned in the Air Service in 1924. Commanding officer of 24th Bombardment Squadron February 1940-August 1941. Assistant chief of staff for plans and training at headquarters of Army Air Force October 1941-September 1942. At headquarters of 8th Bomber Command September-December 1942. Brigadier general in December 1942. Commanding general of 97th Bombardment Group, then 5th Bombardment Wing 1943. Deputy commanding general of Fifteenth Air Force March-July 1944. Commanding general of 3rd Bomber Command July 1944-May 1945. Assignments after the war included commanding general of Alaskan Air Command 1946-1949 and Air Defense Command September 1956-February 1961. Retired as lieutenant general in February 1961. Decorations included the Distinguished Service Medal, Silver Star and Distinguished Flying Cross. Died on November 6, 1984.

Auton, Jesse (1904-1952) Born in Fiskburg, Kentucky, on December 1, 1904. B.A. from Georgetown College of Kentucky in 1927. Commissioned in the Air Corps in 1930. Aide to the commanding general of Second Army June 1934-December 1934. Aide and pilot to the assistant secretary of war July 1938-August 1939 and again June 1940-February 1941. Graduated from the Army Industrial College in 1940. Staff officer, later commanding officer of 20th Pursuit Group 1941-1942. Brigadier general in March 1944. Commander of 65th Fighter Wing July 1943-July 1945. Died on March 30, 1952, at Offutt Air Force Base. Decorations included the Legion of Merit, Distinguished Flying Cross, Bronze Star and Purple Heart.

Backus, Edward Nolen (1906-1973) Born in Vernon, Texas, on July 16, 1906. Graduated from Washington and Lee University in 1929. Commissioned in the Air Reserve in 1933. With 16th Bomber Squadron, 27th Bomber Group and Ninth Air Force 1941-1943. Brigadier general in August 1944. Commander of 97th Bomber Wing 1944-1946. Reverted to colonel in March 1946. Retired in August 1961. Decorations included the Silver Star, Legion of Merit, two Distinguished Flying Crosses and two Air Medals. Died on March 30, 1973.

Banfill, Charles Yawkey (1897-1966) Born in Bonifay, Florida, on September 5, 1897. Enlisted service 1916-1918. Commissioned in the aviation section of the Signal Corps Reserve in 1918 and the Air Service in 1920 upon being called to active duty. Graduated from Command and General Staff School in 1936 and the Army War College in 1940. With military intelligence division of the War Department General Staff January 1941-June 1942. Commandant of Military Intelligence Training Center June 1942-January 1945. Brigadier general in February 1944. Director of intelligence at Eighth Air Force January 1945-August 1945. At headquarters of Army Air Force August 1945-February 1946. Assignments after the war included commandant of Armed Forces Staff College November 1947-July 1950. Retired in July 1953. Decorations included the Legion of Merit and Bronze Star. Died on March 13, 1966.

Barber, Edward (1900-1965) Born in Covington, Kentucky, on May 8, 1900. Attended the University of Cincinnati. Commissioned in the Coast Artillery Corps in 1921. Graduated from Command and General Staff School in 1939 and the Army War College in 1940. With the War Department General Staff July 1940-November 1941, the Army War College staff November 1941-February 1942 and Army Ground Forces February 1942-February 1943. Brigadier general in September 1943. Commanded the 59th Antiaircraft Artillery Brigade 1943-1945. Assignments after the war included deputy commandant of the Air War College 1948-1949. Retired in September 1951. Decorations included the Bronze Star and Commendation Ribbon. Died on January 28, 1965.

Barcus, Glenn Oscar (1903-1990) Born on July 25, 1903, in Genoa, Illinois. Commissioned in the cavalry reserve following graduation from the University of Illinois at Champaign in 1924. Transferred to the Air Corps and earned his wings in February 1927. Commanding officer of 22nd Pursuit Squadron February 1940-March 1941. Plans and training officer of the Puerto Rican Region of 6th Interceptor Command March 1941-March 1942. Commanding officer of the Trinidad Region of 6th Interceptor Command March-April 1942. At headquarters of Army Air Force April-December 1942. Wing commander of Philadelphia Air Defense Wing December 1942-April 1943. Brigadier general in May 1943. Commander of 1st Fighter Command April 1943-April 1944. Commanding general of 64th Fighter Wing April 1944-February 1945 then 12th Tactical Air Command February 1945-August 1946. Assignments after the war included commanding general of Fifth Air Force June 1952-May 1953, commander of Air Training Command May 1953-July 1954 and chief of staff of U.S. European Command April 1957 until retirement as lieutenant general in July 1960. Decorations included the Distinguished Service Medal, Legion of Merit, Distinguished Flying Cross, Bronze Star, Air Medal and Commendation Ribbon. Died on December 9, 1990.

Barker, John DeForest (1897-1986) Born in St. Albans, Vermont, on March 25, 1897. Enlisted service with Vermont National Guard 1916-1918. Commissioned in the Bureau of Military Aeronautics in 1918. Graduated from Command and

General Staff School in 1936 and the Army War College in 1938. Chief of training division at the War Department General Staff May-September 1942. Assistant chief of staff of Twelfth Air Force 1942-1943. With the War Department General Staff again in 1943. Instructor at Army Navy Staff College August-November 1943. Brigadier general in May 1944. Retired in August 1953. Decorations included the Distinguished Service Medal and Legion of Merit. Died on October 1, 1986.

Barnes, Earl Walter (1902-1979) Born in Crawford, Nebraska, on August 23, 1902. Commissioned in the Air Service from West Point in 1925. Graduated from Command and General Staff School in 1937. Served with 31st, 52nd and 53rd Pursuit Groups August 1940-July 1942. Executive officer of 26th Fighter Command July-November 1942. Brigadier general in August 1943. Assistant commandant of Army Air Force School of Applied Tactics November 1942-August 1943. Deputy commander, then commanding general of 13th Fighter Command August 1943-October 1945. Assignments after the war included commanding general of Thirteenth Air Force October 1945-January 1946, deputy commander of Tactical Air Command 1953-1956, and chief of staff of Far East Command 1956-1957. Retired as lieutenant general in September 1957. Decorations included two Distinguished Service Medals and the Distinguished Flying Cross. Died on May 23, 1979.

Bartholf, John Charles Palmer (1891-1969) Born in Plattsburg, New York, on October 26, 1891. B.A. from Harvard in 1913. Commissioned in the infantry in 1913. Transferred to the Aviation Section of the Signal Corps in 1916. Graduated from Command and General Staff School in 1925. Served in the Canal Zone 1925-1927. Instructor with the New York National Guard July 1934-August 1939. Duty with 29th Infantry 1939-1940. Professor of military science and tactics at Drexel Institute September 1940-August 1942. Executive officer at headquarters of Third Army 1942-1944. Brigadier general in April 1943. Duty at headquarters of Fourth Army December 1944 until retirement in October 1945. Died on September 22, 1969.

Bartron, Harold Arthur (1894-1975) Born in Frankfort, Indiana, on September 17, 1894. Enlisted service in the Marine Corps 1912-1916. Commissioned in the aviation section of the Signal Corps in 1918. Duty with the 13th Squadron, 2nd Pursuit Group, including the St. Mihiel and Argonne offensives August 1918-February 1919. Discharged then commissioned in the U.S. Army in October 1920. Commanding officer of 1st Area Service Command, then commanding general of Army Air Forces Service Command, North African Theater of Operations of Operations October 1942-August 1944. Brigadier general in June 1943. Commander of Fairfield Area, Air Service Command September 1944-November 1945. Retired in January 31, 1948. Decorations included the Legion of Merit. Died on May 21, 1975.

Beach, Maurice Milton (1903-1987) Born on April 1, 1903, in Caro, Michigan. Enlisted service in the Air Service 1923-1937. Commissioned in the Air Reserve in 1925 while on active duty in an enlisted status. Called to active duty in 1940. Served at Wright Field 1940-1942. Commanding officer of 10th Transport Group, then 53rd Troop Carrier Wing 1942-1945. Brigadier general in April 1945. Retired in January 1949. Decorations included the Legion of Merit. two Distinguished Flying Crosses, the Bronze Star and Air Medal. Died on January 17, 1987.

Beaman, Bartlett (1891-1947) Born in Princeton, Massachusetts, on July 20, 1891. B.A. from Harvard in 1913. Commissioned in the aviation section of the Officers Reserve Corps in 1918. Active duty with the 12th Aero Squadron in World War I, including the Meuse-Argonne campaign. Discharged in 1919. Recalled to active duty as a major in the office of the chief of the Air Corps February 1941-March 1942. Special observer in England, then executive officer of 1st Provisional Bombardment Wing, finally chief of staff of 1st Air Division in Eighth Air Force March 1942-November 1945. Brigadier general in February 1944. Died on November 14, 1947. Decorations included the Distinguished Service Medal, Legion of Merit, Bronze Star and Air Medal.

Beau, Lucas Victor Jr. (1895-1986) Born on August 3, 1895, in New York, New York. Enlisted service in the New York National Guard and the Signal Corps, aviation section 1916-1918. Commissioned in the Air Service in 1918. Assistant chief, then chief of the personnel division, headquarters of the Air Corps March 1940-February 1942. Commanding officer of San Bernardino Air Depot 1942-1943. Brigadier general in April 1943. Chief of staff of Air Service Command November 1943-March 1945. Commanding general of Medical Air Transport Service March-September 1945. Retired as major general in August 1955. Decorations included the Legion of Merit. Died on October 22, 1986.

Beebe, Eugene Harold (1906-1992) Born on September 27, 1906, in Utica, Nebraska. Graduated from the University of Idaho in 1928. Commissioned in the Air Corps in 1929. Executive assistant to General Henry H. Arnold July 1941-July 1942. Group commander of 302nd, 308th and 346th Bomb Groups July 1942-November 1943. Brigadier general in November 1943. Staff officer at Southeast Asia Command, war planning division November 1943-August 1944. Acting commanding general of Continental Air Forces December 1944 until retirement in November 1945. Died on September 25, 1992.

Beebe, Royden Eugene Jr. (1908-1959) Born on December 14, 1908, in Fort Douglas, Utah. Commissioned in the cavalry from West Point in 1931. Transferred to the Air Corps in 1933. Assistant to the assistant chief of staff for operations, Third Air Force 1941-1942. Brigadier general in June 1942. Assistant, then director of operations for Allied Air Forces Southwest Pacific 1942-1944. Chief of staff for operations, then chief of staff of Far East Air Forces 1944-1945. Member of U.S. Strategic Bombing Survey 1945-1946. Died as major general on

April 29, 1959, from a heart attack while playing golf at Andrews Air Force Base. Decorations included the Distinguished Service Medal and Legion of Merit.

Berman, Morris (1891-1945) Born in New York, New York on August 10, 1891. Enlisted in the U.S. Army in 1912. Commissioned in the infantry in 1917. Transferred to the Air Service in 1920. Commanding officer of the Philippine Air Depot at Camp Nichols December 1923-January 1925 then Second Observation Squadron at Kindley Field, Philippines 1925-1926. Chief of the civilian personnel branch at Wright Field August 1937-May 1940. Commanding officer of the Air Depot, then 482nd base headquarters, finally Air Depot Control Area Command, all at Ogden, Utah, 1940-1943. Brigadier general in September 1943. Commander of San Antonio Air Service 1943-1944. Assigned to U.S. Strategic Air Forces in Europe November 1944 until his death there on November 11, 1945.

Bertrandis, Victor Emile (1893-1961) Born in San Francisco, California, on May 14, 1893. Attended St. Mary's College. Commissioned in the Sanitary Corps in 1918 and the Air Service in 1920. Resigned in 1929. Recalled to active duty as major, Air Corps Reserve, in 1942. Commanding officer of 4th Air Depot Group, then 5th Air Service Command October 1942-January 1944. Brigadier general in June 1944. Commander of Far Eastern Service Command July-October 1944. Chief of the maintenance division at Air Technical Service Command November 1944-July 1945. Relieved of active duty in January 1946. Decorations included the Distinguished Service Medal and Air Medal. Died on March 18, 1961.

Bevans, James Millikin (1899-1977) Born in San Francisco, California, on October 12, 1899. Attended West Point 1917-1918 and Princeton 1918-1921. Commissioned in the field artillery in 1918. Graduated from Command and General Staff School in 1938. Brigadier general in March 1943. Assistant chief of staff for personnel on the Air Staff 1943-1945. Major general in February 1944. Retired in October 1951. Decorations included the Distinguished Service Medal, Legion of Merit and Bronze Star. Died on May 1, 1977.

Beverley, George Hendricks (1897-1988) Born in Amarillo, Texas, on May 27, 1897. Attended Texas A&M. Commissioned in the Bureau of Military Aeronautics in 1918. Instructor with the Massachusetts National Guard in 1933. Graduated from Command and General Staff School in 1938. Director of technical inspection at headquarters Army Air Force in 1942. Commanding officer of 2nd, then 1st Air Service Area Command 1942-1943. Brigadier general in June 1943. Commander of 51st Troop Carrier Wing 1943-1944 then 15th Air Force Service Command March-October 1944. Air service inspector at Air Materiel Command 1944-1945. Commanding general of San Antonio Materiel Command 1945-1947. Retired in July 1949. Decorations included two Legions of Merit. Died on September 15, 1988.

Bissell, Clayton Lawrence (1896-1972) Born in Kane, Pennsylvania, on July 29, 1896. LL.B. from Valparaiso University Law School in 1917. Commissioned in the aviation section of the Signal Corps in 1918. Served with 148th Fighter Squadron, then commanding officer of 638th Fighter Squadron in France in World War I. Assistant to Brigadier General Billy Mitchell 1921-1924. Graduated from Command and General Staff School in 1933, the Army War College in 1934 and the Naval War College in 1939. With Stilwell in China 1941-1942. Brigadier general in April 1942. Commanding general of Tenth Air Force 1942-1943. Major general in March 1943. Chief of Army Air Force intelligence 1943. Assistant chief of staff for intelligence, U.S. Army 1943-1945. Retired in October 1950. Decorations included the Distinguished Service Cross, Distinguished Service Medal, Silver Star, Distinguished Flying Cross and Air Medal. Author of *History of U.S. Army Air Corps* (1923). Died on December 29, 1972.

Blackburn, Thomas Welch (1892-1964) Born in Gane Hill, Arkansas, on April 29, 1892. Attended State University School 1910-1911 and State Normal School 1911-1912. Enlisted service 1917-1918. Commissioned in the Bureau of Military Aeronautics in 1918. Served with the Fourth Pursuit Group, Second Army in France April 1918-July 1919. Operations officer at Clark Field, Philippines 1929-1931. Assistant to the chief of the Aviation Bureau 1937-1939. Acting chief of the aviation division May-July 1939. Group operations officer with 19th Bombardment Group July 1939-May 1941. Executive officer of Fourth Air Base Command at March Field June 1941-February 1942 then Ninth Interceptor Command February-June 1942. Chief of staff of a bombardment wing July-November 1942. Brigadier general in December 1942. Commanding general of Twelfth Fighter Command 1942-1943, 31st Flying Training Wing April 1943-February 1944 and Third Fighter Command March 1944-February 1946. Reverted to colonel in February 1946 and retired in April 1952. Died on September 27, 1964.

Booth, Charles Loomis (1901-) Born in East Orange, New Jersey, on June 30, 1901. Commissioned in the field artillery from West Point in 1924. Transferred to the Air Corps in 1941. Assistant chief of staff of Eighth Air Force January-November 1942. Assistant chief of staff of Northwest African Air Forces November 1942-December 1943. Brigadier general in November 1943. Deputy commanding general of Mediterranean Air Forces May 1944-June 1945. Retired in January 1947. Decorations included two Legions of Merit and the Bronze Star. Resides in Washington, DC.

Born, Charles Franklin (1903-1979) Born in Racine, Wisconsin, on April 24, 1903. Attended St. John's Academy 1920-1924. Commissioned in the cavalry from West Point in 1928. Instructor at West Point 1937-1939 and 1939-1940. Commanding officer of 5th Bombardment Squadron July 1940-August 1941, 9th Bombardment Group in Panama 1941-1943 and Antilles Air Command 1943-1944. Brigadier general in March 1943. Assistant chief of staff, then deputy commanding general of Fifteenth Air Force 1944-1945. Chief of operations and training, then chief of staff at Continental Air Forces 1945-1946. Assignments after the war included commanding general of Second Air Force 1946-1947. Retired as major general in October 1955. Decorations included the Distinguished Service Medal, two Legions of Merit, the Distinguished Flying Cross and three Air Medals. Died on May 24, 1979.

Borum, Fred S. (1892-1978) Born in Winchester, Illinois, on April 25, 1892. Attended Kendall College in 1912. Commissioned in the aviation section of the Signal Corps in 1918. Graduated from the Army Industrial College in 1939. Chief of the field service section, office of the chief of the Air Corps 1939-1941. Assistant chief of staff for supply at headquarters of the Army Air Force December 1941-April 1942. Brigadier general in September 1942. Commander of 1st Troop Carrier Command 1942-1943. Commanding general of 4th Bomb Wing in 1943. Headed the supply division at 15th Air Service Command 1943-1944 then at headquarters Air Service Command in 1944. Major general in 1944. Commanding general of Miami Air Technical Service Command 1944-1945. Retired in April 1954. Decorations included the Legion of Merit and two Commendation Ribbons. Died on October 24, 1978.

Bradley, Follett (1890-1952) Born in Omaha, Nebraska, on February 12, 1890. Graduated from USNA in 1910. Commissioned in field artillery, U.S. Army in 1911. Transferred to the Air Service in 1920. Graduated from the Army War College in 1932 and the Naval War College in 1933. With War Department General Staff 1934-1935. Brigadier general in October 1940. Commander of 13th Composite Wing 1940-1941. Commanding general of 3rd Bomber Command in 1941 and First Air Force in 1942. Major general in February 1942. Undertook a special mission to Russia with the rank of minister 1942-1943. Inspector at headquarters Army Air Force in 1944. Retired in April 1944. Decorations included the Distinguished Service Cross, Distinguished Service Medal, Silver Star and Distinguished Flying Cross. Died on August 4, 1952.

Brady, Francis M. (1896-1969) Born in Yonkers, New York, on July 7, 1896. Commissioned in the infantry in 1917. Transferred to the Air Service in 1925. Graduated from Command and General Staff School in 1931 and the Army War College in 1936. Served with the War Department General Staff September 1938-April 1939. Brigadier general in February 1942. Retired in January 1947. Decorations included the Distinguished Service Cross, two Silver Stars, two Legions of Merit, the Bronze Star and Purple Heart. Died on October 26, 1969.

Brandt, Carl Amandus (1906-1961) Born on January 9, 1906, in Fort Niebrara, Nebraska. Commissioned in the field artillery from West Point in 1930. Transferred to the Air Corps in 1931. Commanding officer of Fifth Air Force Service Command in 1943 and 90th Bombardment Group in 1944. Commander of Far East Air Forces Combat Replacement Training Center in 1944. Brigadier general in June 1945. Commanding general of 13th Bomber Command in 1945. Deputy commander then chief of staff of Thirteenth Air Force 1945-1946. Retired as major general in 1961. Decorations included the Distinguished Service Medal, two Legions of Merit, the Distinguished Flying Cross, two Air Medals and the Commendation Ribbon. Died on December 23, 1961.

Branshaw, Charles Egbert (1895-1949) Born in Fairhaven, Vermont, on August 6, 1895. Enlisted service with the Colorado National Guard 1916-1917. Commissioned in the aviation section of the Signal Corps in 1917. Served with the AEF in World War I. Graduated from Air Corps Tactical School in 1935. Commanding officer of the Hawaiian Air Depot April 1936-September 1938. Executive officer of Sacramento Air Depot 1938-1939. Army Air Corps representative at Douglas Aircraft Plant March 1939-December 1940. Supervisor at the Western Air Corps Procurement Division December 1940-March 1943. Brigadier general in May 1942. Commanding general of Army Air Force Material Command March 1943-July 1944. Major general in June 1943. District supervisor for Army Air Force Technical Training Command at Coral Gables July 1944 until retirement in December 1944. Decorations included the Distinguished Service Medal and Legion of Merit. Died on May 8, 1949.

Brant, Gerald Clark (1880-1958) Born in Charlton, Iowa, on June 29, 1880. Commissioned in the cavalry from West Point in 1904. Commandant of Pennsylvania Military College 1911-1913. Graduated from the Army War College in 1923. Executive officer to the assistant secretary of war in 1927. Commanding general of 3rd and 2nd Air Wings 1935-1938. Commandant of Army Air Corps Technical Schools 1938-1940. Brigadier general in October 1940. Commanding general of Gulf Coast Training Center 1940-1941 then Newfoundland Base 1941-1943. Major general in July 1941. Commanding general of Army Air Force Gulf Coast Training Center 1943-1944. Retired in May 1944. Decorations included the Distinguished Service Medal and Legion of Merit. Died on August 5, 1958.

Breene, Robert G. (1894-1969) Born in Dayton, Ohio, on September 17, 1894. B.S. from Purdue in 1917. Commissioned in the Corps of Engineers, Officers Reserve Corps in 1917. Served with the AEF 1918-1919. Graduated from Command and General Staff School in 1936 then instructor there until 1940. With 3rd Wing, then 3rd Bombardment Group July-December 1940. Chief of staff of Second Air Force December 1940-August 1942. Brigadier general in August 1942. Commanding general of Services of Supply in the South Pacific Area August 1942-July 1944. Major general in April 1943. Deputy commander of Army Air Forces in Pacific Ocean Areas 1944-1945. Commander of Army Air Force Central Flying Training Command 1945-1946. Retired in February 1946. Decorations included the Legion of Merit. Died on February 25, 1969.

Brereton, Lewis Hyde (1890-1967) Born in Pittsburgh, Pennsylvania, on June 21, 1890. Commissioned ensign in the U.S. Navy from USNA in 1911. Resigned to accept a commission in the Coast Artillery Corps. Transferred to the aviation section of Signal Corps. Commanding officer of 2nd and 12th Aero Squadrons, then chief of aviation for I Army Corps in France October 1917-February 1919. Graduated from Command and General Staff School in 1926. Instructor at Command and General Staff School 1935-1939. Commanding officer of 17th Bomb Wing 1939-1941. Brigadier general in October 1940, major general in July 1941. Commanding general of Third Air Force July-December 1941. Commander of Far East Air Forces, then commander in chief of Allied Air Forces Far East, finally commanding general of Tenth Air Force December 1941-March 1942. Commander of Middle East Air Forces, then U.S. Army Forces Middle East March 1942-October 1943. Commanding general of Ninth Air Force October 1943-August 1944. Lieutenant general in April 1944. Commanding general of First Allied Airborne Army April 1944-May 1945, then Third Air Force and First Air Force 1945-1946. Retired in August 1948. Decorations included the Distinguished Service Cross, Distinguished Service Medal, Silver Star, Legion of Merit, Distinguished Flying Cross and Bronze Star. Died on July 20, 1967.

Brett, George Howard (1886-1963) Born on February 7, 1886, in Cleveland, Ohio. Commissioned in the Philippine Scouts in 1910 following graduation from Virginia Military Institute the previous year. Transferred to the aviation section of the Signal Corps in 1915. Graduated from Command and General Staff School in 1930 and the Army War College in 1936. Brigadier general in January 1939. Chief of the materiel division at Wright Field 1939-1941. Major general in October 1940. Chief of the Air Corps May 1941-March 1942. Lieutenant general in January 1942. Deputy supreme allied commander in the Southwest Pacific in 1942. Commanding general of the Caribbean Defense Command 1942-1946. Retired in May 1946. Decorations included two Distinguished Service Medals, the Silver Star and Distinguished Flying Cross. Died on December 2, 1963.

Brooks, John B. (1891-1975) Born in Greenwich, New York, on June 8, 1891. Commissioned in the cavalry in 1912. Transferred to the Air Service in 1920. Graduated from Command and General Staff School in 1925 and the Army War College in 1927. Commanding officer of Clark Field, Philippine Islands 1930-1933. Duty at the War Department General Staff 1933-1937. Commanding officer of Air Corps Primary Flying School 1937-1940. Brigadier general in October 1940. Commanding general of 4th Bomb Wing 1940-1941 then 2nd Bomber Command 1941-1942. Commander of 2nd Ground Air Support Command in 1942. Major general in March 1943. Commanding general of Newfoundland Base Command 1943-1944. Duty with the Organization of the Joint Chiefs of Staff 1944-1945. Commanding general of Seventh Air Force July 1945 until retirement in September 1946. Decorations included the Distinguished Service Medal, Legion of Merit, Distinguished Flying Cross and Air Medal. Died on December 31, 1975.

Burns, Robert Whitney (1908-1964) Born in Stanley, Wisconsin, on September 15, 1908. Attended the University of Wisconsin 1926-1927. Commissioned in the Air Corps in 1928. Adviser to the Air Corps Military Mission to Chile 1940-1943. Assistant chief of staff for operations at 8th Fighter Command, then Eighth Air Force 1943-1945. Brigadier general in June 1945. Commander of 4th Combat Wing and 14th Bomb Wing in 1945. Assignments after the war included commander of Fifth Air Force 1958-1961, chairman of the Inter-American Defense Board 1961-1963, and commanding general of Air Training Command 1963-1964. Retired as lieutenant general in August 1964 and died on September 5, 1964.

Burrows, Paul Edmund (1895-1975) Born in Washington, DC, on August 13, 1895. Enlisted as a flying cadet in 1917. Commissioned in the Air Service in 1918. Served with the 28th Bombardment Squadron at Camp Nichols, Philippines May 1926-May 1927. Instructor with the 321st Observation Squadron, Organized Reserves 1933-1940. Chief of the research division in the office of the chief of the Air Corps July 1940-December 1941. Assigned to headquarters of Air Transport Command December 1941-January 1943. Brigadier general in February 1943. Commanding general of the Caribbean Wing, then European Wing, finally the Domestic Transportation Division of Air Transport Command 1943-1944. Deputy commanding general of Eleventh Air Force in 1945. Reverted to colonel in March 1946 and retired in August 1951. Died on February 2, 1975.

Burwell, Harvey S. (1890-1955) Born in Winsted, Connecticut, on April 20, 1890. B.S. from Norwich University in 1913. Commissioned in the cavalry in 1913. Graduated from Command and General Staff School in 1934. Commanding officer of 19th Bomber Group in 1939. Commanding officer of Wheeler Field 1940-1941 then 14th Pursuit Wing in 1941. Commander of Lowry Field in 1942. Brigadier general in September 1942. Commanding general of Amarillo Army Air Base 1942-1944. Retired in February 1944. Decorations included the Legion of Merit. Died on March 6, 1955.

Butler, William Ormond (1895-1962) Born on September 23, 1895 in Marshall, Virginia. Commissioned in the field artillery from West Point in 1917. Commanding officer of 2nd American Balloon Company, AEF in 1918. Executive officer of Nichols Field, Philippine Islands 1929-1931. Graduated from Command and General Staff School in 1935. Commanding officer of France Field, Panama Canal Zone 1937-1939. Executive officer of 1st Wing in 1940. Chief of staff of Fourth Air Force in 1940, then Air Service Command 1940-1942. Brigadier general in March 1942. Commanding general of Eleventh Air Force March 1942-September 1943. Major general in October 1942. Deputy commanding general of Allied Expeditionary Air Forces in European Theater of Operations 1943-1944. Commanding general of Eastern Flying Training Command 1944-1945 then Sixth Air Force 1945-1946. Retired in January 1946. Decorations included two Legions of Merit. Died on October 29, 1962.

Cabell, Charles Pearre (1903-1971) Born in Dallas, Texas, on October 11, 1903. Commissioned in the field artillery from West Point in 1925. Transferred to the Air Corps in 1931. Graduated from Command and General Staff School in 1940. Observer with the Royal Air Force 1940-1941. Head of photo unit for chief of the Air Corps April 1941-February 1942. Assistant executive for technical planning and coordination, then chief of the Advisory Council in the office of the chief of Air Corps. The council served as a daily sounding board and planning group for General Arnold. Commanding officer of 45th Combat Bomb Wing, Eighth Air Force December 1943-April 1944. Brigadier general in February 1944. Director of plans for U.S. Strategic Air Forces in Europe 1944. Director of operations and intelligence for Mediterranean Allied Air Forces 1944-1945. Attended Yalta Conference as lone staff officer to Field Marshal Harold R. Alexander. Chief of strategy and policy at headquarters of Army Air Force 1945-1946. Assignments after the war included director of the joint staff, Joint Chiefs of Staff 1951-1953, and deputy director of CIA April 1953-January 1962. General in November 1958. Retired as general in January 1962. Decorations included two Distinguished Service Medals, the Legion of Merit, Distinguished Flying Cross, Bronze Star and two Air Medals. Died on May 25, 1971.

Caldwell, Charles Henry (1900-1967) Born on May 28, 1900, in Tampa, Florida. Commissioned in the Air Service from West Point in 1925. Served at Nichols Field, Philippine Islands 1934-1935. Graduated from Air Corps Tactical School in 1936 and the Command and General Staff School in 1937. Assistant operations officer, then operations officer of the 2nd Wing 1938-1940. Executive officer of 3rd Wing 1940-1941. Assistant chief of staff for personnel at Third Air Force then intelligence at Army Air Forces Far East 1941-1942 and personnel at Tenth Air Force 1942-1943. Duty with the War Department General Staff June 1943-January 1944. Chief of staff of First Air Force 1944-1945. Brigadier general in May 1944. Military attache in Buenos Aires 1945-1948. Retired in February 1951. Decorations included the Legion of Merit, Bronze Star and Purple Heart. Died on January 21, 1967.

Candee, Robert C. (1892-1963) Born in Hinsdale, Illinois, on June 4, 1892. B.A. from Cornell in 1915. Commissioned in the cavalry in 1916. Transferred to the Air Service in 1924. Graduated from Command and General Staff School in 1928, the Army War College in 1936 and the Naval War College 1937. Brigadier general in June 1942. Commanding general of 8th Air Support Command of Eighth Air Force 1942-1943. Instructor at Army Navy Staff College 1943-1944. Director of air instruction at Command and General Staff School 1945-1946. Retired in June 1952. Decorations included the Distinguished Service Medal and Legion of Merit. Died on June 23, 1963.

Cannon, John Kenneth (1892-1955) Born on March 9, 1892, in Salt Lake City, Utah. Graduate of Utah Agricultural College in 1914. Commissioned in the infantry Reserve in 1917. Served in the United States during World War I. Completed pilot training in 1922. Graduated from Command and General Staff School in 1935. Brigadier general in February 1942. Commanding general of 12th Air Support Command February 1942-June 1942 then 12th Bomber Command until May 1943. Major general in June 1943. Deputy commanding general of Allied Tactical Air Forces May 1943-December 1943. Commanding general of Twelfth Air Force December 1943-March 1945. Lieutenant general in March 1945. Air commander in chief of Allied Air Forces, Mediterranean Theater of Operations March-May

1945. Commanding general of U.S. Air Forces Europe May 1945-April 1946. Assignments after the war included commanding general of Air Training Command April 1946-March 1950 and commanding general of Tactical Air Command October 1950-March 1954. Retired as general in March 1954. Decorations included four Distinguished Service Medals, the Legion of Merit, Bronze Star and Air Medal. Died on January 12, 1955.

Carr, Lawrence Joseph (1899-1972) Born on April 8, 1899, in Chicago, Illinois. Commissioned in the cavalry from West Point in 1920. Graduated from Command and General Staff School in 1938. In the office of the chief of the Air Corps 1938-1941. Chief of staff of Army Air Force Technical Training Commands at Tulsa and Knollwood 1941-1942. Commanding officer of Boca Raton Field 1942. With Army Air Force School of Applied Tactics 1943. Deputy chief of staff of Seventh Air Force 1943. Chief of staff of Forward Area Command in 1944. Commander of 7th Bomber Command December 1944-October 1945. Brigadier general in June 1945. Retired in August 1946. Decorations included the Distinguished Service Medal, Legion of Merit, Distinguished Flying Cross and two Air Medals. Died on July 24, 1972.

Carter, Warren Rice (1898-1992) Born in Winchell, Texas, on July 31, 1898. Attended Howard Payne College 1915-1916. Commissioned in the Air Service in 1918. Instructor at Air Corps Tactical School 1933-1935. Graduated from Command and General Staff School in 1936 and the Army War College in 1938. Assistant chief of the plans division in the office of the chief of the Air Corps 1938-1941. Commanding officer of Air Corps Advanced Flying School 1941-1942. Brigadier general in October 1942. Assistant chief of staff for intelligence at Army Air Force Training Command in 1942. Chief of staff of Gulf Coast Training Center 1942-1943. Commanding general of San Francisco Fighter Wing 1943-1944, 54th Troop Carrier Wing January-November 1944 and 47th Air Service Area Command 1944-1945. Chief of staff of 15th Troop Carrier Command 1945-1946. Assignments after the war included deputy commander of Tactical Air Command 1946-1947. Retired as major general in January 1955. Decorations included the Distinguished Service Medal and Legion of Merit. Died on August 30, 1992.

Castle, Frederick Walker (1908-1944) Born in Manila, Philippine Islands, on October 14, 1908. Commissioned in the Air Corps from West Point in 1930. Earned his wings in October 1931. Served until February 1934 with 17th Pursuit Squadron, when he returned to civilian life. Recalled to active duty in January 1942 as a captain. Promoted to lieutenant colonel September 1942. He was one of eight officers who accompanied Major General Ira Eaker to England to form Eighth Air Force. Commanded 94th Bomb Group June 1943-April 1944 as colonel, then commanding officer of 4th Combat Bomb Wing. Brigadier general in November 1944. Killed in action on December 24, 1944, his thirtieth bombing mission. Decorations included the Medal of Honor (for staying with his heavily damaged plane to prevent it from hitting friendly troops below and to allow his crew to escape), the Distinguished Service Cross, Legion of Merit, four Distinguished Flying Crosses, four Air Medals and the Purple Heart.

Chaney, James Eugene (1885-1967) Born in Chaney, Maryland, on March 16, 1885. Attended Baltimore City College 1900-1904. Commissioned in the infantry from West Point in 1908. Transferred to the Air Service in 1920. Graduated from Command and General Staff School in 1926 and the Army War College in 1931. In office of the chief of the Air Corps 1931-1934, then assistant chief of the Air Corps in the rank of brigadier general 1934-1938, reverting thereafter to colonel. At Mitchel Field 1938-1940. Brigadier general again in January 1940. Command ing general of Air Defense Command 1940-1941. Major general in October 1940. Air observer in the United Kingdom 1941-1942. Commanding general of U.S. Army Forces British Isles in 1942 and First Air Force 1942-1943. Commanding general of Army Air Force Basic Training Center, Sheppard Field 1943-1944. Commanding general of U.S. Army forces in the battle for Iwo Jima, then commander of U.S. Forces on Iwo Jima. Commanding general of Pacific Base Command in 1945. Retired in July 1947. Decorations included the Distinguished Service Medal and two Legions of Merit. Died on August 21, 1967.

Chappell, Julian Merritt (1909-1993) Born on September 6, 1909, in Americus, Georgia. Commissioned in the Air Corps from West Point in 1931. Duty with 50th Observation Squadron at Luke Field, Hawaii 1934-1936. Operations officer with 89th Reconnaissance Squadron February 1940-February 1941. Commanding officer of 19th Reconnaissance Squadron then executive officer of 12th Bombardment Group February 1941-April 1942. Commanding officer of 89th Troop Group, 50th Troop Carrier Wing May 1942-October 1943 then 50th Troop Carrier Wing October 1943-February 1946. Brigadier general in November 1944. Reverted to colonel in February 1946. Assignments after the war included commanding general of Seventh Air Force 1955-1957. Retired in July 1961. Decorations included the Legion of Merit, two Distinguished Flying Crosses and the Bronze Star. Died on May 26, 1993.

Chauncey, Charles Carl (1889-1991) Born in Joshua, Texas, on October 31, 1889. Enlisted service in the aviation section, Signal Corps 1917-1918. Commissioned in the Officers Reserve Corps in 1918. Graduated from Command and General Staff School in 1936. Assistant operations and intelligence officer at GHQ Air Force July 1936-February 1941. Duty at the War Department General Staff in 1941 and Air Force Combat Command 1941-1942. Chief of staff of Third Air Force May-June 1942. Brigadier general in August 1942. Chief of staff of Eighth Air Force 1942-1943. Chief of staff of Mediterranean Allied Air Forces January 1944-June 1945. Major general in February 1944. Deputy chief of staff at headquarters Army Air Force June 1945-September 1947. Retired in October 1951. Decorations included two Distinguished Service Crosses and the Legion of Merit. Died on August 30, 1991.

Chennault, Claire Lee (1890-1958) Born in Commerce, Texas, on September 6, 1890. Graduated from Louisiana State Normal College. School teacher until 1917, when he attended Officers' Training Camp at Fort Harrison, Indiana and earned a commission in the infantry reserve. Served in the U.S. during World War I. Transferred to the aviation section of the Signal Corps, earned his wings and served as a flight instructor. As a captain he led the Air Corps Exhibition Group known as "Three Men on a Flying Trapeze" 1932-1936. Retired due to deafness in 1937. Recruited by Madame Chiang kai-Shek in late 1937 to organize the Chinese air defenses against Japan, Chennault hired American pilots in 1940 and undertook their training August-December 1941. Over the next seven months the American Volunteer Group, or AVG, more commonly known as "The Flying Tigers," flew numerous missions in China and Burma in P-40 aircraft. Recalled to active duty in April 1942, promoted to brigadier general that month and in July named chief of Army Air Forces China. Major general in March 1943. Commanding general of Fourteenth Air Force March 1943-August 1945. Retired in October 1945. Decorations included two Distinguished Service Medals, the Air Medal and two Distinguished Flying Crosses. Died on July 27, 1958.

Chidlaw, Benjamin Wiley (1900-1977) Born in Cleves, Ohio, on December 18, 1900. Commissioned in the Air Service from West Point in 1922. Graduated from Command and General Staff School in 1937. Technical assistant to the assistant chief of staff for materiel at Air Corps headquarters in 1939. Chief of the engineer section, then experimental engineering branch in the office of the chief of the Air Corps 1939-1943. Chidlaw was responsible for the development of the first jet engine and jet aircraft. Brigadier general in November 1942. Duty with the assistant chief of Air Staff for materiel at Army Air Force headquarters 1942-1943. Deputy commanding general of 12th Tactical Air Command 1944. Commanding general of 22nd Tactical Air Command 1944-1945. Commander of Mediterranean Allied Tactical Forces 1945. Major general in April 1945. Deputy commanding general for operations, then deputy commanding general, finally commanding general of Air Materiel Command 1945-1951. Assignments after the war included commander of Air Research and Development Command 1951-1955. Retired as general in May 1955. Decorations included the Distinguished Service Medal, Legion of Merit, Bronze Star and Air Medal. Died on February 21, 1977.

Clagett, Henry B. (1884-1952) Born on December 19, 1884, in Fort Wayne, Michigan. Commissioned in the infantry from West Point in 1906. Transferred to the Air Service in 1920. Graduated from the Army Industrial College in 1936. Brigadier general in October 1940. Commanding general of 5th Interceptor Command, Philippine Islands 1940-1941. Acting commanding general of U.S. Army Forces Australia December 1941-January 1942. Reverted to colonel in March 1942. Retired in November 1944. Died on November 14, 1952.

Clark, Harold L. (1893-1973) Born in Stillwater, Minnesota, on September 28, 1893. Commissioned in the aviation section of the Signal Corps in 1918. Graduated from Command and General Staff School in 1937. Liaison officer between the Air Corps and the Corps of Engineers in 1942. Commander of 50th Troop Carrier Wing 1942-1945. Brigadier general in September 1943. Retired in July 1946. Decorations included the Distinguished Service Medal, Legion of Merit, Distinguished Flying Cross and two Air Medals. Died on August 23, 1973.

Clark, John Martin (1893-1988) Born in Lockhart, Texas, on November 1, 1893. Attended San Antonio Business College 1910-1913. Commissioned in the aviation section of the Signal Corps in 1917. Commanding officer of Middletown then Sacramento Air Depots 1940-1942. Commander of 4th Air Service Area Command in 1942. Chief of the maintenance division, then commanding general of Tactical Air Service Command 1942-1944. Brigadier general in October 1942. Commanding general of Middletown then Warner-Robins Air Technical Service Commands 1944-1946. Retired in September 1946. Died on January 7, 1988.

Clark, Ray Henry (1896-1955) Born in Gueydan, Louisiana, on September 19, 1896. B.S. from the University of Southern California in 1918. Commissioned in the Air Service in 1918. Post operations officer at Chanute Field July 1938-July 1940. Air Corps technical supervisor at Fairfield Air Depot July 1940-January 1942. Director of technical inspection at headquarters of Army Air Force January-September 1942. Technical supervisor for Tenth Air Force at New Delhi September 1942-October 1943. Commanding officer, then air inspector of air bases in the China-Burma-India Theater of Operations from October 1943. Brigadier general in February 1944. Reverted to colonel in March 1946. Retired in 1953. Decorations included the Legion of Merit and Air Medal. Died on October 27, 1955.

Collier, William Albert (1896-1984) Born in Bristol, England, on January 2, 1896. Commissioned in the aviation section of the Officers Reserve Corps in 1918. Served with the AEF 1918-1919. Instructor at the Infantry School 1925-1928. Graduated from Command and General Staff School in 1935 and the Army War College in 1937. Assistant chief of staff for personnel at headquarters of the I Corps Area 1937-1941. Member of the Infantry Board June 1941-July 1942. Chief of staff of 78th Division, then IV Armored Corps 1942-1943. Chief of staff of XX Corps October 1943-February 1944 then the European Theater of Operations 1944-1946. Brigadier general in November 1944. Retired in August 1954. Decorations included the Distinguished Service Medal, Silver Star, three Legions of Merit, the Distinguished Flying Cross, three Bronze Stars, eight Air Medals and two Commendation Ribbons. Died on September 24, 1984.

Connell, Carl W. (1890-1946) Born on March 16, 1890, in Birmingham, Alabama. Commissioned in the aviation section of the Signal Corps in 1917. Graduated from Command and General Staff School in 1931 and the Army War College in 1937. Commanding officer of 9th Bombardment Group 1937-1940. Commanding officer of Lorinquen Field (Puerto Rico) 1940-1941. Commanding officer of Bangor (Maine) Air Base 1941-1942. Brigadier general in February 1942. Commanding general of Fifth Air Force Service Command 1942-1944 then Army Air

Force Basic Training Center, Amarillo, 1944-1945. Reverted to colonel in November 1945. Died on January 7, 1946.

Connell, Samuel Martin (1897-1981) Born in Warrenton, North Carolina, on July 10, 1897. Attended North Carolina Agricultural and Mechanical College 1914-1916. Commissioned in the aviation section of the Signal Corps in 1917. Commanding officer of 99th Bomber Squadron June 1936-September 1939. Graduated from Command and General Staff School in 1940. Commanding officer of 6th Bombardment Group 1940-1941. Air plans and operations officer at the Department of Puerto Rico 1941-1942. Brigadier general in February 1942. Commanding general of 4th Bomber Command 1942-1944. Deputy commanding general of Fourth Air Force April-October 1944. Retired in November 1946. Decorations included the Distinguished Service Medal. Died on December 18, 1981.

Cook, Orval Ray (1898-1980) Born in West Union, Indiana, on July 27, 1898. Commissioned in the Air Corps from West Point in 1922. Instructor at West Point 1934-1937. Graduated from Command and General Staff School in 1939. With engineering section of production division at Wright Field 1940-1942, then chief of production division 1943-1945. Brigadier general in November 1943. Duty with Far East Air Forces in 1945. Assignments after the war included deputy commander in chief of U.S. European Command April 1954-May 1956. Retired as general in May 1956. Decorations included two Distinguished Service Medals and the Legion of Merit. Died on March 18, 1980.

Coupland, Richard Cox (1893-1988) Born in West Point, Virginia, on December 14, 1893. B.S. from Virginia Military Institute in 1915. Commissioned in the Coast Artillery Corps in 1917. Transferred to Ordnance in 1921. Chief ordnance officer of the Air Corps 1939-1947. Brigadier general in March 1943. Retired as major general in August 1951. Decorations included the Distinguished Service Medal, Legion of Merit and Commendation Ribbon. Died on January 10, 1988.

Cousins, Ralph Pittman (1891-1964) Born on December 1, 1891, in Mexia, Texas. Commissioned in the Cavalry from West Point in 1915. M.S. from Yale in 1922. Graduate of Command and General Staff School in 1933 and the Army War College in 1937. Brigadier general in January 1942, major general in February 1942. Commanding general of Army Air Force Western Flying Training Command 1942-1946. Retired in March 1946. Decorations included the Distinguished Service Medal, Air Medal and Commendation Ribbon. Died on March 15, 1964.

Crabb, Jarred Vincent (1902-1981) Born in Olney, Illinois, on September 18, 1902. B.S. from Purdue in 1925. Commissioned in the Air Corps in 1930. Officer in charge of the base flight section at 27th Pursuit Squadron September 1936-January 1938 then the recruit section at 21st Reconnaissance Squadron September 1938-January 1941. Commander of 14th Reconnaissance Squadron January-

May 1941 and U.S. Army Air Base Newfoundland May-August 1941. Commanding officer of Bombardment Group 1942-1943. Chief of staff of 5th Bomber Command in 1943. With Fifth Air Force 1943-1944. Brigadier general in June 1944. Duty with 5th Bomber Command 1944-1945. Assignments after the war included commanding general of Thirteenth Air Force in 1948. Retired in July 1961 as major general. Decorations included two Distinguished Service Medals, two Legions of Merit, the Distinguished Flying Cross and Air Medal. Died on July 25, 1981.

Craig, Howard Arnold (1898-1977) Born on December 22, 1898, in Philadelphia, Pennsylvania. Enlisted in Signal Corps, aviation section, November 1917. Commissioned in June 1918. Graduated from Command and General Staff School in 1936. Assistant to the chief of Air Corps plans May 1940-February 1942. Assistant chief of Air Staff for plans February-June 1942. Brigadier general in August 1942. Assistant chief of staff, then deputy chief of staff for air of European Theater of Operations in 1942. Commanding general of 12th Air Support Command, then chief of staff of Mediterranean Air Command 1943. Assistant chief of staff at headquarters of Army Air Force 1943-1944. Major general in February 1944. With operations department of the War Department General Staff 1944-1946. Assignments after the war included inspector general of the Air Force 1949-1952 and commandant of the National War College 1952-1955. Retired as lieutenant general in June 1955. Decorations included the Distinguished Service Medal and Legion of Merit. Died on September 14, 1977.

Craigie, Laurence Cardee (1902-1994) Born on January 26, 1902, in Concord, New Hampshire. Commissioned in the Air Service from West Point in 1923. Graduated from the Army Industrial College in 1939. While assigned to the aircraft projects branch at Wright-Patterson Air Base he became the first officer of the U.S. Armed Forces to fly a jet aircraft, the XP-59, in October 1942. Commander of 1st Fighter Command, Boston Air Defense Wing, New York Fighter Wing and 87th Fighter Wing 1943. Brigadier general in September 1943. Commanding general of 63rd Fighter Wing, Twelfth Air Force 1944. Deputy chief, then chief of engineering division at Wright-Patterson 1944-1947. Assignments after the war included deputy chief of staff for development, U.S. Air Force 1951-1954 and Commander Allied Air Forces Southern Europe 1954-1955. Retired as lieutenant general in June 1955. Decorations included two Distinguished Service Medals, the Silver Star, two Legions of Merit, and the Distinguished Flying Cross. Died on February 27, 1994.

Crawford, Alden Rudyard (1900-1978) Born in Mt. Sterling, Illinois, on November 27, 1900. Commissioned in the Air Service from West Point in 1923. Graduated from Command and General Staff School in 1937. Served in the Philippines 1937-1939. Assistant technical executive, then technical executive at the Air Corps materiel division 1939-1942. Chief of staff of the Air Corps Materiel Center 1942-1944. Brigadier general in March 1943. Deputy commander of Army Air Force Service Command 1944-1945. Chief of the research and development division in the office of the chief of Army Air Force 1945-1947. Assignments after the war included commanding general of Twelfth Air Force September 1949-June 1950. Retired as major general in July 1953. Decorations included two Legions of Merit. Died on July 24, 1978.

Curry, John Francis (1886-1973) Born in New York, New York on April 22, 1886. Commissioned in the infantry from West Point in 1908. Transferred to the aviation section of the Signal Corps in 1916. Graduated from Command and General Staff School in 1929. Commandant of Air Corps Tactical School 1931-1935. Graduated from the Army War College in 1936. Duty at the War Department General Staff 1936-1938. Brigadier general in October 1940. Commanding general of Northwest Air District 1940-1941 then Rocky Mountain Technical Training Command in 1941. Commander of the Civil Air Patrol December 1941-March 1942. Commanding general of the 4th District Technical Training Command 1942-1944. President of the Evaluation Board, Mediterranean Theater of Operations 1944-1945. Major general in October 1942. Retired in October 1945. Decorations included the Distinguished Service Medal and Legion of Merit. Died on March 4, 1973.

Curtis, Edward Peck (1897-n/a) Born in Rochester, New York, on January 14, 1897. Attended Williams College 1914-1917. Commissioned in the aviation section of the Officers Reserve Corps in 1917. Served with American Ambulance Field Service in France, then with 95th Aero Squadron in the Chateau-Thierry, St. Mihiel and Meuse-Argonne offensives 1917-1918. Shot down six enemy planes and became an ace. Discharged in May 1919. Called to active duty as major in December 1940. Transferred to the Air Corps in July 1941. At headquarters of Army Air Force July 1941-July 1942. Served with Eighth Air Force July 1942-January 1944. Brigadier general in June 1943. Chief of staff of U.S. Strategic Air Forces in Europe January 1944-June 1945. Major general in June 1945. Returned to inactive status in November 1945. Decorations included the Distinguished Service Cross, Distinguished Service Medal, Silver Star and Legion of Merit.

Darcy, Thomas Connell (1910-) Born in Boston, Massachusetts, on August 12, 1910. Commissioned in the infantry from West Point in 1932. Transferred to the Air Corps in 1934. Commanding officer of Desert Air Task Force in 1943. Chief of staff of 12th Tactical Air Command 1943-1944. Brigadier general in August 1944. Commanding general of 87th Fighter Wing in 1944. Deputy commanding general, then commanding general of 22nd Tactical Air Command 1944-1945. Director of operations and intelligence at Mediterranean Allied Air Forces in 1945. Assistant chief of staff for operations at U.S. Strategic Air Forces 1945-1946. Retired as major general in 1961. Decorations included the Distinguished Service Medal, Legion of Merit, Bronze Star and Air Medal. Resides in Essex, Connecticut.

Dargue, Herbert A. (1886-1941) Born on November 17, 1886, in Brooklyn, New York. Commissioned in the Coast Artillery Corps from West Point in 1911.

Transferred to the Air Service in 1914. Graduated from Command and General Staff School in 1924, the Army War College in 1929 and the Naval War College in 1930. Assistant commandant of Air Corps Tactical School 1934-1938. Brigadier general in October 1938. Commanding general of 19th Wing 1938-1940. Assistant chief of the Air Corps October 1940-July 1941. Major general in July 1941. Commanding general of First Air Force July 1941 until his death on December 12, 1941, in the crash of an Army airplane near Bishop, California. Decorations included the Distinguished Flying Cross.

Davidson, Howard Calhoun (1890-1984) Born on September 15, 1890, in Wharton, Texas. Commissioned in the infantry from West Point in 1913. Transferred to the Air Service in 1916. Commanding officer of Air Service, VII Corps in the AEF during World War I. Air attache in London 1922-1926. Graduated from Command and General Staff School in 1935 and the Army War College in 1940. Brigadier general in April 1941. Commanding general of 14th Fighter Wing 1940-1942. Commanding general of Tenth Air Force in the China-Burma-India Theater of Operations 1943-1945. Major general in January 1944. Retired in June 1946. Decorations included the Distinguished Service Medal, Distinguished Flying Cross, Air Medal and Purple Heart. Died on November 7, 1984.

Davies, Isaiah (1890-1976) Born on July 12, 1890, in Columbus, Kansas. Enlisted service 1912-1917. Commissioned in the Signal Corps in 1917. Transferred to the Air Service in 1920. Assistant commandant of Air Corps Advanced Flying School January 1940-October 1941. At headquarters station complement, Midland, Texas, October 1941-May 1942. Brigadier general in April 1942. Commanding general of 34th Flying Training Wing May 1942-March 1944. Chief of staff of Eleventh Air Force March 1944-October 1945 then Air Training Command 1945-1949. Retired in October 1949. Decorations included the Air Medal and Commendation Ribbon. Died on August 31, 1976.

Davies, John Hubert (1903-1976) Born in Piedmont, California, on October 25, 1903. B.A. from the University of California in 1928. Commissioned in the Air Reserve in 1930. Aide to Brigadier General Gerald C. Brant 1936-1938. Graduated from Air Corps Tactical School in January 1940. Adjutant with 24th Bombardment Squadron in 1940. Served with 27th Bombardment Group June-December 1941. Duty in the Philippines as group commander, then commanding officer of 27th and 3rd Bombardment Groups 1941-1945. Brigadier general in January 1945. Commanding general of 5th and 21st Bomber Commands, then 313th Bombardment Wing in 1945. Reverted to colonel in December 1945. Assignments after the war included commanding general of Alaskan Air Command. Retired in October 1957. Decorations included the Distinguished Service Cross, two Silver Stars, the Legion of Merit and Air Medal. Died on August 20, 1976.

Davis, Michael Frank (1894-1973) Born on March 25, 1894, in New Richmond, Ohio. Commissioned in the Coast Artillery Corps from West Point in 1915. Duty with the Punitive Expedition into Mexico 1916-1917. Served with the AEF in

World War I. Transferred to the Air Service in 1920. Graduated from Army Balloon School in 1921 and the Command and General Staff School in 1927. Assistant to the executive, then acting executive, finally executive to the chief of the Air Corps 1935-1939. Graduated from the Army Industrial College in 1940. Commander of 10th Pursuit Wing 1941-1942. Commanding officer of San Antonio Aviation Cadet Center 1942-1943. Commander of 509th Base Headquarters 1943-1944. Brigadier general in January 1944. Commanding general of 78th Flying Training Wing 1944-1945. Commanding general of Army Air Force Central Flying Training Command, then commander of the Technical School at Boca Raton Airfield 1945-1946. Retired in July 1950. Decorations included the Legion of Merit. Died on August 31, 1973.

Davison, Frederick Trubee (1896-1974) Born in New York, New York on February 7, 1896. B.A. from Yale in 1918, M.A. and LL.B. from Columbia University in 1922. Assistant secretary of war for air 1926-1932. President of the American Museum of Natural History 1933-1951. Called to active duty in June 1941 as colonel. Acting deputy chief of staff of Army Air Force Combat Command June-December 1941 then aide to Lieutenant General Delos Emmons, commanding general of the Hawaiian Department 1941-1943. Chief of the special projects division at headquarters of Army Air Force 1943-1946. Brigadier general in June 1945. Released from active duty in 1946. Decorations included the and Navy Cross and Distinguished Service Medal. Died on November 16, 1974.

DeFord, Earl Hamlin (1890-1976) Born on September 1, 1890 in Stuart, Iowa. LL.B. from Drake University in 1911. Commissioned in the infantry, Officers Reserve Corps in 1917. Graduated from Command and General Staff School in 1935. Instructor, then departmental director at Air Corps Tactical School June 1935-January 1939. Commanding officer of 7th Bombardment Group 1939-1941. Commanding officer of Will Rogers Field 1941-1943. Bomber commander in Alaskan Defense Command 1943. Brigadier general in September 1943. With Allied Expeditionary Air Forces in Europe in 1944. Commanding general of 33rd Flying Training Wing 1944-1945. Commanding general of Sixth Air Force February 1945-February 1946. Reverted to colonel in February 1946. Retired in September 1950. Decorations included the Distinguished Flying Cross and Air Medal. Died on December 4, 1976.

Dillon, Joseph Vincent DePaul (1899-1971) Born on January 4, 1899, in New York, New York. Commissioned in the infantry from West Point in 1920. LL.B. from Georgetown University in 1937, LL.M. in 1939. Transferred to the judge advocate general department in 1939. Assistant professor at West Point 1939-1941. Duty in offices of the judge advocate general and provost marshal general in 1941. Commander of the Provost Marshal General Training Center in 1942. Brigadier general in March 1943. Provost marshal general in North Africa and European Theater of Operations 1943-1945. Assignments after the war included air provost marshal, U.S. Air Force 1948-1953. Retired as major general in July

1953. Decorations included the Legion of Merit and Bronze Star. Died on July 25, 1971.

Doolittle, James Harold (1896-1993) Born on December 14, 1896, in Alameda, California. Attended the University of California. Enlisted in the Army Reserve in October 1917 and commissioned in the aviation section of the Signal Corps in 1920. Flying instructor during World War I. Credited with making the first transcontinental flight in less than 24 hours on September 4, 1922. Resigned his commission in 1930 and entered private industry. Returned to active duty with the Air Corps in July 1940. On April 18, 1942, Doolittle, as a lieutenant colonel, led a group of sixteen B-25 bombers from the deck of the carrier *Hornet* on a bombing raid over Japan. He received promotion to brigadier general the following day. Organized and commanded Twelfth Air Force September 1942-March 1943. Major general in November 1942. Led Northwest Africa Air Force, Fifteenth Air Force, and Eighth Air Force through the end of World War II. Lieutenant general in March 1944. Left the Air Force in May 1946. Decorations included the Medal of Honor. General on the retired list in 1986. Died on September 27, 1993.

Douglass, Robert Wilkins Jr. (1900-1976) Born on March 8, 1900, in Memphis, Tennessee. Commissioned in the infantry from West Point in 1922. Served at France Field, Panama Canal Zone 1926-1929. Graduated from Command and General Staff School in 1937. Duty with 18th Pursuit Group in Hawaii 1937-1939. Air observer in England 1940-1941. Operations officer for Third Air Force 1941-1942. Member of the Permanent Joint Board for Canada-United States Defense in 1942. Brigadier general in September 1942. Served with the 7th Fighter Command 1942-1944. Major general in September 1944. Commander of Seventh Air Force 1944-1945. Duty in the office of the Joint Chiefs of Staff in 1945. Assignments after the war included commanding general of First Air Force October 1945-July 1947 and Eighteenth Air Force April 1951-September 1954. Retired in February 1957. Decorations included the Distinguished Service Medal, Silver Star, Legion of Merit and Bronze Star. Died on May 27, 1976.

Doyle, John Paul (1904-1988) Born on October 1, 1904, in Washington, DC Commissioned in the cavalry from West Point in 1926. Transferred to the Air Corps in 1932. Commanding officer of Post Air Navigation School, Mitchel Field July 1935-September 1938. Commanding officer of 15th Bombardment Squadron February 1940-May 1941. Executive officer of 1st Air Support Command 1941-1943. At headquarters of Fifth Air Force in 1943. Chief of staff, then commanding general of 42nd Bomb Wing 1943-1945. Brigadier general in November 1944. Deputy chief of staff at U.S. Air Forces Europe in 1945. Air liaison officer with Army Ground Forces 1945-1946. Assignments after the war included commanding general of Twelfth Air Force 1946-1947 and commanding general of Twentieth Air Force in 1949. Retired as major general in June 1956. Decorations included the Distinguished Service Medal, two Legions of Merit, the Distinguished Flying Cross, Bronze Star and three Air Medals. Died on August 30, 1988.

Duncan, Asa North (1892-1943) Born in Leighton, Alabama, on March 30, 1892. Commissioned in the cavalry, Alabama National Guard in September 1916. Served with the 91st Aerial Squadron, AEF at the Meuse-Argonne offensive in 1918. Transferred to the Air Service in July 1920. Instructor with the Alabama National Guard 1922-1927. Graduated from Command and General Staff School in 1931. Duty in the office of the chief of the Air Corps 1934-1935. Chief of the personnel division at headquarters Army Air Force 1939-1942. Brigadier general in February 1942. Missing in action on November 17, 1942, in the European Theater of Operations and declared dead the following year.

Duncan, Early Edward Walters (1894-1966) Born on January 1, 1894, in Woodsdale, North Carolina. B.A. from the University of North Carolina in 1917. Commissioned in the cavalry, Officers Reserve Corps in 1917. Transferred to the Air Service in 1920. Graduated from Air Service Tactical School in June 1926. Graduated from Command and General Staff School in 1933. War Department representative with the U. S. Navy staff at Commander Aircraft, Battle Force October 1938-October 1939. Air officer at VIII Corps Area October 1939-May 1940. Military attache in Athens May-June 1940. Executive officer at Technical School, Lowry Field June-November 1940 then commandant of Lowry Field November 1940-April 1942. Commanding officer of Lincoln Air Base April 1942-May 1944 and 24th Composite Wing, European Theater of Operations May-December 1944. Brigadier general in December 1942. Commanding general of Iceland Base Command December 1944-May 1945. Retired in July 1953. Died on October 2, 1966.

Dunton, Delmar Hall (1890-1967) Born on November 1, 1890, in Detroit, Michigan. Enlisted service 1917-1918. Commissioned in the Air Service in 1918. Commanding officer of 27th Reconnaissance Squadron September 1939-October 1940. Commander of Ponce Air Base, Puerto Rico October 1940-April 1941. Commanding officer of Losey Field April 1941-November 1941. Brigadier general in June 1942. Chief of maintenance, then commanding officer of 8th Air Service Command June 1942-June 1943. Major general in March 1943. Deputy commander, then commander of Air Service Command June 1943-December 1944. Retired in March 1945. Decorations included the Legion of Merit. Died on April 14, 1967.

Eaker, Ira Clarence (1896-1987) Born on April 13, 1896, in Field Creek, Texas. B.A. from Southeastern State Teachers College in 1917. Commissioned in the infantry, Officers Reserve Corps in 1917. Transferred to the aviation section of the Signal Corps and earned pilot's wings in 1918. He and Major Carl Spaatz kept a Fokker monoplane named *Question Mark* aloft above Los Angeles a record 150 hours in January 1929. In 1936 he made the first transcontinental flight solely on instruments. Graduated from Command and General Staff School in 1937. Commander of 20th Pursuit Group 1941-1942. Brigadier general in January 1942. Commander of 8th Bomber Command July 1942-December 1942. Major general in September 1942. Commanding general of Eighth Air Force December 1942-January 1944. Lieutenant general in September 1943. Commander of Mediterranean Allied Air Forces from January 1944 to the end of the war. Assignments after the war included chief of the Air Staff in Washington until his retirement in August 1947. General on the retired list in 1986. Decorations included three Distinguished Service Medals, the Silver Star, Legion of Merit, two Distinguished Flying Crosses and the Air Medal. Inducted into the Aviation Hall of Fame in 1970. Died on August 6, 1987.

Easterbrook, Arthur E. (1893-1952) Born in Amsterdam, New York, on November 4, 1893. Attended the University of Washington 1915-1917. Commissioned in the field artillery, Officers Reserve Corps in 1917. Served in the AEF in World War I. Retired as lieutenant colonel in September 1939. Recalled to active duty in May 1940. Duty at Air Corps Basic Flying School 1940-1941. Assistant chief of staff for personnel at West Coast Training Center, Santa Ana, California 1941-1944. Brigadier general in January 1944. Commander of Santa Ana Army Air Base August 1944 until retirement again in August 1946. Decorations included two Distinguished Service Crosses, the Legion of Merit and Purple Heart. Died on July 24, 1952.

Eaton, William Herbert (1906-1945) Born in Buffalo, New York, on April 29, 1906. B.A. from Williams College in 1928. LL.D. from Harvard in 1931. Practiced law in new York City, then associated with Shell Oil Company 1935-1942. Commissioned captain in May 1942. Transferred to the Air Corps in October 1942. Served as personnel officer at Southeastern Army Air Force Flying Training Command May-August 1942, assistant chief of staff for supply at 4th Bombardment Wing, Eighth Air Force August-September 1942, and chief of the movement control section at Twelfth Air Force in the European and North African Theaters of Operations 1942-1943. Executive to the assistant chief of staff for supply (movement and shipping) at Twelfth Air Force July 1943-January 1944. Assistant to the assistant chief of staff for supply, then assistant chief of staff for supply at headquarters Army Air Force in the Mediterranean Theater of Operations January 1944-February 1945. Brigadier general in January 1945. Killed in action in France on February 6, 1945. Decorations included the Legion of Merit.

Echols, Oliver Patton (1892-1954) Born in Charlottesville, Virginia, on March 4, 1892. Attended Virginia Polytechnic Institute 1908-10 and the University of Virginia 1910-1913. Commissioned in the aviation section of the Signal Corps in 1916. Served with the AEF 1917-1919, including the St. Mihiel, Champagne-Marne, Aisne-Marne and Meuse-Argonne offensives. Graduated from the Army Industrial College in 1926. Graduated from Command and General Staff School in 1934. Chief engineer at Materiel Division 1934-1938. Graduated from the Army War College in 1939. Assistant chief, then chief of the materiel division 1939-1947. Brigadier general in October 1940, major general in February 1942. Retired in February 1947. Decorations included two Distinguished Service Medals, the Legion of Merit and Purple Heart. Died on May 15, 1954.

Edwards, Idwal Hubert (1895-1981) Born in Freedom, New York, on April 5, 1895. Commissioned in the infantry, Officers Reserve Corps in 1917. Transferred to the Air Service in 1918. Graduated from Command and General Staff School in 1935 and the Army War College in 1938. Commanding officer of Randolph Field 1941-1942. Brigadier general in May 1942. Assistant chief of staff for training on the War Department General Staff May 1942-May 1943. Major general in February 1943. Chief of staff for operations in the European Theater of Operations 1943. Deputy commander of U.S. Air Forces in the Mediterranean Theater of Operations 1944-1945. Assignments after the war included commandant of Air University 1951-1953. Retired as lieutenant general in February 1953. Decorations included two Distinguished Service Medals and the Legion of Merit. Died on November 25, 1981.

Egan, John Franklin (1898-) Born on November 7, 1898, in New York, New York. Commissioned in the Air Service, Officers Reserve Corps in 1919. Enlisted service during World War I in the Aviation Section, Signal Reserve. Commissioned in the Air Service in October 1918. Discharged in January 1919 and joined the Air Reserve. Commissioned in the U.S. Army in 1928. Flight commander with 94th Pursuit Squadron at GHQ Air Force July 1938-May 1939. Graduated from Air Corps Tactical School in August 1939. Again with 94th Pursuit Squadron, August-November 1939. Commanding officer of 40th Pursuit Squadron November 1939-December 1940. Group adjutant, then commanding officer of 49th Pursuit Group January-May 1941. Assistant to the chief of staff of First Air Force, then assistant chief of staff for operations, later officer in charge of pursuit training at 1st Fighter Command May 1941-February 1943. Fighter group commander in the China-Burma-India February-September 1944. Brigadier general in March 1944. Commanding general of 5320th Air Defense Wing (Provincial) in India April-July 1944. Army Air Force personnel district commander July-September 1944. Commanding general of 77th and 33rd Flying Training Wings 1944-1946. Retired in September 1946. Decorations included the Silver Star. Resides in Winter Park, Florida.

Emmons, Delos Carleton (1888-1965) Born in Huntington, West Virginia on January 17, 1888. Commissioned in the infantry from West Point in 1909. Served on the Mexican border in 1916. Transferred to the aviation section of the Signal Corps in 1917. Graduated from Command and General Staff School in 1934. Brigadier general in June 1936. Commanding general of 1st Wing 1936-1939. Major general in March 1939. Commanding general of GHQ Air Force 1939-1941. Lieutenant general in October 1940. Commander of the Air Force Combat Command June-December 1941. Commander of the Hawaiian Department ten days after Pearl Harbor until May 1943. Commanding general of Western Defense Command May 1943-June 1944 then the Alaskan Department June 1944-June 1946. Retired in June 1948. Decorations included three Distinguished Service Medals, two Legions of Merit, the Distinguished Flying Cross and Air Medal. Died on October 5, 1965.

Ent, Uzal Girard (1900-1948) Born on March 3, 1900, in Northumberland, Pennsylvania. Enlisted service in the infantry 1917-1919. Commissioned in the Air Service from West Point in 1924. Graduated from the Command and General Staff College in 1938. Military attache in Lima, Peru, July 1939-October 1942. Chief of staff of U.S. Army Forces Middle East in 1942. Brigadier general in May 1943. Commanding general of 9th Bomber Command, Ninth Air Force in 1943. Led 178 B-24s in the bombing raid on oil fields at Ploesti, Romania, on August 1, 1943. Commanding general of Second Air Force 1943-1946. Major general in June 1944. Seriously injured in the crash of a bomber in October 1944. Retired in 1946. Decorations included the Distinguished Service Cross, two Distinguished Service Medals, the Legion of Merit, two Distinguished Flying Crosses and two Air Medals. Died on March 5, 1948.

Esposito, Vincent Joseph (1900-1965) Born in Brooklyn, New York, on April 29, 1900. Enlisted service 1918-1925. Commissioned in the Air Corps from West Point in 1925. Graduated from Command and General Staff School in 1939. With the War Department General Staff 1943-1946. Brigadier general in June 1945. Assignments after the war included professor at West Point 1947-1963. Retired in November 1963. Decorations included the Distinguished Service Medal. Chief editor of *The West Point Atlas of American Wars* (1959). Died on June 10, 1965.

Estabrook, Merrick Gay Jr. (1886-1947) Born in Boston, Massachusetts, on July 12, 1886. B.A. from Harvard in 1909. Commissioned in the aviation section, Officers Reserve Corps in 1917. Attended Cornell University in 1917 and Massachusetts Institute of Technology in 1918. Commissioned in the U.S. Army in 1920. Depot supply officer at the Philippine Air Depot 1925-1927. Graduated from the Army Industrial College in June 1936. Commanding officer of Fairfield Air Depot October 1939-February 1943 then commander of Fairfield Air Depot Control Area Command February 1943 until retirement in August 1944. Brigadier general in September 1943. Died on December 19, 1947.

Eubank, Eugene Lowry (1892-n/a) Born in Mangum, Oklahoma, on December 2, 1892. Commissioned in the aviation section of the Officers Reserve Corps in 1918. Graduated from Air Corps Tactical School in 1931 then instructor there 1934-1935. Graduated from the Command and General Staff School in 1938. Commanding officer of 34th Bomb Squadron 1939-1940 then 19th Bomb Group 1941-1942. Brigadier general in August 1942. Commander of 2nd Bomber Command 1942-1943. Executive director of the Army Air Force Board 1943-1944. Assistant to deputy commander for operations at Eighth Air Force 1944-1945. Commanding general of 3rd Air Division in the European Theater of Operations in 1945 then Army Air Force Proving Ground Command 1945-1946. Assignments after the war included commanding general of Thirteenth Air Force 1946-1948. Retired as major general in December 1954. Decorations included the Distinguished Service Medal, Silver Star, two Distinguished Flying Crosses, the Bronze Star and Purple Heart.

Evans, Frederick William (1898-1975) Born in Lawrence, Massachusetts, on March 8, 1898. Commissioned in the aviation section of the Officers Reserve Corps in 1918. Instructor at Air Corps Tactical School 1934-1937. Graduated from Command and General Staff School in 1938. Duty with the War Department General Staff in 1942. Brigadier general in December 1942. Director of war organization and movement at headquarters Army Air Force 1942-1943. Commanding general of 1st Troop Carrier Command October 1943-August 1944 the Combat Cargo Task Force, Eastern Air Command 1944-1945. Served with Army Air Force in the China Theater of Operations July 1945-February 1946. Assignments after the war included commanding general of Second Air Force July 1946-June 1947. Hospitalized then retired as major general in February 1948. Decorations included two Distinguished Service Medals, the Legion of Merit and Distinguished Flying Cross. Died on December 14, 1975.

Everest, Frank Fort (1904-1983) Born in Council Bluffs, Iowa, on November 13, 1904. Commissioned in the field artillery from West Point in 1928. Instructor at Air Corps Technical School September 1939-August 1941. With plans division of the War Department General Staff 1941-1942. Liaison officer to the aircraft commander, then commanding officer of 11th Heavy Bomb Group, and finally Army Air officer on the staff of General MacArthur at headquarters of U.S. Army Forces in the South Pacific 1942-1944. Brigadier general in June 1944. At headquarters Army Air Force 1944-1946. Assignments after the war included commanding general of Fifth Air Force 1951-1952, deputy commander of Tactical Air Command 1952-1953, director of the joint staff, Joint Chiefs of Staff 1953-1954, deputy chief of staff for operations, U.S. Air Force 1954-1957, commander in chief of U.S. Air Forces Europe 1957-1959 and commander of Tactical Air Command 1959-1961. Decorations included two Distinguished Service Medals, the Silver Star, Legion of Merit, Distinguished Flying Cross and Air Medal. Died on October 10, 1983.

Fair, Ford Larimore (1898-1946) Born in Fort Wayne, Indiana, on July 9, 1898. Enlisted service 1917-1919. Commissioned in the Air Corps in 1927. Duty with 3rd Pursuit Squadron in the Philippine Islands 1932-1935. Graduated from Air Corps Tactical School in 1936 and the Command and General Staff School in June 1937. Squadron adjutant at 1st Observation Squadron July 1937-August 1940. Division air officer at 1st Armored Division August 1940-January 1941. Materiel and parachute officer with 22nd Bombardment Group then executive officer and inspector with 13th Bombardment Group in 1941. Assistant chief of the strategic planning section, air war plans division at headquarters of the Army Air Corps November 1941-March 1942. Member then deputy chief of the logistics group in the operations division of War Department General Staff March 1942-January 1943. Deputy chief of staff of Army Air Force Antisubmarine Command January-November 1943. Duty with Third Tactical Air Division November 1943-June 1944. Commanding officer of 313th Base Unit, Tactical Air Divison then 1st Tactical Air Divison 1944-1945. Brigadier general in November

1944. Reverted to colonel in November 1945. Killed in an aircraft accident on November 1, 1946.

Fairchild, Muir Stephen (1894-1950) Born in Bellingham, Washington, on September 2, 1894. Enlisted service 1916-1918. Commissioned in the Signal Corps, aviation section 1918. Graduated from the Army Industrial College in 1936 and the Army War College in 1937. Director of air tactics and strategy at the Air Corps Tactical School 1939-1940. With plans division of the War Department General Staff 1941. Named first secretary of the Air Staff in June 1941. Brigadier general in August 1941. Director of military requirements for the Air Corps March-November 1942. Major general in August 1942. Member of Joint Strategic Survey Committee of Joint Chiefs of Staff November 1942-January 1946. Assignments after the war included commandant of Air University 1946-1948 and vice chief of staff, U.S. Air Force May 1948 until his death at Fort Myer on March 17, 1950. Decorations included the Distinguished Service Medal, Legion of Merit, Distinguished Flying Cross and Purple Heart.

Farman, Ivan Lonsdale (1902-1990) Born on January 2, 1902, in Oakland, California. B.S. from California Institute of Technology in 1926. Commissioned in the Air Corps in 1930. Weather officer at March Field July 1939-March 1940. Commanding officer of 1st Weather Squadron 1940-1941. Regional control officer in the 1st Weather Region in 1941 and at Newfoundland Base Command 1941-1942. Commanding officer of 8th Communications Squadron in 1942. Regional control officer at Presque Isle in 1943. Chief of intelligence security, then wing commanding officer, finally commanding general of Army Airways Communications System 1943-1945. Brigadier general in April 1945. Retired in June 1957. Decorations included the Distinguished Service Medal and Air Medal. Died on June 26, 1990.

Farthing, William Eugene (1892-1964) Born in Gainesville, Texas, on August 7, 1892. B.S. from Texas A&M in 1914. Commissioned in the Corps of Engineers, Officers Reserve Corps in 1917. Transferred to the Air Service in 1920. Served in the Canal Zone 1922-1925. Graduated from Command and General Staff School in 1928 then instructor there 1931-1935. Graduated from the Army War College in 1937. Assistant chief of the plans section in the office of the chief of the Air Corps July 1937-August 1940. Commanding officer of Hickham Field, Hawaii in 1941 then Seventh Air Force Base Command December 1941-October 1942. Brigadier general in April 1942. Commanding general of Seventh Air Force in 1942 then Atlantic Overseas Air Technical Service Command 1943-1945. Retired as major general in August 1952. Decorations included the Legion of Merit, Commendation Ribbon and Purple Heart. Died on March 12, 1964.

Fechet, James Edmon (1877-1948) Born on August 21, 1877, in Fort Ringgold, Texas. Attended the University of Nebraska 1895-1897. Enlisted service in Cuba during Spanish American War. Commissioned in the Cavalry in 1901. Served with Pershing's Punitive Expedition into Mexico in 1916. Commanding officer of flying schools at Belleville, Illinois, Arcadia, Florida and Kelly Field 1917-1924. Assistant chief of the Air Corps 1925-1927. Chief of the Air Corps December 1927 until retirement in December 1931. Recalled to active duty in the office of the chief of the Air Corps during World War II. Decorations included the Legion of Merit and Purple Heart. Died on February 10, 1948.

Fickel, Jacob Earl (1883-1956) Born in Des Moines, Iowa, on January 31, 1883. Attended Des Moines College 1899-1902. Enlisted service 1904-1907. Commissioned in the Aviation Section of the Signal Corps in 1907. Became the first aerial gunner in 1910. Served at headquarters of the Air Service in World War I. Graduated from Command and General Staff School in 1926 and the Army War College in 1931. Staff officer at IX Corps Area 1936-1939. Commanding officer of 1st Wing at GHQ Air Force in 1939. Brigadier general in December 1939. Assistant chief of the Air Corps then commander of the Southwest Air District in 1940. Major general in October 1940. Commanding general of Fourth Air Force in 1941, 3rd District Technical Training Command in 1942, Eastern Technical Training Command 1943-1944 and Western Technical Training Command 1945-1946. Retired in August 1946. Decorations included the Distinguished Service Medal. Died on August 7, 1956.

FitzGerald, Shepler Ward (1884-1953) Born in Burden, Kansas, on November 11, 1884. LL.B. from George Washington University in 1907. Commissioned in the Coast Artillery Corps in 1911. Transferred to the Air Service in 1920. Served in the training section at headquarters of the Air Service, AEF in France December 1917-April 1918. Air Service Commander for First Army in 1919. Graduated from Air Corps Tactical School in June 1931 and the Army War College in 1932. Commanding officer of Luke Field, Hawaii September 1938-January 1939 then air base commander at Hickam Field January 1939-August 1940. Duty with 5th Air Base Group August 1940-February 1941 then in the inspector general's department February 1941-May 1942. Brigadier general in April 1942. Commanding general of African Middle East Wing, Air Transport Command and commanding general of U.S. Army Forces Central Africa June 1942-June 1943. Commander of Army Air Force Radio School Number Four at Sioux Falls 1943-1946. Retired in November 1946. Decorations included the Legion of Merit, Bronze Star and Air Medal. Died on January 10, 1953.

Fitzmaurice, James Michael (1900-1983) Born on August 23, 1900, in Bucyrus, Ohio. Commissioned in the Air Corps from West Point in 1923. Duty in the Panama Canal Zone 1928-1931. Graduated from Air Corps Tactical School in 1939. Commanding officer of 13th Bombardment Command 1943. Chief of staff of Thirteenth Air Force 1943-1944. Brigadier general in November 1944. Commanding general of Third Air Force Staging Command, then 1st Staging Command 1944-1946. Retired in December 1949. Decorations included two Legions of Merit. Died on May 22, 1983.

Flood, William J. (1895-1977) Born in Peoria, Illinois, on July 15, 1895. Attended George Washington University 1916-1917, National University 1919-1921 and St. Louis University in 1925. Commissioned in the aviation reserve in 1917. Served in the AEF 1917-1919. Commanding officer of 19th Airship Company 1927-1929. Graduated from Air Corps Tactical School in 1935. Assistant chief of staff for supply at Hawaiian Air Force November 1940-October 1941. Commander of Wheeler Field, Hawaii 1941-1942. Chief of staff of Seventh Air Force June 1942 until retirement in May 1946. Brigadier general in February 1943. Decorations included the Legion of Merit, Bronze Star, Air Medal and Purple Heart. Died on March 20, 1977.

Forrest, Nathan Bedford (1905-1943) Born on April 7, 1905, in Memphis, Tennessee. Attended Georgia Institute of Technology 1923-1924. Commissioned in the Air Corps from West Point in 1928. Graduated from Air Corps Technical School in April 1931. Assigned to the 78th Pursuit Squadron, Panama Canal Zone April 1931-November 1934 and the 17th Attack Group July 1936-September 1939. Graduated from Air Corps Tactical School in December 1939. Duty with the 17th Bombardment Group December 1939-February 1941. Executive officer of 5th Bombardment Wing February 1941-January 1942 then 2nd Bomber Command January-February 1942. Plans and training officer with Eleventh Air Force February-June 1942. Chief of staff of Second Air Force June 1942-May 1943. Brigadier general in November 1942. Assigned to Eighth Air Force, London in May 1943. Reported missing on an air mission over Kiel, Germany, on June 14, 1943, he was officially listed as killed in action one year later. Decorations included the Distinguished Service Cross and Purple Heart.

Frank, Walter Hale (1886-1968) Born in Humphrey, New York, on April 23, 1886. Commissioned in the infantry from West Point in 1910. Transferred to the Air Service in 1917. Executive officer to the chief of the Air Corps 1920-1924. Graduated from Command and General Staff School in 1926 and the Army War College in 1931. Chief of staff of GHQ Air Force 1938. Brigadier general in September 1938. Commanding general of 18th Wing 1938-1940. Commanding general of Interceptor Command, Third Air Force 1941-1942. Major general in October 1941. Commanding general of Eighth Air Force Service Command June-November 1942, then Army Air Force Service Command November 1942-July 1944. Member of the Army Pearl Harbor Board 1944. Special assistant to General Henry H. Arnold November 1944-September 1945. Retired in December 1945. Decorations included the Distinguished Service Medal, Legion of Merit and Air Medal. Died on March 30, 1968.

Fritch, Donald Fowler (1900-1985) Born in Attleboro, Massachusetts, on September 10, 1900. Attended Northfield University. Commissioned in the field artillery in 1921 then transferred to the Air Corps. Squadron officer with 24th Pursuit Squadron at France Field, Canal Zone 1929-1930. Graduated from Air Corps Tactical School in 1937 and Command and General Staff School in 1938. Assigned to the office of the chief of the Air Corps July 1938-July 1941. Assistant chief of staff of Materiel Command at headquarters Army Air Force July 1941-July 1943. Duty with the War Department General Staff 1943-1944. Chief of staff at headquarters Army Air Force in the Mediterranean Theater of Operations 1944-1945. Brigadier general in January 1945. Reverted to colonel in November 1947 and retired in September 1948. Decorations included the Bronze Star. Died on October 25, 1985.

Fritz, Lawrence George (1896-1970) Born in Marine City, Michigan, on August 7, 1896. Attended Michigan State College 1915-1917. Enlisted service in the Army 1917-1918. Commissioned in the Air Reserve in 1924. Pursued a career in commercial aviation 1925-1938. Mustered into federal service in April 1942 as captain. Assistant chief of staff for operations, Air Transport Command 1942-1943. Commander of North Atlantic Wing, then North Atlantic Division 1943-1946. Brigadier general in June 1944. Retired in January 1946. Decorations included the Distinguished Service Medal, Legion of Merit and Air Medal. Died on October 4, 1970.

Gaffney, Dale Vincent (1895-1950) Born in Methuen, Massachusetts, on February 18, 1895. Enlisted service with the Massachusetts National Guard 1915-1918. Commissioned in the Air Service in 1920. Served at France Field, Canal Zone 1925-1928. Commandant of cadets at Air Corps Advanced Flying School 1929-1935. Graduated from the Command and General Staff School in 1937. Duty overseeing cold weather testing at Ladd Field, Alaska April 1940-April 1943. Brigadier general in September 1943. Commander of the Alaskan Wing July 1943-June 1946. Died on March 23, 1950. Decorations included the Distinguished Service Medal, Legion of Merit, Distinguished Flying Cross and Commendation Ribbon.

Galloway, Floyd Emerson (1890-1955) Born in Falmouth, Kentucky, on September 11, 1890. Attended the University of Kentucky 1911-1914. Commissioned in the infantry in 1917. Duty with the 31st Infantry in Siberia in 1918, the Philippine Islands in 1920 and the Czechoslovakian Repatriation Service June-October 1920. Transferred to the Air Service in December 1922. Aide and personal pilot to the assistant secretary of war July 1928-March 1929. Graduated from Air Corps Tactical School in June 1933. Commanding officer of 91st Observation Squadron July 1936-August 1937. Graduated from the Command and General Staff School in June 1938. Commanding officer of Bolling Field June 1938-September 1939. Graduated from Army War College in June 1940. Commanding officer of Air Corps Primary Flying School June 1940-March 1941 then commander of Albrook Field, Panama Canal Zone March-October 1941. Commanded Bolling Field, Maxwell Field and Crissy Field 1941-1943. Brigadier general in November 1942. Reverted to colonel in May 1943. Retired in May 1947. Died on September 22, 1955.

Gardner, Grandison (1892-1973) Born in Pine Valley, Utah, on September 18, 1892. B.S. from Utah State College in 1914. Commissioned in the aviation section of the Signal Corps in 1917. M.S. from Massachusetts Institute of Technology in 1928. Instructor and student at Air Corps Tactical School in 1933-1937. Operations officer, then executive officer of 19th Bomb Group 1937-1939. Duty at the Air Corps materiel division 1939-1940. Military air observer in England in 1940. Duty at Wright Field 1940-1942. Commander of Proving Ground Command March 1942-July 1945. Brigadier general in August 1942. Deputy to the chairman of the U.S. Strategic Bombing Survey 1945-1946. Retired as major general in August 1954. Decorations included the Distinguished Service Medal and Legion of Merit. Died on January 19, 1973.

Gates, Byron Elihu (1895-1970) Born in Aberdeen, South Dakota, on May 6, 1895. Attended the University of Montana in 1915. Enlisted as a flying cadet, then commissioned in the Air Service in 1920. Instructor at Air Service Advanded Flying School February 1924-January 1926. Duty with 28th Bombardment Squadron at Camp Nichols, Philippine Islands January 1926-April 1928. Graduated from Air Corps Tactical School in 1935 then instructor there until 1938 and again 1939-1940. With the plans division, office of the chief of the Air Corps 1940-1941, then the division of management control 1942-1945. Brigadier general in June 1943. Senior Air Force member of U.S. Military Mission to Brazil 1945-1947. Retired as major general in May 1955. Decorations included the Legion of Merit. Died on April 18, 1970.

George, Harold Huston (1892-1942) Born on September 14, 1892, in Lockport, New York. Enlisted service 1916-1917. Completed training on Curtis biplane in 1917 and commissioned in the Signal Corps, aviation section. Duty with 185th and 139th Aero Squadrons August 1918-November 1918 during World War I. Qualified as an ace for downing five German planes in combat. Graduated from Command and General Staff School in 1938. Brigadier general in May 1941. Commanded all air units in the Philippines and accompanied MacArthur to Australia when he escaped from Manila early in World War II. Killed in an airplane accident near Darwin on April 29, 1942. Decorations included the Distinguished Service Cross.

George, Harold L. (1893-1986) Born in Somerville, Massachusetts, on July 19, 1893. Attended George Washington University. Commissioned in the cavalry, Officers Reserve Corps in 1917. Transferred to the aviation section of the Signal Corps the following year. With 163rd Bomb Squadron at Meuse-Argonne offensive in World War I. Instructor at Air Corps Tactical School 1932-1936. Graduated from Command and General Staff School in 1937. Commander of 2nd Bomb Group, the first unit to be equipped with the B-17, 1937-1941. Assistant chief of staff for war plans on the Air Staff 1941-1942. Brigadier general in April 1942, major general in August 1942. Commanding general of Air Corps Ferrying Command, later redesignated Air Transport Command 1942-1946. Lieutenant general in March 1945. Retired in December 1946. Decorations included the Distinguished Service Medal, Legion of Merit, Distinguished Flying Cross and Air Medal. Died on February 24, 1986.

Gerhart, John Koehler (1907-1981) Born in Saginaw, Michigan, on November 27, 1907. Graduated from the University of Chicago in 1928. Commissioned in the Air Corps in October 1929. Flight test pilot at Wright Field 1939-1942. Assistant chief of staff for operations at Eighth Air Force April 1942-June 1943. Commander of 95th Bomb Group, then the 93rd Bomb Group 1943-1946. Brigadier general in January 1945. Assignments after the war included commanding general of Twelfth Air Force 1956-1957, deputy chief of staff for plans and programs, U.S. Air Force 1957-1962 and commander in chief of North American Air Defense Command 1962-1965. Retired as general in March 1965. Decorations included three Silver Stars, the Legion of Merit, Distinguished Flying Cross, Bronze Star and three Air Medals. Died on January 14, 1981.

Giles, Barney McKinney (1892-1984) Born in Mineola, Texas, on September 13, 1892, twin brother of Benjamin Franklin Giles. Attended East Texas College and the University of Texas. Enlisted service as flying cadet 1917-1920. Commissioned in the Air Service in July 1920. Graduated from Command and General Staff School in 1938. Head of inspection section in the office of the chief of the Air Corps 1938-1941. Commander of 4th Air Service Area Command 1941-1942. Brigadier general in January 1942. Commanding general of 4th Bomber Command 1942-1943. Major general in September 1942. Commanding general of Fourth Air Force 1943. Assistant to chief of the Air Staff, then chief 1943-1945. Lieutenant general in April 1944. Commanding general of Army Air Forces Pacific Ocean Areas April-October 1945. Assignments after the war included commanding general of U.S. Strategic Air Forces Pacific 1945-1946. Retired in June 1946. Decorations included. Died on May 10, 1984.

Giles, Benjamin Franklin (1892-1974) Born in Mineola, Texas, on September 13, 1892, the twin brother of Barney McKinney Giles. Commissioned in the infantry, Officers Reserve Corps in 1917. Entered active duty in 1920, underwent flight training, and earned his wings in 1924. Instructor with the California National Guard 1935-1938. Graduated from Command and General Staff School in 1939. Chief of aviation division for National Guard Bureau 1939-1941. Commander of Greenland Base Command, then Eastern Canada Base Command 1941-1943. Brigadier general in August 1942. Commanding general of 15th Troop Carrier Command, then U.S. Army Forces Africa-Middle East Theater of Operations 1943-1946. Major general in May 1944. Retired in August 1946. Decorations included two Distinguished Service Medals, the Legion of Merit and Air Medal. Died on November 30, 1974.

Gilkeson, Adlai Howard (1893-1959) Born on January 25, 1893, in Lansdale, Pennsylvania. Commissioned in the infantry from West Point in 1915. Served with the 1st Aero Squadron in the Punitive Expedition into Mexico 1916-1917. Involved in Air Service training in the U.S. during World War I. Commanding officer of Clark Field, Philippine Islands 1921-1925. Graduated from Air Corps Tactical School in 1932 and the Command and General Staff School in 1939. Commander of Air Defense Canal Zone 1939-1942. Brigadier general in February

1942. Commanding general of fighter commands in the U.S. and China-Burma-India Theater of Operations 1942-1945. Retired in 1953. Decorations include the Legion of Merit, Distinguished Flying Cross and two Air Medals. Died on November 2, 1959.

Gillmore, William E. (1876-1948) Born in Lorain, Ohio, on November 29, 1876. Attended West Point 1896-1899. Commissioned in the infantry in 1901. Transferred to the Air Service in 1920. Brigadier general in July 1926 as assistant chief of the Air Corps 1926-1930. Retired in June 1930. Recalled to active duty July-September 1943. Died on November 7, 1948.

Glenn, Charles Roland (1891-1970) Born in Independence, Iowa, October 16, 1891. M.D. from Jefferson Medical College in 1914. Commissioned in the Medical Corps, U.S. Army in 1918. Ward surgeon at Fort William McKinley, Philippine Islands July 1919-July 1921. Post surgeon at Albrook Field, Canal Zone July 1935-June 1937. Station surgeon at Air Corps Tactical School July 1937-December 1939. Air base surgeon at Moffett Field December 1939-April 1941. Surgeon for West Coast Air Corps Training Center April 1941-July 1942 then Army Air Force Flying Training Command July 1942-August 1944. Brigadier general in October 1943. Deputy air surgeon of the Army Air Force 1944-1945. Retired in January 1951. Died on October 6, 1970.

Glenn, Edgar Eugene (1896-1955) Born in Kansas City, Kansas, on October 27, 1896. Attended the University of Illinois 1917-1918. Commissioned in the aviation section of the Signal Corps in 1918. Flight instructor 1918-1919. Duty in the Panama Canal Zone 1923-1925. Professor at Georgia Institute of Technology 1926-1927. Graduated from Command and General Staff School in 1936. Staff officer with 2nd Wing 1937-1940. Special observer in England 1941-1942. Brigadier general in December 1942. Chief of staff of 1st Wing in 1942 and Fourteenth Air Force in 1943. Chief of staff and deputy commander of First Air Force March 1945-March 1946. Reverted to colonel in February 1946. Patient at Walter Reed Army Hospital prior to retirement in January 1954. Decorations included the Distinguished Service Medal, Legion of Merit, Distinguished Flying Cross, Air Medal and Purple Heart. Died on March 9, 1955.

Goodrich, Donald Reuben (1894-1945) Born in Marshall, Michigan, on October 17, 1894. Commissioned in the Air Service in 1920. Duty in the Philippines with 2nd Observation Squadron February 1927-September 1929. Graduated from Army Industrial College in 1931 and Air Corps Tactical School in 1938. Executive officer of the military personnel division, office of the chief of the Air Corps 1940-1942. Commanding officer of 3rd Air Service Area Command August 1942-March 1943. Chief of staff of Eighth Air Force Service Command in 1943. Brigadier general in February 1944. Assistant deputy commander for materiel in the European Theater of Operations March-December 1944. Commanding officer of San Antonio Technical Service Command January-March 1945. At headquarters Army Air Force March 1945 until his death there on July 12, 1945

Gordon, John Clarence (1906-1992) Born on January 6, 1906, in Yellow Pine, Alabama. Commissioned in the Air Corps from West Point in 1931. Assistant chief of staff for operations at Air Service Command, China-Burma-India Theater of Operations 1944-1945. Brigadier general in April 1945. Assigned to headquarters Air Materiel Command 1945-1949. Retired in March 1949. Decorations included the Legion of Merit, Bronze Star, Air Medal and Commendation Ribbon. Died on April 22, 1992.

Goss, Wentworth (1903-1971) Born in Peoria, Illinois. on January 23, 1903. Commissioned in the Air Corps in 1928. Duty with the 28th Bombardment Squadron, Phillipine Islands 1930-1933. Aide-de-camp to Brigadier General Delos S. Emmons November 1936-December 1941. Chief of the fighter division, office of the director of air defense, Army Air Force in 1942. Deputy chief of staff at Seventh Air Force 1942-1943. Assistant plans officer at Pacific Air Forces 1943-1945. Brigadier general in March 1945. Retired in July 1957. Decorations included the Legion of Merit. Died on February 23, 1971.

Grant, David Norvell Walker (1891-1964) Born in Richmond, Virgina, on May 14, 1891. M.D. from the University of Virginia. Commissioned in the Medical Corps in 1916. Post surgeon at Barksdale Field 1936-1939. Chief of the medical division, office of the chief of the Air Corps 1939-1941. Air surgeon for the Air Corps, then Army Air Force 1941-1946. Brigadier general in June 1942, major general in September 1943. Retired in April 1946. Decorations included the Distinguished Service Medal. Died on August 15, 1964.

Gravely, William Seymour (1888-1956) Born in Martinsville, Virginia, on March 30, 1888. Attended Virginia Polytechnic Institute. Commissioned in the field artillery in 1917. Duty with 2nd Observation Squadron, then 3rd Pursuit Squadron in the Philippine Islands 1922-1924. Instructor at the Air Service Advanced Flying School 1925-1930. Graduated from Command and General Staff School in 1936. Served in the Canal Zone as plans and training officer, then intelligence officer of a wing, then assistant chief of staff for operations and intelligence in the Panama Canal Department, finally deputy chief of staff of Caribbean Air Forces October 1939-October 1942. Chief of staff of 7th Air Support Command in the North African Theater of Operations 1942-1944. Brigadier general in January 1944. Commander of 74th and 37th Flying Training Wings August 1944-May 1945. Retired in September 1945. Died on July 25, 1956.

Graves, Davis Dunbar (1903-1945) Born in Buffalo, New York, on August 29, 1903. B.A. from Stanford University in 1927. Commissioned in the Air Corps in 1929. Served with the 78th Pursuit Squadron, Panama Canal Zone June 1934-July 1935. Adjutant at 19th Composite Wing, Panama Canal Zone July-December 1936 then Bolling Field July 1937-October 1939. Operations officer with 23rd Composite Group October 1939-January 1940. Graduated from Air Corps Tactical School in March 1940. Operations officer at Orlando Air Base December 1940-July 1941. Commanding officer of 56th Pursuit Group, Third International

Command July 1941-June 1942. Regional commander for New York, 1st Fighter Command June 1942-January 1943. Commanded Air Fighter Wing, North African Theater of Operations 1943-1944. Brigadier general in January 1944. Missing on a flight over Italy on February 8, 1944 and declared dead on February 9, 1945.

Griswold, Francis H. (1904-) Born in Erie, Pennsylvania, on November 5, 1904. Attended Columbia and Ohio State. Commissioned in the Air Corps in 1930. Commanding officer of 35th Pursuit Squadron in 1940 and 33rd Pursuit Group November 1940-April 1941. Executive officer of 4th Interceptor Command April-August 1941. Assistant to the assistant chief of staff for intelligence at 10th Pursuit Wing August-October 1941. Chief of the training section, then the fighter division at headquarters Army Air Force 1942-1943. Acting chief of staff, then chief of staff of 8th Fighter Command in the European Theater of Operations July 1943-August 1944. Brigadier general in March 1944. Commanding general of 8th Fighter Command August-October 1944. Chief of staff of 2nd Bombardment Division in Europe 1944-1945. Retired as lieutenant general.

Gross, Mervin Eugene (1900-1946) Born in Bowyer, South Carolina, on February 16, 1900. Commissioned in the Air Corps from West Point in 1922. Instructor at West Point 1928-1932. Chief of requirements at headquarters of Army Air Force 1939-1944. Brigadier general in September 1943. Chief of staff of the China Theater of Operations 1945-1946. Commandant of the Air Institute of Technology April 1946 until his death in an aircraft accident in Kentucky on October 18, 1946. Decorations included two Distinguished Service Medals.

Gross, William Milton (1908-1972) Born on August 29, 1908, in St. Joseph, Missouri. Commissioned in the Air Corps from West Point in 1934. Assistant operations officer at Chanute Field October 1937-January 1938. Post and squadron armament officer at Clark Field, Philippines 1938-1940. Assistant post operations officer, then operations officer at Bolling Field 1940-1942. Acting assistant chief of staff for supply, then intelligence at Eighth Air Force Staging Area 1942-1943. Commanding officer of 1st Combat Wing, Eighth Air Force 1943-1945. Brigadier general in May 1944. Commanding general of 1st Bomb Wing in 1945. Retired as major general in 1964. Decorations included two Silver Stars, three Distinguished Flying Crosses, the Bronze Star, four Air Medals and the Purple Heart. Died on February 2, 1972.

Grow, Malcolm Cummings (1887-1960) Born in Philadelphia, Pennsylvania, on November 19, 1887. M.D. from Jefferson Medical College in 1909. Served as captain, Medical Corps, in the Russian Imperial Army 1915-1917. Commissioned in the Medical Reserve Corps in 1921. Post surgeon at Chilkost Barracks, Alaska 1925-1927. Chief flight surgeon of the Air Corps 1934-1939. Brigadier general in September 1943. Director of medical services at U.S. Strategic Air Forces 1942-1945. Retired as major general in November 1949. Decorations included two Distinguished Service Medals, the Legion of Merit and Bronze Star. Died on October 20, 1960.

Hackett, Frank Dennis (1889-1951) Born in Brainard, Minnesota, on August 11, 1889. Attended Cornell University and Massachusetts Institute of Technology. Commissioned in the Air Service in 1920. Served with the 3rd Pursuit Squadron at Clark Field, Philippines 1922-1924. Graduated from Air Corps Tactical School in 1929. Post engineering officer at March Field, California 1939-1941. Commanding officer of 4th Air Base Group January-October 1941. Commandant of Air Corps Advanced Flying School from 1941. Brigadier general in January 1945. Reverted to colonel in March 1946. Retired in September 1948. Decorations included the Legion of Merit. Died on September 4, 1951.

Haddon, Julian Buckner (1894-1958) Born in Pleasant Hill, Missouri, on October 28, 1894. Commissioned in the aviation section of the Signal Corps in 1918. Duty with 3rd Pursuit Squadron in the Philippines 1925-1927. Graduated from Air Corps Tactical School in 1933 then secretary of the school July 1934-August 1937. Graduated from the Army Industrial College in 1938. Commanding officer of the 91st School Squadron at Maxwell Field 1938-1940 then the Southeast Air Corps Training Center November 1940-January 1942. Commanded Craig Field January-October 1942. Brigadier general in September 1942. Commanding general of Army Air Force Technical Training School October 1942-March 1943, 14th Air Force Service Command March-August 1943, the China-Burma-India Army Air Force Training Command 1943-1945 and the Army Air Force Eastern Flying Training Command 1945-1946. Retired in February 1946. Died on April 16, 1958.

Hale, Willis Henry (1893-1961) Born in Pittsburg, Kansas, on January 7, 1893. Enlisted service in the Philippines 1913-1917. Commissioned in the infantry in 1917. Aide-de-camp to Major General Harry C. Hale in Tientsin, China in 1917 and the AEF 1917-1919. Professor of military science and tactics at Yale 1920-1923. Transferred to the Air Corps in 1924. Graduated from Air Corps Tactical School in 1928, the Command and General Staff School in 1934 and Army War College in 1937. Inspector general of the Hawaiian Department 1939-1940. Brigadier general in January 1942. Commander of Seventh Air Force 1942-1944. Major general in June 1942. Commanding general of Air, Forward Areas of Pacific Ocean Areas, then deputy commander for operations at Army Air Force Pacific Ocean Areas 1944-1945. Commanding general of Fourth Air Force June 1945-October 1947. Assignments after the war included commanding general of Ninth and First Air Forces 1949-1950 and Continental Air Command 1951-1952. Retired in October 1952. Decorations included the Navy Cross, Distinguished Service Medal, two Legions of Merit, the Distinguished Flying Cross, Bronze Star and Air Medal. Died on March 25, 1961.

Hall, William Evans (1907-1984) Born in McAlester, Oklahoma, on October 22, 1907. Commissioned in the field artillery from West Point in 1929. Special assistant to the air inspector, Army Air Force 1941-1942. Secretary of the Air Staff, Army Air Force 1942-1943. Brigadier general in April 1943. Chief of the American Mission to Bulgaria 1943-1945. Deputy commanding general of Fifteenth Air Force in 1945. Assignments after the war included commanding general of Fourth Air Force 1951-1952 and commander of Continental Air Command 1957-1961. Retired as lieutenant general in September 1961. Decorations included the Distinguished Service Medal, two Legions of Merit, the Bronze Star and Air Medal. Died on May 30, 1984.

Hanley, Thomas James Jr. (1893-1969) Born on March 29, 1893, in Coshocton, Ohio. Commissioned in the infantry from West Point in 1915. Graduated from Command and General Staff School in 1930. Brigadier general in May 1942. Commanding general of Southeast Air Force Training Center 1943-1944. Major general in June 1943. Commanding general of Air Service Command, then Army Air Forces India-Burma Theater of Operations 1944-1946. Assignments after the war included commanding general of Eleventh Air Force 1946-1948. Retired in 1952. Decorations included the Distinguished Service Medal and two Legions of Merit. Died on March 9, 1969.

Hansell, Haywood Shepherd Jr. (1903-1988) Born in Fort Monroe, Virginia, on September 28, 1903. B.S. from Georgia Tech in 1924. Commissioned in the Air Reserve in 1928. Instructor at Air Corps Tactical School 1935-1938. Graduated from Command and General Staff School in 1939. Duty in the public relations section, then the foreign intelligence section, finally the air war plans division, office of the chief of the Air Corps 1938-1942. With the War Department General Staff in 1942. Brigadier general in August 1942. Commanding general of 3rd then 1st Bomb Wing 1942-1943. Duty at headquarters Army Air Force 1943-1944. Commanding general of 25th Bomber Command August 1944-January 1945 and 38th Flying Training Wing in 1945. Retired in December 1946. Recalled to active duty in July 1951. Chief of the mobilization division, office of the deputy chief of staff for operations, U.S. Air Force 1951-1953. Major general in September 1952. Decorations included the Distinguished Service Medal, Silver Star, Legion of Merit, Distinguished Flying Cross and Air Medal. Died on November 14, 1988.

Harbold, Norris Brown (1906-1993) Born on July 14, 1906, in Fort Niobrara, Nebraska. Commissioned in the field artillery from West Point in 1928. Commander of 80th Flying Training Wing 1943-1944. Brigadier general in February 1944. Chief of staff, then commanding general of 3rd Air Division, Eighth Air Force 1944-1945. Assistant chief of staff for intelligence, then commanding general of U.S. Army Strategic Air Forces in 1945. Retired as major general in August 1957. Decorations included two Distinguished Service Medals, two Legions of Merit, the Distinguished Flying Cross and Bronze Star. Died on August 12, 1993.

Hardin, Thomas Oates (1894-1968) Born in Mexia, Texas, on October 15, 1894. Served with the 101st Aero Squadron, AEF 1917-1919. Commissioned in the Air Service Reserve in 1922. Resigned in 1929 to enter commercial aviation. Pilot with American Airlines 1930-1938. Recalled to active duty as lieutenant colonel in 1942. At Ferrying Command headquarters in 1942. Deputy commander of African, then Middle East Wing of Air Transport Command 1942-1943. Commanding officer of Eastern Sector of India-China Wing, West Coast Wing and Central Pacific Wing 1943-1945. Brigadier general in January 1944. Returned to inactive status but recalled once again in 1947 to head the Air Force Air Reserve Division. Decorations included the Distinguished Service Medal and Distinguished Flying Cross. Died on October 18, 1968.

Harmon, Hubert Reilly (1892-1957) Born on April 3, 1892, in Chester, Pennsylvania, brother of Millard Fillmore Harmon. Commissioned in the Coast Artillery Corps from West Point in 1915. Earned his wings in 1917. Graduated from Command and General Staff School in 1935 and the Army War College in 1938. On the War Department General Staff 1938-1940. Commanding officer of Advanced Flying School at Kelly Field 1940-1941. Brigadier general in September 1941. Commanding general of Gulf Coast Air Corps Training Center 1941-1942. Major general in February 1942. Commander of Sixth Air Force 1942-1943. Commanding general of Thirteenth Air Force 1943-1944. Commander of Army Air Force Personnel Distribution Command, then deputy chief of staff for personnel, Army Air Force 1945-1946. Assignments after the war included commanding general of Sixth Air Force 1946-1947. Retired as lieutenant general in February 1953. Recalled to active duty by President Eisenhower to be the first superintendent of the Air Force Academy 1954-1956. Retired a second time in July 1956. Decorations included two Distinguished Service Medals, the Legion of Merit and Distinguished Flying Cross. Died on February 22, 1957.

Harmon, Millard Fillmore (1889-1945) Born on January 19, 1889, in Fort Mason (San Francisco), California, brother of Hubert Reilly Harmon. Commissioned in the infantry from West Point in 1912. Earned his wings in 1916. With 1st Aero Squadron in the Punitive Expedition into Mexico 1916-1917. Flew with a French aviation unit in combat in World War I. Graduated from Command and General Staff School in 1923 and the Army War College in 1925. Brigadier general in October 1940. Commander of Gulf Coast Training Center, then 7th Pursuit Wing and 11th Wing 1940. Air observer in England January-June 1941. Major general in July 1941. Commanding general of the Interceptor Command, Fourth Air Force July-December 1941. Chief of the Air Staff, Army Air Force January-June 1942. Commanding general of U.S. Army Forces South Pacific, then Army Air Forces Pacific Ocean Areas July 1942-February 1945. Lieutenant general in February 1943. Lost on a flight over the Pacific on February 26, 1945. Decorations included three Distinguished Service Medals and the Distinguished Flying Cross.

Harms, Henry William (1887-1945) Born in Wentworth, South Dakota, on November 25, 1887. Commissioned in the Air Service from West Point in 1912. Served with the AEF in World War I. Duty in the office of the chief of the Air Corps 1920-1923 and 1926-1929. Brigadier general in October 1940. Commanding general of B-29 bases in the U.S. 1941 until his death in Riverside, California on June 4, 1945.

Harper, Robert Wells (1900-1982) Born in Seattle, Washington, on November 7, 1900. Commissioned in the infantry from West Point in 1924. Transferred to the Air Corps in 1928. Graduated from Command and General Staff School in 1938. Tactical officer at West Point 1940-1942. Assistant chief of the Air Staff, Army Air Force 1942-1944. Brigadier general in February 1943, major general in February 1944. Represented the Army Air Force at the military government in Germany 1944-1947. Assignments after the war included commanding general of Air Transport Command 1947-1948 and Air Training Command 1948-1954. Retired as lieutenant general in June 1954. Decorations included two Distinguished Service Medals and two Legions of Merit. Died on December 7, 1982.

Harris, Harold Ross (1895-1988) Born in Chicago, Illinois, on December 20, 1895. B.S. from California Institute of Technology in 1917. Commissioned in the Air Service in 1917. Served as chief of flight section, Army Air Corps 1920-1925. Pioneered use of the parachute when his airplane collapsed in flight in 1922 and he parachuted safely to earth. Resigned in 1926. Employed in general aviation 1926-1941. Called to active duty in 1942. Chief of staff of Air Transport Command 1942-1946. Brigadier general in June 1945. Released from active duty in 1946. Decorations included the Distinguished Service Medal, Legion of Merit and Air Medal. Died in 1988.

Harris, Ray Guy (1891-1971) Born in Aquilla, Texas, on July 11, 1891. Attended Decatur Baptist College in 1908 and the University of Texas in 1918. Commissioned in the aviation section of the Signal Corps, Officers Reserve Corps in 1918. Graduated from Air Corps Tactical School in 1939. Commander of Midwestern District, Army Air Force Air Training Service Command 1942-1945. Brigadier general in February 1943. Reverted to colonel in March 1946. Retired in October 1947. Decorations included the Distinguished Service Medal. Died on October 25, 1971.

Hawkins, John Reynolds (1899-1947) Born in Prescott, Arkansas, on November 30, 1899. Commissioned in the Air Corps from West Point in 1924. Flying instructor 1927-1930 and 1932-1936. Graduated from Air Corps Tactical School in 1937 and the Command and General Staff School in 1938. Operations officer of the fighter group at Selfridge Field 1938-1941. Commanding officer of 31st Fighter Group 1941-1942. Chief of staff of 12th Fighter Command then 12th Air Support Command Decemeber 1942-July 1943. Commander of 64th Fighter Wing, Twelfth Air Force 1943-1944. Brigadier general in January 1944. Chief of the Air Force Mission to Chile at the time of his death in an aircraft accident in Peru on October 10, 1947. Decorations included the Legion of Merit, Distinguished Flying Cross and Purple Heart.

Hayes, Wolcott Paige (1894-1967) Born in Washington, DC, on December 17, 1894. Attended the University of Wisconsin 1914-1916 and Colby College 1916-1917. Commissioned in the cavalry in 1917. Transferred to the Air Service in 1920. Designated aviator in 1921. Graduated from Air Corps Tactical School in

1933. Duty with 65th Service Squadron in Hawaii 1933-1935. Air officer for the IV Corps Area May 1935-July 1940. Assistant commandant, then commandant of Air Corps Tactical School July 1940-February 1944. Brigadier general in October 1942. Commanding general of Antilles Air Command 1944-1945. Hospitalized until retirement in December 1945. Died on August 24, 1967.

Haynes, Caleb Vance (1895-1966) Born in Mount Airy, North Carolina, on March 15, 1895. L.L.B. from Wake Forest College in 1917. Commissioned in the Air Service in 1920. Commanding officer of 49th Bomber Squadron July 1936-January 1940, during which he was awarded a world's record and the MacKay Trophy for attaining the highest altitude with the greatest payload, as well as load distance (2,000 kilograms for 5,000 kilometers) in 1939. Commanding officer of 41st Reconaissance Squadron in 1940. Aide to Brigadier General Follett Bradley October-December 1940. Commanding officer of 26th Bomb Group in Puerto Rico 1941-1942 then Bomber Command, China Air Task Force June-October 1942. Brigadier general in October 1942. Commanding general of India Air Task Force 1942-1943 and 1st Bomber Command 1943-1945. Retired in April 1952. Decorations included the Distinguished Service Medal, two Silver Stars, the Legion of Merit, four Distinguished Flying Crosses, two Air Medals and three Commendation Ribbons. Died on April 5, 1966.

Hegenberger, Albert Francis (1895-1983) Born on September 30, 1895, in Boston, Massachusetts. Attended Massachusetts Institute of Technology. Enlisted service 1917-1918. Commissioned in the aviation section of the Signal Corps in 1920. Together with Lieutenant Lester J. Maitland flew a tri-motor Fokker named *Bird of Paradise* non-stop from Oakland to Hawaii in 25 hours and 50 minutes, a distance of 2,418 miles, on June 28, 1927 - the first time such a flight had been made. Graduated from Air Corps Tactical School in 1938 and the Command and General Staff School in 1939. Operations officer of 18th Wing, then the Hawaiian Air Force 1940-1941. Commanding officer of 11th Bomb Group, then 18th Bombardment Wing, finally 7th Bomber Command April 1941-July 1942. Commander of 2nd Bomber Command in 1942. Brigadier general in September 1943. Chief of staff of Second Air Force, then Fourteenth Air Force 1943-1945. Commanding general of Tenth Air Force in 1945. Retired as major general in September 1949. Decorations included two Distinguished Flying Crosses and the Legion of Merit. Died on August 31, 1983.

Hewitt, Leland Ross (1896-1967) Born in Mansfield, Louisiana, on July 12, 1896. Commissioned in the aviation section of the Officers Reserve Corps in 1917. Duty with 3rd Pursuit Squadron in the Philippines July 1931-May 1934. Graduated from Air Corps Tactical School in 1935 and Command and General Staff School in 1936. Director of flying at Air Corps Primary Flying School July 1936-July 1940. Executive officer of West Coast Air Corps Training Center 1940-1941. Commandant of Air Corps Advanced Flying School 1941-1943. Brigadier general in February 1943. Commanding general of 35th Flying Training Wing February 1943-March 1944 then 37th Flying Training Wing March-

November 1944. Chief of staff of Western Flying Training Command 1944-1946. Retired in March 1946. Decorations included the Legion of Merit. Died on July 26, 1967.

Hill, Edmund Walton (1896-1973) Born in New London, Connecticut, on April 26, 1896. Attended Case School of Applied Science 1914-1915 and Massachusetts Institute of Technology 1916-1917. Commissioned in the infantry in 1917. Transferred to the Air Service in 1920. Graduated from Command and General Staff School in 1931 and the Army War College in 1939. Air inspector, Army Air Force 1941-1942. Commanding general of U.S. Army Forces Northern Ireland in 1942. Brigadier general in August 1942. Commanding general of Eighth Air Force Composite Command December 1942-August 1944 and U.S. Air Forces in Russia 1944-1945. Major general in January 1945. Coordinator of the Inter-American Defense Board 1945-1946. Retired in October 1946. Decorations included the Legion of Merit, Bronze Star and Air Medal. Died on May 1, 1973.

Hoag, Earl Seeley (1895-1968) Born in Sioux City, Iowa, on May 30, 1895. Commissioned in the aviation section of the Officers Reserve Corps in 1918. Graduated from Air Corps Tactical School in 1936. Executive officer of the 1st Wing July 1937-January 1940. Duty with the War Department General Staff July 1940-March 1943. Brigadier general in June 1943. Served in Air Transport Command as executive officer, then commanding general of Africa-Middle East Wing, India-China Wing and the European Division March 1943-August 1945. Duty with the War Department General Staff again 1945-1947. Retired as major general in February 1953. Decorations included the Distinguished Service Medal, Legion of Merit, Air Medal and Commendation Ribbon. Died on March 3, 1968.

Hodges, James Pratt (1894-1992) Born in Oakley, Maryland, on October 7, 1894. Attended Georgia Institute of Technology in 1917. Commissioned in the aviation section of the Signal Corps in 1918. Flying instructor in World War I. Instructor at Air Corps Tactical School 1919-1923 and the Coast Artillery School 1930-1934. Graduated from the Command and General Staff School in 1936. Assistant chief of staff at GHQ Air Force 1936-1940. Commanding officer of 21st Reconaissance Squadron 1940-1941 and 29th Bomb Group 1941-1942. Chief of staff of 3rd Bomber Command in 1942. Commanding general of 2nd Bomb Wing September 1942-August 1944. Brigadier general in October 1942, major general in May 1944. Assistant chief of staff for intelligence, Army Air Force 1944-1945. Commanding general of Western Flying Training Command July-December 1945. Assignments after the war included commanding general of First Air Force February 1951 until retirement in September 1951. Decorations included two Distinguished Service Medals, the Silver Star, Distinguished Flying Cross and Air Medal. Died on July 19, 1992.

Hood, Reuben Columbus Jr. (1907-1985) Born in Atlanta, Georgia, on April 12, 1907. B.S. from Georgia Institute of Technology in 1928. Commissioned in the Air Corps in 1929. Graduated from Air Corps Tactical School in 1935. Executive officer of 10th Pursuit Wing February-November 1941. Member of the Military Mission to Cairo in 1942. Chief of supply, then chief of staff, finally commanding officer of Air Service Command, China-Burma-India Theater of Operations 1942-1944. Brigadier general in November 1943. Deputy chief of staff, supply division at Air Service Command and Air Technical Service Command in 1944. Duty in the office of the assistant chief of staff for plans, Army Air Force September-December 1944. Assistant chief of staff for intelligence at Contintinental Air Force in 1945. Assignments after the war commanding general of Caribbean Air Command June 1953-June 1956. Retired in June 1959. Decorations included the Distinguished Service Medal, two Legions of Merit, the Distinguished Flying Cross, Air Medal and Commendation Ribbon. Died on April 2, 1985.

Hopkins, Frederick Mercer Jr. (1895-1978) Born in New York, New York, on June 8, 1895. B.S. from New York University in 1926. Commissioned in the Coast Artillery Corps, Officers Reserve Corps in 1918. Assistant professor of military science and tactics at New York University September 1926-August 1930. Assistant commandant of the Air Corps Engineer School 1932-1936. Graduated from Command and General Staff School in 1938. Instructor at Air Corps Tactical School 1938-1940. Assistant executive officer, then chief of materiel division in the office of the chief of the Air Corps 1940-1942. Brigadier general in September 1942. Chief of facilities section of the Materiel Command 1942-1943. Chief of redistribution at headquarters of Army Air Force 1943-1945. Staff officer with U.S. Army Strategic Air Forces in the Pacific Theater of Operations in 1945. Retired in August 1951. Decorations included the Distinguished Service Medal and Legion of Merit. Died on January 22, 1978.

Hornsby, Aubrey (1895-1981) Born in Eclectic, Alabama, on January 8, 1895. Attended the University of Alabama 1915-1916 and Southern University 1916-1917. Commissioned in the field artillery, Officers Reserve Corps in 1917. Served with the AEF 1918-1919. Transferred to the Air Service in 1920. Commanding officer of 3rd Pursuit Squadron at Clark Field, Philippine Islands June 1930-August 1932. Commanding officer of Air Corps Basic Flying School August 1940-December 1942 then 30th Flying Training Wing 1942-1943. Brigadier general in February 1943. Commanding general of 32nd Flying Training Wing 1943-1945 and Eastern Technical Training Command March 1945-February 1946. Retired in August 1947. Decorations included the Distinguished Service Medal and Legion of Merit. Died on May 22, 1981.

Houghton, Junius Henry (1892-1980) Born on August 21, 1892, in Titusville, Pennsylvania. Commissioned in the infantry from West Point in 1916. Executive officer and supply officer at Barksdale Field 1939-1940. Graduated from Air Corps Tactical School in 1940. Commanding officer of Jackson Army Air Base 1941-1942 and 3rd Air Base Depot, European Theater of Operations 1943-1944. Director of supply at Air Service Command, Strategic Air Forces Europe January 1944-October 1945. Brigadier general in September 1944. Reverted to colonel in

January 1946 and retired in June 1950. Decorations include the Legion of Merit and Bronze Star. Died on December 20, 1980.

House, Edwin Jacob (1895-1969) Born on July 6, 1895, in Syracuse, New York. Commissioned in the infantry from West Point in 1917. Duty in Hawaii 1922-1925. In the plans division, office of the chief of the Air Corps 1930-1934. Commanding officer of 1st Pursuit Group 1937-1938. Graduated from the Command and General Staff School in 1939. Commanding officer of France Field, Canal Zone, 1939-1941. Commanding general of Antilles Air Command 1941-1943. Brigadier general in March 1942, major general in February 1943. Commanding general of 12th Air Support Command 1943-1944 then Army Air Force Tactical Center at Orlando March 1944 until retirement in October 1945. Decorations included two Distinguished Service Medals and two Legions of Merit. Died on October 18, 1969.

Hovey, Burton Murdock Jr. (1905-1978) Born in Haliflax, Nova Scotia, on July 7, 1905. Enlisted service 1923-1927. Commissioned in the Air Corps in 1927. Graduated from Air Corps Tactical School in 1940. Commandant of the Air Corps Basic Flying School 1941-1943. Commander of Norfolk Air Defense Wing 1943. Commanding officer of 303rd Fighter Wing 1943-1944. Brigadier general in September 1944. Deputy commanding general of 26th Tactical Air Command 1944-1945. Commanding general of Berlin Air Command in 1945. Retired as major general in February 1957. Decorations included two Legions of Merit and the Bronze Star. Died on December 10, 1978.

Howard, Clinton Wilbur (1890-1970) Born on November 27, 1890, in Campello, Massachusetts. Commissioned in the field artillery from West Point in 1915. Served with Pershing in the Punitive Expedition into Mexico 1916-1917. Graduated from the Army Industrial College in 1936 and the Army War College in 1937. With the War Department General Staff 1939-1941. Commanding officer of Morris Field (North Carolina) then chief of staff of Third Air Force 1941-1942. Brigadier general in December 1942. Chief of staff of Army Air Force Technical Training Command, then commanding general of Sacramento Air Service Command 1943 until retirement in August 1946. Died on January 19, 1970.

Hoyt, Ross Gordon (1893-1983) Born in Travers City, Michigan, on March 12, 1893. Attended Olivet College and the University of Michigan. Enlisted service 1914-1917. Commissioned in the Coast Artillery Corps in 1917. Transferred to the Air Service in 1920. Graduated from Air Corps Tactical School in 1920. Professor of military science and tactics at Kamehemeha Schools, Hawaii September 1922-February 1923. Refueling officer for the *Question Mark*, piloted by Captain Ira C. Eaker, during its marathon endurance flight over Los Angeles January 1-7, 1929. Set a world record with a solo flight of 48 hours between New York City and Nome, Alaska in July 1929. Duty with 20th Pursuit Group 1939-1940. Commanding officer of Oklahoma City Air Base 1940-1941 then Luke Air Force Base September 1941-February 1943. Brigadier general in June 1943. Fighter wing commander in the European Theater of Operations 1943-1944. Retired in April 1944. Died on April 7, 1983.

Huglin, Harold Quiskey (1906-1975) Born on September 22, 1906, in Fairfield, Iowa. Attended Parsons College. Commissioned in the Air Corps from West Point in 1929. Commanding officer of 90th and 78th Bomber Squadrons 1940-1941. Operations officer at 3rd Bomb Group April-August 1941. Assistant chief of staff for intelligence at Air Force Combat Command January-March 1942. Duty with the directorate of bombardment, Army Air Force March 1942-February 1943. Assistant chief of staff for intelligence at 3rd Bomb Wing, then commanding officer of 100th Bomb Group in 1943. Chief of staff, then commanding officer of 13th Combat Bomb Wing September-December 1943, then 92nd and 13th Combat Bomb Wings January 1944-July 1945. Brigadier general in January 1945. Deputy chief of staff, then chief of staff of U.S. Air Forces Europe 1945-1947. Retired as major general in July 1959. Decorations included the Silver Star, two Legions of Merit, the Distinguished Flying Cross, Bronze Star, Air Medal and two Commendation Ribbons. Died on November 24, 1975.

Hunter, Frank O'Driscoll (1894-1982) Born in Savannah, Georgia, on December 8, 1894. Enlisted service 1917-1918. Commissioned in the Signal Corps, aviation section, Officers Reserve Corps and flew with 103rd Aero Squadron, AEF 1918-1919, participating in the St. Mihiel and Meuse-Argonne offensives and becoming an ace for downing eight German planes. Transferred to the U.S. Army in 1920. Air attache in Paris, then London May-December 1940. Commanding officer of 23rd Composite Group 1940-1942. Brigadier general in April 1942. Commanding general of 8th Fighter Command 1942-1943. Major general in November 1943. Commanding general of First Air Force 1943-1946. Retired in March 1946. Decorations included five Distinguished Service Crosses, the Distinguished Service Medal and Distinguished Flying Cross. Presented the CBE in the name of King George VI of England. Hunter Air Force Base at Savannah, Georgia, was named in his honor in 1950. Died on June 27, 1982.

Hutchinson, Donald Robert (1909-1989) Born in Cleveland, Ohio, on January 5, 1909. B.S. from Case School of Applied Science in 1931. Commissioned in the Air Reserve in 1932. Served in the Panama Canal Zone 1932-1934. Resigned in 1934 then commissioned again in the Air Corps in 1936. Duty in Darwin, Australia, in 1942. Commanding officer of 49th Fighter Group, then chief of staff of 5th Fighter Command 1942-1943. Commanding officer of 3rd Air Task Force in 1944. Brigadier general in June 1944. Chief of staff of Fifth Air Force 1944-1945 then Far East Air Force and Allied Air Forces Southwest Pacific Area 1945-1946. Retired in June 1962. Decorations included two Distinguished Service Medals, the Distinguished Flying Cross and Air Medal. Died on July 23, 1989.

Hutchison, David William (1908-1982) Born on May 21, 1908, in Mineral Point, Wisconsin. Commissioned in the Air Corps from West Point in 1931. Commanding officer of 6th Photo Group, 91st Reconaissance Wing, 508th Bomb

Wing and 514th Composite Wing 1943-1947. Brigadier general in April 1945. Assignments after the war included commanding general of Seventeenth Air Force 1952-1954 and Ninth Air Force 1958-1961. Retired as major general in June 1961. Decorations included the Distinguished Service Medal, Silver Star, two Distinguished Flying Crosses, two Air Medals and the Purple Heart. Died on September 25, 1982.

Ignico, Robert Victor (1894-1982) Born in Boston, Massachusetts, on October 14, 1894. Attended Washington & Lee University 1914-1917. Commissioned in the aviation section of the Signal Corps in 1917. Duty at Philippine Islands Air Depot 1923-1925. Graduated from the Army Industrial College in 1932. Chief of staff of 13th Composite Command February 1940-May 1941. Duty with Air Service Command 1941-1942. Commander of 11th Air Service Command 1942-1944. Brigadier general in September 1942. Commanding general of Spokane Air Depot August 1944-December 1945. Retired in June 1952. Decorations included two Legions of Merit, the Air Medal and Commendation Ribbon. Died on November 15, 1982.

Israel, Robert Scott Jr. (1907-) Born on July 27, 1907, in San Antonio, Texas. Commissioned in the field artillery from West Point in 1928, then transferred to the Air Corps. Brigadier general in August 1944. Commanding general of 22nd Tactical Air Command 1945-1946. Retired in July 1958. Decorations included the Legion of Merit and Bronze Star. Resides in St. Petersburg, Florida.

Jamison, Glen Clifford (1899-1973) Born on September 3, 1899, in Richmond, Kansas. Commissioned in the Air Corps from West Point in 1923. Instructor at Kelly Field 1933-1935. Operations officer of Air Corps Advanced Flying School 1935-1938. Assigned to the engineering section at headquarters of the Air Corps 1939-1942. Duty with Tenth Air Force in India, then chief of staff of Thirteenth Air Force in the South Pacific in 1942. Brigadier general in May 1943. Commanding general of 8th Bomber Command June-August 1943. In the plans division, office of the assistant chief of the Air Corps 1943-1946. Retired in December 1949. Decorations included two Legions of Merit and the Distinguished Flying Cross. Died on January 30, 1973.

Johnson, Davenport (1890-1963) Born on March 28, 1890, in Tyler, Texas. Commissioned in the infantry from West Point in 1912. Served in the invasion of Vera Cruz in 1914 and with the 1st Aero Squadron in the Punitive Expedition into Mexico in 1916. Saw action in the Meuse-Argonne offensive as commanding officer of 95th Aero Squadron in the AEF in 1918. Graduated from the Command and General Staff School in 1926. Instructor at Air Corps Tactical School 1926-1928. Graduated from Army War College in 1929. Brigadier general in August 1941. Assistant to the chief of the Air Corps 1940-1941. Major general in August 1941. Duty with the Caribbean Command 1941-1942. Commander of Sixth Air Force March-November 1942. Director of military personnel in the Air Corps 1942-1943. Commanding general of Second Air Force in 1943. Commanding general of Eleventh Air Force 1943-1945. Retired in November 1945. Decorations included the Silver Star, Legion of Merit, Distinguished Flying Cross, Air Medal and Purple Heart. Died on October 21, 1963.

Johnson, Harry Anton (1893-1978) Born in Litchfield, Minnesota, on June 29, 1893. Graduated from the University of Minnesota. Commissioned in the aviation section of the Signal Corps in 1918. Graduated from Air Corps Tactical School in 1933, Command and General Staff School in 1936 and the Army War College in 1938. Instructor at Naval War College in 1940. Chief of the training section, office of the chief of the Air Corps in 1941. Duty with the War Department General Staff 1942. Chief of staff of Sixth Air Force 1942-1943. Brigadier general in December 1942. Staff officer at headquarters of SHAEF 1943-1944. Commanding general of Eleventh Air Force Service Command in Alaska July-November 1944, then deputy commanding general of Eleventh Air Force 1944-1945. Assignments after the war included chief of staff, then commanding general of Tenth Air Force July 1946-April 1952. Retired in June 1953. Decorations included two Legions of Merit, the Distinguished Flying Cross and two Air Medals. Died on May 1, 1978.

Johnson, Leon William (1904-) Born on September 13, 1904, in Columbia, Missouri. Commissioned in the infantry from West Point in 1926. M.S. from California Institute of Technology in 1936. Earned his wings and transferred to the Air Corps in 1930. Assistant chief of staff for operations, Eighth Air Force, January 1942-January 1943. Commander of 44th Bomb Group January-September 1943. On August 1, 1943, he led the unit of B-24s, nicknamed the "Eight Balls," in one of five elements of a massive attack against the oil refineries at Ploesti, Romania. His actions earned him the Medal of Honor. Brigadier general in November 1943. Commanded the 14th Combat Bomb Wing from September 1943 until the war ended. Assignments after the war included commanding general of Continental Air Command January 1952-April 1956 and air deputy to the Supreme Allied Commander in Europe August 1957 until retirement as general in July 1961. Decorations included the Medal of Honor, three Distinguished Service Medals, the Silver Star, Legion of Merit, two Distinguished Flying Crosses and four Air Medals. Resides in McLean, Virginia.

Jones, Aaron Edward (1889-1963) Born in Cincinnati, Ohio, on September 26, 1889. B.D. from Kenyon College in 1912. Commissioned in the aviation section of the Signal Corps in 1917. Graduated from Air Corps Tactical School in 1936. Brigadier general in October 1942. Chief of procurement division, Army Materiel Command then assistant chief of staff for materiel and services at headquarters Army Air Force 1942-1946. Retired in May 1946. Decorations included the Legion of Merit. Died on July 25, 1963.

Jones, Junius Wallace (1890-1977) Born on April 3, 1890, in Jackson, Louisiana. Commissioned in the Coast Artillery Corps from West Point in 1913. Graduated from Command and General Staff School in 1929, the Army War College in 1930 and Naval War College in 1934. Commandant of Air Corps

Technical School 1934-1938. Air inspector in the office of the inspector general of the Air Corps 1938-1941. Brigadier general in February 1941. Commanding general of 5th Air Support Command 1941-1942. With Army Air Force Technical Training Command 1942-1943. Air inspector at headquarters of Army Air Force 1943-1948. Retired as major general in April 1952. Decorations included two Distinguished Service Medals, two Legions of Merit and the Air Medal. Died on February 14, 1977.

Kane, Clarence Peyton (1890-1964) Born on April 9, 1890, in San Francisco, California. Attended San Francisco Law School 1913-1916. Commissioned in the infantry, Officers Reserve Corps in 1917. Transferred to the Air Service in 1918. Graduated from Army Balloon School in 1921. Assigned to the American Embassy in Tokyo July 1926-May 1928. Duty at the Hawaii Air Depot 1935-1937. Graduated from the Army Industrial College in 1938. Duty at the Air Corps Materiel Division 1939-1941 then at Air Materiel Command in 1942. Chief of Air Force security in the Field Service Command July-December 1942. Assistant chief of the supply division at Air Service Command in 1943. Brigadier general in June 1943. Commanding general of Rome then Fairfield Air Service Command 1943-1944. Served with Air Service Command at U.S. Strategic Air Forces Europe in 1944. Commanding general of Air Technical Service Command Europe December 1944-June 1945 then Atlantic Overseas Service Command July 1945-July 1946. Reverted to colonel and retired in October 1946. Brigadier general on the retired list in July 1948. Decorations included the Distinguished Service Medal. Died on November 11, 1964.

Kauch, Robert (1894-1967) Born in Philadelphia, Pennsylvania, on July 14, 1894. Attended Franklin Institute. Commissioned in the infantry, Officers Reserve Corps in 1916. Transferred to the Air Service in 1920. Duty in the Philippines 1925-1927. With 12th Observation Group, then 12th Observation Command 1933-1936. In plans and training division in the office of the chief, Air Corps 1939-1940. Assistant director, then director of the Air Corps Band at Maxwell and Eglin Fields 1940-1941. Commanding officer of 1st Air Service Command 1941-1942. Duty with Ninth Air Force 1942-1943. Brigadier general in February 1943. Commanding general of Medical Air Transport Command 1943-1944. Chief of the air installations division of Army Air Force September 1944-October 1947. Retired in June 1948. Decorations included the Legion of Merit. Died on April 7, 1967.

Kennedy, John Carroll (1893-1977) Born in New York on November 28, 1893. LL.M. from New York University in 1925. Commissioned in the aviation section of the Signal Corps Reserve in 1918 then the Air Service in July 1920. Served in France during World War I. Duty with 66th Service Squadron in the Philippine Islands January 1929-October 1930. Commanding officer of 12th Observation Squadron 1935-1939. Graduated from the Air Corps Tactical School in 1939. Military observer in London in 1941. Commanding officer of the 73rd Observation Group then the 77th Observation Group November 1941-September 1943.

Assigned to U.S. Army Forces China 1943-1945. Brigadier general in January 1945. Retired in 1950. Died on August 2, 1977.

Kenney, George Churchill (1889-1977) Born on August 6, 1889, in Yarmouth, Nova Scotia. Commissioned in the Air Service in 1917. Served with the 91st Aero Squadron in World War I. Graduated from Command and General Staff School in 1927 and the Army War College in 1933. Brigadier general in January 1941. Commander of Air Corps Experimental Depot January 1941-April 1942. Major general in April 1942. Commanding general of Fourth Air Force April-July 1942. Lieutenant general in September 1942. Commanding general of Fifth Air Force September 1942-June 1944, then Southwest Pacific Allied Air Forces June 1944-March 1945. General in March 1945. Commander of Allied Air Forces Pacific March 1945 until war's end. Assignments after the war included commander of Strategic Air Command April 1946-October 1948. Decorations included two Distinguished Service Crosses, two Distinguished Service Medals, the Silver Star, two Distinguished Flying Crosses and the Bronze Star. Author of *General Kenney Reports* (1948), *The MacArthur I Know* (1951), *The Saga of Pappy Gunn* (1959) and *Dick Bong, Ace of Aces* (1960). Died on August 9, 1977.

Kepner, William Ellsworth (1893-1982) Born on January 6, 1893, in Miami, Indiana. Graduated from Command and General Staff School in 1937. Enlisted service in the U.S. Marine Corps 1909-1913. Commissioned in the cavalry, Indiana National Guard in 1916. Transferred to the infantry in 1917. Commanded a company and battalion in the Meuse-Argonne, Aisne, Champagne, Marne and St. Mihiel campaigns in World War I. Transferred to the Air Service in 1920. Balloon observer and dirigible pilot 1920-1930. Executive officer of Air Defense Command 1940-1941. Commanding officer of 1st Air Support Command 1941-1942. Brigadier general in February 1942. Commanding general of 4th Fighter Command, then Fourth Air Force 1942-1943. Major general in April 1943. Commanding general of 8th Fighter Command 1943-1944. Commanding general of 2nd Bomb Division, Eighth Air Force 1944-1945. Assignments after the war included commander in chief of Alaskan Command 1950-1953. Retired as lieutenant general in February 1953. Decorations included the Distinguished Service Cross, Distinguished Service Medal, Legion of Merit, Distinguished Flying Cross, Bronze Star, Air Medal and Purple Heart. Died on July 3, 1982.

Kessler, Alfred August Jr. (1898-1956) Born on August 3, 1898, in Union Hill, New Jersey. Commissioned in the infantry from West Point in 1918 prematurely for service in World War I then following the war returned and graduated with the class of 1922. Duty in the Philippine Islands 1924-1926. M.S. from Massachusetts Institute of Technology in 1932. Graduated from Air Corps Tactical School in December 1939. Commanding officer of 95th Bombardment Group and 13th Bombardment Wing, Eighth Air Force April 1943-March 1944. Brigadier general in May 1944. Commanding general of Eastern Command, U.S. Tactical Air Forces in the Soviet Union March-October 1944. Military attache in Sweden

1944-1947. Assignments after the war included commanding general of Fourth Air Force September 1952 until retirement as major general in February 1955. Decorations included the Distinguished Service Medal, Silver Star, two Legions of Merit, the Distinguished Flying Cross, two Air Medals and the Commendation Ribbon. Died on November 30, 1956.

Kiel, Emil Charles (1895-1971) Born in Manitowoc, Wisconsin, on September 25, 1895. Attended Stout Institute 1915-1917. Commissioned in the Signal Corps, aviation section in 1918. Instructor at Air Corps Tactical School 1932-1936. Duty with the operations training division at War Department General Staff 1940-1941 then in the office of the chief of the Air Corps in 1941. Chief of staff of Fourth Air Force December 1941-June 1944. Brigadier general in April 1943. Commanding general of 318th Fighter Wing June-July 1944. Again chief of staff of Fourth Air Force July-November 1944. Deputy commanding general then chief of staff of Eighth Air Force November 1944-October 1945. Retired in July 1953. Decorations included the Distinguished Service Medal, Legion of Merit, Bronze Star and Commendation Ribbon. Died on November 4, 1971.

Kimble, Frederick Von Harten (1895-1978) Born on August 10, 1895, in Portland, Oregon. Commissioned in the infantry from West Point in 1918. Aide to the assistant secretary of war, then White House aide 1929-1934. Graduated from Command and General Staff School in 1936. Instructor at Air Corps Tactical School 1936-1940. Again a White House aide 1940-1941. Commanding officer of Tuskegee Flying School in 1942. Commander of 27th Flying Training Wing 1942-1944. Brigadier general in April 1943. Commanding general of Tinian Island 1944-1946. Retired in February 1953. Decorations included two Legions of Merit. Died on August 19, 1978.

Kincaid, Alvan Cleveland (1892-1968) Born in Orleans, Indiana, on September 25, 1892. Attended Indiana University. Commissioned in the infantry, Officers Reserve Corps in 1917. Transferred to the Air Service in 1920. Served at headquarters of the Air Corps 1935-1938. Graduated from Command and General Staff School in 1939. Executive officer, then assistant commandant of Air Corps Technical School 1939-1941. Commanding officer of Army Air Base, Roswell, New Mexico 1941-1942. Assistant chief of staff of West Coast Army Air Force Training Center 1942-1943. Brigadier general in February 1943. Commanding general of 37th Flying Training Wing February 1943-March 1944. Chief of staff of 9th Tactical Air Command April-December 1944 then deputy chief of staff until May 1945. Chief of staff of U.S. Air Forces Europe June 1945-March 1946. Assignments after the war included commanding general of Twelfth Air Force September 1948-May 1949, Twentieth Air Force June 1949-July 1950 and Fourth Air Force September-December 1950. Retired as major general in Septemeber 1952. Decorations included the Distinguished Service Medal, Silver Star, Legion of Merit, Bronze Star and Purple Heart. Died on January 31, 1968.

Kissner, August Walter (1906-1973) Born on February 8, 1906, in New Haven, Connecticut. Commissioned in the Air Corps from West Point in 1928. Duty at headquarters of the Air Corps 1940-1943. Chief of staff of 3rd Bombardment Division, Eighth Air Force 1943-1944. Chief of staff of 20th Bomber Command, Twentieth Air Force in 1944. Brigadier general in February 1944. In plans division of Strategic Air Forces Europe 1944-1945. Chief of staff to General Curtis LeMay in 21st Bomber Command in 1945. Retired as major general in July 1958. Decorations included two Distinguished Service Medals, the Silver Star, Legion of Merit and Air Medal. Died on July 10, 1973.

Knapp, Robert Duane (1897-1994) Born in Moreland, Georgia, on December 26, 1897. Attended Alabama Polytechnic Institute. Enlisted service 1917-1918. Commissioned in the Air Service in 1920. Director of flying training at Kelly Field 1934-1937. Graduated from Air Corps Tactical School in 1938. Executive officer of 2nd Wing, then GHQ Air Force, and commanding officer of 38th Bombardment Group 1940-1942. Commanding officer of 21st Bombardment Group, then group commander of 321st Bombardment Group in 1942. Assigned to the Third Bomber Command July-September 1942. Group commander of the 321st Bombardment Group September 1942-December 1943. Commanded 12th Bomber Command December 1943-September 1944. Brigadier general in February 1944. Commander of 57th Bombardment Wing 1944-1945. Reverted to colonel in November 1945. Retired in September 1953. Decorations included the Distinguished Service Medal, Silver Star, Distinguished Flying Cross, Bronze Star and eight Air Medals. Died on April 25, 1994.

Knerr, Hugh Johnson (1887-1971) Born in Fairfield, Iowa, on May 30, 1887. Attended Midland College 1900-1904. Graduated from USNA in 1908. Commissioned in the U.S. Navy and served 1908-1912. Transferred to the Coast Artillery Corps of the U.S. Army in 1912, then the Air Corps in 1917. Graduated from the Army War College in 1931. Chief of staff at GHQ Air Corps 1937-1938. Retired as colonel in May 1939. Returned to active duty in 1942. Deputy commander of Air Service Command 1942-1944. Brigadier general in June 1943, major general in March 1944. Commander of 8th Air Service Command then Air Service Command, Strategic Air Forces in Europe in 1944. Deputy commanding general of U.S. Air Forces Europe 1944-1945. Commanding general of Air Technical Service Command 1945-1946. Assignments after the war included inspector general of the Air Force June 1947-September 1949. Retired in October 1949. Decorations included the Distinguished Service Medal, two Legions of Merit, the Bronze Star and Commendation Ribbon. Died on October 26, 1971.

Kraus, Walter Francis (1894-1977) Born in New York, New York, on February 3, 1894. Attended Columbia University 1911-1915. Commissioned in the Coast Artillery Corps in 1917. Attended Massachusetts Institute of Technology 1925-1926. Brigadier general in April 1942. Chief of staff of Army Air Force Flying Training Command 1942-1944. Commanding general of Central Flying Training Command 1944-1945. Major general in March 1945. Chief of staff of Army Air

Force Flying Training Command 1945-1946. Retired in April 1946. Decorations included the Distinguished Service Medal and Legion of Merit. Died on July 13, 1977.

Krogstad, Arnold Norman (1885-1982) Born in Lansboro, Minnesota, on August 28, 1885. Commissioned in the infantry from West Point in 1909. Transferred to the Signal Corps, aviation section in 1916. Graduated from Air Corps Tactical School in 1933, The Army Industrial College in 1934 and the Army War College in 1935. Commanding officer of the Air Corps Advanced Flying School 1936-1938. Brigadier general in March 1938. Commanding general of 2nd Wing 1938-1941. Commanding general of 1st Bomber Command 1941-1942. Commanding general of 2nd District, Army Air Force Technical Training Command, then Army Air Force Technical Training Command Schools, finally 5th District 1942-1944. With Army Air Force Technical Training Command at Coral Gables February 1944 until retirement in July 1944. Died on January 17, 1982.

Kuter, Laurence Sherman (1905-1979) Born on May 28, 1905, in Rockford, Illinois. Commissioned in the Air Corps from West Point in 1927. Flew alternate wing position with Captain Claire L. Chennault's forerunner to the Thunderbirds, the "Flying Trapeze," in 1933. On the War Department General Staff 1939-1941. Member, along with Lauris Norstad and Charles P. Cabell, of General Arnold's advisory council. Assistant secretary of the War Department General Staff November 1941-February 1942. Promoted from lieutenant colonel to brigadier general in February 1942. Commanding general of 1st Bomb Wing October 1942-January 1943. Commanding general of Allied Tactical Air Forces in North Africa January-May 1943. Assistant chief of the Air Staff May 1943-May 1945. Major general in February 1944. Represented General Arnold at the Yalta and Malta conferences in 1945. Assignments after the war included the first commander of Military Air Transport Service, commonly known as MATS, in 1948, commanding general of Far East Air Forces, later renamed Pacific Air Forces 1955-1957 and commander in chief of North American Air Defense Command August 1959 until retirement as general in July 1962. Decorations included three Distinguished Service Medals, the Legion of Merit and Bronze Star. Died on November 30, 1979.

Lackland, Frank Dorwin (1884-1943) Born in Fauquier County, Virginia, on September 13, 1884. Commissioned in the District of Columbia National Guard in 1905. With 11th Infantry 1911-1913 at San Antonio, then 1913-1914 at Fort Russell, Wyoming. Transferred to aviation section of the Signal Corps in 1917. Served in the U.S. during World War I. Graduated from Command and General Staff School in 1931. In the plans division at Air Corps headquarters 1934-1935. Brigadier general in December 1939. Commanding general of 1st Wing 1939-1942. Retired on June 30, 1942. Died on April 27, 1943. Lackland Air Force Base, San Antonio, was named in his honor in 1947.

Landon, Truman Hempel (1905-1986) Born on February 11, 1905, in Maryville, Missouri. Commissioned in the Coast Artillery Corps from West Point in 1928. Transferred to the Air Corps and earned his wings in 1930. Graduated from Air Corps Tactical School in 1939. Commanding officer of 38th Reconaissance Squadron 1939-1942. Commander of 7th Bomber Command 1942-1945. Brigadier general in February 1943. Assignments after the war included the inspector general, U.S. Air Force 1954-1956, deputy chief of staff for personnel, U.S. Air Force 1959-1961 and commander in chief of U.S. Air ForceE June 1961 until retirement as general in August 1963. Decorations included the Distinguished Service Medal, Legion of Merit and three Air Medals. Died on January 27, 1986.

Langmead, Edmund Clarence (1894-1978) Born in Cleveland, Ohio, on September 3, 1894. Commissioned in the Air Service in 1921. Graduated from Air Corps Tactical School in 1936 and Army Industrial College in 1937. Executive officer in the engineering section, materiel division, office of the chief of the Air Corps November 1940-February 1942. Staff officer in the supply division, Army Air Force February-December 1942. Chief of the aircraft division, then logistics division at Army Air Force headquarters in 1943. Air officer with Allied Expeditionary Air Force September 1943-October 1944. Brigadier general in May 1944. Commanding general of 1st Tactical Air Service Command October-December 1944. Deputy commanding general of 1st Tactical Air Force December 1944-June 1945. Chief of the supply division at headquarters Army Air Force 1945-1946. Reverted to colonel in February 1946. Retired as major general in September 1954. Decorations included the Legion of Merit and Bronze Star. Died on September 18, 1978.

Larson, Westside T. (1892-1977) Born on April 18, 1892, in Vernalis, California. Attended Polytechnic College of Engineering. Commissioned in the Air Service in 1920. Awarded the Mackay Trophy in 1933. Assistant plans and operations officer at GHQ Air Corps 1940-1941. Commanding officer of 13th Bombardment Group 1941. Commanding officer of 1st Bomber Command 1942. Brigadier general in March 1942. Commander of Third Air Force 1943-1945. Major general in November 1943. Commanding general of 8th Fighter Command in 1945. Hospitalized in October 1945 and retired in July 1946. Decorations included the Distinguished Service Medal. Died on March 7, 1977.

Lawrence, Charles White (1901-1982) Born on March 28, 1901, in Parkville, Missouri. Commissioned in the Air Service from West Point in 1923. Duty with 7th Observation Squadron in the Canal Zone 1929-1931. Instructor at Air Corps Primary Flying School in 1931 then with the Texas National Guard 1939-1940. Materiel officer then executive officer of 29th Bomb Group December 1940-March 1941. Duty with 3rd Air Support Command then 3rd Fighter Command 1941-1942. Director of academic training at Fighter Command School May 1942-November 1943. Commanding officer of 99th Bomb Group December 1943-January 1944. Commander of 5th Bombardment Wing 1944-1945. Brigadier general in June 1944. Retired in September 1952. Decorations included the Distinguished Service Medal, Legion of Merit, two Distinguished Flying Crosses and twelve Air Medals. Died on November 10, 1982.

Lacey, Julius Kahn (1904-1992) Born in Elizabethtown, Tennessee, on September 18, 1904. B.S. from the University of Tennessee in 1927. Commissioned in the Air Corps Reserve in 1930. M.S. from Massachusetts Institute of Technology in 1936. Assigned to 2nd Weather Region July 1937-November 1940. Duty in the office of the chief, then the weather directorate at headquarters of the Air Corps 1941-1943. Served with Second Air Force January-June 1943. Brigadier general in June 1944. Commanding officer of 103rd Combat Bomb Wing, 384th Bomb Group and 92nd Combat Bomb Wing in 1943. Commanding general of 94th Combat Bomb Wing December 1943-May 1945. Deputy commanding general, then commanding general of Second Air Force 1945-1946. Retired as major general in October 1957. Decorations included two Silver Stars, the Legion of Merit, two Distinguished Flying Crosses and three Air Medals. Died on July 5, 1992.

Lawson, Laurence Augustus (1896-1951) Born in Menominec, Michigan, on August 8, 1896. Commissioned in the Air Service in 1920. Trained as a balloon pilot. Graduated from Air Corps Tactical School in 1940. Executive officer, then assistant commandant of the Air Corps Technical School 1940-1942. Commanding officer of Army Air Force Training School 1942-1945. Brigadier general in November 1942. Duty with Tenth Army August 1945-May 1946. Reverted to colonel and retired in May 1946. Died on October 27, 1951.

Lee, Robert Merrill (1909-) Born on April 13, 1909, in Hinsdale, New Hampshire. Commissioned in the Air Corps from West Point in 1931. Aide to Major General Adna R. Chaffee 1939-1940. Commanding officer of 7th Observation Group 1941-1942. Chief of staff of 1st Air Support Command 1943-1944. Deputy commander for operations of Ninth Air Force 1944-1945. Brigadier general in February 1945. Assignments after the war included commanding general of Twelfth Air Force 1953-1957, commanding general of Ninth Air Force 1957-1958, vice commander, then commander of Air Defense Command 1959-1963 and air deputy to the Supreme Allied Commander in Europe 1963-1966. Retired as general in July 1966. Decorations included two Distinguished Service Medals, the Legion of Merit, Bronze Star and Air Medal. Resides in Melbourne, Florida.

Lee, William Lecel (1903-1976) Born in Weatherford, Texas, on July 18, 1903. B.S. from Texas A&M in 1927. Enlisted service with the Texas National Guard 1922-1927. Commissioned in the field artillery, Officers Reserve Corps in 1927. Organized the Philippine Air Force 1935-1938. Operations officer at Kelly Field 1938-1940. Served with 2nd and 22nd Bombardment Groups 1940-1941. Supervisor of training for the B-26 Group 1941-1943. Commanding officer of 49th Bomb Wing 1943-1945. Brigadier general in November 1944. Assignments after the war included vice commander, then commander of 13th Air Force in the Philippines 1952-1956. Retired in July 1959. Decorations included the Distinguished

Service Medal, Distinguished Flying Cross and Air Medal. Died on February 26, 1976.

LeMay, Curtis Emerson (1906-1990) Born in Columbus, Ohio, on November 15, 1906. B.C.E. from Ohio State University in 1927. Commissioned in the Air Corps in 1929. Commander of the 305th Bomb Group, then the Third Bomb Division 1942-1943. Brigadier general in October 1943. Major general in March 1944. Commanding general of 20th Bomber Command in the China-Burma-India Theater of Operations August 1944-July 1945. He oversaw the conversion of B-29 bombers from high altitude to low-level missions against the Japanese homeland armed with fire bombs. A raid composed of 335 B-29s on March 9, 1945, carried out the single most destructive military mission in history against Tokyo. Assignments after the war included command of U.S. Air Forces Europe in 1948, during which he oversaw airlifts in the Berlin blockade, commander in chief of Strategic Air Command 1948-1957 and vice chief, then chief of staff of U.S. Air Force 1957-1965. Retired in February 1965. Decorations included the Distinguished Service Cross, three Distinguished Service Medals, the Silver Star, three Distinguished Flying Crosses and four Air Medals. Died on October 2, 1990.

Lincoln, Rush B. (1881-1977) Born on December 8, 1881, in Boone, Iowa. Enlisted service 1903-1907. B.S. from Iowa State College in 1916. Commissioned in the infantry in 1907. Graduated from the Balloon School in 1921, Command and General Staff School in 1923 and the Army War College in 1925. Brigadier general in October 1940. Commanding general of Air Corps Technical Training Command October 1940-February 1942. Major general in July 1941. Commanding general of Air Services Australia at headquarters of Army Air Forces South Pacific Area 1942-1944. Retired in August 1944. Decorations included the Legion of Merit. Died on February 25, 1977.

Lindsay, Richard Clark (1905-) Born in Minneapolis, Minnesota, on October 31, 1905. Attended Carlton College and the University of Minnesota. Commissioned in the infantry reserve in 1928. Earned his wings in 1929. Duty with war plans division of the War Department General Staff 1941-1943. Member of Joint War Plans Committee, then chief of combined joint staff division of Army Air Force 1943-1945. Brigadier general in September 1944. Assistant chief of staff for plans at Twentieth Air Force, then Pacific Air Command in 1945. Assignments after the war included commander of Allied Air Forces Southern Europe 1957-1960. Retired as lieutenant general in April 1960. Decorations included the Distinguished Service Medal, two Legions of Merit, the Bronze Star and two Commendation Ribbons.

Longfellow, Newton (1890-1970) Born in Chicago, Illinois, on January 1, 1890. Attended the University of Minnesota. Commissioned in the Air Service in 1920. Commanding officer of 88th Reconaissance Squadron 1936-1940. Commanding officer of 30th Bombardment Group at New Orleans Air Base 1941-1942. Served with Fourth Air Force, 4th Bomber Command, 1st Provisional Bomb Wing and

2nd Bomb Wing in 1942. Brigadier general in October 1942. Commanding general of 8th Bomber Command 1942-1945. Reverted to colonel in November 1945 and retired in January 1950. Decorations included the Legion of Merit. Died on May 1, 1970.

Loutzenheiser, Joe L. (1899-1945) Born in Canton, Ohio, on February 5, 1899. Commissioned in the cavalry from West Point in 1924. Transferred to the Air Corps. Graduated from Air Corps Tactical School in 1937 and the Command and General Staff School in 1938. Chief of operations division at War Department General Staff 1942-1945. Brigadier general in August 1944. Killed in an airplane crash at Okinawa on October 7, 1945. Decorations included the Distinguished Service Medal and Legion of Merit.

Lowe, Thomas Merritt (1901-1962) Born on March 2, 1901, in Buena Vista, Georgia. Commissioned in the Air Service from West Point in 1923. Graduated from Air Corps Tactical School in 1936 and the Command and General Staff School in 1940. Served at headquarters of the Army Air Force 1941-1943. Deputy chief of staff of Eighth Air Force 1943-1944 then Army Air Forces Mediterranean Theater of Operations January 1944-October 1945. Brigadier general in January 1945. Retired in June 1948. Decorations included the Legion of Merit and Bronze Star. Died on September 23, 1962.

Luedecke, Alvin Roubal (1910-) Born in El Dorado, Texas, on October 10, 1910. B.S. from Texas A&M in 1932. Commissioned in the field artillery in 1932. Earned his wings in 1934. Assistant military attache for air at San Jose, Costa Rica January 1940-August 1942. Executive air officer at the office of Military Intelligence Service, Quarry Heights, Canal Zone in 1942. Chief of the operations branch, then Latin-American branch at American Intelligence Command 1942-1943. Deputy commander of 39th Bombardment Group, then executive officer of 16th Bombardment Training Wing in 1943. Assistant chief of staff for operations, plans, training and intelligence, then deputy chief of staff of Army Air Force in the India-Burma Theater of Operations August 1943-November 1944. Brigadier general in August 1944. Deputy chief of the Air Staff then assistant chief of staff for operations, plans, training and intelligence in the China Theater of Operations 1944-1945. Retired as major general in 1958. Decorations included two Legions of Merit, the Bronze Star and Commendation Ribbon. Resides in Bryan, Texas.

Lundberg, George G. (1892-1981) Born in Titusville, Pennsylvania, on October 19, 1892. B.S. from the University of Pennsylvania in 1916. Commissioned in the aviation section of the Signal Corps in 1918. Brigadier general in September 1943. Commanding general of Air Service Command, Middletown, Pennsylvania, Eighth Air Force Service Command, Antilles Air Command and Pacific Overseas Air Materiel District 1943-1946. Reverted to colonel in April 1946. Retired in November 1949. Decorations included the Legion of Merit. Died on January 12, 1981.

Lynch, Edmund Clayton (1900-) Born on December 15, 1900, in Philadelphia, Pennsylvania. Commissioned in the Air Service from West Point in 1922. Graduated from Command and General Staff School in 1938. Assistant to assistant chief of staff for operations at Air Force Combat Command July 1938-April 1939 then Langley and Bolling Fields until March 1942. Executive officer in the personnel division of WDGS September 1942-June 1943 then chief of the enlisted branch until November 1944. Brigadier general in November 1944. Commanding general of 3rd Tactical Air Division 1944-1945. Assignments after the war included commanding general of Eleventh Air Force, Alaska 1945-1948. Retired as major general in February 1953. Decorations included two Legions of Merit. Assistant professor at the University of Texas 1956-1971. Resides in Austin, Texas.

Lynd, William Elmer (1893-1968) Born in Santa Fe, Kansas, on September 10, 1893. Enlisted service 1916-1917. Commissioned in the field artillery in 1917. Attended the University of Washington 1919-1920. Graduated from Command and General Staff School in 1933 and the Army War College in 1934. Duty with the plans division in the office of the chief of the Air Corps 1935-1937. Graduated from the Naval War College in 1938. Commanding officer of Wheeler Field, Hawaii July 1939-July 1940. Air officer at GHQ Air Corps 1940-1941. Brigadier general in March 1942. Commanding general of 2nd Air Support Command, then 7th Bomber Command 1942-1943. On the staff of commander in chief Pacific Fleet in 1943. Major general in September 1943. Commanding general of Fourth Air Force 1944-1946. Retired in December 1946. Decorations included the Silver Star, two Legions of Merit, the Distinguished Flying Cross, two Air Medals and the Purple Heart. Died on November 14, 1968.

Lyon, Alfred Jefferson. (1892-1942) Born in Coeur d'Alene, Idaho, on August 23, 1892. Enlisted service with the Idaho National Guard 1910-1913. B.S. from the University of Idaho in 1917. Commissioned in the aviation reserve in 1918. M.S. from Massachusetts Institute of Technology in 1921. Instructor with the organized reserves in the V Corps Area January 1930-January 1931. Served at Wright Field 1931-1935. Graduated from Air Corps Tactical School in 1936, Army Industrial College in 1937 and the Army War College in 1938. Duty again at Wright Field in 1938. Instructor at the Army War College 1938-1939. In the office of the chief of the Air Corps September 1939-December 1942 with a two-month tour as special observer in London May-June 1942. Brigadier general in May 1942. Died on December 1, 1942.

Lyon, Edwin Bowman (1892-1971) Born on December 8, 1892, in Las Cruces, New Mexico. Attended State College (Mesilla Park, New Mexico) 1904-1910. Commissioned in the cavalry from West Point in 1915. With Pershing in the Punitive Expedition into Mexico 1916-1917. Transferred to the Air Service in 1920. Instructor at Air Corps Tactical School 1924-1926. Graduated from Command and General Staff School in 1927 and the Army War College in 1932. Commanding officer of Randolph Field July 1937-August 1940. Commandant of the Air Corps Basic Flying School September 1940-June 1941. Brigadier general in July

1941. Commanding general of 19th Bomber Wing in 1941 then 6th Bomber Command September 1941-May 1943 and Antilles Air Command in 1943. Deputy to commanding general of Army Air Force Flying Training Command May 1944-March 1945. Commanding general of Air Forces Mid Pacific 1945-1946. Retired as major general in July 1952. Decorations included the Legion of Merit and Air Medal. Died on August 11, 1971.

Mace, Harold Loring (1907-1946) Born in Lake Helen, Florida, on October 10, 1907. Attended the University of Florida 1926-1928. Commissioned in the Air Reserve in 1929 and the U.S. Army in 1930. Served at Nichols Field, Philippine Islands with 65th Service Squadron and 4th Composite Group 1936-1938. Instructor at Air Corps Basic Flying School 1938-1942. Director of training at Army Air Force Basic Fyling School 1942-1943. Deputy commander of 56th Bombardment Training Wing 1943-1944. Brigadier general in November 1944. Commanding general of 98th Bombardment Wing 1944-1945. Died on January 20, 1946, in the Pacific Area. Decorations included the Distinguished Flying Cross and three Air Medals.

Manning, Timothy J. (1905-) Born on May 30, 1905, in Superior, Wisconsin. Attended Omaha University 1920-1922. General manager of Union Pacific Railroad 1929-1937. President of Manning Transportation Company 1937-1942. Commissioned in the Army Air Force as captain in 1942. Brigadier general in November 1944. Commanding general of 51st Troop Carrier Wing in the Mediterranean Theater of Operations 1944-1945. Decorations included the Silver Star, Legion of Merit and Air Medal. *

Marriner, Alfred Warrington (1891-1959) Born in Chicago, Illinois, on August 16, 1891. Attended the University of Illinois. Commissioned in the Signal Corps, aviation section in 1918. Graduated from Air Corps Tactical School in 1938 and AIC in 1939. Communications equipment officer in the office of the assistant chief of the Air Staff 1940-1943. Brigadier general in June 1943. Deputy air signal officer at Allied Expeditionary Air Forces October 1943-April 1944. Communications officer for Mediterranean Allied Air Forces 1944-1946. Retired in April 1946. Decorations included two Legions of Merit. Died on December 5, 1959.

Martin, Frederick LeRoy (1882-1954) Born in Liberty, Indiana, on November 26, 1882. B.S. from Purdue in 1908. Commissioned in the Coast Artillery Corps in 1908. Director of military aeronautics, Washington, DC 1918-1919. Transferred to the Air Service in 1920. Commanding officer of the Air Service around the world flight April 6-30, 1924. Graduated from Command and General Staff School in 1926 and the Army War College in 1935. Brigadier general in January 1937. Commanding general of 3rd Wing, GHQ Air Force April 1937-October 1940. Major general in October 1940. Commanding general of Hawaiian Air Force November 1940-December 1941, Second Air Force February-May 1942 and 2nd District, Army Air Force Central Technical Training Command June

1942-January 1944. Retired in July 1944. Decorations included the Distinguished Service Medal and Legion of Merit. Died on February 23, 1954.

Matheny, William Albert (1902-1984) Born in Carrington, North Dakota, on June 5, 1902. B.S. from Marquette University in 1926. Commissioned in the Air Corps in 1929. Graduated from Air Corps Tactical School in 1935. Member of the Pan-Am goodwill flight 1938-1939. Commanding officer of 1st Reconaissance Squadron 1941-1942 and 307th Bomb Group 1942-1943. Brigadier general in November 1943. Commanding general of 8th Bomber Command, Southwest Pacific Area 1943-1945. Deputy commanding general of Air Training Command March-August 1945. Duty in the office of the assistant chief of staff for intelligence, Army Air Force 1945-1946. Retired in July 1959. Decorations included the Distinguished Service Medal, Legion of Merit, two Distinguished Flying Crosses and the Air Medal. Died on April 26, 1984.

Maxwell, Alfred Rockwood (1906-) Born on May 29, 1906, in Seattle, Washington. Commissioned in the Air Corps from West Point in 1928. Duty with the 2nd Observation Squadron in the Philippines January 1935-February 1938. M.S. from Massachusetts Institute of Technology in 1940. Assistant commandant of the Air Corps Engineering School. Duty at headquarters of the Army Air Force 1942-1943. Assigned to U.S. Strategic Air Forces in the European Theater of Operations 1944-1945. Brigadier general in March 1945, major general in June 1945. Retired in May 1957. Decorations included the Distinguished Service Medal, two Legions of Merit and the Bronze Star. Resides in Arlington, Virginia.

Maxwell, Earl (1904-1984) Born in Sparta, Illinois, on August 9, 1904. M.D. from Washington University School of Medicine in 1928. Commissioned in the Medical Corps in 1928. Graduated from Army Medical School in 1930 and the School of Aviation Medicine in 1932. Served at Gorgas Hospital, Canal Zone September 1936-October 1939 then station hospital at Barksdale Field 1939-1940. Base surgeon at Savannah Army Air Base 1940-1942. Surgeon, then chief surgeon at U.S. Army Forces South Pacific Area July 1942-February 1946. Brigadier general in January 1944. Reverted to colonel in February 1946. Retired in August 1958. Died on April 26, 1984.

McBlain, John Ferral (1900-1967) Born on November 14, 1900, in Washington, DC Commissioned in the infantry from West Point in 1920. Graduated from the Command and General Staff School in 1938. Assistant to the chief of training section in the office of the chief of the Air Corps 1938-1942. Wing commander at Southeast Flying Training Command 1942-1943. Graduated from Army-Navy Staff College in 1943. Brigadier general in April 1943. Commanding general of 30th Flying Training Wing 1943-1944. Deputy chief of staff of Southeast Asia Command January-August 1944. Deputy commanding general, then commanding general of 3rd Tactical Air Command September 1944-March 1945. Chief of staff of Eastern Flying Training Command March-July 1945. Retired as major general in October 1956. Decorations included the Distinguished Service Medal and Legion of Merit. Died on October 22, 1967.

McCauley, James Wayne (1900-1958) Born in Jedsonia, Arkansas, on September 24, 1900. Attended the University of Arkansas 1921-1922. B.A. from Ouachita College in 1925. Commissioned in the infantry in 1923. Commanding officer of 55th Pursuit Group October 1939-December 1941, Portland Air Defense Wing December 1941-August 1942 and Seattle Air Defense Wing August 1942-November 1943. Commander of 70th Fighter Wing November 1943-July 1945. Brigadier general in June 1944. Commanding general of 3rd Tactical Air Command July-October 1945 then 14th Tactical Air Command October 1945-February 1946. Reverted to colonel in February 1946. Brigadier general again in September 1951. Died of a heart attack on March 9, 1958. Decorations included two Legions of Merit and the Air Medal.

McClelland, Harold Mark (1892-1965) Born in Tiffin, Iowa, on November 4, 1892. B.S. from Kansas State University in 1916. Commissioned in the infantry in 1917. Graduated from Air Corps Tactical School in 1936 and Command and General Staff School in 1937. Duty in the operations and training division of War Department General Staff 1938-1941. Assistant chief of staff at the Special Army Observer Group in London May-December 1941 then U.S. Forces British Isles December 1941-July 1942. Brigadier general in April 1942. Air communications officer of the Army Air Force July 1942-April 1946. Major general in June 1945. Retired in August 1951. Decorations included the Distinguished Service Medal and Legion of Merit. Died on November 18, 1965.

McConnell, John Paul (1908-1986) Born on February 7, 1908, in Booneville, Arkansas. Commissioned in the Air Corps from West Point in 1932. Earned his wings in 1933. Duty with 50th Observation Squadron in Hawaii 1937-1939. Assistant executive in the office of the chief of Army Air Force January-May 1942. Chief of staff of Army Air Force Technical Training Command May 1942-June 1943. Deputy chief of staff of Army Air Force Training Command June 1943-November. Chief of staff of China-Burma-India Air Forces Training Command November 1943-February 1944. Deputy commander of the Third Tactical Air Force in India, then the Southeast Asia Air Command in Ceylon 1944-1945. Brigadier general in August 1944. Chief of staff of Tenth and Fourteenth Air Forces 1945-1946. Assignments after the war included commanding general of Second Air Force 1957-1961, vice commander in chief of Strategic Air Command 1961-1962, deputy commander in chief of U.S. European Command 1962-1964 and vice chief of staff, then chief of staff, U.S. Air Force 1964-1969. Retired as general in February 1969. Decorations included the Distinguished Service Medal, four Legions of Merit, the Distinguished Flying Cross, Bronze Star and Air Medal. Died on November 21, 1986.

McCormick, John Halliday (1903-1992) Born on September 26, 1903, in Gallipoli, Ohio. Commissioned in the Signal Corps from West Point in 1925. Transferred to the Air Corps in 1930. Graduated from the Command and General Staff School in 1940. Air officer at IX Corps Area February-May 1940. Duty in the military personnel division, office of the chief of the Air Corps June 1940-March 1942. Deputy assistant chief of staff for personnel at Army Air Force 1942-1945. Brigadier general in May 1944. Assistant chief of staff for personnel at U.S. Army Forces Europe May 1945-July 1947. Retired as major general in 1956. Decorations included the Distinguished Service Medal, Legion of Merit and Bronze Star. Died on July 24, 1992.

McCoy, George Jr. (1904-1950) Born on March 31, 1904, in Napavine, Washington. Commissioned in the Air Corps from West Point in 1927. Duty at headquarters Army Air Force 1942-1943. Brigadier general in November 1943. Commanding general of Service Command, Thirteenth Air Force 1943-1944. Chief of the communications division at headquarters Army Air Force 1944-1945. Chief of staff of Sixth Air Force in 1945. Reverted to colonel in February 1946. Killed in an aircraft accident in Oregon on October 16, 1950. Decorations included the Legion of Merit and Air Medal.

McDaniel, Arthur B. (1895-1943) Born in San Antonio, Texas, on August 13, 1895. LL.B. from the University of Texas in 1917. Commissioned in the infantry in 1917 and transferred to the Air Service in 1922. Member of the Pan-American goodwill flight 1926-1927. Graduated from the Command and General Staff School in 1936 and Army War College in 1939. Brigadier general in March 1942. Commanding general of 3rd Reconaissance Command 1942-1943. Died on December 26, 1943. Decorations included the Distinguished Flying Cross.

McDaniel, Carl Brown (1901-) Born in Franklin, Texas, on April 23, 1901. Enlisted service 1919-1923. Commissioned in the Air Service in 1923. Commanding officer of 20th Bombardment Squadron at GHQ Air Force in 1940. Director of training at Air Corps Advanced Training School 1940-1941. Commanding officer of Air Corps Basic Flying School, then Army Air Force Combat Crew School 1941-1942. Commanding officer of Hendricks Field July 1942-September 1943. Brigadier general in November 1943. Commanding general of 76th Flying Training Wing 1943-1945. Deputy commander, then chief of staff of Seventh Air Force at Saipan and Okinawa July 1945-July 1947. Retired in November 1953. Decorations included two Legions of Merit, the Bronze Star, Air Medal and two Commendation Ribbons.

McDonald, George Clement (1892-1969) Born in Philadelphia, Pennsylvania, on April 27, 1892. Commissioned in the aviation section of the Signal Corps in 1918. Graduated from the Command and General Staff School in 1938. Plans, operations and intelligence officer at 2nd Wing, GHQ Air Force July 1938-February 1939. Assistant military attache in London April 1939-October 1940. Duty in the office of the chief of the Air Corps 1940-1941 then assistant to the assistant chief of staff for operations, Army Air Force 1941-1942. Duty with War Department General Staff March-September 1942. Intelligence officer for Eighth

Air Force, Twelfth Air Force, Northwest African Air Forces and Mediterranean Allied Air Forces September 1942- February 1944. Brigadier general in February 1944. Director of intelligence at U.S. Air Forces Europe 1944-1946. Retired as major general in October 1950. Decorations included the Distinguished Service Medal, Legion of Merit and Bronze Star. Died on April 24, 1969.

McDonald, Thomas Benton (1907-1982) Born on June 19, 1907, in Cumberland, Maryland. Commissioned in the Air Corps from West Point in 1929. Assistant engineering officer at San Antonio Air Depot 1937-1940. Chief of maintenance at Middletown Depot 1940-1943. Duty with Air Service Command 1943-1944. Brigadier general in March 1945. Commanding general of India-Burma Air Service Command in 1945. Retired as major general in August 1959. Decorations included the Distinguished Service Medal, three Legions of Merit and the Air Medal. Died on June 20, 1982.

McDonnell, John Chilton (1887-1971) Born in Baltimore, Maryland, on November 9, 1887. B.S. from Loyola College in 1908. Commissioned in the Cavalry in 1912. Transferred to the Air Service in 1915. With the 1st Aero Squadron on the Punitive Expedition into Mexico 1916-1917. Served with III Corps, Third Army in France in World War I. Graduated from Command and General Staff School in 1935. Commanding officer of 3rd Attack Group, then 3rd Bombardment Group 1938-1940. Brigadier general in October 1940. Commanding general of 7th Pursuit Wing December 1940-March 1941. Commanding general of 1st Interceptor Command March 1941 until retirement in June 1943. Died on December 18, 1971.

McGinnis, Harold Alling (1893-1986) Born in Murrayville, Illinois, on November 26, 1893. LL.B. from the University of Chicago in 1916. Commissioned in the Air Service in 1918. Graduated from AIC in June 1929. M.B.A. from Harvard in 1931. Graduated from Air Corps Tactical School in June 1936. Assistant inspector general at GHQ Air Force October 1939-July 1942. Inspector general at Eighth Air Force 1942-1944. Deputy chief of staff for maintenance and supply at Second Air Force from 1944. Brigadier general in November 1944. Retired in September 1948. Decorations included the Legion of Merit. Died on February 20, 1986.

McKee, William Fulton (1906-1987) Born on October 17, 1906, in Chilhowie, Virginia. Commissioned in the Coast Artillery Corps from West Point in 1929. Battalion commander in the 71st Coast Artillery 1941. At headquarters of Army Air Force 1942-1945. Brigadier general in February 1945. Chief of staff, then commanding general of the European Division of Air Transport Command 1945-1946. Assignments after the war included vice commander of Air Materiel Command 1953-1961, commander of Air Force Logistics Command 1961-1962 and vice chief of staff, U.S. Air Force 1962-1964. Retired as general in July 1964. Decorations included two Distinguished Service Medals and the Commendation Ribbon. Died on February 28, 1987.

McMullen, Clements (1892-1959) Born in Largo, Florida, on February 5, 1892. Attended Washington and Lee University 1907-1911. Commissioned in the aviation section of the Signal Corps in 1918. Completed record flight from New York to Buenos Aires in five days in February 1930. Operations officer at GHQ Air Corps 1936-1937. Graduated from the Command and General Staff School in 1938. Chief engineer at San Antonio Air Depot July 1938-March 1941 then commanding officer March 1941-January 1942. Commanding officer of Third Air Service Command January-August 1942. Brigadier general in August 1942. Commanding general of the Overseas Division of Air Service Command November-December 1942. Chief of the maintenance division at headquarters of Air Service Command 1942-1944. Major general in April 1943. Commanding general of Air Service Command July-August 1944 then Far Eastern Air Service Command October 1944-December 1945. Retired in February 1954. Decorations included two Distinguished Service Medals, the Air Medal and Commendation Ribbon. Died on January 9, 1959.

McNarney, Joseph Taggart (1893-1972) Born on August 28, 1893, in Emporium, Pennsylvania. Commissioned in the infantry from West Point in 1915. Served successively as commanding officer of the 1st Corps Observation Group, head of Air Service with the 3rd Corps and on the staff of the chief of Air Service in the First Army during the Chateau Thierry, St. Mihiel and Meuse-Argonne offensives in World War I. Graduated from Command and General Staff School in 1926 and the Army War College in 1930. Instructor at the Army War College 1933-1935. Served with the war plans division of the War Department General Staff 1939-1941. Brigadier general in April 1941. Member of the Roberts Commission investigating the Pearl Harbor disaster 1941-1942. Major general in January 1942. Deputy chief of staff, U.S. Army March 1942-October 1944. Lieutenant general in June 1942. Deputy, then acting supreme allied commander in the Mediterranean Theater of Operations October 1944-December 1945. General in March 1945. Assignments after the war included commanding general of U.S. Forces in Europe December 1945-May 1947 and commander of Air Materiel Command 1947-1949. Retired as general in January 1952. Decorations included five Distinguished Service Medals and the Legion of Merit. Died on February 1, 1972.

McNaughton, Kenneth Perry (1903-1975) Born on June 18, 1903, in Kent County, Michigan. Commissioned in the field artillery from West Point in 1926. District supervisor of Army Air Force Western Flying Training Command 1939-1941. Brigadier general in September 1942. Chief of staff of Army Air Force Training Command 1942-1945. Chief of staff of Strategic Air Forces on Guam in 1945. Assignments after the war included vice commander of Far East Air Forces 1953-1956. Retired as major general in July 1956. Decorations included two Legions of Merit and the Bronze Star. Died on June 16, 1975.

Meloy, Vincent J. (1895-1960) Born in Brooklyn, New York, on December 8, 1895. Commissioned in the aviation section of the Signal Corps in 1917. Flight commander with the Pan-American goodwill flights to South America in 1938. Commanding officer of 29th Bomb Group May 1940-January 1941. Assigned to Third Air Force January-November 1941. Commanding officer of the Caribbean Wing, Air Transport Command January-October 1943. Brigadier general in September 1943. Commanding general of the Africa-Middle East then North African Wing November 1943-July 1944. Commanding general of Truax Field July 1944-January 1946. Retired in April 1946. Decorations included the Legion of Merit. Died on December 10, 1960.

Meyers, Bennett Edward (1897-n/a) Born in Buffalo, New York, on March 29, 1897. Attended the University of California 1914-1918. Enlisted service as an aviation cadet 1917-1918. Commissioned in the Air Service in 1920. Graduated from the Army Industrial College in 1931. Brigadier general in February 1942. Deputy assistant chief of staff for aircraft procurement, maintenance and transport at headquarters Army Air Force 1942-1944. Deputy director of Air Technical Service Command 1944-1948. Major general in February 1945. Dismissed from the Air Force on July 16, 1948, following a felony conviction in U.S. District Court.

Miller, Henry Jervis Friese (1891-1949) Born on September 10, 1891, in Alloways, New Jersey. Commissioned in the cavalry from West Point in 1915. With the Punitive Expedition into Mexico 1916-1917. Served in the aviation section of the Signal Corps in the AEF in 1918. Brigadier general in July 1941. Chief of Air Service Command 1941-1942. Major general in February 1942. Chief of Army Materiel Command in the European Theater of Operations 1943-1944. Retired in November 1944 as colonel. Brigadier general on the retired list in October 1948. Died on January 7, 1949.

Miller, Leland Wilbur (1894-1959) Born in Galesburg, Kansas, on November 26, 1894. Enlisted service with the Nebraska National Guard 1909-1913 and in the U.S. Army 1917-1918. Attended Purdue University 1915-1917. Commissioned in the Air Corps in 1931. B.S. from George Washington University in 1932. M.B.A. from Harvard in 1933. Budget and fiscal officer in the office of the chief of the Air Corps 1936-1942. Brigadier general in May 1942. Deputy chief of staff of Eighth Air Force 1942-1943. Budget and fiscal officer of the Army Air Force 1943-1946. Retired in May 1946. Decorations included the Distinguished Service Medal. Died on September 7, 1959.

Miller, Lester Thomas (1894-1969) Born on September 24, 1894, in Marietta, Ohio. B.A. from Marietta College in 1916. Commissioned in the infantry in 1917. Assistant executive officer to the chief of the Air Corps, then head of public relations at headquarters of the Air Corps 1938-1939. Commander of Wright Field October 1939-December 1941. Assigned to Air Service Command 1942-1944. Brigadier general in August 1942, major general in June 1943. Chief of the supply division at Air Technical Service Command 1944-1946. Retired in August 1946. Died on March 24, 1969.

Mollison, James Alexander (1897-1970) Born in Smith Center, Kansas, on July 9, 1897. Commissioned in the Air Service in 1920. Graduated from Command and General Staff School in 1940. Chief of staff of Hawaiian Air Force 1940-1941. Commander of 2nd Air Service Command in 1942. Brigadier general in November 1942. Chief of personnel training division at Air Service Command 1942-1944. Commanding general of Fifteenth Air Force Service Command October 1944-August 1945. Commanding general of Army Air Forces in the Mediterranean Theater of Operations August 1945-November 1945. Retired in June 1948. Decorations included the Distinguished Service Medal and Bronze Star. Died on February 4, 1970.

Moore, Aubry Lee (1901-1980) Born in Frost, Texas, on August 4, 1901. B.S. from Texas A&M in 1923. Commissioned in the field artillery reserve in 1923. Transferred to the Air Corps in 1929. Assistant to the chief of plans division, Air Corps 1939-1941. Section chief at headqaurters Army Air Force 1941-1942 then deputy chief of the Air Staff 1942-1943. Assistant chief of staff for operations, plans, training and intelligence in the China-Burma-India Theater of Operations October 1943-January 1944. Brigadier general in February 1944. Chief of staff of Tenth Air Force January 1944-October 1945. Retired in March 1953. Decorations included the Legion of Merit, Distinguished Flying Cross, Bronze Star and Air Medal. Died on June 9, 1980.

Moore, Ernest (1907-1981) Born on December 23, 1907, in Vienna, Illinois. Commissioned in the Air Corps from West Point in 1931. Attended Massachusetts Institute of Technology 1936-1937. Deputy chief of staff of Hawaii Army Air Forces 1942. Chief of staff, then commanding general of 7th Fighter Command 1942-1945. Brigadier general in August 1944. Assignments after the war included vice commander of Military Air Transport Service 1954-1957 and commanding general of Third Air Force July 1957 until retirement as major general in November 1961. Decorations included three Distinguished Service Medals, three Legions of Merit, two Distinguished Flying Crosses, the Bronze Star, Air Medal and Commendation Ribbon. Died on April 7, 1981.

Morris, Edward Moses (1895-1969) Born in Marinette, Wisconsin, on December 21, 1895. B.S. from City College of New York in 1919. Commissioned in the aviation section of the Signal Corps in 1918. Graduated from Air Corps Tactical School in 1939. Brigadier general in September 1942. Commanding general of 4th Fighter Command in 1943, 7th Fighter Command in 1944, 318th Fighter Wing and Fourth Air Force in 1945. Retired in December 1945. Decorations included the Distinguished Service Cross, Legion of Merit and Bronze Star. Died on January 19, 1969.

Morris, Joseph Theodore (1894-1980) Born in Punxsutawney, Pennsylvania, on April 17, 1894. B.S. from Pennsylvania State College in 1917. Attended West Point 1917-1918. Commissioned in the Air Service in 1920. Stationed at Luke Field, Hawaii 1928-1929. Engineer officer at Rockwell Air Depot June 1935-January 1940. Duty with the materiel division at headquarters of the Air Corps 1940-1941. Assistant chief of staff for plans and projects at Air Service Command December 1941-December 1942. Brigadier general in September 1942. Assistant chief of the maintenance division at Air Service Command January-June 1943. Commander of Eighth Air Force Depot Area July-December 1943. Deputy commanding general of Eighth Air Force Service Command December 1943-February 1944. Director of maintenance at Air Service Command, European Theater of Operations February 1944-February 1945. Commanding general of Eighth Air Force Service Command in 1945. Retired in July 1953. Decorations included the Legion of Merit, Bronze Star and two Commendation Ribbons. Died on May 21, 1980.

Morse, Winslow Carroll (1904-1990) born in Ovid, Michigan, on April 4, 1904. B.A. from the University of Redlands in 1928. Commissioned in the Air Corps in 1930. Duty with the 3rd Pursuit Group in the Philippines September 1934-February 1937. Commanding officer of Army Air Force Proving Ground at Elgin Field 1941-1943. Chief of staff, then commander of Army Air Force Proving Grounds Command in 1943. Commanding general of Chinese-American Composite Wing in the China-Burma-India September 1943-April 1945. Brigadier general in August 1944. Commander of Boca Raton Field 1945-1946. Retired in November 1959. Decorations included the Distinguished Flying Cross and Air Medal. Died on November 14, 1990.

Myers, Charles Trovilla (1900-1976) Born on February 10, 1900, in Mannington, West Virginia. Commissioned in the Air Corps from West Point in 1923. Duty in the Philippines 1929-1931. Assistant chief of staff for training in Army Air Force Central Flying Training Command 1941-1943. Brigadier general in November 1943. Commanding general of 77th Flying Training Wing 1943-1944. Chief of staff of Twelfth Air Force 1944-1945. Commanding general of Army Air Forces in the Mediterranean Theater of Operations in 1945. Commanding general of 33rd Flying Training Wing 1945-1946. Assignments after the war included commanding general of Thirteenth Air Force 1948-1949 and commander of Air Training Command 1954-1958. Retired as lieutenant general in July 1958. Decorations included the Distinguished Service Medal, two Legions of Merit, the Bronze Star and Air Medal. Died on September 27, 1976.

Naiden, Earl Larue (1894-1944) Born on February 2, 1894, in Woodward, Iowa. Commissioned in the cavalry from West Point in 1915. Transferred to the Air Service in 1916. Served with the Punitive Expedition into Mexico 1916-1917. Saw combat with AEF in World War I. Graduated from Command and General Staff School in 1920. Director of instruction, then assistant commandant of Air Service Tactical School 1923-1926. Graduated from the Army War College in

1927. Instructor at the Army War College 1929-1933. Chief of staff of the Ferry Command in China-Burma-India Theater of Operations March-July 1942. Brigadier general in January 1942. Chief of staff of Tenth Air Force July-September 1942 then duty at Southeast Air Force Training Center at Maxwell Air Force Base September-November 1942. Reverted to colonel in November 1942. Died while on active duty on September 20, 1944.

Nelson, Morris Robert (1901-1985) Born on January 20, 1901, in Corydon, Iowa. Commissioned in the Air Service from West Point in 1926. Operations and intelligence officer with 30th Pursuit Group July 1939-January 1941. Executive officer at Hamilton Field january-June 1941. Operations officer for 4th Interceptor Command June 1941-February 1942. Director of tactics and techniques at the Fighter School February-June 1942. President of the Air Defense Board at headquarters Army Air Force July-October 1942 then chairman April-June 1943. Duty with 1st Fighter Command July-December 1943. Commander of 305th Fighter Wing, Fifteenth Air Force 1944-1945. Brigadier general in March 1945. Retired as major general in October 1959. Decorations included four Legions of Merit, the Distinguished Flying Cross and two Air Medals. Died on February 9, 1985.

Netherwood, Douglas Blakeshaw (1885-1943) Born in Birmingham, England, on February 4, 1885. B.S. from Agricultural and Mechanical College of Texas in 1908. Enlisted service 1908-1911. Naturalized in 1910. Commissioned in the Coast Artillery Corps in 1911. Completed flying training in 1914. Served with the 2nd Aero Squadron in the Philippine Islands 1916-1917. Graduated from Army Industrial College in 1925. M.B.A. from Harvard in 1927. Graduated from Air Corps Tactical School in 1932. Air officer in the Department of the Philippines 1932-1934. Graduated from Army War College in 1936. Assistant director, then director of the Air Corps Board June 1936-February 1940. Commanding officer of Air Base, Mitchell Field in 1940. Brigadier general in October 1940. Wing commander in the Panama Canal Zone 1940-1941. Commander of Baer Field, Indiana in 1941. Reverted to colonel on December 25, 1941. Died on August 19, 1943, en route to Pope Field from Orlando, Florida.

Newman, James Bryan Jr. (1896-1959) Born on July 10, 1896, in Talladegh, Alabama. Commissioned in the Corps of Engineers from West Point in 1918. B.S. from Massachusetts Institute of Technology in 1921. Graduated from Command and General Staff School in 1940. Chief of buildings and grounds division of Army Air Force 1942-1943. Brigadier general in September 1943. Engineer at Eighth Air Force 1943-1944. Commanding general of 9th Engineer Command, Ninth Air Force 1944-1945. Division engineer at South Atlantic Division, Department of Engineers 1945-1946. Retired in October 1946 as colonel. Brigadier general on the retired list in 1948. Decorations included the Distinguished Service Medal and Legion of Merit. Died on February 7, 1959.

Norstad, Lauris (1907-1988) Born on March 24, 1907, in Minneapolis, Minnesota. Commissioned in the cavalry from West Point in 1930. Transferred to the

Air Corps in 1931. Duty in intelligence division of GHQ Air Force 1940-1942. Adviser to General Arnold in 1942. Assistant chief of staff of Twelfth Air Force August 1942-December 1943. Brigadier general in March 1943. Director of operations in Mediterranean Allied Air Forces December 1943-August 1944. Chief of staff of Twentieth Air Force, which was under the direct command of General Arnold August 1944-June 1946. He had responsibility of planning the two atomic bomb attacks on Japan. Major general in June 1945. Assignments after the war included commander of U.S. Air Forces Europe 1950-1953, air deputy to the Supreme Allied Commander in Europe 1953-1956 and SACEUR November 1956 until retirement as general in January 1963. Decorations included three Distinguished Service Medals, two Silver Stars and two Legions of Merit. President, then chairman of Owens-Corning Fiberglass Corporation 1967-1977. Died on September 12, 1988.

Nowland, Bob Edward (1891-1974) Born in Peoria, Illinois, on March 10, 1891. Attended the University of California. Commissioned in the aviation section, Officers Reserve Corps in 1918. Graduated from Air Corps Tactical School in 1937 and Command and General Staff School in 1938. Instructor with the California National Guard 1938-1939. Base adjutant at March Field 1939-1940. Duty in the personnel division of the War Department General Staff 1940-1943. Brigadier general in February 1943. Commanding general of 28th Flying Training Wing February-July 1943. Chief of staff of Air Transport Command August 1943-July 1944. Commanding general of the ferrying division at Air Transport Command 1944-1946. Retired in April 1950. Decorations included the Distinguished Service Medal. Died on September 18, 1974.

Nugent, Richard Emmel (1902-1979) Born in Altoona, Pennsylvania, on December 12, 1902. Commissioned in the infantry from West Point in 1924. Transferred to the Air Corps in 1930. Graduated from Command and General Staff School in 1939. Head of flying cadet section at headquarters of Air Corps 1940-1941. Assistant military attache for air at London in 1941. Again at Air Corps 1941-1942. With the War Department General Staff 1942-1943. Brigadier general in June 1943. Chief of staff of Eastern Defense Command in 1943. Assistant chief of staff for operations of Ninth Air Force 1943-1944. Commander of 29th Tactical Air Command 1944-1945. Assignments after the war included deputy chief of staff for personnel, U.S. Air Force 1950-1951. Retired as lieutenant general in August 1951. Decorations included two Distinguished Service Medals, the Legion of Merit, Bronze Star and Air Medal. Died on November 5, 1979.

O'Donnell, Emmett Jr. (1905-1972) Born in Brooklyn, New York, on September 15, 1905. Commissioned in the infantry from West Point, where he acquired the nickname "Rosie," in 1928. Assistant football coach at West Point 1934-1938. Commanding officer of 14th Bomb Squadron 1941-1942. Operations officer of Far East Air Forces, then assistant chief of staff of Tenth Air Force 1942-1943. Member of General Arnold's advisory group 1943-1944. Brigadier general in February 1944. Commander of 73rd Bomb Wing 1944-1945. Assignments after the war commanding general of Fifteenth Air Force 1948-1953, deputy chief of staff for personnel, U.S. Air Force 1953-1959 and commander in chief of Pacific Air Forces 1959-1963. Retired in July 1963. Decorations included the Distinguished Service Cross, Distinguished Service Medal, Silver Star, four Distinguished Flying Crosses and two Air Medals. Died on December 26, 1972.

Old, Archie J. Jr. (1906-1984) Born in Farmersville, Texas, on August 1, 1906. Attended Trinity University and the University of Texas at Austin 1924-1927. Enlisted service in Texas National Guard 1930-1932. Commissioned in the Air Corps in 1932. Resigned in February 1933. Returned to active duty in September 1940. Duty with the 29th Bomb Group 1940-1942. Commanding officer of 96th Bomb Group September 1942-December 1943 and 45th Combat Bomb Wing December 1943-July 1945. Brigadier general in November 1944. Commanding general of the Southwest Pacific Wing of Air Transport Command 1945-1946. Assignments after the war included commanding general of Fifteenth Air Force. Retired as lieutenant general in July 1965. Decorations included the Distinguished Service Cross, Distinguished Service Medal, two Silver Stars, the Legion of Merit, five Distinguished Flying Crosses, nine Air Medals and the Purple Heart. Died on March 24, 1984.

Old, William Donald (1901-1965) Born on November 21, 1901, in Uvalde, Texas. B.S. from Texas A&M in 1924. Commissioned in the Air Service in 1924. Graduated from the Command and General Staff School in 1937. Commanding officer of 43rd Bomb Squadron February 1940-January 1941. Assistant to the air officer at GHQ Air Force March 1941-February 1942. Assistant chief of staff for intelligence, then chief of staff at Tenth Air Force May 1942-September 1943. Brigadier general in February 1943. Commanding general of American Air Command Number One, then Troop Carrier Command, India Theater of Operations September 1943-June 1944. Commanding general of 1st Troop Carrier Command August 1944-August 1945. Assignments after the war included commanding general of Ninth Air Force 1947-1949, commanding general of Alaskan Air Command 1950-1952. Retired in August 1954. Decorations included the Distinguished Service Medal, Silver Star, Legion of Merit, two Distinguished Flying Crosses and the Air Medal. Died on June 28, 1965.

Olds, Robert (1896-1943) Born in Woodside, Maryland, on June 15, 1896. Commissioned in the aviation section of the Officers Reserve Corps in 1917. Instructor with the AEF 1918-1919. Served in Hawaii 1919-1923. Graduated from Air Corps Tactical School in 1928 and the Command and General Staff School in 1935. Commanding officer of 2nd Bombardment Group March 1937-January 1940. During this time he led seven Flying Fortresses on a flight from the U.S. to Rio de Janeiro in February 15-27, 1938, earning the Mackay and Harmon trophies. Assistant to the chief of plans division, office of the chief of the Air Corps 1940-1941. Commanding officer of Air Corps Ferrying Command 1941-1942. Brigadier general in January 1942, major general in May 1942. With Third and Second Air Forces 1942-1943. Duty at headquarters of Army Air Force February

1943 until his death on April 28, 1943. Decorations included the Distinguished Service Medal and Distinguished Flying Cross.

Oliver, Robert Chaffee (1902-1966) Born on May 1, 1902, in Manila, Philippine Islands. Commissioned in the field artillery from West Point in 1923. Graduated from Command and General Staff School in 1937. Instructor at Air Corps Tactical School 1937-1940. Chief of staff of air missions in Africa, the Middle East and India 1941-1942. Brigadier general in December 1942. Commanding general of Air Service Command in China-Burma-India Theater of Operations 1942-1944. Commanding general of 56th Combat Crew Training August 1944-August 1945. Assignments after the war included commander of Thirteenth Air Force 1947-1948. Retired in 1953. Decorations included the Distinguished Service Medal, Legion of Merit, Air Medal and five Commendation Ribbons. Died on January 13, 1966.

O'Neill, Raymond Edward (1894-1947) Born in Port Townsend, Washington, on May 31, 1894. B.S. from the University of Washington in 1916. Commissioned in the infantry in 1917. Served with the 20th Machine Gun Battalion in France 1918-1919. Transferred to the Air Service in 1920. Instructor at Air Corps Flying School 1926-1927 and Air Corps Tactical School 1934-1936. Executive officer of Chanute Field August 1939-October 1940. Commandant of Air Corps Technical School June 1941-August 1942. Commanding officer of Air Corps Training Command at Chanute Field 1942-1946. Brigadier general in September 1942. Reverted to colonel in February 1946. Died in an aircraft accident on May 20, 1947.

Ott, Isaac William (1903-1976) Born in Osyka, Mississippi, on April 6, 1903. B.A. from the University of Kentucky in 1927. Commissioned in the Air Corps in 1929. Served at France Field, Canal Zone 1935-1937, Middletown Air Depot 1937-1939, Wright Field 1939-1941 and Duncan Field 1941-1943. Brigadier general in March 1944. Commander of Central Air Depot Area, European Theater of Operations 1944-1945. Retired in August 1946. Decorations included the Distinguished Service Medal, Legion of Merit and Bronze Star. Died on March 7, 1976.

Owens, Ray L. (1891-1948) Born in Chillicothe, Missouri, on April 7, 1891. Attended Moore's Normal School 1908-1910. Public school teacher 1912-1917. Commissioned in the field artillery in 1918, then the Air Service in 1920. Served in the Philippines with 2nd Observation Squadron 1922-1924. Graduated from Command and General Staff School in 1938. Deputy chief of staff, then chief of staff of Second Air Force 1941-1942. Assistant chief of staff at headquarters of the Air Corps and with U.S. Army Forces South Pacific Area in 1942. Brigadier general in December 1942. Commanding general of Service Command on Fiji 1942-1943. Chief of staff of Thirteenth Air Force July 1943-January 1944. Deputy chief of staff, Army Air Force 1944-1945. Commanding general of Miami District, Personnel Distribution Command June 1945 until retirement in April 1946. Died on August 16, 1948.

Parker, James Edmund (1896-1946) Born on August 9, 1896, in Anniston, Alabama. Attended Marion Military Institute 1916-1917. Commissioned in the field artillery from West Point in 1919. Transferred to the Air Service in 1920. Brigadier general in December 1942. Commanding general of 3rd Bomber Command 1942-1944. Major general in November 1944. Commanding general of Fourth Air Force 1944-1945. Commanding general of Twentieth Air Force 1945 until his death in an aircraft accident in Formosa on March 19, 1946. Decorations included the Distinguished Service Medal, two Legions of Merit and the Bronze Star.

Partridge, Earle Everard (1900-1990) Born on July 7, 1900, in Winchendon, Massachusetts. Enlisted service with 79th Division 1918-1919, including the St. Mihiel and Meuse-Argonne campaigns. Commissioned in the Air Service from West Point in 1924. Graduated from Command and General Staff School in 1938. With war plans division of the War Department General Staff 1941-1942. Brigadier general in December 1942. Commander of New York Air Defense Wing, then operations officer of Northwest African Air Forces, finally chief of staff of 12th Bomber Command and Fifteenth Air Force in 1943. Major general in May 1944. Deputy commander of Eighth Air Force 1944. Commander of 3rd Bomb Division 1944-1945. Commander of Eighth Air Force 1945-1946. Assignments after the war included commanding general of Fifth Air Force 1948-1951, commander of Air Research and Development Command 1951-1953, deputy chief of staff for operations, U.S. Air Force 1953-1954, commander of Far East Air Forces 1954-1955 and commander in chief of Continental Air Defense Command 1955-1959. Retired in July 1959. Decorations included the Distinguished Service Cross, two Distinguished Service Medals, the Silver Star, Legion of Merit, three Distinguished Flying Crosses, three Bronze Stars and ten Air Medals. Died on September 7, 1990.

Peabody, Hume (1893-1984) Born on November 24, 1893, in Shinglehouse, Pennsylvania. Commissioned in the cavalry from West Point in 1915. Professor of military science and tactics at the University of California 1923-1928. Graduated from Air Corps Tactical School in 1929 and Command and General Staff School in 1931. Assistant commandant of Air Corps Tactical School 1931-1934. Graduated from the Army War College in 1935. Duty in Hawaii with 18th Composite Wing 1935-1937. At GHQ Air Force 1939-1941. With 2nd Air Support Command 1941-1942. Brigadier general in April 1942. Intelligence officer on the Air Staff, Army Air Force in 1942. Commandant of Army Air Force School of Applied Tactics 1942-1944. Commanding general of Eastern Fighter Command 1945-1946. Retired in October 1946. Decorations included the Distinguished Service Medal and Legion of Merit. Died on January 1, 1984.

Peck, Walter Raymond (1896-1965) Born on January 15, 1896, in Lima, Ohio. Attended West Point 1916-1917. Commissioned in the Philippine Scouts in 1917. Transferred to the Air Service in 1922. Commanding officer of 32nd Bomb Squadron July 1937-August 1939. Instructor with the 41st Division 1939-1940.

Operations officer at McChord Field September 1940-March 1941. Commanding officer of 17th Bombardment Group March 1941-March 1942. Commanding officer of Army Air Base Wendover Field March-July 1942. Commander of 17th Bombardment Wing July 1942-September 1943. Brigadier general in June 1943. Commanding general of Combat Crew Replacement Group at Eighth Air Force 1943-1944, 96th Combat Bomb Wing May 1944-August 1945 and 462nd Army Air Force Base Unit 1945-1946. Retired in September 1948. Decorations included the Silver Star, Legion of Merit, two Distinguished Flying Crosses, the Bronze Star and two Air Medals. Died on December 24, 1965

Perrin, Edwin Sanders (1905-1946) Born in Custer, South Dakota, on October 15, 1905. Attended the University of Nebraska 1923-1925. Commissioned in the Coast Artillery Corps from West Point in 1930. Transferred to the Air Corps in 1931. Graduated from the Command and General Staff School in 1933. M.S. from the University of Michigan in 1937. Duty with the Air Corps Material Division 1937-1941. Military air observer in the Middle East January 1941-September 1942. Brigadier general in June 1942. Commanding general of 4th Air Service Area Command October 1942-June 1943. Deputy chief of the Air Staff at headquarters Army Air Force 1943-1944. Reverted to major in May 1945. Died on November 17, 1946.

Phillips, James Frederick (1900-1973) Born in Cambridge, Idaho, on February 25, 1900. B.S. from the University of Iowa. Commissioned in the Corps of Engineers in 1923. Served in the Canal Zone 1927-1928. Commanding officer of 2nd Observation Squadron, Philippine Islands February 1936-May 1937. Assistant project officer in the experimental engineering section, Wright Field July 1940-July 1942. Assigned to the Materiel Command July 1942-August 1945. Brigadier general in January 1945. Assistant to the commanding general of Far Eastern Air Service Command August-October 1945. Retired as major general in March 1953. Decorations included the Legion of Merit. Died on February 5, 1973.

Powell, James Franklin (1893-1983) Born in Fort Monroe, Virginia, on August 30, 1893. B.S. from Virginia Polytechnic Institute in 1916. Commissioned in the Coast Artillery Corps in 1917. Graduated from the Balloon School in 1921. Graduated from the Command and General Staff School in 1935. Chief of the material planning section, then the statistical section in the office of the chief, AAC January 1940-January 1942. Assistant chief of staff for supply at Army Air Force Training Command in 1944. Commanding officer of 31st then 57th Flying Training Wing in 1944. Deputy chief of staff, then chief of staff at Army Air Force Training Command October 1944-March 1946. Brigadier general in March 1945. Retired as major general in July 1953. Decorations included two Legions of Merit and three Commendation Ribbons. Died on March 25, 1983.

Power, Thomas Sarsfield (1905-1970) Born in New York, New York on June 18, 1905. Attended Cooper Union (New York City) 1924-1928. Enlisted service in the Air Corps 1928-1929. Commissioned in the Army Air Corps in 1929.

Served at Nichols Field in the Philippines 1936-1938. Graduated from Air Corps Tactical School in 1941. Assistant operations officer at Western Command Army Air Force Training Center 1941-1942. Inspector of Fort Worth Flying Training Center 1942-1943. Commanding officer of 40th Bomb Group 1943-1944. Director of operations for Second Air Force in 1944. Deputy commander of 304th Bomb Wing, then 314th Bomb Wing 1944-1945. Brigadier general in January 1945. Planned and led a contingent of 334 B-29 bombers to fire bomb Tokyo on March 9, 1945, the most devastating attack in history. Assignments after the war included commander of Air Research and Development Command 1954-1957 and commander in chief of Strategic Air Command 1957-1964. Retired as general in November 1964. Decorations included two Distinguished Service Medals, the Silver Star, two Legions of Merit, the Distinguished Flying Cross, Bronze Star, two Air Medals and two Commendation Ribbons. Died on December 6, 1970.

Powers, Edward Michael (1892-1977) Born in LeRoy, Illinois, on September 4, 1892. Attended the University of Illinois in 1918. Commissioned in the U.S. Army in 1918. Transferred to the Air Service in 1920. Graduated from the Command and General Staff School in 1938. Chief of the engineering section, office of the chief of the Air Corps October 1939-May 1942. Member of the Joint Production Survey Committee 1943-1944. Deputy assistant chief of staff for materiel, maintenance and distribution at headquarters Army Air Force June 1944-May 1945. Major general in June 1945. Acting assistant chief of staff for materiel, maintenance and distribution at headquarters Army Air Force 1945-1947. Retired in March 1949. Decorations included the Distinguished Service Medal. Died on January 4, 1977.

Pratt, Henry Conger (1882-1966) Born in Fort Stanton, New Mexico, on September 2, 1882. Commissioned in the cavalry from West Point in 1904. Transferred to the Air Service in 1920. Graduated from the Army War College in 1924. Brigadier general in July 1930. Assistant chief of the Air Corps July 1930-July 1934. Commander of 2nd Wing 1935-1937. Brigadier general again in January 1937. Commandant of the Air Corps Tactical School 1937-1938. Commanding general of 23rd Brigade 1938-1940. Major general in October 1940. Commanding general of II Corps December 1940-August 1941, III Corps Area 1941-1942, Trinidad Sector 1942-1943, Antilles Department in 1943, Southern Defense Command in 1944 and Western Defense Command 1944-1945. Retired in September 1946. Decorations included two Distinguished Service Medals. Died on April 6, 1966.

Prentiss, Paul Hyde (1895-1953) Born on March 26, 1895, in Newark, New Jersey. Attended Bowdoin College 1914-1915. Designated aviator in June 1918. Commissioned in the U.S. Army in 1920. Instructor at Air Corps Primary Flying School 1923-1925. Commanding officer of 38th Reconaissance Squadron 1937-1940 then 374th Troop Carrier Group 1941-1942. Troop carrier wing commander May 1943-March 1944. Brigadier general in September 1943. Commander of 54th Troop Carrier Wing March-August 1944. Commanding general of

Far East Air Force Service Command August-November 1944. Reverted to colonel in February 1946. Decorations included the Distinguished Service Medal, Silver Star, Distinguished Flying Cross and Air Medal. Died on July 22, 1953.

Quesada, Elwood Richard (1904-1993) Born in Washington, DC on April 13, 1904. Attended the University of Maryland and Georgetown University. Commissioned in the Air Reserve in 1925. Began active duty in 1927. Aide-de-camp to Major General James E. Fechet, chief of the Air Corps 1928-1929. Member of the crew aboard *Question Mark* January 1-7, 1929, together with Ira C. Eaker and Carl Spaatz. Aide to the assistant secretary of war 1932-1933, the administrator of the N.R.A. in 1935 and the secretary of war in 1936. Graduated from Command and General Staff School in 1937. Commanding officer of 33rd Pursuit Group 1941-1942. Commander of Philadelphia Region, 1st Fighter Command in 1942. Brigadier general in December 1942. Commanding general of 1st Air Defense Wing 1942-1943 and 9th Fighter Command 1943-1944. Major general in April 1944. Commanding general of 9th Tactical Air Command 1944-1945. Assignments after the war included commanding general of Third Air Force, which became Tactical Air Command 1946-1948. Retired as lieutenant general in October 1951. Decorations included two Distinguished Service Medals, the Legion of Merit, Distinguished Flying Cross, three Air Medals and the Purple Heart. Died on February 9, 1993.

Ramey, Howard Knox (1896-1945) Born in Waynesboro, Mississippi, on October 14, 1896. Attended Mississippi A&M College 1915-1917. Commissioned in the aviation section of the Signal Corps in 1917. Commanding officer of 6th Photo Section in the Philippine Islands January-October 1925 then intelligence officer October 1925-February 1927. Instructor at Air Corps Advanced Flying School 1928-1931. Graduated from Air Corps Tactical School in 1934 and the Command and General Staff School in June 1936. Operations officer and assistant chief of staff for intelligence with 1st Wing June 1936-January 1941 then deputy chief of staff at 4th Air Force January 1941-August 1942. Brigadier general in September 1942. Commanding general of 4th Bomber Command, then 5th Bomber Command 1942-1943. Missing in action over New Guinea in March 1943 and declared dead on November 19, 1945. Decorations included the Distinguished Service Medal and Legion of Merit.

Ramey, Roger Maxwell (1903-1963) Born in Emblem, Texas, on September 9, 1903. Attended North Texas Teachers College 1921-1924. Commissioned in the infantry from West Point in 1928. Deputy chief of staff of Seventh Air Force 1941. Commanding officer of 43rd Bomber Group in 1943. Brigadier general in July 1943. Commanding general of 5th Bomber Command in 1943. Commanding general of 38th Flying Training Wing in 1944. Chief of staff of 21st Bomb Command in 1944. Commanding general of 58th Bomber Wing 1945-1946. Assignments after the war included commander of Eighth Air Force 1946-1950, commanding general of Fifth Air Force 1954-1956 and vice commander of Air Defense Command 1956-1957. Retired in January 1957. Decorations included the

Distinguished Service Cross, three Distinguished Service Medals, the Legion of Merit, Distinguished Flying Cross and Commendation Ribbon. Died on March 4, 1963.

Randall, Russell Edward (1902-1992) Born on January 14, 1902, in Lynn, Massachusetts. Attended Massachusetts Institute of Technology 1920-1921. Commissioned in the Air Service from West Point in 1925. Instructor at West Point 1930-1934. Senior instructor at Air Corps Advanced Flying School 1937-1939. In the Canal Zone 1940-1942. Brigadier general in September 1942. Commanding general of Seattle Air Defense Wing October-December 1943 then 4th Fighter Command December 1943-April 1944. Chief of staff of Fourth Air Force June-July 1944. Deputy commanding general of Tenth Air Force July-September 1944. Commanding general of West China Raiders 1944-1945. Member of the Air Force Liaison Mission to China October 1945-April 1946. Retired in November 1949. Decorations included the Distinguished Service Medal, two Legions of Merit and the Distinguished Flying Cross. Died on March 14, 1992.

Rawlings, Edwin William (1904-) Born in Milroy, Minnesota, on September 11, 1904. B.A. from Hamline University in 1927. Commissioned in the Air Corps in 1930. Duty in the materiel, maintenance and distribution divisions at Wright Field, with a break to receive an M.B.A from Harvard 1935-1944. Chief of readjustment division at Air Technical Service Command 1944-1945. Brigadier general in January 1945. Assignments after the war included commander of Air Materiel Command July 1951 until retirement as general in February 1959. Decorations included the Distinguished Service Medal, Distinguished Flying Cross and Commendation Ribbon.

Reed, Walter J. (1892-1963) Born in St. Paul, Minnesota, on November 7, 1892. B.S. from Columbia University in 1917. Commissioned in the aviation section of the Signal Corps in 1917. Commanding officer of 1st Balloon Company, AEF 1917-1919. Graduated from Command and General Staff School in 1939. In the office of the chief of the Air Corps 1939-1942. Brigadier general in December 1942. Commandant of Army Air Force Technical School 1942-1943. Commanding general of 7th Air Service Command 1943-1945. Retired in February 1945. Decorations included the Legion of Merit. Died on July 8, 1963.

Reinartz, Eugen Gottfried (1889-1969) Born in Liverpool, Ohio, on December 27, 1889. M.D. from the Medical College of Philadelphia in 1916. Commissioned in the Medical Corps in 1917. Commandant of the School of Aviation Medicine 1941-1946. Brigadier general in December 1942. Retired in October 1946. Died on July 29, 1969.

Richardson, William Lloyd (1901-1973) Born on December 14, 1901, in Saginaw, Michigan. Commissioned in the Coast Artillery Corps from West Point in 1924. Served at Fort Milla, Philippine Islands 1936-1938. Graduated from the Command and General Staff School in 1939. Instructor at West Point 1939-1941.

Assigned to the operations division of the War Department General Staff 1941-1942. Duty with Eighth Air Force 1942-1943. Brigadier general in March 1943. Commanding general of 51st Coast Artillery Brigade in 1943. Commanding general of 9th Air Defense Command of Ninth Air Force 1943-1945. Retired as major general in July 1954. Decorations included the Distinguished Service Medal, Legion of Merit and Commendation Ribbon. Died on March 21, 1973.

Ridenour, Carlyle Howe (1893-1971) Born in Denver, Colorado, on April 8, 1893. B.S. from California Institute of Technology in 1918. Commissioned in the Signal Corps in 1918. Transferred to the Air Service in 1920. Commanding officer of 11th Bombardment Squadron 1936-1938. Chief of the maintenance branch at Wright Field in 1938. Graduated from Command and General Staff School in 1939. Inspector officer in Central Air Corps Procurement District 1940-1942. Chief of staff of 12th Bomber Command, Eighth Air Force in 1942. Brigadier general in June 1943. Commanding general of 47th Bombardment Wing 1943-1944. Air inspector at Air Technical Service Command March-November 1944. Retired in March 1945. Decorations included the Silver Star, Distinguished Flying Cross, four Air Medals and the Purple Heart. Died on August 27, 1971.

Ritchie, William Ludlow (1902-1980) Born on April 1, 1902, in Helena, Arkansas. Commissioned in the field artillery from West Point in 1925. Graduated from Command and General Staff School in 1940. Personnel and supply officer with 25th Bomb Group 1940-1941. Squadron commander in 2nd Bomb Group in 1941. Assistant chief of staff for intelligence at Air Force Combat Command July 1941-March 1942. Duty with the operations division of the War Department General Staff 1942-1944. Member of U.S. Military Mission to U.S.S.R. 1944-1946. Brigadier general in March 1945. Retired in 1951. Decorations included the Distinguished Service Medal, Legion of Merit and Air Medal. Died on August 17, 1980.

Rives, Tom Christopher (1892-1975) Born in Montgomery, Alabama, on December 3, 1892. B.S. from Alabama Polytechnic Institute in 1916. Served as lieutenant in Alabama National Guard 1915-1919. Commissioned in the Signal Corps in 1920. M.S. from Yale in 1927. Graduated from the Army Industrial College in 1938. Chief of radio communications in the research and development division, office of the chief signal officer July 1940-August 1941. Assistant to the chief, then chief of the research and development division, office of the chief signal officer 1941-1943. Chief engineer in the office of the commanding general of the Air Corps October 1943-July 1945. Brigadier general in September 1944. Served with Air Materiel Command 1945-1949. Retired in June 1949. Decorations included the Distinguished Service Medal and Legion of Merit. Died on June 17, 1975.

Roosevelt, Elliott (1910-1990) Born on September 23, 1910, in New York, New York. Aviation editor for Hearst Newspapers 1933-1935. Vice president, then president of Hearst Radio 1935-1939. President of Texas State Network,

Inc., 1938-1940 Called to active duty as captain in the Air Corps in October 1940. Assigned to the industrial war plans section of the Air Corps materiel division at Wright Field in 1940. Duty with a reconnaissance squadron in 1941 then instruction in aerial navigation September-December 1941. Rated aircraft observer with 6th Reconnaissance Squadron in 1942. Served with 3rd Photographic Group in 1942, at headquarters Army Air Force in 1943 and at headquarters Eighth Air Force as commanding officer of a reconnaissance wing in 1944. Brigadier general in February 1945. Assigned to headquarters Army Air Force until released from active duty in August 1945. Decorations included the Distinguished Flying Cross, Legion of Merit and Air Medal. Died in October 27, 1990.

Royce, Ralph (1890-1965) Born on June 28, 1890, in Marquette, Michigan. Commissioned in the infantry from West Point in 1914. Assistant military attache in London in 1941. Brigadier general in April 1941. Commander of Southeast Air Corps Training Center 1942-1943. Major general in June 1942. Commanding general of First Air Force in 1943. Commanding general of U.S. Forces Middle East 1943-1944. Deputy commander of Ninth Air Force March-October 1944. Commanding general of First Tactical Air Force 1944-1945. Retired in June 1946. Decorations included the Distinguished Service Cross, Distinguished Service Medal, two Legions of Merit and the Distinguished Flying Cross. Died on August 7, 1965.

Rudolph, Jacob Herman (1886-1960) Born on March 25, 1886, in Milwaukee, Wisconsin. Commissioned in the infantry in 1908. Served with 29th Infantry in the Philippines 1908-1909 and in the Panama Canal Zone 1915-1917. Graduated from Air Service Pilots School in 1921 and Air Corps Tactical School in 1929. Graduated from Command and General Staff School in 1931 and the Army War College in 1935. Director of the Air Corps Board 1935-1938. Brigadier general in October 1940. Duty at the Hawaiian Department 1940-1942. Commanding general of 4th Air Support Command April 1942-January 1943, then Spokane Air Depot Control Area of Air Service Command January 1943 until retirement in July 1944. Died on March 19, 1960.

Rush, Hugo Peoples (1900-1979) Born on September 13, 1900, in West Willow, Pennsylvania. Commissioned in the infantry from West Point in 1920. Commander of 44th Bombardment Group 1941-1942. Chief of staff of 15th Bomber Command in 1942. Commander of 98th Bomber Group, then 47th Bombardment Wing 1942-1945. Brigadier general in September 1944. Retired in August 1951. Decorations included the Distinguished Service Medal, Silver Star, Legion of Merit, Distinguished Flying Cross and four Air Medals. Died on February 1, 1979.

Russell, Clinton Warden (1891-1943) Born on May 6, 1891, in Hico, Texas. Commissioned in the infantry from West Point in 1913. Served with the 1st Aero Squadron in the Punitive Expedition into Mexico 1916-1917 and in the U.S. during World War I. Graduated from the Command and General Staff School in

1925, then instructor there until 1929. Graduated from Army War College in 1930 and Naval War College in 1931. Served with the War Department General Staff 1931-1935. Chief of staff at GHQ Air Force March 1939-January 1941. Brigadier general in October 1940. Duty in the office of the chief of the Army Air Force in 1942. War Department liaison officer in the office of Admiral Ernest J. King in 1943. Died on March 23, 1943.

Ryan, William Ord (1891-1980) Born on August 10, 1891, in San Antonio, Texas. Commissioned in the cavalry from West Point in 1914. With the Punitive Expedition into Mexico 1916-1917 and the AEF in World War I. Chief of staff of the Hawaiian Air Force 1940-1941. Brigadier general in April 1941. Commanding general of the West Coast Division of Air Defense Command 1941-1942. Commanding general of the Pacific Division of Air Transport Command 1943-1946. Major general in January 1945. Retired in September 1946. Decorations included the Silver Star, Legion of Merit and Air Medal. Died on March 18, 1980.

Samford, John Alexander (1905-1968) Born in Hagerman, New Mexico, on August 29, 1905. Attended Columbia University 1923-1924. Commissioned in the field artillery from West Point in 1928. Transferred to the Air Corps in 1929. Assistant chief of staff of Third Air Force 1941-1942. Deputy chief of staff of Eighth Air Force, then 8th Bomber Command 1943-1944. Brigadier general in January 1944. Chief of staff of Eighth Air Force January-October 1944. Deputy assistant chief of staff, Army Air Force 1944-1947. Assignments after the war included deputy director, then director of National Security Agency 1956-1960. Retired as lieutenant general in November 1960. Decorations included the Distinguished Service Medal and two Legions of Merit. Died on November 20, 1968.

Sanders, Homer LeRoy (1904-) Born in Marshall, Texas, on July 25, 1904. Attended Rice Institute 1922-1926. Enlisted service in Texas National Guard 1923-1928. Commissioned in the Air Reserve in 1928. Commander of 51st Fighter Group 1941-1943. Brigadier general in August 1944. Commander of 100th Fighter Wing 1944-1947. Assignments after the war included vice commander of Continental Air Command 1957-1959. Retired as major general in March 1959. Decorations included the Silver Star, two Legions of Merit, the Bronze Star, Distinguished Flying Cross and two Air Medals. Resides in Albuquerque, New Mexico.

Sanders, Richard C. (1915-1976) Born in Salt Lake City, Utah, on August 19, 1915. B.S. from the University of Utah in 1937. Commissioned in the field artillery in 1937. Transferred to the Air Corps in 1939. Known as the "bombardment brain of the Ninth Air Force," he became a brigadier general in June 1944, at age 28 the youngest general or flag officer in the U.S. Armed Forces in World War II. Reverted to colonel in April 1946. Retired in July 1950. Decorations included the Distinguished Service Medal, two Silver Stars, two Distinguished Flying Crosses and the Air Medal. Died on September 20, 1976.

Saunders, Laverne George (1903-1988) Born on March 21, 1903, in Stratford, South Dakota. B.A. from the University of South Dakota in 1924. Commissioned in the infantry from West Point in 1928. Transferred to the Air Corps in 1929. Instructor and assistant football coach at West Point 1931-1939. Commanding officer of 23rd Bomb Squadron in 1940 and 11th Bomb Group 1940-1943. Brigadier general in December 1942. Commanding general of 7th Bomber Command Jan-March 1943. Chief of staff of Seventh Air Force March-June 1943. Assistant chief of staff for intelligence, then commanding general of 58th Bomb Wing June 1943-July 1944. Commanding general of 20th Bomber Command from 1944. Retired in February 1947. Decorations included the Navy Cross, Distinguished Service Medal, Silver Star, two Legions of Merit, the Distinguished Flying Cross, Bronze Star, Air Medal and two Purple Hearts. Died on November 16, 1988.

Saville, Gordon Philip (1902-1984) Born in Macon, Georgia, on September 14, 1902. Attended the University of Washington, Antioch College and the University of California. Commissioned in the infantry, Officers Reserve Corps in 1923. Transferred to the Air Corps in 1927. Military air observer in England in 1940. Director of air defense for the Air Corps in 1941. Brigadier general in November 1942. Chief of staff of Mediterranean Air Command in 1943. Commander of 12th Fighter Command 1943-1944. Commanding general of Air Forces in Southern France, 3rd Tactical Air Command and deputy commander of Air Transport Command in 1945. Chief of air section of U.S. Military Mission in Rio de Janeiro 1945-1948. Assignments after the war included commanding general of Air Defense Command 1948-1950. Retired as major general in July 1951. Decorations included two Distinguished Service Medals, the Legion of Merit, Bronze Star, Distinguished Flying Cross and Air Medal. Died on January 31, 1984.

Scanlon, Martin Francis (1889-1980) Born in Scranton, Pennsylvania, on August 11, 1889. Attended the University of Pennsylvania 1908-1909 and Cornell University 1910-1911. Commissioned in the infantry in 1912. Transferred to the Air Service in 1916. Assistant military attache in Rome 1923-1927. Graduated from the Command and General Staff School in 1929. Assistant military attache in London 1929-1933 then military attache 1936-1941. Brigadier general in October 1940. Assistant chief of the Air Staff 1941-1942. Commanding general of U.S. Air Command Number Two in Australia May-September 1942. Duty with West Coast Army Air Force Training Command 1942-1944. President of the Army Air Force Evaluation Board August 1944-April 1946. Reverted to colonel in March 1946. Retired in February 1948. Decorations included the Distinguished Service Medal, Silver Star, Legion of Merit and Air Medal. Died on January 26, 1980.

Schlatter, David Myron (1901-1973) Born in Fostoria, Ohio, on November 21, 1901. Commissioned in the Air Service from West Point in 1923. Graduated from Command and General Staff School in 1939. Director of training at West Coast Air Corps Training Center 1940-1942. Duty at headquarters of Air Corps 1942-1943. Brigadier general in September 1943. Deputy chief of staff of Ninth Air

Force in 1944. Commanding general of American components of Allied Expeditionary Air Forces in 1944. Duty at headquarters of the European Theater of Operations 1944-1945. Major general in January 1945. Deputy commandant of Air University 1945-1948. Assignments after the war included commander of Allied Air Forces in Southern Europe 1951-1954 and commandant of the Armed Forces Staff College 1954-1957. Retired as lieutenant general in July 1957. Decorations included two Distinguished Service Medals, the Legion of Merit, Bronze Star and Air Medal. Died on December 14, 1973.

Schneider, Max F. (1896-1975) Born on June 11, 1896, in Cincinnati, Ohio. Commissioned in the aviation section of the Officers Reserve Corps in 1918. Graduated from the Army Industrial College in 1937, the Naval War College in 1938 and the Army War College in 1939. Member of the Air Corps Board at Maxwell Field July 1939-August 1941. Chief of the supply section at headquarters Army Air Force 1941-1942. Supply officer with Twelfth Air Force August 1942-March 1943 then assistant chief of staff of Twelfth Air Force Service Command March-June 1943. Deputy director of maintenance and supply at Mediterranean Air Command June-September 1943. Deputy to the air inspector at headquarters Army Air Force 1943-1946. Brigadier general in January 1945. Retired in July 1953. Decorations included two Distinguished Service Medals, two Legions of Merit and the Commendation Ribbon. Died on April 27, 1975.

Schramm, Ned (1896-1983) Born on August 23, 1896, in Burlington, Iowa. Enlisted service 1917-1918. Commissioned in the Air Service in 1920. Commanding officer of 36th Pursuit Squadron 1936-1941. Commanding officer of Puerto Rico Region and 6th Fighter Command 1941-1943. Brigadier general in June 1943. Commander of San Francisco Fighter Wing in 1943. Commander of 71st Fighter Wing 1943-1944, briefly 9th Air Defense Command, then 71st Fighter Wing again 1944-1945. Retired in June 1949. Decorations included the Legion of Merit and Bronze Star. Died on March 15, 1983.

Schulgen, George Francis (1900-1955) Born on April 23, 1900, in Traverse City, Michigan. B.S. from Michigan Agricultural College in 1922. Commissioned in the Air Service in 1924. Graduated from Command and General Staff School in 1939. In operations division of the War Department General Staff, then assistant secretary 1941-1943. Brigadier general in June 1943. Wing commander, then chief of staff of First Air Force 1943-1944. Staff member of Southwest Pacific Area, then Southeast Asia Command 1944-1945. Duty with the civil affairs division in the office of the chief of the Army Air Force 1945-1947. Retired in June 1948. Decorations included the Legion of Merit. Died on February 16, 1955.

Smith, Albert Daniel (1887-1970) Born on February 6, 1887, in Farley, Missouri. Enlisted service with 22nd Infantry 1904-1907 and the aviation section 1915-1916. Commissioned in the Signal Corps, Officers Reserve Corps in 1917. Active duty 1917-1920. Retired in 1923. Recalled to active duty as captain in 1940. Operations officer at Albuquerque Air Base 1940-1942. Commander of the

Eastern Sector of Air Transport Command 1942-1943. Base commander, North American Theater of Operations 1943-1945. Brigadier general in March 1944. Decorations included two Legions of Merit. Died on January 20, 1970.

Smith, Cyrus Rowlett (1899-) Born on September 9, 1899, in Minerva, Texas. Attended the University of Texas 1920-1924. President of American Airlines 1935-1942. Resigned to enter the Army Air Force as colonel in April 1942. Chief of staff to Lieutenant General Harold L. George, commanding general of Air Transport Command, 1942-1944. Brigadier general in October 1942. Deputy commander of Air Transport Command in the China-Burma-India Theater of Operations 1944-1945. Major general in September 1944. Returned to civilian life in June 1945. Decorations included the Distinguished Service Medal, Legion of Merit and Air Medal.

Smith, Frederic Harrison Jr. (1908-1980) Born at Fort Monroe, Virginia, on June 30, 1908. Commissioned in the field artillery from West Point in 1929. Commanding officer of 36th Pursuit Group, then 8th Pursuit Group 1939-1942. Chief of staff of Fifth Air Force 1942-1944. Brigadier general in November 1943. Chief of operations at Allied Expeditionary Air Forces in 1944. Commander of 5th Fighter Command in 1945. Assignments after the war included commanding general of Fifth Air Force 1956-1958, commander of Air Training Command 1958-1959, commander of Fourth Allied Tactical Air Force 1959-1961, commander in chief of U.S. Air Forces Europe August 1959-June 1961 and vice chief of staff, U.S. Air Force 1961-1962. Retired as general in June 1962. Decorations included four Distinguished Service Medals, the Legion of Merit, two Air Medals and the Commendation Ribbon. Died on May 28, 1980.

Smith, Joseph (1901-1993) Born in Scranton, Pennsylvania, on October 31, 1901. Commissioned in the cavalry from West Point in 1923. Assistant to assistant chief of staff for operations at GHQ Air Corps, then at operations division of the War Department General Staff 1940-1943. Senior Air Corps member of Joint War Plans Commission of the Joint Chiefs of Staff 1943-1944. Brigadier general in May 1944. Chief of staff of Third Air Force, then 20th Bomber Command 1944-1945. Assistant chief of staff for plans, Army Air Force in 1945. Chief of staff, then deputy commandant of Air University 1945-1946. Assignments after the war included commander of Military Air Transport Service 1951-1958. Retired as lieutenant general in June 1958. Lieutenant general in July 1952. Decorations included two Distinguished Service Medals, two Legions of Merit and the Bronze Star. Died on May 19, 1993.

Smith, Lotha A. (1894-1970) Born on January 8, 1894, in Kentucky. Commissioned in the aviation section of the Signal Corps in 1917. Instructor at Air Corps Tactical School 1934-1938. Commanding officer of Air Provisional Group Alaska in 1940. Acting assistant chief of staff for operations at 4th Air District in 1941. Commanding officer of Hammer Field December 1941-March 1943 and Army Task Force, Pacific April-December 1943. Served with Seventh Air Force as field inspector 1943-1944 and assistant chief of staff for plans February-December 1944. Brigadier general in January 1945. Retired in June 1950. Decorations included the Legion of Merit and Bronze Star. Died on April 11, 1970.

Smith, Luther Stevens (1901-1974) Born in Wadeville, North Carolina, on March 1, 1901. Attended the University of North Carolina 1918-1920. Commissioned in the Air Corps from West Point in 1924. Junior executive to the chief of the Air Corps 1936-1940. Director of training at Southeast Air Forces Training Center 1940-1941. Executive assistant to the chief of Army Air Force 1941-1942. Director of individual training at headquarter Army Air Force in 1942. Brigadier general in November 1942. Commander of 33rd Flying Training Wing 1943-1944. Director of military missions to Central and South America in 1944-1945. Chief of civil affairs at headquarters Army Air Force in 1945 then U.S. liaison for protocol at Allied Control Authority, Berlin June 1945 until retirement in August 1946. Decorations included the Legion of Merit. Died on May 28, 1974.

Snavely, Ralph A. (1898-) Born in Aurora, Missouri, on January 5, 1898. B.A. from State Teachers College in 1921. Commissioned in the Air Corps in 1923. Graduated from Command and General Staff School in 1937. Instructor at Air Corps Tactical School July 1937-June 1938 then chief of the bomb section September 1938-June 1939 and instructor in bomber aviation July 1939-June 1940. Instructor at the Command and General Staff School November 1940-May 1941. Assistant chief of staff for intelligence at Fourth Air Force September 1942-March 1943. Graduated from Army and Navy Staff College in 1943. Commanding officer of Los Angeles Fighter Wing March-August 1943 and December 1943-March 1944, then 319th Night Fighter Wing April-December 1944. Brigadier general in November 1944. Commanding general of Air Task Force Austria December 1944-February 1945, then the air division of 15th Army Group in Austria February 1945-March 1947. Retired in July 1953. Decorations included the Legion of Merit and Bronze Star. Resides in Fulton, Texas.

Sneed, Albert Lee (1884-1967) Born in Conway, Arkansas, on April 24, 1884. Attended the University of Alaska 1902-1904. Commissioned in the infantry from West Point in 1908. Foreign duty in the Philippines 1909-1910, Hawaii 1913-1914, Turkey 1922-1923 and again in the Philippines 1934-1937. Retired in December 1938. Recalled to active duty in World War II. Commanding officer of Maxwell Field February 1941-January 1942 then U.S. Air Command Number One with Allied Air Forces Australia February-September 1942. Brigadier general in June 1942. Commanding general of Army Air Force Technical School 1942-1943, Lowry Field April 1943-November 1944 and Army Air Force Technical Training Command November 1944 until retirement again in June 1946. Decorations included the Silver Star and Legion of Merit. Died on November 25, 1967.

Sorensen, Edgar Peter (1893-1967) Born in Glenville, Minnesota, on March 11, 1893. B.S. from the University of Washington in 1915. Transferred to the aviation section of the Signal Corps in 1917. M.S. from Massachusetts Institute of

Technology in 1925. Graduated from Command and General Staff School in 1937. Director of the Air Corps Board at Maxwell Field 1937-1940. Commandant of Air Corps Tactical School 1940-1941. Duty in the intelligence division at headquarters Army Air Force July 1941-September 1943. Brigadier general in April 1943. Commanding general of Sixth Air Force May 1944-January 1945. Staff officer, then chief of the services division at U.S. Strategic Bombing Survey January-September 1945. Retired in August 1948. Decorations included the Bronze Star. Died on December 22, 1967.

Spaatz, Carl (1891-1974) Born on June 28, 1891, in Boyertown, Pennsylvania. Commissioned in the infantry from West Point in 1914. Early in his career acquired the nickname of "Tooey." Flew with the 1st Aero Squadron in the Punitive Expedition into Mexico 1916-1917 and the 2nd Pursuit Group in France 1918, where he downed three enemy planes. Commander of the *Question Mark*, a tri-motor Fokker, as it demonstrated in-flight refueling by flying a total of 11,000 miles above Los Angeles on January 1-7, 1929. Captain Ira C. Eaker and Lieutenant Elwood R. Quesada accompanied Major Spaatz. Graduated from Command and General Staff School in 1936. Executive officer of the 2nd Wing 1939-1939. Executive officer, then assistant to the chief of the Air Corps 1939-1940. Brigadier general in October 1940. Head of plans division, then chief of the Air Staff 1940-1942. Major general in January 1942. Chief of the Army Air Force Combat Command January-June 1942. Commanding general of Eighth Air Force July-December 1942. Commanding general of Twelfth Air Force, then Northwest African Air Force, finally deputy commanding general of Mediterranean Allied Air Forces in 1943. Lieutenant general in March 1943. Commander of U.S. Strategic Air Forces in Europe, then in the Pacific Theater of Operations January 1944-October 1945. Assignments after the war included commander of the Army Air Force, then first chief of staff, U.S. Air Force 1946-1948. Retired as general in June 1948. Decorations included the Distinguished Service Cross, four Distinguished Service Medals, the Legion of Merit, Distinguished Flying Cross and Bronze Star. Died on July 14, 1974.

Spry, James Wrathall (1900-1983) Born on March 12, 1900, in Grantsville, Utah. Commissioned in the Air Corps from West Point in 1922. Served with 3rd Pursuit Squadron, Philippine Islands August 1924-February 1927. Assistant to the chief of the inspection section. office of the chief of the Air Corps September 1936-September 1939. Assistant chief of staff for supply at Air Service Command June 1940-April 1943. Commanding officer of Miami Air Depot in 1943. Brigadier general in November 1943. Chief of staff of Air Service Command in China-Burma-India Theater of Operations 1943-1945. Commanding general of Air Technical Service Command April-December 1945. Retired as major general in January 1957. Decorations included the Distinguished Service Medal, Legion of Merit, Air Medal and two Commendation Ribbons. Died on November 15, 1983.

Stearley, Ralph Francis (1898-1973) Born on July 25, 1898, in Brazil, Indiana. Commissioned in the Cavalry from West Point in 1919. Attended Yale 1920-1921. Graduated from Air Corps Tactical School in 1935 and Command and General Staff School in 1936. Assistant executive officer in the office of the chief of the Air Corps 1940-1942. Military intelligence officer at Flying Training Command in 1942. Commanding general of 1st Tactical Air Division, Ninth Air Force 1943-1944. Brigadier general in September 1943. Head of operations for First Allied Airborne Army 1944-1945. Commander of the air section at Fifteenth Army Theater of Operations General Board 1945-1946. Assignments after the war included commanding general of Fourteenth Air Force 1948-1950 and Twentieth Air Force in the Korean War 1950-1953. Retired as major general in February 1953. Decorations included two Distinguished Service Medals, the Legion of Merit, Bronze Star, Air Medal and Commendation Ribbon. Died on February 3, 1973.

Stenseth, Martinus (1890-1979) Born in Heiberg, Minnesota, on June 11, 1890. Commissioned in the Air Service in 1920. Assistant military attache in Latvia and Finland May-September 1940. Administrative inspector at Moffett Field September 1940-May 1941. Base commander at Air Corps Gunnery School in Las Vegas 1941-1943. Brigadier general in April 1943. Commanding general of 36th and 82nd Flying Training Wings June 1943-April 1945 then U.S. Forces Ireland May-December 1945. Reverted to colonel in April 1946 and retired in June 1950. Decorations included the Distinguished Service Cross, Silver Star and two Legions of Merit. Died on June 25, 1979.

Stone, Charles Bertody III (1904-1992) Born at Fort McPherson, Georgia, on March 8, 1904. Commissioned in the infantry from West Point in 1927. Duty at headquarters of Army Air Force 1941-1943 and the China-Burma-India Theater of Operations 1943-1944. Brigadier general in November 1943. Chief of staff, then commanding general of Fourteenth Air Force 1945-1946. Major general in August 1945. Assignments after the war included commanding general of Second Air Force in 1946, comptroller of the Air Force 1951-1955 and commander of Continental Air Command 1955-1957. Retired as lieutenant general in June 1957. Decorations included two Distinguished Service Medals, two Legions of Merit, the Distinguished Flying Cross and two Bronze Stars. Died on May 17, 1992.

Stowell, James Somers (1900-1978) Born on June 17, 1900, in Syracuse, New York. Commissioned in the infantry from West Point in 1924. Transferred to the Air Corps in 1927. Duty in the Philippines July 1930-July 1932. Instructor at Air Corps Technical School 1932-1936. Graduated from Air Corps Tactical School in June 1937 and Command and General Staff School in 1938. Director of training at Air Corps Basic Flying School March 1941-January 1942. Organized and commanded the officer candidate school for the Army Air Force January-July 1942. Chief of staff of 1st District, Air Force Technical Training Command July-September 1942. Commanding officer of Tarrant Field, Texas 1942-1943. Commander of Central African Wing of Air Transport Command 1943-1944. Brigadier general in June 1944. Commanding general of North Africa Division, Air Transport Command 1944-1945 then North Atlantic Wing, Air Transport Command September 1945-January 1946. Retired as major general in May 1955. Decorations included the Distinguished Service Medal, Legion of Merit and Air Medal. Died on December 23, 1978.

Strahm, Victor Herbert (1895-1957) Born in Nashville, Tennessee, on October 26, 1895. Attended Western Kentucky Teachers College 1911-1915 and the University of Kentucky 1915-1917. Commissioned in the aviation section of the Signal Corps in 1917. Flew with the AEF in World War I and became an ace with five downings of German airplanes. Attended the University of Wisconsin 1919-1920. Graduated from Command and General Staff School in 1936 and the Army War College in 1939. Brigadier general in October 1942. Chief of staff of Ninth Air Force 1942-1945. Commanding general of Army Air Force Central Flying Training Wing September-November 1945. Retired in February 1953. Decorations included the Distinguished Service Cross, Silver Star and Legion of Merit. Died on May 11, 1957.

Stratemeyer, George Edward (1890-1969) Born on November 24, 1890, in Cincinnati, Ohio. Commissioned in the infantry from West Point in 1915. Graduated from Command and General Staff School in 1932 and the Army War College in 1939. Attached to the aviation section of the Signal Corps in 1916. Transferred in 1920. With the 1st Aero Squadron in Columbus, New Mexico 1916-1917. Instructor at West Point 1924-1929 and Command and General Staff School 1932-1936. Head of training and operations division at headquarters Army Air Force 1940-1941. Brigadier general in August 1941. Executive officer to General Henry H. Arnold 1941-1942. Major general in June 1942. Chief of Air Staff 1942-1943. Commanding general of Army Air Forces in China-Burma-India Theater of Operations 1943-1946. Assignments after the war included commanding general of Air Defense Command, Continental Air Command and Far East Air Forces 1946-1951. Retired as lieutenant general in January 1952. Decorations included the Distinguished Service Cross, four Distinguished Service Medals, the Distinguished Flying Cross and two Air Medals. Died on August 9, 1969.

Streett, St. Clair (1893-1970) Born in Washington, DC on October 6, 1893. Commissioned in the aviation section of the Signal Corps in 1917. Commander of the Alaskan flight, New York to Nome and back in 1920. Graduated from Command and General Staff School in 1934 and the Army War College in 1935. Served in the miscellaneous and operations sections of War Department General Sstaff August 1935-June 1939. Graduated from the Naval War College in 1940. Commanding officer of 11th Bomb Group July 1940-April 1941. Plans and training officer with the Hawaiian Department April 1941-January 1942. Brigadier general in March 1942. Again with the War Department General Staff February-December 1942. Major general in December 1942. Commanding general of Third Air Force 1942-1943, Second Air Force September 1943-January 1944, Thirteenth Air Force Task Force in the Southwest Pacific Area April-June 1944 and

Thirteenth Air Force June-December 1944. Deputy commander of Continental Air Command January 1945-March 1946. Assignments after the war included deputy commander of Air Materiel Command October 1949-December 1951. Retired as major general in February 1952. Decorations included three Distinguished Service Medals, the Legion of Merit, Distinguished Flying Cross, Air Medal and Purple Heart. Died on September 28, 1970.

Strickland, Auby Casey (1895-1969) Born in Braggs, Alabama, on December 17, 1895. Attended Alabama Polytechnic Institute 1914-1917. Commissioned in the infantry in 1920. Transferred to the Air Corps in 1924. Co-pilot of the airplane that refueled the *Question Mark* during its endurance flight over Los Angeles in January 1929. Commanding officer of 13th Attack Squadron August 1937-June 1939. Graduated from Air Corps Tactical School in 1939 then commanding officer of 35th Pursuit Group 1939-1941. Commanding officer of Paine Field, Everett, Washington 1941-1942. Brigadier general in August 1942. Commander of 9th Fighter Command 1942-1943. Governor of Pantelleria Island July-October 1943. Duty at headquarters of Allied Expeditionary Air Forces 1943-1944. Commander of 318th Fighter Wing 1944-1945. President of the Army Air Force Board in 1945. Retired in July 1953. Decorations included the Distinguished Service Medal and Legion of Merit. Died on August 16, 1969.

Strother, Dean Caldwell (1908-) Born in Winfield, Kansas, on February 12, 1908. Attended Southwestern College 1925-1927. Commissioned in the infantry from West Point in 1931. Commanding officer of Thirteenth Air Force Fighter Command 1942-1943. Brigadier general in May 1943. Commanding general of the Solomon Islands Fighter Command 1943-1944. Commander of 306th Fighter Wing 1944-1945. Commanding general of West Coast Wing, Air Transport Command 1945-1946. Assignments after the war included commander of Twelfth Air Force, then Fourth Allied Tactical Air Forces in Central Europe 1951-1953, deputy chief of staff for operations, U.S. Air Force 1958-1962, U.S. representative to the NATO Millitary Committee 1962-1965 and commander in chief of North American Air Defense Command 1965 until retirement as general in July 1966. Decorations included three Distinguished Service Medals, the Silver Star, two Legions of Merit, the Distinguished Flying Cross and two Air Medals. Resides in Colorado Springs.

Sullivan, Charles Wesley (1893-1975) Born in Peoria, Illinois, on June 15, 1893. Attended the University of Illinois. Enlisted service with the Signal Corps Reserve 1917-1918. Commissioned in the aviation section in 1918. Flight instructor at Air Corps Primary School November 1926-July 1928. Graduated from Air Corps Tactical School in June 1933 and the Command and General Staff School in June 1939. Assistant chief of the inspection division, office of the chief of the Air Corps July 1939-August 1941. Assistant air inspector at headquarters Army Air Force 1941-1942. Chief of the air section in the office of the inspector general of the Army Air Force June 1942-May 1943. Chief of the air transport division at headquarters Army Air Force May-November 1943. Brigadier general in November 1943. Air inspector at Air Training Command 1943-1945. Retired in June 1953. Died on November 26, 1975.

Taylor, Willis Ratcliffe (1897-1945) Born on February 24, 1897, in Parkersburg, West Virginia. Enlisted service as flying cadet 1917-1918. Commissioned in the aviation section of the signal reserve in 1918. Stationed at Clark Field, Philippine Islands May 1921-May 1923 and adjutant at France Field, Panama Canal Zone December 1934-July 1936. Commanding officer of 27th Pursuit Squadron June 1937-June 1939. Graduated from Air Corps Tactical School in August 1939. Executive officer of 1st Pursuit Group 1939-1941 and 2nd Interceptor Command April-December 1941. Commanding officer of 5th Interceptor Command December 1941-March 1942. Commanding officer of Fighter Command School from March 1942. Brigadier general in October 1942. Reverted to colonel in April 1943. Died in the Canal Zone on June 14, 1945.

Taylor, Yantis Halbert (1898-1956) Born in Bartlett, Texas, on July 29, 1898. Commissioned in the Air Service in 1926. Flying instructor at Kelly Field 1926-1930. Graduated from Command and General Staff School in 1938. Instructor at Lambert Field 1938-1940. Director of flying at Barksdale Field 1940-1941 then director of training at Craig Field in 1941. Commanding officer of Spence Field 1941-1942. Chief of staff of 47th Bomber Wing in 1943. Deputy commander, then commanding officer of 306th Fighter Wing 1943-1945. Brigadier general in June 1945. Retired in December 1949. Decorations included the Legion of Merit, Distinguished Flying Cross, Bronze Star and three Air Medals. Died on December 22, 1956.

Thatcher, Herbert Bishop (1909-1986) Born on May 1, 1909, in East Orange, New Jersey. Commissioned in the infantry from West Point in 1932. Commanding officer of 97th Observation Squadron 1940-1941. Operations officer, then executive officer of 3rd Bomb Group 1941-1942. Commanding officer of 323rd Bomb Group 1942-1943. Commander of wings in the 8th and 9th Bomber Commands 1943-1944. Brigadier general in June 1944. Assistant chief of staff for operations at Allied Expeditionary Air Forces 1944-1945. Assignments after the war included chief of staff of United Nations Command Korea 1961-1963 and commander of Air Defense Command 1963 until retirement in July 1967. Decorations included the Silver Star, two Legions of Merit, two Distinguished Flying Crosses, the Bronze Star, nine Air Medals and two Purple Hearts. Died on June 11, 1986.

Thomas, Arthur (1894-n/a) Born on January 2, 1894, in Zanesville, Ohio. LL.B. from St. Louis University in 1917. Commissioned in the aviation section of the Officers Reserve Corps in 1917 and the Air Service, U.S. Army in 1920. Instructor at Air Service Balloon and Airship School 1922-1924. Served in the Philippines 1925-1927. Graduated from Air Corps Tactical School in 1933. Assistant to the assistant chief of staff for supply at GHQ Air Force August 1938-March 1942. Assigned to War Department General Staff March-June 1942, as Army Air Force liaison officer to the Services of Supply then chief of staff of 12th Army Air Force

Service Command in 1942. Commander of 3rd Air Service Area in Sicily in 1943. Brigadier general in February 1944. Commanding general of 12th Army Air Force Service Command in 1944. Assistant chief of staff for supply then deputy commander for administration, Army Air Force in the Mediterannean Theater of Operations in 1945. Duty at headquarters of Air Technical Training Command in 1945 then deputy commanding general, supply, at headquarters Air Materiel Command 1945-1946. Retired in February 1953. Decorations included two Legions of Merit and the Bronze Star.

Thomas, Charles Edwin Jr. (1896-1969) Born in Atlanta, Georgia, on April 8, 1896. Attended Georgia Institute of Technology 1914-1917. Commissioned in the Air Corps in 1918. Graduated from the Army Industrial College in 1935 and the Army War College in 1937. Instructor at Air Corps Tactical School 1937-1940. Aviation observer on the staff of Admiral Halsey in 1940. Commander of Warner Robbins Air Service Command 1941-1944. Brigadier general in September 1943. Deputy commander of 21st Bomber Command, then Army Air Forces Pacific Ocean Areas 1944-1945. Assignments after the war included commanding general of Fourteenth Air Force 1950-1952. Retired in January 1955. Decorations included two Legions of Merit and the Commendation Ribbon. Died on March 13, 1969.

Timberlake, Edward Julius (1909-1990) Born at Fort Hunt, Virginia, on November 10, 1909. Brother of Patrick Weston Timberlake. Commissioned in the infantry from West Point in 1931. Adjutant of 6th Bomb Squadron 1940-1941. Commanding officer of 66th Bomb Squadron 1941-1942, then 93rd Bomb Group 1942-1943. The 93rd became known as "Ted's flying circus" in combat in Europe. Brigadier general in October 1943. Commanding general of 201st Combat Wing 1943-1944. Major general in January 1944. Commanding general of 20th Combat Bomb Wing 1944-1945. Assignments after the war included chief of staff, then commanding general of Fifth Air Force 1949-1951, commanding general of Ninth Air Force 1951-1957, deputy chief of staff for personnel, U.S. Air Force 1961-1962 and commanding general of Continental Air Command July 1962 until retirement as lieutenant general in June 1965. Decorations included two Distinguished Service Medals, the Silver Star, two Legions of Merit, two Distinguished Flying Crosses and three Air Medals. Died on September 30, 1990.

Timberlake, Patrick Weston (1901-1983) Born at Fort Greble, Rhode Island, on December 25, 1901. Brother of Edward Julius Timberlake. Commissioned in the field artillery from West Point in 1923. Transferred to the Air Corps in 1928. Graduated from Command and General Staff School in 1939. Duty with materiel division at headquarters of the Air Corps 1939-1942. Commander of 9th Bomber Command 1942-1943. Brigadier general in November 1942. Director of operations and plans, then chief of staff of Mediterranean Air Command 1943-1944. Deputy chief of the Air Staff 1944-1945. Chief of staff, then commanding general of Eighth Air Force 1945-1946. Assignments after the war included commander of Allied Air Forces in Southern Europe 1955-1957. Retired as lieutenant general in July 1957. Decorations included two Distinguished Service Medals, two Legions of Merit and the Bronze Star. Died on October 18, 1983.

Tinker, Clarence Leonard (1887-1943) Born in Elgin, Kansas, on November 21, 1887. Commissioned in the infantry following graduation from Wentworth Military Academy in 1912. Chief of the aviation division, National Guard Bureau 1936-1939. Commanding officer of 27th Bomb Group 1939-1940. Brigadier general in May 1940. Commanding general of 3rd Interceptor Command January-November 1941. Major general in January 1942. Commander of Army Air Forces in Hawaii December 1941-June 1942. Died on June 7, 1943, when his B-24 crashed into the sea near Wake Island.

Todd, Walter Edwin (1906-1978) Born in Gonzales, Texas, on June 25, 1906. Attended the University of Texas in 1923. Commissioned in the field artillery from West Point in 1928. Member of the Air Staff, then the War Department General Staff 1942-1944. Assistant chief of staff for operations in Eighth Air Force 1944-1945. Brigadier general in November 1944. Military attache in Moscow 1945-1947. Assignments after the war included chief of staff of U.S. Forces Korea 1957-1958 and commandant of Air University 1958-1961. Retired in July 1961. Decorations included two Distinguished Service Medals, the Legion of Merit, Distinguished Flying Cross, Commendation Ribbon and Air Medal. Died on February 13, 1978.

Tourtellot, George Platt (1895-1946) Born on November 5, 1895, in Dows, Iowa. Attended Carroll College 1915-1917. Commissioned in the Air Service in 1918. Served with combat pursuit units in France and germany 1918-1919. Duty at Wheeler Field, Hawaii 1930-1933. Commanding officer of 35th Pursuit Group 1940-1941. Executive officer of 2nd Interceptor Command in 1942. Commanding officer of 111th Fighter Command in 1942. Commander of 24th Composite Wing 1942-1944. Brigadier general in February 1943. Commanding general of 72nd Fighter Wing in 1944. Assigned to headquarters Army Air Force in 1945. Died on October 28, 1946. Decorations included the Air Medal.

Travis, Robert Falligant (1904-1950) Born in Savannah, Georgia, on December 26, 1904. Commissioned in the field artillery from West Point in 1928. Commanding officer of 29th Bomb Group 1941-1942. Commanding officer of 15th Bomb Wing 1942-1943. Brigadier general in May 1943. Commanding general of 1st Bomber Command, then 41st Combat Wing of Eighth Air Force 1943-1944. Commanding general of 17th Bomber Operational Training Wing 1944-1946. Assignments after the war included commanding general of Pacific Air Command 1948-1949. Killed in an airplane accident at Fairfield-Suisun Air Force Base on August 6, 1950. The base was renamed Travis Air Force Base in his honor in October 1950. Decorations included the Distinguished Service Cross, three Silver Stars, four Distinguished Flying Crosses, four Air Medals, the Commendation Ribbon and Purple Heart.

Tunner, William Henry (1906-1983) Born in Elizabeth, New Jersey, on July 14, 1906. Commissioned in the field artillery from West Point in 1928. With the Ferrying Command 1941-1942. Commanding officer of the Ferrying Division of Air Transport Command 1942-1943. Brigadier general in July 1943. Commanding general of Air Transport Command in the China-Burma-India Theater of Operations 1943-1945. Commanding general of the Atlantic Division of Military Air Transport Service, formed when Air Transport Command merged with Naval Air Transport 1945-1948. Assignments after the war included commanding general of the Berlin Airlift 1948-1949, commander in chief of U.S. Air Forces Europe 1953-1957 and commander of Military Air Transport Service 1958-1960. Retired as lieutenant general in May 1960. Decorations included the Distinguished Service Cross, four Distinguished Service Medals, the Legion of Merit, Distinguished Flying Cross and two Air Medals. Died on April 6, 1983.

Turner, Howard McMath (1902-1965) Born in Avoca, Iowa, on February 21, 1902. Commissioned in the Air Corps from West Point in 1924. Earned his wings in 1925. Instructor at Primary Flying School, Brooks Field 1928-1931. White House aide in 1938. Graduated from Air Corps Tactical School in 1940. Commander of 4th Staff Squadron 1941-1942. Pilot aide to the secretary of war 1942-1943. Commander of 1st Air Division, Eighth Air Force June 1943-October 1944. Brigadier general in June 1944. Commanding general of 1st Bombardment Division, Eighth Air Force 1944-1945. Major general in March 1945. Assignments after the war included member of the United Nations truce team in the Korean War 1951-1952 and commanding general of First Air Force 1952 until retirement in 1954. Decorations included the Distinguished Service Medal, two Silver Stars, two Legions of Merit, the Distinguished Flying Cross, Bronze Star and two Air Medals. Died on June 25, 1965.

Twining, Nathan Farragut (1897-1982) Born on October 11, 1897, in Monroe, Wisconsin, brother of Merrill Barber Twining, who became a general in the U.S. Marine Corps. Enlisted service with Oregon National Guard June 1916-September 1916, and March 1917-June 1917. Commissioned in the infantry from West Point in 1919. Graduated from Command and General Staff School in 1937. In the office of the chief of the Air Corps 1940-1942. Brigadier general in June 1942. Chief of staff of Allied Forces South Pacific 1942-1943. Commanding general of Thirteenth Air Force, then air commander of the Solomon Islands, finally commanding general of Fifteenth Air Force 1943-1944. Major general in February 1943. Commander of Mediterranean Allied Strategic Air Forces 1944-1945. Lieutenant general in June 1945. Commanding general of Twentieth Air Force August-October 1945. Assignments after the war included commander of Air Materiel Command 1945-1947, commanding general of Alaskan Command 1947-1950, deputy chief of staff, U.S. Air Force May-October 1950, vice chief of staff, then chief of staff, U.S. Air Force 1950-1957 and chairman of the Joint Chiefs of Staff 1957-1960. Retired as general in September 1960. Decorations included two Distinguished Service Medals, two Legions of Merit, the Distinguished Flying Cross, Bronze Star and two Air Medals. Died on March 29, 1982.

Upston, John Edwin (1890-1952) born in Tawas City, Michigan, on September 9, 1890. Commissioned in the aviation section in 1918. Served with the 63rd Service Squadron then 25th Bombardment Squadron at France Field, Panama Canal Zone March 1923-February 1926. White House aide 1928-1930. Graduated from Air Corps Tactical School in 1935, the Command and General Staff School in 1937 and Army War College in 1939. Served with War Department General Staff March 1942-February 1944. Brigadier general in December 1942. Operations officer, then chief of staff of 20th Bomber Command in 1944. Duty in the China-Burma-India 1944-1945. Assignments after the war included commanding general of Fourth Air Force 1948-1950. Retired in September 1950. Decorations included the Distinguished Service Medal, Legion of Merit and Air Medal. Died on August 18, 1952.

Upthegrove, Fay Roscoe (1905-1992) Born on Janaury 28, 1905, in Port Allegheny, Pennsylvania. Commissioned in the infantry from West Point in 1927. Commandant of Air Corps Basic Flying School at Moffett Field in 1939. Commanding officer of 99th Bomb Squadron 1939-1940. Materiel officer, then executive officer of 22nd Bomb Squadron 1940-1941. Executive officer, then commanding officer of 38th Bomb Squadron 1941-1942. Executive officer, then commanding officer of 308th Bomb Group in 1942. Commanding officer of 39th Bomb Group in 1942, 99th Bomb Group 1942-1943 and 304th Bomb Wing January 1944-July 1945. Brigadier general in September 1944. Commanding general of 76th Flying Training Wing August-October 1945. Assignments after the war included commanding general of Twentieth Air Force 1953-1955. Retired as major general in July 1957. Decorations included the Distinguished Service Medal, Silver Star, Legion of Merit, two Distinguished Flying Crosses and ten Air Medals. Died on January 8, 1992.

Usher, George Luke (1899-1974) Born in New York, New York, on March 3, 1899. Enlisted service 1916-1917. Commissioned in the field artillery, Officers Reserve Corps in 1917. Transferred to the aviation section of the Signal Corps later that year. Flew with the 135th Aero Squadron in the St. Mihiel and Meuse-Argonne offensives 1918-1919. Commanding officer of 66th Service Squadron at Camp Nichols, Philippine Islands 1927-1929. Commanding officer of Moffett Field, 9th Air Base Group, West Coast Training Center and Army Air Force Materiel Center at Wright Field 1939-1945. Brigadier general in February 1943. Commanding general of Camp Davis in 1945. Reverted to colonel in November 1945. Retired in March 1950. Decorations included two Legions of Merit and the Air Medal. Died on April 28, 1974.

Vanaman, Arthur William (1892-1987) Born on May 9, 1892, in Millville, New Jersey. B.S. from Drexel Institute in 1915. Commissioned in the Signal Corps in 1917. Attended Massachusetts Institute of Technology in 1918. Graduated from the Army Industrial College in 1936 and the Army War College in 1937. Air attache in Berlin 1937-1941. Brigadier general in March 1942. Commander of

Army Air Force Materiel Center 1942-1943 and Oklahoma City Air Service Command April 1943-March 1944. Major general in March 1944. Commanded San Antonio Air Service Command March-May 1944. Assistant chief of staff for operations at Eighth Air Force May-June 1944. Prisoner of war in Germany June 1944-April 1945. Deputy chief of staff for prisoner of war affairs with U.S. Strategic Air Forces May-June 1945. Commanding general of Mobile Air Technical Service Command June-December 1945. Retired in May 1954. Decorations included three Legions of Merit, the Bronze Star, Air Medal, two Commendation Ribbons and the Purple Heart. Died on September 14, 1987.

Vandenberg, Hoyt Sanford (1899-1954) Born on January 24, 1899, in Milwaukee, Wisconsin. Commissioned in the Air Corps from West Point in 1923. Graduated from Command and General Staff School in 1936 and the Army War College in 1939. In plans division, then operations and training officer in the office of the chief of the Air Corps 1939-1942. Chief of staff of Twelfth Air Force, then Northwest Africa Strategic Air Force 1942-1943. Brigadier general in December 1942. Deputy chief of the Air Staff at headquarters Army Air Force 1943-1944. Major general in March 1944. Deputy commander of Allied Expeditionary Air Forces, then commanding general of Ninth Air Force 1944-1945. Lieutenant general in March 1945. Assistant chief of staff for operations, Army Air Force 1945-1946. Assignments after the war included chief of the intelligence division of the War Department General Staff, then director of the Central Intelligence Group (predecessor of the Central Intelligence Agency) 1946-1947, deputy commander and chief of staff of Army Air Force, then vice chief and of staff of U.S. Air Force 1947-1953. Retired as general in June 1953. Decorations included two Distinguished Service Medals, the Silver Star, Legion of Merit, Distinguished Flying Cross and five Air Medals. Died on April 2, 1954.

Vincent, Clinton Dermott (1914-1955) Born on November 29, 1914, in Gale, Texas. Commissioned in the field artillery from West Point in 1936. Completed flying training and transferred to the Air Corps in October 1937. Executive officer of American Air Base Command, China-Burma-India Theater of Operations, February-November 1942, then operations officer, later executive officer, China Air Task Force, November 1942-March 1943. Acting chief of staff, later commander of forward echelon, then chief of staff of Fourteenth Air Force. Brigadier general in June 1944, at age 29 the second youngest American general or flag officer in World War II. Reverted to colonel after the war. Commanded wings at Napier Field and Randolph Field August 1945-August 1946. Died suddenly on July 6, 1955 at Colorado Springs, Colorado. Decorations included the Distinguished Service Medal, Silver Star, Legion of Merit, two Distinguished Flying Crosses, four Air Medals and the Purple Heart.

Walker, Kenneth Newton (1898-1945) Born in Cerrillos, New Mexico, on July 17, 1898. Enlisted service as flying cadet December 1917-November 1918. Commissioned in the Signal Corps, aviation section in November 1918. Graduated from Command and General Staff School in 1935. Operations officer of 5th

Bombardment Group 1938-1939. Executive officer at Hickam Field 1939-1940. Commanding officer of 18th Pursuit Group 1940-1941. Assistant chief of the plans division, office of the chief of the Air Corps 1941-1942. In operations division of the War Department General Staff in 1942. Brigadier general in June 1942. Commanding general of 5th Bomber Command September 1942 until missing in action over Rabaul, New Britain, on January 5, 1943. Declared dead on December 12, 1945. Decorations included the Medal of Honor and Legion of Merit. Roswell Army Air Field was renamed Walker Air Force Base in his honor in June 1949.

Walsh, Robert LeGrow (1894-1985) Born on July 25, 1894, in Walla Walla, Washington. Commissioned in the cavalry from West Point in 1916. Transferred to the Signal Corps, aviation section. Flew with the 22nd Aero Squadron at St. Mihiel and Meuse-Argonne offensives in World War I. Graduated from Command and General Staff School in 1929, the Army Industrial College in 1939 and the Army War College in 1940. Brigadier general in June 1942. Served at headquarters of Army Air Force 1942-1943. Major general in September 1943. Commanding general of Armed Forces Security Agency 1943-1944. At headquarters of Army Air Force again 1944-1945. Retired as major general in February 1953. Decorations included two Distinguished Service Medals and the Legion of Merit. Died on June 23, 1985.

Walton, Leo Andrew (1890-1961) Born on October 7, 1890, in Salem, Oregon. Commissioned in the cavalry from West Point in 1915. With Pershing on the Punitive Expedition into Mexico 1916. Transferred to the Air Service in 1920. Graduated from Command and General Staff School in 1938. Commanding officer of Air Corps Advanced Flying School 1940-1942. Brigadier general in October 1942. Chief of staff of West Coast Air Force Training Center 1942-1944. Briefly with Sixth Air Force November 1944-February 1945. Air inspector for Army Air Force in the China Theater of Operations 1945-1946. Assignments after the war included commanding general of Fourteenth Air Force 1946-1948. Retired as major general in June 1949. Decorations included the Legion of Merit and Bronze Star. Died on September 7, 1961.

Wash, Carlyle Hilton (1893-1943) Born on October 15, 1893, in Minneapolis, Minnesota. Commissioned in the cavalry from West Point in 1913. Served with the Punitive Expedition into Mexico 1916-1917. Transferred to the Air Service in 1917. Served in World War I. Graduated from the Command and General Staff School in 1936. Brigadier general in October 1940. Special observer in England in 1941. Commanding general of 2nd Interceptor Command 1941-1942, Third Air Force June-November 1942 and 2nd Air Support Command December 1942 until his death from an airplane accident in Alabama on January 26, 1943. Decorations included the posthumous Legion of Merit.

Weaver, Walter Reed (1885-1944) Born in Charleston, South Carolina, on February 23, 1885. Commissioned in the infantry from West Point in 1908. Commandant of flying cadets at Wilbur Wright Field in 1917. Organized the U.S. Army Aviation Mechanic School 1917-1918. Director of aviation mechanic training in the office of the chief of the Air Service in 1919. Received his wings in 1920. Attended Harvard University in 1924. Commanding officer of Maxwell Field 1927-1931. Chief of the plans and information division in the office of the chief of the Air Corps 1932-1933. Graduated from Army Industrial College in 1933. Commanding officer of Langley Field 1937-1939. Commandant of the Air Corps Tactical School in 1939. Brigadier general in October 1940. Commanding general of Southeast Air Corps Training Center, Maxwell Air Base in 1940. Acting chief of the Air Corps December 1941-March 1942. Commanding general of Army Air Force Technical Training Command March 1942 until retirement in December 1943. Decorations included the Distinguished Service Medal. Died on October 27, 1944.

Webster, Robert Morris (1892-1972) Born in Boston, Massachusetts, on October 19, 1892. Commissioned in the Air Service in 1918. Graduated from Command and General Staff School in 1938. Chief of the training section in the office of the chief of the Air Corps 1938-1942. With operations division of the War Department General Staff March-August 1942. Brigadier general in September 1942. Commanding general of 1st Air Support Command 1942-1943. Commanding general of 42nd Bombardment Wing 1943-1944. Major general in November 1944. Commander of Allied forces in Sardinia, then deputy commander of Twelfth Air Force 1944-1945. Assignments after the war included commanding general of Air Transport Command 1946-1947 and commanding general of First Air Force 1947-1949. Retired as major general in October 1954. Decorations included two Distinguished Service Medals, the Silver Star, Legion of Merit and two Air Medals. Died on February 28, 1972.

Weddington, Leonard Dickson (1895-1961) Born in Childress, Texas, on October 8, 1895. Commissioned in the Air Service, Officers Reserve Corps in 1918. Served in Hawaii June 1920-June 1923. Graduated from Air Corps Tactical School in 1938. Again in Hawaii at Wheeler and Bellows Fields March 1941-March 1942. Acting deputy chief of staff, then chief of staff of Seventh Air Force Service Command, Central Pacific Area March 1942-August 1944. Commander of 6th Air Service Command 1944-1945. Brigadier general in June 1945. Returned to the U.S. and hospitalized, then retired in June 1946. Decorations included the Legion of Merit, Distinguished Flying Cross, two Bronze Stars and the Purple Heart. Died on May 26, 1961.

Weikert, John Maurice (1898-1991) Born on September 29, 1898, in Gettysburg, Pennsylvania. Commissioned in the Air Service from West Point in 1923. Graduated from Command and General Staff School in 1937. Instructor at West Point 1937-1939. Commanding officer of Stewart Field 1941-1943. Assigned at headquarters of Commander in Chief Pacific Fleet 1943-1944. Commanding general of 7th Fighter Wing 1944-1946. Brigadier general in March 1945. Retired as major general in July 1953. Decorations included four Legions of Merit, the Bronze Star and Purple Heart. Died on January 2, 1991.

Weir, Benjamin Grant (1891-1991) Born on July 25, 1891, in Springfield, Ohio. Commissioned in the infantry from West Point in 1915. Transferred to the Air Service in 1917. Served in the Philippines as commanding officer of 4th Composite Group 1922-1924. Graduated from Army Industrial College in 1926 and the Command and General Staff School in 1932. Instructor at the Infantry School 1932-1936. Duty at Albrook Field, Canal Zone September 1936-December 1938. Air Corps instructor at Fort Benning July-December 1942. Served with Twelfth Air Force 1943-1944. Inspector at U.S. Strategic Air Forces 1944-1945. Brigadier general in January 1945. Reverted to colonel in March 1946. Brigadier general on the retired list in 1948. Decorations included the Legion of Merit and Bronze Star. Died on April 11, 1991.

Welsh, William Warren (1893-1960) Born in Alma, Colorado, on September 16, 1893. Attended the University of Texas in 1918. Commissioned in the Air Service in 1918. Staff officer, chief of staff and commanding general of Southeast Air Corps Training Center 1940-1943. Brigadier general in September 1942. Acting chief of staff of Army Air Force Training Command July 1943-September 1944. Assistant chief of the Air Staff for training 1944-1946. Retired in June 1946. Decorations included the Distinguished Service Medal, Legion of Merit and Commendation Ribbon. Died on July 28, 1960.

Wetzel, Emery Scott (1907-1988) Born on October 21, 1907 in Billings, Montana. Commissioned in the field artillery from West Point in 1929. Transferred to the Air Corps and earned his wings in 1930. Head of enlisted section of military personnel in the office of the chief of Army Air Force 1941-1945. Brigadier general in November 1944. Assistant chief of staff for personnel at U.S. Army Strategic Air Forces in the Pacific, then Far East Air Forces 1945-1948. Assignments after the war included chief of staff of United Nations Command Korea 1959-1961. Retired as lieutenant general in August 1961. Decorations included the Distinguished Service Medal, two Legions of Merit and the Bronze Star. Died on May 4, 1988.

Weyland, Otto Paul (1902-1979) Born in Riverside, California, on January 27, 1902. B.S. from Texas A&M in 1923. Commissioned in the Air Service in 1923. Graduated from Command and General Staff School in 1939. Assistant to the chief of aviation division, National Guard Bureau 1939-1941. Commanding officer of 16th Pursuit Group 1941-1942. Deputy director of air support at headquarters of Army Air Force 1942-1943. Brigadier general in September 1943. Commanding general of 84th Fighter Wing 1943-1944. Commanding general of 14th Tactical Air Command, providing air support to Patton's Third Army, 1944-1945. Patton called Weyland "the best damn general in the Air Corps." Major general in January 1945. Assistant commandant of Command and General Staff School 1945-1946. Assignments after the war included commanding general of Far East

Air Forces June 1951-May 1954 then commanding general of Tactical Air Command May 1954 until retirement as general in July 1959. Decorations included two Distinguished Service Medals, the Silver Star, Distinguished Flying Cross, Legion of Merit, Bronze Star and Air Medal. Died on September 2, 1979.

White, Thomas Dresser (1901-1965) Born in Walker, Minnesota, on August 6, 1901. Commissioned in the infantry in July 1920, one of the youngest graduates in history. Studied the Chinese language at Peking 1927-1931. Assistant military attache for air in Moscow and Rome 1934-1937. Military attache in Brazil 1940-1942. Assistant chief of staff, then chief of staff of Third Air Force 1942-1943. Brigadier general in November 1942. Assistant chief of staff for intelligence at headquarters Army Air Force in 1944. Deputy commander of Thirteenth Air Force September 1944-June 1945. Commanding general of Seventh Air Force 1945-1946. Assignments after the war included commanding general of Fifth Air Force 1947-1948, director of plans, then deputy chief of staff for plans, U.S. Air Force 1951-1953, vice chief, then chief of staff of U.S. Air Force 1953-1961. Retired as general in June 1961. White was proficient in Italian, Russian, Spanish, Chinese, Greek and Portuguese languages. Decorations included two Distinguished Service Medals and two Legions of Merit. Died on December 22, 1965.

Whitehead, Ennis Clement (1895-1964) Born in Westphalia, Kansas, on September 3, 1895. Attended the University of Kansas 1915-1917. Commissioned in the aviation section of the Signal Corps in 1917. Resigned in 1919 to return to the University of Kansas, from which he earned a B.E. in 1920. Commissioned in the Air Service that year. Graduated from Command and General Staff School in 1938. Duty with the War Department General Staff 1938-1941. Commanding officer of advanced flying training 1941-1942. Brigadier general in June 1942. Deputy commander, then commanding general of Fifth Air Force 1942-1945. Major general in March 1943 and lieutenant general in June 1945. Commanding general of Far East Air Forces 1945-1949. Assignments after the war included commanding general of Continental Air Command, then Air Defense Command 1949-1951. Retired as lieutenant general in July 1951. Decorations included the Distinguished Service Cross, two Distinguished Service Medals, the Silver Star, Distinguished Flying Cross and two Air Medals. Died on October 12, 1964.

Whitten, Lyman Perley (1897-1989) Born in Malden, Massachusetts, on March 25, 1897. Commissioned in the Air Service in 1918. B.S. from Massachusetts Institute of Technology in 1920. Graduated from the Command and General Staff School in 1937. Chief of the planning branch October 1938-April 1939, chief of the field service section, supply division April 1939-November 1940 and chief of the maintenance section, supply division in the office of the chief of the Air Corps November 1940-November 1941. Assistant to the commanding general of Air Service Command, then director of base services at headquarters Army Air Force November 1941-July 1943. Brigadier general in December 1942. Air Corps member of the Joint Logistics Committee, Combined Chiefs of Staff 1943-1944. Commanding general of Army Air Force Service Command, Mediterranean

Theater of Operations 1944-1945. Assistant chief of staff for supply in the European Theater of Operations 1945-1946. Retired as major general in June 1956. Decorations included the Distinguished Service Medal, two Legions of Merit and the Bronze Star. Died on September 29, 1989.

Wilkins, Paul California (1895-1968) Born in Angels Camp, California, on September 27, 1895. Attended the University of California 1916-1917. Commissioned in the Air Service in 1918. Stationed at Luke Field, Hawaii 1924-1926. Air Corps supply officer, then post chemical officer at Air Corps Advanced Flying School 1940-1941. Commanding officer of Kelly Field July 1941-July 1942. Commanding officer of San Antonio Air Depot 1942-1944. Brigadier general in May 1943. Assigned to Air Service Command March 1944 until retirement in August 1944. Decorations included the Legion of Merit. Died on June 12, 1968.

Williams, John Gordon (1896-1957) Born in Beacon, New York, on June 19, 1896. Attended Cornell University 1915-1917. Commissioned in the aviation section of the Signal Corps in 1918. Served at France Field, Panama Canal Zone in 1919 and Clark Field, Philippine Islands with the 3rd Pursuit Squadron 1926-1928. Air Corps technical adviser at Middleton Air Depot June 1938-November 1941. Assistant chief of staff for materiel, then chief of staff at Southeast Army Air Force Training Center 1941-1942. Duty with 28th Flying Training Wing December 1942-February 1943. Brigadier general in February 1943. Commanding general of 29th Flying Training Wing 1943-1945. Major general in January 1944. Commanding general of 1st Tactical Air Force Service Command April-July 1945. Chief of the flight operations division in the office of the assistant chief of Army Air Force 1945-1946. Retired in February 1950. Decorations included the Legion of Merit. Died on April 17, 1957.

Williams, Paul Langdon (1894-1968) Born in Detroit, Michigan, on April 16, 1894. B.A. from Stanford University in 1917. Commissioned in the Air Service in 1921. Commanding officer of 90th Attack Squadron June 1937-September 1940. Operations officer, then commander of 3rd Attack Group 1939-1941. Commander of 27th Bombardment Group July 1941-May 1942 then 51st Troop Carrier Wing in 1942-1943. Commanding general of 12th Air Support Command January-June 1943. Brigadier general in March 1943. Commanding general of 51st Troop Carrier Wing June 1943-February 1944 then 9th Troop Carrier Command 1944-1946. Major general in August 1944. Assignments after the war included commanding general of Third, Ninth, Second and Tenth Air Forces 1946-1950. Retired in April 1950. Decorations included the Distinguished Service Medal, Legion of Merit, two Distinguished Flying Crosses and the Air Medal. Died on March 3, 1968.

Williams, Robert Boyd (1901-1977) Born in Albany, Texas, on November 9, 1901. B.S. from Texas A&M in 1923. Commissioned in the Air Service in 1923. Graduated from Command and General Staff School in 1936. Operations officer with 2nd Bomb Group 1937-1939. Commanding officer of 49th Bomb Squadron

1939-1940. Military observer in London September 1940-January 1941. Commanding general of 2nd Bomber Command, then 1st Bomber Command 1941-1943. Brigadier general in September 1942. Commander of 1st Bomber Division July 1943-October 1944. Major general in May 1944. Commanding general of Second Air Force 1944-1946. Retired in June 1946. Decorations included the Distinguished Service Cross and Distinguished Service Medal. Died on February 10, 1977.

Wilson, Donald (1892-1978) Born in Hiner Mill, West Virginia on September 25, 1892. Attended Baltimore Polytechnic Institute 1906-1909. With the Baltimore and Ohio Railroad 1910-1916. Commissioned in the Maryland National Guard in 1917 and served on the Mexican border 1916-1917 and in France with the 29th Division in 1918. Graduated from Command and General Staff School in 1936. Director of the department of tactics and strategy at Air Corps Tactical School 1936-1940. Duty in the office of the chief of the Air Corps 1940-1941, then the War Department General Staff 1941-1942. Brigadier general in June 1942. Chief of staff of Allied Forces Southwest Pacific Area, then Fifth Air Force 1942-1944. Assigned to headquarters Army Air Force 1944-1945. Major general in March 1945. Commanding general of Army Air Force Proving Ground Command 1945-1946. Retired in March 1947. Decorations included two Distinguished Service Medals. Died on June 21, 1978.

Wilson, Russell Alger (1906-1944) Born in Dixon Springs, Illinois, on December 18, 1906. Commissioned in the Signal Corps from West Point in 1928. Qualified as aviator in March 1932. Graduated from Air Corps Tactical School in 1937. Commanding officer of 13th Reconaissance Squadron January-August 1941. Assistant to the assistant chief of staff for intelligence at Air Force Combat Command August 1941-March 1942. Executive officer, then commanding general of 4th Bombardment Wing April 1942-March 1944. Brigadier general in February 1944. Lost on a mission over Berlin on March 6, 1944. Decorations included the Distinguished Service Cross, Silver Star and two Air Medals.

Wolfe, Kenneth Bonner (1896-1971) Born in Denver, Colorado, on August 12, 1896. Enlisted service as a flying cadet in aviation section of the Signal Corps January 1918 until commissioned that July. Graduated from Command and General Staff School in 1937. Chief of the production engineering section at Wright Field, responsible for development of the B-29 1939-1943. Brigadier general in March 1942. Commanding general of 58th Bomb Wing 1943-1944. At Wright Field 1944-1945. Assignments after the war included deputy chief of staff for materiel, U.S. Air Force 1949-1951. Retired as lieutenant general in June 1951. Decorations included two Distinguished Service Medals. Died on September 20, 1971.

Wood, Jack Weston (1907-1994) Born in Faribault, Minnesota, on January 2, 1907. Attended Kansas City Junior College 1925-1927. Commissioned in the Air Corps in 1929. Served in Hawaii 1935-1937. Graduated from Air Corps Tactical

Bomber Group, and 20th Combat Bomber Wing 1942-1944. Took part in the massive air raids on Ploesti in August 1943. Brigadier general in November 1944. Assigned to SHAEF December 1944-May 1946. Retired in October 1959. Decorations included the Distinguished Service Cross, Distinguished Flying Cross, Bronze Star and two Air Medals. Died on July 18, 1994.

Wood, Myron Ray (1892-n/a) Born in Salinas, California, on December 4, 1892. Attended the University of Colorado. Commissioned in the aviation section of the Signal Corps in 1918. Assistant to the head of the plans division, office of the chief of the Air Corps in 1939. Chief of aircraft production branch in the office of the under secretary of war 1939-1940. Chief of the aircraft section in the procurement division of Services of Supply 1941-1942. Chief of Air Force Supply in the European Theater of Operations September 1942-1946. Brigadier general in June 1943.

Woodbury, Murray Clarke (1899-1978) Born in Burlington, Vermont, on October 7, 1899. Attended Norwich University 1917-1920. Commissioned in the aviation section of the Officers Reserve Corps in 1918. Called to active duty in 1928. Earned his wings in 1930. Served at Luke Field and Schofield Barracks, Hawaii January 1932-November 1935. Graduated from Air Corps Tactical School in April 1940. Commanding officer of 10th Transportation Group 1940-1941, 6th and 52nd Air Base Groups September 1941-March 1942, 50th Fighter Group March-September 1942, Norfolk Air Defense Wing September 1942-March 1943 and 5th Air Defense Wing March-June 1943. Brigadier general in February 1944. Reverted to colonel in March 1946. Retired in January 1954. Decorations included two Legions of Merit, the Distinguished Flying Cross, Bronze Star, and two Air Medals. Died on June 25, 1978.

Wooten, Ralph Hudson (1893-1969) Born in Independence, Mississippi, on August 30, 1893. B.S. from Texas A&M in 1916. Commissioned in the infantry in 1917. Attended the School of Military Aeronautics, University of Tennessee in 1918. Graduated from the Command and General Staff School in 1935 and Army War College in 1937. Duty with the operations and training division at War Department General Staff 1937-1938. Military attache in Chile 1938-1941. Assigned to the military intelligence division of the War Department General Staff July-September 1941. Brigadier general in February 1942. Commanding general of Army Air Force Technical Training Command March 1942-January 1943. Commanding general of Sixth Air Force Service Command, then chief of staff and later commanding general of Sixth Air Force February 1943-May 1944. Major general in May 1944. Commanding general of U.S. Army Forces South Atlantic, then Pacific 1944-1945. Assignments after the war included commanding general of Seventh Air Force May-December 1947. Retired in September 1948. Decorations included the Distinguished Service Medal, Legion of Merit and Bronze Star. Died on November 10, 1969.

Wurtsmith, Paul Bernard (1906-1946) Born in Detroit, Michigan, on August 9, 1906. Attended the University of Detroit 1924-1927. Enlisted service as a flying cadet August 1927-June 1928. Commissioned in the Air Corps in June 1928. Served with 17th, 41st, 50th and 49th Pursuit Groups September 1939-November 1942. Commanding officer of 5th Fighter Command November 1942-February 1945. Brigadier general in February 1943. Commanding general of Thirteenth Air Force January 1945-July 1946. Major general in March 1945. At headquarters of Strategic Air Command July 1946 until his death on September 13, 1946, when his B-25 crashed into a mountain near Asheville, North Carolina Wurtsmith Air Force Base was named in his honor in 1953. Decorations included two Distinguished Service Medals, the Silver Star, Distinguished Flying Cross and Air Medal.

York, John Y. Jr. (1890-1971) Born in Yorkville, West Virginia, on April 10, 1890. B.S. from West Virginia University in 1913. J.D. from the University of Michigan in 1916. Commissioned in the Air Service in 1917. Served at Fort Mills and Camp Nichols, Philippine Islands 1922-1924. Graduated from Air Service Balloon and Airship School in June 1926. Graduated from the Army Industrial College in 1927. M.B.A. from Harvard in 1919. Graduated from the Army War College in 1938. Duty with the plans division in the office of the chief of the Air Corps April 1941-June 1942. Member of the Munitions Board 1942-1946. Brigadier general in September 1943, major general in November 1944. Retired in January 1946. Decorations included the Distinguished Service Medal. Died on July 29, 1971.

Yount, Barton Kyle (1884-1949) Born in Troy, Ohio, on January 18, 1884. Attended Ohio University 1902-1903. Commissioned in the infantry from West Point in 1907. Transferred to the aviation section of the Signal Corps in 1917. Graduated from the Army Industrial College in 1935 and the Army War College in 1936. Commander of 18th Composite Wing 1936-1938. Brigadier general in September 1936. Commanding general of Air Corps Training Center, Randolph Field, 1938-1939. Assigned to headquarters of the Air Corps responsible for all training 1939-1940. Major general in October 1940. Commander of Panama Canal Department Air Forces, then Southeast Air District 1940-1941. Commanding general of West Coast Air Corps Training Center July 1941-March 1942. Commanding general of Army Air Force Training Command March 1942 until retirement in June 1946. Lieutenant general in September 1943. Decorations included two Distinguished Service Medals and the Legion of Merit. Died on July 11, 1949.

3

National Guard of the United States

Alexander, George Murrell (1889-n/a) Born in Virginia on August 1, 1889. Commissioned in the Virginia National Guard following graduation from Virginia Military Institute in 1909. Active duty in the Regular Army June 1916-January 1917 and July 1917-July 1919. Recalled to active duty in January 1941 as brigadier general and commander of 91st Infantry Brigade. Assistant deputy provost marshal at headquarters of European Theater of Operations August 1943-March 1945. Released from active duty in July 1945. Retired in August 1949. Decorations included the Purple Heart.

Andersen, Wilhelm Arthur (1894-n/a) Born in Maui, Hawaii, on July 22, 1894. Attended St. Louis College, Honolulu 1904-1912. Enlisted service 1917-1919. Commissioned in the infantry, Hawaiian National Guard in 1919. Called to active duty as colonel in October 1940. Commanding officer of 289th Infantry at Schofield Barracks, Hawaii 1940-1942. Brigadier general in November 1942. Reverted to colonel in May 1943. Released from active duty in December 1945.

Anderson, Alexander Edward (1889-1942) Born in New York City on November 23, 1889. Enlisted service in the New York National Guard 1910-1912. Commissioned in the infantry in August 1912. Served on the Mexican border in 1916 and with the 165th Infantry in France during World War I. Brigadier general in August 1938. Recalled to active duty at Fort McClellan in October 1940. Commanding general of 86th Infantry Division November-December 1942. Major general in December 1942. Died on December 24, 1942. Decorations included the Distinguished Service Cross and Distinguished Service Medal. Died in 1942.

Baker, Frayne (1891-1968) Born in Bismarck, North Dakota, on August 26, 1891. Commissioned in the Quartermaster Reserve Corps in 1917. Rose to colonel in the Indiana National Guard and called to active duty in January 1941. Brigadier general in August 1941. Commanding general of 68th Infantry Brigade, 34th Division June 1941-January 1942. Commanding general of 32nd Infantry Division January 1942-April 1942. Deputy chief of staff of U.S. Army Forces

Pacific February 1943-June 1946. Returned to inactive duty in October 1946. Decorations included the Distinguished Service Medal, Legion of Merit, Bronze Star. Died on August 3, 1968.

Barker, Harold Richards (1891-1965) Born in Providence, Rhode Island, on August 4, 1891. Commissioned in the Rhode Island National Guard in 1916. Brigadier general in the Rhode Island National Guard in November 1940. Called to active duty in February 1941 as commanding general of 43rd Infantry Division Artillery. Returned to inactive duty in June 1946. Decorations included two Silver Stars, the Legion of Merit, Bronze Star and Air Medal. Died on May 30, 1965.

Beightler, Robert Sprague (1892-1978) Born in Marysville, Ohio, on March 21, 1892. Attended Ohio State University 1909-1912. Enlisted service with 4th Ohio Infantry 1911-1914. Commissioned in the infantry in 1914. Duty overseas with 166th Infantry of 42nd (Rainbow) Division in World War I. Discharged in 1919 and entered the National Guard. Graduated from Command and General Staff School in 1939. Brigadier general in August 1940, major general in October 1940. Recalled to active duty as commanding general of 37th Infantry Division, one of the earliest units sent into action in the Pacific, October 1940-February 1946. Commanding general of 5th Service Command 1946-1947, 5th Armored Division 1948-1949 and the Ryukyus Command 1951-1953. Retired in July 1953. Decorations included two Distinguished Service Medals, the Silver Star, Legion of Merit, two Bronze Stars and the Purple Heart. Died on February 12, 1978.

Birkhead, Claude Vivian (1880-1950) Born in Phoenix, Oregon, on May 27, 1880. Attended Fort Worth University 1898-1899. Admitted to Texas Bar in 1899. Practiced law in San Antonio 1904-1941 except for service with the 131st Field Artillery in the AEF 1917-1919. Brigadier general in the Texas National Guard in 1923, major general in September 1936. Called to active duty in November 1940 as commanding general of 36th Division. Commanding general of internal security forces in 3rd Service Command in 1942. Retired in June 1942. Appointed brevet lieutenant general in Texas National Guard upon retirement in May 1948. Died on November 19, 1950.

Bowen, Charles Francis (1889-1977) Born in Manchester, New Hampshire, on January 13, 1889. Commissioned in the New Hampshire National Guard in 1918. Served with the 32nd Division in the AEF 1918-1919. Secretary to the governor of New Hampshire 1937-1939. Brigadier general in September 1940. Federal service as adjutant general of New Hampshire 1940-1947. Continued as adjutant general until 1954. Decorations included the Silver Star, Legion of Merit and Commendation Ribbon. Died in 1977.

Brock, Ronald Cornelius (1895-1984) Born in Coudersport, Pennsylvania, on June 25, 1895. Enlisted service in the Regular Army 1917-1919. Saw action with the AEF at the St. Mihiel and Meuse-Argonne offensives. Commissioned in the field artillery, New York National Guard, in 1921. Called to active federal service as commanding officer of the 106th Field Artillery 1940-1943. Brigadier general in April 1943. Commanding general of the 65th Infantry Division Artillery 1943-1945. Released to inactive duty at the end of the war. Died on October 29, 1984.

Brown, Ames T. (1890-1961) Born in Boston, Massachusetts, on November 3, 1890. Commissioned in the infantry, New York National Guard, in 1915. Served with the 106th Infantry at Ypres-Lis and Somme engagements in 1918. Discharged in 1919 then commissioned in the New York National Guard again in 1924. Brigadier general in February 1940 as adjutant general of New York. Director of Selective Service, New York October 1940-September 1947. Retired in November 1950. Decorations included the Distinguished Service Medal, Silver Star, Commendation Ribbon and Purple Heart. Died on May 19, 1961.

Buchanan, Kenneth (1892-1967) Born in Chicago on August 30, 1892. B.S. from the University of Illinois in 1917. Commissioned in the coast artillery reserve in 1917. Commissioned in the Illinois National Guard in 1920. Called to active duty as lieutenant colonel in 1936. In the supply division of the War Department General Staff April 1936-August 1939. Aide to General George C. Marshall 1939-1940. Duty with National Guard Bureau in 1940. At GHQ U.S. Army September 1940-May 1942. Brigadier general in May 1942. Assistant division commander of 28th Infantry Division May 1942-August 1944 then 9th Infantry Division August-October 1944. Reverted to colonel in October 1944. Brigadier general, Illinois National Guard in 1947. Retired in 1952. Decorations included the Legion of Merit and Bronze Star. Died on April 12, 1967.

Buzzell, Reginald William (1894-1959) Born in Quebec, Canada on March 22, 1894. Enlisted service with the Vermont Infantry 1914-1919. Commissioned in the infantry, Vermont National Guard in December 1919. Colonel and regimental commander in August 1938. Entered federal service in February 1941. Brigadier general in July 1942. Assistant commanding general of the Infantry Replacement Training Center at Camp Croft July 1942-April 1943. Commanding general, then assistant commanding general of Infantry Replacement Training Center at Camp Wheeler April 1943-January 1946. Released from active duty in January 1946. Assistant division commander of 43rd Infantry Division, Vermont National Guard October 1946 until retirement in July 1951. Died on January 23, 1959.

Carter, Ellerbe Winn (1884-1972) Born on March 23, 1884, in Louisville, Kentucky. B.A. from Fredricksburg College (Virginia) in 1904. LL.B. from the University of Virginia in 1907. Practiced law in Virginia and Louisville 1910-1916. Enlisted service in the First Kentucky Infantry 1911-1912. Commissioned in the infantry, Kentucky National Guard in 1912. Served on the Mexican border 1916-1917 and with the field artillery in the AEF during World War I. Brigadier general, Kentucky National Guard in July 1934 as commanding general of 63rd Field Artillery Brigade. Inducted into federal service with the 63rd in January 1941. Commanding general of 57th Field Artillery Brigade, 32nd Division December 1941-January 1942 then artillery commander of 7th Division January 1942-

February 1943. Assistant commander of Field Artillery Recruit Training Command at Fort Bragg February 1943-March 1946. Released from active duty in March 1946 and retired in June 1948. Died on October 11, 1972.

Cheshire, Godfrey (1893-n/a) Born in Charlotte, North Carolina, on January 21, 1893. Attended the University of the South. Commissioned in the Coast Artillery Corps, North Carolina National Guard in 1916. Served on active duty during World War I. Commanding officer of 113th Field Artillery, 30th Division September 1940-May 1941. Brigadier general in May 1941. Commanding general of 55th Field Artillery Brigade May 1941-April 1942. Assigned to headquarters of I Corps and VI Corps in 1942. Reverted to colonel in August 1942. Released from active duty in March 1944.

Clemens, Paul Bernard (1882-1960) Born on September 4, 1882, in Superior, Wisconsin. Enlisted service in the Wisconsin National Guard 1901-1906. Commissioned in the infantry, Wisconsin National Guard in 1906. Served on active duty during the Mexican border crisis in 1916 and as a military intelligence officer with the 32nd Division, AEF in World War I. B.Ph. from the University of Wisconsin in 1922, M.Ph. in 1927. Graduated from Command and General Staff School in 1929. Brigadier general in Wisconsin National Guard February 1929. Called to active duty as brigadier general in October 1940. Commanding general of 64th Infantry Brigade 1940-1942. Director of defense activities for the VII Corps Area from 1942. Released to inactive duty in 1944 and retired in June 1948. Decorations included the Distinguished Service Medal. Died on October 31, 1960.

Coane, Ralph Waldo (1891-n/a) Born on October 17, 1891, in Oakland, California. B.S. from the University of California in 1913. Commissioned in the field artillery, California National Guard, in 1918. Called to active duty with the 144th Field Artillery in February 1941. Brigadier general in March 1942. Commanding general of 41st Infantry Division Artillery March 1942-July 1944. Hospitalized for battle wounds until November 1944 then assigned to Special Troops, Fourth Army until retirement in March 1946. Decorations included the Purple Heart.

Colburn, Albert Edward (1895-n/a) Born on August 18, 1895, in Somersworth, New Hampshire. Graduated from Virginia Military Institute in 1918. Served on active duty in the Regular Army 1918-1919. Commissioned in the infantry, New Hampshire National Guard in October 1924. Graduated from Command and General Staff School in 1938. Called to active duty as commander of the 197th Coast Artillery 1940-1942. Brigadier general in May 1942. Commanding general of 40th Antiaircraft Artillery Brigade in Australia 1942-1945. Released from active duty as colonel in March 1946. Retired in October 1952. Decorations included the Bronze Star.

Collins, Stewart Garfield (1880-n/a) Born in St. Cloud, Minnesota, on October 29, 1880. B.S. from the University of Minnesota in 1904. Commissioned in the

4th Infantry, Minnesota National Guard in 1918. Appointed colonel and commanding officer of 151st Field Artillery in July 1940. Brigadier general in December 1940 as commander of 59th Field Artillery Brigade. Called to active duty in February 1941. Commanding general of 68th Brigade, 34th Division 1941-1942. Released from active duty in March 1942 and retired in November 1942.

Collins, Vivian Bramble (1883-1955) Born on April 15, 1883, in Plant City, Florida. Graduated from St. Louis College of Pharmacy in 1905. Commissioned in the Coast Artillery Corps, Florida National Guard in 1909. Served on active duty on the Mexican border June 1916-April 1917 and as a battalion commander with the 124th Infantry in World War I. Brigadier general in the Florida National Guard in June 1928. Served on active duty as head of the Florida Selective Service System March 1941-June 1946. Retired as major general in April 1947. Died in 1955.

Compere, Ebenezer Lattimore (1880-1963) Born on February 26, 1880, in Witcherville, Arkansas. Commissioned in the infantry, Arkansas National Guard in 1905. B.A. from Ouachita College (Arkansas) in 1906. LL.B. from the University of Arkansas in 1911. Served as colonel in World War I. Brigadier general as adjutant general of Arkansas April 1929-June 1937. Called to active duty in December 1940 as adjutant general of Arkansas for the duration of the war. Brigadier general, AUS in March 1941. Died in February 1963.

Conelly, Ludwig Shaner (1883-n/a) Born on August 29, 1883, in Kingston, Ohio. Commissioned in the infantry, Ohio National Guard in 1916. Served on active duty during the Punitive Expedition into Mexico in 1916 and with the 37th Division, AEF 1918-1919. Brigadier general, Ohio National Guard in January 1929 as commanding general of the 73rd Infantry Brigade. Entered federal service in October 1940. Served with the Army Group in Washington and the War Department Dependancy Board until June 1943, then the Replacement and School Command at Birmingham, Alabama until released from active duty in August 1945. Decorations included the Silver Star, Bronze Star and two Purple Hearts.

Cramer, Kenneth Frank (1894-1954) Born in Gloversville, New York, on October 3, 1894. B.Litt. from Princeton in 1916, M.A. in 1917. Commissioned in the infantry, Officers Reserve Corps in 1917. Served with 310th Infantry in France at the St. Mihiel and Meuse-Argonne offensives in 1918. Wounded in action and taken prisoner of war on November 5, 1918. Discharged in June 1919. Joined the Connecticut National Guard in May 1931. Assistant adjutant general of Connecticut in January 1939. Colonel of the 169th Infantry, Connecticut National Guard in November 1940. Called to active duty in February 1941. Assistant division commander of 24th Infantry Division 1941-1946. Brigadier general in July 1942. Major general in July 1946. Commanding general of 43rd Infantry Division 1946-1947. Chief of the National Guard Bureau September 1947-1954. Died of a heart attack on February 20, 1954 while hunting in Germany. Decorations included four

Silver Stars, the Legion of Merit, Bronze Star, Air Medal, Commendation Ribbon and Purple Heart.

Culbertson, Albert L. (1884-1956) Born on June 1, 1884. Commissioned in the infantry, Illinois National Guard in 1904. Wounded in combat in World War I. Brigadier general in June 1940. Called to active federal service as commander of the 66th Infantry Brigade, 33rd Division from March 1941. Decorations included the Purple Heart. Died in 1956.

Curtis, Charles Clarence (1893-1960) Born in Wisconisco, Pennsylvania, on October 29, 1893. Enlisted service with the 4th Pennsylvania Infantry on the Mexican border in 1916 and with the AEF in 1917-1919. Commissioned in the Pennsylvania National Guard in 1920. Colonel and commander of the 213th Regiment in 1938. Entered federal service in September 1940. Brigadier general in December 1941. Commander of an antiaircraft artillery brigade composed of National Guard and Regular Army regiments 1941-1943. Duty at the Antiaircraft Artillery Training Center, Fort Bliss October 1943-January 1944. Commander of 51st Antiaircraft Artillery Brigade 1944-1946. Relieved from active duty in March 1946. Major general, Pennsylvania National Guard in December 1947. Decorations included the Legion of Merit and Bronze Star. Died on June 24, 1960.

Dean, Herbert Reynolds (1882-1970) Born on September 8, 1882 in Providence, Rhode Island. Enlisted service in the Rhode Island Militia 1899-1911. Commissioned in the cavalry, Rhode Island National Guard in 1911. Active duty with Troop A in Mexico in 1916 and the 43rd Field Artillery in 1918. Returned to the insurance business after World War I but remained active in the national guard. Commander of 68th Field Artillery Brigade April 1930-February 1931. Adjutant general of Rhode Island February 1931-February 1941. Brigadier general in March 1937. Called to active duty October 1940 as director of Selective Service for Rhode Island, serving until October 1945. Major general upon retirement in February 1946. Decorations included the Distinguished Service Medal. Died on March 21, 1970.

Easley, Roy Woodson (1891-1985) Born on February 13, 1891, in Frankfort, Kentucky. Attended Cumberland College 1909-1911. Commissioned in the Quartermaster Corps in 1917. Served on active duty during World War I. Joined the Kentucky National Guard in 1921. Chief of police, then director of public safety for the city of Louisville 1926-1934. Brigadier general in July 1941 as commanding general of the 75th Infantry Brigade. Assistant division commander of 38th Infantry Division from February 1942. Reverted to colonel and released from active duty in June 1945. Died on November 25, 1985.

Eckfeldt, Roger Weed (1891-n/a) Born in New Bedford, Massachusetts, on October 31, 1891. Enlisted service with the 1st Massachusetts Field Artillery 1909-1912 and 1916-1917. B.A. from Harvard in 1913. Commissioned in the field artillery, Massachusetts National Guard in 1917. Civilian career in investment banking 1926-1941. Brigadier general in November 1934. Commanding general of 51st field artillery Brigade of 26th Division, Massachusetts National Guard, 1934-1939. Major general in November 1939. Called to active duty in January 1941. Commanding general of 26th Infantry Division 1941-1943. Member of the War Department Dependence Board August 1943 until released from active duty in October 1945.

Edmonds, James E. (1879-1969) Born on December 17, 1879, in New Orleans, Louisiana. B.A. from the University of Mississippi in 1900. Commissioned in the field artillery in 1916. Active duty 1916-1919. Managing editor of the New Orleans *Times-Picayune* 1920-1940. Brigadier general and major general in the Louisiana National Guard 1923-1940. Called to active duty in 1941. Commanding general of Camp Lee 1941-1943. Returned to inactive status in 1943. Decorations included the Legion of Merit. Died on July 16, 1969.

Edwards, Heber L. (1897-1962) Born in Park River, North Dakota, on June 16, 1897. Enlisted service with 1st North Dakota Infantry on the Mexican border 1916-1917. Commissioned in the infantry, North Dakota National Guard in 1920. LL.B. from the University of North Dakota in 1927. Appointed adjutant general of North Dakota in February 1937. Graduated from Command and General Staff School in 1939. Appointed director of the Selective Service System of North Dakota in October 1940. Called to federal service as brigadier general in February 1941 and served until returned to inactive duty in July 1947. Major general in May 1954. Retired in June 1957. Decorations included the Legion of Merit and Commendation Ribbon. Died on October 18, 1962.

Egleston, Nathaniel Hillyer (1884-1981) Born on February 13, 1884, in Elizabeth, New Jersey. B.A. from Williams College (Massachusetts) in 1906. LL.B. from New York Law School in 1908. Enlisted service in the cavalry 1907-1915. Commissioned in the cavalry, New York National Guard in 1915. Brigadier general, New York National Guard in January 1933 as commanding general of 51st Cavalry Brigade. Major general in July 1940 as commander of 21st Cavalry Division. Called to active duty as brigadier general in September 1940 in command of 102nd Coast Artillery Brigade. Returned to inactive status in January 1946 and retired in February 1948. Decorations included two Silver Stars and the Purple Heart. Died on January 7, 1981.

Esteves, Luis Raul (1893-1958) Born in Aguadilla, Puerto Rico, on April 30, 1893. Commissioned in the infantry from West Point in 1915. Served on the Mexican border in 1916. Instructor at First Officers Training Camp, Puerto Rico 1917-1918. Resigned in June 1919 and commissioned in the Puerto Rico National Guard in 1920. Colonel and regimenal commander 1924-1939. Appointed the adjutant general of Puerto Rico as brigadier general in February 1939. Entered federal service as commanding general of Puerto Rican Mobile Forces in October 1940. Major general in December 1948. Retired in 1957. Decorations included the Legion of Merit. Died on March 12, 1958.

Evans, Henry Cotheal (1895-1976) Born on September 17, 1895, in Baltimore, Maryland. B.A. from Johns Hopkins in 1917. Commissioned in the field artillery in 1917. Saw action with the 1st Division, AEF at Montelier-Noyon, Aisne-Marne, St. Mihiel and Meuse-Argonne 1917-1919. Resigned in 1921 and joined the Maryland National Guard. Called to active duty as colonel in the 29th Infantry Division in 1941. Assistant commandant of the Field Artillery Training Center in 1942. Brigadier general in August 1942. Commanding general of 76th Infantry Division Artillery 1942-1946. Reverted to inactive status in 1946. Later commanded 29th Infantry Division Artillery, then the division 1947-1954. Decorations included the Distinguished Service Cross and Silver Star. Died on February 17, 1976.

Eversburg, Eugene O. (1891-n/a) Born on September 12, 1891, in Texas. Commissioned in the infantry, Texas National Guard in 1915. Served on active duty during the Mexican border crisis May 1916-May 1917 and during World War I. Called to active federal service with the 141st Infantry in November 1940. Brigadier general in July 1941. Reverted to colonel on December 12, 1941.

Fish, Irving Andrews (1881-1948) Born in Racine, Wisconsin, On August 25, 1881. Attended the University of Wisconsin 1899-1904. Practiced law after 1904. Commissioned in the Wisconsin National Guard and served 1903-1916. Served in the U.S. Army in the Punitive Expedition into Mexico and in World World I. Brigadier general, Wisconsin National Guard in July 1927. Major general in the Wisconsin National Guard in December 1938. Called to active duty in October 1940. Commanding general of the 32nd Division October 1940-January 1944. Member of the secretary of war's Separation Board until June 1945. Died on April 25, 1948.

Fleming, Raymond Hartwell (1889-1974) Born in Waxahachie, Texas, on July 5, 1889. B.A. from Trinity University in 1915. Enlisted service in the Louisiana National Guard on the Mexican border 1916-1917. Commissioned in the field artillery in 1917. Served with the 141st Field Artillery in the AEF 1917-1919. Discharged after the war and entered the Louisiana National Guard. Adjutant general of Louisiana as major general 1928-1948. Brigadier general, U.S. Army in February 1940. Director of Selective Service in Louisiana 1940-1947. Major general in October 1942. Chief of the Army Division, National Guard Bureau 1948-1950. Acting chief, then chief of the National Guard Bureau September 1950 until released from active duty in February 1953. Adjutant general of Louisiana 1952-1956 and 1960-1964. Decorations included the Distinguished Service Medal. Died on November 23, 1974.

Frazier, Thomas Alexander (1894-1969) Born in Chattanooga, Tennessee, on October 31, 1894, the son of former governor and U.S. Senator James B. Frazier. B.A. from Vanderbilt in 1917. Commissioned in the 11th Cavalry in 1917. Saw action with First Army, AEF at Aisne-Marne, St. Mihiel and Meuse-Argonne in

1918. Discharged in 1919. Private law practice 1920-1939. Appointed adjutant general of Tennessee in January 1939. Brigadier general and director of Selective Service for Tennessee in September 1940. Released from active duty in September 1945. Died on May 2, 1969.

Fuller, Howard Ellsworth (1892-1975) Born on July 12, 1892, in Pawtucket, Rhode Island. B.S. from Dartmouth in 1915. Commissioned in the infantry in 1917. Served with the AEF 1917-1918. Discharged in 1919 and joined the Officers Reserve Corps in 1920. LL.B. from Boston University Law School in 1920. Transferred to the Massachusetts National Guard in 1923. In private law practice 1923-1941. Entered active duty as colonel in January 1941 and commanding officer of the 182nd Infantry until 1943. Brigadier general in October 1942. Director of training then commanding general of the Infantry Replacement Training Center, Fort McClellan November 1943-December 1944. Member of the secretary of war's Separation Board 1944-1945. Died on December 8, 1975.

Grahl, Charles Harry (1894-1981) Born on September 23, 1894, in Council Bluffs, Iowa. Enlisted service with 3rd Infantry, Iowa National Guard 1914-1921. Commissioned in the infantry, Iowa National Guard, in 1921. Assistant adjutant general of Iowa 1927-1932. Brigadier general as adjutant general in January 1932. Called to active service in December 1940 as state director of selective service. Released from federal service in July 1947. Decorations included the Distinguished Service Medal, Legion of Merit and Commendation Ribbon. Died on February 16, 1981.

Grayson, Thomas Jackson (1896-1962) Born in Mobile, Alabama, on May 5, 1896. Commissioned in the infantry in 1917. Saw action with the AEF in World War I. Wounded in action on October 2, 1918. Brigadier general in the Mississippi National Guard in July 1933. Called to active duty in October 1940 as director of Mississippi Selective Service. Served until released to inactive status in June 1942. Decorations included the Distinguished Service Cross and Purple Heart. Died on April 6, 1962.

Guerre, Louis Francis (1884-1966) Born on July 29, 1884, in New Orleans, Louisiana. Attended Louisiana State University. Commissioned in the infantry, Louisiana National Guard, in 1907. Served on the Mexican border in 1916. Commissioned in the Regular Army in 1917. Served with the 39th Division during World War I. Brigadier general in the Louisiana National Guard in 1934. Called to active duty as brigadier general in November 1940. Commanding general of 61st Infantry Brigade, 31st "Dixie" Division 1940-1942. Director of the internal security division in the VII Corps Area 1942-1944. Commanding general of Camp Claiborne 1944-1945. Released from active duty in October 1945. Decorations included the Legion of Merit. Died on August 21, 1966.

Guthner, William E. (1884-1951) Born in Germany on December 1, 1884. Enlisted service with the 6th Cavalry 1902-1905. Commissioned in the infantry in

1917. Graduated from Command and General Staff School in 1929. Brigadier general, Colorado National Guard in February 1934. Director of public safety in Denver, Colorado 1934-1940. Called to active federal service in September 1940 as commanding general of 89th Infantry Brigade, 45th Division until 1942. Assigned to the VI Corps Area 1942-1945. Retired in June 1948. Died on January 24, 1951.

Haffner, Charles Christian Jr. (1895-n/a) Born on March 15, 1895, in Bloomville, Ohio. Commissioned in the field artillery, Illinois National Guard in 1917. Served with the field artillery in the AEF in 1918. B.A. from Yale University in 1919. In the banking industry in Chicago 1927-1933, then with R.R. Donnelly & Sons 1927-1933. Brigadier general, Illinois National Guard in September 1940. Called to active duty in March 1941 as commanding general of 58th Field Artillery Brigade. Major general in December 1942. Commanding general of 103rd Division 1944-1945 then the Infantry Advanced Replacement Training Center at Camp Rucker in 1945. Released from active duty in August 1945.

Hardy, David P. (1890-1957) Born on May 24, 1890, in Petaluma, California. B.S. from the University of California in 1912. High school teacher and deputy superintendent of schools in San Francisco 1912-1916. Enlisted service with the California National Guard on the Mexican border 1914-1917. Commissioned in the Coast Artillery Corps, California National Guard in 1917. Entered federal service as commanding officer of 250th Coast Artillery in Alaska September 1940-December 1941. Brigadier general in November 1941. Commanding general of harbor defenses at Chesapeake Bay 1941-1942. Training duty at Camp Pendleton, Camp Maxie and Camp Ord 1942-1945. Deputy commander of XXXVI Corps 1945-1946. Released from federal service in February 1946. Died while attending the national rifle matches at Camp Perry, Ohio, in September 1957.

Haskell, William N. (1878-1952) Born in Albany, New York, on August 13, 1878. Commissioned in the cavalry from West Point in 1901. Served in the Philippines 1901-1902. Graduated from Infantry and Cavalry School in 1904 and Army Staff College in 1905. Again in the Philippines 1906-1907 and 1912-1914. Regimental commander in Mexico 1916-1917. Assistant chief of staff of 77th Division, then chief of operations and deputy chief of staff at Second Army, AEF in World War I. Chief of the American relief mission to Russia 1921-1923. LL.D. from Georgetown University in 1925. Resigned from the Army and appointed major general and commander of the New York National Guard in January 1926. Called to active duty as commanding general of 27th Division in October 1940 and served until released to inactive status in July 1942. Director of civil protection for the state of New York in 1942. Lieutenant general upon retirement in August 1942. Died on August 13, 1952.

Hawkins, Sion Boone (1887-n/a) Born on August 19, 1887, in Americus, Georgia. Enlisted service with the 4th Regiment, Georgia National Guard 1904-

1918. Attended the University of Georgia. Commissioned in the infantry, Officers Reserve Corps in 1918. Served with the 82nd Division in the AEF 1918-1919. Discharged in 1919. Joined the Georgia National Guard in 1926. Brigadier general, Georgia National Guard in March 1941 as adjutant general of Georgia. Called to active duty as director of selective service for Georgia and served from May 1941.

Henninger, Guy Nelson (1895-1977) Born in Shelton, Nebraska, on July 16, 1895. B.S. from the University of Nebraska in 1918. Enlisted service in the Aviation Section of the Signal Reserve Corps in 1918. Commissioned in the Aviation Section in 1919. Appointed adjutant general of Nebraska in January 1939. Brigadier general in November 1939. Called to active federal service and assigned as director of Selective Service for Nebraska in October 1940. Released from active duty in June 1947. Decorations included the Distinguished Service Medal and CR. Died on October 30, 1977.

Hervey, Harcourt (1892-1970) Born in Los Angeles, California, on September 2, 1892. B.A. from the University of California in 1916. Commissioned in the field artillery in 1916. Served with the AEF 1916-1918. Resigned in 1920. Affiliated with the California National Guard in 1922. Brigadier general in July 1937. Called to active federal service in March 1941. Commanding general of 80th Infantry Brigade March-April 1941 then 65th Field Artillery Regiment until September 1942. Commander of 40th Infantry Division Artillery from September 1942. Decorations included the Purple Heart. Died on September 26, 1970.

Hollar, Gordon Cloyd (1887-1963) Born on December 7, 1887, in Sioux City, Iowa. Enlisted service in Iowa National Guard 1907-1913. Commissioned in the infantry, Iowa National Guard in 1913. Served on the Mexican border 1916-1917. Chief of police in Sioux City 1930-1934, then commissioner of public safety 1935-1938. Member of the Iowa Tax Commission 1939-1941. Brigadier general, Iowa National Guard in October 1940. Called to active duty as brigadier general in February 1941. Commanding general of 67th Infantry Brigade February 1941-August 1942. Deputy provost marshal for Services of Supply in the European Theater August 1942-January 1946. Died on September 28, 1963

Howe, William Francis (1888-n/a) Born on December 16, 1888, in Dorchester, Massachusetts. Graduated from Yale University in 1913. Enlisted service with the Massachusetts National Guard 1914-1916. Commissioned in the field artillery, Massachusetts National Guard in 1917. Battery commander in 102nd Field Artillery, AEF 1917-1919. Brigadier general, Massachusetts National Guard in November 1939. Called to active duty as brigadier general January 1941. Commanding general of 51st Field Artillery Brigade 1941-1942. Reverted to colonel in September 1942. Commandant of Army Schools, then professor of military science and tactics at Yale University from 1943.

Hutchison, Joseph Carson (1894-1982) Born on September 17, 1894, in Cross Hill, South Carolina. B.A. from Wofford College in 1915. Enlisted service in the field artillery 1917-1919. Commissioned in the infantry, Florida National Guard in 1921. Called to active duty as brigadier general in November 1940. Commanding general of 62nd Infantry Brigade 1940-1942. Assistant division commander of 31st Infantry Division 1942-1946. Returned to inactive status in 1946. Major general as commanding general of 48th Infantry Division, Florida National Guard in 1951. Decorations included the Silver Star, Legion of Merit, Bronze Star and Air Medal. Died on December 7, 1982.

Immell, Ralph Maxwell (1894-n/a) Born on September 11, 1894, in Blair, Wisconsin. Graduate of the University of Wyoming in 1928. LL.B. from the University of Wisconsin in 1921. Commissioned in the infantry, Wisconsin National Guard in 1917. Commander of the 53rd Cavalry Brigade in 1938. Adjutant general of Wisconsin in 1940. Brigadier general, Wisconsin National Guard in January 1941. Called to active duty as colonel in October 1942. Served at headquarters of Services of Supply October-December 1942. Commanded installation number two, Atlantic Base Section January-June 1943, general depot number two, Eastern Base Section in the North African Theater June-July 1943 and the center district, Mediterranean Base Section 1943-1944. Brigadier general, AUS in January 1944. Commanding general of Peninsula Base Section, North African Theater June-October 1944 then deputy commander of the Continental Advance Section, European Theater October 1944-July 1945. Assigned to the War Department General Staff from July 1945. Major general in September 1945. Decorations included the Distinguished Service Medal and Legion of Merit.

Johnson, Harry Hubbard (1895-n/a) Born in Eagle Lake, Texas, on April 11, 1895. Attended Texas A&M University. Commissioned in the infantry, Texas National Guard in 1917. Served on active duty with the AEF 1917-1919, including the Meuse-Argonne offensive. Called to active duty as lieutenant colonel in November 1940. Executive officer of 124th Cavalry 1940-1941. Commanding officer of 112th Cavalry September-November 1941. Brigadier general in November 1941. Commander of 2nd Cavalry Brigade November 1941-January 1942. Commanding general of 56th Cavalry brigade 1942-1943. Major general in February 1943. Commanding general of 2nd Cavalry Division 1943-1944. Allied military governor in Rome in 1944. Commanding general of 93rd Infantry Division 1944-1945. Released from active duty in November 1946.

Jones, Edwin Whiting (1896-1956) Born in Huntsville, Alabama, on December 7, 1896. B.S. from the University of Alabama in 1918. Commissioned in the engineer reserve in 1918. Served with the Corps of Engineers, Officers Reserve Corps 1918-1922. Civil engineer 1919-1941. Called to active duty as colonel in the 151st Engineer Regiment of the Alabama National Guard in January 1941. Brigadier general in July 1942. Commanding general of Army Post Nome, Alaska 1942-1944. Duty with the chief of engineers 1944-1945. Decorations included the Legion of Merit. Died in 1956.

Kernan, Redmond Francis (1895-1982) Born on November 9, 1895, in New Jersey. Commissioned in the field artillery from West Point in 1917. Served with the AEF in 1918. Resigned in 1922 and entered the New York National Guard. J.D. from Fordham University in 1927. Called to active duty as colonel in October 1940. Chief of staff of 27th Division, then commanding general of 52nd field artillery Brigade 1940-1942. Brigadier general in January 1942. Served in Saipan 1942-1944. Member of the War Department Special Staff 1945-1946. Released from active duty in January 1947. Decorations included the Bronze Star. Died on June 15, 1982.

Key, William Shaffer (1889-1959) Born in Dudleyville, Alabama, on October 6, 1889. Enlisted service 1907-1910 then commissioned in the Georgia National Guard in 1910. Served on the Mexican border 1916-1917 and attained colonel with the AEF 1918-1919. Warden at Oklahoma State Penitentiary 1924-1927. Brigadier general in August 1928, major general in April 1937. Called to active duty as commanding general of 45th Division in September 1940 and served until October 1942. Provost marshal general at the European Theater October 1942-June 1943. Commanding general of U.S. Forces Iceland June 1943-December 1944. Chief of U.S. Military Control Commission Hungary December 1944-August 1946. Returned to inactive status in August 1946. Decorations included two Distinguished Service Medals, the Legion of Merit, Bronze Star and Commendation Ribbon. Died on January 5, 1959.

King, Woods (1900-1947) Born on January 31, 1900, in Cleveland, Ohio. B.A. from Williams College in 1919. Commissioned in the field artillery, Ohio National Guard in 1919. Commanding officer of 107th Cavalry 1936-1941. Called to active duty in March 1941. Served with the China Combat Command. Brigadier general, AUS in June 1945. Retired in June 1946. Decorations included the Distinguished Service Medal and Legion of Merit. Died on January 15, 1947.

Kreber, Leo Myron (1896-1973) Born in Akron, Ohio, on August 15, 1896. Commissioned in the field artillery from West Point in 1918. Resigned from the Regular Army in 1922 and commissioned in the 62nd Field Artillery Brigade, Ohio National Guard. Entered federal service in October 1940. Brigadier general in May 1941. Commanding general of 37th Infantry Division Artillery 1942-1946. Released from active service in June 1946. Major general in November 1946. Commanding general of 37th Infantry Division, Ohio National Guard 1946-1949. Adjutant general of Ohio 1949-1959. Retired in 1959. Decorations included the Distinguished Service Medal, Silver Star, two Legions of Merit, the Bronze Star, Air Medal and Purple Heart. Died on September 5, 1973.

Lawton, Samuel Tilden (1884-1961) Born in Peoria, Illinois, on April 1, 1884. LL.B. from John Marshall Law School in 1905. Commissioned in the cavalry, Illinois National Guard in 1912. Federal service 1916-1919. Brigadier general in March 1936, major general in June 1940. Called to active duty in 1941. Commanding general of 33rd Infantry Division March 1941-April 1942. Commanding general of Great Lakes Sector, Central Defense Command, then Sault St. Marie Military Area 1943-1944. Member of the War Department Dependency Board 1944-1945. Retired as lieutenant general. Died in January 1961.

Ledbetter, Louis A. (1890-n/a) Born in Gainesville, Texas, on July 5, 1890. LL.B. from the University of Oklahoma in 1912. Commissioned in the Oklahoma National Guard in 1918. Adjutant general of Oklahoma 1938-1940. Brigadier general in July 1940. Called to active duty in September 1940 as commanding general of 90th Infantry Brigade. Reverted to colonel in May 1942 and continued on active duty until October 1944.

Lewis, Joseph H. (1888-1968) Born on March 28, 1888, in Washington, DC. Commissioned in the Michigan National Guard in 1912. Graduated from National Guard courses at AWC in 1925 and Command and General Staff School in 1926. Brigadier general in November 1940. Called to active duty in April 1941. Commanding general of 72nd Field Artillery Brigade 1941-1943. Reverted to inactive status as colonel in August 1943. Died in 1968.

Logan, Francis Vincent (1891-n/a) Born in Boston, Massachusetts, on July 16, 1891, the son of Brigadier General Lawrence J. Logan. Commissioned in the infantry, Massachusetts National Guard, in April 1917. Brigadier general in April 1939. Called to active duty in November 1940 as brigadier general, AUS. Commanding general of 52nd Infantry Brigade, 26th Division 1941-1942. Assistant division commander of 26th Infantry Division December 1942-April 1943. Assistant commanding general of the Infantry Replacement Training Center at Camp Croft from April 1943.

Lowry, Sumter de Leon Jr. (1893-n/a) Born on August 27, 1893, in St. Augustine, Florida. Graduate of Virginia Military Institute in 1914. Commissioned in the infantry, Florida National Guard in 1914. Federal service on the Mexican border 1916-1917 and with 124th Infantry, 31st Division 1917-1919. Brigadier general as commanding general of 56th Filed Artillery Brigade in December 1934. Called to active duty in November 1940. Commanding general of 31st Infantry Division Artillery 1940-1944. Duty at headquarters of Army Ground Forces January-March 1945, then assistant commanding general at the Infantry Replacement Training Center, Camp Livingston March 1945 until released from active duty in September 1945. Major general in September 1946. Retired as lieutenant general in 1952. Decorations included the Distinguished Service Medal and Bronze Star.

March, William A. (1884-1963) Born on January 1, 1884, in Pennsylvania. C.E. from Princeton in 1908. Commissioned in the infantry, Pennsylvania National Guard in 1913. Called to federal service in January 1941. Brigadier general, Pennsylvania National Guard in February 1941. Commanding general of 73rd Field

Artillery Brigade July 1941-September 1942. Reverted to colonel in September 1942. Died on July 3, 1963.

Marchant, Trelawney E. (1887-1950) Born in Lexington, South Carolina, on May 11, 1887. Graduate of Draughons Business College in 1911. Enlisted service in the National Guard 1905-1910. Commissioned in the South Carolina National Guard in 1910. Duty on the Mexican border 1916-1917 and with the AEF in France 1917-1919. Brigadier general in 1932. Graduated from Command and General Staff School in 1940. Called to active duty as brigadier general in September 1940. Commander of 59th Infantry Brigade 1940-1942. Commanding general of Sault St. Marie District at Fort Brady May-December 1942. Duty with 5th Service Command from December 1942. Died in 1950.

Marlin, William Lloyd (1882-1959) Born on October 17, 1882, in Covington, Ohio. Commissioned in the infantry, Ohio National Guard in 1911. Served on active duty with the Third Infantry during World War I and on occupation duty with the 6th and 90th Divisions. Mayor of Covington 1920-1921. With Veterans Administration 1922-1940. Brigadier general, Ohio National Guard in December 1936 as commanding general of 62nd Field Artillery Brigade. Called to active duty in October 1940 in command of 74th Infantry Brigade. Released from active duty in September 1942. Retired in October 1946. Decorations included the Distinguished Service Cross and Purple Heart. Died on June 17, 1959.

Martin, Edward (1879-1967) Born on September 18, 1879, in Ten Mile, Pennsylvania. Enlisted in the Pennsylvania National Guard in 1898 and served with the 10th Pennsylvania Volunteer Infantry in the Spanish-American War. B.A. from Waynesburg College in 1901. Commissioned in 1901. Served with the Punitive Expedition into Mexico June-October 1916. Saw action with the 109th and 110th Regiments in France 1917-1919. Brigadier general, Pennsylvania National Guard in August 1922. Auditor general of Pennsylvania, then treasurer 1925-1933. Major general, Pennsylvania National Guard June in 1939. Adjutant general of Pennsylvania 1939-1941. Called to active duty as commanding general of 28th Division February 1941-January 1942. Retired in April 1942. Decorations included two Distinguished Service Crosses and two Purple Hearts. Governor of Pennsylvania 1943-1947. U.S. senator 1947-1958. Died on March 19, 1967.

McConnel, Mervin Gilbert (1882-1948) Born in Parma, Idaho, on December 29, 1882. Attended the University of Idaho. Commissioned in the field artillery, Idaho National Guard in 1909 and in the field artillery, Officers Reserve Corps in 1917. Served on active duty with the AEF in World War I. Brigadier general, Idaho National Guard in 1936, Regular Army in October 1940. Called to active duty with the adjutant general department as director of the Idaho National Guard in October 1940. Retired in November 1946. Decorations included the Legion of Merit. Died on April 29, 1948.

McLain, Raymond Stallings (1890-1954) Born on April 4, 1890, in Washington County, Kentucky. Attended Hills Business College in 1909. Commissioned in the infantry, Oklahoma National Guard in 1916. Graduated from Command and General Staff School in 1938. Brigadier general, Oklahoma National Guard in June 1937. Called to active duty in September 1940. Commanding general of 45th Infantry Division Artillery, then 30th Infantry Division Artillery 1940-1944. Major general in August 1944. Commanding general of 90th Infantry Division in 1944. Commanding general of XIX Corps 1944-1945. Lieutenant general in June 1945. Assistant chief of information, then chief of information, U.S. Army 1946-1949. Comptroller of the Army 1949-1952. Retired in March 1952. Decorations included two Distinguished Service Crosses, two Distinguished Service Medals, the Silver Star and two Bronze Stars. Died on December 14, 1954.

Means, Lewis M. (1890-1971) Born on July 15, 1890, in Camden County, Missouri. Enlisted service April-August 1917. Commissioned in the infantry following graduation from the First Officers Training Camp at Fort Riley in August 1917. Served on active duty until discharged in February 1919. Commissioned captain in the Missouri National Guard in 1922. Commanding officer of the 138th Infantry as major in 1923. Appointed adjutant general of Missouri in 1937 by Governor Stark and commissioned brigadier general in May 1938. Called into federal service in December 1940. Commanding general of 70th Infantry Brigade, 35th Division 1940-1942. Reverted to colonel in August 1942. Died on June 8, 1971.

Miltonberger, Butler Buchanan (1897-1977) Born on August 31, 1897, in North Platte, Nebraska. Enlisted service in Mexico and with the AEF in WWI. Commissioned in the infantry, Nebraska National Guard in 1923. He was serving as battalion commander in the 134th Infantry Regiment when mobilized in December 1940. Commanded the 134th Infantry Regiment May 1941-February 1945. Brigadier general in February 1945. Assistant division commander of 35th Division 1945-1946. Major general in February 1946. Chief of the National Guard Bureau 1946-1947. Retired in August 1947. Decorations included the Distinguished Service Medal and Silver Star. Died on March 23, 1977.

Mittelstaedt, Richard Eugene (1884-1973) Born on April 28, 1884, in San Francisco, California. Commissioned in the infantry, California National Guard in 1905. Served on active duty in World War I. Brigadier general, California National Guard in November 1938. Called to active duty in March 1941. Commanding general of 79th Infantry Brigade, 40th Division March-December 1941. Commander of San Diego Sub-Sector December 1941-April 1942. Assistant division commander of 40th Infantry Division in 1942. Commanding general of Maui District 1943-1944. Commander of Infantry Replacement Training Center at Camp Roberts from June 1944. Died in September 1973.

Myers, Diller S. (1887-1947) Born on November 21, 1887, in Illinois. Commissioned in the Illinois National Guard in 1912. Colonel in the California National Guard in 1924, brigadier general in August 1938. Called to active duty in March

1941 as commanding general of 65th Infantry Brigade, 33rd Division. Served until July 1942, when he reverted to colonel. Decorations included the Silver Star. Died on May 12, 1947.

Newton, Henry Carlton (1896-1981) Born on July 7, 1896, in Rankin, Illinois. Commissioned in the field artillery, California National Guard in 1918. Attended the University of Southern California 1919-1921. With the California National Guard 1921-1939. Plans and training officer at Armed Forces Replacement Training Center 1940-1941. Commanding officer of Officers Orientation School for the Armored Command at Fort Knox 1941-1942. Brigadier general in September 1942. Commanding general of Combat Command "A," 12th Armored Division 1943-1944. Staff officer at SHAEF 1944-1945. Retired in July 1956. Decorations included two Legions of merit, the Bronze Star and Commendation Ribbon. Died on November 20, 1981.

O'Brien, Maxwell A. (1890-n/a) Born in Chicago, Illinois, on November 21, 1890. LL.B. from the University of Iowa in 1914. Commissioned in the cavalry, Iowa National Guard in June 1920. Practiced law in Des Moines, Iowa. Assistant attorney general of Iowa 1924-1928. Commanding officer of 113th Cavalry from April 1936. Called to active duty in January 1941. Brigadier general, AUS in January 1942. Assistant division commander of 4th Motorized Infantry Division January 1942-November 1943. Reverted to inactive status in September 1945.

Opie, Evarts Walton (1893-n/a Born on September 13, 1893, in Staunton, Virginia. Attended Staunton Military Academy 1908-1911. Enlisted service in Virginia National Guard 1907-1911. In the newspaper business in Staunton 1911-1941. Commissioned in the infantry, Virginia National Guard in 1916. Served on active duty in World War I. Graduated from National Guard course at Command and General Staff School in 1936. Called to active duty as colonel in 1941. Commanding officer of 116th Infantry 1941-1942. Brigadier general in September 1942.

Page, John Watt (1882-1961) Born on February 20, 1882, in Manchester, Vermont. Enlisted service in the Massachusetts National Guard 1899-1901 and the Colorado National Guard 1903-1905. Commissioned in the infantry, Texas National Guard in 1907. Businessman in Fort Worth 1902-1940. Brigadier general in January 1940 as adjutant general of Texas. Active federal service as Texas director of selective service December 1940-March 1943. Retired in April 1947. Decorations included the Legion of Merit and Commendation Ribbon. Died in October 1961.

Paxton, Alexander Gallatin (1896-1974) Born in Vicksburg, Mississippi, on October 4, 1896. B.A. from Washington and Lee University in 1917. Commissioned in the field artillery, Officers Reserve Corps in 1917. Member of the Mississippi National Guard 1926-1940. Called to active duty in November 1940 as commanding officer of 114th Field Artillery. Chief of staff of 31st Infantry Division February- July 1942. Brigadier general in August 1942. Commanding general of 33rd Infantry Division Artillery 1942-1945. Released from active service in November 1945. Major general as commanding general of 31st Infantry Division, Mississippi National Guard in July 1948. Decorations included the Legion of Merit, Bronze Star and Air Medal. Died on August 11, 1974.

Penington, Carlos A. (1878-n/a) Born in Wilmington, Illinois, on May 3, 1878. Enlisted service with the West Virginia Volunteer Infantry during the Spanish-American War then in the Washington National Guard until 1909. Commissioned in the Coast Artillery Corps, Washington National Guard in 1909. Called to federal service in August 1917 and served on quartermaster duty in the AEF until discharged in August 1919. Affiliated with the field artillery reserve, then the Washington National Guard. Brigadier general in the Washington National Guard in August 1934. Called to active duty in September 1940. Commanding general of 66th Field Artillery Brigade until retirement on December 16, 1941.

Perrine, Nat Smith (1894-1952) Born on July 16, 1894, in Fort Worth, Texas. Attended Texas Agricultural and Mechanical College. Commissioned in the infantry, Texas National Guard in 1917. Served with the 142nd Infantry in France in 1918. Graduated from the National Guard course at the Command and General Staff School in 1933. Assigned to the military intelligence division of the War Department General Staff November 1933-November 1937. LL.B. from Washington College of Law in 1927. Commanding officer of 142nd Infantry November 1940-August 1942. Served as brigadier general, AUS August 1942 until released from active duty in November 1946. Died on August 11, 1952.

Persons, John Cecil (1888-1974) Born in Atlanta, Georgia, on May 9, 1888. LL.B. from the University of Alabama in 1910. Practiced law in Tuscaloosa, Alabama, 1910-1915. Commissioned in the infantry in 1917. Served on active duty with the AEF in World War I. In the banking industry in Tuscaloosa 1919-1939. Brigadier general in the Alabama National Guard as commander of the 62nd Infantry Brigade 1930-1939. Called to active duty as major general and commander of 31st Division November 1940-May 1948. Retired as lieutenant general in May 1948. Decorations included the Distinguished Service Cross and Distinguished Service Medal. Died on December 24, 1974.

Powell, Clifford Ross (1893-1973) Born on July 26, 1893, in Lumberton, New Jersey. Enlisted service with the New Jersey National Guard 1913-1914. Commissioned in the infantry in 1917 and transferred to the Aviation Section later that year. Served on active duty with the 9th Bombardment Group, AEF at Oise-Aisne, St. Mihiel and Meuse-Argonne. Pursued a career in banking in New Jersey. Member of the New Jersey House of Representatives 1922-1928 and the Senate 1928-1939. Brigadier general, New Jersey National Guard in February 1937, major general in June 1939. Graduated from the national guard course at Command and General Staff School in 1940. Called to active federal service in September 1940. Commander of Fort Dix October 1940-March 1941. Commanding general of 44th Division 1941-1942. Reverted to colonel in September 1942. Decorations included the Purple Heart. Died on March 28, 1973.

Pyron, Walter Braxton (1882-1951) Born in Mecklenburg County, North Carolina, on April 10, 1882. Enlisted service in the Texas National Guard 1905-1909. Commissioned in the cavalry, Texas National Guard in 1921. Commanding general of 56th Cavalry Brigade August 1938 until induction into federal service as brigadier general in November 1940. Served in the office of the under secretary of war 1941-1942 and briefly at headquarters of the Services of Supply in 1942. An oil company executive in civilian life, Pyron was selected to head the Army-Navy Oil Board in July 1942 and served there until released from active duty in October 1945. Retired in April 1947. Decorations included the Legion of Merit. Died on January 8, 1951.

Reckord, Milton A. (1879-1975) Born in Harford County, Maryland, on December 28, 1879. Enlisted service with Maryland National Guard 1901-1903. Commissioned in the First Maryland Infantry in 1903. Served on the Mexican border in 1917 and in the AEF 1917-1918. Saw action at Meuse-Argonne in command of the 115th Infantry Regiment. Appointed adjutant general of Maryland in 1920. Brigadier general of the line in February 1924 and major general in April 1934. Commanded the 29th Division 1934-1941. Called to federal service in February 1941. Commanding general of III Corps Area January 1942-December 1943. Duty as theater provost marshal in the European Theater 1943-1945. Served in the office of the chief of staff, U.S. Army June-October 1945. Decorations included four Distinguished Service Medals and the Bronze Star. Died on September 9, 1975.

Rilea, Thomas Edward (1895-1959) Born on May 5, 1895, in Chicago, Illinois. Enlisted service with the Third Oregon Infantry 1914-1916. B.S. from Oregon Institute of Technology in 1916. Commissioned in the adjutant general department in 1918. Served at GHQ, AEF 1918-1919. Discharged from federal service in 1919. Graduated from the national guard course at the Army War College in 1929. Brigadier general, Oregon National Guard in January 1931. Called to active duty in September 1940. Commander of 82nd Infantry Brigade 1941-1942. Assistant division commander of 41st Infantry Division 1942-1943. Commander of Army Services of Supply Base at Sydney, Australia 1943-1945. Commanding general of the Infantry Replacement Training Center at Fort McClellan 1945-1946. Decorations included the Distinguished Service Medal, Bronze Star, Commendation Ribbon and Purple Heart. Died on February 3, 1959.

Robinson, Donald Brandt (1891-n/a) Born on June 14, 1891, in Kansas City, Missouri. Enlisted service in the Minnesota National Guard 1909-1917. Commissioned in the 6th Infantry, Minnesota National Guard in 1922. Graduated from the National Guard course, Command and General Staff School in 1939. Brigadier general in December 1940. Called to active duty in January 1941. Commanding general of 101st Coast Artillery Brigade January 1941-April 1944 then the 62nd Antiaircraft Artillery Brigade April-August 1944.

Rollins, Francis Willard (1893-n/a) Born on December 1, 1893, in Springfield, Massachusetts. Attended Brown University 1912-1914. Commissioned in the field artillery, Rhode Island National Guard in 1917. Served on active duty on the Mexican border in 1917 and in the AEF during World War I. including the Aisne-Marne, St. Mihiel, Oise-Marne and Meuse-Argonne engagements. Called to active duty as brigadier general in September 1942. Assigned to the Field Artillery Replacement Training Center at Camp Roberts October 1942-January 1943. Commanding general of 66th Division Artillery 1943-1945.

Rose, Edward Clark (1892-1967) Born on December 2, 1892, in Trenton, New Jersey. Graduated from Penn State University in 1914. LL.D. from Rider College. Served with 35th Division Artillery in the AEF 1917-1919. Commissioned in the ordnance department, Officers Reserve Corps in 1920. Transferred to the Quartermaster Corps, New Jersey National Guard in 1924. Brigadier general and commander of 69th Field Artillery Brigade in August 1938. Called to federal service in September 1940 and releases from active duty in September 1941. Re-entered federal service as colonel in October 1942. Liaison officer with the British Fourteenth Army in the China-Burma-India Theater of Operations 1942-1944. Chief of transportation in the CBI Theater of Operations 1944-1945. Brigadier general again in February 1945. Separated from active service in December 1945. Major general, New Jersey National Guard in March 1949. Decorations included the Distinguished Service Medal and Legion of Merit. Died in 1967.

Rose, William Irwin (1898-1954) Born on September 8, 1898, in Worcester, Massachusetts. Enlisted service with the Massachusetts National Guard 1916-1918. Discharged in July 1919 then commissioned in the 104th Infantry, Massachusetts National Guard in 1920. Brigadier general Massachusetts National Guard in January 1937 as commanding general of 51st Infantry Brigade. Called to active duty in September 1940. Commanding general of U.S. forces at Efate, New Hebrides and Espiritu Santo 1942-1943. Commanding general of Provisional Island Command South Pacific July 1943-December 1944. Training officer at Infantry Replacement Training Center, Camp Fannin 1944-1946. Released from active service in November 1946. Major general, Massachusetts National Guard in February 1958. Decorations included the Legion of Merit and Bronze Star. Died on June 9, 1954.

Ross, Ogden J. (1893-1968) Born on April 6, 1893, in Troy, New York. Graduate of Albany Law School in 1915. Enlisted service in the 2nd Infantry November 1910-March 1917. Commissioned in the infantry, New York National Guard in 1917. Served on active duty with the AEF in World War I 1917-1919. Wounded in September 1918. Member of the governor's staff 1923-1937. Brigadier general in September 1940 as commander of 53rd Infantry Brigade. Called to active duty as brigadier general and commanding general of the 53rd Infantry in

October 1940. Released from active service in May 1946. Major general, New York National Guard in April 1953. Retired in April 1957. Decorations included the Silver Star and Purple Heart. Died on October 27, 1968.

Russell, Henry Dozier (1889-1972) Born on December 27, 1889, in McDonough, Georgia. B.A. from the University of Georgia in 1912 and LL.B. in 1914. Commissioned in the infantry, Georgia National Guard in 1916. Served on the Mexican border in 1916 and with the 31st Division in France 1917-1918. Released from federal service in 1919 then commissioned colonel in the infantry, Georgia National Guard in May 1921. Brigadier general, Georgia National Guard in January 1923, major general in September 1932. Called to active duty in September 1940 as commanding general of 30th Division. Assigned to headquarters of I Corps, then assistant commanding general of Replacement and School Command in Birmingham in 1942. Member of 5th section, field agencies, War Department Manpower Board 1943-1944 then the Pearl Harbor Board 1944-1945. Released from active duty then commanding general of 48th Division, Georgia National Guard. Retired in 1951. Died on December 31, 1972.

Safay, Fred A. (1897-1952) Born on June 15, 1897, in Jacksonville, Florida. Attended Florida Military Academy 1916-1917. Commissioned in the infantry, Florida National Guard in 1920. Sanitation officer with the Florida Health Department 1923-1938, then director 1938-1940. Colonel and commanding officer of 124th Infantry when called to active duty in November 1940. Brigadier general in September 1942. Reverted to colonel in August 1943, released from active duty in October 1944 and retired in June 1946. Died on January 4, 1952.

Saltzman, Charles Eskridge (1903-1994) Born on September 19, 1903, in Mindanao, Philippine Islands, the son of Major General Charles M. Saltzman. Attended Cornell University 1920-1921. Commissioned in the Corps of Engineers from West Point in 1925. Resigned from the Army and joined the New York National Guard in 1930. Member of the New York Stock Exchange 1935-1940. Recalled to active duty as lieutenant colonel in 1940. Deputy chief of staff of 5th Army and 15th Army Group 1943-1945. Brigadier general in January 1945. Released from active service in July 1946. Assistant secretary of state 1947-1949. Under secretary of state for administration 1954-1955. Retired as major general in September 1967. Decorations include the Distinguished Service Medal and Legion of Merit. Died on June 16, 1994.

Sands, William Hamilton (1892-1978) Born on May 13, 1892, in Richmond, Virginia. Attended Richmond College 1906-1908, Carnegie Institute of Technology 1908-1910 and the University of Virginia 1915-1916. Commissioned in the field artillery, Virginia National Guard in 1917. Served with the 80th Division, AEF in World War I. Practiced law in Norfolk 1916-1940. Graduated from the National Guard course, Command and General Staff School in 1929. Brigadier general in November 1939. Commanding general of 54th Field Artillery Brigade, 29th Division. Called to active duty as brigadier general in February 1941. Commanding general of 29th Infantry Division Artillery 1941-1945. Retired as major general in May 1954. Decorations included two Silver Stars, two Legions of Merit, three Bronze Stars, the Commendation Ribbon and Purple Heart. Died on July 4, 1978.

Scott, Donnell Everett (1887-n/a) Born on March 3, 1887, in Graham, North Carolina. Enlisted service 1904-1906. B.S. from Davidson College in 1907. Commissioned in the infantry, North Carolina National Guard in 1906. Served in the AEF April 1918-March 1919. Brigadier general in January 1937. Called to active duty as brigadier general in September 1940. Commanding general of 60th Infantry Brigade September 1940-February 1942 then the Internal Secruity Force at District One, 3rd Service Command from February 1942. Decorations included the Silver Star.

Smith, Benjamin Mitchell (1900-1949) Born in Hull, Alabama, on September 10, 1900. Enlisted service 1919-1922. Commissioned in the infantry, Alabama National Guard in 1922. Graduated from the Command and General Staff School in 1936. Brigadier general in January 1939. Federal service as adjutant general and director of selective service for Alabama October 1940-January 1945.

Stackpole, Edward J. Jr. (1894-1967) Born on June 21, 1894, in Harrisburg, Pennsylvania. Graduated from Yale in 1915. Twice wounded while serving with the Regular Army in the AEF 1917-1918. Commissioned in the infantry, Pennsylvania National Guard in 1921. Brigadier general in June 1933, major general in February 1940. Called to active duty as brigadier general in September 1940. Commanding general of 56th Infantry Brigade, 28th Division 1941-1943. Member of field agencies, War Department Manpower Board 1943-1945. Decorations included the Distinguished Service Cross and two Purple Hearts. Author of six volumes on the Civil War. Died in October 1967.

Story, Walter P. (1883-1957) Born on December 18, 1883, in Bozeman, Montana. Attended Eastman College in 1902. Enlisted service in the infantry in World War I. Commissioned in the California National Guard in 1920. Brigadier general in July 1926. Graduated from the Army War College in 1933. Major general in July 1937. Commanding general of IX Corps Area 1940-1941. Called to active duty in March 1941. Commanding general of 48th Division March-September 1941. Relieved due to protracted illness. Retired in July 1942. Died on June 19, 1957.

Thomas, Amos S. (1882-n/a) Born in Milwaukee, Wisconsin, on August 30, 1882. Enlisted service in the Nebraska National Guard Cavalry 1897-1902. Attended the University of Nebraska 1900-1902. Commissioned in the Nebraska National Guard in 1902 LL.B. in 1909. Practiced law in Nebraska 1909-1941. Commissioned in the cavalry, Officers Reserve Corps in May 1917. Served with the AEF 1918-1919. Graduated from the Army War College in 1925. Brigadier general in the Nebraska National Guard in August 1932. Called to active duty in

December 1940. Served at headquarters of VII Corps 1940-1941. Assistant division commander of 8th Infantry Division November 1941-January 1942. Commanding general of the Southern Security District, 9th Service Command January-September 1942 then Camp White, Oregon until March 1945. Retired in August 1946.

Tobin, Ralph C. (1890-1957) Born on May 5, 1890, in New York. Enlisted service with 7th Infantry June 1916-November 1918. Commissioned in the infantry, Regular Army in November 1918. Served with the AEF 1918-1919. Graduated from the National Guard course at the Army War College in 1930. Called to active duty as colonel and commanding officer of 207th Coast Artillery in February 1941. Brigadier general in August 1942. Released from active duty in December 1946. Retired as major general in May 1954. Died on August 5, 1957.

Troland, Thomas Edison (1893-n/a) Born on January 22, 1893, in New London, Connecticut. Commissioned in the Coast Artillery Corps, Connecticut National Guard in 1920. Brigadier general in November 1940 as commanding general of 85th Brigade. Quartermaster general on the staff of Governor Baldwin 1939-1941. Ordered into federal service in February 1941. Commanding general of 85th Infantry Brigade, 43rd Division 1941-1942. Organized the provisional military police command at 1st Service Command 1942-1943. Attended the Command and General Staff School April-June 1943. Served with Security District Five, 1st Service Command 1943-1945. Released from active duty in December 1945. Retired in January 1952 as major general.

Tupper, Tristram (1886-1954) Born on September 11, 1886, in Caroline County, Virginia, the brother of Katherine Tupper, George C. Marshall's second wife. LL.B. from New York Law School in 1912. Enlisted service 1916-1917. Commissioned in the Corps of Engineers, New York National Guard in 1917. Served with the 22nd Engineers on the Mexican border then the 102nd Engineers in the AEF in 1918. Discharged in March 1919. Novelist and screen writer 1919-1940. Called to active duty as lieutenant colonel with the 27th Division in October 1940. Aide to Major General William N. Haskell 1940-1941. Public relations officer at headquarters of the Armored Force 1941-1943 then headquarters of the European Theater of Operations May 1943-September 1944. Brigadier general in November 1943. Public relations officer for Sixth Army Group September 1944-October 1945. Released from active duty in October 1945. Decorations included the Silver Star. Died on December 30, 1954.

Weatherred, Preston Alonzo (1884-1967) Born in Occala, Texas, on August 11, 1884. LL.B. from the University of Texas in 1908. Commissioned in the infantry, Texas National Guard in 1902. Practiced law 1908-1939 except for active service as commanding officer of 1st Battalion, 2nd Texas Infantry in Mexico 1916-1917 and commanding officer of 132nd Machine Gun Battalion, 36th Division, AEF in 1918. Graduated from the Army War College in 1922. Called to active duty as brigadier general in July 1939 as commanding general of 72nd Brigade, 36th Division and served until released from active duty in September 1942. Co-author of *Pointers for Infantry Troop Leaders* (1940). Died in 1967.

White, Miller Grieve (1895-1987) Born on July 28, 1895, in Macon, Georgia. Enlisted service with the 42nd Division, AEF in World War I as the sergeant-major of a machine-gun battalion. Commissioned in the infantry, Georgia National Guard in 1921. Called to active duty in July 1937. Served at the War Department General Staff 1937-1942. Brigadier general in September 1942. Selected by General George C. Marshall as deputy chief of staff for personnel in September 1942 and served until August 1944. Major general in June 1943. Assistant chief of staff for personnel in the North African Theater of Operations 1944-1945 then deputy chief of staff for U.S. forces in the European Theater of Operations 1945-1948. Retired in June 1955. Decorations included two Distinguished Service Medals and the Purple Heart. Died on October 26, 1987.

Whiteaker, Robert Olando (1882-1959) Born in Sherman, Texas, on December 16, 1882. Enlisted service in the Texas National Guard 1899-1916. Commissioned in the cavalry, Texas National Guard in 1916. Commanded a battery of the 132nd Field Artillery, 36th Division during World War I. Brigadier general in April 1938. Called to active duty in November 1940 as commanding general of 72nd Field Artillery Brigade, 36th Division. Appointment as brigadier general terminated in February 1942 and he accepted a commission as colonel, AUS. Served with the Corps of Engineers in the Lower Mississippi Valley Division 1942-1943. Retired from the National Guard in 1946 as major general. Died on April 26, 1959.

Wilfong, Albert E. (1885-n/a) Born on April 25, 1885, in Vermont. Commissioned in the infantry, Vermont National Guard in 1913. Federal service in Mexico in 1917. Transferred to the cavalry in 1921. Brigadier general in February 1940 as commanding general of 65th Filed Artillery brigade, 40th Division. Called into federal service in March 1941.

Williams, John Francis (1887-1953) Born on January 7, 1887, in Wilkes-Barre, Pennsylvania. Enlisted service with 2nd Missouri Infantry 1903-1904. Attended the University of Missouri 1908-1911. Commissioned in the infantry, Missouri National Guard in 1917. Active duty with the 128th Machine Gun Battalion, AEF at Vosges, St. Mihiel, Meuse-Argonne and Verdun 1918-1919. Ordered to active duty in January 1936 in the National Guard Bureau. Major general and chief of the National Guard Bureau 1940-1946. Retired in July 1946. Decorations included the Distinguished Service Medal. Died on May 29, 1953.

Wing, Leonard Fish (1893-1945) Born in Ira, Vermont, on November 12, 1893. Enlisted service 1917-1918. Commissioned in the Vermont National Guard in 1919. Brigadier general in July 1938. Called to active federal service in February 1941. Commander of the 86th Infantry Brigade 1941-1942. Assistant division commander of 43rd Infantry Division February 1942-October 1943. Major general in September 1943. Commanding general of 43rd Infantry Division October 1943-October 1945. Died of a heart attack on December 19, 1945. Decorations included the Distinguished Service Medal, Silver Star, Legion of Merit and Bronze Star.

Wood, Eric Fisher (1889-1962) Born on January 4, 1889, in New York City. B.A. from Yale in 1910. Served with the American Ambulance Corps in France in 1915-1916 and as major in the British Army in 1917, wounded at the Battle of Arros. Commissioned in the infantry, Regular Army in 1918 as assistant chief of staff of 8tth Division. Wounded at the Meuse-Argonne offensive in 1918. Commissioned in the infantry, Pennsylvania National Guard in 1922. Graduated from the National Guard course, Command and General Staff School in 1936. Brigadier general in December 1940. Called to federal service in February 1941. Served at Indiantown Gap, Pennsylvania 1941-1942 and the U.S. Army Reclassification Center at Fort Benning from 1942. Decorations included the Legion of Merit and two Purple Hearts. Author of *The Writing on the War* (1916) and *Biography of Leonard Wood* (1920). Died on October 4, 1962.

Woodcock, Amos Walter Wright (1883-1964) Born in Salisbury, Maryland, on October 29, 1883. B.A. from St. John's College in 1903. Enlisted service 1904-1907. Commissioned in the infantry, Maryland National Guard in 1907. LL.B. from the University of Maryland in 1910 and M.A. from Harvard in 1912. Served with 1st Maryland Infantry on the Mexican border in 1916 and in the 58th Infantry Brigade with the AEF 1918 in the Verdun and Meuse-Argonne offensives. LL.D. from Washington University in 1932. Special assistant to the United States Attorney General 1933-1934. President of St. John's College 1934-1937. Brigadier general in November 1936 as commander of 58th Brigade, Maryland National Guard. Served on active duty February 1941-August 1942. Again special assistant to the United States attorney general involved in prosecuting Japanese war criminals December 1945-March 1946. Died on January 18, 1964.

Yenter, Raymond A. (1887-n/a) Born on August 17, 1887. Saw federal service in Mexico 1916-1917. Commissioned in the cavalry, Iowa National Guard in 1921. Brigadier general in March 1936. Called to federal service in February 1941. Commanding general of 75th Field Artillery Brigade from February 1941.

4

The United States Navy

Acuff, Jasper Terry (1898-1973) Born on March 29, 1898, in Fayetteville, Tennessee. Commissioned from Annapolis in 1921. Instructor at Annapolis 1928-1930. Graduated from the Naval War College in 1934. Served aboard the *Tennessee* 1941-1942. Commanding officer of the *Kaskakia* 1943-1944. Staff officer with Service Squadron Eight, Pacific Fleet May 1944-January 1945. Commander of Service Division 102, Service Squadron Ten 1945-1946. Commodore June 30, 1945. Reverted to captain in February 1946 and retired in July 1952. Decorations included the Distinguished Service Medal. Died on April 1, 1973.

Adams, John Clausel (1893-1981) Born on October 9, 1893, in Jackson, Alabama. M.D. from the University of Alabama in 1917. Commissioned in the Medical Corps in 1917. Attended Navy Medical School 1917-1919. Chief of the Aviation Medicine Division, Bureau of Medicine and Surgery 1937-1946. Commodore in April 1945. Assistant chief of the Bureau for aviation 1946-1947. Rear admiral in December 1946. District medical officer at Fifth Naval District 1947-1949. Retired in April 1949. Decorations included the Legion of Merit. March 22, 1981.

Agnew, William John Clarke (1891-1955) Born on December 6, 1891, in High Falls, New York. Attended Long Island College Hospital 1910-1911. M.D. from the University of Vermont in 1914. Commissioned in the Medical Corps in 1917. Duty at Canacao Naval Hospital, Philippines 1930-1932. Head of the personnel division at the Bureau of Medicine and Surgery September 1938-November 1944. Rear admiral in September 18, 1942. Assistant chief of the Bureau November 1944-December 1946. District medical officer in the Eleventh, Fourteenth and Ninth Naval Districts 1946-1951. Commanding officer of National Naval Medical Center at Bethesda October 1951 until retirement in May 1952. Decorations included the Legion of Merit. Died on January 26, 1955.

Ainsworth, Walden Lee (1886-1960) Born on November 10, 1886, in Minneapolis, Minnesota. Graduated from Annapolis in 1910 and commissioned in 1912. Served aboard the *Florida* at the occupation of Vera Cruz in 1914. Commanding officer of the *Paul Jones* 1927-1928. Instructor at Annapolis September 1928-June 1931. Duty at Fifteenth Naval District, Panama Canal Zone 1933-1935. Professor of naval science and tactics at Tulane University 1938-1940. Commander of Destroyer Squadron Two July 1940-December 1941. Commanding officer of the *Mississippi* 1941-1942. Rear admiral in December 1941. Commander of Destroyers, Pacific Fleet 1942-1943, Cruiser Division Nine January 1943-October 1944 and Cruisers and Destroyers Pacific Fleet October 1944-July 1945. Commandant of Fifth Naval District 1945-1948. Vice admiral upon retirement in December 1948. Decorations included the Navy Cross, Distinguished Service Medal and two Legions of Merit. Died on August 7, 1960.

Albright, Paul Morris (1894-n/a) Born on March 26, 1894, in Alburtis, Pennsylvania. M.D. from the University of Pennsylvania in 1917. Commissioned in the Medical Corps in 1917. Served with the 1st Marine Brigade at Port au Prince 1927-1929. Executive officer at Naval Hospital Pearl Harbor 1941-1942. Commanding officer of Naval Hospital Quantico October 1942-January 1944. Rear admiral in July 1942. Commanding officer of Naval Hospital Long Beach 1944-1945. Staff surgeon at Okinawa naval operating base in 1945 then at Commander in Chief Pacific Fleet October 1945-March 1946. Commanding officer of Naval Hospital Corona, California March 1946-January 1947. Assistant chief of the Bureau of Medicine and Surgery 1947-1948. District medical officer at Eleventh Naval District 1948-1953. Retired as vice admiral in May 1953. Decorations included the Bronze Star.

Allen, Ezra Griffin (1885-1952) Born on March 11, 1885, in Scranton, Pennsylvania. Graduated from Annapolis in 1907 and commissioned in 1909. Commanding officer of the *Sultana* and the *Walkina* operating in French waters in World War I. Aide to Admiral William S. Sims in 1918. Commanding officer of the *Belknap* in 1919. Graduated from the Naval War College in 1920. Aide to Admiral Edward W. Eberle 1922-1923 and Rear Admiral William A. Moffett 1924-1926. Graduated from the Army War College in 1929. Commanding officer of the *Bridge* in 1933. Aide to the commander of Battle Force 1936-1938. Budget officer for the Navy Department July 1938-July 1946. Rear admiral in October 1941. Retired in November 1946. Decorations included the Navy Cross. Died on January 4, 1952.

Allen, William Henry (1878-1951) Born on June 28, 1878, in Florence, South Carolina. Attended South Carolina College 1894-1896. Graduated from Annapolis in 1901 and commissioned in 1903. Commanding officer of the *Flusser* October 1911-August 1912 then the *Ammen* August 1912-May 1913. Commanding officer of the *Yorktown* August-December 1918, then the *Nansemond* March-September 1919. Commanding officer of the *Sirius* then the *Aroostook* May 1922-February 1923. Graduated from the Naval War College in 1925. Assistant commandant Sixth Naval District June 1925-March 1927. Commanding officer of the *Denver* March 1927-November 1928. Commander of Destroyer Squadron Two, Battle Force 1932-1934. Commandant of Sixth Naval District May-August

1934. Commander of the Yangtze Patrol, Asiatic Fleet 1934-1937. Rear admiral in November 1934. Member of the General Board June 1937-March 1938. Commandant of the Sixth, Seventh and Eighth Districts March 1938-July 1942. Commandant of Sixth Naval District 1942. Retired in July 1942. Decorations included the Legion of Merit. Died on February 9, 1951.

Anderson, Thomas Carlyle (1886-n/a) Born on October 2, 1886, in Sheffield, Iowa. B.A. from Morningside College in 1908, M.D. from the University of Michigan in 1914. Medical practice in South Dakota 1914-1917. Commissioned in the Medical Corps in 1917. Duty at the naval hospital in Pearl Harbor 1917-1919. Served with the Third Marine Brigade in China in 1928 and at the naval hospital in Canacao, Philippines. Assigned to the naval hospital in Philadelphia November 1939-February 1942 then commanding officer of the naval hospital in Norfolk 1942-1943. Fleet surgeon for the Pacific Fleet 1943-1945. Commodore in April 1945, rear admiral in January 1946. Commander of the National Naval Medical Center at Bethesda 1946-1948. Retired in November 1948. Decorations included the Legion of Merit.

Anderson, Walter Stratton (1881-1981) Born on October 4, 1881, in Carlinville, Illinois. Graduated from Annapolis in 1903 and commissioned in 1905. Post graduate study in naval ordnance 1906-1907. Gunnery officer, then executive officer aboard the *Arizona* in World War I. Graduated from the Naval War College in 1921. Naval attache in London 1934-1936. Rear admiral in July 1936. Commander of Cruiser Division Four 1937-1939. Director of naval intelligence 1939-1941. Commander of battleships in the Pacific Fleet 1941-1942. President of the Naval Board of Inspection and Survey 1942-1944. Commandant of 7th Naval District 1944-1945. Vice admiral in April 1945. Retired in March 1946. Decorations included the Legion of Merit. Died on October 24, 1981.

Andrews, Adolphus (1879-1948) Born on October 7, 1879, in Galveston, Texas. Attended the University of Texas 1896-1897. Graduated from Annapolis in 1901 and commissioned in 1903. Aide to the superintendent of Annapolis 1911-1914. Gunnery officer aboard the *Michigan* at Vera Cruz, Mexico, in 1914. Executive officer of the *Mississippi* and commanding officer of the *Massachusetts* during World War I. Graduated from the Naval War College in 1920. Senior aide to President Harding in 1922, then President Coolidge 1923-1926. Chief of staff of the Battle Force in 1933. Rear admiral in January 1934. Chief of staff of United States Fleet 1934-1935. Chief of the Bureau of Navigation 1935-1938. Commander of the Scouting Force as a vice admiral 1938-1941. Commandant of the Third Naval District 1941-1942. Commander of Eastern Sea Frontier February 1942-November 1943. Vice admiral in May 1942. Retired in November 1943. Decorations included the Distinguished Service Medal. Died on June 19, 1948.

Andrus, Carlton Leverett (1888-n/a) Born on February 10, 1888, in Monrovia, California. Commissioned in the Medical Corps in 1917. Chief of the planning division at the Bureau of Medicine and Surgery 1939-1946. Commodore in April

1945. Assistant chief of the Bureau for planning and logistics June 1946-January 1947. Rear admiral in December 1946. Commanding officer of the medical center on Guam 1947-1948. Retired in February 1950. Decorations included the Legion of Merit.

Antrim, Archie Arthur (1892-n/a) Born on June 29, 1892, in Arlington, Nebraska. Enlisted service 1910-1918. Commissioned in the Supply Corps in 1918. Duty with the U.S. Navy in Australia 1942-1943. Rear admiral in September 1943. Officer in charge of the logistics planning division at the Bureau of Supplies and Accounts November 1943-October 1945. Duty on the staff of Commander Service Force Pacific Fleet 1946-1948. Officer in charge of Navy Ships Store, Brooklyn 1948-1950. Commander of Naval Supply Depot June 1950-March 1954 then Naval Supply Center, Norfolk 1954-1956. Retired as vice admiral in April 1956. Decorations included the Legion of Merit and Navy Commendation Medal.

Austin, Bernard Lige (1902-1979) Born on December 15, 1902, in Wagener, South Carolina. Commissioned from Annapolis in 1924. Commanding officer of the submarine *R-11* 1934-1937. Naval observer in London 1940-1941. Commanding officer of the *Woolsey* in 1942 and the *Foote* in 1943. Commander of Destroyer Division Forty-Six in 1943 and Destroyer Squadron Fourteen in 1944. Operations officer on the staff of the commander of destroyers in the Pacific in 1944. Commodore in December 1944. Assistant chief of staff for administration at headquarters Pacific Fleet 1944-1945. Navy member of the State, War and Navy Coordinating Committee 1945-1946. Assignments after the war included director of the Joint Staff 1956-1958, commander of Second Fleet 1958-1959, deputy chief of naval operations for plans and policy 1959-1960 and president of the Naval War College July 1960-July 1964. Retired as vice admiral in August 1964. Decorations included two Navy Crosses, two Distinguished Service Medals, the Legion of Merit and Bronze Star. Died on September 21, 1979.

Badger, Oscar Charles (1890-1958) Born on June 26, 1890, in Washington, DC. Attended St. John's College 1905-1907. Graduated from Annapolis in 1911 and commissioned in 1913. Earned the Medal of Honor at Vera Cruz in April 1914. Graduated from the Naval War College in 1939. Chief of staff to Admiral Ernest J. King December 1940-October 1941. Commanding officer of the *North Carolina* 1941-1942. Rear admiral in April 1942. Assistant chief of naval operations for logistics 1942-1944. Commander of Service Squadrons, South Pacific Force in 1944 then Battleship Division Seven 1944-1945. Commander of Task Force 31 in 1945. Assignments after the war included commander of Eastern Sea Frontier 1950-1952. Retired as admiral in July 1952. Decorations included the Medal of Honor, Navy Cross, Distinguished Service Medal and two Legions of Merit. Died on November 30, 1958.

Badt, Harry Asher (1884-1967) Born on September 22, 1884, in Tyler, Texas. Graduated from Annapolis in 1908. Aboard the *Annapolis* at Vera Cruz in 1914. M.S. from Columbia in 1916. Duty aboard the *Minneapolis* on convoy duty in the

Atlantic and the *Arizona* in British waters during World War. Instructor at Annapolis 1926-1928. Commanding officer of the *Nokomis* 1928-1930. Instructor again at Annapolis 1930-1933. Graduated from the Naval War College in 1938. Commanding officer of the *Tuscaloosa* 1938-1940. Duty with the Bureau of Naval Personnel as director of enlisted personnel 1940-1942 then director of special projects 1942-1946. Commodore in September 1944. Retired in April 1947. Decorations included the Legion of Merit. Died on September 7, 1967.

Bagley, David Worth (1883-1960) Born on January 8, 1883, in Raleigh, North Carolina. Graduated from Annapolis in 1904 and commissioned in 1906. Aboard the *Rhode Island* in the world cruise of the Battle Fleet 1907-1909. Flag lieutenant to the commander in chief of China Station during the revolution 1911-1912. Commanding officer of the destroyer *Jacob Jones* in World War I. Naval attache in Holland 1919-1920. Rear admiral in April 1938. Commandant of Mare Island Navy Yard 1938-1941. Commander of Battleship Division Two January-April 1942. Commandant of Fourteenth Naval District April 1942-March 1943 and Eleventh Naval District March 1943-January 1944. Vice admiral in February 1944. Again commandant of Fourteenth Naval District November 1944-July 1945. Member of the International Defense Board August 1945-March 1947. Admiral upon retirement in April 1947. Decorations included the Distinguished Service Medal. Died on May 25, 1960.

Baker, Wilder Dupuy (1890-1975) Born on July 22, 1890, in Topeka, Kansas. Commissioned from Annapolis in 1914. Served aboard submarine *L-11* in British waters in World War I. Commanding officer of *L-3* 1919-1920, *S-11* and *T-2* in 1923 and *S-13* July 1923-May 1924. Commanding officer of the *Kidder* 1926-1928. Assistant naval attache in London 1935-1936. Aide to the commander of Special Service Squadron 1936-1937. Professor of naval science and tactics at Yale 1939-1940. Commander of Destroyer Squadron 31 November 1940-March 1942. Commander officer of the *North Carolina* 1942-1943. Rear admiral in July 1942. Commander of Cruiser Division One June 1943-March 1944. Chief of staff to the commander 2nd Fast Carrier Task Force Pacific Fleet July 1944-October 1945. Retired as vice admiral in August 1952. Decorations included the Distinguished Service Medal, Silver Star, Legion of Merit and Bronze Star. Died on November 10, 1975.

Baldwin, Frank (1880-1959) Born on November 19, 1880, in Pennington, New Jersey. Commissioned in the Supply Corps in 1906. Served with U.S. Navy railway batteries at the Aisne-Marne and Meuse-Argonne offensives in World War I. Graduated from the Naval War College in 1937. Officer in charge of Naval Cost Inspection Service August 1941-June 1943, then director until retired in December 1944. Rear admiral in September 1942. Recalled to active duty as director of the Cost Inspection Service 1944-1950. Retired again in June 1950. Died on October 19, 1959.

Ballentine, John Jennings (1896-1970) Born on October 4, 1896, in Hillsboro, Ohio. Commissioned from Annapolis in 1918. Served aboard battleships in World War I. Designated a naval aviator in 1920. Commanding officer of the *Long Island* in 1942, then the *Bunker Hill* 1942-1943. Rear admiral in April 1943. Deputy commander of Naval Air Forces in the Pacific, then commander of Division Seven in Third Fleet 1944-1945. Assignments after the war included commander of Sixth Fleet 1949-1951 and Air Force, Atlantic Fleet 1951-1954. Admiral upon retirement in May 1954. Decorations included three Legions of Merit and the Bronze Star. Died on May 21, 1970.

Barbey, Daniel Edward (1889-1969) Born on December 23, 1889, in Portland, Oregon. Graduated from Annapolis in 1912. Chief of war plans division in the Bureau of Navigation 1937-1940. Chief of staff and aide to the commander of the Service Force and Amphibious Force in the Atlantic Fleet in 1941. Established the amphibious warfare section of the Navy Department in 1942 and oversaw development of the Landing Ship, Dock (LSD) and Landing Ship, Tank (LST). Rear admiral in December 1942. Commander of the VII Amphibious Force in the Seventh Fleet January 1943-November 1945, during which time his forces landed more than one million men in 56 separate operations. Vice admiral in June 1944. Assignments after the war included commander of Seventh Fleet, then Atlantic Amphibious Forces, finally the Caribbean Sea Frontier 1945-1950. Retired in June 1951. Decorations included the Navy Cross, three Distinguished Service Medals and the Legion of Merit. Died on April 11, 1969.

Bass, Ivan Ernest (1877-1967) Born on July 29, 1877, in Carley, Mississippi. Graduated from Annapolis in 1901 and commissioned in 1903. Engineering officer at Boston Navy Yard in World War I. Rear admiral in March 1934. Naval inspector of machinery at Newport News Shipbuilding Company 1934-1939. Member of the U.S. Navy Compensation Board 1939-1941. Retired in August 1941. Recalled to active duty in January 1942. Member of the Compensation Board 1942-1944 and the Contract Settlement Review Board 1944-1947. Retired again in December 1947. Died on November 1, 1967.

Bates, Richard Waller (1892-1973) Born on January 16, 1892, in San Francisco, California. Commissioned from Annapolis in 1915. Executive officer of the *Cincinnati* 1918-1919. M.S. from Columbia University in 1922. Commanding officer of the *Clark* 1938-1940. Graduated from the Naval War College in 1941, then member of the staff until 1943. Commanding officer of the *Minneapolis* 1943-1944. Staff officer with the Pacific Fleet, then chief of staff of the bombardment group in Third Fleet and Seventh Fleet 1944-1945. Commodore in April 1945. Chief of staff of Battleship Squadron One, then commander of motor torpedo boats in the Pacific Fleet in 1945. Chief of staff of the Philippine Sea Frontier 1945-1946. Retired in May 1949. Decorations included the Navy Cross and three Legions of Merit. Died on December 26, 1973.

Battle, Charles Eugene Jr. (1887-1970) Born on June 15, 1887, in Oglethorpe, Georgia. Graduated from Annapolis in 1910 and commissioned in 1912. Commanding officer of the *Chase* in 1921 and the *Selfridge* 1924-1927. Aide to Rear Admiral William H. Standley October 1930-June 1932 then Rear Admiral Edward C. Kalbfus 1932-1933. Staff officer at the Naval War College 1933-1935. Graduated from the Naval War College in 1939. Commanding officer of the *Quincy* June 1941-May 1942. Chief of staff to Commander Service Force, Atlantic Fleet 1942-1945. Commodore in April 1944. Retired in July 1948. Decorations included the Navy Cross and Legion of Merit. Died on September 22, 1970.

Baughman, Cortlandt Chesterfield (1884-1976) Born on December 12, 1884, in West Newton, Pennsylvania. Graduated from Annapolis in 1907. Served aboard the *Maine* on the world cruise of the Battle Fleet 1907-1908 and at the occupation of Nicaragua in 1912. Aide to the military governor of Santo Domingo 1916-1919. Duty in Havana 1923-1924. Commanding officer of the *Farenholt* 1924-1925. Assistant governor of Samoa 1929-1930. Commanding officer of Destroyer Squadrons Twelve and Eleven 1933-1934. Commanding officer of the *Cincinnati* 1936-1937 and the *New Mexico* June 1939-January 1941. Commanding officer of the Receiving Station Pearl Harbor 1941-1942. Director of special activities in the Bureau of Naval Personnel 1942-1943. Commodore in September 1943. Commander of Naval Operating Base Londonderry September 1943-September 1944 then Naval Operating Base Trinidad 1944-1946. Retired in November 1946. Decorations included the Bronze Star. Died on September 16, 1976.

Beardall, John Reginald (1887-1967) Born on February 7, 1887, in Sanford, Florida. Graduated from Annapolis in 1908 and commissioned in 1910. Served aboard the *Vermont* at the occupation of Vera Cruz in April 1914. Aboard the *Kansas* and *New Hampshire* in World War I. Graduated from Naval War College in 1933. Aide to the secretary of the navy 1936-1939. Commanding officer of the *Vincennes* 1939-1941. Aide to President Roosevelt April 1941-January 1942. Rear admiral in November 1941. Superintendent of Annapolis January 1942-August 1945. Retired in November 1946. Decorations included two Legions of Merit. Died on January 4, 1967.

Beary, Donald Bradford (1888-1966) Born on December 4, 1888, in Helena, Montana. Graduated from Annapolis in 1910 and commissioned in 1912. M.S. from Columbia University in 1917. Commander of the destroyers *Ramlik* and *Lamson* in World War I. Commanding officer of the *Talbot, Parrott* and *Sumner* April 1921-September 1923. Instructor at Annapolis 1928-1930 then aide to the superintendent 1930-1931. Graduated from the Naval War College in 1937. Commanding officer of the *Richmond* 1938-1939. Aide to the superintendent of Annapolis 1939-1941. Commanding officer of the *Mount Vernon* in 1941. Rear admiral in December 1941. Commandant of Naval Operating Base Iceland 1942-1943. Commander of Fleet Operational Training Command, Atlantic Fleet 1943-1944. Commander of Service Squadron Six November 1944-April 1946. Assignments after the war included president of the Naval War College 1948-1950. Retired as vice admiral in October 1950. Decorations included the Navy Cross, Distinguished Service Medal, Legion of Merit and Bronze Star. Died on March 7, 1966.

Beatty, Frank Edmund (1894-1976) Born on June 17, 1894, in Washington, DC. Commissioned from Annapolis in 1916. B.S. from Massachusetts Institute of Technology in 1922. Served aboard the *New York* in World War I. Commanding officer of the *Long* 1933-1934. Aide to Commander Destroyers, Scouting Force 1934-1935. Executive officer of the *Augusta* March 1940-February 1941. Aide to the secretary of the navy 1941-1943. Rear admiral in January 1943. Commanding officer of the *Columbia* April 1943-July 1944. Commander of U.S. forces in the Aruba-Curacao area 1944-1945. Retired as vice admiral in June 1951. Decorations included the Navy Cross, two Legions of Merit and the Bronze Star. Died on November 12, 1976.

Beauregard, Augustin Toutant (1885-1951) Born on December 1, 1885, in San Antonio, Texas. Graduated from Annapolis in 1907 and commissioned in 1908. Member of the staff at Pacific Fleet 1916-1917. Naval aide to the president of Uruguay during his visit to the U.S. in 1918. Naval aide to President Hoover on his South American tour 1928-1929. Naval attache in Paris, then Madrid 1934-1936. Chief of the U.S. naval mission to Brazil 1939-1941. Rear admiral in April 1941. Naval attache in Rio de Janeiro 1941-1942. Retired in November 1942. Decorations included the Legion of Merit. Died on April 8, 1951.

Behrens, William Wohlsen (1898-1965) Born in Lancaster, Pennsylvania, on June 6, 1898. Enlisted service 1917-1919. Commissioned in 1919. Commanding officer of the *Iuka* in 1932 and the *Southard* 1936-1937. Aide to the commandant of the Philadelphia Navy yard June 1937-March 1939. Commanding officer of the *Cimarron* 1939-1940. Executive officer of the *Concord* July 1940-July 1942. Duty at the Bureau of Naval Personnel 1942-1943. Commanding officer of the *Houston* December 1943-July 1945. Commodore in August 1945. Commander of the Naval Training Center, Bainbridge, Maryland 1945-1947. Retired as rear admiral in July 1947. Decorations included the Navy Cross and Purple Heart. Died on January 27, 1965

Bellinger, Patrick Nieson Lynch (1885-1962) Born in Cheraw, South Carolina, on October 8, 1885. Graduated from Annapolis in 1907 and commissioned in 1909. Became one of the first seven naval aviators in 1912. Participated in the invasion of Vera Cruz in 1914. Set an altitude record of 10,000 feet in 1915. Commander of Hampton Roads Naval Air Station in World War I. Accompanied by Lieutenant Marc A. Mitscher, Bellinger piloted one of three navy seaplanes that attempted to cross the Atlantic in 1919. His and another plane were forced down in fog near the Azores, but a plane piloted by Lieutenant Albert C. Read completed the flight. Commander of Patrol Wing Two in Honolulu 1940-1942. Rear admiral in November 1941 and the senior naval officer present at the attack.

His was the first message to be transmitted: "Air raid, Pearl Harbor - this is no drill." Commander of all patrol wings in the Pacific Fleet May-August 1942. Chief of staff to Admiral Ernest J. King August 1942-March 1943. Commander of Atlantic Fleet Air Force 1943-1947. Vice admiral in October 1943. Retired in October 1947. Decorations included the Navy Cross and Distinguished Service Medal. Died on May 29, 1962.

Bennett, Andrew Carl (1889-1971) Born on December 17, 1889, in Goodland, Kansas. Commissioned from Annapolis in 1912. Commanding officer of the submarine *L-11* in Irish waters 1917-1918. Commanding officer of *R-24* and *S-16* 1918-1922. Instructor at Annapolis 1933-1936. Commanding officer of the *Savannah* 1940-1942. Rear admiral in May 1942. Commander of Advance Group, Amphibious Force July 1942-February 1943 then Navy Operating Base, Iceland in 1943. Retired in November 1946. Decorations included the Navy Cross and two Legions of Merit. Died on November 29, 1971.

Benson, Howard Hartwell James (1888-1975) Born on October 8, 1888, in Baltimore, Maryland, the son of Admiral William S. Benson. Graduated from Annapolis in 1909 and commissioned in 1911. Commanding officer of the submarine *H-2* 1913-1916 then the *Guinevere, Corona, Noma* and *Roe* 1917-1918. Commanding officer of the *Buchanan* 1919-1920 then the *Yarnell* February-March 1920 and the *Howard* March-September 1920. Instructor at Annapolis 1920-1922. Commanding officer of the *S.P. Lee* June-October 1922 then the *Sloat* May 1927-June 1929. Graduated from the Naval War College in 1930. Instructor at Annapolis 1930-1932. Commanding officer of the *Sapelo* in 1932 and acting commanding officer of the battleship *Tennessee* in 1934. Graduated from the Army War College in 1935. Commanding officer of the *Holland* June 1936-July 1938 then the *Reina Mercedes* 1938-1941 and the *Washington* April 1941-July 1942. Chief of staff to Commandant Seventh Naval District 1942-1945. Commodore in November 1944. Chief of staff to Commander Gulf Sea Frontier 1945-1946. Retired in November 1946. Decorations included the Navy Cross and Legion of Merit. Died on January 28, 1975.

Berkey, Russell Stanley (1893-1985) Born on August 4, 1893, in Goshen, Indiana. Commissioned from Annapolis in 1916. Served aboard the *New York* during World War I. Aide to Admiral William V. Pratt 1929-1932. Commanding officer of the gunboat *Panay* on the Yangtze River 1933-1934. Graduated from the Naval War College in 1939. Assistant commandant of U.S. Naval Base Iceland 1941-1942. Commanding officer of the *Santa Fe* 1942-1943. Rear admiral in November 1942. Commander of Cruiser Division Fifteen in 1943. Commander of curisers in the Seventh Fleet, then Task Forces 74 and 75 December 1943-July 1945. Chief of public relations for the Navy Department August 1945-May 1947. Assignments after the war included commander of Seventh Fleet in 1949. Admiral upon retirement in September 1950. Decorations included the Navy Cross, Distinguished Service Medal and three Legions of Merit. Died on June 17, 1985.

Bernhard, Alva Douglas (1886-1955) Born on March 9, 1886, in Enterprise, Pennsylvania. Graduated from Annapolis in 1909 and commissioned in 1911. Aide to the commandant of Washington navy Yard in 1917. Commanding officer of the *Bailey, Radford* and *Dent* 1919-1920 then the *Litchfield* 1924-1926. Commanding officer of Naval Air Station Colo Solo, Canal Zone 1929-1931. Chief of staff to Commander Aircraft, Scouting Force 1937-1939. Commanding officer of the carrier *Lexington* 1939-1940. Commander of Patrol Wings, Atlantic Fleet April 1942-March 1943. Rear admiral in September 1942. Commander of Task Force 22 in 1943. Staff officer with Commander in Chief Pacific Fleet October 1943-January 1945. Commander of Naval Air Bases, Eleventh Naval District 1945-1946. Vice admiral upon retirement in November 1946. Died on July 24, 1955.

Bidwell, Abel Trood (1885-1980) Born on September 19, 1885, in Bellefonte, Pennsylvania. Graduated from Annapolis in 1908 and commissioned in 1910. Executive officer of the *Birmingham* in convoy duty, then commanding officer of the *Gregory* during World War I. Commanding officer of the *Chicago* 1938-1939. Director, then assistant chief of personnel at the Bureau of Navigation 1940-1942. Rear admiral in October 1941. Retired in October 1942. Died on August 1, 1980.

Bieri, Bernhard Henry (1889-1971) Born on June 24, 1889, in Walnut Lake, Minnesota. Graduated in 1909 and commissioned in 1911. Served aboard the *Texas* 1915-1919. Commanding officer of the *Corry* 1921-1925. Graduated from the Naval War College in 1936. Staff officer with Commander Battleships in 1938, Battle Force in 1939 and Commander in Chief United States Fleet 1939-1940. Commanding officer of the *Chicago* 1941-1942. Rear admiral in April 1942. Again on staff of Commander in Chief United States Fleet 1942-1945. Assignments after the war included deputy chief of naval operations 1945-1946 and commander of U.S. Naval Forces Mediterranean 1946-1948. Retired as vice admiral in June 1951. Decorations included the Legion of Merit. Died on April 10, 1971.

Bisset, Andrew Gustave (1893-1976) Born on October 4, 1893, in Washington, DC. C.E. from Lafayette College in 1915. Commissioned in the Civil Engineer Corps in 1917. Officer in charge of construction at Annapolis 1936-1939. Public works officer at Portsmouth Navy Yard 1939-1941. Commander of seabees in South Pacific and Okinawa operations 1942-1945. Commodore in October 1944. Reverted to captain in December 1945. Rear admiral in May 1948. District engineer at Fifth Naval District 1948-1950. Vice admiral upon retirement in July 1950. Decorations included the Distinguished Service Medal and Legion of Merit. Died on January 24, 1976.

Blakely, Charles Adams (1879-1950) Born on October 1, 1879, in Whitley County, Kentucky. Served as a sergeant with the Second Kentucky Volunteer

Infantry in the Spanish-American War. Graduated from Annapolis in 1903 and commissioned in 1905. Served at Vera Cruz during the occupation in April 1914. Commanding officer of the *O'Brien* in European waters during World War I. Designated a naval aviator in 1936. Rear admiral in November 1936. Commandant of Pensacola Naval Air Station 1936-1937. Commander of the Second Carrier Division in 1937, then all patrol plane squadrons in the Navy 1937-1939. Vice admiral in June 1939. Commander of Aircraft, Battle Force 1939-1940. Commandant of the Eleventh Naval District 1940-1941. Retired in October 1942. Decorations included the Distinguished Service Medal. Died on September 12, 1950.

Blandy, William Henry Purnell (1890-1954) Born on June 28, 1890, in New York, New York. Commissioned upon graduation from Annapolis in 1913. Served aboard the *Florida* in the Vera Cruz invasion and during World War I. Member of U.S. naval mission to Brazil 1930-1934. Head of gunner section in the fleet training division, office of the chief of naval operations 1936-1938. Commanding officer of the *Utah* 1938-1940. Member of the Navy Department Antiaircraft Board 1940-1941. Chief of the Bureau of Ordnance 1941-1943. Rear admiral in May 1942. Commander of Amphibious Group One, Pacific Fleet January 1944-July 1945. Commander of cruisers and destroyers in the Pacific Fleet July-November 1945. Assignments after the war included deputy chief of naval operations for special weapons November 1945-December 1946, commander of Eighth Fleet December 1946-February 1947 and commander of the Atlantic Fleet February 1947 until retirement as admiral in February 1950. Decorations included four Distinguished Service Medals. Died on January 12, 1954.

Bloch, Claude Charles (1878-1967) Born on July 13, 1878, in Woodbury, Kentucky. Graduated from Annapolis in 1899 and commissioned in 1901. Served aboard the *Newark* and the *Wheeling* during the Philippine insurrection and the Boxer Rebellion 1900-1901. Aide and flag lieutenant to Commander in Chief Pacific Fleet 1907-1909. Assistant chief of the Bureau of Ordnance 1918-1921, then chief as rear admiral 1923-1927. Commanding officer of the *California* 1927-1929. Graduated from the Naval War College in 1929. Rear admiral again in July 1931. Commander of Cruisers, Battle Force 1932-1933. Judge advocate general of the Navy 1934-1936. Commander of Battleship Division Two June 1936-January 1937. Admiral in January 1937. Commander of the Battle Force 1937-1938. Commander in chief of U.S. Fleet 1938-1940. Commandant of Eleventh Naval District 1940-1942. Retired in August 1942. Recalled to active duty on the General Board in World War II. Decorations included the Navy Cross. Died on October 4, 1967.

Boak, James Earl (1891-1956) Born on April 6, 1891, in Hughesville, Pennsylvania. Commissioned from Annapolis in 1914. Served aboard the *Georgia* at the occupation of Vera Cruz in April 1914 and the *Rowan* in Irish waters during World War I. Commanding officer of the *Morris* 1920-1921. Instructor at Annapolis 1921-1923. Commanding officer of the submarine *R-18* 1924-1926. Again instructor at Annapolis August 1926-June 1929. Commanding officer of the *Patoka Gilmer* 1931-1932. Duty in the office of the chief of naval operations May-July 1942 then at Naval Air Station Moffett Field 1942-1943. Commander of Naval Base Espiritu Santo February 1943-March 1944. Commodore in January 1944. Commander of Naval Base Manus, Admiralty Islands 1944-1945 then Naval Repair Base San Diego July-September 1945. Retired in November 1947. Decorations included the Legion of Merit. Died on March 31, 1956.

Bogan, Gerald Francis (1894-1973) Born on July 27, 1894, in Mackinac Island, Michigan. Commissioned from Annapolis in 1916. Served aboard the *Birmingham* on convoy duty 1917-1918. Instructor at Annapolis 1923-1924. Designated a naval aviator in 1925. Navigator, then executive officer of the *Yorktown* 1938-1940. Commanding officer of Naval Air Station Miami 1940-1942. Commanding officer of the *Saratoga* October 1942-June 1943. Rear admiral in December 1942. Commander of Naval Air, Tenth Fleet June-October 1943, Fleet Air Norfolk October 1943-January 1944, Carrier Divisions 25, 11 and 4 1944-1945. Assignments after the war included commander of Air Force, Atlantic Fleet 1946-1948. Retired as vice admiral in February 1950. Decorations included the Navy Cross, two Distinguished Service Medals and the Legion of Merit. Died on June 8, 1973.

Boone, Joel Thompson (1889-1974) Born in St. Clair, Pennsylvania, on August 29, 1889. M.D. from Hahnemann Medical College in 1913. Commissioned in the Naval Reserve Medical Corps in April 1914. Served with a Marine battalion in Haiti 1915-1916. With the 6th Marine Regiment in France 1917-1919. Awarded the Medal of Honor at Vierzy on July 19, 1918. Medical officer aboard the presidential yacht *Mayflower*, then physician to the White House 1922-1933. Aboard the *Saratoga*, then the *Argonne* 1938-1940. Senior medical officer at San Diego Naval Air Station 1940-1943. Commander of the naval hospital in Seattle 1943-1945. Commodore in March 1945. Fleet medical officer of the Third Fleet 1945-1946. Assignments after the war included inspector general of the Naval Medical Bureau March 1950 until retirement in November 1950 as vice admiral. Decorations included the Medal of Honor, Distinguished Service Cross, five Silver Stars, the Bronze Star and three Purple Hearts. Died on April 2, 1974.

Bottom, John Thomas Jr. (1899-1983) Born on May 16, 1899, in Denver, Colorado. Commissioned from Annapolis in 1920. Commanding officer of the *Gridley* then the *Salinas* 1938-1941. Graduated from the Naval War College in 1941. Duty in the office of chief of naval operations 1941-1942. Staff officer with Commander in Chief United States Fleet 1942-1943. Commander of Destroyer Squadron 48 July 1943-September 1944. Staff officer with Commander Destroyers, Pacific Fleet 1944-1945. Commodore in April 1945. Commander of Task Flotilla One attached to Destroyers, Pacific Fleet May 1945-March 1946. Retired as rear admiral in July 1949.Decorations included the Silver Star and Bronze Star. Died on October 9, 1983.

Boundy, James William (1907-) Born on June 26, 1907, in Seattle, Washington. B.B.A. from the University of Washington in 1930. Commissioned in the Supply Corps in 1930. Served in the Philippines 1936-1937. Staff officer with Commander Support Force, Atlantic Fleet 1941-1942. Supply officer at Chief of Air Operational Training, Jacksonville 1942-1943 then Commander Air Force, Pacific Fleet 1943-1945. Commodore in July 1945. Fleet supply officer at Commander Service Force, Pacific Fleet 1945-1946. Reverted to captain in 1946, Graduated from NWC in 1949. Rear admiral again in April 1955. Force supply officer with Commander Service Force, Pacific Fleet 1955-1957. Director of supply management policy in the office of the secretary of defense 1957-1958. Chief of the Bureau of Supplies and Accounts August 1958-May 1961. Special assistant to the secretary of the navy May 1961 until retirement in December 1961. Decorations included the Distinguished Service Medal, Legion of Merit and Navy Commendation Medal.

Bowen, Harold Gardiner (1883-1965) Born on November 6, 1883, in Providence, Rhode Island. Graduated from Annapolis in 1905 and commissioned in 1907. M.A. from Columbia University in 1914. Assistant chief, then chief of the Bureau of Engineers 1931-1939. Rear admiral in June 1938. Director of the Naval Research Laboratory 1939-1942. Special assistant to the under secretary, then secretary of the navy 1942-1947. Vice admiral in July 1946. Retired in June 1947. Decorations included the Distinguished Service Medal. Died on August 1, 1965.

Bowne, William Rainear (1878-1956) Born in Bordentown, New Jersey, on May 21, 1878. Attended Annapolis 1897-1898. Commissioned in the Supply Corps in 1901. Aide to Rear Admiral Thomas Washington 1923-1925. Graduated from the Naval War College in 1929. Duty at the Naval Clothing Depot in Brooklyn 1939-1941. District supply officer in Third Naval District August 1941-June 1946. Commodore in April 1945. Retired in May 1942 but continued on active duty until June 1946. Died on March 9, 1956.

Brainard, Roland Munroe (1886-1967) Born on May 17, 1886, in Annapolis, Maryland. Graduate of Annapolis in 1906 and commissioned in 1908. Served aboard the *Louisiana* during the world cruise of the Battle Fleet 1907-1908. Aide to the Commander in Chief Pacific Fleet 1919-1921. Commanding officer of the *LaValette* October 1925-August 1926 and the *Detroit* 1933-1934. Chief of staff to Commander Battleships, Battle Force 1937-1938 then Battle Force 1938-1939. Director of the ships movement division in the office of the chief of naval operations July 1939-March 1942. Rear admiral in July 1940. Commander of the Amphibious Force, Atlantic Fleet March-April 1942 then Task Force 24 April 1942-April 1943. Vice admiral in June 1942. Senior member of the Joint Production Survey Committee, Joint Chiefs of Staff 1943-1945. Retired as vice admiral in November 1943 but continued on active duty until the end of the war. Decorations included the Distinguished Service Medal. Died on December 28, 1967.

Braine, Clinton Elgin Jr. (1894-1951) Born on December 9, 1894, in New York, New York. Commissioned from Annapolis in 1916. Duty with the Bureau of Ordnance 1938-1941. Commanding officer of the *Memphis* 1941-1942. Chief of staff of Fourth Fleet 1942-1945. Commodore in April 1944. Commanded Naval Base Newport 1945-1946. Retired in May 1949. Decorations included three Legions of Merit. Died on January 12, 1951.

Braisted, Frank Alfred (1889-1981) Born on February 12, 1889. in Detroit, Michigan. Graduated from Annapolis in 1909 and commissioned in 1911. M.S. from Columbia University in 1916. Commanding officer of the *Beale* in 1918. Graduated from the Naval War College in 1930. Commanding officer of the *Trenton* 1937-1939. Director of naval reserves in the Ninth Naval District 1939-1940. Commander of the Transport Service Force in the Pacific Fleet 1940-1942. Rear admiral in August 1942. Commander of the Operational Training Command in the Pacific Fleet 1943-1944. Commandant of naval operating bases at Guantanamo and Bermuda 1944-1946. Retired in March 1951. Decorations included the Legion of Merit. Died on December 24, 1981.

Brand, Charles Lees (1887-1953) Born on November 11, 1887, in Worcester, Massachusetts. Graduated from Annapolis in 1910 and commissioned in 1912. M.S. from Massachusetts Institute of Technology in 1915. Stationed at Philadelphia Navy Yard 1915-1920. Staff officer at the Battle Force 1925-1927. Head of the construction division at Bureau of Ships 1932-1936. Commander of Boston Navy Yard 1938-1942. Rear admiral in November 1941. Assistant chief of design and shipbuilding in the Bureau of Ships 1942-1949. Retired in May 1949. Decorations included the Distinguished Service Medal. Died on April 18, 1953.

Briggs, Henry Mixer (1891-1966) Born on May 11, 1891, in New Hampton, Iowa. Commissioned from Annapolis in 1913. Served aboard the *Vermont* at the invasion of Vera Cruz in 1914 and aboard the *Cummings* in European waters during World War I. Instructor at Annapolis 1925-1927. Graduated from the Naval War College in 1935 then a member of the staff there until 1937. Duty in the Bureau of Naval Personnel 1939-1942. Professor of naval science and tactics at Brown University 1943-1944. Staff officer with Commander Caribbean Sea Frontier 1944-1945 then chief of staff February-June 1945. Commodore in February 1945. Staff officer with Commander in Chief Atlantic Fleet 1945-1946. Retired in December 1946. Died on February 27, 1966.

Brinser, Harry Lerch (1876-1945) Born on November 11, 1876, in Middletown, Pennsylvania. Graduated from Annapolis in 1899 and commissioned in 1901. Served aboard the *Santiago* at the battle of Santiago Bay in the Spanish-American War. Commanding officer of the *Columbia* and the *Mercury* in World War I and the *Rigel* 1922-1925. Graduated from the Naval War College in 1928. Commanding officer of the *Mississippi* 1930-1932. Rear admiral in September 1932. Director of Navy Yards October 1932-May 1935. Commander of Cruiser Division Four 1935-1937. President of the Board of Inspection and Survey July 1937-

December 1940. Retired in December 1940. Recalled to active duty in World War II as inspector of naval material in New York City. Served December 1941 until his death on December 9, 1945. Decorations included the Navy Cross and Legion of Merit.

Briscoe, Robert Pearce (1897-1968) Born on February 19, 1897, in Centreville, Mississippi. Commissioned from Annapolis in 1919. Instructor at Annapolis 1929-1931. Duty in China 1931-1933. Again instructor at Annapolis 1934-1937. Navigator on the *Mississippi* 1937-1939. Assistant director of the Naval Research Laboratory 1939-1941. Commanding officer of the *Prometheus* 1942-1943. Commander of Destroyer Squadron Five in 1943. Staff officer with United States Fleet 1944-1945. Rear admiral in April 1945. Commander of operational development for the Atlantic Fleet 1945-1948. Assignments after the war included deputy chief of naval operations 1954-1956 and commander of Allied Forces Eastern Atlantic and Mediterranean 1956-1958. Retired as admiral in January 1959. Decorations included the Navy Cross, Distinguished Service Medal and two Legions of Merit. Died on October 14, 1968.

Bristol, Arthur Leroy Jr. (1886-1942) Born on July 15, 1886, in Charleston, South Carolina. Graduated from Annapolis in 1906 and commissioned in 1908. Served aboard the *Illinois* during the world cruise of the Battle Fleet 1907-1909. Assistant naval attache in Berlin 1912-1913. Commanding officer of the *Terry* then the *Jarvis* 1913-1915. Aide and flag secretary to Commander Destroyer Force, Atlantic Fleet 1916-1917 then Commander Cruiser Force, Atlantic Fleet 1917-1918. Commanding officer of the Breckinridge 1919-1920 then the *Overton* 1920-1921. Aide to Commander Scouting Fleet May-December 1924. Member of the Naval Mission to Brazil January 1925-October 1926. Designated naval aviator in March 1929. Naval attache in London October 1931-March 1934. Commanding officer of the carrier *Ranger* 1934-1936. Rear admiral in July 1939. Commander of Patrol Wing Two, Aircraft, Scouting Force then Carrier Division One, United States Fleet 1939-1940 and Patrol Wings, United States Fleet 1940-1941. Commander of Support Force, Atlantic Fleet March 1941-February 1942. Vice admiral in February 1942. Commander of Task Force Four until his death from coronary thrombosis aboard *the Prairie* in Argentia, Newfoundland, on April 20, 1942. Decorations included the Navy Cross and Distinguished Service Medal.

Brittain, Thomas Baldwin (1898-1974) Born on December 13, 1898, in Annapolis, Maryland. Commissioned from Annapolis in 1920. Instructor there 1925-1927. On patrol duty on the Yangtze River the summer of 1927. Again instructor at Annapolis 1930-1933 and 1936-1938. Commanding officer of the *Shaw* 1938-1941. Professor of naval science and tactics at Tulane University January 1941-January 1943. Commanding officer of the *Monrovia* in 1943. Commander of Transport Division Six September 1943-January 1945. Commodore in November 1944. Commander of Transport Squadron 17 in 1945. Vice admiral upon retirement in February 1955. Decorations included the Silver Star, four Legions of Merit, the Bronze Star and Navy Commendation Medal. Died on April 12, 1974.

Broshek, Joseph John (1886-1957) Born on November 1, 1886, in New Bedford, Massachusetts. Graduated from Annapolis in 1908. M.S. from Columbia University in 1915. Served aboard the *George Washington* during World War I. Aide to Admiral Joseph Strauss 1921-1922. Duty at Naval Station Cavite, Philippines 1922-1923. Assigned to New York Navy yard June 1937-December 1941. Rear admiral in October 1941. Served with the Bureau of Ships 1941-1945. Retired in October 1946. Decorations included the Distinguished Service Medal. Died on June 2, 1957.

Brown, Clarence John (1895-1973) Born on January 15, 1895, in Plum City, Wisconsin. B.S. from the University of Wisconsin in 1915. Commissioned in the Medical Corps in 1917. Medical inspector with the Haitian constabulary 1918-1921. Served at Naval Station Guam 1926-1928 and Guantanamo Bay Naval Station 1941-1942. Rear admiral in September 1942. Duty at Naval Hospital Philadelphia 1942-1944. Staff officer with Commander Twelfth Fleet 1944-1945. Assignments after the war included deputy chief of the Bureau of Medicine and Surgery January 1951-May 1954. Retired as vice admiral in May 1954. Decorations included the Distinguished Service Medal and two Legions of Merit. Died on August 28, 1973.

Brown, John Herbert Jr. (1891-1963) Born on October 12, 1891, in Canton, Pennsylvania. Commissioned from Annapolis in 1914. Commanding officer of submarines *C-2* and *G-4* in World War I, then *N-5* and *R-2* 1919-1921, *S-42* 1924-1927 and the *Narwhal* May 1930-May 1933. Graduated from the Naval War College in 1940. Commanding officer of the *Richmond* 1941-1942. Commander of Submarine Squadron Four June 1942-November 1943. Rear admiral in January 1943. Commander of Submarine Training Command 1943-1945. Vice admiral upon retirement in February 1954. Decorations included two Distinguished Service Medals and the Legion of Merit. Died on June 10, 1963.

Brown, Wilson (1882-1957) Born on April 27, 1882, in Philadelphia, Pennsylvania. Graduated from Annapolis in 1902 and commissioned in 1904. Instructor at Annapolis 1907-1908. Aide to the commandant of the New York Navy yard 1911-1913. Staff officer with Admiral William S. Sims and commanding officer of the *Parker* during World War I. Commanding officer of the *Blakeley* 1919-1920. Aide to Commander Destroyer Squadrons, Battle Fleet 1924-1926. Naval aide to President Calvin Coolidge 1926-1929. Commanding officer of the *California* 1932-1933. Chief of staff at the Naval War College 1933-1934. Naval aide to President Herbert Hoover 1934-1936. Rear admiral in July 1936. Commander of the Training Squadron, Scouting Force May 1936-February 1938. Superintendent of Annapolis 1938-1941. Vice admiral in February 1941. Commander of Scouting Force, Pacific Fleet February 1941-July 1942. Commandant of the First Naval District 1942-1943. Aide to President Roosevelt February 1943-1944. Retired in December 1944. Decorations included the Navy Cross and Distinguished Service Medal. Died on January 2, 1957.

Browne, Davenport (1895-1988) Born on March 10, 1895, in Bradford, Connecticut. Commissioned from Annapolis in 1917. Served aboard the *Delaware* during World War I, with the British Grand Fleet, and later in Haitian waters. Aide to Commander Battleship Division Three, Atlantic Fleet then Division Seven, Pacific Fleet 1921-1924. Commanding officer of the *Hale* 1933-1935. Duty in the Bureau of Navigation July 1939-October 1941. Commanding officer of the *Chaumont* 1941-1943. Fleet Personnel Officer, Service Force, Subordinate Command Pacific Fleet then assistant chief of staff for personnel with the Western Sea Frontier 1943-1946. Commodore in April 1945. Retired in November 1946. Decorations included the Navy Commendation Medal. Died on August 26, 1988.

Bruce, Bryson (1886-1961) Born on March 20, 1886, in Garden Grove, Iowa. Graduated from Annapolis in 1907 and commissioned in 1909. M.S. from Columbia University in 1914. Served in Shanghai 1926-1928. Duty in the inspection division, office of chief of naval operations 1938-1941 then the administrative division of the Bureau of Ships July 1941-June 1942. Rear admiral in April 1941. Chief of the office of procurement and material, Navy Department in 1942. Supervisor of shipbuilding at Cramp Shipbuilding Company, Philadelphia then New York Shipbuilding Corp. October 1942 until retirement in November 1946. Died on April 17, 1961.

Bruns, Henry Frederick (1889-1947) Born on November 24, 1889, in Whites Creek, West Virginia. Commissioned in the Civil Engineer Corps from Annapolis in 1911. B.S. from Rensselaer Polytechnic Institute in 1914. Public works officer at Naval Base Guantanamo Bay 1916-1917. Duty at Navy Yard Pearl Harbor 1928-1930 and again 1938-1941. Public works officer at Naval Operating Base San Diego January-April 1942. Superintendent engineer at Area Six, San Francisco 1942-1945. Rear admiral in July 1943. Director of the Atlantic Division, then the Eastern Pacific Division of the Bureau of Yards and Docks August 1945 until his death on January 20, 1947. Decorations included the Legion of Merit.

Bryan, George Sloan (1884-1964) Born on December 23, 1884, in Scotland Neck, North Carolina. Graduated from Annapolis in 1906 and commissioned in 1908. Commanded the *Monocacy* 1915-1916. Aide and flag lieutenant to Commander in Chief Asiatic Fleet May 1917-June 1918. Commanded the *Yarborough* 1925-1926. Graduated from the Naval War College in 1928. Commanding officer of the *Melville* 1929-1931 and the *Maryland* 1935-1936. Chief of staff to Commander Scouting Force June 1936-July 1937. Hydrographer of the Navy 1938-1940. Retired in June 1941 but continued on active duty. Rear admiral in March 1942. Released from active duty in August 1946. Decorations included the Navy Cross and Legion of Merit. Died on July 13, 1964.

Bryant, Carleton Fanton (1892-1987) Born on November 29, 1892, in New York, New York. Commissioned from Annapolis in 1914. M.S. from Lehigh University in 1921. Commanding officer of the *Oahu* in 1932 and the *Stewart* in

1934. Inspector of ordnance at Cavite, Philippine Islands 1934-1935. Commanding officer of the *Charleston* 1937-1939 and the *Arkansas* 1941-1943. Rear admiral in September 1942. Commander of Battleship Division Five, Atlantic Fleet May 1943-October 1944. Commander of Fleet Operations Training Command October 1944-December 1945. Vice admiral upon retirement in July 1946. Decorations included the Distinguished Service Medal and three Legions of Merit. Died on April 11, 1987.

Buck, Walter Albert (1895-1955) Born on June 4, 1895, in Oskaloosa, Kansas. B.S. from Kansas State University in 1913 and M.S. in 1916. Commissioned in the Supply Corps in 1917. M.B.A. from Harvard in 1924. Graduated from AIC in 1933 then instructor there until 1936. Executive officer of Navy Finance and Supply School 1938-1941. Staff officer with Commander Support Force Atlantic Fleet March 1941-February 1942. Duty in the office of procurement and material, Navy Department in 1942. Rear admiral in March 1943. Supply officer at Philadelphia Navy Yard January 1943-April 1944. Assigned to the office of the assistant secretary of the navy 1944-1945. Chief of the property disposition branch, material division April-October 1945. Retired in March 1948. Decorations included two Legions of Merit and the Navy Commendation Medal. Died on June 12, 1955.

Buckmaster, Elliott (1889-1976) Born on October 18, 1889, in Brooklyn, New York. Commissioned from Annapolis in 1912. Served aboard the *New Jersey* at the occupation of Vera Cruz in 1914 and the *Tacoma* on convoy duty during World War I. Aide to the commandant of Portsmouth Navy yard 1927-1929. Commanding officer of the *McFarland* 1929-1931 and the *Farragut* 1934-1936. Qualified as naval aviator in 1937. Executive officer of Fleet Air Base Coco Solo, Canal Zone in 1938. Commander of Naval Air Station Pearl Harbor August 1939-January 1941. Commanding officer of the carrier *Yorktown*, sunk at the Battle of Midway. Rear admiral in May 1942. Commander of Naval Air Station Norfolk July-October 1942. Chief of air primary training 1942-1943. Commandant of Naval Air Center December 1943-January 1945. Commander of Western Carolinas and South China naval forces in 1945. Vice admiral upon retirement in November 1946. Decorations included two Distinguished Service Medals. Died on October 10, 1976.

Bunker, Charles Waite Orville (1882-1958) Born on February 23, 1882, in Viroqua, Iowa. M.D. from Cornell in 1905. Commissioned in the Medical Corps in 1907. Staff officer for the United States High Commissioner to Turkey 1923-1925. Graduated from the Naval War College in 1936. Commanding officer of Naval Medical School 1941-1942 and the National Naval Medical Center at Bethesda February 1942-October 1944. Rear admiral in June 1942. Retired in October 1944. Died on September 17, 1958.

Bunkley, Joel William (1887-1967) Born on July 3, 1887, in Macon, Georgia. Graduated from Annapolis in 1909 and commissioned in 1911. Served with the

Naval Railway Battalion in France in World War I. Aide to the commander of the Destroyer Force, Atlantic Fleet 1919-1920. Aide to the Commander in Chief Asiatic Fleet 1923-1924. Commanding officer of the *Pruitt, Childs* and *Banner* 1924-1926 then the *Wood* and *Greer* 1928-1930. Member of U.S. Naval Mission to Argentina 1934-1937. Commander of Destroyer Squadron Ten 1938-1939. Commanding officer of the *California* 1940-1942, sunk during the attack on Pearl Harbor. Retired as rear admiral in July 1942 and immediately recalled to active duty as supervisor of New York harbor until retirement again in January 1946. Decorations included the Navy Cross and Legion of Merit. Died on December 10, 1967.

Burke, Arleigh Albert (1901-) Born on October 19, 1901, in Boulder, Colorado. Graduated from Annapolis in 1923. M.S. from the University of Michigan in 1931. Commanding officer of destroyer *Mugford* 1939-1940. With Bureau of Ordnance 1940-1943. Commander of Destroyer Squadron 23 1943-1945, where he earned the nickname "31-Knot Burke" during campaigns at Bougainville and Buka, October-November 1943. Commodore in October 1944. Chief of staff to Vice Admiral Marc A. Mitscher in 1945. Chief of staff to commander of the Atlantic Fleet 1945-1947. Assignments after the war included director of strategic plans division, Navy Department 1952-1954. Named by President Eisenhower as chief of naval operations over the heads of more than 90 senior admirals and served as chief of naval operations August 1955 until retirement as admiral in August 1961, a term longer than anyone in history. Decorations included the Navy Cross, three Distinguished Service Medals, the Silver Star, four Legions of Merit and the Purple Heart. Resides in Bethesda, Maryland.

Burrough, Edmund Weidmann (1890-1962) Born on October 28, 1890, in Camden, New Jersey. Commissioned from Annapolis in 1914. Commanding officer of the *L-2, B-1, Monadnock* and *B-2* 1918-1919. M.S. from Columbia University in 1921. Commanding officer of *S-26* 1923-1925. Staff officer at the Naval War College 1936-1938. Duty with the war plans division, office of the chief of naval operations 1940-1942. Commanding officer of the *Cleveland* 1942-1943. Rear admiral in April 1943. Staff officer with Commander in Chief United States Fleet 1943-1945. Assistant chief of naval operations for logistics plans July-December 1945. Vice admiral upon retirement in November 1952. Decorations included two Legions of Merit. Died on May 8, 1962.

Busbey, Leroy White Jr. (1897-1952) Born on March 7, 1897, in Washington, DC. Commissioned from Annapolis in 1918. Commanding officer of *S-16* 1922-1923. Instructor at Annapolis 1923-1925. Commanding officer of the *Bernadou* 1935-1937 and the *Gridley* 1937-1938. War plans officer at Fifth Naval District July 1938-October 1940. Executive officer of the *Arkansas* 1940-1942 then commanding officer of the *Alcor* April-July 1942. Operations officer for Service Force Atlantic Fleet July 1942-August 1943. Commanding officer of the *Salt Lake City* 1943-1944 then American Naval Forces Aruba November 1944-

January 1946. Commodore in December 1944. Rear admiral upon retirement in July 1949. Decorations included the Silver Star and Legion of Merit. Died on February 27, 1952.

Butler, Henry Varnum (1874-1957) Born on March 9, 1874, in Paterson, New Jersey. Graduated from Annapolis in 1895 and commissioned in 1897. Aide to Captain Charles V. Gridley aboard the *Olympia* at the Battle of Manila Bay in the Spanish-American War. Served aboard the *Buffalo* during the Boxer Rebellion and commanding officer of the *Mindora* in the Philippine Insurrection of 1901. Aide to Admiral George Dewey 1907-1911. Captain of the port at Panama, Canal Zone 1914-1915. Commanding officer of the *San Francisco* attached to the British Grand Fleet in World War I. Commanding officer of the *Michigan* in 1921 and the *Saratoga* 1926-1927. Rear admiral in 1927. Chief of staff to the Commander in Chief United States Fleet 1927-1929. Superintendent of the Naval Gun Factory 1931-1934. Vice admiral in April 1935. Commander of Aircraft, Battle Force 1935-1936. Commandant of Sixth, Seventh and Eighth Naval Districts 1936-1938. Retired in April 1938. Recalled to active duty in March 1942. Administrative officer in the office of the secretary of the navy March 1942-October 1944. Decorations included the Distinguished Service Medal. Died on August 6, 1957.

Byrd, Richard Evelyn Jr. (1888-1957) Born in Winchester, Virginia, on October 25, 1888. Attended Virginia Military Institute and the University of Viriginia. Graduated from Annapolis in 1912. Qualified as a naval aviator in 1918. Commander of a patrol squadron in Canada during World War I. Instrumental in planning the 1919 flight to Europe of three Navy flying boats. Attached to Donald B. MacMillan's Arctic expedition in 1924. With Bernt Balchen as his co-pilot Byrd made the first flight over the North Pole in the *Josephine Ford* on May 9, 1926. Both men were awarded the Medal of Honor. Led an expeditiion to Antarctica 1928-1930 and established a base known as "Little America." Byrd, Balchen and two others made the first flight over the South Pole on November 29, 1929. Rear admiral, retired, in December 1929. Commanded a second expedition to Antarctica 1933-1935, during which he nearly died from carbon monoxide poisoning while alone in a weather observation shack for five months in the winter of 1934. Recalled to active duty on the staff of Admiral Ernest J. King in World War II. After the war he made another expedition to Antarctica 1946-1947 and in 1955 became head of Operation Deep Freeze. Made his last flight over the South Pole in January 1956. Decorations included the Medal of Honor, Navy Cross and Distinguished Service Medal. Author of *Skyward* (1928), *Little America* (1930), *Discovery* (1935) and *Alone* (1938). Died on March 11, 1957.

Calhoun, William Lowndes (1884-1963) Born on July 13, 1884, in Palatka, Florida, a great grandson of Vice President John Calhoun. Graduated from Annapolis in 1906 and commissioned in 1908. Commanding officer of the submarine *L-7* 1916-1917 and the *Farragut* in 1917. Commander of Submarine Base Coco Solo, Canal Zone 1918-1919. Commanding officer of the *Young* in 1923. Graduated from the Naval War College in 1930. Instructor at Annapolis 1930-

1932. Commanding officer of the *Rochester* 1932-1933 and the *California* 1937-1938. Rear admiral in November 1938. Chief of staff to Commander Battleships, Battle Force 1938-1939. Duty at the Naval War College 1939-1940. Commander of Base Force, United States Fleet 1940-1942. Commander of Service Force Pacific Fleet February 1942-March 1945. Vice admiral in June 1942. Commander of South Pacific Force March-October 1945. Retired in December 1946. Decorations included two Legions of Merit. Died on October 19, 1963.

Callaghan, Daniel Judson (1890-1942) Born in San Francisco, California, on July 26, 1890. Graduated from Annapolis in 1911 and commissioned in 1913. Naval aide to President Roosevelt 1938-1941. At Pearl Harbor as commanding officer of the *San Francisco* on December 7, 1941. Chief of staff to Vice Admiral Robert L. Ghormley January 1942-November 1942. Rear admiral in October 1942. Commander of a task force of cruisers and destroyers on escort duty. Killed when a shell from a Japanese battleship struck the bridge of his flagship off Guadalcanal on November 13, 1942. Decorations included a posthumous Medal of Honor.

Callaghan, William McCombe (1897-1991) Born on August 8, 1897, in Oakland, California, the brother of Rear Admiral Daniel Callaghan. Commissioned from Annapolis in 1919. M.S. from Columbia University in 1925. Instructor at Annapolis 1936-1939. Commanding officer of the *Reuben James* then executive officer of the *Henderson* 1936-1939. Duty in the ships' movements section, office of the chief of naval operations 1939-1942. Staff officer with Commander in Chief Pacific Fleet July 1942-May 1944. Rear admiral in August 1943. Commanding officer of the Missouri 1944-1945. Rear admial in May 1945. Duty on the staff of Commander in Chief Pacific Fleet May-July 1945. Assistant chief of naval operations for transportation 1945-1948. Assignments after the war included command of Amphibious Force, Pacific Fleet December 1952-March 1954, Naval Forces Far East 1954-1956 and Western Sea Frontier November 1956-March 1957. Retired as vice admiral in March 1957. Decorations included the Legion of Merit. Died on July 8, 1991.

Camerer, Clyde Bradley (1882-1959) Born on August 20, 1882, in Kinmundy, Illinois. M.D. from St. Louis University School of Medicine in 1909. Commissioned in the Medical Corps in 1909. Duty as brigade surgeon with the Third Provisional Brigade in Haiti and Cuba April 1917-June 1919. Graduated from the Naval War College in 1935. Served at the Naval Hospital, Puget Sound 1937-1940. Medical officer in command of Naval Hospital Canacao, Philippines April 1940-October 1941 then Naval Hospital Parris Island October 1941-February 1944. District medical officer at Ninth Naval District 1944-1945 then Fourteenth Naval District February 1945 until retirement in April 1946. Rear admiral in April 1945. Died on May 12, 1959.

Campbell, Edward Hale (1872-1946) Born on October 4, 1872, in South Bend, Indiana. Graduated from Annapolis in 1893 and commissioned in 1895. Judge advocate general of the Navy as captain in 1907. Commanding officer of the *New Orleans* 1915-1016 and the *Charleston* 1916-1917. Graduated from the Naval War College in 1920. Judge advocate general of the Navy as rear admiral 1925-1929. Commander of the Special Service Squadron 1929-1930. Commandant of Thirteenth Naval District 1931-1934. Commander of the Scouting Force as vice admiral 1934-1935. Commandant of Twelfth Naval District 1935-1936. Retired in November 1936. Recalled to active duty May-August 1942 to serve at Thirteenth Naval District. Decorations included the Navy Cross. Died on December 11, 1946.

Carlson, Milton Oren (1895-1977) Born on January 11, 1895, in Minneapolis, Minnesota. Commissioned from Annapolis in 1916. M.S. from Massachusetts Institute of Technology in 1923. Aboard the *Stewart* during the landing at Shanghai in 1925. Aide to Rear Admiral Orin G. Murfin May 1930-June 1931. Commanding officer of the *Charleston* 1939-1940. Duty at New York Navy Yard January 1941-February 1944. Commodore in October 1944. Commander of 5th Amphibious Force then Transport Squadrons 32. 13 and 37 1944-1946. Rear admiral upon retirement in August 1947. Decorations included three Legions of Merit and two Bronze Stars. Died on February 2, 1977.

Carney, Robert Bostwick (1895-1990) Born in Vallejo, California, on March 26, 1895. Graduated from Annapolis in 1916. Served aboard the *Dixie* and the *Fanning* in World War I. Instructor at Annapolis 1923-1925. Commanding officer of the *Sirius* 1937-1938. In the office of the secretary of the navy 1938-1940. Chief of staff of the Support Force Atlantic Fleet 1941-1942. Commanding officer of the *Denver* 1942-1943. Rear admiral in December 1942. Chief of staff to Admiral William F. Halsey, commander of the South Pacific area, then Third Fleet 1943-1946. Assignments after the war included commander of the Second Fleet in 1950, U.S. Naval Forces in the Eastern Atlantic and Mediterranean 1950-1951, commander in chief of NATO forces in the Mediterranean, then NATO forces in Southern Europe 1951-1953 and chief of naval operations August 1953 until retirement as admiral in August 1955. Decorations included the Navy Cross, four Distinguished Service Medals, the Legion of Merit and Bronze Star. Died on June 25, 1990.

Carpender, Arthur Schuyler (1884-1960) Born on October 24, 1884, in New Brunswick, New Jersey. Graduated from Annapolis in 1908 and commissioned in 1910. Served aboard the *Minnesota* during the world cruise with the Battle Fleet 1907-1908. Adjutant with the 1st Marine Regiment at the occupation of Vera Cruz in 1914. Commanding officer of the *Fanning* in 1917. His ship sank the first German u-boat in World War I. Commanding officer of the *Maddox* 1921-1922 and the *McDonough* in 1928. Chief of staff to the Commander Destroyers, Scouting Force 1936-1937. Commanding officer of the *Northampton* 1937-1938. Professor of naval science and tactics at Northwestern University 1938-1939. Rear admiral in December 1941. Commander of Destroyers, Atlantic Fleet 1941-

1942 then Southwest Pacific Force September 1942-November 1943. Commandant of Ninth Naval District January 1944-March 1946. Admiral upon retirement in November 1946. Decorations included two Distinguished Service Medals and two Legions of Merit. Died on January 10, 1960.

Carroll, Penn Leary (1886-1961) Born on February 17, 1886, in Minden, Louisiana. Graduated from Annapolis in 1909 and commissioned in 1911. Served aboard the *Balch* at the invasion of Vera Cruz in 1914. M.S. from Columbia University in 1916. M.S. from Massachusetts Institute of Technology in 1917 and Harvard in 1917. Commanding officer of the *Fox, Gilmer* and *Toucey* August 1920-May 1921. Member of the U.S. Military Mission to Brazil 1923-1925. Aide to Commander in Chief Asiatic Fleet 1927-1929. Graduated from the Naval War College in 1930 then staff officer there until 1932. Commodore in July 1945. Deputy chief of staff to Commander Seventh Fleet July 1945-April 1946. Retired in December 1947. Decorations included the Legion of Merit and Bronze Star. Died on December 3, 1961.

Carson, John Hazard (1896-1976) Born on April 13, 1896, in Spartanburg, South Carolina. Commissioned from Annapolis in 1916. Served with the Atlantic Fleet in World War I. M.S. from Massachusetts Institute of Technology in 1924. Commanding officer of the *Dewey* 1936-1937. Duty at the Navy Proving Ground, Dahlgren, Virginia, 1937-1940. Executive officer of the *New Mexico* 1940-1941. Operations officer on the staff of the commander of cruisers in the Battle Force, then Southwest Pacific Forces 1941-1943. Commanding officer of the *Boston* 1943-1944. Rear admiral in March 1944. Commander of U.S. Naval Torpedo Station, Newport 1944-1946. Retired as vice admiral in April 1958. Decorations included two Bronze Stars and the Navy Commendation Medal. Died on February 1, 1976.

Carter, Andrew Francis (1883-1966) Born on January 17, 1883, in Little Rock, Arkansas. Graduated from Annapolis in 1905 and commissioned in 1907. Commanding officer of the *Monocacy* June 1914-September 1916. Aide to Admiral William S. Benson 1916-1919. Commanding officer of the *Herbert* December 1919-January 1920. Resigned in January 1920 and joined the Naval Reserve. Called to active duty in March 1942 as executive officer of the Army-Navy Petroleum Board, office of the chief of naval operations. Commodore in July 1943 and rear admiral in June 1944. Retired again in March 1946. Decorations included the Navy Cross and Distinguished Service Medal. Died on August 2, 1966.

Carter, James Benham (1896-1985) Born on December 28, 1896, in Ozark, Arkansas. Commissioned from Annapolis in 1919. Designated naval aviator, lighter-than-air, in March 1927. Pilot aboard the dirigible *Los Angeles* 1927-1928. Served aboard the destroyer *Edsall* during Yangtze River operations in 1931. Aide to Commander Base Force, United States Fleet 1933-1934. Instructor at George Institute of Technology ROTC 1936-1938. Commanding officer of the *Reid* June 1938-May 1941. Attended the Naval War College in 1941 then staff member there until June 1943. Duty with Commander in Chief Pacific Fleet as member of the war plans division then assistant chief of staff for operations 1943-1945. Commodore in November 1944. Retired in July 1949. Decorations included the Legion of Merit. Died on April 1, 1985.

Carter, William Joseph (1893-n/a) Born on April 19, 1893, in Dillon, South Carolina. B.A. from Wofford College in 1913 then attended Cornell University. Commissioned in the Supply Corps in 1917. M.B.A. from Harvard in 1926. Served with the Bureau of Supplies and Accounts August 1937-October 1946, from June 1942-March 1945 as assistant chief of the Bureau and chief 1945-1946. Rear admiral in September 1942, vice admiral in August 1946. Retired in October 1946. Decorations included the Distinguished Service Medal.

Carter, Worrall Reed (1885-1975) Born on January 11, 1885, at sea aboard the American sailing ship *Storm King*. Graduated from Annapolis in 1908 and commissioned in 1910. Commanding officer of the submarines *C-5* November 1911-September 1912, *D-3* September 1912-September 1913. M.S. from Columbia University in 1915. Commanding officer of *L-11* August 1915-June 1917. Member of the U.S. Navy Mission to Brazil 1925-1926. Commanding officer of the *Osborne* September 1927-June 1929. Instructor at Annapolis 1929-1931. Commanding officer of the *Nokomis* July 1931-May 1933 and the *Marblehead* 1936-1938. Commandant of the Guantanamo Bay Naval Station June 1938-August 1940. Commander of Submarine Squadron Four October 1940-January 1941. Chief of staff of Battleships, Battle Force 1941-1942. Commander of U.S. Naval Advanced Base South Pacific Area October 1942-June 1943 then North Pacific Area June-October 1943. Commodore in June 1944. Commander of Service Squadron Ten January 1944-July 1945. Rear admiral upon retirement in February 1947. Decorations included the Distinguished Service Medal and Legion of Merit. Died on July 22, 1975.

Cary, Robert Webster Jr. (1890-1967) Born on August 18, 1890, in Kansas City, Missouri. Commissioned from Annapolis in 1914. Awarded the Medal of Honor for heroism following a boiler explosion on the *San Diego* on January 21, 1915. Aide to Commander Naval Forces Eastern Mediterranean 1919-1920 and Commandant Norfolk Navy Yard 1921-1924. Commander of Battleship Division Three 1925-1927. Aide to Commander Battleships, Battle Force 1930-1932. Commanding officer of the *Jacob Jones* 1932-1934. Graduated from the Naval War College in 1935 then member of the staff there until 1937. Executive officer of the *Chicago* June 1939-December 1940. Duty in the office of the chief of naval operations January 1941-January 1943. Commanding officer of the *Savannah* and the *Brooklyn* February 1943-May 1944. Commander of the Naval Training and 1944. Rear admiral upon retirement in December 1946. Decorations included the Medal of Honor, Navy Cross, five Legions of Merit, the Navy Commendation Medal and Purple Heart. Died on July 15, 1967.

Cassady, John Howard (1896-1969) Born on April 3, 1896, in Spencer, Indiana. Commissioned from Annapolis in 1919. Designated a naval aviator in 1928. Assistant naval attache in Rome 1937-1939. Operations officer on the staff of the commander of Aircraft, Atlantic Fleet 1940-1941. Chief of staff to the commander of the Operational Training Command at Jacksonville 1941-1942. Commanding officer of the *Saratoga* 1943-1944. Rear admiral in August 1943. Assistant deputy chief of naval operations for air 1944-1945. Commander of Carrier Division Four, Atlantic Fleet 1945-1946. Assignments after the war included deputy chief of naval operations (air) January 1950-May 1952, commander of Sixth Fleet 1952-1954 and commander in chief Naval Forces Eastern Atlantic and Mediteranean 1954-1956. Retired as admiral in May 1956. Decorations included three Legions of Merit. Died on January 25, 1969.

Cather, David Clark (1879-1944) Born on December 19, 1879, in Clearbrook, Virginia. M.D. from the University of Pennsylvania in 1903. Commissioned in the Medical Corps in 1904. Duty at Naval Hospital Canacao, Philippines during World War I. Senior medical officer at Submarine Base Coco Solo, Canal Zone August 1928-July 1930. Graduated from the Naval War College in 1931. Medical officer in command of Naval Hospital Puget Sound 1935-1939. Rear admiral in January 1939. Inspector of Medical Department Activities, Pacific Coast 1939-1942. Retired in December 1942. Died on June 25, 1944.

Cecil, Charles Purcell (1893-1944) Born on September 4, 1893, in Louisville, Kentucky. Commissioned from Annapolis in 1916. Served aboard the *Yankton* in escort duty during World War I. Aide to Commandant Sixth Naval District 1922-1924. Aide to Commander Battleship Divisions Three and Four 1929-1930. Commanding officer of the *Greer* September 1935-February 1936 and the destroyer *Cummings* 1936-1938. Commander of Destroyer Division Eleven then Destroyer Squadron Five June 1941-October 1942. Commanding officer of the *Helena* when it was sunk in the Kula Gulf on July 6, 1943. Commander of a unit of the Seventh Fleet Amphibious Force 1943-1944. Rear admiral in June 1944. Killed along with 18 others in the crash of a Navy transport plane while taking off from an island in the Pacific on July 31, 1944. Decorations included two Navy Crosses and the Bronze Star.

Chambers, William (1884-1951) Born on August 25, 1884, in Philadelphia, Pennsylvania. M.D. from Jefferson Medical College in 1907. Commissioned in the Medical Corps in 1908. Served aboard the *Morro Castle* and with the Third Regiment, U.S. Marines at Vera Cruz in 1914. Served with the Marine Detachment at Peking 1916-1917, the 13th Regiment, Fifth Brigade, U.S. Marines in the AEF in 1918, and again in Peking 1921-1922. Graduated from the Naval War College, then designated a flight surgeon in 1926. Director of the American Scientific Mission to Haiti 1933-1934. Medical officer in charge of Naval Hospital Canacao, Philippines 1936-1938 then Naval Medical School July 1938-July 1940 and Naval Hospital San Diego 1940-1942. Rear admiral in September 1942. District medical officer at Fourteenth Naval District 1942-1943. Inspector of medical department activities in the Southwest Pacific Areas 1943-1944. Medical officer in charge of the National Naval Medical Center at Bethesda September 1944-November 1946. Retired as vice admiral in November 1946. Decorations included the Distinguished Service Medal and Navy Commendation Medal. Died on March 29, 1951.

Chandler, Theodore Edson (1894-1945) Born on December 26, 1894, in Annapolis, Maryland. Commissioned from Annapolis in 1915. Served aboard the destroyer *Conner* in World War I. M.S. from the University of Michigan in 1922. Commanding officer of the *Pope* 1929-1930. Graduated from the Army Industrial College in 1931. Commanded the *Buchanan* 1934-1935. Assistant naval attache in Paris, Madrid and Lisbon 1935-1938. Commanding officer of the *Omaha* 1941-1943. Rear admiral in October 1942. Commander of U.S. forces in Aruba and Curacao April 1943-July 1944. Commander of Cruiser Division Two, Battleship Division Two and Cruiser Division Four July 1944-January 1945. Died on January 7, 1945, the result of enemy action while liberating Luzon. Decorations included the Navy Cross, Distinguished Service Medal, Silver Star and Legion of Merit.

Chantry, Allan J. Jr. (1883-1959) Born on April 15, 1883, in Malvern, Iowa. Graduated from Annapolis in 1906 and commissioned in 1908. M.S. from Massachusetts Institute of Technology in 1910. Instructor at Annapolis 1923-1927. Graduated from the Naval War College in 1936. Head of the design and construction division, Navy Department 1936-1939. Rear admiral in October 1938. Manager of the industrial department at Philadelphia Navy Yard September 1939-December 1945. Retired in April 1946. Decorations included the Legion of Merit. Died on April 9, 1959.

Chapline, Vance Duncan (1887-1970) Born on September 19, 1887, in Red Cloud, Nebraska. Graduated from Annapolis in 1909 and commissioned in 1911. Commanding officer of the *Preble* October 1914-May 1916. Commanded the *Burrows, Harvard* and *Fairfax* during World War I in Irish waters. Aide to Commander Squadron Five, Patrol Force Atlantic Fleet then aide for operations to Commander Naval Forces in France in 1918-1919. Commanding officer of the *Reid* April 1919-June 1921 and the Philadelphia September 1939-September 1941. Director of the Naval Reserve division in the Bureau of Navigation 1941-1942. Director of the fleet maintenance division in the office of the chief of naval operations February 1942-May 1946. Rear admiral in April 1945. Retired in November 1946. Decorations included the Navy Cross and Legion of Merit. Died on August 21, 1970.

Charlton, Alexander Mark (1887-1971) Born on July 19, 1887, in Omaha, Nebraska. Graduated from Annapolis in 1908 and commissioned in 1910. Served aboard the *Texas* in World War I. Member of the Naval Mission to Brazil 1926-1930. Staff officer with the Battle Force 1931-1933 then the Asiatic Fleet 1935-

1937. Industrial manager at Puget Sound Navy Yard 1940-1943. Rear admiral in October 1941. Inspector for Naval Materiel in Chicago 1943-1944. Member of the executive committee of the Army and Navy Munitions Board, then head of the production branch in the office of procurement and material 1944-1946. Retired in October 1946. Decorations included the Legion of Merit. Died on July 11, 1971.

Christie, Ralph Waldo (1893-1987) Born on August 30, 1893, in Somerville, Massachusetts. Commissioned from Annapolis in 1915. M.S. from Massachusetts Institute of Technology in 1923. Commanding officer of the submarines *C-1* January 1918-February 1919 and the *R-6* August-December 1920. M.S. from Massachusetts Institute of Technology in 1923. Commanding officer of the S-1 in 1923 and the S-17 in 1924. Commander of Submarine Division Fifteen January 1939-December 1940 then Submarine Squadron Twenty 1940-1942. Rear admiral in November 1942. Duty at Naval Torpedo Station Newport January-March 1943 then commander of Submarines, Southwest Pacific 1943-1945. Commandant of Puget Sound Navy Yard February 1945-January 1948. Vice admiral upon retirement in August 1949. Decorations included the Distinguished Service Medal, Silver Star and Legion of Merit. Died on December 19, 1987.

Church, Albert Thomas (1882-1954) Born on April 6, 1882, in Idaho City, Idaho. Graduated from Annapolis in 1905 and commissioned in 1907. Staff officer with Admiral William S. Sims at American Naval Forces Europe in World War I. Served aboard the *Louisiana* at Vera Cruz in 1914. Fleet engineer, then aide to Commander in Chief Battle Fleet 1923-1927. Duty in the shore establishments division, office of the assistant secretary of the navy 1937-1939. Rear admiral in June 1938. Director of the naval engineering experiment division at Annapolis October 1939-September 1944. Retired in January 1945. Decorations included the Legion of Merit. Died on March 14, 1954.

Church, Gaylord (1885-1965) Born on August 14, 1885, in Meadville, Pennsylvania. Graduated from Annapolis in 1909 and commissioned in the Civil Engineer Corps in 1911. Staff officer with naval governor of the Virgin Islands 1917-1919. Duty at the Naval Station, Canal Zone 1926-1928 then Cavite, Philippine Islands 1932-1934. Duty at Philadelphia Navy Yard 1937-1942. Rear admiral in September 1942. Superintending civil engineer of Area Number Three 1943-1945. Retired in November 1945. Decorations included the Legion of Merit. Died on January 12, 1965.

Clark, David Henderson (1899-1982) Born on February 25, 1899, in Henderson, Kentucky. Commissioned from Annapolis in 1919. M.S. from Columbia University in 1925. Naval personnel officer at the Bureau of Engineers then Bureau of Ships 1938-1940. Duty with the design division, Bureau of Ships 1940-1941. Fleet engineering officer of the staff of Commander in Chief Pacific Fleet 1941-1942. Assistant fleet maintenance officer at Pacific Fleet 1942-1943. Rear admiral in July 1943. Planning officer at Boston Navy Yard 1943-1946. Retired in July 1953. Decorations included the Legion of Merit. Died on September 3, 1982.

Clark, Joseph James (1893-1971) Born on November 12, 1893, in Pryor, Oklahoma. Attended Oklahoma A&M College. Commissioned from Annapolis in 1918. Served aboard the cruiser *North Carolina* in World War I. Instructor at Annapolis 1923-1924. Designated naval aviator in March 1925. Executive officer of Fleet Air Base, Pearl Harbor 1937-1939 then Jacksonville Naval Air Station 1940-1941. Executive officer of the *Yorktown* May 1941-February 1942. Duty in the Bureau of Aeronautics February-June 1942 then commanding officer of the *Suwanee* November 1942-February 1943 and the new Yorktown 1943-1944. Rear admiral in January 1944. Task group commander operating with the First and Second Fast Carrier Task Groups, Pacific Fleet February 1944-June 1945. Chief of Naval Air Intermediate Training Command 1945-1946. Assignments after the war included commander of First Fleet March-May 1952, then Seventh Fleet during the Korean War 1952-1953. Admiral upon retirement in December 1953. Decorations included the Navy Cross, two Distinguished Service Medals, the Silver Star and Legion of Merit. Died on July 13, 1971.

Clarke, Horace Donald (1892-1957) Born on May 15, 1892, in Eagle Grove, Iowa. Commissioned from Annapolis in 1915. Served aboard the *Pennsylvania* 1917-1919. Aide and flag secretary to Commander Battleship Division Four, Battle Fleet September 1924-November 1925. Aide to the superintendent, then instructor at Annapolis 1927-1930 and 1933-1936. Commanding officer of the destroyer *Selfridge* 1936-1938. Graduated from the Naval War College in 1939. Commanded Destroyer Squadron 83 September 1939-May 1940 and Destroyer Division 16 1940-1941. Head of the ordnance and gunnery department at Annapolis May 1941-February 1943. Commanding officer of the *Idaho* 1943-1944. Assistant chief of staff to Commandant Twelfth Naval District September 1944-January 1945. Commodore in April 1945. Commander of Naval Training Station at Norfolk February 1945-February 1946. Reverted to captain in August 1947. Rear admiral upon retirement in December 1947. Decorations included the Legion of Merit. Died on May 11, 1957.

Cluverius, Wat Tyler Jr. (1874-1952) Born on December 25, 1874, in New Orleans, Louisiana. Graduated from Annapolis in 1896 and commissioned in 1898. Served aboard the *Maine* 1897-1898 and survived its sinking in Havana Harbor on February 15, 1898. Took part in the Spanish-American War and, aboard the *Solace*, in the Philippine Campaign in 1900. Commanding officer of the *Alvarado* and the *Sandoval* 1901-1902. Commanding officer of the battalion aboard the *North Dakota* during the occupation of Vera Cruz in 1914. Commanding officer of the *Dubuque* in 1915. Instructor at Annapolis 1915-1917. Commanded the *Shawmut* in mine laying duties in the Atlantic during World War I then the *Baltimore* in 1919. Commandant of midshipmen at Annapolis 1919-1921. Graduated from the Naval War College in 1922. Rear admiral in May 1928. Commandant of the Norfolk Navy Yard 1928-1930. Commander of Battleship Division Two, Scouting Fleet June-November 1930. Chief of staff to Commander in Chief United States Fleet 1930-1932. Commandant of Ninth Naval District September 1932-March 1935. Commander of the Base Force, United States Fleet 1935-1937. Commandant of Fourth Naval District June 1937-January 1939. Retired in January 1939. Recalled to active duty in the office of the secretary of the navy in World War II. Decorations included the Distinguished Service Medal. Died on October 28, 1952.

Cobb, Calvin Hayes (1889-1961) Born on November 21, 1889, in Kittery, Maine. Graduated from Annapolis in 1911. Served aboard the Minnesota at the civilian uprising in Guantanamo, Cuba in 1912 and at Vera Cruz in 1913. Commanding officer of the *Duncan* during World War I 1916-1919. Commanded the destroyers *Monaghan, Drayton* and *Walker* in 1919 then the *Percival* July 1922-April 1925. Commanding officer of the *Billingsley* and the J. Fred Talbott 1927-1930. Assistant naval attache in Paris, Lisbon and Madrid August 1930-May 1933. Commanding officer of the Nitro 1939-1940. Duty at Annapolis 1940-1942. Commanding officer of the battleship Mississippi June-November 1942. Rear admiral in November 1942. Commander of Service Squadron South Pacific 1942-1944. President of the Naval Examining and Retiring Board 1944-1945. Commander of Naval Forces Ryukyus January-August 1945. Commandant of U.S. Naval Base Philadelphia 1945-1946. Vice admiral upon retirement in November 1946. Decorations included the Navy Cross and Legion of Merit. Died on March 29, 1961.

Cochrane, Edward Lull (1892-1959) Born on March 18, 1892, in Mare Island, California, the son of Brigadier General Henry C. Cochrane, USMC. Commissioned from Annapolis in 1914. Served aboard the *Rhode Island* at the invasion of Vera Cruz in 1914. M.S. from Massachusetts Institute of Technology in 1920. Staff officer with the Scouting Force 1933-1935. Graduated from the Naval War College in 1939. Assistant to the chief of the design division in the Bureau of Ships 1939-1940. Assistant naval attache in London in 1940. Head of the preliminary design branch in the Bureau of Ships 1941-1942. Rear admiral in November 1942. Chief of the Bureau of Ships November 1942-October 1946. Vice admiral in April 1945. Retired in November 1947. Decorations included the Distinguished Service Medal. Died on November 13, 1959.

Coman, Robert Grimes (1887-1963) Born on September 17, 1887, in Trempealeau, Wisconsin. Graduated from Annapolis in 1909 and commissioned in 1911. Commanding officer of the *Truxtun* 1914-1915, the *Hamilton* 1919-1920 and the destroyers *Farquhar, Twiggs* and *Sloat* in 1921. Commanding oficer of the *Reno* February 1927-March 1928. District communication officer at Fourteenth Naval District, Pearl Harbor 1928-1931. Graduated from the Army Industrial College in 1935. Commanding officer of the *Vestal* 1937-1938 and the battleship *New Mexico* January-September 1941. Commander of Receiving Station

Philadelphia 1941-1942 then Transport Division Three, Amphibious Force, Atlantic Fleet April-December 1942. Commanded Task Force 19, Amphibious Force December 1942-February 1943 then Service Force, Seventh Fleet 1943-1944. Duty at Twelfth Naval District September 1944-March 1945 then with Commander Western Sea Frontier 1945-1946. Commodore in April 1945. Retired in November 1946. Decorations included the Legion of Merit. Died on September 29, 1963.

Combs, Lewis Barton (1895-n/a) Born on April 7, 1895, in Manchester Center, Vermont. Attended Rensselaer Polytechnic Institute. Commissioned in the Civil Engineer Corps in 1917. Treaty engineer in Haiti 1919-1924. Public works officer at Ninth and Sixteenth Naval Districts 1932-1937. Duty at the Bureau of Yards and Docks June 1937-January 1938 then assistant chief of the bureau until February 1946. Director of the Atlantic Division, Bureau of Yards and Docks March 1946-October 1947. Rear admiral in July 1942. Retired in December 1947. Decorations included the Distinguished Service Medal. Resides in New York.

Comstock, Merrill (1895-1980) Born on April 29, 1895, in Jamestown, North Dakota. Commissioned from Annapolis in 1917. Commanding officer of the submarines K-7 and R-22 March 1922-May 1924. Instructor at Annapolis 1926-1928. Commanding officer of the submarine Cachalot December 1933-June 1936. Graduated from the Naval War College in 1939. Commanded Submarine Division 13, then Submarine Squadron 7, Atlantic Fleet 1939-1942. Duty in the office of the chief of naval operations June 1942-November 1943. Chief of staff to Commander Submarine Force, Pacific Fleet 1943-1945. Commodore in October 1944. Commander of Submarine Training Pacific July-December 1945. Retired in July 1949. Decorations included the Legion of Merit and Navy Commendation Medal. Died on December 3, 1980.

Conolly, Richard Lansing (1892-1962) Born on April 26, 1892, in Waukegan, Illinois. Commissioned from Annapolis in 1914. Served aboard the *Smith* in World War I. M.S. from Columbia University in 1922. Instructor at Annapolis 1925-1927. Commanding officer of the *Case* August 1929-May 1930 then the *Dupont* in 1930. Aide to Commander Cruisers, Scouting Force May 1933-April 1935. Again instructor at Annapolis 1936-1939. Commander of Destroyer Squadron Seven, then Six May 1939-April 1942. Staff officer in the office of the chief of naval operations and Commander in Chief United States Fleet 1942-1943. Rear admiral in July 1942. Duty with the Amphibious Force, Atlantic Fleet March-October 1943 then the Pacific Fleet October 1943-July 1944. Commander of Group 3, Amphibious Force, Pacific Fleet 1944-1945. Assignments after the war included commander of Twelfth Fleet September 1946-January 1947, commander in chief of U.S. Naval Forces Eastern Atlantic and Mediterranean 1947-1950 and president of the Naval War College 1950-1953. Retired as admiral in November 1953. Decorations included the Navy Cross, Distinguished Service Medal and Legion of Merit. Died in the crash of an American Airlines jet at La Guardia Airport on March 1, 1962.

Cook, Arthur Byron (1881-1952) Born on December 11, 1881, in Evansville, Indiana. Graduated from Annapolis in 1905 and commissioned in 1907. Flag lieutenant to the commander in chief Atlantic Fleet in World War I. Commanding officer of the *Long* 1919-1921 and the *Niagara* 1927-1928. Designated a naval aviator in September 1928. Commanding officer of the *Langley* in 1928. Assistant chief of the Bureau of Aeronautics 1931-1934. Commanding officer of the *Lexington* 1934-1936. Rear admiral in June 1936. Chief of the Bureau of Aeronautics 1936-1939. Commander of Aircraft, Scouting Force 1939-1941 then Aircraft, Atlantic Fleet 1941-1942. Chief of Naval Air Operational Training May 1942-August 1943. Vice admiral in July 1943. Commandant of Tenth Naval District August 1943-May 1944. Retired in December 1944. Decorations included the Legion of Merit. Died on January 11, 1952.

Cooke, Charles Maynard (1886-1970) Born on December 19, 1886, in Fort Smith, Arkansas. B.S. from the University of Arkansas in 1905. Graduated from Annapolis in 1910 and commissioned in 1912. Commanding officer of submarines *E-2* 1915-1916 and *R-2* and *S-5* 1919-1920. Commander of Submarine Division Eleven May 1931-May 1933. Graduated from the Naval War College in 1934. Commandant of the Guantanamo Bay Naval Station 1934-1936. War plans officer with the United States Fleet 1936-1938. Commanding officer of the *Pennsylvania* February 1941-June 1942. Rear admiral in June 1942. Assistant chief of staff (plans) to Commander in Chief United States Fleet 1942-1945. Vice admiral in September 1944. Assignments after the war included commander of Seventh Fleet December 1945-February 1948. Retired as admiral in May 1948. Decorations included the Distinguished Service Medal. Died on December 24, 1970.

Cooke, Henry David (1879-1958) Born on September 21, 1879, in Washington, DC. Graduated from Annapolis in 1903. Wounded by Moro rebels while on patrol duty in the Philippines in 1904. Commissioned in 1905. Served aboard the *Virginia* in the world cruise of the Battle Fleet 1907-1908. Instructor at Annapolis 1908-1912. Commanding officer of the *Henley* 1914-1915 and the *Kanawha, Jenkins, Allen* and *Harding* during World War I. Commanding officer of the *Melville* 1930-1931. Commandant of midshipmen at Annapolis 1931-1932. Commanding officer of the *Oklahoma* 1932-1934. Chief of staff to the commandant of the Naval War College 1934-1937. Captain of the yard at Boston Navy Yard 1937-1939. Rear admiral upon retirement in June 1939. Continued on active duty in the office of the chief of naval operations 1939-1942 and as Convoy Commodore March 1942-May 1945. Decorations included the Navy Cross and Purple Heart. Died on July 7, 1958.

Cooley, Thomas Ross Jr. (1893-1959) Born on June 26, 1893, in Grass Valley, California. Commissioned from Annapolis in 1917. Served aboard the *Florida*, which operated with the British Grand Fleet during World War I. Instructor at Annapolis 1922-1924 and 1927-1929. Aide and flag lieutenant to Commander Special Service Squadron 1929-1931, participating in the second Nicaraguan campaign. Again instructor at Annapolis 1937-1940. Commanding officer of the *Executor* 1941-1942. Duty in the Bureau of Naval Personnel June 1942-April 1944. Rear admiral in March 1943. Commanding officer of the *Washington* April-November 1944. Commander of Battleship Division Six, Pacific Fleet 1944-1945. Vice admiral upon retirement in July 1952. Decorations included the Legion of Merit and two Navy Commendation Medals. Died on November 28, 1959.

Cotter, Carl Henry (1892-1965) Born on July 11, 1892, in Bay City, Michigan. B.S. from the University of Michigan in 1916. Commissioned in the Civil Engineer Corps in 1918. Treaty engineer in Haiti January 1920-June 1924. Public works officer at Naval Operating Base, Norfolk December 1940-April 1942 then superintending civil engineer of Area Number Three 1942-1943. Director of the Pacific Division, Bureau of Yards and Docks February 1943-June 1945. Rear admiral in June 1943. Vice chief of the material division, office of the assistant secretary of the navy December 1945-December 1946. Retired in March 1947. Decorations included the DSM, LM and Navy Commendation Medal. Died on October 9, 1965.

Cox, Ormond Lee (1883-1968) Born on October 16, 1883, in Rix Mills, Ohio. Graduated from Annapolis in 1905 and commissioned in 1907. Engineer officer aboard the *Nevada* 1916-1918. Head of the design division in the Bureau of Engineers 1927-1932. Director of the U.S. engineering experimental station at Annapolis 1933-1939. Rear admiral in May 1938. Supervisor of shipbuilding at Newport News Naval Shipyard July 1939-May 1946. Retired in October 1946. Decorations included the Legion of Merit. Died on April 16, 1968.

Craven, Thomas Tingey (1873-1950) Born in July 8, 1873, in Vallejo, California. Graduated from Annapolis in 1896 and commissioned in 1898. Served aboard the *Massachusetts* and the *Eagle* in the Spanish-American War and at Manila 19001-1901. Commanding officer of the *Sacramento* in European waters 1917-1918. Served in France 1918-1919. Commanding officer of the *Maryland* 1925-1927. Director of naval communications 1927-1928. Commandant of 9th Naval District 1928-1929. Commander of Battleship Division One in 1933. Rear admiral in February 1928. Commander of Battleship Divisions, United States Fleet 1934-1935. Commandant of 13th Naval District 1935-1937. Retired in August 1937. Recalled to active duty in May 1942 to be superintendent of the New York State Maritime Academy. Retired again as vice admiral in April 1946. Decorations included the Distinguished Service Medal. Died on April 5, 1950.

Crawford, George Clifford (1897-1993) Born on July 9, 1897, in Old Fort, North Carolina. Commissioned from Annapolis in 1921. Commanding officer of the submarine *S-34* October 1931-March 1934 then the Perch November 1936-June 1939. Officer in charge of the Submarine School, New London 1940-1941. Naval observer in London 1941-1942. Commander of Submarine Division 43 March-June 1943. Chief of staff to Commander Submarine Force Atlantic Fleet 1943-1944. Commander of Submarine Squadron 24 August 1944-March 1945.

Assistant chief of staff for personnel at Fourth Naval District April-June 1945. Commodore in June 1945. Chief of staff to Commander Submarine Forces, Pacific Fleet June-September 1945. Retired in April 1958. Decorations included two Legions of Merit. Died on July 21, 1993.

Crisp, Frederick Grafton (1892-1970) Born on March 21, 1892, in Baltimore, Maryland. Commissioned from Annapolis in 1913. M.S. from Massachusetts Institute of Technology in 1917. Served at New York Navy Yard 1917-1921. Duty in the industrial department at Navy Yard Cavite, Philippines 1936-1937. Mnager of the Mare Island Navy Yard July 1940-February 1944. Rear admiral in June 1942. Director of the division of shore establishments and civilian personnel in the office of the assistant secretary of the navy 1944-1946. Retired in October 1947. Decorations included two Legions of Merit. Died on December 9, 1970.

Cronin, Joseph Campbell (1899-1972) Born on December 3, 1899, in Geneva, Alabama. Commissioned from Annapolis in 1921. Designated naval aviator in April 1926. Duty at Coco Solo Fleet Air Base, Canal Zone 1932-1935. Commanding officer of Naval Air Station Sitka, Alaska 1938-1940. Navigator aboard the Saratoga April 1940-July 1941. Chief of staff to Commander Patrol Wing One 1941-1942. Commander of Memphis Naval Reserve Air Base September 1942-November 1943. Commanding officer of the Tulagi December 1943-May 1945. Commodore in April 1945. Chief of staff to Commander Battleship Squadron Two, Pacific Fleet May-December 1945. Rear admiral upon retirement in June 1951. Died on June 13, 1972.

Crosse, Charles Washburn (1885-1951) Born on April 12, 1885, in Sun Prairie, Wisconsin. Graduated from Annapolis in 1907 and commissioned in 1909. Instructor at Annapolis 1913-1915. Navigator, then executive officer of the *Charleston* during World War I. Graduated from the Naval War College in 1930. Commanding officer of the *Gold Star* stationed at Guam 1930-1932 then the *Marblehead* April 1935-November 1936. Aide to the commandant of midshipmen at Annapolis 1937-1939. Commander of Subordinate Command, Service Force Pacific Fleet June 1941-December 1944. Rear admiral in January 1942. Hospitalized then retired in May 1945. Decorations included the Legion of Merit. Retired in May 1945. Died on April 21, 1951.

Curts, Maurice Edwin (1898-1976) Born on March 25, 1898, in Flint, Michigan. Served as a midshipman aboard the *Nevada* in World War I. Commissioned from Annapolis in 1920. M.S. from Harvard in 1928. Commanding officer of the *Case* 1938-1939. Communications officer for the United States Fleet 1939-1944. Rear admiral in November 1943. Chief of staff of the 1st Carrier Task Force, Pacific Fleet in 1945. Assignments after the war included commander of Cruisers Fleet 1955-1957 and Commander in Chief Pacific Fleet January 14-January 31, 1958. Retired as admiral in April 1960. Decorations included the Distinguished Service Cross, Navy Cross, Distinguished Service Medal, Silver Star, Legion of Merit and Bronze Star. Died on February 16, 1976.

Daubin, Freeland Allyn (1886-1959) Born on February 6, 1886, in Lamar, Missouri. Graduated from Annapolis in 1909 and commissioned in 1911. Commanding officer of the submarines *C-4* 1913-1914, *L-1* in 1916 and *U-111* 1919-1920 and the *Barry* and the *Sturtevant* 1923-1926. Instructor at Annapolis 1931-1934. Commander of Destroyer Division Four July 1934-June 1936, Destroyer Squadron Six June 1939-January 1941 and Submarine Base Pearl Harbor January 1941-February 1942. Rear admiral in November 1941. Commander of Submarines, Atlantic Fleet 1942-1944. Commandant of New York Navy Yard 1944-1945. Retired in March 1948. Decorations included the Distinguished Service Medal and Legion of Merit. Died on October 24, 1959.

Davidson, Lyal Ament (1886-1950) Born on December 12, 1886, in Muscatine, Iowa. Graduated from Annapolis in 1910 and commissioned in 1912. Served aboard the *New Hampshire* at the invasion of Vera Cruz in 1914 and the *Kansas* during World War I. M.S. from Columbia University in 1917. Aide to Commandant Eleventh Naval District 1931-1934. Commander of 9th Destroyer Division 1934-1936. Commanding officer of the *Relief* 1938-1939 and the *Omaha* 1939-1940. Instructor at the University of Michigan ROTC July 1940-December 1941. Rear admiral in November 1941. Commander of Cruiser Division Eight, Atlantic Fleet 1942-1944. Commander of Task Force 86 July-October 1944. Duty in the office of the chief of naval operations as member of the State-War-Navy Coordinating Committee 1945-1946. Vice admiral upon retirement in June 1946. Decorations included two Distinguished Service Medals and two Legions of Merit. Died on December 29, 1950.

Davis, Arthur Cayley (1893-1965) Born on March 14, 1893, in Columbia, South Carolina. Attended the University of Nebraska 1909-1911. Commissioned from Annapolis in 1915. M.S. from the Univesity of Chicago in 1922. Qualified as naval aviator in 1923. Head of the plans division at the Bureau of Aeronautics 1936-1939. Commanding officer of the *Langley* June 1939-June 1940. Aviation officer on the staff of Commander in Chief Pacific Fleet July 1940-June 1942. Rear admiral in July 1942. Commander of Carrier Division Five July-October 1942, Carrier Replacement Squadron, Atlantic Fleet November-December 1942 and Fleet Air Atlantic December 1942-February 1943. Assistant chief of staff to Commander in Chief Atlantic Fleet February 1943-August 1944. Chief of staff to Commander Fifth Fleet 1944-1945. Commander of Carrier Division Five August-October 1945. Assignments after the war included director of the Joint Staff, Joint Chiefs of Staff 1949-1952. Admiral upon retirement in November 1955. Decorations included three Navy Crosses, two Distinguished Service Medals and three Legions of Merit. Died on February 10, 1965.

Davis, Glenn Benson (1892-1984) Born on January 2, 1892, in Norwalk, Ohio. Commissioned from Annapolis in 1913. Commanding officer of the *Blakely* June 1932-June 1934. Executive officer of the *Philadelphia* September 1937-June 1939. Duty at the Bureau of Ordnance June 1939-January 1940 then assistant chief of ordnance January 1940-July 1942. Commanding officer of the *Washing-*

ton July 1942-April 1943. Rear admiral in September 1942. Commander of Battleship Division Eight April 1943-March 1945. Inspector general of Western Sea Froniter March-July 1945. Deputy commander of Western Sea Frontier July 1945-January 1946. Vice admiral upon retirement in June 1953. Decorations included the Navy Cross and two Legions of Merit. Died on September 9, 1984.

Davis, Milton Smith (1880-1955) Born on January 28, 1880, in San Francisco, California. Graduated from Annapolis in 1903 and commissioned in 1905. Commanding officer of the *Fox, Rowan* and *Paul Jones* March 1908-December 1909. Served aboard the *Maryland* in the occupation of Vera Cruz in 1914. Commanding officer of the *Shaw* during World War I. Graduated from the Naval War College in 1922. Commanding officer of the *Medusa* 1925-1926. Staff officer at the Naval War College June 1931-May 1934. Commanding officer of the *Tennessee* June 1934-November 1935. Inspector of naval material, San Francisco August 1937-June 1939. Retired in June 1939. Recalled to active duty as port director, then regional shipping director, Naval Transportation Service, Twelfth Naval District 1939-1945. Commodore in September 1944. Retired again in March 1945. Decorations included the Navy Cross. Died on September 4, 1955.

Davis, Ralph Otis (1891-1967) Born on January 19, 1891, in Litchfield, Illinois. Commissioned from Annapolis in 1914. Commanding officer of the submarines *H-4* 1918-1919, *L-4* 1919-1920 and *S-17* 1923-1924. Executive officer of the *Indianapolis* May 1938-June 1942. Served briefly at Annapolis in 1942. Rear admiral in October 1942. Commander of Rear Echelon, Amphibious Force Pacific Fleet 1943-1944, Training Command, Amphibious Forces Pacific Fleet in 1944 and Amphibious Group 13, Pacific Fleet 1945-1946. Vice admiral upon retirement in January 1953. Decorations included three Legions of Merit and the Bronze Star. Died on December 15, 1967.

Davison, Ralph Eugene (1895-1972) Born on September 12, 1895, in St. Louis, Missouri. Commissioned from Annapolis in 1916. Head of the administrative division in the Bureau of Aeronautics June 1937-June 1939. Chief of staff to Commander Aircraft, Scouting Force June 1939-October 1940 and Commander Aircraft, Atlantic Squadron 1940-1941. Chief of the plans division at the Bureau of Aeronautics 1941-1942 then assistant chief of the bureau May 1942-November 1943. Rear admiral in November 1942. Commander of Carrier Air Support Group 1943-1945. Commanded the Air Operational Training Command 1945-1946. Vice admiral upon retirement in July 1948. Decorations included the Distinguished Service Medal and two Legions of Merit. Died on February 14, 1972.

Dees, Randal Euesta (1893-1972) Born on October 8, 1893, in Crystal Springs, Mississippi. B.S. from Mississippi College in 1912. Commissioned from Annapolis in 1917. Commanding officer of the *Flussser* and *Sharkey* October 1920-September 1922. Aide to the naval governor of Guam July 1929-July 1931. Instructor at Annapolis June 1936-June 1939. Commanding officer of the *Winslow* 1939-1941. Staff officer at the Naval War College June 1941-June 1943. Commanding officer of the *Pensacola* 1943-1944. Staff officer with Commander Service Force, Pacific Fleet June 1944-May 1946. Rear admiral upon retirement in July 1949. Decorations included the Silver Star and two Legions of Merit. Died on July 25, 1972.

DeLany, Walter Stanley (1891-1980) Born on January 21, 1891, in Reading, Pennsylvania. Commissioned from Annapolis in 1912. Commanding officer of the *Paulding* June 1919-July 1920. Commander of Destroyer Division Seven, Battle Force 1938-1939. Chief of staff to Commander Cruisers, Battle Force May 1939-February 1941. Assistant chief of staff for operations for Commander in Chief Pacific Fleet 1941-1942. Commanding officer of the cruiser *New Orleans* June-November 1942. Rear admiral in May 1942. Assistant chief of staff for readiness at Commander in Chief United States Fleet November 1942-August 1945. Head of the operational readiness section, office of the chief of naval operations September 1945-January 1946. Retired as vice admiral in February 1953. Decorations included two Legions of Merit. Died on September 21, 1980.

Denebrink, Francis Compton (1896-1987) Born on June 22, 1896, in Chicago, Illinois. Commissioned from Annapolis in 1917. Aide to the superintendent of Annapolis 1922-1923. Naval aide at the White House 1926-1928. Commanding officer of the *McCormick* in 1930. Graduated from the Naval War College in 1932. Senior aide to the chief of naval operations in 1942. Commanding officer of the *Brooklyn* 1942-1943. Rear admiral in March 1943. Chief of staff to the Commander Fleet Operational Training, Atlantic Fleet 1943-1944. Commander of Fleet Operational Training Command, Pacific Fleet 1944-1945. Assignments after the war included commander of Military Sea Transport Service 1952-1956. Retired as vice admiral in July 1956. Decorations included the Distinguished Service Medal and three Legions of Merit. Died on April 8, 1987.

Denfeld, Lewis Emil (1891-1972) Born in Westboro, Massachusetts, on April 13, 1891. Graduated from Annapolis in 1912. Aboard destroyers involved in escort duty in the Atlantic during World War I. Aide to Admiral William D. Leahy, the chief of naval operations, 1937-1939. Commander of Destroyer Division Eighteen, then Destroyer Squadron One 1939-1941. Staff officer with commander of the Atlantic Fleet Support Force. Assistant chief of the Bureau of Navigation 1942-1945. Rear admiral in May 1942. Commander of Battleship Division Nine in 1945. Assignments after the war included chief of naval personnel 1945-1946, commander in chief of the Pacific Fleet February-December 1947 and chief of naval operations December 1947-October 1949. An active and vocal participant in the "revolt of the admirals," Denfeld was relieved from duty and retired as admiral in March 1950. Decorations included the Distinguished Service Medal and two Legions of Merit. Died on March 28, 1972.

Deyo, Morton Lyndholm (1887-1973) Born on July 1, 1887, in Poughkeepsie, New York. Commissioned from Annapolis in 1911. Commanding officer of the *Morris* July 1919-June 1920, the *Sloat* 1929-1930 and the *Upshur* 1930-1932.

Assistant hydographer of the Navy April 1939-February 1940. Aide to the secretary of the navy 1940-1941. Commander of Destroyer Squadron Eleven April-September 1941. Commanding officer of the *Monticello* in 1942. Rear admiral in May 1942. Commander of Destroyers, Atlantic Fleet 1943-1944 then Cruiser Division 13, Pacific Fleet September 1944-November 1945. Vice admiral upon retirement in August 1949. Decorations included two Navy Crosses, the Distinguished Service Medal and Legion of Merit. Died on November 10, 1973.

Dickeman, Charles Theodore (1894-1976) Born on August 11, 1894, in New York City. B.S. from Cooper Union Institute of Technology in 1917. Enlisted service in the U.S. Army 1917-1919. Served with 302nd Engineers, AEF and wounded at Oise-Aisne offensive in September 1918. Commissioned in the Civil Engineer Corps in 1921. Duty at U.S. Naval Station Tutuila, Samoa November 1932-July 1934. Served at New York Navy Yard and Pearl Harbor October 1939-November 1941. Member of the U.S. Military Mission to North Africa 1941-1942. Officer in charge of Naval Advance Base Depot at Davisville, Rhode island November 1942-December 1943. Director of the advance base department in the Bureau of Yards and Docks December 1943-July 1945. Commodore in July 1945. Retired in October 1947. Decorations included the LM and PH. Died on February 25, 1976.

Dillon, Wallace Myron (1895-1965) Born on July 18, 1895, in Talladega, Alabama. Commissioned from Annapolis in 1918. Naval attache at Mexico City August 1938-June 1941. Executive officer of the *Lexington* August 1941-January 1942. Chief of staff to Commander Patrol Wing Two at Pearl Harbor January-July 1942. Commander of Naval Air Station Kaneohe Bay, Hawaii July 1942-May 1943. Commanding officer of the *Langley* as part of Vice Admiral Marc Mitscher's Task Force 58 June 1943-September 1944. Commander of Naval Air Base Okinawa November 1944-October 1945. Commodore in April 1945. Rear admiral upon retirement in November 1946. Decorations included two Legions of Merit, the Distinguished Flying Cross and Purple Heart. Died on April 4, 1965.

Dismukes, Douglas Eugene (1869-1949) Born on October 1, 1869, Macon, Mississippi. Commissioned from Annapolis in 1890. Served in the Spanish-American War. Commanding officer of the *Petrel* in the Haiti campaign in 1911. Served in Panama 1913-1914. Commanding officer of the *Nevada* in 1922. Commandant of Portsmouth Naval Yard 1923-1925. Retired as rear admiral in 1925. Recalled to active duty as commandant of Maine Maritime Academy 1942-1945. Decorations included the Distinguished Service Medal. Died on December 2, 1949.

Dodd, Harold (1890-1968) Born on November 10, 1890, in New York City. Commissioned from Annapolis in 1912. M.S. from Columbia University in 1924 and LL.B. from George Washington University in 1930. Graduated from the Naval War College in 1940. Commanding officer of the *Honolulu* June 1940-August 1942. Chief of staff to Commandant Naval Operating Base Trinidad September

1942-May 1943. Commandant of Naval Operating Base Rio de Janeiro May 1943-June 1944. Commodore in June 1944. Chief of the U.S. Naval Mission to Brazil June 1944-October 1945. Retired in June 1949. Decorations included the Legion of Merit. Died on August 5, 1968.

Dow, Jennings Bryan (1897-1970) Born on January 2, 1897, in Bowling Green, Ohio. Commissioned from Annapolis in 1919. Duty with Sixteenth Naval District, Cavite, Philippines January 1928-June 1929. Officer in charge of the radio division, Bureau of Engineerings June 1938-January 1940 then the Naval Radio and Sound Laboratory at Eleventh Naval District June-October 1940. Assistant naval attache in London November 1940-April 1941. Chief of the radio and sound division, Bureau of Ships 1941-1945. Commodore in June 1945. Director of the electronics division, then assistant chief in the Bureau of Ships June 1945-November 1946. Retired in January 1947. Decorations included the Legion of Merit and Navy Commendation Medal. Died on February 20, 1970.

Downes, John Jr. (1879-1954) Born on November 16, 1879, in Boston, Massachusetts. Graduated from Annapolis in 1901 and commissioned in 1903. Commanding officer of the *Pocahontas* 1918-1919 and the *Bridgeport* 1919-1921. Commander of Submarine Division One 1924-1926. Graduated from the Naval War College in 1929. Commanding officer of the *Detroit* 1929-1931. Director of the Naval Reserve 1931-1934. Rear admiral in February 1935. Commander of Carrier Division Seven, Scouting Force January 1937-July 1938. President of the Naval Examining Board, then the Naval Retiring Board July 1938-August 1940. Commandant of Ninth Naval District in 1940-1943. Retired in December 1943. Decorations included the Legion of Merit. Died on February 9, 1954.

Doyle, Austin Kelvin (1898-1970) Born on November 7, 1898, in Staten Island, New York. Commissioned from Annapolis in 1919. Qualified as a naval aviator in 1922. Commander of air groups on the *Saratoga* 1939-1940. Duty with the Bureau of Aeronautics 1941-1942. Commander of the *Nassau* 1942-1943 then commandant of Bermuda Naval Base 1943-1944. Commanding officer of the *Hornet* August 1944-1945. Rear admiral in August 1945. Assignments after the war included Caribbean Sea Frontier 1952-1954 and chief of Naval Air Training 1954-1957. Admiral upon retirement in August 1958. Decorations included two Navy Crosses, the Distinguished Service Medal and two Legions of Merit. Died on July 12, 1970.

Draemel, Milo F. (1884-1971) Born on May 31, 1884, in Fremont, Nebraska. Graduated from Annapolis in 1906 and commissioned in 1908. Flag lieutenant to Commander Battleship Force in 1918. Commanding officer of the *Boggs* July 1921-June 1922 and the *Selfridge* 1922-1923. Graduated from the Naval War College in 1926. Commanding officer of the *Holland* June 1931-June 1933. Instructor at the Naval War College 1933-1936. Commandant of midshipmen at Annapolis 1937-1939. Rear admiral in December 1939. Commander of Destroyer Flotillas One and Two 1940-1941. Chief of staff to the Commander in Chief Pacific Fleet December 1941-June 1942. Commander of Amphibious Force, Pacific Fleet in 1942. Commandant of Fourth Naval District September 1942-March 1946. Retired in August 1946. Decorations included the Distinguished Service Medal and Legion of Merit. Died on March 25, 1971.

Dreller, Louis (1897-1970) Born on March 6, 1897, in Portsmouth, New Hampshire. B.S. from the University of New Hampshire in 1918. Commissioned in 1918 for engineering duty only. M.S. from Columbia University in 1925. Duty in the design division, Bureau of Enginnering June 1936-January 1941. Force engineer officer for Commander Scouting Force, Pacific Fleet 1941-1942. Assigned to the Brazilian Navy 1942-1945. Rear admiral in July 1943. Retired in July 1951. Decorations included the Legion of Merit and Navy Commendation Medal. Died on May 8, 1970.

DuBose, Laurance Toombs (1893-1967) Born on May 21, 1893, in Washington, DC. Commissioned from Annapolis in 1913. Commanding officer of the *Lansdale* August 1921-April 1922. Instructor at Annapolis 1929-1932. Commanding officer of the *Schenck* June 1932-June 1934. Again instructor at Annapolis 1934-1937. Graduated from the Naval War College in 1940. Commanding officer of the *Portland* in 1942. Rear admiral in September 1942. Chief of staff to Commander in Chief U.S. Naval Forces Europe 1942-1943. Commander of Cruiser Division 13 May 1943-January 1945. Commandant of Sixth Naval District 1945-1948. Assignments after the war included chief of naval personnel 1951-1953 and commander of Eastern Sea Frontier February 1953 until retirement as admiral in June 1955. Decorations included three Navy Crosses, three Legions of Merit and two Commendation Ribbons. Died on July 11, 1967.

Duncan, Donald Bradley (1896-1975) Born on September 1, 1896, in Alpena, Michigan. Commissioned from Annapolis in 1917. M.S. from Harvard in 1926. Executive officer of Naval Air Station Pensacola June 1938-March 1941. Commanding officer of the *Long Island* June-December 1941. Staff officer with Commander in Chief United States Fleet December 1941-November 1942. Commanding officer of the *Essex* December 1942-November 1943. Rear admiral in March 1943. Assistant chief of staff for plans with Commander in Chief United States Fleet May 1944-July 1945. Commander of Carrier Division Four July-November 1945. Assignments after the war included deputy chief of naval operations 1950-1951 and vice chief of naval operations 1951-1956. Retired as admiral in March 1957. Decorations included the Legion of Merit and Navy Commendation Medal. Died on August 9, 1975.

Duncan, Jack Harlan (1894-1966) Born on September 21, 1894, in Ozark, Missouri. Commissioned from Annapolis in 1918. Aide to the commandant of Sixteenth Naval District June-August 1921. Aide to Admiral William H. Standley 1930-1934. Commanding officer of the *Roper* July 1935-January 1937. Graduated from the Naval War College in 1939. Commanding officer of the *Sangamon* October 1940-August 1942. Rear admiral in December 1942. Naval attache to

Moscow December 1942-November 1943. Reverted to captain in November 1943. Commanding officer of the *Phoenix* in 1944. Commanding officer of naval command, strategic service units in the State and War Departments 1945-1946. Vice admiral upon retirement in July 1948. Decorations included the Navy Cross, two Legions of Merit and the Navy Commendation Medal. Died on August 21, 1966.

Dunn, Charles Alfred (1885-1961) Born on October 14, 1885, in Warrensburg, Missouri. Commissioned from Annapolis in 1908. Industrial manager at New York Navy Yard 1934-1940. Superintendent of shipbuilding at Electric Boat Company, New London July 1940-March 1942. Rear admiral in December 1940. Fleet maintenance officer with Commander Service Force, Pacific Fleet March 1942-May 1944. Supervisor of shipbuilding in New York 1944-1945 and assistant deputy administrator for maintenance and repair in the War Shipping Administration in 1945. Retired in July 1947. Decorations included the Legion of Merit. Died on June 13, 1961.

Durgin, Calvin Thornton (1893-1965) Born on January 7, 1893, in Palmyra, New Jersey. Commissioned from Annapolis in 1916. Commanding officer of the *Wright* May-June 1939. Commander of Utility Wing, Base Force June 1939-June 1940. Duty with the plans division, Bureau of Aeronautics 1940-1942. Commanding officer of the *Ranger* May 1942-March 1943. Rear admiral in February 1943. Commander of Fleet Air Quonset Point 1943-1944, Task Group, Atlantic Fleet June-October 1944, Carrier Division 29, Pacific Fleet October-December 1944 and Escort Carrier Group, Pacific Fleet December 1944-November 1945. Assignments after the war included deputy chief of naval operations for air May 1949-March 1950. Retired as vice admiral in September 1951. Decorations included the Distinguished Service Medal and three Legions of Merit. Died on March 25, 1965.

Duvall, Elmer Ellsworth Jr. (1894-1980) Born in Baltimore, Maryland, on October 10, 1894. Commissioned from Annapolis in 1918. Commanding officer of the *Noa* in 1934 and the *Hovey* 1934-1937. Duty at the Naval Observatory 1937-1940. Commanding officer of the *Bowditch* in 1940. Convoy commander with Twelfth Naval District 1941-1942. Commanding officer of the *Kitty Hawk* June 1942-June 1943. Served in the office of chief of naval operations 1943-1944. Chief of staff to Commander Service Squadron Ten August 1944-June 1945. Commodore in June 1945. Commander of Service Division 101 June-August 1945. Rear admiral upon retirement in July 1949. Decorations included the Legion of Merit and Navy Commendation Medal. Died on December 1, 1980.

Edgar, Campbell Dallas (1889-1961) Born on August 23, 1889, in Washington, DC. Commissioned from Annapolis in 1912. Instructor at Annapolis 1919-1921. Duty at Naval Station Tutuila, Samoa April 1924-July 1925. Commanding officer of the *Smith Thompson* August 1931-July 1933. Communications officer at Sixteenth Naval District July 1933-August 1934. Executive officer of the *Louisville* June 1937-June 1939. Radio materiel officer at New York and Pearl Harbor. Commanding officer of the *William P. Biddle* February 1941-September 1942. Commander of Transport Divisions Five, Eleven and Three, Amphibious Force Atlantic Fleet September 1942-October 1943. Commodore in September 1943. Commander of Transports, 11th Amphibious Force, Pacific Fleet 1943-1945 then Transport Squadron 19 January-July 1945. Duty at Puget Sound Navy Yard 1945-1946. Rear admiral upon retirement in January 1947. Decorations included the Legion of Merit and Distinguished Flying Cross. Died on June 24, 1961.

Edwards, Richard Stanislaus (1885-1956) Born on August 1, 1885, in Philadelphia, Pennsylvania. Graduated from Annapolis in 1907 and commissioned in 1909. Commanding officer of the submarine *C-3* in 1913. Instructor at Annapolis 1914-1917. Served aboard the *Kentucky, Kansas* and *Arkansas* during World War I. Aide to Commander Battleship Squadron One 1919-1921. Commanding officer of the *Wood* August 1924-June 1926. Aide to Commander in Chief Battle Fleet April-September 1931. Staff officer at Command and General Staff School 1931-1934. Graduated from the Naval War College in 1935. Commander of Submarine Base New London June 1937-June 1940. Commanding officer of the *Colorado* June-October 1940. Commander of Submarines, Patrol Force 1940-1941 then Submarines, Atlantic Fleet February-December 1941. Rear admiral in May 1941. Deputy chief of staff and aide to Commander in Chief United States Fleet December 1941-October 1944 then Deputy Commander in Chief United States Fleet 1944-1945. Vice admiral in August 1942, admiral in April 1945. Assignments after the war included commander of the Western Sea Frontier 1946-1947 then Pacific Reserve Fleet January 1947 until retirement in July 1947. Decorations included the Navy Cross and Distinguished Service Medal. Died on June 2, 1956.

Emmet, Robert Rutherford Morris (1888-1977) Born on January 27, 1888, in New Rochelle, New York. Graduated from Annapolis in 1908 and commissioned in 1910. Commanding officer of the *Bainbridge* 1923-1926. Graduated from the Naval War College then naval attache in The Hague in 1927. Commanding officer of the *Taylor* May 1931-May 1933. Staff officer at the Naval War College 1936-1938. Commanding officer of the *Texas* June 1938-May 1940. Chief of staff to Commander Atlantic Squadron May-November 1940. Commander of Transports, Amphibious Force Atlantic Fleet May 1942-January 1943. Commander of the Naval Training Center at Great Lakes, Illinois January 1943-October 1945. Commodore in September 1944. Retired as rear admiral in August 1946. Decorations included the Navy Cross and Distinguished Service Medal. Died on July 6, 1977.

English, Robert Henry (1888-1943) Born on January 16, 1888, in Warrington, Georgia. Attended Georgia Institute of Technology 1904-1906. Commissioned from Annapolis in 1912 following graduation the previous year. Commanding officer of the submarines *D-3* and *O-4* Mar 1916-May 1919 and the *Fulton* May

1921-July 1922. Chief of staff to Commander Submarine Force, United States Fleet May 1938-April 1939. Commanding officer of the cruiser *Helena* June 1941-March 1942. His ship was hit by a torpedo during the attack on Pearl Harbor. Commander of Submarine Squadron Four March-May 1942. Rear admiral in May 1942. Commander of Pacific Fleet Submarine Force May 1942 until his death from an airplane crash at Boonville, California, on January 21, 1943. Decorations included the Navy Cross and Distinguished Service Medal.

Fahrion, Frank George (1894-1970) Born on April 17, 1894, in Pickens, West Virginia. Commissioned from Annapolis in 1917. M.S. from Massachusetts Institute of Technology in 1924. Served on the staff of Commander in Chief Asiatic Fleet May 1934-June 1937 then the Naval Torpedo Station at Newport June 1937-January 1940. Commanding officer of the *Warrington* January 1940-March 1941. Commander of Destroyer Division Three March 1941-February 1942. Chief of staff to Commander Destroyers, Battle Force February-December 1942. Inspector of naval ordnance at Naval Torpedo Station, Newport February 1943-August 1944. Rear admiral in February 1943. Commanding officer of the *North Carolina* October 1944-February 1945. Commander of Cruiser Division Four February 1945-January 1946. Assignments after the war included command of the Destroyer Force Atlantic Fleet July 1950-January 1952 and Amphibious Force Atlantic Fleet January 1952-May 1956. Admiral upon retirement in May 1956. Decorations included three Legions of Merit and two Bronze Stars. Died on January 16, 1970.

Fairfield, Arthur Philip (1877-1946) Born on October 29, 1877, in Saco, Maine. Attended Bowdoin College 1895-1897. Served aboard the *Columbia* in the Spanish-American War. Graduated from Annapolis in 1901 and commissioned in 1903. Instructor at Annapolis 1906-1909. Commanding officer of the *McDougal* and the *Gregory,* then staff officer with Admiral William S. Sims in London in World War I. Commanding officer of the *Argonne* in 1922 and the *Chester* 1930-1932. Graduated from the Naval War College in 1933. Assistant chief of the Bureau of Navigation May 1933-April 1935. Rear admiral in September 1934. Commander of Cruiser Division Seven 1935-1936. Member of the General Board 1937-1938. Assistant to chief of naval operations June 1938-July 1939. Commander of Battleship Division Three, Battle Force July 1939-January 1941. Retired as vice admiral in November 1941. Decorations included the Navy Cross. Died on December 14, 1946.

Farber, William Sims (1885-1963) Born on March 16, 1885, in Frankfort, Indiana. Graduated from Annapolis in 1907 and commissioned in 1909. Served at Vera Cruz in 1914. Aide to the Commander in Chief Atlantic Fleet July 1921-July 1922. Commanding officer of the *Reuben James* July 1925-September 1927. Head of the department of seamanship and flight tactics at Annapolis September 1927-June 1930. Aide to the Commander in Chief United States Fleet November 1930-October 1931. Graduated from the Army Industrial College in May 1933. Commanding officer of the *Louisville* December 1935-June 1937. Graduated from the Naval War College in 1938 then staff officer there until August 1939. Commanded Destroyer Squadron 41 September 1939-October 1940 then U.S. Naval Mine School October 1940-May 1941. Head of the fleet maintenance division in the office of the chief of naval operations May 1941-October 1943. Rear admiral in September 1941. Deputy chief of naval operations (logistics) October 1943-June 1946. Retired as vice admiral in December 1946. Decorations included the Distinguished Service Medal and Legion of Merit. Died on February 5, 1963.

Fechteler, William Morrow (1896-1967) Born in San Rafael, California, on March 6, 1896. Graduated from Annapolis in 1916. Served aboard the *Pennsylvania* in World War I. With the Bureau of Naval Personnel 1942-1943. Commanding officer of the *Indiana* 1943-1944. Rear admiral in December 1944. Commander of Amphibious Group Eight in Seventh Fleet 1944-1945. Assignments after the war included commander of battleships and cruisers in the Atlantic Fleet 1946-1947, deputy chief of naval operations for personnel 1947-1950, commander in chief of the Atlantic Fleet 1950-1951, chief of naval operations 1951-1953 and commander in chief of NATO Forces Southern Europe 1953-1956. Retired in July 1956. Decorations included three Distinguished Service Medals, the Legion of Merit and Bronze Star. Died on July 4, 1967.

Fife, James Jr. (1897-1975) Born on January 22, 1897, in Reno, Nevada. Commissioned from Annapolis in 1918. Commanding officer of the submarine *N-7* February-July 1920, the *R-19* February-October 1921, the *R-18* November 1921-August 1923, the *Monocacy* December 1927-June 1928 and the *Hatfield* April 1932-July 1933. Duty at the Bureau of Navigation August 1933-May 1935. Commanding officer of the *Nautilus* June 1935-December 1937. Commander of Submarine Division 12 December 1937-June 1938. Officer in charge of the Submarine School at New London June 1938-August 1940. Assistant naval attache in London September 1940-April 1941. Duty in the office of the chief of naval operations (naval intelligence) April-August 1941. Commander of Submarine Division 62 September-October 1941. Chief of staff to Commander Submarines, Asiatic Fleet December 1941-December 1942. Commander of Task Force 42 December 1942-March 1944. Rear admiral in April 1943. Assistant planner with Commander in Chief United States Fleet, March-November 1944. Commander of Submarines Southwest Pacific and Task Force 71 November 1944-December 1945. Assignments after the war included commander of Submarine Force, Atlantic April 1947-June 1950, deputy chief of naval operations July 1950-March 1953 and deputy Commander in Chief, Mediterranean March 1953-August 1955. Admiral upon retirement in August 1955. Decorations included three Distinguished Service Medals and the Air Medal. Died on November 17, 1975.

Fink, Beauford Wallace (1900-1968) Born on July 31, 1900, Bloomfield, Missouri. Commissioned in the Civil Engineer Corps from Annapolis in 1922. M.C.E. from Rensselaer Polytechnic Institute in June 1927. Assistant public works officer at Navy Yard Cavite, Philippine Islands April 1932-October 1934 and Navy Yard Bremerton February 1938-June 1940. Resident officer in charge of construction at all naval defense construction in Washington and Oregon June 1940-May 1941. Staff officer with Commander Mine Squadron Six, Base Force Pacific Fleet May 1941-February 1942. Assistant director, then director of the construction division, Bureau of Yards and Docks, February 1942-October 1943. Head of construction section at Commander in Chief Pacific Fleet and Pacific Ocean Areas October 1943-February 1946. Commodore in April 1945. Reverted to captain in March 1946 and retired in September 1949. Decorations included two Legions of Merit. Died on November 12, 1968.

Fischler, Peter Kalsh (1895-1950) Born on September 10, 1895, in Wellsboro, Pennsylvania. Commissioned from Annapolis in 1917. Commanding officer of the destroyers *Meredith, Breckenridge, Bell* and *Robinson* October 1919-June 1922. Executive officer, then commanding officer of the *Putnam* June 1922-February 1924. Instructor at Annapolis February 1924-June 1926 and June 1929-June 1931. Commanding officer of the *Preble* July 1936-May 1937 then the *Farragut* May 1937-June 1938. Executive officer of the *Wyoming* May 1940-January 1941. Operations officer on the staff of Commander Train, Patrol Force January 1941-March 1942. Assistant chief of staff at Commander Service Force, Atlantic Fleet March 1942-August 1942. Staff officer with Commander in Chief United States Fleet, August 1942-February 1944. Rear admiral in May 1943. Commanding officer of the *Alaska* February 1944-January 1945. Commander of Battleship Division Five January 1945-June 1945. Assistant chief of staff for logistics at Commander in Chief Pacific Fleet June 1945-February 1946. Died on July 14, 1950. Decorations included the Legion of Merit, Bronze Star and two Navy Commendation Medals.

Fisher, Charles Willis (1880-1971) Born on October 27, 1880, in New York, New York. Graduated from Annapolis in 1901 and commissioned in 1903. M.S. from Massachusetts Institute of Technology in 1907. Aide to Commander U.S. Naval Forces in France September 1918-October 1919. Duty with the shore establishments division, office of the assistant secretary of the navy September 1935-September 1939. Director of shore establishments, Navy Department 1939-1942. Rear admiral in October 1941. Duty in the office of the secretary of the navy 1942-1944. Retired in November 1944. Decorations included the Navy Cross and Legion of Merit. Died on October 8, 1971.

Fitch, Aubrey Wray (1883-1978) Born in St. Ignace, Michigan, on June 11, 1883. Graduated from Annapolis in 1906 and commissioned in 1908. Served aboard the *Wyoming*, attached to the Grand Fleet, during World War I. Qualified as a naval aviator in 1930. Graduated from the Naval War College in 1938. Commanding officer of Pensacola Naval Air Station 1938-1940. Rear admiral in July 1940. Commander of Patrol Wing Two, then Carrier Division One 1940-1941. As commander of a task force in the Pacific, Fitch joined forces with Rear Admiral Frank Jack Fletcher on May 7-8, 1942, in the Battle of the Coral Sea. The first battle at sea where opposing ships exchanged no gunfire, it turned the tide of advance by the Japanese. Commander of all aircraft in the South Pacific

Fleet in 1942, then commander of all air forces of the United States the following year. Vice admiral in December 1943. Deputy chief of naval operations for air in 1944. Superintendent of Annapolis August 1945-January 1947. Retired in July 1947 as admiral. Decorations included the Distinguished Service Medal, Legion of Merit and Distinguished Flying Cross. Died on May 22, 1978.

Fite, William Conyers (1882-1963) Born on January 3, 1882, in Carterville, Georgia. Cadet at USMA 1900-1902. Resigned in September 1902. Commissioned assistant paymaster in the Navy in 1903. Supply officer for Sixth and Seventh Naval Districts June 1933-June 1936. Rear admiral in October 1933. Supply officer at Mare Island Navy Yard 1936-1940. Officer in charge of the Navy Purchasing Office in San Francisco July 1940-July 1942. Officer in charge of Oakland Naval Supply Depot 1942-1945. Retired in June 1945. Died on April 1, 1963.

Flanagan, Henry C. (1891-1964) Born on September 9, 1891, in Desota Parish, Louisiana. Attended Teachers College in Richmond, Kentucky. Enlisted service 1915-1918. Commissioned in 1918. M.S. from the University of California in 1934. District communication officer and commanding officer of outlying naval radio stations March 1937-October 1940. Executive officer of the *Fuller* November 1940-August 1942 then the *Fomalhaut* August 1942-July 1943. Assigned to the *President Hayes* July-December 1943. Commander of the Administrative Command, Amphibious Forces Pacific Fleet 1944-1946. Commodore in October 1944. Retired in July 1946. Decorations included the Silver Star and two Bronze Stars. Died on Septemeber 26, 1964.

Flanigan, Howard Adams (1889-1967) Born on January 23, 1889, in New York City. Graduated from Annapolis in 1910 and commissioned in 1912. Served at Vera Cruz in 1914. Commanding officer of the *Rowan* in World War I, the *Barney* December 1920-December 1921, the *Bainbridge* December 1921-June 1922, the *Paul Jones* June 1922-June 1924 and the *Chewink* January 1924-May 1926. Retired in August 1936. Executive vice president of the New York World's Fair 1936-1941 and chairman of New York Dock Company 1941-1942. Called to active naval service in the office of the chief of naval operations May-June 1941. Assistant naval attache in London June 1941-September 1942. Duty with U.S. Naval Forces Europe November 1942-December 1944. Commodore in April 1944. Director of the Naval Transportation Service December 1944-November 1945. Rear admiral in April 1945. Decorations included the Navy Cross, Distinguished Service Medal and Legion of Merit. Died on March 30, 1967.

Fletcher, Frank Jack (1885-1973) Born in Marshalltown, Iowa, on April 29, 1885. Graduated from Annapolis in 1906 and commissioned in 1908. Participated in the Vera Cruz occupation and earned the Medal of Honor in April 1914. Commanding officer of the *Benham*, a destroyer, during World War I. Graduated from the Naval War College in 1930 and the Army War College in 1931. Aide to the secretary of the navy 1933-1936. Staff officer at the Bureau of Personnel 1938-1939. Rear admiral in November 1939. Commander of Cruiser Division

Three in the Atlantic Fleet 1939-1941. Commander of a task force that joined with Rear Admiral Aubrey W. Fitch in the Battle of the Coral Sea on May 7-8, 1942, the first sea battle fought entirely in the air. Vice admiral in June 1942. Commander of naval forces in the North Pacific 1943-1945. Chairman of the General Board 1945 until retirement and promotion to admiral in May 1947. Decorations included the Medal of Honor, Navy Cross, Distinguished Service Medal and Purple Heart. Died on April 25, 1973.

Forster, Otto Marquard (1889-1961) Born on May 24, 1889, in St. Louis, Missouri. Commissioned from Annapolis in 1912. Served at naval headquarters in Brest, France in 1919. Commanding officer of the *Kane* October 1926-September 1928, the *Biddle* July 1930-February 1931, the *Simpson* June-December 1931 and the *Parrott* December 1931-September 1933. Graduated from the Naval War College in 1935. Officer in charge of the branch hydrographic office September 1939-May 1940. Commander of Inshore Patrol at Thirteenth Naval District June-October 1940. Commanding officer of the *Harris* October 1940-February 1943. Commanded the Navy Personnel Distribution Center at Pleasanton, California February 1943-July 1944 and the U.S. Naval Training and Distribution Center at Shoemaker, California July 1944-September 1946. Commodore in October 1944. Retired in November 1946. Decorations included two Navy Commendation Medals. Died on December 13, 1961.

Fort, George Hudson (1891-1975) Born on August 23, 1891, in Lumpkin, Georgia. Graduated from Annapolis in 1912 and commissioned in 1914 after an obligatory two years at sea. Commanding officer of the *Henley* June-July 1919, the submarine *S-25* July 1923-September 1925 and the *Borie, Paul Jones* and *Hamilton* June 1928-February 1931. Graduated from the Naval War College in May 1938. Commanding officer of Destroyer Division Two, Battle Force May 1938-June 1940. Head of the department of mathematics at Annapolis June 1940-June 1942. Rear admiral in May 1942. Commanding officer of the *North Carolina* June-December 1942. Commanded a task group of amphibious units which landed assault troops on New Georgia and Treasury, Russell and Green Islands December 1942-April 1944, Landing Craft Flotillas South Pacific in 1944, Amphibious Group Five July-October 1944 and Training Command, Amphibious Forces, Pacific Fleet January 1945-June 1946. Vice admiral upon retirement in September 1953. Decorations included the Navy Cross, Distinguished Service Medal and Legion of Merit. Died on July 21, 1975.

Foster, Edwin Dorsey (1896-1979) Born on February 17, 1896, in Cape May Court House, New Jersey. BA from Princeton University in 1924. Commissioned assistant paymaster in the Supply Corps in June 1917. Disbursing and commissary officer at Queenstown, Ireland November 1917-August 1919 then at Naval Station Tutuila, America Samoa December 1924-August 1926. M.B.A. from Harvard University in June 1933. Graduated from Army Industrial College in June 1937. Officer in Charge of the war plans division, Bureau of Supplies and Accounts June 1937-June. Supply officer to Commander Aircraft, Scouting Force,

Commander Aircraft, Atlantic Squadron, and Commander Aircraft, Patrol Force June 1939-April 1942. Aviation supply officer at Naval Aircraft Factory, Philadelphia December 1942-June 1943. Rear admiral in June 1943. Supply officer in command of the Naval Aviation Supply Depot, Philadelphia July 1943-July 1946. Assignments after the war included chief of naval material October 1949 until retirement as vice admiral in January 1951. Decorations included the Legion of Merit. Died on June 14, 1979.

Foster, Paul Frederick (1889-1972) Born on March 25, 1889, in Wichita, Kansas. Attended the University of Idaho, 1905-1906. Graduated from Annapolis in 1911 and commissioned in 1913. Earned the Medal of Honor during the invasion of Vera Cruz in April 1914. Commanding officer of the submarines *G-4* February 1916-September 1917 and the *AL-2* March-July 1918. Officer in charge of the Navy Recruiting Bureau, the principal publicity office for the Navy June 1921-January 1924. He oversaw development of the first Navy radio programs and the first productions of Navy publicity films for newsreels. Resigned in March 1929 and entered the Naval Reserve. Recalled to active duty in December 1941, he was the first man to receive all three of the navy's highest awards and except for Rear Admiral Richard E. Byrd he was the only officer in the U.S. Navy who had been awarded the Medal of Honor, Navy Cross and Distinguished Service Medal up to the outbreak of World War II. Duty in the logistics plans division, office of the chief of naval operations February 1942-August 1943. Assistant naval inspector general August 1943-December 1946. Rear admiral in January 1944. Vice admiral upon retirement in December 1946. Decorations included the Medal of Honor, Navy Cross, Distinguished Service Medal and Legion of Merit. Died on January 31, 1972.

Fox, Charles Welford (1894-1975) Born on December 5, 1894, in Baltimore, Maryland. Enlisted service 1913-1917. Commissioned in the Supply Corps in 1919. Served at U.S. Naval Air Station Moutchic Lacanau, France in World War I. Assistant to the supply officer at Mare Island Navy Yard July 1938-June 1940. Supply officer on the *Enterprise* July 1940-September 1942. Officer in Charge of the aviation supply division, Bureau of Supplies and Accounts September 1942-June 1944 then the Aviation Supply Office in Philadelphia June 1944-April 1945. Commodore in December 1944. Supply officer in command of Naval Supply Depot Mechanicsburg, Pennsylvania April 1945-May 1946. Assignments after the war included chief of naval material October 1951 until retirement as vice admiral in August 1953. Decorations included two Legions of Merit. Died on November 4, 1975.

Friedell, Wilhelm Lee (1883-1958) Born on August 22, 1883, in Texarkana, Arkansas. Graduated from Annapolis in 1905 and commissioned in 1907. Commanding officer of the *Villalobos* January 1910-October 1911. Instructor at Annapolis March 1912-April 1914. Commanding officer of the *C-3* June 1914-September 1916 and the *Bushnell* November 1916-February 1919. Again instructor at Annapolis August 1919-June 1921. Commanding officer of *Rainbow* June

1922-September 1923. Again instructor at Annapolis September 1923-June 1926. Commanded Submarine Division 11 then Submarine Division, Battle Fleet June 1926-June 1928. Graduated from the Naval War College in June 1929. Commanding officer of the *Colorado* February 1936-July 1937. Chief of staff to Commandant Fourteenth Naval District, Pearl Harbor August 1937-May 1938. Rear admiral in June 1938. Commander of Minecraft, Battle Force May 1938-June 1939, Submarine Force, United States Fleet June 1939-November 1940 and Submarines, Scouting Force November 1940-January 1941. Commandant of Navy Yard Mare Island February 1941-January 1944 then Eleventh Naval District January 1944-January 1946. Retired in May 1946. Decorations included the Navy Cross and two Legions of Merit. Died on January 27, 1958.

Furer, Julius Augustus (1880-1963) Born on October 9, 1880, in Mosel, Wisconsin. Graduated from Annapolis in 1901 and commissioned in 1903. M.S. from Massachusetts Institute of Technology in 1905. In charge of the sub chaser program in World War I. Staff officer with commander in chief Pacific Fleet 1919-1921. Member of the naval mission to Brazil 1923-1927. Head of the navy yard at Cavite, Philippine Islands 1928-1930. Technical assistant to naval attaches in London, Paris, Rome and Berlin 1935-1938. General inspector at the Bureau of Ships 1938-1941. Rear admiral in October 1941. Head of research and development for the Navy Department 1941-1944. Retired in November 1944. Decorations included the Navy Cross and Legion of Merit. Died on June 5, 1963.

Furlong, William Rea (1881-1976) Born on May 26, 1881, in Washington County, Pennsylvania. Graduated from Annapolis in 1905 and commissioned in 1907. M.A. from Columbia University in 1914. Staff officer with Rear Admiral Frank Friday Fletcher at the invasion of Vera Cruz in 1914. Gunnery observer with the British Grand Fleet then staff officer with Admiral William S. Sims in London during World War I. Commanding officer of the *West Virginia* 1936-1937. Staff officer with Admiral Arthur J. Hepburn, commander in chief United States Fleet in 1937. Chief of the Bureau of Ordnance August 1937-February 1941. Rear admiral in June 1938. Commander of Minecraft, Battle Force in 1941. Commandant of Pearl Harbor Navy Yard December 12, 1941-May 1945. Retired in June 1945. Died on June 2, 1976.

Gaffney, John Jerome (1891-1947) Born on March 5, 1891, in Charleston, South Carolina. B.A. from the College of Charleston in 1912. Commissioned in the Supply Corps in 1912. Served in China waters 1913-1916 and the Virgin Islands 1920-1923. Attended Brooklyn Law School 1925-1926. Staff officer with commander Aircraft, Battle Force 1939-1941. Supply officer at Pearl Harbor July 1941-July 1943. Rear admiral in June 1943. District supply officer at Fourteenth Naval District 1943-1945. Supply officer in charge of Oakland Naval Supply Depot August 1945-May 1947. Died on November 21, 1947. Decorations included the Legion of Merit.

Gallery, Daniel Vincent Jr. (1901-1977) Born on July 10, 1901, in Chicago, Illinois. Commissioned from Annapolis in 1921. Designated a naval aviator in 1927. Chief of the aviation section in the Bureau of Ordnance 1938-1941. Naval attache for air in London in 1941. Commanding officer of the Fleet Air Base at Reykjavik, Iceland, 1941-1943. Commanding officer of the *Guadalcanal* and a group of five destroyer escorts on anti-submarine patrols in the Atlantic 1943-1945. Rear admiral in February 1944. His task force encountered a German submarine, the U-505, off the northwestern coast of Africa on June 4, 1944, and forced it to the surface where the crew abandoned ship. As the submarine began to sink Gallery ordered it boarded, the first capture of an enemy warship at sea since 1815. Its sea cocks were closed and the U-505 was towed to Bermuda. Retired in November 1960. Author of *Clear the Decks!* (1951), *Twenty Million Tons Under the Sea* (1956), *Eight Bells and All's Well* (1965) and *Now Hear This!* (1965). Died on January 16, 1977.

Gardner, Matthias Bennett (1897-1975) Born on November 28, 1897, in Washington, DC. Commissioned from Annapolis in 1919. Served aboard the destroyer *Drayton* on convoy duty during World War I. Designated naval aviator in June 1922. Graduated from Air Corps Tactical School in 1927. With Lieutenants Aaron P. Storrs and Frederick M. Trapnell he formed an acrobatic group known as the "Three Flying Fish" 1930-1931. Officer in charge of the aviation section, ship's movement division in the office of the chief of naval operations June 1938-June 1940. Executive officer of the *Wright* 1940-1941. Chief of staff to Commander Aircraft, Scouting Force then Commander Aircraft, South Pacific 1941-1942. Duty with the plans division, office of the Commander in Chief United States Fleet December 1942-October 1943. Rear admiral in July 1943. Commanding officer of the *Enterprise* 1943-1944. Commanded Carrier Division Eleven, then Seven July 1944-May 1945. Assistant chief of staff for plans, office of the Commander in Chief United States Fleet May-October 1945. Assignments after the war included commander of Second Fleet, then Sixth Fleet 1950-1952, deputy chief of naval operations for air, then operations, finally plans and policy May 1952-August 1956. Admiral upon retirement in August 1956. Decorations included the Distinguished Service Medal, Legion of Merit and Bronze Star. Died on August 24, 1975.

Gatch, Thomas Leigh (1891-1954) Born on August 9, 1891, in Salem, Oregon. Attended Oregon State College before entering Annapolis. Commissioned from Annapolis in 1912. LL.B. from George Washington University in June 1922. Commanding officer of the *Percival* and the *Wickes* May 1927-May 1929. Instructor at Annapolis May 1929-June 1933. Assistant to the judge advocate general of the navy June 1935-April 1938. Commanded Destroyer Division Four April 1938-July 1940. Again assistant to the judge advocate general July 1940-March 1942. Commanding officer of the *South Dakota* March 1942-June 1943. Rear admiral in September 1942. He was wounded in the Battle of Santa Cruz and hospitalized for three weeks. Duty at headquarters United States Fleet July-

August 1943. Judge advocate general of the Navy September 1943-November 1945. Commanded Service Force Atlantic Fleet November 1945-June 1947. Vice admiral in December 1945. Retired in September 1947. Decorations included two Navy Crosses and the Purple Heart. Died on December 16, 1954.

Gehres, Leslie E. (1896-n/a) Born on January 13, 1896, in Newark, New York. Enlisted service in the naval militia 1914-1918. Commissioned in the Naval Reserve Force in 1918. Designated naval aviator in August 1927. Trained and led "The Nine High Hats," a nine-plane acrobatic formation in 1929. Operations officer on the staff of Commander Carrier Division Two July 1937-June 1938. Air officer on the *Ranger* May-December 1939. Executive officer at Naval Air Station Pearl Harbor January 1940-October 1941. Commander of Patrol Wing Four 1941-1943. Commodore in July 1943. Commander of Fleet Air Wing Four 1943-1944. Reverted to captain in August 1944. Commanding officer of the *Franklin* 1944-1945. Commander of Naval Air Station San Diego July 1945-August 1948. Director of naval officer procurement in Los Angeles September 1948 until retirement in May 1949. Decorations included the Navy Cross, two Legions of Merit, the Distinguished Flying Cross and Purple Heart.

Ghormley, Robert Lee (1883-1958) Born in Portland, Oregon, on October 15, 1883. Graduate of the University of Idaho in 1902. Graduated from Annapolis in 1906 and commissioned in 1908. Served with the battleship force of the Atlantic Fleet, then in the office of the chief of naval operations during World War I. Graduated from the Naval War College in 1938. Rear admiral in October 1938. Director of war plans division in the Navy Department, then assistant to the chief of naval operations 1938-1940. Naval observed in London 1940-1942. Vice admiral in September 1941. Commander of South Pacific Forces April-October 1942, with responsibility for planning and executing the invasion of the Solomon Islands. Commandant of the Fourteenth Naval District 1943-1944. On the staff of Admiral Harold R. Stark, commander of U.S. Naval Forces in Europe, 1944-1945, then commander of U.S. Naval Forces German Waters May 1945 until retirement in August 1946. Decorations included the Distinguished Service Medal and Legion of Merit. Died on June 21, 1958.

Giffen, Robert Carlisle (1886-1962) Born on June 29, 1886, in West Chester, Pennsylvania. Attended La Salle Institute in Chicago and the University of Notre Dame. Graduated from Annapolis in 1907 and commissioned in 1909. Commanding officer of the *Trippe* January 1917-March 1918, the *Schley* June 1918-August 1919 and the *Sacramento* July 1927-August 1928. Commander of Destroyer Squadron Forty-Five August 1928-September 1929. Commanding officer of the *Neches* June 1932-June 1934 and the *Savannah* August 1937-May 1940. Director of the naval reserve policy division in the office of the chief of naval operations September 1940-March 1941. Commander of Cruiser Destroyer Division Seven March 1941-November 1942. Rear admiral in October 1941. Duty with Commander in Chief Pacific Fleet November 1942-March 1944 including commander of Cruiser Division Six during raids on Truk and Saipan. Vice admiral in March

1944 while serving as Commander Caribbean Sea Frontier. Commandant of Tenth Naval District May 1944-August 1945. Commander Service Force Atlantic Fleet August 1946 until retirement in September 1946. Decorations included the Navy Cross two Distinguished Service Medals and the Legion of Merit. Died on December 10, 1962.

Gillette, Claude Sexton (1886-1959) Born on February 1, 1886, in Chicago, Illinois. Graduated from Annapolis in 1909 and commissioned in 1911. Served in the Bureau of Ordnance. June 1934-May 1937. Executive officer of the *Omaha* June 1937-July 1939. Professor of naval science and tactics at Annapolis September 1939-June 1941. Graduated from the Naval War College in December 1941. Served in the office of chief of naval operations December 1941-February 1942. Commanding officer of the *Tuscaloosa* February 1942-April 1943. Commanded Naval Ordnance Plant Center Line, Michigan May 1943-October 1944. Chief of staff to Vice Admiral J.L. Kauffman, Commander Philippine Sea Frontier October 1944-August 1945. Commodore in June 1945. Retired as rear admiral in November 1946. Decorations included the Legion of Merit. Died on September 27, 1959.

Ginder, Samuel Paul (1895-1959) Born on February 15, 1895, in Altoona, Pennsylvania. Commissioned from Annapolis in 1916. Designated naval aviator (seaplane) in August 1921. Flag lieutenant and flag secretary to Commander Aircraft Squadrons Scouting Fleet June 1925-October 1925. Executive officer of Fleet Air Base Coco Solo, Canal Zone April 1935-May 1937 then the *Langley* June 1937-June 1939. Commanding officer of NAS Anacostia June 1939-July 1940, the *Curtiss* July 1940-December 1941 and NAS Trinidad, British West Indies December 1941-August 1942. Commandant of the Naval Air Center, Seattle August 1942-April 1943. Rear admiral in December 1942. Commanding officer of the *Enterprise* April-October 1943. Commander of Carrier Task Group Four operating as a unit of Task Force Fifty-Eight October 1943-June 1944 and Carrier Transport Squadron Pacific Fleet June 1944-January 1946. Retired in June 1951. Decorations included two Legions of Merit. Died on July 17, 1959.

Gingrich, John Edward (1897-1960) Born on February 23, 1897, in Dodge City, Kansas. Attended the University of Kansas. Commissioned from Annapolis in 1919. Instructor Annapolis at June 1925-May 1927. Commanding officer of the *Algorma* June 1932-April 1934. Aide and flag secretary on the staff of Commander Battleship Division Three June 1937-July 1939. Navigator aboard the *New Mexico* August 1939-August 1940. Aide to the under secretary of the navy August 1940-May 1944 and aide to the secretary of the navy May-July 1944. Commanding officer of the *Pittsburgh* October 1944-September 1945. Assignments after the war included chief of staff to Commander in Chief Pacific Fleet July 1949-October 1951, deputy chief of naval operations (administration) February 1953-August 1953 and chief of Naval Material until retirment as admiral in October 1954. Decorations included the Distinguished Service Medal, Silver Star and two Legions of Merit. Died on May 26, 1960.

Glass, Richard Pollard (1898-1987) Born on October 19, 1898, in Lynchburg, Virginia. Commissioned from Annapolis in 1919. Aide to Commandant Fifth Naval District, Norfolk April 1935-April 1936. Executive officer of the *Charleston* July 1936-April 1938 and gunnery gfficer on the *Louisville* April 1938-May 1939. Duty at the Bureau of Navigation June 1939-December 1941. Graduated from the Naval War College in June 1942. Commanding officer of the *Brazos* July 1942-July 1943. Graduated from Command and General Staff School in November 1943. Staff officer with Commander Third Fleet, South Pacific Force (Admiral Halsey) November 1943-June 1944. Assistant chief of staff for plans and logisitics, then chief of staff and aide on the staff of Commander South Pacific Area and South Pacific Force June 1944-February 1945. Commodore as deputy commander South Pacific Area and South Pacific Force April-November 1945. Retired as rear admiral in October 1954. Decorations included two Legions of Merit. Died on June 27, 1987.

Glassford, William A. Jr. (1884-1958) Born on June 6, 1884, in San Francisco, California. Graduated from Annapolis in 1906 and commissioned in 1908. Commanding officer of the *Davis* March-July 1909 and the *Paul Jones* September 1911-May 1912. Instructor at Annapolis July 1912-June 1914. Again commanding officer of the *Paul Jones* January 1915-November 1916. Commanding officer of the *Shaw* August-December 1918, the *Chauncey* December 1918-September 1919, the *Radford* September-December 1919, the *Montgomery* December 1921-March 1922, the *Pecos* May 1922-January 1923 and the *Tracy* January 1923-June 1924. Graduated from the Naval War College in 1932. Duty with the Argentine Navy January 1935-October 1937. Commanding officer of the *Maryland* December 1937-March 1939. Commander of the Yangtze Patrol March 1939-December 1941. Rear admiral in July 1939. Commanded Task Force Five of the Asiatic Fleet December 1941-January 1942 and U.S. Naval Forces Southwest Pacific January-May 1942. Commandant of Sixth Naval District June-December 1942. Headed U.S. Military Mission to Dakas, French West Africa December 1942-April 1943. Brief duty at the Bureau of naval Personnel April-June 1943. Vice admiral in May 1943. Returned to Dakar as personal representative of the President to the governor of French West Africa with title of minister, then appointed deputy in French West Africa to Supreme Commander Allied Expeditionary Forces (General Eisenhower) 1943-1944. Deputy commander of U.S. Naval Forces in Europe for Occupied Countries September 1944-April 1945. Commander of Eighth Fleet April 1945- December 1945. Retired in March 1947. Decorations included two Distinguished Service Medals. Died on July 30, 1958.

Glover, Cato Douglas (1897-1988) Born on September 15, 1897, in Centerville, Alabama. Attended Marion Institute and the University of Alabama. Commissioned from Annapolis in 1919. Designated naval aviator in December 1922. M.S. from Massachusetts Institute of Technology in June 1931. Commanded Fighter Squadron Three June 1936-June 1937. Tactical officer on the staff of Vice Admiral E. J. King, Commander Aircraft Battle Force June 1937-June 1939.

Assistant naval attache for air in Paris and Lisbon then acting naval attache on the staff of Ambassador Leahy to the Vichy Government 1939-1941. Special aviation adviser to chief of naval operations March 1941-May 1942. Executive officer of the *Saratoga* May-September 1942. Commanding officer of the *Barnes* September 1942-July 1943. Assistant war plans officer on the staff of Commander in Chief Pacific Fleet July 1943-July 1944. Commanding officer of the *Enterprise* July 1944-December 1944. Head of the Pacific planning section, plans division, at headquarters United States Fleet December 1944-August 1945. Chief of staff to Commander Air Force, Pacific Fleet August 1945-October 1946. Assignments after the war included the first director of the Joint Staff, Joint Chiefs of Staff October 1947-August 1949 and the first chief of staff to the newly authorized NATO Command, Supreme Allied Commander Atlantic August 1951-May 1953. Admiral upon retirement in September 1957. Decorations included the Navy Cross, Silver Star and two Bronze Stars. Died on November 5, 1988.

Glover, Robert Ogden (1894-1976) Born on July 3, 1894, in Norfolk, Virginia. Commissioned from Annapolis in 1915. M.S. from Columbia University in June 1923. Aide and flag secretary on the staff of Commander Destroyer Squadrons Scouting Fleet June 1929-July 1930. Commanding officer of the *Pope* May 1933-April 1935. Senior naval aide in the White House July 1935-June 1937. Graduated from the Naval War College in May 1938. Engineer officer on the staff of Commander Scouting Force June 1938-December 1940. Duty in the war plans division, office of the chief of naval operations January 1941-February 1942. Served at headquarters of Commander in Chief United States Fleet February-December 1942. Rear admiral in July 1942. Commanding officer of the *Massachusetts* December 1942-September 1943. Assistant director of the logistics plans division, office of the chief of naval operations October 1943-July 1944. Commander of Service Force Seventh Fleet July 1944-August 1945 and Service Squadron Seven August 1945-January 1946. Retired in September 1948. Decorations included the Distinguished Service Medal. Died on May 20, 1976.

Good, Howard Harrison (1888-1963) Born on August 12, 1888, in Warren, Indiana. Commissioned from Annapolis in 1912. Commanding officer of the *Renshaw* December 1921-May 1922. Aide and flag secretary on the staff of Commander Destroyer Squadrons Pacific Fleet May 1922-July 1923. Comm-anding officer of the *Truxton* October 1926-May 1929. Aide and flag secretary to Commander Yangtze Patrol January 1936-March 1938. Duty in the planning division, Bureau of Navigation March 1938-July 1941. Commanding officer of the *New Orleans* July 1941-June 1942. Rear admiral in May 1942. Commander of Cruiser Division Five June 1942-January 1943. Assigned to the Bureau of Naval Personnel January-May 1943. Director of the base maintenance division, office of the chief of naval operations June 1943-March 1946. Vice admiral upon retirement in September 1950. Decorations included two Legions of Merit and the Navy Commendation Medal. Died on August 12, 1963.

Good, Roscoe Fletcher (1897-1973) Born on March 13, 1897, in Fostoria, Ohio. Commissioned from Annapolis in 1919. Qualified for submarine duty in July 1921. M.S. from Columbia University in 1926. Commanding officer of the *S-17* in 1928. Navigator on the *Arkansas* May 1937-May 1938. Served aboard the *Tuscaloosa* June 1938-June 1939. Staff officer with Commander Cruisers, Battle Force June 1939-February 1941, Commander in Chief Pacific Fleet February 1941-August 1943 and Commander in Chief United States Fleet August 1943-October 1944. Rear admiral in September 1943. Commanding officer of the *Washington* October 1944-June 1945. Commander of Cruiser Division Six July-August 1945. Assignments after the war included deputy chief of naval operations (logistics) March 1953-September 1956 and commander of Naval Forces Japan September 1956 until retirement as admiral in March 1958. Decorations included two Legions of Merit and the Navy Commendation Medal. Died on February 26, 1973.

Graf, Homer William (1894-1970) Born on February 16, 1894, in Chicago, Illinois. Commissioned from Annapolis in 1915. Commanding officer of the *Roper* June 1934-July 1935. Navigator on the *Salt Lake City* July 1935-April 1937. Duty in the technical divison, office of the chief of naval operations May 1937-January 1940. Executive officer of the *Tennessee* Janaury 1940-January 1941. Commanding officer of the *Cincinnati* January 1941-May 1942. Aide to the superintendent of Annapolis May 1942-May 1943. Chief of staff to Commander Seventh Fleet May 1943-October 1944. Commodore in November 1944. Commander of Transport Squadron Nineteen November 1944-December 1945. Retired in December 1948. Decorations included the Legion of Merit. Died on March 12, 1970.

Grant, Vernon Francis (1894-1966) Born on July 8, 1894, in Chicago, Illinois. Commissioned from Annapolis in 1917. Served aboard the *Delaware* and the *Arkansas*, both of which operated with the British Grand Fleet in World War I. Aide to Commander Squadron Two, Destroyer Force February-September 1919. Designated naval aviator in November 1920. Instructor at Pensacola Air Station 1922-1925 then Annapolis 1928-1930. Retired in July 1939. Recalled to active duty in World War II. Duty in the Bureau of Aeronautics 1939-1940 then the Naval Aircraft Factory at Philadelphia Navy Yard November 1940-January 1943. Air officer at Thirteenth Naval District January-March 1943. Commander of Naval Air Station Johnston Island 1943-1944. Air commander then commander of Majuro Atoll February-October 1944. Commodore in October 1944. Commanded Naval Air Bases Guam then Naval Air Bases Saipan 1944-1945. Retired again in April 1946. Decorations included the Legion of Merit and Bronze Star. Died on March 9, 1966.

Gray, Augustine Heard (1888-1981) Born on November 10, 1888, in Boston Massachusetts. Graduated from Annapolis in 1910 and commissioned in 1912.

Commanding officer of the submarines *D-1* and *L-2* 1915-1917. Aide to Commander Train, Atlantic Fleet March 1919-July 1921. Graduated from the Naval War College in 1935. Adviser to the Argentine Navy 1937-1939. Commanding officer of the *New Orleans* December 1939-August 1941. Duty with the Bureau of Navigation 1941-1942. Commanded Transport Division Five, Pacific Fleet then Service Squadron Eight July 1942-September 1945. Commodore in February 1944. Retired in January 1947. Decorations included two Legions of Merit. Died on October 5, 1981.

Greenslade, John Wills (1880-1950) Born on January 11, 1880 in Bellevue, Ohio. Graduated from Annapolis in 1899 and commissioned in 1901. Served on the *Montgomery* in the Spanish-American War and in the Philippines during the insurrection 1899-1902. Commanding officer of the *Housatonic* in World War I. Commander of Mine Squadron One 1923-1925. Head of the operations department at the Naval War College 1926-1928. Commanding officer of the *Pennsylvania* 1928-1929. Chief of staff of Battleship Divisions 1929-1930. Aide to the secretary of the navy 1930-1932. Rear admiral in May 1932. Commander of the Submarine Force 1932-1934, Battleship Division Two in 1937 and Battleships, United States Fleet 1938-1939. Member of the General Board 1939-1941. Commandant of Twelfth Naval District April 1941-January 1944. Vice admiral in May 1942. Retired February 1, 1944. Decorations included two Distinguished Service Medals and the Legion of Merit. Died on January 6, 1950.

Greer, Marshall Raymond (1896-1981) Born on March 1, 1896, in Riverside, North Carolina. Commissioned from Annapolis in 1918. Served aboard the *North Dakota* on escort duty in the Atlantic during World War I. Designated naval aviator in December 1921. Graduated from the Naval War College in 1935. Aviation officer on the staff of Commander Cruisers, Scouting Force 1938-1939. Adviser to the Argentine Navy January 1940-December 1941. Commanding officer of the *Wright* then the *Core* 1942-1943. Commandant of the Naval Air Center at Hampton Roads November 1943-August 1944. Rear admiral in August 1943. Commanding officer of the *Bunker Hill* 1944-1945. Commander of Aircraft, South Pacific Force January-May 1945 then Fleet Air Wing 18 May-December 1945. Vice admiral upon retirement in July 1953. Decorations included the Silver Star and two Legions of Merit. Died on August 12, 1981.

Griffin, Robert Melville (1890-1976) Born on May 23, 1890, in Washington, DC. Graduated from Annapolis in 1911 and commissioned in 1913. Served aboard the *Cushing* and *Aylwin* in the Atlantic during World War I. Duty as junior naval aide in the White House in 1921. Commanding officer of the *Marcus* October 1923-October 1926. Graduated from the Naval War College in 1932 then staff member there until 1934. Commanding officer of the battleship *New York* December 1938-May 1940. Duty in the office of the chief of naval operations 1940-1942. Rear admiral in December 1941. Director of Naval Transportation Service March 1942-March 1943. Commanded Battleship Division Three

1943-1944. Commandant of the Puget Sound Navy Yard June-November 1944 then Thirteenth Naval District 1944-1945. Retired as vice admiral in June 1951.Decorations included the Navy Cross and Legion of Merit. Died on January 30, 1976.

Gunther, Ernest Ludolph (1887-1948) Born on September 7, 1887, in Louisville, Kentucky. Graduated from Annapolis in 1909 and commissioned in 1911. Served aboard the battleship *Texas* during the occupation of Vera Cruz in 1914. Aide to Commander Reserve Force, Atlantic Fleet then Commander Division Four, Battleship Force 1916-1917. Commanding officer of the *Isabel* and the *Jarvis* in the Atlantic during World War I. Commanding officer of the *Elliott* 1919-1921. Commanding officer of the *Somers* December 1923-June 1926. Naval attache in Chile 1931-1934. Designated naval aviator in March 1936. Commanding officer of the *Wright* 1936-1937. Commander of Fleet Air Base Coco Solo in 1937. Commanding officer of the carrier *Yorktown* June 1939-February 1941. Commander of San Diego Naval Air Station 1941-1943. Rear admiral in March 1943. Commanded Fleet Air South, Pacific Fleet 1944-1945 and Air Force Pacific Fleet February 1945-March 1946. Died at his home on March 27, 1948, while awaiting retirement. Decorations included the Navy Cross.

Gygax, Felix Xerxes (1884-1977) Born on March 30, 1884, in Twin Creek, Kansas. Graduated from Annapolis in 1907 and commissioned in 1909. Aide to the commander of the Battle Force, then Commander in Chief United States Fleet 1926-1927. Secretary of the war plans division in the office of the chief of naval operations 1927-1928. Aide to Admiral Charles F. Hughes, the chief of naval operations 1928-1930. Professor of naval science and tactics at the University of California 1932-1935. Commanding officer of the cruiser *Augusta* 1935-1937. Director of the Naval Reserve 1937-1940. Rear admiral in December 1940. Commander of Cruiser Division Three, Pacific Fleet 1940-1941. Commandant of Norfolk Naval Yard in August 1941-October 1944. Commandant of First Naval District 1944-1945. Relieved for age in April 1945 and retired in August 1946. Died on February 24, 1977.

Haggart, Robert Stevenson (1891-1966) Born on April 7, 1891, in Salem, New York. Commissioned from Annapolis in 1912. Commanding officer of the *Hull* December 1917-December 1918. Instructor at Annapolis September 1919-August 1922. Commanding officer of the *William B. Preston* June 1933-August 1934. Professor of naval science and tactics at Georgia School of Technology August 1935-June 1938. Executive officer of the *Chicago* June 1938-June 1939. Commanding officer of the *Pyro* June 1939-July 1940. Professor of naval science and tactics at the University of Oklahoma July-September 1940 then the University of North Carolina September 1940-December 1941. Graduated from the Naval War College in 1942. Commanding officer of the *Tennessee* June 1942-March 1944. Commander of Naval Training Center at San Diego April 1944-January 1948.

Commodore in September 1944. Retired in July 1949. Decorations included the Navy Cross and two Navy Commendation Medals. Died on July 17, 1966.

Hall, John Leslie Jr. (1891-1978) Born on April 11, 1891, in Williamsburg, Virginia. Commissioned from Annapolis in 1913. Commanding officer of the *Schenck* in 1920. Instructor at Annapolis October 1920-June 1922. Commanding officer of the *Childs* December 1928-May 1930. Instructor at Annapolis May 1930-May 1933. Commanding officer of the *Asheville* January 1935-April 1936. Commander of Destroyer Division 15 April 1936-March 1937. Graduated from the Naval War College May 1938 then member of the staff there until June 1940. Commanding officer of the *Arkansas* June 1940-April 1941. Operations officer on the staff of Commander Battleships, Atlantic Fleet May 1941-March 1942. Chief of staff and aide to Commander Cruiser Division Seven, Atlantic Fleet September-November 1942. Rear admiral in May 1942. Commander of the West African Sea Frontier Force at Casablanca 1942-1943 then Amphibious Force Northwest African Waters February-November 1943. Command Eleventh Amphibious Force November 1943-October 1944 and Amphibious Group Twelve, Amphibious Forces Pacific Fleet October 1944-September 1945. Assignments after the war included commandant of Armed Forces Staff College, Norfolk March 1948-July 1951 and commander of Western Sea Frontier August 1961 until retirement as admiral in May 1953. Decorations included two Distinguished Service Medals and two Legions of Merit. Died on March 6, 1978.

Halloran, Paul James (1896-1971) Born on June 26, 1896, in Norwood, Massachusetts. B.S. from Dartmouth College in 1919. M.Ss from Thayer School of Civil Engineering in 1920. Commissioned in the Civil Engineer Corps in 1921. Duty with the enginer-in-chief, Republic of Haiti 1926-1929. Public works officer at Naval Station Tutuila, Samoa July 1937-April 1939, Norfolk Navy Yard April 1939-January 1942 and Naval Operating Base Newport, Rhode Island January 1942-June 1943. Island commander of a naval construction brigade June 1943-November 1945. Commodore in April 1945. Retired as rear admiral in September 1948. Decorations included two Legions of Merit and the Navy Commendation Medal. Died on February 14, 1971.

Halsey, William Frederick Jr. (1882-1959) Born in Elizabeth, New Jersey, on October 30, 1882. Graduated from Annapolis in 1904 and commissioned in 1906. Aboard the *Kansas* during the worldwide cruise of "the great white fleet" 1907-1909. Commanding officer of the *Benham* and the *Shaw,* based in Ireland, during World War I. Naval attache in Berlin, Norway, Denmark and Sweden 1922-1924. Graduated from the Naval War College in 1933 and the Army War College in 1934. Became a naval aviator in March 1935. Commanding officer of the *Saratoga* 1935-1937. Commander of Pensacola Naval Air Station 1937-1938. Rear admiral in March 1938. Commander of Carrier Division Two, then Carrier Division One 1938-1940. Vice admiral in June 1940. Commander of aircraft in the Battle Force 1940-1942. At sea when Japan attacked Pearl Harbor, he led a task force in the attack on Kwajalein on February 1, 1942, the first U.S. offensive of the war in the Pacific. Succeeded Vice Admiral Robert L. Ghormley as commander of the South Pacific Force in October 1942. Admiral in November 1942. Commander of Third Fleet June 1944-December 1945, during which his forces often practiced his motto "Hit hard, hit fast, hit often." On September 2, 1945, Japan formally surrendered aboard his flagship *the Missouri* in Tokyo harbor. Fleet Admiral in December 1945. Retired in December 1946. Decorations included the Navy Cross and five Distinguished Service Medals. Died on August 16, 1959.

Hanson, Edward William (1889-1959) Born on February 12, 1889, in Alexandria, Minnesota. Graduated from Annapolis in 1911 and commissioned in 1912. Commanding officer of the *Quiros* January 1916-May 1917, the *Piscataqua* May-June 1917, the *Dale* July 1917-June 1918, the *Burrows* in 1919, the *Monocacy* in 1921 and the *Pecos* 1922-1923. Graduated from the Naval War College in May 1935. Commanding officer of the *Erie* July 1936-April 1938. Commandant of Naval Station Tutuila, Samoa June 1938-July 1940. Commanding officer of the *Indianapolis* August 1940-July 1942. Duty in the office of procurement and material, office of the assistant secretary of the navy July 1942-August 1943. Rear admiral in August 1943. Commander of Battleship Division Nine August 1943-April 1945. Acting commandant of Fourteenth Naval District April 1945-July 1946. Vice admiral upon retirement in February 1951. Decorations included the Navy Cross Legion of Merit and Bronze Star. Died on October 18, 1959.

Hardison, Osborne Bennett (1892-1959) Born on December 22, 1892, in Wadesboro, North Carolina. B.A. from the University of North Carolina in 1911. Commissioned upon graduation from Annapolis in 1916. Qualified as naval aviator in June 1923. Instructor at Annapolis November 1925-August 1927. Aviation officer in the ships movements division, office of the chief of naval operations June 1936-June 1938. Executive officer of the *Ranger* June 1938-June 1939. Aviation officer on the staff of Commander Battle Force then fleet aviator on the staff of Commander in Chief United States Fleet June 1939-July 1940. Commanding officer of NAS Anacostia July 1940-September 1941. Aide to the assistant secretary of the navy for air September 1941-October 1942. Commanding officer of the *Enterprise* October 1942-April 1943. Rear admiral in November 1942. Commander of Fleet Air South Pacific April 1943-January 1944. Chief of Naval Air Primary Training Command January 1944-September 1945. Vice admiral upon retirement in January 1955. Decorations included the Navy Cross and two Legions of Merit. Died on February 16, 1959.

Hargrave, William Walker (1887-1969) Born on September 6, 1887, in Tazewell, Virginia. B.S. from Washington and Lee University in 1907. M.D. from the Medical College of Virginia, University of Virginia in 1912. Commissioned in the Medical Reserve Corps in 1913. Executive officer of U.S.Naval Hospital Canacao, Philippine Islands 1937-38. Medical director at Naval Hospital Great Lakes August 1938-July 1939. Medical officer at Naval Hospital Philadelphia August 1939-February 1941. Fleet medical officer on the staff of Commander

Train, Atlantic Fleet February 1941-June 1942. Medical officer in command of U.S. Naval Hospital Pensacola June 1942-July 1943. Medical officer in command of Naval Hospital Pearl Harbor, the largest military hospital outside the continental United States, July 1943-February 1945. Duty in the Bureau of Medicine and Surgery March 1945-January 1946. Commodore in April 1945. Retired in October 1949. Decorations included the Legion of Merit. Died on January 23, 1969.

Harper, John (1890-1975) Born on August 15, 1890, in Philadelphia, Pennsylvania. M.D. from Medical-Surgical College of Philadelphia in 1913. Commissioned in the Medical Reserve Corps in August 1915. Graduated from Naval Medical School in 1916. Chief of medical service at Naval Hospital, Washington January 1937-April 1938. Executive officer of Naval Medical School April 1938-August 1940. Medical officer in command of the newly commissioned National Naval Medical Center at Bethesda, Maryland February 1942-December 1943. Rear admiral in May 1942. Medical officer in command of Naval Hospital Corps School December 1943-June 1944. Again medical officer in command of National Naval Medical Center June 1944-April 1945. Served at the Bureau of Medicine and Surgery April-September 1945. Retired in June 1951. Decorations included the Legion of Merit. Died on July 29, 1975.

Harrill, William Keene (1892-1962) Born on May 3, 1892, in Knoxville, Tennessee. Commissioned from Annapolis in 1914. Aide to Commander Mine Force Atlantic Fleet 1917-1919. Designated naval aviator in December 1921. Aide to the assistant secretary of the navy for aeronautics June 1927-June 1929. Assistant naval attache in London May 1937-January 1939. Commanding officer of the *Wright* 1939-1940. Commander of Patrol Wing One July 1940-June 1941. Commanding officer of the *Ranger* 1941-1942. Rear admiral in July 1942. Commander of Fleet Air Alameda September 1942-January 1944 then Fleet Air West Coast January-March 1944 and August 1944-January 1945 (his command was interrupted by an emergency appendectomy). Commander of the Marshall-Gilbert Islands Area February 1945-January 1946. Vice admiral upon retirement in June 1951. Decorations included the Navy Cross and three Legions of Merit. Died on May 11, 1962.

Hart, Thomas Charles (1877-1971) Born in Davison, Michigan, on June 12, 1877. Graduated from Annapolis in 1897 and commissioned in 1899. Commanding officer of a force of seven submarines, based in Ireland, during World War I. Graduated from the Naval War College in 1923 and the Army War College in 1924. Rear admiral in September 1929. Commander of submarines in the Pacific and Atlantic fleets 1929-1931. Superintendent of Annapolis 1931-1934. Commander of the cruiser division in the Scouting Force 1934-1936. Member of the General Board 1936-1939. Admiral in July 1939. Commander of the Asiatic Fleet July 1939-June 1942, escaping by submarine from his headquarters at Cavite in Manila Bay on December 25, 1941. Retired in July 1942 but immediately recalled to active duty on the General Board. Retired again in February 1945 to accept appointment to an unexpired seat in the U.S. Senate from Connecticut until December 1946. Decorations included two Distinguished Service Medals. Died on July 4, 1971.

Hartigan, Charles Conway (1882-1944) Born on September 13, 1882, in New York. Graduated from Annapolis in 1906 and commissioned in 1908. Awarded the Medal of Honor for heroism during the invasion of Vera Cruz in April 1914. Commanding officer of the *Cassin* in 1918. Duty with the U.S. Naval Mission to Brazil 1919-1921 and 1925-1927. Naval attache in Peking 1929-1932. Commanding officer of the hospital ship *Relief* August 1932-June 1934. Graduated from the Naval War College in 1937. Commanding officer of the *Oklahoma* 1937-1939. Duty in the office of the chief of naval operations as member then chairman of the executive committee of the U.S. Antarctic Service December 1939-June 1941. Retired in June 1941 but continued on active duty until June 1942. Decorations included the Medal of Honor. Died on February 25, 1944.

Hartley, Henry (1884-1953) Born on May 8, 1884, in Bladensburg, Maryland. Enlisted service 1901-1913. Commissioned in 1917 during World War I. Commanding officer of the submarine chasers *Number 253, Number 21* and *Number 342* October 1917-September 1918. Commanding officer of *Eagle Number 60* 1919-1921 then the *Falcon* 1924-1928. Executive officer of the *Constitution* April 1932-June 1934. Technical aide to Rear Admiral Cyrus W. Cole July-September 1939 during the salvage of the submarine *Squalus.* Commanding officer of the *Arcturus* June 1941-September 1942 then the *Susan B. Anthony* 1942-1943. Duty with the Fleet Operational Training Command Atlantic August 1943-June 1944. Commanding officer of the *Chester* July 1944-July 1945. Commodore in June 1945. Commander of Service Squadron Ten July 1945-March 1946. Rear admiral upon retirement in May 1947. Decorations included the Navy Cross, Distinguished Service Medals, three Legions of Merit and the Navy Commendation Medal. Died on March 6, 1953.

Hayler, Robert Ward (1891-1980) Born on June 7, 1891, in Sandusky, Ohio. Commissioned from Annapolis in 1914. Served aboard the *Georgia* in the Mexican Campaign in 1914 and the *Oklahoma* during World War I. Commanding officer of the destroyers *Breese* and *Howard* 1921-1922. Aide to Commander Destroyer Squadrons 1927-1929. Office in charge of Naval Torpedo Station Alexandria, Virginia, August 1939-July 1941 then inspector of ordnance there until July 1942. Commanding officer of the *Honolulu* July 1942-March 1944. Rear admiral in January 1943. Commanded Cruiser Division Twelve March 1944-March 1945. Member of the General Board 1945-1947. Vice admiral upon retirement in June 1951. Decorations included three Navy Crosses, the Silver Star, two Legions of Merit and three Bronze Stars. Died on November 17, 1980.

Heim, Schuyler Franklin (1884-1972) Born on January 14, 1884, in Plymouth, Indiana. Graduated from Annapolis in 1907 and commissioned in 1909. Served aboard the *Nebraska* during the world cruise of the Battle Fleet 1907-1908 and the *Charleston* in World War I. Commanding officer of the destroyers *Simpson* 1920-1921, the *MacLeish* January-October 1921, the *Hull* 1921-1923 and the *Rizal* on the Yangtze River 1926-1928. Graduatd from the Naval War College in 1930 and the Army Industrial College in 1934. Commanding oficer of the *Richmond* 1936-1937. Commanded Destroyer Squadron 30, then 33 1939-1940. District port director at Eleventh Naval District December 1940-June 1942. Commander of Naval Operating Base Terminal Island June 1942 until retirement in November 1946. Commodore in September 1944. Decorations inluded the Legion of Merit. Died on February 2, 1972.

Hellweg, Julius Frederick (1879-1973) Born on March 16, 1879, in Baltimore, Maryland. Graduated from Annapolis in 1900 and commissioned in 1902. Commanding officer of the *Burrows* 1911-1913, the *Wilkes* 1916-1917, the *Pocahontas* July 1917-January 1918, the *Marietta* January-October 1918, the former German battleship *Ostfriesland* in 1920, and the cruiser *Columbia* October 1920-June 1921. Assistant to Commandant Fifth naval District 1921-1922. Graduated from the Naval War College in 1924. Commanding officer of the Oklahoma 1928-1930. Retired in June 1935. Recalled to active duty in World War II as superintendent of the U.S. Naval Observatory until April 1947. Commodore in September 1944. Decorations included the Navy Cross. Died on March 10, 1973.

Hendren, Paul (1889-1957) Born on November 10, 1889, in Vashti, North Carolina. Commissioned from Annapolis in 1913. Served aboard the *New Hampshire* during the invasion of Vera Cruz in 1914. Fleet personnel officer on the staff of Commander Scouting Force 1928-1931. Graduated from the Naval War College in 1932 and the Army Industrial College in 1933. Commanded Destroyer Division Eleven 1938-1940. Served in the office of the chief of naval operations 1940-1942. Commanding officer of the *Philadelphia* August 1942-October 1943. Rear admiral in January 1943. Hospitalized until March 1944. Served briefly in the Bureau of Naval Personnel and the office of the naval inspector general March-September 1944. Commander of Service Squadron South Pacific Force 1944-1945. Decorations included four Legions of Merit and the Navy Commendation Medal. Vice admiral upon retirement in August 1949. Died on November 28, 1957.

Hepburn, Arthur Japy (1877-1964) Born on October 15, 1877, in Carlisle, Pennsylvania. Graduated from Annapolis in 1897 and commissioned in 1899. Commanding officer of the *Agamemnon* (formerly the German ship Kaiser Wilhelm II) in 1917 and the *West Virginia* 1925-1926. Director of naval intelligence July 1926-September 1927. Chief of staff to Commander Battleship Divisions Battle Fleet, then Commander Battle Fleet, finally Commander in Chief United States Fleet 1927-1930. Rear admiral in June 1929. Graduatd from the Naval War College in 1931. Commanded the Submarine Force United States Fleet May 1931-June 1932. Commandant of Fourth Naval District 1933-1934. Commanded Destroyers Battle Force June 1934-April 1935. Vice admiral in April 1935.

Commander of Scouting Force United States Fleet 1935-1936. Admiral in June 1936. Commander in chief United States Fleet June 1936-January 1938. Commandant of Twelfth Naval District February-July 1938. Director of the Office of Public Relations Navy Department May-November 1941. Retired in November 1941. Recalled to active duty in World War II. Director of public relations in the office of the secretary of the navy from 1942. Decorations included the Distinguished Service Medal. Died on May 31, 1964.

Herlihy, Joseph Lee (1902-) Born on February 7, 1902, in Somerville, Massachusetts. Commissioned in the Supply Corps following graduation from Annapolis in 1924. Served aboard the *Pittsburgh* during the Yangtze River Campaign in 1928. Duty at Tutuila, Samoa 1935-1937. M.B.A. from Harvard in 1939. Fleet fuel officer, Service Force Pacific Fleet 1939-1942. Graduated from the Army and Navy Staff College in 1943. Commodore in April 1944. Supply officer for the Pacific Fleet 1944-1945. Reverted to captain in 1945. Retired as rear admiral in July 1959. Decorations included the Legion of Merit and Bronze Star.

Hewitt, Henry Kent (1887-1972) Born in Hackensack, New Jersey, on February 11, 1887. Graduated from Annapolis in 1907 and commissioned in 1909. Commanding officer of the *Cummings*, then the *Ludlow*, during World War I. Graduated from the Naval War College in 1929. Commander of Cruiser Division Eight in 1940. Rear admiral in December 1940. Commander of the Amphibious Force in the Atlantic Fleet April 1942-February 1943, responsible for the amphibious landing in Morocco in early November 1942. Vice admiral in November 1942. Commander of Eighth Fleet February 1943-August 1945. He planned and directed landings at Sicily in July 1943, at Salerno in September 1943 and at St. Raphael and St. Tropez in August 1944. Admiral in April 1945. Commander of Twelfth Fleet 1945-1946. Retired in March 1949. Decorations included two Navy Crosses and the Distinguished Service Medal. Died on September 15, 1972.

Higgins, John Martin (1899-1973) Born on August 13, 1899, in Madison, Wisconsin. Commissioned from Annapolis in 1922. Aide to the commandant of the Twelfth Naval District 1939-1940. Commanded Destroyer Divisions 22 and 22 then Destroyer Squadron Six October 1942-May 1944. Commander of Destroyer Squadron 62 1944-1945 then Destroyer Flotilla Three May-December 1945. Commodore in April 1945. Retired in September 1961. Decorations included the Navy Cross, Distinguished Service Medal, Silver Star and two Legions of Merit. Died on December 7, 1973.

Hill, Harry Wilbur (1890-1971) Born on April 7, 1890, in Oakland, California.Graduated from Annapolis in 1911. Served aboard the *Texas* and the *Wyoming* attached to the British Grand Fleet in World War I. Aide to Commander Division Seven Atlantic Fleet then Division Six Pacific Fleet in 1919. Aide to the chief of naval operations November 1919-March 1923 then the Commander in Chief United States Fleet in 1925. Commanding officer of the destroyer *Dewey* October 1934-June 1935. Graduated from the Naval War College in 1938. War plans officer on the staff of Commander in Chief United States Fleet June 1938-February 1940 then duty in the war plans division, office of the chief of naval operations until January 1942. Commanding officer of the *Wichita* January-September 1942. Rear admiral in April 1942. Commanded Battleship Division Four 1942-1943 then Amphibious Group Two September 1943-April 1945. Vice admiral in April 1945. Commanded amphibious forces at Okinawa April-June 1945 and the landing of Sixth Army in Japan August-September 1945. Assignments after the war included commandant of the National War College 1947-1949 and superintendent of Annapolis 1950-1952. Admiral upon retirement in May 1952. Decorations included three Distinguished Service Medals. Died on July 19, 1971.

Hiltabidle, William Orme Jr. (1896-1986) Born on November 2, 1896, in Glyndon, Maryland. Commissioned in the Civil Engineer Corps in 1921. Graduated from the Army Industrial College in 1933. Assistant public works officer at Pearl Harbor Navy Yard 1935-1937 and November 1941-June 1943. Public works officer at Naval Operating Base Newport 1943-1944. Island engineer on Guam April 1944-September 1945. Commodore in April 1945. Retired as vice admiral in November 1952. Decorations included the Legion of Merit, Bronze Star and Navy Commendation Medal. Died on February 12, 1986.

Hipp, Thomas Earle (1894-1973) Born on October 29, 1894, in Newberry, South Carolina. Graduated from the Citadel in 1914 and commissioned in the Supply Corps in 1917. Naval aide at the White House 1926-1929. Supply and accounting officer at Jacksonville Naval Air Station 1940-1942. Duty at the Bureau of Supplies and Accounts 1942-1945. Rear admiral in March 1943. Retired in July 1955. Decorations included the Legion of Merit. Died on December 6, 1973.

Holden, Carl Frederick (1895-1953) Born on May 25, 1895, in Bangor, Maine. Commissioned from Annapolis in 1917. Served aboard the *Burrows,* which operated in European waters during World War I. M.S. from Harvard in 1924. Flag lieutenant to Commander Destroyer Force Scouting Fleet 1924-1927. Commanding officer of the *Tarbell* 1932-1934 then the *Ramapo* 1937-1938. Executive officer of the *Pennsylvania* 1941-1942. He was present at the attack on Pearl Harbor. Communication officer then director of communications in the office of the chief of naval operations 1942-1943. Commanding officer of the *New Jersey* May 1943-January 1945. Rear admiral in August 1943. Briefly at the Bureau of Naval Personnel then commander of Cruiser Division 18 July-December 1945. Vice admiral upon retirement in July 1952. Decorations included the Legion of Merit and Bronze Star. Died on May 18, 1953.

Holloway, James Lemuel Jr. (1898-1984) Born on June 20, 1898, in Fort Smith, Arkansas. Commissioned from Annapolis in 1919. Served aboard the destroyer *Monaghan* in French waters during World War I. Aide to Commander Battleship Division Two, Scouting Fleet 1928-1930. Graduated from the Naval War College then aide to the president 1930-1932. Aide to Commander Cruisers

Scouting Force 1933-1934. Commanding officer of the *Hopkins* June 1934-June 1935 and the *Sirius* July-September 1939. Chief of staff to Commander Atlantic Squadron 1939-1940. Duty in the office of the chief of naval operations 1940-1942. Commander of Destroyer Squadron Ten May 1942-March 1943. Staff officer with Fleet Operational Training Command Atlantic Fleet March-September 1943. Director of training office of the chief of naval personnel 1943-1944. Commanding officer of the battleship *Iowa* November 1944-August 1945. Assignments after the war included superintendent of Annapolis 1947-1950, chief of naval personnel 1953-1958 and Commander in chief of Naval Forces Eastern Atlantic and Mediterranean February 1958 until retirement as admiral in April 1959. Decorations included the Distinguished Service Medal and two Legions of Merit. Died on January 11, 1984.

Holmes, Ralston·Smith (1882-1966) Born on June 5, 1882, in Yonkers, New York. Graduated from Annapolis in 1903 and commissioned in 1905. Member of a landing force ashore in Haiti in October 1914 while assigned to the cruiser *Tacoma* April 1914-May 1915. Commanding officer of the presidential yacht *Mayflower* and naval aide to the White House February 1920-December 1922. Member of the U.S. Naval Mission to Brazil in 1923. Graduated from the Naval War College in 1928. Naval attache in Rome September 1928-June 1930. Commanding officer of the *Cincinnati* 1930-1931. Chief of staff to Commander Cruisers, Scouting Force September 1931-June 1932. Commandant of midshipmen at Annapolis July 1932-March 1935. Chief of staff to Commander Battle Force 1935-1937. Rear admiral in October 1936. Director of naval intelligence April 1937-June 1939. Commander of Destroyer Flotilla One, Battle Force then Destroyers, Battle Force 1939-1940. Member of the General Board August 1940-December 1941. Commandant of Eleventh Naval District December 1941-December 1942. Retired in January 1943. Decorations included the Navy Cross and Legion of Merit. Died on January 4, 1966.

Hooper, Stanford Caldwell (1884-1955) Born on August 16, 1884, in Colton, California. Graduated from Annapolis in 1905 and commissioned in 1907. Appointed Fleet Radio Officer in 1912, he became known as the "Fleet Wireless Officer of the Navy." Served aboard the Utah at the invasion of Vera Cruz in 1914. Commanding officer of the Fairfax during World War I convoy duty. During the period 1915-1928 he was the guiding hand to the development of radio in the Navy and oversaw the development of worldwide land stations that provided the first communication between the Navy ashore and the Navy at sea. Director of naval communications 1928-1934. Chairman of the Naval Research Committee 1934-1941. Rear admiral in June 1938. Technical assistant to the vice chief of naval operations 1942-1943. Retired in January 1943 but continued on active duty until June 1945. Recipient of the gold medal from the Franklin Institute in 1945. Decorations included the Navy Cross. Died on April 6, 1955.

Hoover, John Howard (1887-1970) Born on May 15, 1887, in Seville, Ohio. Graduated from Annapolis in 1907 and commissioned in 1909. Duty in London and Scotland 1918-1919. Commander of Submarine Division Eight and Nineteen at the Panama Canal Zone March 1924-July 1926. Designated naval aviator in May 1929. Graduated from the Naval War College in June 1932. Commanding officer of Naval Air Station San Diego June 1932-June 1934. Chief of staff to Commander Aircraft, Base Force 1934-1935. Commanding officer of the *Langley* June 1935-July 1936. Graduated from the Army War College in 1937. Commanding officer of Naval Air Station Norfolk July 1937-June 1938 then the *Lexington* June 1938-June 1939. Chief of staff to Commander Aircraft, Battle Force June 1939-June 1941. Rear admiral in July 1941. Commandant of Tenth Naval District and commander of the Caribbean Sea Frontier July 1941-August 1943. Vice admiral in January 1943. Commander of Carrier Division Four and Task Force 56 August 1943-April 1944, Forward Area Central Pacific April 1944-July 1945, Marianas July-August 1945 and Fleet Air West Coast August 1945-January 1946. Admiral upon retirement in July 1948. Decorations included the Navy Cross and three Distinguished Service Medals. Died on December 2, 1970.

Horne, Frederick Joseph (1880-1959) Born on February 14, 1880, in New York City. Graduated from Annapolis in 1899 and commissioned in 1901. Instructor at Annapolis 1904-1906. Commanding officer of the *Rainbow* 1914-1915. Naval attache in Tokyo January 1915-March 1919. Commanding officer of the *Von Steuben* May-October 1919. Aide to the Commandant Portsmouth Navy Yard 1921-1922. Graduated from the Naval War College in 1923 and the Army War College in 1924. Commanding officer of the *Omaha* June 1924-January 1926. Qualified as a naval aviation observer in June 1926. Commanding officer of the *Wright* 1927-1928 then the *Saratoga* April 1929-September 1930. Commander of Aircraft, Scouting Force 1930-1931. Chief of staff to Commandant Fourteenth Naval District July 1931-June 1933. Rear admiral in February 1933. Commander of Train Squadron, Base Force then commander of Base Force 1933-1934. Member of the Naval Examining Board June 1934-March 1935. Commander of Cruiser Division Six then Aircraft, Base Force 1935-1936. Commander of Aircraft, Battle Force June 1936-January 1938. Member of the General Board 1938-1941. Assistant chief of naval operations December 1941-March 1942 then vice chief 1942-1945. Admiral in December 1944. Retired in August 1946. Decorations included the Navy Cross Distinguished Service Medal and Legion of Merit. Died on October 18, 1959.

Howard, Herbert Seymour (1884-1977) Born on August 5, 1884, in Buffalo, New York. Graduated from Annapolis in 1904 and commissioned in 1906. Served aboard the *Cleveland* during the Cuban pacification campaign 1905-1906. M.S. from Massachusetts Institute of Technology in 1909. Aide to Commander Scouting Fleet July 1925-June 1927. Graduated from the Naval War College in 1928. Assistant naval atache in London Paris Rome the Hague and Berlin June 1932-August 1935. Supervisor of shipbuilding at the New York Shipbuilding Corporation February 1939-June 1941. Rear admiral in February 1941 to date from November 1937. Head of the design division at the Bureau of Ships 1941-1942 then director of the David W. Taylor Model Basin at Carderock, Maryland November

1942-September 1946. Retired in September 1946. Decorations included the Legion of Merit. Died on January 12, 1977.

Hundt, Lester Thomas (1897-n/a) Born on November 22, 1897, in New York City. B.A. from the City College of New York in 1917. Enlisted service 1917-1918. Commissioned in the Naval Reserve Flying Corps in 1918. Designated naval aviator in November 1918. Served as aviation member of the U.S. Naval Mission to Brazil June 1925-December 1926. Aide and flag secretary to Commander Aircraft Squadrons Scouting Fleet May 1928-November 1929. Executive officer then commanding officer of the seaplane tender *Pocomoke* January 1941-April 1942. Director of training in the Bureau of Aeronautics 1942-1943. Commanding officer of the *Monterey* June 1943-April 1944. Commandant of the Naval Air Training Center at Pensacola May-September 1944 then commander of Naval Air Training Bases 1944-1947. Commodore in December 1944. Retired in July 1947. Decorations included the Legion of Merit.

Hunt, Daniel (1889-n/a) Born on October 4, 1889, in Ripley, Mississippi. Attended the University of Mississippi and Tulane University then earned an M.D. from Jefferson Medical College. Commissioned in the Medical Corps in 1913. Served at the Naval Station Tutuila, Samoa 1921-1923. Force medical officer on the staff of Commander Base Force July 1939-January 1940 then force surgeon on the staff of Commander Battle Force January 1940-March 1941. Senior medical officer at the Washington Navy Yard March-November 1941 then medical officer in command of Naval Hospital Puget Sound Navy Yard and Norfolk Naval Hospital 1941-1943. District medical officer at Twelfth Naval District September 1943-August 1945. Rear admiral in June 1943. Retired in December 1950. Decorations included the Commendation Ribbon.

Hussey, George Frederick Jr. (1894-1983) Born on June 15, 1894, in Brookline, Massachusetts. Commissioned from Annapolis in 1916. Served aboard the *Pennsylvania* in the Atlantic during World War I. Aide and flag secretary to Commander Battleship Division Three June 1923-January 1925 then Commander Battleship Divisions Battle Fleet and Commander in Chief Battle Fleet June 1928-May 1929. Commanding officer of the *Zane* 1934-1935 then the *Decatur* June 1935-June 1936. Commanded Destroyer Division 24 then Division 51 June 1939-January 1941. Commander of Mine Squadron Three 1941-1942. Director of the production division Bureau of Ordnance June 1942-September 1943. Rear admiral in January 1943. Assistant chief then chief of the Bureau of Ordnance 1943-1947. Vice admiral in December 1945. Retired in December 1947. Decorations included the Distinguished Service Medal. Died on April 17, 1983.

Hustvedt, Olaf Mandt (1886-1978) Born on June 23, 1886, in Chicago, Illinois. Graduated from Annapolis in 1909 and commissioned in 1911. M.S. from George Washington University in 1914. Served abaord the *New York* while attached to the British Grand Fleet in World War I. Commanding officer of the *Burns* 1922-1924. Aide to Commander Battleship Divisions Battle Fleet 1928-1929. Commanding officer of the *Detroit* July 1938-April 1939. Graduated from the Naval War College in 1941. Commanding officer of the battleship *North Carolina* April-October 1941. Rear admiral in November 1941. Chief of staff to Commander in Chief Atlantic Fleet 1941-1943 then commander of Battleships Atlantic Fleet May 1943-December 1944. Member of the General Board 1944-1945. Vice admiral upon retirement in March 1945. Decorations included two Legions of Merit. Died December 22, 1978.

Ihrig, Russell Million (1895-1986) Born on December 15, 1895, in Springville, Utah. Commissioned from Annapolis in 1918. Commanding officer of the *Heron* March 1928-February 1929. Assigned to the naval reserve division in the Bureau of Navigation June 1939-November 1941. Commanding officer of the *Cimarron* January 1942-October 1943. Staff oficer with Commander in Chief Pacific Fleet October 1943-June 1945. Commodore in November 1944. Reverted to captain in June 1945. Commanding officer of the *Canberra* July 1945 until retirement in January 1947. Decorations included the Navy Cross and Legion of Merit. Died on December 15, 1986.

Ingersoll, Royal Eason (1883-1976) Born on June 20, 1883, in Washington, DC. Graduated from Annapolis in 1905 and commissioned in 1907. Served aboard the *Connecticut* in the world cruise of the Battle Fleet 1907-1909. Duty with the communications section, office of chief of naval operations during World War I. Graduated from the Naval War College in 1927. Staff duty in the office of chief of naval operations 1930-1933 and again 1935-1938. Rear admiral in May 1938. Commander of Cruiser Division 6 1938-1940. Assistant to chief of naval operations 1940-1942. Commander-in-chief of Atlantic Fleet January 1942-November 1944. Vice admiral in January 1942, admiral in July 1942. Commander of Western Sea Frontier and deputy chief of naval operations November 1944 until retirement in August 1946. Decorations included the Navy Cross and Distinguished Service Medal. Died on May 20, 1976.

Inglis, Thomas Browning (1897-n/a) Born on November 19, 1897, in Petoskey, Michigan. Commissioned from Annapolis in 1918. Served aboard the *Kearsarge* in the Atlantic in World War I. M.S. from Harvard in 1924. Aide to Commander in Chief Battle Fleet July 1926-September 1927. Commanding officer of the *Hatfield* 1934-1935. Duty in the communications division office of the CNO 1937-1940. Executive officer of the Texas 1940-1941. Commanding officer of the *Algorab* June 1941-March 1942. Deputy director of naval communications 1942-1943. Commanding officer of the *Birmingham* August 1943-May 1945. Commodore in April 1945. Deputy director then chief of naval intelligence 1945-1949. Vice admiral upon retirement in January 1952. Decorations included the Navy Cross, Silver Star, Bronze Star and Purple Heart.

Ingram, Jonas Howard (1886-1952) Born in Jeffersonville, Indiana, on October 15, 1886. Graduated from Annapolis in 1907 and commissioned in 1909. Turret officer aboard the *Arkansas* during the Vera Cruz invastion in April 1914, earning the Medal of Honor. Aide and flag lieutenant to Admiral Hugh Rodman 1917-1921. Graduated from the Naval War College in 1940. Commanding officer of the *Tennessee* 1940-1941. Rear admiral in January 1941. Commander of the cruiser division in the Atlantic Fleet (later designated South Atlantic Force) 1941-1944. Vice admiral in February 1942, admiral in November 1944. Commander of the Atlantic Fleet November 1944 until retirement in April 1947. Decorations included the Medal of Honor, Navy Cross and three Distinguished Service Medals. President of the All America Football Conference 1947-1949. Died on September 10, 1952.

Irish, James McCredie (1885-1970) Born on July 25, 1885, in Utica, New York. Graduated from Annapolis in 1908 and commissioned in 1912. M.S. from Columbia University in 1915. Assistant chief of the Bureau of Engineering June 1936-July 1940. Head of the design division, Bureau of Ships 1940-1941. Supervisor of shipbuilding in Third Naval District June 1941-April 1944. Rear admiral in September 1942. Assistant chief of the Office of Procurement and Material May 1944-October 1945. Retired in November 1946. Decorations included the Legion of Merit. Died on March 29, 1970.

Jackson, Milton C. (1898-1984) Born on December 14, 1898, in Port LaVaca, Texas. Commissioned from Annapolis in 1922. Resigned in June 1926 and entered the Naval Reserve. Appointed lieutenant commander in December 1940. Called to active duty in December 1941. Assigned to the office of the port director, Fourth Naval District 1941-1942. Served on the staff of Commander U.S. Naval Forces Europe August 1942-May 1945. Assistant director of the Naval Transportation Service June-November 1945. Commodore in 1945. Returned to inactive status in December 1945. Decorations included the Navy Commendation Medal. Died on August 20, 1984.

Jacobs, Randall (1885-1967) Born on December 12, 1885, in Danville, Pennsylvania. Graduated from Annapolis in 1907 and commissioned in 1909. Aide to the commander in chief of the Atlantic Reserve Fleet 1913-1914. Commanding officer of the *Henley, Gamble, Delphy and Boggs* 1918-1919. Commanding officer of the *Utah* 1932-1934 and the *Tuscaloosa* 1937-1938. Chief of staff to the commander of Cruisers, Scouting Force 1938-1939. Assistant chief of the Bureau of Navigation 1939-1940. Commander of Train, Atlantic Fleet in January-December 1941. Rear admiral in April 1941. Chief of the Bureau of Navigation (renamed the Bureau of Naval Personnel in 1942) December 1941-September 1945. Vice admiral in February 1944. Retired in November 1946. Decorations included the Distinguished Service Medal. Died on June 19, 1967.

Jacobson, Jacob Harry (1894-1951) Born on December 10, 1894, in Frankfort, Michigan. Commissioned from Annapolis in 1917. Served aboard the *Ohio* in the Atlantic during World War I. M.S. from Massachusetts Institute of Technology in 1924. Executive officer of the *Colorado* March 1941-February 1942 then commanding officer of the *Wharton* until November 1942. Commanding officer of the *Milwaukee* 1942-1943. Duty in the Bureau of Ordnance July 1943-January 1945. Commander of Naval Operating Base Leyte, Philippine Islands 1945-1946. Commodore in April 1945. Retired in July 1949. Died on November 5, 1951.

James, Jules (1885-1957) Born on February 14, 1885, in Pittsylvania County, Virginia. Graduated from Annapolis in 1908 and commissioned in 1910. Naval aide at the White House 1913-1914. M.S. from Columbia University in 1916. Navigator then executive officer of the *Rochester* during World War I. Aide and flag lieutenant to Admiral Hilary P. Jones December 1918-August 1922. Assistant naval attache in Paris 1923-1926. Commanding officer of the *Edsall* 1927-1928. Naval aide to the governor genral of the Philippines February-December 1928. Graduated from the Naval War College in 1932. Commanded Destroyer Division Six Battle Force 1932-1934. Department head at Annapolis June 1934-June 1937. Commanding officer of the cruiser *Philadelphia* 1937-1939. Duty in the office of naval intelligence November 1939-March 1941. Commander of Naval Operating Base Bermuda 1941-1943. Rear admiral in November 1941. Commandant of Sixth Naval District May 1943-August 1945. Vice admiral upon retirement in November 1946. Decorations included the Legion of Merit. Died on March 12, 1957.

Jenkins, Samuel Power (1893-1975) Born on June 3, 1893, in Evansville, Indiana. Commissioned from Annapolis in 1915. Served aboard the *Florida* which operated with the British Grand Fleet during World War I. Executive officer of the *Mullany* during operations in Nicaragua July-August 1927. Commanding officer of the gunboat *Helena* and the destroyer *Stewart* on China patrol 1931-1932. Instructor at Georgia Institute of Technology ROTC 1933-1935. Commanding officer of the Perkins September 1936-June 1937. Duty at Annapolis 1937-1940. Commander of Destroyer Division Eight Battle Force 1940-1941. Commanding officer of the *Atlanta* May 1942-February 1943. During the battle for Guadalcanal in November 1942, Rear Admiral Norman Scott, who had his flag on the *Atlanta,* was killed and the ship was sunk. Duty in the office of the chief of naval operations 1943-1944. Commanded Transport Division 35 July 1944-April 1945. Commodore in April 1945. Commander of Transport Squadron 22 April-October 1945. Reverted to captain in October 1945. Rear admiral upon retirement in October 1947. Decorations included the Navy Cross, Legion of Merit and Purple Heart. Died on June 10, 1975.

Jennings, Ralph Edward (1897-1970) Born on June 14, 1897, in New York City. Commissioned from Annapolis in 1919. Designated naval aviator in 1929. Aviation member of the Board of Inspection and Survey July 1936-May 1939. Navigator then air officer of the *Yorktown* 1939-1941. Duty with the inspection division in the office of the chief of naval operations December 1941-April 1943. Commanding officer of the *Copahee* April 1943-January 1944 then the *Yorktown* February-September 1944. Rear admiral in December 1944. Commander of Carrier Divisions 29 and 12 then Carrier Training Squadron Pacific 1944-1945. Vice admiral upon retirement in July 1953. Decorations included the Legion of Merit and Bronze Star. Died on March 23, 1970.

Johnson, Alfred Wilkinson (1876-1963) Born on November 18, 1876, in Philadelphia, Pennsylvania. Commissioned from Annapolis in 1901 following an obligatory two years at sea. Served aboard the New York during the Philippine insurrection 1901-1903. Instructor at Annapolis 1907-1910. Commanded the destroyers *Benham, Downes, Conyngham* and *Kimberly* 1914-1918. Commanded Air Force Atlantic Fleet 1920-1921. Assistant chief of the Bureau of Aeronautics 1923-1925. Commanding officer of the cruiser *Richmond* January 1926-November 1927. Director of naval intelligence 1927-1930. President of the National Board of Elections in Nicaragua in 1930. Commanding officer of the *Colorado* 1931-1932. Assistant chief of the Bureau of Navigation January 1932-May 1933. Rear admiral in February 1933. Commander of Patrol Plane Squadrons United States Fleet 1933-1935. Member of the General Board June 1935-January 1938. Commanded the Atlantic Squadron United States Fleet 1938-1939. Again a member of the General Board November 1939-December 1940. Vice admiral upon retirement in December 1940. Recalled to active duty in January 1942 to serve as U.S. naval delegate to the Inter-American Defense Board March 1942-August 1945. Retired again in August 1945. Decorations included the Distinguished Service Medal and Legion of Merit. Died on December 5, 1963.

Johnson, Isaac Cureton (1881-1960) Born on June 20, 1881, in Evergreen, Louisiana. Attended Louisiana State University. Graduated from Annapolis in 1904 and commissioned in 1906. Commanding officer of the *Remlik* and the *Nomo* 1917-1918. District commander at Brest, France in 1918. Commanding officer of the *Porter* in 1918. Commanding officer of the *Twiggs* January 1919-January 1920. Graduated from the Naval War College in 1922. Commander of Destroyer Divison 32, Destroyers Squadrons Battle Fleet July 1923-April 1925. Commander of Submarine Division 12 Control Force June 1928-June 1930. Naval attache in Japan September 1930-June 1933. Commanding officer of the *Salt Lake City* 1934-June 1935. Inspector of ordnance at Naval Torpedo Station June 1935-April 1939. Retired in June 1939. Recalled to active duty in June 1941. Assigned to Eleventh Naval District, January 1942-June 1945. Rear admiral in February 1942. Returned to retired status in June 1945. Decorations included the Navy Cross. Died on April 3, 1960.

Johnson, Lee Payne (1886-1964) Born on October 26, 1886, in Concord, North Carolina. Graduated from Annapolis in 1909 and commissioned in 1911. Served aboard the *Connecticut* during the occupation of Vera Cruz in 1914. Instructor at Annapolis 1915-1917. Served abord the *Conyngham* in Irish waters during World War I. Commanding officer of the *Balch* August 1918-May 1919 the Aulick July 1919-August 1920 the destroyers *Tingey, Gamble* and *Bulmer* 1920-1921 and the minelayers *Luce, Rizal* and *Montgomery* June 1930-March 1932. Inspector of ordnance at the Naval Ammunition Depot Balboa Canal Zone 1937-1939. Graduated from the Naval War College in 1940. Commanding officer of the *Tuscaloosa* May 1940-February 1942. Chief of staff to Commander Amphibious Force, Atlantic Fleet March 1942-May 1944. Commander of the Naval Ordnance Plant York Pennsylvania June 1944-March 1946. Commodore in August 1944. Retired in August 1944 but continued on active duty until March 1946. Decorations included the Navy Cross and two Legions of Merit. Died on April 5, 1964.

Johnson, Lucius Warren (1882-1968) Born on June 24, 1882, in Staten Island, New York. D.D.S. from the University of Pennsylvania in 1903 and M.D. in 1907. Commissioned in the Medical Corps in 1907. Duty in Guam, Vladivostock and Queenstown, Ireland during World War I. Director of the Public Health Service in Haiti May 1928-February 1931. Assigned to the Naval Hospital San Diego March 1937-May 1938 then the Bureau of Medicine and Surgery May 1938-September 1940. Medical officer in command at Naval Mobile Base Hospital, New York September 1940-April 1941. Again at the Bureau of Medicine and Surgery April-May 1941. Medical officer in command of Naval Hospital Pensacola May 1941-June 1942. Served at Naval Air Station Moffet Field June 1942-June 1943. Rear admiral in September 1942. Medical officer in command of Base Hospital Number Six August-October 1943. District medical officer at Fourteenth Naval District October 1943 until retirement in 1946. Died on January 13, 1968.

Jones, Carl Henry (1893-1958) Born on June 17, 1893, at Jones Mill, Alabama.Commissioned from Annapolis in 1914. Served aboard the Washington duirng the Vera Cruz occupation in 1914 and the Haitian Campaign July-December 1915. Commanding officer of the submarines A-2 and A-7 in the Philippine Islands 1917-1918. Again in the Philippines as gunnery officer of the Marblehead 1927-1930. Assistant operations officer with Battle Force, United States Fleet 1938-1939. Executive officer of the *Maryland* July 1939-July 1940. Duty in the Bureau of Ordnance 1940-1942. Commanding officer of the *Maryland* January-December 1943. Rear admiral in November 1943. Commanded Gilbert Islands Subordinate Area 1943-1944. Commandant of Norfolk Navy Yard October 1944-November 1945. Vice admiral upon retirement in November 1946. Decorations included the Navy Commendation Medal. Died on September 1, 1958.

Jones, Claud Ashton (1885-1948) Born on October 7, 1885, in Fire Creek, West Virginia. Graduated from Annapolis in 1906 and commissioned in 1908. Awarded the Medal of Honor for his actions following the destruction by tidal wave of the *Memphis* on August 29, 1916. Served aboard the *Indiana* during the world cruise of the Battle Fleet 1907-1909. M.S. from Harvard in 1913. Assistant naval attache in London, Paris, Rome, Berlin and the Hague 1924-1925. Aide to Commander Battleships Divisions Battle Fleet 1929-1930. Fleet engineer officer with Commander in Chief Battle Fleet 1930-1931. Assistant to the chief of the Bureau of Engineering September 1931-June 1936. Head of the shipbuilding division at Bureau of Ships June 1940-January 1942. Rear admiral in October 1941. Assistant chief of procurement and material 1942-1944. Director of the Naval

Experiment Station at Annapolis September 1944-December 1945. Retired in June 1946. Decorations included the Medal of Honor and Legion of Merit. Died on August 8, 1948.

Jones, James Cary (1892-1957) Born on March 2, 1892, in Huntsville, Alabama. Commissioned from Annapolis in 1913. Served aboard the *Oklahoma* during World War I while attached to the British Grand Fleet. Aide to Commander Destroyer Squadrons Battle Fleet 1926-1929 then Commander Battleship Division Four Battle Force Commander Battle Battle Force and Commander Battle Force 1930-1933. Commanded Destroyer Division 19 Battle Force 1935-1938. Chief of staff to Commander Cruisers Pacific Fleet then Commander Allied Naval Forces Southwest Pacific January 1941-November 1943. Rear admiral in May 1942. Commander of Destroyers Atlantic Fleet January-September 1944 then Cruiser Division Seventeen 1944-1945 and U.S. Naval Forces Eastern Japan in 1945. Senior U.S. naval delegate to the Inter-American Defense Board 1945-1947. Vice admiral upon retirement in April 1954. Decorations included four Legions of Merit. Died on Janaury 12, 1957.

Joy, Charles Turner (1895-1956) Born in St. Louis on February 17, 1895. Commissioned from Annapolis in 1916. Aboard the *Pennsylvania* during World War I. M.S. from the University of Michigan in 1922. Member of the staff at Annapolis 1937-1940. Staff officer with the Scouting Force in 1941 and Task Force Eleven in 1942. Commanding officer of the *Louisville* in 1942. Rear admiral in December 1942. Head of Pacific plans division in U.S. Fleet 1943-1944. Commander of Cruiser Division Six 1944-1945, then Amphibious Group Two in 1945. Assignments after the war included commander of U.S. Naval Forces in the Far East, then United Nations Naval Forces 1949-1951, including the amphibious landing at Inchon in September 1950, senior United Nations delegate to the armistice talks 1951-1952 and superintendent of Annapolis August 1952 until retirement as admiral in July 1954. Decorations included the Distinguished Service Cross, two Distinguished Service Medals and five Legions of Merit. Author of *How Communists Negotiate* (1955). Died on June 6, 1956.

Jupp, Stanley Dexter (1894-1973) Born on August 4, 1894, in Detroit, Michigan. Commissioned from Annapolis in 1918. Served aboard the destroyer *Flusser* during World War I. M.S. from Columbia University in 1924. Commanding officer of the submarine *S-44* 1926-1928. Instructor at Annapolis 1933-1936. Executive officer of Naval Station Guam May 1939-May 1941. Commanding officer of the *Griffin* 1941-1942. Commandant of the Naval Operating Base Auckland, New Zealand October 1942-January 1944. Commodore in October 1943. Commanding officer of the *Idaho* 1944-1945. Retired in June 1949. Decorations included the Legion of Merit. Died on June 11, 1973.

Kalbfus, Edward C. (1877-1955) Born on November 24, 1877, in Mauch Chunk, Pennsylvania. Graduated from Annapolis in 1899 and commissioned in 1901. Instructor at Annapolis 1904-1906. Fleet engineer and aide to Commander in Chief Atlantic Fleet in the occupation of Vera Cruz in 1914. Commanding officer of the *Pocahontas* and the *Iowa* in 1918 then the *Trenton* April 1924-June 1926. Graduated from the Naval War College in 1927. Commanding officer of the *California* 1929-1930. Chief of staff to Commander Battleships, Battle Fleet 1930-1931. Rear admiral in July 1931. Commander of Destroyers, Battle Force December 1931-June 1934. President of the Naval War College June 1934-December 1936. Commander of Battleships, Battle Force December 1936-January 1938. Vice admiral in January 1937, admiral in January 1938. Commander of Battle Force January 1938-June 1939. Again president of the Naval War College June 1939-December 1941. Retired in December 1941 but continued on active duty as president of the Naval War College until June 1942, then member of the General Board November 1942-July 1944 and Director of Naval History July 1944-May 1946. Decorations included the Navy Cross and Legion of Merit. Died on September 6, 1955.

Kauffman, James Laurence (1887-1963) Born on April 18, 1887, in Miamisburg, Ohio. Graduated from Annapolis in 1908 and commissioned in 1910. Commanding officer of the destroyer *Hopkins* May 1912-November 1914, operating in Mexican waters in 1914. Commanding officer of the *Patrol* July-August 1917 and the *Jenkins* June-December 1918 in Irish waters during World War I then the *Barney* March 1919-November 1920. Aide and flag secretary to Commander in Chief Battle Fleet then United States Fleet 1923-1926. Member of the U.S. Naval Mission to Brazil 1927-1931. Graduated from the Naval War College in 1934. Commanding officer of the *Memphis* 1936-1938. Captain of the yard at Mare Island Navy Yard January 1938-January 1940. Commanding officer of sixteen over-age destroyers, later given to the British, operating on the coast of Texas and Mexico 1940-1941. Commander of Destroyers, Support Force, Atlantic Fleet March-September 1941. Member of the General Board October-December 1941. Rear admiral in January 1942. Established then commanded the Naval Operating Base in Iceland in 1942. Commandant of Seventh Naval District June 1942-February 1943. Duty at headquarters of Commander in Chief United States Fleet February 1943-January 1944. Commander of Destroyers, Pacific Fleet and Cruisers, Pacific Fleet January-October 1944. Commander of the Philippine Sea Frontier November 1944-May 1946. Vice admiral in April 1945. Retired in May 1949. Decorations included the Navy Cross, Distinguished Service Medal, three Legions of Merit and the Navy Commendation Medal. Died on October 21, 1963.

Keleher, Timothy Jerome (1885-1962) Born on February 17, 1885, in Perth Amboy, New Jersey. Graduated from Annapolis in 1908 and commissioned in 1910. M.S. from Columbia University in 1917. Commanding officer of the *Jenkins* January 1918-January 1919. Aide and fleet engineer on the staff of Commander Scouting Fleet 1929-1930. Head of the marine engineering department at Annapolis 1938-1941. Inspector of naval material at Third Naval District May-December 1941. Chief of the Navy section on the Army-Navy Munitions Board 1941-1943. Rear admiral in June 1942. Retired in July 1943. Continued on active duty in the office of procurement and material until January 1944. Decorations included the Navy Cross. Died on July 23, 1962.

Keliher, Thomas Joseph Jr. (1893-1953) Born on March 5, 1893, in Boston, Massachusetts. Commissioned from Annapolis in 1916. Served aboard the *Oklahoma*, which operated with the British Grand Fleet during World War I. Commanding officer of the *Hart* in 1930. Graduated from the Naval War College in 1938 then a member of the staff there until 1940. Commanded Destroyer Divisions 17 and 5 then Destroyer Squadron 3, Pacific Fleet June 1940-June 1942. Operations officer on the staff of Commander in Chief Pacific Fleet 1942-1944. Commanding officer of the *Indiana* March 1944-May 1945. Commodore in June 1945. Commander of Service Division 104 and Service Force Pacific Fleet July 1945-February 1946. Rear admiral upon retirement in June 1949. Awards included two Legions of Merit. Died on February 18, 1953.

Kelley, Frank Harrison (1889-1953) Born on February 26, 1889, in New Haven, Connecticut. Graduated from Annapolis in 1910 and commissioned in 1912. Commanding officer of the *Stoddart* in 1923 and the *Milwaukee* 1938-1939. Professor of naval science and tactics at the University of Minnesota and Marquette University 1939-1941. Commanding officer of the *West Point*, formerly the luxury liner America, May 1941-April 1943. Commandant of Naval Training Center Farragut, Idaho 1943-1946. Commodore in September 1944. Rear admiral upon retirement in December 1946. Decorations included the Bronze Star. Died on November 19, 1953.

Kelly, Monroe (1886-1956) Born on July 30, 1886, in Norfolk, Virginia. Graduated from Annapolis in 1909 and commissioned in 1911. Commanded the Submarine Base, Hampton Roads 1923-1925. Member of the U.S. Naval Mission to Brazil 1927-1931. Commanding officer of the *J. Fred Talbot* 1931-1932. Instructor at Annapolis 1933-1936. Commanding officer of the *Nitro*, then the *Richmond* 1936-1938. Naval attache in the Hague August 1938-July 1940. Duty in the office of the chief of naval operations 1940-1941. Staff officer with Commander Train, Atlantic Fleet April-July 1941 then commander of Train Squadron Five 1941-1942. Rear admiral in November 1941. Again in the office of the chief of naval operations March-May 1942 then assistant chief of staff to Commander in Chief United States Fleet until August 1942. Commander of Battleships, Atlantic Fleet 1942-1943. Commandant of New York Navy Yard May 1943-November 1944 then commandant of Third Naval District until 1948. Vice admiral upon retirement in August 1948. Decorations included the Distinguished Service Medal and Legion of Merit. Died on August 29, 1956.

Kendall, Henry Samuel (1896-1963) Born on April 19, 1896, in Baltimore, Maryland. Commissioned from Annapolis in 1917. Served aboard the *Mississippi* during World War I. Designated naval aviator in December 1922. Commander of Seattle Naval Air Station June 1935-June 1937. Graduated from the Naval War College in 1940 then remained there as a staff officer until March 1941. Commanded Patrol Wing Three at Coco Solo, Canal Zone March-June 1941. Inspector of naval aircraft at Curtis Wright Corporation July-November 1941. Commanding oficer of the Curtiss 1941-1942 then Fleet Air Wing One April 1942-February 1944. Rear admiral in January 1944. Commander of the Air Technical Training Command 1944-1945 then Carrier Division 24 June 1945-March 1946. Vice admiral upon retirement in July 1952. Decorations included the Legion of Merit. Died on November 7, 1963.

Kennedy, Sherman Stewart (1888-1961) Born on September 16, 1888, in Saginaw, Michigan. Graduated from Annapolis in 1909 and commissioned in 1911. M.S. from Columbia University in 1916. Served aboard the *Virginia* during World War I. Engineer officer at the Naval Station Cavite, Philippine Islands 1930-1932 then on the staff of Commander Battleships, Battle Force and Commander Battle Force 1935-1937. Planning officer at Mare Island Navy Yard 1937-1940. Duty at New York Navy Yard August 1940-December 1941 then manager of the yard until April 1945. Rear admiral in May 1942. Director of the shore division in the Bureau of Ships April-November 1945. Retired in July 1948. Decorations included the Legion of Merit. Died on November 4, 1961.

Kessing, Oliver Owen (1890-1963) Born on December 6, 1890, in Greensburg, Indiana. Commissioned from Annapolis in 1914. Served aboard the *Huntington* during World War I. Instructor at Annapolis 1926-1929. Commanding officer of the *Alden* 1934-1935. Again duty at Annapolis 1937-1940. Commanding officer of the *Chaumont* January 1940-November 1941. Duty in the office of the chief of naval operations and the Bureau of Aeronautics 1941-1942. Commanded the preflight training school at the University of North Carolina May-November 1942. Commander of naval bases at Tulagi, Bougainville, Ulithi Atoll, Manila and Yokosuka November 1942-September 1945. Commodore in August 1944. Rear admiral upon retirement in June 1947. Decorations included three Legions of Merit and the Bronze Star. Died on January 31, 1963.

Ketcham, Dixwell (1899-1993) Born on December 2, 1899, in Buena Park, Illinois. Commissioned from Annapolis in 1920. Designated naval aviator in December 1922. Aide and flag secretary to Commander Aircraft Squadrons, Scouting Fleet 1929-1930 then Commander Carrier Division One November 1930-June 1931. Chief of staff to Commander Aircraft, Scouting Force October 1940-May 1941. Duty in the plans division of the Bureau of Aeronautics June 1941-August 1943. Commanding officer of the Chenango 1943-1944. Rear admiral in November 1943. Commander of Fleet Air Wing One September 1944-May 1945 and Carrier Division 27 May 1945-January 1946. Vice admiral upon retirement in November 1949. Decorations included the Legion of Merit. Died on July 7, 1993.

Kidd, Isaac Campbell (1884-1941) Born in Cleveland, Ohio, on March 26, 1884. Commissioned from USNA in 1884. Served aboard the *New Jersey* on the world cruise of the Battle Fleet 1907-1909. Assigned to the staff of Commander in Chief Atlantic Fleet during World War I. Chief of staff of Battleships, United

States Fleet 1940-1941 then commander of the Battleship Division, United States Fleet from 1941. Killed aboard his flagship the *Arizona* during the Japanese attack on Pearl Harbor on December 7, 1941. Awarded a posthumous Medal of Honor.

Kiefer, Dixie (1896-1945) Born on April 4, 1896, in Blackfoot, Idaho. Commissioned from Annapolis in 1919. Designated naval aviator in December 1922. M.S. from Massachusetts Institute of Technology in 1929. Executive officer of the *Wright* 1941-1942 then the *Yorktown* February-June 1942, when the *Yorktown* was lost during the Battle of Midway. Hospitalized until January 1943 for injuries suffered on the *Yorktown*. Commanded Naval Air Station Olathe, Kansas January-August 1943. Chief of staff to the Chief of Naval Air Primary Training Command 1943-1944. Commanding officer of the *Ticonderoga* May 1944-1945. Commander of Naval Air Bases, First Naval District April-November 1945. Commodore in May 1945. Killed in a plane crash near Beacon, New York, on November 11, 1945. Decorations included the Navy Cross, Distinguished Service Medal, Silver Star and Purple Heart.

Kiland, Ingolf Norman (1895-1992) Born on March 26, 1895, in Sioux Falls, South Dakota. Commissioned from Annapolis in 1916. Served aboard the *Sterett* in Irish waters during World War I. M.S. from Columbia University in 1923. Commanding officer of the *Schenck* June 1934-December 1935. Commanding officer of the *Crescent City* December 1941-November 1942. Commanded Transport Division Two, Amphibious Force 1942-1943. Duty in the office of the Command in Chief United States Fleet April 1943-October 1944. Rear admiral in September 1944. Commander of Group Seven, Amphibious Force 1944-1945. Retired as vice admiral in April 1957. Decorations included the Navy Cross, Distinguished Service Medal and two Legions of Merit. Died on March 10, 1992.

Kilpatrick, Walter Kenneth (1887-1949) Born on October 29, 1887, in New York. Graduated from Annapolis in 1908 and commissioned in 1910. Graduated from the Naval War College in 1922. Commanding officer of the *Doyen* 1923-1925 and the *Hatfield* 1925-1927. Graduated from the Army War College in 1928. Commanding officer of the *Bushnell* 1928-1929. Aide and flag secretary to Commander in Chief Asiatic Fleet 1929-1931. Duty in the office of naval intelligence January-June 1938. Commanding officer of the *Chester* July 1938-February 1940. Chief of staff to Commander Cruisers, Scouting Force February 1940-January 1941, Commandant Twelfth Naval District January-December 1941, Commander Pacific Southern Naval Coastal Frontier December 1941-April 1943 and Commander in Chief Atlantic Fleet May 1943-August 1945. Rear admiral in July 1942. Deputy commander of Western Sea Frontier August 1945 until retirement in August 1946. Decorations included the Distinguished Service Medal and two Legions of Merit. Died on September 26, 1949.

Kimmel, Husband Edward (1882-1968) Born in Henderson, Kentucky, on February 26, 1882. Graduated from Annapolis in 1904 and commissioned in 1906.

Served aboard the *Georgia* during the world cruise of the Battle Fleet 1907-1909. Wounded during the occupation of Vera Cruz in April 1914. Aide to Assistant Secretary of the Navy Franklin D. Roosevelt in 1915. Served with the Grand Fleet in World War I. Rear admiral in November 1937. Staff duty at the Navy Department 1937-1939. Commander of Cruiser Division Seven, then cruisers in the Battle Force 1939-1941. Named commander in chief of the United States Fleet over the heads of many senior flag officers and elevated to admiral in February 1941. The senior officer present at Pearl Harbor on December 7, 1941, he was relieved of his command ten days later and retired in March 1942 as rear admiral. The Roberts Commission declared him guilty of dereliction of duty in 1942, but a naval court of inquiry found no mistakes in judgment. Author of *Admiral Kimmel's Story* (1955). Died on May 14, 1968.

King, Ernest Joseph (1878-1956) Born in Lorain, Ohio, on November 23, 1878. Graduated from Annapolis in 1901 and commissioned in 1903. Commanding officer of the *Terry* during the occupation of Vera Cruz in April 1914. Staff officer with the commander of the Atlantic Fleet 1916-1922. Designated a naval aviator in 1928. Graduated from the Naval War College in 1933. Named chief of the Bureau of Aeronautics in 1933. When President Roosevelt could not find a qualified flag officer who also knew how to fly he promoted King to rear admiral in November 1933. Commander of Aircraft, Battle Force as vice admiral 1938-1939. Member of the General Board 1939-1940. Admiral in February 1941 as commander of the Atlantic Fleet. Ten days after Pearl Harbor he replaced Admiral Husband E. Kimmel as commander in chief U.S. Fleet. The following March King relieved Admiral Harold R. Stark as chief of naval operations and became the first officer to simultaneously hold the top two positions in the Navy. He directed all activies of the Navy during World War II, becoming a five-star Fleet Admiral in December 1944 and relinquishing the post of chief of naval operations to Admiral Chester W. Nimitz in November 1945. King went on inactive status until 1950, when he had limited duty as an advisor to the secretary of the navy. Decorations included the Navy Cross and three Distinguished Service Medals. Died on June 25, 1956.

Kingman, Howard Fithian (1890-1968) Born on May 5, 1890, in Hillsboro, North Dakota. Commissioned from Annapolis in 1911. Graduated from the Naval War College in 1924. Aide and flag lieutenan to Commander in Chief Battle Fleet September 1925-September 1926 then Commander in Chief United States Fleet September 1926-October 1927. Commanding officer of the *Doyen* November 1927-August 1928. Assistant naval attache in London August 1928-October 1930. Senior aide in the White House January 1934-August 1935. Duty at Third Naval District June 1937-May 1939. Commander of Destroyer Squadron Five May 1939-May 1941. Assistant director of naval intelligence May 1941-January 1943. Commander of Battleship Division Two, Pacific Fleet January 1943-November 1944. Rear admiral in February 1943. Commander of Panama Sea Frontier, commandant of Fifteenth Naval District and commander of Southeast Pacific Sea Forces November 1944-July 1945. Commander of Battleship Division

Nine July-November 1945. Assignments after the war included command of Third Fleet November 1945-November 1946. Retired as vice admiral in February 1947. Decorations included three Legions of Merit, the Bronze Star and two Navy Commendation Medals. Died on July 4, 1968

Kinkaid, Thomas Cassin (1888-1972) Born in Hanover, New Hampshire, on April 3, 1888. Graduated from Annapolis in 1908 and commissioned in 1910. Served aboard the *Arizona* in World War I. Graduated from the Naval War College in 1930. Commanding officer of the *Indianapolis* 1937-1938. Naval attache in Rome, then Belgrade 1938-1941. Rear admiral in November 1941. Commander of Cruiser Division Six, then the "Enterprise Task Force" 1941-1943, taking part in offensives against the Gilbert, Marshall, Wake, Bougainville and Marcus islands and the battles of the Coral Sea, Midway and Santa Cruz. Commander of naval forces in the North Pacific January-November 1943. Vice admiral in June 1943. Commander of Seventh Fleet, and General MacArthur's naval commander, November 1943-November 1945. Admiral in April 1945. Assignments after the war included commander of the Eastern Sea Frontier January 1946 until retirement in May 1950. Decorations included four Distinguished Service Medals and the Legion of Merit. Died on November 17, 1972.

Kirk, Alan Goodrich (1888-1963) Born in Philadelphia, Pennsylvania on October 30, 1888. Graduated from Annapolis in 1909 and commissioned in 1911. Served at the Naval Proving Ground at Dahlgren, Virginia, in World War I. Naval aide at the White House 1920-1921. Graduated from the Naval War College in 1929, then instructor there until 1931. Staff officer in the Battle Force, then U.S. Fleet 1937-1939. Naval attache in London 1939-1941. Chief of naval intelligence in 1941. Commanded a division of destroyer escorts in the Atlantic Fleet October 1941-March 1942. Rear admiral in November 1941. Returned to London as naval attache March 1942-February 1943. Commander of the Amphibious Force, Atlantic Fleet February 1943-October 1944. He had command of U.S. naval task forces on D-Day. Vice admiral in May 1945. Retired as admiral in March 1946. Decorations included the Distinguished Service Medal and two Legions of Merit. Ambassador to Belgium, then minister to Luxemourg 1946-1949. Ambassador to the Soviet Union April 1949-October 1951 and the Republic of China May 1962-April 1963. Died on October 15, 1963.

Kitts, Willard Augustus III (1894-1964) Born on April 14, 1894, in Oswego, New York. Commissioned from Annapolis in 1916. B.S. from Massachusetts Institute of Technology in June 1922. Commanding officer of the *McCormick* April 1935-June 1936. Head of the fire control section in the Bureau of Ordnance June 1936-June 1939. Executive officer of the *Salt Lake City* June 1939-January 1941. Gunnery officer on the staff of Commander in Chief Pacific Fleet January 1941-September 1942. Commanding officer of the *Northampton* September 1942-January 1943 and the *Nevada* January-July 1943. Rear admiral in January 1943. Head of the production division in the Bureau of Ordnance July 1943-March

1946. Retired as vice admiral in June 1951. Decorations included the Navy Cross and three Legions of Merit. Died on November 21, 1964.

Klein, Grover Cleveland (1892-1965) Born on July 14, 1892, in Georgetown, Ohio. Commissioned from Annapolis in 1916. Served aboard the *Hancock* in the Dominican Campaign and World War I. M.S. from Massachusetts Institute of Technology in 1921. Instructor at Annapolis 1925-1927. Duty at Sixteenth Naval District, Cavite, Philippines 1934-1936. Production officer at New York Navy Yard June 1941-January 1944. Rear admiral in December 1942. Commander of U.S. Naval Shipyard Mare Island 1944-1947. Retired in June 1951. Continued on active duty until Novenber 1952. Decorations included two Legions of Merit. Died on September 26, 1965.

Knowles, Herbert Bain (1894-1976) Born on March 20, 1894, in North Newburg, Maine. Commissioned from Annapolis in 1917. Commanding officer of the *S-6* September 1922-August 1924, the *S-37* December 1926-October 1929 and the *Bass* August 1931-June 1934. Instructor at Annapolis June 1934-May 1936. Commanding officer of the *Neches* April 1938-July 1939. Operations officer at Fourteenth Naval District July 1939-December 1941. Commanding officer of the *Heywood* December 1941-October 1943. Commander of Transport Division Eighteen October 1943-January 1945 then Transport Squadron Twelve and Transport Division 34 January 1945-January 1946. Commodore in October 1944. Reverted to captain in January 1946. Rear admiral upon retirement in September 1947. Decorations included five Legions of Merit. Died on March 3, 1976.

Korns, Virgil Eben (1899-1976) Born on June 6, 1899, in Holmesville, Ohio. Commissioned from Annapolis in 1919. Instructor at Annapolis October 1925-July 1927 and August 1935-May 1938. Graduated from the Naval War College in 1931. Commanding officer of the *Hannibal* June 1939-July 1940. Damage control officer on the *Saratoga* July 1940-June 1941. Duty in the office of the chief of naval operations June 1941-August 1943. Chief of staff to Commander Landing Craft and Bases Europe August 1943-June 1945. Commodore in August 1944. Staff officer with Commander in Chief Pacific Fleet July 1945-September 1946. Retired in June 1949. Decorations included two Legions of Merit. Died on December 7, 1976.

Kraus, Sydney Moses (1887-1969) Born on July 16, 1887, in Peru, Indiana. Graduated from Annapolis in 1908. M.S. from Columbia University in 1916. Crossed the Atlantic as a naval observer on the dirigible *Los Angeles* October 12-15 1925. Duty in the Bureau of Aeronautics October 1926-February 1931 and March 1936-March 1943 as head of the material branch. Rear admiral in October 1941. Bureau of Aeronautics representative in the Third Naval District 1943-1947. Retired in January 1948. Died on April 28, 1969.

Kurtz, Thomas Richardson (1881-1956) Born on October 31, 1881, in Minneapolis, Minnesota. Graduated from Annapolis in 1901 and commissioned in 1903.

Aide to Commander Atlantic Torpedo Fleet 1911-1913 then the superintendent of Annapolis 1915-1916. During World War I he was executive officer of the *Illinois* and commanding officer of the *Wakiva II.* Aide to Commander Patrol Force, Atlantic Fleet 1917-1919 then Commander Squadron Four, Battleship Force January-April 1919. Commanding officer of the *Chicago* April-July 1919. Assistant chief of staff to Commander in Chief Atlantic Fleet 1919-1921. Commandant of midshipment at Annapolis June 1921-March 1924. Commanding officer of the *Galveston* 1924-1926. Assistant chief of the Bureau of Navigation June 1928-August 1929. Retired in August 1929. Recalled to active duty in February 1942. Commodore in April 1944. Chief of staff of Eastern Sea Frontier 1942-1945. Retired again in September 1945. Decorations included the Navy Cross and Legion of Merit. Died on March 6, 1956.

Laning, Richard Henry (1883-1963) Born on September 25, 1883, in Osaka, Japan of American parents. Commissioned in the Medical Corps in 1911. Served in China with units of the Asiatic Fleet 1912-1913 then at the American Legation in Peking 1914-1915. Duty at Port-au-Prince, Haiti 1922-1926. Medical officer in command of Philadelphia Naval Hospital 1942-1943. Rear admiral in June 1943. District medical officer at First Naval District 1943-1944. Inspector of medical department activities at Fourteenth Naval District October 1944-August 1945 then district medical officer at Third and Twelfth Naval Districts 1945-1946. Retired in August 1946. Decorations included the Legion of Merit. Died on April 9, 1963.

Lannon, James Patrick (1878-1953) Born on October 12, 1878, in Alexandria, Virginia. Graduated from Annapolis in 1902 and commissioned in 1904. Awarded the Medal of Honor at Vera Cruz in 1914. Instructor at Annapolis August 1909-August 1911. Commanding officer of the *Nashville* December 1917-January 1919 and the *Helena* August 1923-October 1924. War plans office at Sixteenth Naval District October 1924-August 1925. Liaison officer in the office of the governor general of the Philippines August-October 1925. Commanding officer of the *Concord* August 1928-June 1930. Chief of staff and aide to Commandant Third Naval District New York January 1936-June 1937. Retired as captain in June 1937. Recalled to active duty in December 1941. President of the General Court Martial Board, Washington, DC. December 1941-February 1945. Rear admiral in February 1942. Decorations included the Medal of Honor and Navy Cross. Died on March 12, 1953.

Leahy, William Daniel (1875-1959) Born in Hampton, Iowa, on May 6, 1875. Graduated from Annapolis in 1897 and commissioned in 1899. Served aboard the *Oregon* in the Spanish-American War and later saw service in the Philippine Insurrection and the Boxer Rebellion. Commanding officer of the *Nevada* in World War I. Chief of the Bureau of Ordnance as rear admiral 1927-1931. Commander of destroyers in the Scouting Force 1931-1932. Chief of the Bureau of Navigation 1933-1935. Vice admiral in March 1935. Commander of battleships in the Battle Force March 1935-April 1936. Admiral in April 1936 as commander of the Battle

Force. Chief of naval operations January 1937 until retirement in July 1939. Governor of Puerto Rico 1939-1940. Ambassador to the Vichy government in France 1940-1942. Recalled to active duty as chief of staff to President Roosevelt in 1942. Fleet Admiral in December 1944. Remained as chief of staff to President Truman after Roosevelt's death in April 1945. Retired a second time in March 1949. Decorations included the Navy Cross and three Distinguished Service Medals. Author of *I Was There* (1950). Died on July 20, 1959.

Leary, Herbert Fairfax (1885-1957) Born on May 31, 1885, in Washington, DC, the son of Rear Admiral Richard Phillips Leary, Annapolis Class of 1863. Graduated from Annapolis in 1905 and commissioned in 1907. Commanding officer of the *Lamson* December 1911-May 1912 and the *Preston* May-October 1912. Liaison officer with the French Fleet August-September 1917. Duty with U.S. Naval Forces Europe in 1917. Served on a number of boards including the Joint Army and Navy Board to consider the use of gas in naval warfare in 1918. Commanding officer of the *Harvard* and the *Corsair* in 1919. Assistant naval attache in London with duties also in Paris, Rome, Berlin and The Hague May 1924-April 1925. Aide to Commander Destroyer Squadrons, Battle Fleet June 1926-October 1928. Graduated from the Naval War College in May 1932. Commanding officer of the *Portland* May 1932-June 1934. Chief of staff and aide to Commander Battle Force, United States Fleet April 1937-January 1938. Rear admiral in June 1938. Director of fleet training, office of the chief of naval operations June 1939-February 1941. Commander of cruisers, Battle Force and Commander Cruiser Division Nine February-December 1941. Commanded naval forces of the Australian-New Zealand Area December 1941-April 1942 then U.S. Naval Forces Southwest Pacific April-September 1942 and Task Force One, Pacific Fleet September 1942-April 1943. Commandant of Fifth Naval District May-November 1943. Commander of Eastern Sea Frontier November 1943-September 1945. Retired in June 1946. Retired as vice admiral in June 1946. Decorations included the Navy Cross, Silver Star and two Legions of Merit. Died on December 3, 1957.

Le Breton, David McDougal (1884-1973) Born on August 12, 1884, in San Francisco, California. Graduated from Annapolis in 1904 and commissioned in 1906. Served aboard the *Rhode Island* during the world cruise of the Battle Fleet 1907-1909. Aide to Admiral George Dewey 1914-1917. Commanding officer of the *Aylwin* 1917-1918 and the Ingraham 1918-1919. Naval attache in Madrid 1921-1923 then the Hague January-June 1923. Aide to Commander Battleship Divisions, Battle Fleet 1923-1925. Graduated from the Naval War College in 1929. Commanding officer of the *Hannibal* 1929-1931. Naval attache in Paris May 1931-May 1934. Commanding officer of the Portland 1934-1936. Chief of staff to Commandant Fourteenth Naval District January 1936-May 1937. Chief of staff to Commander in Chief May 1937-March 1938. Rear admiral in August 1937. Commanded the Yangtze Patrol 1938-1939. Again at the Naval War College 1939-1940. Commanded Squadron 40-T June-October 1940, Battleship Division Five, Battle Force 1940-1941 and Battleships, Atlantic Fleet June-December 1941. President of the Board of Inspection and Survey December

1941-November 1942, then the Naval Examining Board 1942-1943. Commandant of Fifth Naval District 1943-1946. Retired in October 1946. Decorations included the Navy Cross. Died on September 6, 1973.

Lee, Willis Augustus Jr. (1888-1945) Born on May 11, 1888, in Kentucky.
Graduated from Annapolis in 1908 and commissioned in 1910. Member American
rifle team in the 1920 Olympic Games at Antwerp, Belgium and recipient of nine
gold, two silver and two bronze medals. Commanding officer of the *Fairfax* and
William B. Preston September 1920-June 1924 and the *Lardner* October 1927-
June 1928. Graduated from the Naval War College in May 1929. Commanding
officer of the *Concord* October 1936-July 1938. Operations officer, then chief of
staff to Commander Cruisers, Battle Force July1938- May 1939. Assistant director, then director of the division of fleet training June 1939-February 1942. Chief
of staff to Commander in Chief United States Fleet December 1941-June 1941.
Commander of Battleship Divison Six, Battleships Pacific Fleet and Battleship
Squadron Two June 1941 until his death on August 24, 1945, of a heart attack on
board a launch taking him to his flagship. Rear admiral in March 1942, vice admiral in March 1944. Decorations included the Navy Cross, two Distinguished
Service Medals and the Legion of Merit.

Leighton, Frank Thompson (1885-1943) Born on September 2, 1885, in Tunk-
hannock, Pennsylvania. Graduated from Annapolis in 1909 and commissioned in
1911. Commanding officer of the *Claxton* 1919-1920, the *Somers* 1929-1930 and
the *Buchanan* April 1930-September 1931. Graduated from the Naval War College in 1934. Commander of Destroyr Division Five June 1934-April 1936.
Commanding officer of the *Louisville* 1938-1940. Duty in the office of the chief
of naval operations December 1940-February 1942. Commandant of Eighth Naval
District April-November 1943. Rear admiral in November 1942. Died on November 23, 1943.

Lewis, Spencer Steen (1888-1952) Born on January 8, 1888, in Calvert, Texas.
Graduated from Annapolis in 1910 and commissioned in 1912. Commanding offi-
cer of the *Patterson* October 1917-September 1918 and the *Herbert* March-
November 1921. Executive officer of the *Cleveland* August 1925-January 1928
and member of the landing force ashore at Bluefields, Puerto Cabezas and Rio
Grande, Nicaragua in 1926 and 1927. Aide to Commandant Third Naval District
January 1928-July 1930 and Commander Scouting Force December 1931-1932.
Graduated from the Naval War College in May 1939. Commanding officer of the
Cincinnati May 1939-January 1941. Chief of staff to Commander Cruisers,
Scouting Force January 1941-November 1942. Rear admiral in August 1942.
Duty with Commander in Chief United States Fleet November 1942-March 1943.
Chief of staff to Commander U.S. Naval Forces Northwest African Waters March
1943-July 1945 then Commander U.S. Naval Forces Europe July 1945- January
1947. Vice admiral upon retirement in October 1947. Decorations included the
Navy Cross, two Distinguished Service Medals and three Legions of Merit. Died
on June 26, 1952.

Libby, Ruthven Elmer (1900-1986) Born on December 22, 1900, in Spokane, Washington. Commissioned from Annapolis in 1922. M.S. from Columbia University in 1931. Executive officer of the *MacDonough* February 1937-May 1938. Engineering officer on the *Northampton* May 1938-July 1939. Duty with the Bureau of Engineering July 1939-November 1940. Assistant naval attache in London December 1940-August 1941. Staff officer with Commander in Chief Atlantic Fleet September-December 1941. Aide to Commander in Chief United States Fleet December 1941-March 1923. Commander of Destroyer Squadron One March 1943-January 1944 then Destroyer Squadron Fifty-Six and Destroyer Division 111 January-October 1944. Served in the planning section, office of the chief of naval operations October 1944-March 1945. Commodore in April 1945. Senior Naval Member Joint War Plans Committee, Joint Chiefs of Staff April 1945-February 1946. Assignments after the war included U.N. delegate to the Korean Truce Talks November 1952-June 1953, Commander Battleship Cruiser Force Atlantic Fleet May 1954-January 1956, Deputy chief of naval operations (Fleet Operations and Readiness) May-August 1956, Deputy chief of naval operations (Plans and Policy) August 1956-June 1958 and Commander First Fleet June 1958 until retirement as vice admiral in May 1960. Decorations included six Legions of Merit. Died on July 28, 1986.

Litch, Ernest Wheeler (1897-1967) Born on November 22, 1897, in Boston, Massachusetts. Commissioned from Annapolis in 1919. Designated naval aviator in January 1924. Naval aide on the staff of Commanding General GHQ Air Force September 1938-March 1939. Navigator and later head of the air department on the *Ranger* April 1939-March 1941. Staff officer with Commander Support Force Atlantic Fleet March- August 1941. Special naval observer at Laugherne, Ireland August 1941-February 1942. Assistant naval attache in London February-August 1942. Commanding officer of Naval Reserve Aviation Base, Detroit September 1942-March 1943. Chief of staff and aide to Commander Naval Air Operational Training Command, Jacksonville March 1943-March 1944. Commanding officer of the *Lexington* April 1944-January 1945. Commander of Carrier Division 12 January-April 1945 and Carrier Division 26 April-October 1945. Assignments after the war included Commander Naval Forces Marianas July 1951-April 1954. Vice admiral upon retirement in July 1954. Decorations included four Legions of Merit and the Navy Commendation Medal. Died on February 14, 1967.

Lockwood, Charles Andrews Jr. (1890-1967) Born on May 6, 1890, in Midland, Virginia. Commissioned from Annapolis in 1912. Commanding officer of the *A-2* and the *B-1* December 1914-July 1917, the *Monadnock* September 1917-April 1918, the *G-1* and *N-5* October 1918-February 1919 and the ex-German submarine *UC-97* March-August 1919. Commanding officer of the *R-25* and *S-14* August 1919-June 1922 and the *Quiros* June 1922-March 1923. Executive officer of the *Peary* and commanding officer of the *Smith Thompson* October 1923-July 1924 then the *V-3* May 1926-December 1928. Member of the U.S. Naval Mission to Brazil December 1928-February 1931. Instructor at Annapolis June 1933-August 1935. Duty in the office of the chief of naval operations September 1937-June 1939. Chief of staff to Commander Submarine Force, United States Fleet June 1939-February 1941. U.S. naval attache in London 1941-March 1942. Commander of Submarines Southwest Pacific April 1942-February 1943 then Submarines Pacific Fleet February 1943-December 1945. Retired as vice admiral in September 1947. Decorations included three Distinguished Service Medals, the Legion of Merit and the Navy Commendation Medal. Died on June 6, 1967.

Loomis, Donald Wood (1895-1958) Born on July 15, 1895, in Milwaukee, Wisconsin. Commissioned from Annapolis in 1917. Survived the sinking of the *San Diego* in July 1918. Instructor at Annapolis September 1923-June 1925. Commanding officer of the *Twiggs* November 1936-April 1937 and the *Monaghan* APril 1937-June 1938. War plans officer on the staff of Commandant Sixth Naval District July 1938-March 1941. Executive officer of the *Pensacola* April 1941-October 1942. Commanding officer of the *Harry Lee* October 1942-March 1943. Commander of Transport Division Seven, Atlantic Fleet March-November 1943 and Transport Divison Twenty, Pacific Fleet November 1943-October 1944 Commodore in October 1944. Commander of Transport Squadron Eleven and Transport Division Thirty-One October 1944-September 1945. Rear admiral upon retirement in July 1949. Decorations included five Legions of Merit and the Bronze Star. Died on August 4, 1958.

Lowe, Frank Loper (1891-1963) Born April 17, 1891, in Monticello, Arkansas. Commissioned from Annapolis in 1914. Commanding officer of the *Kennison* November 1920-October 1921. Aide and flag secretary to Commander Destroyer Squadrons, Pacific Fleet October 1921-June 1922. LL.B. from George Washington University Law School in 1925. Aide and flag secretary to Commander Naval Forces Europe October 1926-September 1928. Assigned to the office of the Judge Advocate General July 1922-July 1925 and October 1928-April 1930. Attorney general for the government of American Samoa September 1931-May 1933. Commanding officer of the *Flusser* 1936-1938. Duty with the war plans division, office of the chief of naval operations October 1938-November 1941. Naval liaison officer with the U.S. Army November 1941-January 1942. Commanding officer of the *Pensacola* January 1942-March 1943. Duty in the office of the chief of naval operations March 1943-January 1944. Assistant judge advocate general of the Navy January 1944-August 1945. Rear admiral in August 1945, vice admiral upon retirement in August 1945. Decorations included the Navy Cross. Died on July 28, 1963.

Lowry, Frank Jacob (1888-1955) Born on February 15, 1888, in Cresco, Iowa. Graduated from Annapolis in 1911 and commissioned in 1913. Commanding officer of the *Pensacola* 1922-1925. Graduated from the Naval War College in May 1926. Professor of naval science and tactics at the University of California, Berkeley August 1929-June 1931. Commanding officer of the *Hale* July 1931-July 1933. Assigned to the officer personnel division in the Bureau of Navigation March 1938-September 1940. Commanding officer of the *Minneapolis* October

1940-September 1942. Rear admiral in August 1942. Executive officer, then commander of Naval Training Center, Great Lakes November 1942-February 1943. Commander of Moroccan Sea Frontier Forces, Casablanca, French Morocco February-September 1943. Commander of Landing Craft and Bases, American Forces Northwest African Waters September-October 1943 then Eighth Amphibious Force October 1943-October 1944 and Amphibious Group October 1944-August 1945. Vice admiral upon retirement in March 1950. Decorations included the Navy Cross, Distinguished Service Medal, two Legions of Merit and the Navy Commendation Medal. Died on March 26, 1955.

Lyle, Alexander Gordon (1889-1955) Born on November 12, 1889, in Gloucester, Massachusetts. Graduated from Baltimore College of Dentistry in 1912 and commissioned in the Dental Corps. Earned the Medal of Honor and the Silver Star as a lieutenant commander serving on the French front in World War I. Graduated from the Army Industrial College in May 1937. Assigned to the Naval Dispensary Washington, DC June 1937-February 1940, NAS Pensacola February 1940-February 1941 and NAS Quonset Point March 1941-April 1943. Rear admiral in March 1943, the first man of the Dental Corps of any armed service to make flag rank. Inspector of dental materials in the Medical Supply Depot, Brooklyn April-September 1943. Inspector of dental activities for the Navy, Bureau of Medicine and Surgery September 1943-June 1945. Assistant chief of the Bureau of Medicine and Surgery for Dentistry June 1945-April 1947. Retired as vice admiral in August 1948. Decorations included the Medal of Honor, two Silver Stars and the Navy Commendation Medal. Died on July 15, 1955.

Magruder, Cary Walthall (1886-1967) Born on April 7, 1886, in Vicksburg, Mississippi. Graduated from Annapolis in 1908 and commissioned in 1910. Commanding officer of the *Perkins* March-August 1916, the *Preston* 1916-1918 and the *Lansdale* October 1918-November 1919. Aide to Commandant New York Navy Yard 1919-1921 then Commander Battleship Force, Atlantic Fleet 1921-1923. Commanding officer of the *Yarborough* 1926-1928. Graduated from the Naval War College in 1929. Commanding officer of the *Trenton* 1936-1937. Chief of staff to Commander Battleships, Battle Force 1939-1941. Commander of Naval Training Station Newport May 1941-March 1945. Commodore in September 1944. Reverted to captain in March 1946 and retired in May 1946. Decorations included the Navy Cross. Died on November 17, 1967.

Mahoney, John Joseph (1891-1953) Born on September 18, 1891, in Worcester, Massachusetts. Commissioned from Annapolis in 1915. Commanding officer of the *Perry* December 1918-June 1919. Executive officer then commanding officer of the *Dupont* February 1920-September 1921. Instructor at Annapolis September 1921-August 1924 and January 1927-June 1929. Commanding officer of the Decatur June 1934-June 1935 and the *Kanawha* April 1936-May 1937. Commanded Destroyer Division 61 September 1939-March 1940. Assistant chief of staff and operations officer on the staff of Commander Atlantic Squadron, Battle Fleet March 1940-January 1941. Member of the General Board January 1941-

February 1943. Commanding officer of the *Wichita* March 1943-April 1944. Chief of staff and aide to Commander Operational Training Command, Atlantic Fleet May-September 1944. Commodore in September 1944. Commander of Naval Operating Base Guantanamo Bay, Cuba September 1944-December 1945. Rear admiral upon retirement in July 1949. Decorations included the Legion of Merit. Died on March 20, 1953.

Manahan, Stewart Allan (1887-1972) Born on March 1, 1887, in Chicago, Illinois. Graduated from Annapolis in 1909 and commissioned in 1911. Commanding officer of the *Severn* November 1913-September 1915, the *Parrott* November 1923-August 1925 and the *Humphreys* August 1929-December 1930. Member of the Naval Mission to Brazil 1936-September 1938. Commanding officer of the *Memphis* December 1938-May 1940. Marine superintendent in the office of the governor of the Panama Canal May 1940 until retirement in November 1946. Commodore in April 1945. Decorations included the Legion of Merit. Died on January 3, 1972.

Mann, William Leake Jr. (1884-1953) Born on July 26, 1884, in Georgetown, Texas. M.A. from Southwestern University of Texas in 1903, Ph.D. in 1904. M.D. from Harvard in 1908. Commissioned in the Medical Corps in 1911. Medical director for Gendarmerie d'Haiti 1919-1922. Commanding officer of Naval Hospital Corpus Christi, Texas 1940-1942. Medical officer in command of Naval Medical Research Institute 1942-1945. Rear admiral in June 1943. Retired in November 1945. Decorations included the Navy Commendation Medal. Died on June 12, 1953.

Manning, John Joseph (1894-1962) Born on July 16, 1894, in Troy, New York. B.S. from Rensselaer Polytechnic Institute in 1915. Commissioned in the Civil Engineer Corps in 1917. Public works officer at Naval Station Guantanamo Bay, Cuba July 1918-August 1920, Navy Yard Pearl Harbor September 1930-August 1933 and Navy Yard Philadelphia and Fourth Naval District, Philadelphia September 1936-September 1937. Head of the fleet facilities division in the Bureau of Yards and Docks and later director of the construction department September 1937-November 1942. Rear admiral in July 1942. Director of the Atlantic division, Bureau of Yards and Docks November 1942-June 1945 then the Eastern-Pacific Division June-November 1945. Assignments after the war included chief of the Bureau of Yards and Docks November 1945 until retirement as vice admiral in December 1949. Decorations included the Distinguished Service Medal, Legion of Merit and Bronze Star. Died on September 5, 1962.

Maples, Houston Ledbetter (1896-1980) Born on March 4, 1896, in Scottsboro, Alabama. Commissioned from Annapolis in 1917. Instructor at Annapolis September 1922-September 1924, September 1927-March 1930, June 1934-June 1936 and June 1938-October 1940. Duty at Naval Station Tutuila, Samoa April 1931-September 1932. Executive officer of the *Melville* April 1937-June 1938 and commanding officer of the *Sabine* November 1940-December 1942. Commander of Naval Base Guadalcanal December 1942-May 1943. Staff officer with Commander Service Squadron, South Pacific Force May-July 1943. Served with the logistics plans division, office of the chief of naval operations Septembert 1943-April 1945. Senior naval officer with the U.S. Military Mission to Russia and Naval Attache in Moscow April 1945-June 1947. Rear admiral in May 1945. Retired in January 1948. Decorations included the Navy Commendation Medal. Died on February 15, 1980.

Marquart, Edward John (1880-1954) Born on March 11, 1880, in Valparaiso, Indiana. Graduated from Annapolis in 1902 and commissioned in 1904. Commanding officer of the *Breck* May 1924-July 1927. Naval attache in the Hague July 1931-June 1933. Commanding officer of the *Nokomis* May 1935-May 1937. Duty in the hydrographic office, Bureau of Navigation May 1937-January 1939. Commanding officer of the *Augusta* March 1939-May 1941. Assistant commandant of Fourth Naval District May 1941-January 1943. Chief of staff to Commander Caribbean Sea Frontier January 1943-January 1945. Rear admiral in January 1936. Deputy commander of Forward Area, Central Pacific and Marianas January-December 1945. Retired in April 1944 but continued on active duty until June 1946. Decorations included the Legion of Merit. Died on November 4, 1954.

Marshall, Edward Lester (1892-1966) Born on January 14, 1892, in Lynn, Massachusetts. Attended Tufts College. Commissioned in the Civil Engineer Corps in June 1917. Public works officer at Naval Station Tutuila, Samoa April 1926-September 1927 and Navy Yard Cavite, Philippine Islands September 1934-June 1936. Duty at the Bureau of Yards and Docks August 1937-1941. Director of the finance and operating department at the Bureau of Yards and Docks in 1941. Chief inspector in the Bureau of Yards and Docks 1942-1946. Rear admiral in January 1943. Retired in November 1948. Decorations included the Legion of Merit. Died on January 26, 1966.

Martin, Charles Franklin (1892-1975) Born on January 4, 1892, in Augusta, Georgia. Attended the College of Charleston. Commissioned from Annapolis in 1914. Qualified in submarines in December 1919. Commanding officer of the *K-8* June-December 1920, the *R-8* December 1920-July 1921 and the *S-19* December 1923-June 1926. Commander of Submarine Division Eleven 1935-1937, then Submarine Squadron Three, Submarine Division Eleven and Submarine Base Coco Solo, Canal Zone in 1937. Chief of the administrative division in the office of the judge advocate general June 1938-January 1941. Commanding officer of the *Henderson* January 1941-October 1942. Duty in the office of the chief of naval operations October 1942-April 1944. Commodore in May 1943. Commanding officer of the *Pennsylvania* April 1944-June 1945. Commander of Naval Base Manus Island June 1945-April 1946. Rear admiral upon retirement in November 1946. Decorations included the Legion of Merit and Navy Commendation Medal. Died on January 19, 1975.

Martin, Harold Montgomery (1896-1972) Born on January 18, 1896, in Bay Mills, Michigan. Attended the University of Illinois. Commissioned from Annapolis in 1918. Designated naval aviator in December 1921. Force aviation officer on the staff of Commander Scouting Force 1938-1940. Commanding officer of NAS Kaneche Bay, Oahu February 1941-July 1942, NAS Midway Island July 1942-September 1943 and the *San Jacinto* September 1943-October 1944. Chief of staff and aide to Commander Air Force, Atlantic Fleet October 1944-March 1945. Commanded Carrier Division Twenty-Three March-September 1945. Assignments after the war included command of Carrier Divisions Two and Five April 1947-November 1948, command of First and Seventh Fleets February 1951-April 1953 and Commander Air Force, Pacific April 1953 until retirement as admiral in February 1956. Decorations included the Distinguished Service Medal Silver Star and two Legions of Merit. Died on December 3, 1972.

Mason, Charles Perry (1891-1971) Born on January 12, 1891, in Harrisburg, Pennsylvania. Graduated from Annapolis in 1912 and commissioned in 1914. Qualified as naval aviator in June 1917. Officer in charge of inspection and test of airplanes at NAS Paulliac, France June-November 1918, where he flew the first American built seaplanes powered with single and twin-engined Liberty motors. Commanding officer of NAS Key West January-October 1919. Organized the first seaplane patrol squadron of the Pacific Fleet 1920-1921. Commanding officer of Jacksonville Naval Air Station September 1940-May 1942. Rear admiral in May 1942. Commanding officer of the *Hornet* June-December 1942. Commanded Task Group December 1942-February 1943 then Naval Air Training Center, Corpus Christi July-December 1943. Chief of Naval Air Intermediate Training Command at NAS Pensacola 1943-1944 then commander of Naval Air Training Bases, Corpus Christi September 1944-May 1945. Commander of Naval Air Bases Fourteenth Naval District, Pearl Harbor May 1945-April 1946. Vice admiral upon retirement in April 1946. Decorations included the Navy Cross, Silver Star and Legion of Merit. Died on August 13, 1971.

Mathews, James Thomas (1891-1947) Born on November 6, 1891, in Marion, South Carolina. Commissioned from Annapolis in 1913. C.E. from Rensselaer Polytechnic Institute in May 1918. Treaty engineer in the Republic of Haiti October 1919-January 1921. Public works officer at Naval Operating Base San Diego July 1937-January 1942. Superintendent civil enginer in Area IV, New Orelans 1942-1946. Rear admiral in June 1943. Decorations included the Legion of Merit. Died on December 14, 1947.

Mayo, Arthur Henry (1884-n/a) Born on June 9, 1884, in Ottawa, Ontario. Graduated from the Army & Navy Academy in 1911. Commissioned in the Supply Corps in 1911. Aide on the staff of the military governor of Santo Domingo August 1918-January 1922. Duty in the Bureau of Supplies and Accounts April 1936-March 1940. Supply and accounting officer at NAS San Diego April 1940-January 1943. Supply officer in command of Naval Supply Depot, Oakland January 1943-August 1945. Rear admiral in July 1943. Retired in November 1946. Decorations included the Legion of Merit.

McCain, John Sidney (1884-1945) Born on August 19, 1884, in Carroll County, Mississippi. Graduated from Annapolis in 1906 and commissioned in 1908. Commanding officer of the *Sirius* July-September 1926 and the *Nitro* June 1931-April 1932. Qualified as naval aviator in August 1936. Commander of aircraft squadrons and attending craft at Fleet Air Base Coco Solo, Canal Zone August 1936-May 1937. Commanding officer of the Ranger May 1937-July 1939, NAS San Diego July 1939-January 1941. Rear admiral in February 1941. Commanded Aircraft, Scouting Force January 1941-May 1942 and Aircraft, South Pacific and South Pacific Force May-October 1942. Chief of the Bureau of Aeronautics October 1942-August 1943. Vice admiral in July 1943. Deputy chief of naval operations (air) August 1943-August 1944. Commander of Second Carrier Task Force, Pacific Fleet August 1944-September 1945, where he operated with Admiral Halsey's Third Fleet as Task Force 38. Died at his home in Coronado on September 6, 1945. Posthumous promotion to admiral in September 1945. Decorations included the Navy Cross, three Distinguished Service Medals and the Navy Commendation Medal.

McCandless, Byron (1881-1967) Born on September 5, 1881, in Endicott, Nebraska. Attended the University of Colorado. Graduated from Annapolis in 1905 and commissioned in 1907. Aide to the chief of naval operations May 1915-August 1916 then Secretary of the Navy Josephus Daniels 1916-1917. Commanding officer of the Caldwell 1917-1920 then the *Parrott* and January 1922-August 1923. Instructor at Annapolis August 1923-July 1926. Commanding officer of the *Brazos* May 1927-June 1928. Graduated from the Naval War College in May 1929. Director of the training division in the Bureau of Navigation May 1929-December 1930. Commanding officer of the *Raleigh* December 1930-January 1933. Chief of staff to Commander Destroyers, Battle Force March 1935-January 1937. Commanding officer of the *Rigel* January 1937 until retirement in June 1940. Recalled to active duty in World War II as commandant of Naval Repair Base, San Diego until retirement again in September 1946. Commodore in October 1943. Decorations included the Navy Cross and Legion of Merit. Died on May 30, 1967.

McCann, Allan Rockwell (1896-1978) Born on September 20, 1896, in North Adams, Massachusetts. Commissioned from Annapolis in 1917. Commanding officer of the *K-6* May-September 1920, the *N-4* and *L-3* January 1921-June 1922, the *R-21* June 1922 until her decommissioning in June 1924, the *S-46* October 1926-May 1929 and the *Bonita* August 1931-June 1934. Duty in the design division of the Bureau of Construction and Repair July 1929-July 1931, where he developed a submarine escape apparatus and rescue chamber known as "the bell." Assisted in salvaging the *Squalus* May 1939-April 1941 which sank during a trial run off Portsmouth. Commander of Submarine Squadron Seven, Atlantic Fleet May 1941-January 1943. Rear admiral in March 1943. Commander of Submarine

Squadron Six April-September 1943. Assigned to the fleet main-tenance divison in the office of the CNO September 1943-July 1944. Commanding officer of the *Iowa* July-November 1944. Chief of staff to Commander Tenth Fleet December 1944 until Tenth Fleet was dissolved in June 1945. Commander Task Force 68 June-August 1945 during the presidential trip to Berlin. Assistant chief of staff (operations) to Commander in Chief United States Fleet August-October 1945. Assignments after the war included Commander Submarine Force, Pacific Fleet December 1945-September 1948. Vice admiral upon retirement in May 1950. Decorations included two Legions of Merit, the Bronze Star and Navy Commendation Medal. Died on February 22, 1978.

McCrea, John Livingstone (1891-1990) Born on May 29, 1891, at Marlette, Michigan. Commissioned from Annapolis in 1915. Served aboard the battleship *New York* in World War I. Aide to Admiral Hugh Rodman, commander in chief Pacific Fleet 1919-1921. J.D. from George Washington University in 1929. Aide to the commander of Special Service Squadron 1929-1931 then the judge advocate general of the Navy 1932-1934. Executive officer of the *Pennsylvania* 1938-1940. Aide to Admiral Harold R. Stark, the chief of naval operations October 1940-January 1942. Naval aide to President Roosevelt January 1942-February 1943. Commanding officer of the *Iowa* 1943-1944. Rear admiral in August 1944 (to date from November 1942). Commander of Cruiser Division One 1944-1945. Assignments after the war included deputy chief of naval operations for administration 1946-1947 and deputy commander in chief Pacific Fleet 1948-1949. Retired in June 1953. Decorations included two Legions of Merit. Died on January 25, 1990.

McCullough, Richard Philip (1881-1966) Born on February 14, 1881, in Round Brook, New Jersey. Graduated from Annapolis in 1904 and commissioned in 1906. Commanding officer of the *Lydonia* October 1917-June 1918, the *Machias* June-August 1918, the *Scorpion* May 1919-December 1920, the *Bridge* August 1924-November 1925, the *Argonne* July 1928-June 1929 and the *Arctic* June 1929-February 1930. Member of the Board of Inspection and Survey, Pacific Coast Section September 1931 until retirement in January 1932. Recalled to active duty as district intelligence officer, Twelfth Naval District December 1939-January 1943. Rear admiral in February 1942. Served in the overseas branch, Office of War Information January 1943 until retirement a second time in June 1945. Decorations included the Distinguished Service Medal. Died on February 22, 1966.

McDonnell, Edward Orrick (1891-1960) Born on November 13, 1891, in Baltimore, Maryland. Graduated from Annapolis in 1912 and commissioned in 1914. Awarded the Medal of Honor at Vera Cruz in 1914. Qualified as naval aviator in March 1915. Served with Commander U.S. Forces Operating in European Waters 1917 -1918 in active air combat in France and Italy. Duty at U.S. Naval Headquarters London November-December 1918. Resigned in January 1920 and entered the Naval Reserve. Recalled to active duty in World War II. Naval observer on the first flight of Pan American Airways to New Zealand, Australia and Dutch East Indies August-September 1940. Duty with the chief of the Bureau of Aeronautics October-December 1940. Assistant naval attache in London January-March 1941 then Peking, China May-June 1941. Commanding officer of NAS New York July 1941-February 1943. Rear admiral in December 1942. Chief of staff and aide to Commandant Naval Air Training Center, Corpus Christi June 1943-February 1944. Commanding officer of the *Long Island* May-December 1944 and the *Nehenta Bay* December 1944-November 1945. Vice admiral upon retirement in December 1951. Decorations included the Medal of Honor, three Navy Crosses, the Bronze Star and Air Medal. Killed in a plane crash on January 31, 1960. A destroyer escort, *USS Edward McDonnell (DE-1043)*, was named in his honor.

McFall, Andrew Calhoun (1893-1988) Born on February 6, 1893, in Darlington, South Carolina. Commissioned from Annapolis in 1916. Qualified as naval aviator in November 1920. Instructor at Annapolis June-October 1925. Aide to Admiral Harry E. Yarnell, Commander Aircraft Squadrons, Scouting Fleet 1925-1926. Commanding officer of Torpedo Squadron One July 1929-April 1931. Executive officer of the *Enterprise* July 1938-June 1940. Commander of Patrol Wing Four July 1940-June 1941, NAS Quonset Point, Rhode Island June 1941-October 1942, and the *Hornet* in October 1942. He had reported aboard but not yet assumed command when the aircraft carrier was lost in the Battle of Santa Cruz Islands on October 26, 1942. Rear admiral in February 1943. Commander of Carrier Division Twenty-Two February-July 1943. Chief of Naval Air Operational Training Command at NAS Jacksonville August 1943-February 1945. Commander of Fleet Air Wing Two February 1945 until retirement in March 1946. Decorations included the Legion of Merit. Died on October 25, 1988.

McIntire, Ross T. (1889-1959) Born on August 11, 1889, in Salem, Oregon. Attended the University of Oregon 1907-1912. M.D. from Willamette University in 1912. Commissioned in the Medical Corps Reserve in 1912. Postgraduate studies at Washington University in 1921 and the University of Pennsylvania in 1928. Instructor at the Naval Hospital, Washington, DC 1931-1934. Concurrently White House physician 1935-1938. Rear admiral in December 1938. Surgeon general of the Navy 1938-1946. Vice admiral in February 1944. Retired in April 1947. Decorations included the Distinguished Service Medal. Died on December 8, 1959.

McLean, Heber Hampton (1899-1971) Born on December 9, 1899, in Plano, Texas. Commissioned from Annapolis in 1920. Commanding officer of the *S-45* 1930-1933 and the *Pike* 1935-1938. Duty with the Bureau of Mavigation 1939-1940. Served aboard the *Minneapolis* 1940-February 1941. Assistant operations officer on the staff of Commander in Chief Atlantic Fleet February 1941-May 1942. Commander of a submarine division and squadron then chief of staff to Commander Submarines Southwest, Pacific Fleet May 1942-November 1944. Rear admiral in March 1944. Commanding officer of Submarine Base New London November 1944-December 1945. Vice admiral upon retirement in December 1954. Decorations included three Legions of Merit. Died on September 9, 1971.

McMahon, Frederick William (1898-1986) Born on February 23, 1898, in New Haven, Connecticut. Enlisted service August 1915-June 1916. Comm-issioned from Annapolis in 1919. Designated naval aviator in 1922. Assistant air officer on the *Lexington* June 1938-May 1940. Duty with the Bureau of Aeronautics May 1940-October 1942. Staff officer with Air Force Pacific Fleet October 1942-January 1943. Commanding officer of the *Suwanee* January 1943-January 1944. Commodore in December 1944. Deputy commander of Air Force Pacific Fleet December 1944-September 1945. Assignments after the war included commander of Air Force Atlantic Fleet May 1954-June 1956 and Eastern Sea Frontier June 1956 until retirement as vice admiral in January 1959. Decorations included the Distinguished Service Medal Legion of Merit Bronze Star and Commendation Ribbon. Died on January 26, 1986.

McMillen, Fred Ewing (1882-1959) Born on April 11, 1882, in Springfield, Missouri. Graduated from Annapolis in 1904 and resigned that year. Commissioned in the Supply Corps in 1907. Collector of customs and captain of the port of Petit Goave and Miragoane, Haiti September 1915-May 1916. Duty at the Naval Supply Depot, Naval Operating Base Norfolk, Virginia March 1936-July 1940. Officer in charge of supplies and accounts at First Naval District, Boston July-November 1940. Supply officer at Boston Navy Yard November 1940-December 1942. Rear admiral in December 1942. Chief of the field branch, Bureau of Supplies and Accounts, Cleveland December 1942-January 1946. Retired in August 1946. Decorations included the Legion of Merit. Died on September 17, 1959.

McMorris, Charles Horatio (1890-1954) Born on August 31, 1890, in Wetumpka, Alabama. Graduated from Annapolis in 1912 and commissioned in 1914. Commanding officer of the *Walke* June-July 1919. Instructor at Annapolis September 1925-May 1927. Commanding officer of the *Shirk* May 1927-February 1930 during the second Nicaraguan Campaign then the *Elliott* February-July 1930. Graduated from the Naval War College in May 1938. Operations officer on the staff of Commander Scouting Force, United States Fleet May 1938-October 1939. Operations officer at the Hawaiian Department October 1939-January 1941. War plans officer on the staff of Commander in Chief Pacific Fleet February 1941-April 1942. Rear admiral in May 1942. Commanding officer of the *San Francisco* May-November 1942. Commander of Cruiser Task Force Eight December 1942-June 1943. Chief of staff and aide to Commander in Chief Pacific Fleet and Pacific Ocean Areas June 1943-February 1946. Vice admiral in September 1944. Retired in September 1952. Decorations included the Navy Cross, two Distinguished Service Medals and the Legion of Merit. Died on February 11, 1954.

McNair, Laurance North (1884-1964) Born on May 30, 1884, in Warsaw, New York. Graduated from Annapolis in 1905 and commissioned in 1907. Commanding officer of the *Chauncey* November 1908-September 1911. Instructor at Annapolis January 1912-June 1913. Commanding officer of the *Ericsson* December 1917-May 1918 and the *Chauncey* October 1918-June 1923. Acting chief of staff to Commander Destroyer Squadrons, Battle Fleet June 1923-July 1924. Comm-anding officer of the *Reina Mercedes* July 1924-January 1927. Assistant commandant of Fifteenth Naval District, Balboa, Panama Canal Zone November 1928-June 1930. Commanding officer of the *Richmond* July 1931-April 1933. Naval attache in Rome July 1933-June 1936. Commanding officer of the *Tennessee* 1936-1937. Chief of staff and aide to Commander Destroyers, Scouting Force 1937-July 1938. Graduated from the Naval War College in 1931. Captain of the yard at New York Navy Yard July-December 1940. Retired as captain in June 1941 but continued on active duty. Again naval in Rome March 1941-May 1942. Member of the U.S. Naval Mission to Peru August 1942- February 1946. Rear admiral in February 1943. Retired in March 1947. Decorations included the Navy Cross and Legion of Merit. Died on October 8, 1964.

Meade, Robert Heber (1905-1977) Born on May 8, 1905, in Newark, New Jersey. Attended Stevens Institute of Technology. Commissioned from Annapolis in 1926 and transferred to the Civil Engineer Corps in 1929. M.S. from Rensselaer Polytechnic Institute in 1930. Public works officer at Marine Barracks, Quantico 1934-1937 and Fleet Air Base, Fourteenth Naval District June 1937-May 1939. Served in the aviation section of the Bureau of Yards and Docks May 1939-November 1940. Public works officer at NAS Jacksonville November 1940-March 1942. Officer in charge of construction at Norman, Oklahoma March-October 1942. Executive officer at Naval Construction Centers Camp Allen and Camp Peary October 1942-March 1943. Officer in charge of First and Seventh Naval Construction Brigades April 1943-May 1945. Commodore in April 1945. Assignments after the war included chief of the Bureau of Yards and Docks and chief of Civil Engineers November 1955-December 1957. Retired as rear admiral in August 1959. Decorations included two Legions of Merit and the Air Force Commendation Medal. Died on December 23, 1977.

Mecleary, Howard Blaine (1884-1972) Born on September 1, 1884, in Philadelphia, Pennsylvania. Graduated from Annapolis in 1908 and commissioned in 1910. Instructor at Annapolis September 1914-March 1917. Commanding officer of the *Stewart* March 1923-August 1924. Graduated from the Naval War College in June 1927. Commanding officer of the *Sands* June 1927-June 1928 and the *Omaha* September 1936-November 1937. Chief of staff and aide to Commandant Fourteenth Naval District, Pearl Harbor May 1938 until retirement in July 1939. Recalled to active duty as port director at Fourth Naval District November 1939-June 1940. Commander of the Inshore Patrol at Philadelphia June 1940-May 1941 and at Cape May May 1941-October 1943. Commanding officer of Section Base and U.S. Naval Base Cape May-October 1943 then U.S. Naval Advance Base, Espiritu Santo, New Hebrides December 1943-July 1945. Commodore in

December 1944. Released from active duty in November 1945. Decorations included the Legion of Merit. Died on August 31, 1972.

Melhorn, Kent Churchill (1883-1978) Born on December 9, 1883, in Kenton, Ohio. Attended Ohio Northern University 1901-1902. M.D. from the University of Pennsylvania in 1906. Commissioned in the Medical Corps in 1907. Graduated from Naval Medical School in 1908. Served in the Dominican Campaign with Fourth Regiment, U.S. Marines 1916-1917 and at Port au Prince, Haiti 1920-1922. Director general of Haitian Department of Public Health April 1927-September 1930. Commanding medical officer of the *Relief* March 1935-March 1936. Force surgeon on the staff of Commander Battle Force June 1939-January 1940. Fleet medical officer with Commander in Chief United States Fleet January 1940-January 1941. Assigned to the Bureau of Medicine and Surgery January-April 1941. Medical officer in command of Navy Medical Supply Depot, New York April 1941-March 1946. Rear admiral in September 1942. Retired in April 1946. Decorations included the Legion of Merit. Died in 1978.

Merrill, Aaron Stanton (1890-1961) Born on March 26, 1890, in Stanton, Mississippi. Graduated from Annapolis in 1912 and commissioned in 1914. Commanding officer of the *Harvard* March-June 1919. Aide to Rear Admiral Mark L. Bristol, U.S. High Commissioner at Constantinople, Turkey November 1919-August 1923. Commanding officer of the *McCormick* and the *Elcano* 1924-1926 then the *Williamson* November 1929-June 1932. Aide to the assistant secretary of the navy June 1933-May 1934. Naval attache in Santiago, Chile August 1936-May 1938. Graduated from the Naval War College June 1939. Commander of Destroyer Division Seventeen June 1939-June 1940 then Destroyer Squadron Eight 1940-1941. Professor of naval science and tactics at Tulane University 1941-1942. Commanding officer of the *Indiana* April 1942-February 1943. Rear admiral in February 1943. Commander of Task Force 36.2 February 1943-April 1943 then Commander Cruiser Destroyer Division Twelve April 1943-March 1944. Director of the office of public relations June 1944-April 1945. Vice admiral upon retirement in November 1947. Decorations included the Navy Cross, Distinguished Service Medal, two Legions of Merit and the Navy Commendation Medal. Died on February 28, 1961.

Merring, Harry Lloyd (1888-1965) Born on November 25, 1888, in Rathbone, New York. Commissioned from Annapolis in 1913. Served aboard the *Sampson* in Irish waters during World War I. Commanding officer of the *Hazelwood* April-December 1919, then the *Isherwood* and *Breckinridge* 1927-1930. Commanding officer of the *Nitro* 1938-1939. Retired in July 1939. Recalled to active duty in October 1939. Port director at Thirteenth Naval District 1939-1940 then contracting officer of the Bureau of Ordnance 1940-1946. Rear admiral in November 1944. Released to inactive duty in August 1946. Decorations included the Legion of Merit. Died on December 25, 1965.

Michael, Stanley John (1897-1984) Born on June 30, 1897, in Cincinnati, Ohio. Commissioned from Annapolis in 1919. Designated naval aviator in March 1925. Instructor at NAS Pensacola December 1931-June 1934. Duty in the hydrographic office, Navy Department June 1937-March 1940. Commanding officer of the *Goldsborough* March 1940-June 1941, the *Matagorda* June 1941-July 1942, Patrol Wings Atlantic Fleet July 1942-January 1943 and Fleet Air Wing 12 January-February 1943. Commandant of NAS Jacksonville February-September 1943. Commanding officer of the *Nassau* September 1943-April 1944 and the *Cabot* May 1944-February 1945. Commodore in December 1944. Commander of Naval Air Bases, Twelfth Naval District 1945-1947. Rear admiral upon retirement in July 1949. Decorations included two Navy Crosses and two Legions of Merit. Died on December 12, 1984.

Miles, Arthur Clark (1893-1972) Born on March 9, 1893, in Denver, Colorado. Commissioned from Annapolis in 1916. M.S. from Massachusetts Institute of Technology in June 1920. Designated naval aviator in December 1922. Duty at NAS San Diego July 1937-July 1941. Director of the procurement division, Bureau of Aeronautics 1941-1944. Rear admiral in December 1942. Staff officer with Commander Air Force, Pacific Fleet August-November 1944. Bureau of Aeronautics general representative, Central District, Dayton November 1944-December 1945. Retired as vice admiral in June 1951. Decorations included the Legion of Merit. Died on December 19, 1972.

Miller, Harold Blaine (1903-1992) Born on January 4, 1903, in Newton, Iowa. Commissioned from Annapolis in 1924. Designated naval aviator in November 1926. Executive officer and commanding officer of Patrol Squadron Five June 1938-June 1940. Aide and flag secretary on the staff of Commander Carrier Division One June 1940-February 1941 then Commander Support Force, Atlantic Fleet March-October 1941. Commanding officer of the Flag Unit of the Support Force October 1941-February 1942. Head of the training literature section in the Bureau of Aeronatuics March 1942-Novembver 1943. Naval attache for air in London November 1943-September 1944. Public relations officer on the staff of Commander in Chief Pacific Fleet September 1944-April 1945. Rear admiral in April 1945, the youngest in the U.S. Navy, as director of the Office of Public Relations June 1945-July 1946. Retired in November 1946. Decorations included two Legions of Merit. After retirement he was vice president of Trans World Airlines, director of information at the American Petroleum Institute and director of public relations for Pan American World Airways. Author of *Navy Wings*. Died on May 15, 1992.

Mills, Earle Watkins (1896-1968) Born on June 24, 1896, in Little Rock, Arkansas. Attended the University of Arkansas 1913-1914. Commissioned from Annapolis in 1918. M.S. from Columbia University in 1924. Aide and flag lieutenant on the staff of Commander in Chief United States Fleet September 1930-August 1932. Duty in the design and construction division of the Bureau of Ships 1933-1937. Engineering officer on the staff of Commander Destroyers, Battle

Force June 1937-August 1939. Head of the design and construction division 1939-1940. Assistant naval attache in London 1940-1941. Assistant chief of the Bureau of Ships as rear admiral November 1942-November 1945. Assignments after the war included chief of the Bureau of Ships November 1946-March 1949. Retired as vice admiral in March 1949. Decorations included the Distinguished Service Medal. Died on August 25, 1968.

Mills, George Henry (1895-1975) Born on August 5, 1895, in Rutherfordton, North Carolina. Commissioned from Annapolis in 1918. Designated naval aviator in June 1932. Tactical officer on the airship *Macon,* rescued when lost at sea off Point Sur, California on February 12, 1935. Naval observer aboard German airship *Hindenburg* in August 1936. Gunnery officer on the *Yorktown* November 1936-June 1939. Executive officer then commanding officer at NAS Lakehurst July 1939- July 1941. Commander of Airship Patrol Group One January-December 1942. Commander of Fleet Airships, Atlantic Fleet July 1943-July 1945. Commodore in September 1943. Reverted to captain in July 1945. Retired in July 1949. Decorations included the Legion of Merit. Died on October 24, 1975.

Minter, James Morgan (1882-1943) Born on August 23, 1882, in Monroe County, Georgia. Graduated from the University of the South in 1903. Commissioned in the Medical Corps in 1906. Sanitary engineer of Haiti November 1920-May 1923. Medical officer in command of Naval Hospital Pearl Harbor May 1936-August 1938. Medical officer in command of Naval Hospital San Diego and Hospital Corps School August 1938-August 1940. Assigned to Annapolis August 1940-February 1942. Rear admiral in September 1941. Died on May 11, 1943 while on active duty.

Mitchell, David Wilson (1891-1983) Born on August 24, 1891, in St. Clairsville, Ohio. Attended Ohio Wesleyan University. Commissioned in the Supply Corps in 1917. M.S. from Harvard University in June 1928. Duty at Naval Station St. Thomas 1928-1930. Supply officer on the the the *Nevada* March 1937-June 1939. Served in the Bureau of Supplies and Accounts June 1939-June 1942. Assistant to the supply officer at Boston Navy Yard June-December 1942 then supply officer there December 1942-September 1944. Supply officer for Commander Service Force, Atlantic Fleet September 1944-July 1945. Commodore in April 1945, rear admiral in June 1945. Duty with the general liaison office between the Navy Department and the Branch of Supplies and Procurement July-November 1945. Retired in April 1949. Decorations included the Bronze Star. Died on April 4, 1983.

Momsen, Charles Bowers (1896-1967) Born on June 21, 1896, in Flushing, Queens, New York. Commissioned from Annapolis in 1919. Commanding officer of the *O-15, R-24* and *S-1* June 1923-June 1927. Developed the "Momsen Lung," a submarine safety test unit June 1929-September 1932. Officer in charge of experimental diving at Navy Yard Washington, DC August 1937-September

1939. Commanding officer of the *Sirius* September 1939-October 1941. Duty at Fourteenth Naval District, Pearl Harbor October 1941-July 1942. Assistant chief of staff and war plans officer with Commander Hawaiian Sea Froniter July 1942-February 1943. Commander of Submarine Squadron Two February-November 1943 and Submarine Squadron Four November 1943-June 1944, the first U.S. submarine "wolf packs" to operate in enemy waters. Rear admiral in October 1943. Duty in the office of the chief of naval operations June-December 1944. Commanding officer of the *South Dakota* December 1944-July 1945. Staff officer with Commander in Chief United States Fleet responsible for preparing plans for the invasion of Japan July 1945-October 1945. Assignments after the war included Commander Submarine Force, Pacific Fleet May 1951-May 1953 and Commander Joint Task Force Seven April 1954 until retirement as vice admiral in September 1955. Decorations included the Navy Cross, Distinguished Service Cross, Distinguished Service Medal, three Legions of Merit, the Air Force Commendation Medal and the Navy Commendation Medal. Died on May 25, 1967.

Montgomery, Alfred Eugene (1891-1961) Born on June 12, 1891, in Omaha, Nebraska. Graduated from Annapolis in 1912 and commissioned in 1914. Commanding officer of the *F-1* June-December 1917 and the *R-20* Ocvtobert 1918-September 1920. Designated naval aviator in June 1922. Senior aide on the staff of Commander Aircreaft Squadrons, Scouting Fleet June-October 1924. Commanding officer of NAS Seattle August 1930-May 1932 and NAS Anacostia July 1934-February 1936. Executive officer of the *Ranger* November 1936-June 1938 and NAS San Diego July 1938-July 1939. Head of the flight division in the Bureau of Aeronautics July 193-June 1940. Commanding officer of the *Ranger* June 1940-June 1941. Chief of staff and aide to Commander Aircraft, Atlantic Fleet June 1941-June 1942. Rear admiral in May 1942. Commanding officer of NAS Corpus Christi June-November 1942, Naval Air Training Center November 1942-August 1943, Carrier Division Twelve August 1943-March 1944, Carrier Division Three March 1944-January 1945, Fleet Air West Coast January-July 1945 and Air Force, Pacific Fleet July 1945-August 1946. Assignments after the war included Commander Fifth Fleet August 1946-January 1947. Retired as vice admiral in June 1951. Decorations included the Navy Cross, three Distinguished Service Medals and two Legions of Merit. Died on December 15,1961.

Moon, Don Pardee (1894-1944) Born on April 18, 1894, in Kokomo, Indiana. Commissioned from Annapolis in 1916. M.S. from the University of Chicago in 1921. Officer in charge of the drafting room at the Naval Gun Factory October 1927-July 1929, where he served as U.S. Navy representative on the National Screw Thread Commission. Commanding officer of the *John D. Ford* September 1934-February 1937 and Destroyer Division 15 February-June 1937. Graduated from the Naval War College in May 1938 then staff duty there until May 1940. Commander of Destroyer Division Fifteen June 1940-December 1941 then Destroyer Squadron Eight December 1941-November 1942. Staff officer with Commander in Chief United States Fleet November 1942-January 1944. Commanded a task group of the Eighth Amphibious Force January 1944 until his death in the Mediterranean Area on August 5, 1944. Decorations included the Distinguished Service Medal and Legion of Merit.

Moosbrugger, Frederick (1900-1974) Born on October 9, 1900, in Philadelphia, Pennsylvania. Commissioned from Annapolis in 1923. Submarine qualified in December 1929. Instructor at Annapolis April 1931-June 1934 and June 1937-June 1939. Gunnery officer on the *Tennessee* June 1939-April 1941. Commanding officer of the *McCall* April 1941-May 1942 and Destroyer Divisions 11 and 12 May 1942-September 1943. Staff officer with the Operational Training Center Pacific November 1943-June 1944. Commanded Destroyer Squadron 63 and Commander Destroyer Division 125 August-December 1944. Commodore in April 1945. Commander of Destroyers, Pacific Fleet and Task Flotilla Five May-December 1945. Vice admiral upon retirement in October 1956. Decorations included the Navy Cross, Distinguished Service Medal, Legion of Merit and Navy Commendation Medal. Died on October 1, 1974.

Moran, Edmund Joseph (1893-1957) Born on August 15, 1893, in Brooklyn, New York. Enlisted service 1917-1918. Commissioned in the Naval Reserve in 1918. Active duty 1918-1921. Called to active duty in April 1942 as lieutenant commander. Served at headquarters of Eastern Sea Frontier 1942-1943. Commodore in July 1943. With the War Shipping Administration December 1943-November 1945. Rear admiral in November 1945. Retired in December 1947. Decorations included the Legion of Merit. Died in 1957.

Moreell, Ben (1892-1978) Born in Salt Lake City on September 14, 1892. B.S. from Washington University in 1913. Commissioned in the Civil Engineer Corps in June 1917. Served in the Azores during World War I. Executive officer to the chief engineer, department of public works in Haiti 1920-1924. Attended Ecole Nationale des Ponts et Chausses in Paris 1932-1933. Chief of the Bureau of Yards and Docks as well as the Civil Engineer Corps as rear admiral December 1937-November 1945. Beginning in December 1941 he organized the Construction Battalions, known as the Seabees, whose motto "Can Do" reflected the exceptional effort they put forth in building a variety of naval installations throughout the Pacific during the war. Vice admiral in February 1944. Chief of the Material Division November 1945 until retirement in September 1946. In June 1946 Moreell became the first staff corps officer, and the first officer not a graduate of Annapolis, to be promoted to four-star admiral. Decorations included two Distinguished Service Medals and the Legion of Merit. Died on July 30, 1978.

Morgan, Gail (1893-1973) Born on April 7, 1893, in Porter's Falls, West Virginia. Commissioned from Annapolis in 1916. Designated naval aviator in August 1921. Aide to Commander in Chief Battle Fleet May 1930-August 1932. Graduated from the Naval War College in June 1938. Commanding officer of Fleet Air Base Coco Solo, Canal Zone July 1938-February 1939. Executive officer of the *Saratoga* June 1940-May 1941. Duty in the office of the CNO May-August 1941. Commander of NAS Argentia, Newfoundland and commandant of Naval Operating Base August 1941-December 1942. Commanding officer of NAS Quonset Point December 1942-September 1943. Instructor at the American Embassy in Ankara, Turkey January-August 1944. Commodore in September 1944. Commander of Naval Operating Base Midway September 1944-September 1945. Reverted to captain in October 1945. Retired in June 1949. Decorations included the Bronze Star. Died on December 8, 1973.

Nelson, Roger Eastman (1902-) Born on August 31, 1902, in Ishpeming, Michigan. Graduated from Annapolis in 1922. Recruit training officer at Great Lakes naval Training Station 1939-1941. Navigator on the *Texas* May 1941-August 1942. Executive officer of the *Vulcan, Delta* and *Edward Rutledge* 1942-1943. Commanding officer of Group Four, LST Flotilla Two in European waters February 1943-January 1945. Commander of Naval Operating Base Guam 1945-1946. Commodore in July 1945. Rear admiral in September 1949 upon retirement. Decorations included two Legions of Merit and the Bronze Star. Resides in Carlisle, Pennsylvania.

Newton, John Henry (1881-1948) Born on December 13, 1881, in Pittston, Pennsylvania. Graduated from Annapolis in 1905 and commissioned in 1907. Commanding officer of the *Patterson* 1915-1917. Commanding officer of Destroyer Flotillas, Queens Town, Ireland October 1917-May 1918 and Naval Air Station Whiddy Island, Ireland May-June 1918. Commanding officer of the *Maury* 1918-1919. Graduated from the Naval War College in 1925. Commanding officer of the *Trenton* June 1931-June 1933. Rear admiral in June 1938. Commander of Cruiser Division Four 1939-1940, Cruiser Division Five 1940-1941 and Cruisers, Scouting Force 1941-1942. Deputy Commander in Chief Pacific Ocean Areas then South Pacific Area 1943-1944. Vice admiral in October 1943. Commander of South Pacific Area then inspector general for Pacific Fleet 1944-1945. Retired in May 1946. Decorations included the Navy Cross, Distinguished Service Medal and Legion of Merit. Died on May 2, 1948.

Nibecker, Paul Braids (1898-1980) Born on August 26, 1898, in Independence, California. Commissioned from Annapolis in 1919. M.S. from Massachusetts Institute of Technology in 1923. Duty in the Bureau of Construction and Repair June 1935-June 1939. Production officer at Puget Sound Navy Yard February 1943-December 1946. Rear admiral in October 1943. Retired in July 1954. Decorations included the Legion of Merit. Died on June 30, 1980.

Nicholson, Charles Ambrose, II (1895-1991) Born on April 15, 1895, in Utica, New York. Commissioned from Annapolis in 1919. M.S. from Massachusetts Institute of Technology in 1922. Assembly and repair officer at Naval Air Station Pensacola 1940-1941. Naval observer in London 1941-1942. Duty at Naval Air Station Pearl Harbor March 1942-October 1943. Rear admiral in July 1943. Material officer at Commander Fleet Air Western District 1943-1945. Duty with the Western District 1945-1946. Retired in September 1951. Decorations included the Legion of Merit. Died on July 21, 1991.

Nimitz, Chester William (1885-1966) Born in Fredericksburg, Texas, on February 24, 1885. Graduated from Annapolis in 1905 and commissioned in 1907. Chief of staff to the commander of Submarines, Atlantic Fleet during World War I. Graduated from the Naval War College in 1923. Rear admiral in June 1938 as commander of a cruiser then a battleship division 1938-1939. Chief of the Bureau of Navigation June 1939-December 1941. Admiral in December 1941 as commander in chief of the Pacific Fleet, replacing Admiral Husband E. Kimmel. He exercised command of all land, sea and air forces in the Pacific Ocean areas throughout the war. Fleet Admiral in December 1944. Assignments after the war included chief of naval operations December 1945 until retirement in December 1947. Decorations included four Distinguished Service Medals. Co-author of *Sea Power, a Naval History* (1960). Died on February 20, 1966.

Nixon, Elliott Bodley (1889-1952) Born on October 26, 1889, in New York, New York. Commissioned from Annapolis in 1913. Commanding officer of the *Reid* January-November 1922. Aide to Commander Destroyer Squadrons, Atlantic Fleet 1922-1924. Commanding officer of the *Sicard* 1926-1929. Duty in the office of naval intelligence 1938-1941. Commanding officer of the *Louisville* February 1941-September 1942. District intelligence officer at Seventh Naval District 1942-1945. Chief of staff to Commander Fourth Fleet January-August 1945. Commodore in April 1945. Chief of staff to Commandant Tenth Naval District August 1945 until retirement in June 1949. Died on August 8, 1952.

Noble, Albert Gallatin (1895-1980) Born on December 14, 1895, in Preston, Texas. Commissioned from Annapolis in 1917. Commanding officer of the *Dallas* 1935-1936 and the *Cassin* 1936-1937. Gunnery officer on the staff of Commander Battle Force June 1937-January 1940. Duty with the Bureau of Ordnance 1940-1943. Rear admiral in April 1943. Chief of staff to Commander Amphibious Force, Pacific Fleet 1944-1945. Commander of Amphibious Group Eight March 1945-May 1946. Assignments after the war chief of the Bureau of Ordnance 1947-1950 and chief of naval material 1950-1951. Admiral upon retirement in October 1951. Decorations included the Navy Cross, two Distinguished Service Medals and four Legions of Merit. Died on February 22, 1980.

Noyes, Leigh (1885-1961) Born on December 15, 1885, in St. Johnsbury, Vermont. Graduated from Annapolis in 1906 and commissioned in 1908. Commanding officer of the *Biddle* 1919-1920. Graduated from the Naval War College in 1923. Member of the U.S. Naval Mission to Brazil 1926-1929. Commanding officer of the *Richmond* August 1934-March 1936. Designated a naval aviator in March 1937. Commanding officer of the *Lexington* 1937-1938. Chief of staff to Commander Aircraft, Battle Force 1938-1939. Rear admiral in July 1939. Director of naval communications 1939-1942. Commander of Task Force 16, Pacific Fleet in 1942. His flagship, the carrier *Wasp,* sank on September 15 after being struck by three torpedoes. Senior member of the Board of Inspection and Survey

1942-1946. Vice admiral upon retirement November 1946. Decorations included the Navy Cross, Legion of Merit and Purple Heart. Died on March 24, 1961.

Nuber, Horace David (1894-n/a) Born on July 28, 1894, in Washington, DC. B.A. from Wesleyan University in 1916. Commissioned in the Supply Corps in 1917. Supply officer on the *Texas* 1939-1940 and on the staff of Commander Patrol Force Atlantic Fleet 1940-1941. Fleet supply officer, Atlantic Fleet March-April 1941. Assistant supply officer at Oakland Supply Depot 1941-1942. Office in charge of supply, accounting and disbursing for U.S. naval forces in New Zealand April 1942-March 1943. Assigned to the Bureau of Ships April-June 1943. Served in the Bureau of Supplies and Accounts as purchasing officer, assistant chief and deputy chief 1943-1946. Rear admiral in March 1945. Retired in January 1947. Decorations included the Distinguished Service Medal and Navy Commendation Medal.

Ofstie, Ralph Andrew (1897-1956) Born on November 16, 1897, in Eau Claire, Wisconsin. Commissioned from Annapolis in 1918. Naval aide at the White House 1924-1927. Assistant naval attache in Tokyo August 1935-November 1937. Navigator on the *Enterprise* 1938-1939. Operations officer on the staff of Commander Carrier Division One then Commander Battle Force 1939-1941. Assistant naval attache in London April 1941-March 1942. Aviation officer on the staff of Commander in Chief Pacific Fleet 1942-1943. Rear admiral in July 1943. Commander of Carrier Task Group 22 and Carrier Division 26 in 1944 the Carrier Division 23 in 1945. Chief of staff to Commander Air Force, Atlantic Fleet April-August 1945. Assignments after the war as vice admiral included commander of First Fleet June 1952-March 1953, deputy chief of naval operations for air 1953-1954, and Commander Sixth Fleet December 1954 until his death on November 18, 1956. Decorations included the Navy Cross, two Distinguished Service Medals, the Silver Star and four Legions of Merit.

Oldendorf, Jesse Barrett (1887-1974) Born on February 16, 1887, in Riverside, California. Graduated from Annapolis in 1909 and commissioned in 1911. Commanding officer of the *Decatur* 1925-1927. Graduated from the Naval War College in 1929 and the Army War College in 1930. Commanding officer of the *Houston* 1939-1941. Staff officer at the Naval War College August 1941-February 1942. Commander of U.S. Forces Aruba-Curacao Area February-July 1942. Rear admiral in June 1942. Commander of Naval Operating Base Trinidad 1942-1943, a task force of the Atlantic Fleet May-November 1943 and Cruiser Division Four January-December 1944. Vice admiral in December 1944. Commander of Battleship Squadron One 1944-1945. Assignments after the war included commander of Western Sea Frontier 1947-1948. Admiral upon retirement in September 1948. Died on April 27, 1974.

Overesch, Harvey Edward (1893-1973) Born on January 20, 1893, in Lafayette, Indiana. Attended Purdue University in 1911. Commissioned from Annapolis in 1915. Commanding officer of the *Monocacy* February-June 1929. Served at the

American Legation in Peking, then commanding officer of the *Philip*, navigator on the *Oklahoma* and commanding officer of the *Cuyama* June-1934-June 1937. Brief duty in office of chief of naval operations 1937-1938. Naval attache at the American Legation in Peking April 1938-May 1940. Commanding officer of Destroyer Division Ten, Destroyers, Battle Force June 1940-September 1941 then Destroyer Squadron Five, Pacific Fleet September 1941-June 1942. Commandant of midshipmen at Annapolis June 1942-December 1943. Commanding officer of the *San Francisco* December 1942-March 1945. Served briefly in the Bureau of Ordnance March-May 1945. Commodore in April 1945. Chief of staff and aide to Commander Hawaiian Sea Frontier & Fourteenth Naval District May 1945-January 46. Vice admiral upon retirement in May 1946. Decorations included the Legion of Merit, Bronze Star and two Commendation Ribbons. Died on January 20, 1973.

Owen, George Thomas (1895-n/a) Born on September 15, 1895, in White Pine, Tennessee. Attended George Washington University. Commissioned in the naval reserve in 1918. Active duty 1918-1919. Appointed in Regular Navy in 1921. Commander of Patrol Wing 5, Aircraft, Base Force then commander of Patrol Wing 5, Aircraft Scouting Force September 1937-May 1938. Executive officer, then commanding officer of Fleet Air Base, Coco Solo, Canal Zone 1938-1939. Executive officer of the seaplane tender *Curtiss* 1940-1942. Commanded Patrol Wing 5, Patrol Wings, Atlantic Fleet March-November 1942, Argentia Naval Air Station (Newfoundland) November 1942-January 1943 and Corpus Christi Naval Air Station February 1943-March 1944. Commodore in May 1944. Commander of Fleet Air Wing 15, Port Lyautey Naval Air Station and Fleet Air Wing 5 1944-1945. Reverted to captain in July 1945 and retired in November 1948 as rear admiral. Decorations included the Silver Star and Legion of Merit.

Owen, John Paul (1889-1954) Born on January 29, 1889, in Milford, Missouri. M.D. from Saint Louis University Medical School in 1913. Commissioned in the Medical Corps Reserve in 1915. Transferred to the Regular Navy in 1917. Duty at Naval Hospital Washington, DC March 1936-May 1939. Fleet surgeon on the staff of Commander in Chief Asiatic Fleet June 1939-August 1941. Assigned to the Bureau of Medicine and Surgery August 1941-February 1942. Commanding officer of Naval Hospital Quantico with additional duty as medical aide to the commanding general of Marine Barracks February 1942-October 1942 then Naval Hospital Mare Island November 1942-March 1945. Commodore in April 1945. Medical officer on the staff of Commander Seventh Fleet April 1945-November 1945. Retired as rear admiral in April 1948. Decorations included two Legions of Merit. Died on January 15, 1954.

Pace, Ernest Milton Jr. (1891-1969) Born on April 23, 1891, in Calvert, Texas. Commissioned from Annapolis in 1912. M.S. from Massachusetts Institute of Technology in 1916. Duty in the Bureau of Aeronautics as the first Inspector of Naval Aircraft on the Pacific Coast 1923-1938. Duty with Division Two on the *Yorktown* July 1938-March 1939 then at the Bureau of Aeronautics March 1939-

June 1940. Manager of the Naval Aircraft Factory at Philadelphia June 1940-December 1941. Director of material then special assistant to the chief of the Bureau of Aeronautics, 1941-1944. Rear admiral in May 1942. Bureau of Aeronautics general representative for the Western Division November 1944-August 1945. Member of the Joint Production Survey Committee at Commander in Chief United States Fleet August 1945-October 1945. Retired in July 1948. Decorations included the Legion of Merit. Died on March 6, 1969.

Paine, Roger Warde (1887-1964) Born on September 7, 1887, in Springfield, Ohio. Graduated from Annapolis in 1911 and commissioned in 1913. M.S. from Columbia University in 1920. Commanding officer of the *Delphy* November 1921-July 1922. Designated Engineering Duty Only Officer in 1932. Assistant head, later head of design division in the Bureau of Engineering July 1934-August 1938. Planning Officer at Boston Navy Yard, in charge of design and procurement of material for all Navy Yard built destroyers August 1938-February 1942. Duty in the office of Shore Establishments, Navy Department February-April 1942. Manager of the industrial department at Pearl Harbor Navy Yard May 1942-October 1944. Rear admiral in June 1942. Deputy chief of the production branch, office of procurement and material (later Material Division), in the office of the assistant secretary of the navy November 1944-November 1945. Retired in October 1949. Decorations included two Legions of Merit. Died on May 3, 1964.

Palmer, John Roy (1889-1963) Born on March 30, 1889, in Ethlyn, Missouri. Commissioned from Annapolis in 1913. Commanding officer of the *Moody* January 1921-March 1921. Instructor at Annapolis September 1926-June 1929. Duty at Naval Torpedo Station, Newport March 1937-June 1940. Commanding officer of the battleship *Utah* June 1940-July 1941. Production officer at the U.S. Naval Gun Factory, Washington, DC August 1941-September 1944. Commander of Transport Division 54 November 1944-February 1945. Duty with Training Command, Amphibious Forces Pacific Fleet February-March 1945. Commodore in April 1945. Served at the Bureau of Naval Personnel 1945-1946. Retired in September 1947. Awards included the Legion of Merit. Died on September 29, 1963.

Penn, Albert Miller (1885-1947) Born on September 11, 1885, in Laredo, Texas. Graduated from Annapolis in 1908 and commissioned in 1910. Duty in the planning division of New York Navy Yard 1936-1940. Manager of the yard at Charleston Navy Yard, the first yard to employ women in building and fitting out fighting ships 1940-1943. Rear admiral in May 1942. Manager of Norfolk Navy Yard September 1943-December 1944. Director of the industrial survey division, office of the secretary of the navy December 1944-September 1945. Retired in November 1945 but remained on duty in the Bureau of Ships until May 1946. Died on September 19, 1947.

Pennoyer, Frederick William Jr. (1892-1971) Born on November 11, 1892, in East Orange, New Jersey. Commissioned from Annapolis in 1915. Transferred to the Construction Corps in December 1918. M.S. from Massachusetts Institute of

Technology in 1920. Designated a naval aviator in October 1923. Assistant naval attache in Rome May 1931-May 1934. Assembly and repair officer at San Diego Naval Air Station July 1934-April 1937. Headed the engineering division in the Bureau of Aeronautics May 1937-October 1940. Assistant naval attache for air and special observer at the American Embassy in London October-December 1940. Material officer on the staff of Commander Support Force, Atlantic Fleet March 1941-February 1942. Duty in the office of procurement and material and in the Bureau of Aeronautics March-October 1942. Rear admiral in July 1942. Staff officer with Commander Air Force, Pacific Fleet October 1942-August 1944 then fleet aircraft maintenance officer September 1944-November 1945. Vice admiral upon retirement in July 1950. Decorations included two Legions of Merit, the Air Medal and Navy Commendation Medal. Died on January 21, 1971.

Perry, John (1897-1972) Born on July 29, 1897, in Greenville, South Carolina. Attended Clemson College. Commissioned from Annapolis in 1919. Designated naval aviator in June 1923. Commanded the *Williamson* October 1938-November 1939. Executive officer at Naval Air Station, then duty establishing Naval Air Station Kodiak, Alaska November 1939-March 1941 and commanding officer of NAS Kodiak June 1941-August 1942. Chief of staff to Commander Fleet Air West Coast October 1942-April 1944. Rear admiral in October 1943. Commanding officer of the *Belleau Wood* April 1944-January 1945. Commander of Fleet Air Wing Two, Commander in Chief Pacific Fleet January-July 1945 then Fleet Air Wing One July 1945- January 1946. Assignments after the war included command of Task Force 77 during the Korean War 1951-1952. Vice admiral upon retirement in February 1959. Decorations included the Distinguished Service Medal, Silver Star and Legion of Merit. Died on August 7, 1972.

Perry, John Richard (1899-1955) Born on May 24, 1899, in Waco, Texas. Attended Rice Institute. Enlisted service October 1918-June 1919. Commissioned in the Civil Engineer Corps from Annapolis in 1923. B.C.E. and M.C.E. from Rensselaer Polytechnic Institute June 1925 and June 1927 respectively. Duty at Naval Station Guantanamo Bay November 1927-June 1930, Sixteenth Naval District July 1936-August 1938 and at the Bureau of Yards & Docks August 1938-August 1944. Commodore in October 1944. Officer in charge of 2nd Naval Construction Brigade 1944-1945. Duty on the staff of Commander Service Force Pacific Fleet, deputy commander of Construction Forces Seventh Fleet, then commander of Construction Troops Seventh Fleet until reverted to captain in September 1945. Died of a heart attack on September 25, 1955. Decorations included two Legions of Merit.

Pettengill, George Tilfort (1877-1959) Born on October 25, 1877, in Boise, Idaho. Graduated from Annapolis in 1898 and commissioned in 1900. Served aboard the *New York* and the *Puritan* in the Spanish-American War and in Tientsin during the Boxer Rebellion 1900-1901. Assigned to the British Grand Fleet in World War I. Commander of the Asiatic Destroyer Squadron 1922-1923. Naval attache in Peking 1925-1927. Commanding officer of the *Tennessee* 1928-1929.

Graduated from the Naval War College in 1930. Rear admiral in October 1930. Commander of the Submarine Force, Battle Fleet 1930-1931 then the Mine Force 1931-1932. Commander of the Base Force, United States Fleet 1934-1935. Commander of Battleship Division Two, Battle Force 1935-1936. Commandant of Washington Navy Yard 1936-1941 then Potomac River Naval Command until retirement in November 1941. Recalled to active duty as commander of Naval Ordnance Plant at Charles, West Virginia in November 1942-March 1946. Decorations inluded the Navy Cross and Legion of Merit. Died on January 11, 1959.

Phillips, Wallace Benjamin (1888-1961) Born on November 29, 1888, in Greensboro, North Carolina. Graduated from Annapolis in 1911 and commissioned in 1913. Commanding officer of the *Manley* operating from Queenstown, Ireland during World War I. Commanding officer of the *Laub* July-November 1919. District intelligence officer in the Third Naval District November 1935-June 1937. Graduated from the Naval War College in 1938. Executive officer of the *Arizona* June 1938-September 1939. Operations officer with Commander Base Force September 1939-June 1940. Duty in the office of chief of naval operations June 1940-June 1941. Commanding officer of the *Barnett* June 1941-September 1942. Commanded the transport division, Amphibious Force, Atlantic Fleet September 1942-May 1945. Commodore in October 1943. Commander of Administrative Command, Amphibious Forces, Pacific Fleet 1945-1946. Rear admiral upon retirement in December 1946. Decorations included the Legion of Merit. Died on June 20, 1961.

Phillips, William Kearney (1894-1986) Born on March 11, 1894, in Tullahoma, Tennessee. Commissioned from Annapolis in 1918. Commanding officer of submarines *R-24* June-December 1921, *S-21* 1923-1924 and *S-38* August 1926-March 1928 then the *Peary* March 1928-July 1929. Designated naval aviator in 1931. Intelligence officer at Fifteenth Naval District, Balboa, Canal Zone June 1937-May 1940. Commanding officer of the *Sampson* June 1940-January 1941. Commander of Destroyer Division 53 January-September 1941. Escort commander with Commander Task Force 24 September 1941-May 1942 then commander of Destroyer Division 26 May-June 1942 and Destroyer Squadron 31 June 1942-February 1943. Commanding officer of the *Oakland* July 1943-August 1944. Rear admiral in September 1943. Chief of staff to Commander Cruisers and Destroyers, Pacific Fleet then commander of Cruiser Division 18 August 1944-October 1945. Assignments after the war included chief of staff to Commander in Chief Pacific Fleet September 1952-October 1953 and commander of First Fleet 1953-1955. Admiral upon retirement in August 1955. Decorations included the Distinguished Service Medal, two Silver Stars, two Legions of Merit and two Commendation Ribbons. Died on October 10, 1986.

Pickhardt, Adolf Von Scheven (1891-1947) Born in New York, New York on December 13, 1891. Commissioned from Annapolis in 1913. Commanding officer of the *Peary* July 1929-February 1932. Personnel and material officer at Third Naval District June 196-March 1939. Executive officer of the *New Mexico* then executive officer of the *Detroit* July 1939-December 1940. Brief duty in the office of chief of naval operations December 1940-May 1941. Naval attache in Berlin, Germany May-December 1941. Interned with the American diplomatic group at Bad Nauheim until May 20, 1942. Deputy director of naval intelligence June 1942-May 1944. Staff officer with Commander Hawaiian Sea Frontier May-September 1944. Chief of staff to Commander Naval Forces Germany October 1944-January 1945 then Task Force 124 January-June 1945. Chief of staff to Commander U.S. Naval Forces Northwest African Waters July-September 1945. Commodore in July 1945. Retired in May 1946. Died on June 30, 1947.

Pihl, Paul Edward (1898-1991) Born on July 19, 1898, in Paxton, Illinois. Commissioned from Annapolis in 1920. M.S from Massachusetts Institute of Technology in 1924. Designated naval aviator in August 1928. Engineering officer on staff of Commander Aircraft, Battle Force January-June 1938. Assistant naval attache in Berlin, Stockholm, Copenhagen, the Hague, Oslo and Helsingfors, Finland June 1938-April 1941. Duty in the procurement division, Bureau of Aernoautics 1941-1944. Head of the logistical organization planning unit in the office of chief of naval operations January-November 1944. Commodore in December 1944. Assistant chief of staff for logistics at headquarters of Western Sea Frontier 1944-1946. Reverted to captain in March 1946. Retired in April 1953. Decorations included two Legions of Merit and the Navy Commendation Medal. Died on July 18, 1991.

Pope, Ralph Eaton (1876-1959) Born on December 7, 1876, in Waupaca, Wisconsin. Graduated from Annapolis in 1899 and commissioned in 1901. Served in Mexico 1911-1917 and in Europe during World War I. Commanding officer of the *Martha Washington* in 1919, the *Galveston* in 1921, and the *Antones* 1923-1924. Graduated from the Naval War College in 1927. Commanding officer of the *Memphis* 1927-1929. Assistant chief of the Bureau of Navigation 1931-1932. Chief of staff to Commander Battleships, Battle Force then Commander Battle Force 1932-1934. Rear admiral upon retirement in June 1934. Recalled to active duty in 1942. Decorations included the Navy Cross. Died on May 13, 1959.

Popham, William Sherbrooke Jr. (1892-1977) Born on May 8, 1892 in Perth Amboy, New Jersey. Commissioned from Annapolis in 1914. Commanding officer of submarines *O-6* July 1920-May 1921 and *S-2* May 1921-August 1923 then the *Worden* April-September 1928. Duty in the office of naval intelligence 1937-1940. Commanded Destroyer Division One June 1940-December 1941. Professor of naval science and tactics at the University of North Carolina 1941-1944. Duty with the Amphibious Training Command, Pacific Fleet July-September 1944 then commander of Transport Division 2, Transport Division 32 and Transport Squadron 15 until October 1945. Commodore in May 1945. Rear admiral upon retirement in January 1947. Decorations included the Legion of Merit. Died on August 14, 1977.

Powell, Paulus Prince (1892-1963) Born on April 25, 1892, in Woodview, Virginia. Commissioned from Annapolis in 1913. Aide to Commander Naval Forces Europe 1923-1925. Commanding officer of the *Scorpion* November 1925-August 1926. Operations officer for Commander in Chief Asiatic Fleet 1934-1935. Graduated from the Naval War College in 1937. Member of the U.S. Naval Mission to Brazil July 1937-1939. Executive officer of the *Arizona* September 1939-May 1940 then commanding officer of the *Omaha* June 1940-1941 and the *Mount Vernon* February 1942-October 1943. Chief of staff to Commander Third Amphibious Force 1943-1946. Commodore in October 1944. Rear admiral upon retirement in January 1947. Decorations included two Legions of Merit. Died on July 31, 1963.

Pownall, Charles Alan (1887-1975) Born on October 4, 1887, in Atglen, Pennsylvania. Commissioned from Annapolis in 1912. Temporary command of the *Reid* in April 1914 to convoy Major General Funston's forces to Vera Cruz and serve in the bombardment and occupation of that city. M.S. from Columbia University in 1917. Commanding officer of the *Vedette* and *Roe* in 1918. Aide to Commander Naval Forces Europe in 1918. Commanding officer of the *John D. Ford* in 1921. Designated naval aviator in 1927. Chief of staff to Commander Aircraft, Base Force June 1936-June 1937. Duty at the Bureau of Aeronautics as head of the flight division 1937-1938. Commanding officer of the *Enterprise* December 1938-April 1941 then Norfolk Naval Air Station April 1941-May 1942. Rear admiral in December 1941. Commanded Patrol Plane Replacement Squadrons, Patrol Wings Pacific Fleet May 1942-July 1943 then Carrier Division Three August 1943-January 1944. Commander of Air Force, Pacific Fleet February-September 1944. Chief of Naval Air Training Command, Pensacola 1944-1946. Retired as vice admiral in November 1949. Decorations included the Navy Cross, Distinguished Service Medal, Legion of Merit and Navy Commendation Medal. Died on July 19, 1975.

Price, John Dale (1892-1957) Born on May 18, 1892, in Augusta, Arkansas. Attended the University of Arkansas. Commissioned from Annapolis in 1916. Designated naval aviator in 1920. He made the first night landing aboard a U.S. Navy aircraft carrier and the first cross-deck takeoff while serving aboard the *Langley* in the summer of 1931. Executive officer, then commanding officer of Naval Air Station Anacostia June 1937-May 1939. Commanded Patrol Wing Three on Coco Solo, Canal Zone 1939-1941. Commanding officer of the *Pocomoke* April-July 1941. Commander of Patrol Wing Eight August 1941-May 1942 then Naval Air Station Jacksonville 1942-1943. Rear admiral in February 1943. Commanded Fleet Air Wings Two then One February 1943-July 1945. Commandant of Naval Operating Base, Okinawa July 1945-March 1946. Assignments after the war included commander of Air Force, Pacific Fleet 1946-1948, deputy chief of naval operations (air) January 1948-May 1949, vice chief of naval operations 1949-1950 and chief of Naval Air Training at NAS Pensacola May 1950-June 1954. Admiral upon retirement in June 1954. Decorations included the Navy

Cross, two Legions of Merit and the Distinguished Flying Cross. Died on December 18, 1957.

Purnell, William Reynolds (1886-1955) Born on September 6, 1886, in Bowling Green, Missouri. Graduated from Annapolis in 1908 and commissioned in 1910. Commanding officer of the *Patterson, Lamson* and *Montgomery* 1917-1919 then the *Cuyama* 1934-1936. Secretary of the General Board April 1936-December 1938. Commanding officer of the *New Orleans* January-December 1939. Chief of staff and aide to Admiral Thomas C. Hart, Commander in Chief Asiatic Fleet 1939-1942 then Vice Admiral W.A. Glassford, Commander Naval Forces Southwest Pacific January-April 1942. Rear admiral in November 1941. Commanded U.S. Naval Forces Western Australia May-June 1942. Assistant chief of staff, then deputy chief of staff, office of Commander in Chief United States Fleet June 1942-October 1943. Assistant chief of naval operations (material) 1943-1945. Hospitalized prior to retirement in October 1946. Decorations included the Navy Cross and two Distinguished Service Medals. Died on March 5, 1955.

Pye, William Satterlee (1880-1959) Born on June 9, 1880, in Minneapolis, Minnesota. Graduated from Annapolis in 1901 and commissioned in 1903. Served as fleet tactical and war plans officer, Atlantic Fleet during World War I. Commanded Division 31, Destroyer Squadron Eleven, Battle Fleet 1923-1924 and during the disaster at Point Honda, California on September 8, 1923 in which seven destroyers were lost. Commanding officer of the *Oglala* April 1927-March 1929. Head of the U.S. Naval Mission to Peru March 1929-March 1932. Commanding officer of the *Nevada* April 1932-April 1933. Graduated from the Naval War College in 1935. Director of the war plans division in the office of the chief of naval operations April 1935-June 1936. Rear admiral in June 1936. Assistant to the chief of naval operations 1936-1937. Commander of Destroyers, Scouting Force then Battle Force July 1937-January 1940. Commander of Battleships, Battle Force then commander of Battle Force 1940-1942. Vice admiral in June 1942. President of the Naval War College October 1942-December 1945. Retired in July 1944 but continued on active duty. Decorations included the Navy Cross and Legion of Merit. Died on May 4, 1959.

Pyne, Frederick Glover (1879-1962) Born on June 5, 1879, in Central Falls, Rhode Island. Commissioned in the Supply Corps in 1901. Rear admiral in October 1930. Supply officer at Philadelphia Navy yard 1932-1935 then officer in charge of the Navy Purchasing Office, New York 1935-1938 and the Naval Finance and Supply School in Philadelphia July 1938-February 1941. General inspector of the Supply School 1941-1943. Retired in July 1943 but remained on active duty until December 1944. Died on April 15, 1962.

Quigley, William Middleton (1890-1957) Born on July 9, 1890, in Brooklyn, New York. Commissioned from Annapolis in 1913. Commanding officer of the submarines *A-7* May 1915-April 1916, the *F-3* 1917-1918 and the *O-16* 1918-1919. Commanding officer of the *Delaware* July 1919-April 1921, the *S-2* April

1921-January 1922 and the *Sigourney* in 1922. Aide to Rear Admiral Samuel S. Robison, military governor of Santo Domingo April-November 1922. Commanding officer of the *Argonaut* 1928-1931. Instructor at Annapolis 1935-1937. Commanding officer of the *Holland* 1938-1940. Chief of the U.S. Naval Mission to Peru October 1940-August 1942. Duty with the Amphibious Force, Atlantic Fleet 1942-1943. Commander of Naval Bases South Solomons then Forward Area, Central Pacific May 1943-January 1945. Commodore in October 1943. Commanded Naval Base Port Hueneme 1945-1946. Retired in September 1946. Decorations included the Legion of Merit. Died on April 21, 1957.

Quynn, Allen George (1894-1971) Born on June 16, 1894, in Baltimore, Maryland. Commissioned from Annapolis in 1915. Instructor at Annapolis October 1927-June 1933 then assistant commandant of midshipmen June 1933-June 1936. Commanding officer of the *Mindanao* June 1936-March 1937 then the *Asheville* March 1937-July 1938. Member of the Naval Examining Board 1938-1940. Operations officer then chief of staff to Commander Base Force, Pacific 1940-1943. Duty in the office of the chief of naval operations February-October 1943. Chief of staff to Commander Service Force, Pacific Fleet then Commander Eastern Sea Frontier 1943-1949. Commodore in April 1944, rear admiral upon retirement in June 1949. Decorations included the Distinguished Service Cross and Legion of Merit. Died on June 17, 1971.

Radford, Arthur William (1896-1973) Born in Chicago on February 27, 1896. Commissioned from Annapolis in 1916. Served aboard the *South Carolina* in World War I. Designated a naval aviator in 1920. Commanding officer of Seattle Naval Air Station 1937-1940. Executive officer of the *Yorktown* 1940-1941. Director of aviatioin training in the Bureau of Aeronautics December 1941-April 1943. Rear admiral in December 1942. Commander of the Northern Carrier Group July 1943-May 1944. Assistant deputy chief of naval operations for air May-November 1944. Commander of Carrier Division Six 1944-1945. Assignments after the war included deputy chief of naval operations for air 1946-1947, commander of Second Task Fleet February 1947-January 1948, vice chief of naval operations January 1948-April 1949, commander of the Pacific Fleet 1949-1953, during which time Radford was a prominent and vocal member of the "revolt of the admirals," and chairman of the Joint Chiefs of Staff, the first naval officer to hold the position, July 1953 until retirement in August 1957. Decorations included three Distinguished Service Medals and two Legions of Merit. Died on August 17, 1973.

Ragsdale, Van Hubert (1892-1953) Born on August 9, 1892, in Toccoa, Georgia. Commissioned from Annapolis in 1916. Designated naval aviator in June 1921. Graduated from the Naval War College in 1939. Executive officer of the *Enterprise* June 1939-June 1940. Commanded the utility wing on the *Rigel* June 1940-March 1941. Head of the personnel division, Bureau of Aeronautics March 1941-May 1943. Rear admiral in December 1942. Staff officer with Commander Carrier Division One May-July 1943. Commanded Carrier Division 22 1943-1944 and Fleet Air Alameda July 1944-June 1945. Deputy commander of Western Sea Frontier 1945-1946. Underwent treatment at the Naval Hospital, Bethesda October 1947 until August 1948. Vice admiral upon retirement in August 1948. Decorations included the Legion of Merit and two Commendation Ribbons. Died on October 11, 1953.

Ramsey, DeWitt Clinton (1888-1961) Born on October 2, 1888, at Whipple Barracks, Arizona. Commissioned from Annapolis in 1912. Designated a naval aviator in May 1917. Duty durign World War I as inspection officer at Naval Air Station France and member of the Inter-Allied Armistice Commission. Graduated from the Naval War College in 1937. Fleet aviation officer on staff of Commander in Chief United States Fleet then Commander Battle Force 1937-1938. Executive officer of the *Saratoga* June 1938-April 1939. Duty at the Bureau of Aeronautics as head of the plans division 1939-1941 and assistant chief of the Bureau July 1941-May 1942. Rear admiral in May 1942. Commanding officer of the *Saratoga* and participated in Coral Sea and Midway battles May-October 1942. Commanded a task force, his flag on the *Saratoga*, that included the British aircraft carrier *Victorious* and marked the first time that such units of the two navies had worked together November 1942-August 1943. Chief of the Bureau of Aeronautics August 1943-June 1945. Chief of staff to Commander Fifth Fleet June 1945-November 1945. Assignments after the war included deputy Commander in Chief Pacifc Fleet and Pacific Ocean Areas November 1945-January 1946, vice chief of naval operations 1946-1948, Commander in Chief Pacific Fleet January-April 1948 and High Commissioner of the Trust Territory of the Pacific Islands April 1948 until retirment in May 1949. Decorations included the Navy Cross and two Distinguished Service Medals. Died on September 7, 1961.

Ray, Herbert James (1893-1970) Born on February 1, 1893, in Milwaukee, Wisconsin. Commissioned from Annapolis in 1914. Instructor at Annapolis September 1921 thru June 1923. Commanding officer of the *Farenholt* January-July 1926. Instructor at Annapolis August 1936-June 1938. Graduated from the Naval War College in 1939. Executive officer of the *Quincy* June 1939-March 1941. Chief of staff to Commandant Sixteenth Naval District 1941-1942. Naval advisor and head of war plans on the staff of Supreme Commander Southwest Pacific Area, General MacArthur March 1942-April 1943. He escaped with MacArthur from Corregidor to Mindanao on board a motor torpedo boat. Duty at headquarters of Commander in Chief United States Fleet April-September 1943. Commanding officer of the *Maryland,* one of the "ghosts" of Pearl Harbor which had been repaired and returend to duty with the Pacific Fleet October 1943-December 1944. Deputy director of the naval division, U.S. Group Control Council for Germany in Berlin December 1944-June 1946. Commodore in June 1945. Retired as rear admiral in June 1949. Decorations included the Distinguished Service Medal, two Silver Stars, two Legions of Merit and the Bronze Star. Died on December 3, 1970.

Read, Albert Cushing (1887-1967) Born in Lyme, New Hampshire on March 2, 1887. Graduated from Annapolis in 1907 and commissioned in 1909. Designated a naval aviator in March 1916. Commanding officer of Bay Shore Naval Air Station, then Miami Naval Air Station during World War I. Pilot of one of three Navy-Curtiss seaplanes that took off from Rockaway, Long Island, for a flight across the Atlantic on May 8, 1919. The NC-1 with Lieutenants Patrick N.L. Bellinger and Marc A. Mitscher and the NC-3 with Commander John H. Towers both went down in dense fog near the Azores, but Read in NC-4 made to Lisbon on May 27, setting a record of 53 hours and 58 minutes total flying time in the first transatlantic flight. Graduated from the Naval War College in 1923, then instructor there one year. Commanding officer of the *Saratoga* 1938-1940. Commander of Pensacola Naval Air Station 1940-1941. Rear admiral in December 1941. Chief of air technical training 1942-1944. Commander of Fleet Air, Atlantic Fleet 1944-1945. Retired in September 1946. Decorations included four Navy Crosses, the Distinguished Service Medal and Legion of Merit. Died on October 10, 1967.

Reed, Edward Urbane (1884-n/a) Born on May 1, 1884, in Wilkes Barre, Pennsylvania. Commissioned in the Medical Corps in 1905. M.D. from the University of Pennsylvania Medical School in 1905. Graduated from Naval medical School in 1906. Duty at Naval Station Tutuila, Samoa 1911-1913 and in Haiti with the Marine Expeditionary Force 1915-1916. Served aboard the battleships Ohio and Florida during World War I. Commanding officer of the Naval Hospital on Guam 1922-1925. District medical officer at Twelfth Naval District 1940-1943 then Third Naval District 1943-1945. Rear admiral in June 1943. President of the Naval Retiring Board 1945-1946. Retired in August 1946.

Rees, John Frank (1898-1966) Born on October 9, 1898, in North Vernon, Indiana. Commissioned from Annapolis in 1920. Graduated from the Naval War College in 1933. Commanding officer of the *Flusser* 1938-1940 and the *Cuyama* July 1940-June 1941. Attended Command and General Staff School, Army Air Force School of Applied Tactics and Army and Navy Staff College 1941-1943. Chief of the transportation section on the staff of Commander in Chief Pacific Fleet October 1943-July 1945. Commodore in April 1945. Retired in July 1949. Decorations included the Legion of Merit. Died on November 14, 1966.

Reeves, Joseph Mason (1872-1948) Born in Tampico, Illinois, on November 20, 1872. Graduated from Annapolis in 1894 and commissioned in 1896. Commanded battleships *Maine* and *Kansas* in the Atlantic during World War I. Naval attache in Rome 1919-1921. Graduated from the Naval War College in 1925. Rear admiral in June 1927. Adviser to the U.S. degation at the Geneva Disarmament Conference in 1927. Commander of naval air 1927-1931. Commander of Mare Island Navy Yard in 1932. Commander of Battle Fleet as admiral 1933-1934. Commander in Chief United States Fleet June 1934 until retirement in December 1936. Recalled to active duty in May 1940 to serve on various boards, he was a member of the Roberts Commission that investigated in 1942 the attack on

Pearl Harbor. Retired a second time in 1946. Decorations included the Navy Cross, Distinguished Service Medal and Legion of Merit. Died on March 25, 1948.

Reichmuth, Ferdinand Louis (1884-1978) Born on April 11, 1884, in Beloit, Kansas. Graduated from Annapolis in 1906 and commissioned in 1908. Aide to the governor of Guam September 1908-January 1909. Served in the Bureau of Ordnance throughout World War I. Aide on the staff of Vice Admiral W.R. Shoemaker, Commander Battleship Force, Pacific Fleet July 1921-December 1922. Graduated from the Naval War College in June 1926. Commanding officer of the *Cuyama* July 1926-May 1927. Aide to Commandant Twelfth Naval District July 1928-May 1931. Commanding officer of the *Chaumont* May 1931-April 1933. Chief of staff and aide to Commander Battleships, Battle Force March 1936-May 1937. Commanding officer of the *Mississippi* May 1937-April 1938. Captain of the yard at the Washington Navy Yard May 1938-June 1940. Rear admiral in May 1940. Commander of Destroyers, Atlantic Squadron June-November 1940 then Destroyers, Patrol Force November 1940-February 1942. Vice admiral in February 1942. Commander of Service Force, Atlantic February-August 1942. Commandant of Washington Navy Yard September 1942-November 1945. Retired in August 1946. Decorations included the Legion of Merit. Died on August 16, 1978.

Reifsnider, Lawrence Fairfax (1887-1956) Born on November 26, 1887, in Westminster, Maryland. Commissioned from Annapolis in 1912 .Commanding officer of the submarines *C-1* 1915-1916, *E-2* 1917-1918 and *O-5* October 1918-April 1919. Aide to the superintendent of Annapolis 1925-1928. Commanding officer of the *Corry* 1929-1930, the *Broome* February-October 1930 and the *Evans* October-November 1930. Graduated from the Naval War College in 1936. Officer in charge of public relations, division of naval intelligence 1936-1938. Commanding officer of the *Memphis* January 1938-January 1939. Chief of the U.S. Naval Mission to Colombia 1939-1941. Commander of Transport Division Five October 1941-May 1942 then Transport Division Ten May-July 1942. Commander of Transport Group, South Pacific 1942-1943. Rear admiral in January 1943. Commanded Amphibious Group Four 1944-1945. Vice admiral upon retirement in December 1949. Decorations included the Navy Cross, three Distinguished Service Medals and the Legion of Merit. Died on May 16, 1956.

Reinicke, Frederick George (1888-1969) Born on April 8, 1888, in Tripoli, Iowa. Commissioned from Annapolis in 1912. Served aboard the *Galveston* with the Asiatic Fleet 1913-1916. Commanding officer of the destroyer *Aylwin* 1917-1919, on anti-submarine patrol in the English Channel. Commanding officer of the *Taylor* July-October 1919. Instructor at Annapolis 1919-1921 then manager of athletics 1929-1931. Graduated from the Naval War College in 1932. Commanding officer of the *Tulsa* July 1932-January 1935. Retired in June 1939 but recalled to active duty that October. Port director at the Third Naval District 1939-1945.

Commodore in May 1943. Returned to inactive status in August 1945. Decorations included the Navy Cross and Legion of Merit. Died on November 22, 1969.

Richards, John Kelvey Jr. (1891-1959) Born on April 20, 1891, at Ironton, Ohio. Commissioned from Annapolis in 1914. Served on the *Jacob Jones* when it was sunk on December 6, 1917. Executive officer of the *Jouett* then commanding officer of the *Lamson* December 1918-March 1919, the *Jarvis* May-June 1919 and the *Jouett* June-July 1919. Aide to the governor of Guam July 1925-February 1927. Commanding officer of the *John D. Ford* November 1927-July 1928. Aide and flag secretary to Commander Cruisers, Scouting Force April 1932 until retirement in June 1933. Recalled to active duty in July 1940. Executive officer of U.S. Naval Reserve Midshipmen's School July 1940-July 1941 then commanding officer 1942-1944. Commander of Officer Training Center, New York August 1944-1946. Commodore in September 1944. Returned to inactive duty in 1946. Decorations included the Silver Star. Died on July 24, 1959.

Richardson, Clifford Geer (1892-1987) Born on January 2, 1892, in Attleboro, Massachusetts. Commissioned from Annapolis in 1915. Commanding officer of the submarine *O-10* May 1924-August 1926 and *S-14* October 1928-May 1931. Gunnery officer on the *Tuscaloosa* March 1934-April 1936. Commanding officer of the *Sirius* APril 1936-January 1937. Staff officer with Marine Corps Schools May 1937-August 1939. Executive officer of the *Helena* September 1939-March 1941. Commanding officer of the *Nitro* March-June 1941. Professor of Naval Science and Tactics Naval Reserve Officers Training Corps Unit of Rensselaer Polytechnic Institute June 1941-August 1942. Staff officer with Commander Sixth Amphibious Force August 1942-September 1943. Commanded Transport Divison Eleven September 1943-January 1944, Transport Divison Seven January-October 1944 and Transport Squadron Fourteen October 1944-July 1945 Commodore in November 1944. Reverted to captain in July 1945. Rear admiral upon retirement in July 1949. Decorations included three Legions of Merit. Died on August 26, 1987.

Richardson, Lawrence Baxter (1897-1969) Born on January 13, 1897, in Swampscott, Massachusetts. Commissioned from Annapolis in 1917. Transferred to the Constructions Corps in September 1918. M.S. from Massachusetts Institute of Technology in June 1921. Designated naval aviator in August 1929. Served at the Naval Aircraft Factory in Philadelphia June 1935- May 1938. Director of the procurement division, Bureau of Aeronautics May 1938-July 1941. Duty in the assembly and repair office at NAS San Diego August 1941-November 1942. Material officer at Fleet Air West Coast December 1942-November 1943. Rear admiral in November 1943. Assistant chief of the Bureau of Aeronautics November 1943-March 1946. Retired in December 1946. Decorations included the Legion of Merit. Died on July 6, 1969.

Richey, Thomas Beall (1887-1949) Born on November 24, 1887, in Capon Road, Virginia. Graduated from Annapolis in 1909 and commissioned in 1911.

Transferred to the Construction Corps in June 1912. M.S. from Massachusetts Institute of Technology in June 1914. Officer in charge of the production division at the New York Navy Yard June 1934-June 1941. Rear admiral in November 1941. Manager of Norfolk Navy Yard 1941-1943. Member of the Joint Production Survey Committee and the Technical Industrial Intelligence Committee, Combined Chiefs of Staff October 1943 until retirement in January 1944. Died on March 30, 1949.

Ricketts, James Brewerton (1902-1979) Born on August 11, 1902, in at New Rochelle, New York. Commissioned in 1924. Transferred to the Supply Corps in October 1935. Asstant to the supply officer at NAS Pearl Harbor December 1937-December 1939. Supply officer on the *Tippecanoe* December 1939-January 1941. Disbursing and supply officer on the *Augusta* January 1941-May 1942. Assistant to the aviation supply officer in the Bureau of Supplies and Accounts May 1942-April 1943 and the Naval Aircraft Factory in Philadelphia April-September 1943. Served aboard the carrier *Wasp* September 1943-March 1944. Supply officer at the Naval Operational Training Command, NAS Jacksonville April 1943-June 1945. Commodore in July 1945. Staff officer with Commander Air Force, Pacific Fleet June 1945-June 1948. Retired as rear admiral in July 1961. Decorations included the Navy Commendation Medal. Died on December 13, 1979.

Riggs, Ralph Smith (1895-1981) Born on June 20, 1895, in Paris, Texas. Commissioned from Annapolis in 1917. Commanding officer of *USS EAGLE Number 2* November 1918-March 1919 and the *Zane* April 1933-June 1934. Commanding officer of the *Arctic* June 1938-June 1939. Aide to the assistant secretary of the navy June 1939-October 1941. Commanded Destroyer Division Two, Pacific Fleet November 1941-August 1942 then Destroyer Squadron Fourteen August 1942-July 1943. Rear admiral in June 1943. Chief of staff to Commander Destroyers, Pacific Fleet July 1943-February 1944. Commanding officer of the *South Dakota* March-November 1944. Commander of Cruiser Division Twelve November 1944-January 1946. Vice admiral upon retirement in August 1951. Decorations included the Navy Cross, three Legions of Merit and two Bronze Stars. Died on April 28, 1981.

Ring, Morton Loomis (1894-1963) Born on April 1, 1894, in Athens, New York. Commissioned in the Supply Corps from Annapolis in 1915. Staff officer to the military governor of Santo Domingo July 1922-September 1924. Duty in the Bureau of Supplies and Accounts June 1937-June 1943. Rear admiral in April 1943. District supply officer at Thirteenth Naval District July 1943-July 1944. Chief of the supply section, logistics division on the staff of Commander in Chief Pacific Fleet and Pacific Ocean Areas August 1944-September 1945. Retired in July 1952. Decorations included the Legion of Merit. Died on November 30, 1963.

Robbins, Thomas Hinckley Jr. (1900-1972) Born on May 11, 1900, in Paris, France. Commissioned from Annapolis in 1919. Instructor at Annapolis August

1925-August 1927. Designated naval aviator in December 1928. Commanding officer of the *Sandpiper* October 1933-August 1935. Aviation officer on the staff of the Naval War College May 1937-June 1939. Navigator of the *Lexington* June 1939-November 1940. Aviation officer on the staff of Commander Scouting Force and Commander Task Force Three November 1940-November 1941. Liaison officer between the office of the chief of naval operations and the Commanding General Army Air Forces December 1941-February 1942. Aviation plans officer for Commander in Chief United States Fleet March 1942-January 1943. Chief of staff to Commander Fleet Air Quonset Point January-June 1943. Naval aviation officer on the staff of the Army and Navy Staff College June 1943-November 1944. Rear admiral in December 1943. Temporary duty with Commander Air Force, Pacific Fleet November 1944-January 1945 then commanding officer of the *Lexington* January 1945-November 1945. Retired in January 1962. Decorations included two Legions of Merit and the Army Navy Commendation Medal. Died on December 11, 1972.

Robertson, Marion Clinton (1886-1953) Born on September 30, 1886, in Calvert, Texas. Graduated from Annapolis in 1909 and commissioned in 1911. Graduated from the Army War College in June 1933. Head of the department of ordnance and gunnery at Annapolis June 1937-November 1939. Commanding officer of the *Chicago* December 1939-February 1941. Chief of staff to Commander Scouting Force, Pacific Fleet February 1941-July 1942. Brief duty with Commander Western Sea Frontier March-October 1942. Director of naval officer procurement October 1942-April 1943. Chief of staff to Commandant Fourteenth Naval District April 1943-October 1944. Commodore in April 1944. Duty with the Bureau of Naval Personnel November 1944-March 1945 then Commander U.S. Naval Forces Europe March 1945-November 1945. Rear admiral upon retirement in August 1947. Decorations included two Legions of Merit and the Navy Commendation Medal. Died on November 19, 1953.

Robinson, Arthur Granville (1892-1967) Born on May 21, 1892, in Brooklyn, New York. Commissioned from Annapolis in 1913. Commanding officer of the *Robinson* May 1920-February 1921 and the *Monocacy* and *Palos* 1924-1927. Duty at the Bureau of Ordnance June 1938-March 1940. Commanding officer of the *Marblehead* 1940-1942. Rear admiral in June 1942. Commander of Allied Forces Aruba-Curacao Area June 1942-April 1943 then the Trinidad Sector of Caribbean Sea April 1943-June 1944. President of the Board of Inspection and Survey July 1944-March 1945 then commander of U.S. Naval Ports and Bases Germany March-November 1945. Vice admiral upon retirement in June 1951. Decorations included the Navy Cross, two Legions of Merit and two Commendation Ribbons. Died on February 1, 1967.

Robinson, Robert Edmund Jr. (1898-1977) Born on October 5, 1898, in Galveston, Texas. Commissioned from Annapolis in 1919. Officer in charge of the ordnance design division at the Naval Gun Factory, Washington, DC, March 1940-February 1944. Chief of staff to Commander North Pacific Force and Alaskan Sea Frontier February 1944-September 1945. Commodore in April 1945. Retired in July 1949. Decorations included the Legion of Merit. Died on January 1, 1977.

Robinson, Samuel Murray (1882-1972) Born on August 13, 1882, in Eulogy, Texas. Graduated from Annapolis in 1903 and commissioned in 1905. Served aboard the *Vermont* in the world cruise of the Battle Fleet 1908-1909. Executive officer of the *Jupiter* when she became the first naval vessel to transit the Panama Canal in 1915. Assigned to the design division of the Bureau of Steam Engineering during World War I and again June 1921-April 1927. Engineer-in-chief and chief of the Bureau of Engineering with accompanying rank of rear admiral in October 1936. Senior Member of the Compensation Board April 1938-September 1939. Chief of the Bureau of Engineering for a second term September 1939-June 1940. Upon the consolidation of the Bureau of Engineering and Bureau of Construction and Repair as the Bureau of Ships in June 1940 he became the first chief of the newly established bureau. Vice admiral in January 1942. Chief of the office of procurement and material January 1942-September 1945. Admiral in August 1945. Retired in January 1946. Decorations included the Distinguished Service Medal. Died on January 1, 1972.

Rockwell, Francis Warren (1886-1979) Born on July 28, 1886, in South Woodstock, Connecticut. Graduated from Annapolis in 1908 and commissioned in 1910. Instructor at Annapolis September 1914-March 1917. Commanding officer of the *Winslow* June-December 1918 and the *Thatcher* January-February 1919. Instructor at Annapolis July 1920-June 1924 and again 1926-1929. Commanding officer of the *Robert Smith* and *Dorsey* June 1929-May 1935 then the *Medusa* June 1935-June 1936. Duty in the budget office of the Navy Department June 1936-May 1939. Commanding officer of the *Nevada* May 1939-July 1941. Rear admiral in October 1941. Commandant of the Sixteenth Naval District November 1941-April 1942. Commanded Amphibious Force, Pacific Fleet August 1942-November 1943. President of the Naval Examining Board with additional duty as member of the Board of Decorations and Medals November 1943-March 1944. Commander of the Amphibious Training Command, U.S. Atlantic Fleet March 1944-June 1945. Senior member of the Board of Inspections and Survey, Pacific Coast Section August 1945-April 1948. Vice admiral upon retirement in August 1948. Decorations included the Navy Cross, Distinguished Service Medal, Silver Star and two Legions of Merit. Died on January 2, 1979.

Rodgers, Bertram Joseph (1894-1983) Born on March 18, 1894, in Pittsburgh, Pennsylvania. Commissioned from Annapolis in 1916. Commanding officer of the *H-8* and the *R-8* September 1919-June 1923. Designated naval aviator in June 1928. Commanding officer of the destroyer *Blakeley* 1934-1935 and the *Selfridge* June 1938-July 1940. Graduated from the Naval War College in May 1941. Duty in the war plans division, office of the chief of naval operations May 1941-February 1942 then office of the Commander in Chief United States Fleet February 1942-January 1943. Rear admiral in January 1943. Commanding officer of the

Salt Lake City in 1943. Senior United States planning officer on the staff of Supreme Allied Commander Southeast Asia 1943-1944. Commander of Task Group Twenty Eight, Amphibious Force April 1944-February 1946. Vice admiral upon retirement in April 1956. Decorations included the Navy Cross, two Distinguished Service Medals and the Legion of Merit. Died on December 1, 1983.

Rosendahl, Charles Emery (1892-1977) Born on May 15, 1892, in Chicago, Illinois. Commissioned from Annapolis in 1914. Instructor at Annapolis September 1921-April 1923. Designated naval aviator in November 1924. Commanding officer of the *Los Angeles* May 1926-June 1930 and the dirigible *Akron* October 1931-June 1932. Commanded NAS Lakehurst, New Jersey June 1934-September 1938. Executive officer of the *Milwaukee* September 1938-May 1940. Served in the office of the secretary of the navy May 1940-February 1941 then the office of the chief of naval operations February 1941-April 1942 in connection with lighter-than-air projects. Special assistant to the chief, Bureau of Aeronautics April-September 1942. Rear admiral in July 1942. Commanding officer of the *Minneapolis* September 1942-April 1943. Chief of Naval Airship Training at NAS Lakehurst May 1943-July 1946 where he supervised the building of many blimps used in submarine patrolling along Atlantic and Pacific coasts. Vice admiral upon retirement in November 1946. Decorations included the Navy Cross, Distinguished Service Medal and Distinguished Flying Cross. Retired in November 1946. Died on May 17, 1977.

Rowcliff, Gilbert Jonathan (1881-1963) Born on July 22, 1881, in Peoria, Illinois. Graduated from Annapolis in 1902 and commissioned in 1904. Naval aide at the White House for Presidents Teddy Roosevelt and William Howard Taft November 1908-November 1910. Duty with Commander Battleship Force Two in World War I. Graduated from the Naval War College in May 1920. Instructor at Annapolis June 1925-June 1928. Commanding officer of the *Cincinnati* July 1928-June 1930. Commander of Naval Training Station Newport, Rhode Island July 1930-May 1933 then Destroyer Squadron Four, Battle Force June 1933-June 1934. Director of naval communications June 1934-June 1936. Rear admiral in January 1936. Judge advocate general of the navy June 1936-June 1938. Commander of Cruisers, Scouting Force July 1938-February 1941. Member of the General Board March 1941 until retirement in August 1945. Decorations included the Navy Cross. Died on July 14, 1963.

Rowe, Gordon (1896-1974) Born on January 12, 1896, in Buffalo, New York. Commissioned from Annapolis in 1917. Commanding officer of *Eagle Number 33* November 1918-March 1919. M.S. from Harvard University in June 1924. Designated naval aviator in June 1925. Commanding officer of the *Kane* May 1933-June 1935. Operations officer for aircraft squadrons based at Coco Solo, Canal Zone April 1936-January 1938. Executive officer of the *Wainwright* June 1939-May 1940 then Naval Operating Base Norfolk May 1940-July 1941. Commander of Patrol Wing Four July-December 1941 then NAS Palmyra Island December 1941-August 1942. Air officer on the staff Commander Hawaiian Sea Frontier

August 1942-February 1943. Commanding officer of the *Ranger* February 1943-April 1944. Commodore in April 1944. Commander of Fleet Air Quonset Point April 1944-October 1945. Rear admiral upon retirement in November 1946. Decorations included two Legions of Merit. Died on September 3, 1974.

Royal, Forrest Betton (1893-1945) Born on February 10, 1893, in New York, New York. Commissioned from Annapolis in 1915. M.S. from Massachusetts Institute of Technology in 1924. Administrative aide to the chief of naval operations, Admiral William H. Standley July 1933-May 1936. Commanding officer of the *Porter* August 1936-June 1938. Graduated from the Naval War College in 1939. Member of U.S. Naval Mission to Brazil 1939-1941. Commanded the *Milwaukee* 1941-1942. Rear admiral in October 1942. Served with the Combined Chiefs of Staff 1942-1944. Commander of Amphibious Group Six June 1944-January 1945. Died of a heart attack on board his flagship on June 18, 1945. Decorations included the Distinguished Service Medal.

Royar, Murrey Levering (1894-1985) Born on November 22, 1894, in Los Angeles, California. B.S. from the University of California. Commissioned in the Supply Corps in June 1917. Accounting officer at Navy Yard Cavite, Philippine Islands February 1920-November 1921. M.B.A. from Harvard in June 1924. Supply officer on the *Saratoga* June 1938-April 1940. Senior assistant to the supply officer at Washington Navy Yard May 1940-May 1942. Officer-in-charge of the maintenance division in the Bureau of Supplies and Accounts May 1942-February 1944 then the accounting group of the Bureau February-November 1944. Rear admiral in June 1943. General inspector for the Supply Corps November 1944-April 1945. Assignments after the war included chief of naval material as vice admiral October 1954 until retirement in February 1956. Decorations included the Legion of Merit. Died on December 26, 1985.

Ruddock, Theodore Davis Jr. (1892-1989) Born on December 23, 1892, in Anderson, South Carolina. Commissioned from Annapolis in 1914. Senior aide and operations officer on the staff of Commander Destroyer Flotilla One, Battle Force June 1938-June 1939. Commander of Destroyer Division Six, Battle Force June 1939-July 1940. Director of the production division in the Bureau of Ordnance July 1940-July 1942. Rear admiral in September 1942. Assistant chief of the Bureau of Ordnance July 1942-September 1943. Commanding officer of the *Massachusetts* September 1943-April 1944. Commander of Battleship Division Four April 1944-January 1945. Duty in the office of the vice chief of naval operations April 1945-February 1946. Vice admiral upon retirement in June 1951. Decorations included two Navy Crosses, two Silver Stars, five Legions of Merit, two Bronze Stars and the Purple Heart. Died on August 11, 1989.

Ryden, Roy Warren (1882-1956) Born on February 27, 1882, in Des Moines, Iowa. Graduated from Annapolis in 1903 and commissioned in 1905. Transferred to the Construction Corps in 1906. M.S. from Massachusetts Institute of Technology in June 1908. Attached to Naval Station Olongapo, Philippine Islands

September 1915-March 1918. Superintendent of the mechanical division of the Panama Canal, Balboa, Canal Zone August 1921-June 1924. Graduated from the Naval War College in May 1925. Aide on the staff of Rear Admiral Ashley H. Robertson, Commander Scouting Fleet. May 1927-May 1929. Again superintendent of the mechanical division of the Panama Canal June 1929-July 1934. Graduated from the Army Industrial College in June 1935. Rear admiral in October 1936. Manager of the industrial department at Norfolk Navy Yard October 1936-June 1941. Supervisor of shipbuilding at New York Shipbuilding Corporation, Camden, New Jersey July 1941-January 1946. Retired in August 1946. Decorations included the Legion of Merit. Died on August 16, 1956.

Sallada, Harold Bushnell (1895-1977) Born on January 23, 1895, in Williamsport, Pennsylvania. Commissioned from Annapolis in 1917. Served aboard the *Vermont* in World War I. Designated naval aviator in August 1921. Aide and flag secretary to Commander Aircraft Squadrons Battle Fleet 1930-1931. Executive officer of the *Wasp* April 1940-February 1941. Commanding officer of the *Albemarle* 1941-1942. Director of the planning division, Bureau of Aeronautics April 1942-September 1943. Rear admiral in March 1943. Organized and commanded the Pacific Fleet Amphibious Forces Support Aircraft 1943-1944. Commanded Carrier Divisions 26 and 6 March-November 1944 then the Marshalls-Gilberts Area 1944-1945. Chief of the Bureau of Aeronautics June 1945-May 1947. Assignments after the war included Deputy Commander in Chief Pacific Fleet 1947-1948 and Commander Air Force, Pacific Fleet January 1948-October 1949. Admiral upon retirement in October 1949. Decorations included three Legions of Merit. Died on April 25, 1977.

Sample, William Dodge (1898-1945) Born on March 9, 1898, in Buffalo, New York, the son of Brigadier General W.R. Sample. Commissioned from Annapolis in 1919. Served aboard the *Henderson* and the destroyers *Dixie, Trippe* and the *Wilkes* during World War I and the gunboat *Pampanga* in China in 1922. Designated naval aviator in June 1923. Aide and flag secretary to Rear Admiral John Halligan 1932-1934. Operations officer on the staff of Commander Aircraft, Battle Force 1939-1940. Superintendent of aviation training at Pensacola July 1940-March 1941 then executive officer of Pensacola Naval Air Station 1941-1942. Commanding officer of the *Santee* 1942-1943. Duty at headquarters of United States Fleet March 1943-April 1944. Rear admiral in August 1943. Commanding officer of the *Intrepid* then the *Hornet* April-August 1944. Commanded Carrier Division 27 1944-1945 then Carrier Division 22 February-October 1945. Lost at sea on a flight near Wakayama, Japan on October 2, 1945. Decorations included four Legions of Merit. The destroyer escort *Sample* was named in his honor in 1964.

Schade, Henry Adrian (1900-1992) Born on December 3, 1900, in St. Paul, Minnesota. Commissioned from Annapolis in 1923. M.S. from Massachusetts Institute of Technology in 1928. D.E. from the Technische Hochschule in Berlin in 1937. Duty in the office of the supervisor of shipbuilding at Newport News

Shipbuilding and Dry Dock Company August 1937-December 1941 then the Bureau of Ships January 1942-January 1945. Commodore in December 1944. Headed a Naval Technical Mission to Paris then Germany in 1945. Retired in February 1949. Decorations included two Legions of Merit. Died on August 12, 1992.

Schaeffer, Valentine Hixson (1897-1983) Born on May 29, 1897, in Dayton, Ohio. Commissioned from Annapolis in 1919. Served aboard the *Caldwell* in the Irish Sea during World War I. Designated naval aviator in December 1921. Duty at Fleet Air Base Coco Solo, Canal Zone 1931-1933. Director of the maintenance division at Bureau of Aeronautics June 1939-June 1942. Commanded Fleet Air Wing Eight 1942-1943. Commanding officer of the *Bataan* August 1943-August 1944. Commodore in October 1944. Chief of staff to Commander Seventh Fleet October 1944-May 1945. Reverted to captain after the war. Rear admiral upon retirement in July 1949. Decorations included the Legion of Merit. Died on December 19, 1983.

Schuirmann, Roscoe Ernest (1890-1971) Born on December 17, 1890, in Chenoa, Illinois. Commissioned from Annapolis in 1912. Duty at Sixteenth Naval District, Cavite, Philippine Islands 1922-1923. Commanding officer of the *Mahan* November 1924-October 1927. Technical adviser at the London Naval Conference 1935-1936. Administrative aide to the chief of naval operations 1936-1937. Commander of Destroyer Division Five July 1937-June 1939. Director of the central division, office of the chief of naval operations 1939-1942. Rear admiral in May 1942. Commanding officer of the battleship *Idaho* August 1942-February 1943. Assistant chief of staff to Commander in Chief United States Fleet 1943-1944, duty with Commander U.S. Naval Forces Europe November 1944-April 1945 then deputy commander of Naval Forces Europe (for occupied countries) April-August 1945. Duty with the Bureau of Naval Personnel August 1945-January 1946. Retired in June 1951. Died on July 27, 1971.

Scott, Norman (1889-1942) Born on August 10, 1889, in Indianapolis, Indiana. Commissioned from Annapolis in 1913. Executive officer of the destroyer *Jacob Jones* when it was sunk by an enemy submarine in December 1917. Briefly aboard the *Melville* in January 1918. Naval aide to President Woodrow Wilson September 1918-March 1919. Commanding officer of *Eagle Number Two* then *Eagle Number One* 1919-1920. Duty at Fourteenth Naval District, Pearl Harbor 1921-1923 then aide to the commandant 1923-1924. Aide to Commander Battle Fleet 1924-1927. Instructor at Annapolis 1927-1930. Commanding officer of the *Macleish* and *Paul Jones* 1931-1932. Graduated from the Naval War College in 1935. Member of the U.S. Naval Mission to Brazil February 1937-November 1939. Commanding officer of the *Pensacola* 1939-1942. Duty in the office of the chief of naval operations January-May 1942. Rear admiral in May 1942. Commander of Task Force 18 May-November 1942. Killed aboard *USS Atlanta* during the Battle of Savo Island on November 13, 1942. Decorations included the

Medal of Honor and Purple Heart. The *Norman Scott (DD-690)* was named in his honor in 1943.

Settle, Thomas Greenhow Williams (1895-1980) Born on November 4, 1895, in Washington, DC. Commissioned from Annapolis in 1919. Served aboard the Sampson in Irish waters in the closing months of World War I. M.S. from Harvard in 1924. Commanding officer of the airship *J-3* in 1924. Member of the navy team in the National Elimination Balloon Races 1927-1930, setting a world record for distance of 952 miles in 43 hours and 2 minutes. On Novembr 20, 1933 he set a record for altitude in a balloon of 61,236 feet. Commanding officer of the *Palos* on Yangtze patrol in 1934. Acting consul at Chunking 1934-1935. Commanding officer of the *Whipple* 1935-1937 then fleet communications officer to Commander in Chief Asiatic Fleet 1937-1938. Executive officer of Lakehurst Naval Air Station August 1938-June 1939. Graduated from the Naval War College in May 1940 then a member of the staff there until 1941. Chief of staff to Commander Cruiser Division Two May-July 1941 then Cruiser Division Eight and Cruisers, Atlantic 1941-1942. Duty in the Bureau of Aeronautics May 1942-September 1943. Commanded Fleet Airships, Pacific 1943-1944. Commanding officer of the *Portland* March 1944-July 1945. Rear admiral in August 1945. Assignments after the war included chief of Naval Airship Training and Experimentation 1946-1947, vice chief of naval material October 1949-January 1951 and commander of Amphibious Force, Pacific Fleet 1954-1956. Retired as vice admiral in December 1957. Decorations included the Navy Cross, Legion of Merit and Bronze Star. Died on April 28, 1980.

Shafroth, John Franklin (1887-1967) Born on March 31, 1887, in Denver, Colorado. Graduated from Annapolis in 1908 and commissioned in 1910. Served aboard the *Virginia* in the world cruise of the Battle Fleet in 1908. Executive officer of the *Jenkins* during the occupation of Vera Cruz in 1914. Commanding officer of the *Terry* then commander of Submarine Chaser Detachment Three during World War I. Commanding officer of the destroyers *Waters, Upshur* and *Philip* 1919-1920. Aide to the Commander Special Service Squadron April 1922-July 1923 then the Commander in Chief United States Fleet 1923-1925. Graduated from the Naval War College in 1926 then instructor there until 1927. Commanding officer of the *Reina Mercedes* 1935-1938 then the *Indianapolis* August 1938-August 1940. Rear admiral in November 1941. Assistant chief of the Bureau of Navigation 1941-1942. Commander of Cruiser Division Three January 1942-June 1943. Deputy commander of the South Pacific Area 1943-1944. Inspector general of the Pacific Fleet March-December 1944. Commander of Battleship Division Eight 1944-1945 then Task Group 34.8.1 July-December 1945. Vice admiral upon retirement in April 1949. Decorations included the Navy Cross and four Legions of Merit. Died on September 1, 1967.

Sharp, Alexander Jr. (1885-1975) Born on August 13, 1885, in Washington, DC. Graduated from Annapolis in 1906 and commissioned in 1908. Served aboard the *Minneapolis* during the Cuban Pacification Expedition in 1906 and the

Connecticut in the world cruise of the Battle Fleet 1907-1909. Commanding officer of the *Paul Jones* 1914-1915, the *Downes* September 1918-April 1919 and the destroyers *Bailey* and *John D. Edwards* 1919-1921. Graduated from the Naval War College in 1924. Commanding officer of the *Ludlow* and the *Gamble* 1929-1931, the *Concord* 1933-1935 and the Idaho 1938-1939. Director of the naval districts division, office of the chief of naval operations September 1939-November 1941. Rear admiral in July 1940. Commander of Battleship Division Five 1941-1942, Battleships, Atlantic Fleet April-August 1942, Service Force, Atlantic Fleet August 1942-October 1944 and Minecraft, Pacific Fleet 1944-1945. Retired as vice admiral in September 1946. Decorations included two Distinguished Service Medals. Died on June 20, 1975.

Shelley, Tully (1892-1966) Born on September 9, 1892, in Washington, DC. Commissioned from Annapolis in 1915. Served aboard the *Wyoming* during the world cruise of the Battle Fleet 1907-1909. Commanding officer of the *H-4* in 1921. Instructor at Annapolis 1931-1934. Aide to the Commander Special Service Squadron 1934-1935. Duty in the central division, office of the chief of naval operations 1936-1939. Senior aide to the Commander in Chief Asiatic Fleet June 1939-April 1940. Executive officer of the *Marblehead* 1940-1941. Again in the office of the chief of naval operations September 1941-February 1943. Commanding officer of the Augusta 1943-1944. Assistant naval attache, then naval attache in London 1944-1949. Commodore in April 1945. Rear admiral upon retirement in July 1949. Decorations included the Legion of Merit and Bronze Star. Died on September 6, 1966.

Sherman, Forrest Percival (1896-1951) Born in Merrimack, New Hampshire, on October 30, 1896. Attended Massachusetts Institute of Technology 1912-1913. Commissioned from Annapolis in 1918. Served on the *Murray* and the *Nashville* in European waters during World War I. Qualified as naval aviator in 1922. Graduated from the Naval War College in 1927. Instructor at Annapolis 1930-1931. Fleet aviation officer, United States Fleet 1937-1940. Duty in the office of the chief of naval operations 1940-1942. Commanded the carrier *Wasp* in 1942. Aide and chief of staff to Vice Admiral John H. Towers, commander of the Pacific Fleet Air Forces 1942-1943. Rear admiral in April 1943. Deputy chief of staff to Admiral Chester W. Nimitz 1943-1945. Assignments after the war included deputy chief of naval operations 1945-1948, commander of Sixth Fleet 1948-1949 and chief of naval operations November 1949 until his death on July 22, 1951 from a heart attack while in Naples, Italy. Decorations included the Navy Cross, Distinguished Service Medal and Legion of Merit.

Sherman, Frederick Carl (1888-1957) Born on May 27, 1888, in Port Huron, Michigan. Graduated from Annapolis in 1910 and commissioned in 1912. Commanding officer of the *H-2* 1916-1917 and the *O-7* 1918-1919 on patrol duty in the Atlantic during World War I. Commander of Submarine Division Nine 1921-1924. Graduated from the Naval War College in 1925. Commander of Destroyer

Divisions Eight and One 1933-1934. Aide to the Commandant of Eleventh Naval District 1934-1935. Designated a naval aviator in 1936. Commander of Patrol Wing Three at Coco Solo, Canal Zone 1938-1939. Again graduated from the Naval War College in 1940. Commanding officer of the *Lexington* June 1940-April 1942. The ship was lost at the Battle of the Coral Sea. Rear admiral in April 1942. Assistant chief of staff to the Commander in Chief United States Fleet August-November 1942. Commander of Carrier Task Force Sixteen and Carrier Division Two 1942-1944. Commander of Fleet Air West Coast March-August 1944. Commander of Task Group 58.3 1944-1945. Vice admiral in July 1945. Commander of First Carrier Task Force, Pacific Fleet July 1945-January 1946. Assignments after the war included command of the Fifth Fleet January-September 1946. Admiral upon retirement in March 1947. Decorations included three Navy Crosses, three Distinguished Service Medals and the Legion of Merit. Died on July 27, 1957.

Short, Edwin Thomas (1891-1958) Born on January 4, 1891, in Astoria, Oregon. Commissioned from Annapolis in 1914. Commanding officer of *A-3* August 1915-July 1917, then the *K-8, R-12* and *S-35* 1918-1922. Instructor at Annapolis 1923-1925 and the University of California ROTC 1928-1930. Commanding officer of the *Cushing* 1936-1938. Training officer in the naval reserve division, Bureau of Navigation 1938-1942. Executive officer of the Naval Training Station, Bainbridge October 1942-July 1944. Commander of Transport Divisions 30, 42 and 70 1944-1946. Commodore in April 1945. Reverted to captain and retired as rear admiral in June 1949. Decorations included the Legion of Merit. Died on January 24, 1958.

Short, Giles Elva (1896-1973) Born on March 25, 1896, in Lohrville, Iowa. Commissioned from Annapolis in 1919. Served aboard the *Conyngham* in Irish waters in World War I. Designated a naval aviator in June 1922. Commander of Patrol Squadron Five at Coco Solo, Canal Zone in 1934. Commanding officer of the *Patoka* 1939-1940. Graduated from the Naval War College in 1941 then staff officer there until 1942. Commodore in July 1943. Commanding officer of the *Bogue* September 1942-August 1943. Commander of Naval Operating Base Midway Island 1943-1944. Commanding officer of the *Intrepid* February-December 1945. Rear admiral upon retirement in July 1949. Decorations included the Legion of Merit. Died on July 1, 1973.

Simard, Cyril T. (1895-1976) Born in Pleasanton, California, on August 3, 1895. Enlisted service in the Naval Reserve 1917-1918. Commissioned in the Naval Reserve Flying Corps in 1918 and designated a naval aviator in October that year. Duty as San Diego Naval Air Station 1938-1941. Established and commanded the Midway Island Naval Air Station June 1941-July 1942. Commanding officer of Naval Air Station Whidbey Island 1942-1943 then Naval Air Bases Thirteenth Naval District November 1943-December 1945. Commodore in October 1944. Commander of Fleet Air Wing One 1945-1946. Reverted to captain in March 1946 and retired as rear admiral in January 1947. Decorations included the

Distinguished Service Medal and Navy Commendation Medal. Died on October 29, 1976.

Simpson, Rodger Whitten (1898-1964) Born on June 4, 1898, in Portland, Oregon. Commissioned from Annapolis in 1921. Gunnery officer on the *Memphis* 1939-1941. Commanding officer of the *Mahan* March 1941-March 1943. Commander of Destroyer Squadron Twelve 1943-1944. Duty with San Diego Shakedown Group, Fleet Operational Training Command, Pacific June 1944-April 1945. Commodore in April 1945. Task Flotilla Commander, Destroyers, Pacific Fleet April-November 1945. Commander of Fleet Training Group, Western Pacific February 1946-May 1948. Retired as rear admiral in June 1951. Decorations included two Navy Crosses, the Silver Star and Legion of Merit. Died on December 10, 1964.

Slarrow, Malcolm Gordon (1891-1958) Born on May 18, 1891, in Bel Air, Maryland. B.S. from George Washington University in 1913. Commissioned in the Supply Corps in 1916. Fleet logistics officer with Commander Base Force, United States Fleet 1939-1940, supply officer for Commander Destroyers, Battle Force April 1940-May 1941, supply officer in command of Naval Supply Depot, Naval Operating Base Norfolk 1941-1945. Rear admiral upon retirement in February 1953. Decorations included the Legion of Merit and Navy Commendation Medal. Died on September 29, 1958.

Small, Ernest Gregor (1888-1944) Born on November 5 1888 in Waltham Massachusetts. Commissioned from Annapolis in 1914. Served aboard the *Duncan* in Irish waters during World War I. Instructor at Annapolis 1920-1923. Commanding officer of the *Brooks* 1924-1926. Aide to the Commander Battleship Division Four 1928-1929 and Commander Scouting Force June 1929-May 1931. Commander of Destroyer Division Nine July 1939-March 1940. Instructor at Annapolis 1940-1942. Commanding officer of the *Salt Lake City* April 1942-January 1943. War plans officer on the staff of Commander in Chief Pacific Fleet January-August 1943. Commander of Cruiser Division Five as rear admiral 1943-1944. Hospitalized in August 1944 and died on December 26, 1944. Decorations included the Navy Cross, Distinguished Service Medal and three Legions of Merit. The destroyer *Ernest G. Small (DD-838)* was named in his honor in 1945.

Smeallie, John Morris (1886-1947) Born on September 5, 1886, in Amsterdam, New York. Graduated from Annapolis in 1905 and commissioned in 1907. Commander of Destroyer Division 39 1926-1929. Commanding officer of the *Indianapolis* 1932-1935. Graduated from the Naval War College in 1937. Chief of staff to Commander Scouting Force 1937-1939. Rear admiral in June 1938. Commandant of Sixteenth Naval District May 1939-December 1940. Hospitalized in 1941 and retired in April 1942. Died on November 23, 1947.

Smith, Allan Edward (1892-1987) Born January 19, 1892, in Detroit, Michigan. Commissioned from Annapolis in 1915. Served aboard the *New York* during

World War I. LL.B. from George Washington University in 1930. Aide to Commander Light Cruiser Division Two, Scouting Force 1930-1932. Commanding officer of the *Jacob Jones* June 1932-June 1933. Graduated from the Naval War College in 1938 then member of the staff until September 1939. Commander of Destroyer Division Three June 1940-March 1941. Operations officer for Commander Battle Force 1941-1942. Chief of staff to Commander Task Force One, Pacific Fleet May-September 1942. Duty at headquarters of Commander in Chief United States Fleet 1942-1943. Rear admiral in November 1942. Commanding officer of the *South Dakota* September 1943-March 1944. Commanded Cruiser Division One March-July 1944. Commandant of Seventeenth Naval District July-August 1944. Commander of Cruiser Division Five 1944-1945 then Service Squadron Ten July 1945-January 1946. Assignments after the war included of Cruisers, Atlantic Fleet 1948-1950 and United Nations Blockade and Escort Force, Pacific Fleet September 1950-July 1951. Vice admiral upon retirement in February 1954. Decorations included the Distinguished Service Medal and five Legions of Merit. Died on July 2, 1987.

Smith, Harold Travis (1887-1956) Born on June 7, 1887, in Minneapolis, Minnesota. Graduated from Annapolis in 1909 and commissioned in 1911. Engineering aide to Commander Submarine Force, Atlantic Fleet March-October 1918. Aide to Commander Light Cruiser Divisions, Scouting Force 1930-1932. Assistant supervisor of shipbuilding, then supervisor at Bethlehem Steel Company 1940-1944. Rear admiral in November 1941. Fleet maintenance officer for Commander in Chief Pacific Fleet April 1944-July 1946. Retired in November 1946. Decorations included the Legion of Merit. Died on January 12, 1956.

Smith, Oscar Jr. (1887-1969) Born on January 8, 1887, in Wilkes-Barre, Pennsylvania. Graduated from Annapolis in 1908 and commissioned in 1910. Served aboard the *Machias* during the Vera Cruz occupation in 1914 and the *Virginia* and the *Utah* during World War I. Aide to Commander in Chief Asiatic Fleet 1925-1927. Instructor at Annapolis 1927-1930. Commanding officer of the *Fulton* 1930-1931. Graduated from the Naval War College in 1933. Again instructor at Annapolis 1935-1938. Commanding officer of the *Honolulu* June 1938-July 1940. Duty in the war plans division, office of the chief of naval operations 1940-1941. Officer in charge of Atlantic Fleet School November 1941-February 1942. Again in the office of the chief of naval operations 1942-1943. Commodore in April 1943. Commander of Special Task Force One, United States Fleet April 1943-March 1944 then Special Air Task Force March-December 1944. Deputy chief of staff, then chief of staff to Commander in Chief Atlantic Fleet December 1944-November 1946. Retired in June 1947. Decorations included three Legions of Merit. Died on July 9, 1969.

Smith, William Henry (1895-1971) Born on February 9, 1895, in Boston, Massachusetts. B.S. in civil engineering from Massachusetts Institute of Technology in 1915. Commissioned in the Civil Engineer Corps in 1917. Duty with the Bureau of Yards and Docks 1930-1934, during which time he designed the ARD-1, the Navy's floating dry dock used extensively in World War II. U.S. delegate to the Sixteenth International Navigation Congress in 1935. Public works officer at the New York Navy Yard September 1937-April 1942. Superintending civil engineer for Area II April-October 1942. Chairman of the Facility Reviw Committee of the War Production Board 1942-1943. Duty in the Bureau of Yards and Docks as director of the planning and design department, chief planning officer assistant chief for research and development and director of the Atlantic Division 1943-1948. Rear admiral in April 1945. Retired in March 1948. Decorations included the Legion of Merit. Died on August 21, 1971.

Smith, William Ward (1888-1966) Born on February 8, 1888, in Newark, New Jersey. Graduated from Annapolis in 1909 and commissioned in 1911. Served aboard the *Monterey* during the Chinese revolution in 1912 and the destroyers *Downes* and *Allen* in 1918 in Irish waters. Commanding officer of the *Fairfax* 1919-1920 the *Herbertin* 1920 and the *Williamson* 1923-1925. Aide and flag secretary to Commander Scouting Fleet 1925-1926. Commanding officer of the *Sacramento* 1929-1931. Aide to the Commander in Chief United States Fleet 1935-1936. Duty at Annapolis 1936-1939 as head of the mathematics department. Commanding officer of the *Brooklyn* May 1939-February 1941. Chief of staff to Commander in Chief Pacific Fleet 1941-1942. Commanded Cruiser Task Forces Eleven Eight and Seventeen January-December 1942. Rear admiral in April 1942. Director of Naval Transportation Service January 1943-February 1945. Vice admiral in March 1945. Commander of the Service Force Pacific Fleet March-November 1945. Retired in October 1946. Member, then chairman of the U.S. Maritime Commission October 1946-April 1949. Decorations included the Distinguished Service Medal and Navy Commendation Medal. Died on May 30, 1966.

Snyder, Charles Philip (1879-1964) Born on July 10, 1879, in Charleston, West Virginia. Graduated from Annapolis in 1900 and commissioned in 1902. Instructor at Annapolis 1905-1907 and 1910-1913. Commanding officer of the *Oregon* 1917-1918 the transport *Mongolia* June-September 1918 and the *Minneapolis* 1918-1919. Graduated from the Naval War College in 1925 then member of the staff there until 1926. Commanding officer of the *Argonne,* the *Concord* and the battleship *Tennessee* 1926-1927. Commandant of midshipmen at Annapolis 1928-1931. Chief of staff to Commander Battleships United States Fleet then Commander in Chief United States Fleet August 1932-June 1934. Rear admiral in March 1933. Commanded Cruiser Division Six 1935-1937. President of the Naval War College 1937-1939. Commander of Battleships, Battle Force as vice admiral 1939-1940 then Battle Force as admiral February 1940-April 1941. Member of the General Board 1941-1942. Served as naval inspector general June 1942-April 1946. He retired in August 1943 but continued on active duty until relieved in March 1947. Decorations included the Navy Cross and Distinguished Service Medal. Died on December 3, 1964.

Solberg, Thorvald Arthur (1894-1964) Born on February 17, 1894, in Mason, Wisconsin. Commissioned from Annapolis in 1916. Served aboard the *Tacoma* on escort duty in World War I. M.S. from Columbia University in 1923. Engineering officer on the staff of Commander Battle Force July 1939-April 1941. Duty as special naval observer in London 1941-1944 then in the Bureau of Ships March 1944-October 1946. He was promoted to rear admiral in 1945 with a date of rank in December 1942. Retired in June 1951. Decorations included the Legion of Merit. Died on May 16, 1964.

Soucek, Apollo (1897-1955) Born on February 24, 1897, in Lamont, Oklahoma. Commissioned from Annapolis in 1921. Designated naval aviator in October 1924. Set a world's altitude record for land planes of 43,166 feet on June 4, 1930. Assistant to the chief of the personnel division at the Bureau of Aeronautics 1938-1940. Navigator on the Yorktown May 1940-June 1941 then air officer and executive officer of the *Hornet* October 1941 until the ship was lost in the Battle of Santa Cruz Islands on October 26 1942. Assistant chief of staff for operations to Commander Aircraft, Pacific Fleet January-June 1943. Chief of staff to the Chief of Naval Air Intermediate Training Command then deputy chief of naval air training 1943-1945. Rear admiral in July 1944. Assignments after the war included commanding officer of the *Franklin D. Roosevelt* October 1945-January 1946, commander of Carrier Division Three January 1952-June 1953 and chief of the Bureau of Aeronautics 1953-1955. Hospitalized in February 1955 he retired as vice admiral on July 1 and died on July 22, 1955. Decorations included the Silver Star, two Legions of Merit and the Bronze Star. Died on July 22, 1955.

Sowell, Ingram Cecil (1889-1947) Born on August 3, 1889, in Lawrenceburg, Tennessee. Commissioned from Annapolis in 1914. Commanding officer of the submarine *K-2* on patrol duty in the Azores during World War I. Instructor at Annapolis 1925-1927. Commanding officer of the *Henshaw* and the *Wasmuth* 1927-1930. Graduated from the Naval War College in 1935. Officer in charge of Recruiting Training School 1938-1940. Commanding officer of the Concord January 1940-January 1942. Established and commanded Naval Air Station Farragut Idaho 1942-1943. Rear admiral in April 1943 (to date from September 1942). Commandant of the Naval Operating Base at Bermuda April 1943-October 1944. Commanded Battleship Divisions Five, Four and Three October 1944-June 1946. Died on December 21, 1947, while serving as general inspector of the Atlantic Fleet. Decorations included the Navy Cross and Legion of Merit.

Sprague, Clifton Albert Furlow (1896-1955) Born in Dorchester, Massachusetts, on January 8, 1896. Commissioned from Annapolis in 1918. Served aboard the cruiser *Wheeling* on patrol duty in the Mediterranean during World War I. Designated naval aviator in August 1921. Graduated from the Naval War College in 1939. Commanding officer of the *Tangier* November 1939-June 1942. Air officer on staff of Commander Gulf Sea Frontier 1942-1943. Commanded the second *Wasp* 1943-1944 then Carrier Division Twenty-Five August 1944-August 1945.

Vice admiral upon retirement in November 1951. Decorations included the Navy Cross and four Legions of Merit. Died on April 11, 1955.

Sprague, Thomas Lamison (1894-1972) Born on October 2, 1894, in Lima, Ohio. Commissioned from Annapolis in 1918. Served aboard the *Cleveland* on patrol and convoy duty in World War I. Commanding officer of the *Montgomery* January-November 1920. Designated naval aviator August 1921. Aide to Commander Cruiser Division Three 1931-1932. Superintendent of aviation training at Naval Air Station Pensacola 1937-1940. Executive officer of the *Ranger* June 1940-July 1941. Commanding officer of the *Pocomoke* 1941-1942 and *the Charger* March-December 1942. Chief of staff to Commander Fleet Air Quonset and Commander Air Force Atlantic Fleet 1942-1943. Rear admiral in April 1943. Commanding officer of the *Intrepid* August 1943-March 1944. Commander of Fleet Air Alameda March-July 1944 then Carrier Divisions 22 and 3 July 1944-August 1945. Assignments after the war included deputy chief, then chief of naval personnel 1946-1949 and Commander Air Force, Pacific Fleet as vice admiral 1949-1952. Admiral upon retirement in April 1952. Decorations included the Navy Cross, Distinguished Service Medal, Legion of Merit and Bronze Star. Died on September 17, 1972.

Spruance, Raymond Ames (1886-1969) Born in Baltimore on July 3, 1886. Graduated from Annapolis in 1907 and commissioned in 1909. Served aboard the *Minnesota* in world cruise of the Battle Fleet 1907-1909. Commanded the *Aaron Ward* 1919-1921. Staff officer with U.S. Naval Forces Europe 1924-1925. Graduated from the Naval War College in 1927 then instructor there 1931-1932 and 1935-1938. Rear admiral in December 1939. Commandant at Tenth Naval District 1940-1941. Commanded Cruiser Division Five, Pacific Fleet 1941-1942. Chief of staff, then deputy commander of the Pacific Fleet 1942-1943. Vice admiral in May 1943. Commander of the Central Pacific Area 1943-1945. Admiral in February 1944. Succeeded Nimitz as commander of the Pacific Fleet in November 1945 but relinquished command to Admiral John H. Towers in December in order to become president of the Naval War College. Retired in July 1948. Decorations include the Navy Cross and three Distinguished Service Medals. Served as ambassador to the Philippine Islands 1952-1955. Died on December 13, 1969.

Standley, William Harrison (1872-1963) Born on December 18, 1872, in Ukiah, California. Graduated from Annapolis in 1895 and commissioned in 1897. Staff officer, then commandant of midshipmen at Annapolis 1916-1919. Graduated from the Naval War College in 1921. Rear admiral in November 1927. Director of fleet training 1927-1928. Assistant chief of naval operations 1928-1930. Commander of destroyer squadrons in the Battle Fleet 1930-1931. Commander of cruiser divisions in the Scouting Force 1931-1933. Vice admiral in January 1932. Commander of the Battle Force as admiral May-July 1933. Chief of naval operations July 1933 until retirement in January 1937. Recalled to active duty briefly in 1942 to serve on the Roberts Commission investigating the disaster at Pearl Harbor. Ambassador to the Soviet Union February 1942-September 1943. Recalled to active duty again with the Office of Strategic Services 1944-1945. Decorations included the Distinguished Service Medal. Died on October 25, 1963

Stanley, Emory Day (1881-1968) Born on November 16, 1881, in Hooper, Nebraska. B.A. from the University of Nebraska in 1904. Commissioned in the Supply Corps. Duty at Naval Station Olongapo, Philippine Islands 1911-1913. Fleet supply officer on the staff of Commander in Chief Asiatic Fleet 1936-1938. Adviser to the minister of marines in Peru 1938-1940. Duty at the Bureau of Supplies and Accounts 1940-1941. Supply officer in command of Naval Supply Depot, Bayonne, New Jersey April 1941-December 1945. Rear admiral in September 1942. Retired in December 1945. Decorations included the Navy Commendation Medal. Died on February 8, 1968.

Stark, Harold Raynsford (1880-1972) Born in Wilkes-Barre, Pennsylvania, on November 12, 1880. Graduated from Annapolis in 1903 and commissioned in 1905. Aide to Admiral William S. Sims 1917-1919. Aide to the secretary of the navy 1930-1933. Rear admiral in November 1934. Chief of the Bureau of Ordnance 1934-1937. Commander of Cruiser Division Three in the Battle Force 1937-1938. Commander of all cruisers in the Battle Force, as vice admiral, July 1938-August 1939. Admiral in August 1939. Selected chief of naval operations by President Roosevelt over the heads of more than fifty senior flag officers and served August 1939-March 1942. Replaced by Admiral Ernest J. King following the investigation into the Pearl Harbor in which Stark was severely criticized for not supplying Admiral Husband E. Kimmel with intelligence just prior to the Japanese attack. Commanded U.S. Naval Forces Europe March 1942-August 1943. Retired in April 1946. Decorations included the Distinguished Service Medal. Died on August 20, 1972.

Stevens, Leslie Clark (1895-1956) Born on February 19, 1895, in Kearney, Nebraska. B.A. from Nebraska Wesleyan University in 1913. Commissioned from Annapolis in 1918. Served aboard the *Wyoming, Kansas, Georgia* and *Balch* during World War I. M.S. from Massachusetts Institute of Technology in 1922. Designated naval aviator in August 1924. Assistant naval attache in London 1934-1937. Duty in the Bureau of Aeronautics June 1937-April 1944. Rear admiral in July 1943. Member of the staff of Commander Air Force, Pacific Fleet 1944-1945 and Commander Naval Forces Germany August-December 1945. Assistant chief of the Bureau of Aeronautics for research, development and engineering 1945-1947. Assignments after the war included naval attache in Moscow August 1947-October 1949. Vice admiral upon retirement in August 1951. Decorations included the Legion of Merit. Died on November 30, 1956.

Stone, Earl Everett (1895-1989) Born on December 2, 1895, in Milwaukee, Wisconsin. Commissioned from Annapolis in 1918. Served aboard the *Cleveland* on escort duty during World War I. Aide to Commander Base Force, Pacific Fleet 1919-1923. M.S. from Harvard in 1925. Aide to Commander Battleship Division Four 1926-1928 and Commander in Chief United States Fleet 1930-1932. Commanding officer of the *Long* and the *Aylwin* June 1935-June 1938. Communications war plans officer in the office of the chief of naval operations 1938-1941. Executive officer of the *California* then the *Utah* February 1941-October 1942. Assistant director of naval communications 1942-1944. Commanding officer of the battleship *Wisconsin* April 1944-March 1945. Commodore in April 1945. Assistant chief of staff for communications on the staff of Commander in Chief Pacific Fleet 1945-1946. Retired as rear admiral in January 1958. Decorations included three Legions of Merit and the Navy Commendation Medal. Died on September 24, 1989.

Struble, Arthur Dewey (1894-1983) Born in Portland, Oregon, on June 28, 1894. Commissioned from Annapolis in 1915. Served in the office of the chief of naval operations 1939-1940. Commanding officer of the *Trenton* 1941-1942. Again in the office of the chief of naval operations in 1942-1943. Rear admiral in October 1942. Chief of staff of Task Force 122 in the Twelfth Fleet November 1943-August 1944. Commander of Amphibious Group Two 1944-1945. Assignments after the war included command of the Amphibious Force, Pacific Fleet 1946-1948, deputy chief of naval operations 1948-1950 and commander of the Seventh Fleet May 1950-March 1951. The Seventh blockaded Korea early in the Korean War and supported the landings at Inchon and Wonsan. Commander of the First Fleet 1951-1952 and the Eastern Sea Frontier in 1956. Admiral upon retirement in July 1956. Decorations included the Distinguished Service Cross, Distinguished Service Medal and Legion of Merit. Died on May 1, 1983.

Stuart, Harry Allen (1882-1950) Born on June 16, 1882, in Tazewell, Virginia. Graduated from Annapolis in 1904 and commissioned in 1906. Served aboard the *Vermont* during the world cruise of Battle Fleet 1907-1908. Navigator of the *Louisiana* 1917-1918. Aide to Commander Scouting Fleet 1923-1924. Director of Naval Petroleum Reserve, Navy Department June 1933-June 1944. Rear admiral in May 1939. Retired in March 1943 but continued on active duty until June 1944. Died on June 14, 1950.

Stump, Felix Budwell (1894-1972) Born in Clarksburg, West Virginia, on December 15, 1894. Commissioned from Annapolis in 1917. Aboard the *Cincinnati* in World War I. Designated a naval aviator in 1920. M.S. from Massachusetts Institute of Technology in 1924. Served in the Bureau of Aeronautics 1937-1940. Executive officer of the *Enterprise* 1940-1941. Commanding officer of the *Langley* 1941-1942. Staff officer in the Asiatic Fleet in 1942. Air officer of the Western Sea Frontier 1942-1943. Commanding officer of the *Lexington* in 1943. Rear admiral in May 1943. Commanded Carrier Division Twenty-Four 1944-1945. Chief of naval air technical training June 1945-December 1948. Assignments after the war included commander of Air Force, Atlantic Fleet December 1948-April 1951, Second Fleet 1951-1953 and Pacific Fleet, then commander in chief of the Pacific Command in the reorganization in 1957, until retirement as admiral in August 1958. Decorations included the Distinguished Service Medal, the Silver Star and three Legions of Merit. Died on June 13, 1972.

Styer, Charles Wilkes (1897-1976) Born on May 4, 1897, in Fort Niagara, New York. Commissioned from Annapolis in 1918. Served aboard the *Columbia* during World War I. Commanding officer of the submarines *L-2, L-3* and *K-5* 1920-1922. M.S. from Columbia University in 1924. Commanding officer of the *Cuttlefish* June 1934-May 1937. Commander of Submarine Division 16 December 1939-February 1941. Chief of staff to Commander Submarines Pacific Fleet 1941-1942. Commanded Submarine Squadron Ten August 1942-August 1943. Rear admiral in April 1943. Commanding officer of Submarine Base New London January-November 1944. Commander of Submarines Atlantic Fleet 1944-1946. Retired in June 1948. Decorations included four Legions of Merit. Died on August 20, 1976.

Sullivan, William Aloysius (1894-1985) Born on August 27, 1894, in Lawrence, Massachusetts. Attended Phillips Andover Academy and Massachusetts Institute of Technology. Commissioned in the Construction Corps in 1917. Served at Portsmouth Navy Yard during World War I. Duty in the industrial department at Naval Station Cavite, Philippines 1928-1930. Superintending constructor at Shanghai August 1934-August 1937. Assistant naval attache in London 1940-1941. Head of the salvage section of the Bureau of Ships April 1941-May 1943. Commodore in May 1943. Chief of Navy Salvage 1943-1944. Staff officer with Commander U.S. Ports and Bases France June 1944-February 1945. Officer in charge of clearing the Manila harbor February-August 1945. Rear admiral upon retirement in May 1948. Decorations included the Distinguished Service Medal and Legion of Merit. Died on September 6, 1985.

Taffinder, Sherwood Ayerst (1884-1965) Born on March 18, 1884, in Council Bluffs, Iowa. Graduated from Annapolis in 1906 and commissioned in 1908. Served aboard the *El Occidente* during World War I. Graduated from the Naval War College in 1923. Instructor at Annapolis 1923-1924. Served with the Peruvian Navy 1924-1926. Captain of the port at Balboa, Canal Zone 1927-1930. Commanding officer of the *Sapelo* August 1930-March 1962 and the *Texas* 1935-1936. Director of the ships' movement division office of the chief of naval operations December 1936-May 1939. Chief of staff to Commander Battle Force then Commander in Chief United States Fleet 1939-1941. Rear admiral in July 1940. Commanded Cruiser Division Five February-September 1941. Duty in the office of the chief of naval operations 1941-1942. Commandant of Puget Sound Navy Yard March 1942-October 1943 then Thirteenth Naval District 1943-1944. Vice admiral in December 1944. Commander of Service Force, Atlantic Fleet December 1944-July 1945. Commandant of Fourteenth Naval District 1945-1946. Retired in January 1947. Decorations included three Legions of Merit. Died on January 25, 1965.

Talbot, Frank Russell (1897-1980) Born on November 7, 1897, in Cornwall-on-Hudson, New York. Commissioned from Annapolis in 1921. M.S. from Columbia University in 1928. Instructor at Annapolis 1935-1938 and 1941-1943. Commanding officer of the *George Clymer* July 1943-December 1943. Commander of

Transport Division Eight January-October 1944. Deputy chief of staff of the naval detachment at headquarters Tenth Army 1944-1945. Commodore in April 1945. Reverted to captain in September 1945. Rear admiral upon retirement in June 1951. Decorations included two Legions of Merit. Died on November 2, 1980.

Tarbuck, Raymond Dombill (1898-1986) Born on May 4, 1898, in Pennsylvania. Commissioned from Annapolis in 1921. Commodore in April 1945. Rear admiral upon retirement in July 1950. Decorations included two Legions of Merit and the Navy Commendation Medal. Died on November 15, 1986.

Tarrant, William Theodore (1878-1972) Born on July 28, 1878, in Black Hawk, Mississippi. Graduated from Annapolis in 1898 and commissioned in 1900. Served aboard the *New Orleans* in Cuban waters in the Spanish-American War and the Brooklyn during the Philippine Insurrecton. Instructor at Annapolis 1903-1905 and 1906-1909. Commanding officer of the *Wilhelmina* in 1918 the Oregon January-June 1919 and the *Marblehead* June-August 1919. Aide to the Commandant of Puget Sound Navy Yard 1919-1921. Graduated from the Naval War College in 1922. Commanding officer of the *Baltimore* and the *Ludlow* 1922-1924 then the Arizona 1927-1928. Chief of staff to Commander Scouting Force 1928-1929. Rear admiral in October 1930. Chief of staff to Commander in Chief United States Fleet 1930-1932. Commander of Cruiser Division Four 1932-1933. Commandant of Eleventh Naval District 1933-1936. Commander of the Scouting Force 1936-1938. Commandant of First Naval District 1938-1942. Vice admiral in June 1942. Retired in August 1942. Decorations included the Legion of Merit. Died on July 29, 1972.

Taussig, Joseph Knefler (1877-1947) Born on August 30, 1877, in Dresden, Germany. Graduated from Annapolis in 1899 and commissioned in 1901. Served in the Boxer Rebellion 1900-1901 and in World War I. Served aboard the *Kansas* in the world cruise of Battle Fleet 1907-1908. Aide to his father, Rear Admiral Edward D. Taussig 1908-1909 then Rear Admiral Charles Vreeland 1909-1911. Commanding officer of the *Ammen* July 1911-April 1912, the *Wadsworth* 1915-1917 and the destroyer *Little* 1917-1918. Graduated from the Naval War College in 1920. Commanding officer of the *Great Northern* (renamed the *Columbia*) August 1921-April 1922 then the *Cleveland* 1922-1923. Assistant chief of staff to Admiral Hilary P. Jones, Commander in Chief United States Fleet February-July 1923. Instructor at the Naval War College 1923-1926. Commanding officer of the Trenton 1926-1927. Again at the Naval War College as chief of staff October 1927-May 1930. Commanding officer of the *Maryland* 1930-1931. Rear admiral in July 1931. Chief of staff to Vice Admiral Richard H. Leigh, Commander Battleships, Battle Force then Commander in Chief United States Fleet February 1931-May 1933. Commander of Cruisers, Scouting Force June 1937-May 1938. Commandant of Fifth Naval District 1938-1941. Vice admiral upon retirement in September 1941. Recalled to active duty in 1943 as a member of the Procurement and Review Board and the Naval Clemency and Prison Inspection Board August 1943-October 1946. Decorations included the Distinguished Service Medal. Co-author of *Our Navy: A Fighting Team.* The *Joseph K. Taussig DE-1030* was named in his honor. Died on October 29, 1947.

Taylor, Henry George (1885-1973) Born on June 3, 1885, in Philadelphia, Pennsylvania. Graduated from Annapolis in 1908 and commissioned in the Civil Engineer Corps in 1910. M.S. from Rensselaer Polytechnic Institute in 1913. Served at Naval Station Cavite, Philippines 1928-1931. Public works officer at Norfolk Navy Yard 1934-1938 and Twelfth Naval District 1938-1942. Superintending civil engineer of Area Five, Chicago April 1942-May 1946. Rear admiral in September 1942. Retired in November 1946. Decorations included the Legion of Merit. Died on May 19, 1973.

Thebaud, Leo Hewlett (1890-1980) Born on February 15, 1890, in Madison, New Jersey. Commissioned from Annapolis in 1913. Served aboard the *Wyoming* at Vera Cruz in 1914. Commanding officer of the *Paul Jones* in the Atlantic in World War I and the *Bainbridge* in 1921. Instructor at Annapolis 1922-1925. Commanding officer of the *James K. Paulding* 1926-1928. Aide to Commander Cruiser Division Four Scouting Force 1931-1933. Assistant naval attache in Paris Madrid and Lisbon August 1933-September 1935. Commanding officer of the *Clark* May 1936-June 1938. Duty with the executive department at Annapolis 1938-1940. Commander of Destroyer Squadrons 27 and 13 July 1940-March 1942 then Task Force 24 1942-1943. Rear admiral in June 1942. Commanding officer of the *Boise* February-November 1943. Commanded Cruiser Division 10 1943-1944. Assistant chief of staff for intelligence and director of naval intelligence September 1944-September 1945. Assignments after the war included the naval inspector general September 1946-July 1949. Vice admiral upon retirement in March 1952. Decorations included the Navy Cross, four Legions of Merit and the Navy Commendation Medal. Died on April 18, 1980.

Theiss, Paul Seymour (1890-1956) Born on October 6, 1890, in Washington, DC. Graduated from Annapolis in 1912 and commissioned in 1914. Served aboard the *Allen* in Irish waters during World War I. Commanding officer of the *Paul Hamilton* 1927-1929 and the *Borie* on Yangtze patrol 1929-1931. Commanding officer of the *Fuller* November 1940-December 1942. Commanded Transport Division 14 December 1942-August 1943. Chief of staff to Commander Fifth Amphibious Force Pacific Fleet 1943-1944. Commodore in April 1944. Commander of Amphibious Forces, Pacific Fleet April 1944-October 1945. Rear admiral upon retirement in July 1949. Decorations included the Navy Cross, Distinguished Service Medal and two Legions of Merit. Died on June 3, 1956.

Theobald, Robert Alfred (1884-1957) Born on January 25, 1884, in San Francisco. Graduated from Annapolis in 1907 and commissioned in 1909. Served aboard the Wisconsin on the world cruise of the Battle Fleet 1908-1909. Commanding officer of the destroyer *Walke* 1915-1916 operating with the Marine Force early in the Dominican Republic campaign. Gunnery officer on the *New*

York in World War I. Present at the surrender of the German Fleet at Scapa Flow in November 1918. Commanding officr of the *Radford* then the *Noa* 1922-1924. Graduated from the Naval War College in 1935 then staff officer there until 1937. Chief of staff to Commander Destroyers, Battle Force 1932-1934. Commanding officer of the *Nevada* 1937-1939. Chief of staff to Admiral Claude C. Bloch, Commander in Chief United States Fleet 1939-1940. Rear admiral in September 1940. Commanded Cruiser Division Three Destroyer Flotilla One and Destroyers, Pacific Fleet 1940-1943. Commandant of the First Naval District January 1943-October 1944. Retired in February 1945. Died on May 13, 1957.

Thomas, George Carroll (1881-1957) Born on May 27, 1881, in Lima, Pennsylvania. P.D. from Philadelphia College of Pharmacy and Science in 1902. M.D. from Jefferson Medical College in 1906. Commissioned in the Medical Corps in 1907. Served at the Naval Station on Guam 1914-1916 and Submarine Base New London during World War I. Duty with the First Brigade, U.S. Marines at Port au Prince, Haiti 1924-1926. Medical officer in command of the Naval Hospital Washington, DC December 1935-June 1939, the Naval Hospital at Annapolis 1939-1942 and the Naval Hospital San Diego September 1942-July 1943. Rear admiral in June 1943. District medical officer at Eleventh Naval District 1943-1944. Retired in August 1944 but remained on active duty as chief of the professional division at the Bureau of Medicine and Surgery until April 1946. Decorations included the Navy Commendation Medal. Died on November 17, 1957.

Thomas, William Nathaniel (1892-1971) Born on March 21, 1892, in Rankin County, Mississippi. B.A. from Millsaps College in 1912 and B.D. from Seashore Divinity School in 1914. Ordained in the Methodist Episcopal Church, he held pastorates in Mississippi 1910-1917. Commissioned in the Chaplain Corps in 1918. Assistant chaplain at Annapolis August 1924-October 1927. Served in the Fourteenth Naval District, Honolulu November 1929-July 1932 then aboard the *West Virginia* 1932-1933. Chaplain at Annapolis May 1933-July 1945. Rear admiral in July 1945. Chief of chaplains 1945-1949. Retired in September 1949. Decorations included the Legion of Merit. Died on April 26, 1971.

Tisdale, Mahlon Street (1890-1972) Born on December 6, 1890, in Wenona, Illinois. Graduated from Annapolis in 1912 and commissioned in 1914. Served aboard the cruiser *Salem* at the invasion of Vera Cruz in 1914. Aide and flag secretary to Commander Patrol Force, Atlantic Fleet then Commander U.S. Naval Forces in France during World War I. Aide to the superintendent of Annapolis June 1921-May 1925. Commanding officer of the *Farenholt* 1926-1928. Aide to the assistant secretary of the navy June 1932-May 1933. Commanding officer of the *Vestal* and the *Chester* 1939-1941. Commandant of midshipmen at Annapolis April 1941-May 1942. Rear admiral in May 1942. Commanded Cruiser Task Force Sixteen July 1942-January 1943 then Destroyers, Pacific Fleet January 1943-January 1944. Commandant of Mare Island Navy Yard 1944-1947. Vice admiral upon retirement in November 1947. Decorations included two Navy

Crosses, the Distinguished Service Medal and three Legions of Merit. Died on July 1, 1972.

Todd, Forde Anderson (1881-1971) Born on February 20, 1881, in Anderson, South Carolina. Graduated from Annapolis in 1904 and commissioned in 1906. Served aboard the *Idaho* during the blockade of Mexico and as adjutant of the occupying force at Verz Cruz in 1914. Executive officer of the presidential yacht *Mayflower* and naval aide to the President 1914-1915. Served aboard the *Utah* which operated with the British Grand Fleet during World War I. Commanding officer of the destroyer *Swasey* 1919-1920. Aide to Commander Battleship Division, Battle Fleet 1923-1925. Naval attache in Rome November 1926-October 1928. Graduated from the Naval War College then staff officer there until May 1933. Commanding officer of the *Idaho* 1933-1935. Commandant of midshipmen at Annapolis April 1935-December 1937. Rear admiral in January 1938. President of the General Court Martial Board 1938-1940. Commander of Cruiser Division Eight, Battle Force and commander of Atlantic Squadron then again president of the General Court Martial Board in New York City until retirement in May 1941. Recalled to active duty in World War II May 1942-October 1946. Died on August 5, 1971.

Towers, John Henry (1885-1955) Born in Rome, Georgia, on January 30, 1885. Attended Georgia School of Technology 1901-1902. Graduated from Annapolis in 1906 and commissioned in 1908. Designated a naval aviator in August 1911, the third naval officer to qualify. While stationed at the Navy's first naval air station at Annapolis he set a world endurance record for seaplanes in October 1912. Commanding officer of the naval air unit at Vera Cruz in April 1914. Assistant naval attache in London 1914-1916. Commanded the flight of three Navy-Curtiss seaplanes that took off from Rockaway, Long Island, on a flight across the Atlantic on May 8, 1919. Towers in NC-3 and NC-1, with Lieutenants Marc A. Mitscher and Patrick N.L. Bellinger, were forced down in fog near the Azores but Lieutenant Commander Albert C. Read completed the first transatlantic flight later in the month. Assistant naval attache in London again 1923-1925. Instructor at the Naval War College 1933-1934. Rear admiral in December 1939. Chief of the Bureau of Aeronautics 1939-1942. Vice admiral in October 1942. Commander of the Air Force, Pacific Fleet 1942-1944. Deputy to the commander of the Pacific Fleet in 1944. Commanded Second Carrier Task Force of Task Force 38, then Task Force 38, and finally Fifth Fleet in 1945. Assignments after the war included command of the Pacific Fleet November 1945 until retirement as admiral in December 1947. Decorations included the Navy Cross, Distinguished Service Medal and Legion of Merit. Died on April 30, 1955.

Train, Harold Cecil (1887-1968) Born on October 15, 1887, in Kansas City, Missouri. Graduated from Annapolis in 1909 and commissioned in 1911. Served as executive officer on the *Siboney* on transport duty in 1918. Commanding officer of the *Borie* in 1924. Aide to the Commander in Chief Asiatic Fleet 1924-1925. Commanding officer of the *Parrott* October 1925-July 1926. Naval aide to

President-elect Herbert Hoover during his trip through Central and South America November 1928-January 1929. Aide to the Commander in Chief United States Fleet in 1932. Commanding officer of the *Vestal* June 1936-January 1937. Duty in the Bureau of Navigation 1937-1940. Commanding officer of the *Arizona* February 1940-February 1941. Chief of staff to the Commander Battle Force 1941-1943. Rear admiral in March 1942. Commandant of Fifteenth Naval District September 1943-June 1944. Duty with the Joint Post-War Committee of the Joint Chiefs of Staff 1944-1946. Retired in May 1946. Decorations included two Legions of Merit and the Navy Commendation Medal. Died on September 7, 1968.

Trexel, Carl Alvin (1892-n/a) Born on May 4, 1892, in Des Moines, Iowa. Attended the University of Iowa. Commissioned in the Civil Engineer Corps in 1917. Duty at Port au Prince 1920-1923 as assistant to the engineer in chief of Haiti. Public works officer at the Cavite Naval Station, Philippines 1928-1932. Duty at the Bureau of Yards and Docks November 1936-December 1942 then the logistics plans division office of the chief of naval operations 1942-1944. Rear admiral in January 1943. Director of the Alaskan Division Bureau of Yards and Docks September 1944-1947. Decorations included the Legion of Merit and two Navy Commendation Medals. Retired in April 1950.

Turner, Richmond Kelly (1885-1961) Born in Portland, Oregon, on May 22, 1885. Graduated from Annapolis in 1908 and commissioned in 1910. Served aboard several battleships in World War I. Designated a naval aviator in 1927. Member of the staff at the Naval War College 1935-1938. Commanding officer of the *Astoria* 1938-1940. Director of the war plans division in the Navy Department 1940-1942. Rear admiral in December 1941. Commanded amphibious forces in the South Pacific area 1942-1943. On August 9, 1942, Turner's forces were attacked by a Japanese task group near Savo Island and within a half hour four cruisers were lost, one of the worst defeats the Navy has suffered. Commander of Fifth Amphibious Force in the Central Pacific area 1943-1945. Planned and executed amphibious landings including Tarawa, Kwajalein, Guam, Iwo Jima and Okinawa. Vice admiral in February 1944. Commander of Amphibious Forces, Pacific in 1945. Admiral in May 1945. U.S. naval representative on the United Nations military staff committee 1945-1947. Retired in July 1947. Decorations included the Navy Cross and four Distinguished Service Medals. Died on February 12, 1961.

Van Deurs, George (1901-1984) Born on July 25, 1901, in Portland, Oregon. Commissioned from Annapolis in 1921. Designated naval aviator in January 1924. Served at the Asiatic Station September 1929-June 1932 including duty aboard the *Jason* on Yangtze patrol. Commanding officer of Patrol Squadron 23 at Pearl Harbor March 1939-August 1941. Assistant superintendent, then superintendent of aviation training at Corpus Christi Naval Air Station 1941-1943. Duty with the Commander Air Force, South Pacific as plans officer then chief of staff May 1943-May 1945. Commodore in April 1945. Chief of staff to Commander Battleship Squadron One 1945-1946. Rear admiral upon retirement in June 1951.

Decorations included three Legions of Merit and the Navy Commendation Medal. Died on August 6, 1984.

Van Hook, Clifford Evans (1886-1975) Born on April 10, 1886, in Washington DC. Graduated from Annapolis in 1909 and commissioned in 1911. Served aboard the *New Jersey* during the invasion of Vera Cruz in 1914 and served as adjutant of the adjutant of the ship's Landing Force Battalion during the occupation. Instructor at Annapolis 1915-1917. Executive officer of the *Cushing* and commanding officer of the *Lamson* during World War I. Commanding officer of the *Cowell* March-December 1919 and the *Breck* December 1919-July 1921. Aide to the president of the Naval War College December 1921-June 1923. Member of the U.S. Naval Mission to Brazil 1927-1931. Graduated from the Army War College in 1934. Commanding officer of the hospital ship *Relief* February-October 1937 then the *Portland* June 1940-January 1942. Rear admiral in November 1941. Commandant of Naval Operating Base Balboa, Canal Zone 1942-1943. Deputy commander of Seventh Fleet November 1943-November 1945. Retired in May 1948. Decorations included the Navy Cross, two Distinguished Service Medals and the Legion of Merit. Died on November 28, 1975.

Van Keuren, Alexander H. (1881-1966) Born on March 9, 1881, in Howell, Michigan. Graduated from Annapolis in 1903 and commissioned in 1905. Transferred to the Construction Corps in 1906. M.S. from Massachusetts Institute of Technology in 1908. Graduated from the Naval War College in 1926. Rear admiral in July 1936. Superintending constructor at the New York Shipbuilding Corporation 1936-1937. Industrial manager of the Philadelphia Navy Yard April 1937-September 1939. Chief of the Bureau of Construction and Repair 1939-1940 then assistant chief of the Bureau of Ships June 1940-December 1941. Chief of the Bureau of Ships January-October 1942. Director of the Naval Research Laboratory, Washington, DC 1942-1945. Retired in April 1945. Decorations included the Legion of Merit. Died on July 4, 1966.

Vernou, Walter Newhall (1878-1955) Born on February 10, 1878, at Fort Leonard, Kansas. Graduated from Annapolis in 1901 and commissioned in 1903. Served as a Naval Cadet aboard the *Newark* during the Spanish-American War. Instructor at Annapolis 1906-1906. Commanding officer of the *Beale* 1914-1917 then the *Sigourney* May-August 1918 and October 1918-January 1919. Again instructor at Annapolis 1919-1921. Chief of staff to Commander in Chief Asiatic Fleet 1925-1927. Staff officer at the Naval War College October 1927-May 1930. Commanding officer of the *Northampton* 1930-1932. Naval aide to the President of the United States 1932-1934. Rear admiral in September 1934. Graduated from the Naval War College in 1935. Commander of Cruiser Division Three, Battle Force March 1935-June 1936 then Cruisers, Battle Force 1936-1937. Commandant of Fifteenth Naval District September 1937-August 1939. Commander of Battleship Division Two 1939-1941. Senior member of the Board of Inspection and Survey Pacific Coast Section January 1941-January 1942. Vice admiral upon retirement in March 1942. Decorations included the Distinguished Service Medal. Died on May 23, 1955.

Vickery, Howard Leroy (1892-1946) Born in Bellevue, Ohio, on April 20, 1892. Commissioned from Annapolis in 1915. Served aboard the *Charleston* in World War I. M.S. from Massachusetts Institute of Technology in 1921. Graduated from the Army Industrial College in 1934. Staff member, then assistant to the chairman, finally a member and vice chairman of the U.S. Maritime Commission 1937-1945. Rear admiral in February 1942 and vice admiral in October 1944. Vickery oversaw the construction of nearly 40 million gross tons of merchant shipping during the war, including the "Liberty" and "Victory" ships. Retired in December 1945. Decorations included the Distinguished Service Medal. Died on March 21, 1946.

Wagner, Frank Dechant (1893-1966) Born on August 22, 1893, in Pottstown, Pennsylvania. Commissioned from Annapolis in 1915. Designated naval aviator in December 1921. Aviation officer on the staff of Commander in Chief United States Fleet 1934-1936. Commanding officer of the *Langley* June 1940-September 1941. Commanded Aircraft, Asiatic Fleet 1941-1942. Director of Naval Air Transport Service June-October 1942. Rear admiral in July 1942. Commander of Fleet Air Seattle 1942-1943. Assistant to the deputy chief of naval operations (air) July 1943-April 1944. Commander of Carrier Division Five Pacific Fleet April-June 1944 then Aircraft Seventh Fleet July 1944-November 1945. Vice admiral upon retirement in July 1950. Decorations included two Distinguished Service Crosses and the Legion of Merit. Died on January 6, 1966.

Warlick, William Walter (1895-1981) Born on May 25, 1895. in Childress, Texas. Enlisted service in U.S. Navy 1913-1914 aboard the cruiser *Maryland* off the coast of Mexico during the Vera Cruz incident in April 1914. Commissioned from Annapolis in 1918. Instructor at Annapolis September 1923-June 1925 where he prepared one of the first Annapolis textbooks on naval aviation. Graduated from the Naval War College in 1930. Commanding officer of the *Jacob Jones* April 1932-April 1933. Again instructor at Annapolis April 1933-August 1934. Aide and flag secretary to Commander Battleship Division Two September 1934-1935 then Commander Cruiser Division Force, April 1935-June 1937. Instructor with the NROTC unit at Harvard University July 1937-May 1940. Commanding officer of the *McDougal* June 1940-October 1941. Commander of Destroyer Division 15 October 1941-June 1942 then Destroyer Squadron 7, June 1942-July 1942. Duty with the plans division of United States Fleet July 1942-January 1943 and the logistics plans division, office of the chief of naval operations January 1943-September 1943. Staff officer with Commander in Chief Pacific Fleet September 1943-April 1944. Commanding officer of the *Massachusetts* April 1944-May 1945. Commodore in April 1945. Again staff officer with Commander in Chief Pacific Fleet May 1945-October 1945. Rear admiral upon retirement in November 1947. Decorations included the Legion of Merit and Bronze Star. Died on November 1, 1981.

Wellings, Augustus Joseph (1897-1956) Born on February 3, 1897, in Chelsea, Massachusetts. Commissioned from Annapolis in 1919. M.S. from Massachusetts Institute of Technology in 1927. Duty at Naval Gun Factory, Washington Navy Yard June 1935-June 1937. Gunnery officer on the *California* June 1937-April 1939. Commanding officer of the *Arctic* April 1939-May 1940. Inspector of naval material at Bethlehem Steel Company May 1940-October 1942. Director of inspection administration in the office of procurement and material, executive office of the secretary of the navy October 1942-July 1945. Commodore in April 1945. Retired as rear admiral in July 1954. Decorations included two Legions of Merit and the Navy Commendation Medal. Died on November 29, 1956.

Wentworth, Ralph Strafford (1890-1980) Born on December 18, 1890, in Brockton, Massachusetts. Graduated from Annapolis in 1912 and commissioned in 1914. Instructor at Annapolis 1919-1921. Aide to Rear Admiral A.H. Scales while he was Commander Battleship Division Seven, Atlantic Fleet then Commandant of Fourth Naval District June 1921-October 1925. Executive officer, then commanding officer of the *Nenshaw* October 1925-June 1927. Commanding officer of the *Decatur* June 1931-June 1932 and the *Hull* October 1934-April 1936. Commanded Destroyer Division Five, Battle Force April 1936-February 1937. Graduated from the Naval War College June 1938 then member of the staff there until December 1939. Commanding officer of the *Nashville* January 1940-April 1941. Special naval observer in London under Vice Admiral Robert L. Ghormley May 1941-August 1942. Assistant naval inspector general August 1942-April 1943. Commodore in April 1943. Retired in November 1946. Died on September 13, 1980.

Weyler, George Lester (1886-1971) Born on May 24, 1886, in Emporia, Kansas. Graduated from Annapolis in 1910 and commissioned in 1912. Commanding officer of the *Lawrence, Hull, Hopkins* and *Preble* early in World War I. Aide to Commander Atlantic Section, Fifteenth Naval District April 1918-March 1919. LL.B. from Geogetown University Law School in June 1922. Commanding officer of the *Moody* July 1927-June 1930 then the *Trevor* in 1930. Aide to the superintendent of Annapolis 1931-1933. Naval attache in Peru August 1935-June 1937. Graduated from the Naval War College in May 1938. Commanding officer of the *Vestal* and *Detroit* June 1938-July 1940. Commandant of the Naval Station Guantanamo Bay, Cuba September 1940-March 1944. Rear admiral in August 1942. Commander of Battleship Division Three March 1944-August 1945. Vice admiral upon retirement in November 1946. Decorations included the Navy Cross and two Legions of Merit. Died on August 6, 1971.

Whiting, Francis Eliot Maynard (1891-1978) Born on February 10, 1891, in New York City. Commissioned from Annapolis in 1914. Commanding officer of the *Bulmer* and executive officer of the *Edsall* and *Hannibal* September 1924-August 1925 then commanding officer of the *Sylph,* a yacht assigned for use by the secretary of the navy August 1925-February 1926. Commanding officer of the

Goff June 1928-January 1931. Commander of Destroyer Division Eight September 1938-May 1940. Director of recruiting at the Bureau of Navigation June 1940-March 1942. Rear admiral in May 1942. Commanding officer of the *Massachusetts* March-December 1942. Commander of Southeast Pacific Force December 1942-October 1943 then the Alaskan Sector October 1943-April 1944. First commandant of the Seventeenth Naval District, which included Alaska and the Aleutian Islands April-August 1944. Commander of Cruiser Division Fourteen, Pacific Fleet August 1944-May 1945. Island commander of Saipan and commandant of Naval Operating Base Saipan May 1945-January 1946. Vice admiral upon retirement in August 1947. Decorations included three Legions of Merit, two Bronze Stars and two Navy Commendation Medals. Died on June 7, 1978.

Whitney, John Perry (1900-1974) Born on September 25, 1900, in Brooklyn, New York. Commissioned from Annapolis in 1922. Designated naval aviator in May 1925. Graduated from the Army Industrial College in June 1938. Duty in the plans division of the Bureau of Aeronatucis June 1938-March 1940. Commanding officer of the *Clemson* March 1940-March 1942. Operations officer at the Bureau of Aeronautics May-October 1942. Director of the aviation division in the office of the chief of naval operations October 1942-November 1943. Commanding officer of the *Kitkun Bay* November 1943-December 1944. Director of Naval Air Transport Service December 1944-February 1945. Chief of staff to the newly designated Commander Naval Air Transport Service 1945-1946. Commodore in April 1945. Assignments after the war included vice commander of Military Air Transport Service as rear admiral June 1948-March 1951 and chief of Naval Air Basic Training at NAS Pensacola April 1952-November 1953. Vice admiral upon retirement in March 1955. Decorations included the Navy Cross, Distinguished Service Medal, Bronze Star and Navy Commendation Medal. Died on February 4, 1974.

Wilcox, John Walter Jr. (1882-1942) Born on March 22, 1882, in Millidgeville, Georgia. Graduated from Annapolis in 1905 and commissioned in 1907. Aide to Commandant Third Naval District May-September 1917. Commanding officer of the *Yacona* October 1917-January 1918, the *Roper* October 1919-July 1920 and the *Boggs* and *Waters* in 1920. Graduated from the Naval War College in May 1924. Commanding officer of the *Hopkins* June 1923-May 1924 and the *Camden* June 1929-May 1931. Instructor at Annapolis July 1931-July 1934. Commanding officer of the *Chester* July 1934-June 1935. Commander of the Special Service Squadron September 1938-September 1940. President of the Board of Inspection and Survey September 1940-November 1941. Commander of Battleships, Atlantic Fleet as rear admiral November 1941-March 1942. His flagship departed Casco Bay on March 25, 1942 and encountered exceptionally foul weather in the Atlantic two days later. On March 27, 1942, Wilcox was swept overboard and lost at sea.

Wilkinson, Theodore Stark (1888-1946) Born on December 22, 1888, in Annapolis, Maryland. Graduated from Annapolis in 1909 and commissioned in 1911.

Awarded the Medal of Honor for leading a landing party from the *Florida* during the invasion of Vera Cruz in April 1914. Duty with the Bureau of Ordnance in World War I. Commanding officer of the *Mississippi* in 1941. Director of naval intelligence 1941-1942. Rear admiral in April 1942. Commander of Battleship Division Two 1942-1943. Deputy commander of the South Pacific Force in 1943. Commanded the Third Amphibious Force 1944-1945. Vice admiral in August 1944. Wilkinson received orders to the Joint Strategic Survey Committee of the Joint Chiefs of Staff in January 1946 but he drowned on February 21, 1946, when his automobile drove off a pier in Norfolk, Virginia. Decorations included the Medal of Honor and three Distinguished Service Medals.

Willcutts, Morton Douglas (1889-1976) Born on March 10, 1889, in Carthage, Indiana. B.S. from Indiana University in 1914 and M.D. in 1916. Commissioned in March 1917 in the Medical Corps, Naval Reserve Force. Transferred to the Regular Navy in September 1917. Chief of surgical service at Naval Hospital Canacao, Philippine Islands 1922-1923. Medical officer at the American Legation Peking, China December 1932-May 1935, one of the first American Navy doctors to treat victims of the Japanese aggression. Chief of surgery at Naval Medical School May 1935-April 1940. Medical officer on the *Wasp* April 1940-April 1941. Chief of surgery, then executive officer and finally medical officer in command at Naval Hospital San Diego June 1941-April 1945. He supervised the development of the hospital into the world's largest naval medical center which became a reconstruction and rehabilitation base for veterans of the Pacific. Commodore in April 1945. Fleet medical officer for Fifth Fleet April 1945-November 1945. Assignments after the war included medical officer in command of National Naval Medical Center at Bethesda July 1948 until retirement as vice admiral in December 1946. Decorations included the Legion of Merit and Navy Commendation Medal. Died on September 26, 1976.

Williams, Henry (1877-1973) Born on August 12, 1877, near Hagerstown, Maryland. Graduated from Annapolis in 1898 and commissioned in 1900. Rear admiral in October 1930. Manager of Philadelphia Navy Yard May 1935-April 1937. Assistant to the chief of the Bureau of Construction and Repair April 1937-June 1940 when the bureau was combined with the Bureau of Engineering and designated the Bureau of Ships and he was named head of the administrative division of the Bureau of Ships. Administrative officer in the office of the secretary of the navy July 1941 until retirement in September 1941. Continued on active duty as special sssistant to Vice Admiral Samuel M. Robinson, chief of the office of procurement and material until January 1946. Decorations included the Navy Commendation Medal. Died on July 6, 1973.

Willson, Russell (1883-1948) Born on December 27, 1883, in Fredonia, New York. Graduated from Annapolis in 1906 and commissioned in 1908. Flag lieutenant to Admiral Henry T. Mayo, Commander in Chief Atlantic Fleet during World War I. Commanding officer of the *Southard* June 1919 and the destroyers *Cole* and *Mason* June 1919-May 1921. Graduated from the Naval War College in

1924. Member of the U.S. Naval Mission to Brazil March 1927-December 1930. Head of the Department of Seamanship and Navigation at Annapolis July 1932-March 1935. Commanding officer of *Pennsylvania* April 1935-October 1936. U.S. naval attache in London January 1937-January 1939. Rear admiral in January 1939. Commander of Battleship Division One May 1939-February 1941. Superintendent of Annapolis February-December 1941. Chief of staff to Commander in Chief United States Fleet December 1941-September 1942. Deputy Commander in Chief United States Fleet 1942-1943. Retired as vice admiral in January 1943 but retained on active duty at headquarters Commander in Chief United States Fleet until relieved of all active duty in February 1946. Decorations included the Navy Cross and two Distinguished Service Medals. Died on June 6, 1948.

Wilson, George Barry (1892-1949) Born on March 27, 1892, in Norfolk, Virginia. Commissioned from Annapolis in 1914. M.S. from Columbia University in June 1921. Executive officer on the *Honolulu* March 1938-July 1940. Duty in the detail section of the officer personnel division, Bureau of Navigation July 1940-June 1942. Commanding officer of the *Alabama* August 1942-March 1943. Rear admiral in October 1942. Chief of staff to Commander U.S. Navy Forces March 1943-April 1945. President of the Naval Examining Board April-June 1945. Chief of staff to Commander Eastern Sea Froniter June 1945 until retirement in November 1946. Decorations included the Legion of Merit. Died on December 4, 1949.

Wiltse, Lloyd Jerome (1891-1984) Born on September 11, 1891, in Mitchell, South Dakota. Commissioned from Annapolis in 1914. Commanding officer of the submarine *R-3* July 1920-November 1921. Naval escort to accompany the body of President Warren G. Harding from San Francisco to Washington, DC in August 1923. Naval aide to the White House November 1923-September 1925. Duty in the Bureau of Navigation May 1937-November 1938. Recorder of the Selection Board November 1938-June 1940. Executive officer of the *Idaho* July 1940-January 1941. Commanding officer of the *Detroit* January 1941-April 1942. Assistant chief of staff for administation to Commander in Chief Pacific Fleet and Pacific Ocean Areas April 1942-September 1943. Rear admiral in October 1942. Commander of Cruiser Division Eleven September 1943-August 1944 then Division Ten August 1944-January 1946. Vice admiral upon retirement in April 1947. Decorations included the Navy Cross, two Legions of Merit and the Bronze Star. Died on February 1, 1984.

Womble, John Philip Jr. (1900-1956) Born on December 13, 1900, in Atlanta, Georgia. Commissioned from Annapolis in 1920. Commanding officer of the *Dale* Janaury 1939-February 1941. Executive officer of the *Dobbin* February 1941-August 1942. Director of field administration training activities for the Bureau of Naval Personnel September 1942-May 1944. Commander of Destroyer Squadron 52 June 1944-October 1944 then Commander Destroyers Pacific Fleet until March 1945. Commodore in April 1945. Commander of Task Flotilla Two April

1945-October 1945. Died on October 5, 1956. Decorations included the Silver Star, three Legions of Merit, the Distinguished Flying Cross and Navy Commendation Medal.

Wood, John Enos (1892-1964) Born on March 11, 1892, in Newark, Delaware. Enlisted service in the Naval Forces of Pennsylvania 1917-1917. Called to active duty in April 1917. Commissioned in June 1920. Supply officer on the *Scorpion,* the flagship of U.S. Naval Detachment Operating in Turkish Waters 1924-1926. Assistant to the supply officer on the *Augusta* September 1935 November 1937 then the supply officer at Washington Navy Yard November 1937-October 1940. Supply officer on the *Maryland* October 1940-March 1942. Supply and accounting officer at NAS Coco Solo, Canal Zone March 1942-January 1943. Rear admiral in December 1943. Supply officer on the staff of Commander Air Force, Atlantic Fleet January 1943-July 1944. Officer in charge of the aviation supply division, Bureau of Supplies and Accounts August 1944-April 1945. Supply officer in command of the Naval Aviation Supply Depot, Philadelphia May 1945-January 1947. Retired in April 1954. Decorations included the Legion of Merit. Died on February 9, 1964.

Wood, Ralph Frederic (1890-1958) Born on July 6, 1890, in Goshem, Indiana. Graduated from Annapolis in 1911 and commissioned in 1913. Commanding officer of the *Shark* September 1913-April 1915. Instructor at Annapolis July 1919-November 1920. Designated naval aviator in August 1921. Commander of NAS Coco Solo, Canal Zone May 1922-March 1924. Executive officer, then commanding officer of NAS Pensacola May 1931-June 1933. Graduated from the Naval War College in June 1934. Executive officer of the *Lexington* then aide for aviation on the staff of Commandant Ninth Naval District June 1934-October 1938. Commanding officer of the *Wright* 1938-1939 and the *Ranger* 1939-1940. Commander of NAS Seattle July 1940-July 1942 then Carrier Replacement Squadron, Pacific Fleet as rear admiral July-August 1942. Commander of Aircraft, Southwest Pacific Force August 1942-July 1943 then Fleet Air Seattle July 1943-August 1944. Commandant of Seventeenth Naval District, Kodiak, Alaska August 1944-March March 1946. Retired in October 1946. Decorations included the Legion of Merit. Died on November 29, 1958.

Woodson, Walter Browne (1881-1948) Born on October 18, 1881, in Lynchburg, Virginia. Graduated from Annapolis in 1905 and commissioned in 1907. LL.B. from George Washington University Law School in 1914. Director of the ships movements division, office of the chief of naval operations 1918-1919. Commanding officer of the *Bernadou* and *Dickerson* 1919-1921. Graduated from the Naval War College in 1922. Commanding officer of the *Houston* June 1934-June 1935. Chief of staff to Commander in Chief Asiatic Fleet June 1935-November 1936. Naval aide to the President of the U.S. September 1937-June 1938. Rear admiral and judge advocate general of the Navy 1938-1943. Retired in September 1943. Died on April 22, 1948.

Woodward, Clark Howell (1877-1967) Born on March 4, 1877, in Atlanta, Georgia. Graduated from Annapolis in 1899 and commissioned in 1901. Particated in the Spanish-American War in 1898 and the Phillipine and Boxer Campaigns in 1901. Navy representaative at the Panama-Pacific International Exposition in San Francisco 1914-15. Member of the U.S. Naval Mission to Brazil 1921-1922 then the U.S. Naval Mission to Peru 1923-1926 where he held the rank of rear admiral in the Peruvian Navy. Commanding officer of the *Milwaukœ* 1926-1928. Served in the office of the governor of the Panama Canal April 1928-June 1931. Commander of Cruiser Division Three, Scouting Force as rear admiral then Commander of Cruisers, Battle Force 1931-1932. Special representative of the President of the U.S. to supervise elections in Nicaragua 1932-1933. Commander of Destroyers, Battle Force March 1935-June 1937. Commandant of Third Naval District October 1937-March 1941. Retired in April 1941 and recalled to active duty in June 1941. Navy representative on the Federal Board for Civilian Protection and assistant director of the office of civilian defense in charge of plant protection June 1941-June 1942. Duty in the office of the under secretary of the navy June 1942 until October 1946. Died on May 29, 1967.

Wotherspoon, Alexander Somerville (1892-1976) Born in Utica, New York on December 2, 1892. Commissioned from Annapolis in 1915. Instructor there June 1922-June 1924. Commanding officer of the *Bernadou* June 1930-July 1931. Duty at Naval Gun Factory, Washington Navy Yard June 1936-November 1940. Member of the Advisory Commission Council of National Defense December 1940-January 1942. Inspector of Ordnance Plant, Center Line, Michigan with additional duty as Naval Inspector of Ordnance at the Pontiac Division of General Motors Corporation and Chrysler Corporation January 1942-June 1943. Commanding officer of the *Louisville* June-December 1943. Duty in Twelfth Naval District, San Francisco December 1943-June 1944. Served at headquarters of Training Command Amphibious Force, Pacific Fleet June-September 1944. Commander of Transport Division A September-November 1944 and Transport Division Forty-Seven November 1944-April 1945. Commodore in April 1945. Commanded Transport Squadron Twenty-Three June 1945-December 1945. Retired as rear admiral in June 1949. Decorations included the Legion of Merit and Bronze Star. Died on March 9, 1976.

Wright, Carleton Herbert (1892-1973) Born on June 2, 1892, in New Hampton, Iowa. Commissioned from Annapolis in 1912. Duty at Naval Bases 17 and 18, Ivergordon and Inverness, Scotland April-November 1918. M.S. from George Washington University in June 1920. Operations officer on the staff of Commander Scouting Force, United States Fleet June 1936-July 1938. Inspector of ordnance at Naval Mine Depot, Yorktown, Virginia July 1938-May 1941. Commanding officer of the *Augusta* May 1941-June 1942. Rear admiral in May 1942. Commander of Cruisers Task Force Two July 1942-January 1943. Director of the base maintenance division, office of the chief of naval operations January 1943-August 1943. Commander of Cruiser Division Four August 1943-January 1944.

Commandant of Twelfth Naval District January 1944-March 1946. Vice admiral upon retirement in October 1948. Decorations included the Navy Cross, Legion of Merit and Bronze Star. Died on June 27, 1973.

Wynkoop, Thomas Pilmore Jr. (1896-1983) Born on December 27, 1896, in Philadelphia. Commissioned from Annapolis in 1918. Served on the destroyer *Manley* in World War I. Duty at Cavite Naval Station in the Philippines 1928-1930. Member of the U.S. Naval Mission to Brazil 1939-1941. Assigned to the Bureau of Ships 1941-1944. Rear admiral in June 1943. Commandant of Norfolk Naval Ship Yard 1944-1946. Retired in March 1949. Decorations included the Legion of Merit and Navy Commendation Medal. Died on September 15, 1983.

Yarnell, Harry Ervin (1875-1959) Born on October 18, 1875, in Independence, Iowa. Graduated from Annapolis in 1897 and commissioned in 1899. Served on the *Oregon* in the Spanish-American War and the *Yorktown* in the Philippine insurgency and the Boxer Rebellion. Served at the invasion of Vera Cruz in April 1914. Graduated from the Naval War College in 1915. Commanded the *Nashville* in 1917 and served on the staff of Admiral William S. Sims in 1918. First commanding officer of the United Steamship *Saratoga* 1927-1928. Rear admiral in August 1928. Chief of the Bureau of Engineering 1928-1931. Commander of Aircraft Squadrons, Battle Fleet 1931-1933. Commandant of Navy Station Pearl Harbor 1933-1936. Commander in chief Asiatic Fleet as admiral 1936-1939. Retired in November 1939. Recalled to active duty in the office of the secretary of the navy as advisor to the Chinese Military Mission November 1941-January 1943 and again June 1943-December 1944 in the office of the chief of naval operations. Admiral in July 1942. Retired in December 1944. Decorations included the Navy Cross and Distinguished Service Medal. Died on July 7, 1959.

Yates, Charles Moulding (1884-1964) Born on October 21, 1884, in Palmyra, Wisconsin. Enlisted service in the Navy January 1903-September 1904. Graduated from Annapolis in 1908 and commissioned in 1910. Commanding officer of the *Shark* in 1912 and the *F-2* November 1913-October 1915. Graduated from the Naval War College June 1929. Commanding officer of the *Arctic* June 1934-June 1936. Served at the Bureau of Navigation June 1936-June 1939. Commanding officer of the *San Francisco* June 1939-May 1941. Duty in the office of the chief of naval operations July 1941-February 1942 then Commander in Chief United States Fleet February-October 1942. Professor of naval science and tactics at Brown University October 1942-April 1943. Commodore in April 1943. Commandant of Naval Operating Base Oran, Algeria from April 1943. Decorations included two Legions of Merit. Retired in January 1947. Decorations included the Legion of Merit. Died on November 14, 1964.

Ziroli, Humbert William (1893-1979) Born on September 21, 1893, in Fall River, Massachusetts. Commissioned from Annapolis in 1916. Commanding officer of the submarine *S-4* September 1921-May 1924. Instructor at Annapolis May 1930-June 1933. Commanding officer of the *Simpson* June 1933-April 1934 and the *Narwahl* April 1934-April 1936. Graduated from the Naval War College in May 1939. Executive officer of the *Philadelphia* May 1939-June 1941. Head of modern languages at Annapolis July 1941-February 1943. Commanding officer of the *Brooklyn* February-October 1943. Commodore in November 1943. U.S. member of the Allied Control Commission in Rome November 1943-June 1947. Retired as rear admiral in December 1947. Decorations included three Legions of Merit. Died on October 20, 1979.

5

The United States Marine Corps

Ames, Evans Orchard (1895-1982) Born on January 12, 1895, in Boston, Massachusetts. Studied law at the University of San Francisco. Commissioned in 1917. Served overseas in Haiti 1923-1925, China in 1927 and 1937, and the Philippines 1938-1939. Duty at Marine Corps Schools January 1941-December 1942. Commanding officer of 21st Marines, Third Marine Division January 1943-March 1944. Chief of staff and deputy commander of Supply Service, Fleet Marine Force, Pacific March 1944-January 1946. Brigadier general in May 1945. Major general upon retirement in February 1947. Decorations included two Legions of Merit and the Bronze Star. Died on March 17, 1982.

Barrett, Charles Dodsen (1885-1943) Born on August 16, 1885, in Henderson, Kentucky. Commissioned in 1909. Served at the occupation of Vera Cruz in 1914, at Nieder Bieber, Germany April-August 1919, and in Santo Domingo 1921-1922. Graduated from the Ecole Superieure de Guerre in 1929. Instructor at Marine Corps Schools 1929-1933. Duty in the war plans section, office of the chief of naval operations 1936-1939. Commanding officer of 5th Marines, First Marine Brigade August 1939-June 1940. Director of the plans and policies division and the assistant commandant of the Marine Corps November 1941-March 1942. Brigadier general in December 1941. Commanding general of Third Marine Brigade March-September 1942 then the 3rd Marine Division September 1942-September 1943. Commanding general of the First Marine Amphibious Corps, September-October 1943. Major general in October 1943. Accidentally killed on October 8, 1943. Decorations included the Distinguished Service Medal.

Blake, Robert (1894-1983) Born on August 17, 1894, in Seattle, Washington. Graduated from the University of California in 1917. Commissioned in 1917. Served with the Army of Occupation in Germany 1918-1919. Instructor at Marine Corps Schools January 1920-April 1922. Commanding officer of 2nd Battalion, Second Marine Brigade, Nicaragua in 1928 then with the electoral mission in Nicaragua 1929 and 1932. Instructor at Marine Corps Schools December 1932-June 1934. Duty in the office of naval intelligence September 1937-June 1940. Graduated from the Naval War College in 1941. Commanded Fifth Marine Regiment 1941-1942, Tenth Defense Battalion June 1942-June 1943 and Marine Defense Group June-August 1943. Brigadier general in October 1942. Chief of staff of 3rd Marine Division August 1943-February 1944. Command of 21st Marine Regiment February-July 1944. Deputy Island Commander 1944-1945. Marine deputy chief of staff of Tenth Army on Okinawa June-November 1945. Commanding general of Occupation Forces November 1945-June 1946. President of the Post-War Personnel Reorganization Board June-October 1946. Assignments after the war included inspector general, U. S. Marine Corps 1946-1949. Major general upon retirement in June 1949. Died on October 2, 1983. Decorations included two Navy Crosses, the Distinguished Service Cross, Silver Star, Legion of Merit and Bronze Star.

Bourke, Thomas Eugene (1896-1978) Born on May 5, 1896, in Saverna Park, Maryland. B.S. from St. John's College in 1916. Enlisted service in the U.S. Army 1916-1917. Commissioned in 1917. Duty in the Virgin Islands 1917-1919 and Nicaragua 1922-1924. Assigned to the war plans division at headquarters U.S. Marine Corps 1931-1934. Graduated from the Army War College in June 1936. Served at the Navy Yard at Pearl Harbor 1938-1940. Brigadier general in June 1943. Commanding general of 24th Corps Artillery (U.S. Army) 1943-1944. Major general in February 1944. Commanding general of 5th Marine Division 1945-1946. Lieutenant general upon retirement in November 1946. Decorations included the Legion of Merit and two Bronze Stars. Died on January 5, 1978.

Brewster, David Lukens Shoemaker (1887-1945) Born on December 31, 1887, in Washington, D.C.. Commissioned in 1910. Designated naval aviator in 1917. Instructor at Marine Corps School, 1925-1926. Served in Santo Domingo and the Nicaraguan Campaign 1928-1929. Duty with the 4th Marines in China 1932-1935. Commanding officer of the Barracks Detachment at New River, North Carolina in 1941. Brigadier general in April 1943. Assigned to First Marine Amphibious Corps 1943-1944. Chief of staff of Administrative Command 1944-1945. Relieved of all duty due to illness in June 1945. Died on July 10, 1945.

Brice, William Oscar (1898-1972) Born on December 10, 1898, in Columbia, South Carolina. B.S. from the Citadel in 1921. Enlisted service in the Army in the latter part of World War I. Commissioned in 1921. Qualified as naval aviator in 1924. Served with Scouting Squadron One in Guam and China June 1925-November 1927. Graduated from Air Corps Tactical School in August 1937. Commander of Scouting Squadron One August 1937-June 1939. Instructor at Pensacola June 1939-August 1941. Operations officer with Marine Aircraft Group Two August-December 1941. Commanding officer of Marine Aircraft Groups 12 and 14 March 1942-January 1944. Executive officer in the division of plans and policies, headquarters U.S. Marine Corps 1944-1945. Brigadier general in January 1945. Assignments after the war included deputy commander of Fleet Marine Force Pacific October 1951-March 1952, director of Marine Corps Aviation April 1952-July 1955 and commanding general of Fleet Marine Force Pacific July 1955-1956. General upon retirement in July 1956. Decorations included the Distinguished Service Medal, Legion of Merit, Bronze Star and Air Medal. Died on January 30, 1972.

Campbell, Harold Denny (1895-1955) Born on March 30, 1895, in Middlesex, Vermont. B.S. from Norwich University in 1917. Commissioned in 1917. Served in France 1917-1919. Designated a naval aviator in 1921. Duty in Haiti and Santo Domingo in 1923. Recipient of the Schiff Award in 1926 for the world's record number of air hours without an accident. Graduated from Air Corps Tactical School in 1929. Duty in Guam in 1930. Air officer for Fleet Marine Force 1935-1939. Advisor to Lord Mountbatten in the China-Burma-India Theater of Operations 1942-1943. Brigadier general in April 1943. Commanding general of 4th and 2nd Marine Air Wings 1943-1944 then Marine Corps Air Bases and 9th Marine Air Wing 1944-1945. Major general upon retirement in November 1946. Decorations included the Legion of Merit and Purple Heart. Died on December 29, 1955.

Cates, Clifton Bledsoe (1893-1970) Born on August 31, 1893, in Tiptonville, Tennessee. LL.B. from the University of Tennessee in 1916. Commissioned in 1917. Twice wounded while serving with 6th Marines in the AEF at Verdun, Belleau Woods, Aisne-Marne, St. Mihiel and Meuse-Argonne. Aide-de-camp to President Woodrow Wilson 1919-1923. Duty in Shanghai 1929-1932. Graduated from Army Industrial College in 1932. Again in Shanghai with the 6th Marines 1937-1939. Graduated from the Army War College in 1939. Brigadier general in April 1940. Commanding general of 1st Marines at Guadalcanal in 1942. Commandant of Marine Corps Schools 1943-1944. Major general in February 1944. Commanding general of 4th Marine Division July 1945-November 1945. Assignments after the war included commandant of the Marine Corps 1948-1952. Unable to retire due to a peculiarity of the law regarding his age, he reverted to lieutenant general and served again as commandant of Marine Corps Schools until retirement as general in July 1954. Decorations included the Navy Cross, two Distinguished Service Crosses, two Distinguished Service Medals, two Silver Stars, the Legion of Merit and two Purple Hearts. Died on June 4, 1970.

Cauldwell, Oscar Ray (1892-1959) Born on August 24, 1892, in Nyesville, Indiana. Attended Wabash College. Commissioned in the Marine Corps from Annapolis in 1916. Duty in France 1917-1918. Instructor at Marine Corps Schools 1919-1921 and 1925-1927. Served in Haiti 1924-1925 and 1928-1930. Graduated from Command and General Staff School in 1928. Commandant of the Ecole Militaire of the Garde d'Haiti August 1930-July 1933. Graduated from the Army War College in June 1934 and the Naval War College in May 1935. Assigned to the war plans section, Fleet Marine Force November 1935-May 1939. Member of the staff at the Naval War College May 1940-March 1942. Commanding officer of Third Marines June-August 1942. Brigadier general in September 1943. Assistant division commander September 1943-January 1944. Commanding general of Training Command, Fleet Marine Force April 1944-May 1946. Major general upon retirement in May 1946. Decorations included the Silver Star and Purple Heart. Died on September 8, 1959.

Clement, William Tardy (1894-1955) Born on September 27, 1894, in Lynchburg, Virginia. B.S. from Virginia Military Institute in 1914. Commissioned in 1917. Served in Haiti 1917-1919. Duty with the American Legation guard in Peking 1923-1925 then Shanghai 1927-1929. Instructor at Marine Corps Schools 1934-1938. Battalion commander with 5th Marines 1938-1940. Fleet Marine officer for the Asiatic Fleet aboard the *Augusta* and the *Houston* 1940-1941. Assigned to Fourth Marines on Bataan in 1942. Major general in October 1942. Escaped before the fall of Corregidor. Staff officer with Naval Forces Europe 1942-1943. Brigadier general in April 1942. Assistant commandant, then commandant of Marine Corps Schools 1943-1944. Assistant division commander of 6th Marine Division 1944-1945. Commander of the Third Fleet landing force in Japan in 1945. Lieutenant general upon retirement in May 1952. Decorations included the Navy Cross, three Legions of Merit, the Bronze Star and Navy Cross. Died on October 17, 1955.

Creesy, Andrew Elliott (1893-1974) Born on November 7, 1893, in Beverly, Massachusetts. Commissioned from Annapolis in 1917. Served with the 13th Regiment Marines in France September 1918-July 1919 then the Second Provisional Brigade in the Dominican Republic July 1919-June 1922. Instructor at Marine Corps Schools July 1924-September 1926. Aide to the American High Commissioner to Haiti then a member of the Gendarmerie d' Haiti September 1926- June 1929. Graduated from Command and General Staff School in 1931. Again instructor at Marine Corps Schools July 1931-June 1933. Supply officer and force quartermaster at Fleet Marine Force April 1939-April 1941. Division quartermaster at 1st Marine Division April 1941-January 1942. Corps quartermaster at Amphibious Corps Atlantic Fleet January 1942-February 1943, I Marine Amphibious Corps February-August 1943 and V Amphibious Corps August 1943-January 1944. Officer in charge of the general supply section at headquarters U.S. Marine Corps January-August 1944. Brigadier general in May 1944. Commander of Forward Echelon and First Field Service Command, Fleet Marine Force Pacific August 1944-May 1945. Director of supply at Fleet Marine Force Pacific May-November 1945. Major general upon retirement in July 1951. Decorations included the Legion of Merit and Bronze Star. Died on December 11, 1974.

Cumming, Samuel Calvin (1895-1983) Born on October 14, 1895, in Kobe, Japan. B.S. from Virginia Military Institute in 1917. Commissioned in 1917. Served with the Fifth Marine Regiment in France 1917-1920. Overseas duty in Haiti 1922-1926, China 1927-1928 and the Virgin Islands 1929-1931. Graduated from Command and General Staff School and the Army War College. Instructor at Marine Corps Schools 1935-1936. Force Marine Officer in the Scouting Force 1937-1940. Assigned to headquarters U.S. Marine Corps 1940-1943. Brigadier general in September 1942. Commanding officer of 25th Marine Regiment July

1943-April 1944. Assistant division commander April-September 1944. Chief of staff of Marine Barracks September 1944-November 1946. Major general upon retirement in November 1946. Decorations included three Silver Stars and two Purple Hearts. Died on January 14, 1983.

Curtis, Merritt Barton (1892-1966) Born on August 31, 1892, in San Bernardino, California. B.A. from the University of California at Berkeley in 1916. Commissioned in 1917. Served in Haiti 1920-1923. LL.B. from George Washington University in 1927. Post paymaster at the American Legation in Peking October 1927-December 1929. Instructor at Marine Corps Schools June 1931-June 1934. Served with the Fourth Marine Regiment in Shanghai April 1936-October 1937. Executive officer of the Paymaster Department at headquarters U.S. Marine Corps July 1941-December 1944. Brigadier general in May 1944. Paymaster at Fleet Marine Force Pacific December 1944-August 1946. Chief of the disbursing branch at headquarters U.S. Marine Corps August 1946 until retirement in June 1949. Died on May 16, 1966.

Cushman, Thomas Jackson (1895-1972) Born on June 27, 1895, in St. Louis, Missouri. Attended the University of Washington 1913-1917. Enlisted service 1917-1918. Commissioned in 1918. Designated naval aviator in June 1919. Duty with the First Brigade Marines in Haiti May 1929-August 1931. Graduated from Army Air Corps Technical School in 1932 and Tactical School in 1936. Assigned to the Marine Barracks at Quantico June 1939-August 1941 then the Marine Corps Air Station January 1942-August 1943. Chief of staff of Marine Aircraft Wings September 1943-May 1944. Brigadier general in December 1943. Commanding general of Fourth Marine Base Defense Aircraft Wing May-August 1944. Major general in June 1944. Assistant Wing Commander, Aircraft Fleet Marine Force September-October 1944. Commanding general of Forward Area, Aircraft Fleet Marine Force Pacific November 1944-April 1945 then Marine Base Cherry Point May 1945-March 1947. Chief of staff, Aircraft Fleet Marine Force Pacific May-July 1947. Deputy commander of Fleet Marine Force Pacific August 1947-May 1949 then Air, Fleet Marine Force Pacific and First Marine Air Wing June 1949-July 1950. Commanding general, tactical air commander and again commanding general of First Marine Air Wing 1950-1953. Deputy commander of Fleet Marine Force Pacific 1953-1954. Lieutenant general upon retirement in February 1954. Decorations included the Distinguished Service Medal, two Legions of Merit and the Bronze Star. Died in 1972.

DeCarre, Alphonse (1892-1977) Born on November 15, 1892, in Washington, DC. Commissioned in 1913. Served in Haiti 1915-1916 and Oriente, Cuba 1916-1917, then with the Fifth Regiment, France in 1917-1919. Duty in Nicaragua, the Dominican Republic and China in the 1920-1925. Graduated from the Naval War College in 1926. Served again in China 1937-1938. Commanding officer of Marine Barracks Puget Sound June 1941-July 1942. Brigadier general in August 1942. Assigned to 2nd Marine Division at Guadalcanal 1942-1944. Major general upon retirement in June 1946. Decorations included the Navy Cross, Distinguished Service Medal, Silver Star and Purple Heart. Died on May 3, 1977.

del Valle, Pedro Augusto (1893-1978) Born on August 28, 1893, in San Jose, Puerto Rico. Commissioned from Annapolis in 1915. Served with the 2nd Provisional Marine Brigade in Haiti 1916-1917 and participated in the capture of Santo Domingo City in 1916. Commanding officer of the Marine detachment aboard the *Texas* during World War I. Aide-de-camp to Major General Joseph H. Pendleton 1923-1924. Duty with the Gendarmerie d'Haiti May 1926-August 1928. Served with the Second Brigade in Nicaragua June-November 1930 and January 1931-July 1933. Assistant naval atache in Rome October 1935-June 1937. Graduated from Army War College in June 1938. Duty in the operations and training division at headquarters U.S. Marine Corps 1938-1941. Regimental commander with First Marine Division March 1941-April 1943 then commander of Marine forces on Guadalcanal and Tulagi May-July 1943. Brigadier general in August 1942. President of the Marine Corps Equipment Board September 1943-March 1944. Major general in January 1944. Commanding general of III Corps Artillery April-September 1944 then First Marine Division November 1944-August 1945. Served at headquarters U.S. Marine Corps as inspector general and director of personnel 1945-1946. Lieutenant general upon retirement in October 1946. Decorations included the Distinguished Service Medal and two Legions of Merit. Died on April 28, 1978.

Denig, Robert Livingston (1884-1979) Born in Clinton, New York, on September 29, 1884. Attended the University of Pennsylvania 1903-1905. Commissioned in 1905. Served with Fifth Marines, 3rd and 2nd Divisions in the AEF 1917-1918 and in Nicaragua 1930-1931. Brigadier general in June 1941. Director of Marine Corps public relations 1941-1945. Retired in December 1945. Decorations included the Distinguished Service Cross, Navy Cross, Legion of Merit and two Purple Hearts. Died on July 25, 1979.

Edson, Merritt Austin (1897-1955) Born on April 25, 1897, in Rutland, Vermont. Attended the University of Vermont 1915-1917. Commissioned in 1917. Served with 11th Marines 1918-1919. Qualified as naval aviator in 1922. Expeditionary duty in Guam 1923-1925 and Nicaragua 1927-1929. Instructor at Marine Corps Schools 1929-1931. Duty with 4th Marines at Shanghai 1937-1939. At headquarters U.S. Marine Corps 1939-1941. Commanding officer of 1st Raider Battalion February-September 1942 and 5th Marines on Guadalcanal, where he earned the Medal of Honor, September 1942-July 1943. Chief of staff of 2nd Marine Division on Tarawa August 1943-January 1944. Brigadier general in December 1943. Assistant division commander of 2nd Marine Division January-August 1944. Chief of staff of Fleet Marine Force Pacific September 1944-July 1945 then commanding general of Service Command there July-December 1945. Assigned to the staff of chief of naval operations 1946-1947. Major general upon retirement in August 1947. Decorations included the Medal of Honor, two Navy Crosses, the Silver Star and two Legions of Merit. Died on August 14, 1955.

Erskine, Graves Blanchard (1897-1973) Born on June 28, 1897, in Columbia, Louisiana. Attended Louisiana State University. Enlisted service in the Louisiana National Guard. Commissioned in 1917. Served with the 6th Marines at Aisne-Marne, St.-Mihiel, Belleau Wood and Soissons in World War I. Wounded in action at Marbache. Served in Haiti in 1921, Santo Domingo 1922-1924 and Nicaragua 1928-1930. Executive officer of the embassy guard at Peking 1935-1937. Brigadier general in March 1941. Assigned to Quantico March-December 1941. Chief of staff of V Amphibious Corps 1942-1943. Chief of amphibious training for the Pacific Fleet 1943-1944. Major general in February 1944, Commanding general of 3rd Marine Division on Iwo Jima in 1945. Personal representative of the secretary of labor as head of the Retraining and Reemployment Administration 1945-1947, retaining his Marine Corps rank. Assignments after the war included commanding general of Fleet Marine Force Atlantic 1951-1953. General upon retirement in July 1953. Served in the office of the secretary of defense June 1953-1961. Decorations included the Distinguished Service Medal, Silver Star, two Legions of Merit and the Purple Heart. Died on May 21, 1973.

Farrell, Walter Greatsinger (1897-1990) Born on June 4, 1897, in San Francisco, California. Attended the University of Illinois. Enlisted service in the Illinois National Guard and Marine Corps Reserve 1916-1917. Commissioned in 1917. Served with the AEF during World War I, including the Meuse-Argonne offensive. Duty in Haiti 1919-1920. Designated naval aviator in 1921. Again in Haiti 1923-1924. Served in China in 1928 and Guam 1928-1930. Graduated from the Naval War College in 1934. Instructor at Marine Corps Schools 1936-1939. Duty with Second Marine Aircraft Group in San Diego 1940-1941. Assistant naval attache in London 1941-1942. Chief of staff of Second Aircraft Wing July 1942-November 1943. Commander of Marine Aircraft, Hawaiian Area in 1944. Brigadier general in March 1944. Deputy commander of Naval Air Bases in the Eleventh Naval District, then commanding general of the Third Marine Aircraft Wing November 1944-January 1946. Major general upon retirement in November 1946. Decorations included the Silver Star and Bronze Star. Died on October 11, 1990.

Fegan, Joseph Charles (1886-1949) Born on November 6, 1886, in Dallas, Texas. Commissioned in 1909. Served in Panama 1909-1910, Cuba in 1913, the Philippines in 1916 and 1917-1918 and Santo Domingo 1923-1924. Commander of the Department of the North at Cap Haitien, Haiti 1929-1932. Graduated from the Naval War College in 1936. Commanded the 4th Marines at Shanghai August 1938-December 1939. Director of Marine Corps Reserve 1940-1941. Brigadier general in February 1942. Commander of Camp Pendleton 1942-1944. Major general in September 1942. Commanding general of Marine Corps Department of the Pacific May 1944 until retirement in August 1945. Decorations included the Distinguished Service Medal. Died on May 26, 1949 from injuries suffered in an automobile accident five days earlier.

Fellows, Joseph Howard (1897-1980) Born on April 16, 1897, in Washington D.C. Attended George Washington University. Enlisted in the Marine Corps Reserve in August 1917 and commissioned that October. Wounded in action while serving with the Fifth Marine Regiment in France in 1918. Duty in Santo Domingo 1920-1923. Instructor at Marine Corps Schools June 1925-June 1927. Served in Nicaragua in 1928. Graduated from Army Industrial College in June 1930 and the Naval War College in May 1939. Assigned to the Quartermaster Department at headquarters of the Marine Corps 1939-1942. Plans Officer for Commander Service Squadron, South Pacific Area and South Pacific Force June 1942-November 1943. Executive assistant to assistant chief of staff for logistics at Commander in Chief Pacific Fleet December 1943-December 1945. Brigadier general upon retirement in June 1949. Decorations included the Legion of Merit, Bronze Star and Purple Heart. Died on February 26, 1980.

Geiger, Roy Stanley (1885-1947) Born on January 25, 1885, in Middleburg, Florida. LL.B. from John B. Stetson University in 1907. Commissioned in 1909. Served in Nicaragua the Philippine Islands 1912-1913 and in Peking 1913-1916. Designated naval aviator in June 1917. Commanding officer of Squadron A, 1st Marine Aviation Force in France in World War I. Duty with the Marine Aviation Force in Haiti 1919-1921. Graduated from Command and General Staff School in 1925. Again in Haiti 1925-1927. Graduated from the Army War College in 1929. Head of Marine Corps aviation 1931-1935. Brigadier general in October 1941. Assistant naval attache for air in London 1941-1942. Director of Allied air operations on Guadalcanal in 1942. Major general in August 1942. Commanding general of 1st Marine Amphibious Corps 1943-1945. Lieutenant general in June 1945. Commanding general of Tenth Army in 1945. Represented the U.S. Marine Corps at the formal Japanese surrender aboard the *Missouri* in Tokyo Bay September 2, 1945. Assignments after the war included commanding general of Fleet Marine Force Pacific 1945-1946. Died on January 23, 1947. Decorations included two Navy Crosses, three Distinguished Service Medals, the Distinguished Flying Cross and Air Medal. Promoted to general posthumously by the 80th Congress in January 1947.

Gregory, Maurice Clinton (1881-1949) Born on October 9, 1881, in Cresco, Iowa. Enlisted in U.S. Marine Corps in February 1905. Appointed second lieutenant in June 1917. Post quartermaster with the legation guard at Managua, Nicaragua October 1920-June 1922. Assigned to the Guardia Nacional de Nicaragua December 1928-June 1931. Post quartermaster at Marine Corps Base, Quantico then San Diego May 1935-June 1940. Depot quartermaster for the Depot of Supplies, Philadelphia June 1940-September 1945. Brigadier general in May 1944. Retired in September 1945. Died on October 27, 1949.

Hall, Elmer E. (1890-1958) Born in Rocky Bar, Idaho, on April 20, 1890. Attended the University of Oregon 1910-1913. Enlisted in U.S. Marine Corps May 1917 and commissioned in 1918. Played for the Mare Island Marines in the 1918 Rose Bowl game. Served with the Thirteenth Marine Regiment in France in World War I. Head coach in 1926, 1929-1930, 1933 and 1939-1940. Commanding officer of Second Engineer Battalion at Pearl Harbor. Commanding officer of

18th Engineers, chief of staff of the 2nd Marine Division, commander of the Eighth Regiment and liaison officer to the Personnel Department at headquarters U.S. Marine Corps 1942 until retirement in 1946. Brigadier general in May 1945. Decorations included the Legion of Merit and Navy Commendation Medal. Died on September 22, 1958.

Harrington, Samuel Milby (1882-1948) Born on November 13, 1882, in Annapolis, Maryland. B.A. from Yale in 1909. Commissioned in 1909. Served with the First Brigade Marines in the Philippines in 1913, at the American Legation in Peking, China 1913-1916, on expeditionary duty in Santo Domingo June-December 1916 and as Department Commander in the Haitian Gendarmerie 1922-1925. Instructor at Marine Corps Schools 1926-1927. Assistant chief of Guardia Nacional de Nicaragua 1927-1929. Graduated from the Naval War College in 1935. Commanding officer of Fifth Marine Regiment 1937-1938 then executive officer of First Marine Brigade 1938-1939. President of the Naval Examining Board December 1939-July 1941. Brigadier general in January 1940. Commandant of Marine Corps Schools June 1941-January 1943. Retired January 1943 but continued on active duty. President of the Marine Corps Equipment Board April-July 1943 and the Permanent General Court Martial Board July 1943-February 1945. Decorations included the Distinguished Service Medal. Died on March 31, 1948. Died on March 31, 1948.

Harris, Field (1895-1967) Born on September 18, 1895, in Versailles, Kentucky. Commissioned from Annapolis in 1917. Served with the Third Provisional Brigade at Guantanamo Bay, Cuba 1917-1919 and at the Marine Barracks, Naval Station Cavite, Philippine Islands December 1919-June 1922. LL.B. from George Washington University in 1925. Qualified as naval aviator in 1928. Graduated from the Naval War College in May 1939. Assistant naval attache in Cairo 1941-1943. Brigadier general in February 1942. Chief of staff to Commander Aircraft, Guadalcanal April-July 1943. Commander of Aircraft, Northern Solomons 1943-1944 then commander of air in the Green Island Operation February-April 1944. Director of Marine Aviation 1944-1948. Major general in September 1944, lieutenant general upon retirement in July 1953. Decorations included two Distinguished Service Medals, four Legions of merit, the Bronze Star, Air Medal and Commendation Ribbon. Died on December 21, 1967.

Hart, Franklin Augustus (1894-1967) Born on September 16, 1894, in Cuthbert, Georgia. B.S. from Alabama Polytechnic Institute in 1915. Commissioned in 1917. Served with the National Guard on the Mexican border during the Punitive Expedition in 1916, the Marine detachment aboard the *Vermont* in the Atlantic Fleet 1917-1918 and with a machine gun battalion the 5th Brigade in France 1918-1919. District commander of Santo Domingo City, Guardia Nacional Dominicana September 1919-November 1921. Instructor at Marine Corps Schools May 1924-June 1926 and again in 1929. District commander of the constabulary detachment, Garde d'Haiti August 1930-May 1933 then assistant chief of staff May 1933-July 1934. Officer in charge of the war plans section at headquarters Marine Corps 1937-1938. Graduated from the Army War College in June 1939. Chief of the planning section at Marine Corps Base, San Diego June 1939-July 1940. Commanding officer of First Battalion, Eighth Marines July 1940-June 1941. Assistant naval attache in London June-September 1941 then special naval observer September 1941-October 1942. Chief of the future plans section, United States Fleet October 1942-June 1943. Commanding officer of 24th Marine Regiment, Fourth Marine Division June 1943-August 1944. Brigadier general in August 1944. Assistant division commander of 4th Marine Division August 1944-September 1945. Assignments after the war included commanding general of Fleet Marine Force Pacific January 1952-1954. General upon retirement in August 1954. Decorations included the Navy Cross, Legion of Merit and Bronze Star. Died on June 22, 1967.

Hermle, Leo David (1890-1976) Born on June 30, 1890, in Hastings, Nebraska. B.A. from the University of California in 1914, J.D. in 1917. Commissioned in 1917. Served with 6th Marines, 2nd Division in the AEF in World War I. Instructor at Marine Corps Schools June 1928-May 1930. Assigned to the constabulary detachment, Garde d'Haiti May 1930-August 1934. Assistant adjutant and inspector at headquarters Marine Corps August 1934-August 1938. Graduated from the Army War College in June 1939. Executive officer of the Sixth Marines 1939-1941 then commanding officer June 1941-August 1942. Brigadier general in April 1940. Chief of staff and assistant division commander of 2nd Marine Division August 1942-January 1944. Major general in September 1942. Administrative deputy at V Amphibious Corps January-April 1944. Assistant division commander of 5th Marine Division April 1944-June 1945. Deputy island commander on Guam and the Marianas June 1945-February 1946. Lieutenant general upon retirement in September 1949. Decorations included the Navy Cross, Distinguished Service Cross, Distinguished Service Medal, two Silver Stars, the Legion of Merit, Bronze Star, Commendation Ribbon and two Purple Hearts. Died on January 21, 1976.

Hill, Walter Newell (1882-1955) Born in Haverhill, Massachusetts, on September 29, 1882. Attended Harvard University 1900-1904. Commissioned in 1904. Expeditionary duty in Cuba October-November 1906, in China October 1911-January 1912 and with the occupation of Vera Cruz in 1914, where he earned the Medal of Honor. Served in Haiti August 1915-December 1916 and St. Thomas April 1926-June 1928. Graduated from the Army War College in June 1928. Brigadier general in September 1938. Retired in September 1938. Returned to active duty in December 1941. Assigned to headquarters Marine Corps 1942-1945. Decorations included the Medal of Honor. Died on June 29, 1955.

Hill, William Pendleton Thompson (1895-1965) Born on February 22, 1895, in Vinita, Oklahoma. B.S. from the University of Oklahoma in 1917. Commissioned in 1917. Designated naval aviator in October 1917. Served in the Azores 1917-1918, Peking 1926-1929 and with the Garde d'Haiti 1933-1934. Instructor at Marine Corps Schools 1936-1938. Liaison officer during the construction of

Camp Lejeune April 1941-May 1943. Officer in charge of the supply division in the Quartermaster Department June 1943-January 1944. Brigadier general in January 1944 as quartermaster general of the Marine Corps, a position he held until retirement in January 1955. Major general in April 1945. Decorations included the Distinguished Service Medal. Died on December 6, 1965.

Holcomb, Thomas (1879-1965) Born on August 5, 1879, in New Castle, Delaware. Commissioned in 1900. Aide to Major General George Barnett, commandant of the Marine Corps, in 1917. Served in the AEF in 1918 as battalion commander in the 6th Marines at Chateau-Thierry and executive officer of 6th Marines at St. Mihiel and Meuse-Argonne. Graduated from Command and General Staff School in 1925. Commanding officer of Marines at the American legation in Shanghai 1927-1930. Graduated from the Naval War College in 1931 and the Army War College in 1932. Brigadier general in February 1935. Commandant of Marine Corps School 1935-1936. Major general in November 1946. Commandant of the Marine Corps 1936-1943. Lieutenant general in January 1942, the first marine to wear three stars. Retired in December 1943 and promoted to full general, the first Marine to be so honored. Decorations included the Navy Cross, four Silver Stars and the Purple Heart. Ambassador to the Union of South Africa April 1944-May 1948. Died on May 24, 1965.

Howard, Archie Franklin (1892-1964) Born on January 29, 1892, in Clay Center, Kansas. Commissioned from Annapolis in 1915. Foreign duty included Siberia in World War I and China, Santo Domingo, the Philippine Islands and Panama Canal Zone. Graduated from Command and General Staff School and the Naval War College. Assistant commandant, then commandant of Marine Corps July 1939-May 1941. Chief of staff of I Marine Amphibious Corps May 1941-July 1943. Brigadier general in August 1942. Island commander at Guadalcanal and New Guinea July 1943-June 1944. Major general in July 1944. Commanding general of Marine Corps Base San Diego 1944-1946. Retired in November 1946. Decorations included the Distinguished Service Medal. Died on June 24, 1964.

Hunt, Leroy Philip (1892-1968) Born on March 17, 1892, in Newark, New Jersey. Attended the University of California 1911-1913. Commissioned in March 1917. Served with the 5th Marine Regiment in France in World War I. Wounded at the Aisne-Marne offensive in 1918. Graduated from the Naval War College in 1939. Force Marine officer on the *California* May 1939-February 1941. Brigadier general in January 1940. Commander of Special Service Troops of the 2nd Marine Division February-June 1941. Commanded 5th Marines, 1st Marine Division June 1941-September 1942. Assistant division commander of 2nd Marine Division September 1942-September 1944. Major general in February 1944. Commanding general of I Army Corps 1944-1946. Assignments after the war included commanding general of the Department of the Pacific 1947-1949 and commanding general of Fleet Marine Force Atlantic 1949-1951. General upon retirement in July 1951. Decorations included the Navy Cross, Distinguished Service Cross,

Silver Star, Legion of Merit, Bronze Star and Purple Heart. Died on February 8, 1968.

Jacobsen, Arnold Windom (1892–1970) Born on May 9, 1892, in Walnut, Ohio. Commissioned from Annapolis in 1916. LL.B. from George Washington University School of Law in 1924. Served with First Marine Brigade in Haiti 1932–1934. Instructor at Marine Corps Schools 1935–1936. Assistant to the quartermaster, U.S. Marine Corps July 1940–December 1942. Commander of the Depot of Supplies at San Francisco 1942–1946. Brigadier general in April 1944, major general upon retirement in July 1946. Decorations included the Silver Star and Legion of Merit. Died on March 22, 1970.

James, William Capers (1896–1974) Born on June 22, 1896, in Florence, South Carolina. Graduated from the Citadel in 1917. Commissioned in 1917. Served with the Second Provisional Brigade of Marines at Santo Domingo 1917–1919. Duty in Cuba 1922–1924 and with the Nicaraguan Expedition 1927–1928. Graduated from the Naval War College in 1937. Duty with the American Embassy in Peking 1937–1938. Secretary to the commandant of the Marine Corps 1939–1942. Served with the First Marine Division in the Solomons June–December 1942. Assigned to Camp Lejeune January–April 1943 then commanding officer of Marine Corps Base San Diego 1943–1944. Brigadier general in July 1944. Deputy chief civil affairs officer on Tinian 1944–1945. Commander of the forward echelon, Fleet Marine Force January–June 1945. Assistant director of personnel at headquarters U.S. Marine Corps July 1945 until retirement in November 1946. Died on September 30, 1974.

Johnson, Byron Fillmore (1894–n/a) Born on November 15, 1894, in Elk Falls, Kansas. Enlisted service 1917–1918. B.S. from the University of Minnesota in 1920. Commissioned in 1918 and served as an instructor at Officer Training Camp, Quantico until discharged in September 1919. Returned to the Marine Corps in 1921. Duty with the Third Brigade in China 1927–1928. Designated naval aviator in January 1929. Served in Nicaragua with the Second Marine Brigade 1930–1931. Graduated from Command and General Staff School in 1935. Naval attache in Bogota January 1941–March 1944. Served at the Marine Air Station, Cherry Point March–November 1944. Commander of Third Marine Aircraft Wing 1944–1945. Brigadier general in January 1945. Deputy commander of the First Marine Aircraft Wing August 1945–March 1946. Major general upon retirement in November 1946. Decorations included the Distinguished Flying Cross.

Jones, Louis Reeder (1895–1973) Born on June 29, 1895, in Philadelphia, Pennsylvania. Enlisted service 1914–1917. Commissioned in 1917. Served with the Sixth Marine Regiment in France in World War I, including the Aisne-Marne and St. Mihiel offensives. Duty with the Fourth Marine Regiment in Shanghai February 1927–January 1930. Instructor at Marine Corps Schools 1935–1938 then director of the Correspondence School May 1938–June 1939. Served at Parris Island 1939–1942. Commanding officer of the 23rd Marine Regiment September

1942-August 1944. Brigadier general in October 1942. Assistant division commander of the First Marine Division October 1944-September 1945. Participated
in the occupation of North China 1945-1946. President of the Marine Corps
Equipment Board June 1946-June 1949. Major general upon retirement in June
1949. Decorations included the Navy Cross, two Silver Stars, three Legions of
Merit and the Purple Heart. Died on February 2, 1973.

Keyser, Ralph Stover (1883-1955) Born on May 10, 1883, in Thoroughfare,
Virginia. Enlisted service in the U.S. Army 1902-1905. Commissioned in 1905.
Served at the American Embassy in Tokyo 1912-1913. Commanded a battalion of
the Fifth Marine Regiment and served as assistant chief of staff of 2nd Division,
AEF in World War I. Participated in the St. Mihiel and Meuse-Argonne offensives. Commanding officer of the Marine detachment at Managua, Nicaragua
1924-1925. Retired in February 1937 and promoted to brigadier general. Recalled
to active duty in April 1941. Served as director of the Marine Corps research division then assistant to the commandant 1941-1942. Retired in October 1942 as
major general. Decorations included the Navy Cross, Distinguished Service
Medal, two Silver Stars and the Purple Heart. Died on April 19, 1955.

Kingman, Matthew Henry (1890-1946) Born on March 1, 1890, in Humestown,
Iowa. B.S. from Virginia Military Institute in 1913. Commissioned in November
1913. Served in France and with U.S. Army Occupation Forces in Germany July
1917-July 1919. Instructor at Marine Corps Schools 1921-1922. Duty in Haiti
1923-1926 and Nicaragua May-July 1927. Brigade executive officer at 2nd Brigade, Fleet Marine Force August 1938-January 1939. Retired as colonel in April
1940. Recalled to active duty in February 1942. Brigadier general in March 1942.
Tactical instructor with 2nd Marine Division 1942-1944. Service with the Office
of Strategic Services in 1944. Retired a second time in October 1944. Decorations included the Silver Star and Purple Heart. Died on November 16, 1946.

Larkin, Claude Arthur (1891-1969) Born on June 21, 1891, in Garfield, Washington. Enlisted service 1915-1917. Commissioned in 1917. Served in Cuba, Haiti
and China. Designated naval aviator in April 1930. Assistant naval attache for air
in London in 1941. Commander of Marine Aircraft Group 21 1941-1943. Brigadier general in June 1942. Commanding general of Third Marine Aircraft Wing
December 1943-April 1944. Deputy commander of air operations in the Northern
Solomons April-August 1944 then commander of Third Marine Aircraft Wing
again August-December 1944. Commanding general of Marine Fleet Air, West
Coast 1945-1946. Major general in April 1945, lieutenant general upon retirement
in March 1946. Decorations included the Legion of Merit and Purple Heart. Died
on November 2, 1969.

Larsen, Henry Louis (1890-1962) Born on December 10, 1890, in Chicago, Illinois. Commissioned in 1913. Expeditionary duty in Cuba, Haiti, Santo Domingo
and Mexico 1914-1916. Served in the AEF 1917-1919. Duty in Nicaragua 1928-
1930. Attended the Ecole Superieure de Guerre 1932-1934. Brigade commander

on Samoa 1941-1942. Brigadier general in December 1941. Military governor of Samoa January 1942-June 1943. Major general in September 1942. Commander of Camp Lejeune June 1943-July 1944. Island commander on Guam July 1944-May 1946. Lieutenant general upon retirement in November 1946. Decorations included two Distinguished Service Crosses, the Distinguished Service Medal and three Silver Stars. Died on October 2, 1962.

Little, Louis McCarty (1878-1960) Born on January 16, 1878, in New York City. B.S. from Rensselaer Polytechnic Institute 1895-1899. Commissioned in 1899. Served in the Boxer Rebellion in 1900, the Philippine Insurrection 1900-1902 and with the Battle Fleet in its world cruise 1907-1909. Duty with the Marine Provisional Brigade in Cuba in 1911 and the American legation in Peking 1913-1917. Assigned to the naval planning section at headquarters of U.S. Naval Forces in Europe during World War I. Served in Haiti with the First Provisional Brigade 1919-1921. Graduated from the Naval War College in 1921 and the Army War College in 1923. Commander of the American legation guard in Peking 1924-1927. Again in Haiti as commander of First Marine Brigade 1931-1934. Brigadier general in January 1934. Assistant to the commandant, U.S. Marine Corps May 1935-1937. Major general in July 1935. Commanding general of Fleet Marine Force June 1937-September 1939 then Marine Barracks 1939-1942. Retired in February 1942. Died on July 16, 1960.

Long, Earl Cecil (1883-n/a) Born on November 4, 1883, in Clayton, New Jersey. Attended the University of California 1901-1905. Commissioned in 1909. Served overseas in Nicaragua, Mexico, France in World War I and China. Marine Corps representative to the Golden Gate International Exposition in San Francisco 1938-1940. Assistant chief of staff for supply at headquarters of Department of the Pacific 1940-1943. Brigadier general in September 1942. Commanding general of supply service, I and V Marine Amphibious Corps 1943-1944 then Service Command, Fleet Marine Force Pacific 1944-1945. Major general in November 1944. Commanding general of Marine Base San Diego 1945-1946. Retired in August 1946. Decorations included the Legion of Merit.

Marston, John (1884-1957) Born on August 3, 1884, in Somerset County, Pennsylvania. Attended the University of Pennsylvania 1901-1904. Commissioned in 1908. Served aboard the *Michigan* at Vera Cruz in 1914. Civil administrator in Haiti 1915-1918. Commander of the Marine detachment in Nicaragua 1922-1924 then area commander 1932-1933. Student then director of Marine Corps Schools 1933-1934. Director of personnel at headquarters U.S. Marine Corps 1934-1937. Commander of Marine forces in Northern China 1937-1939. Brigadier general in October 1939. Chief of staff of Department of the Pacific in 1940. Commander of infantry in 2nd Marine Division in 1941. Commanding general of U.S. forces in Iceland 1941-1942. Major general in March 1942. Commanding general of 2nd Marine Division April 1942-April 1943, the Department of the Pacific 1943-1944 and Camp Lejeune 1944-1946. Retired in August 1946. Died on November 25, 1957.

McKittrick, William Lake (1897-1984) Born on June 30, 1897, in Pelzer, South Carolina. B.S. from the Citadel in 1918. Commissioned in 1918. Served with the Second Provisional Brigade in the Dominican Republic 1919-1921. Qualified as naval aviator in 1923. Duty in Haiti 1923-1925 and Nicaragua 1931-1932. Aviation officer in the war plans section at headquarters U.S. Marine Corps 1939-1941. Commanding officer of Marine Air Group 24 February 1942-March 1944 then chief of staff of First Marine Air Wing March-November 1944. Brigadier general in January 1945. Assistant director of Marine Corps aviation January 1945-June 1947. Major general upon retirement in October 1951. Decorations included the Legion of Merit and Bronze Star. Died on March 27, 1984.

Merritt, Lewie Griffith (1897-1974) Born on June 26, 1897, in Ridge Spring, South Carolina. B.S. from the Citadel in 1917. Commissioned in 1917. Served with the Second Provisional Brigade in Santo Domingo June 1917-August 1918 and the AEF October 1918-August 1919. Designated naval aviator in January 1924. LL.B. from George Washington University in June 1928. Duty in Haiti 1928-1903. Graduated from Command and General Staff School in May 1933. Observer in England 1940-1942. Commander of Service Group, Marine Air Wings Pacific May-September 1942. Brigadier general in October 1942. Commanding general of Fleet Marine Air, West Coast 1942-1945 then First Marine Aircraft Wing 1945-1946. Major general upon retirement in June 1947. Decorations included the Legion of Merit and Bronze Star. Died on March 24, 1974.

Miller, Ivan W. (1898-n/a) Born on July 16, 1898, in Versailles, Ohio. Commissioned from Annapolis in 1920. Qualified as naval aviator in 1921. M.S. from MIT in 1924. Served with the First Marine Brigade at Port au Prince, Haiti 1926-1928. Assigned to Nicaragua and Haiti 1932-1934. Commanding officer of Marine Corps Air Station Quantico 1941-1943. Assistant chief of staff, then chief of staff of four section, Marine Aircraft South Pacific February-June 1944, then Aircraft, Fleet Marine Force Pacific June 1944-July 1945. Brigadier general in January 1945. Commanding general of Marine Corps Air Stations at Miramar and El Toro 1945-1947. Retired as major general in October 1951. Decorations included the Legion of Merit.

Miller, Lyle Holcombe (1889-n/a) Born on March 10, 1889, in Athens, Michigan. B.A. from Albion College. Commissioned in 1914. Served with the 13th Marines in the AEF September 1918-July 1919. Graduated from Command and General Staff School in 1927. Battalion commander with Fourth Marines in Shanghai 1932-1934. Graduated from the Naval War College in 1941. Assigned to 2nd Marine Division 1941-1942. Chief of staff of Amphibious Force, Pacific Fleet March-April 1942 then Defense Force, Samoan Group April 1942-March 1944. Brigadier general in August 1942. Lengthy hospitalization prior to retirement in June 1945. Decorations included the Legion of Merit.

Mitchell, Ralph Johnson (1891-1970) Born on September 25, 1891, in New Britain, Connecticut. Commissioned from Annapolis in 1915. Qualified as naval aviator in 1921. Established and built the Naval Air Station in Guam 1921-1923. Graduated from Air Corps Tactical School in 1927 and Command and General Staff School in 1928. Commander of aircraft squadrons in Nicaragua 1929-1931. Graduated from the Naval War College in 1933. Commander of 2nd Marine Aircraft Group 1935-1939. Director of aviation at headquarters U.S. Marine Corps March 1939-April 1942. Brigadier general in March 1942, major general in September 1942. Assistant to the commandant of the Marine Corps for aviation April 1942-November 1943. Commander of Aircraft, Solomon Islands 1943-1944. Commanding general of Marine Corps Air Base Cherry Point, then Second Marine Air Wing 1945-1947. Lieutenant general upon retirement in May 1948. Decorations included two Distinguished Service Medals, two Legions of Merit, the Distinguished Flying Cross and two Air Medals. Died on May 31, 1970.

Moore, James Tillinghast (1895-1953) Born on September 5, 1895, in Barnwell, South Carolina. B.S. from the Citadel in 1916. Commissioned in 1916. Served with the Second Provisional Brigade, Santo Domingo 1916-1919. Qualified as naval aviator in 1921. Executive officer of Aircraft Squadrons, Third Marine Brigade, China March 1927-September 1928. Duty at Naval Station, Guam September-November 1928. Graduated from Air Corps Tactical School in July 1930. Squadron commander on St. Thomas 1935-1937. Graduated from the Naval War College in 1938. Executive officer of First Marine Aircraft Group 1938-1939. Force air officer with Fleet Marine Force July 1939-October 1940. Member of the U.S. Aviation Mission to Peru October 1940-October 1942, where he was named commanding general of the Peruvian Air Force. Brigadier general in September 1942. Commanding general of Fourth Marine Aircraft Base Defense Wing October 1942-May 1943. Chief of staff, then deputy commander, finally commanding general of First Marine Air Wing May 1943-July 1944. Commanding general of Second Marine Air Wing July 1944-February 1945 then Aircraft, Fleet Marine Force Pacific February 1945-August 1946. Major general in February 1944. Retired in November 1946. Decorations included Distinguished Service Medal and Legion of Merit. Died on November 10, 1953. Died on November 10, 1953.

Moses, Emile Phillips (1880-1965) Born on May 27, 1880, in Sumter, South Carolina. Attended the University of South Carolina 1896-1899 and Georgia Institute of technology 1901-1902. Commissioned in 1904. Served with the expeditionary forces in Nicaragua and Cuba in 1912 and in Peking and Shanghai 1927-1929. Graduated from the Army War College in 1930 and the Naval War College in 1931. Again in China with the Fourth Marines at Shanghai 1932-1934. Chief of staff of Fleet Marine Force 1935-1938. Brigadier general in February 1939. President of the Marine Corps Equipment Board 1939-1941. Commanding general of Marine Barracks at Parris Island September 1941-April 1944. Major general in September 1942. Retired in May 1944. Died on December 22, 1965.

Mulcahy, Francis Patrick (1894-1973) Born on March 9, 1894, in Rochester, New York. Ph.B. from Notre Dame in 1914. Commissioned in 1917. Served with the AEF in 1918 and in Haiti in 1925. Graduated from Air Corps Tactical School in 1928 and Command and General Staff School in 1929. Duty in Nicaragua 1931-1932. Graduated from the Naval War College in 1936. Served in St. Thomas, Virgin Islands 1938-1940. Brigadier general in July 1941. U.S. naval observer in Libya and Egypt 1941-1942. Commander of 2nd Marine Air Wing including all Allied air forces on Guadalcanal December 1942-February 1943. Chief of staff to Commander Air Forces, Solomon Islands February-April 1943. Major general in February 1944. Commanding general of Marine Fleet Air, West Coast May-September 1944 then Aircraft, FMF Pacific 1944-1945. Hospitalized in 1945. Lieutenant general upon retirement in April 1946. Decorations included the Distinguished Service Medal. Died on December 11, 1973.

Nimmer, David Rowan (1894-1975) Born on October 14, 1894, in St. Louis, Missouri. Enlisted service 1912-1918 and commissioned in 1918. Resigned his commission in 1919 but returned to active duty in the Marine Corps as a captain in April 1921. Instructor at Marine Corps Schools 1927-1929. Overseas duty with the Fourth Marine Regiment in Shanghai 1929-1930, the American Legation in Peking, China 1931-1932, where he learned the Russian language, and as assistant naval attache in Moscow 1932-1934. Operations officer with the 1st Marine Division 1937-1939. Commanding officer of Marine Corps Base, Cuba 1939-1942 then Ninth Defense Battalion (Pacific) October 1942-April 1943. Duty with the Joint War Plans Committee of the JCS, Commander in Chief United States Fleet 1943-1944. Brigadier general in February 1944. Commander of Third Amphibious Corps Artillery 1944-1945. Major general upon retirement in July 1947. Decorations included the Legion of Merit. Died on August 23, 1975.

Noble, Alfred Houston (1894-1983) Born on October 26, 1894, in Federalsburg, Maryland. B.A. from St. John's College in 1917. Commissioned in 1917. Served with 6th Marines in France and Germany 1917-1919. Duty in the Virgin Islands 1919-1922. Instructor with Marine Corps Schools 1925-1927 and 1930-1932. Chief of staff of 1st Marine Brigade in Haiti 1932-1934. Assistant commandant of Marine Corps Schools 1937-1939. Battalion commander in 5th Marines 1940-1941. Brigadier general in August 1940. Director of the plans and policy division at headquarters U.S. Marine Corps in 1941. Chief of staff of 3rd Division 1942-1943. Major general in September 1942. Chief of staff of I Marine Amphibious Corps 1943-1944. Commanding general of Training Command at Camp Lejeune 1945-1946. Retired in November 1956. Decorations included the Navy Cross, Distinguished Service Cross, two Legions of Merit, two Silver Stars and the Commendation Ribbon. Died on September 27, 1983.

Ostermann, Edward Albert (1882-1969) Born on November 23, 1882, in Columbus, Ohio. Attended Ohio Northern University. Commissioned in 1907. Enlisted service in the U.S. Army as a chief trumpeter 1899-1902 and 1904-1905. Earned the Medal of Honor at Fort Liberte, Haiti for action on October 24, 1915 as a first lieutenant. Wounded during the Haitian Campaign 1930-1931. Brigadier general in February 1939. Adjutant and inspector of the Marine Corps 1939-1943.

Major general upon retirement in January 1943. Decorations included the Medal of Honor. Died on May 18, 1969.

Peck, DeWitt (1894-1973) Born on May 29, 1894, in Bakersfield, California. Commissioned from Annapolis in 1915. Served in Haiti 1915-1916. Company commander with 5th Marines in the AEF in World War I. Duty in Cuba 1922-1924. Instructor at Marine Corps Schools in 1925. Graduated from Command and General Staff School in 1928. Intelligence officer with the Nicaraguan Electoral Mission in 1929. Again instructor at Marine Corps Schools 1931-1933. Graduated from the Naval War College in 1936 then instructor there until 1937. Commander of the Fourth Marines in Shanghai, China November 1939-March 1941. Assigned to headquarters Commander in Chief United States Fleet March 1941-May 1942. Brigadier general in March 1942. Assistant chief of staff for war plans to Commander South Pacific Area and South Pacific Force May 1942-July 1943. Director of the Marine Corps division of plans and policies 1943-1944. Major general in January 1944. Assistant commandant of the Marine Corps 1944-1945. Commanding general of 1st Marine Division August 1945-1946. Retired in November 1946. Decorations included two Legions of Merit and the Purple Heart. Returned to active duty in 1953 and served as deputy director of manpower utilization in the Department of Defense. Died on January 13, 1973.

Pepper, Robert Houston (1895-1968) Born on April 22, 1895, in Georgetown, Delaware. B.A. from the University of Delaware in 1917. Commissioned in 1917. Served with the First Provisional Brigade in Haiti December 1917-December 1919 and aide to the Haiti High Commissioner May 1922-August 1924. Assigned to the war plans division at headquarters, U.S. Marine Corps July 1935-June 1939. Battalion commander with 15th Marines June-October 1939 then Third Defense Battalion, Fleet Marine Force October 1939-August 1940. Executive officer, then commanding officer of 11th Marines August 1940-February 1944. Brigadier general in December 1943. Chief of staff at Camp Lejeune April 1944-May 1945. Commanding general of V Amphibious Corps Artillery, Fleet Marine Force Pacific June 1945-October 1945. Assignments after the war included commanding general of 3rd Marine Division 1952-1953 and 1st Marine Division in Korea May-July 1954, commanding general of Fleet Marine Force Pacific August 1954-September 1955 then Department of the Pacific 1955-1957. Retired as lieutenant general in September 1957. Decorations included the Legion of Merit and two Commendation Ribbons. Recalled to active duty in 1964 to head the Pepper Board which studied the role of women Marines in peacetime. Died on June 1, 1968.

Pfeiffer, Omar Titus (1895-1979) Born on November 24, 1895, in Toledo, Ohio. B.A. from the University of Minnesota in 1917. Commissioned in 1917. Served with the Atlantic Fleet in World War I then the Second Provisional Brigade in the Dominican Republic August 1919-November 1921. Company commander at Marine Barracks, Guam March-December 1925 then expeditionary duty in Shanghai December 1925-October 1927. Assigned to Pearl Harbor June

1930-July 1931 then Fourteenth Naval District July 1931-March 1933. Graduated from the Naval War College in May 1937. Duty in the war plans section at Marine Barracks, Quantico May 1937-April 1941. Assistant war plans officer with Commander in Chief Pacific Fleet April 1941-June 1943 then staff Marine officer at Commander in Chief United States Fleet June 1943-November 1945. Brigadier general in October 1942. Duty in the office of the chief of naval operations November 1945-February 1946. Fleet Marine officer with Commander Seventh Fleet February 1946-May 1947. Commanding general of Fleet Marine Force Western Pacific May-October 1947. Chief of staff of Marine Barracks and Marine Training and Replacement Command, Camp Pendleton October 1947-July 1948. Major general upon retirement in May 1950. Decorations included the Legion of Merit and Bronze Star. Died on March 1, 1979.

Pickett, Harry Kleinbeck (1888-1965) Born on January 9, 1888, in Ridgeway, South Carolina. B.S. from the Citadel in 1913. Commissioned in 1913. Served in Guam March 1915-August 1917 then with the 11th Regiment in France September 1918-July 1919. Brigadier general in January 1942, major general in September 1942. Commanding general of Troop Training Unit, Training Command Amphibious Forces, Pacific Fleet May 1943-July 1946. Retired in November 1, 1946. Decorations included two Legions of Merit. Died on March 19, 1965.

Price, Charles Frederick Berthold (1881-1954) September 18, 1881, in Hamburg, Germany. C.E. from Pennsylvania Military College in 1902. Commissioned in 1906. Expeditionary duty in Cuba September 1906-December 1908, Nicaragua and Panama Canal Zone 1909-1910 and the occupation of Vera Cruz in 1914. Battalion commander in the AEF in 1918. Instructor at Marine Corps Schools in 1923. Overseas duty with the American Legation in Peking 1925-1927, the American Electoral Mission in Nicaragua 1928 and 1930-1932, and with the Fourth Marines at Shanghai, China April 1935-November 1938. Assigned to the Naval Examining Board at headquarters, U.S. Marine Corps 1938-February 1941. Brigadier general in August 1940. Commanding general of the Department of the Pacific February-November 1941 then 2nd Marine Division November 1941-April 1942. Major general in February 1942. Commanded the Defense Force, Samoan Group April 1942-May 1944. Commander of San Diego Area and Marine Training and Replacement Command May 1944-1948. Lieutenant general upon retirement in October 1948. Decorations included the Distinguished Service Medal and Legion of Merit. Died in January 1954.

Puryear, Bennet Jr. (1884-1982) Born on January 9, 1884, in Richmond, Virginia. Attended Texas A&M 1903-1905. Commissioned in 1905. Duty in Isle of Pines, Cuba 1906-1909 and in the Philippine Islands 1911-1914. Served with the 5th Marines, 2nd Division in the AEF 1917-1919. Quartermaster for the Gendarmerie d'Haiti July 1925-July 1928. Brigadier general in March 1942. Assigned to the Quartermaster Department at headquarters, U.S. Marine Corps 1942-1944. Major general upon retirement in May 1944. Decorations included the Navy Cross, Legion of Merit and Purple Heart. Died on February 11, 1982.

Putnam, Russell Benjamin (1878-1959) Born on January 7, 1878, in Abbeville, Louisiana. B.S. from Centenary College in 1894 and M.E. from Cornell University in 1901. Commissioned in 1904. Expeditionary duty with the First Brigade Marines in the Philippine Islands 1909-1912, in Nicaragua 1912-1914, during the occupation of Vera Cruz in 1914, with the First Brigade Marines in Haiti 1915-1916, in the Dominican Republic with the Second Provisional Brigade Marines 1916-1917 and again in Haiti 1919-1921. Served in the office of the paymaster general, United States Marine Corps October 1935-1938. Brigadier general in May 1938 as paymaster of the Marine Corps 1938-1942. Retired in February 1942. Died on May 29, 1959.

Rea, Leonard Earl (1897-) Born on March 14, 1897, in Auburn, New York. Enlisted in April 1917 and commissioned in 1918. Wounded in action during service in France and Germany during World War I. Discharged in July 1919. Returned to active duty in May 1921. Commanding officer of the Marine detachment at Chinandega, Nicaragua July-December 1928 then duty with the Nicaragua National Guard May 1931-February 1933. Post, brigade and division quartermaster January 1937-May 1941. Assistant to the officer in charge then officer in charge of the supply division of the Quartermaster Department, headquarters U.S. Marine Corps 1941-1943. Executive officer of the Quartermaster Department at headquarters, Marine Corps 1943-August 1946. Brigadier general in May 1944. Depot quartermaster at Depot of Supplies August 1946-October 1950. Chief of the supply branch at headquarters, Marine Corps October 1950 until retirement as major general in November 1953. Decorations included the Navy Cross, Distinguished Service Cross, two Silver Stars, the Legion of Merit and Purple Heart.

Riley, William Edward (1897-1970) Born on February 2, 1897, in Minneapolis, Minnesota. Attended College of St. Thomas. Commissioned in 1917. Twice wounded in action while serving with the Sixth Marine Regiment in France September 1917-December 1918. Foreign duty in Haiti, Puerto Rico, Santo Domingo and Cuba 1919-1925. Instructor at Marine Corps Schools July 1926-July 1928. Company commander with the Gendarmerie d'Haiti July 1928-June 1931. Graduated from Command and General Staff School in May 1933. Instructor at Northwestern University Naval ROTC May 1933-May 1935. Graduated from the Naval War College in May 1940. Squadron Marine officer then fleet Marine officer with Atlantic Squadron May 1940-April 1942. Duty with the war plans division at headquarters of Commander in Chief United States Fleet 1942-1943. Brigadier general in April 1943. Assistant war plans officer at Commander South Pacific Area and South Pacific Force July 1943-June 1944. Assistant chief of staff at Commander Third Fleet June 1944-May 1945. Major general and commander of the 3rd Marine Division May-December 1945. Lieutenant general upon retirement in June 1951 but continued on active duty until 1953. Decorations included the Distinguished Service Medal, Legion of Merit, two Silver Stars, the Navy Cross and two Purple Hearts. Died on April 28, 1970.

Robinson, Ray Albert (1896-1976) Born on June 1, 1896, in Los Angeles, California. Attended the University of Southern California. Commissioned in October 1917. Served with the 13th Marine Regiment in France September 1918-July 1919. Duty at Marine Barracks, Pearl Harbor September 1921-December 1923 then on the staff of the Commanding General Third Marine Brigade, Shanghai January 1927-March 1929. Commander of Marine Forces North China and the embassy detachment at Peking May 1939-June 1941. Officer in Charge of the personnel section, headquarters Marine Corps June 1941-January 1944. Brigadier general in April 1943. Chief of staff of 3rd Marine Division January-October 1944 then 5th Division October 1944-June 1945. Assistant division commander of 5th Marine Division June 1945-March 1946. Assignments after the war included commander of 2nd Marine Division June 1950-December 1951 and commanding general of Fleet Marine Force Atlantic November 1956-November 1957. General on retirement in November 1957. Decorations included two Legions of Merit and the Bronze Star. Died March 26, 1976.

Rockey, Keller Emrick (1888-1970) Born on September 27, 1888, in Columbia City, Indiana. B.S. from Gettysburg College in 1909. Attended Yale University Forestry School 1910-1911. Commissioned in 1913. Served with 5th Marines, 2nd Marine Division in the AEF during World War I. Assigned as major in the Gendarmerie d'Haiti 1919-1922. Graduated from Command and General Staff School in 1926. Instructor at Marine Corps Schools 1926-1928. Battalion commander in Nicaragua 1928-1929. Staff officer with the Battle Force 1937-1939. Duty in the office of the chief of naval operations 1939-1941. Chief of staff of 2nd Marine Division 1941-1942. Brigadier general in August 1942, major general in August 1943. Director of the plans and policy division at headquarters U.S. Marine Corps 1943-1944. Commanding general of 5th Marine Division 1944-1945 and V Amphibious Corps 1945-1946. Assignments after the war included commanding general of Fleet Marine Force Atlantic 1947-1949 and Department of the Pacific 1949-1950. Retired as lieutenant general in September 1950. Decorations included two Navy Crosses and two Distinguished Service Medals. Died on June 6, 1970.

Rogers, Ford Ovid (1894-1972) Born on March 23, 1894, in Waco, Texas. Attended Annapolis 1913-1917. Commissioned in the Marine Corps in 1917. Designated a naval aviator, he saw action with the AEF in World War I. Served in the Dominican Republic 1922-1924 and Haiti 1929-1931. Commanding officer of the Marine Air Station, St. Thomas 1941-1942. Chief of the U.S. Naval Aviation Mission to Peru 1942-1945. Brigadier general in November 1943. Commanding general of Third Marine Aircraft Wing then duty with the Air Defense Command Okinawa 1945-1946. Major general upon retirement in November 1946. Decorations included the Navy Cross. Died on September 12, 1972.

Rogers, William Walter (1893-1976) Born on December 25, 1893, in Thorntown, Indiana. B.S. from Miami University of Ohio in 1914. Enlisted service 1917-1918 in the AEF. Commissioned in 1918. Seriously wounded in the Meuse-

Argonne offensive on October 7, 1918. Assigned to the plans and policies division at headquarters U.S. Marine Corps 1941-1943. Chief of staff of the Fourth Marine Division August 1943-August 1944. Duty with V Marine Amphibious Corps 1944-1946. Brigadier general in January 1945, major general upon retirement in December 1946. Decorations included the Distinguished Service Medal, two Silver Stars and the Purple Heart. Died on October 15, 1976.

Rowell, Ross Erastus (1884-1947) Born on September 24, 1884, in Ruthven, Iowa. Attended Iowa State University 1901-1903 and the University of Idaho 1904-1905. Commissioned in 1906. Overseas assignments included Cuba 1906-1909, Nicaragua 1914-1916, again in Cuba 1917-1918 and Haiti in 1918. Qualified as naval aviator in 1923. Director of Marine Corps aviation 1935-1939. Brigadier general in August 1939, the first Marine aviator to achieve that rank. Naval attache in Havana 1939-1940. Commanding officer of Marine Squadrons at Naval Air Station San Diego June 1940-April 1941. Major general in January 1942. Commanding general of Marine Aircraft Wings in the Pacific Fleet July 1942-October 1944. Member of the U.S. Aviation Mission to Peru 1944-1946. Retired in November 1946. Decorations included the Distinguished Service Medal and Distinguished Flying Cross. Died on September 6, 1947.

Rupertus, William Henry (1889-1945) Born in Washington, D.C., on November 14, 1889. Enlisted service in the District of Columbia National Guard 1907-1910. Graduated from the United States Revenue Cutter Service School in 1913 and commissioned in the Marine Corps. Served in Haiti 1920-1924. Graduated from Command and General Staff School in 1926. Duty with the American Legation in Peking 1929-1933 then the Fourth Marines in Shanghai 1937-1938. Commanded the Marine Barracks in Washington, D.C. 1938-1940. Assistant division commander of the First Marine Division 1941-1943. Brigadier general in January 1942, major general in July 1943. Commander of the First Marine Division July 1943-November 1944. Commandant of Marine Corps Schools until his death on March 25, 1945. Decorations included the Navy Cross.

Sanderson, Charles Roosa (1882-1961) Born on June 25, 1882, in Washington, D.C. Attended George Washington University. Commissioned in 1904. Aide to the governor of Puerto Rico 1904-1907. Duty in the Philippines October 1908-October 1910 and Nicaragua 1912-1913. Served with the Second Provisional Brigade in Santo Domingo 1920-1922 and Nicaragua 1928-1929. Quartermaster at the Philadelphia Depot of Supplies July 1936 until retirement in June 1939. Recalled to active duty in June 1940 and assigned to the purchase division of the Quartermaster Department. Brigadier general in December 1944. Retired again in December 1945. Decorations included the Distinguished Service Medal and Legion of Merit. Died on December 22, 1961.

Sanderson, Lawson Harry McPherson (1895-1979) Born on July 22, 1895, in Shelton, Washington. Attended the University of Washington. B.A. from the University of Montana in 1917. Commissioned in 1917. Qualified as a naval aviator in

1917. Served in the AEF 1917-1918, where he pioneered dive bombing. Occupation duty in Haiti 1919-1921 and 1923-1924 then Nicaragua 1927-1930. Expeditionary duty in Puerto Rico, the Virgin Islands and China 1934-1941. Operations officer in the 1st Marine Aircraft Wing 1941-1942. Commanding officer of Marine Air Group Eleven January 1943-September 1944. Brigadier general in June 1944. Commander of Marine Fleet Air West Coast September 1944-May 1945 then 4th Marine Aircraft Wing 1945-1946. Major general upon retirement in December 1951. Decorations included the Legion of Merit. Died on June 11, 1979.

Schilt, Christian Frank (1895-1987) Born on March 18, 1895, in Richland County, Illinois. Attended Rose Polytechnic Institute 1915-1917. Commissioned in 1918. Served at Ponta Delgada, Azores with the 1st Marine Aeronautical Company during World War I. Qualified as a naval aviator in 1919. Expeditionary duty in Santo Domingo October 1919-February 1920. Served with Marine Aviation Forces, Haiti August 1920-October 1922 and with Observation Squadron 7-M, Managua, Nicaragua November 1927-August 1929. Earned the Medal of Honor as a first lieutenant at Quilali, Nicaragua in 1928. Graduated from Air Corps Tactical School in June 1934. Executive officer of Marine Corps Air Station St. Thomas May 1938-June 1940. Assistant naval attache for air in London May-August 1941. Engineer and supply officer then assistant chief of staff of 1st Marine Aircraft Wing August 1941-September 1942. Commander of Marine Aircraft Group Eleven and Strike and Search Patrol Commands, Solomon Islands in 1943. Commanding officer of Marine Corps Air Station, Cherry Point September 1943-March 1944. Chief of staff then commander of 9th Marine Aircraft Wing April-December 1944. Brigadier general in June 1944. Island commander on Peleliu February-August 1945. Commanding general of Air Defense Command August-October 1945. Assignments after the war included assistant commandant of the Marine Corps for air July 1955-April 1957. General upon retirement in April 1957. Decorations included the Medal of Honor, Distinguished Service Cross, Legion of Merit, Bronze Star, Distinguished Flying Cross and five Air Medals. Died on January 9, 1987.

Schmidt, Harry (1886-1968) Born on September 25, 1886, in Holdrege, Nebraska. Commissioned in 1909. Attended Nebraska State Normal College. Commissioned in August 1909. Stationed at Marine Barracks, Guam January 1911-September 1912. Duty with the expeditionary force in China November-December 1911. Served in the Philippines October 1912-April 1913. Instructor at Marine Corps Schools 1923-1926. Duty with the Sixth Regiment in China April-September 1927 then the Second Brigade in Nicaragua February 1928-June 1929. Graduated from Command and General Staff School in June 1932. Regimental pay officer with the Expeditionary Force, Shanghai September 1934-April 1936. Chief of staff of Second Marine Brigade, Shanghai June 1937-June 1938. Executive and personnel officer at headquarters, Marine Corps July 1938-January 1942 then assistant to the commandant of the Marine Corps January 1942-August 1943. Brigadier general in October 1941, major general in September 1942. Commanding general of 4th Marine Division August 1943-July 1944 then V Amphibious Corps July 1944-February 1946. Assignments after the war included commanding general of Marine Training and Replacement Command February 1946-July 1948. General upon retirement in July 1948. Decorations included the Navy Cross, three Distinguished Service Medals, the Legion of Merit and Bronze Star. Died on February 10, 1968.

Shepherd, Lemuel Cornick, Jr. (1896-1990) Born on February 10, 1896, in Norfolk, Virginia. Commissioned from Virginia Military Institute in 1917. With 5th Marine Regiment in battles of Aisne-Marne, St. Mihiel and Meuse-Argonne in World War I. Aide to Major General John A. Lejeune, commandant of the Marine Corps, 1920-1922. With 4th Marine Regiment in China 1927-1929. Stationed in Haiti 1930-1934. Graduate of the Naval War College in 1937. Staff officer at Marine Corps Schools 1939-1942. Commanding officer of 9th Marine Regiment March 1942-January 1943. Assistant commander of the 1st Marine Division January 1943-April 1944. Brigadier general in July 1943. Commanding general of 1st Provisional Marine Brigade April-September 1944. Major general in September 1944. Commander of 6th Marine Division September 1944-November 1946. Assignments after the war included assistant commandant of the Marine Corps November 1946-June 1950, commanding general of Fleet Marine Force Pacific June 1950-December 1951, and commandant of the Marine Corps January 1952 until retirement as general in January 1956. Decorations included the Navy Cross, Distinguished Service Cross, two Distinguished Service Medals, two Silver Stars, two Legions of Merit and three Purple Hearts. Died on August 6, 1990.

Silverthorn, Merwin Hancock (1896-1985) Born on September 22, 1896, in Minneapolis, Minnesota. Attended the University of Minnesota 1914-1917. Enlisted service 1917-1918. Commissioned in 1918. Served in the AEF 1918-1919. Duty with the Gendarmerie d'Haiti 1923-1926. Instructor at Marine Corps Schools 1936-1937. Graduated from the Naval War College in 1938. Force Marine officer with the Scouting Force 1939-1941. Brigadier general in June 1942. Member of the Joint U.S. Strategic Committee, JCS 1942-1943. Major general in April 1943. Chief of staff of III Amphibious Corps 1944-1945 then Fleet Marine Force Pacific 1945-1946. Assignments after the war included assistant commandant of the Marine Corps 1950-1952. Retired as lieutenant general in July 1954. Decorations included the Navy Cross, Distinguished Service Cross, Distinguished Service Medal, two Silver Stars, the Legion of Merit, Commendation Ribbon and Purple Heart. Died on August 14, 1985.

Smith, Holland McTyeire (1882-1967) Born on April 20, 1882, in Seale, Alabama. Graduated from Alabama Polytechnic Institute 1901. LL.D. from the University of Alabama in 1903. Practiced law two years in Montgomery. Commissioned in 1905. Overseas duty in the Philippines 1906-1908 and 1912-1914, Panama 1909-1910, and Dominican Republic 1916-1917, during which he earned the nickname "Howlin' Mad" Smith. Saw combat in the Aisne-Marne, St. Mihiel, Oise and Meuse-Argonne campaigns in World War I. Graduated from the Naval War College in 1921. At headquarters of the Marine Corps 1937-1939. Brigadier general in August 1939. Assistant to the commandant April-September 1939. Commander of 1st Marine Brigade September 1939-August 1942. Major general in February 1941. Commanding general of Amphibious Force, Atlantic Fleet, then Pacific Fleet September 1942-July 1944. Lieutenant general in February 1944. Commanding general of Fleet Marine Force Pacific July 1944-July 1945 then Camp Pendleton July 1945 until retirement as general in August 1946. Author of *Coral and Brass*, 1949. Decorations included the Purple Heart. Died on January 12, 1967.

Smith, Joseph Thomas (1895-1965) Born on August 11, 1895, in Livermore, California. B.A. from the University of California in 1917. Commissioned in 1917. Foreign duty on Guam 1918-1920, in the Virgin Islands 1923-1925, Nicaragua in 1928 and Shanghai 1937-1938. Chief of staff of Third Marine Brigade Pacific, commanding officer of South Pacific Echelon and deputy chief of staff of Fleet Marine Fleet Pacific during World War II. Brigadier general in April 1943. Major general upon retirement in November 1946. Decorations included the Legion of Merit and Bronze Star. Died on May 27, 1965.

Smith, Julian Constable (1885-1975) Born on September 11, 1885. B.A. from the University of Delaware in 1907. Commissioned in 1909. Served at Camp Elliott in the Canal Zone 1912-1914, at Vera Cruz in 1914 and in Santo Domingo 1915-1916. Instructor at Marine Corps Schools 1918-1919. Commanding officer of 2nd Machine Gun Battalion, 6th Marines in Cuba in 1919. Again instructor at Marine Corps Schools 1928-1930. Chief of staff of Nicaraguan National Guard detachment 1930-1933. Operations officer with 7th Marines 1933-1934. Member, then director of operations and training division at headquarters U.S. Marine Corps 1935-1938. Chief of staff of 1st Brigade 1938-1940. Chief of staff to commanding general of Marine Barracks at Quantico 1940-1941. Brigadier general in March 1941, major general in October 1942. Commanding general of Fleet Marine Force Training Schools October 1942-May 1943, 2nd Marine Division 1943-1944 and expeditionary troops of the Third Fleet April-December 1944. Commander of the Department of the Pacific then Marine Corps Recruit Depot at Parris Island 1944-1946. Lieutenant general upon retirement in December 1946. Decorations included the Navy Cross and two Distinguished Service Medals. Died on November 5, 1975.

Smith, Oliver Prince (1893-1977) Born on October 26, 1893, in Menard, Texas. Graduated from the University of California at Berkeley in 1916. Commissioned in May 1917. Instructor at Marine Corps Schools, Quantico 1932-1933 and again 1936-1939. Staff officer with Fleet Marine Force Pacific 1939-1940. Commanded a battalion of the 6th Marine Regiment 1940-1942. At headquarters U.S. Marine Corps 1942-1943. Battalion commander in the 5th Marine Regiment, 1st Division, then assistant commanding general in of the division January-November 1944. Brigadier general in April 1944. Deputy chief of staff of Tenth Army November 1944-June 1945. Commandant of Marine Corps Schools June 1945-April 1948. Assignments after the war included commanding general of Fleet Marine

Force Atlantic July 1953 until retirement as general in September 1955. Decorations included the Distinguished Service Cross, two Distinguished Service Medals, the Silver Star, two Legions of Merit and the Bronze Star. Died on December 25, 1977.

Thomas, Gerald Carthrae (1894-1984) Born on October 29, 1894, in Slater, Missouri. Attended Illinois Wesleyan University 1915-1917. Enlisted service 1917-1918 include combat at Verdun, Belleau Wood, St. Mihiel and Meuse-Argonne. Commissioned on the battlefield in 1918. Overseas duty in Haiti 1919-1920 and Peking 1935-1937. Assistant operations officer at 1st Marine Division 1941-1942 then chief of staff to Major General Alexander Vandegrift on Guadalcanal September 1942-July 1943. Brigadier general in December 1943. Director of plans and policies at headquarters U.S. Marine Corps January 1944-June 1947. Assignments after the war included commanding general of 1st Marine Division 1951-1952 and assistant commandant of the Marine Corps 1952-1954. General upon retirement in December 1955. Decorations included the Distinguished Service Cross, two Distinguished Service Medals, the Silver Star and Purple Heart. Died on April 7, 1984.

Torrey, Philip Huston (1884-1968) Born on July 18, 1884, in Fort Douglas, Utah. Attended Lehigh University 1902-1903 and the University of Montana in 1904. Commissioned in 1905. Served in Cuba 1906-1909 and again 1911-1912, then Mexico in 1915 and Haiti 1920-1922 and 1929-1931. Graduated from the Naval War College in 1938. Commandant of Marine Corps Schools July 1939-January 1941. Brigadier general in November 1939. Commanding general of Infantry Forces, First Marine Brigade January-June 1941. Acting commanding general, then commanding general of 1st Marine Division June 1941-March 1942. Major general in November 1941. Director of the division of reserve, headquarters Marine Corps March 1942-1944. Major general in April 1942. Commandant of Marine Corps Schools 1944-1946. Retired in August 1946. Died on June 7, 1968.

Turnage, Allen Hal (1891-1971) Born on January 3, 1891, in Farmville, South Carolina. Attended the University of North Carolina. Commissioned in 1913. Foreign duty with the First Brigade in Haiti 1915-1918. Commanding officer of a machine gun battalion in the Fifth Marine Brigade in France in 1918. Instructor at Marine Corps Schools 1918-1922. Assigned to the Gendarmerie d'Haiti 1922-1925 and the American Embassy in Peking 1939-1941. Director of the division of plans and policies, headquarters Marine Corps April 1941-June 1942. Brigadier general in May 1942. Commander of Base and Training Center, Camp Lejeune June-October 1942. Major general in September 1942. Assistant division commander of 3rd Marine Division October 1942-September 1943. Commanding general on Guadalcanal September 1943-September 1944. Director of personnel at headquarters, Marine Corps 1944-1945. Assistant commandant of the Marine Corps 1945-1946. Assignments after the war included commanding general of Fleet Marine Force Pacific May 1946-January 1948. General upon retirement in

January 1948. Decorations included the Navy Cross, Distinguished Service Medal and Legion of Merit. Died on October 22, 1971.

Underhill, James Latham (1891-1991) Born on June 12, 1891, in San Francisco, California. B.S. from the University of California in 1913. Commissioned in 1913. Commanding officer of the Eighth Separate Battalion in France in October 1918. Duty at the American Legation in Managua, Nicaragua in 1919. Instructor at Marine Corps Schools October 1921-June 1922. Judge advocate, then post quartermaster at Cavite, Philippine Islands 1925-1926. Assigned to Shanghai, China as plans and training officer in 1927, commanding officer of the Third Battalion in 1928 and commander of Sixth Marines 1937-1938. Executive officer to the adjutant and inspector, headquarters Marine Corps 1939-1942. Major general in September 1942. Commanding general of Marine Corps Base, San Diego April 1942-March 1943. Commander of East Coast Echelon, 4th Marine Division April-August 1943. Assistant division commander of 4th Marine Division August 1943-August 1944. Island commander on Tinian August-November 1944. Deputy commander, then inspector general of Fleet Marine Force Pacific 1944-1945. Lieutenant General upon retirement November 1946. Decorations include Legion of Merit and Bronze Star Medal. Died on October 7, 1991.

Upshur, William Peterkin (1881-1943) Born on October 28, 1881, in Richmond, Virginia. B.S. from Virginia Military Institute in 1902. Attended the University of Virginia Law School 1902-1903. Commissioned in 1904. Foreign duty with expeditionary forces in Cuba October 1906-1907, in Panama June-August 1908, the First Brigade Marines in the Philippines in 1912, the American Legation in Peking 1914-1915, and as company commander in the Second Regiment, Haiti 1915-1918 where he earned the Medal of Honor for action against hostile Cacos bandits at Fort Liberte. Additional foreign duty with the 13th Regiment Marines in France September 1918-August 1919, at Naval Station, St. Thomas July-August 1921 and the First Brigade Marines in Haiti 1922-1924. Graduated from Command and General Staff School in 1925, the Naval War College in 1932 and the Army War College in 1933. Officer in Charge of the Marine Corps Reserve, headquarters Marine Corps 1937-1939. Major general in October 1939. Commanding general of Marine Corps Base and Fleet Marine Force San Diego 1939-1942 then Department of the Pacific January 1942 until his death in an airplane crash near Sitka, Alaska on August 18, 1943 while on an inspection tour of his command. Decorations included the Medal of Honor.

Vandegrift, Alexander Archer (1887-1973) Born on March 13, 1887, in Char-lottesville, Virginia. Attended the University of Virginia 1906-1908. Enlisted in the Marine Corps in 1908 and commissioned in 1909. Overseas duty in Cuba and Nicaragua in 1912, Canal Zone in 1913, Vera Cruz, Mexico in 1914, Haiti 1915, again 1916-1918 and 1919-1923. With the Marine Expeditionary Force in China 1927-1929 and again 1935-1937. Secretary, then assistant to Major General Thomas Holcomb, commandant of the Marine Corps 1937-1941. Brigadier general in April 1940, major general in March 1942. Assistant commander, then commanding general of 1st Marine Division 1942-1943. Lieutenant general in July 1943. Commanding general of I Marine Amphibious Corps July-November 1943. Commandant of the Marine Corps January 1944-January 1948. General in March 1945, the first active duty four-star general in the Marine Corps. Retired in March 1949. Decorations included the Medal of Honor, Navy Cross and Distinguished Service Medal. Died on May 8, 1973.

Vogel, Clayton Barney (1882-1964) Born on September 18, 1882, in Philadelphia. Graduated from Rutgers University in 1904. Commissioned in 1904. Foreign duty with the American Legation in Peking 1906-1909, then the Second Regiment of the Expeditionary Brigade in the Canal Zone in 1910 and Cuba in 1911. Special White House Aide 1911-1912. Inspector with the Haitian Constabulary 1916-1918. Chief of staff to the Commandant, Nicaraguan National Guard May 1929-June 1930 then the Commandant, Garde d'Haiti November 1930-August 1934. Brigadier General in March 1937. The adjutant and inspector of the Marine Corps March 1937-September 1939. Commanding general of the Second Marine Brigade September 1930-February 1941. Major general in May 1941. Commanding general of 2nd Marine Division February-November 1941 then Amphibious Corps, Pacific Fleet November 1941-October 1942. Commanding general of I Marine Amphibious Corps October 1942-August 1943 then Fleet Marine Force San Diego Area August 1943-May 1944. Commanding general of Marine Barracks, Parris Island May 1944-January 1946. Retired in January 1946. Died on November 26, 1964.

Walker, John Thaddeus (1893-1955) Born on September 15, 1893, in Azle, Texas. B.S. from Texas Agricultural and Mechanical College. Commissioned in 1917. Served with Fifth Marine Regiment in France 1917-1918. Duty in the Dominican Republic 1920-1922. Aide to the Commandant Norfolk Navy Yard 1922-1925. Instructor at Marine Corps Schools 1928-1932. Duty in Haiti July 1932-September 1934. Again instructor at Marine Corps Schools 1938-1940. Chief of the plans section at Marine Corps Base San Diego 1940-1941. Naval observer in Cairo July-December 1941. Operations officer with 2nd Marine Division January-June 1942. Commander of 22nd Marines 1942-1944. Brigadier general in October 1942. Chief of staff of First Provisional Brigade March-December 1944. Assistant director of personnel at headquarters U.S. Marine Corps December 1944-May 1945. Assistant division commander of 2nd Marine Division 1945-1946. Retired as lieutenant general in July 1954. Decorations included the Navy Cross, Legion of Merit and Bronze Star. Died on February 27, 1955.

Wallace, William Jennings (1895-1977) Born on August 6, 1895, in Church Hill, Maryland. B.S. from Washington College in 1918. Commissioned in 1918. Served with the Second Provisional Brigade in Santo Domingo 1918-1921. Designated naval aviator in 1922. Became the first Marine aviator to land and take off from an aircraft carrier. Served in China 1925-1929. Executive officer of Marine Air Group 21 in Hawaii in 1941. Commanding officer of Marine air groups at

Midway and Guadalcanal in 1942. Chief of staff then commanding general of Marine Air West Coast 1943-1946. Brigadier general in January 1944. Assignments after the war included director of aviation, U.S. Marine Corps 1948-1950. Lieutenant general upon retirement in July 1952. Decorations included the Distinguished Service Medal, Legion of Merit, Bronze Star and Purple Heart. Died on July 7, 1977.

Waller, Littleton Waller Tazewell, Jr. (1886-1967) Born in Norfolk, Virginia, on September 18, 1886. Attended Annapolis. Commissioned in 1907. Served at the invasion of Vera Cruz in 1914 and with the Fourth Marine Brigade at Belleau Wood 1917-1918. Resigned in 1925 and joined the Marine Corps Reserve. Called to active duty in June 1941 as lieutenant colonel. Officer in charge of target practice at headquarters U.S. Marine Corps 1941-1943 then director of personnel February 1943-September 1944. Brigadier general in September 1942, the first reservist in the Marine Corps to rise to that rank. Commanding general of naval bases in Fourteenth Naval District 1944-1946. Retired as major general in June 1946. Decorations included the Navy Cross and Purple Heart. Died on April 14, 1967.

Watson, Thomas Eugene (1892-1966) Born on January 18, 1892, in Oskaloosa, Louisiana. Attended Penn College 1911-1912. Commissioned in 1916. Served in the Dominican Republic 1916-1919 and 1919-1920, with the Third Marine Brigade in Tientsin 1927-1928, again in the Dominican Republic 1930-1931 and in Nicaragua 1931-1933. Graduated from the Army War College in 1938. Duty in the war plans division at headquarters U.S. Marine Corps 1938-1942. Served in Western Samoa as commander of the 3rd Marine Brigade 1942-1943 and Tactical Group One 1943-1944. Brigadier general in August 1942, major general in January 1944. Commanding general of 2nd Marine Division April 1944-July 1945. Director of personnel, U.S. Marine Corps August 1945-June 1946. Assignments after the war included commanding general of Fleet Marine Force Pacific January 1948-April 1950. Retired in July 1950 as lieutenant general. Decorations included two Distinguished Service Medals. Died on March 6, 1966.

Whitehead, Frank (1888-1950) Born on January 4, 1888 in Camden, New Jersey. Enlisted service in the Marine Corps 1908-1917. Commissioned in 1917. Served with the Fifth Marines in France during World War II and was twice wounded in action. Duty at Pearl Harbor 1924-1926. Graduated from the Army Industrial College in June 1937. Brigade quartermaster of the Second Marine Brigade in Shanghai August 1937-April 1938. Instructor then commandant of the Army Industrial College 1941-1942. Assigned to the plans division in the office of the Commander in Chief United States Fleet January-June 1942 then at headquarters U.S. Marine Corps June 1942-May 1944. Brigadier general upon retirement in May 1944. Recalled to active duty in the division of plans and policies at Marine Corps headquarters until January 1946. Decorations included the Distinguished Service Cross, Navy Cross and Purple Heart. Died on July 21, 1950.

Williams, Seth (1880-1963) Born on January 19, 1880, in Foxboro, Massachusetts. Enlisted service with the Vermont National Guard 1901-1903. B.S. from Norwich University in 1903. Commissioned in 1903. Foreign service prior to World War I included the Philippine islands, France, Guam, China and Panama. Officer in charge of building Marine Barracks Quantico, Virginia during World War I. Commanding officer of Depot of Supplies at San Francisco October 1923-November 1926 and Philadelphia 1930-1937. Brigadier general in December 1937. Quartermaster of the Marine Corps 1937-1944. Major general in March 1942. Retired in February 1944. Died on July 29, 1963.

Woods, Louis Earnest (1895-1971) Born on October 7, 1895, in Fredonia, New York. Attended Syracuse University. Commissioned in 1917. Designated naval aviator in June 1922. Served in Haiti 1924-1926 and 1933-1934. Graduated from the Naval War College in May 1941. Chief of staff of First Marine Aircraft Wing May 1941-June 1943. Brigadier general in October 1941, major general in September 1942. Director of Marine Corps Aviation 1943-1944 then Fourth and Second Marine Aircraft Wings until November 1945. Lieutenant general upon retirement in July 1951. Decorations included the Distinguished Service Medal and two Legions of Merit. Died on October 20, 1971.

Worton, William Arthur (1897-1973) Born on January 4, 1897, in Boston, Massachusetts. Attended Harvard University and Boston University Law School. Commission in the Massachusetts Naval Militia in 1917. Served with the Sixth Marine Regiment in the AEF in 1918, including the Aisne-Marne offensive where he was seriously wounded. A Chinese linguist, he saw duty in China 1922-1926, 1927-1929 and 1931-1937. Brigadier general in October 1942. Assistant division commander of the Third Marine Division 1942-1945 then chief of staff of III Amphibious Corps June 1945-September 1946. Major general upon retirement in June 1949. Died on July 26, 1973.

Wright, Raymond Race (1892-1964) Born on February 5, 1892, in Council Bluffs, Iowa. Commissioned from Annapolis in 1915. Served in Santo Domingo in 1916 and Haiti 1916-1921. Brigade paymaster of the Second Marine Brigade in Nicaragua 1928-1930. Graduated from the Naval War College in 1936. Brigadier general in January 1942. Paymaster general of the Marine Corps February 1942-August 1946. Major general in June 1945. Retired in December 1946. Decorations included the Legion of Merit. Died on February 19, 1964.

6

The United States Coast Guard

Chalker, Lloyd T. **(1883-1981)** Born on December 4, 1883, in Mobile, Alabama. Graduated from the Coast Guard Academy in 1903 and commissioned in 1906. Commanding officer of the *Modoc* and *Ericsson* 1924-1928 then the *Saranac* October 1930-August 1931. Chief of the personnel section at Coast Guard headquarters August 1931-September 1934 then head of the aviation division and assistant chief of operations 1940-1942. Rear admiral in March 1942. Assistant commandant until retirement as vice admiral in July 1946. Decorations included the Legion of Merit. Died on March 12, 1981.

Covell, Leon Claude (1877-1960) Born in Middleville, New York, on December 2, 1877. Attended George Washington University prior to accepting appointment as cadet in the Coast Guard in June 1900. Commissioned in June 1902. Between 1915 and 1926 commanded the *Unalga, Snohomish, Zara, Mackinas, Gresham* and *Bear*. Assistant commandant of the Coast Guard December 1931-January 1942. Rear admiral in May 1939. Retired in January 1942. Recalled to active duty as commander of the Coast Guard Training Station 1943-1945. Retired a second time as vice admiral in April 1945. Decorations included the Legion of Merit. Died on November 20, 1960.

Derby, Wilfrid Neville (1889-1973) Born on December 4, 1889, in Newark, New Jersey. Appointed cadet in 1908, commissioned ensign in 1911. Instructor at the Coast Guard Academy during World War I. Except for two months as commanding officer of the *Wakefield* in 1941, he had duty at Coast Guard headquarters October 1935-June 1942. District Coast Guard Officer, First Naval District, June 1942-August 1947. Commodore in June 1943, rear admiral in July 1945. Duty at the Coast Guard Academy August 1947-September 1950. Vice admiral upon retirement in September 1950. Died on January 12, 1973.

Donohue, Robert (1886-n/a) Born on August 23, 1886. Served as chief of the division of personnel at Coast Guard headquarters during World War II. Rear admiral in June 1942. Retired in June 1946.

Eaton, Philip Bentley (1887-1958) Born on January 24, 1887, in Elkins, New Hampshire. Attended Webb Institute of Naval Architecture 1905-1908. Graduated from the Coast Guard Academy and commissioned in 1908. Rear admiral in November 1943. Assistant engineer-in-chief at headquarters U.S. Coast Guard 1943-1945. Retired in September 1946. Died on May 18, 1958.

Farley, Joseph Francis (1889-1974) Born in Oxford, Ohio, on June 22, 1889. Commissioned from the Coast Guard Academy in 1912. Commanding officer of the destroyers *McCall* and *Wilkes* March 1928-September 1930 then the *Pontchartrain* and *Modoc* 1933-1937. Chief of the communications office at Coast Guard headquarters 1937-1942. District Coast Guard Officer at Eighth Naval District in New Orleans June 1942-December 1943. Commodore in June 1943 and rear admiral in November 1943. Chief of operations then chief personnel officer at Coast Guard headquarters 1943-1945. Appointed commandant with promotion to admiral in January 1946. Served until retirement in January 1950. Decorations included the Legion of Merit. Died on November 25, 1974.

Farwell, Lorenzo Chase (1878-1966) Born in Boston, Massachusetts, on June 5, 1878. Graduated from Massachusetts Nautical Training School in 1897. Appointed cadet engineer in the Coast Guard May 1902 and commissioned the following month. On recruiting duty in New York City during World War I. Engineer-in-chief at Coast Guard headquarters 1930-1931 then engineer at the New York Division June 1934-July 1942. Retired as rear admiral in July 1942. Recalled to active duty later that month. Engineer officer, then procurement officer at Third Naval District 1942-1943. Died on April 10, 1966.

Finlay, Gordon Thomas (1886-n/a) Born in Battle Creek, Michigan, on September 12, 1886. Commissioned from the Coast Guard Academy in 1909. Commanding officer of the *Noma* October 1918-July 1919 and the *Shaw* May-September 1928. Executive officer at the Coast Guard Academy 1931-1934. Commanding officer of the *Shoshone* June 1934-October 1937. Commanded the Honolulu District July 1939-June 1940, the Chicago District August 1940-May 1941 and again the Honolulu District May 1941-October 1942. District Coast Guard Officer at Fifth Naval District 1942-1944. Commodore in June 1943, rear admiral in June 1945. Commander of Eighth Coast Guard District August 1945 until retirement as vice admiral in June 1948.

Gorman, Frank Joseph (1891-1962) Born in Washington, DC, on November 3, 1891. Cadet at the Coast Guard Academy 1910-1913. Commissioned in 1913. Served aboard the *Manning* and the *Seneca* during World War I. Chief finance officer at Coast Guard headquarters 1936-1945, with additional duty as chief supply officer 1943-1945. Rear admiral in June 1942. Chief planning and control officer at Coast Guard headquarters 1945-1946. Retired in July 1946. Died on May 11, 1962.

Hottel, James Freeman (1876-1973) Born in Washington, DC, on November 24, 1876. Commissioned from the Coast Guard Academy in April 1898. Commanding officer of the *Snohomish, McCulloch, Manhattan* and *Tallapoosa* August 1911-May 1916, the *Haida* 1921-1924 and the *Morthland* 1927-1929. Commander of the Northwestern Division July 1929-January 1930. Commander of the Eastern Area and Captain of the Port of New York 1934-1935. Commanding officer of Fort Trumbull Training Station July 1937-October. Retired as rear admiral in December 1940. Recalled to active duty with the War Shipping Administration in August 1942. Retired again in November 1946. Died on January 7, 1973.

Johnson, Harvey Fletcher (1882-n/a) Born in Wheatley, Arkansas, on August 27, 1882. Graduated from Cornell University in 1906 and the U.S. Revenue Cutter School in 1908. Commissioned in the Coast Guard in February 1908. Served on convoy duty during World War I. Served repeated tours of duty in the office of the engineer-in-chief 1919-1936. Appointed engineer-in-chief of the Coast Guard in May 1936. Rear admiral in May 1939 with appointment to an additional four years as engineer-in-chief.

Jones, Edward Darlington (1885-1954) Born on May 8, 1885, in Williamsburg, Virginia. Cadet at the Coast Guard Academy 1904-1906. Commissioned in 1906. Served in command of ships performing convoy duty in World War I. Chief communications officer at Coast Guard headquarters and superintendent of the Coast Guard Academy July 1935-June 1940. Commander of the Honolulu District June 1940-June 1941. Liaison officer with Department of the Navy June 1941-March 1942. Rear admiral in March 1942. Pacific Coast coordinator of Coast Guard activities 1942-1944. Retired in October 1946. Died on May 2, 1954.

Molloy, Thomas Marcus (1874-1945) Born in Worcester, Massachusetts, on June 4, 1874. B.S. from Worcester Polytechnic Institute. Appointed a cadet in the Coast Guard in August 1897. Commissioned ensign in 1899. Commanding officer of the *Rambler* and *Nokomis* on escort duty during World War I. Commanded the international ice patrol in 1929, then commanding officer of the *Cayuga* 1932-1933. Duty in the New York Division 1937-1938. Retired as rear admiral in July 1938. Recalled to active duty in May 1941. Served at Coast Guard headquarters until a second retirement shortly before his death on October 11, 1945.

Park, Charles Abraham (1882-1966) Born on November 30, 1882, in New Lexington, Ohio. C.E. from Ohio State University. Assigned as the quartermaster deputy at large at Fort D.A. Russell 1908-1911. Chief engineer for the U.S. Lighthouse Service 1933-1935. Deputy commissioner of lighthouses 1935-1939. Operations officer at Coast Guard headquarters 1939-1942 then chief operations officer from July 1942. Rear admiral in May 1943. Died in 1966.

Parker, Stanley Vincent (1885-1968) Born on October 26, 1885, in Cincinnati, Ohio. Cadet in U.S. Revenue Cutter Service (forerunner of the Coast Guard) 1904-1906. Commissioned in 1906. Underwent flight training at Naval Air Station Pensacola 1917, designated naval aviator and Coast Guard aviator number 7. Commanding officer of naval air stations at Key West, Florida, December 1917-August 1918 and Rockaway, New York, August 1918-May 1919. Senior Coast Guard officer, in various roles, at San Francisco 1937-1942. Rear admiral in March 1942. Coordinator of port security for Atlantic and Gulf coasts February 1942-June 1942, then District Coast Guard Officer at Third Naval District June 1942-September 1945. Commander of Western Area, Coast Guard, September 1945- November 1947. Vice admiral upon retirement in November 1947. Died on July 15, 1968.

Pine, James (1885-1953) Born on October 19, 1885, in Cincinnati, Ohio. Commissioned from the Coast Guard Academy in 1908. Commanding officer of the *May* and the *Zeelandia* during World War I. Duty at Coast Guard headquarters 1932-1934. Executive officer of the Coast Guard Academy 1934-1937 then superintendent 1940-1947. Rear admiral in June 1942, the first superintendent to hold flag rank. Retired in August 1947. Decorations included the Legion of Merit. Died in 1953.

Roach, Philip Francis (1881-1976) Born on February 11, 1881, in Sedalia, Colorado. Cadet 1904-1907. Commissioned in 1907. During World War I commanded *SS Lydonia* in European waters. Chairman of the Permanent Board 1938-1942. District captain of the port officer, then District Coast Guard Officer at Twelfth Naval District April 1942-February 1945. Commodore in June 1943. Rear admiral upon retirement in March 1945. Died on March 8, 1976.

Rose, Earl Gray (1887-1982) Born in Lithopolis, Ohio, on November 9, 1887. Attended Ohio State University 1907-1910. Appointed cadet in the U.S. Revenue Cutter Service in 1910. Commissioned in 1913. Served as commanding officer of the *Rambler* on merchant convoy escort duty off the coast of France during World War I. Commanding officer of the *Tampa* in 1934 when she rescued the crew of the *Morro Castle* which sank off the coast of New Jersey. Supervised convoys and provided air-sea rescue services during World War II. Commodore in November 1943, rear admiral in 1946. Headed the office of operations at Coast Guard headquarters at retirement in 1949. Decorations included the Navy Cross and Legion of Merit. Died on October 20, 1982.

Smith, Edward Hanson (1889-1961) Born on October 29, 1889, in Vineyard Haven, Massachusetts. Attended Massachusetts Institute of Technology. Cadet at the Coast Guard Academy 1910-1913. Commissioned in 1913. On convoy escort duty in the Atlantic in World War I. M.A. in 1924 and Ph.D. in 1930 from Harvard. Member of the scientific staff during the Graf Zeppelin Polar flight in 1931. Commander of the Greenland Naval Patrol 1942-1943. Rear admiral in June 1942. Commander of 24th Task Force November 1943-July 1945. District Coast

Guard Officer at Third Naval District July 1945 until retirement in June 1950. Decorations included the Distinguished Service Medal. Died on October 29, 1961.

Waesche, Russell Randolph (1886-1946) Born on January 6, 1886, in Thurmont, Maryland. Commissioned in 1906. Served aboard the *Mohawk, Morrill, Tahoma, Snohomish* and *Rush* prior to commanding the *Arcata* October 1911-November 1912 and the *Pamlico* November 1912-February 1915. Served at Coast Guard headquarters February 1915-August 1919. Commanding officer of the *Snohomish,* the *Bothwell* 1920-1924, *USS Beale* 1924-1926 and the *Tucker* 1926-1927. Gunnery officer on staff of the Commander, Destroyer Force 1927-1928. Thereafter served at Coast Guard headquarters as chief ordnance officer 1928-1932, then liaison officer with Navy Department War Plans Division February 1932-June 1932, finally aide to the commandant June 1932-June 1936. Appointed commandant and promoted from commander to rear admiral in June 1936. Vice admiral in March 1942, admiral in April 1945. Retired in January 1946 and died on October 17, 1946.

Webster, Edward M. (1889-n/a) Born in Washington, DC, on February 28, 1889. Graduated from the Coast Guard Academy in 1912. Served on active duty 1912-1918. Staff member with the Federal Communications Commission 1934-1938 then assistant chief engineer there 1938-1942. Recalled to active duty in 1942. Chief of the communications division, office of operations at Coast Guard headquarters June 1942-October 1945. Retired as commodore in 1946. Awards included the Legion of Merit.

Appendix 1

SUMMARY OF BIRTHPLACES AND BIRTHDATES

Appendix 1.a
Birthplaces of World War II Generals and Flag Officers

State	Army	Army Air Force	National Guard	Navy	Marine Corps	Coast Guard	Total
AL	30	8	4	9	1	1	53
AK	1						1
AZ	11						
AR	18	6	1	9		1	35
CA	35	11	3	20	5		75
CO	15	3		4		1	23
CT	18	3	1	4	1		27
DE	4			1	2		7
FL	7	4	3	2	1		17
GA	32	10	4	12	1		59
HI	2						2
ID	5	2	1	3	1		12
IL	63	21	7	19	2		112
IN	43	8		18	3		72
IA	36	15	2	19	4		76
KS	40	12		9	2		63
KY	26	4	3	7	2		42
LA	18	3	2	4	3		30
ME	11	1		4			16
MD	25	5	3	18	4	1	56
MA	56	15	6	25	5	3	110
MI	34	17		17	1	1	70
MN	25	13	1	8	2		49
MS	17	3	1	10			31
MO	49	8	2	14	3		76
MT	3	1	1	1			6
NE	26	5	2	8	2		43
NV	2			1			3
NH	9	2	2	4		1	18
NJ	26	8	4	15	3	1	57
NM	6	5					11
NY	103	31	6	47	5	1	193
NC	26	6	3	10			45
ND	7	1	2	2			12
OH	54	22	6	21	4	4	110
OK	5	2		2	1		10
OR	10	2	1	9			22
PA	76	25	6	42	3		152

Birthplaces of World War II Generals and Flag Officers

State	Army	Army Air Force	National Guard	Navy	Marine Corps	Coast Guard	Total
RI	8	1	3	2			14
CC	17	2	2	11	8		43
SD	17	4		2			23
TN	25	5	1	6	1		13
TX	50	37	7	16	4		114
UT	9	6		2	1		18
VT	8	3	3	2	2		18
VA	57	11	4	15	7	1	95
WA	15	7		2	3		27
WV	9	5		6			20
WI	20	10	3	12			45
WY	10		1				11
DC	36	6	1	17	5	3	68
FB*	26	4	8	5	3		46

*Foreign born

Appendix 1.b
Birthdates of World War II Generals and Flag Officers

Year	Army	Army Air Force	National Guard	Navy	Marine Corps	Coast Guard	Total
1869	1			1			2
1870	1						1
1871							
1872	1			3			4
1873				1			1
1874	3			2			5
1875	4			2			6
1876	4	1		3		1	9
1877	12	1		9		1	23
1878	13		2	7	2		26
1879	17		3	8	1		29
1880	17	1	3	9	3	1	34
1881	24	1	1	14	3	1	44
1882	29	2	8	16	6	2	63
1883	35	1	4	13	2	1	56
1884	21	6	10	25	5		67
1885	38	4	1	24	3	3	73
1886	52	7		26	3	2	90
1887	52	6	7	26	2	2	95
1888	62	2	3	22	3		92
1889	68	7	7	24	2	4	112
1890	65	22	7	22	4		120
1891	83	16	8	28	4	1	140
1892	102	31	6	33	8		180
1893	95	27	10	27	6		165
1894	101	24	9	32	10		176
1895	97	29	9	28	15		178
1896	70	22	5	25	5		127
1897	40	11	3	22	9		85
1898	43	12	1	20	2		78
1899	38	10		9			57
1900	26	23	2	8			59
1901	26	14		3			43
1902	19	14		4			37
1903	12	15	1	1			29
1904	5	17					22
1905	3	13		1			17
1906	3	17					20

Birthdates of World War II Generals and Flag Officers

Year	Army	Army Air Force	National Guard	Navy	Marine Corps	Coast Guard	Total
1907	4	11		2			17
1908	2	8					10
1909	2	5					7
1910	2	3					5
1911	1						1
1912							
1913							
1914		1					1
1915		1					1

Appendix 2

GENERAL AND FLAG OFFICERS WHO DIED DURING WORLD WAR II

Appendix 2.a
United States Army General Officers

Name	Circumstances and Date
Charles H. Barth Jr.	Killed in an airplane crash in Iceland on May 3, 1943
Gustav J. Brann Jr.	Missing in action in the Mediterranean, March 17, 1945
Simon B. Buckner Jr.	Killed in action on Okinawa on June 18, 1945
Gordon De L. Carrington	Died on August 21, 1944
Harry D. Chamberlin	Died on September 29, 1944
Malin Craig	Died on July 25, 1945
James L. Dalton II	Killed by a sniper at Luzon on May 16, 1945
William O. Darby	Killed in action in Italy on April 30, 1945
Donald A. Davison	Died in India on May 6, 1944
Claudius M. Easley	Killed in action on Okinawa on June 19, 1945
Guy O. Fort	Executed by the Japanese on November 9 or 13, 1942
Creswell Garlington	Died on March 11, 1945
John Gardner	Died on October 11, 1944
Lloyd H. Gibbons	Died on April 7, 1945
James F.C. Hyde	Died of a heart attack on August 7, 1944
Stonewall Jackson	Killed in a plane crash on October 13, 1943
Charles L. Keerans Jr.	Killed on an air mission over Sicily on July 11, 1943
Walter G. Layman	Died in the United Kingdom on September 24, 1944
Vicente Lim	Executed by the Japanese in late 1944 or early 1945
Albert K.B. Lyman	Died in Hawaii on August 17, 1942
Frank C. Mahin	Killed in a plane crash in Tennessee on July 24, 1942
Alan McBride	Died while a POW in the Philippines on May 9, 1944
Leslie J. McNair	Killed by an Allied bomb at St. Lo on July 23, 1944
Paul W. Newgarden	Killed in a plane crash in Tennessee on July 14, 1944
Edwin D. Patrick	Died from wounds in action on Luzon on March 14, 1945
William D. Powell	Died in China on October 6, 1943
Don F. Pratt	Killed in a glider crash at Normandy on June 6, 1944
Thomas E. Roderick	Died in Africa on September 21, 1944
Theodore Roosevelt Jr.	Died in Cherbourg, France on July 12, 1944
Maurice Rose	Killed in action in Germany on March 30, 1945
Edmund W. Searby	Killed in action in France on September 14, 1944
Edwin M. Watson	Died on February 20, 1945

Appendix 2.b
United States Army Air Force General Officers

Name	Circumstances and Date
James R. Anderson	Killed in a plane crash at Kwajalein on February 26,1945
Frank M. Andrews	Killed in a plane crash in Iceland on May 3, 1943
Frederick W. Castle	Killed in action on December 24, 1944
Herbert A. Dargue	Killed in a plane crash in California, December 12,1941
Asa N. Duncan	Missing in action in Europe on November 17, 1942
William H. Eaton	Killed in action in France on February 6, 1945
Nathan B. Forrest	Killed in action over Kiel, Germany on June 14, 1943
Harold H. George	Killed in a plane crash in Australia on April 29, 1942
Donald R. Goodrich	Died on July 12, 1945
David D. Graves	Missing in action over Italy
Millard F. Harmon	Lost on a flight over the Pacific on February 26, 1945
Henry W. Harms	Died on June 4, 1945
Alfred J. Lyon	Died on December 1, 1942
Arthur B. McDaniel	Died on December 26, 1943
Earl L. Naiden	Died on September 20, 1944
Douglas B. Netherwood	Killed in a plane crash in Florida on August 19, 1943
Robert Olds	Died on April 28, 1943
Howard K. Ramey	Missing in action over New Guinea in March 1943
Clinton W. Russell	Died on March 23, 1943
Willis R. Taylor	Died in the Canal Zone on June 14, 1945
Clarence L. Tinker	Killed in a plane crash at Wake Island on June 7, 1943
Kenneth N. Walker	Missing in action over Rabaul on January 5, 1943
Carlyle H. Wash	Killed in a plane crash in Alabama on January 26, 1943
Russell A. Wilson	Killed in action over Berlin on March 6, 1944

Appendix 2.c
United States Navy Flag Officers

Name	Circumstances and Date
Arthur L. Bristol Jr.	Died of a heart attack on April 20, 1942
Daniel J. Callaghan	Killed in action at Guadalcanal on November 13, 1942
Charles P. Cecil	Killed in a plane crash in the Pacific on July 31, 1944
Theodore E. Chandler	Killed in action liberating Luzon on January 7, 1945
Robert H. English	Killed in a plane crash in California on January 21, 1943
Willis A. Lee Jr.	Died of a heart attack on August 24, 1945
Frank T. Leighton	Died on November 23, 1943
Don P. Moon	Died in the Mediterranean area on August 5, 1944
Norman Scott	Killed in action at Savo Island on November 13, 1942
Ernest G. Small	Died on December 26, 1944
John W. Wilcox	Swept off his ship and lost at sea on March 27, 1942

Appendix 2.d
United States Marine Corps General Officers

Name	Circumstances and Date
Charles D. Barrett	Accidentally killed on October 8, 1943
David L.S. Brewster	Died on July 10, 1945
William H. Rupertus	Died of a heart attack on March 25, 1945
William P. Upshur	Killed in a plane crash in Alaska on August 18, 1943

Index

About the Authors

R. MANNING ANCELL, a former broadcast journalist and magazine publisher, is vice president for communications at the Greater Washington Society of Association Executives. He is co-author of *Who Will Lead?* (Praeger, 1995).

CHRISTINE M. MILLER, formerly a professor and director of admissions, is a marketing communications manager for MCI government markets in McLean, Virginia. She holds a Ph.D. from Northwestern University.

ISBN 0-313-29546-8

90000>

EAN

9 780313 295461

HARDCOVER BAR CODE